ALSO BY TAYLOR BRANCH

Pillar of Fire: America in the King Years 1963–65
Parting the Waters: America in the King Years 1954–63
Labyrinth (with Eugene M. Propper)
The Empire Blues
Second Wind (with Bill Russell)
Blowing the Whistle: Dissent in the Public Interest (with Charles Peters)

TAYLOR
BRANCH

AT
CANAAN'S
EDGE

America
in the
King Years
1965–68

Simon & Schuster
New York   London
Toronto   Sydney

SIMON & SCHUSTER
Rockefeller Center
1230 Avenue of the Americas
New York, NY 10020

For information about special discounts for bulk purchases,
please contact Simon & Schuster Special Sales at
1-800-456-6798 or business@simonandschuster.com

Photography Consultant: Kevin Kwan

Manufactured in the United States of America

10 9 8 7 6 5 4 3 2 1

Library of Congress Cataloging-in-Publication Data
Branch, Taylor.
   At Canaan's edge : America in the King years, 1965–68 / Taylor Branch.
      p.   cm.
   1. African Americans—Civil rights—History—20th century.   2. Civil
rights movements—United States—History—20th century.   3. King, Martin
Luther, Jr., 1929–1968.   4. United States—History—1961–1969.   I. Title.
E185.615.B67   2006
323.1196'073 009046—dc22   2005040177
ISBN-13: 978-0-684-85712-1
ISBN-10: 0-684-85712-X

Photo credits will be found on page 1040.

For Macy and Franklin
And for Diane Nash

CONTENTS

III. CROSSROADS IN FREEDOM AND WAR

IV. PASSION

INTRODUCTION

$NONVIOLENCE$ is an orphan among democratic ideas. It has nearly vanished from public discourse even though the most basic element of free government—the vote—has no other meaning. Every ballot is a piece of nonviolence, signifying hard-won consent to raise politics above firepower and bloody conquest. Such compacts work more or less securely in different lands. Nations gain strength from vote-based institutions in commerce and civil society, but the whole architecture of representative democracy springs from the handiwork of nonviolence.

America's Founders centered political responsibility in the citizens themselves, but, nearly two centuries later, no one expected a largely invisible and dependent racial minority to ignite protests of steadfast courage—boycotts, sit-ins, Freedom Rides, jail marches—dramatized by stunning forbearance and equilibrium into the jaws of hatred. During the short career of Martin Luther King, Jr., between 1954 and 1968, the nonviolent civil rights movement lifted the patriotic spirit of the United States toward our defining national purpose.

James Madison, arguing in 1788 to ratify the novel Constitution of the United States, called upon "every votary of freedom to rest all our political experiments on the capacity of mankind for self-government." This revolutionary premise challenged the once universal hierarchy of rulers and subjects along with its stubborn assumption that a populace needs discipline by superior force or authority. Madison also prescribed a bold commitment to the wisdom of citizens at large. This public trust surfaces in close elections, when it becomes more than a theoretical article of faith that the power of a great nation can turn on the last trickle of marginal voters to the polls. Without "virtue in the people," wrote Madison, "no theoretical checks, no form of government, can render us secure."

There remains debate about the relative sturdiness of self-governance and public trust as bedrock features of constitutional design. Is democracy more vulnerable to a loss of collective will or to deficiencies in popular judgment? Rulers from China and elsewhere scoff that both ideals are impossibly unstable for a long run measured in dynasties, and doubters within democracy itself push for authoritarian shelter. However, nonviolent pioneers from the civil rights era stand tall in the commitment to govern oneself and develop political bonds with strangers, rather than vice versa. Teenagers and small children sang freedom songs in the Birmingham jail. Workshops trained nonviolent pilgrims to uphold democratic beliefs against the psychology of enemies. Demonstrators faced segregationist oppressors in the utmost spirit of disciplined outreach, willing to suffer and even die without breaking witness for civil contact. Bob Moses, the mystical student leader, recruited college volunteers to endure scapegoat brutality during the Mississippi Freedom Summer of 1964. On its first night, one of three lynch victims haunted the surrounding posse with his last words. "Sir, I know just how you feel," Michael Schwerner told a Klansman about to pull the trigger.

Martin Luther King famously exhorted the nation to "rise up and live out the true meaning of its creed," but he paid tribute to vanguard students for teaching him that oratory alone was not enough. He reinforced a cry for democracy with political sacrifice, and dreams of brotherhood collided in his anguished voice with the cruelties of race. To combat distortions in historical perception, King balanced an imperative for equal votes with the original prophetic vision of equal souls before God. He grounded one foot in patriotism, the other in ministry, and both in nonviolence. The movement he led climbed from obscurity to command the center stage of American politics in 1963, when President John F. Kennedy declared racial segregation a moral issue "as old as the Scriptures and . . . as clear as the American Constitution." A year later, after President Lyndon Johnson signed a landmark law to abolish segregation by sex as well as race, King accepted the Nobel Peace Prize. "I believe that unarmed truth and unconditional love will have the final word in reality," he said, echoing the Founders' lyrical hopes for freedom. "But what," wrote Madison, "is government itself but the greatest of all reflections on human nature? If men were angels, no government would be necessary."

In this third, concluding volume on America in the King Years, King has willed himself from the pinnacle of acclaim straight to "the valley" of a new campaign to seek voting rights for black people. By early 1965, he has been beaten and arrested again through two months of arduous demonstrations in Selma, Alabama—highlighted once more by children marched to jail, with a young black man shot to death in a vigil—and has attracted very little notice. For all its resonant success to win the courtesies of democracy, the freedom movement has evoked lethal opposition at the color line of political power—the vote—from a nation that long ago enshrined but essentially forgot a Fifteenth Amendment guarantee of this most fundamental right.

Marchers stand here on the brink of violent suppression in their first attempt to cross Selma's Edmund Pettus Bridge, after which thousands of ordinary Americans will answer King's overnight call for a nonviolent pilgrimage to Selma. Three of them will be murdered, but the quest to march beyond Pettus Bridge will release waves of political energy from the human nucleus of freedom. The movement will transform national politics to win the vote. Selma will engage the world's conscience, strain the embattled civil rights coalition, and embroil King in negotiations with all three branches of the United States government. It will revive the visionary pragmatism of the American Revolution.

In adjacent Lowndes County, where no member of the black majority has dared to vote, sharecroppers will risk their lives to enter politics. Torment over distant Vietnam will destroy a historic collaboration between King and Lyndon Johnson at the signal divide from the 1960s—whether to pursue democracy by force of arms. Actors on all sides will confront persistent blind spots of violence and race. At their best, like the Founders, allies of the nonviolent movement will turn rulers and subjects into fellow citizens. Literally and figuratively, they still change the face of the country we inherit.

AT
CANAAN'S
EDGE

I

Selma:
The Last Revolution

CHAPTER 1

Warning

February 28, 1965

TERROR approached Lowndes County through the school system. J. T. Haynes, a high school teacher of practical agriculture, spread word from his white superiors that local Klansmen vowed to kill the traveling preacher if he set foot again in his local church. This to Haynes was basic education in a county of unspoiled beauty and feudal cruelty, where a nerve of violence ran beneath tranquil scenes of egret flocks resting among pastured Angus cattle. Across its vast seven hundred square miles, Lowndes County retained a filmy past of lynchings nearly unmatched, and Haynes tried to harmonize his scientific college methods with the survival lore of students three or four generations removed from Africa—that hens would not lay eggs properly if their feet were cold, that corn grew only in the silence of night, when trained country ears could hear it crackling up from the magic soil of Black Belt Alabama.

Lessons about the Klan arrived appropriately through the plainspoken Hulda Coleman, who had run the county schools since 1939 from a courthouse office she inherited from her father, the school superintendent and former sheriff. After World War II, when Haynes had confided to Coleman that the U.S. Army mustered him out from Morocco with final instructions to go home and vote as a deserving veteran, she explained that such notions did not apply to any colored man who valued his safety or needed his job in her classrooms. Haynes stayed on to teach in distinguished penury with his wife, Uralee, daughter of an engineer from the Southern land-grant colleges, loyally fulfilling joint assignment to what their Tuskegee professors euphemistically called a "problem county." Not for twenty years, until Martin Luther King stirred up the Selma voting rights movement one county to the west, did Negroes even discuss the franchise. There had been furtive talk since January about whether Haynes's 1945 inquiry or a similarly deflected effort by an aged blind preacher qualified as the last attempt to register, but no one remembered a ballot actually cast by any of the local Negroes who comprised 80 percent of the 15,000 residents in Lowndes County.

Despite ominous notices from Deacon Haynes, Rev. Lorenzo Harrison was keeping his fourth-Sunday commitment when the sound of truck engines roared to a stop outside Mt. Carmel Baptist on February 28, 1965. Panic swept through the congregation even before investigating deacons announced that familiar Klansmen were deployed outside with shotguns and rifles. Harrison gripped the pulpit and stayed there. He lived thirty miles away in Selma, where he knew people in the ongoing nonviolent campaign but was not yet involved himself, and now he switched his message from "How can we let this hope bypass us here?" to a plea for calm now that "they have brought the cup to the Lord's doorstep." He said he figured word would get back to white people that he had mentioned the vote in a sermon. Haynes reported that some of the Klansmen were shouting they'd get the out-of-county nigger preacher before sundown, whether the congregation surrendered him or not.

Harrison kept urging the choir to sing for comfort above the chaos of tears and moans, with worshippers cringing in the pews or hunched near windows to listen for noises outside, some praying for deliverance and some for strength not to forsake their pastor even if the Klan burned the whole congregation alive. There were cries about whether the raiding party would lay siege or actually invade the sanctuary, and Harrison, preaching in skitters to fathom what might happen, said he had been braced for phone threats, night riders—almost any persecution short of assault on a Sunday service—but now he understood the saying that bad surprises in Lowndes could outstrip your fears. Deacons said they recognized among the Klansmen a grocer who sometimes beat debtors in his store, a horseman who owned ten thousand acres and once shot a young sharecropper on the road because he seemed too happy to be drafted out of the fields into the Army, then with impunity had dumped the body of Bud Rudolph on his mother's porch. There was Tom Coleman, a highway employee and self-styled deputy who in 1959 killed Richard Lee Jones in the recreation area of a prison work camp. Such names rattled old bones. Sheriff Jesse Coleman, father of Klansman Tom and school superintendent Hulda, successfully defied the rare Alabama governor who called for state investigation in a notorious World War I lynching—of one Will Jones from a telegraph pole by an unmasked daytime crowd—by pronouncing the whole episode a matter of strictly local concern.

Noises outside the church unexpectedly died down. Uncertain why or how far the Klan had withdrawn, deacons puzzled over escape plans for two hundred worshippers with a handful of cars and no way to call for help—barely a fifth of the county's households had telephone service, nearly all among the white minority. A test caravan that ferried home sick or infirm walkers ran upon no ambush nearby, and a scout reported that the only armed pickup sighted on nearby roads belonged to a known non-Klansman. The task of evacuating Harrison fell to deacon John Hulett, whose namesake slave ancestor was said to have founded Mt. Carmel Baptist in the year Alabama gained statehood, 1819. Hulett, a former agriculture student under deacon Haynes, was considered a man of substance because he farmed his own land instead of sharecropping and once had voted as a city dweller in Birmingham. He recruited a deacon to drive Harrison's car, put the targeted reverend down low in the back seat of his own, and by late afternoon led a close convoy of all ten Mt. Carmel automobiles some fifteen miles north on Route 17 to deliver him to an emergency way station at Mt. Gillard Missionary Baptist Church on U.S. Highway 80, where Harrison's father was pastor.

Celebrations at the transfer were clandestine, urgent, and poignant, being still in Lowndes County. Until Hulett pulled away to attend the stranded congregation back at Mt. Carmel, Harrison kept muttering in terrified regret that one of them had to follow through on this voting idea no matter what. "If I have to leave, you take it," he told Hulett with a tinge of regret, as though cheating his own funeral.

Just ahead lay fateful March, with a crucible of choice for Martin Luther King and President Lyndon Johnson. The Ku Klux Klan would kill soon in Lowndes County, but its victims would be white people from Michigan and New Hampshire. Lowndes would inspire national symbols. It would change Negroes into black people, and deacon John Hulett would found a local political party renowned by its Black Panther emblem. Beyond wonders scarcely dreamed, Reverend Harrison would vote, campaign, and even hold elected office for years in Selma, but never again in the twentieth century would he venture within ten miles of Mt. Carmel Church.

CHAPTER 2

Scouts

February 28–March 1, 1965

SOME fifty miles from Mt. Carmel, on the other side of Selma, James Bevel was preaching against an outbreak of fear in Perry County that same Sunday. He recited from the twelfth chapter of Acts about how King Herod of Judea had "laid violent hands" upon the followers of the Jesus movement by killing "James the brother of John with the sword," and how Herod, seeing that his vengeance pleased the public, "proceeded to arrest Peter also." The modern Herod was Governor George Wallace of Alabama, said Bevel, and the modern martyr James was Jimmie Lee Jackson, whose name was bound in grief to the crowd at Zion's Chapel Methodist because he had walked with them from this same church in a night vigil that had been set upon by state troopers under Colonel Al Lingo. Even the segregationist *Alabama Journal* called the ensuing mayhem "a nightmare of State Police stupidity and brutality," as officers first shot out streetlights, disabled news cameras for cover, and beat reporters into the hospital or distant retreat, which compelled a *New York Times* correspondent to report the ensuing rampage by ear: "Negroes could be heard screaming and loud whacks rang through the square." An officer put two bullets into the stomach of Jimmie Lee Jackson, a twenty-six-year-old pulpwood worker whose application to register for the vote had been rejected five times.

"I'm not worried about James any more!" Bevel cried from the pulpit, two days after Jackson died as the first martyr of the current campaign for the vote. "I'm concerned about Peter." Only twenty-eight himself, Bevel sang out in the spitfire tenor of a gifted Baptist orator—more original than King, believed many admirers of both—wearing the denim overalls common to those who came into the nonviolent movement as students, and on his head a yarmulke that marked him for an eccentric identification with the Hebrew prophets. By Peter, Bevel meant all those left behind "to be cowed and coerced and beaten and even murdered," yet to prevail by spirit. He said he had gone out into the countryside only hours after the death on Friday and found Jackson's mother still bandaged from the attack and his battered grandfather, Cager Lee, still pronouncing himself fit for the next march. Bevel said that while he should be accustomed by now to such plainspoken courage, somehow the exposure to Jimmie Lee Jackson's family "is falling kind of hard on me." He shifted his biblical text to the story of Esther, a Queen of ancient Persia who had concealed her Hebrew identity until a courtier's plot moved her to "go unto the king, to make supplication unto him, and to make request before him for her people." Just so, said Bevel, voteless Negroes should honor Jimmie Lee Jackson by hazarding a mass pilgrimage of several days to petition the ruler of Alabama. "We must go to Montgomery and see the king!" he shouted. "Be prepared to walk to Montgomery! Be prepared to sleep on the highway!" He preached the congregation into full-throated shouts of call and response.

Bevel returned to Selma that evening and was repeating his challenge when Rev. Lorenzo Harrison burst through the doors at Brown Chapel AME. A commotion ran through the packed congregation of seven hundred until Rev. L. L. Anderson brought the fugitive into the pulpit to tell of being chased from his church in Lowndes County that day. Harrison clung to bravado on the edge of hysteria. He declared that he would have stayed on to face the threats—and would go back—except that his deacons had paid him three months' severance pay of a hundred dollars. "I said you ought not to be crying, you should be like men!" he shouted. "I told them I was not leaving because I was afraid, but because I can't fight white folks and black folks at the same time!" Then Harrison himself broke down.

Rev. Anderson reacted in a fury: "I want the world to know that in Alabama you are through running Negro preachers out of their pulpits!" He reminded the crowd that terror almost this extreme had paralyzed Selma itself until less than two years ago, during the national upheaval over King's 1963 demonstrations in Birmingham, when the young civil rights worker Bernard Lafayette had persuaded Anderson, over the strenuous objections of his deacons, to open Tabernacle Baptist for the first church meeting about the right to vote, and Sheriff Jim Clark had brought intimidating deputies right into the Tabernacle sanctuary. Despite this early trauma, the Selma movement had grown slowly into a thundering witness, with nearly four thousand demonstrators jailed since King arrived in January of 1965. Anderson vowed to carry this newfound courage into the harshest surrounding countryside.

In a cable to headquarters, FBI observers downplayed the excitement from Lowndes County as a dubious tale "inasmuch as Harris [sic] could furnish no description of any vehicle that the white people were traveling in and could not furnish any description of the whites that allegedly contacted the deacons in his church." More accurately, agents reported from private sources that James Bevel was distraught over Harrison's flight. Recently, he and colleague Andrew Young had turned up glimmers of interest as they scouted into Lowndes County along Highway 80, ducking into makeshift sharecroppers' stores with low tin roofs and walls of rough-cut timber, where chamber pots and drinking dippers hung for sale, telling nonplussed customers that "Dr. King asked us to come down here like Caleb and Joshua, to survey the land and look for the giants." Most contacts hastily vanished, and no church yet dared to open its doors for a meeting about the vote, but one deacon had promised "to do what I can." A farmer had said he heard talk of Dr. King on his television, and others warily had gauged whether local whites might tolerate registration if Negroes confined themselves to small groups. Now the preemptive raid showed that such timid interest was betrayed already to the Klan, and shock threatened to reseal the most isolated part of Alabama behind its firewall of legend at the county line. One dire consequence for Bevel was that the pragmatic Martin Luther King might not approve his desperate new resolve to walk fifty-four miles from Selma to Montgomery, through Big Swamp and the expanse of Lowndes County.

* * *

KING WAS returning to Alabama by way of Atlanta that Sunday, from a fund-raising excursion to California. "My few days here are a refreshing contrast to Selma," he told a crowd in Los Angeles, trying to look past the bubble of crisis that traveled with him. Because of death threats from callers who identified themselves with a newly formed Christian Nationalist State Army, a hundred Los Angeles police officers guarded his appearances at Temple Israel, Victory Baptist Church, and the Hollywood Palladium. News stories tracked a manhunt for the cultish group's leader, who was said to have stolen more than a half-ton of dynamite. Reporters pressed King to confirm rumors that Attorney General Nicholas Katzenbach had just warned him personally of other murder plots in Alabama, and they bombarded him with questions about the assassination of Malcolm X the previous Sunday in New York. Did King suspect a conspiracy? Had he made arrangement for succession if "something should happen" to him? Was he afraid that support for the doctrine of nonviolence was evaporating nationwide? In his sermon at Victory Baptist, King decried popular culture that made heroes of fast guns and raised even children to think of dissent by murder. "This disturbs me," he said, "because I know violence is not the answer."

A charged atmosphere both galvanized and polarized press attention. When King defined nonviolence in a Los Angeles interview as a leadership discipline for public conduct, and said he could in good conscience defend his family from attack in their home, a local Negro newspaper excoriated him as "the biggest hypocrite alive" for excluding his own loved ones from the suffering witness he prescribed, and declared that his nonviolence itself failed the Malcolm X standard of manhood. In New York, by contrast, the normally reserved *Times* reacted to Malcolm's death with open scorn for a "pitifully wasted" life marked by "ruthless and fanatical belief in violence."

King made his way through Atlanta back to Alabama for a few hours of domestic refuge at the home of Dr. Sullivan Jackson, Selma's only Negro dentist, where he knew he would find the small guest bedroom stocked for him with Jackson's spare clothes in his size, including suits and underwear, plus matching pajamas and a twin bed for his movement companion, Rev. Ralph Abernathy. King regularly teased himself for failing to persuade Jackson to join the nonviolent demonstrations— "I flunked on you, Sully"—but he valued the respite of well-worn hospitality. Dr. Jackson's wife, Jean, was a childhood friend of Abernathy's wife, Juanita; her great-aunt had been one of Coretta King's music teachers. College ties and pulpit connections extended social bonds among the families that cushioned King's reentry to the Selma campaign. He knew of Jimmie Lee Jackson's death, which doctors had predicted before King left for California, but now he learned of the newly proposed march to Montgomery. He knew to expect danger on his scheduled tour of the outlying rural areas on Monday morning,

March 1—one of only two days per month when Alabama law required courthouses to be open for voter registration—but now he learned of the Klan raid in Lowndes County. Aides argued that it was suicidal futility for King to venture there with personal appeals for white officials to accept Negro applicants, and some traced anticipated disaster on several fronts to the lunatic streak in James Bevel.

Doubts about Bevel were legion in King's inner circle. Bevel himself claimed to hear voices. His rival, Hosea Williams of Savannah, regularly denounced Bevel to King as unstable, even though Williams himself had pioneered night marches through Klan towns in a semitrance that inspired playful remarks about side effects from the metal plate still in his head, courtesy of war wounds in Germany. Wyatt Walker, chief of staff from 1960 until 1964, had resigned from movement service in part because King refused his insistent demands to fire Bevel for insubordinate mischief. King had indulged Bevel, saying the movement required a touch of madness—"maladjustment," he called it in sermons—in order to crusade against the entrenched structure of racial caste in America from a base of powerless, nonviolent Negroes. Indeed, King was in Selma largely on a quixotic leap urged upon him since the Birmingham church bombing eighteen months earlier, when Bevel and his wife, Diane Nash Bevel, had concocted a grand design to answer the heinous crime by securing the right to vote for Negroes. Vowing never to rest until they succeeded, the couple had made a life's pact out of anguish intensified by their pivotal roles in urging King's Birmingham movement to use students, adolescents, and finally small children in great numbers—girls mostly, many even younger than the four victims in the church bombing—in the May 1963 demonstrations that at last overwhelmed the national and international conscience about segregation. While King knew that Bevel walked a thin edge between prophetic genius and self-destruction, the record of astonishing nonviolent breakthroughs made him slow to reject any of Bevel's schemes as crazy or immature.

King encountered new rumbles of amateur diagnosis about Bevel, who had been discovered wandering Selma's streets in the predawn hours on Friday, evicted by his wife from their lodgings at the Torch Motel. In one sense, friends considered the evident crackup a minor surprise compared with the mismatched wedding three years earlier between the unabashedly skirt-chasing Mississippi Baptist preacher and the reserved Catholic puritan from Chicago—Hotspur and Joan of Arc.

Introduced in nonviolent college workshops, where Nash emerged from the sit-ins of 1960 as the iron-willed leader of Nashville's vanguard student organization, they had achieved by harrowing common experience a spiritual respect that overcame their sniping incompatibility. Through the birth of two children, Nash had remained oblivious to her husband's rascally effusions—blind to quips and rumors, dismissing one direct complaint from a movement colleague that Bevel had seduced his wife. In Selma, earlier in February, when Sheriff Clark had boiled over against the voting rights demonstrations and punched Bevel with his nightstick, then had him jailed, his cell stripped bare and hosed with cold water at night until Bevel ran a high fever from viral pneumonia, Nash mounted a telephone blitz to the Justice Department that prompted Clark to transfer the prisoner to a hospital, where Nash found him shackled and chained to the bed. Another round of calls and door banging by Nash secured Bevel's release, leaving friends puzzled anew over her ferocious loyalty and the mysterious personal chemistry of opposites.

Now King found the couple fractured, reticent in shock. Each insisted that personal casualties were incidental to the larger campaign for the vote, and other members of King's staff knew little as yet about the precipitating incident late Thursday night when Nash had found a baby-sitter for the children and slipped into the back of a nightspot to observe Bevel keeping one of his assignations rather than his promise to come home. Later, when she contradicted his alibi about car trouble, Bevel had struck her, in the face. "How dare you, lie to me and then hit me!" Nash shouted, so angry that she remained dry-eyed all night, which surprised her as a departure from her habit of crying privately through anxiety before demonstrations. She went instead to a lawyer, but the harsh realities of divorce made her hesitate. Nash remained partly under the spell of Bevel, who, always on the offensive, folded the conflict into a teaching tool for their ongoing commitment to answer the Birmingham church bombing. Citing Nash herself, ironically, he presented nonviolence as a kind of nuclear science by which truth properly applied could release stupendous healing energy in the larger society.

King knew there was calculated political strategy in Bevel's method, beyond his mystical exuberance and personal demons, and that the real target of the proposed journey to Montgomery was not Governor Wallace but the national government in Washington. For nine years now, since the Montgomery bus boycott of 1955–56, King's cohorts had experimented with the spiritual and political arts required to nurture a small inspiration, such as the arrest of Rosa Parks, into a movement of sufficient scope to make America "rise up and live out the true meaning of its creed," as he put it in his signature "dream" speech. For King, this meant steering a course that took account not only of Bevel's state of mind and the residual strength of the jailgoers in Selma, plus the likely effect of Lorenzo Harrison's flight into the mass meeting, but also the response from national leaders a world apart.

* * *

BY FAR the most critical figure for him to read was President Lyndon Johnson, whose relations with King contrasted sharply with President John F. Kennedy's sympathetic, sophisticated aloofness. Whereas Kennedy had charmed King while keeping him at a safe distance, harping in private on the political dangers of alleged subversives in the civil rights movement, Johnson in the White House was intensely personal but unpredictable—treating King variously to a Texas bear hug of shared dreams or a towering, wounded snit. After the assassination in Dallas, Johnson had burst with urgent intimacy in a telephone call, promising to show King "how worthy I'm going to try to be of all of your hopes," and the new President indeed played skillfully upon national mourning to enact the landmark Civil Rights Act of 1964. Then Johnson had turned suddenly coy and insecure. Having consciously alienated the century-old segregationist base of his Democratic Party, he refused to see King, pretended he had nothing to do with his own nominating convention, and lashed out privately at both King's Negroes and white Southerners. Just as suddenly, after his landslide election in November, Johnson had rushed past King's congratulations to confide a crowning ambition to win the right for Negroes to vote. "That will answer seventy percent of your problems," he had said in January, rehearsing at breakneck speed speeches he urged on King to dramatize the idea that every American should "have a right to vote just like he has a right to fight, and that we just extend it whether it's a Negro or whether it's a Mexican or who it is." King, on his heels, had mumbled approval. He did not mention that he was headed to Selma for that very purpose—knowing that Johnson would not welcome his tactics of street protest—and the President kept pressing him to aim higher than conventional civil rights goals such as a Negro Cabinet officer. "There's not gonna be anything, though, doctor, as effective as all of 'em votin'," Johnson had told King. "That'll get you a message that all the eloquence in the world won't bring. . . . I think this will be bigger, because it will do things that even that '64 act couldn't do."

More recently, Johnson's mood had turned prickly again. When a haggard King placed an ad in the February 5, 1965, *New York Times*— THIS IS SELMA, ALABAMA. THERE ARE MORE NEGROES IN JAIL WITH ME THAN THERE ARE ON THE VOTING ROLLS—and posted bond to confer in Washington, White House aides had scolded him for presuming upon Johnson's schedule, adding to the grave burdens of state. Johnson had set for King an appointment with underlings, then concocted an "accidental" meeting at which he insisted upon his prerogative to choose the content and moment for any voting rights bill. This last encounter had put King back on edge with Johnson. Before he left California on Sunday, February 28, King called intermediaries to urge that prominent citizens send telegrams on his behalf, beseeching Johnson for federal protection of his life against death threats the next day in Alabama. He had no way of knowing that FBI agents overheard his call through a wiretap on the phone of his lawyer in New York, Clarence Jones, or that FBI Director J. Edgar Hoover reacted to the intercept by maneuvering to escape such duty. Nor could King realize how sharply Johnson felt the tenterhooks of two fateful decisions that same weekend.

The President ordered his staff to evaluate a proposal to suspend local literacy tests, and to provide for direct registration by federal officials, in those areas of the country where Negroes voted drastically under their percentage of the population. Senior speechwriter Horace Busby promptly warned that white Southern voters would deplore such drastic measures as "a return to Reconstruction." More broadly, a stand for the rights of poorly educated and illiterate Negroes "will be unpopular far outside the South" as a "most radical intervention" in state affairs, Busby argued, and would jeopardize generations of accumulated public trust by touching the hot-button fear of government domination. Busby's objections circulated on Sunday, and Attorney General Nicholas Katzenbach wrote a pained reply. Katzenbach himself strongly opposed any new civil rights initiative as premature. He believed the country had just begun to digest the law of 1964—moving toward gradual compliance in public accommodations but still segregated, now illegally, in nearly all schools and employment sectors, including the news media and government itself. He feared that another controversial race law would undermine the daunting task of enforcement, and meanwhile would snarl the Congress for months of a second consecutive year. Reluctantly, however, Katzenbach turned aside from Busby's tempting position that it was wiser to outlaw the "abuse" by state officials of their rightful duty to set standards for voters. Such abuse was forbidden already by statutes across two centuries, he said, but local officials consistently delayed, thwarted, and evaded prosecution by the Justice Department in dozens of recent marathon cases. He saw only a remote chance to win effective remedy under arrangements that "leave control of voting machinery in state hands," given the pervasive obstacles in Southern statehouses and courtrooms. "Therefore," Katzenbach concluded, "while I agree with Mr. Busby that the political consequences of the proposed message are serious, I see no alternative." If Johnson really meant to secure the right of Negroes to vote, he must try to extend the reach of national government and trust posterity to judge whether the result enhanced freedom or tyranny.

*   *   *

KATZENBACH'S MEMORANDUM landed on Monday at the White House, where officials bemoaned a simultaneous choice about whether American power should and could shape political order halfway around the world. In a cocoon of official secrecy, President Johnson was ending his own tormented war of decision before most people recognized anything of significance about distant Vietnam. "The game now is in the fourth quarter and it's about 78 to nothing," he had lamented on Friday to Secretary of Defense Robert McNamara. Beneath public assurances of stability, Johnson faced a bleak reality that guerrilla armies were defeating the partitioned South, and would unify Vietnam under Communist rule unless the United States swiftly intervened. Worse, his military experts advised that a commitment of blood and treasure could stave off immediate disaster in South Vietnam—but little more. Classified military projections stubbornly refuted the ingrained presumption that a flick of American power would prevail in backward Vietnam, and strategic plans failed to predict lasting success by warfare of any design, scale, or duration. Johnson, trapped between looming humiliation and futile war, erupted in moments of primal fury against resignation to Communist victory. This to him was spineless surrender and political suicide for the leader of a great power, because American voters would "forgive you for anything except being weak." Yet he also recoiled from a vision of bloody stalemate, saying, "this is a terrible thing we're getting ready to do," and that the prospect of sending American soldiers into Asia "makes the chills run up my back."

Bad weather still delayed the start of sustained bombing against North Vietnam, destined to last eight years, which Johnson had approved secretly on February 13 amid warnings of impending collapse in the South. (It was this crisis that had shortened his patience for King's visit from Selma.) In the interim, another military coup by South Vietnamese allies installed the latest of six chronically unstable governments over the past eighteen months. Nerves tightened, the President made the best of a decision no longer deferred. "Now we're off to bombing those people and we're over that hurdle," he told McNamara privately. "And I don't think anything is gonna be as bad as losing, and I don't see any way of winning, but I would sure want to feel that every person that had an idea, that his suggestion was fully explored."

On Monday, March 1, when McNamara explained the latest weather postponement and obtained clearance to "go ahead tonight" with the first of the new air attacks, he found the President transfixed by a report in the *New York Times* of plans for these continuous air strikes as well as ground troops to follow. "Am I wrong in saying that this appears to be almost traitorous?" Johnson asked shortly before noon. News about Vietnam decisions risked disclosure of the mountainous doubt and brutally frank pessimism inside his government—with Johnson and most of his advisers skeptical of airpower in this guerrilla war, with General Maxwell Taylor, ambassador in South Vietnam and America's most illustrious active soldier, warning sharply against the introduction of American troops. Almost any candor about actual deliberations would erase the appearance of sovereign control, violating Johnson's first rule of successful politics. He ached to introduce the conflict matter-of-factly, confidently, and even as quietly as possible, and pleaded with McNamara that Monday morning to track down those leaking war news to the press. "Somebody ought to be removed, Bob," he said in a voice choked with emotion. "I just, you just can't, you can't exist this kind of thing . . . you just can't exist with it."

By then, a draining twelve hours since Los Angeles, King began registration day in Alabama with an explicit prophecy of relief in the national arena. "We are going to bring a voting bill into being in the streets of Selma, Alabama," he told a late-morning crowd at Brown Chapel AME Church, the twin-steepled gathering point for demonstrations in Selma. "President Johnson has a mandate from the American people." Then he led an orderly double file of some three hundred volunteers on the familiar short walk through downtown Selma—a left turn from the church, two short blocks south on Sylvan Street, right on Alabama Avenue for five blocks to the Dallas County courthouse. Sheriff's deputies blocked the head of the line at the steps, and across the street, buffered behind a line of city police officers, clumps of reporters and bystanders waited to see what reception lay in store. Sheriff Clark had employed tactics of selective or mass arrest, elaborate stalls, and various forms of harassment including one surprise dispersal of some two hundred adolescent Negro demonstrators by forced march behind cattle prods for three miles, out beyond the city limits to the Cosby-Carmichael gravel pit. A cold rain fell steadily this Monday on observers and demonstrators alike. King, wearing a raincoat and felt hat, passed words of encouragement down the line of aspiring voters along the sidewalk.

*   *   *

DURING THIS wait in Selma, a slow accumulation of Negroes caused a hush to fall around the Lowndes County courthouse. As many as thirty-seven conspicuously nervous citizens arrived to mingle outside in the rain, unsure how or where to find the registrars and hesitant to enter without knowing. People stared from windows around the courthouse square. The Negroes formed a volunteer delegation of five that wandered the imposing halls, hats off, pausing at doorways. One of the white secretaries spoke to an office companion, asking, "Who is that little fella who keeps walking through the courthouse?" This gave John Hulett an opening to inquire about the registrars. He received no reply, but white men soon appeared to shoo the group back outside with a notepad and instructions to have all who wanted to register write down their names and come back in two weeks.

The Negro group huddled under the eaves for furtive debate. Were these really the registrars? If so, why did familiar white men including car dealer Carl Golson decline to identify themselves by name or title? They "refused to know their own selves," later recalled Elzie McGill, a fifty-nine-year-old railroad worker who came with his daughter Lillian from the White Hall area around Mt. Gillard Church, where preacher Lorenzo Harrison had taken refuge the previous day. McGill did not know Hulett or his carload from Mt. Carmel Baptist very well—indeed, many in White Hall thought Negroes from Hulett's Gordonville area down Highway 17 spoke with an odd accent. They had been able to agree across community lines to show up this registration day in spite of the Klan scare, like regular citizens, with no outside civil rights workers to provoke the courthouse powers more than necessary. Such caution seemed especially prudent after the officials made goading remarks about whether the Negroes expected Martin Luther King to be the current local voter who would stand for their "good blood," meaning vouch for their character, as local law required for each new registrant. This barrier helped confine Negro voting to the mists of faith for things unseen, which allowed for disagreement about the notepad. Some worried that those who signed would be marked for retribution. Others said they were identified already by standing there in daylight, and that non-signers would be targeted as defiant, or as weak. Emma and Matthew Jackson of White Hall led a majority who signed, and Hulett's small delegation returned inside to deliver the notepad so they could leave.

* * *

In SELMA, where the line of potential registrants stretched more than a block around on Lauderdale Street by early afternoon, King knocked on the closed courthouse door and beseeched Sheriff Clark for shelter from the rain. Reporters pressed forward to hear some of their exchange. "In the name of humanity," King called out, "we are asking you to let them come inside." He said there was room for them to wait in the corridors and stairwells. "In the name of common sense," Clark replied, "they will have to stay out there until their numbers are called." The numbers, mandated by federal court, were the recent fruit of legal pounding by lawyers from the civil rights movement and the Justice Department, designed to prevent manipulation in the order of service and to discourage all-day filibusters by the registrars. Sheriff Clark improvised this day by calling out numbers for the registrar's office in a slurred whisper, then announcing that those who missed the call forfeited their number and must go to the back of a separate line for a new one. He dueled the movement staff in logistical maneuver until King led most of the sodden crowd in retreat back to Brown Chapel. No one knew whether any new applicants would be accepted as registered voters, if so, how many, or how long it would take to find out. These were separate, uphill battles. On balance, however, reporters judged the day's effort a success for the demonstrators. There were no arrests or casualties, and 266 people managed to finish the complicated application process—twice the previous record.

A small caravan of reporters and federal observers followed King out of Selma for an afternoon pilgrimage to outlying areas, first south to the Wilcox County seat of Camden, which had been named in 1842 for the city in South Carolina. Many of the early Wilcox settlers brought from South Carolina the zeal of its famous "fire-eaters," who championed slavery and secession toward the Civil War in an era when one isolated Unionist balefully observed that his state was "too small to be a republic and too large to be an insane asylum." Although no Negro had voted in Wilcox County since an accommodating barber* in 1901, the white minority still raised apoplectic cries from time to time. One prominent local senator issued a proclamation that the racial voting margin— "2,250 whites registered, AND NOT ONE NEGRO"—would be unsafe against "the onrushing black horde" without new character requirements, which he advocated as "our only hope for white supremacy, our only hope for peace, our only protection against a race war." Ghosts of yesteryear remained close in a county that had no electric lights until 1925, where temperament flickered between homespun gentility and raw tribal aggression. Ben Miller, elected on an anti-Klan platform as "the sturdy oak of Wilcox," took a cow with him to supply milk at the governor's mansion in 1930. Four years later into the Depression, a posse of mounted whites liquidated chattel liens in Wilcox County by seizing every crop, chicken, wagon, and plow from sixty-eight families of Negro sharecroppers, then setting them adrift on the Alabama River. Some of those who survived still never had seen a water faucet when King arrived at the Camden courthouse in 1965. He walked along a line of two hundred Negroes waiting in the rain—"Doin' all right. How you feeling?"—and sought out P. C. "Lummie" Jenkins, county sheriff since 1937. Voluble and commanding, boasting that he had never carried a gun, Jenkins fretted about wasted time for everybody. To be registered, he said, each applicant needed not only to pass the literacy and citizenship tests but also to present a current local voter who would vouch for good character.

"Well, how about you acting as voucher?" asked King.

"I'm not allowed," Jenkins replied. Elected officials were barred in order to avoid conflicts over vote trading.

"Mind if I look around town for vouchers?" asked King.

"Inquire around," Jenkins invited. He called King "preacher," and candidly advised that it might not "look right" for anyone to sponsor these new voters.

---

* The barber, Frank Beck, defended segregation during the uproar over Booker T. Washington's dinner invitation from Theodore Roosevelt. By accepting, Beck was quoted to say, Washington flirted with social equality and "let the President tempt him to walk in paths untried. Goodbye, Booker!" A white newspaper defended Beck's last, lone Negro vote as a safe reward, saying he "always votes the Democratic ticket."

Practiced, jovial banter masked the edge of tension. One awed woman would summarize in her words King's quiet plea for them to put away anything that could cause harm or excuse violence: "Don't even carry a hair clamp in your head." Those in line eyed the fifty wet Alabama state troopers who stood vigil over them with guns and nightsticks, many knowing that a similar detachment had run violently amok in nearby Perry County when Jimmie Lee Jackson was shot. King himself was keenly aware of intensified threats against him, partly from Attorney General Katzenbach's confidential notice that two riflemen intended to shoot him on his previous visit to the counties around Selma. He climbed a stoop at the jail to pay tribute to those who "turned out in the rain" where no Negro had voted for decades. "This is a magnificent thing," he told those in line. Only ten were allowed to apply for registration, but this was a seismic number in Wilcox County. "Keep walking, children," King called out in his familiar closing from the spirituals. "Don'cha get weary."

* * *

THERE WAS no public spectacle at the last stop. The sleepy courthouse lawn was drained of everything but fear when King arrived at Hayneville, where John Hulett's group had been sent away hours ago. Lowndes County shared a South Carolina heritage with adjacent Wilcox but ranked higher on the intimidation scale. The county seat was named for Robert Y. Hayne, once South Carolina's junior U.S. senator to John C. Calhoun, the county itself for South Carolina congressman William Lowndes, namesake relative of Alabama's own fire-eating Senator William Lowndes Yancey, who in 1848 had advanced a Southern demand to extend slaveholding rights throughout newly settled territories. Racial solidarity remained a prime civic duty among local whites, resting on memories and practices that sometimes were peculiar or invisible to outsiders. No merchant in Lowndes County would sell Marlboro cigarettes or Falstaff beer, for instance, because of a report from the 1950s—unnoticed or long forgotten everywhere else—that the companies once made donations to the National Association for the Advancement of Colored People (NAACP). Mysteriously, the lone official who halted King's party in the courthouse corridor refused to give his name or title. He did allow that other Negroes might have come to the courthouse on their own that day. If they did, he added, they wanted nothing to do with outsiders.

King replied that local people had asked for help, but were frightened. "We had heard that if we work here, there would be violence," he said.

"I heard there would be violence, too," said the man. "And you can agitate that. Everywhere you have been, there has been violence."

King sparred about seeking justice instead of trouble. As minutes passed, his persistently mild words echoed down the hallway and the man's temper seemed to rise. Asked about religion, he said he was a Methodist but demanded to know what Christianity had to do with the vote. Asked about the county's voting procedures, he said testily that the information was reserved for county citizens.

"We don't understand," said King.

"You are damned dumb, then, if you don't understand," the man said angrily. Photographers snapped a picture of him pointing an index finger closely at King's nose as he denounced him for interfering where he had no business. "None of you can help the Negroes of Lowndes County," he said to Abernathy, Andrew Young, and observers close by. After he declared the courthouse closed and walked away, reporters identified the pointer as car dealer Carl Golson, a former state senator and one of three county registrars.

King returned safely from the outlying counties late Monday afternoon, March 1, completing a circuit of better than a hundred miles. He crossed the Alabama River over the Edmund Pettus Bridge into Selma on U.S. Highway 80, by the same route that Lorenzo Harrison had fled from Lowndes County into the previous night's mass meeting. The deposed minister was fired from his regular job as a bush-hog operator for a construction company.

FBI agents cabled headquarters that their personal observations "revealed no incidents throughout day." They reported that King left Sullivan Jackson's house after supper for Brown Chapel, arriving at 8:28 P.M. Monday evening, but he did not follow his usual practice of slipping into the pastor's study before making an entrance to the mass meeting. James Bevel was exhorting a crowd of five hundred to be ready for a foot pilgrimage all the way to Montgomery, and King debated how and when to respond from the pulpit. Still undecided whether to embrace or deflect the call for such prolonged, vulnerable exposure on Alabama highways, he hesitated for six minutes on the steps outside the church, then climbed back in his car to catch a night flight from the Montgomery airport.

CHAPTER 3

Dissent

March 2–5, 1965

KING landed in Washington for Tuesday's hundred-year anniversary observance at Howard University, which had been chartered under the Freedmen's Bureau and named for its first appointed head under Abraham Lincoln, Union General Oliver Howard. In full academic regalia, he delivered a reprise on his Nobel Peace Prize lecture from December—urgently recommending nonviolence to combat what he called mankind's three related scourges of racial injustice, poverty, and war. He spoke broadly on survival and moral progress in a shrinking world, and reacted to sketchy reports of that day's first massive U.S. air strike under a new policy of sustained military attack upon North Vietnam. "I know that President Johnson has a serious problem here, and naturally I am sympathetic to that," King told the Howard convocation, but said he saw no solution in violence. "The war in Vietnam is accomplishing nothing."

King's first public comment about Vietnam, like his speech at Howard, escaped notice in a press climate that looked to him for confrontational stories about race in the South. Attention to the war itself remained muted by later standards: a one-inch story noted that two deaths that week brought the number of Americans killed through five years of military support to 402, including 124 who perished in accidents. In some respects, neither King nor President Johnson wanted to advertise inner conflict about strategy. Johnson made sure that the United States and South Vietnam made no formal announcement of the new bombing policy, nor of the actual strike earlier that day by 104 Air

Force jets, six of which were lost, and reporters were obliged to piece together the story indirectly. King, for his part, did not mention his apprehensions about the proposed march out of Selma any more than he dwelled on the forty policemen who stood guard around him on the Howard campus because of numerous death threats received in Washington. If he was not safe at a Negro college in Lincoln's capital, what could be gained by an exposed hike through rural Alabama?

Privately, King spent Tuesday in the capital seeking counsel about his dilemma. He arranged to meet with his Northern advisers later that week and sought another audience with President Johnson. Events pushed him to decide, but disputes and confusion made him hesitate. Bad weather delayed his return flight through Atlanta to Montgomery on Wednesday morning, March 3, and he circled in the air while two thousand mourners filed past Jimmie Lee Jackson's casket at Brown Chapel in Selma. King missed the morning service there, as well as the thirty-mile procession by hearse and caravan northwest from Selma to Perry County, but reached Jackson's hometown of Marion in time to join the afternoon funeral procession that moved into Zion's Chapel Methodist through an overflow crowd of nearly a thousand Negroes standing outside. Some four hundred people were packed into the tiny structure of rough-cut planks, built for half that number. Jackson's mother, Viola, and his eighty-two-year-old grandfather, Cager Lee, wept openly in the front pews, still bearing signs of violence from the attack on the march out of this church two weeks earlier.

King was accustomed to funerals, and normally kept his trained composure in the pulpit, but a correspondent noted that "a tear glistened from the corner of his eye as he rose to speak." Recycling the text of his brief eulogy for the young girls killed by dynamite in their Birmingham church, he parceled out blame for the funeral among the hatred in some segregationists, the passivity in moderates, the "timidity" of the federal government, and "the cowardice of every Negro" who "stands on the sidelines in the struggle for justice." He acknowledged the unfathomable depth of the moment—"At times life is hard, hard as crucible steel"—and reached high and wide for consolation. "God still has a way of wringing good out of evil," he said. "History has proven over and over again that unmerited suffering is redemptive." Finally, King added a personal tribute with a conclusion that also addressed his own dilemma. "Jimmie Lee Jackson is speaking to us from the casket," he said, "and he is saying to us that we must substitute courage for caution. . . . We must not be bitter, and we must not harbor ideas of retaliating with violence. We must not lose faith in our white brothers."

King recessed behind the pallbearers out through the courthouse square, past the café where Jackson had been shot, out of town on muddy roads to Heard Cemetery. "More than 1,000 walked three miles in rain to bury him on a pine hill," the *New York Times* recorded simply of Jackson's interment. Some of those in the long line had marched in the Selma campaign since January, including nine-year-old Sheyann Webb, whose example had melted the fearful nonparticipation of her parents. "What time they be marchin'?" her father asked her at last, and John Webb walked memorably this day in a new suit so thin that rain rinsed its blue dye all through his white shirt. The humblest citizens of two counties mingled in a burial procession that stretched nearly half a mile, confronting reminders of lethal, semiofficial violence in such numbers as to invite greater leaps of faith. King passed word to schedule the fifty-four-mile march from Selma to Montgomery. He set the starting date for Sunday, March 7, only four days away, and Bevel announced the first detailed plans that night in Selma. Again, however, King decided not to speak at the mass meeting. To give himself some wiggle room about Lowndes County, he told reporters that he might break away from the four-day pilgrimage and rejoin its conclusion in Montgomery.

* * *

KING RUSHED to catch a plane for New York, leaving behind the frantic logistical preparations and ferocious debates that were triggered by his commitment to the Sunday march. Staff members of the Student Nonviolent Coordinating Committee (SNCC) branded his announcement another high-handed betrayal by King of their working agreement to make joint decisions. At a crisis staff meeting in Selma, Fay Bellamy voiced the prevailing opinion that the proposed march would be a publicity stunt. Bellamy was twenty-six. Gripped by news images of the Birmingham church bombing, she had made her way east from San Francisco in search of the movement, and in January had secured her first field assignment among roughly a dozen SNCC workers added to Selma since King opened his campaign there, grabbing space willy-nilly on cots and bedrolls in SNCC's Freedom House at 2021 Eugene Street, with no telephone and virtually no heat, drawing a weekly SNCC paycheck of $9.64 when lucky. She and other newcomers absorbed SNCC's five-year institutional memory of subdued grievance against King—

that he reaped public glory from their sacrifice as shock troops since the sit-ins and Freedom Rides, that his hit-and-run celebrity priesthood undercut their long-term efforts to build local leadership. By natural temperament, or out of emotional exhaustion from prolonged exposure to suffering, they also chafed against the nonviolent doctrines SNCC shared publicly with King and his preacher-based Southern Christian Leadership Conference (SCLC). In February, Bellamy had introduced herself to Malcolm X at Tuskegee and boldly importuned him to discuss alternatives to nonviolence in Selma, scaring people for and against the movement. She and most SNCC colleagues, having fought rearguard battles against the innovation of night marches before Jimmie Lee Jackson was killed in one, saw King's plan as an invitation to punishment on a grand scale. Lacking the means to stop it, however, they were sharply divided about whether to split the movement by public dissent, and tactical arguments raged until project director Silas Norman arranged for the national officers of SNCC to address the emergency issue Friday night in Atlanta.

* * *

IN MONTGOMERY, where an opposing war council convened behind closed doors, Governor George Wallace and his deputies, especially Colonel Al Lingo of the state troopers, debated a surprise suggestion to let the march go forward unmolested. Staff advisers explained the scheme as a mousetrap for King. They proposed to lure his group onto the highway and then stop all vehicular traffic between Selma and Montgomery behind trooper roadblocks. Not even reporters would be allowed to follow, except on foot, and King's ragtag pilgrims would find themselves cut off from motorized support or relief, facing fifty miles of hostile country. Press secretary Bill Jones confidently predicted that the Negroes would abandon voting rights and limp back to Selma as the "laughingstock of the nation." The Alabama officials warmed to the propaganda value of defeating King with a shrewdly tailored version of what he wanted, and chortled over refinements such as temporary signs to mark Highway 80 as a "Jefferson Davis footpath" for these pedestrians. By midnight Thursday, Wallace approved deceptive news leaks that Alabama would *not* allow Sunday's march to leave Selma. This feint might induce Negroes to show up low on water and travel supplies, expecting no march, and it gave Wallace a strong position for maneuver if he changed his mind about the laughingstock option.

* * *

IN NEW YORK, at 12:31 P.M. on Thursday, March 4, FBI surveillance agents carefully noted that Stanley Levison rode an elevator to the forty-third floor of the Americana Hotel and walked into Room 4323, where Andrew Young and King's travel aide Bernard Lee were waiting. The agents recorded that King himself arrived at 12:56 from a speaking engagement before a federation of Jewish women, followed by King's lawyer Clarence Jones at 1:25 and actor Ossie Davis at 3:20. Since Saturday, when Davis had delivered the principal eulogy for Malcolm X, agents had intercepted conversations over the wiretapped phone lines of Jones in which Davis worried about threats against King's life in Alabama, saying, "We cannot afford to lose him at this juncture." These spare gleanings were flashed to headquarters and distilled from the FBI point of view into an overnight warning to President Johnson that forthcoming requests for federal protection of King would be subversive in origin. Director Hoover's note included boilerplate allegations: Clarence Jones had reportedly belonged to a suspect college youth group, and a source in 1963 had called Ossie Davis a Communist.

A separate letter from Hoover, hand-delivered to the White House and classified secret, reported that King was resuming contact with Stanley Levison a year and a half after breaking off all communication under heavy pressure from President Kennedy. Hoover had source information that Levison had been a Communist fund-raiser in the early 1950s, which he preserved secretly as the official predicate not only for the pressure through Kennedy and for the authorized wiretaps on Jones, King, and others who knew Levison, but also for Hoover's extralegal harassment of King. Alerted by wiretaps, for instance, FBI headquarters only the day before had instructed the head of the Boston office to try to scuttle a "Martin Luther King Day" scheduled for April by arranging a derogatory briefing about King for Governor John Volpe of Massachusetts, "on a highly confidential basis and with the proviso that under no circumstances may there ever be any attribution to the FBI."

FBI surveillance agents lacked an opportunity to plant microphone bugs in the Americana walls that could record these two-day deliberations behind closed doors. Wiretaps on telephones missed celebrations over the return of Levison to the inner circle, but they did pick up undercurrents of friction as the volunteer advisers readjusted to King's closest white friend in the movement. Since February, when he insisted that the advisers "clear" Levison back into their informal councils—saying he still regretted giving in to the government's arbitrary and unprincipled banishment, whether or not it helped secure passage of the 1964 Civil Rights Act—King had ached to resume his late-night telephone chats. Levison, a lifelong activist and semiretired investor, was bluntly straightforward and yet avuncular by nature. "Escalation [in Southeast Asia] in the manner recently conducted is more suited to small boys than great powers," he advised President Johnson two weeks earlier in a typically brief, handwritten letter. "Walter Lippman[n] is one hundred percent right in asserting that our national interests are not critically involved in the jungles of Viet Nam, particularly since our naval power is unhampered off its shores. Your election was characterized by the clearest mandate for peace since World War II. Please execute it fearlessly."

Clarence Jones arrived at the Americana with his own draft letter for President Johnson "to express my vigorous dissent and alarm over the conduct of present United States foreign policy in South Vietnam." Jones differed markedly from Levison in style—more formal and polished, from upbringing in a chauffeur's household and hard-won training in entertainment law—yet gravitated to him in the current alignment of the Northern council. Assuming that Wallace would stop Sunday's march, which could not thereafter reach Montgomery without federal intervention, the advisers heatedly debated ways to apportion risk and hardship among people from different worlds. Should they postpone for safety while seeking a federal protective order? Or try to march, perhaps to rally support by enduring another mass incarceration, and then go to court?

Levison opposed the quest of his "twin" Jewish adviser, Harry Wachtel, to become the designated liaison with Attorney General Katzenbach, in a side dispute that awkwardly followed Wachtel's assignment to cajole Levison back from exile. Granted, King's Washington representative Walter Fauntroy was out of his depth on legislative matters before Congress, but Wachtel was too eager to replace the young Negro minister rather than develop Fauntroy's voice alongside Wachtel's influence as a Wall Street law partner. Together with Jones, Levison similarly criticized Bayard Rustin's tendency of late to dismiss student complaints about the Selma movement as naive or obstructionist. With Rustin, architect of the 1963 March on Washington, Wachtel pushed King toward a larger role in national politics while Levison and Jones tilted for patchwork unity in the protest movement. Where one side saw colleagues limiting King, the other thought he was being used.

King chose a path through the counsel of strong-willed advisers. He took Walter Fauntroy with him late Friday afternoon to the White House, past a line of uniformed American Nazis on Pennsylvania Avenue with picket signs—"Down With Martin Luther Koon," "Who Needs Niggers"—to a contrasting welcome in the Fish Room of the West Wing. Then, alone with President Johnson, he followed Wachtel's advice to argue that any effective voting rights bill must include an iron-clad provision to replace local officials with registrars accountable to the President. Johnson agreed that legislation was a better route to securing Negro voting rights than a proposed constitutional amendment, which would be slow, difficult to ratify, and redundant to the existing Fifteenth Amendment, but he declined to go beyond his public promise to submit a voting rights "message" to Congress. King, for his part, did not ask the President explicitly to submit a new bill, nor did he ask for federal marshals to protect the march on Sunday, so as not to force Johnson to ask for postponements and conditions, or to oppose such a protest altogether. Instead, King emerged from the White House Friday evening to emphasize carefully that he and Johnson had shared their respective troubles and come tantalizingly close to a common agenda. "The President told me that Senator [Everett] Dirksen had made a commitment to support a voting rights bill," King told reporters of the pivotal Republican leader, but he could not say what bill or when. He missed his scheduled flight home that night and scrambled for a later one. Airline sources told FBI agents that King had a reservation from Atlanta to Montgomery at 8:35 A.M. Sunday, in time to reach Selma for the march.

* * *

IN THE basement of Frazier's soul food café, near its Atlanta headquarters, the national executive committee of SNCC convened before ten o'clock Friday night with a convoluted debate about the rules of procedure—bylaws, credentials, determination of a quorum, standing to vote—that ran well past midnight, punctuated by a shout of "Who the hell is Robert, anyway?" from Courtland Cox, who noted wryly that the author of the book on parliamentary order was not a SNCC member. For five years, as they confronted race questions that long befuddled elder statesmen, the young SNCC activists had made decisions by informal consensus born of a common willingness to go to jail and risk their lives, which also winnowed out frivolous leadership claims. Cox, a veteran strategist out of Howard University, lamented a loss of family camaraderie that had accelerated since SNCC's 1964 Freedom Summer project in Mississippi. Disagreements festered over whether the project was a model for revolutionary change or a mistaken venture into national politics, and internal governance was paralyzed by collisions of numbers and ideology—how to apportion the influence of burgeoning staff members against the hoped-for participation of the poorest Negroes. Nearly a hundred of the summer volunteers had been inspired to stay on, which more than doubled the permanent staff and threatened to swamp SNCC with mostly white students from Northern colleges.

Beneath SNCC's vanguard devotion to racial harmony, anxieties about group control were concealed as issues of class or geography, and Bob Moses, one of the few SNCC leaders who addressed internal racial hostilities, had vanished in a cloud of paradox since his stunning withdrawal announcement at the previous meeting. Moses was the anti-King within SNCC. By immersing himself for years in the persecution of rural Mississippi, and subordinating his Harvard education to folk wisdom, he acquired stature that defined grassroots SNCC culture. By speaking softly, he gained a voice within SNCC far stronger than King's classical oratory. By eschewing the priestly hierarchy of King's leadership, he became a quiet icon who could pull off Freedom Summer—a desperate gamble to pierce national conscience through the sacrifice of elite students. By lifting up the innate capacities of all citizens, he helped discover pathbreaking democratic leaders such as an unlettered orator from Mississippi, Fannie Lou Hamer, but at least five colleagues followed his example to their martyrdom in Mississippi despite his insistence that they all make their own decisions. While classmates finished their degrees back on campus, Moses carried the moral weight of these losses plus the heavy expectations that he alone could bridge the growing fissures between sharecroppers, saints, and sharp-tongued dialecticians—until, breaking down in the midst of a February SNCC debate, he tried to escape his charisma by conducting a mysterious final ceremony of wine and cheese, during which he renounced his own name. Contenders threw up questions more urgently in his absence. What did it mean now to be a Student Nonviolent Coordinating Committee, and who should decide?

A ruling from the chair suspended procedural wrangles to hear from the new Selma project director. Silas Norman had left Wisconsin the previous summer to be a clandestine literacy tutor for potential voters in Selma, where he lost his cover when subjected to Sheriff Clark's cattle prod during a spontaneous demonstration, then joined SNCC in the fall and came to preside over the local office as it swelled during King's campaign. With a rich deep voice and precise diction, ingrained from family training in Augusta, Georgia,* Norman recommended that SNCC provide a minimum level of cooperation with the march on Sunday—lend walkie-talkies for logistics on the road, contribute cooking utensils, and handle medical support—which could be done merely by contacting volunteer nurses and doctors already on the way from New York. While making clear that the Selma project had opposed Bevel's plan altogether, Norman tempered criticism in his first presentation to national officers. "We have to go," he said, partly out of deference to SNCC's public alliance with King.

In response, several officers rushed past his caution to ask why SNCC should participate at all. Norman's predecessor in Selma called the march a "joyride" for King's fund-raising apparatus at the expense of local Negroes. Executive Director James Forman, SNCC's organizational mainstay since 1961, raised the most basic issue by asking whether there could be validity in any movement for the right to vote in Alabama. To succeed required principled commitment and action from the federal government, for which hope had drained very low within SNCC by the end of Freedom Summer, and without such hope, deliberate sacrifice and risk looked pointless. Forman and others suggested that SNCC needed to find a more independent course. The executive committee voted to spell out its broader dissent against the strategy in Selma, and Norman spent what little remained of Friday night with Ivanhoe Donaldson, a quick-witted movement veteran of Jamaican descent, drafting a letter to Martin Luther King. It was Donaldson whose lecture at the University of Wisconsin had mesmerized Norman with transforming tales of suffering and mirth from SNCC's era of classical nonviolence, so much so that he resolved to leave his graduate studies in microbiology to come south. Only a year later, they collaborated in an attempt to explain the swift passing of a generation inside the movement.

* Norman's younger sister Jessye, then a student at Howard University, would become a noted opera singer.

CHAPTER 4

Boxed In

March 6, 1965

PRESIDENT Johnson labored under
pressure at the White House on Saturday. "Good God, I'd rather hear
your voice than Jesus this morning," he told his bosom friend Richard
Russell of Georgia, chairman of the Senate Armed Services Committee.
Russell had been breathing through a tracheotomy tube for a month,
hospitalized with emphysema and pulmonary edema, and Johnson
oozed genuine sympathy in his habitual prelude to serious business.
"Dick, I haven't got anybody left like you," said the President. "I've
said more prayers about you than I have said since Lady Bird threatened
to divorce me two years after we were married . . . and I'm so glad
you've come through." He offered to send an Air Force plane to move
Russell during recuperation—"it'll go above the clouds and everything"—then plunged into his quandary about combat troops in Vietnam. Having commenced regular bombing, and established airbases to
support it, Johnson was withholding final authority to send Marines to
protect the bases. "I guess we got no choice, but it scares the death out of
me," he said.

Russell agreed on both counts. "These Marines, they'll be killing a
whole lot of friendly Vietnamese," he told Johnson from his sickbed in a
raspy drawl. "They're gonna shoot everything that comes around those
airplanes. They've been trained to do that. And that's their business."

"Airplanes ain't worth a damn, Dick," said Johnson. He and Russell
swapped stories on the futility of sending bombers over jungle targets.
"Hell, I had a hundred and sixty of 'em over a barracks of twenty-seven

buildings," said Johnson, "and they set two on fire. It's the damnedest thing I ever saw and the biggest fraud." Bombing only "lets you get your hopes up," he added, "that the Air Force is gonna defend us."

"No, they're not at all," said Russell. "Not at all. I know they're not."

Summarizing "the great trouble I'm under," Johnson told Russell that "a man can fight if he's got, if he can see daylight down the road somewhere, but there ain't no daylight in Vietnam."

"There's no end to the road," Russell concurred.

"The more bombs you drop, the more nations you scare," said the President. "The more people you make mad, the more embassies you get mad—"

"We gon'," Russell interrupted. "We gon' wind up with the people mad as hell at us that we're saving by being in there. . . . It's the biggest and worst mess I ever saw in my life. You couldn't have inherited a worse mess."

"Well, if they'd say I inherited it, I'd be lucky," Johnson lamented. "But they all say I created it, and you know . . ."

The President paused, then snapped back to pleasantries at manic full speed. "You go get well and come back and I got a big bed for you and I want to see you and I got three women want to see you," he said, signing off with regards from his wife, Lady Bird, and their two daughters.

Johnson alternated on Saturday between his morose stall on the Marine orders and hot pursuit of his legislative agenda. He called Vice President Hubert Humphrey to pepper him with lobbying instructions on the record number of 104 bills before Congress, stressing those that had languished in controversy for as long as forty years, such as landmark proposals to establish a medical care system (Medicare) for the elderly and provide the first federal assistance to public education. "If we don't pass anything but education, and medical care, and Appalachia," Johnson said, referring to his poverty bill, "we have had a record that the Congressmen can be reelected on."

The normally loquacious Humphrey struggled to squeeze in a word. "Well, Mr. President, I'll go right up there and be right on 'em all afternoon," he said.

"You just be on 'em the next four years," Johnson prodded. Urgency was his theme. More than once he exhorted his assembled Cabinet not to waste his landslide popular margin of 16 million votes from the 1964 election, predicting that he would lose strength in the polls at the rate of a million votes per month, and he told Martin Luther King of his hurry "to get these big things through" in a brief window of historic opportunity "before the vicious forces concentrate."

Now the President told Humphrey there could be no excuses: "We're smarter than they are," he said. "We've got more energy, we can work faster, we got all the machinery of the government." He dangled a vision of glory for Humphrey from a presidential mandate to handle Congress, which Johnson said Kennedy had denied to him for fear that he, the former Senate leader, would get public credit for success. "You're the first vice president in the country that had responsibility for the—I don't care if it's the Humphrey-Johnson program," Johnson declared. He personalized the quest for key votes such as that of Representative Edith Green, reducing her qualms about federal aid for education to a stubborn rivalry with a fellow Oregonian in Congress. "She hates [Senator Wayne] Morse," advised the President, instructing Humphrey to court Green from every angle. "Lady Bird just took her to Florida," he said. "I've had her down here. I've bragged on her. But she is just a mean woman, and she's gonna whip you, and if she does, why then I'm gonna get you in the five-cent cigar business."

* * *

In Selma, early Saturday afternoon, Rev. L. James Rongstad of St. John's Lutheran Church tried to head off a surprise intervention by white people from cities across Alabama. He found seventy-two of them assembled as inconspicuously as possible at Knox Reformed Presbyterian, an old mission congregation established for Negroes in the white part of town, and gained entry to deliver a warning speech that emphasized the Golden Rule. "We did not interfere in your problems, and we do not need your interference in our problems," said Rongstad, who beseeched them not to provoke further conflict or violence. He addressed a fellow Lutheran minister personally, reminding Rev. Joseph Ellwanger that he was a graduate of Selma's Albert G. Parrish High School and that crossing lines in a hometown race crisis would upset Ellwanger's childhood friends, not to mention his parents, who still lived just three blocks away and were members of Rongstad's congregation. To tighten the pressure, he read a proclamation that only by genuine conversion, not politics or trouble, could the people of Alabama reach the desired "wholehearted willingness to love our neighbors as ourselves." It was signed by the Negro minister of a local Lutheran congregation and by the man who recently replaced Ellwanger's father as head of the Alabama Lutheran Academy and College (for Negroes). The clear message to Ellwanger, who pastored an all-Negro congregation in Birmingham, was that he should not "go native" beyond the missionary boundaries of the Lutheran Church, lest he endanger the Negroes themselves and repudiate his own father's tradition of religious service.

"We are not here to point the finger at Selma," Ellwanger replied. "We are here to point the finger at the state and at the nation." He led the white demonstrators from the church in eighteen groups of four, spaced thirty feet apart so as to avoid violating the local parade ordinance. Marjorie Linn walked beside him, despite some grumbling in the group that it was neither wise nor chivalrous to honor the request of an inexperienced woman to share the lead. The prevailing view was that no one else was any more prepared than Linn, a reporter for a suburban newspaper outside Birmingham, and that she fairly represented the women who had worked for this moment since one of them stood up during a semiclandestine speech by King's aide Hosea Williams to ask how they could help the Selma movement, and Williams had invited them to "take some warm white bodies down there and show that you care." A handful of women from the Alabama Human Relations Council had mounted a ten-day telephone blitz to recruit these assorted freethinkers—scientists from the U.S. rocket program in Huntsville, a professor of dentistry, a Methodist minister whose dog had been poisoned after sermons favorable to integration, several dozen Unitarians, the head of the university art department in Tuscaloosa—who agreed to go to jail, if necessary, though none had been arrested before and Ellwanger himself never had joined a racial demonstration.

They walked twelve blocks, from the church on Jefferson Davis Avenue to Broad Street, Selma's main thoroughfare, down past the bustling Saturday shoppers, who generally ignored them. Turning right on Alabama Avenue toward the Dallas County courthouse, those in front confronted roughly a hundred hostile white people with pipes, clubs, and chains—"most of them sturdily built and roughly dressed," noted a reporter. They came alive with catcalls at their first sight of Ellwanger's group, in sharp contrast with the five hundred Negroes who stood across the street in silent contemplation, and some amazement, waiting to behold a white delegation from Alabama make public witness on their behalf. One minute later, as recorded by FBI agents, a battered jalopy stopped in the street with a deafening roar from a throaty engine. Its driver jumped out, threw up the hood, and poured a viscous

liquid over the carburetor that sent clouds of acrid smoke billowing outward, first choking and screening the Negroes, then wafting with a shift
of wind back over the angry whites. A few of the Negroes stifled laughter over this whimsical turn of menace, which somehow encouraged the
Ellwanger group forward.

Chief Deputy Sheriff L. C. Crocker stopped them at the corner of
Lauderdale Street, just before the courthouse. With a hand held up for
silence, he read a telegram from Dr. Edgar Homrighausen, president of
the Southern District Lutheran Church, Missouri Synod, declaring that
"in no way does Rev. Ellwanger represent the church." For Ellwanger,
this stinging disavowal was unusually swift and public but consistent
with previous edicts from Homrighausen, who was effectively his
bishop. Before the large funeral for the girls killed in the Birmingham
church bombing, Homrighausen had served notice that Ellwanger's
presence at the Baptist service would violate the ban on "unionism," or
joint worship with those outside the fold of Lutheran doctrine. Ellwanger had attended anyway, at the request of his Negro Lutheran
parishioner who was father to one of the victims, and this first public
witness had marked him not only as an isolated white face in Birmingham police photographs but as a dissident within his ministry. "Insofar
as his goal is freedom for all under just legislation, we agree," Homrighausen's telegram continued, "but we do not concur with or sponsor
his philosophy or action of demonstration in this instance."

Deputy Crocker finished reading and loudly addressed Ellwanger.
"What do you think of that?" he asked.

"He is entitled to his opinion, but we are here to make clear our position," Ellwanger replied, asking to pass by. Crocker shrugged, and motioned with a withering look of pity to a place on the courthouse steps
near the crowd of roughnecks. Once assembled there, Ellwanger tried
to shout out a prepared statement that "there are white people in Alabama who will speak out. . . . We consider it a shocking injustice that
there are still counties in Alabama where there are no Negroes registered to vote . . ." His words were lost, FBI agents cabled headquarters,
as "the whites hooted and yelled to such an extent that statement could
not be heard." Ellwanger's group tried to rise above the hecklers by
singing "America the Beautiful," only to be drowned out again by a
spirited rendition of "Dixie." Louder still, Negroes across the street
joined spontaneously in "We Shall Overcome." Above the cacophony of
competing songs, some angry bystanders shouted threats to throw Ell-

wanger's race traitors into the nearby Alabama River, and others made lewd comments on their imagined sexual preferences. "Tears trickled down the cheeks of some of the women," reported an AP correspondent, "as the crowd cursed, insulted, and jeered them."

Wilson Baker, Selma's director of public safety, hurried through the yelling crowd to Ellwanger's side and spoke into his ear, saying he knew his parents and that it would be wise to return by way of Church Street rather than double back through the unruly whites to Broad Street. "You'd best hurry up," Baker advised.

With the help of others nearby, Ellwanger skipped forward to the concluding lyrics they were determined to reach: ". . . and crown thy good with brotherhood, from sea to shining sea." Then, as he led the marchers forward toward Church Street, angry whites darted in to jostle those behind, and James Robinson grabbed one of two SNCC photographers walking next to the lines. Baker shoved his way through again to arrest Robinson, a member of the violently anti-Negro and anti-Jewish National States Rights Party, who had become a familiar figure in Selma since slugging Martin Luther King after the first voting rights demonstration in January. While Baker stared down the surrounding crowd, the photographers broke away to friends in a passing car, only to have several dozen of Robinson's cohorts surround them and begin rocking the car to turn it over. They had lifted one set of wheels waist high before Baker arrived to place another man under arrest, which allowed the car to pull away.

Ellwanger's group escaped the Selma mob toward more subtle retributions ahead. The Methodist minister who had lost his dog would lose his pulpit, and Marjorie Linn would lose her job as well as a car, which vandals soon pushed from a parking space over a steep embankment. For the time being, they shared immense relief at Knox Reformed Presbyterian Church, both crying and laughing at the comic inspiration of James Bevel's sermon of praise about the celestial meaning of a freedom march by white people. Joyce Ellwanger, pregnant with her first child, made it back to the church in the embattled rear of the line, where her husband had placed her in hope of greater safety. Ironically, in view of Wilson Baker's exertions, she carried a placard saying, "Decent Alabamans Protest Police Brutality," but Baker himself made a similar point when he reported breathless to his boss, Selma's mayor, Joe Smitherman, and learned that Smitherman had agreed to let Governor Wallace handle the next day's march toward Montgomery. Enraged, Baker said

Wallace's people would brutalize the demonstrators no matter what they promised.

Baker fulminated, threatening to resign. He was a shrewd, sophisticated police leader in the region—a former college professor, mortician, and amateur Bible scholar, known as "Captain Baker" for his commanding presence (offset by a morbid, quirky fear of housecats), and as "The Fat Man" for his nervous compulsion to eat "anything that won't bite back." When Smitherman expressed a novice mayor's trust in Wallace as his towering political mentor, Baker replied that Wallace could not control Sheriff Jim Clark or his "posse" of volunteer militia if he tried. Clark's primitive itch to attack Negroes was so strong that he had journeyed to Perry County just to be on hand for the night riot of troopers when Jimmie Lee Jackson was killed, and Colonel Al Lingo of the state troopers was as bad or worse in the estimation of Baker, who accused Smitherman of naively abandoning their pact to defeat Martin Luther King by his own nonviolent methods. Their strategy was to defend a kind of progressive segregation by restrained law enforcement, protecting Selma's reputation along with King's demonstrators from the violent propensities of Sheriff Clark. If the Negroes must be stopped, Baker preferred to arrest them with his officers before they could reach Clark's jurisdiction, which included the courthouse and all county areas outside the city limits. For Smitherman, however, that option would require him to break his commitment to Wallace and take on himself the burden of legal and political opposition to King.

A parallel debate raged privately at the governor's mansion, where soundings on the "laughingstock" plan had turned out badly for George Wallace. Legislators bridled at his notion of relying upon weakness and natural privation to vanquish the protesters. Some doubted that Colonel Lingo could safeguard the marchers long enough to fail, and State Representative Bill Edwards specifically advised that his Lowndes County constituents included stoutly independent sharpshooters and dynamite experts who would never defer to any complicated jujitsu plan regarding Negroes. Wallace reconsidered the blockade option just as a counterstroke landed from the opposing camp. From Atlanta about noon on Saturday, Martin Luther King issued a statement that if the Sunday marchers were stopped, they would "lie down in the road" and seek relief from the federal government. While Wallace recognized that this could be a bluff, he recoiled from being drawn into what would be an uneven standoff with President Johnson. To raise the stakes against King, he summoned a four o'clock news conference to forbid a contest of any kind. "There will be no march between Selma and Montgomery," Wallace announced personally, saying he had instructed Colonel Lingo to "take whatever steps necessary" to prevent it. His aides quickly secured a public endorsement from Mayor Smitherman that "Negroes should not be permitted to make this senseless march."

* * *

OPTIONS CLOSED upon President Johnson that Saturday afternoon, March 6, once Secretary McNamara reported that Vietnamese Communist units had been sighted near the new airbase at Da Nang. The Joint Chiefs were expecting two Marine battalions to guard the installation, and McNamara, anxious about vulnerability and blame, pressed for final approval to send them.

"The answer is yes, if there's no other alternative," the President replied. He consoled himself by reciting one estimate that predicted less than even odds of a big land war in Asia, but fretted to McNamara over the "psychological impact" of landing Marines as the first full combat units in Vietnam. "I know every mother is gonna say, 'Uh, oh. This is it,' " he complained, adding that Americans pictured the Marine soldier as "a guy that's got a dagger in his hand, and it's going to put the flag up."

Johnson recalled the firestorm reaction to a White House press announcement that Marines were dispatched into Mississippi the previous June, to search for the three civil rights workers who disappeared on the first day of the SNCC summer project. "I damn near had to evacuate the White House," he said.

"I know it," said McNamara.

They had calmed that uproar by swiftly substituting Navy units for the Marines, the President recounted—"When I said the boy with the white jersey is coming in, it was a helluva lot of difference"—and he groped for a comparable gesture in Vietnam. If the Joint Chiefs required Marines for the task, he suggested, perhaps they should soften the name by calling them military police.

"Well, these aren't MPs," said McNamara. "We can't call 'em that, but we can call 'em security battalions."

"Well, can't you call 'em security battalion and say 'similar to MPs'?" Johnson persisted.

"No, sir," said McNamara. "We can't really say that, but we can say security. That's clear enough. They're quite different from the MPs, and all the press knows it. And it would—we'd just be accused of falsifying the story."

"All right," Johnson said glumly. He swallowed with an audible gulp. "Well, we'll just go with it. And we know what we're walkin' into. Rather than havin' it said, 'well, we wanted protection for our planes and you wouldn't give it to us,' then, my answer is yes but my judgment's no."

"Well, I agree with you," said McNamara. He said he had stressed his own reluctance while clearing the move with Senate Majority Leader Mike Mansfield, a strong private opponent of military involvement in Vietnam. "I said, 'I'm cold as hell to this myself,' " McNamara told the President, " 'and I'm just telling you that the field commanders recommend it, and can't think of any other solution, and I'd like to know what you think.' Said I hate to see this done. And then he, well, we went on, and I was—what I was trying to do was to push him around to reluctantly agreeing, and I got him sort of half-agreed, but he'll fall off it if anybody attacks him. I'm sure of that."

"When are you gonna issue the order?" Johnson interrupted.

"Well, it should go out this afternoon," said McNamara. "I'm just so scared something is going to happen out there."

"When are you gonna announce it?"

"Well, we'll make it late today so it'll miss some of the morning editions," said McNamara, "and then there's no afternoon edition on Sunday." He said he would handle the public notice so as to minimize attention.

The President emitted a quiet, loony laugh as McNamara conceded that combat troops inevitably would generate headlines. "You're tellin' *me?*" Johnson moaned as his goodbye. McNamara sent cables spurring pre-mobilized shipments of Marines to land within thirty-six hours, but held back the Pentagon news release until nightfall.

* * *

AT FRAZIER's café in Atlanta, Friday's SNCC debate about Selma lasted well into Saturday night. Back and forth, amending its draft letter for Martin Luther King, the executive committee swerved from narrow defenses of organizational turf to the broadest misgivings of purpose. Communications director Julian Bond proposed that the letter be stripped of argumentation simply to notify King where SNCC would and would not cooperate with the march to Montgomery. To Courtland Cox, however, the point of the letter was to express the depth of SNCC's ideological dissent, and James Forman sought to spell out a fundamental difference in working technique. Whereas King conducted dangerous street demonstrations for the vote, SNCC was supporting a challenge in the U.S. House of Representatives to unseat Mississippi's five members on the constitutional ground that their elections in 1964 had excluded Negroes. Whereas King tried to negotiate voting rights with the Johnson administration, Silas Norman and others of SNCC proposed for disenfranchised Negroes to submit their own voting bill as a claim of full citizenship.

Forman defined SNCC methods as safer and closer to the people, but critics reminded him that Bob Moses himself had opposed the Mississippi congressional challenge as a siren song, saying it lured grassroots workers into the maw of Washington's publicists, lawyers, and politicians. Others questioned Mississippi as a model when veteran SNCC workers were migrating to other states, weary of contentions there since Freedom Summer. Moses, now calling himself Bob Parris, refused for a time to speak with white people and was disappearing into Alabama—away from the extra, prodigal distractions of holdover white volunteers. Five of them, including Dennis Sweeney of Stanford and Ursula Junk of Germany, had just been jailed with forty Negroes in McComb, Mississippi, and reports to SNCC headquarters indicated that the arresting officers "roughly handled the white workers" with special abuse.

Almost alone at Frazier's, SNCC chairman John Lewis spoke in favor of the march to Montgomery. Steadfast and unassuming, Lewis was respected within SNCC and had been elected national chairman for three consecutive years. Yet opinion crystallized against him as though Lewis somehow personified contradictory arguments about SNCC's nature. He had been a founder of SNCC five years earlier at the age of twenty, coming from a Nashville chapter so steeped in nonviolent commitment that it embodied SNCC's upstart boast through the sit-ins and Freedom Rides into Mississippi—that students stepped forward to risk their lives where King hung back to preach. Bernard Lafayette, Lewis's roommate at ministerial school in Nashville, had established a Selma project for SNCC back in 1962, first sleeping alone in cars when no Negro family would house a civil rights worker. Lewis had been arrested before King in Selma, and more often, and he came from a sharecropping family of ten children in nearby rural Alabama. Lewis was the ideal SNCC representative to oppose King's strategy, but he turned grassroots credentials against his exhausted cohorts instead. "If these people want to march, I'm going to march with them," he insisted. "You decided what you want to do, but I'm going to march."

Rancor surged on both sides. SNCC members accused Lewis of defying and misrepresenting his own organization. Wounded, Lewis argued that SNCC was "abandoning these people" in violation of its cardinal commitment to stand with them in danger. Some retorted that King could hoodwink the masses into false moves, and suggested that it was better to melt back among the people as organizers, like trade unionists. While a few called it an ideological retreat to dedicate themselves blindly to the material ambitions of the poor, saying many Negroes wanted only "a house on a hill and two Cadillacs," others said SNCC now embraced transforming goals from outside the American system. One member asked pointedly "why we bother with the vote at all," which expressed the disillusionment of young SNCC workers who had suffered for the national promise of equal rights and still felt its rawest shortcomings up close. To hope for fundamental change only "sets the stage" for another letdown, one executive committee strategist wrote in preparation for the meeting. They were still being jailed because of an "emasculated" 1964 Civil Rights Act, added SNCC's research director Jack Minnis, who foresaw no chance that a strong voting rights law could be passed, signed, upheld, and enforced. "Therefore," he concluded, "I think it illusory to the point of fatuity to suppose that any purpose we avow would be served by trying to get still another voting bill passed by Congress." Such skepticism about government was the dominant new mood within SNCC, making Lewis too earnest and steadfast by contrast—too much like King—and the religious optimism of his nonviolence had worn too thin to invite another beating in Selma.

Still at an impasse, the executive committee voted toward midnight to disapprove of the march officially but allow workers to participate "as individuals," so long as they did not imply SNCC's sanction. The committee stopped short of voting Lewis out of the chairmanship, which would have advertised an internal split, and the members knew better than to try to restrain him by persuasion or edict. Lewis, for his part, turned from reproach to the practical problem of getting to Selma by morning on his own, with no help from the executive committee. Lacking a car or driver's license, he managed to recruit Wilson Brown, a young member of the communications staff who had a white Dodge, and also Bob Mants of Atlanta. Mants, during high school, had been drawn to the excitement of the Atlanta SNCC headquarters near his home, first as a volunteer janitor, then as "captain" of posters for the Freedom Hops at the Simpson Road skating rink, and briefly in bone-chilling demonstrations. Now twenty-one, still captivated by movement people, Mants seized the chance to get away from his premed studies at Morehouse College, never dreaming that a Selma weekend would lead him to spend his life in Lowndes County. Escorting Lewis, he and Wilson Brown reached SNCC's Freedom House in Selma by dawn, and napped before the march in sleeping bags on the floor.

CHAPTER 5

Over the Bridge

March 7, 1965

A chorus of automobile horns sounded through the Carver housing project at mid-morning on Sunday, March 7, as some two hundred people from Perry County rolled up to Brown Chapel safe, relieved, and ready, many of them veterans of Wednesday's funeral march for Jimmie Lee Jackson. Their arrival soon registered in a room at the courthouse marked by a prominent sign—"Quiet Please, We Are Trying To Monitor Three Radios"—where Sheriff Clark's female deputies relayed reports to city police and Colonel Lingo's state troopers. They wore Confederate flag pins on white blouses, and one of them told a reporter she had taken special pains to be presentable on what figured to be an important day. An incoming transmission crackled: "There's three more cars of niggers crossing the bridge. Some white bastards riding with them." This bulletin referred to the Edmund Pettus Bridge, named for a hometown Confederate general and U.S. senator, which arched from the edge of the Selma business district over the Alabama River toward Montgomery.

Trepidation rose steadily in Andrew Young as he drove past sheriff's cruisers into Selma with a white Episcopal priest, and it jumped when he saw the large crowds of Negroes milling about Brown Chapel, some with knapsacks and bedrolls. Young quickly sought out Hosea Williams and demanded to know why he had not postponed the march until Monday as Martin Luther King had instructed. Rev. P. H. Lewis, pastor of Brown Chapel, heartily seconded Young. He had been a party on the same late-night conference call and could not fathom why

Williams proceeded to whirl around his church all morning with pep talks for arriving marchers. Williams admitted that "Doc" made himself plain against him as the lone holdout—"Hosea, you're not with me, son, you need to pray"—but insisted with his usual swagger that King reauthorized the march once he realized "how well I got this thing organized." He implored Young to check with Bevel, saying Bevel talked recently with King and would vouch for the change if someone could find him.

Young paused in exasperation, knowing that Williams would not lightly invoke the authority of his bitter rival. Since Birmingham, Williams had aspired to Bevel's position as chief action adviser, disparaging him as unstable and devious, a potential usurper against King, and Bevel just as openly denigrated Williams as a thick-headed former pesticide chemist who had no conception of nonviolent strategy beyond "putting niggers in jail to get on TV." King deliberately preserved these and other fierce antagonists in his inner council, which was more than enough to guarantee spirited debate, and Young knew Williams would be loath to exaggerate in a way that opened him to contradiction from Bevel. Still, Young recognized a state of combat agitation in Williams that made him wary from personal experience. In 1963, while visiting anti-segregation demonstrations in Savannah, Georgia, where Williams was then a local leader, Young wound up arrested for the first time. In 1964, sent by King with explicit instructions to dampen incipient protests in St. Augustine, Florida, he walked into a mass meeting only to hear Williams invite "the prettiest girl in the church" to join Young in leading a night march—his first—which soon led to a Klan beating. Young realized that these baptismal trials actually raised his commitment to and his standing within the nonviolent movement, above that of mild-mannered church administrator, but he warned sternly that the stakes in Selma were too high for Williams to dissemble again.

Young sent messengers to retrieve Bevel and retreated to the parsonage next door, fending off urgent inquiries about the schedule. Albert Turner, a bricklayer swept into voting protests only a month ago, served notice that his people from Perry County were resolved to march *somewhere* that day, even if only around Brown Chapel, and many raised questions about the white man in a clerical collar who arrived with Young in place of Martin Luther King. Rev. John B. Morris by coincidence had shared a flight from Atlanta and then joined Young for the drive from Montgomery in haste to follow up on the previous day's drama, which the *New York Times* on page one called "the first time an all-white group of Southerners had demonstrated in the streets for Negro equality." The Ellwanger march came as a welcome surprise to Morris, a founder of the Episcopal Society for Cultural and Racial Unity (ESCRU), as did the nationwide coverage alongside stories about the upcoming Marine deployment to Vietnam.

Regular notice made Selma part of a new vocabulary that the civil rights movement had pushed forward in public discourse since the 1954 *Brown v. Board of Education* decision on schools. There was a photograph of Sheriff Jim Clark in that morning's *New York Times Magazine*, illustrating a published debate from England between writers James Baldwin and William F. Buckley on whether "The American Dream is at the expense of the American Negro." Buckley assailed a tendency to "rush forward and overthrow our civilization because we don't live up to our high ideals," while Baldwin asserted that "the American soil is full of the corpses of my ancestors" for systemic reasons deeper than hateful excess on the fringes of society. "Sheriff Clark in Selma, Alabama cannot be dismissed as a total monster," Baldwin told the Cambridge Union Society in February. "I am sure he loves his wife and children and likes to get drunk. One has to assume that he is a man like me. But he does not know what drives him to use the club, to menace with the gun, and to use the cattle prod."

Sheriff Clark's image also appeared that Sunday morning on national television, explaining that he had started using cattle prods about 1957 and that he had formed his volunteer posse of two hundred men originally to handle labor disputes. To interviewers from the ABC *Issues and Answers* program, Clark asserted that King came to Selma "to satisfy his revenge against me and also to make his personal bank account larger" by stirring trouble over a voting issue that was phony because "nigras are registered pretty much as they desire to." Clark told the television audience that public harassment had driven him to move his wife and children into the jail for security, though there had been "no attempts on my life as yet." Locally, every half-hour on Selma radio, his voice urged citizens to stay in their homes that Sunday, and Clark in person—back from taping *Issues and Answers* the previous day in Washington—was driving from the Montgomery airport with Colonel Al Lingo toward a staging ground on the east side of Pettus Bridge, outside city limits, where their men saddled horses and issued equipment that included wide-nozzle tear gas spray guns and launching rifles for tear gas canisters.

Word of the tear gas spread rapidly among the marchers, who tried to calm themselves as they filled out mimeographed notification forms in and around Brown Chapel. Some suggested that they try to elude the troopers by taking a more northerly route on Alabama Highway 14 instead of U.S. 80 over Pettus Bridge, but local ministers L. L. Anderson and F. D. Reese said it was foolhardy to hope that demonstrators on foot could outflank motorized officers. Dr. Alfred Moldovan of New York, one of ten volunteer doctors and nurses from the Medical Committee for Human Rights, gathered prospective marchers for impromptu speeches about the medical properties of tear gas. "It is not a dangerous gas, usually," he said. "It blinds you temporarily and drives you into a panic. If tear gas hits you, go off to the side of the road and stand quietly. Don't panic." Frank Soracco, a young white Californian, added a roving speech for nonviolent discipline, saying that panic could make them look like a mob and give the troopers an excuse to do their worst. Having canvassed, improvised, and gone to jail in Selma since December, Soracco resolved that morning to be in the midst of whatever developed—a choice that fell within SNCC's grudging vote of tolerance but isolated him among fellow staff workers, most of whom regarded march preparations with censure from a distance.

* * *

SHORTLY AFTER noon, John Lewis arrived at Brown Chapel to find Young, Bevel, and Williams darting about in agitated huddles. Bevel had endeared himself for once to Williams (who said later he "could have kissed him"), by confirming that King wanted to supersede the instructions he gave early that morning when he sent Young alone to the Atlanta airport, and now to reauthorize the march. Before a nonplussed Lewis, they debated whether to confirm the change with King in light of the formidable opposition across Pettus Bridge, and if so how to penetrate the screen of Daddy King's loyal deacons at Ebenezer Church where King was preaching in a lengthy service. They all knew that King's father and co-pastor for years had employed a mix of sly ministrations and histrionic bluster to discourage his son from taking movement risks—this time scolding him for neglecting Ebenezer, coaxing him to fulfill his primary duties as a pastor, and finally claiming a sudden illness that Daddy King said rendered him so weak that his son must stay in Atlanta to take his place in the pulpit. Hosea Williams conceded that he lacked the clout to get an emergency phone message to

King during worship, but he did manage to pull Ralph Abernathy from his service at West Hunter Street Baptist in Atlanta and beg intercession on behalf of the "thousands" Williams declared had showed up ready to march.

Abernathy in turn pushed through to King by phone during the Ebenezer service, as did Young and Bevel from Selma. They said postponement would be dispiriting, especially for the large turnout from Perry County, which more than offset the advantage of waiting until King could be there on Monday. Bevel reiterated that if five hundred people went to jail today, five hundred more should go tomorrow. No matter what the result, he said, their effort almost certainly would need repeating, and King was better saved for the building phases in days ahead, as in Birmingham. King consented. He stipulated that two of his three deputies should stay out of the march to handle follow-up logistics. They retired to flip coins simultaneously, and Williams, by showing the only heads, became the odd-man-out to lead the march in King's place. Their usual banter defied the solemnity of what was to come. Young congratulated Williams for not hoodwinking him to the front a third time, and Williams accused Bevel of rigging the toss against him.

Hastily, they reviewed contingencies of nonviolent practice for the volunteers assembled in Brown Chapel. If stopped, they would sit in prayer until arrested or tear-gassed, which would provide ample ground to seek relief in federal court. Young told reporters that King decided to stay in Atlanta once Governor Wallace announced his intention to block the march, the better to seek political support in the North. Lewis read a statement about why they were marching. He carried a backpack stocked haphazardly for a short trip to jail, with an apple, an orange, a toothbrush, and a copy of *American Political Traditions*. After a final chorus of "God Will Take Care of You," Lewis and Hosea Williams led the way from Brown Chapel at 1:40 P.M. Sunday—only to run into a glowering Wilson Baker, who, having resigned and unresigned that morning in renewed infighting among segregationists, required them to abide by every scintilla of the parade ordinances until he could bid them good riddance from his jurisdiction. The marchers repaired to the playground of Carver Homes for an anticlimactic interval to form roughly twenty-four squads of twenty-five, each with a staff person to maintain proper spacing, and they stepped off again two abreast at 2:18 P.M., followed by a vehicular train that reflected their meager expectation of reaching outdoor bivouac: a flatbed truck with four portable toilets, two ambulances for the medical committee volunteers, and three borrowed hearses for supplies.

* * *

SQUADS CLOSED ranks as the march line turned out of Selma as never before, climbing on the left sidewalk up the long slope of an empty Pettus Bridge. Police officers held up the ambulances and hearses, saying the roadway was closed to traffic, and a state administrator served notice that the out-of-state volunteers were not licensed to dispense medical care in Alabama. Diane Nash, patrolling the rear of the march line for stragglers, was drawn into a dispute over the legal status of Red Cross armbands and the meaning of "emergency treatment" in one section of the state code, but the support vehicles remained stranded as the front of the line reached the overarching steel girders at the crest of the bridge, nearly a hundred feet above river waters that were choppy from the crisp March winds.

Down the bridge before Lewis and Williams opened a vista of forbidding reception. In the middle distance, a wall of trooper cruisers blocked all four lanes of Highway 80. Closer, a reserve of some 150 troopers, sheriff's deputies, and possemen mingled behind a front line of twenty-five troopers about two hundred yards beyond the foot of the bridge—the possemen in khaki jackets and white helmets, fifteen of them mounted on horseback, the troopers in blue uniforms and blue helmets. Scores of white spectators jammed the parking lot of "Chicken Treat, Home of the Mickey Burger," some standing on parked cars, across the highway from several dozen Negroes who gathered cautiously behind an old school bus. Near the front line, outside the showroom of Lehman Pontiac, troopers guarded an observation area reserved for journalists and several of the twenty FBI observers scattered around Selma.

With the march line sighted on the bridge, a buzz about rumors and source reports died down in the observation area. FBI communications were sifting two death threats out of Chicago alone, one falsely claiming that a hired gunman spotted King in Selma. A television correspondent who knew better took King's absence as confirmation of his political soundings on "some sort of power struggle" behind the scenes, in which the more militant SNCC students reportedly had imposed the Sunday march upon an unwilling King. At least one network camera operator, without knowing that SNCC's executive committee actually was renouncing the march as King's folly,* adapted in his own pragmatic way to the volatile confusion of cross-racial journalism in Selma. He dutifully followed the instructions of troopers and deputies who promised to guarantee his safety, but also wore a new athletic supporter and protective cup to guard against a repeat of earlier attacks from the same uniformed authorities. On foot, and from makeshift perches, the camera crews gathered images that soon obliterated a host of preoccupations while lifting some details into lore—that Hosea Williams claimed under his breath to have captured such bridges in Germany, that one tipsy marcher near the front had to be steadied over the crest, that Lewis and Williams eyed a possible destination below in the Alabama River and confessed softly to each other that neither could swim.

What the machines recorded as Williams and Lewis continued methodically down the slope was an eerie silence, broken by the snorting of horses. After they had covered roughly a hundred yards of level ground, a quietly spoken order ahead introduced unnerving new sights and sounds to the marchers: snapping noises that swept along the barrier line ahead as officers secured otherworldly gas masks of bug-eyed goggles and elongated rubber snouts. Williams and Lewis halted the march line at a separation of fifty feet when an unmasked trooper stepped forward with a bullhorn. "It would be detrimental to your safety to continue this march," said Major John Cloud, a scholarly-looking deputy to Al Lingo. "And I'm saying that this is an unlawful assembly. You are to disperse. You are ordered to disperse. Go home or go to your church. This march will not continue. Is that clear to you? I've got nothing further to say to you."

"May we have a word with the major?" asked Hosea Williams. Without amplification, his voice was barely audible to the journalists nearby.

"There is no word to be had," replied Cloud. He gave the marchers two minutes to withdraw, and the lines faced each other silently in front of Haisten's Mattress and Awning Company. Lewis and Williams looked straight ahead, wearing light and dark raincoats, respectively, each with a buttoned tab collar pushing forward his necktie. Behind Lewis, Bob Mants stood motionless in an overcoat and collegiate scarf,

---

* "We strongly believe that the objectives of the march do not justify the danger and the resources involved," declared the SNCC letter mailed to King that day. A stand-in signed Lewis's name.

wearing "high-water pants" that were stylish on the Atlanta University campuses, stopping five inches above the ankle. Behind Williams stood Albert Turner in rural denim, carrying a stuffed backpack that evidenced the hope of the Perry County marchers to sustain themselves all the way to Montgomery. Mants and Turner wore the jaunty Sluggo cap, also known as the Big Apple hat.

After one minute and five seconds, Major Cloud addressed his front unit without the bullhorn: "Troopers, advance." The blue line of elephantine masks moved forward with slow, irregular steps, overlapping and concentrating to curl around the front ranks of marchers. With nightsticks held chest high, parallel to the ground, the troopers pushed into the well-dressed formation, which sagged for nearly four suspended seconds until the whole mass burst to the rear, toppling marchers with accelerating speed as troopers hurtled over and through them. Almost instantly, silence gave way to a high-pitched shriek like the war cry of Indians in Hollywood movies, as the march line screamed and white spectators thrilled, some waving encouragement alongside the charge. John Lewis shot out of the mass at an angle, leaning oddly as he sank to the ground in five steps, felled by a truncheon blow to the head. A clattering of horses' hooves on pavement signaled the general deployment of Alabama reserves and raised the volume of the pulsing shrill yell. Two troopers in the forward tangle stumbled over bodies into a heap and came up swinging clubs. The sharp report of guns sounded twice on the first launch of tear gas, one round reportedly fired by Sheriff Clark himself. A canister landed behind a moving wave of chaos that had not yet registered all the way back up Pettus Bridge toward Selma, where some marchers in the distance still knelt in prayer as instructed. From the tangle in the foreground, a Negro woman came spilling out to the side, pursued by one masked trooper and struck by two others she passed. Three ducking Negro men crossed toward nowhere with an injured woman they carried by arms and a leg, her undergarments flapping. Horsemen and masked officers on foot chased marchers who tried to escape down along the riverbank, herding them back. The cloud of tear gas from canister and spray darkened toward the mouth of the bridge, obscuring all but the outlines of a half-dozen figures on the ground and scattered nightsticks in the air.

*   *   *

FROM A corner pay phone in Selma, SNCC worker Lafayette Surney was describing the departure when distant bedlam sounded and the first

marchers streamed back over the bridge. The contact at SNCC headquarters in Atlanta transcribed Surney's first words of alarm at 3:15
P.M., Selma time: "State Troopers are throwing tear gas on them. A few
are running back. A few are being blinded by tear gas." Nearby, Rev.
John Morris heard radio news bulletins on the attack and jumped from
his car to see refugees flee past. With James Bevel and Andrew Young,
he pitched into Diane Nash's efforts to extricate the blockaded medical
teams. Injured marchers came to them instead, and the ambulances and
hearses overflowed also with victims of blows inflicted by waiting teams
of possemen who fell upon retreating marchers once they reached
downtown Selma. Surney's account generated notes by the minute in
Atlanta. At 3:16 P.M.: "Police are beating people on the streets. Oh,
man, they're just picking them up and putting them in ambulances.
People are getting hurt pretty bad." At 3:17 P.M.: "Ambulances are
going by with their sirens going. People are running, crying, telling
what's happening." Atlanta SNCC workers crowded around the wide-
area telephone service phone receiver to hear the riveting noises in the
background.

Marchers in flight back to Selma collided with one another in the
mists of choking tear gas. Many clung to the bridge railing on the sidewalk to escape the mounted possemen who swung clubs or homemade
flails of rubber hose laced with spikes, then jumped through gaps back
into the roadway to run more freely, dodging troopers and possemen on
foot. Third-grader Sheyann Webb, swept into the air by her armpits,
wiggled and hollered for Hosea Williams to put her down because he
could not carry her as fast as she could run.

"Here come the white hoodlums," Lafayette Surney reported to Atlanta over SNCC's WATS line at 3:25 P.M. "I'm on the corner of one of
the main streets. A lady said they tried to kill her." Surney, a young
movement veteran from Ruleville, Mississippi, was soon injured himself in the pell-mell retreat toward Brown Chapel.

Dr. Moldovan and two nurses broke away from the blockade by force
of will, and the only ambulance to make it out of Selma on the original
line of march crossed to find a thinning civilian battlefield on the far side
of the bridge, littered with abandoned purses, umbrellas, hats, packs,
shoes, and prostrate human forms, several with spewing tear gas canisters close by. The heavy gas curled thickly above and around the grass in
the dividing strip of Highway 80. Gasping through damp cloths, the
medical workers found Amelia Boynton near the point of the first

trooper surge. Boynton, who formally had invited King to reinforce a stalled voting rights campaign in Selma, lay immobile from blows but somewhat protected from fumes by a borrowed rain hat that had slipped down over her face. The owner of the rain hat sat woozy nearby. Margaret Moore, a pioneer schoolteacher who had offered Bernard Lafayette the first toehold of a civil rights project in 1962—indoor lodging—at first resisted the ambulance for fear of white people jeering her rescue, but Moore and Boynton rode into Selma on Moldovan's first trip.

By 3:30 P.M., more than a hundred troopers, possemen, and sheriff's deputies pursued the marchers over the mile back to the neighborhood around Brown Chapel, where they attacked stragglers in a frenzy. Some drove their quarry indoors; others yelled for Negroes to come out. Down the block, troopers threw one teenager through a ground-floor window into the basement of First Baptist Church. In the Carver housing project, John Webb cried with his shotgun trained on the door from the couch, where his daughter Sheyann said she could not stop shaking. Across the way, Frank Soracco did not stop running until he collapsed bruised and gassed in the upstairs bathroom of his host family, locking the door. Outside, Sheriff Clark fired one of many canisters into a home. Wilson Baker, who saw mounted possemen urge their horses up the steps of Brown Chapel to take swings, confronted the sheriff in front of reporters, demanding that Clark stop the show of force and move "your cowboys" out of the city. "I've already waited a month too damn long about moving *in!*" Clark defiantly replied, and Baker, helpless to control the blood lust in some of his own men, let alone Clark, waved police officers out of the area with resignation.

At 3:32 P.M. from Brown Chapel, a wobbly John Lewis tried to summarize the shocking attack firsthand over a new connection to the SNCC line in Atlanta. "I've never seen anything like it in my life," he said. "They are shooting gas, acid. One very old lady I know has a broken arm." A female SNCC worker took the phone to report that Lewis "has a small hole in his head," and dispatched him over his protest to a makeshift first-aid center. "We have a problem," she announced at 3:40 P.M. "The guys are not nonviolent any more. They're ready to fight. About two or three busloads of possemen are in front of the church beating people, throwing tear gas." Leaders ventured outside to plead for calm. Andrew Young challenged would-be gunmen to compare their rusty weapons with the opposing arsenal. Bevel pleaded with teenagers not to let the attackers "off the hook" by throwing rocks.

Sheriff Clark and most of the assorted authorities soon paraded back and forth on deserted Sylvan Street, jittery but with horses at a walk. A local reporter followed one detachment that searched out the large number of Negroes who had been curious about the march but now sat frozen in their cars. Although the *Selma Times-Journal* remained a segregationist newspaper, to the point that Monday's edition would muffle the worldwide news from home beneath a banner headline of a more congenial lead story—"Johnson Asks Congress to Intensify Fight on Crime"—its editors did publish straightforward observations on the inside pages. "Members of the posse beat on the hoods of the automobiles with their nightsticks and pointed their clubs at the drivers, shouting, 'Get the hell out of town! Go on, I mean it! We want all the Niggers off the streets!' The Negroes all left without protest," the unsigned story concluded. "Thirty minutes after the marchers' encounter with the troopers, a Negro could not be seen walking the streets."

* * *

REPORTERS FOLLOWED the aftermath into the parsonage next door to Brown Chapel. "Negroes lay on the floors and chairs, many weeping and moaning," wrote Roy Reed for the *New York Times*. "A girl in red slacks was carried from the house screaming. Mrs. Boynton lay semiconscious on a table." Doctors and nurses worked feverishly through more than a hundred patients, bandaging heads, daubing eyes, shipping more serious cases to the only local hospital that would treat them—Good Samaritan, a Catholic mission facility run by the Edmundite Order in a Negro neighborhood. By relay of ambulance and hearse, they ferried patients there until fifty-eight of them occupied every surface, including the floor of the employee dining room, and then eight more went down a dirt road to the humble Burwell Infirmary. Operated since 1926 by Mrs. Minnie B. Anderson, it served primarily as a nursing home for twenty-five long-term residents, including a 108-year-old woman and a sixty-two-year-old man who could move only his hands, plus a maternity unit with one old incubator and a charity ward for abandoned children—all jammed, with only one vacant bed. Two practical nurses, just back from Pettus Bridge themselves, cheerfully made room on the floor and used a respirator all night to keep one asthmatic man alive until the tear gas cleared from his lungs.

Lafayette Surney found John Lewis at Good Samaritan two hours after the rampage, admitted for a fractured skull. FBI agents reported the most common injuries to be lacerations and broken bones, but Lewis and Surney alike saw more suffering from tear gas that still seeped out of the patients' saturated clothes. "Tear gas—that's the baddest thing," recorded the note-taker in Atlanta when Surney called the Atlanta WATS line from the hospital. SNCC headquarters swarmed in mobilization. Julian Bond, snatched from home, issued two bulletins by 5:30 P.M. and offered taped excerpts of the dramatic WATS-line reports to radio stations. Four carloads of SNCC workers were driving to Selma from Jackson, Mississippi. Ivanhoe Donaldson and Courtland Cox were bargaining in a Piper Cub with a rattled pilot who agreed to drop them quickly at a tiny landing strip outside Selma, while James Forman harangued officials at Hertz to meet them with a rental car. Forman hired a second emergency charter flight for experienced fieldworkers including Stokely Carmichael, who, after three summers and a full year in Mississippi, was by coincidence in Atlanta looking for transfer into Alabama. Forman also left repeated telephone messages for Martin Luther King, whose secretary said he was deep in conference over the crisis, and he sent a telegram to ABC executives in New York protesting the "misstatements and distortions which [Sheriff] Clark disseminated today through the nationwide facilities of your TV network. We shall expect to hear from you without delay."

The ABC News film crew raced network competitors in a cavalry relay dictated by broadcast technology before videotape or satellite transmission. They drove around the troopers blockading Highway 80 at the first chance, then on through Lowndes County to the Montgomery airport and flights through Atlanta to New York, bearing canisters of undeveloped film to lab technicians rushed in for Sunday night work. Before nine o'clock—eight o'clock in Selma—news executives privately viewed footage from Pettus Bridge while their network signal disseminated the scheduled television premiere of *Judgment at Nuremberg,* which had won two Academy Awards and nine more nominations in 1961. Actor Spencer Tracy was in the kitchen of temporary quarters where his character, an unvarnished Maine judge, was newly arrived to try magistrates of the Third Reich for war crimes. As a married couple of dutiful but thoroughly cowed German house servants served him milk and a cheese sandwich, Tracy gently probed for clues about life under Hitler—asking about daily habits and hardships, then about local parades and the giant Nazi rallies held every year in Nuremberg. "I'm just curious," he said. "I'd like to know." The servants evasively replied that they were "only little people" who avoided politics and had suffered greatly in the war. Tracy asked whether they had ever heard of Dachau, not far away.

"How, how can you ask if we know anything about that?" the servant wife implored, trembling.

"I'm sorry," said Tracy.

"Hitler did some good things," she conceded. "I won't say he didn't do some good things. He built the autobahn. He gave more people work. But . . . the *other* things, we know nothing about that. Very few Germans did."

"And if we *did* know," added the husband, "what could we do?"

Tracy paused over the equivocation. Correspondent Frank Reynolds broke in upon this film conversation shortly after nine o'clock to announce news from Selma, and ABC's bonanza audience of forty-eight million unsuspecting viewers transferred from the mystery of Holocaust atrocities nestled among good Germans to real-life scenes of flying truncheons on Pettus Bridge. ABC News executives let the footage run nearly fifteen minutes—as long as Sheriff Clark had appeared on *Issues and Answers*—before resuming the film. CBS and NBC aired similar bulletins during regular programming, but the Nuremberg interruption struck with the force of instant historical icon.

President Johnson, who received word during a small social dinner at the White House, decided to block it out until morning. He neither made nor received phone calls and retired promptly, but Lady Bird Johnson recorded her husband's "cloud of troubles" in her diary entry for the night: "Now it is the Selma situation . . . and the cauldron is boiling."

She also quoted his private lament to friends that evening about Vietnam: "I can't get out. I can't finish it with what I have got. So what the hell can I do?" Johnson's two rising worries converged almost to the minute, as the first Marine amphibian tractors touched Red Beach 2 at 9:03 P.M. Washington time, which was 9:03 Monday morning across the International Dateline in Vietnam. Squad leader Garry Parsons of Springfield, Illinois, led Battalion Landing Team 3/9 ashore near Da Nang. Ten-foot swells hampered the debarkation, crushing one soldier's chest between a ship transport and a landing craft, but the battalion assembled at 9:18 and marched up the beach between welcoming lines of Vietnamese children, who hung a garland of flowers around the neck of Brigadier General Frederick J. Karch, commander of the 9th Marine Expeditionary Brigade, in ceremonies of optimism and relief.

No one, including President Johnson, foresaw America's first loss of a war, any more than the day's tear gas victims pictured Selma as the last great thrust of a movement built on patriotic idealism. It was a turning point. The tide of confidence in equal citizenship had swelled over decades to confront segregation as well as the Nazis, and would roll forward still, but an opposing tide of resentment and disbelief rose to challenge the overall direction of American politics, contesting the language of freedom.

Martin Luther King struggled in seclusion to secure something positive from the day's harsh repulse. Resolving first to mobilize "a renewed march from Selma to Montgomery," he issued a statement that night from Atlanta and asked aides to bring Rev. F. D. Reese to the telephone of the pastor's office in Brown Chapel. Reese was president of the Dallas County Voters League, the host group in Selma founded by Amelia Boynton and her late husband.

"Mr. President, I understand you are having trouble over there," said King, with fraternal understatement intended to comfort Reese.

"Yeah, we do," said Reese. With Bevel, Young, Williams, and L. L. Anderson, he was preaching perseverance to a mass meeting of 450 wounded and numb.

"Well," said King, "I'm gonna put out a call for help."

CHAPTER 6

The Call

March 8, 1965

THE rout on Pettus Bridge ignited a week of passionate struggle about fundamental and historic issues. Would the pent-up conflict about Negro voting rights be settled in the streets, the courts, the legislatures, or not at all, and would results favor the primacy or subordination of states? King's swift appeal that Sunday night pushed the focus toward gathering drama rather than a finite sensation that was likely to fade. "He Reveals Plans to Lead a New March To-morrow," declared the front page of Monday's *New York Times,* beneath headlines and a graphic picture from Selma. "King Calls for Another Try," announced the *Washington Post.*

Surrounded by newspapers in his bed, President Johnson made his first call Monday morning for a briefing on hospital casualties and King's intentions. Attorney General Katzenbach volunteered the awk-ward news of the FBI's only active intervention during the charge of troopers and possemen: jailing three white men, including the serial at-tacker James Robinson, for assaulting an FBI agent. "I didn't give the arrests any publicity last night," said Katzenbach. "That didn't look right, Mr. President, from a public viewpoint, you know—all the Ne-groes that were beat up and the people we arrested were the people who beat up the FBI agent." Worse, the circumstances recalled FBI director J. Edgar Hoover's public accusation in November that Martin Luther King was "the most notorious liar in the country." To justify his impul-sive outburst, Hoover oddly had cited a complaint by King two years earlier that FBI agents too often were native Southerners who stood aloof while Negro demonstrators were brutalized. Now the three white attackers in Selma had mistaken FBI agent Dan Doyle of Little Rock for a reporter taking notes and pictures from the sidewalk—and had stolen his camera. The federal prosecution would be scuttled quietly to avoid attention to the FBI's selective perception of duty, as Katzenbach, who considered Hoover to be actively senile, knew better than to suggest fault in the FBI's hypersensitive founding Director. If public discussion of race was stilted, Hoover was taboo.

President Johnson simply tuned out FBI controversy as unproductive. "Do you know Wallace very well?" he asked, and the Attorney General said no one did. "The senators say they can't get to Wallace at all," he reported.

Johnson proposed former Tennessee governor Buford Ellington as a possible go-between with Wallace, based on personal history and chemistry. The President vowed to send Ellington, the newly installed head of federal disaster relief, over to Katzenbach's office within the hour to begin figuring out how to prevent repeated violence against the next King march. "Just have to be mighty quiet," he instructed.

Quiet was difficult to achieve. Picket lines sprang up outside the Justice Department before Ellington could get there. Katzenbach received a small delegation of preachers from the local chapter of King's SCLC, and by the time their leader emerged to tell reporters that he deflected their request for protection by U.S. marshals, three SNCC students darted into Katzenbach's office to sit in for the same objective. "It did not take the Attorney General long to get us policemen up here to throw us out," shouted Frank Smith as he was being dragged down a corridor. "Why can't he give us some protection in Alabama?" Katzenbach broke away to salvage one piece of the day's regular schedule—his formal introduction to the U.S. Supreme Court, hurried and sheepish in a rented morning coat—and returned to find twenty SNCC students encamped outside his fifth-floor office at the Justice Department.

"Our basic difficulty is we have no communication with Wallace at all," President Johnson complained that afternoon to Senator Lister Hill of Alabama. He confided that Buford Ellington had found Wallace to be vaguely interested in "a way out" but close-mouthed and opaque, determined not to appear weak before Negro protest. Discreetly, Johnson did not tell Senator Hill that Ellington also warned of a duplicitous streak to Wallace's folksy manner ("You can't trust him . . . you talk to him, you don't know what he's gonna say that you said . . . there's an element of danger in talking with George"), but Hill made essentially the same point. "That damn little Wallace," he warned Johnson, would find a theatrical way to magnify himself, just as he had stood in the schoolhouse door against integration "to show the people of Alabama that he fought to the bitter end." Wallace would maneuver to make Johnson appear the instigator of federal tyranny and racial chaos, Hill predicted, so that "the people down home gotta think well, my God, he [Johnson] just moved in there and took over for this King."

Hill offered Johnson sympathy but no advice. Johnson likened his razor's choice to Vietnam. "I had to send the Marines in yesterday," he said.

"It's a helluva dilemma," said Hill about Alabama. He bemoaned his home crisis as though the Asian conflict did not yet register for him.

Johnson disclosed reports already reaching the White House that the wave of protest against Wallace was strong. "This fella's sent out wires all over the United States, King has, askin' everybody to come in there for the march tomorrow," he said. "And they're fifty Protestant ministers from Washington, D.C., for instance, chartered an airplane, and they're gettin' ready to go, and they're flying in and coming by bus and everything else from all over the country."

* * *

THE WASHINGTON charter was the work of glacial church bureaucracies accelerated to lightning speed. One of King's telegrams calling for a "ministers' march to Montgomery"* scarcely arrived on Monday at the New York office of the National Council of Churches before ten church executives vowed to be in Selma by 8:30 the next morning. The board of the Council's Commission on Religion and Race (CORR), which had been created after the breakthrough anti-segregation marches of 1963 by Birmingham's Negro children, voted to buttress King's appeal with its own press release and mass telegrams, and by midday, the council's chapter in the greater Washington area chartered an airplane to accom-

---

* "No American is without responsibility," King's wire declared. "All are involved in the sorrow that rises from Selma to contaminate every crevice of our national life. The people of Selma will struggle on for the soul of the nation, but it is fitting that all Americans help to bear the burden. I call, therefore, on clergy of all faiths, representatives of every part of the country, to join me for a ministers' march to Montgomery on Tuesday morning, March 9th. In this way all America will testify to the fact that the struggle in Selma is for the survival of democracy everywhere in our land."

modate the prominent clergy whose instant mobilization attracted notice from the White House staff.

Reporters bombarded the Washington archdiocese wanting to know whether Roman Catholics would be permitted to go on the charter flight, since the hierarchy had forbidden participation of priests and nuns in all previous demonstrations, including the 1963 March on Washington. In a frenzy of church politicking, amid rumors that fervent clergy might break church discipline if refused, Archbishop Patrick O'Boyle reluctantly granted an exception "just this once," and astonished Catholics rushed to join Protestants at the airport. At least two of them, Monsignor George L. Gingras and Father Geno Baroni, either missed or evaded calls from Auxiliary Bishop John Spence trying to revoke their mission on the ground that the Bishop of Alabama was withholding the required consent. Once word flashed through the diocese that Vatican protocol was breached, a helpful secretary at one Baltimore parochial school buzzed the classroom intercom with a message for a sympathetic teacher: "Sister Cecilia, do you want to go to Selma?" She did.

National officers of the Episcopal Church responded to King's telegram on Monday by voting to sidestep their ecclesiastical rules. Presiding Bishop John Hines notified Bishop C. C. J. Carpenter of Alabama that Tuesday's march in Selma qualified as a "recognized ecumenical activity" in light of previous resolutions of support for the voting rights movement, and therefore needed no sanction by the local bishop. "By nightfall," Hines reported to his executive council, "several hundred persons were on their way to Selma" over the heated objections of Bishop Carpenter, who formally protested the outside clergy as a threat to established church governance. Carpenter denounced the pending Selma march as "a foolish business and a sad waste of time." Defying him, nine Episcopal priests crowded into one Selma motel room late Monday and made room on the floor for Harris Wofford, an assistant director of the Peace Corps and one of the few white people who had gone south to support the fledgling bus boycott in Montgomery nine years earlier.

Some religious leaders drew on prior experience to jettison ordinary life. Presbyterian ministers Metz Rollins and Robert Stone, who had coordinated a revolving picket line of outside clergy for six months in Hattiesburg, Mississippi, departed for Selma with their call lists. Theologian Robert McAfee Brown hastily arranged a cross-country flight after word of King's telegram interrupted his class at Stanford University. One of Brown's cellmates from a 1961 Freedom Ride in Florida, Rabbi Israel "Sy" Dresner, went on his own to Newark airport and ran into an AME Zion minister and two other clergy from previous journeys South. They rented a car from Atlanta that night and found themselves "scared witless" to be driving in an interracial group through rural Georgia and Alabama. Dresner, answering King's appeals to shore up stalemated campaigns, had survived inspirational but harrowing incarcerations with handfuls of pioneer clergy in Albany, Georgia, and St. Augustine, Florida.

Scattered veterans of the movement joined a larger wave of newcomers who broke barriers of habit and inhibition. A Negro student named Jesse Jackson jumped on a cafeteria table at Chicago Theological Seminary shouting, "Pack your bags," and preached on the gospel challenge beyond the classroom until seven white classmates piled into a van for the long drive to Alabama, with carloads of CTS students and faculty stretched behind. In Philadelphia, an Episcopal priest coordinating a radio appeal tried to discourage one volunteer by observing that women were neither safe nor welcome and that Jesus had no female disciples, but the Jewish caller said she heard that Christians also had no east or west, male or female, and soon said goodbye to her husband and five nonplussed children.

*   *   *

SENATOR LEVERETT Saltonstall urgently summoned Assistant FBI Director Cartha "Deke" DeLoach at noon on Monday, shaken by the eruption of support for King's cause in his home state of Massachusetts. There were spontaneous rallies and petition drives in Boston, spurred by hourly television reports from Selma. More than a hundred Unitarian leaders from the reformed Puritan tradition of old Harvard were scrambling to reach Alabama. One pious and independent student at the Episcopal Theological School in Cambridge modified his prior interpretation that the rules of order required aspiring priests to defer to the Bishop of Alabama. First, he justified a personal donation to one seminarian's wife who wanted to march, and later, during the day's recital of the Magnificat prayer— "He hath scattered the proud in the imagination of their hearts. He hath put down the mighty from their seats and exalted them of low degree . . ."—received as a "decisive, luminous, Spirit-filled epiphany" that even students should witness like the saints, with their bodies. He joined ten other Episcopal seminarians who juggled tests and papers, raced through Lawrence Hall dormitory to solicit travel money, dashed off notes to family, and then jammed aboard a flight with the Boston Unitarians in the chain reaction that rattled politicians. Senator Saltonstall privately told DeLoach that "pressure is mounting" in Boston for him to sponsor a testimonial dinner for King, and suggested that he felt misled by the FBI. In the year since he had helped block an honorary degree at Springfield College, by spreading the FBI's clandestine allegations that King was a philandering, subversive fraud, Salstonstall noted pointedly to DeLoach that the target of scorn had received the Nobel Peace Prize and several invitations to meet privately with the President of the United States.

The senator's complaint did not faze the FBI's polished chief of political liaison and publicity. DeLoach replied that Saltonstall was overlooking the subtle fact that President Johnson never allowed himself to be alone with King. Although this was untrue, and in any case a minor point, Senator Saltonstall dared not seem naive in the face of the FBI's command of political secrets, and he claimed instead to have wondered about that very detail. "I told Saltonstall there was no change in King," DeLoach reported back to J. Edgar Hoover. "I told him that King was a phony through and through and that obviously he would never change."

The animus at the top of the FBI's political hierarchy was oblivious to law or the swells of public opinion. Professionally, Director Hoover cultivated King as the fearsome dark symbol of the latest twentieth-century threat to tranquillity on Main Street America—succeeding immigrants, Depression gangsters, Nazis, and Communists—but he also modified some of his strict bureaucratic regimen to vent a personal disparagement of King as a "burrhead." Hoover revised internal communications about the latest threats to kill King if he marched on Tuesday in Selma—one via the Secret Service about two alleged gunmen out of Detroit, another about a killing squad from the Coushatta, Louisiana, Ku Klux Klan—and vetoed plans to give a routine warning to King. "No," Hoover scrawled on one memo, and on another ordered agents "not to tell King anything." He reminded top officials of a previous order to exclude King from the standard advisory to the targets of threats, and explicitly confined FBI notice to Sheriff Clark and other local authorities of dubious protective value. The exclusion order gained for Hoover the satisfaction of avoiding any contact with King that might suggest recognition or service to a fellow citizen on the part of the FBI. To offset the small risk of being challenged, he vacuumed up useful information *about* King from agents whose training and distance buffered them from political applications at FBI headquarters.

*   *   *

FBI AGENTS recorded that at 10:30 P.M. that same Monday, March 8, King entered Brown Chapel to address nearly a thousand people still gathered there in the nightly mass meeting. James Bevel was preaching again from the Book of Ruth about their unfinished quest to "go and see the king" George Wallace in Montgomery, insisting that yesterday's blood vindicated the practice of nonviolence. "Any man who has the urge to hit a posseman or a State Trooper with a pop bottle is a fool," cried Bevel. "That is just what they want you to do. Then they can call you a mob and beat you to death." A sudden hush ran through the church to announce King's unseen arrival, and Bevel stood aside in the pulpit for a five-minute ovation of welcome above a breakout rendition of "Battle Hymn of the Republic."

King delivered a tribute to Sunday's march. He mingled an apology for missing it with a reminder of the travails that buffeted him, too, quoting poet Langston Hughes ("Life for me ain't been no crystal stair"), and vowing that the threat of death could not stop them now. "If a man is 36 years old, as I happen to be," he said, "and some great truth stands before the door of his life . . . and he refuses to stand up because he wants to live a little longer and he's afraid that his home will get bombed or he's afraid that he will lose his job, he's afraid that he will get shot or beaten down by State Troopers, he may go on and live until he's 80, but he's just as dead at 36 as he would be at 80. And the state of breathing in his life is merely the announcement of an earlier death of the spirit." King roused the crowd for the next day on Pettus Bridge. "We must let them know that if they beat one Negro they are going to have to beat a hundred," he declared, "and if they beat a hundred, then they are going to have to beat a thousand."

King recognized fresh hope in the first fifty traveling clergy who reached Selma and were ushered to seats in the front pews. One by one, he asked them to stand and introduce themselves. From the Washington charter flight, Methodist bishop John Wesley Lord expressed shock over the photographs from Pettus Bridge. "I hear that Dr. Martin Luther King was calling for white ministers to come and march," he said. "And I am a white minister. You could say that I heard the Macedonian call."

Toward midnight in Washington, President Johnson prodded one of his top assistants about frenzied efforts to prevent repetition of Sunday's violence. "The Negroes are still meeting in the church in Selma with Martin Luther King," Bill Moyers reported. He said Governor Wallace had just proposed covertly through the intermediary Buford Ellington that the President assume responsibility in Selma by federalizing the National Guard. However, since Wallace undoubtedly would denounce that very move as power-mad tyranny against his state, Moyers added that Attorney General Katzenbach was concentrating on the alternative of getting the Negroes to cancel Tuesday's march. "The question is," Moyers said crisply, "do you want to be informed when King calls back?"

"Yep," said Johnson. "But I would take a much tougher line than we're going to with him." The President was disturbed by news footage of Katzenbach kneeling in shirtsleeves to plead with the young sit-ins to leave his office corridor after business hours, and by shots later that night of them telling the cameras that they would gladly desist if the U.S. marshals hauling them out of the Justice Department were dispatched instead to protect constitutional rights in Selma. Johnson attributed the protest to orchestration by King. "I think it's outrageous what's on TV," he said. "It looks like that man's in charge of the country and taking it over." He told Moyers to remind King of Monday's bargaining and "take a very firm line with him."

*   *   *

FOR THE remainder of a long hard night, Johnson's intermediaries wrestled earnestly with King over prospects for the voting rights movement. Each said the other could tip a precarious balance from disastrous collision just ahead to historic triumph. Johnson's side demanded a peaceful respite to shore up national consensus, while King insisted he was "too deeply committed" to call off the march without tangible signs of support from Washington. The balance of nerves seesawed as they exchanged blandishments, professions of respect, and outright threats, but only hints of their struggle seeped outside private councils. About two o'clock Tuesday morning, agents notified FBI headquarters that King reportedly had agreed to confine any march that day to the city limits of Selma—thus avoiding another confrontation across Pettus Bridge. Lawyer Harry Wachtel suspected from parallel talks that Attorney General Katzenbach did not "have his heart" fully in the pressure he applied, but advisers told King by telephone conference that the tenderfoot church elders could not walk far toward Montgomery, anyway.

An hour later, agents gleaned from wiretapped conference calls that King seemed resolved to lead his columns back into the maw of Alabama troopers after all, in spite of Wallace, Johnson, or his own admitted fear of snipers, saying he must keep faith with the marchers. He knew a host of new ones were careening toward Selma through makeshift points of transit, oblivious to his second thoughts. The Episcopal seminarians were mostly too giddy to sleep before catching a bus from Atlanta, having risen Monday morning for classes in Massachusetts and next coming to rest in King's own private office at SCLC, staring at his books and mementos, the males bedded down on the floor and Judith Upham of St. Louis on his leather couch. Some of the Boston Unitarians dozed in the Hertz rental office at the Atlanta airport until a connecting flight early Tuesday, March 9—Henry Hampton* on a chair, James Reeb on a divan, Orloff Miller on the floor.

President Johnson called Bill Moyers at home before breakfast. "What happened with Martin Luther King?" he asked. A baby cried in the background as Moyers explained that he had not awakened the President because he had heard from Attorney General Katzenbach only at four o'clock and again just now. He summarized the marathon negotiations by reporting that King was "very fearful for his life" and "really wanted" to cooperate, but "couldn't get out of at least a token march." So the administration still faced a double bind. "Any effort to put a federal presence in there will only likely cause Wallace to feel that he's being pressured and confronted, and he might go in the wrong direction," Moyers told the President. In case of renewed violence, however, the White House would face difficult questions about "how does it look if things go wrong and we've done nothing more" than on Sunday? Moyers described the situation as "very tenuous." He said their intermediaries were working both sides to reduce the chances of conflagration—"Ellington is at this very moment talking to Wallace"—and "the best we can do now is hope."

The President did not fulminate against King as he had done the

---

* Hampton, the first black executive hired by the Unitarian Universalist Association, later became creator and executive producer of *Eyes on the Prize,* an acclaimed television documentary series about the civil rights movement that aired on the Public Broadcasting System beginning in 1986.

night before. He had a politician's respect for pressure, and very likely realized that the tide of reaction to Sunday's march was beyond push-button control. Johnson had added political nuance to his "tougher line" on King by sending in former governor LeRoy Collins of Florida, the head of the new Community Relations Service created by the 1964 Civil Rights Act. Before dawn, Collins landed at Craig Air Force Base in one of the two-engine jets reserved for presidential use and proceeded to briefings from Assistant Attorney General John Doar, head of the Justice Department's Civil Rights Division, who since Sunday had pulled nearly all his staff lawyers into Selma. Collins and Doar drove that morning in a white military sedan to the home of Selma's Negro dentist, Sullivan Jackson, and Jean Jackson knocked apologetically on the door of her front bedroom to tell King that "a man from the President" was there to see him.

CHAPTER 7

Devil's Choice

March 9, 1965

KING and Ralph Abernathy stumbled into the living room in Dr. Jackson's matching burgundy pajamas, followed by colleagues who had been trying to sleep on sofas, rugs, and even in the tub of the bathroom, which James Bevel called his crisis "suite" since the forced separation from his wife ten days earlier. King's inner circle had endured the night of emergency bulletins and fierce internal debate, briefly relieved by one loud bang that brought panicked sentries running to find the bed collapsed under a conclave and King convulsed with laughter, attributing the fall to the extra weight of his brother, Rev. A. D. King, who accused Abernathy, who pointed to Hosea Williams, and so on around the sprawled huddle of rotund preachers. Now groggy but gravely composed, King sat at the dining room table to hear John Doar disclose that U.S. District Judge Frank M. Johnson indeed was signing a federal court order to prohibit another voting rights march from Selma until further notice.

King sagged grimly. Only yesterday afternoon, his movement lawyers had filed their petition for Judge Johnson to do the opposite—to forbid Governor Wallace and other Alabama officials from repeating Sunday's violent interference. This stinging reversal went far beyond postponement or denial as the anticipated risk. While King could not claim to be surprised, he was depressed by the very fact that Doar had warned him of such an order and that Attorney General Katzenbach had invoked its likelihood to buttress President Johnson's demand for delay. Suspecting correctly that the President's lawyers and Judge Johnson were to some degree in cahoots, he complained that the order was blatantly unjust and political.

Doar did not try to defend the legal merits. Judge Johnson was issuing the injunction against King on his own initiative, without a motion or pleading from any party to the case, and he was suspending in advance a number of constitutional rights inherent to the march without a word of justification in law or fact. Like Katzenbach, Doar privately agreed with King's lawyers that the injunction would be overturned on appeal, but he knew the issue would be moot long before then. For now, the order carried the full authority of national law—even if Judge Johnson himself believed it was unconstitutional—and Doar stood on this practical advantage as an article of rectitude. "This is a *federal* order," he repeatedly told King across the table. Never in all his civil disobedience had King defied one, in part because the federal courts remained the hope and refuge of the civil rights movement. Federal judges and justices had sustained its victories. Even now they were moving to enforce the 1964 law against entrenched segregation in the states, and Doar warned that King could alienate more than the federal courts if he disobeyed. The Justice Department would be obliged to defend and carry out an order to jail him for contempt, which inevitably would divide the administration and poison chances for voting rights legislation.

All these crushing points Doar could make painfully as King's frequent ally since the sit-ins of 1960. A Republican holdover who had stayed on at Justice to build the huge backlog of civil rights cases across the South, Doar was a pioneer of tenacity and innovation among government lawyers. He traveled endless hours beyond courtrooms and offices to remote areas of near peonage for Negroes, often alone and sometimes warily incognito, gathering evidence independently—to J. Edgar Hoover's everlasting annoyance—that the FBI overlooked or ignored. His newborn son had gone unnamed for six weeks while he followed the maelstrom after the Birmingham demonstrations of 1963, ending with King at the funeral of NAACP martyr Medgar Evers, and Doar, having personally escorted James Meredith through mobs into Ole Miss not on the first try, or even the second try, had earned standing to counsel patience. He spoke tersely in a calming style he brought from small-town practice in Wisconsin. Judge Johnson was a good judge, he said. As King well knew, he had cast the deciding judicial vote to vindicate the bus boycott. The judge was not dismissing King's suit permanently. He was just demanding a suspension of trouble in order to hear evidence. If King called off the march, Doar promised, the Department of Justice would join as a friend of the court to seek protection for the future. No one could say how the judge would rule, of course, but by obeying Judge Johnson's order King might win not only a court-protected march later but also the full backing of the executive branch for a voting rights bill.

King tried to engage Doar's points of law, but his arguments gravitated to moral anguish. He said Judge Johnson's injunction was like "condemning a man for being robbed," and otherwise used language that discomfited government lawyers as overwrought. King saw moral dilemmas where they saw logical relief, and they questioned how he could speak of mere delay as condemnation, especially delay of a potentially suicidal protest. Since King attributed good will to administration officials from President Johnson on down, and readily agreed that the federal government was the essential instrument to establish new freedom to vote, Katzenbach had puzzled through the night about why King agonized about relying on trust for a few days. King, on the other hand, groaned against the convenient assumption that he would give way for a promise. It summoned up a contrasting heritage that made patriotism an act of faith and put a furnace in his troubled voice. "But Mr. Attorney General," King said repeatedly, "you have not been a black man in America for three hundred years." To Doar, as to Katzenbach, he said it was his "duty" to march, and he could not promise to obey the new court order.

Governor Collins waded into the impasse with a personal message from President Johnson. The President felt strongly that Sunday's violence disgraced the United States in the eyes of the world, said Collins. His overriding concern was to prevent more violence that would inflame racial hatreds and threaten stability far beyond Selma. Therefore, quite apart from legal mandates, the President wanted King's people to stay home to guarantee the peace.

This was too much for Rev. Fred Shuttlesworth. "You're talking to the wrong people," he interrupted from the background. Shuttlesworth, the irrepressible movement leader from Birmingham, said Collins was mixed up about who was beating people over the head and who was nonviolent. Did he see the pictures? Shuttlesworth suggested that Collins take up the issue of violence with Governor Wallace and Sheriff Clark. "They're the ones in the disgrace business," he said with his matador's bravado.

Collins retreated from grand exhortation to explore compromise. What if King marched across Pettus Bridge but then turned around? How far could he go and still plausibly claim not to violate the judge's new ban on "attempting to march from Selma, Alabama, to Montgomery, Alabama"? As King responded to various hypothetical options, John Doar squirmed with disapproval. In his view it was worse than improper for Collins to tinker with a court order, as such a course played into the proven strength of segregationist powers. Bitter courtroom experience convinced Doar that any temporary advantage of an "adjustment" to Judge Johnson's order would backfire a hundredfold in the discretionary evasions that the South had refined to minimize Negro voting nearly a century after the Fifteenth Amendment and to keep schools segregated more than a decade after the *Brown* decision. Because the overriding goal in civil rights compliance was to close off loopholes, not create them, many Justice Department lawyers resented the mediating role of the new Community Relations Service as a blatant invitation to political mischief.

Doar withdrew from the talks to avoid any appearance of tacit consent, and Collins left the Jackson home later Tuesday morning to search for Colonel Al Lingo among the state troopers massed on the other side of Pettus Bridge, this time behind an armada of 150 cruisers. His urgent goal now was to answer King's piercing doubt about compromise. "I don't believe you can get those people not to charge into us even if we do stop," King kept saying. King's worst fear was to lose everything—to march just short enough to lose momentum and cohesion within the movement, just far enough to break the injunction and lose any chance of federal alliance, just blindly enough to reap blame on all sides for getting mauled gratuitously in defeat. Such was the accustomed lot of Negroes as recounted by folk wisdom and brash comedians.

* * *

THE MORNING crowd at Brown Chapel was "ominously quiet, oppressively tense," according to a theologian from Chicago. Speakers reviewed the Selma movement to packed congregations at Brown and at First Baptist a block down Sylvan Street, while buses, rental cars, and even taxis from Montgomery continued to spill newcomers into the overflow mass between the two churches. Suitcases and bedrolls were stowed in the Brown parsonage or shuttled to Good Samaritan Hospital, where the Edmundite Catholics alone of white Selma welcomed travelers to sleeping spots laid out on the floor of the maternity ward.

Young Negroes of Selma recruited new arrivals to their family apartments in the Carver housing project nearby, some treating the collared white clergy as celebrities to the extent of asking for autographs, while weary and embarrassed clergy eyed bandaged veterans of Sunday's march as heroes. To one reporter, the "coolest cats in town" were scores of SNCC staff workers who patrolled in radio-equipped cars or sliced through clumps of people to conduct sidewalk classes on nonviolence. One who demonstrated shielding techniques vowed above all else to make sure that "if anyone gets whupped out there today, it ain't gonna be our women." Another told cowed bystanders he had learned to cushion the expected licks by letting his hair grow.

U.S. marshals, arriving after an hour's high-speed drive from Montgomery, fanned out to search for Hosea Williams and the other parties named in the restraining order that Judge Johnson signed just before ten o'clock. Rumors of their mission swept unevenly through assorted demonstrators "numbering between two thousand and twenty-five hundred," by FBI estimate. "Injunctions aren't legal until they are served," James Forman cautioned one group that heard the march was canceled, "and we haven't seen any order." Some who were steeling themselves to face the troopers and tear gas shrugged off any piece of paper as a minor nuisance. Others expressed dismay that federal authority could side with George Wallace. "As far as I'm concerned, the federal government *is* the enemy," Diane Nash said bitterly on the fringes of one argument. The unseen order left James Reeb of the Boston Unitarians paralyzed by the "heavy responsibility deliberately to break the law," as he told a Baptist minister who left him to meditate.

Willie Ricks of SNCC climbed the steps outside Brown Chapel to aim a pep talk at a corner of the milling crowd. "That is *your* bridge!" he shouted. The looming barrier at the Alabama River was fully theirs as a public possession, he declared, and they were free to march right past its memories, its fear—all the limits the Edmund Pettus span called to mind. Ricks sang out with a preacher's cadence in the street language of a seventh-grade dropout who had converted to the Chattanooga sit-ins from a life "stealing hubcaps." Now twenty-two, he had proven himself a gifted motivator in SNCC's jail movements across the South, most recently in Moultrie, Georgia. "If Sheriff Clark tries to stop you," he cried out, "what are you gonna do?" Ricks elicited a series of shouts vowing successively to march through the opposition of the major segregationists, then through Uncle Toms, various judges, "your mama," and finally even fainthearted movement figures. "If Martin Luther King says don't march, what are you gonna do?" he shouted. Ricks had a section of the outdoor crowd so worked up to charge the Pettus Bridge that Andrew Young quietly asked SNCC leaders to tone him down in the interests of control. They refused.

Harris Wofford of the Peace Corps prevailed upon Young to take him to the secluded council in the Jackson home. Alarmed by the undercurrent of defiance in the waiting crowd, he pleaded with King not to let emotion divide the civil rights movement from the federal courts. The pilgrim clergy would understand the reasons for delay, he predicted, and would return to march in Selma whenever the court granted permission. "Do you think people really would?" King asked. Even if all the estimated eight hundred travelers from twenty-two states might forgive him for wasting their sacrifice, he wondered how to re-create the galvanizing jolt of events already being called "Bloody Sunday." King remained noncommittal with Wofford, as with a SNCC delegation that pressed arguments on the other side. James Forman, Silas Norman, and others said Sunday's violence nullified their qualms about King's strategy. Now they rallied to the fundamental right of protest, telling King they could not give that up and hope to win the vote. Their chairman, John Lewis, had just left the hospital with a fractured skull and was outside Brown Chapel defending the people's right to decide. How could King bottle up these people who risked their lives to answer his call?

* * *

Across Selma, the driver of one bus refused to approach the racial showdown being forecast in radio bulletins and discharged passengers at an open field almost two miles from Brown Chapel. The eleven Episcopal seminarians from Cambridge were among those obliged to trudge conspicuously with luggage past Selmians staring from front porches. They joined other latecomers at a staging area in the playground of the Carver housing project, where strangers eventually passed by to collect signed power-of-attorney forms in case of arrest or casualty. Jitters quickened and lapsed over a long wait. The seminarians assumed from a distant sighting of King's entrance that those inside the church must have learned the final plan, but King retreated to the Brown Chapel parsonage to receive a last round of telephone debate on the arcane but gloomy legal implications of *United States v. United Mine Workers* (1946), in which John L. Lewis had been treated harshly for violating an injunction not to strike the coal mines, along with more welcome legal advice not to hamper his defense by specifying his intentions in detail. King embraced ambiguity in discussions that ranged from destiny to personality quirks and political timing. Straddling the conflicts between movement zeal and national authority, he thrashed about for chances to bind them together.

Passions ran more freely away from the eye of decision. In Montgomery, a joint session of the legislature was cheering a guest speaker who sought repeal of the 1964 Civil Rights Act as "unnatural law," and the Alabama House commended Governor Wallace by resolution for stopping "an unruly mob" on Sunday. Among rallies on the other side, Michigan governor George Romney was leading a Joshua-like march of ten thousand people five times around the Detroit federal building, and six hundred picketed a New York City FBI office to demand U.S. protection for Negro voting rights in Alabama. In Washington, sit-ins at the Justice Department grew nearly tenfold from the twenty-odd of the previous day, and on the White House sidewalk marched seven hundred pickets, including mothers with baby carriages and one novel placard: "Johnson Is Goldwater in Disguise." The President, distracted from strategy talks on education and a grand ceremony to sign the Appalachian Regional Development Act, veered into a private soliloquy on the urgency of Negro voting rights that astounded six top congressional leaders, including four Southerners. "Good Lord, Mr. President," gasped Speaker John McCormack of Massachusetts, "why don't you say that to the people?"

"At the right time I will," said Johnson.

In Selma, long past lunch, the Episcopal seminarians found themselves hungry and partially separated. Jonathan Daniels, the student with scruples about treading on the authority of the local bishop, wandered off in search of a candy bar, leaving Judith Upham to watch the gear they had pared down to a minimum for the walk to Montgomery. A sudden roar signaled King's emergence and brought Daniels running back empty-handed to hear the indistinct drone of a bullhorn far ahead. "Almighty God, thou has called us to walk for freedom, even as thou did the children of Israel," King began in prayer from the steps of Brown Chapel. When he finished, freedom chants soared above what the New York Times called "a great rustling" in the lines. As aides tried to dress the columns two abreast, King shouted for them to stay on the shoulder of the road and not to panic. "I say to you this afternoon that I would rather die on the highways of Alabama than make a butchery of my conscience," he cried out through the bullhorn, and a cheer spread rearward. His final, rhythmic sentences urged nonviolence. "If you can't be nonviolent, don't get in here," he said. "If you can't accept blows without retaliating, don't get in the line."

At 2:17 P.M., as recorded by FBI observers, King stepped off, and competing songs broke out along the long chain waiting to follow. Ahead, a moving cloud of reporters noted that some white bystanders motioned for calm while others muttered or shouted insults. "You son of a bitch!" yelled one man at King. "You want to vote—why don't you act like a human being?" King said nothing, until a breathless Governor Collins jumped from his government sedan for an emergency walking conference. "They" had promised not to attack, Collins confided, so long as the march kept to the route they marked on the crudely drawn street map he handed to King. Collins emphasized the importance of keeping strictly on the path, which puzzled King because the map prescribed the simple, normal route for voting rights marches toward the courthouse as far as Broad Street, where a leftward turn ascended Pettus Bridge. King could only guess that Governor Wallace and his troopers needed to pretend that he was submitting to orders as a kind of salve for their aroused martial instincts, which were loath to let the renewed march of Negroes go unpunished. Or perhaps they meant to jostle his fear by advertising interest in his movements. In any case, King's worries went beyond trusting the flimsy, irrational promise of the map. He still doubted that he could control the entire diverse crowd to follow him in retreat if he reached the far side of the bridge. "I'll do my best," he told Collins, who rushed back across the bridge with a parting vow to do the same. He would stand close to Colonel Lingo and Sheriff Clark as a federal presence to inhibit violence, risking the appearance of complicity if he failed.

On Broad Street, at the foot of Pettus Bridge, Deputy U.S. Marshal Stanley Fountain confronted King with a raised hand and a signed copy of Judge Johnson's court order. As he formally read the full text of some six hundred judicial words ("This cause is now submitted on the verified complaint. . . . Negroes to register and become voters . . . attempted a march along the public highway on March 7. . . . Plaintiffs say they desire to resume. . . . In consideration of the foregoing . . . plaintiffs and other members of their class, and those acting in concert with them, be and each is hereby enjoined and restrained . . ."), King's eyes drifted until Fountain began to explain the practical effects. "I am aware of the order," he said, snapping to. He hesitated, then waived ceremonial speech in favor of a simple request to move forward.

Fountain stood aside at the flashpoint of commitment. "I intend in no way to interfere with your movement," he announced, formalizing the choice of federal authorities not to repress the march in advance, like Alabama. "Let's go," said King. FBI agents recorded that he "ignored" the court order at 2:35 P.M. and led the climb up Pettus Bridge, the ranks closing beyond the Selma line to four abreast. A dismayed John Doar stood by, knowing that every step opened the marchers to a contempt judgment that would shift the federal government toward an unwelcome alliance with Alabama.

* * *

SILENCE AND bright sunshine fell on the second march to crest the bridge high above the Alabama River, as though re-creating Sunday's instant history on a larger scale. More than twice as many blue helmets spanned Highway 80 on the flatland below, from a deployment to Selma that the local newspaper put at five hundred Alabama troopers. Major Cloud stood a short distance behind his previous position to accommodate some 150 foreign and domestic journalists who crowded along the shoulders, and again confronted the approaching lines with orders to disperse. King sparred briefly over rights, then secured from Cloud a brief truce for prayerful decision. The front ranks knelt at his beckoning, and a wave of dry-throated marchers sank slowly behind them for nearly a mile to six ambulances poised in the rear, far past earshot of Ralph Abernathy's public prayer—"We come to present our bodies as a living sacrifice . . ." A few skeptics stood on lookout near the front, peeking. One bruised, blue-collar veteran of Sunday wore his construction helmet as a precaution.

Attorney General Katzenbach called the White House at 2:56 P.M. "We're at the critical moment," he told Bill Moyers. "I'll keep you posted." Chain-smoking cigarettes at his desk, Katzenbach monitored a speaker phone connected by open line to John Doar. Noise crackled above static. "What's that applause?" asked Katzenbach.

"They're cheering the white women," Doar replied. Two dignitaries, initially held back in case of another preemptive charge by troopers, slowly made their way into the standoff on the arm of Rev. Farley Wheelwright. Newspapers would identify them as Mrs. Paul Douglas, wife of the Democratic senator from Illinois, and Mrs. Charles Tobey, widow of the late Republican senator from New Hampshire—both wearing dress gloves and hats, one in pearls. Tobey's daughter, psychiatrist Belinda Strait, had been among the medical volunteers overwhelmed on Sunday. "And now one of them is talking to King," Doar reported.

From another roadside telephone, on through concluding prayers by Bishop Lord and Rabbi Dresner, Colonel Lingo exchanged information and orders over an open line to Governor Wallace. As the marchers began to rise again from the pavement, some singing the movement standard "We Shall Overcome" and others easing forward with scattered cheers, Major Cloud executed a surprise maneuver. "Troopers, withdraw!" he shouted, and the officers swung back from the center of the road with their portable barricades. To the horror of bystanders Doar and Collins, the way to Montgomery lay open.

King stood stunned at the divide, with but an instant to decide whether this was a trap or a miraculous parting of the Red Sea. If he stepped ahead, the thrill of heroic redemption for Bloody Sunday could give way to any number of reversals—arrests, attacks, laughingstock exhaustion in hostile country—all with marchers compromised as flagrant transgressors of the federal order. If he stepped back, he could lose or divide the movement under a cloud of timidity. If he hesitated or failed, at least some of the marchers would surge through the corridor of blue uniforms toward their goal.

"We will go back to the church now!" shouted King, peeling around. Abernathy and the congressional wives fell in, as did James Farmer of the Congress of Racial Equality (CORE) and Rev. Robert Spike, head of the National Council of Churches' Commission on Religion and Race. Andrew Young stationed himself at the point to wave oncoming marchers into a turnaround loop. SNCC leaders James Forman and Silas Norman, who had moved ahead, wheeled to catch up from behind, utterly perplexed. From the roadside, Governor Collins remained petrified that a stray gunshot from angry whites or a runaway marcher could break the spell of disengagement. Doar exclaimed over the telephone that there was a switch, gaining momentum. "Now I'm sure," he told the Attorney General. "The crowd's turning back." Katzenbach called the White House with the news. FBI agents dryly notified headquarters that King retreated at 3:09 P.M., five minutes after greeting Mrs. Douglas.

Collins was euphoric. "If I hadn't done anything else in my lifetime," he would record confidentially a decade later, "I had something to feel good about." In Washington, Katzenbach numbly withdrew from the commotion of his own office to ponder the government's future stance toward the entangled parties. "Now I want to think about this awhile," he said. For those returning to Selma across Pettus Bridge, a geyser of emotion blended joy with rage. A Roman Catholic priest cried out, "Thank you, Lord." Tears welled up in some who felt spared recurrent terror, while others sobbed over the letdown from a transcendent moment. Rev. Edwin King, who had been jailed and beaten and defrocked for integration in Mississippi, cried fitfully over a U-turn he considered a disastrous waste of moral courage, and forever lost trust in Martin Luther King. James Forman and other SNCC leaders fretted about treachery and betrayal of an unprecedented nonviolent army that had been stoked to march or die. Silas Norman, having set aside his fear and strategic dissent to join this time, sagged with fresh humiliation for being swept along backward without knowing why, and vowed never again to march in Selma. Willie Ricks moaned over the suddenness, believing that with any preparation the SNCC organizers could have bolted past King to steal most of the march. When an elder cautioned that leadership division was lethal for minorities, Ricks and others launched a spirited rendition of "Ain't Gonna Let Nobody Turn Me 'Round." Their sarcasm was well disguised by the metaphorical optimism of the traditional movement hymn as it wafted along the lines.

Outpourings from the front ranks doubled back past those still wondering what had happened beyond the bridge. Some of the Episcopal seminarians mumbled, "Well, crud," fighting anticlimax. Back outside Brown Chapel, stuck once again in the overflow crowds, they absorbed movement lore that no showdown was ever simple and no tactical move above criticism from those who bore witness in demonstrations. They welcomed the dramatic arrival by charter flight of the first Episcopal bishop, James Pike of California, who offered an apology that he was too late to march—but censured him for self-importance when he hurried off again moments later. They observed the manpower that still poured into Selma, including two new planeloads of clergy from the Midwest, and sifted rumors of leadership disputes about how and when to use them.

Inside the church, King described the truncated march as "the greatest demonstration for freedom, the greatest confrontation so far in the South." A young man rose from the pews with a rare challenge: "Why didn't we just sit down in the highway and wait until the injunction was lifted?" King replied indirectly, omitting practicalities and legal details to insist that the voting rights movement would not rest until marchers reached Montgomery by the thousands. In his turn from the pulpit, James Forman raised a collateral discontent. "I've paid my dues in Selma," he declared. "I've been to jail here, I've been beaten here, so I have the right to ask this: why was there violence on Sunday and none on Tuesday? You know the answer. They don't beat white people. It's Negroes they beat and kill." A Selma Negro addressed an undertone of Forman's diagnosis. "You're right, they didn't beat us today because the world was here with us," he said. "But that's what we want. Don't let these white people feel that we don't appreciate their coming." Leaders tried to elevate the unsettled mood with upbeat sermons and youth songs, such as "I've Got the Love of Jesus in My Heart."

* * *

LUGGAGE AND opinions crossed in all directions outside. Most of the senior seminarians caught rides toward an airport, hurrying back to finish thesis papers for graduation. Notice passed by word of mouth drew upward of fifty Unitarians to a five o'clock caucus outside the church, where discussion of extending their vigil led some to retrieve suitcases from cars bound for Atlanta and stow them again in the parsonage. One group wandered down Sylvan Street into Amelia Boynton's insurance office, which doubled as SCLC headquarters, seeking tips on where to have supper.

"Do you prefer to eat with your own kind?" Diane Nash asked politely. When they expressed a desire instead for integrated facilities, if they existed, she smiled and directed them to a small restaurant with two names and an informal address, Southern style. Local people all called it "Eddie's," but strangers needed to look for a hand-lettered "Walker's Café" sign on the round Coca-Cola ad above an exterior window. There the Unitarians found a dinner atmosphere of millennial rarity. Columnist Jimmy Hicks of the *New York Amsterdam News* sat with Negro reporters from Chicago, pointing out prominent intellectuals scattered among the regular clientele of day laborers. "Imagine a Harvard theologian eating soul food," joked one of them. Unitarian Clark Olsen recognized at a nearby table a fellow resident of Berkeley, California, in Mario Savio, whose experience as a summer volunteer in Mississippi had spurred him into leadership of the ongoing Free Speech Movement at the Berkeley university campus, making Savio arguably the first nationally known white student of the civil rights era. The Unitarians avoided the tins of snuff and jars of pigs' feet on the counter, but savored the last plates of fried chicken, turnip greens, and cornbread from a kitchen stripped clean. Above the jumble of conversations, a jukebox recycled the prophetic anthem of the late pop star Sam Cooke, "A Change Is Gonna Come."

* * *

IN WASHINGTON, much relieved about Selma, President Johnson decided not to drop by a private dinner for departing Treasury Secretary Douglas Dillon because the Metropolitan Club was strictly segregated. He turned full attention to the ninth of ten war briefings aimed to reach every member of Congress in groups of roughly fifty apiece. "The most important thing I can say to you about South Vietnam," Secretary of State Dean Rusk told them in the Blue Room at the White House, is that "there are no tricks in it, nothing up our sleeves, no essential facts being concealed." Defense Secretary McNamara reviewed operations, including a massive naval patrol that stopped 350,000 Vietnamese per year on the 72,000 junks in the coastal waters of South Vietnam, of whom 2,000 were removed as suspects and "about 150 have proven to be Vietcong." The President praised McNamara for taking a 90 percent pay cut "just to come here and serve his President," and launched an appeal for Congress to maintain the solidarity of its support resolutions on Vietnam, which had passed by combined votes of 502–2. On past eight o'clock, Alabama time, Johnson described himself as a man with few of the answers and all of the burdens—"you just got one President, whether you like it or not"—who "needs all the help he can possibly get, and all the sympathy he can possibly get."

It was dark in Selma when two of the Unitarian ministers emerged from Walker's Café. Orloff Miller smoked a cigar on the sidewalk, waiting with Clark Olsen while James Reeb called Boston to tell his wife that he had decided to stay over another day. When Reeb joined them, Olsen pushed slightly ahead. Having arrived from California minutes too late for the afternoon's "turnaround" march, he wanted badly to honor the contributions of church members who had financed his cross-country travel, and was anxious to find out what was scheduled for Wednesday. Less than a block from the restaurant, footsteps sounded behind and a hard voice called, "Hey, niggers. Hey, you niggers." Olsen hastened a few steps, then turned to see one white man rush from behind and bring a club to the side of Reeb's head with a left-handed baseball swing, felling him. Two others kicked Miller after he dropped protectively to the pavement, and a fourth pummeled Olsen about the face. The attackers vanished in seconds, one of them shouting, "Now you know what it's like to be a real nigger."

Diane Nash called a doctor and Burwell Infirmary as soon as the three ministers stumbled through the door. Reeb appeared to be relatively unscathed compared with the bleeding friends who supported him on either side, but he was frightened and incoherent. Nash summoned one of the funeral home hearses that had served as ambulances for the two marches across Pettus Bridge. Dr. William Dinkins met them at Burwell, where Reeb spoiled X-rays from the portable machine by involuntarily jerking his head. From the look of his glazed eyes, Dinkins announced that Reeb must be transferred to an emergency neurosurgery unit ninety miles away in Birmingham, but a call to alert the hospital ran into notice that a $150 fee would be required for admission. Dinkins and the ministers did not have that much. Reeb vomited and lapsed into unconsciousness. Nash secured the money, and the ambulance roared off under siren until the right rear tire went flat a few miles north of Selma. Dinkins ordered driver Morris Anderson to ride the rim to a place where it was safe for a mixed group of whites and Negroes to call for a replacement ambulance.

This was not easy. Cars cruised ominously back and forth past the crippled ambulance in the parking lot of a radio station where Anderson used to work. One of Sheriff Clark's deputies stopped, shined a flashlight inside to question the racially mixed occupants, and refused Clark Olsen's desperate request to provide escort. It was too late for whites to retract or deny their protest, even to save a life, and Dr. Dinkins, who often soared above Negro status in his own Piper Cub, sporting a leather helmet and white silk scarf, could only wait trembling on the ground. Past 9:30, two hours after the attack, the driver of the second ambulance belatedly arrived. He abandoned an effort to hot-wire its balky siren to life, and sped north again in silence. Reeb's fellow ministers braced him around the highway curves because the stretcher stays were broken.

* * *

"THEY CAME here from other sections of the country," King told the hushed crowd at Brown Chapel, receiving whispered bulletins from grave-looking couriers. "I think two of them were from Boston, the Rev. Miller and the Rev. Reeb—and the Rev. Reeb was the one, I believe, who was very seriously injured—James Reeb, and I believe he's from Boston." He paused in prayer for "these brothers who came here to be with us today," recognized the pilgrim clergy, whose ranks had thinned so that all of them now fitted into the front pews, and saluted a delegation of "our brothers in the adjoining county, Wilcox—not a single Negro registered." King said forces might "rearrange our plans a bit" but could never retard their determination to secure the vote. "Now next week we're going to the statehouse in Montgomery," he declared, "but *tomorrow* we're going to the courthouse in Selma and we ask for your participation." FBI agents recorded that he surrendered the pulpit at 10:30 P.M. Of the remaining Episcopal seminarians, Judith Upham and Jonathan Daniels next found themselves recruited by eager young Negroes who escorted them to shelter with families in the Carver apartment project. Bone tired, they slept past the appointed march time of 9:15 and bolted up in panic, not yet savvy to the movement's padded timetable.

CHAPTER 8

The Ghost of Lincoln

March 10–12, 1965

JAMES Reeb's name commanded national headlines on Wednesday morning, March 10. Details of the dramatic ambush—how the three ministers took a wrong turn in the dark past a reputed Klan hangout called the Silver Moon diner—eclipsed brooding controversies about the abbreviated march, and fresh cascades of emotion swelled the reaction to Sunday's televised violence. Of the many newcomers who filed into Brown Chapel that morning, one Catholic philosopher from Missouri's Fontbonne College was mystified to behold in the pulpit "a squat figure in blue jeans and a bizarre beanie," then guessed from the ensuing shower of parables and entertainment that "one of Martin Luther King's most articulate spokesmen" must be concealing himself in an outfit of "local color." James Bevel coached the crowd to sort through every proposed action for constructive purpose. "We are testifying," he said. "Remember that. Some people have a hard time understanding nonviolence." Bevel claimed an immense untapped power for the doctrine to break down barriers when people willing to suffer worked hard to frame questions of justice unambiguously. "If nonviolence can work in Alabama," he declared, "it can work in South Africa."

At 12:47 P.M., Rev. L. L. Anderson led the crowd of five hundred outside to a roadblock under a chinaberry tree less than a block down Sylvan Street, where Mayor Joseph Smitherman, backed by a line of policemen, declared a permanent blockade. "You can make all the statements you want," added Public Safety Director Wilson Baker, "but you are not going to march." Behind Baker, flanked by deputies and posse-men, Sheriff Clark wore a white helmet and his trademark button pledging "Never" to abandon segregation. Behind them formed a loose reserve of one hundred Alabama troopers.

Thus began a marathon standoff. Sister Antona, a Negro nun from St. Louis, was the first to take a bullhorn to deliver a simple statement about why she had made the journey. One by one, more than thirty speakers stepped forward for nearly two hours—a rabbi from New Jersey, a student from Yale, a priest from Minnesota. At four o'clock, when members of an ecumenical delegation headed home to Missouri in two chartered airplanes, they were such an instant phenomenon that the powerful St. Louis radio station KMOX put Sister Antona and five other "nuns of Selma" directly on the air with stories that drew a flood of more than twenty thousand phone calls. Listeners from forty states variously praised them as national saviors and denounced them for perverting their image of a nun's cloistered purity. In Selma, Ralph Abernathy announced at dusk that the stymied marchers would keep vigil all night for the comatose James Reeb. Jesse Jackson, having arrived from Chicago in the van packed with divinity students, moved briskly among leaders of the weary veterans and new reinforcements, asking, "What do you want *my people* to do?" Wilson Baker strung a clothesline across Sylvan Street to mark a boundary line, and Selma teenagers swiftly improvised verses to the tune of "The Battle of Jericho": "We got a rope that's a Berlin Wall, Berlin Wall . . . in Selma, Alabama. . . . We're gonna stand here 'til it falls. . . . Hate is the thing that built the wall. . . . Love is the thing that will make it fall . . ." Headlights from the state troopers' idling cruisers silhouetted them behind the long clothesline.

The pilot of a commercial flight radioed ahead for a Birmingham taxi to meet his airplane on the runway so as to spare Marie Reeb the ordeal of pushing through photographers at the terminal. Hospital escorts took her promptly to the surgical recovery room where her husband lay in the midst of life support machines with a tracheotomy tube in his throat. By evening, with the help of friends, she managed to compose herself to speak briefly with reporters arranged in three tiers around the hospital auditorium. They had agreed to minimize her stress by submitting seven questions in advance through ABC correspondent Edgar Needham, ending with the most difficult. "I told the children this morning as soon as they woke up that their father had been hurt," she replied. "The younger ones did not fully understand, but the thirteen-year-old was quite upset." Retreating to wait in a reserved space near the recovery room, she found a bouquet of yellow roses with a note of condolence from President and Mrs. Johnson.

The President, back in Washington from a day trip to Camp David, called Attorney General Katzenbach later Wednesday night. "This minister's gonna die, isn't he?" asked Johnson.

"Yes, sir," said Katzenbach.

"Is he already dead?" asked Johnson.

When Katzenbach said it was a matter of hours, Johnson pushed for specific actions the administration could take to meet another crescendo of unrest. Katzenbach, having apologized profusely for recommending that the President make no public statement about Bloody Sunday until a legislative proposal was ready ("Forget it," Johnson told him), presented measures that were not quite ready. That day's draft of a voting rights message was unsatisfactory. "It just doesn't sing yet," Katzenbach said. He was consulting privately with Judge Frank Johnson ("I think the judge is going to be pretty good"), but could not say so. His feverish negotiations toward a voting rights bill with Senator Everett Dirksen, who again controlled the critical Republican swing vote, had irritated Senator Mike Mansfield to the point that the Democratic Majority Leader threatened revolt over being taken for granted. "He's too polite to say that," Katzenbach reported, "but that's what he felt." As to law enforcement, the Attorney General said he was eager to press federal charges for Sunday's violence against Alabama officials, including Sheriff Clark ("I'm a little more reluctant with Lingo because it touches the governor"), but the Department was struggling to identify specific defendants from FBI evidence. "I just sent seven more lawyers down there," he reported. Johnson spurred Katzenbach forward on all these options, and resolved to "take the cork out of the bottle" by confiding his plans to civil rights groups and religious leaders in the Oval Office, before their protests could escalate. "I don't mind meeting with them," he said. Katzenbach believed the somber reality of Reeb's impending death could help "keep the rowdies down."

* * *

WILDCAT REBELLIONS already were defying such hopes in Montgomery, where a supervised field trip shifted within hours into what the press called a "pee-in" outside the Alabama state capitol. Earlier on Wednesday, a convoy of cars and chartered buses arrived bearing seven hundred student members of the Tuskegee Institute Advancement

League, with faculty chaperones and bag lunches packed by university cafeteria workers. Governor Wallace refused to see their representatives or receive their carefully drawn petition for Negro voting rights, which came as a shock to the delegation. The rebuff convinced one student leader that Tuskegee students were "no different from other black people—the country people, the people of Selma, anywhere." Indignant speeches at the outdoor rally developed into a free-form debate about their condition, punctuated by clashes with the constricting rings of police and state troopers who pushed them back and forth between their respective jurisdictions at the foot of the capitol property. Against the pleas of the highly agitated dean of students, James Forman and other circulating SNCC leaders convinced about two hundred students to stage a sit-down strike for the governor's attention. Some hand-holding couples wrenched apart over the sudden option to extend a college day-trip into uncharted insurrection. The majority who returned as scheduled with the dean put the Tuskegee campus into an upheaval, and the dwindling number who held their ground into the night, prevented from returning if they left, eventually broke through inhibitions to relieve themselves where they stood—female students squatting within clusters of friends faced outward. They sought shelter from rain after midnight by breaking into the nearby First Baptist Church—Ralph Abernathy's old "Brick-a-day" church, built by ex-slaves, where the Freedom Riders of 1961 had been besieged. Forman resolved Thursday morning to "radicalize" the Alabama movement from a new SNCC base in Montgomery, animated by what the *New York Times* reported as "open contempt" for King's conduct in Selma.

Eight blocks away, in a federal courtroom swamped with reporters, King testified as the first witness in Judge Frank Johnson's hearing on the proposed march to Montgomery. Lawyers for Governor Wallace and Sheriff Clark made him admit that he marched on Tuesday in spite of Judge Johnson's injunction, "even after a marshal read you the order." When they pressed him to acknowledge that he had denounced the order as "unjust," King shifted uneasily. "Yes, I did," he said. The judge interrupted the lawyers to claim the fight as his own, ruling that guilt for contempt was a matter "between this court and the alleged contemptors." Removing his glasses, he stared down from the bench to question King directly about his conversations with Governor Collins and how far he had marched beyond Pettus Bridge. Most pointedly, he asked King about a "report I have received from the Justice Department" that after the march was confronted by troopers, "they were pulled away and that their automobiles were removed while y'all were still there, is that correct?"

"That is correct," said King.

"And then did you go forward, or did you turn and go back?" asked Judge Johnson.

"We turned around and went back to Selma," said King.

"After the troopers had pulled back?"

"That is correct," said King.

"And at that point there were no troopers in front of you?"

"That is correct," said King. Heads nodded in the courtroom. The contest turned on clashing interpretations of his behavior as compliance, defiance, or shame.

Judge Johnson sternly demanded silence from spectators and admonished both sides to maintain decorum through their badgering hostilities. To circumvent his orders requiring the use of courtesy titles such as "Dr." and "Mr.," lawyers for Alabama never referred to or addressed King by name.

* * *

In Washington that same Thursday morning, Secret Service Agent Rufus Youngblood rushed into President Johnson's living quarters to inform him that twelve demonstrators had launched a sit-in downstairs. With security already heightened by the perpetual picket lines outside the gates, the alarm would be enough to generate two diagrams on the front page of the next day's *New York Times* showing how the six young Negroes and six whites had accomplished the first recorded penetration of the White House, posing as tourists. The President sought advice from his aides Lee White, Bill Moyers, and Jack Valenti, as well as Youngblood—the agent who had covered him famously during the gunfire into the Dallas motorcade—then vetoed the standing procedure to eject the demonstrators by force. Instead, he ordered Youngblood to keep them sealed off in the East Wing corridor where they had ensconced themselves, and divert all foot traffic elsewhere. Not even Mrs. Johnson was allowed the peek she desired, but White House maids could serve coffee to advance nature's encouragement for them to leave. With that, the President departed for the Cabinet Room to begin his civil rights audiences with a group of Negro newspaper publishers.

In Montgomery, before Judge Johnson recessed his hearing for the day, Willie Ricks reported to Atlanta over the SNCC WATS line that

"Bevel and Forman almost came to blows in the church." They were in Dexter Avenue Baptist, the prim little church at the foot of the capitol hill where King had been pastor during the bus boycott. Forman had led a tired remnant of the Tuskegee Institute Advancement League group there from First Baptist to join students newly recruited by Ricks from Alabama State, the local Negro college, along with some traveling students and clergy—mostly white—gathered up from the Montgomery airport on their way to Selma. Bevel barged in from Selma to challenge their clarity of purpose. "What did you set out to do?" he asked. He induced several people to say they were responding to publicity about Selma. "Then why are you *here* in Montgomery?" shouted Bevel. "Why don't you go to Selma and find out what people see as the next logical step in a nonviolent campaign to win the vote?" He said their "foolishness" in Montgomery could undercut the national drama building from Selma with an image of angry Negroes who broke into their own churches and urinated in the street. Bevel sat down in the front row and heckled Forman's efforts to refute him. Forman said Bevel was taking the same side as the hateful racists who had abused their right to demonstrate. "Demonstrate for *what?*" cried Bevel. He accused Forman of controlling the crowd by keeping it uninformed, which brought their dispute to a boil.

"I decided to stop trying to talk," Forman later wrote of the moment. If he launched into "the whole history of King's actions in Selma," he knew Bevel would dismiss his grievances as rivalry in the guise of strategy. Instead, Forman announced that he was resuming the demonstration at the capitol by himself if necessary. "Anybody who wants to come with me can do so," he said. Four SNCC staff members and one student followed him out the door. A cordon of Montgomery police officers manhandled Forman and dragged all five to jail. Shortly thereafter, officers fell upon the others as they tried to slip away to Selma—seizing Bevel and the first few students, driving the remaining two hundred back into the church with billy clubs that inflicted several wounds. Forman and Bevel wound up in neighboring cells, their differences swallowed up until they posted bail.

By late Thursday afternoon in Washington, only two of twelve demonstrators had voluntarily departed from their sit-in positions along the primary entry corridor at the White House. President Johnson, running out of time before fifty-odd members of Congress were due for the tenth briefing reception on Vietnam, gave Agent Youngblood and several aides detailed instructions for removing the intruders with minimum public notice. While he diverted the press with a brief stop elsewhere by motorcade, Johnson directed, they were to assemble integrated teams of police officers—not federal agents—to haul away the occupiers in small groups out of different gates to different precinct stations in unmarked cars. That being precisely done, the arriving legislators passed no jarring sights of disorder on their way into the White House, but sounds from the continuous picket line outside the gates did penetrate the walls of the East Room, where Johnson made prefacing remarks on the parallel crisis in Selma. "The ghost of Lincoln," he said, "is moving up and down the corridors rather regularly these days."

The President introduced the Attorney General to explain the judgment he had just rendered at a press conference initiated and scripted by Johnson—that state and local officials had used "totally unreasonable force" on Sunday. "I have no question that federal law was violated," Katzenbach declared in the administration's first substantive response to Pettus Bridge. "We are going to bring charges against those whom we can identify as violators." This message drew a stinging cross-examination from several legislators, including Representative John Bell Williams of Mississippi, who blasted Katzenbach for siding with Communist agitators to trample on the rights of the South. McNamara and Rusk were having an easier time explaining the administration's war moves in Vietnam when an aide handed President Johnson a note that James Reeb had been pronounced dead at 6:55 P.M., Alabama time. "Lyndon and I excused ourselves for a helpless, painful talk with Mrs. Reeb," recorded Lady Bird Johnson. The President insisted that a presidential C-140 airplane take the widow and Reeb's father back home when they were ready, and he consoled them for fifteen long minutes about their personal loss for a just cause. "But what is there to say?" Mrs. Johnson added in her diary. "When we went upstairs we could hear the Congressional guests and the music still playing below; and out in the front the chanting of the Civil Rights marchers. What a house. What a life."

* * *

WILSON BAKER, unshaven and haggard from lack of sleep, announced Reeb's death Thursday night to several hundred Selma Negroes and visiting clergy still standing vigil at the "Berlin Wall" clothesline on Sylvan Street. Behind them, dripping from a second day of steady cold rain, a banner still hung above the Brown Chapel doorway from Jimmie Lee

Jackson's funeral on March 3: "Racism Killed Our Brother." Prayers and song verses recognized Reeb as the second martyr of the Selma campaign until interrupted by another object hurled from the distance, which struck a demonstrator from Wisconsin in the forehead. Baker helped send him off to Good Samaritan for treatment, maintaining a rapport of gruff civility across his barrier even though he had prevented the demonstrators from building tent shelters—city code, he said—which left them and their patchwork bed of air mattresses soaked in the mud beneath umbrellas, blankets, and flattened cardboard boxes on sticks. ("I'm a segregationist," Baker told one reporter, "but if I was a nigger I'd be doing just what they're doing.") He pledged solemnly to the crowd—as he had promised the Justice Department already—that he would file first-degree murder charges within an hour of Reeb's death against the four Selma men he had identified as the assailants, one of whom had seventeen prior arrests. When he returned, the bandaged Wisconsin man was already back among demonstrators, who sang between their diversions of fatigue, such as street dances, grandiose debates about fasts to the death, and naps in the dry Brown Chapel pews.

Governor Collins rushed back to Selma that evening to buffer emotional eruptions from Reeb's death—only to become disturbed himself by an encounter with Lola Bell Tate, a teenage girl he found on the floor of the Brown Chapel parsonage. Dr. Dinkins explained as he worked to stop the bleeding that a .22 caliber bullet had pierced her lip and knocked out a tooth, but luckily had been too spent to cause more damage. Tate was the third victim so far of potshots fired into the street vigil. Collins made his way back outside past the clothesline and Baker's police officers to the commander of the state troopers, asking why he deployed his armed men to face inward with weapons trained on the demonstrators rather than upon the marauders who fired and hurled projectiles from the darkness behind. Receiving no satisfactory answer, Collins recovered his official neutrality and went off to seek a negotiated truce that would relax the vigil in return for a one-time memorial service for Reeb at the courthouse. He and his assistants discovered that tear gas grenades had been set off beneath their government sedan. "They attempted to drive it," reported the *New York Times,* "but were forced to get out after half a block, their eyes watering."

At FBI headquarters, officials maneuvered to minimize the bureau's public exposure. When both the White House and Justice Department requested an FBI escort for Marie Reeb in Birmingham, Assistant Director DeLoach fended off the courtesy duty with an exaggerated claim that all Alabama agents were "working around the clock in the Selma area." This earned him a personal commendation from J. Edgar Hoover, who mandated instead a security review of the Justice Department aide suspected to have originated the escort idea. Simultaneously, to forestall any "numbers game" about FBI performance, DeLoach dodged a request to disclose how many agents were assigned to Selma. There were enough to get results, he told White House press secretary George Reedy, but Katzenbach's press conference late Thursday pitched the Bureau's internal machinery into reverse alarm. Well into the night, headquarters grilled employees about how the Attorney General could promise federal prosecutions before the FBI provided "any information whatsoever . . . indicating that any of the police officers involved in the brutal beating of the marchers on Sunday March 7, 1965 had been identified." Panicky agents "emphatically stated that they had no knowledge," and parroted the accepted line that matching troopers or deputies with thousands of photographs "has been difficult due to the fact a large majority were wearing gas masks." When supervisors wrung from the head of the Mobile office an admission that he had shared interim results with John Doar, and thus taken initiative for which "he has no written record of authorization," the FBI's disciplinary apparatus isolated and removed him by morning.

* * *

THE SEVERAL crises converged toward showdown on Friday, March 12. In Selma, where rain fell so hard that only eighty at a time maintained the vigil outdoors, the last of the Chicago theology students left for home—Jesse Jackson with a mild case of pneumonia—but newcomers replaced them several times over. Seventy Catholics arrived that day from Chicago alone, and the annual meeting of the Unitarian-Universalist Association adjourned en masse to Selma from Boston, where the symphony honored Reeb with the same piece it had played after the Kennedy assassination, Gluck's "Dance of the Blessed Spirits."

Wilson Baker could not keep his agreement with Governor Collins to secure permission for a memorial service at the Selma courthouse, because his boss, Mayor Smitherman, moved steadily against him into a political alliance with Sheriff Clark, bending to local voters angered by the "appeasement" of Tuesday's march. On his own, Baker did cut down the "Berlin Wall" with his pocketknife that afternoon. Although he emphasized that there still would be no marches, demonstrators eagerly cut up pieces of the clothesline as souvenirs of a symbol removed. They raised freedom chants along with prayers of conviction that nonviolence would overcome the barriers to Montgomery. The rain finally stopped. Young people invented new verses for their song: "The invisible wall is a Berlin Wall. . . . The troopers' cars are a Berlin Wall . . ."

In Montgomery, a large truck pulled up outside temporary SNCC headquarters with a surprise delivery of tents, helmets, cooking utensils, and assorted survival equipment. Silas Norman berated Forman for spending many thousands of scarce SNCC dollars unilaterally toward a "grandstand" campaign that the organization had rejected a week earlier. SNCC leader Cleveland Sellers was stunned to learn that Forman had put out a "nationwide call" to Montgomery, mimicking King. Forman, in turn, was dismayed to learn that Stokely Carmichael and seventy Tuskegee recruits abandoned the occupation of Dexter Avenue Baptist as a foothold for demonstrations, under pressure from Bevel and church trustees who cut off the electricity and water. Meanwhile, at federal court in Montgomery, Assistant Attorney General John Doar was "plainly astonished," according to the *New York Times,* to hear his own FBI witness blurt out—against the grain of his testimony, and without being asked—that Alabama troopers were "justified in using tear gas" on Bloody Sunday. Unbeknownst to Doar or spectators, rookie agent James M. Barko had misinterpreted the Bureau's overnight dragnet about helping Doar, and soon felt corrective discipline straight from Hoover's office for putting the FBI on any side of public controversy about race. Doar, arguing in support of King's petition for a protected march, tried to recover by offering into evidence a three-minute news film of the violence on Pettus Bridge, and Judge Johnson, visibly affected by footage he had never seen, called a recess as soon as courtroom lights were restored. His demeanor confirmed instincts within Governor Wallace's inner circle that the judge and the whole country were tilting against them. "The niggers are like cats," one legislator told a reporter. "They always land on their feet." Late Friday, yearning to regain public initiative, Wallace wired President Johnson for an appointment to address "some of the greatest internal problems ever faced by this nation."

Undercover agents scattered through the outdoor lines for the White House tour on Friday to prevent a recurrence of the previous day's sit-in. For better than four hours, through lunch, President Johnson sat in the Cabinet Room flanked by Katzenbach and Vice President

Humphrey, listening to stories about voting rights from more than three dozen men—a few young activists* and a delegation of clergy from a mammoth ecumenical assembly convened by the Commission on Religion and Race. Many had been to Selma, including Rev. Joseph Ellwanger of the white Alabamian's march and Rev. Robert Spike from the "turnaround" march on Tuesday. The President took notes. His joke fell flat when he remarked that the picket lines outside were "violatin' *my* civil rights" by keeping his daughters from doing their homework, and the audience grew restless when Humphrey recited all the past achievements for which Johnson deserved credit. "Why has it taken so long for you to send a voting rights bill to Congress?" Episcopal Bishop Paul Moore asked bluntly. Stung, Johnson said it was not easy to fashion a constitutional bill that would pass a Congress dominated by hostile Southern committee chairmen, and also deliver the franchise effectively to five million Negroes where all previous measures had failed. When Spike and his delegation returned to the Lutheran Church of the Reformation on Capitol Hill, where the CORR's nationwide convocation of three thousand clergy itself made front-page news, their reports of impatience with Johnson drew cheers, but descriptions of an "anguished" President received skeptical comments about an LBJ "snow job."

Back in the Oval Office, Johnson called for his dog Blanco but found him sick from a rabies shot. To stimulate interest in an upbeat topic, he took Laurence Rockefeller of the White House Conference on Natural Beauty down to the press room—only to find that nearly all the reporters had rushed outside to watch officers haul away two dozen demonstrators who had been rooted out of the tour line but now sat in Pennsylvania Avenue during rush hour, plus a handful of white women who had slipped through the northwest gate to lie facedown on the White House driveway. Johnson told the remaining journalists they could ask Rockefeller anything they wanted, but got few takers. When one of them mentioned that Governor Wallace reportedly was asking to see him, Johnson pounced. Even before the telegram from Alabama was received, his staff arranged and announced a summit conference for the next morning.

---

* Including Lester McKinney of SNCC, William Higgs of the MFDP, Rev. Jefferson Rogers of SCLC, and Hubert (Rap) Brown of the Nonviolent Action Group at Howard University.

CHAPTER 9

Wallace and the Archbishop

March 13–15, 1965

ON Saturday, March 13, President Johnson prepared for Wallace first by consulting his Secretary of Defense about the heavy pressure from the lobbying clergy to dispatch U.S. soldiers to Alabama. "They all say, 'we want troops,' " Johnson told McNamara. But troops, he said, really meant sending "some young boy who's just been drafted or joined in," and who lacked the ability to handle prosecutions or complex racial entanglements. "Troops don't do any of that, and we don't know that we've got enough troops but what he [Wallace] could match them if he just called in everybody that he could get." Johnson added that Katzenbach had "thirty-three lawyers" working on the legal ramifications of using troops in Selma, "all of whom are in this field, and all of them recommend against it."

McNamara concurred. "Beyond all the arguments you've given, Mr. President, Selma is just one point," he said. "You have Mississippi, Louisiana, and the rest of Alabama to take care of. You got this bill coming up next week, and troops leave a bitter taste in the mouths of all the people that are in those three states, and in the mouths of all the senators."

As applied to Vietnam as well as Selma, these were profound, treacherous distinctions of politics and war. Johnson also leaned against sending civilian U.S. marshals to Selma, which was the option that Martin Luther King strongly preferred. King saw the enforcement mission of marshals as corrective and constructive—treating violent segregationists as errant fellow citizens, with rights—whereas the military mission of soldiers tended to dehumanize opponents into enemies. For King, even armed marshals were easier to square with nonviolence than soldiers, but Johnson worked from practical experience rather than abstraction. Behind the myth of Wyatt Earp, he saw the typical U.S. marshal as a patronage hack with very little training. "He's just a fellow that carried some senator's suitcase," the President told McNamara, "and there are just a hundred or so of 'em in the whole United States."

Johnson wanted to rely on seasoned FBI agents as long as possible. DeLoach, his FBI liaison officer, had promised him that the Bureau would bring evidence to prosecute a hundred of the troopers who had run roughshod over the marchers on Sunday. "While this FBI man was getting his head beat in with a club, he was taking pictures . . . and he got them all on their horses," the President told McNamara. "We can't identify 'em with gas masks on, but we've got their horses, and we're identifying the horses they rode." McNamara expressed no reservations about such a fantastic stalling yarn, which the Bureau would discard when pressure eased, and if he detected a rare gullibility in Johnson he refrained from saying so. Instead, he assured the President that he had troop units on alert for rapid deployment, and endorsed Johnson's reluctance to use them in a political crisis. "If we did anything wrong in the past two or three years on this," said McNamara of previous crises in Birmingham and at Ole Miss, "it was to introduce troops too early, and they escalate to a higher level of violence."*

With Governor Wallace waiting in the Cabinet Room, Johnson summoned Attorney General Katzenbach alone into his private bathroom while he sat on the toilet. This was Katzenbach's first exposure to a legendary Johnsonian practice, which power analysts interpreted as a submission drill for squeamish aides such as McGeorge Bundy. To Katzenbach, who may have been eligible for such treatment himself as an Ivy Leaguer, Johnson's manner seemed wholly one of raw urgency about Wallace, stripped of pretense. "What should I ask him to do?" Johnson demanded.

Katzenbach stammered. "I don't know," he said. "What do you want him to do?"

"Write down six things for me," Johnson commanded—make a list,

---

* McNamara here contradicted prevailing judgment. At Little Rock in 1957, and more so at Ole Miss in 1962, most of the violence occurred before rather than after the deployment of U.S. Army troops.

put numbers on it. "I don't give a damn how outrageous they are," he said.

Katzenbach found a pad in the Oval Office. The President glanced at the hastily composed list when he emerged minutes later, then pocketed it on the way to greet the Wallace entourage. There he remarked effusively on Lady Bird's Alabama roots and made a point of introducing the renowned Secret Service agent Rufus Youngblood as a native Georgian, which reminded him to send for an agent born in Alabama. He grandly announced that George Wallace had at least one thing in common with Martin Luther King, namely, that they were the only two people cheeky enough to ask him for an appointment and notify the press before the request reached the White House, which King had done on leaving the Selma jail in February. Bantering about Southern manners and a President's prerogatives, he waved off Wallace's apologies with assurances that he was glad to see him. The summoned Secret Service agent arrived, whereupon Johnson beamed, "Lem, I want to introduce you to your governor."

The President soon invited Wallace and one aide to retire privately with him and Katzenbach. He guided the diminutive Wallace to sink low in one of the cushioned sofas in the Oval Office, then pulled his favorite rocking chair close enough to rub knees as he towered over his guest. "Well, governor," said Johnson, "you wanted to see me?"

Wallace defined the problem as malcontent demonstrators trained in Moscow or New York. "You cannot deal with street revolutionaries," he said. "You can never satisfy them. First it's a front seat on the bus. Next it's a takeover of parks. Then it's public schools. Then it's voting rights. Then it's jobs. Then it's distribution of wealth without work." For fifteen minutes, he described the hardships created by subversive demonstrators for Alabama and Washington alike, then exhorted President Johnson to join with him in a dutiful alliance to restore public order. "Finally, Mr. President, I'd like to thank you for the opportunity to let me come here," Wallace concluded, with comments about the White House and other national symbols that bordered on awe.

Johnson never took his eye off Wallace. His accent thickened as he expressed his own distaste for demonstrations, to the point that Wallace's aide later claimed he said "nigger" outright instead of the drawled Southern "nigra." "Those goddam nigras have kept my daughters awake every night with their screaming and hollering," said Johnson, then slowly shifted from the faults of the demonstrators to their grievances. "You can't stop a fever by putting an icepack on your head," he told Wallace, and brutality was no good to "get at the cause" of the fever, of course. "I know you're like me, not approving of brutality," said Johnson. He brushed off Wallace's quibbles about the word "brutality" by snapping his fingers for photographs of the violence on Pettus Bridge. Johnson secured a numb agreement that brutality injured the United States even if Wallace qualified the cause of it, then mused sadly about how the governor strayed so far from his progressive record in public service. "Why are you off on this black thing?" he asked. "You ought to be down there calling for help for Aunt Susie in the nursing home."

The President soared off into New Deal memories of hooking up the first electricity in hardscrabble rural Texas so families at last could see at night and farmers could live past forty and farm women could iron clothes without first heating a metal slab in the fire. He rhapsodized on his plans to establish Medicare and attack hopelessness in Appalachia. He said Wallace could do a lot to educate the poor of both races in Alabama—"Your president will help you"—if he would stop harkening back to 1865 and look instead to his legacy for 2065. "What do you want left when you die?" Johnson intoned. "Do you want a great big marble monument that reads, 'George Wallace—He Built,' or do you want a little piece of scrawny pine board that reads, 'George Wallace—He Hated'?"

Seymore Trammell loyally intervened to say his boss had come there to discuss the growing menace of Communist demonstrations, but he failed to relieve Wallace from the grip of LBJ's treatment. The President slowly turned and "looked at me like I was some kind of dog mess," Trammell recalled, then handed him a pencil from the coffee table. "Here, take notes," Johnson ordered. Picking the most far-fetched item from Katzenbach's list, he offered Wallace a suggestion to "turn off those demonstrations in a minute" by announcing his commitment to desegregate all of Alabama's public schools: "You and I go out there right now in front of those television cameras."

Wallace looked stricken. On the defensive about his tombstone, he parried the notion by saying that he lacked the power to do so under Alabama law.

Johnson sparred with Wallace through the items on Katzenbach's list: a pledge of obedience for federal court orders, a commitment to law enforcement without brutality, a declaration of support for the protected right of peaceful assembly, and a call for biracial meetings between Alabama whites and Negroes. "Are you getting this down?" he prodded Trammell, and finally suggested that Wallace simply affirm the principle of universal suffrage.

Wallace replied that everybody in Alabama could vote already if they were registered. In that case, Johnson pressed, say everybody including nigras could be registered. "I don't have that power, Mr. President," said Wallace. "Under Alabama law it belongs to the county registrars."

"Don't you shit me, George Wallace," Johnson said sternly. Then he grinned slyly to register a sore point from the 1964 election: "You had the power to keep the President of the United States off the [Alabama] ballot. Surely you have the power to tell a few poor county registrars what to do."

They emerged after three hours and fifteen minutes to tell a crush of reporters outside the West Wing lobby that they had enjoyed a frank exchange of views. Wallace called the President "a great gentleman, as always," and then departed, confiding glumly to assistants on his homeward flight that "when the President works on you, there's not a lot you can do." White House aides, by contrast, shelved contingency plans to contain an ugly scene if "the meeting has gone badly," and later recorded that Johnson's performance left Wallace "sort of cowed and pliable—of course, it didn't last more than two days." Johnson himself gobbled a bowl of soup before announcing outdoors at his thirty-eighth press conference that he would submit voting rights legislation next week. Asked what he had told Wallace, he revealed the last three suggestions from Katzenbach: "First, I urged that the Governor publicly declare his support for universal suffrage." Asked why he had waited a week to respond publicly to Sunday's violence, Johnson asserted that he had received a suitable proposal only hours earlier. "I have plotted my course," he said. From the Rose Garden, the freedom chants of a thousand pickets still could be heard beyond the Pennsylvania Avenue gates.

* * *

A SMALL airplane identified as the "Confederate Air Force" buzzed low over Selma's blockaded vigil on its fifth continuous day, dropping leaflets that advised white citizens to fire local Negroes—"an unemployed agitator ceases to agitate"—and to support a defense fund for the alleged murderers of James Reeb. Morale suffered on both sides of the line below. Bands of frustrated demonstrators slipped around Wilson Baker's front ranks toward the courthouse, only to need rescuing by Baker himself from more hostile whites lurking in the rear. Uniformed officers occasionally weakened under the prolonged barrage of nonvio-

lent freedom songs that were personalized for them at close quarters—
"I love badge number forty-seven . . ." Some answered questions about
hobbies and trivia, or even expressed confusion about their duty, and a
few commanders reportedly asked to have their men relieved by the Alabama National Guard. Sheriff Clark rallied his possemen and Lingo's
troopers to block the first surge of a march to honor Reeb on March 14,
but he relented under a truce with Baker to allow small parties through
the lines for the limited purpose of attending Sunday worship downtown. Two fresh acquaintances from the vigil arranged to meet at the
doorstep of First Presbyterian, where ushers turned them away because
one was a Negro. At Central Baptist, much of the large congregation
evacuated or avoided the sanctuary until the deacons safely refused several racially mixed groups.

At St. Paul's Episcopal, Rev. Frank Mathews missed his own service
because of an ulcerous stomach that was aggravated by the expected arrival of twenty aspiring worshipers from the "Berlin Wall," led by collared clergy. When Rev. John Morris and others had provided a courtesy
notice of their intention, Mathews responded by asking whether they
thought it would be Christian to bring guests with measles. In his absence, the awkward debate about an appropriate analogy for multiracial
worship resumed in confrontation on the church steps. Seminarian
Jonathan Daniels acknowledged the frayed nerves all around as signs of
genuine spiritual conflict, but theological issues were so urgent to him
that he frankly expressed worry about how the leaders of St. Paul's
could hope to secure any standing within Episcopal canon law or any
personal comfort from the deeper imperatives of faith.

For Judith Upham, the only other Boston seminarian who had remained all week in Selma, distress focused more on the tactical disadvantage of having within their group some local people in dirty blue
jeans who displayed little respect for Episcopal tradition. She was embarrassed by her own wish that all the Negroes among them could be
like the impeccably educated Ivanhoe Donaldson of SNCC, who had
been raised Anglican in Jamaica. Finally, the phalanx of ushers and
vestrymen from St. Paul's concocted a "nonracial" policy to admit all the
clergy but none of the laymen, including Donaldson. Those blockaded
on the church steps retreated to Brown Chapel rather than submit to the
mandated division. Three regular members of St. Paul's walked out of
the delayed service to protest the refusal of worship, opening battle
within a congregation that included many of Selma's most prominent
citizens.

At St. Mark's Episcopal in Washington, Rev. William Baxter preached about his own Selma journey to a congregation that included the Johnson and Humphrey families, as observances spilled widely to mark the week since Pettus Bridge. From San Jose, California, and Beloit, Wisconsin, marchers set off on fifty-mile treks to honor the impeded course from Selma to Montgomery. Twenty-seven ministers conducted a service of reconciliation at the Alamo in San Antonio, Texas, and a thousand people in New Orleans marched through hostile crowds to advocate voting rights. In Massachusetts, twenty thousand attended a "Rally for Freedom" on Boston Common, while opponents burned a ten-foot cross in the fabled revolutionary town of Lexington. A relay of eighteen freedom runners left from New York's George Washington Bridge bound for Washington, and nuns from the Sisters of Charity, in military formation and Puritan-style habits, joined a procession of 15,000 through Harlem to hear addresses by John Lewis, James Forman, and Bayard Rustin. From All Souls Unitarian Church in Washington, where James Reeb had served as assistant pastor until 1964, the morning service emptied into a spontaneous march down Sixteenth Street that gathered another crowd of 15,000 into Lafayette Park for speakers, including Fannie Lou Hamer of Mississippi. "Her plump face shining in the sun," reported the normally staid *New York Times,* "she shouted in her mighty voice: 'It's time now to stop begging them for what should have been done one hundred years ago. We have stood up on our feet, and God knows we're on our way!' "

Noise from Lafayette Park filtered across the street into the Cabinet Room where President Johnson convened seven congressional leaders Sunday afternoon. "You made the White House fireproof but not soundproof," he observed wryly in the midst of a sober prediction that more would die like Reeb until the government secured the right to register and vote for all citizens "except those in mental institutions." Senate leaders Mike Mansfield and Everett Dirksen each pressed Johnson not to seem panicky in the face of demonstrations. "This is a deliberate government," said Dirksen. "Don't let those people say, 'we scared him into it.' " Perhaps by prearrangement, House leaders argued that a presidential address to the nation would instill relief rather than panic. "I think it would help," said Majority Leader Carl Albert of Oklahoma, and Speaker John McCormack invited Johnson to address a joint session of Congress. They fixed Tuesday evening as the earliest practicable time for the President to put his proposals into speech form, but Attorney General Katzenbach allowed that the "unpredictable" King might try to resume the march from Selma earlier the same day. To preclude being upstaged, the leaders resolved to advance the date to Monday—the next evening. Bill Moyers called in emergency help from church leader Robert Spike as well as political strategist Louis Martin, the former publisher of Negro newspapers who worked for Democratic presidents since FDR. Johnson commandeered writers to work through Sunday night, including Horace Busby, author of Johnson's treasured 1963 civil rights speech at Gettysburg. Busby dismissed the Justice Department draft as "junk," but the weekend rewrites fared so poorly that the President yanked in a startled new speechwriter, Richard Goodwin, to begin Monday morning from a blank page.

*   *   *

THAT MARCH 15, as the third calendar Monday of the month, was a day specified in Alabama law for voter registration. At the Lowndes County seat in Hayneville, where surprised officials simply had told Negro aspirants to go away two weeks earlier, registrar Carl Golson consulted widely to prepare this time. He no longer required applicants to produce a testament of character from a current voter, because this custom, as applied selectively to Negroes, was deemed a legal albatross with the Justice Department and the newspapers now in an uproar over voting—especially for a county where no Negro had been registered for at least sixty years. Like the registrars of neighboring counties such as Wilcox, Golson balanced this concession with a special new arrangement for Negro applicants. When more than twenty did present themselves that morning a second time—all from the pioneer thirty-seven who had signed their names to the sheet on March 1—Golson redirected them to line up on a side street about two hundred yards from the courthouse, outside the old county jail.

None of the applicants had ever been inside the long-abandoned relic of local punishment. A scouting trip by John Hulett and Frank Miles turned up no booby traps or obvious signs of ambush, but did little to calm apprehensions. Just inside the front door, to the left, the old indoor gallows stood with a rope slung over the yardarm. Jesse "Note" Favors reported that a deputy sheriff mused to him, "I wonder if that old thing still works." Mattie Lee Moorer noticed items other than the rope that seemed to be freshly placed props of crude but resonant intimidation: a shotgun leaned against the wall, a pint of unlabeled whiskey on a bare table in the cellblock. A news photographer later captured the registrar administering a test to a lone applicant at this table beneath the glare of three naked light bulbs. Sidney Logan, who had ventured alone on Tuesday to witness the "turnaround" march in Selma, stayed on outside as a reassuring presence for those obliged to wait under the gaze of passersby. Of the seventeen who completed the registration test by the end of the day, Logan would be rejected weeks later along with fourteen others, and two—John Hulett and the blind preacher, John C. Lawson—would become the first registered Negroes since the reign of England's Queen Victoria. These numbers were a pittance, and very likely a strategic move by county officials to remove the stigma of absolute racial exclusion. In Lowndes County, however, even the fifteen who persevered to failure vindicated Sidney Logan's scouting report from Selma that wonders must be afoot.

*   *   *

CAREFULLY REMOVED from his public schedule that Monday, President Johnson convened the Joint Chiefs and his top national security officials to hear the report of a ten-day, "final" diagnostic mission to Vietnam. Army General Harold K. "Johnny" Johnson, a survivor of the Bataan Death March and three years in a Japanese POW camp, exceeded his own reputation for tough-minded realism by predicting that it would take 500,000 U.S. soldiers five years to "arrest the deterioration" in the military situation. As the President's chosen leader for the on-site review, he recommended a twenty-one-point program featuring large, immediate troop deployments to forestall what National Security Adviser McGeorge Bundy now secretly called the Vietcong's "current expectation of early victory." Assistant Defense Secretary John McNaughton, who had accompanied the delegation as McNamara's chief strategic thinker on Vietnam, was equally candid in his top secret apportionment of U.S. war motives: "70% to avoid a humiliating defeat . . . 20% to keep SVN [South Vietnam] (and then adjacent territory) from Chinese hands, 10% to permit the people of SVN to enjoy a better, freer way of life."

The report stunned the assembled commanders in the White House. Even McNamara, who had recommended the mission in order to solidify official support for gradual troop deployments, professed shock to hear the accepted difficulties projected into large, blunt numbers, and the President blanched at the implications of such a war. He warned thunderously against leaks of the sensitive material, then lashed out as though there must be a way to change the projections rather than fulfill them. "Kill more Vietcong," he ordered the Joint Chiefs.

President Johnson dismissed the military conclave to keep a Monday afternoon appointment with columnist Walter Lippmann, who represented the opposite pole of his Vietnam predicament. Lippmann was warning in print that military escalation was leading to unnecessary, avoidable disaster: "The reappraisal of our present policy is necessary, I submit, because the policy is not working and will not work." Over lunch with President and Mrs. Johnson in the White House residence, and then alone with Johnson in the Oval Office, the nation's foremost public intellectual pressed for national debate about Vietnam to prepare the public for a political compromise. "Your policy is all stick and no carrot, Mr. President," said Lippmann. "You're bombing them without offering any incentive for them to stop fighting." Johnson replied genuinely that he loathed the war and would do almost anything to escape it, but said the Vietnamese Communists were offering him no carrots either, short of a reciprocal invitation to leave.

The two men argued for competing versions of a middle course in Vietnam—contained war versus negotiated settlement—both of which rested on wishful thinking or fiction. Lippmann probably guessed this, and Johnson certainly knew so from the consistently grim assessments within his own government. Nevertheless, the President favored either course over his actual choice between major war and collapse of the American position. He was keenly aware that Lippman himself publicly ruled out American withdrawal from Vietnam,* which only reinforced Johnson's political instinct that no President could risk "unmanly" surrender. Honesty about Vietnam would touch off a war stampede and upheaval over blame for weakness, Johnson figured, along with dissent against the notion that humiliation could justify war. He resolved instead to contain political division separately from the conflict itself, using secrecy as a first defense.

Privately, Johnson railed against Lippmann's call for open national debate ("He doesn't understand that I'm debatin' it every night," Johnson told Moyers). In person, he presented himself to Lippmann as a reluctant warrior seeking to win in Vietnam by the minimal application of violence, and he entertained belief that Lippmann's suggested "peace initiative" might yield a surprise settlement. The President buzzed McGeorge Bundy: "Mac, I've got Walter Lippmann over here, and he says

---

* "Before saying any more about this," Lippmann wrote that week, "let me say at once that this does not mean that we can or should withdraw our troops, abandon our clients in Saigon, retire from the theater and give up the effort to safeguard the independence of the Indochinese states."

we're not doing the right thing. Maybe he's right." Lippmann was elated by the positive reception, which relieved his anxiety about being ostracized after decades of access to Presidents.

President Johnson reverted briefly to his domestic crisis. Hours before the address to Congress, pages of a new draft were spilling one by one from the office where speechwriter Richard Goodwin had locked himself from the frantic attentions of presidential aides—chiefly Moyers, Katzenbach, and Jack Valenti, with supporting experts and ad hoc advisers. Somewhat to their chagrin, Johnson had insisted upon Goodwin as his last-minute substitute even though he was an urbane Kennedy holdover of the pedigree the President often disparaged as "a Harvard," known for his dialectical encounter with Cuban revolutionary Ernesto "Che" Guevara and starkly ill-suited to the Texas folkways that Johnson applied to politics. Still, after seeing Lippmann, the President lobbed a hand grenade into the speech stew by buzzing Goodwin ex cathedra with a story from his formative experience as a teacher of young Mexican-Americans in Cotulla, Texas. "I just wanted to remind you," he signed off abruptly. Johnson saw in Goodwin an outsider with a gift for words, fit for the task of quick-mixing a bubble of presidential memory into the framework of Negro voting rights. "A liberal Jew," he lectured Valenti, "has his hand on the pulse of America."

* * *

BACK FROM weekend speeches in Chicago, a conflicted Martin Luther King hesitated too long in Judge Frank Johnson's courtroom to address the James Reeb memorial service at two o'clock Monday afternoon. If he went to Selma, he could not make it back to Montgomery in time to catch a flight to Washington for the joint session of Congress that night. Since White House operators had tracked him down with President Johnson's personal invitation, some around King argued that his first obligation was to be visible in the House chamber as an emissary of the voting rights movement. To go to Washington, however, King must renege on commitments not only in Selma but also in Montgomery, where he remained a witness under subpoena. On this fourth day of hearings, Major Cloud defended the conduct of his troopers on March 7 ("I never saw any violence," he testified), and one of Sheriff Clark's deputies disclosed in passing that two of those charged in the Reeb murder were the men who had tried the carburetor smokescreen three days earlier during the march of white Alabamians. Even this small surprise, linking a sinister event with antecedents that had seemed silly, was a reminder of what King called the "tiptoe stance" in the psychology of minorities. Uncertainty recommended that he take nothing for granted, including Judge Johnson's decision on the legal status of the suspended march from Selma. Finishing that quest was now the movement's test of its competence as well as its cause, and by this light King's first duty was to tend to the plaintiff's case through expected completion on Tuesday.

He lingered in Montgomery also to keep internal rifts from exploding in the press. So troubled was King that he solicited from Clarence Jones what arrived just then as a fourteen-page telegram defending him from charges "in some quarters" that he had "worked with the federal government to bottle up the militancy and indignation of Negroes." Tuesday's mysterious "turnaround" march intensified King's vulnerability to the usual organizational frictions, in part because so many parties had reason to ascribe unflattering motives to him. Federal officials were straining to create for themselves a facade of sovereign control by suggesting that they had throttled King to broker peace. SNCC leaders encouraged the notion that King had connived his way into safe retreat, abandoning to them the trust of the long-suffering people, and reporters were drawn to saucy interpretations that put King under the condescension of his young allies for chessboard deal-making with Johnson and Wallace. Jones's defense was sophisticated but necessarily defensive, and King set it aside to tend higher priorities. Habitually late, he declined the President's invitation, secured an excused absence from Judge Johnson, and sent word to extend the Reeb memorial until he could get to Selma with a eulogy after all.

By four o'clock, recorded a member of King's staff, the crowd in Brown Chapel "got tired and even a little hostile." There had been futile attempts since dawn to circumvent the six-day blockade at the invisible wall, where internecine tensions among the segregationists were reaching the brink of open fisticuffs between Wilson Baker and Sheriff Clark over the latter's refusal to permit a token, pressure-relieving march to the courthouse. Inside, the afternoon service heated with the overflow crowd, which spilled from the aisles into window casements, then over the balcony railings and camera equipment.

With pilgrim travelers far outnumbering local veterans a week after King's mass invitation, spoken tributes recognized a swelling bank of dignitaries—presiding Bishop John Hines of the Episcopal Church, United Auto Workers president Walter Reuther, several members of

Congress, more than a hundred Roman Catholic priests and nuns of different orders, and Archbishop Iakovos, Greek Orthodox Primate for North and South America, who wore a flowing black cassock and carried a gold-tipped pastoral staff. In 1959, Iakovos alone had represented the Eastern hierarchy at its first direct Vatican contact in nine hundred years, opening ecumenical discussion with Pope John XXIII toward removal of the mutual excommunications that had stood between Rome and Istanbul since the year 1054. Here, however, the Archbishop ventured on his own against the advice of his clergy and staff, who worried correctly that he would be called traitor to the quest of marginalized Greeks for full acceptance as Americans. Not a single member of the Orthodox community would appear for scheduled events at his next stop, and Iakovos would find himself alone in a Charleston hotel room, stripped of accustomed pomp, telling hostile callers nationwide that he was compelled to Selma by formative memories of Greek suffering on his native Adriatic islands, under harsh occupation by the Ottoman Turks.

Between hymns at Brown Chapel, one bored reporter counted seven of eighteen bare bulbs burned out from the cross made of lights on the pulpit wall behind Iakovos, and murmurs of disapproval ran through the crowd over the effusions of speech and prayer. "I found myself greatly agitated and sometimes furiously angry at the behavior of my white colleagues," wrote a clergyman from New York. Most speakers gloried in the footsteps of James Reeb's martyrdom. Some abased themselves before the lifetime sacrifice of the local movement, or confessed that they had just learned of Jimmie Lee Jackson, and others winced to hear local Negroes lionized in theological language by strangers who were unsure how to say hello to them in the same pew. Long overdue, a clamor from outside finally announced King's arrival, and relief whipped through the weary crowd. "It suddenly seemed right," the New Yorker decided, "that we should all be there."

* * *

KING IMPROVISED, reaching first to salute Reeb with the lines from *Romeo and Juliet* that Robert Kennedy famously had quoted ("And if he should die/Take his body, and cut it into little stars . . .") for his assassinated brother. "James Reeb was martyred in the Judeo-Christian faith that all men are brothers," added King. "His death was the result of a sensitive religious spirit. His crime was that he dared to live his faith." He joined Reeb's name to predecessors from the movement, summoning up language from his own eulogies back to the funeral of the Birmingham girls bombed in church. Looking beyond the killers as a few "sick, misguided" men, King repeated a question he had asked "a few days ago when we funeralized James Jackson": what could sustain such anonymous hatred? "When we move from the who to the what," he said, "the blame is wide and the responsibility grows." To a Brown Chapel half-filled with prominent clergy, King still began his roll call of shame with indifferent religious leaders and irrelevant churches that kept "silent behind the safe security of stained glass windows." As in Birmingham, he went on to indict the demagoguery and brutality of local officials, the "timidity" of the federal government, and the broad apathy of citizens who nominally owned the country. "Yes," said King, "he was murdered even by the cowardice of every Negro who tacitly accepts the evil of segregation."

He pulled back to soft consolation. "I know our hearts, all the sympathy we can muster, go out to Mrs. Reeb and the children," said King. He called up words from his most shattered moments—"At times, life is hard, as hard as crucible steel"—and cited in ecumenical language "the great affirmations of religion, which tell us that death is not the end."

To lift up a vision of justice "one day," when "our nation will realize its true heroes," King drew upon memories etched in his speeches since the Montgomery bus boycott. He pictured first among future honorees the "old, oppressed, battered Negro women," symbolized by the steadfast walker Mother Pollard, "who responded with ungrammatical profundity to one who inquired about her weariness, 'My feets is tired, but my soul is rested.' " From his awakening tributes to the breakthrough sit-ins and Freedom Rides, he saluted the discipline of nonviolent youth—"faceless, honest, relentless young people, black and white, who have temporarily left behind the temples of learning to storm the barricades of violence." For the first time, he included in his pantheon the "ministers of the gospel, priests, rabbis, and nuns, who are willing to march for freedom, to go to jail for conscience's sake." From the cry of hope in his Letter from Birmingham Jail, he foresaw again a broad, healing realization that all these vexing protesters "in reality" stood for "the most sacred values in our Judeo-Christian heritage, thereby carrying our whole nation back to those great wells of democracy." From the perorations that defined his public voice, King rolled out citations from prophets and patriots to extol a fused source for justice—sacred and secular, equal souls and equal votes—ending this time with Isaiah and Jef-

ferson: " 'Every valley shall be exalted . . . and all flesh shall see it together.' We must work to make the Declaration of Independence real in
our everyday lives."

He claimed only a glimpse of sweetness beyond an age of pangs. "Out
of the wombs of a frail world," said King, "new systems of equality and
justice are being born." There were seeds of hope for "the shirtless and
barefoot people" of a shrinking globe, he said, borrowing from his
Nobel Prize lecture of December. "Here and there an individual or
group dares to love. . . . Therefore, I am not yet discouraged about the
future. . . . So we thank God for the life of James Reeb," King said. "We
thank God for his goodness." As he finished, Sheriff Clark received
mortifying news on the sidewalk outside with Wilson Baker, Hosea
Williams, and James Bevel, after which Baker removed the wooden
barricades across Sylvan Street. Four minutes later, Ralph Abernathy
rushed behind King into the pulpit to announce that U.S. District Judge
Daniel Thomas of Mobile had ordered Clark to permit a limited march
to the courthouse—now! "Grown men wept at the wonder of the moment," recorded a participant, as days of complex machinations by
LeRoy Collins and others seemed to answer King's eulogy. Crowds
surged toward the church doors, sweeping King and the distinctive
Greek Archbishop from handshake recognition that they had met
briefly in Geneva after the bus boycott, on King's first trip abroad.
Iakovos wore a frozen look. A small Negro girl took him by the hand
and said not to worry.

A march of some 3,500 people stepped off at 5:08 P.M., breaking confinement that had introduced people of the local movement to relays of
incoming clergy through six days of rain, bullets, tedium, and song. For
holdovers such as Boston seminarians Judith Upham and Jonathan
Daniels, the unplanned boot camp in nonviolence made this hard-won
release more impressive than the fresh fear of Tuesday, even though the
lines made no attempt to cross Pettus Bridge. Sheriff Clark locked the
courthouse to guard his bastion of local power; behind windows, his five
children watched the twenty-minute memorial ceremony for voting
rights martyrs on the steps below. A photographer captured the extraordinary assembly with a shot destined for the next cover of *Life* magazine. At dusk, with the recessional fading back toward Brown Chapel, a
hand emerged just long enough to remove a mourning wreath King
had left in the courthouse doorway.

CHAPTER 10

And We Shall Overcome

March 15, 1965

IN Montgomery, Stokely Carmichael reported Monday afternoon over the SNCC WATS line that police "with guns" tried to raid the Ben Moore Hotel, where James Forman had set up temporary headquarters. Assured by the manager that the Negro establishment had warded off the assault, Carmichael returned to his fifth-floor outpost to observe SNCC colleagues moving nearly three hundred demonstrators from the nearby campus of Alabama State University, where faculty and deans vainly pleaded and shrieked to dissuade them, past the hotel toward the Alabama capitol ten blocks away. Forman intended to establish a beachhead there, leapfrogging the stalled campaign out of Selma, for more aggressive "second front" forays to demand the attention of Governor Wallace. From his window, Carmichael saw police units with cavalry detachments of sheriff's deputies move slowly from distant points to seal off the march. He rushed downstairs to sound a warning, only to find the hotel doors chain-locked from the outside. He banged helplessly against the exits, then ran back upstairs to watch the converging police repulse the march in the streets below. Skirmishes broke out along the fringes. Horses reared, and officers swung long-handled truncheons.

In the aftermath, SNCC colleagues came upon Carmichael standing dazed on the sidewalk. He said they should have seen this coming. "This is you," he accused Cleveland Sellers, a friend and fellow project director in Mississippi. He could not, or would not, explain himself beyond saying, "Et tu, Brute?" with a vacant cast to his normally infectious grin. Sellers, Willie Ricks, and others knew Carmichael had been troubled since his duels with Bevel inside the besieged Dexter Avenue church. Discounting a remote chance that he was "possuming" to fool them, they recognized signs of the nervous breakdown that had afflicted SNCC workers with far less stress than Carmichael's five years and two dozen trips to jail. Either way, they knew from previous triage to get him swiftly out of town.

Couriers managed to notify Forman a few blocks from the Ben Moore Hotel, where his demonstration settled in a standoff that lasted into Monday evening. Huddled with companions against buildings on a dark street, surrounded by police and the mounted deputies, Forman had scrounged a transistor radio that scratchily could receive President Johnson's address to Congress, but he labored to disseminate his own small news without benefit of eyewitness reporters. Gathering sketchy details of a dozen injuries nearby ("Melzetta Poole, 19, Alabama State, hit in head . . . Eric Stern, U. of Pitt., possible broken jaw . . . Fran Lipton, U. of Michigan, horse kicked her . . . Rev. Gerald Witt, 28, Huntington, Pa. . . ."), he found substitutes for Carmichael's role of calling them through SNCC's communications department in Atlanta to be offered as balancing grist for the official version that otherwise appeared baldly in many newspapers: "300 Negro demonstrators blocking an ambulance . . . throwing stones, bricks and bottles at the deputies, none of whom was hurt seriously . . . violent demonstration about six blocks from the state Capitol." Carmichael himself went numbly but willingly to the Montgomery airport with escorts, headed for the usual therapy of a speaking tour in safe cities. Not for the first time, however, the contrast of bustling normalcy at an airport concourse—travelers with golf clubs, families embracing at the gate—ate through the wounded psyche of a veteran SNCC worker, and Carmichael collapsed on the floor before an astonished police officer. He writhed and screamed beneath friends who sat on him until he was subdued enough to board an airplane for California.

* * *

LADY BIRD Johnson stoically watched her husband flay the pale aides who raced between typewriters carrying pieces of his speech. With a motorcade waiting to transport him to the Capitol for the nine o'clock address, the President berated a distant secretary for typing slowly with "fourteen goddam wooden fingers," and accused Jack Valenti and Bill Moyers of garbling his clearly stated revisions. "Every goddam body around here thinks he's smarter than I am!" he grumbled. When Valenti bared his chest to announce that previous additions already pushed the end of the speech too late to make the TelePrompTer screen in the well of the House, the notoriously sensitive Johnson raved to the doorway against a host of betrayals he saw conspiring to accentuate his cornpone look and ponderous delivery. He composed himself swiftly, however, so that Richard Goodwin—waiting with a speechwriter's rare invitation to ride along, freshly shaved but bleary from the day's crash composition—heard no sound from the arriving sphinx who exuded and commanded silence in the presidential limousine.

President Johnson's concentration sank into script changes that lengthened Goodwin's draft. There was a new section on the provisions of his voting rights bill, for instance, along with words of disapproval for protesters who "holler fire in a crowded theater" or "block public thoroughfares to traffic." Changing his mind, Johnson struck the latter paragraph to avoid misimpression that marginal annoyance reflected his true feeling. Elsewhere, his editing added words and compounded metaphors. Where Goodwin exhorted Americans to "look within our own communities, and our own hearts, and root out injustice there," the final version substituted: "let each of us look within our own hearts and our own communities, and let each of us put our shoulder to the wheel to root out injustice wherever it exists." More substantively, Johnson had deleted a sentence that succinctly joined two causes. To advance freedom, wrote Goodwin, "Americans are risking their lives today in Vietnam—and in Selma." This direct parallel thrust Vietnam as a twin issue that invited questions, such as why the lives risked should be soldiers in one instance, nonviolent Negroes and clergy in the other. Instead, Johnson's team composed a safer general call to "rally now together" in the spirit of common sacrifice, citing traditions of patriotic duty to which "the South made its contribution of honor and gallantry no less than any other region."

At the Capitol, which buzzed more expectantly than usual over a boycott by the entire Mississippi and Virginia delegations along with scattered representatives from other Southern states, the congressional leadership greeted the President as always in the Speaker's chambers, while Mrs. Johnson went to a reserved box in the packed gallery with her daughter Lynda and guests including USIA director Carl Rowan, former Southern governors Buford Ellington and LeRoy Collins, Robert Spike among four prominent clergy from the vigil in Selma, and

FBI director Hoover as the featured trophy on her front row. The President himself, heralded into the House for handshakes down the aisle past Cabinet officers and Supreme Court Justices, on through the ritual standing ovations, stood quiet again with his text at the lectern, before the assembled branches of government and his largest television audience—some seventy million viewers.

* * *

"I speak tonight for the dignity of man and the destiny of democracy," he began slowly.

"I urge every member of both parties, Americans of all religions and of all colors, from every section of this country, to join me in that cause.

"At times history and fate meet at a single time in a single place to shape a turning point in man's unending search for freedom. So it was at Lexington and Concord. So it was a century ago at Appomattox. So it was last week in Selma, Alabama.

"There, long-suffering men and women peacefully protested the denial of their rights as Americans. Many were brutally assaulted. One good man, a man of God, was killed.

"There is no cause for pride in what has happened in Selma. There is no cause for self-satisfaction in the long denial of equal rights of millions of Americans.

"But there is cause for hope and for faith in our democracy in what is happening here tonight.

"For the cries of pain, and the hymns and protests of oppressed people, have summoned into convocation all the majesty of this great government of the greatest nation on earth."

Only a hush greeted the natural pause. The lyrical opening, which followed Goodwin's first draft almost to the word, sucked away the whole range of normal response from a chamber that seemed stunned and on edge, as though mesmerized to witness the gangling, slow-tongued President leaping suddenly to a rhetorical high wire without a net. Johnson, having claimed for Selma a place among historic moments, and pronounced it a test of free government itself, fastened both the moment and the test to the core of the nation's only story. "Rarely in any time does an issue lay bare the secret heart of America itself," he said. "Rarely are we met with a challenge, not to our growth or abundance, or our welfare or our security, but rather to the values and purpose and the meaning of our beloved nation.

"The issue of equal rights for American Negroes is such an issue.

And should we defeat every enemy, and should we double our wealth and conquer the stars and still be unequal to this issue, then we will have failed as a people and as a nation.

"For with a country as with a person, 'What is a man profited if he shall gain the whole world and lose his own soul?' "

Into this pause fell a first lone clap, which spread through the House in tentative applause. Uncommonly, Johnson had pulled off the cadences of Lincoln and the intimacy of a quotation from St. Mark. For that alone he earned credit, and he proceeded to ground the spiritual lilt in the secular base of American ideology. "This was the first nation in the history of the world to be founded with a purpose," he said. "The great phrases of that purpose still sound in every American heart, North and South: 'All men are created equal,' 'government by consent of the governed,' 'give me liberty or give me death . . . ' " Johnson defined his issue by the commitment to freedom, above any dodging confinement of section or race. "There is no Negro problem," he said, "there is only an American problem, and we are met here tonight as Americans . . . to *solve* that problem."

The address marched steadily through history into the thicket of modern politics. Johnson decried the "harsh fact" that "men and women are kept from voting simply because they are Negroes." He told plain stories to illustrate. "No law that we now have on the books—and I have helped to put three of them there*—can ensure the right to vote when local officials are determined to deny it," he asserted, then outlined his new bill to "strike down restrictions to voting in all elections—federal, state, and local—which have been used to deny Negroes the right to vote." To confront the issue of federalism, he offered defenders of states' rights a simple way to nullify the brunt of enforcement: "Open your polling places to all of your people. Allow men and women to register and vote whatever the color of their skin. Extend the rights of citizenship to every citizen of this land." But he pledged no more to defer the nation's constitutional mandate where states historically condoned tyranny. "We have already waited a hundred years and more," President Johnson declared, "and the time for waiting is gone."

The senior House Democrat, the seventy-seven-year-old Emanuel

* Johnson referred to the laws of 1957, 1960, and 1964, which ended a drought in civil rights acts since Reconstruction. He supported the first two as Senate Majority Leader, and signed the third as President.

Celler of Brooklyn, rose to his feet and a standing ovation spread in waves with the conviction that Johnson was committing hard mechanics of government to his beguiling patriotic music. Above isolated cheers, the noise hung long enough that network cameras slowly panned to broadcast what the *New York Times* called "remarkable views of the reaction of Congress": Celler clapping with hands high above his head, Senator Mike Mansfield visibly shaking with emotion, Senator Sam Ervin of North Carolina "sitting with arms folded in massive disapproval." For White House aide Jack Valenti, waiting desperately with a stopwatch, the panning cameras posed one of two threats of searing disgrace.

When couriers arrived with TelePrompTer tape composed from the only copy of revisions after page twelve, Valenti beseeched cameramen by whisper to focus closely on the podium, then crept unpictured through the well of the House to feed the tape into the TelePrompTer before the President ran naked off his partial text.

The vote was essential to the "far larger movement" of American Negroes to "secure for themselves the full blessings of American life," Johnson resumed. "Their cause must be our cause, too," he said slowly, placing his hands on the lectern. "Because it is not just Negroes, but really it's all of us, who must overcome the crippling legacy of bigotry and injustice. And—we—shall—overcome."

No one stood. Applause battled disbelief and renewed astonishment to hear such words from the first Southern President in a century. When it registered that Johnson with unmistakable intent had adopted the signature phrase of Negro protest, a Southern representative on the floor quietly muttered, "Goddam," and fell numb. To friends in the U.S. Senate, Richard Russell sadly pronounced his dear friend and protege "a turncoat if there ever was one." Watching in Selma, Mayor Joseph Smitherman recoiled as from "a dagger in your heart." Still puzzled later, he said, "You know, the South is very patriotic, but it just destroyed everything you'd been fighting for." Blocks away from Smitherman on Lapsley Street, pandemonium erupted in the living room of Sullivan and Jean Jackson, where colleagues of Martin Luther King stared at Johnson's image and shouted to each other, "Can you believe he said that?"

King himself, from an armchair drawn close to the Jackson television, wordlessly occupied a charged space apart. The address for him already was more than an answered prayer. Not only did Johnson embrace the fused spiritual and patriotic grounding of the nonviolent movement, but he committed the national government to vindicate its long-suffering promise of equal citizenship. A tear rolled down King's cheek.

He watched the President lift up by adaptation more themes of his message for and from the movement. "The real hero of this struggle is the American Negro," Johnson told his audience. "And who among us can say that we would have made the same progress were it not for his persistent bravery, and his faith in American democracy?" His address in the House chamber burst through resistance to applause as Johnson raised the stakes still higher. "The time of justice has now come," he declared. "And when it does, I think that day will brighten the lives of every American. For Negroes are not the only victims." He told the story he had urged on Goodwin only hours before, of his first job teaching Mexican-American children of Cotulla, Texas. "My students were poor, and they often came to class without breakfast, hungry," said the President. "And they knew even in their youth that pain of prejudice. They never seemed to know why people disliked them. But they knew it was so . . .

"Somehow you never forget what poverty and hatred can do when you see its scars on the hopeful face of a young child.

"I never thought then in 1928 that I would be standing here in 1965 . . . that I might have the chance to help the sons and daughters of those students, and to help people like them all over this country. But now I do have that chance, and I let you in on a secret: I—mean—to—use—it."

A second standing ovation answered the peek behind the veneer of Johnson as oil-state politician. Its personal revelation added consistency to the surprise force of the voting rights address, and tumultuous acclaim engulfed the President's exit from the House floor. "Manny, I want you to start hearings tonight," he shouted to Celler through a sea of outstretched arms. Beaming, electrified, he waved off the Judiciary chairman's abashed reply that the voting rights bill—not yet introduced—was rushed for next week. *This* week," said Johnson. "And hold night sessions, too."

Noise collapsed to quiet adrenaline in the presidential limousine. No one spoke for blocks. "Jack, how did I do?" the President finally asked. Goodwin and Moyers shrank from the enormity of the question, but Valenti was ready with stabilizing facts of the White House trade: thirty-six interruptions for applause consuming eight minutes, forty seconds; total delivery time, forty-five minutes, twenty seconds.

CHAPTER 11

Half-Inch Hailstones

March 15–17, 1965

APOCALYPSE briefly wore a smile of dizzy surprise. "There cannot be anyone alive," wrote columnist Murray Kempton, "who knows the names of all the children who carried us and Mr. Johnson to the place where he stood last night." The *Atlanta Constitution* surrendered to the "unanswerable detail" of Johnson's argument for Negro voting rights, and many Southern newspapers frankly expressed awe for his unabashed idealism. "Rarely has the American conscience been so deeply stirred," said the *Houston Post.* In the *New York Times,* James Reston hailed Johnson's gift for oratorical ambush, saying he "waited out his critics . . . to channel all these emotions and struggles into legislation at the right moment." Other public voices offered gasps instead of the usual guarded appeals to reason. Joseph Alsop saluted "the speech of a big man dealing with a big problem in a big, bold way." William S. White opposed Johnson's voting rights bill as a violation of state prerogatives "at the very heart of this Republic," but he openly admired the sudden revelation of a President who "lifts this terrible pack uncomplainingly upon his back."

Past midnight, then all day Tuesday, President Johnson harvested the tribute of potentates turned gushy. Chicago mayor Richard Daley called to praise the address as "terrific, magnificent, and impressive," adding that all his aldermen and precinct captains agreed. "They said one of the greatest they've seen," the mayor reported. "Do more of them. That's what people want to hear from you. God bless you and Mrs. Johnson." The President kept interjecting, "Bless your heart, Dick," as Daley bubbled on: "One of the greatest presentations on this subject since Lincoln. Talked about the government. Talked about the people. Obey the law, the Constitution. Know your duty. This is the only way to treat people . . . above all they had hope on that television. . . . May the Lord continue to give you good health. I'll be talking to you."

IBM president Tom Watson wanted to discuss Selma instead of Johnson's search for a new Secretary of the Treasury. "That was a terrific speech you made last night, sir," he said. "I think that thrilled the whole nation."

"I don't know," Johnson replied. "Did the best I could." Down-home modesty evaporated as the President recited the exact running count of White House response: 1,436 pro telegrams and 82 cons. He read the text of a stirring wire from Harry Truman, repeating the ex-President's name with warm satisfaction, and rose to full dramatic ardor in reliving for Watson how he had coaxed Republicans to their feet through his peroration about teaching Mexican-American children. "I just put my head back and I'd look at them," said Johnson, "and I'd look at the camera. They looked at all the damn cameras on them, and I wish you'd seen them get up."

He and Watson roared with laughter. "I saw them get up," said Watson, "but I didn't know how you pulled it off."

"Yeah, that, that's what I was doing," beamed Johnson.

"I'll be darned," said Watson.

"They all of them had glue in their britches, and they were just *stuck*, and they wouldn't come at all," Johnson boasted. "And when they saw that camera start circling around on 'em, that little red light—it was the funniest thing I ever saw."

"Well, that was a stroke of genius," said Watson. "Well, they damn well *ought* to have gotten up, because it was magnificent."

Before the end of the day, Johnson applied the full energy of boyish celebrations to hard business. He summoned Vice President Humphrey and the entire Democratic leadership of the House—Speaker John Mc-Cormack, Majority Leader Carl Albert, Majority Whip Hale Boggs, and all eighteen assistant majority whips—for a strategy session on his determination to use the cresting tide of national support to secure four new cornerstones in American law: federal aid to education, Medicare, voting rights, and immigration reform. The fourth and least heralded bill would replace the Chinese Exclusion Act of 1882 among others back to the nation's first immigration law in 1790, all heavily restricting immigrants by race or nationality to the favored "stock" of northern Europe. Johnson's reform sought to limit newcomers by number but not by origin, which promised slowly to absorb all the world's faces and cultures under the Constitution. Each of the bills established a landmark national commitment—to the young, the elderly, minorities, and even aspiring foreigners. Together they extended America's distinctive horizontal bonds of popular strength, in keeping with the founding principle of equal citizenship.

Johnson exhorted the House leaders to pass these four above all others. This year, he said, while the momentum of Selma augmented the political mandate of the 1964 election. He worked them over, then retired upstairs in the White House to dicker toward the same goal with Senate Republican leader Everett Dirksen.

* * *

Seminarians Judith Upham and Jonathan Daniels suffered an acute letdown when Selma woke up Tuesday unchanged. They debated whether speeches and tumultuous marches were more than vanishing noise, and agreed that demonstrations were "sort of stupid"—making a spectacle of themselves to communicate a simple point in a stubborn world. Outside Brown Chapel, where James Bevel told morning crowds he hoped to have court permission soon to march to Montgomery, eager new arrivals tried to circumvent the blockades. Negro seminarians from Atlanta confronted Sheriff Clark, and a group of three hundred sat for hours in witness on Sylvan Street. Upham and Daniels meant to go back to school, but missed another departing bus. Paralyzed—"blinded," wrote Daniels—they could not bring themselves to wrap up Selma in one "slam-bam" visit, like tourists in ministry, and it registered within hours that they could leave only on a solemn pledge to return for keeps. "The imperative was too clear," Daniels explained in a letter, "the stakes were too high, my own identity was called too nakedly into question . . . and the road to Damascus led, for me, back here." Liberated by resolve, they headed for Boston just long enough to drop seminary for the term and pack Upham's Volkswagen.

They passed through confusion at the Montgomery airport, where SNCC recruiters intercepted pilgrims bound for Selma and diverted them to downtown Montgomery. From Jackson Baptist Church, James Forman led a crisis march of some six hundred students to answer Monday night's violent siege near the Ben Moore Hotel, which had gone virtually unnoticed. They intended to deliver a voting rights petition to Governor Wallace, but police blockaded them at the corner of Decatur Street and Adams Avenue. Montgomery County sheriff Mac Sim Butler led a charge of fifteen mounted horsemen into the standoff, "wearing a cowboy hat"—wrote an observer confirmed by photographs—"and swinging a cane by the tip end." Howls and screams sounded. One handful of demonstrators protectively circled Forman, many clutching a telephone pole until blows forced them to scatter backward. Helmeted possemen followed the horses on foot. A rabbi among the demonstrators spun from a yard with a lit cigar between his teeth, holding a sheaf of papers with one arm and the legs of a wounded Negro girl with the other; a SNCC worker in bib overalls and a dress shirt held her shoulders, shouting, "Can we get a doctor?" When one blow struck a skull in an eerie moment of quiet, "the sound of the nightstick carried up and down the block," wrote correspondent Roy Reed for the *New York Times.* "Across Decatur Street, the larger crowd was almost hysterical. . . . When the smaller group was routed, the mounted officers waded into the larger one."

The demonstrators retreated to the street outside Jackson Baptist, where an exasperated Bevel, having rushed over from Selma, dragged Forman aside to find out why he invited such punishment. Couldn't he tell from the President's speech that the right-to-vote movement was on the brink of success? An equally exasperated Forman dismissed the address as empty politics. "That cracker was just talkin' shit," he said.

"Naw, the man was preaching," said Bevel.

They muted their ongoing dispute for the benefit of a shaken crowd. From atop a wooden crate, Bevel preached nonviolence and suggested that they save themselves for a more decisive march. Forman followed with an argument that LBJ must guard the right to petition for voting rights until he could deliver them. They stepped down to wait for Martin Luther King to arrive for mediation. The crowd cheered both of them. There were students from Tuskegee, Alabama State, and local high schools, plus mostly white travelers still holding up "One Man-One Vote" placards with identifying signs from nineteen scattered schools, including Antioch, Spokane, Wilberforce, Harvard, Carnegie Tech, Duke, and Wayne State.

* * *

THE IMPACT of Selma reverberated worldwide, with responses to new events feeding off others in the pipeline. In Budapest that Tuesday, embattled under Communist rule, the Hungarian Council of Churches celebrated the twentieth anniversary of liberation from Hitler by a letter of appreciation to King ("We are deeply astonished at the death of Rev. James J. Reeb . . ."). From one campus alone, which already had sent some people to Selma and fifty others to picket the White House, another 250 Wayne State University students joined Governor Romney of Michigan for a second Tuesday march of ten thousand around the federal building in downtown Detroit. Some of these gathered afterward for discussion at the home of the Episcopal chaplain, where a number resolved to leave immediately by caravan for Alabama. "Prior to today I felt that any personal contribution I might offer to those individuals in Selma was of little or no consequence. . . ." wrote one of them. "Nevertheless, upon reading the content of our president's speech today, I am no longer able to sit by while my people are suffering. . . . I examined carefully my own possible reaction if I were one of the Selma victims, not just a spectator." By "my people," Viola Liuzzo meant fellow citizens. She was the daughter of a Tennessee coal miner, now a married part-time student nearly forty, with five children, and by nature determined. When all the other student volunteers canceled or postponed their trip by morning, Liuzzo, over the fearful protest of her family, headed south in her Oldsmobile alone.

Also on Tuesday at Wayne State, Alice Herz realized she had left the original of her protest leaflet in a commercial copying machine. Afraid the authorities would intercept it and stop her, Herz abandoned plans to carry out her demonstration on the campus where she had taught German after fleeing first from Berlin in 1933, then as a refugee west through wartime internment camps in France and Cuba. With her materials, she hastily boarded an outbound bus along Detroit's Grand River Street. Herz was a bookworm, a trilingual freelance writer, retired kindergarten proprietor, and ardent admirer of Martin Luther King. She had pushed her way into the 1963 rally at Cobo Hall to hear an early rendition of his "I Have a Dream" speech, which Michigan devotees considered superior to the famous version in Washington. She had joined the first giant march around Detroit's federal building on March 9, and could not believe that an American President who so eloquently endorsed the cause of Selma since then could withstand a jolting appeal to stop an incipient war. Herz exited the bus near a parking lot, stuffed her mouth with cotton, poured two cans of Energine dry cleaning fluid over her head, and struck a match. Left behind in her handbag near the flames, the copied leaflets denounced "hatred and fear, deliberately whipped up during the last twenty years," and accused President Johnson of having "declared his decision and already started to enact it," to make war in Vietnam. "GOD IS NOT MOCKED," wrote Herz. "To make myself heard I have chosen the flaming death of the Buddhists. . . . May America's Youth take the lead toward LIFE!"

Against her will, the eighty-two-year-old body of Alice Herz struggled ten days before she succumbed to burns. She had confided nothing of the plan to her sole surviving child, even though they had been lifelong pacifists together at the urging of her late husband, Paul (a conscript in Kaiser Wilhelm's army), and apartment-mates since his death in 1928. Tuesday evening at the hospital, supported by a co-worker from the Detroit public library, Helga Herz managed to say that her mother had been very upset by the bombing of Vietnam since February. She received a note in the next day's mail begging forgiveness: "When you understand why I've done this, you will accept it. Don't cry and don't complain. I'm not doing this out of despair but out of hope for mankind." A book of Alice Herz's worldwide correspondence would be published a decade later in Holland—"A holy courage must animate more and more American souls," she had written a Japanese philosopher in 1952—but America's first Vietnam peace casualty sank invisibly among freakish news squibs.

*   *   *

PUBLIC SENSATION did rise from the late mass meeting in Montgomery, despite great efforts to forge a working compromise. King secured a large church from the network of pastors who had refused SNCC, and Forman agreed to emphasize the goal of national action as symbolized by the twice-deferred march from Selma. "There's only one man in this country that can stop George Wallace and those posses," he told the overflow crowd at Beulah Baptist. "We can present thousands and thousands of bodies in the streets if we want to . . . but a lot of these problems will not be solved until that shaggedy old place called the White House begins to shake, and gets on the phone and says, 'Now listen, George, we're coming down there and throw you in jail if you don't stop that mess!' " Over rippling cheers, Forman let slip his corrosive doubts. "This problem goes to the very *bottom* of the United States," he shouted, "and you know, I said it today and I'll say it again. If we can't sit at the table, let's *knock* the fuckin' legs off! Excuse me."

Forman caught himself instantly and nodded with sheepish, ingrained respect for the nuns present, but a single obscene word dominated his message. Observers shivered with delight or disapproval over the lapse from the movement's wholesome public discipline, ending a day that Forman later marked as a watershed—"the last time I wanted to participate in a nonviolent demonstration." King came behind him with a fiery speech that concealed the breach. "The cup of endurance has run over," he declared, then steered outrage over the horseback brutality into enthusiasm for massive nonviolent witness behind him and Forman the next day.

* * *

EARLY WEDNESDAY, Attorney General Katzenbach called to prod Judge Frank Johnson on the case that had bottled up the long march from Selma for eight days running. Now that the President had announced the government's position, and a voting rights bill was being delivered just then to Congress, Katzenbach pushed to relieve rather than contain the pressure. He asked when the Justice Department could expect a ruling.

"It won't be forthcoming," the judge replied—not until he felt certain the order would be backed.

"Backed?" said Katzenbach. "Well, I think we can back it."

"I don't care what you think," the judge said sternly. He wanted a guarantee of enforcement to bind the contending parties, lest his imposed settlement fail in a vacuum of finger pointing between the various levels of government. "It won't be fair to the court and to the people to have an order that does not have support," he added.

"All right, you have my assurance," said Katzenbach. Washington would fill any default of duty by state or local officials.

"I don't want your assurance, Mr. Katzenbach," insisted the judge. "I want it from the president. I want to know before I issue this order."

Katzenbach signed off to call the White House.

Not far from Judge Johnson's chambers in Montgomery, King, Forman, and Silas Norman led nearly two thousand people on a mile-long walk to Sheriff Butler's office at the county courthouse. Students clustered around King as a human shield from the threat of snipers, but rows of police officers guarded the long procession in a stark reversal. For the third time in March, following Bloody Sunday and the attack on James Reeb, a spasm of national publicity put Alabama on the defensive and masked strains within the civil rights movement. Two large photographs on the front page of the *New York Times* showed "mounted possemen" and "club-wielding deputies" pounding integrated ranks of young demonstrators. Other photographs on an inside page were captioned, "Taking Refuge" and "Cry for Help." Wednesday's *Washington Post* carried eleven separate dispatches on the Alabama crisis. One of the few unrelated stories on its front page told of South Korean diplomats who apologized to guests turned away from a formal luncheon for their visiting foreign minister, saying they had sent invitations without realizing that Washington's National Press Club banned females from the dining room.

In Montgomery, a chagrined local prosecutor already had excused the previous day's rampage as unworthy of the capital city, saying, "We are sorry there was a mix-up and a misunderstanding of orders." He invited King and Forman into the courthouse to negotiate new protest procedures with local officials, including Sheriff Butler, who had discarded his cowboy hat. John Doar observed for the Justice Department. The crowd waited outside through the whole afternoon, upbeat and singing in spite of a steady rain. "Police protection was thoroughly organized" against aggressive hecklers on the sidewalks, wrote one astonished demonstrator. Fifty miles away in Selma, meanwhile, FBI agents counted 586 people who braved the elements for an outdoor prayer rally. Half-inch hailstones fell as Hosea Williams exhorted the mix of travelers and local stalwarts to hold on. "I'm not interested in criticizing Sheriff Clark," he shouted. "I'm interested in *converting* Sheriff Clark!"

In Montgomery, emerging at 5:15 P.M. on Wednesday, King and Forman shared a megaphone to deliver a progress report from the steps of the courthouse. Local officials had agreed to sign a statement of regret for Tuesday's violence, they said, and to forswear the use of the unaccountable possemen for law enforcement. They thanked the rainsoaked crowd for putting a "historic occasion" within reach, and urged them all to find shelter as talks continued into the night. "There are points that we agree on, and there are still points that we must negotiate," King announced, then paused as Andrew Young pushed through to speak in his ear. His face changed. News cameramen expectantly buzzed reporters near him to clear the view—"get the mike down, get the mike down."

"Let me give you this statement which I think will come as a source of deep joy to all of us," King called out. "Judge Johnson has just ruled that we have a legal and Constitutional right to march from Selma to Montgomery!" Rolling cheers erupted over the last words.

CHAPTER 12

Neutralize Their Anxieties

March 17–20, 1965

JUDGE Johnson advised stunned lawyers for Alabama that they could catch a plane to New Orleans within the hour to seek an emergency stay in the Fifth Circuit. He assumed rightly that they would hurry, because his order prescribed a window of little more than a week to complete the fifty-mile march. Rushing just as hard to get started, King fixed Sunday for the third attempt to cross Pettus Bridge. This allowed movement workers only three days to improvise bivouac logistics along Highway 80.

On Thursday, as Governor Wallace's lawyers argued their appeal to block them, the U.S. Senate debated and passed an extraordinary resolution to send the day-old voting rights bill to the Judiciary Committee with instructions to report it back for floor action no later than April 9, the hundredth anniversary of Appomattox. "I am opposed to every word and every line in the bill," declared Judiciary chairman James Eastland of Mississippi, protesting the usurpation of his traditional prerogative to set the timetable for legislation. Against him rose the leadership of both parties, with Vice President Humphrey formally presiding and many senators praising the Selma demonstrators for steadfast commitment to democratic principles. "As American citizens, they have faith in America," said Republican John Sherman Cooper of Kentucky, "and we must sustain that faith." Only thirteen senators voted against the resolution, including one—Republican Margaret Chase Smith of Maine—who opposed sending the bill to committee even for three weeks.

A Soviet cosmonaut burst into news bulletins as the first human to walk in space. "I didn't experience fear," Colonel Alexei Leonov said on reentry to his orbiting spacecraft, Voshkod 2, "only a sense of infinite expanse and depth of the universe." At the White House, once a graceful response was framed for the latest setback in the space race, Johnson delegated to his confidential go-between Buford Ellington the task of securing from Governor Wallace a commitment to protect the Selma march as ordered by the court, but Attorney General Katzenbach soon interrupted with bad news from Ellington that the elusive Wallace was asking for help. With Deputy Defense Secretary Cyrus Vance, who was preparing U.S. troop deployments in case Alabama balked altogether, Katzenbach and Ellington coached Johnson for a showdown phone call calculated to draw upon his mesmerizing personal dominance of Wallace on Saturday.

The governor came on the line at full gallop against marchers "pourin' in from all over the country . . . nuns and priests, and got hundreds of bearded beatniks in front of my capitol now." Just two days ago, he said, "it was James Forman suggesting in front of all the nuns and priests that if they, anybody went in the café and they wouldn't serve 'em, to kick the fuckin' legs of the tables off . . . that kind of intemperate remarks, and inflames people, you know . . . and I'm gonna do everything that I can, but now, all I want to say quite frankly is that they've been stirred up by a lot of things, and I know you don't want anything to happen that looks like a revolution, but if these people keep pouring in here . . . why, it's gonna take you, it's gonna take everybody in the country to stop something."

President Johnson worked in a calming volley of words about cooperating peacefully with the march as ordered by the court. "Let's get it over as soon as we can," he said. "And let's don't, uh, when you talk about a revolution, that uh, that really, that really upsets us all."

Wallace made sure Johnson knew he meant polar threats from two kinds of revolutionaries: outsiders who pressed for the Negro vote by "wantin' the federal government to take the state over," and Alabamians on his side who wanted to annul federal authority on issues touching race. "Of course, if I was a revolutionary, I probably could invite a quarter of a million people to come help us," he said. "But of course I don't want anything like that at all. I don't want people to get hurt."

"I know," Johnson said.

The President seemed chastened by the blunt talk of revolution, and

Wallace resumed the offensive with tales of white Alabama as victim rather than oppressor, suffering nearly unbearable cases of interracial flirting. "A Negro priest yesterday asked all the patrolmen what their wives were doing," he told Johnson. "Uh, reckon some of their friends could have dates with their wives, you know, tryin' to provoke 'em, those kind of things, you know, and we're tellin' 'em just *take* all that stuff." The marching and agitating in Selma had been getting worse for eight weeks, Wallace complained, rushing hotly to warn again that "if this matter continues on and on and on . . . if they're gonna just stay in this state eight weeks and congregate fifty thousand strong a day, then uh, we're going to have a revolution." He checked himself. "Well, I don't mean that, as you say, [to] use the word 'revolution,' " he said. "We just gonna have trouble."

Johnson pleaded several times for Wallace to call out the Alabama Guard so the federal government would not have to intrude, but Wallace parried with a steady refrain. "Here's what I'll do," he said. "I will, we're gonna keep *close touch* with the situation."

The President brought Katzenbach, then Ellington, on the phone to push in tandem for a more definitive commitment. "George, are you by yourself?" asked Ellington, suspecting that Wallace might not want political colleagues to hear him pledge to protect race mixers under federal pressure.

When Wallace parried again, Johnson tried an edge of disgust. "You don't need to talk to me any more," he announced, saying he had a Treasury nomination to finish before he flew home to Texas that afternoon. "I thought Governor Ellington and y'all had kind of, had a, uh a meeting of the minds on it," he added in a plaintive tone.

"Well, we'll have a meeting of the minds, Mr. President," said Wallace, giving ground. "I'll do whatever it takes. If it takes ten thousand Guardsmen, we'll have them. I'll use—do whatever is necessary. And I won't uh, wait too late. Of course, you know—"

"That's okay," said Johnson, pouncing. "That's good. And you keep in touch with Buford." Wallace signed off with two hours left to prepare an address to the Alabama legislature.

* * *

In Montgomery, legislative leaders escorted Governor Wallace into the House chamber precisely on cue for live statewide television at 6:30 P.M. His speech needed only sixteen minutes to draw from many wells of emotional resistance, beginning with ridicule. He read a long list of mobile support equipment already requested by the Selma organizers, including nine three-hundred-gallon water trailers and two rubbish trucks, then denounced the marchers as a mob. "And it is upon these people, and upon their anarchy," said Wallace, "that a federal judge, presiding over a mock court, places a stamp of approval." Nurtured by the "collectivist press," they served a "foreign philosophy" that aimed to "take all police powers unto the central government," he declared. "And sadly, the Negroes used as tools in this traditional type of Communist street warfare have no conception of the misery and slavery they are bringing to their children."

Wallace turned from "words of alarm, not that I have anything against proper alarm," to the poignant retreat of the Lost Cause. "I do not ask you for cowardice," he said, "but I ask you for restraint in the same tradition that our outnumbered forefathers followed." He urged Alabamians to "exercise that superior discipline that is yours," obey the order "though it be galling," and leave the march alone. "Please stay home," he pleaded. "Let's have peace." He presented scornful forbearance as the utmost patriotic sacrifice, but he could not bring himself to allow protection by any Alabama authority. "The federal courts have created this matter," he declared, and therefore he would call on Washington to "provide for the safety and welfare of the so-called demonstrators." Thunderous cheers answered his concluding appeal—"I have kept faith with you . . ."—for voters to stand behind the people's governor. The *Montgomery Advertiser* recorded that "several women in the audience were in tears." Friday's *Birmingham News* proclaimed, "Wallace Has Finest Hour."

Flashes from Montgomery kept the Marine helicopter stalled on the White House lawn. "I've been leavin' since 3:30, messing with that son of a bitch," President Johnson fumed to Buford Ellington after nine o'clock Thursday night, "and he is absolutely treacherous."

Ellington vowed never to speak to Wallace again. "Well, you know I *told* you—"

The President interrupted to quote from the speech. "I'm, I'm not going to be double-crossed this way," he told Ellington. "I'm gonna issue a statement here that kinda burns his tail."

Wallace struck first. Johnson called Attorney General Katzenbach at ten, sputtering with frustration that he had been about to summon reporters when "in comes this goddam wire" asking the President to police the march with five thousand civilian federal workers, such as marshals and prison guards.

The request was "ridiculous," said Katzenbach, "as Governor Wallace knows perfectly well," but the maneuver neatly sidestepped all National Guard options as political poison in Alabama. If Wallace called out the Guard himself, he would assume defense of Negroes he demonized to popular acclaim; if he refused, he would invite federal command and with it blame for surrender. If Johnson now suggested that Wallace was "reneging" on his commitment to use the Guard as necessary, the governor would simply reply that he preferred civilians. "That's what he'll say," Katzenbach predicted. He advised Johnson to scrap his statement of rebuke and compose a straightforward reply: that federal civilian employees were unprepared and unsuited for the emergency, being scattered in assorted agencies nationwide, whereas the ten thousand members of the Alabama National Guard were on hand, "trained and equipped for this purpose."

"Uh, and if he won't call them out, we will," the President suggested.

"And uh, if he's unable to maintain law, we will," Katzenbach added.

Johnson shouted for his secretary Marie Fehmer to get on the line for dictation that bounced back and forth for ten minutes before he took off for Andrews Air Force Base. He called the FBI from the plane "in a highly agitated condition about the situation in Alabama," Director Hoover advised his executives, and the President reached the LBJ Ranch before two o'clock Friday morning.

* * *

FOR KING, Wallace's speech was background radio news in a long night of related collisions. With the victory of Judge Johnson's order, pressure spiked on many fronts, including where to camp Sunday on the first night out of Selma. No sooner did a volunteer at last offer a farm near the highway than Dallas County officials rushed James Minter to court with an ironclad argument that Anderson Watts was merely his sharecropper of twenty years and could not grant such permission. The Selma courthouse swarmed with word of imminent suits by the city and the local bus company to collect massive damages from Negro leaders over the economic effect of demonstrations. Familiar signs of spite hollowed optimism among movement veterans who had learned to be wary on the brink of hard-won public success. Retaliatory violence had charred celebrations consistently in the past, with bombs detonated soon after the bus boycott, sit-ins, Birmingham campaign, and March on Washington.

The usual infighting rubbed so raw as to provoke a rare eruption of temper from King, against SNCC's Willie Ricks in Montgomery. With

James Forman, Ricks had organized student pickets that held ground outside the capitol for several hours Thursday, menaced by a larger "Niggers Go Home" counterdemonstration of whites. When police arrested eighty-four of the students for sitting down on the sidewalk, three hundred new demonstrators—mostly travelers on their way to Selma—marched to the courthouse to denounce the jailing as a violation of the new protest agreement. At midnight, the most persistent thirty-six were jailed themselves, joining the others, and arguments seethed into the morning over the priority of this crisis.

What upset King was a passing encounter with three female students from Alabama State who wore helmets from the huge batch that Forman had imported for SNCC's "second front" campaign. When he complimented the distinctive look, one of them replied, "You need one." Another added, "You better get you one."

King stopped. "Willie Ricks told you to say that," he said. When he pressed the students to confirm his guess, they ran off instead to Ricks, whom they knew, saying King was a paranoid celebrity who thought Ricks controlled his fate.

Hours later, King spotted Ricks on a fringe of the marathon strategy session. "Come here, son," he said, pulling him close. "I've been out here fighting a long time, and I know what I'm doing. You can't hurt me." His tone hushed the room. King preached that Cain had killed Abel but Ricks couldn't hurt him. "Remember that," he said. "I was Martin Luther King before you were Willie Ricks, and I'll be Martin Luther King long after you're gone."

Ricks stood silent as King "went off on me," but his SNCC colleagues lit into King's surrogates. Forman accused Andrew Young of undermining SNCC's militancy in order to please Washington. He said King's SCLC staff sacrificed integrity even to get creature comforts for the march, such as port-o-potties and walkie-talkies. "I've known people who sold out for a car or money," he shouted, "but never for toilets!"

"Jim, why don't you just tell everybody that you hate Dr. King?" Young retorted. He said Forman was consistent only in branding King wrong.

Most observers recoiled from the disputes, but King's host in Montgomery tried to reassume his role from the bus boycott as volunteer "bodyguard." Richmond Smiley, whose family included trustees who had shut off the water and electricity to drive Forman's demonstrators from Dexter church, was appalled to watch young rowdies berate his old pastor. He offered more than once to bounce them from his house, but King checked him, having recovered his amiable thick skin under fire. "No, that's not the way," he said as he held mostly aloof, intervening to let the clashes play out. At dawn, with Forman departed after a half-hearted truce rendition of "We Shall Overcome," King addressed his own staff and friends. "Well brothers, if there's going to be a divorce, SNCC will have to initiate it," he announced. "And if they do, I'll be just like Rockefeller's wife when she discovered that Happy* was pregnant." He paused for effect, then added, "I'll not say a word." His primly comic allusion relieved stress with a splash of laughter.

On Friday in New York, while monitoring wiretaps on civil rights advisers, FBI agents overheard Bayard Rustin urge King to renounce SNCC publicly as a political liability. King deflected. Rustin believed from personal experience that King avoided personal conflict, especially severances and goodbyes, out of weakness. King saw it differently, arguing that he was bound to SNCC by necessity and principle. With his own small staff crushed by an avalanche of assignments, he saw the SNCC veterans as a unique human resource—intrepid, task-oriented loners, accustomed to the threat of violence and qualified to create instant miracles everywhere from crowd control to tent construction. Through Hosea Williams, he assigned much of the logistics and communication over the fifty-four miles to SNCC's Ivanhoe Donaldson. Having survived many jailings and one threat of death from an irate Mississippi officer with a pistol to his head, Donaldson could disregard the scorn of some SNCC colleagues for "the Reverend's show." He had skipped the March on Washington and now claimed indulgence to be in the middle of a gigantic movement event. "Everybody's entitled to one in a lifetime," he joked.

Donaldson pitched into the chaos of Selma, where crowds jostled journalists, camping supplies littered church basements, and farm pickups needed to be commandeered into a truck transport system. For a celebrity concert that Harry Belafonte planned near Montgomery on the last night of the march, he began figuring how to rig an outdoor soundstage out of stacked coffin crates from Selma's Negro funeral homes. Donaldson and SNCC's Frank Soracco undertook the delicate

---

* New York governor Nelson Rockefeller replaced his wife of thirty-two years with campaign volunteer Margaretta "Happy" Murphy, which many believed cost him the 1964 Republican presidential nomination.

assignment of winnowing the aspiring marchers to comply with Judge Johnson's order, which specified that unlimited hosts at the beginning and end of the five-day trek must be constricted to three hundred designated marchers for the middle passage through Lowndes County, where Highway 80 narrowed to two lanes. This requirement posed logistical nightmares for the thousands who must confine themselves to one segment of the march, or suspend participation for several days in hostile country, and the choice of each coveted spot among the "elite" three hundred put Donaldson and Soracco into Solomon's hot seat. They organized a census to gather information on physical fitness and movement service, then weighed competing claims among local Negroes and eminent visitors alike. They selected Rev. F. Goldthwaite Sherrill of Ipswich, Massachusetts, to represent Episcopalians, for instance, and reserved 250 places for Alabamians who had marched on or before Bloody Sunday.

King's trust in two SNCC workers to compile the sensitive roster muted widespread rumors of estrangement. "Arguments take place in any family," Donaldson told reporters. "They don't mean disunity." He complained that the press was "confusing people who want to support both organizations." A syndicated column by Rowland Evans and Robert Novak on Thursday lumped John Lewis with James Forman as "two hotheaded extremists" who had imposed their will upon King. By agreeing to resume the Selma march, the column charged, King had "capitulated," "abdicated," and "knuckled under" to a SNCC group "substantially infiltrated by beatnik left-wing revolutionaries, and—worst of all—by Communists." For King, the only grain of truth in the attack was that he did consider some recent SNCC demonstrations to be expressions of rivalry and rage, without constructive purpose. He had vented privately to colleagues that the students lacked a sense of "political timing" and maneuvered selfishly to "get a martyr" for SNCC in Alabama, but he resisted advice to rebuke them publicly. In essence, King worried that some SNCC leaders were falling away from nonviolence—from its disciplined commitment to rise above human proclivities to denigrate and separate, strike back, demonize, and incite—but he could not say so without betraying nonviolence himself. Instead, he told Rustin and others that he would work hard to communicate with SNCC leaders "sufficiently to neutralize their anxieties." King acknowledged that stinging impatience with him had contributed to historic, creative sacrifice by students, notably the sit-ins and Freedom

Rides, and he knew their attitudes toward Selma were varied and volatile. Forman, for all his bluster, agreed to suspend demonstrations in Montgomery until the march was over.

*   *   *

STOKELY CARMICHAEL returned to Alabama from his "two-day nervous breakdown" with a novel remedy in mind. His experimental motto was "use King," in contrast with what he called James Forman's "fight King," and various other stances within SNCC such as "ignore King" (Silas Norman), "be King" (John Lewis), and "cooperate selectively with King" (Ivanhoe Donaldson). To challenge King's appeal for mass mobilization was futile and destructive, Carmichael decided, but he thought SNCC workers might harness the popular response for their own grassroots work. On Friday, he drove into the wilds with a stack of leaflets for the upcoming march. He took along Bob Mants, who was just back from a wrenching journey home to tell his parents that he was intact after Bloody Sunday but must drop out of Morehouse College to rejoin SNCC. Outside the all-Negro Lowndes County Training School, Carmichael and Mants waved leaflets and SNCC buttons at departing students who avoided them. One student bus driver furtively signaled interest before principal R. R. Pierce expelled the visitors with notice that he had called police. Deputy Sheriff "Lux" Johnson overtook Carmichael and Mants less than two miles away and ordered them back for investigation at the school, where a state trooper already waited with the overwrought Pierce. Students and teachers gawked from a distance as Carmichael pulled the receiver cord of a CB radio from his Mississippi SNCC car and transmitted his location and ETA in brisk radio jargon.

Two teachers soon carefully followed the departing caravan to find out whether the deputy and the trooper really would let the intruders go free. Seventeen-year-old John Jackson, expecting correctly that he would lose his job as bus driver, sped home with leaflet evidence that Martin Luther King was coming to Lowndes County whether people believed it or not, as promised by these "Freedom Riders" who had appeared in a stick-shift Plymouth with a long whip antenna. His parents, Matthew and Emma Jackson, slipped away that night to discuss providential signs on a word-of-mouth summons from William Cosby. Since Cosby was considered exposed already by the visit to his store of "Joshua's scouts" (Andrew Young and James Bevel) nearly a month ago, they gathered first at the home of Frank Haralson to settle upon the safest spot, free of vulnerable mortgage and secluded from known stooges. Rocena Haralson stayed behind to feed those who decided not to walk or drive across the way to the Haralson country store for the county's first political meeting of Negroes.

Nearly thirty people, most of whom had tried to register Monday at the old jail, organized themselves as the Lowndes County Christian Movement for Human Rights (LCCMHR). The name, adapted from Fred Shuttlesworth's group in Birmingham, was suggested by John Hulett, who accepted the lead role with open trepidation—partly to honor the goodbye plea of his pastor, Lorenzo Harrison, in flight from the local Klan. As secretary the founders chose Lillian McGill, who had met King during the bus boycott while working as a maid in Montgomery. Her father, Elzie, a railroad worker, was elected treasurer. Farmer Charles Smith of Calhoun served as vice chairman and chief orator, reciting scripture from his locally celebrated memory. A teacher in 1930 had begged him to take his gift for literature beyond the heights of eight grade, but Smith had turned away from impractical academics to marry Ella Mae, who had since borne them nine children.

Carmichael and Mants crept out of Lowndes County with eyes fixed on cruisers in the rearview mirror, fighting cocky mirth as well as fear. Mants brimmed with admiration for Carmichael's quick-witted fake transmission, from well out of range, which may have puffed them up as aliens best left alone. They found Selma so overrun with early arrivals from the North that King's own staff allowed demonstrations of restless enthusiasm. Some three hundred new visitors, arrested for picketing Mayor Smitherman's home, refused release and insisted on being confined at the Negro Community Center, albeit with some exits unlocked. Jammed together, strangers acquainted themselves by ecumenical exchange that wore on until one New Yorker "almost began to feel up to my ears with the religion, with the intense religion bit." Some overnight prisoners tried folk dancing. "This is stupid," said their reluctant jailer, Wilson Baker, who groused to reporters that "at least we had good music when the Negroes were demonstrating."

*   *   *

OTHER MARCH volunteers more than filled the Friday mass meeting at Brown Chapel. "No white churchman is going to be free until you're free," declared Rev. C. Kilmer Myers, suffragan Bishop of Michigan, who was called briefly to the pulpit along with a second Episcopal bishop, George Millard of San Francisco. Rev. F. D. Reese of Selma proclaimed applications still open for three hundred stalwarts "with good hearts, good feet, good minds, people who are willing to go all the way" to Montgomery. He announced that provisions, protections, and camp-sites all remained in doubt: "we might sleep on the highway, I don't know." Reese called the movement a jumbled leap beyond full grasp— "you will never know what it means"—but envisioned a universal grandchild looking back some day on Selma, "trying to find a channel through which he can direct his own life," and "something within him would say, 'You've got to *go*.' "

James Bevel followed with a featured address that mingled Selma history with provocative skeins of entertainment. He described a staff journey for King into Rochester, New York, after racial disturbances the previous summer, and being asked "what's wrong with Negroes— they've gone crazy all over the country? And I said, 'Do you know Ne-groes?' They said, 'Oh, yeah, we know our Negroes.' 'What Negroes do you know?' " To much laughter, Bevel recounted efforts to educate white city fathers about race by taking Kodak executives "down on the corner with me" to listen to a local jukebox: "I can't get no sleep, and it's crowded on the street / I got to move, I got to find myself a quieter place." Bevel quoted the soul tune by Garnet Mimms & the Enchanters, then recalled in Brown Chapel, "I said, 'Do you hear what he's saying? If you listen to him sing in the spring time, he'll tell you what he's gonna do in the summer.' " He preached seriously for a time on the danger of another "letdown" period in history, as after the Civil War. "You cannot legislate deals and go home without dealing with sicknesses in society," Bevel shouted. Something was wrong when Sheriff Clark "will take two or three hundred Negro children and run 'em down the highway for six miles and leave 'em in the country," or when sight of a pastor like James Reeb enraged a community to homicide. "Unless we profoundly address ourselves to the hate in the white community," he added, a vot-ing rights bill "won't have any meaning. So we have a job to do. I'm gonna do my job." He turned to Bishop Myers on the podium. "I'm gonna give you a suggestion, bishop," said Bevel. "Call your missionar-ies from Africa." Above startled laughter, he called out impishly, "Lots of people in Africa are killing folks, but at least when they kill some-body, they're trying to get a meal! Sheriff Clark, he doesn't *need* a meal."

King stayed away from the mass meeting to battle arrangements for the ordeal just ahead. Through Andrew Young, he sent an urgent re-quest for Rabbi Abraham Heschel to join the first day's exodus. "By all means," Heschel replied from New York, "but I have a problem with Shabbat." Orthodox Jewish practice banned regular activities including travel until the close of sabbath at dusk on Saturday, which made it impossible to reach Selma in time. Conflict gnawed at Heschel, the scion of a long line of Hasidic rebbes from Poland, who had fled Europe ahead of Nazi persecution. Across the chasm between their respective backgrounds, he and King had found seeds of a surprising bond at a historic Chicago conference on religion and race in 1963, when they brought almost interchangeable sermons on the claims of prophetic justice. Each had railed against a national religious climate of resigned, trivial piety, prodding some two thousand eminent clergy to inflict healing discomfort on the world's racial divisions. "To act in the spirit of religion is to unite what lies apart," Heschel had proclaimed, "to remember that humanity as a whole is God's beloved child." Now that a flood of response at last descended upon Selma, Heschel consulted fellow authorities about Talmudic exceptions for saving and risking lives, and whether dire circumstances might permit a person of frail health to modify strict Shabbat prohibitions by substitute ritual, such as pushing elevator buttons with the point of an elbow.

*   *   *

HELICOPTERS AND motorcades shuttled a sleep-deprived President Johnson to visit friends at five different ranches on his first day home in Texas. From Washington, aides bombarded him in transit with pressure to initiate troop movements in Alabama Friday night. Against Johnson's political desire to conceal or delay all moves until his own press announcement on Saturday, Pentagon commanders warned that the advance concentration of Army transport planes was "likely to leak some time during the night anyway," and government lawyers advised that his formal signature must precede even preliminary notice to call out the Alabama National Guard. "Cy Vance strongly—repeat: strongly—insists he needs full day tomorrow in order to mesh Guard with regular Army," Bill Moyers cabled. The President, giving in, flew from Judge A. W. Moursund's late supper to work on documents amassed at the LBJ Ranch.

Johnson signed the two necessary orders at 1:28 and 1:30 A.M. Saturday, resting on precedent dating back to George Washington's suppression of the Whiskey Rebellion in 1792, and veterans beneath Alabama flight paths soon recognized the loud drone of C-130 aircraft. Sixty-eight of them landed through the night at either end of the march route—the 720th MP Battalion at Craig Air Force Base just outside Selma, from Fort Hood, Texas, and the 503rd MP Battalion at Maxwell Air Force Base near Montgomery, from Fort Bragg, North Carolina. The President retired at three o'clock and was awakened at 6:34 to prepare for his morning press conference. Outdoors, with Lady Bird sitting nearby under a shawl, he declared it an "unwelcome duty" to assume any part of a state's responsibility for public order. He said nearly four thousand assorted soldiers would be ready by Sunday, along with two field hospitals he hoped would not be needed. "Over the next several days the eyes of the nation will be upon Alabama," said Johnson, "and the eyes of the world will be on America." He invoked Lincoln's confidence that Americans would be "touched by the better angels of our nature."

* * *

IN SELMA, nearly two hundred clergy formed at midday on Saturday for what Bishop Myers of Michigan called "somewhat of a family quarrel" among the nation's Episcopalians. They walked one block toward St. Paul's Church before a police blockade stopped them and Wilson Baker announced that Bishop C. C. J. Carpenter of Alabama refused permission for visiting bishops to hold Communion service at any altar within his diocese. He waved off their explanations of canon law. "Don't talk to me," he said. "I'm not the bishop. I'm not even an Episcopalian." Besides, Baker added, he could not "for your own sake" let a march venture near the hostile possemen downtown.

The columns turned back to Brown Chapel, where the bishops conducted Communion services on the sidewalk with vessels borrowed from an Episcopal mission for Negroes in Birmingham. The rhythmic chants of their liturgy echoed among charged sounds and spectacles against the grain of normalcy, like a New Orleans funeral. Local children spurred clergymen in piggyback rides on the playground. A one-legged man on crutches stared from the church steps, wearing a yarmulke. Twenty-four portable toilets sat on a row of flatbed trucks parked on the street. Someone announced that homemade sausages and fifty more sandwiches were ready from the volunteer cooks inside, where Viola Liuzzo processed newcomers at one of the welcome tables less than a day after her own arrival from Wayne State. Army Specialist E-4 Hank Thomas wandered carefully in civilian clothes, avoiding recognition. A charter member of SNCC—one of the thirteen original Freedom Riders, Stokely Carmichael's cellmate nearly four years ago at

Mississippi's notorious Parchman Penitentiary—Thomas did not want to explain to nonviolent comrades why he had accepted Army conscription, even as a medic, nor admit to any stray military officer that he had slipped his pass from Fort Benning for one last taste of the movement before shipping out to Asia with the First Air Cavalry.

"By late Saturday," wrote march participant and historian Charles Fager, "green army jeeps had begun rolling through Selma, dropping off soldiers carrying rifles tipped with fixed bayonets at street corners along the route to the armory." Behind them came Alabama National Guard vehicles with "U.S." painted freshly on the sides to advertise federalized command. A *New York Times* correspondent found the atmosphere among the soldiers "not particularly tense." Festive hymns pulsed from Brown Chapel, where both Bevel and Diane Nash were to give evening speeches, but one Boston College student walked alone into segregationist ambush from an alley: beaten to the ground, yanked up by his hair, sliced on the right cheek with a razor blade.

FBI agents reported the Leo Haley incident ("required three stitches") to Washington among threats and warnings outside the usual conduits. A secretary at the Justice Department, then a lawyer, each reported an anonymous caller who said he owned a small plane and would "get that damn nigger Martin Luther King" from the air. Director Hoover, immensely relieved that military units had drawn the exposed security duties, pitched his Bureau with compensatory enthusiasm into intelligence work behind the lines. "Immediately contact airlines, railroads, bus lines, informants, contacts in Negro and other organizations," he ordered, and a response "from all of our field offices" advised on Saturday that "a total of 1,856 persons are already in Selma or actually have departed and are en route." They included ten priests from Connecticut and thirty-five Southern Methodist University students on a Greyhound bus from Dallas. Another sixty-three groups "totaling 1,011 in number" were said to be getting ready. Behind these absurd specifics—a standard FBI requirement in case Hoover wanted to assume a precisely omniscient pose—the report hedged with confidential sources estimating thousands "on standby" or coming "on their own."

A more comprehensive, fourteen-page FBI analysis prepared Director Hoover for Saturday night's annual Gridiron Club dinner. Assistant Director DeLoach summarized the Bureau's massive file of suspicious "Connections and Affiliations" on the part of NAACP director Roy

Wilkins, dating back to the 1930s—clippings from the Communist Party's *Daily Worker* newspaper quoting him against colonialism and for the Scottsboro Boys, informants who branded Wilkins an outright Communist or follower of a "Communist line," an agent who overheard him remark in 1944 that Japanese immigrants had been "the best truck farmers in America." Still, DeLoach reported that Wilkins had been reliably anti-Communist during the Cold War, and, most important, had praised the Director without fail. Thus briefed, dressed formally in the required white tie and tails, Hoover accepted his assigned seat next to Wilkins for the capital's stag ritual of political satire. They joined Vice President Humphrey, the entire Cabinet, four Supreme Court Justices, the Joint Chiefs of Staff, nearly a hundred members of Congress, and assorted celebrity guests including rookie pro quarterback Joe Namath—leaving one seat conspicuously empty in the Statler Hilton ballroom.

News stories speculated that President Johnson, ever sensitive to caricature, had contrived his Texas retreat expressly to avoid the obligation to smile through the merciless barbs reserved for the chief executive on Gridiron Club night. Members of the Washington press corps lampooned all powers in a spirited musical revue. One reporter impersonated Secretary McNamara in rimless glasses and hair slicked back perfectly like his facts, singing to the tune of "Heat Wave":

> We're havin' a small war, a hole in the wall war
> The Buddhists are risin', it isn't surprisin'
> The natives will say they can can Khanh
> We're fightin' 'round Saigon, wish bygones were bygone
> And though we can fight there, displaying our might there
> They certainly could can Khanh

Freshman senator Robert Kennedy watched himself struggle as an elfin schoolboy to master the shift in national diction since his brother's assassination. "Today, ah'm all the way with LBJ," his character drawled with Bostonian vowels that diminished until a Senate tutor exclaimed, "Ah thank he's got it," and the whole cast broke into an LBJ fandango to the tune of "The Rain in Spain."

* * *

THERE WERE no skits about the Selma influx of Negroes and clergy, which resisted humanizing parody more than Vietnam or Dallas. Outsiders to the movement remained inhibited, uninformed, and sullen to such extremes that the South's largest newspaper literally struck itself dumb. By sudden corporate edict, the *Atlanta Journal and Constitution* resolved to boycott the final march in Alabama notwithstanding the proud regional credo on its front page: "Covers Dixie Like the Dew." Top editors Ralph McGill and Eugene Patterson nursed glasses of whiskey in Atlanta, glumly stupefied that they were forbidden to send even one reporter to join the legions of worldwide press. They dismissed as a smokescreen the fluctuating rationale for the order—worries about libel suits, admonishments to hold back until newsworthy violence occurred.

"Gene, let's go over and catch the bus down to Selma," said McGill. He proposed to sneak off that night and write dispatches as though they were front-line reporters again.

Patterson restrained his illustrious mentor, who, since becoming editor of the *Constitution* in 1938, had wrestled with the race issue in prize-winning columns—sometimes accepting segregation in the hope of moderate reform, sometimes chafing against acquiescence as "the most melancholy aspect" of Southern life. "Pappy, that would be an open rebellion," Patterson warned. They would have to resign if they could not get stories into their own newspaper, he said, and likely be fired if they could, especially since many of their reporters already knew of the ban on coverage of the march.

To his later regret, Patterson talked them out of rash defiance. They ached instead for the biggest Southern story of their lifetime, which portended a wholly different order with some five million newly enfranchised voters, and consoled themselves with visions of the runaway assignment. "Damn, it would be fun," said McGill.

CHAPTER 13

To Montgomery

March 21–24, 1965

FRED Calhoun, parish custodian at Our Lady of the Universe, picked up a presumed box of trash and heard it ticking. He set the box carefully on the ground and hurried inside to early Sunday mass. Father Edward Foster appealed for calm. Catholic discipline did not permit mass to be abandoned once begun, he said, and besides, Negroes were accustomed to bombs on Dynamite Hill. Foster led a procession outside to complete the service on a portable altar, while Birmingham police relayed an emergency appeal to U.S. Army units on alert for the Selma march. By the time a demolition team arrived from the Third Army's 142nd Ordnance Detachment (Explosives Disposal) at Fort McClellan, two more ticking green boxes were discovered nearby—one at a mortuary owned by A. G. Gaston, whose motel had been bombed while hosting King and his staff in 1963, another at the home of attorney Arthur Shores, which had been bombed twice during that campaign to break segregation. Master Sergeant Marvin Byron and Specialist 6 Robert Presley manually disarmed the first bomb of fifty-eight sticks of dynamite (forty whole, eighteen partial) set to go off at noon, and then, observed a *New York Times* correspondent from a distance, "dashed up the hill to Mr. Shores's house."

Alarms from Birmingham flashed through temporary command posts in Selma and Montgomery over special hotlines into the Pentagon War Room. Bulletins by other channels heightened morning chaos in the Selma home where Wilson Baker himself more than once crawled under the floor joists to check for threatened bombs. Jean Jackson coped by turning out specialized breakfasts from her kitchen—eggs sunny-side-up for King, with the yolks semigooey and the whites firmly "to-gether," as he put it, no toast or bacon for the bearded rabbi on the front sofa, only crackers and an egg poached separately in a clean pan. Nobel Laureate Ralph Bunche, whose stomach condition was aggravated by nerves, received cottage cheese and scrambled eggs without salt. Jack-son stepped over sleepers, including a doctor posted outside her small "VIP" bedroom, amid subdued and exotic pandemonium. Abraham Heschel, the rabbi, made a space at a window for morning prayers in Hebrew; a bishop prayed nearby in another language, probably Latin. A blanket, a pipe, and trademark orange peelings marked the spot where James Forman had slept under the dining room table. King made teas-ing estimates about how long Ralph Abernathy's imminent "grand en-trance" would monopolize the bathroom, which drove Bevel to retrieve his pillow from the tub. Staff members and government officials pushed inside among long-lost friends.

FBI agents recorded that King's party reached the crowds outside Brown Chapel at 10:58 A.M. Selma time, already late. Burke Marshall, retired from the Justice Department but present as President Johnson's personal emissary, radioed estimates that the march would be delayed at least another hour pending arrival of expected dignitaries and an over-due charter plane from Germany. At First Baptist, doctors completed medical exams on the three hundred people chosen to make the ex-tended march. On the steps of Brown Chapel, clergy of varied traditions used megaphones to deliver a series of homilies—Heschel from the He-brew scriptures. A high delegation of Episcopalians returned from St. Paul's, rebuffed again by churchmen who defended with dogged scholasticism a vestry policy of open worship for "all but Negro laity." A delegation of Hawaiians arrived waving aloft a huge banner—"Hawaii Knows Integration Works"—and distributing garlands of traditional leis. King wore one around his neck as he knelt to pose with two of his favorite marching third-graders, Sheyann Webb and her friend Rachel West, after they led a freedom song.

At 12:15 P.M., Attorney General Katzenbach funneled to the White House a disagreement between Army intelligence, which predicted that the march "will be moving out" before one o'clock, and his own Justice Department officials, who agreed with Hoover's FBI that it would take longer, maybe ruinously past two, which would make it impossible to reach camp before dark. A correspondent for *The New Yorker* noted marchers talking wryly among themselves about the movement's own private time zone called "C. P. T., Colored People Time." Nevertheless, Bevel and Andrew Young dressed the billowing front ranks into columns roughly of six, marshals in armbands squeezed the formation half a mile back down Sylvan Street, and the whole contraption lurched forward at 12:46 P.M. Photographers took portraits from the back rails of an open truck moving slowly in advance. Camera crews carried enough spare film to support a continuous shot of the leaders, as it was already a whispered joke that the networks would fire anyone who missed impact footage of a sniper's shot. Ivanhoe Donaldson posted a moving shield of volunteer marshals slightly ahead of King on both flanks, without his permission, to minimize direct sight lines.

With nineteen jeeps and four military trucks in rear escort, and two helicopters hovering above, the march of three thousand followed the usual short route downtown. Hostile males among the spectators were quieter than at previous demonstrations, more inclined to heckle from their cars. One in a red roadster played "Dixie" at full volume, as broadcast just then by a cooperative radio station. Another aired a sarcastic "Bye, Bye, Blackbird" over four loudspeakers. Demonstrative females seemed comparatively undaunted by the intervening rows of Army MPs. Two matrons in their fifties shouted to each other in mock discovery: "You ever seen a white nigger?" "*Look* at the white niggers!" A well-dressed woman got out of her Chrysler at an intersection, stalked forward, stuck out her tongue decisively, then drove off. A mother with two small children led a chorus of inquisition about the sexual appetites of female marchers. What nuns in particular "heard concerning their chastity out of the mouths of the white women of Alabama," wrote two observers for *The Saturday Evening Post,* "cannot be transmitted in public print."

More esoteric dissent shunned the great sendoff. Famously within the movement, Silas Norman shellacked the floor of the Selma SNCC office. Consistent with his promise not to lapse again from SNCC's debated consensus weeks earlier—that the proposed march to Montgomery was a pointless captive of King's showboat national politics—Norman never would claim a place in historic commemorations decades later, and this day he tended chores in studied disregard for the tumult passing by the window outside. Well up ahead, at a rump press conference on the courthouse steps, Sheriff Clark pointed out John Doar with his predecessor Burke Marshall alongside the approaching front ranks. "The federal government has given them everything they wanted," Clark said morosely, to dispirited assent from fifty shelved possemen in the background.

* * *

THE LINES turned left at Broad Street, away from Sheriff Clark and up Pettus Bridge for the third time since March 7. At the crest in full uniform waited Brigadier General Henry Graham, an everyday Realtor from Birmingham, who twice before had followed orders dutifully to safeguard historic transitions—rescuing trapped Freedom Riders cooperatively with John Doar in 1961, integrating the University of Alabama through Nicholas Katzenbach's nationally televised confrontation with Governor Wallace in 1963. Graham issued commands shifting primary escort duty from the 720th MP Battalion to his own federalized Alabama National Guard, 31st Infantry Division, and the march lines started downward through brisk winds above the Alabama River. Bright sunshine already had raised temperatures well above overnight lows near freezing. No blockade of troopers loomed ahead. By coincidence, seminarians Jonathan Daniels and Judith Upham approached Selma from the opposite direction at the end of their long return drive from Massachusetts. Heading up Pettus Bridge, they waved a salute to the last columns coming down to the flat ground on the Montgomery side.

Fearful tedium evaporated, recorded a journalist, "and the march entered another mood—jubilation." Assistant Peace Corps Director Harris Wofford trotted among latecomers to join a rear contingent of high school students who clapped in ragtime to a hymn: "I'm gonna march when the spirit say march . . . sing when the spirit say sing . . . vote when the spirit say vote . . . die when the spirit say die." Reporters counted at least four other songs going simultaneously over the extended line to the front. An exhilarated Rabbi Heschel "felt my legs were praying," and kept pace with a couple from California who pushed the youngest participant in a stroller. The oldest marcher—Jimmie Lee Jackson's eighty-two-year-old grandfather, Cager Lee—waved blithely to unfriendly stares from the shoulders of Highway 80. National Guard jeeps leapfrogged forward to stop traffic for security at rural intersections, where FBI agents photographed seventeen cars decorated with crudely whitewashed signs, including one marked "Coonsville, USA" that cruised in tandem with a state trooper.

Security forces scrambled briefly when a tethered horse, frightened by helicopter noise, pulled up a road sign and galloped wildly toward the march with the metal post clanging behind on the pavement. Roughly two miles out, a federal observer who saw distant marchers felled as though by a scythe signed off Border Patrol radio to investigate on foot—"I'm going out of service!"—then returned minutes later to broadcast a chagrined all-clear. "Apparently," he said, "the Negroes just decided to take a break all of a sudden, and just started lying down on the grass." After the reclining multitude ate bologna sandwiches— King in a dark suit, overcoat, and new hiking boots—hard pavement troubled the march more than danger. Backpacks grew heavy and assorted protections awkward—yellow hardhats, umbrellas, one football helmet. For stragglers who dropped from the lines by the score, sore and sick, marshals arranged transport back to Selma in private automobiles with National Guard escorts.

Justice Department officials debated whether and how to streamline the cumbersome relay for excess marchers due to be shipped back to Selma for the night. John Doar argued that federal assistance beyond court-mandated security would undermine the department's impartial advocacy for voting rights. Deputy Attorney General Ramsey Clark overruled him. Safe meant smooth, he said, and the President wanted no effort spared. From maps showing that tracks passed near the first overnight campsite, Clark contacted officials of the Western Alabama Railroad by radio to hire a special train. Callers promptly threatened to blow it up. Hushed emergency orders halted the run fifteen miles outside Montgomery until Army units could fan out along bridges and trestles ahead.

Seven miles out of Selma, the march was obliged to detour south to the closest available Negro freehold in Dallas County. The front ranks that stepped into David Hall's field at 5:07 P.M. found advance workers bustling to raise four large field tents, including one for women donated by the International Ladies Garment Workers Union. Federalized Guardsmen from Alabama's 156th MPs took up positions around the perimeter. Professor Elwyn Smith of Pittsburgh Theological Seminary arrived after dusk in a yellow Hertz truck with three tons of supper— spaghetti, cornbread, pork and beans—prepared by cooks at Green Street Baptist and transported in king-sized galvanized garbage cans by Smith's round-the-clock food crew of twelve. Vehicles evacuated day marchers directly to Selma or across Highway 80 to the rendezvous junction of Tyler, where the nine-car train special loaded a thousand people at 75 cents apiece for an express trip into Selma, arriving at 8:45 P.M. Leaders canceled meetings at the campsite so that a remnant of some four hundred could try to bed down, plagued by a shortage of blankets and only one oil-barrel fire against the cold. "A few marchers made their way to the loft of a barn beside the Hall farmhouse, to profit from the heat given off by the animals in the stalls below," wrote Renata Adler for *The New Yorker.* "Five guinea hens perched in a tree outside the barn. The march's security patrol wandered about with walkie-talkies."

* * *

BEFORE MIDNIGHT, Bill Moyers notified President Johnson from the White House that Army demolition teams had disarmed a total of four large bombs at Negro sites in Birmingham. Two more turned up Monday, as the President finished an extended Texas weekend of rest by manic exuberance. He told a yarn about how he had begun a penniless rebellion trip at the age of seventeen by charging cases of pork and beans surreptitiously to his father, so that for weeks "we ate pork and beans three times a day, for breakfast, lunch, and dinner" on the runaway hitchhike to California. "I guess that's why I like them so much now," he said, exhorting hesitant guests through a reprise menu at the LBJ Ranch. A twenty-car motorcade of Secret Service agents, friends, and reporters chased dust at high speeds across the Texas Hill Country into a breathless, jarring skid behind Johnson, who stopped to call his foreman about a newborn goat kid that lay abandoned in the road.

* * *

PROFESSOR SMITH's food truck stirred camp with galvanized cans of oatmeal before six o'clock Monday for an early start. Marchers shivered awake to 28 degrees with heavily frosted ground; by noon, many were stripping down to T-shirts in the bright cool of Alabama's early spring, and, having covered another seven miles, some walked barefoot to soothe aching feet. From the Pentagon, McNamara's special assistant Joe Califano circulated the first bihourly bulletin to top government officials: "There are about 392 people in the column, of which approximately 45 are white. . . . During the last hour, a bus from Selma brought 40 fresh marchers to the group and returned 40 tired marchers to Selma." Helicopters buzzed a lone Piper Cub that dived toward the march but swerved off course to drop thousands of yellow segregationist leaflets into the desolate woods around Soapstone Creek. The military escort "noticeably increased" before the Lowndes County boundary, reported the *Washington Post*. A demolition team took lead position ahead of the press truck, reinforced by eight new Army jeeps and several staff cars. Major General Carl Turner, provost marshal of the Army, emerged to walk now and then on the shoulder.

At the next rest stop, dissent greeted Andrew Young's announcement that lines must pare down to comply with Judge Johnson's limit of three hundred. Nonselected teenagers protested that it should be a Negro march to reflect their long record of sacrifices in Selma. A white woman agreed, and Young was obliged to compose a mini-sermon on two points: first, that whites offered practical protection as lightning rods for attention, second, that it would be unprincipled to exclude them. As he did, Ivanhoe Donaldson and the marshals culled their chosen Negro veterans by county: 157 from Dallas (Selma), eighty-nine from Perry (home of Jimmie Lee Jackson), twenty-one from Wilcox, fifteen from Marengo. There were none from Lowndes. Beyond the few outsiders already designated, such as Episcopalian "Goldy" Sherrill, Hosea Williams compacted a final category of "Dr. King's Special Guests" to ten, including Harris Wofford and an aide to U.S. Senator Daniel Inouye of Hawaii. Buses returned to Selma with some hundred people— exhilarated, resentful, relieved, some vowing to be back—from the spot where Highway 80 narrowed to two lanes for twenty-two miles through Lowndes County.

"Pick it up, now!" shouted King. FBI agents counted 308 marchers, twenty-two of them white. Califano's "Report No. 2 as of 1400" told McNamara and Katzenbach that one-third were female, and noted the late arrival of SNCC's John Lewis among columns that moved three abreast over Big Swamp Creek on a narrow ribbon of land, through "opaque waters dotted with lily pads and floating algae," wrote Charles Fager, "dead trees standing with the bark gone and the wood weathered smooth, long strands of gray moss fluttering," then gently back up into dry and lonely square miles of scrub pasture, barely green.

Openness made the sun unexpectedly cruel, so that 250 of the marchers needed medical treatment by nightfall for sunburn and heatstroke. King removed his green marching hat with earflaps and placed it on John Lewis, saying he needed to protect his shaved head wound from Bloody Sunday. Negro teenagers wrote "VOTE" on their foreheads with thick white sun cream. Sister Mary Leoline of Kansas City, the only nun to walk the whole way, wilted inside a layered habit with a starched wimple that framed her round face, puffy and burned severely red. Jim Leatherer, a settlement house worker from Saginaw, Michigan, hopped on one leg with crutches, hands and armpits raw, lips cracked from the sun. Freed of Selma's street hecklers, who had mocked him with a parade cadence of "Left, left, left," he disclosed miles along that he sometimes challenged female companions not to be put off by his fleshy right stump, causing Worth Long of SNCC to howl with semi-feigned indignation that white men stooped to guilt hustling, which was controversial within the movement as applied to white women. Leatherer said he was a democrat. Bevel and others coerced him into the medical van for spells of rest, but marshal Soracco chased weary dawdlers off a latrine truck as bad for morale. An itinerant local preacher of seventy-two years urged the teenagers forward, asking why they needed five days to go fifty-four miles. "I'm used to walking," he said with bravado. "I could do it in a day and a half."

*   *   *

BYSTANDERS IN the landscape were scarce until the columns approached the invisible hamlet of Trickem Fork. From the shade of two oak trees that rose on the horizon, a score of Negroes moved to the center of Highway 80, having waited four hours. Will Jackson, seventy-five, unaccountably left the door of his prized pickup standing wide open to peer intently back toward Selma. Twenty-two years earlier, he had stood numb near the courthouse lawn in Hayneville as his young daughter Mary Lee wrestled to the ground and choked a wealthy white farmer for putting his arm around her again. With former Sheriff Woodruff refusing the farmer's pleas for help, saying he had brought the scrap on himself, Mary Lee Jackson had won scars of lifelong conflict—proudly vindicating family lessons never to run from a fight of honor, but fleeing permanently for Detroit within days, sadly aware what it would cost her father and brothers to defend her in Lowndes County. Her mother, Mary Jane, who had wailed through the public commotion, now absorbed as revelation the slowly advancing host of helicopters, jeeps, marchers, trucks, soldiers, medical vans, and reporters. "Lordy!" she cried. "I didn't ever thought I'd seen anythin' like this!"

Mattie Lee Moorer threw her arms around King's neck, singing a biblical hymn of ancestors about "numbers no man can know." She later recalled that he "got right in with it" on the music, but complained that "the ladies took Dr. King away from me." The elderly swirled about— Mattie Ruth Mallard, Will Jackson's brother Gully, and Lula May, among "1800s people" born in the last century—and barefoot children scampered from the trees to be part of the excitement.

"I done kissed him!" cried one of the older women, in tears.

"Who? Who you done kissed?" shouted others.

"The Martin Luther King," said Juanita Huggins. "I done kissed the Martin Luther King!" A strong singer, Huggins launched a new song: "Lord, I Cannot Stay on This Highway by Myself."

Andrew Young tried to keep the columns moving past the knot of emotion. "Look at that!" he called out, asking reporters to notice the broken windows and missing roof shingles of Mt. Gillard Missionary Baptist Church, just off the highway. "That's why we're marching." Young urged the Lowndes County residents to keep seeking the vote. While some reporters tried to interview them on the road, others who lingered to inspect the church discovered to their amazement that the unmarked shack nearby on brick stilts was the functioning public school for Negroes, Rolen Elementary, with an outhouse, rusty corrugated roof, rotted steps, and patches of Alabama license plates nailed askew over holes in the floor. Jesse "Note" Favors told reporters he had helped plant the overhanging oak trees as a student in 1931, when the saplings "weren't no bigger 'round than my wrists."

Coretta King joined the march late Monday from a concert in North Carolina, bringing newspaper accounts that she and King read side by side down the highway. LeRoy Collins fell alongside as mediator, bringing details of Governor Wallace's latest efforts to restrict the final rally in Montgomery. Near White Hall, more Lowndes County residents waved and even cheered the march. Napoleon Mays, a deacon at Mt. Gillard and distant relative of Morehouse College president Benjamin Mays, joined the ranks with a small flock of nieces, nephews, and his own children. Frank Haralson hastened boldly from a pine tree to greet the columns head-on, extending his hand. Ralph Abernathy asked whether he had ever seen Martin Luther King.

"No, sir," said Haralson.

"Well, you're shaking hands with him now," said Abernathy. Haralson drew himself up into a wide-eyed stare.

"Will you march with us?" King asked gently.

"I'll walk one step, anyway," Haralson replied. On his cane, which supported an imperfectly healed broken leg, he walked the last two and a half of Monday's sixteen miles to camp in a cow pasture infested with red ants. Workers from one of the volunteers committees poured kerosene on the mounds, and actor Pernell Roberts of the television show *Bonanza* helped raise the four tents. Rosie Steele, a seventy-eight-year-old widow, confided to a Negro reporter what had changed her mind about opening the property she had accumulated during World War II, "when prices was up" at her country store. Steele recalled "telling my daughter the other day" that to her, President Johnson had been "just another white Southerner when I heard him talking about Vietnam," but then came the speech about Selma, "saying we had the right to vote, to march clear to Montgomery if we wanted to," and she decided she could not refuse King's scouts. "If the president can take a stand," said Steele, "I guess I can, too."

After dark, a teenager sneaked under a tent flap and asked nervously how to start a youth movement like Selma's in Lowndes County. Some restless marchers sneaked the other way past military sentries to gather outside the country store. A convoy of eight white college students pulled up and got out of their cars, prompting security marshals, including a minister from New Jersey, to join the standoff. Asked what they wanted, one curious visitor said, "I don't know," and an awkwardly honest conversation turned sour on the question of motive. Students from Tennessee and Georgia concluded that the march aimed for hatred, not freedom, saying they heard white families were firing their maids. A student from Alabama insisted that the male marchers were being paid $15 a day, and recited precise lightning gossip that one female marcher was hospitalized already with $1,500 in her pockets from sleeping with forty-one niggers. To incredulous requests for names and verification, he politely shrugged, "Well, actually, ma'am, she bled to death."

King broke away twice from the Lowndes County bivouac. With Abernathy, he rode back to Jean Jackson's kitchen in Selma and soaked blistered feet in a tub. After returning to overnight at Steele's campsite, he excused himself to raise funds for the march by a quick charter flight to Cleveland. "Mr. Young is in charge until his return," Califano's Pentagon "Report No. 6" advised in Washington, where President Johnson, back from Texas, watched the successful space launch of Gemini 3. Military control of the Alabama protection mission passed "at 0600" from Selma's Team Alpha to Team Bravo based in Montgomery, Califano noted, adding that early rains caused trouble with mud: "One latrine truck is still stuck but should be on the road shortly."

At 10:25 Tuesday morning, the Lowndes County skies opened. "It hit with drops as big as quarters, pouring down on them with a great clap of sound," wrote one journalist from a trail car, "and coming back off the blacktop and crushed-gravel highway in a spray as high as their knees." Scattered white hecklers shouted from umbrellas that "a nigger won't stay out in the rain," but the lines slowed only until the continuing deluge saturated clothes and bedrolls beyond worry. Teenagers picked up the cadence for an uninhibited wet march. "A few youngsters put on cornflakes boxes for hats," reported the *New York Times.* "Their freedom songs rang out louder than ever." An old minister added merriment with a spontaneous shouted prayer of thanks to "Reverend Abernickel" for leading the exodus by flood, even though Abernathy did not march in King's absence. Halfway to Montgomery, on request from John Doar through Pentagon channels, Guardsmen in splattered ponchos along the route obediently turned outward toward the countryside, acknowledging external rather than internal danger.

*   *   *

WHILE MEETING with the House leadership, President Johnson first deflected a call from columnist Drew Pearson. "Just tell him no—tell him I've got the Security Council right after . . . this is just the worst day of the year for me," he whispered to the operator, but changed his mind to give Pearson a soft, off-the-record telephone monologue on Vietnam ("I can't send up a white flag") that ran on for fifteen minutes and pushed him late for a photograph visit. To British foreign minister Michael Stewart and his arriving entourage, Johnson continued seamlessly that some people wanted him to "bomb the hell out of China," some wanted him to run yellow, and Barry Goldwater, his defeated Republican opponent in 1964, wanted him to defoliate North Vietnam with nuclear bombs to "clear the brush where I can see" infiltrators on the trails. "Sometimes I just get all hunkered up like a jackass in a hailstorm," Johnson told the nonplussed diplomats, veering between picaresque anecdote and masterful synopsis well into the appointed time for Stewart to deliver a luncheon speech elsewhere. "He is power sublimated, like Niagara Falls," U.S. ambassador to England David K. E. Bruce recorded in his diary. "He read a long letter from an American soldier in Vietnam to his 'Mom,' strongly supporting American policy. . . . The cameramen made their onslaught in two waves. Then the Foreign Minister was released, after ninety minutes of an experience he is never likely to forget."

Johnson started a late lunch with Secretary McNamara as "Report No. 7" from the Pentagon tracked the Selma march across the turnoff to

Hayneville. "It is still raining," Califano advised. On cue from the carrier *Intrepid,* the President broke away to congratulate Gemini 3 astronauts Virgil Grissom and John Young for completing three earth orbits in five hours to Atlantic Ocean splashdown only sixty miles off target. Shortly thereafter, as crews removed the immense bank of temporary cameras from the Oval Office, he received a decisive conference call from the House Speaker's caucus about legislative negotiations on the bill to create Medicare. "I think we've got you something," reported committee chairman Wilbur Mills.

"Wonderful," said Johnson. He reviewed the agreement by imaginary inquiry: "All right now, my doctor . . . he pumps my stomach out to see if I've got any ulcers . . . does he charge what he wants to?"

"No, he can't quite charge what he wants to," replied the administration's chief negotiator, Wilbur Cohen. Medical bills would be routed through insurance companies—"somebody like Blue Shield"—in a compromise arrangement "to be sure the government wasn't regulating the fees directly." Patients would pay a percentage of the costs.

"All right," said Johnson. "That keeps your hypochondriacs out." He cross-examined the negotiators on their mechanism to mollify the doctors and insurance companies without breaking the new Medicare budget, then pressed for a vote before each group mobilized against the shared revenue stream. "Now remember this," he instructed Cohen. "Nine out of ten things I get in trouble on, is because they lay around. . . . It stinks, it's just like a dead cat on the door. . . . You either bury that cat or get some life in it." He reminded House Speaker John McCormack of a saying by his predecessor, Sam Rayburn, that a finished committee report was a dead cat "stinkin' every day. And let's get it passed before they can get their letters in." He spurred on Majority Leader Carl Albert, and promised Wilbur Mills to cover the projected costs without deficit, saying "four hundred million is not going to separate us friends when it's for health, when it's for sickness, because there's a greater demand, and I know it, for this bill than for all my other program put together . . . and it will last longer." Johnson told Mills a soft Texas yarn while munching a bit of sandwich, then worked himself back up to his war cry: "And for God's sake, don't let the dead cat stand on your porch! Mr. Rayburn used to say they stunk and they stunk and they stunk." Mills averred that his own method was to seize the voting majority, by which time the President was purring again. "I know where you learned it," he said. "Let me talk to the Speaker."

* * *

THE ALABAMA marchers sloshed that afternoon into campsite three, which the FBI classified as "a sea of mud" on pastureland owned by Birmingham entrepreneur A. G. Gaston at the eastern end of Lowndes County. Army demolition units sank to their ankles combing the field for bombs. The logistics committee located level high ground to pitch only two of the four field tents, which were uninhabitable until donated bales of hay and straw could be heaved from trucks by chain relay and spread into flimsy rafts of dryness. Conditions blotted out group activities including a "community sing" for morale. Folksinger Odetta found Pete Seeger curled up asleep.

Episcopal priest Morris Samuel of Los Angeles recruited seminarian Jonathan Daniels among extra security marshals for a night of stress. One marcher who broke down into shouts and seizures was hauled off to treatment for "emotional exhaustion." Another fell violently ill, and FBI inspector Joseph Sullivan only partly calmed fears of deliberate food poison by tracing a strange taste to extra creosote cleaner in a rented water truck, which previously had hauled sewage. (The U.S. Army supplied water the rest of the way, despite the misgivings of some marchers and the legal scruples of John Doar.) Wet Guardsmen on perimeter duty broke discipline to call people "nigger," and one reportedly spit in the face of a priest. A Northern white pilgrim, desperate for sleep, quarreled vainly with the perpetual singers, shouting, "You goddam kids, shut up!" Two photographers scuffled for position to catch a tilted Unitarian, who had dozed off seated, at the instant he toppled into the muck.

In Cleveland that evening, a police guard arrested one of twenty-eight pickets at the Hotel Sheraton for charging with a Confederate flag up to King's room on the ninth floor. Downstairs in the giant banquet hall, energy from compressed history piled newer agendas ahead of recent ones. King told 2,200 paying guests that proceeds intended to honor his Nobel Prize would be used to defray SCLC's $50,000 cost for the Selma-to-Montgomery march, and that beyond a second landmark law on segregation he looked soon to address "unjust conditions" of race nationwide, outside the South. "In the world as it is today," he said, "America can no longer afford an anemic-type democracy." The governor of Ohio sent a personal donation to the banquet for presentation by Negro publisher William Walker, whose family in Selma once owned the café where Rev. James Reeb ate supper before the ambush two Tuesdays earlier. Ohio's largest newspaper, the *Plain Dealer,* highlighted blistered feet on the front page—"Dr. King, in Cleveland, Tries Not to Limp"—and reported as a breakthrough that the diocese authorized Catholic clergy to march over the objections of the Alabama archbishop. Well after midnight, King and his traveling aide Bernard Lee made room for two Ohio priests on the chartered flight back to Montgomery by way of Pittsburgh and Atlanta.

The Alabama columns followed Andrew Young out of Gaston's pasture before seven o'clock Wednesday morning, mostly soggy and miserable but relieved to be on the move. Jonathan Daniels hitched a ride back to the rearguard bustle of Selma and the clutter of signs posted throughout Brown Chapel—"All those who wish to take hot baths, contact Mrs. Lilly"—looking for sleep after all-night security duty. His seminary companion Judith Upham crossed in the other direction to join the ranks past the first mile, where Highway 80 opened to four lanes and the court order no longer restricted numbers. The march doubled to 675 people by nine o'clock. Those with transistor radios heard descriptions of the last close-up photographs transmitted from the exploratory satellite Ranger 9 before crash impact on the moon crater Alphonsus, and station WHHY broadcast news of fresh resolutions by the Alabama legislature declaring the march to be a pestilence of sex orgies and vulgar language, specifying that "young women are returning to their respective states apparently as unwed expectant mothers." John Lewis joked to reporters that segregationists were preoccupied with interracial sex, which was "why you see so many shades of brown on this march." Harris Wofford "almost welcomed the wild charges" as relief from sentimentality, noting privately that some Northerners babbled naively about the rustic glory of abject poverty, like "Peace Corps Volunteers during their first week abroad."

* * *

WITH ABERNATHY and Coretta, King rejoined the columns at eleven o'clock in Montgomery County, beyond the Lowndes boundary about halfway through Wednesday's sixteen miles. He welcomed some of the constant arrivals who had swelled the ranks above a thousand, dropped off by bus and car—long-lost preacher friends from Crozer Seminary, a Jewish delegation from the Anti-Defamation League. The grime of bedraggled permanent marchers dispersed in a sea of clean new faces and fresh shirts, some unwisely attached to suitcases. FBI agents recorded the presence of more celebrities—singer Tony Bennett, actor

Anthony Perkins and his wife—among numbers that doubled again before thunderstorms at 1:30 drenched lines stretched more than a mile. Coming out of open country, they passed Montgomery's Dannelly Airport, headquarters for military escort Team Bravo, where officials processed a rash of unseen threats to firebomb the women's tent, blow up Dexter Avenue Baptist Church, and to shoot King from the roof of a downtown building. By three o'clock the lead vehicles approached campsite four at the City of St. Jude, a Catholic compound on the outskirts of Montgomery. "The latest estimates ran between 4,000 and 5,000 just before entering the bivouac area," Joseph Califano informed government leaders from the Pentagon.

Above the drone of helicopters, nuns and schoolchildren of St. Jude sang with crowds of Negroes from the surrounding neighborhood, greeting not only the marchers from Highway 80 but also thousands who converged for Thursday's final push to the capitol. C. Vann Woodward and John Hope Franklin arrived in a delegation of twenty prominent historians. A trainload of 117 Washingtonians, stranded all night by balky crews on their Atlanta–West Point special, hiked wearily from the railroad station. Two hundred students came straight from Kilbey State Prison and nearby jails, released on bond a week after James Forman's Montgomery demonstrations. Assorted columns filed for hours into the fenced grounds of St. Jude with "a grandeur that was almost biblical," reported the *New York Times*. Even troubles acquired epic scale. Hands passed food above heads jammed close on a St. Jude lawn trampled to mud. Pastors joined volunteers trying to repair a failed generator. Poles snapped on two of the field tents.

CHAPTER 14

The Stakes of History

March 24–25, 1965

OUT of a Wednesday afternoon nap, President Johnson called Henry Cabot Lodge about filling a Republican vacancy at the new Communications Satellite Corporation, saying he refused to let him "sit on your tail up there in Boston" while Republicans were out of power. "I got lots of Republican votes 'cause you weren't nominated," he teased, alluding to massive gains in his Goldwater race above the stiff competition from the GOP's Richard Nixon–Henry Cabot Lodge ticket of 1960, and he complained that the Republican National Committee made it hard for him to hire top-quality government executives. "Dogs," he called their suggested political appointments— "somebody somebody's owned for twenty years out in Ohio or somewhere . . . or somebody that hates everything"—and Lodge agreed, "Just deadbeats, yes." Above all, Johnson cooed and wooed the Republican scion to "lead them down a good path of public service," back in harness. "I waked up here, and I just thought of something out of heaven almost," he said, opening a barrage of flattery about how badly he missed contact with a peer statesman to "walk around with our dog and philosophize some, because I get pretty lonesome around here sometimes." In passing, he asked for confidential advice about replacing General Maxwell Taylor in Lodge's former post as U.S. ambassador to South Vietnam.

Lodge answered briskly that Vietnam needed "a politically minded civilian" of stature. "There are a lot of things that a military man just doesn't see," he argued, though conceding that Johnson rightly had sent

Taylor as "your number one soldier" to neutralize Vietnam as a campaign issue in 1964. "I certainly will, will think about it," Lodge promised, then stopped, chuckled, and coughed. "But maybe the thing to do is to send me back."

"Well, might be," Johnson replied. "Might be, might be." Lodge said he spoke fluent French and knew how to handle the military, which was "very important out there." Johnson renewed his pitch for the COMSAT board, masking any targeted recruitment for Vietnam with a general enthusiasm that betrayed no hint of his prior disparagement of Lodge. On becoming President sixteen months earlier in Dallas, he had flayed Lodge to confidants as an overbred patrician, telling Senator Richard Russell that he "ain't worth a damn" and Senator William Fulbright that he had "things screwed up good" in Vietnam. Johnson blamed Lodge for conniving like Lady Macbeth in the fateful coup against South Vietnamese President Ngo Dinh Diem. McNamara considered him a self-important "loner," and Russell whispered to Johnson that Lodge "thinks he's emperor out there . . . dealing with barbarian tribes."

What had changed since was Johnson, not Lodge. Now that the President himself grimly had "crossed the Rubicon" on direct intervention, as Ambassador Taylor put it, Lodge's impulse to command looked more necessary than inept. "The Vietnamese have no tradition of national government," he had advised Johnson recently as a secret consultant. "They do not do it well." Still regarding Communist subversion as an apocalyptic danger—"a bigger threat than the nuclear"—Lodge urged the President to ignore or work around the Vietnamese government rather than "hamper ourselves by the classic, diplomatic idea that for us to deal with anything below the national level is interference in internal affairs." By contrast, Ambassador Taylor consistently opposed the introduction of U.S. ground troops as politically and militarily self-defeating. Not only would the prospect of American rescue "sap the already flaccid purpose of the Vietnamese" military, he feared, but Vietnamese civilians would come to resent and resist the "white-faced soldier, armed, equipped and trained as he is," as successor to the hated French colonialists. Taylor offered Johnson a soldier's loyal realism, but Lodge offered boundless confidence, plus partisan cover as a Republican of presidential stature.

"Don't you mention this other thing to another human," the President instructed.

"Can I call you tomorrow?" asked Lodge.

"I wish you would," said Johnson. "Call me early in the morning as you can."

* * *

FACULTY ORGANIZERS had averted the wrath of the state legislature by moving their planned "work moratorium" out of regular class time at the University of Michigan, and relieved administrators helped female dorm students secure permission to stay out late Wednesday night in Ann Arbor. This boosted attendance, as did the theatrical energy of needlers who showed up chanting "Better Dead Than Red," with sarcastic signs of "Defoliate the Arb, Deflower the Thetas," and "Drop the Bomb." Still, no one expected more than a small fraction of the three thousand students who overflowed ten volunteer seminars on aspects of the Vietnam War—basic geopolitics, revolutions in Asia, theories of guerrilla warfare, history of American involvement. Hecklers and curious couples alike stayed on to question professors debating as citizens. In one of the featured lectures, Arthur Waskow was presenting the war as misguided—"we have not yet learned that the political freedom of the Vietnamese people cannot be advanced by a military policy"—when helmeted police evacuated Angell Hall because of bomb threats. The whole assembly moved outside before midnight to loudspeakers set up in the snow, first to hear Waskow complete his lament that "we might have to pay the cost of our delay." He quoted Thomas Jefferson's premonition on blinkered democracy and slavery: "I tremble for my country when I reflect that God is just."

By then in Montgomery, the afternoon's celebration was deteriorating into confusion on the verge of panic. Equipment failure left the St. Jude campsite almost entirely in darkness, and a crowd grown from ten thousand close to thirty thousand by FBI estimate jammed against the makeshift stages until some fifty-seven people collapsed of illness, exhaustion, or injury. Marshals pushed through with twenty of them on stretchers before the jerrybuilt sound system sputtered to life late in the evening, allowing Harry Belafonte to sing one of his signature calypso hits, "Jamaica Farewell." To restore order and spirits, Belafonte presented a midnight gala featuring Nina Simone, Alan King, Billy Eckstine, Johnny Mathis, the Chad Mitchell Trio, Leonard Bernstein, James Baldwin, and many others. Coretta King read a Langston Hughes poem in a rare joint appearance with her husband, saluting the large contingent of marchers from her native Perry County—"I was born and reared just eighty miles from here . . ." Before the rally ended at two o'clock, overflow marchers dispersed through Montgomery to seek dry pallets in Negro homes and church pews. Viola Liuzzo of Detroit slept in her car. King withdrew to Richmond Smiley's home for another contentious late staff meeting. From predawn flights—a delegation of 293 landing at 4:45 A.M. from Burbank Air Terminal, for instance, and charters bearing four hundred people from New York City alone—a long line of rumbling buses stirred the campsite before breakfast.

In Ann Arbor, meanwhile, six hundred students lasted all through the night, extending the Vietnam seminars until the university tower struck eight o'clock Thursday morning. A contagion was spreading already from the advance buzz about the first "T-Day" or "Teach Day," which had been proposed less than two weeks earlier on the conscious model of SNCC's Freedom Schools from the 1964 Mississippi Summer Project. The "teach-in" phenomenon instantly acquired a name from another antecedent in the movement, and would crisscross major universities even more rapidly than the sit-ins of 1960 leapt between Negro colleges. Columbia University in New York hosted a Vietnam teach-in the very next day, Wisconsin the next week. Within two months, there would be simultaneous teach-ins on more than a hundred campuses.

* * *

IN WASHINGTON, Lodge indeed called the White House early: "Good morning, sir, how did you sleep?" As President Johnson replied that he was already going through reports on the Alabama march—"Today's the big day . . . very potentially dangerous"—Lodge promptly announced his readiness to serve again as ambassador in South Vietnam. The President regretted that he had to send anyone "back in the swamp holes," but reported that he and his top advisers were overjoyed to learn of Lodge's willingness. "McNamara was just almost ecstatic last night . . . said it just solves all of our problems," Johnson declared. He urged Lodge to keep quiet for a few months—"don't even say to anybody that we even talked"—until Taylor's replacement could be arranged as routine. From there, Johnson interrupted a telephone briefing on Alabama to console Attorney General Katzenbach personally—"it's been an ordeal, I know"—warning him about the risk of heavy cigarette consumption through the late-night vigils.

"I am smoking too many of them, Mr. President," Katzenbach confessed. He asked for personal advice about how Johnson had quit tobacco, looking to find "the guts" to do so when pressure relented. If they could get through the grand finale on the steps of Wallace's capitol, Katzenbach reported hopefully, "I think King would like to take a little rest—he's got some sore feet." Johnson dissected legislative prospects on the voting rights bill, then soon called young Senator Edward Kennedy about the upcoming 750th anniversary of the Magna Carta at Runnymeade field, where Queen Elizabeth would dedicate "an acre of English ground" in memory of President Kennedy. He invited Kennedy to represent the United States along with Robert Kennedy and their widowed sister-in-law, Jacqueline, at the royal ceremony in May. Kennedy responded warmly, and joked about how hard it could be to reach his brother "in that remote area, as you probably know." (Concluding a perilous expedition in the Far Yukon Territory, Senator Robert Kennedy only the day before had planted three PT-109 tie clasps at the summit of the previously unnamed and unclimbed Mt. Kennedy.) Johnson traded quips with the younger brother, then switched still laughing to fraternal challenge. "Where is my immigration bill, goddam it?" he roared. Kennedy, still merry but sputtering, said his allies in the Judiciary Committee had "lost four weeks" to intervening hearings on voting rights. Johnson exhorted him to push immigration in tandem, while Selma had the Southern senators on their heels about racial exclusion.

From the Pentagon, Joseph Califano wrote Thursday morning that the "Army force of 2,966 personnel has been split into three teams": roadblock units along the march route, security deployments at the rally site, reserves to the north and east. "The tents have been taken down and the camp site is being policed," advised his "Report No. 12" as of ten o'clock in Washington, which in Montgomery was the scheduled start time of nine. Moving to the White House Situation Room, Califano prepared a bulletin an hour later that "some 2,000/4,000 marchers are now milling around, unorganized," with the start delayed in light rain, and he scrawled a hasty addendum on delivery to President Johnson: "11:35 A.M. Still milling around. Est. 10,000 people."

*   *   *

STALLED AMID Army jeeps at a roadblock, Bernard Lee remonstrated with soldiers that Dr. King's party must turn into the St. Jude campsite to start the march. Andrew Young jumped from the car to do the same, and finally the light-skinned Ralph Bunche unfolded from the back seat with the aplomb of an international executive.

"I'm Dr. Bunche, undersecretary of the United Nations," he told the posted sergeant. "Here for the march."

"Sorry, sir," replied the sergeant. "This is not the United Nations. My orders are no left turn."

As King emerged to ask Lee what was wrong, a Montgomery police motorcycle arrived under siren through traffic piling up behind. The officer brusquely interrupted the sergeant's explanation of the impasse. "You danged fool," he said, pointing in recognition of King. "This is the man. Let him through!"

The car inched forward into the teeming grounds at St. Jude, full of competitive teasing about the relative impotence of pastoral reason and the United Nations, with ironic jokes about whether the rescuing policeman was old enough to have arrested King when he lived in Montgomery. Discussions of rank churned less happily around marshals Ivanhoe Donaldson and Frank Soracco as they distributed bright orange vests to the three hundred stalwarts who had marched the whole fifty miles, calling out, "Make way for the originals." Newcomers surged around them at the point of formation, demanding extra vests for parallel status. Some said they belonged up front with fellow preachers, or claimed promised rewards—"our president told us Dr. King wanted us to march with him"—and a few refused outright to march behind "kids."

The young orange vests asserted themselves with the pluck that had made Selma High School a manpower center for demonstrations since 1963. "All you dignitaries got to get behind me," shouted seventeen-year-old Profit Barlow. "I didn't see any of you fellows in Selma, and I didn't see you on the way to Montgomery. Ain't nobody going to get in front of me but Dr. King." His cohorts confirmed pretenders by their clean footwear and shooed them toward the rear.

Roy Wilkins of the NAACP set an example for the recognized national leaders. "You fellows deserve to go first," he told the orange vests, in a gesture that calmed frayed nerves through untimely distraction from waiting deputies of the Montgomery County Sheriff's Department. They intercepted King to serve summons on several legal actions before he could leave Alabama: a preliminary injunction against boycotts, an action by the Selma Bus Line for recovery of lost revenue, a suit by the city of Selma for damages and reimbursement of public expenditures during demonstrations, all with duplicate paperwork for defendants Abernathy, Young, and Lewis. When King did join the march line, the tentative accommodation of leaders was swamped by an anonymous surge toward him from all sides. Marshals struggled to adapt by placing the younger orange vests well ahead of King as an honor vanguard, followed by an open space for the photographers, then King and Abernathy with front-row leaders Wilkins, A. Philip Randolph, Bunche, Hosea Williams, Lewis, Bevel, and Fred Shuttlesworth, plus Coretta and Juanita Abernathy, followed by Amelia Boynton, Cager Lee, and Marie Foster among more senior orange vests, James Forman, the entertainers, and a host of clergy including Orloff Miller, James Reeb's last dinner companion.

*   *   *

THEY EMBARKED nearly two hours late, almost noon in Washington. Marchers toward the front still jostled self-consciously for position, some hoisting important organizational banners. Rosa Parks found herself shoved several times to the sidewalk, where she stood until a marshal who knew her came along to make a fuss about getting her in the march. "I *was* in it, but they put me out," Parks complained. She dropped back where placement was more relaxed. Of those content to wait for the crowded campsite to thin out, Viola Liuzzo asked a priest of St. Jude to take her into the high church tower to watch the line stretch into the distance beneath fading helicopters and light Army planes. Suddenly agitated, Liuzzo confessed fear of a contorted segregationist plot to assassinate George Wallace and blame the civil rights movement. She calmed down to waft along with the rearguard marchers, carrying her purse and shoes.

"It required one hour and 40 minutes to pass a starting point," FBI agents reported from an observation post, "and a head count tallied approximately 12,000 marchers." A greater number joined spontaneously or from staging areas at many of the 104 road-blocked intersections along the last four miles into Montgomery, passing sights that made a fresh impression on most marchers but for some touched depths of an odyssey come home. From St. Jude hospital, where Coretta had given birth to the Kings' first two children, the path moved into Negro neighborhoods down Oak Street past Holt Street Baptist Church, where King at twenty-six had addressed the first mass meeting of the bus boycott more than nine years earlier. Families waved from ramshackle homes. "Many cried," wrote a correspondent. Belafonte turned to companions and said, "This is it. If I could sing what's in the hearts and minds of these people, I'd be happy."

The columns streamed down Mobile Street into a downtown business district that was eerily deserted. Governor Wallace had proclaimed a "danger" holiday for female state employees, and major businesses placed newspaper advertisements endorsing his stay-home message. From an office building at the corner of Lee and Montgomery, marchers were showered with leaflets picturing King in 1957 at Tennessee's Highlander Center, labeled "MARTIN LUTHER KING AT COMMUNIST TRAINING SCHOOL." King himself doubtless had forgotten what he actually said in his speech* celebrating the twenty-fifth anniversary of Highlander, but he knew well that Tennessee had persecuted the South's pioneer interracial retreat to the brink of extinction, and that Governor Wallace among others made the photograph the centerpiece of an attack campaign springing up nationally on highway billboards.

From a high window in the federal building, where four years earlier a horrified John Doar had watched mobs beat integrated Freedom Riders at the bus station, Frank Johnson witnessed a political demonstration for the first time in his life; he and a fellow judge measured two hours for the lines to pass the Jeff Davis Hotel. By temperament, Judge Johnson bristled against all street politics for the implication that justice was not yet available through the courts, but he came to exempt from private censure this one messy proof of "something special about democracy: that it can never be taken for granted."

Around the fountain at Court Square, where Rosa Parks had boarded her segregated bus home from work on the day in 1955 when her arrest started the boycott, the route opened broadly for the last six blocks up the hill toward the Palladian white dome of the Alabama state capitol. Soldiers stood behind wooden barricades on both sides of Dexter Avenue. Jim Leatherer of Saginaw thumped along in weary exultation, nodding, "I believe in you, I believe in democracy," but he shook a crutch defiantly at elderly white hecklers in a distant window. A student in the lines received what amounted to a carefree effusion from the circumspect John Doar: "You're only likely to see three great parades in a lifetime, and this is one of them."

To the right at the final intersection stood prim Dexter Avenue Bap-

* "Men hate each other because they fear each other," King had said on September 2, 1957. "They fear each other because they don't know each other. They don't know each other because they can't communicate with each other. They can't communicate with each other because they are separated from each other." Rosa Parks and Aubrey Williams, Lyndon Johnson's New Deal boss at the National Youth Administration, were among those present for King's speech on the meaning of segregation.

tist Church, organized nine decades earlier in the former Harwell Mason slave pen, on whose bulletin board, snug at the base of the capitol grounds, the vagabond sage Vernon Johns had scandalized whites and Negroes alike by posting sermon titles such as "Segregation After Death" and "When the Rapist Is White," during the Korean War. Daddy King, having once begged his son not to follow the chewed-up Johns into the employ of "preacher-eating" Dexter deacons, now converged with the first marchers at the site of King's first pastorate, along with Coretta's parents, Obadiah and Bernice Scott.

At a right angle to the church, a line of Alabama troopers barred access to state property across the wide neck of pavement where Dexter Avenue dead-ended into Bainbridge Street. Reserve troopers faced down the capitol hill from steps rising behind, and Governor Wallace had installed conspicuously on the marble plaza above a final protective barrier. To prevent "desecrating" political touch by Negroes and integrationists, plywood temporarily covered the bronze floor emblem on the spot where Jefferson Davis swore an oath to become the first Confederate President in February of 1861.

Andrew Young climbed aboard a flatbed truck below. "This is a revolution, a revolution that won't fire a shot. . . ." he called over loudspeakers. "We come to love the hell out of the State of Alabama." Rally host Abernathy entertained the thickening mass of arrivals with a wry commentary on flags. Refining rumors that a black mourning banner would fly above an evacuated capitol—and erroneous FBI intelligence that Wallace would raise the Soviet hammer and sickle "to show that socialism has taken over"—he described the Alabama and Confederate battle flags waving over the dome, with Old Glory struck down, and guessed mischievously that Alabamians had misplaced their country or forgotten its national anthem. "Let's teach 'em the words!" Abernathy shouted, turning the crowd away from the dome to see American flags waving thickly above the marchers coming up Dexter Avenue.

"The Star-Spangled Banner" spilled into "Blowin' in the Wind," "Go, Tell It on the Mountain," and "This Land Is Your Land" among patriotic folk songs and spirituals led by singers grouped around the cluster of microphones—Odetta, Leon Bibb, Oscar Brand, Len Chandler in a pith helmet, Joan Baez barefoot in a velvet dress. "Great day! Great day! Great day!" Belafonte shouted among them, above reports that marchers *still* were filing out of St. Jude. Mary Travers, of the trio Peter, Paul and Mary, kissed him on the cheek.

Calls besieged corporate headquarters in New York to protest the visible contact between blond Travers and darkly West Indian Belafonte, which "makes a Southerner's blood run hot." A station manager in Charlotte, North Carolina, threatened CBS News president Fred Friendly with an organized revolt of affiliates unless he removed offensive "propaganda" from the network feed. Friendly and his vice presidents battled blinking telephone lights until the half-hour break, and then an opposing flood of calls denounced the switch from historic Montgomery back to regular soap operas.

For ninety minutes, while executives straddled promises to resume the live broadcast from Alabama, television viewers missed the raw chemistry of a mass meeting that lurched between tedium and surprise. "I look worse than anybody else on this stage," said bricklayer Albert Turner on behalf of Perry County. "That's because I marched fifty miles." Some prostrate orange vests could not be roused even for a nod to admiring celebrities, while others agitated to inject extra speakers into the all-male procession on the scheduled program. Amelia Boynton of Selma read a petition intended for Wallace. Rosa Parks, coaxed forward to thunderous applause, recalled hiding from the Klan as a small child. "My family was deprived of the land that they owned," she said softly. "I am handicapped in every way." Faltering, she said others could put it all better into words.

*   *   *

"THEY TOLD us we wouldn't get here," King called out that afternoon. "And there were those who said that we would get here only over their dead bodies." Already he strayed from lyrical prepared remarks about their long march from Selma "through desolate valleys and across the trying hills," to claim validation for the competent and concrete result. "But all the world today knows that we *are* here," he declared extemporaneously, "and we are standing before the forces of power in the State of Alabama, saying, 'We ain't gonna let nobody turn us around.' " Tepid response greeted a pause, and his deep opening tones continued at the slow pace of practiced salutation, inviting concentration rather than excitement. From the flatbed, wearing boots and a conservative dark suit, his plain necktie in a formal Windsor knot, King looked over heads massed down the gentle slope of Dexter Avenue to Court Square. As once before at the March on Washington, but never again in his lifetime, cameras from every network transmitted the full speech nationwide.

He pronounced it fitting that the Selma campaign should end in Montgomery, where domestic nonviolent resistance had been born as an idea "more powerful than guns or clubs," to spread and grow for eight years until the witness of jailed children in Birmingham aroused the nation "from the wells of its democratic spirit" to provide Negroes "some part of their rightful dignity" in the Civil Rights Act of 1964. "But without the vote, it was dignity without strength," King added, and "once more the method of nonviolent resistance was unsheathed." He sketched the arduous, lonely vote drive in Alabama to its point of crisis, and said with deliberation: "There never was a moment in American history more honorable and more inspiring than the pilgrimage of clergymen and laymen of every race and faith, pouring into Selma to face danger at the side of its embattled Negroes." King saluted President Johnson's "sensitivity to feel the will of the country" and his forthrightness to recognize "the courage of the Negro for awakening the conscience of the nation," then summarized the Alabama movement thus far. "From Montgomery to Birmingham, from Birmingham to Selma, from Selma back to Montgomery," he said, "the trail wound in a circle long and often bloody. Yet it has become a highway up from darkness."

"*Yes,* sir," answered scattered voices.

"So I stand before you this afternoon with the conviction that segregation is on its deathbed in Alabama," King announced, projecting a spur of energy, "and the only thing uncertain about it is how costly the segregationists and Wallace will make the funeral."

A wave of cheers rolled over an applause line that King had refined with fellow preachers since graduate school. By the rules of oratory, he usually followed the quickening moment of introduction with an anecdote or scriptural passage to frame an accessible question ahead, but here he detoured instead into a troublesome corner of history. "Racial segregation as a way of life did not come about as a natural result of hatred between the races immediately after the Civil War," King asserted, citing arguments published by Yale historian C. Vann Woodward in his acclaimed book, *The Strange Career of Jim Crow.* Southern states had permitted biracial voting for two decades after the end of Reconstruction in 1877—seating nearly a hundred elected Negro legislators in North and South Carolina alone—and for a time white supremacists themselves had ridiculed the crippling inconvenience of Jim Crow proposals.

King left his script briefly again—"I want you to follow me through here"—to beg patience for abstractions that were remote to dedicated marchers and many scholars, let alone television viewers. What had changed toward the end of the nineteenth century, he argued, was that the fledgling Populist Party, with its potential voting alliance of "poor white masses" and Negroes, had provoked the "emerging bourbon interests" to take drastic action. "Through their control of the mass media," said King, with a hint of conspiracy, they campaigned shrewdly and sensationally for "laws that made it a crime for Negroes and whites to come together as equals at any level. And that did it."

"*Yes,* sir," called a lone voice from the huge crowd.

The mechanical vocabulary of labor materialism and class politics was new in King's public speech, and perhaps reflected partial drafts from Bayard Rustin among the advisers huddled on the flatbed. He rephrased his interpretation of Woodward's book in biting religious language at the edge of blasphemy. "If it may be said of the slavery era that the white man took the world and gave the Negro Jesus," King continued, "then it may be said of the Reconstruction Era that the Southern aristocracy took the world and gave the poor white man Jim Crow . . . a psychological bird that told him that no matter how bad off he was, at least he was a white man better than the black man."

"*Yes,* sir," answered voices.

"He ate Jim Crow . . . and his children too learned to feed upon Jim Crow," said King. Against the threat of free ballots, political powers engineered the segregated society. "They segregated Southern churches from Christianity," he declared. "They segregated Southern minds from honest thinking. And they segregated the Negro from everything!" Cheers erupted briefly from portions of the crowd. Most remained silent, however, as though confounded.

King's unexpected, unfinished diagnosis rested on notions of raw political economy beyond his established pulpit. He drew a direct line from Reconstruction to the Selma march as twin crossroads in the patriotic history of freedom, a century apart, and warned by analogy of pitfalls in this second opportunity to "build a great society." Inspiration and goodwill were not enough to stabilize new democracy born in traumatic sacrifice, because reactive fears would threaten not only empirical gains but the political vocabulary of self-government itself. After the Civil War, to undermine the three new freedom amendments in the Constitution, Americans broadly had distorted Reconstruction to accommodate a romantic view of white supremacy. Such pitfalls in history, while mysterious and beguiling, went to "the very origin, the root cause of segregation," King said. Professor Woodward called them "strange," in his restrained description of the decades when Southern states had come to fasten upon Negroes, and themselves, a segregation so thorough as to banish any fraternal organization with bylaws that allowed members of difference races to address each other as "brother."

* * *

KING EMPHASIZED the stakes of historical choice. "We've come a long way since that travesty of justice was perpetrated on the American mind," he told the rally. "James Weldon Johnson put it eloquently. He said:

> 'We have come over a way that with
> Tears has been watered.
> We have come, treading our path through the
> Blood of the slaughtered.' "

The crowd fell silent as King touched bottom. Whatever had created segregation from slavery, both durable beyond the life span of totalitarian inventions since, he looked unflinching at the consequences. Far from crafting artificial comfort for white listeners, he was quoting a portion of Johnson's "Lift Every Voice and Sing" that recalled degradation too harshly for many slave descendants themselves. Often omitted from performance, the middle stanza of the accepted "Negro National Anthem" evoked formless ghosts of the ancient Middle Passage into slavery, with sharp echoes more recently from the eras of lynching and Civil War. Outside Fort Pillow, Tennessee, where his Confederates massacred surrendered black troops, General Nathan Bedford Forrest had written straightforwardly in his battle report: "The river was dyed red with the blood of the slaughtered for 200 yards." The wife of the white Union commander interceded with Abraham Lincoln on behalf of fresh sister widows who, as fugitive chattel under state laws, had no more right to veterans' benefits than did animals or furniture, and Congress, answering Lincoln's proposal to treat ex-slave orphans and widows "as though their marriages were legal," granted family status to Negroes by law passed on July 2, 1864, a century to the day ahead of the Civil Rights Act that abolished segregation in the summer before Selma.

In Montgomery, King continued from the hymn:

"Out of the gloomy past,
'Til now we stand at last
Where the white gleam
Of our bright star is cast."

His mood snapped forward: "Today I want to tell the city of Selma."
"Tell 'em, now," came a shout.
"Today I want to say to the State of Alabama."
"*Yes,* sir."
"Today I want to say to the people of America, and the nations of the world, that we are not about to turn around. We are on the move now. Yes, we are on the move, and no wave of racism can stop us."
"*Yes,* sir."
"We are on the move now. And the burning of our churches will not deter us. We are on the move now . . ." His voice rose steadily in pitch as he pictured an inexorable move through obstacle and sacrifice, then shifted his drumbeat phrase to a march. "Let us march on segregated housing," King intoned. "Let us march on segregated schools, until. . . . Let us march on poverty, until. . . . Let us march on ballot boxes, until we send men . . . who will not fear to 'do justice, love mercy, and walk humbly with thy God.' "

After embellishing the march on ballot boxes seven times near the peak of his baritone register, King slowed to give respite. "There is nothing wrong with marching in this sense," he said. "The Bible tells us that the mighty men of Joshua merely walked about the walled city of Jericho, and the barriers for freedom came tumbling down." He quoted words of the old slave spiritual slowly and intimately in dialect, "just as they were given us:

'Joshua fit de battle of Jericho
Joshua fit de battle of Jericho . . .
Go blow dem ram horns, Joshua cried
Course de battle am in my hand.' "

King asked his listeners to honor the "unknown, long gone black bard" with a worthy reply. "The battle is in our hands," he said. "We can answer with creative nonviolence the call to higher ground." He lifted up personal memories of Montgomery's bus boycotters as "wondrous signs of our times, so full of hope . . . the faces so bright," and added to the answering roll the names of martyrs down to Jimmie Lee Jackson and

James Reeb. "The patter of their feet . . . is the thunder of the marching men of Joshua, and the world rocks beneath their tread," he sang out solemnly. "My people, my people, listen. The battle *is* in our hands."

King paused briefly, having run out of prepared text. He improvised first to answer persistent appeals by critics and bystanders for an end to troubling agitation. He rejected their rhetorical image of prior tranquillity, saying normalcy had shrugged off brutal terror and merely frowned over bombed churches. "It is normalcy all over Alabama that prevents the Negro from becoming a registered voter," he said. His distinctive, anguished voice heated the word "normalcy" into an improbable engine of speech momentum, fired fifteen times over ten consecutive sentences. "The only normalcy that we will settle for is the normalcy that allows judgment to run down like waters and righteousness like a mighty stream," King shouted, transposing the prophet Amos. He rushed on from memory to make three final appeals for nonviolence in the struggle to build "a society at peace with itself," then spoke to yearnings within. "I know you are asking today, how long will it take?" he confessed. "Somebody's asking, how long will prejudice blind the visions. . . . Somebody's asking . . ."

Only then did King let loose words that would be remembered from the zenith of the freedom movement. Nearly everything else soon dissipated in the flux of perception on all sides. Inside the capitol, Governor Wallace watched three television sets and peeked at the future electorate through an aide's window blinds, so as not to be seen shuttered in his own office. Outside, King's presentation cut across tender seams of comfort and color among his own sympathizers—too black in tone, too nonviolent, too dark and tendentious in warning from Reconstruction history against another slow erosion of hope. The preserved record of King's speech would be messier than his hastily thrown-together text, reflecting an era in upheaval. Passages were adjusted or skipped. What lasted in print* was not what he said. What lasted in memory was not what he wrote in advance.

"How long will justice be crucified and truth buried?" King cried out

---

* The sanctioned anthology of King's major works (1986) shifts nonviolence to the past tense, from "can transform" in the actual speech to "transformed." It omits the first and last blocks of the delivered speech advocating nonviolence ("And so I plead with you . . ."). Also omitted in the preserved version are King's entire discussion of Reconstruction and Jim Crow, his peroration on normalcy, and his recitals of "Lift Every Voice" and "The Battle of Jericho," among other passages. Some of the errors and abridgments appeared first in excerpts compiled overnight by the *New York Times*.

in Montgomery. "I come to say to you this afternoon, however difficult the moment, however frustrating the hour, it will not be long. Because truth crushed to earth will rise again. How long? *Not* long! Because no lie can live forever. How long? *Not* long! Because you shall reap what you sow. How long?"

Already shouts echoed and anticipated his refrain at a driving pace, above cries of encouragement and a low roar of anticipation. King dispensed with the names of the authors from his treasured string of classical quotations, to streamline a final run of oratory into ninety seconds. *"Not* long!"

"Not long!" answered a female voice above the others.

" 'Truth forever on the scaffold, wrong forever on the throne,' " he recited in passion from the poet James Russell Lowell. " 'Yet that scaffold sways the future and / Behind the dim unknown stands God / Within the shadow, keeping watch above his own.' How long? *Not* long! Because the arc of the moral universe is *long,* but it bends toward justice. How long? *Not* long! Because mine eyes have seen the glory of the coming of the Lord. He is trampling out the vintage where the grapes of *wrath* are stored. He has loosed the fateful lightning of his *terrible* swift sword. His truth is marching on."

King kept on at a gallop through another stanza of the "Battle Hymn." He slowed only to hurl himself into selected words, trembling at the limit, and to climb still higher through a spoken chorus.

> "He has sounded forth the trumpet that shall *never* call retreat
> He is sifting out the *hearts* of men before his judgment seat
> Oh, be swift my soul to answer him, be *jubilant* my feet
> Our God is marching on
> Glory! Hallelujah!
> Glory! Hallelujah!
> Glory! Hallelujah!"

Crowd noise dropped away until this third cannon cry of "Glory," then spilled over the end of the long march.

> "Glory! Hallelujah!
> His truth is marching on!"

CHAPTER 15

Aftershocks

March 25–30, 1965

BROADCASTS faded from Montgomery with Ralph Abernathy leading tributes to King in the background. "Who is our leader?" he kept shouting over the loudspeakers. "God bless him!" He cultivated cheers of genuflection with a characteristic zeal that grated on SNCC activists, in part for Abernathy's embrace of reflected praise. "I know of no other woman in America who has suffered as much as she has for freedom," he declared with a closing nod to his wife, Juanita. "She is not a speaker very much, but she can kiss me!" Abernathy dismissed the crowd with reminders of their printed march instructions to disperse quietly and rapidly—"Stragglers must not remain"—so as to empty the city of potential targets before dark. "Within ten minutes," reported an eyewitness with some exaggeration, "Dexter Avenue was cleared of all but the press and the troopers."

In Washington, President Johnson ducked into the Cabinet Room to tease reporters reeling under a volley of announcements from top government officials: notice of a multibillion-dollar trade shift and a hundred-mayor summit meeting, an offer of massive economic aid to North Vietnam if violent conflict should cease, plus a statement that the Ranger space mission had found "two or three places" where astronauts might land on the moon. "God have mercy on your souls," quipped Johnson, who had ordered a "heavy budget of news" to reclaim national attention after the march. Former governor Collins of Florida admitted to the assembled press that the federal agencies around Montgomery remained largely segregated, and pledged specific reform. This was a mild version of what Collins had just told the Cabinet secretaries in their closed meeting, with Johnson's encouragement. Repeated intercession with local white ministers yielded only a few willing to preach "against rowdiness," and none yet who would "go so far as to speak up for brotherhood," Collins confessed, and his mediators encountered heavy resistance from white Alabama contacts "conditioned to think of the federal government and of the march leadership as forces of evil." Collins told the reporters that he and Attorney General Katzenbach hoped for a "respite" from months of racial tension.

In Montgomery, seminarian Jonathan Daniels knelt quietly on the pavement among thinning crowds beneath the capitol. Having encountered one of his Boston professors among the hundreds of Episcopal clergy at the march, Daniels asked for and received a formal blessing to stay behind on what he conceived as a religious mission, forgoing the remainder of the school term. He and companion Judith Upham loaded Upham's Volkswagen with teenagers returning to Selma for stored belongings. Two volunteer drivers, collecting others who needed rides, recognized Viola Liuzzo of Detroit among the sick and footsore nearby at a makeshift clinic in Dexter Avenue Baptist Church. When she asked about her Oldsmobile, which she had donated all week to the transportation committee, they advised candidly that the car had been reassigned more than once in all the confusion, and further that she should hasten to retrieve it because the current driver was rumored to have no license.

Liuzzo roused herself. By late afternoon, she spotted her Oldsmobile packed with departing marchers at the St. Jude staging area. She took the steering wheel from nineteen-year-old volunteer Leroy Moton, saying politely that she wanted to practice for the long journey back to Michigan. On the way to Selma, after they dropped a man from New York at the Montgomery airport, two cars tailgated them with bright headlights flashing. Liuzzo tried to calm her passengers with feisty comments about a lack of good sense in hostile white people, speeding up and slowing down evasively until the pursuers dropped away. She and Moton arrived safely at Brown Chapel with a Negro man from Selma and three white females from Pennsylvania. They rested, then started a final run to gather marchers stranded in Montgomery.

An "action team," or "missionary squad," of four Birmingham Klansmen suffered letdown instead of relief. They had harassed marchers along the route into Montgomery, and once came close to dragging off a Negro who ventured into a gasoline station, but real or imagined military patrols stymied them. Then, on their way to check for lapses of security in Selma, they had been stopped on Highway 80 by an Alabama trooper, and Klansman Eugene Thomas had been obliged to display a police auxiliary badge and two special deputy commissions to get off with a warning ticket about the glass-pack muffler on his car. At Selma's Silver Moon Café, they were brooding over the collapse of a day they had built up among themselves as the biggest ever, when Elmer Cook, one of three men charged in the beating death of James Reeb on the sidewalk just outside the Silver Moon, dropped by to visit the out-of-towners whose presence caused a stir. "I did my job," said Cook, patting them on the back. "Now you go and do yours." While he asked nothing, and said no more, his encouragement helped the Birmingham team look for renewed opportunities after dark. They briefly targeted isolated pedestrians near Brown Chapel, only to break away at the sight of a National Guard jeep with a mounted machine gun. At a stoplight on Broad Street, noticing the occupants of a car with Michigan plates, one of them sharply remarked, "Well, I'll be damned." Energized, they speculated about lewd acts the racially mixed couple must have in mind, and Eugene Thomas said, "This looks like some of the brass."

The Klansmen followed Liuzzo and Leroy Moton over Pettus Bridge back toward Montgomery. Thomas told his companions to conceal their number by ducking beneath the window line. Of the two Klansmen lying across the back seat, one promised the other a gift trophy of "the nigger's sport coat" from the car ahead. "This is it," they said, peeking to fathom painful delays once they cleared congestion east of Selma. They slowed down past Craig Air Force Base, where it appeared briefly that the Oldsmobile might turn off for shelter, then dropped back again when they passed the state trooper radar unit that had stopped them two hours earlier, its dome light twirling alongside another detained car on the two-lane portion of Highway 80. After that, with the quarry in flight well above the speed limit, the Klansmen did not overtake them for miles into the rural isolation of Lowndes County. Collie Wilkins shouted for Thomas not to bang the Oldsmobile off the road, lest their own car be identified by paint and chrome chips. Thomas handed him a pistol from the glove box. William Eaton and Tommy Rowe drew theirs. Over one hilly straightaway, jammed against rolled-down windows on the passenger side, they held on for a passing run with three guns poked into the howling wind.

Leroy Moton was absorbed with the radio dial, making an effort to accept Liuzzo's hope that the pursuers might be "some of our own people," when glass exploded over the front seat. Realizing that the car still hurtled along with Liuzzo slumped under the wheel, he grabbed from the side and steered blindly off the right shoulder over violent bumps to a tilted stop along the embankment of a fenced pasture. Moton managed to turn off the engine and headlights, blacked out for some time from the look of Liuzzo's dead face, then ran toward Montgomery. Not for several miles of empty night did a truck come along driven by a Disciples of Christ minister from Richmond, California, Leon Riley, who backed up to investigate the frantically waving, blood-splattered young beanpole—nearly six feet four, less than 140 pounds. Pulled aboard the open flatbed, Moton screamed that the forty assorted marchers should lie low across each other and cover their heads. He collapsed on sight of the first headlights, saying they looked like the shooters' car circling back again, and there was furious debate before they agreed to stop in Lowndes County even long enough to let two nieces of Napoleon Mays jump off for home, crying with fear.

President Johnson called Katzenbach within two hours about bulletins moving on the newswires. "The woman is from Michigan?" he asked.

"From Michigan, yeah," said Katzenbach.

"Somebody out from the—out *ambushed* 'em or something?"

"Yes," said Katzenbach, adding that he did not yet know the extent of the woman's injuries or "any further details."

"I didn't wake you up, did I?" asked the President.

Katzenbach laughed. He said he had asked the FBI to have a full report to the White House before breakfast, but the President could not wait to do something. Even mediation, he told Katzenbach—sending Governor Collins back overnight—was "worth a damn in theory, to succeed military intervention."

Just before one o'clock, President Johnson startled the overnight duty officer at FBI headquarters with a personal call for an update. Night supervisor Harold Swanson was rousted to give the President basic facts at 1:07, then again at 1:11 A.M. The Michigan victim was deceased, autopsy underway, bullet fragments and a clipboard headed "transportation committee" recovered from the car. Swanson emphasized that FBI inspector Joe Sullivan, in Selma for the Reeb case, commanded the investigation and already had secured the Liuzzo crime scene. Johnson admired Sullivan for his work on the murders of the three civil rights workers the previous summer in Mississippi, but he demanded news at any hour.

At 1:49 A.M., Diane Nash bulldozed a telephone call into FBI headquarters with notice that Leroy Moton had been jailed in Selma. Beyond the blatant injustice of it, she warned of the grave danger to the only known witness in the shooting, especially if Alabama authorities managed to get him transferred to the jurisdiction of the crime in Lowndes County. Supervisor Swanson refused Nash's request to track down John Doar for her, but he did find out that Inspector Sullivan already knew about Moton. With Sullivan's approval, Moton was being interviewed by FBI agents in the protective custody of Wilson Baker, safe from the Klan and Lowndes County, as well as from Sheriff Clark.

Swanson contacted Sullivan later with a terse announcement: "The president just called me and said you should work all night."

* * *

LONG EXPERIENCE inside the FBI enabled Sullivan to sense something extraordinary before morning on Friday. The buzz of a high-profile investigation mysteriously shifted elsewhere. Colleagues undercut him instead of competing to help. High officials summoned to headquarters in the night were evasive, and only reluctantly did a friend confide that Birmingham agents had commandeered the FBI action on his case.

Director Hoover carefully emitted the bare minimum of his radioactive secret before breakfast, calling the White House residence to tell President Johnson that the case was nearly solved because the FBI had "one of our men *in* the car." Inaccurately, Hoover said the insider "of course had no gun and did no shooting." He continued in breathless staccato that the killers planned to "throw the guns into the blast furnace where they work, in those steel mills down there, and that's what we're laying for now, to uh, head off these individuals when they come to work this morning and shake 'em down. . . . We've got the informant in the office, and we're talking to him, because uh, uh, he's scared to death, naturally, because he fears for his life." The Director assured President Johnson that Inspector Sullivan had taken charge of the investigation.

Johnson thanked Hoover—"As usual, you're right on top of it"—and asked about the difference between an infiltrator and an informant. "You hire someone? And they join the Klan and keep—"

"We only go to someone who's is, who is in the Klan," Hoover replied, "and persuade him to work for the government. Uh, we pay him for it. Sometimes they demand a pretty high price, and sometimes they don't. Now, for instance, in those three bodies we found in Mississippi, we had to pay thirty thousand dollars for that." In Alabama, the informant was "not a regular agent of the Bureau," but "fortunately he happened to be in on this thing last night," said Hoover. "Otherwise, we'd be looking for a needle in a haystack."

President Johnson hung up the telephone and looked blankly at his aides. "Do you know Hoover had a guy, an informer, in that car that shot her?" he asked.

Johnson immediately called Katzenbach to test his knowledge: "Looks like we'll be pretty much on top of this one, doesn't it?"

"I say, I haven't heard a lot," Katzenbach confessed. The entire Justice Department knew nothing of Hoover's secret, like Inspector Sullivan himself, and would remain sealed from its background.

"They had an informant in the car," the President announced. He said the FBI was waiting to pick up the killers.

"Oh, that's good," said Katzenbach. Asked whether the President should speak directly with Liuzzo's widower, Anthony Liuzzo, in Detroit, he advised a careful test of the FBI's negative recommendation. Johnson agreed. He tasked White House lawyer Lee White to make a preliminary call, with instructions loaded toward FBI warnings that Liuzzo was dangerously bitter. Minutes later, White reported with surprise that he found Liuzzo to be "much in control of himself, very relaxed, and sounded like a pretty fine fellow." Liuzzo was grieving with five children, and "had a few unkind things to say about Wallace," White told Johnson, but "he was in sort of a reflective mood and wanted to know where do we go from here now. . . . My judgment, sir, is that if you did call him, that he's gonna be reasonable and not in any sense uncontrollable or wild."

Hoover, meanwhile, called Attorney General Katzenbach to say "we have to move very rapidly" to break the Liuzzo case, and that Justice Department lawyers needed to draw up charges to hold the suspects. He accepted Katzenbach's suggestion that only Doar was near enough to be mobilized instantly. Hoover tersely disclosed that there was an FBI informant. He explained with some exaggeration that President Johnson knew the substance ahead of the Attorney General only because he had called Hoover personally three or four times since midnight. For Katzenbach, the FBI Director added shocking arguments why the

President should avoid the Liuzzo family, which Hoover promptly dictated to his top executives in a memo headed "9:32 A.M.": "I stated the man himself doesn't have too good a background and the woman had indications of needle marks in her arms where she had been taking dope; that she was sitting very, very close to the Negro in the car; that it had the appearance of a necking party." Katzenbach did not react to Hoover's slanderous Klan fantasy dressed as evidence,* but neither did he ask a single question about the FBI's surprise informant in the murder car. Naively, or protectively, he formed an impression that Rowe had only a casual relationship with the FBI until turning state's evidence after the crime. Like President Johnson, Katzenbach wanted to believe that the FBI discovered a miraculous star witness, and Hoover zealously aimed suspicion at the victim Liuzzo instead.

President Johnson reached Hoover again minutes later, at 9:36, to say he was under heavy pressure to return Mr. Liuzzo's phone call. The delay was making adverse news with an army of reporters camped in the Detroit home, waiting for reaction from the White House. Johnson wanted to know if Hoover knew "any reason why I shouldn't, because in your file he's a Teamster man."

"Yes, he's a Teamster man," said Hoover. His voice tumbled through stops and starts: "I wouldn't say bad character, but he's uh, uh, well known out there as being one of the Teamsters' strong arm there, and uh, this woman his wife, uh we found on they, on her body, uh numerous uh needle points indicating that she may have been taking dope." Hoover said Johnson should delegate the call to an aide.

"White's already talked to him," said the President.

"Oh, he has?" said Hoover, taken aback. He promised quickly to send word on arrests in Alabama.

"Please do," urged Johnson, "because they're runnin' me crazy over here."

"All right, I'll, I'll get word down there right away," said Hoover. He offered the President hurried images of the dragnet—multiple stake-outs, the killers' red Impala under surveillance in a yard—along with jumbled observations about motive. The Klan conspiracy was "pretty

* An FBI agent, not medical examiner Paul E. Shoffeitt, speculated that one glass nick in Liuzzo's arm "was observed as though a needle was recently used." The toxicology report found no evidence of drugs. Hoover's other slurs were similarly baseless. Against common sense and Moton's testimony, he adopted the Klan informant's stereotype of mixed Selma marchers as a "necking party."

well planned out" since the Reeb murder, Hoover told Johnson, but he mitigated the ambush as a product of circumstance: "They accidentally ran onto this car by reason of the fact that this colored man was, was snugglin' up uh, uh, pretty close to the white woman who was driving." He thought it would be safe to make a statement from the White House within the next hour.

The President instructed Hoover to grab the Attorney General when he was ready and "the two of you ride over and let the television cover you as you come in." This, he added with understatement, "might be a little dramatic."

"Well, I'll, I'll speed this thing up right away," replied Hoover as Johnson signed off. The Director scrambled the FBI, but first he called Katzenbach to lobby one last time against Liuzzo. The President should "hold off until after the case is broken," Hoover told Katzenbach, "and then he could consider whether he wants to call the man and extend condolences."

Many years later, when documents and tape recordings of these transactions became available to scholars, Johnson would not be alive to say how consciously he was goading Hoover toward decisive commitment. The President had a recognized gift for subtle manipulation. He never acknowledged Hoover's clear sensitivity about the Liuzzo call, nor his vulgarity. Among Hoover biographers, Richard Gid Powers would cite the Liuzzo comments in 1987 as evidence of Hoover's core beliefs about civil rights: "paternalistic at best, mean-spiritedly racist at worst." From a more complete record in 1998, Liuzzo biographer Mary Stanton would conclude that Hoover's disparagement came also from a desperate need to minimize disclosure about his informant. If the first nationwide image of Liuzzo were a White House phone call with sympathetic relatives, stamping her as a martyred heroine, pressure to explain her death might unearth potentially ruinous secrets—beginning with the fact that the informant Gary Thomas Rowe had asked for and received prior FBI approval to ride with Thursday's action squad, as he had been doing for nearly five years of unsolved crimes by the Birmingham Klan.

"Hoover panicked," wrote Stanton. He clawed against Liuzzo to seize the hero's mantle for his Bureau. Most certainly he did not disclose that Liuzzo, in unmailed letters recovered from her car, said she had been inspired to Selma by Johnson's March 15 address to Congress. Johnson, for his part, recognized how hard it was for Hoover to expose

FBI performance to outside accountability. The Director had not surrendered the informant's name even to him, let alone the public, as would be required for any criminal trial. Johnson pushed Hoover to guarantee at least that much.

* * *

THE PRESIDENT initiated a record White House news day that pre-empted nationwide television three times before lunch. First, Johnson brought top congressional leaders from the Oval Office to thank them on camera for nearing passage of Medicare. He ambushed the bill's chief remaining obstacle, Senator Harry Byrd of Virginia, by asking whether such momentous legislation deserved at least a vote in committee. When Byrd conceded that nothing urgent stood in the way of consideration, Johnson pressed in a televised display of his full-bodied lobbying style: "So when the House acts and it is referred to the Senate Finance Committee, you will arrange for prompt hearings and thorough hearings?" Byrd lamely committed himself, and the President soon led the way outside to welcome a helicopter bearing Gemini 3 astronauts Virgil Grissom and John Young for a medal ceremony in the East Room.

Only NBC of the three networks stayed afterward to broadcast the astronauts' parade down Pennsylvania Avenue. CBS executives were congratulating themselves for the choice not to bump *Search for Tomorrow,* their popular and lucrative regular show, when the White House issued yet another presidential news standby. White House press secretary George Reedy refused to confirm whether the alert involved the Liuzzo case. Reporters frantically gathered clues. Word came from Detroit that Johnson called the Liuzzo house at 12:30, unsuccessfully—Liuzzo had collapsed after a sleepless night and the family decided not to wake him—and from Washington that the Director's limousine was sighted on White House grounds. Television screens were yanked back to the presidential seal just before the announced entrance at 12:40, and network executives knew they had guessed correctly when President Johnson emerged flanked by Katzenbach and Director Hoover himself. The President announced the four arrested suspects by name. He called for a national campaign against "the terrorists of the Ku Klux Klan," and congratulated the FBI for breaking the case within twenty-four hours. "I cannot express myself too strongly in praising Mr. Hoover," he said. These actions dwarfed other news, generating triple-tiered headlines and five separate photographs on the front page of the *New York Times.*

Inside the FBI, triumph gave way to renewed crisis when reporters questioned why Gary Thomas (Tommy) Rowe did not appear with the other three suspects Friday afternoon for arraignment. Rowe, the informant, had returned secretly to the crime scene with trusted FBI handlers, and was trying to remember where along Highway 80 they had thrown shell casings out the car windows. Terrified, Rowe procrastinated on a razor's edge. The longer he remained separate from fellow Klansmen in jail, the more suspicion he invited upon himself as the government agent among them, but he did not want to leave his FBI protection. Finally, at 5:25 P.M., Rowe arrived handcuffed for arraignment in full Klan character, snarling at reporters and his FBI handlers alike. Attorney Matt Murphy, who identified himself by title as Klonsel for the Alabama Klan, secured the defendants' immediate release on $50,000 bond and withdrew with a Grand Titan and an Exalted Cyclops to grill Rowe, who survived on his wits. Rowe said the FBI must have traced the action team through the warning ticket from the state trooper. He said with some truth that FBI agents had isolated him in custody all day, mixing threats and inducements to make him turn state's evidence. Rowe claimed to be resisting gallantly. Klonsel Murphy said they could impeach any prosecution with evidence of tampering and "bribes." Klan leaders reserved suspicion of Rowe, but let him go home.

The FBI's secret survived also in news coverage, with only one remote item questioning "an unexplained four-hour delay" in Rowe's arraignment. Teams of agents diligently collected forensic evidence, and actually did find the spent shell casings along Highway 80. Edicts from FBI headquarters spurred them on, balanced by internal warnings to suppress all hints of an informant. One memo from Hoover's office bluntly instructed that "all agents must keep their mouths shut." A top official told supervisors that the Bureau had "no need or reason to explain what we are doing and the less said the better." Hoover added a handwritten order: "I want no comments nor amplifications made in Ala. or here, as President has made his statement & it ends there."

Political work continued behind the bulwark of Johnson's announcement. Granting an audience to a newly elected congressman from Oregon, who volunteered loyalty by denouncing all criticism of the FBI from either King or the Warren Commission, Hoover reviewed at length his decision to call King the nation's most notorious liar. Also, on the Friday of the Liuzzo arrests, FBI intelligence agents secretly delivered to federal mediator LeRoy Collins a poisonously targeted report. From mountains of telephone intercepts, supervisors isolated one remark by Coretta King to her husband. She thought Collins, while marching briefly with them on Monday, had revealed himself to be "blinded by prejudice" in pushing King to accommodate white Montgomery's desired limits on the final rally. FBI supervisors highlighted her comment as an insult to Collins, obtained from an unspecified reliable source. With Hoover's approval, on assurance that Collins was "a long-time admirer of the Director and the Bureau," they attached a compendium of the FBI's top secret allegations against King as a philandering subversive. The package, in the guise of friendly caution against false allies, served notice to Collins that national security authorities intercepted his private communications with people branded unfit. This sour message complemented rude adjustments for the ex-governor back home in Florida, where a barber of long service refused to cut his hair because he was consorting with Negroes.

A final alarm rattled over the UPI national ticker at 2:26 P.M. on Saturday with a quotation from Sheriff Clark. "The FBI had that car under surveillance," he said of the Birmingham Klan squad. To reporters badgering him about the latest Alabama civil rights murder, Clark guessed about how federal agents solved the case so quickly, then shifted blame to the FBI for failure to share information that might have averted the murder. This UPI item rocketed upward through FBI headquarters, and by 9:45 P.M. a public statement dismissed the Clark statement as "a malicious lie." Accurately, the FBI official denied that agents had the Klan car under active surveillance on the day of the murder. The rebuttal, like Hoover's subsequent report to Katzenbach—"I had to blast the story of the Sheriff down there as a lie . . ."—seized upon an error in Clark's guesswork to obfuscate the FBI's inside knowledge of the plot. Omitting prior communications, including the approval for Rowe to join the Klan mission, which would have raised thorny issues about why the car was *not* under surveillance, the headquarters spokesperson declared that the Bureau "promptly disseminated all information which came to its knowledge," then solved the crime overnight. Only a "totalitarian" FBI could have done more, he said, and Director Hoover modestly refused such power.

The single FBI statement sufficed. DeLoach wisely advised colleagues to ignore any future attacks from Clark, who was at best a discredited segregationist, lest Hoover's prestige kindle a "feud" story. The ever-vigilant Hoover took advantage of respite in the Liuzzo case to burnish the fabled discipline of his headquarters bureaucracy. He tasked inspectors to explain why it took seven hours to react on Saturday, which nearly had pushed the vital press reaction into another day's news cycle. From time stamps on every document, inspectors made sure that intake scanners had met rigorous deadlines for culling out sensitive material, and that routers and messengers had met their deadlines for delivering flagged items to top officials—every seven minutes on workdays, every hour on weekends. Hoover's own secretary insisted that she had pouched the Clark story to Hoover "immediately," as her intake stamp of 4:16 P.M., less than two hours after it moved on the UPI wire, demonstrated. Executives defended every detail of their conduct, but the inspectors inevitably discovered correctable lapses. There were missing time stamps in DeLoach's political shop, for instance, and one unfortunate assistant admitted leaving for home late Saturday without noticing Clark documents on his desk.

The FBI enjoyed a feast of glory in the news, which one of DeLoach's assistants called "another vindication of the propriety of the Bureau's press release procedures." The *New York Times* saluted Hoover with a crowning profile as "an authentic American folk hero . . . the incorruptible idol of generations of American youngsters and the symbol of the 'honest cop' to millions of their elders." The "spectacular feat" of the Liuzzo arrests was especially sweet for Hoover, said the *Times,* because it repaired "a few cracks . . . in the previously impenetrable armor of his public esteem." Reviewing Hoover's forty-eight continuous years at the Justice Department, the profile found that Hoover had demanded only two things since 1924 as the FBI's first and only Director: absolute control, and freedom from politics. With no hint that these conditions might be incompatible, especially over time, or that they violated the most basic principles of constitutional self-government, the *Times* concluded that Hoover had used his iron hand to build "an impressive monument to efficiency and integrity."

Martin Luther King sent Hoover a telegram of thanks. "Let me congratulate you and the FBI for this speedy arrest of the accused assassins of Mrs. Liuzzo," he wrote. "The agents assigned to Alabama have done an outstanding job of containing the tremendous violence and savagery which runs rampant under this surface of Alabama life. There is still much work to be done." The explicit reference to Alabama agents was a signal of conscious apology, as Hoover had justified his "notorious liar" outburst by King's one publicized criticism of FBI performance in Alabama. Nevertheless, Hoover refused any reply to King—gloating, gracious, or pro forma. Even acknowledgment "would only help build up this character . . . tie us in with him, and put us under obligation to him," wrote DeLoach for the executives. They decided not to confirm to reporters that the King telegram existed.

*   *   *

KING FLEW west to preach on Sunday, March 28, at Grace Cathedral in San Francisco, then drove to a local television station. Producers had agreed to film him from there in a special edition of *Meet the Press* if he promised to withhold from NBC's competitors any newsworthy comments about a post-Selma boycott of Alabama products. King acceded. Experience taught him that the national news shows tended to provoke controversy from perspectives at odds with the movement, toward the extreme of treating him as a houseboy, and he knew better than to expect a discussion of Selma's place in history. Still, the opening question sprang from deep ambush.

"First," King replied on the air, "I would say that the march was not silly at all."

Panelist Lawrence Spivak insisted that the evaluation—"this was his word"—came from Harry Truman, who believed the "silly" march could not accomplish "a darn thing" except make a big scene. The same former President who lionized President Johnson for his speech about Selma scorned the movement itself, personified by King.

Spivak next suggested that the Selma marches were superfluous to any voting rights bill. "Wouldn't you have gotten it whether or not you marched?" he asked.

"The demonstration was certainly for the voting rights bill," King carefully replied. He could not cite the engine force of the movement without risking losing the votes of those in Congress who needed to claim untainted judgment, free of pressure by minority groups. So he tied the Selma campaign to multiple goals. "There have been untold bombings of homes and churches," he said. "Again, nothing has been done about this on the whole. We were marching there to protest these brutalities, these murders and all of the things that go along with them, as much as to gain the right to vote."

Panelists doubted King's personal commitment to nonviolence, and worried about disorders beyond his control: "How deeply do you fear the eruption of Negro violence?" One described the Highlander photograph "being plastered all over Alabama billboards," and asked him to explain "whether that was a Communist training school and what you were doing there?" A question put suspicions bluntly, "Have Communists infiltrated the movement?" Others pressed for an end to demonstrations.

King held his own. He said that because people of goodwill had "abdicated responsibility," the movement felt a "moral obligation to keep these issues before the public, before the American conscience, before the mainstream of our nation, that somebody will do something about it. And demonstrations have proved to be the best way to do this."

Organs of mainstream culture divided over Selma. Even as the panelists on national television labored to diminish its unsettling impact, reporters gathered Sunday morning in Selma on advance word that Bishop Carpenter of Alabama had brokered a new policy to comply with Canon 16, Section 4 of Episcopal rules, governing admission for worship. Wilson Baker arrested an armed member of Sheriff Clark's posse who shouted obscenities from the street, as the ushers at St. Paul's Church dutifully seated on the front row a group of sixteen newcomers from Brown Chapel—mostly white clergy from Los Angeles, plus four Negroes, three of them from Selma. Rector Frank Mathews, having urged acceptance in two anguished pastoral letters that week, preached on reconciliation without mentioning the racial conflict. ("That was as bad as my senior sermon in seminary," he said afterward, admitting frayed nerves.) Mathews and several parishioners warmly greeted the visitors, most of whom had been excluded at least once previously in March. Among them, Rev. John Morris hailed "the first breakthrough in Selma not induced by a court order," and seminarian Jonathan Daniels felt a welcome epiphany from the transforming power of church doctrine. "Glory to God in the highest!" he wrote a friend. The *New York Times* covered the service on its front page, headlined "Selma Protestant Church Integrated for First Time," predicting that change would spread from the example.

Morris complained that movement leaders had evacuated too swiftly, leaving hundreds of holdover clergy without direction in Selma. They joined daily demonstrations out of Brown Chapel. Some rallied to James Bevel's call for follow-up action *"now,* while people are still in motion and before fear sets in." SNCC staff members proposed to march again to Montgomery and lay siege this time to Wallace's capital. Others followed new boldness along the march route to Mt. Gillard

Church, where Jesse "Note" Favors spent Sunday afternoon stringing power cords to makeshift spotlights he hung around the perimeter. Sentries used them to keep watch that night over the first mass meeting in Lowndes County. Storekeeper William Cosby presided. Four Sundays after a Klan posse chased a preacher permanently out of the county for mentioning the vote, 170 people showed up to prepare for the legally prescribed odd-Monday registration day on the site opened specially for Negroes, next to the gallows. "Now I hope that tomorrow morning at eight o'clock we'll have the same number at the Lowndes County jailhouse," said Cosby.

The featured speaker at Mt. Gillard, Bernard Lafayette of SNCC, preached on miracles from small beginnings. Though only twenty-six, Lafayette already had served nearly seven years in the vanguard nonviolent movement out of Nashville, acquiring the nickname "Little Gandhi." After incarceration in Mississippi as a Freedom Rider, Lafayette had ventured into Selma to establish the first movement outpost in 1962, when Selma had been nearly as forbidding as Lowndes County. It had required more than six months' patient agitation before the first Negro church dared to host a mass meeting, and Lafayette's work in Selma later informed his young colleagues from Nashville. John Lewis of SNCC scheduled early demonstrations for voting rights there; Bevel and Nash lobbied Martin Luther King to make Selma the base of their massive nonviolent plan to answer the Birmingham church bombing. At Bevel's invitation, Lafayette often had visited the 1965 campaign from Chicago, where he was conducting nonviolent experiments to address de facto segregation. Privately, he warned of "too much leadership concentrated in one place." Publicly, he exhorted the Mt. Gillard crowd to capture the lightning from Selma, which was spreading hope worldwide. Volunteers rose up for Tuesday. Exactly a week after the wondrous host of marchers appeared on Highway 80 with white friends and an armed escort of soldiers, local citizens would dare to gather unprotected where Viola Liuzzo's death car came to rest. Preparations for the leap already made news. "An immediate result of Mrs. Liuzzo's death," reported one story, "will be to move the Alabama Negro movement publicly into Lowndes County."

* * *

PRESIDENT JOHNSON startled his Attorney General by telephone on Monday, March 29. "Nick," he said, "have I ever asked you or suggested to you that you tap a line?"

"No, Mr. President, you never have," said Katzenbach.

"Don't you have to authorize every one to be tapped?" Johnson demanded.

"I authorize every one that the FBI taps," Katzenbach replied. He added that the Pentagon and IRS occasionally tapped phone lines on their own.

"Well, I want them brought to an irreducible minimum, and only in the gravest cases," Johnson thundered. "And I want you to authorize them, and then, by God, I want to know about them. I'm against wiretapping, period."

The catalyst for his outburst was another visit to the White House by syndicated columnist Joe Alsop, this time on Saturday with *New York Times* bureau chief James Reston. Both complained of government harassment by wiretap. Alsop in particular had ranted on the verge of delirium, charging that government agents were shutting off his news sources by spreading scurrilous information about his private life. Johnson told Katzenbach that Alsop was unstable—"just short of the asylum now"—to the point of embarrassing longtime friends in the Washington establishment.

Katzenbach agreed. "I've seen him a couple of times recently, Mr. President," he said. "He is in bad shape. There's no question about it."

The President spoke obliquely of sensitive matters. "Now, I saw the Alsop file," he said. "I don't know how it got over here. I don't know why it got over here. Uh, I saw Alsop's file . . ." He said he had locked it under care of his most trusted secretary, Mildred Stegall—"been with me since '37 or '8"—along with material "in one of our, uh, friend's cases, from what I have seen, that that must be where the evidence comes from, I mean, on Hawaii jaunts and some of those things, California, and uh, uh, with some of the women and that kind of stuff involved. You know who I'm talking about?"

"Yes," said Katzenbach. This was the FBI dossier on King.

"But Joe Alsop's having a change of life," said Johnson. The secret heart of the file was that Soviet KGB agents had entrapped and recorded Alsop in a homosexual tryst in Moscow, after which Alsop, to avoid national security blackmail, had confessed his homosexual life to the CIA and FBI. This happened in 1957, near the Cold War's peak fear of Communist conspiracy. Custom then inhibited reference even to conventional sex within marriage, banning the word "pregnant" through comedy actress Lucille Ball's gestation on her hit television show, and homosexuality still remained taboo beyond mention. Newspapers found euphemisms to report the "lewd conduct" scandal that had banished chief of staff Walter Jenkins from Johnson's White House late in 1964.

Katzenbach gingerly educated the President on the difference between wiretaps, which picked up only phone conversations, and microphone bugs, planted by burglary, which picked up all sounds in a targeted room. He was confident that he controlled the wiretaps, which the FBI called "technical surveillance," or "tesur" for short, and that he had approved only legitimate targets—not including Alsop. "The furthest out one is the one that you referred to," he said, meaning the King wiretap, "which my predecessor [Robert Kennedy] authorized, which I've been ambivalent about taking off."

The Attorney General did not explain the tactical advantage of wiretaps for more intrusive spying—that by telephone interception of travel arrangements, for instance, FBI agents gained advance notice to plant bugs in hotel rooms before King arrived. Uncomfortably, Katzenbach did say he was far less confident of legal accountability for bugs, which the FBI called "microphone surveillance," or "misur." This illicit technique provided the most graphic pay dirt of undercover work. Katzenbach told Johnson that the FBI claimed independent authority "which neither I nor, or my predecessor knew until, oh, in the last couple or three months, there was authority for them occasionally to make a trespass and bug." He said he wanted approval rights for bugs, too, even though gaining such control was a tall order for an Attorney General who had been confirmed only a month. "I'm going to work that out with Mr. Hoover, in writing," vowed Katzenbach, "same as the wiretaps."

President Johnson passed over the distinctions to rail against the secret pressures. "I don't know what legislation you can ask for in that field," he told Katzenbach, "but I've been against it all my life. And I'm a red hot, one million two percent civil liberties man." He mentioned practical motives for respecting the fourth estate. "I don't think we can afford to just let it go unnoticed," said Johnson, "when, when Scotty [James] Reston comes in to plead with the White House." Reston had heard vaguely at the Gridiron Club dinner of agents shadowing his son Richard to keep him off a story. Alsop, ironically, was both the conduit and the victim of much rougher tactics. Based on clandestine FBI allegations, he publicly attacked Martin Luther King as the dangerous, naive tool of Communist spies, in a national column entitled "An Unhappy Secret." At the same time, Alsop blamed both the FBI and KGB for allowing his own secret to fester just beneath public notice. Thirty years later, Alsop biographer Edwin Yoder would unearth documents showing that Hoover periodically "spread the word" of Alsop's homo-sexuality among high officials—especially those who resented Alsop's journalism, Yoder concluded, as they were likely to appreciate the FBI for the top secret tip.

President Johnson kept telling Katzenbach that Alsop may be crazy, "but I like him, and I'm his friend" of thirty years. Now Alsop seemed deeply disturbed, with "the same look in his eye and the same attitude . . . that Phil Graham had the last time I saw him," said the President. (Philip Graham, publisher of the *Washington Post,* committed suicide.) He deplored the personal toll: "I resent this so deeply." As much as he loved power, Johnson decried surveillance as underhanded intimida-tion—"We've had a revolution, I just don't want it"—and repeatedly denounced secret police methods. "I guess you've got to have them in treason [cases] or something," he told Katzenbach. "But I sure, I don't trust anybody on that field. And if I've got to trust somebody in this gov-ernment, I want to trust you."

Johnson plotted in detail how to rein in domestic spies. The next day, March 30, Katzenbach formally ordered Director Hoover to stop exist-ing microphone surveillance and submit future bugging requests for approval by the established legal practice on wiretaps. Only the Presi-dent's surprise initiative and clear mandate allowed him to act deci-sively. Even so, the order met resistance deep within a subterranean government devoted to secrecy and arbitrary authority, which helped generate disillusioning spy scandals for years to come.

*   *   *

MONDAY NIGHT in Detroit, before Tuesday's televised funeral there for Viola Liuzzo, 1,500 people gave a standing ovation to James Leatherer. Wearing his orange marching vest, Leatherer told a memorial service that Liuzzo's sacrifice sent an enduring message to uncertain Ameri-cans: "you have to get off the fence." The crowd stood for Rosa Parks, and cheered a demand for the resignation of Episcopal Rt. Rev. C. C. J. Carpenter. "As Bishop of Alabama," Rev. Carl Sayers accused, "you have been to the flock of Christ a wolf and not a shepherd." Sayers spoke of being turned away from St. Paul's Church on the public instruction of Carpenter. He announced that Suffragan Bishop Kim Myers, also re-buffed in Selma, blessed his demand as an act of religious conscience.

The Rt. Rev. Richard Emrich, Episcopal Bishop of Michigan, emphatically disapproved. He privately reproached both Myers and Sayers for attacking another bishop without his consent, and identified with the travail of Carpenter as a peer at the helm of an embattled institution. Sunday's breakthrough at St. Paul's had withered under siege. With Carpenter's assistant consoling Rev. Mathews about "what a bitter pill it was to you to have to do business with John Morris," the visiting Episcopal clergy, including Morris, returned eagerly to the church house for follow-up consultation (after resolving among themselves, in Judith Upham's favor, a dispute about whether it was proper for a female to join negotiations over church policy). They were dismayed to learn from Mathews that many at St. Paul's understood the mixed service as the one-time price of a bargain for their departure. On the other side, even moderates in the congregation were distressed that the visitors hoped to build continuing fellowship on the divided vote to admit Negroes. Prominent segregationists already resigned from the governing vestry. Church lawyers picked at Carpenter's interpretation of the canon. Only bona fide Episcopalians were guaranteed worship, they said, and ushers were empowered to keep order as they saw fit.

Mathews reserved for his superiors the strength of internal rebellion. "Losing this family would be a terrific financial blow to the parish," he confided to Carpenter's assistant. "They pledge $3,000 a year, and in the past three years have put an additional $7,500 in my discretionary fund . . . but I'll be damned if I'll be bought." He complained that the wife of another resigned vestryman, whose extended family "make up the greatest part of the congregation," was "absolutely 'sick'" with certainty that integrated worship was a Communist conspiracy to enslave white people. "If she is cured," wrote Mathews, "it will be a greater healing miracle than any recorded in the Gospels."

Bishop Carpenter curdled against the movement for overlooking the progressive side of his heritage. His great-grandfather had conducted a pioneer ministry among slaves through four decades, virtually alone among antebellum Southern clergy. Carpenter never had espoused segregation. He saw himself fostering a middle ground between George Wallace and Martin Luther King, only to be rebuked on both sides, and he had been galled to be the first-named addressee on King's famed Letter from Birmingham Jail. As a founding member of the National Council of Churches, who defended the ecumenical body until it "urged the current invasion of Selma and Alabama," Carpenter felt "in the position of having the limb cut out from under me." He seized the victim's perspective to bemoan extreme punishment for sins against Negroes, which he said were "attributed" to the white South by outsiders. "After the nail has been driven all the way in," he wrote Bishop Myers of Michigan, "it is definitely not right to keep pounding on it simply to make the scars deeper." Ever more preoccupied with rulebook decorum, Carpenter denounced Myers to his superior in Michigan for intrusions he found "rude and inexcusable. . . . I do not want him in the Diocese of Alabama until he has learned the rudiments of proper conduct." He disdained the call for his resignation by Rev. Sayers: "I have not answered him at all and would not think of answering him. . . . He obviously is a little fellow who wanted to get some publicity." On this point, Bishop Emrich of Michigan endorsed official hauteur as sound church governance. "When we answer somebody who is in a lower position than ourselves," he wrote Carpenter, "we give him an honor which he does not deserve."

*   *   *

LATE MONDAY night in Washington, President H. E. Maurice Yaméogo presented state gifts from his newly independent African country of Upper Volta, including a red leather saddle and a model village with dwellings that converted to custom-sized holders for American cigarettes. He received an authentic Cochiti Indian tribal drum and a framed painting of the White House viewed from Lafayette Park. As Yaméogo was answering his host's toast of comity between their two nations, an usher crept in with a written note from the Situation Room. President Johnson handed it wordlessly to Secretary of State Rusk, who rushed out.

Minutes earlier, across the morning dateline in Saigon, a Citroën sedan stalled by the riverfront hotel that served as the American embassy. A Vietnamese policeman remonstrated with the driver to move on, then exchanged fatal gunfire when the driver fled instead on the back of a handily passing motorbike, just before an estimated 350 pounds of American-made C-4 plastique explosive—stolen or bought—detonated inside the car. The blast buckled buildings across the street, setting one ablaze, destroyed twenty vehicles, and sent a plume of smoke from the embassy three hundred feet high. Flying glass partially blinded CIA Station Chief Peer da Silva on the second floor, and lacerated Chargé d'Affaires Alexis Johnson on the fifth. Twenty Vietnamese employees were among the dead inside, with nearly two hundred wounded.

After midnight in Washington, President Johnson led a brief flashlight tour of the Lincoln Memorial for President Yaméogo, who praised
Lincoln in a public statement that rejected the Cold War overtures to
Upper Volta by Communist China. Johnson then returned to his office
to monitor the bomb attack in Saigon. Not until daylight did the duty
officer in the Situation Room spell out for him the names of the two
American fatalities, Barbara Robbins, "R-O-B-B-I-N-S of Denver"
(identified in wire stories as "a girl secretary"), and a Navy petty officer—"we're not sure if it's male or female . . . M-A-N-O-L-T-O
Castillo, C-A-S-T-I-L-L-O."

The President called Secretary McNamara, who found small consolation in the prior evacuation of vulnerable Americans—"it does look
good that you pulled the dependents out." McNamara proposed no immediate change in war policy. He reported that he had "cleared up the
policy on taps and surveillance," and had assured James Reston of the
Times that his son was not a spy target. National Security Adviser Mc-
George Bundy next told the President that the White House was
preparing a statement of "firmness and shock" about the embassy bomb.
He said that Henry Cabot Lodge, who was not yet announced as the
next ambassador to South Vietnam, already had called that morning to
urge construction of a new embassy compound in Saigon "with a high
wall around it . . . and treat this as a, as a siege, which is what it is for
working purposes."

Johnson switched abruptly to worries about Bundy's family friend
and fellow New England aristocrat. "Joe Alsop is, in my judgment,
must be going crazy," he said. "Do you think he is or not?"

"I think he's actually at the moment in better shape than he was,"
Bundy replied, but he lamented the latest outburst at the White House
about wiretapping and persecution. "I knew he was going to do this,"
said Bundy. "I told him to shut up about it."

* * *

SOLEMNLY BEFORE noon on Tuesday, timed to coincide with the high
requiem mass in Detroit, a caravan left Selma consisting of an ambulance, a truck, twenty-six cars, and three hearses, headlights on, rolling
east from the Pettus Bridge for twenty-five miles. Less than half the
crowd of five hundred squeezed inside the tiny hillside church,
Wright's Chapel AME Zion, a few hundred yards above the Liuzzo
death site on Highway 80. Honorary pallbearers entered with ten empty
caskets, each bearing the name of a movement victim killed in Alabama

over the past two years, so far with scant sign of interest from state officials—seven during the Birmingham upheavals of 1963,* plus Jackson, Reeb, and Liuzzo from the voting rights campaign.

No local leader or famous orator spoke to the daylight assembly in Lowndes County, and most of the scattered organizers had come lately to steady witness. The children's demonstrations in Birmingham had transformed James Orange from hulking high school drifter to precocious minister of nonviolence. Willie Bolden, the main speaker, had worked as a longshoreman and hotel bellhop until the drama of solo demonstrations by Hosea Williams in Savannah pulled him to join Orange on King's SCLC staff. Rev. L. L. Anderson, who offered the benediction, had defied his own deacons to open Tabernacle Baptist to Bernard Lafayette for the first mass meeting in Selma. "Oh, God," Anderson prayed at Wright's Chapel, "hasten the day when every man—even this hued, flung-down race of mine—can go from one side of this country to the other without being killed."

With Silas Norman of SNCC, James Orange mobilized help to reload the caskets while local citizens, many of whom had heard Lafayette's Sunday sermon about small movement beginnings, refused to say goodbye to some two dozen SNCC workers. Some overheard debates—amid predictions that Mt. Gillard Church would be ashes before May—about assigning Lowndes among new trial projects across the Black Belt of Alabama. They gathered especially around Stokely Carmichael, who was marked locally for speaking "upright" to a state trooper before the great march, and pressed him not to abandon Lowndes for more promising hard cases. "Don't go to Greene County," said Mattie Lee Moorer. "Some of y'all got to stay here." Carmichael took soundings about where he might safely spend the night in the vast rural area of Lowndes County, to gain a foothold. Bob Mants joined him.

The caravan continued into Montgomery. Golden Frinks of North Carolina, at whose home Bevel and Nash had composed their blueprint for the Alabama voting rights campaign, led a brief procession to the capitol on foot. Blocked by guards, pallbearers laid the empty caskets on the marble steps. Bevel, saying, "I pay traffic fines here all the time,"

---

* William Moore, a white Baltimore postman killed on April 23; John Coley, a twenty-year-old shot while standing near Fred Shuttlesworth on September 4, after a bombing at the home of Arthur Shores; Addie Mae Collins, Denise McNair, Carole Robertson, and Cynthia Wesley, the four girls killed in the Birmingham church bombing on September 15; and Virgil Ware, a thirteen-year-old shot randomly from his bicycle by an Eagle Scout on the same day.

talked his way around Governor Wallace's public ban on nonresident "outside agitators" to join the delegation of sixteen Alabamians—fifteen Negro men, plus Rev. Joseph Ellwanger from Selma's "white march" of March 6—who presented an anticlimactic freedom petition to the governor in person. Fifty women conducted a vigil on the steps outside, until black state employees in white servants' jackets hauled away the caskets.

CHAPTER 16

Bearings in a Whirlwind

March 30–April 7, 1965

FROM San Francisco, by way of Los Angeles and Atlanta, King touched down in Detroit long enough to attend Tuesday's high requiem mass for Viola Liuzzo on the second day of mourning as proclaimed by Governor George Romney of Michigan. Forty photographers delayed the funeral to record him among the dignitaries, which featured a rare joint appearance by rival union presidents Walter Reuther of the United Auto Workers and James R. Hoffa of the Teamsters. Afterward, when the crowd filed out of the Immaculate Heart of Mary church behind Viola Liuzzo's maple coffin, one reporter tartly observed that "We Shall Overcome," the recessional hymn, "soon died out because few knew the words."

King and Bernard Lee broke away early to catch a midday flight to New York's JFK Airport. Observed from the gate by FBI surveillance agents, Bayard Rustin and Harry Wachtel rushed them to an afternoon speech in Manhattan and an evening event at Temple Beth El in Great Neck, Long Island. King's mental state alarmed his advisers to the point that Wachtel wanted him to consult a psychiatrist. Always vulnerable to depression at peaks and valleys, King suffered a letdown from Selma that collided with pressure to expand the movement. He displayed a bone-weary paralysis, confessing inability to discern what was important. The advisers found him still in possession of mementos he had promised to Viola Liuzzo's relatives. He had received a windfall gift of $25,000 for SCLC from his passing introduction to Hoffa, but seemed far more agitated about the Teamster president's pained unwillingness to support the call for a boycott of Alabama products.

Wachtel forwarded the papers to Anthony Liuzzo, covering with a note that King had been too upset to deliver them personally. Rustin maneuvered delicately to extricate King from a boycott strategy that he privately called "stupid." On Wednesday, March 31, en route to Baltimore, Rustin blamed the impetuous staff—chiefly Bevel—for announcing in King's name a plan to remake Alabama with momentum from the Selma march. (Unless Governor Wallace acted positively on the freedom petition, said Bevel, "we want the federal government to come in here, register Negroes, and throw out the present government as un-Constitutional.") King had felt obliged to endorse the boycott on *Meet the Press,* which loosed a gale of criticism. The White House issued a statement of nonsupport. The *New York Times* dismissed the proposal as "wrong in principle" and "unworkable in practice." King's political goals "are of course admirable," the editorial stated tersely. "But they can and should be reached by orderly, lawful methods." Other newspapers decried the notion as "vindictive" and "dangerous." Civil Rights leader Whitney Young, executive director of the business-oriented National Urban League, objected that a commercial boycott of one state would require union and business supporters to violate legitimate contracts elsewhere. Radio evangelist Solomon Michaux threw up a picket line around the Lord Baltimore Hotel, where the SCLC board met through the week, protesting that the economic weapon would "throw thousands of Negroes in Alabama out of work and into breadlines."

The irrepressible Bevel denounced critics of the boycott, calling Whitney Young a stuffed shirt "with a fifty-dollar hat on a two-dollar head," but he recognized fateful signs when implementation slipped late on the agenda. Andrew Young proposed instead that SCLC take the nonviolent movement from Selma into the cities of the North, as King himself had suggested, and the board's reluctant approval touched off a crossfire of grumbling. The board of Southern preachers fretted about trying to expand into Northern territory, where they had no base of churches and the established NAACP had bristled repeatedly against competitive intrusion. Bevel wondered what could trouble city Negroes compared with the woes of voteless Southern sharecroppers. Others emphasized a new SCLC program to get at the root of racial conflict through dialogue, separate from protest, by working with distinguished consultants such as anthropologist Margaret Mead and novelist Ralph

Ellison. Rustin, who favored attention to issues of economic justice,* nevertheless stressed a gradual approach to preserve the movement's hard-won coalition. Much of the nation saw race as a matter of gross injustice peculiar to the South, he warned. Too rapid a shift of view would alienate supporters in the North, including the press, which in turn would undermine the historic mobilization of the federal government—"for the first time since 1867"—to support racial equality. "We must not split what we have got for the first time," Rustin told the SCLC board. "No social movement has ever been successful in this country which did not involve as an ally the hard-core white middle classes."

Hosea Williams seized upon Rustin's argument to promote his Summer Community Organization and Political Education, called SCOPE by its acronym, which would import two thousand college students on extremely short notice to register Negro voters across 120 counties of the Black Belt South that summer. King's blessing allowed the SCLC board to embrace the SCOPE alternative more heartily than the Alabama boycott, in a sign that Bevel's hasty proposal already damaged his high standing as a creative strategist. Control of fieldworkers shifted toward Williams, which escalated recriminations between the bitterest antagonists on the headstrong SCLC staff. Williams charged that Bevel tried to dodge the personal witness of nonviolence with grandiose schemes. Bevel countered that Williams had a stunted idea of nonviolence, and that the SCOPE proposal merely copied SNCC's Mississippi Summer Project from the previous year. Williams complained that Bevel campaigned to undermine him with King's executive staff. Loyalists of Williams predicted miracles from his dedication, while others worried about his possessed, domineering bravado. In Baltimore, Williams told FBI agents on the Liuzzo case that he had left all the transportation records from the Selma march in the trunk of a rented car parked somewhere at the Atlanta airport. He ducked subsequent interview requests with a message that the FBI had been nothing but a nuisance, and finally excused persistent agents with a parting comment that his staff had jumped overnight from three to thirty-one people, "and I am busier than Hoover, King, Johnson, or anyone else."

Pressures of the world stage strained an organization steeped in folk-

* "Even if tomorrow Negroes were to become white, they would still be entrapped in their joblessness," Rustin declared earlier in March, as founder of the new A. Philip Randolph Institute to combat poverty.

ways of the pulpit. Board members still made their customary late entrances, and many delivered the required personal donation to SCLC
with an extended, self-centered homily. While Andrew Young reported
that King was demanded as a peacemaker in London, Vietnam, and
even South Africa, board members from Virginia to Florida complained of neglect during the Selma campaign. Rev. Roland Smith of
Atlanta recommended that extra staff be assigned during crises to maintain liaison with the board. Rev. Walter Fauntroy of Washington
warned not to take passage of the voting rights bill for granted. Historian Lawrence Reddick urged support for the upcoming launch of
Head Start among trial federal programs to help poor children learn.
Rev. D. E. King of Kentucky wondered when Negroes would be eligible to enlist in the National Guard units of southern states.

* * *

KING INTERRUPTED the flow of business with a personal request to
"consider seriously and carefully the matter of presidential succession in
SCLC," by formally designating an heir in the event of his demise. "I
know of no one that articulates my ideas more thoroughly than Ralph
Abernathy," he said. Board members first recoiled in shock. Ministers
devoted to funeral oration spoke instead about ways to amend the
SCLC bylaws. Board members who preached often on the nearness of
death—which King invoked for himself by the circumspect phrase
"certain realistic actualities"—took refuge in practical details such as
whether Abernathy should continue also as SCLC's treasurer. Daddy
King channeled resentment of Abernathy into an impassioned speech
about money. He scolded his colleagues over their failure to guarantee
security for his four small grandchildren and Coretta in the event hatred
snatched their provider, his dear son, at the age of thirty-six.

On emergency subcommittees, overwrought board members consulted feverishly about King's morbid surprise. Many knew he had been
depressed before Selma, since the Nobel Prize trip of December and the
realization that Hoover's FBI was blackmailing him toward suicide
with surveillance tapes of his private life. Although King had resolved
to curtail the risk of scandal against the movement by giving up his illicit
consolations—vowing so to some friends with mortified confession, to
others with sighs of resentment—he had succumbed already. Even in
the vortex of twenty-hour days around the marches, he managed travel
with a new black mistress of stylish discretion, who moved easily across
the color line among prominent, mostly wealthy, men. Wild rides gave

way to bouts of self-reproach. The pattern of King's life was exacerbated this time by his piercing failure to keep the high-stakes pledge for his own vulnerable cause, and by parallel discomforts at home. Settlement was imminent in April on Coretta's quest for them to buy a first home in Atlanta after five years as renters, but King still resisted. To him, even a modest house of $10,000 was a haunting luxury, unbecoming his commitment to the poor. His renunciations of material comfort and bourgeois ambition vexed Coretta, especially since his constant journeys most often left her behind with four children in a cramped space. She accommodated what she called the "guilt-ridden" barbs of a man whose "conscience fairly devoured him."

In Baltimore, the *Afro-American* devoted an issue to the SCLC meeting as earth-shattering news and reported its glowing public events by the minute—tribute by Lawrence Cardinal Sheehan at 9:41 P.M., standing ovation for Daddy King six minutes later, entrance by Abernathy at 10:13. By contrast, the dominant *Baltimore Sun* covered the proceedings modestly on the back pages, next to an account of fraud arrests at a local barber school. In private, Rev. C. K. Steele admonished King for springing a chosen heir without prior notice to the board, and small factions stirred against Abernathy. Staff members of King's inner circle staff tended to discount the succession idea as a cosmetic truce between Abernathy and King. They had watched Abernathy mortify King by fits of jealousy at the Nobel ceremonies in Oslo, grasping for an equal share of royal treatment and half the prize money that King resolved to give away. Since then, King had been obliged to beg his sulking colleague to take part in the Selma campaign, and they did not begrudge his right to mollify Abernathy with an empty title, based on wishful presumption that SCLC had a future beyond King. What puzzled them was King's personal attachment. Rustin disparaged Abernathy as a sleepy-headed showboat, but conceded that King could not abide jail "for fifteen minutes" without him. Young, Bernard Lee, and others appreciated Abernathy as a gifted preacher, bonded to King through a base identity in the Negro church. King possessed all Abernathy's raw hunger, thrown against his own leveling obsession with stubborn, flawed human nature. The combination made a furnace of his prophetic voice at full throttle. In repose, it revealed astonishing breadth and beguiling good nature, tinged with depression.

King's aides fully expected him to snap back, as always, to the burden of his indispensable role. A few decided that his ordeals of personal despair and penance in fact were necessary, so that he could renew his inner drive to public sacrifice in the movement. Some advisers pressed him to hurry, and only one argued that they should leave him alone. "Who are we," asked lawyer Harry Wachtel, "to say Martin must go on no matter what the cost?"

The board reconvened to adopt the succession plan. "We must by all means protect his symbolism," said Rev. Fred Shuttlesworth, urging his colleagues to unite behind King. New motions approved insurance and pension benefits for the family. Hosea Williams recommended that something be done to honor Abernathy on his birthday. Bolder members mandated a vacation for King's health, passed a resolution to pay for it, then provided a parallel trip for Ralph and Juanita Abernathy.

Leaving Baltimore, a distressed King sought out Stanley Levison to ask for perspective on his world after Selma.

"Dear Martin," replied Levison, who was still technically in exile from King on the demand of the late President Kennedy. Although King had proclaimed a unilateral "pardon" weeks earlier, Wachtel and others slowly accommodated his full return to their ranks. Even if they could imagine their bosom friend to be a treasonous agent of Soviet influence, bent upon destruction of American freedom, it seemed absurd that the government's murky, lame response was to interdict his volunteer work for King. The separation made sense to them only as naked obeisance to J. Edgar Hoover, but they proceeded with abundant caution because Hoover survived Kennedy. Out of their sight, Hoover stayed on the political offensive by ordering FBI offices to scour future SCOPE workers for subversive backgrounds and to find out whether King had visited Highlander Center more than once. "If we can obtain information disproving King's claims which he recently made before 'Meet the Press,' " Hoover instructed, "we would have some counterintelligence possibility."

Since late 1963, Levison had read to fill hours long devoted to fundraising and other practical services for King. He tried to make up for a weakness in liberal education by studying classical political literature, such as Cervantes, Zola, Hugo, and Tolstoy. He visited gyms in Manhattan to observe the "gentle arts" of jujitsu as a metaphor for nonviolence. He even analyzed popular films, adopting as a motto Humphrey Bogart's statement to predatory mobsters in *The Harder They Fall:* "You can't buy me and you can't scare me." His favorite new author was Victor Hugo, for his ability to summarize "mighty" events in spare language. Hugo called Waterloo "a turning point in the universe."

"Selma was bigger than Birmingham though it was smaller in

scope," Levison wrote King, "because for the first time whites and Negroes from all over the nation joined the struggle in a pilgrimage to the deep south." Whereas Birmingham moved millions "from paper resolutions of support to sympathy," he observed, Selma mobilized "a true cross-section of America." Levison had seen for himself. "In the Montgomery airport I was struck by the unfamiliarity of the participants," he continued. "They were not long-committed white liberals and Negroes. They were new forces from all faiths and all classes . . . from business men to pacifist radicals."

Levison praised "President Johnson's magnificent address" as a vital and necessary expression of popular will, but he insisted that the motive force in history belonged to the movement. "The leadership was yours," he advised, and momentum from Selma made King *"one of the most powerful figures in the country—a leader now not merely of Negroes, but of millions of whites in motion."* He may have underscored the point to lift King from an appealing but relentless modesty that Levison considered a flaw. King was "too humble," he often said, yet far from insecure, and Levison offered his usual unsparing criticism. "The casual manner of proposing [the] boycott, and the impression that this was your central program caused deep disquiet. . . ." he wrote. "It was not the best selection of alternatives for action, and it was not logical to emerge from a struggle for voting rights." By contrast, he sketched the sounder path of historic choices made by Frederick Douglass during and after the Civil War.

"The movement you lead is the single movement in the nation at this time which arouses the finer democratic instincts of the nation," Levison asserted. Laboring to explain why, he focused on method. "Nonviolent direct action was proven by Selma to have even greater power than anyone had fully realized," he wrote. "We would be at fault if we believed our own propaganda that Selma was a terrible expression of brutality and terrorism. Considerable restraint was exercised by the authorities. The degree of violence was shocking and startling, but not extensive." Levison argued that the violence of Birmingham—let alone the spectacle lynchings of recent decades—was much worse, and that the power of Selma arose from the cumulative inspiration of the method itself. Nonviolence evoked courage. When sustained and crafted, it built political engagement almost inexorably. "Someone asked a Negro if he thought they would win," Levison informed King, "and he responded, 'We won when we started.' This is profound."

Levison wrestled with the limits of nonviolence. He could trace its "finer democratic instincts" to thousands of practitioners who risked and absorbed violence without striking back, as their disciplined witness affirmed the daring American theory that people can govern themselves without imposed rulers or guardians. By nearly superhuman forbearance, and a matching faith in common humanity, nonviolent demonstrators invited their own oppressors into the Founders' novel compact of political equals. They challenged hierarchy and heredity, like the original patriots, to transform "the relationship between government and the people," Levison wrote.

For all his balanced wisdom, Levison was not a seer, and his letter to King understated the watershed of Selma. He predicted the overthrow of segregation's "agrarian interests," but not the resulting miracle of Sunbelt prosperity for the South. He believed optimistically that the movement could "go far in changing slum conditions," but he did not foresee corollary ripples of freedom beyond race or economics. Once loosed, doctrines of equality and nonviolent strength resonated broadly against traditional niches of authority. If the depth of potential could be glimpsed in the extraordinary saga of pilgrims to Selma, such as Viola Liuzzo and Jonathan Daniels, the breadth of impact would be felt everywhere from altars and bedrooms to Olympic Games in distant nations. Binding energy from the movement would transform culture and hearth with implications that rattled civil rights leaders themselves, just as the original American Founders had been shaken by a clatter of dollars and frontier brawlers who were not above electing a broomstick, George Washington caustically observed, fearing an excess of democracy in his retirement. Changes beyond imagination soon became commonplace. Inspired by the civil rights movement, a Cincinnati student in 1972 would be ordained the first female rabbi in two thousand years of rabbinical Judaism. "We must face the realities of life," Rabbi Maurice Eisendrath told his board at the Union of American Hebrew Congregations. "Women are here to stay."

Still less did Levison anticipate the spectacular trends of countervailing thought. Both inside and outside the movement, nonviolent politics would drop from scholarly or popular interest at the same time that its inexorable momentum began to spawn lasting achievements. As King warned in his Montgomery speech, revisions of recent history would minimize hope for nonviolent democracy while magnifying its fears. War, even in failure and contradiction, would become again a common measure of freedom, and people sought refuge from unsettled times in what the revolutionary Benjamin Franklin called "a natural inclination in mankind to Kingly Government." A new consensus eventually made people's government the perceived scourge of freedom rather than its unsteady instrument. Phoenix-like, opponents of civil rights landmarks would refine themselves to govern.

King took Levison's long letter on retreat to Jamaica. It was warm counsel for the political maelstrom of his short future. All the twists ahead would be a consequence of, or reaction to, the ten-year crest of the nonviolent movement in March of 1965. Beyond the three years allotted to him, they would shape history into the next century.

II

High Tide

CHAPTER 17

Ten Feet Tall

April 7–May 26, 1965

SCULPTRESS Jimilu Mason despaired of making her subject hold a pose. She tried to shape the bust while President Johnson, seated on a raised platform just outside the Oval Office, gesticulated for an hour to columnist Walter Lippmann about the secret draft of a speech on Vietnam. "I'm going to hold out that carrot you keep talking to me about," he promised. When storms grounded White House helicopters on the evening of April 7, a substitute motorcade whisked Johnson to Baltimore for his nationally televised address from Johns Hopkins University. He welcomed "unconditional discussions" toward peace and offered a "billion dollar American investment" for postwar economic development of the region, including North Vietnam. "The vast Mekong River can provide food and water and power on a scale to dwarf even our own TVA," he declared. "The wonders of modern medicine can be spread through villages where thousands die every year from lack of care. Schools can be established . . ."

All this "and more" would unfold for good once North Vietnam ceased its campaign of "total conquest" in South Vietnam, Johnson pledged. Until then, he presented his nation as a dutiful warrior on "this painful road," standing ready to honor the cause of four hundred Americans who had ended their young lives already "on Vietnam's steaming soil." He announced passive yet steadfast resolve: "We will not be defeated. We will not grow tired." Against unflinching preparations for "a war of unparalleled brutality," he posed lyrical yearnings for peace. Six times Johnson mentioned a dream to end war itself. "It is a very old dream," said the President. "But we have the power and now we have the opportunity to make that dream come true." He struggled almost wistfully with the temptations of martial glory—saying, "the guns and the bombs, the rockets and the warships, are all symbols of human failure"—then closed in the voice of Moses proclaiming his farewell summary of Israel's covenant law: "I call heaven and earth to record this day against you, that I have set before you life and death, blessing and cursing; therefore, choose life."

Critics hailed the threshold speech as a "master stroke." Former President Dwight Eisenhower privately congratulated Johnson for "a very timely and fine move," and welcomed the worldwide political initiative as recognition that an independent South Vietnam could not be maintained "just with bayonets" or "just with white nations." Mail to the White House shifted overnight from 4–1 against U.S. policy in Vietnam to 5–1 in favor, but Johnson mulled over the hostile responses. He sought reassurance the next morning from Arthur "Tex" Goldschmidt, an old friend who served the United Nations as an expert on Mekong River development. Goldschmidt had collaborated with speechwriter Richard Goodwin, and was pleased that the Hopkins audience of sixty million nearly matched the seminal "We Shall Overcome" speech three weeks earlier. His boss, Secretary-General U Thant, already had confided that the message was "wonderful," Goldschmidt told the President, and he had heard "terrific reactions" from lesser U.N. colleagues, "you know, that I talk to in the elevator."

Johnson could not stop reading from his avalanche of telegrams: "Atlanta, Georgia, 'People are sick and tired of your lies about Vietnam. Bring the troops home.' Lubbock, Texas, 'We will back down in Vietnam as we have everywhere else.' . . . Uh, 'your speech tonight was pious nonsense.' . . . Uh, 'Do you really believe that peace can be purchased for a billion?' That's Michigan . . . uh, California, 'a weak-kneed buyout scheme . . . billion-dollar appeasement.' . . . Uh, 'You listened to the wrong advisers. Please ready Encyclopedia America '57. . . .'"

Goldschmidt laughed. He said Johnson was getting hit from both sides.

"I haven't got a damn wire from anybody I know," said the President. "Isn't that odd? Not a one." Political professionals hedged. While Johnson hoped that North Vietnamese leader Ho Chi Minh would choose economic rewards over military punishment, he admitted to himself that he would never negotiate if the positions were reversed. Forlorn, he suggested that Goldschmidt's wife must approve at least of his health legislation.

"She loves it," said Goldschmidt. "We're *both* happy. I mean if you had tried to make the Goldschmidts happy, you couldn't have done better." His wife, Elizabeth Wickenden, had been a social policy advocate since the New Deal, when she and Goldschmidt had introduced a youthful Lyndon Johnson to lifelong friends such as Abe Fortas. Now the President asked that he have her dictate a statement about the passage of Medicare tonight.

"Tonight?" exclaimed Goldschmidt.

"Yeah, we're gonna pass it tonight in the House," said Johnson, chortling over his surprise. "Tell her to give it a little thought and she can call up and dictate it to my secretary. I really want to say it's the finest thing that ever happened to the world."

Historic wonders and woes tumbled over each other. Medicare did pass the House by 110 votes before midnight on April 8. Both education and voting rights cleared Senate hurdles the next day, the centennial of Lee's surrender at Appomattox. In between, Johnson fielded reports through Thursday night about a single Air Force jet fighter that was missing and presumed shot down near the Chinese territory of Hainan Island. He postponed a scheduled trip to Houston, on tenterhooks about military confrontation with Communist China and political backbiting in the Senate, where he feared that the bellicose Thomas Dodd of Connecticut "gets up and says why in the hell did we run, and they knock down our plane and we don't do anything?" Any normal activity would "look awful bad," Johnson worried, "if we had another incident or they bombed or something."

"I believe you can go, Mr. President," said McGeorge Bundy, and Johnson reached "the world's largest air-conditioned room" Friday night to witness the first Major League baseball game ever played indoors. Mickey Mantle's exhibition home run to right-center field triggered the inaugural forty-five-second convulsion of a giant scoreboard that flashed from pinball whirls and rocket flares to electronic cowboys slinging lassos on longhorn steers. The *New York Times* likened the new Houston Astrodome to Roman Emperor Vespasian's cloth-covered amphitheater from the year 70. Innovations included fifty-three luxury boxes with private bars and swivel chairs upholstered in velvet, plus groundskeepers called Earthmen who wore orange space suits. There were flaws to be addressed—the sun-starved death of Tifway Bermuda grass soon introduced plastic AstroTurf—but the domed extravaganza proved a bellwether of the regional economy. That same Friday, the Milwaukee Braves and Detroit Tigers played at a stadium hastily thrown up in Atlanta, according to Mayor Ivan Allen, "on ground we didn't own, with money we didn't have, for a team we hadn't signed." As the Deep South began to escape the commercial shackles of segregation, Allen courted the Braves and a new professional football team to help lift Atlanta into the fifth year of a nationwide boom economy.

Johnson stayed in Texas to dedicate a Job Corps center on Saturday with Sargent Shriver, director of the eight-month-old poverty program. The President confessed to the assembled young trainees that he himself had been a dropout for two years, and he made a teasing lesson of the platform dignitaries by recalling that several had been hungry apprentices in FDR's National Youth Administration, "the job corps of that day"—Governor John Connally for $30 a month, Representative Jake Pickle for $25. "I am not a prophet, or the son of a prophet," said Johnson, but he predicted an era of renewed potential for miracles. Meanwhile, couriers scrambled from Washington with the finished education bill, and on Palm Sunday, April 11, aides hung the presidential seal from a plank table in the yard of the one-room prairie schoolhouse where Johnson had completed eight grades from the age of four. "Come over here, Miss Katie," he said, beckoning his first teacher, long since retired, to sit with him before the press corps.

The new law provided $1.3 billion, which covered only 6 percent of current costs for elementary and secondary schools. It circumvented a long stalemate over church-state issues by targeting the five million poorest students in all schools, whether public or religious, on Johnson's pounded theme: "Poverty has many roots, but the taproot is ignorance." Required local control meant that districts could and would divert funds to less needy students. Still, Johnson waxed euphoric over the breakthrough in federal support for education, ending legislative failures that dated back to 1870 and ran thick since 1946. He mingled at the ceremony with Tomás Coronado and Amanda García among returning admirers from his formative job at Cotulla in 1928. Teacher Johnson had bought a book to drill Coronado in English even though he was the adult janitor. García said Johnson once spanked another student for mimicking his awkward gringo gait, which had made them realize that he, too, was sensitive about humiliation. The President said he would never sign a more important law than the Elementary and Secondary Education Act of 1965. Quoting Thomas Jefferson's admonition to "establish and improve the law for educating the common people," he urged his audience not to "delay in putting it to work."

*   *   *

ON PALM Sunday in Selma, the chief usher at St. Paul's Episcopal stopped a mixed group before 7:30 morning worship. "The bishop says we've got to let you into our church," he advised, "but we don't have to let you receive Communion." Police arrived, and a standoff ensued until Rev. Frank Mathews emerged in robes to guide the ushers down the sidewalk for an intense private discussion. White seminarians Jonathan Daniels and Judith Upham waited with half a dozen charges in question—teenage girls from their host families in the Carver Homes apartments, who had been up since dawn to plait their hair, pull on dress gloves, and practice Communion etiquette. "I may lose my job because of this," Mathews whispered upon his return, "but you can come to the service." With a look that signaled an uneasy compromise with his ushers, he stipulated that they must sit in the back row and receive Communion last. Inside, some members held back from Communion with transparent disgust, as though the intruders had spoiled salvation. Others made a point of welcoming the visitors afterward, while one man made conversation on the steps until he could no longer contain himself. "You goddam scum," he said, and spelled out the word with an intensity that left Upham shaking.

Upham and Daniels carved out their own witness on the fringe of a movement stunned in the afterglow of the great march to Montgomery. They drove to Mobile to buy clerical collars that identified them as seminarians. They spent whole days seeking out the few members of St. Paul's who would exchange words with them. Judge Bernard Reynolds, the chief usher, received them in his chambers at the Dallas County courthouse and explained that they would be welcome in church whenever they did not bring their "nigger trash." Daniels and Upham stifled their rage to discuss church doctrine. "There are still moments when I'd like to get a high-powered rifle and take to the woods," Daniels wrote that week, "but more and more strongly I am beginning to feel that ultimately the revolution to which I am committed is the way of the Cross."

Religious interpretation ran ahead of tactical savvy. The seminarians repeated the knowing buzz of insiders who said Viola Liuzzo had naively endangered herself by interracial travel, but they drove around Selma with half a dozen Negro youngsters stuffed in the Volkswagen. With an Episcopal priest from California and his entire family, including three small children, they ventured into remote Wilcox County and were embarrassed to ask local white people for directions to a voting rights demonstration. Daniels wound up suffering canister burns in the midst of a large crowd being tear-gassed in Camden, where his spirits revived upon personal revelation that hateful Southerners "didn't know what else to do." He conceived "a kind of grim affection" for them—"at least a love that was real and 'existential' rather than abstract."

Young pianist Quentin Lane compounded the lesson before Easter Sunday. Daniels and Upham had met him when Lane's Henry Hudson High School Choir performed at Brown Chapel to honor a classmate killed for participating in the Selma demonstrations. The concert was tenderly charged but hardened to adult reality, as the classmate had been shotgunned by a Negro stepfather enraged against the movement, and white authorities effectively ignored the crime. Lane asked to join the biracial witness at St. Paul's Episcopal, which pitched the seminarians into conflict because they had forecast to Rev. Mathews a breather from the stress of integration. They debated past midnight, then painfully notified Mathews why they would seek worship after all with Lane and four other Negro teenagers. The rector fairly howled against the change as proof of bad faith. He said the Bishop of Alabama himself had relied upon their assurance of relief in a personal negotiation with the governing vestry. The seminarians denied trying to ruin his church. When an exasperated member asked what else their purpose could be, Daniels replied, "We are trying to live the Gospel."

Early on Sunday, April 18, ushers isolated the party of seven on a side aisle of the back row, then confined them during Communion until all others were reseated in their pews. Quietly, with an edge of desperation, Judge Reynolds advised them not to return for the main Easter service at eleven o'clock, and was visibly relieved to hear they would attend the crosstown namesake instead. At St. Paul's Colored Methodist Episcopal Church, Daniels delivered his first public sermon in Alabama, guided by Rev. T. R. Harris and only mildly distracted by encouraging cries of "Preach it, brother." Afterward, he and Upham began a formal letter of inquiry to Episcopal Bishop C. C. J. Carpenter, then ventured into the Negro Elks Club Sunday night. Their month-long presence in Selma made them social novelties around the jukebox until they were eclipsed by the late arrival of SNCC workers from the hinterland. Fascinated, Daniels managed to talk philosophy with Stokely Carmichael.

* * *

THE POLITICAL leaders Upham and Daniels sought to emulate were largely inaccessible. King traveled—"I pray he doesn't get bumped off," wrote Daniels—and the scattered SNCC staff members withdrew three times within a month for a cumulative seven days of internal debate. The commandeered staff car emerged as a new symbol of SNCC disorganization bordering on anarchy. Project directors complained that fieldworkers blithely left rural posts to joyride in Atlanta. "How do you deal with people who tell you they're going to shoot you if you take away their cars?" asked Muriel Tillinghast of Mississippi. Former SNCC chairman Marion Barry traced a loss of communal spirit to the reduction in direct action protest; he lamented that jail-going witness no longer weeded out frivolous politics. Carmichael argued that assorted free spirits—called "floaters"—were merely symptoms of SNCC's lack of a signature program after Freedom Summer of 1964. Some bemoaned an acute leadership vacuum since Bob Moses had changed his name to Parris in his mysterious farewell ceremony two months earlier. Others objected that Moses and his wife, Dona, set a debilitating example by floating anonymously into Birmingham while still on the SNCC payroll. "I will not look for them," announced a peeved Silas Norman. "They must contact me."

Moses missed a three-day SNCC retreat to address the first major rally against the Vietnam War on April 17 in Washington. Colleagues left behind perceived his speech as yet another visionary leap of courage, but the shift of subject highlighted SNCC's division in two respects. First, like the nascent antiwar movement itself, the Washington rally of twenty thousand was composed almost entirely of white people, which raised the hidden issue of racial tensions within a civil rights group that aspired to rise above them. Moses had presided over painful debates about internal hostility even before the Southern movement was flooded with white volunteers who stayed after Freedom Summer, and it was partly to escape the personal and political strain of integrated projects that some sixty SNCC staff members so readily left Mississippi for Selma. Second, the Vietnam speech hazarded a new protest in the arena of national politics, where young SNCC workers—especially Moses—felt beaten down, worn out, and betrayed. Many had come to regard the national government as a stifling enemy. "How many of us are willing to condemn LBJ's voting bill?" urged Courtland Cox, the influential theorist out of Howard University. An analysis by SNCC's research director, Jack Minnis, dismissed the proposed law as "completely fraudulent . . . because the whole racist structure of the enormously complex U.S. government provides those who govern with too many 'outs.' "

SNCC activists broadly rejected the goal of federal action that had anchored the movement's anguished appeals for racial justice. On the brink of history's verdict, they asserted that the landmark civil rights laws would be empty pieces of paper, and their grievance ran deeper than predictions of failure and nonenforcement. Significantly, movement veterans turned sour on the inherent nature of national politics. "Lyndon and Hubert and their friends continue the confidence game that passes for government in the Great Society," wrote Minnis in the April 15 edition of his investigative newsletter, *Life with Lyndon.* The freelance weekly had become a phenomenon within SNCC since January, based on its caustic portrayals of President Johnson as the tool of impersonal forces—chiefly profit and centralized power—behind an empty husk of liberalism. In a fateful irony, this approach mirrored language being crafted by George Wallace and others from the opposite political pole.

SNCC workers vented contradictions. Hard-liners shouted that purists were immorally withdrawn. Purists said hard-liners were immorally engaged. ("They say that since the power structure is so immoral, what we should do to get power is to be sneaky and underhanded ourselves.") A forlorn team of Mississippi workers protested Forman's blatantly inconsistent posture toward the Selma demonstrations—"What in the hell is going on?"—then resigned in frustration. "We destroy each other," wrote one, "but mostly offer each other no comfort." Silas Norman chastised Ivanhoe Donaldson for serving as marshal of the grand Montgomery march even though he opposed it. Mississippians pleaded for Donaldson to return to the grassroots survival projects he championed, only to be shocked when he turned up instead to say he was running SNCC communications director Julian Bond for a seat in the Georgia legislature.

"What will Julian do if he loses?" asked a bewildered staff member.

"I don't know," shrugged Donaldson. He solicited SNCC's first campaign contribution with pragmatic flair, ignoring an ingrained consensus that neckties and electoral politics were paths to corruption. Voters from Atlanta's new 136th district never had been consulted by a candidate, he said, and they deserved better than the nominee decreed by Negro preachers. Also, Bond's name was an asset because of his prominent family and yet his face was unknown, which allowed Donaldson and SNCC co-worker Charlie Cobb to triple the personal reach of the campaign by passing themselves off as the candidate in door-to-door visits. Frank Soracco, who was white, confined his work mostly to headquarters in the back of a wig shop on Hunter Street.

Moses, answering to Parris, dropped by SNCC's final April debate with a meditation on the growing pains of freedom. The movement was opening doors to millions, he said, but there could be no shortcut to institutionalize "the meaningful release of their energy." This he called a central problem for the balance of the twentieth century. He drew sketches of organizational theory as colleagues sat spellbound or puzzled. "If the direction really comes from the bottom," Moses patiently declared, "the people have to get together and hash out what they think are their problems." Including SNCC's problems. Without a deadline. No one called him a floater in person, and several tried to fathom the democratic gist of his message. "People get strength from each other," said Stokely Carmichael.

Rancorous abstraction gave way to divided practice. White SNCC workers drifted away or took up support functions for Negro fieldworkers who ventured deep into isolated territory. The small team in Lowndes County found a freedom house that lacked indoor plumbing, donated by farmer Matthew Jackson of the newly born voting rights group, LCCMHR. From there, Carmichael and Bob Mants slowly canvassed the giant rural county on foot and on borrowed mules, at first claiming victory when frightened Negroes allowed them to come near. An old woman outside Calhoun politely turned them down. "I can't do no registering," she said. "My head done blossomed for the grave." Later, in a small epiphany, an ancient invalid named "Aunt Ida" Bowie announced that she had been expecting them since "I seed y'all up there around Abraham Lincoln"—a reference taken to mean the 1963 March on Washington. She sent relatives to the tiny mass meetings.

Carmichael aimed to burrow deeply into Lowndes. To find others like Aunt Ida he recruited Scott B. Smith, a fieldworker he admired for proven ability to start alone from a roadside drop in a strange county without funds or transportation. Smith was a Chicago street hustler who had come south to volunteer after Bloody Sunday, but he cultivated a backwoods aura by wearing a necklace made of mysterious "haunted" bones—some said deer antlers—and discoursed knowledgeably on the subtle importance of black moonshiners to rural churches. He quickly predicted that the town of Fort Deposit would be the "powder keg" for Lowndes County, where the new project tried to forestall violence by working quietly out of sight. Whatever happened, Carmichael argued, SNCC workers would be foolish to begrudge popular affection for Martin Luther King. He had seen Alabama black people climb over each other just to touch him. "The people didn't know what was SNCC," Carmichael trenchantly observed. "They just said, 'You one of Dr. King's men?' " He urged his colleagues to answer, "Yes, ma'am," and to forge bonds in daily service so that even King would have to "go through the SNCC workers" in the next crisis, making common cause of leadership from top and bottom.

* * *

KING FIRST tested Boston. Beneath giant murals on a theme chiseled into the frieze of the Common Court—"Milestones on the Road to Freedom in Massachusetts"—he addressed a joint session of the legislature on Thursday, April 22. "For one who has been barricaded from the seats of government," he began, "and jailed so many times for attempting to petition legislatures and councils, I can assure you that this is a momentous occasion." Standing galleries cheered his tribute to their slain native son, President Kennedy, for introducing the civil rights bill, and applauded his report that "many communities are now complying . . . with amazing good sense and calm reasonableness." When King touched upon aspects of the "desperate question" that remained, however, observers noticed legislators edging forward, some on overflow camp stools packed in the aisles. "He never mentioned Boston or Massachusetts specifically, but he did stress 'school imbalance' [and] 'de facto segregation,' " reported the *Boston Globe*. "Let me hasten to say," King hedged in the Common Court, "that I come to Massachusetts not to condemn but to encourage. It was from these shores that the vision of a new nation conceived in liberty was born, and from these shores liberty must be preserved."

The thunderous approval that had answered his call to Pettus Bridge still echoed along King's motorcade route to Back Bay. At Temple Israel, for a thousand people on the last night of Passover, he recalled informally that landlords had offered rental lodging to the telephone voice of a new Boston University graduate student in 1951, "at place after place . . . until they found out I was a Negro." By such constriction in real estate, concluded the 1965 Kiernan Report on Education for the commonwealth, 70 percent of all eighty thousand Massachusetts Negroes were cordoned inside the single Boston district of Roxbury, where decay advanced as from a girdled tree. King had toured Roxbury on his way to meet Governor John Volpe and the legislature—climbing into the dilapidated tenement apartment of Betty Jennings, a recent refugee from the segregated South, and speaking to parents through a bullhorn outside Campbell School, where students crowded up to fifty per class. His hardest task was often to prevent the swell of bitterness, he explained at Temple Israel, so as to develop constructive nonviolence. "Every Negro must prepare for 'the Passover of the Future,' " he said.

"Boston is not the worst city in the United States," King told reporters early Friday outside Roxbury's Blue Hill Christian Center. He mentioned people of conscience who had served there, including James Reeb and Mary Peabody, mother of the previous governor, before her jail witness the previous spring in St. Augustine. Rev. Virgil Wood, the former SCLC coordinator in Virginia, presented a choir of recovering alcoholics who had returned from the Montgomery march and now scrubbed Roxbury streets for King's visit. Then, behind closed doors, local leaders exhibited a weak case for a Boston movement. They were "horribly divided along class lines," one conceded. Their nemesis, white school defender Louise Day Hicks, had mobilized more effectively. Some worried that Irish teenagers had stoned the NAACP float in the past two St. Patrick's Day parades, while others discounted prestigious allies. They gave Lieutenant Governor Elliot Richardson a sporting nickname, "I Was With You In Selma," based on a conversational refrain they said he used to finesse talk of race in Boston. King laughed, but he could not lightly risk the support of politicians like Richardson, who indeed went to Selma. The voting rights bill still faced crippling amendments under filibuster, and even settled law would be a fragile base for what King called "creative optimism." Only Wednesday, approaching the eleventh anniversary of the unanimous *Brown* decision, he had told the New York City Bar Association that a mere 1.18 percent of Negro students in the South attended class with any white children.

King emerged two hours late for his first march about conditions in the North, covering three miles out of Roxbury with six hundred police guards and crowds estimated between twenty and fifty thousand. Cold rain drove some to shelter under store awnings along Tremont Street, but most raised umbrellas like King himself for the rally on Boston Common. Within sight of gravestones and monuments for storied heroes of democratic struggle—Samuel Adams, Paul Revere, Crispus Attucks, Robert Gould Shaw, William Lloyd Garrison—he exhorted Americans not to become "a nation of onlookers," then parried questions from reporters in a subsequent rush to the airport. King denied picking on Boston, or worrying over Harry Truman's latest public accusation that he was "a troublemaker," or resenting a diversion of energy to peace issues. "I have no objection to civil rights leaders speaking against war as against segregation," he said, in a comment generating a headline—"King's New Tack: End The Viet War"—that circled back in thank-you telegrams from pacifist friends A. J. Muste and Benjamin Spock, urging him to join their war protests. Distractions from the altar crowded in the same day, as Southern Presbyterians debated a motion to rescind an invitation to King, and two leading churches, St. John's Episcopal of Savannah and First Baptist of Houston, voted to deny admission to Negroes. King complained that his sleeping pills no longer worked and that his vacation felt more like a prison than rest. Aides discussed recommending to him a more drastic psychiatric approach for depression—"not using those words, of course."

* * *

PRESIDENT JOHNSON, asking if he had somehow offended King, remarked toward the end of April that he was falling out of touch with civil rights leaders. "Normally they're tellin' you that you are either playin' hell, or you're doin' a good job," he grumbled to an aide, "and we just haven't heard anything." Johnson wanted help in particular to hire enforcement officials for the equal employment section of the 1964 Civil Rights Act, which took effect in July. Prospective candidates, mindful of their own careers, were shrinking from a task that figured to rankle major employers nationwide. "None of them want to do it," groused Johnson. "I've got to get some good people." He ordered more bundles of his Selma speech shipped to the leaders for distribution to potential recruits.

In downtown Birmingham, seminarian Judith Upham unwisely wore high heels to picket the Bishop of Alabama on Friday, April 30. She took off her shoes to finish four hours' walking with Daniels and three Episcopal priests outside the stone headquarters of the diocese, carrying placards against segregation. Most pedestrians avoided them.

One matron icily wished all their children to be born black, and a few stopped to read or discuss their leaflet of grievance against Bishop Carpenter. He had pressed for "the exact wording" of abusive incidents mentioned in their petition, writing, "I cannot imagine the good people of St. Paul's Church, Selma, using obscene language in your presence." When the seminarians reluctantly complied, saying in a private audience on Tuesday that insults were peripheral to the issue of segregated worship, Carpenter had maintained that they were the ones stuck on extraneous details. The rear pew and last Communion cup were trifles in themselves, he declared, to be embraced as tokens of Christian humility. He advised them to "go to church with eyes closed and just worship the Lord without looking for faults," calling Upham "Old Girl" in a stream of jolly deflection, tinged with sarcasm, that bowled over the seminarians. They wrote him since with recovered grasp—"There is a difference between humility and humiliation . . . you remain in our prayers. Thank you for the good coffee yesterday!"—but Carpenter left them alone on the picket line. Back in Selma, they attended an integrated Catholic service with Jim Leatherer, whose conduct involuntarily repelled Upham as coarsely self-righteous, reminiscent of the bishop, in spite of her contrasting admiration for the one-legged marcher from Saginaw. She wrestled anew with the elusive discipline of brotherhood.

Also on April 30, FBI surveillance agents tracked the arrival of Clarence Jones at the Atlanta airport for the resumption of truce talks between King and SNCC leaders. Singer Harry Belafonte mediated after a ten-day break, and the two sides vented familiar disputes that had become "more dramatic," Belafonte figured, because of attention from Selma. Their session wound up with a cooperative statement between King and Lewis, drafted by James Forman, and a public comment by Belafonte that "these things could not be allowed to fester." Stokely Carmichael told SNCC colleagues that King confessed uncertainty about how to address economic issues ahead. "I think the cats are honest," he said. "Bevel and Belafonte want the boycott. King doesn't." Back in Selma, Carmichael and Scott B. Smith ran into the seminarians again Sunday night at the Elks Club. Smith borrowed $10, and Carmichael said they could be useful in Lowndes County for registration day on May 3.

Daniels and Upham managed to find the domed white courthouse in front of the Hayneville water tower, surrounded by police cruisers and U.S. government sedans in a jam of parked vehicles. They instinctively avoided the local crowds milling about the square for the Monday start of the Viola Liuzzo murder trial, and gravitated to a line of Negroes outside the Old Jail two blocks away. There they met John Hulett, one of the only two Negroes to have passed the registration test, along with a garrulous, electrified version of Carmichael that was scarcely recognizable to the seminarians as the existentialist they knew for offbeat theories of John Brown and Jesus. He pranced about with encouragement in a Caribbean lilt, making light of fancy test words and special intimidations for Negroes, handing SNCC buttons blithely to deputies, but he told Daniels and Upham in a quiet aside that the area was unsafe for white movement workers. They left within an hour. Armed registrars processed sixty of 150 applicants who waited all day, and later accepted nine as a splash in the thimble of new black voters.

Not a single Negro braved attendance at the week-long trial in Hayneville. Robert Shelton, Imperial Wizard of the Alabama Ku Klux Klan, sat next to defendant Collie LeRoy Wilkins at the defense table, and Inspector Joe Sullivan entered with a heavy protective guard for chief witness Gary Thomas Rowe, now revealed as an FBI informant. Sparrows flew through open windows for aerial chases around the high-ceilinged courtroom, sometimes perching on the triangular relic of a prisoners' cage welded into one rear corner, but drama centered upon Klan Klonsel Matt Murphy, first cousin of Mississippi novelist Walker Percy. He bellowed, waved a pistol, and stomped on his hat. Skimming through a cursory defense case that lasted only twenty-one minutes, he pitched himself instead into lurid attacks on the prosecution. Murphy denounced victim Liuzzo as "a white nigger who turned her car over to a black nigger for the purpose of hauling niggers and communists back and forth." He accused Leroy Moton on the stand of shooting Liuzzo himself after interracial sex "under the hypnotic spell of narcotics," and, most heatedly, he impeached star witness Rowe as a liar—"treacherous as a rattlesnake . . . a traitor and a pimp and an agent of Castro and I don't know what all"—for violating his membership oath to guard Klan secrets.

"No one, prosecutor or defense lawyer, had a kind word for the dead woman," reported the *New York Times*. The lead prosecutor acknowledged widespread sentiment to excuse Liuzzo's murder "on the grounds that this woman was riding in a car with a Negro man," but warned against setting a legal precedent that might backfire against segregationist travelers including the jurors themselves. His closing argument—that a not-guilty vote would favor any potential bush-whacker who "sees you driving your Negro maid home, or sees your wife driving her cook home"—was regarded as a creative but futile stretch. With Attorney General Katzenbach privately braced to count even one prosecution vote as a moral victory, the jury made front-page news simply by extending deliberations overnight without reaching swift acquittal, and then on May 7 deadlocked 10–2 for conviction on a charge of manslaughter. Shocked prosecutors vowed to prepare for an-other trial.

Farmer Edmund Sallee said fellow jurors felt "insulted" by Murphy's courtroom antics, including his vicious diatribes against the deceased victim. By failing so far to convict a Klan defendant, the twelve white males did fulfill expectations of avowed segregationists from Lowndes County, but the jury box already had pushed them past visceral images that prevailed elsewhere. The editors of *Ladies' Home Journal,* surprised by poll results showing that 55.2 percent of American women believed Viola Liuzzo "should have stayed home," convened a random sample of Northern women for a discussion forum that skittered tensely through misgivings—with participants objecting most commonly that Liuzzo forsook her children, or could not know enough about issues "outside her back yard," or lacked "her husband's permission," or should have "canceled her newspaper subscription" as a less extreme protest, but also saying, after one woman confessed leaving her children once with a sit-ter for a three-day club trip, that no family could resent an absent hus-band shot for something important, like resisting the Nazis, or that Liuzzo "might have thought her cause was stronger than her husband going to war." The independent embrace of risk by a middle-class mother was yet an unstable new concept, which foreclosed broad inter-est in Liuzzo as a martyr of human scale.

As for Gary Thomas Rowe, the Hayneville jury took a more in-formed view than observers on either side of the civil rights struggle. Several jurors said they could have won over the two holdouts against conviction—hard cases from Fort Deposit—if only Rowe had pleaded guilty to something for his part in the crime. Sophisticated Southerners missed such nuance out of fear and contempt. No lawyer in Alabama wanted to defend Rowe when Klonsel Murphy, vowing to flush him from hiding to face revenge, sued in mid-May for legal fees he claimed Rowe had incurred before defecting from the Klan. Through the American Bar Association, Attorney General Katzenbach prevailed upon Paul Johnston (Harvard '30, Yale Law '33) to represent Rowe, whereupon fellow partners, including his own father and brother, summarily expelled Johnston from his lifelong practice at the Birmingham firm of Cabaniss, Johnston, Gardner & Clark. ("You presently refuse to abide by the unanimous decision of the other members of the firm," stated the letter of severance.) Nationally prominent lawyers and judges commiserated with Johnston from afar. Alabama peers ostracized him to advertise their professional distance from Rowe, who radiated compound controversy as a turncoat Klansman working a race murder for the feds.

Prosecutors seeking justice for Liuzzo stressed the positive side of their linchpin witness, and FBI officials gladly cooperated by concealing Rowe's violent five-year career as a protected federal informant. Not until 1979 would a U.S. Justice Department task force discover that he lied repeatedly under oath about his role in sordid, faction-ridden Klan conspiracies,* and that FBI supervisors covered up all but the bare fact of his former employment. More than two decades later, Birmingham historian Diane McWhorter would examine the detailed mass of Rowe's FBI record, including his reported claim to have killed a black man in 1963, and find it difficult in retrospect to sort out what was understated, condoned, exaggerated, or sanitized. Only one contemporary reporter addressed the Liuzzo trial's glimpse of undercover work by Rowe. "What sorely troubles me, if we accept the prosecution's account of the slaying," wrote Inez Robb, "is the moral aspect of Rowe's presence in the car. . . . Under what kind of secret orders did Rowe work?" Was he expected to join in crime, strictly observe, or try to prevent murder? "It is one woman's opinion" she concluded, "that the FBI owes the nation an explanation of its action in the Liuzzo case."

Robb's May 17 column appeared in 132 newspapers and landed on J. Edgar Hoover's desk with a report finding "no information of a derogatory nature" about Robb. Hoover remembered differently. "Back in the '30s or '40s," he wrote, "she vilified the FBI and me personally when I was in Miami." His note sent FBI officials scurrying a quarter-century back through their files to unearth yellowed confirmation of

---

* Notably, the police-arranged Klan beating of Freedom Riders on May 14, 1961. A news photograph of Rowe pummeling one victim in the Trailways bus station worried control agents, who nevertheless assured FBI headquarters that their informant engaged in no violence.

Hoover's legendary antennae for criticism—a March 5, 1940, Robb column that scolded the top G-man of "the most wonderful brown eyes" for vacationing in mob-controlled spots along Florida's casino Gold Coast while vowing to fight crime. Hoover's deputies, chastened as always, came back with a steely recommendation that DeLoach contact Inez Robb to "set her straight" about Rowe.

"No," Hoover scrawled, countermanding an order that might provoke further inquiry. "She is a 'bitch' & nothing would be gained."

* * *

"BUNDY Is Unable to Appear Because of 'Other Duties,' " headlined a skeptical *New York Times* story on the principal debater's late scratch from the May 15 Vietnam National Teach-In. The *Times* reported that White House officials were "uncomfortable with the need for silence," but "could not in any way discuss Mr. Bundy's whereabouts." (Bundy slipped away for secret truce negotiations in the Dominican Republic, where President Johnson on April 28 had dispatched U.S. troops to quell incipient civil war.) Substitutes took his place before a live audience of five thousand at Washington's Sheraton Park Hotel, connected by patched radio feed to 100,000 listeners at 122 campus teach-ins over thirty-five states. Professor Eric Wolf of Michigan, speaking for the committee that had sprung up from the original teach-in seven weeks earlier, introduced the debate as a "life blood of democracy," vitally needed to resolve contradictory claims that Vietnam policy was at once too complex for the average citizen and as simple as good versus evil. "We are here to serve notice that American citizens are not children," he declared.

Historian Arthur Schlesinger, speaking for the administration's policy, warned that it would be foolish to ignore "the very sure and very terrible consequences of either enlargement or withdrawal" in Vietnam. Enlargement invited World War III, and withdrawal betrayed the students, professors, and intellectuals of Vietnam—"people like ourselves"—who opposed the Vietnamese Communists. Famously, he observed that "if we took the Marines now in the Dominican Republic and sent them to South Vietnam, we would be a good deal better off in both countries." Reporters emphasized the intramural critique of Johnson by a partisan Kennedy Democrat, but the predominantly antiwar crowd booed Schlesinger's overall support for the military commitment to Vietnam. He recommended supplementary moves toward a negotiated settlement that "doesn't promise a perfect solution," and paused to add, "But life is not very satisfactory." Boos turned to silence, then scattered applause. "I welcome this existential endorsement," Schlesinger said wryly.

Like most of the parallel campus debates, the showcase National Teach-In continued for some nine hours after the radio feed. The format limiting speakers to professors and government officials set a muted, academic tone for what columnist Peter Lisagor called a "battle of the eggheads." Daniel Ellsberg, destined to become a historic dissenter in 1971, argued for the State Department that the war could and should be won, while professor Robert Scalapino of Berkeley, standing in for Bundy, proposed a complex program "from the standpoint of maximizing the fundamental interests which you and the non-Communist world hold together."

Across the continent at Berkeley, a more raucous panoply of speakers held forth through intermittent rain the next weekend for nearly thirty-four continuous hours. Professor Scalapino boycotted the largest and longest teach-in as a "travesty" on his home campus that "should be repudiated by all true scholars irrespective of their views on Vietnam." Staughton Lynd of Yale denounced Scalapino for cowardly elitism. Baby doctor Benjamin Spock and British philosopher Bertrand Russell expounded on the threat of nuclear annihilation. Maverick journalist I. F. Stone fielded questions about colonial interventions from the Napoleonic Wars to the Soviet invasion of Hungary, and confronted the fear of "irreversible" Communism—noting from the pattern of police states that "it takes a hell of a long time to get a thaw," but trusting in democratic engagement and free thought ("Jefferson for me is an ultimate and a far greater figure than Lenin") to thaw tyrannies "instead of trying to strangle them with blockades and with hatred." Novelist Norman Mailer conjured up florid images of Lyndon Johnson as a cornpone emperor drawn to Vietnam "out of the pusillanimities of the madnesses of his secret sleep," then swerved through contrarian rhetoric of an isolationist utopia to an "equally visionary" cry for virile combat without high-altitude bombers—"Fight like men! Go in man-to-man against the Vietcong!"—that discomfited some imaginations he had tickled into flight.

Dozens of the Berkeley speakers came grounded in the civil rights movement. Charlie Cobb, fresh from Julian Bond's unheralded victory in the special Georgia primary, read a long poem he had written for a girlfriend about Selma and Vietnam:

So cry not just for Jackson and Reeb
Schwerner Goodman Chaney or Lee
Cry for all mothers
  with shovels
  digging at hovels
  looking for their dead
Cry for all the blood spilled
Of all the people killed
In the standard procedure of the country
  which is not ours . . .

Norman Thomas, the venerable six-time Socialist candidate for President, and a former Presbyterian minister, grieved over his bitter premonition that America's white churches were falling from late conversion on civil rights back to excuse violence in "their familiar role of opposing all wars except the one they are in." Movement comedian Dick Gregory paired the ill omen of Vietnam with California's landslide approval for Proposition 14, which repealed the state's new fair housing law starkly against the grain of the 1964 national election. "Which means," Gregory shouted, "California ain't nothing but Mississippi with palm trees!"

Near adjournment on Saturday night, May 22, Gregory introduced surprise speaker Bob Parris with mysterious, nonspecific praise as one "among the greatest human beings who have ever walked the earth." Murmurs circulated that Parris had dropped the name Moses to shed the burdens of his four pioneer years for SNCC in Mississippi, and his few soft-spoken words were distinctive to others that knew nothing of him: "I saw a picture in an AP release. It said, 'Marine Captures Communist Rebel.' Now I looked at that picture, and what I saw was a little colored boy standing against a wire fence with a big huge white Marine with a gun in his back." Moses implored the Berkeley crowd to approach the issue of political labels personally, first by writing letters—"a lot of you"—to Hazel Palmer, a former maid and future mayor in Mississippi. He gave an address on Farish Street in Jackson and a list of suggested questions: "What did you do? What do you do now? What makes you think that instead of being a cook in somebody's kitchen you could help run a political party?" Through Palmer, he suggested, they could see the South "as a looking glass, not a lightning rod" for deflected troubles, and the peace movement could learn from faceless leaders at home how to gain a picture of Third World faces in Vietnam. "The people in this country believe that they're in Vietnam fighting Communism as the manifestation of evil in the world," said Moses. "That's what they deeply believe. And that's what they read all the time in their newspapers. You've got to be prepared to offer a different reality."

Coverage of the incipient Vietnam protest stoutly resisted association with civil rights. Sunday's *San Francisco Examiner* ignored the marathon Berkeley event altogether. The *New York Times* offered the most substantive account in the mainstream press—"33-Hour Teach-In Attracts 10,000"—leading with the image of "a bleary-eyed, bearded young man whose gray sweatshirt bore the inscription 'Let's Make Love, Not War,' stretched out on the grass," followed by a paragraph on a nearby "girl with straight black hair and bare feet," who "plaintively asked her escort, 'Don't they ever run out of things to say?' "

Strains within the racial movement itself concealed signal lessons about projecting new witness into the prevailing political order, and it scarcely helped that the Berkeley Free Speech Movement had veered notoriously from the quickening battles to support nonviolent volunteers in Mississippi. In March, four days before the Selma Bloody Sunday, a lone fan of the beat comic Lenny Bruce had tested the hard-won political debate plaza with a sign bearing simply the word "FUCK." His arrest energized naughty protest across the spectrum of campus affairs, with jailing soon for a due-process "Fuck Defense Fund," a "Fuck Communism" parade by Cal Conservatives, and a public reading of *Lady Chatterley's Lover* by English majors, also jailed. One leader of the Free Speech Movement convened defense rallies on principle. Some held back, and others tacked against the university for hypocritical indifference to the winning, wildly vulgar "Miss Pussy Galore" entry in a recent fraternity contest. Through April and May, as a statewide chorus of wags mocked the modified "Filthy Speech" Movement, student leaders debated whether the obscenity uproar polluted their cause. One faculty group called them "moral spastics," too enamored of their own flamboyant display to gauge consequence in the world. A few days after the Vietnam teach-in, California Assembly Speaker Jesse Unruh initiated a full investigation of both the "free speech" and "filthy speech" uprisings at Berkeley.

* * *

A BOMB threat evacuated the Americana Hotel in New York before Martin Luther King's speech on May 20. He met privately with Vice President Hubert Humphrey, seeking assurance that the administration had the votes to break the Senate filibuster of the voting rights bill.

Among King's worries was the timing of the SCOPE project he had approved so uneasily, as delays in the anticipated law would ruin hopes for the first mass registration of Negroes that summer, forcing Hosea Williams either to withhold hundreds of new volunteers or fling them unprotected into the maw of Southern sheriffs. King prodded Wachtel to complete a committee "review" of Stanley Levison's pending return to the circle of Northern advisers, and Wachtel stalled in collaboration with Bayard Rustin, believing Levison would regain unfair access to King's ear from his unique personal bond that had encompassed long phone calls from King after midnight.

King was so vexed on a related front that he had prevailed upon Archibald Carey to fly from Chicago to FBI headquarters only the day before, seeking to forestall a press attack rumored for the last week in May. "I interrupted Dr. Carey at this point," DeLoach wrote afterward, "and told him . . . the FBI had plenty to do without being responsible for a discrediting campaign against Reverend King." DeLoach said he countered with a list of King's "derelictions" in criticizing Hoover, then dismissed Carey with a reminder that "King and the other civil rights workers owed the FBI a debt of gratitude they would never be able to repay." Resigned, Carey reported back to King that he should make more effort to praise Hoover. A prominent judge and minister of Daddy King's close acquaintance, Carey had cured the subversive accusations in his own FBI file with single-minded applications of flattery, complete with letters gushing over handshakes and autographed photos with Hoover. He recommended that King confine himself to small talk in the Director's presence. Hoover, for his part, bestowed a rare compliment on DeLoach—"well handled"—and promptly authorized the leak of confidential bug and wiretap information on King to UPI's chief Southern correspondent.

In New York, King emerged at the Americana with a formal lecture on nonviolence for two thousand members of the American Jewish Committee. He tried to combat the popular impression that demonstrators claimed license to break laws in pursuit of "benefits exclusively for the Negro." The civil rights movement came from a larger heritage stretching back through the suffragettes and the Boston Tea Party, he said, and had contributed new civic interactions of broad application, such as the teach-in. Distinguishing between nonviolence and classical civil disobedience, King argued that the former aimed not to defy but to fulfill the Constitution. He pictured democracy itself as a political form of nonviolence, merged and refined in history's slow rise from primitive conquest toward the established vote. "It is an axiom of nonviolent action and democracy that when any group struggles properly and justly to achieve its own rights, it enlarges the rights of all," King asserted. "This element is what makes both democracy and nonviolent action self-renewing and creative."

These were difficult subjects. The speech left enigmatic notice on back pages in New York—"Dr. King Examines Rights and Laws: Says Negro Knows That He Is Part of 'Larger Society' "—as he flew home to Atlanta. Beneath the wave of optimism set loose May 21, when Senator Philip Hart of Michigan filed a cloture petition on voting rights, he preached a haunted sermon on grief. "Disappointment is a hallmark of our mortal life," King observed that Sunday, May 23. He communed with his Ebenezer congregation about wounds beyond reach, sketching the bleakness of people gone cold. "They are too detached to be selfish, and too lifeless to be unselfish," he warned. "Their hands are even unresponsive to the touch of a charming baby." He touched bottom, then cornered despair first by repeating his text from Jeremiah with special emphasis: "This is *my* grief, and I must bear it." Never avoid shame or failure, he counseled, but "put it in the center of your mind and dare— stare daringly at it." From there they could "turn this liability into an asset" by harnessing the energy of pain and reproach. "Never forget, my friends," King told them, "almost anything that happens to us may be woven into the purposes of God." His voice gathered rhythm and strength. As in another trademark sermon, on intractable evil, he listed treasured figures of history who bounced from suffering and penance to glory. "I've been to the mountaintop now," he cried, in words he would repeat for posterity in Memphis. "God allowed me to live these years. It doesn't matter now. Whatever happens now doesn't matter, because I've seen the promised land." He relived a decade in the movement, ending with his march into Montgomery from Selma "to stand right at the place where Jefferson Davis stood and say that the old cradle of the Confederacy is now rocking, and Dixie will one day have a heart, because we are moving now."

On Tuesday, exactly two months after the speech King recalled, a cloture tally of 70–30 in the Senate formally ended the Southern blockade against consideration of the voting rights bill. That night, heavyweight champion Muhammad Ali knocked out favored Sonny Liston in the second minute of their rematch at an old hockey rink in Lewiston, Maine. Some in the meager crowd of three thousand had not yet taken their seats. Many others saw no blows and shouted, "Fake! Fake! Fake!" Stupefied sports journalists divided over a clash of iconic images that turned color and violence inside out—the glistening Ali waving a glove over the prostrate Liston, fallen from a "phantom punch," while "strategy adviser" Stepin Fetchit rejoiced in Ali's corner. Ringside delirium gave lunatic weight to the fabled actor's prediction that Ali would become a national hero, certainly for reporters still blinking from his ambush of their pre-fight banter about "Uncle Tom" humor. "Uncle Tom was not an inferior Negro," Fetchit had corrected, snapping from the "slow-witted darky" character of his Hollywood films since 1927. "He was a white man's child. His real name was MacPherson and he lived near Harriet Beecher Stowe. Tom was the first of the Negro social reformers and integrationists. The inferior Negro was Sambo."

National tempests blended on Wednesday, May 26. McGeorge Bundy returned from the Dominican Republic to Washington, where John Tower of Texas led an outcry for a federal investigation of the sporting "nadir" in Lewiston, charging that the "use of citizen-owned television airways keeps boxing alive in its present highly questionable form." Tower cast one of only two Republican votes that day against final Senate passage of the voting rights bill. Strom Thurmond of South Carolina, before casting the other, eulogized the Senate as the "final resting place of the Constitution and the rule of law, for it is here that they will have been buried with shovels of emotion under piles of expediency, in the year of our Lord, 1965." Defeated Southern Democrats foresaw a "federal dictatorship" over the vote process to cement the economic impoverishment of "garden variety" white people that their leader, Senator Richard Russell of Georgia, pronounced already inevitable from the Civil Rights Act of 1964. Ironically, Russell was one of the few national figures to speak publicly for Muhammad Ali after his conversion to a black Islamic sect, commending his "unpopular" stand against racial integration. The *New York Times,* on the other hand, crusaded for civil rights but disdained both the Lewiston fight and Ali himself* with two front-page stories marshaling disgust—"Clay-Liston

---

* The editors of *Sports Illustrated,* having concluded from studying film of the fight that "a stunning right-handed punch" stopped Liston fairly, criticized the press for raging against the bout's perceived brutality and nonbrutality with indiscriminate zeal that "verged on the hysterical." *Times* reporter Robert Lipsyte was embarrassed that his paper insistently referred to Ali as Cassius Clay, denying him an identity right routinely accorded the users of stage names from Lauren Bacall (Betty Perske) to the Pope.

Fight Arouses Wide Demand for Inquiry"—and a tart editorial hoping the "brief and gentle Clay-Liston encounter" would end "a sport as sick as this one."

With Senate passage of the voting bill, President Johnson publicly gave thanks "on behalf of a heartened nation." He urged swift concurrence in the House, and none doubted the power of his words. Johnson's domestic program commanded "such wide appeal that powerful voices of criticism are virtually nonexistent," and his mastery of political rumblings over Vietnam and the Dominican Republic "only makes Congress seem another pygmy at his feet," *Times* correspondent Tom Wicker wrote that week in a summary essay. For an era of great change, with world stability and even political language in flux, Wicker portrayed Johnson as a colossus of national strength. "Lyndon Johnson, in fact, may be the best John Wayne part ever written," he observed. "[He] seems 20 feet tall—when he really measures no more than 10."

CHAPTER 18

Leaps of Faith

May 27–July 2, 1965

M A S S I V E transitions loomed for summer. Nearly three thousand Southern school districts turned from defensive stall in the federal courts to stampede the sleepiest bureaucracy in Washington. They questioned exactly how to obtain from the U.S. Office of Education a letter certifying each district's compliance with the desegregation provisions of the Civil Rights Act of 1964, as required to be eligible for future appropriations under the giant new education program. "We believe we are entitled to official written guidelines and criteria," one superintendent asserted. Late in April, when Commissioner of Education Francis Keppel issued such rules, lawyers from some of the most resistant areas brazenly declared their districts desegregated already. (Technically, they laid claim to federal money pending their reserved argument that separate schools were the product of "natural" rather than official causes.) These were Wallace people— "screaming and hollering revolution and defiance," confided Governor Carl Sanders, who admitted that they held a strong base in his own state of Georgia.

Sanders privately described his desperate struggle to "put a muzzle on Mr. Wallace . . . to keep this whole section of the country from just following some idiotic leadership." Moderate segregationists would tolerate racially mixed classes in planned stages, he told President Johnson in May, but they could not survive politically if they must integrate the teachers, too. "You know and I know that I couldn't do that with a shotgun," he groaned. Sanders, looking instead to integrate some faculty *meetings* in a few years, said schools would self-destruct before letting the first Negro teacher preside over a classroom of white students. Johnson commiserated effusively. "I know what you've got to do, and God, I just, my heart bleeds for you," he told Sanders, opining that every human being yearned to do right. "But wantin' to do what's right and doing what's right's two different things," said the President, "and sometimes it's a long hill to climb in between." Johnson sidestepped the pressure by rejoicing over the recent delivery to Sanders of a mounted deer head from a hunting trip at the LBJ Ranch, but Sanders called back five days later to seek relaxed terms of compliance for the new school year looming ahead. "I've got my back to the wall, I'm in the corner, and my hands are up," he told Johnson. "I'm just asking for mercy. . . . We're not asking for delay or any suspension of the rules."

Opposing forces whipsawed Commissioner Keppel over the status of the earliest thousand plans submitted to the Office of Education. "Virtually all place the burden of initiating change not on the school boards, the practitioners of segregation, but on their victims," objected NAACP leader Roy Wilkins in mid-May, "the Negro parents and pupils who must bear the financial costs involved and must request and obtain transfer from Negro to white schools." Wilkins called the "freedom of choice" plans a cruel fraud that invited persecution of volunteer families. School boards, on the other hand, complained of nitpicking by federal officials. Lawmakers who had defied the *Brown* decision and filibustered the civil rights bills now denounced the obstruction of laggard bureaucrats. "It is most disturbing to me," wrote Senator Sam Ervin of North Carolina, "that the tireless efforts of Cabarrus County to comply with the Commissioner's order are still frustrated." With enormous consequences in the balance, including possible inoculation against future lawsuits, politicians and school representatives jammed the Office of Education. Pandemonium reigned over makeshift files bulging from cabinets across desks and down along the floor. A handful of legal consultants reinforced the overwhelmed civil servants—mostly second-career school administrators, who normally compiled educational abstracts—and the compliance unit spilled into an office barracks called Temporary S, one of the last surviving emergency structures built near the Capitol for World War II.

Across the Mall, officials finalized parallel campaigns no less daunting. Justice Department lawyers prepared for wholesale redeployment after the voting rights bill, and President Johnson tantalized the president of Howard University, James Nabrit, about hosting a major pronouncement on economic justice issues beyond the end of segregation. Johnson swore Nabrit to silence on pain of cancellation, forbidding even contingency plans to reprint the commencement programs or warn Rev. Walter Fauntroy that a last-minute speaker might displace him. Nabrit nearly burst with anticipation, as no historically Negro college had conferred an honorary degree upon a sitting U.S. President. Mortified, he could only plead ignorance about the purpose of Secret Service agents who scoured his campus on the last day in May.

At Justice, lawyers addressed intergovernmental disputes over the mechanics of superseding local voter registrars across the South. Who would undertake the unwelcome temporary duty, and where would they live? FBI officials resisted assignments to protect recruits, as did the U.S. Marshals Service. Postal authorities objected to a "fortress" concept of rural post offices as registration sites. Representatives from the Civil Service Commission wanted first to test the "easy" voting districts untouched yet by violence, but others insisted on demonstration projects to break the toughest resistance. Negro registrars, while accepted in principle, were tacitly forbidden, and managers worked diligently to prevent human-interest publicity about the pioneer bureaucrats.

Beyond deployment of the registrar corps, the Civil Rights Division of the Justice Department looked to shift its enormous litigation drive from voting rights to school desegregation. The guiding strategy, announced in advance by Attorney General Katzenbach, was that democratization in both these areas needed the coordinated pressure of law and politics. ("*The courts acting alone have failed,*" appellate judges themselves candidly emphasized in a marathon school case.) Title IV of the 1964 Civil Rights Act newly authorized the Justice Department to initiate school desegregation lawsuits, complementing the administrative mandate under Title VI for nondiscriminatory use of federal funds across the board, from schools and hospitals to defense plants.

Katzenbach held back a remnant of the thirty front-line civil rights lawyers for the routine trauma of exceptional events. In Panola County, Mississippi, on June 2, exhorted by Fannie Lou Hamer, seventy Negroes tried to walk the first picket line since the 1930s for improvement of local farm wages ($3 gross per day), and were summarily evicted from privately owned sharecroppers' shacks by prison work gangs, under a local injunction soon to be tested in federal court. That same night, violence struck Bogalusa, Louisiana, where the Justice Department was seeking Title I relief against six holdout restaurants that refused to serve Negroes, and where John Doar, head of the Civil Rights Division, had negotiated for police tolerance of peaceful demonstrations to integrate the city park, public library, and several businesses. Bushwhackers pulled alongside the patrol car of the first two minority officers hired (for police duties restricted to fellow Negroes), and killed Deputy Sheriff O'Neal Moore. Deputy Creed Rogers, surviving shotgun wounds, sent out a radio description that led to the arrest of Klansman Ray McElveen within the hour.

The next morning, at a confidential June 3 briefing for Democratic leaders, President Johnson's grim outlook on Vietnam moved Senator Russell Long of Louisiana to recommend that the United States "face up to the sixty-four-dollar question and bomb China." Senate Majority Leader Mike Mansfield emphatically disagreed. Later that morning, following televised celebrations for the safe launch of the Gemini 4 space mission, the President challenged a delegation of corporate executives to create summer jobs that would get chronically unemployed teenagers "off the streets and behind the [work] bench." He told the executives only partly in jest that St. Peter soon would ask "what you did with your affluence and what you did as a beneficiary of this great system of government." Then, before a quick trip to Chicago, Johnson approved the last-minute draft of his intended agenda on race and released President Nabrit from secrecy into frenzied revision of the next day's graduation ceremony in Washington.

Barriers to freedom were "tumbling down," Johnson told the audience of five thousand at Howard University. "But freedom is not enough." He foresaw a new and "more profound stage" of battle ahead—to seek "not just freedom but opportunity . . . not just equality as a right and a theory, but equality as a fact and as a result." To frame a visionary future, Johnson confronted the past with sweeping metaphors from warfare and sports. "You do not take a person who, for years, has been hobbled by chains, and liberate him, bring him up to the starting line of a race," declared the President, "and then say, 'you are free to compete with all the others,' and still justly believe that you have been completely fair."

Johnson described the remaining handicap as a virulent form of the "inherited, gateless poverty" that stubbornly plagued segments of the whole population, including white families in largest number. Its heritage and prospects were distinct by race, he observed, "for Negro poverty is not white poverty." Captured Africans had landed in the status of products imported for servitude, uniquely by contrast with the self-selected immigrant waves of other new Americans. The non-African arrivals endured hardships far short of chattel slavery or segregation, said Johnson, and none yet faced such ostracism by race and color. He called the distinctive racial animus "a feeling whose dark intensity is matched by no other prejudice in our society."

The speech hushed the crowd. Some brash students trimmed their snickers, having expected the "White Father Texan" to claim tribute from a sea of dark faces for historic victories on their behalf. Instead, Johnson already had abandoned the safer political conceits—that the burden was fading naturally, or peculiar to the South, or manageable by a piece of law—to address what he called "the much grimmer story" of human result. He said most Negroes—the near and distant kin of the achieving graduates before him—remained among the "uprooted and the dispossessed," shut in slums, "losing ground every day," unskilled and poorly educated. "They still are another nation," the President declared. Although he retreated at times to impersonal statistics on unemployment and income, his images closed relentlessly on damaged, unveiled faces. "They are anguishing to observe," he said. "For the Negro they are a constant reminder of oppression. For the white they are a constant reminder of guilt." He charged that "long years of degradation" had broken apart Negro families "on a massive scale," with crippling effect on young children. "This, too, is not pleasant to look upon," said Johnson.

Not since Lincoln's second inaugural had a President confronted the weight of centuries so intimately. Like Lincoln, who lifted up the whole of "American Slavery" as the offense that "all knew" had caused the Civil War "somehow"—not limiting responsibility to Southern slavery, or Confederate treason—Johnson confessed a national legacy still fearfully submerged. Like Lincoln, who quoted Psalm 19 to postulate that four years of untold carnage *still* might not atone for unrequited crimes,* Johnson spoke of penance and resolve. Only an accidental mis-

---

* "Fondly do we hope—fervently do we pray—that this mighty scourge of war may speedily pass away," Lincoln said toward the end of his address on March 4, 1865. "Yet, if God wills that it continue, until all the wealth piled by the bondman's two hundred and fifty years of unrequited toil shall be sunk, and until every drop drawn with the lash, shall be paid by another drawn with the sword, as was said three thousand years ago, so still it must be said, 'the judgments of the Lord, are true and righteous altogether.' "

reading of his text broke the spell, when he pledged to seek specific remedies at a fall conference of experts featuring "Negro leaders of both races." Howard students chuckled over a gaffe that evoked classical DuBois on split identity as well as contemporary jokes about bourgeois Negroes trying to be white. Johnson recovered quickly to extol "the glorious opportunity of this generation to end the one huge wrong of the American nation." Like Lincoln, he embraced freedom in biblical cadence as a builder's quest "to dissolve, as best we can, the antique enmities of the heart, which diminish the holder, divide the great democracy, and do wrong—great wrong—to the children of God."

The June 4 address soon would tear the historical sky like a lightning bolt. Johnson opened new ground on his own, skipping the travail of petitions and demonstrations from the civil rights movement, with bold words the *New York Times* called "remarkable in the history of the Presidency." Martin Luther King saluted Johnson by wire "for your magnificent speech . . . [that] evinced amazing sensitivity." Almost overnight, however, interpretation began to refract. Johnson spoke to and for the whole nation, but at times he adopted a white point of view. He spoke with moral certainty—declaring, for instance, that "white America must accept responsibility" for broken Negro families—but he called for scholarship on baffling mysteries along the racial divide. ("We are not completely sure why this is," he said of the stark, obdurate inequality. "The causes are complex and subtle. . . . Nor do we fully understand all of the problems.") His ambiguities bounced toward opposite conclusions. The *Times* declared the Howard speech a summons to national investment that would make the $1 billion War on Poverty "seem incredibly puny." On the same day, a respected columnist for the *Washington Star* announced that Johnson's real purpose was to lay open "the failure of Negro family life" as the "hitherto most delicate subject" of national concern. "In persuading the Negroes to talk frankly about their own troubles," wrote Mary McGrory, "he hopes they will find solutions of their own." These polar comments were inklings of political mayhem.

Far away in Bogalusa, bushwhackers struck again on the night of the Howard speech. Sheriff Dorman Crowe identified them as "half-witted white kids" incensed by news reports that a Negro would be eligible for state employee survivor's insurance. The attorney general of Louisiana already had disqualified the widow of Deputy O'Neal Moore, ruling that he had not been murdered "while engaged in the direct apprehension of a person," as technically required, and prosecution of Moore's accused killer was securely stalled (the investigation to be reopened more than twenty years later, in 1989), as often occurred in such cases. Even so, said Sheriff Crowe, young attackers, egged on by their parents, shot up his white deputy's home to deter "race traitors" in law enforcement. "These people actually believe in their hearts that the Communists would take over before twelve o'clock if it wasn't for them," he told reporters.

*　*　*

MAMMOTH CHICAGO had swallowed poverty in legions since May 15, 1917, the starting date fixed by publisher Robert Abbott for a modern "Flight Out of Egypt." With shameless tales of balmy winters around the Great Lakes, and with banner headlines about contrasting frost in Georgia and Louisiana ("NEGRO FROZEN TO DEATH IN FIRELESS GRETNA HUT"), his newspaper promoted $3 train tickets to lure refugees from a region that had not yet established its first public high school for Negroes. "SAVED FROM THE SOUTH," the *Chicago Defender* cried to welcome hordes that rode against the flow of the Mississippi River—two thousand reaching the Illinois Central Terminal each day at the peak—hungry to replace war-departed doughboys in factory jobs. Sixty-five thousand emigrants stayed put in Chicago within two years, more than doubling its Negro population, and the staid *Chicago Tribune* recognized the national migration in a scare headline tinged with pride: "HALF A MILLION DARKIES FROM DIXIE SWARM TO THE NORTH TO BETTER THEMSELVES."

The Chicago Real Estate Board reacted swiftly with a 1917 resolution that each block of Negro housing "shall be filled solidly, and that further expansion shall be confined to contiguous blocks, and that the present method of obtaining a single building in scattered blocks be discontinued." Hostility flashed along contested borders even beyond the city beachfront into Lake Michigan, such that when young Negro Eugene Williams floated across an imaginary line extending 29th Street, he was stoned from his swim-raft and drowned on July 27, 1919, touching off wild rumors of gang pillage that came partially true over five days of skittering violence—leaving thirty-eight people dead, twenty-three black and fifteen white, injuring 537 in like ratio—until quelled by 6,500 militia and prolonged summer rains. The Chicago Race Riot of 1919 set the national mark for upheaval in the nativist era of World War I. Like the Black Sox baseball scandal later the same year, and the violent Haymarket labor clashes of 1886, it was an epochal event befitting Chicago's immense blend of rawness and order—vast stockyards, exquisite architecture, giants in violence and art.

Brokers and regulators squeezed Negro migrants southward through 1920s Chicago, past Al Capone's headquarters at the Lexington Hotel. At Café de Champion, the legendary ex-heavyweight Jack Johnson—once hounded from the ring into federal prison for flaunting a white mistress—presided over one of the State Street nightspots where Louis Armstrong and Jelly Roll Morton developed Southern blues into jazz among peers. ("I saw Duke Ellington, Earl Hines, Cassino Simpson, and Art Tatum in a piano playing contest at the Annex Café," recalled one astonished observer.) Singer Cab Calloway enjoyed what he called a "damned comfortable" married life in a bordello not far from all-Negro Olivet Baptist Church, which mushroomed more properly to become the largest Protestant congregation in the United States. With black settlement following a line of least resistance into Jewish Southside Chicago, Greater Bethel AME bought the Jewish Lakeside Club in 1922, and Pilgrim Baptist acquired the landmark structure designed by the firm of Dankmar Adler and Louis Sullivan for Chicago's oldest synagogue, Temple KAM (the Hebrew acronym of *Kehilath Anshe Ma'ariv,* "Men of the West Congregation").

World War II loosed a second, larger northward flood, abetted by International Harvester's publicized field test of a mechanical cotton-picker near Clarksdale, Mississippi, on October 2, 1944. "Each machine did the work of fifty people," wrote poverty historian Nicholas Lemann. Families of obsolete sharecroppers raised the population of Chicago alone by an average of five hundred Negroes every week for twenty consecutive years, and again they followed a settlement pattern cleaved by Jews—this time into West Chicago through the old Maxwell Street ghetto where open-air markets of live chickens and Yiddish newspapers once teemed with half-starved Slavic immigrants in broad-brimmed hats and black overcoats called kapotes, whose plight had moved Jane Addams to create the Hull House community refuge. The desperate energy of Maxwell Street incubated boyhood talent from swing clarinetist Benny Goodman to CBS president William Paley, from gangster accountant Jake "Greasy Thumb" Guzik to Supreme Court Justice Arthur Goldberg. As families gained footholds, the Eastern European Jews built their own schools, clubs, and even hospitals, because their more sophisticated predecessors on the South Side—lumped together as the "German Jews"—systematically excluded them. In turn, the most recent and ragged migration of Southern black people crowded down the stately West Chicago *"Judenstrasse"* of Douglas Boulevard after World War II. They displaced nearly a hundred thousand Jews from the neighborhoods of Lawndale, where fifteen synagogues closed for resale in a single year, 1953. The Hebrew Theological College moved from Lawndale to the suburbs in 1954, just as the bellwether Marshall Field retail stores at last modified company rules that forbade Negro employees.

With dwelling areas subdivided repeatedly into slum density, the onrushing migrants bulged against settlement "confined to contiguous blocks." Elizabeth Wood, the first director of the Chicago Housing Authority, sought to disperse "managed integration" into low-rise housing developments, but mobs a thousand strong, mostly of young white women, besieged new apartments near Midway Airport for two weeks in 1946 to drive out the first two selected families of decorated World War II veterans. Wood persisted until a last Pyrrhic victory in 1954, chronicled for magazine readers by South Africa's anti-apartheid novelist, Alan Paton, when Betty and Don Howard lasted a year in one of the 462 units at Trumbull Park Homes, under police escort to and from work, with windows boarded against mobilized harassment by epithets, rocks, and bombs. ("My people will be in the streets," vowed neighborhood leader Louis Dinnocenzo, "as long as there are Negroes in the project.") With Wood fired, Richard J. Daley first won election as mayor in 1955 over the opposition of Chicago's three major white newspapers. Daley gained the *Defender's* endorsement with a tacit appeal that segregated public housing was better than none, and he gathered his victory margin of 125,000 votes from wards controlled by Negro bosses. As mayor, he used federal dollars to concentrate the most dislocated, unskilled Negroes still more within those wards, most notably in a gargantuan row of twenty-eight sixteen-story brick griddle-stacks down a corridor of South State Street bounded by the new Dan Ryan Expressway. Three-quarters of its first 27,000 residents were children, moving Elizabeth Wood to call such high-rise design "anti-family and anti-humane." Robert Taylor Homes, the world's largest public housing project on completion in 1962, would contain by 1970 two of the three poorest census tracts anywhere in the United States.

Machine politics contained Negro grievance for decades. In 1957, criticized for ignoring the *Brown* decision and the lynch murder of

Chicago's young Emmett Till, Negro ward bosses simply bought enough memberships in the local NAACP chapter—the nation's largest, claiming fifty thousand members—to replace the activist leader Willoughby Abner. He left behind a study of simmering consequence, "De Facto Segregation in the Chicago Public Schools," to be published the next year in the NAACP journal, *The Crisis*. Abner's surveyors found that more than 90 percent of Chicago's schools were effectively segregated. Admitting that de facto segregation was a "comparatively new expression," the *Crisis* study argued that Chicago officials diligently matched districts and teachers by race, in keeping with housing by contiguous blocks.

School Superintendent Benjamin Willis evaded the charge for seven years, first by insisting that his education bureaucracy was oblivious to color and did not even keep such records. When a small group of parents sued in 1961 for the right to transfer their children to less crowded schools near their homes, citing racial discrimination, city lawyers in *Webb v. Board of Education of Chicago* treated race itself as a dubious concept. They advanced a simpler, undisputed cause of crowded public schools—150,000 "extra" students in the past decade, equivalent to the entire student population of Pittsburgh—and defended Willis's efforts to fill the gap by breakneck school construction. The press called him "Big Ben the Builder." Future U.S. Commissioner of Education Francis Keppel, then dean of Harvard's School of Education, praised Willis in 1961 as "an administrative cyclone." Only gradually did independent investigations—some court-ordered, others by prestigious universities—corroborate allegations of managed disparity. White schools had six times the empty space of Negro ones, and one-fifth the burden of half-day "double shift" schedules. Ninety-four percent of new schools since 1955 were mono-racial. Nearly all the city's 189 mobile classrooms—derided as "Willis Wagons" by civil rights pickets—were stationed at all-black schools to absorb more black students.

To settle the 1961 *Webb* case, the Chicago Board of Education agreed in 1963 to conduct the first official head count of schools by race, and to permit—but not initiate—modest relief from unbalanced hardship. The carefully neutral stipulation, that students ranked in the top 5 percent by academic average could seek reassignment to a high school with an honors program, failed to conceal a potential breech of the color line. Seven hundred white parents picketed. More than two thousand held a mass meeting. Willis, who had opposed the settlement as an affront to his authority, successively declared fifteen white high schools ineligible to receive transfers, ducked out a back door to avoid service of court orders, and resigned rather than carry them out. These celebrated gestures sealed Willis as a public champion of white solidarity, causing the board to refuse his resignation, but they coincided with the March on Washington and the Birmingham church bombing—climactic events that shattered distance with opposing emotional force. ("Then came Birmingham," said Chicago civil rights leader Timuel Black, "which changed all space and time.") With a growing minority of crossover whites, nearly three thousand Chicagoans made a pilgrimage to Washington on train rides of heightened identification with the great migrations from the South. Their returning fervor was so widespread and palpable that Mayor Daley instructed Democratic precinct captains to tolerate a one-day protest of local school conditions.

Ten thousand demonstrators marched to the Board of Education on October 22, 1963, calling for the superintendent's resignation with signs that pilloried him as a bigot: "Willis—Wallace What's the Difference?" While such noise was no more than a hiccup in cavernous Chicago, an accompanying silence that same day rattled bystanders and participants alike. Nearly a quarter of a million students boycotted classrooms—224,700 by official figures—on release of the court-ordered count showing that Negroes comprised almost half (46.5 percent) of the 536,163 students in public schools. The enrollment census itself was a flare of startling light on migrant accumulations long in the shadow of public awareness. "Negroes are still a minority in Chicago," the *Tribune* assured readers in an editorial, urging that Mayor Daley and the school board "must refuse to knuckle under to such ultimatums from troublemakers." Protest organizers, for their part, were divided in the giddy aftermath of a near-total boycott that surpassed expectation tenfold. The NAACP and other groups withheld support from a follow-up boycott in 1964, which the Daley organization actively opposed, and debate stagnated on whether the turnout of roughly 150,000 constituted a relative letdown or gain. With civil rights negotiators looking to the retirement of Superintendent Willis in 1965, on expiration of his third four-year contract, general attitudes about Northern poverty and segregation lapsed into rosy disregard. "Many Negroes have improved their lot by moving to the cities," observed *BusinessWeek*. "But many others still live in the rural South." The *Chicago Daily News*, in marked contrast with its support for the Selma demonstrations, dismissed a bad memory of local outbursts that "alternately frightened or bored much of Chicago," and gave thanks that the city's protest coalition "for all effective purposes . . . has expired."

* * *

So LAY the ground on May 27, 1965, when three Daley appointees on the Board of Education switched votes to grant Willis a four-year extension. Front-page news revived spasms of outrage, first in an overnight call from Chicago NAACP leaders for an unprecedented five-day boycott of public schools. Dissenters instantly faulted them for ignoring some thirty other groups in the civil rights coalition. *Jet* magazine reported allied leaders suspicious that "the usually legalistic Chicago NAACP" rushed to escalate a tactic it had derided as waning, counterproductive, and exploitive of school children. King's aide James Bevel, up from Alabama, warned the leadership caucus never to plunge into sacrifice without a movement strategy. Angry voices scorned as wastefully misguided any further protest aimed at "stooges" in education, and dared the coalition to attack the pervasive influence of Mayor Daley. Tempestuous night sessions deadlocked through more than a week of growing recrimination. "Civil rights forces of Chicago are the laughingstock of America!" shouted a coalition delegate on June 5, the night after President Johnson's speech at Howard University.

In frustration, late on Monday, June 7, coalition leader Al Raby left a stalled caucus to carry out a small "pray-in" on the sidewalk—asking for reconsideration of the Willis contract, receiving instead his first trip to jail. Before he could make bail the next day, city lawyers obtained a court injunction barring all the affiliated civil rights groups from any part in a school boycott. When students organized their own walkout on June 10, in numbers estimated upward from sixty thousand, Raby led some of the enjoined adults separately from Soldier Field in a long walk along the edge of defiance—avoiding forbidden school zones, spilling with sympathetic pedestrians into downtown streets, kneeling as a mass in traffic outside City Hall. Mayor Daley announced before the morning of June 11 that there would be no more such marches. Hours later, hemmed in by a police blockade near the perimeter of Grant Park, Raby asked the lines to sit in resistance, and officers hauled away a determined remnant of 252 people, including James Farmer, architect of the 1961 Freedom Rides, who had been a founder of national CORE in Chicago more than twenty years earlier. The *Tribune* called the incident "one of the largest mass arrests" in city annals.

"Who is this man Al Raby?" asked Mayor Daley, in a fit of pique that generated press inquiries and an FBI investigation. He was born in Chicago of Mississippi and Louisiana parents who had met in the World War I migration. In 1935, when Raby was two, his father had fallen ill and died of appendicitis while serving Depression-era guard duty on a mail truck. Shuffled among siblings, Raby dropped out of fourth grade and shined shoes as a truant near the Pershing Hotel. Later, once U.S. Army life brought home the limits of street savvy at minimum literacy, he stuffed himself into small desks through remedial grade school and five years of night classes, to earn a teaching certificate in 1960. In the cause of a colleague fired for her support of the *Webb* suit, he became a charter member of Teachers for Integrated Schools, which rose to prominence within the ad hoc protest coalition on the fresh example of vulnerable teachers. "You don't think these children can be saved," Raby told the Chicago school board of his students at Hess School in Lawndale. "I know they can." To answer the mass arrest of June 11, he joined 196 people handcuffed the next day at the "world's busiest intersection" of State and Madison—mostly first-time detainees full of apprehension about the bare-knuckle reputation of Chicago jails. They included several nuns and Richard Morrisroe, a second-year priest whose mother had emigrated from County Kerry, Ireland, as a governess. Raby, like Morrisroe and many of the 448 people in jail, drew on catalyzing experience three months earlier in Selma. Having answered King's call by long journey to Brown Chapel, and made vigil at the "Berlin Wall" rope, they renewed reciprocal entreaties for King to rally a nonviolent movement in Chicago.

King promised a reply that summer. He still chased appointments through clouds of trouble, behind schedule after a graduation address at Wilberforce College, fending off press inquiries about Communism and more complaints about his staff—lately from clergy scandalized by Bevel's offhand remarks at an ecumenical seminar in Atlantic City that Mary probably was not a virgin and may have conceived Jesus by a Roman soldier—arriving so tardy at Hempstead, New York, on June 13 that distraught Hofstra University officials had been casting about for a substitute commencement speaker, then missing an Ohio reception in his honor, oversleeping, hurrying into robes for graduation at Oberlin College. A dose of levity lingered from the chance selection on King's previous visit there, amid lockdown tension over death threats, of a first question written by a child—"How do you feel about homework?"—

but circumstance stirred new anxiety at the traditionally liberal school founded by abolitionists. "It is not enough to say we must not wage war," King told the Oberlin audience in a reprise of his Nobel Prize lecture. "We must love peace, and sacrifice for it." Beneath thunderous crescendos of approval—widely interpreted as dissent from incipient war in Vietnam—ran undercurrents of respectful discomfort for Secretary of State Dean Rusk, King's fellow honoree on the stage.

In the short interval before yet another graduation speech that week in Ohio—at Antioch College, Coretta's alma mater—King gave instructions in Atlanta to some three hundred SCOPE volunteers to fan out through fifty rural Southern counties. SCOPE's chief trainer and field marshal Hosea Williams introduced Bayard Rustin, who at length introduced Bevel and King. "Negroes have seen what white America has done with its freedom, and are worried," said Bevel, preaching an antidote of nonviolence by "undiscourageable good will." King took a mixed tactical line. Publicly, he emphasized the priority of the SCOPE summer mission, which helped him disengage gracefully from his announced boycott of Alabama. Privately, he urged caution on the mostly white volunteers, charging them to avoid risks of injury and repression that the new voting law soon would reduce. He sought to inspire them for greater possibilities, saying the new voters they met would send ripples of freedom outward from the South.

* * *

WITH COMEDIAN Dick Gregory, prisoner Al Raby managed to send a telegram down the Mississippi: "Greetings from the Chicago movement in the 11th Police Station to our brothers and sisters in the Jackson jail." The wire arrived June 15 along with SNCC chairman John Lewis and two hundred new prisoners joining nearly five hundred already locked overnight in a special stockade. The Mississippi dragnets made front-page news with plainly unsavory details about the treatment of silent marchers to the capitol—hauled away in garbage trucks, confined in livestock barns at the state fairgrounds, some hospitalized for treatment of beatings, all by officers who concealed their badge numbers under electrician's tape. (Charles Marx, deputy chief of the Mississippi Highway Patrol, publicly called the tape a precautionary habit: "We just been doing it ever since this mess started with those Freedom Rides in '61.") Still, reporters drifted away from a story that lacked fresh resonance, in part because of its complex political setting. The Mississippi legislature was quietly repealing a dozen laws that discouraged the

Negro vote—hardly from remorse or concession, but to lay tactical groundwork for a double-joined appeal to void the federal voting law as a moot usurpation of state authority. To protest the "stealth" session, movement organizers from the Mississippi Freedom Democratic Party (MFDP) hastily had redeployed supporters convened in Jackson. June Johnson, the teenager infamously beaten with Fannie Lou Hamer inside the Winona jail two years earlier, was dispatched from Greenwood by her grandmother to find out what happened to her mother, and eventually located her as a fellow prisoner. Parents from New York wrote one white volunteer, who had stayed on since Freedom Summer, that they lied miserably to their friends to avoid trying to explain her incarceration. MFDP chairman Lawrence Guyot urgently wired King for help: "COME TO JACKSON MISS. NOW." A pastor from Huntsville, Alabama, gained entrance to the fairgrounds long enough to be choked in a rolling wall of gas applied by a "fumigation machine." With two church colleagues from the national Commission on Religion and Race, he rushed to testify at a congressional briefing the next day in Washington: "We inspected what we can only describe as a concentration camp."

*　*　*

THE LATEST, and last, civilian government in South Vietnam fell on June 12 to a military junta headed by Vice Marshal Nguyen Cao Ky, who wore pearl-handled pistols and was described by State Department officials as "absolutely the bottom of the barrel." The next day, a classified cable from General Westmoreland raised haunting signs of military collapse: "Thus, we are approaching the kind of warfare faced by the French in the latter stages of their efforts here." This alarm reinforced Westmoreland's new "bombshell" appeal for wholesale American rescue, superseding already the grim calculation from April that measured reinforcements—still being shipped,* not yet announced—would suffice, in McNamara's words, "to protect us against catastrophe." The President bemoaned cumulative, pending requests to raise U.S. troop strength in Vietnam from 33,000 to 175,000 in 1965, "with plans developed," cabled Westmoreland, "to deploy even greater forces, if and when required." Simultaneously, Johnson decried hopes

---

* McNamara warned that news "may begin to leak out, because it is quite a substantial operation to move 15–16000 men, 450 helicopters, 10,000 miles, and get them there within eight weeks from today, roughly."

for a negotiated settlement as fatuous and unrealistic, confiding to Senator Birch Bayh that "the North Vietnamese just said, 'fuck you,' that's exactly what they said," to overtures for talks. "And I don't blame them!" Johnson exclaimed. "I defeated Goldwater by fifteen million [votes]. Now why would I want to give Goldwater half my cabinet? They're winning—why would they want to talk?" A week later, he growled at McNamara over the failure of experts to devise any strategy "except just praying and gasping to hold on during monsoon and hope they'll quit. I don't believe they're ever going to quit."

That night, June 21, McGeorge Bundy debated the Vietnam War on national television, making up for his absence from the May teach-in. His opponent, Columbia professor Hans Morgenthau, stopped short of an argument for American withdrawal, declining to assume straightforward responsibility for Cold War defeat and for the fate of non-Communist Vietnamese. By advocating instead a minimal U.S. intervention, with "face-saving" diplomacy, he became one of many critics and politicians who would open themselves to charges of evasive muddling. Bundy accused Morgenthau of "giving vent to his congenital pessimism," citing his earlier predictions that the Marshall Plan would fail and that the Kennedy administration could not prevent a Communist regime in Laos. "I may have been dead wrong on Laos," Morgenthau replied, "but that doesn't prove that I am dead wrong on Vietnam." He found himself on the defensive, skewered by the very doubt that was abundant inside the White House.

President Johnson cared little that pundits thought Bundy won the showdown. Focused entirely on the ramifications of debate itself, he was furious with Bundy for disregarding direct and indirect warnings that candor pushed the administration toward political minefields. "I'm just against the White House debating," Johnson had told Bundy emphatically. "I'm against us inciting them, and I'm against us inviting them, and I'm against us encouraging it, and I'm against us applauding it." Formal debate set precedent, he warned, and opened pressure for facts. "I don't want you reporting to Mendel Rivers," the President said of the bellicose House committee chairman from South Carolina, reminding Bundy that many like Rivers saw any bad military report as a call for all-out war. (Even moderate House Minority Leader Gerald Ford responded to Johnson's confidential notice of recent air strikes with alarming nonchalance: "Did we use conventional uh, weapons?") The President argued that accepting debate with a professor ("the man with the beard . . . with no responsibility") made it harder for the White House to resist detailed disclosure to elected representatives. Having commended to Bundy the evasive, nonspecific prognosis for Vietnam that McNamara gave Rivers—"There are some things that I'm above you on"—he saw the television debate as rank insubordination. Bill Moyers deflected two or three of his volcanic reactions, as usual, but eventually complied. "The president sent me down to fire you," he told Bundy sheepishly. They reached calm agreement that Bundy would arrange to leave the government by the end of the year.

Johnson groaned under conflicting pressures on Vietnam. "I am pretty depressed reading all these proposals," he told McNamara. The CIA assessment was bleak: "If we succeed in not losing the war during this monsoon season (through October, say), what we will have won is a chance to settle down to a protracted struggle." Undersecretary of State George Ball proclaimed that Johnson faced a "last clear chance" to stop "drifting toward a major war—that nobody wants," and renewed his plea in a flurry of secret papers: "No one can assure you that we can beat the Viet Cong or even force them to the conference table on our terms no matter how many hundred thousand *white foreign* (US) troops we deploy. . . . Once we suffer large casualties we will have started a well-nigh irreversible process. . . . *I think humiliation would be more likely than the achievement of our objectives—even after we had paid terrible costs.*" Also at State, McGeorge Bundy's brother, William, endured "a small state of personal crisis" over Ball's lone explorations about how to make "cutting our losses" palatable to allied nations, and nearly made common cause, but "still could not accept the idea of early American withdrawal." Instead, William Bundy sent President Johnson a "middle way" proposal to hold on in Vietnam without reinforcements. Secretary Rusk, though still reluctant to accept American combat, rushed to the White House a note of distress that his own top aides were flirting with retreat. He warned that failure in Vietnam, by threatening peace commitments worldwide, "would lead to our ruin and almost certainly to catastrophic war." With McNamara, Rusk pushed to restrict the "exceedingly dangerous" knowledge that the Ball position even reached the White House.

The Vietcong announced on June 24 the execution of a captured Army sergeant, Harold G. Bennett, and blew up a floating Saigon restaurant the next day. From a kind of centrifuge, McGeorge Bundy labored to frame rational choice as the secretly lame-duck National Security Adviser. Preliminary disagreements already estranged him from two influential friends in the press: Walter Lippmann, who thought he was deceitfully pro-war, and Joe Alsop, who scorned him as disgracefully timid. ("I've never known him [Alsop] to go to any area where blood could be spilled that he didn't come back and say more blood," Bundy complained to President Johnson. "This is his posture toward the universe.") Inside the government, Bundy and McNamara contained mutual dismay. McNamara winced at Bundy's description of his recommended troop buildup as "rash to the point of folly," and wondered how Bundy could suggest in the same memo an alternative threat of nuclear attack. Bundy, for his part, barely concealed shock that McNamara proposed to send Westmoreland forty-four combat battalions in spite of the military consensus that they could achieve no better than stalemate. "What are the chances of our getting into a white man's war with all the brown men against us or apathetic?" he wrote. "Still more brutally," he asked the President, "do we want to invest 200 thousand men to cover an eventual retreat? Can we not do that just as well where we are?"

Minutes before a morning showdown on July 2, Johnson called former President Eisenhower to ask the nation's most respected general (and Republican) whether it was wise to confine troops within enclaves around airbases in Vietnam. Eisenhower confirmed military advice that such defensive posture made no sense once an "appeal to force" was made. "You think that we can really beat the Vietcong out there?" asked Johnson, in what seemed to Eisenhower a plaintive tone. He encouraged Johnson to go ahead on the combat offensive, with resolve not to be run out of a free country the United States had helped create. Johnson then summoned the contending advisers into the Cabinet Room—McNamara, Ball, Rusk, Bundy—for a cross-examination that ran nearly two hours until he stalled them with orders to scour the earth for alternatives, breaking away to St. Matthew's Cathedral, site of President Kennedy's funeral, for a personal event labeled for still greater secrecy in the White House schedule—"STRICTLY OFF RECORD." A terse public announcement caught the press by surprise once the stoic, tearful family had left Luci Johnson behind for first confession after the baptism that accomplished her conversion to the Catholic faith. "I could not help but think we went in four," Lady Bird painfully recorded in her diary, "and came out three."

The coming of age for the younger daughter, on her eighteenth birthday, also marked exactly ten years since Johnson suffered his 1955 heart attack and one year since he signed the Civil Rights Act of 1964. Under that law, July 2 was the effective date for the Title VII provisions on fair employment, and lawyers for the NAACP Legal Defense Fund filed 476 discrimination complaints when the Equal Employment Opportunity Commission opened for business. To their eventual regret, the lawyers initially emphasized Southern paper and textile mills that were declining, anyway, which hampered compliance, but they also targeted racial discrimination by employers and labor unions nationwide—in companies as large as General Motors, Union Carbide, and U.S. Steel, over practices as esoteric as segregated payroll windows and white-only job-site Bible classes. Another 14,000 complaints would overwhelm the fledgling EEOC over its first eighteen months. Lacking enforcement powers, the five EEOC mediators settled 110 of those complaints in that time, and referred only fifteen to the Justice Department for litigation over such issues as the need to prove discriminatory "intent in the state of mind" at hiring, and over the legitimacy of any specific remedy under law—whether any minimum of Negro jobs could suffice, whether any nonminimum number was a prohibited quota. Most of the early cases stayed in litigation past 1970, but NAACP lawyers would win *Quarles v. Philip Morris* early in 1968. With tobacco unions desegregated by the elimination of Negro locals, a federal appeals court ruled that Philip Morris and the consolidated union must allow seniority to transfer into formerly all-white departments, sparing veteran Negro employees the extra risk of "suicide leap" promotion into newly integrated positions most vulnerable to layoff.

* * *

ONE QUESTION briefly diverted the tumultuous July 2 press conference on the new national commitment to an integrated workforce: "What about sex?"

"Don't get me started," replied Franklin D. Roosevelt, Jr. "I'm all for it." By hinting playfully that duty as first chairman of the EEOC would not hinder his personal life, Roosevelt skirted reminders that Title VII also prohibited employment discrimination by gender.

Nearly all reporters shared Roosevelt's bemusement, although a few publications did warn that any sex reform would undercut the herculean task of breaking caste restrictions for Negroes. The *New York Times* detailed a series of outlandish "possible effects" gleaned from interviews with lawyers: "Executive training programs will have to be opened to women, who are almost universally excluded from them; barbershop owners must be prepared to take job applications from women who want to wield razor and scissors." *The New Republic* magazine bluntly advised the EEOC not to take seriously "a mischievous joke perpetrated on the floor of the House of Representatives." (Southerners had introduced sex equality in a failed, last-minute scheme to kill the civil rights bill with chivalry.)

Some newspapers required prodding under the new law to eliminate racially segregated want-ad sections ("Help Wanted—Colored"). Journals everywhere still divided the want-ads by gender ("Help Wanted—Female," mostly for nurses, typists, and "Girl Friday" assistants), and even the soberest of them made sport of the sex amendment. Both the *Times* and *The Wall Street Journal* published front-page stories about a potential "bunny problem," imagining, as the *Journal* put it, "a shapeless, knobby-kneed male 'bunny' serving drinks to a group of stunned businessmen in a Playboy Club." Another news story in the *Times* mocked a group of women who rallied for access to traditionally male jobs—"Amelia Jenks Bloomer (who gave her name to pantaloons) would have been proud"—and a jocular editorial suggested that Congress might as well "just abolish sex itself."

Within the EEOC, a pose of virile insouciance spared employees from the prospect of opening nearly the entire American workforce by gender as well as race, over decades. "There are some people on this Commission who think that no man should be required to have a male secretary," the staff director announced shortly to the press. "And I am one of them."

CHAPTER 19

Gulps of Freedom

July 2–August 2, 1965

O N July 2, the last of the Mississippi demonstrators obtained bonded release from the makeshift jail at the Jackson fairgrounds. As King passed through Virginia that day, FBI officials were scrambling to fashion a more productive line of attack on him than disappointing wire service profiles in June. These stories had listed King's accomplishments alongside a litany of charges based on FBI leaks, striking a balance that disgusted Director Hoover. ("A 'whitewash' if there ever was one," Hoover scrawled on a widely published UPI release.) To impeach one conclusion reported by the Associated Press—that King lived modestly, whatever his faults, and worked from a small office with "dingy green walls and a bare floor"—headquarters ordered overseas agents to search for wealth King might have concealed in Swiss bank accounts, but this perennial suspicion was proving groundless when Assistant Director DeLoach grasped a different approach. FBI agents retrieved three separate recordings of Ralph Abernathy's Atlanta press conference on otherwise commonplace incidents—a SCOPE volunteer and seven Negroes beaten inside Antioch Baptist Church in Wilcox County, Alabama, two SCOPE volunteers cut by flying glass in Americus, Georgia—to verify the reply to one question about how King's Southern Christian Leadership Conference screened associates for Communist ties. "We will check with FBI men and they will tell us if they have a Communist background," Abernathy exaggerated grandly. "We don't want anything that is pink, much less anything that is red."

A transcript rocketed to Washington within hours, fueled by predatory outrage within the FBI over Abernathy's careless claim to a cooperative relationship. Hoover scribbled a precautionary note that "if I find anyone furnishing information to SCLC he will be dismissed," and DeLoach orchestrated an aggressive campaign to brand Abernathy's statement "absolutely untrue" behind the official stance that all FBI files were strictly confidential. His office distributed sharp, contemptuous statements to press contacts, DeLoach reported to colleagues, "so as to give the lie to Martin Luther King and his ilk." On Hoover's orders, top FBI officials received notice of the media offensive by the close of business on July 2.

These attacks trailed King into Chicago on the night of July 6. A few outlets printed them ("Fast Refutation by FBI"), but most had trouble fashioning news out of a disputed aside by the little-known Abernathy. One Illinois paper conflated the FBI rebuke with a fresh outburst from Mayor Daley, who, exasperated by nineteen days of local civil rights demonstrations, issued his own public charge of subversion on July 2: "We know Communists infiltrate all these organizations." For King, such controversy registered as familiar background nuisance. Flight delays pushed his arrival too late for a scheduled meeting with Al Raby at the Palmer House Hotel, and he was whisked into the ballroom to address the General Synod of the United Church of Christ. He saluted the mass witness of religious Americans over the past two years as an inspirational start. "The actual work to redeem the soul of America is before us," declared King, hinting at constructive tasks across broken barriers of race nationwide. "Not only are millions deprived of formal education and proper health facilities, but our most fundamental social unit—the family—is tortured, corrupted, and weakened by economic injustice," he said. "The church cannot look with indifference upon these glaring evils."

From the crush of a reception among church delegates, King appeared briefly at a press conference. Reporters wanted to know whether he planned to "take over" the upstart civil rights campaign in Chicago, and, strangely, they pressed for his reaction to reports of internecine strife since the previous day's national CORE convention in Durham, North Carolina. King parried both questions, then withdrew for consultations late into the night with his Chicago lawyer Chauncey Eskridge, Al Raby, and local CORE leader Willie Blue. Raby had just filed a complaint with U.S. Education Commissioner Francis Keppel, based on studies since the 1958 *Crisis* report, arguing that Chicago's effectively segregated schools should be "deprived of any and all Federal assistance" pursuant to Title VI of the 1964 Civil Rights Act. This novel petition—the first aimed at a Northern school district—was certain to magnify the stakes of local protest.

As King's staff debated the chances for a Chicago movement, Blue interjected theories about why the national CORE delegates had passed a Vietnam resolution calling for "an immediate withdrawal of all American troops," only to reconsider and table the same measure within hours on a personal appeal from James Farmer. There were grumblings implicating King's speech days earlier at all-Negro Virginia State College. A local reporter had picked up comments on Vietnam—"There is no reason why there cannot be peace rallies like we have freedom rallies. . . . We are not going to defeat Communism with bombs and guns and gases. . . . We must work this out in the framework of our democracy"—which moved over newswires to back pages in several newspapers. Gossip attributed the CORE reversal to hidden maneuvers and rivalries, which drew the press to whiffs of fresh controversy, but an incoming emergency call from Ralph Abernathy—intercepted by the Chicago police "Red Squad"—intervened after midnight with sickening word that Wilson Baker had arrested Rev. F. D. Reese for alleged embezzlement of the donations that had poured into Selma since the marches over Pettus Bridge. Press images of thieving Negro leaders loomed over a voting rights bill that was still stuck between the two houses of Congress.

J. Edgar Hoover was alerted to sensitivities over Vietnam that same evening of July 6. A solicitous call from Attorney General Katzenbach informed him that President Johnson and Secretary Rusk wanted an FBI investigation of the emerging King position on Vietnam, including possible Communist influences. Katzenbach confided that King's most prominent civil rights colleagues, Roy Wilkins and James Farmer, already had disparaged King for Vietnam comments they called wrongheaded and disloyal. For Hoover, the Katzenbach request landed as a welcome reversal by a nominal boss who had resisted his penchant for political intelligence to the point of barely civil relations. Far more important, it signaled a shift by the President, who had ignored scurrilous FBI reports on King since the day he entered the White House. Prior efforts to brand King subversive, which had bounced off Johnson's kindred domestic agenda, acquired sudden new promise across the trenches of the impending foreign war, and Hoover ordered overnight research on the obscure Asian country that might rescue FBI propaganda from flailing jabs at Ralph Abernathy. He delivered the next day a sanctioned, classified paper on "King's injection into the Vietnam situation."

*　*　*

KING ANNOUNCED that morning at the Palmer House that he had agreed "to spend some time in Chicago, beginning July 24." To skeptical questions about the point of demonstrations in a city without segregation laws, he replied that many "persons of good will" did not yet understand the breadth of the nonviolent movement, and that there was "a great job of interpretation to be done" before his first major campaign in the North. "During entire press conference," FBI observers cabled headquarters, "King was not questioned nor did he mention Viet Nam, or make any reference whatsoever to United States foreign policy." Leaving Andrew Young with Bevel to prepare his Chicago canvass, King flew to New York for an afternoon engagement and promptly canceled his evening flight to Los Angeles. There were too many ominous signs radiating over telephone lines, seeping into news—and too many historic changes teetering—for him to be content with guesses about the single most crucial vector in democracy. When an incoming call rang through on July 7 at 8:05 P.M., the White House log recorded Lyndon Johnson's first phone conversation initiated by King.

The President came on the line distant and cold. He grunted without recognition until King confirmed his name: "This is Martin King."

"Yes."

"How do you do, sir?"

"Fine."

"Fine," said King. "Glad to hear your voice."

"Thank you."

Johnson's clipped monosyllables hung until King abandoned pleasantry to ask about the voting rights bill. "I want to get your advice on this," he concluded.

Deference thawed the President. "I'll be glad to," he said, cranking into political calculations of such sustained acceleration that King would speak only one word ("very") over the next ten minutes. Johnson saw the opposing coalition of Republicans and crafty Southerners becoming more potent since Goldwater began to influence Republican leaders in Congress. "They're gonna quit the nigras," he said. "They will not let a nigra vote for them." Their current ploy was "to get a big fight started over which way to repeal the poll tax," he summarized, telling King that the Senate very nearly passed an amendment to abolish poll taxes as a form of racial discrimination, but the administration detected a mousetrap. Vermont had a dormant poll tax law, and Katzenbach warned that segregationists would welcome the amendment as an opening to challenge the overall bill from a state with virtually no Negroes. "They'll bring the case on Vermont," the President told King. "And that'll be the case that they'll take to the Court, and they will not hold that it is discriminatory in Vermont because it is not." Having originally instructed Katzenbach "to get rid of the poll tax any way in the world he could without nullifying the whole law," Johnson said Katzenbach's legal strategy was good politics. He vowed to keep the bill clean, and move separately to speed one of the pending Southern cases by which the Supreme Court was expected to void all poll taxes.

Johnson complained that House liberals could not resist temptation to add a poll tax amendment anyway. "[Speaker John] McCormack was afraid that somebody would be stronger for the Negro than he was," he fumed, "so he came out red hot for complete repeal." The imminent vote could be fatal, he told King, because any slight change in the Senate-passed bill would require a conference committee of both houses of Congress to reconcile differences. "So they get in an argument, and that delays it," he said. "And maybe nothing comes out." Any modified bill must repeat the legislative process in at least one chamber of Congress, and either hurdle a filibuster again in the Senate or "you got to go back to Judge [Howard] Smith" in the House. "You got to get a rule from him, and he won't give you a rule. He, he, he," Johnson sputtered, on the pitfalls of recircumventing the implacable Rules Committee chairman from Virginia. "So you got to file a [discharge] petition and take another twenty-one days . . . and they want to get out of here Labor Day. And they're playin' for that time. Now they been doin' that for thirty-five years that I been here, and I been watchin' 'em do it."

More than once Johnson reminded King of "my practical political problem" with the two Kennedy senators, both of whom supported poll tax repeal. He portrayed himself as a lonely President embattled on a dozen fronts while his civil rights allies were "all off celebratin' "— Wilkins at his convention, labor leaders George Meany and Walter Reuther on vacation, "and you're somewhere else." The opposition was "playin' us," said Johnson, "and we are not parliamentary smart

enough, if you want to be honest—now you asked advice, I'm just tellin'
you." He worked up a lather of shrewdness, rage, and self-pity that tickled King in spite of himself. "They want your wife to go one direction
and you to go the other," said the President.

"Yes," said King, chuckling.

"Then the kids don't know which one to follow," added Johnson.

King laughed as the President rounded through his tactical blueprint. "Well, I certainly appreciate this, Mr. President," he said, adding
softly that he was confident in Katzenbach on "this whole voting bill,"
and that always he had tried to make the movement helpful "as I was
telling you when we started in Alabama."

"You sure have and—" said Johnson. He checked himself, then responded more earnestly to King's personal reminder. "Well, you helped,
I think, to dramatize and bring it to a point where I could go before the
Congress in that night session, and I think that was one of the most effective things that ever happened," he declared. "But uh, you had
worked for months to help create the sentiment that supported it."

"Yes," said King.

"Now the trouble is that fire has gone out," added Johnson, not lingering on sentiment. "We got a few coals on it," he said, then reviewed
his plan to stoke the embers with cedar and "a little coal oil" by full-scale
civil rights lobby for a unified bill in the House.

"Yes, well, this has been very sound," King replied, quickly interjecting "one other point that I wanted to mention to you, because it has
begun to concern me a great deal, in the last uh, few days, in making my
speeches, in making a speech in Virginia, where I made a statement concerning, uh, the Vietnam situation, and there have been some press
statements about it." The President kept silent through King's nervous
monologue denying that he was "engaged in destructive criticism . . .
that we should unilaterally withdraw troops from Vietnam, which I
know is unreasonable." He had been "speaking really as a minister of
the gospel," King said, and wanted to be clear. "It was merely a statement that *all* citizens of good will ought to be concerned about the problem that faces our world, the problem of war," he added carefully, "and
that, although uncomfortable, they ought to debate on this issue." King
coughed. "I just wanted to say that *to* you," he said, "because I felt eventually that it would come to your attention—"

"Well—"

"—and I know the terrible burden and awesome responsibility and decisions that you make, and I know it's complicated," King rushed on, "and I didn't want to add to the burdens because I know they're very difficult."

Johnson paused. "Well, you, you, you're very, uh, uh, helpful, and I appreciate it," he said, stumbling. Then he recovered: "I *did* see it. I *was* distressed. I *do* want to talk to you." He exposed to King his confessional tone about Vietnam, saying he had stalled and hoped to the point that "unless I bomb, they run me out right quick," and stressed the constant toll of war pressure—"well, the Republican leader had a press conference this afternoon, [Gerald] Ford, demanded I bomb Hanoi"—over his twenty months in office. "I've lost about two hundred and sixty—our lives up to now," he told King, "and I could lose two hundred and sixty-five *thousand* mighty easy, and I'm trying to keep those zeroes down."

The President admitted that he was "not all wise" in matters of foreign policy. "I don't want to be a warmonger," he assured King, but neither could he abide defeat in a Cold War conflict. "Now I don't want to pull down the flag and come home runnin' with my tail between my legs," he said, "particularly if it's going to create more problems than I got out there—and it *would,* according to our best judges." Johnson urged King to explore the alternatives at length with Rusk, McNamara, and himself—"I'll give you all I know"—and thanked him for constructive purpose always "in our dealings together." King in turn thanked Johnson for true leadership, and especially—"I don't think I've had a chance"—for his speech after Selma. They parted with pledges of joint zeal to finish the quest for universal suffrage.

At their fleeting, crucial moment of contact on Vietnam, Johnson had minimized his war motive to the point of apology, just as King circumscribed his criticism. Each one said he yearned to find another way, but shied from nonviolent strategies in the glare of the military challenge.

* * *

THE SEMINARIAN Jonathan Daniels reached Selma for a third stay on July 8, this time alone, having completed the semester at Cambridge by submitting overdue papers steeped in religious epiphany. Stark memories had become tools for reflection. He recalled first erasing the hostile stares of Southern strangers simply by switching from Massachusetts to Alabama license tags, with the "Heart of Dixie" state slogan, only to become flushed under the wary looks of Negroes, then mortified by the impression Upham's car advertised along roadways back north through his native New Hampshire. "I wanted to shout to them, 'No, no! I'm *not* an Alabama white,'" Daniels wrote. Yet he identified with white South-erners in turmoil against him, to the point of defending them from showers of condescension at the seminary. Regretting the "self-righteous insanities" of his early weeks in the Alabama Black Belt, he expressed gratitude to his pastoral mentor in Selma, Father Maurice Ouellet of St. Elizabeth's Edmundite mission among Negroes, for mak-ing clear exactly how "he had finally stopped hating" fellow white clergy after twelve years of ostracism and injustice. Daniels carried a se-cret intention to pursue conversion under Ouellet toward the Catholic rather than Episcopal priesthood. He found comfort in the formal liturgy and structured hierarchy of the Roman Church, which had an-chored centuries of cerebral meditation from St. Augustine to Thomas Merton. From his own inner voyage in Alabama, treated variously as a "white nigger," "redneck," and oddball savior, Daniels stretched for an empathy that could reach all human wounds. "It meant absorbing their guilt as well," he wrote of the segregationists, "and suffering the cost which they might not yet even know was there to be paid." He professed new baptism to a living theology beyond fear—"that in the only sense that really matters I am already dead, and my life is hid with Christ in God."

Lonzy and Alice West drove Daniels from the Montgomery airport to apartment 313E at the Carver Homes in Selma, adjacent to Brown Chapel. Many of the ten West children at home squealed with delight over the return of their favorite family guest, even though they had to bunch more tightly on beds and sofas to vacate his old room. Daniels re-tained an open bond with them, particularly the younger ones. He had the wit to join in their fun about the novelty of himself as a white man in Carver Homes. He recognized them as participants in a fearful move-ment, but employed playful nonsense—bouncing them on his knee, twirling them in the air, asking, "Now are you afraid?"—to dispel hard-ships from the grown-up world.

Local powers were reasserting authority in the wake of Selma's great marches. Archbishop Thomas Toolen of Alabama had just banished Father Ouellet to Vermont by edict that made national news, depriving Daniels of personal counsel and the Wests of their family priest. (Lonzy West had converted from the Negro Baptist church a decade earlier, after a stint as Ouellet's parish janitor.) The Dallas County school super-intendent aborted a tense first meeting with Negroes on freedom-of-choice integration by announcing that he would receive only written questions for later study, then refusing to address the Negro parents by courtesy titles rather than first names. In declining also to shake their hands, the superintendent stood curtly on the abstract principle of his free choice, but apologists said he could not survive the political stigma of breaking racial custom. Meanwhile, Mayor Joseph Smitherman stalled the downtown boycott of segregated merchants until it dwindled for lack of result.

Inside a fatigued Selma movement, there were complaints, about self-promotional leadership well before the July 6 embezzlement arrest of Rev. F. D. Reese. A close observer of the emergency perceived him as an amateur trapped between persecutors and opportunists. Ralph Abernathy flew in with an earthy appeal to unite behind Reese even if he was guilty. He ridiculed the idea that white officials, who arrested them for trying to vote, suddenly became trustworthy guardians of the movement's private collections. "I didn't see Mr. Baker put anything in the plate!" he cried. By exercising command of the pulpit—calling for treasured hymns, extolling preachers as inheritors of biblical leadership—Abernathy held off the criticism that bubbled in the pews. "The SNCC people here come on with their taunts about SCLC exploitation and abandonment," one of King's staff members wrote, "and I know it isn't true, but I can't answer them."

Beneath the leadership skirmishes, Daniels pitched himself into experimental projects such as the Selma Free College. Volunteers unpacked books from collection drives organized by spring marchers on their return to home cities—13,000 in the first shipment from students at San Francisco State University, 1,600 from Antioch College, small truckloads from Yale and Brown. To avoid repercussions in white Selma, officials of all-Negro Selma University fearfully declined to accept donations tainted by civil rights (sadly so, as the campus library held fewer than four thousand volumes), whereupon a dozen volunteers catalogued a full lending library for their own improvised summer curriculum. They scrounged a piano for music and folk dance, turned a derelict house into an art gallery, and held large swimming classes in a pond. They nailed wire mesh over windows to control vandalism by the "Green Street Gang" of young Negro boys, who stole supplies and killed mealworms meant to feed the lizards in a nature display assembled by science teacher Mary Alice McQuaid of Colorado State. More pleasantly, the Selma Free College managed overflow attendance in

Gloria Larry's class. Students idolized her poised, movie-star looks, but Larry—a graduate student in comparative literature at Berkeley, who had made her way south with trepidation more than a year after hearing a Bob Moses talk—was nonplussed by the clamor for French lessons instead of demonstrations. Nine-year-old Rachel West eagerly joined her freedom class every morning. West's housemate Daniels, rejoicing to learn that the new teacher was a lifelong Negro Episcopalian, told Larry she had impeccable credentials to renew the campaign for integrated worship at St. Paul's Church.

Daniels resumed his awkward, daily overtures to St. Paul's members at their offices and homes. With members of Silas Norman's local SNCC staff, he also canvassed the poorest sections of East Selma. Households lacked basic nutrition and potable water, as was obvious from surveys taken in the Free College health class, but direct exposure to conditions in see-through shacks often shocked the volunteers. One woman, asked why no male supported her destitute family, placed her hand on the heads of eleven offspring as she recalled absentee fathers out loud. To a numb suggestion that she stop seeing such men in order to qualify for social services, the mother pleaded that children were more precious than a welfare check. Volunteers figured out how to pacify another mother who was too fearful of a doctor, or too distressed by the idea of venturing into white Selma, to accompany Daniels and her two small children to Good Samaritan for emergency treatment of malnutrition and intestinal worms by Dr. Isabel Dumont, a German refugee who had preceded and survived Father Ouellet at the Catholic mission.

Ouellet had feared that Daniels was too naive for such work. From their spring conversations after mass, he thought the seminarian believed too strongly in the power of ideas to reform character—that he could change Rev. Frank Mathews of St. Paul's by dialogue on Christian duty and theology, for instance, whereas Ouellet perceived Mathews to be governed by his coveted social post at Selma's most prestigious church. Now Daniels himself was becoming a relative veteran. He could laugh over poignant absurdities of race while expounding on the difference between foolishness and a childlike tenacity of faith. After one fresh volunteer from California tried to assure strangers that some Negro girls in question were all right because they were under his supervision, only to be chased from the white side of the laundromat by a woman beating him with her shoe, it was Daniels who helped turn the volunteer's fright to relieved hilarity, then to lessons on cultural provocation and risk. He became mentor also to a middle-aged couple who arrived from Long Island for a month's stay. He found them lodging with a nurse in Carver Homes, arranged for them to help teach a geography class, and took them to mass meetings at Brown Chapel, where Rabbi Harold Saperstein twice was asked to speak as a visiting dignitary. From his parallel experience, Daniels tempered disappointment when the Sapersteins were implored by uncomfortable local Jews not to attend services at the temple on Broad Street. He took them into East Selma. He coached them on everyday subtleties such as visits to the post office—how not to stand out more as civil rights workers by trying to hide—and rewarded their progress with an odd announcement: "I think it's all right for you to meet Stokely."

Asked to wait outside a remote, primitive cabin, the Sapersteins first saw Carmichael step from the doorway behind Daniels with a roasted leg of small game. Marcia Saperstein guessed it was possum, her husband thought rabbit, but they were too disoriented to ask. Still rattled from the long drive out of Selma at speeds above eighty—"Never let a car pass you," said Daniels, citing one of Carmichael's paradoxical safety rules—they were absorbing what Daniels told them of the rural SNCC outpost that had lasted four months in Lowndes County without electricity, money, running water, or protection from the Klan.

Maddening hope had seized the Freedom House cabin since July 6, when a Justice Department lawyer stunned Carmichael with notice that local officials agreed to add registration dates and to terminate literacy tests for prospective voters. Was there a trick, or perhaps some deal to mitigate future enforcement of federal law? After spirited debate, the Lowndes County movement resolved to gamble in trust. They appealed to five hundred pioneer applicants since March 1—nearly all of whom had been rejected—to brave another try at the Old Jail in Hayneville. Lillian McGill quit her federal job at the Agriculture Department to canvass nearly around the clock, often with John Hulett, the church deacon who had founded the Lowndes County voting rights movement since rescuing his pastor from the Klan in February. SNCC workers mobilized outside reinforcements including Gloria Larry, who, after morning classes in Selma, ventured out through Big Swamp to help shepherd registration caravans. (When the prim Larry first asked to use the Freedom House bathroom, she endured guffaws as Carmichael merrily pointed her toward the small outhouse in the woods behind.)

There had been serious division also about Daniels. Most project workers opposed the extra dangers and headaches posed by a radioactive white presence in Lowndes, but Carmichael prevailed with the Bob Moses argument that a freedom movement could not throw up barriers of race. He assured Bob Mants, Willie Vaughn, and other SNCC workers that white volunteers would not overrun them as in Mississippi Summer. Carefully, after Daniels, the wonder of a rabbi and wife soon appeared behind knocks on sharecropper doors, wearing business dress in July heat, radiating with news that the trick questions were banished.

Registration lines lurched forward without the literacy exams. "We've fought for the removal of this test for so long it's hard to believe it's really gone," Stokely Carmichael declared in a SNCC press release. Mass meetings at Mt. Gillard Baptist ratcheted up from weekly to nightly for the push, and Carmichael, though far from conventionally religious, preached to high-spirited crowds in the language of the Bible. He imagined from the visionary text of Ezekiel how black folks of Lowndes would rise up dancing like "dry bones" in the valley of Israel, the sinews of life restored.

Hulett presented a separate breakthrough to Mt. Gillard: posted notices that Lowndes County was taking applications for "freedom of choice" assignment to high school. Some argued from the floor that a second front was unwise, but families of nearly fifty children answered the agreed policy of volunteers. Daniels accompanied several to the courthouse for the required forms, which turned out to be nonexistent until Superintendent Hulda Coleman typed her own version. Staff members preserved details of swift, widespread reaction, punctuated by nearby Klan rallies on July 10 and 16, in sworn affidavits collected for the Justice Department. "Buster Haigler sent for me to his house," Cato Lee said of the county's largest private financier. "He took his book out of his pocket, and asked me did I have any children enrolled to go to Hayneville High School." Eli Logan said a white teacher twice advised that "the Ku Klux Klan would be through here next Tuesday" unless Logan took young Stephen's name off the list for twelfth grade. Martha Johnson affirmed that the teacher's son—"the same man who measured my land last year"—said she would "be in a squeeze" if her daughter tried to switch schools. Jordan Gully told how a creditor for farming loans warned that white people were fed up over his daughter's application. "Then he said, 'We didn't bother y'all about registerin'. We didn't bother y'all about goin' to mass meetings,' " recalled Gully. "He told me,

'I'll be goddam if this shit is going over this time. . . . We going to stop it. Don't you ask me for no damn help for nothing.' "

*   *   *

PRESIDENT JOHNSON frantically avoided inertia toward war from the moment in July when he announced the nomination of Henry Cabot Lodge to return as U.S. ambassador to South Vietnam. He moved Bill Moyers to White House press secretary simultaneously, the better to present foreign upheavals ahead, and Moyers dazzled reporters by calling the President right in front of them to resolve a question. To drive the domestic agenda in place of Moyers, Johnson added to his staff Joseph Califano from the Pentagon and Harry McPherson from State. He ordered a verbatim transcript of Califano's first encounters with education officials over the running daily count of delinquent school systems, and then, unsatisfied that Califano was lashing them forward vigorously enough, sprang upon them without warning. "Get 'em! Get 'em!" the President shouted at Commissioner Keppel. "Get the last ones!" Keppel had approved desegregation plans for less than a quarter of three thousand Southern districts, with Lowndes County among a majority of pending new submissions, but Johnson cared most about the four hundred holdouts by late July. He was possessed to break the psychological barrier by inveigling every last district to give up segregation in its own words—almost any words. While this one priority nearly crushed the emergency teams at Temporary S ("We were going absolutely nuts," Keppel recalled), Johnson yanked aides to other tasks. The second time Califano momentarily missed a presidential buzz, an abashed secretary knocked to alert him that Signal Corps technicians were there with orders to install a telephone in the bathroom of his new office.

Johnson shocked former NAACP lawyer Thurgood Marshall with an offer to become Solicitor General of the United States. That same day, the first for Moyers as press secretary, he tried to answer Senator William Fulbright's complaint that the intended nominee to replace Harry McPherson would mean too many senior Negroes at the State Department. "They won't have *any* if I don't name this fella," countered the President. Fulbright narrowed his objection to the particular job, which included managerial control of the prestigious Fulbright scholar exchange program in foreign countries. "It never occurred to me that they were outstanding in the cultural field," he told Johnson. "I mean, after all, they're not. The big universities are not predominantly colored." Fulbright, chairman of the Senate Foreign Relations Committee, argued that participating universities more than governments would recoil if his namesake endeavor were administered by a Negro. "I wouldn't object at all if you made him *Secretary of State,* for that matter," he stressed in a quavering voice, "because I have a rather personal interest in this program."

Fulbright managed to block Johnson's choice for the assistant secretary post, but a bigger appointment commanded public attention upon the sudden death in London of U.N. ambassador Adlai Stevenson. Within hours of an emotional eulogy at Washington Cathedral, the President called Abe Fortas for drinks on the Truman balcony, where he passed along a novel suggestion that Justice Arthur Goldberg might be enticed to leave the Supreme Court for a chance to catalyze a Vietnam settlement at the United Nations. Johnson completed one phase of maneuvers by July 20, the day after Stevenson's burial in Illinois. He announced Goldberg's U.N. appointment in the morning, then called to thank Harvard economist John Kenneth Galbraith for the idea. Ebullient, Johnson said Goldberg was the perfect choice to shatter a political taboo that no Jew could represent the United States at the world body, and he told Galbraith flatly that he would name Thurgood Marshall to a future vacancy on the Supreme Court "after he's Solicitor for a year or two." By then Marshall would have added to the twenty-nine tough cases he had won in the highest court as an NAACP attorney, the President observed, which would make him more than eminently qualified to become the first Negro Justice. "I think we'll break through there like we're breaking through on so many of these things," he said.

* * *

KING TESTED another potential northern site on Saturday, July 24. "If you want a movement to move, you've got to have the preachers behind you," he told an Interfaith Breakfast of 220 clergy in Chicago. Among sixty whites present for the kickoff event were Jews gathered before sabbath services, including the national president of the conservative synagogue association, Rabbi Jacob Weinstein of Temple KAM, who had just returned from an interfaith mission in Saigon with Vietnamese peace petitions directed to King. The Negroes featured a minority of local Baptists thus far willing to defy Rev. J. H. Jackson of Olivet Baptist, the "Negro pope" who in 1961 had branded King an apostate, driving him with two thousand pro–civil rights pastors from the National Baptist Convention. To those familiar with the hidden world of pulpit politics, Rev. Jackson in Chicago loomed a daunting obstacle for his proven exercise of machinelike powers in tandem with Mayor Daley.

King exhorted the religious leaders to "sacrifice body and soul" for the cause astir, then rushed an hour behind schedule into a three-car motorcade bound for Carver Park in far Southside Chicago, with a police escort and a fleet of trailing reporters. The approach of sirens soon released the team of advance SCLC speakers—Abernathy, Bevel, citizenship teacher Dorothy Cotton, Fred Shuttlesworth—toward the rally ahead, where they in turn released the warmup Freedom Singers. King followed with a twenty-minute address on the challenge of de facto segregation. "The Negro is not free anywhere in the United States," he said from the back of a flatbed truck. Al Raby brought a neighborhood leader to brief King on the Robert Taylor Homes project en route to a brick-strewn field at 48th and State Streets, where a second crowd of five hundred was gathered. Uniformed Cub Scouts waited to pass collection buckets.

On through eight speech stops in the lead car, covering 186 miles of city streets before dark, King had the rare extended company of his adviser Bayard Rustin. Always entertaining, sifting rascals and tactical conundrums in his high-spirited Caribbean accent, Rustin addressed King's confluent pressures from experience. He had practiced nonviolence in Northern cities for more than two decades. He knew well the raw methods that Harlem Representative Adam Clayton Powell was using to hamstring competition from King on urban turf, having been driven off King's advisory staff himself in 1960 by Powell's blackmail threats over his homosexuality. From prior work on four continents, Rustin also helped interpret nonviolence in a context of pell-mell slide to distant war. Less than a month before, King had supported the interfaith mission to Vietnam: "Let me commend you. . . . America must be willing to negotiate with all parties. . . . Our guns and our bombs do not prove that we love democracy but that we still believe that might makes right." More than this cablegram, or the stature of Pastor Martin Niemoeller of Wiesbaden, president of the World Council of Churches, Rabbi Weinstein reported that King's nonviolent instructor James Lawson, the only black person among the fourteen delegates, "gave us great prestige and opened many doors to us." Chief among their discoveries in Vietnam was the monk Thich Nhat Hanh, who had sent King a letter on the meaning of self-immolation. The sensational fires were not acts of despair, suicide, or even violence, he argued. Mahayana Buddhism, while abhorring self-destruction, teaches that life is immortal. Candidate monks burn small spots on their bodies at ordination to signify devotion, and immolation expresses merely the extreme degree of constructive hope for a people's salvation above the nihilism of war. "To say something while experiencing this kind of pain," Thich Nhat Hanh wrote, "is to say it with the utmost courage, frankness, determination, and sincerity."

This communication taxed even Rustin's nimble mind for adapting nonviolence across cultures. Witness by flame was "difficult for the Western Christian conscience to understand," the monk's letter conceded, and the interfaith delegation found realistically that the two Vietnamese governments themselves were locked into opposing rationales for conventional terror. Still, from his study of the nonviolent movement against caste in Alabama, Thich Nhat Hanh challenged Americans to reciprocate in Vietnam by applying parallel Buddhist belief that war from any quarter is a greater evil than Communism, capitalism, or colonialism. They should "not allow American political and economic doctrines to be deprived of their spiritual element," he wrote King, quoting a Christian theologian in his personal plea: "You cannot be silent since you have already been in action, and you are in action, because, in you, God is in action, too—to use Karl Barth's expression."

The nonstop Chicago relay ended late Saturday at Friendship Baptist, the former grand Russian synagogue of Anshe Kneseth Israel in Lawndale. When King complained of exhaustion after preaching at two churches Sunday morning, the Freedom Singers improvised an extra hour to cover a breather before motorcades rolled toward six afternoon stops. At a shopping center in Chatham, then in Calumet Park, he urged large middle-class crowds to remember those behind them in the struggle from desperate poverty. "Dives didn't go to hell because he was a millionaire," King explained from the parable in Luke. "He went to hell because he passed Lazarus by." Until dusk, outside Scatchell's BBQ on Pulaski Avenue, King pleaded with listeners to march with him in numbers. "Take a day off on Monday," he cried. "You know, we don't make much money anyhow." Leaving behind most of the entourage to scatter in recruitment, hoping to silence press jibes that recent downtown protests had mustered fewer than a thousand, King ventured seventeen miles north along Lake Michigan to one of the country's wealthiest suburbs. Brown-shirt Nazis were picketing the village green of Winnetka, and police guards had thrown up protective fencing after a bomb threat. Few at the night rally of ten thousand people knew any freedom songs, but Rev. C. T. Vivian, SCLC's director of affiliate chapters, had been holding them with preacher riffs and choruses of "America the Beautiful." King spoke for nearly an hour on the moral imperative to overcome fearful hatred at home and abroad. From dead collapse, he startled Vivian on the way back into Chicago. "You don't think I know what I'm doing when I talk about Vietnam, do you?" King asked.

Vivian muttered questions to stall, then smiled, realizing that King was reading his staff again for unguarded reaction, the way he sampled crowds and cities. King let it go, and Vivian changed the subject. "I just heard that Vernon Johns died," he said.

King sagged. "Johns died?" he asked. "You sure of that?"

Vivian said he was. Like much about the vagabond scholar who had preceded King at Dexter Avenue Baptist in Montgomery, his demise weeks earlier was passing from rumor through fact to legend. It was said that the old man had appeared from somewhere at storied Rankin Chapel of Howard University, without laces in his shoes, to deliver without notes a last sermon entitled "The Romance of Death," then wandered off again to be discovered prostrate by strangers weeks later. A recording survived. "I'm almost afraid to say this, but I can prove to you in less than a second that it's true," Johns had growled to end his lyrical reflections. "Unless a person comes to the place where he wants to die, he has been licked by life."* Vivian knew King had modeled his thematic speech on Lazarus and Dives after the mischievously profound Johns sermon of 1949, "Segregation After Death." From common association, they shared in the car a flood of memorial stories on Johns the peddler and irascible prophet, who once announced a watermelon sale as the chastening benediction for a wedding ceremony that joined two of Dexter's proudest families.

Chicago reporters confronted King after a canceled event early Mon-

---

* "Because he has got to die, and if you have got to do something that you don't want to do, and it's going to be the last thing that you do, then you have been licked. So instead of fearing death, let us learn with the young man who wrote Thanatopsis, not an old man but a young man . . . to approach our graves by living daily so that we can subordinate ourselves to the greatest thing that comes our way, and then the soul will finally throw off the body like a worn-out feather without consequence. Amen."

day as he emerged pasty and feverish from a doctor's office, diagnosed with bronchitis. "I need to rest," he told them, then lagged two hours behind. At lakefront Buckingham Fountain, King climbed a blue truck to address roaring, restless marchers numbered at some twenty thousand. "We sang *Going to Chicago* until there were as many of our people in Chicago as Mississippi," he cried, reviewing the half-century of exodus. "Now we see the results. Chicago did not turn out to be a New Jerusalem . . . but a city in dire need of redemption and reform." With Al Raby, Dick Gregory, and John McDermott of the Catholic Interracial Council, King led a walking mass the full width of Balbo Drive that stretched forward an hour to State Street, Madison, and up LaSalle to City Hall. He offered there a formal prayer for "a greater vision of our task," vowed to be back when needed, and flew to his next trial movement in Cleveland. Mayor Daley, reappearing in Chicago from a hasty trip, adroitly minimized differences with King. "There can be no disagreement that we must root out poverty," Daley announced, "rid the community of slums, eliminate discrimination and segregation wherever they exist, and improve the quality of education."

*   *   *

PRESS SECRETARY Moyers whispered to President Johnson for permission to release simply the names of the men gathered in the Cabinet Room on Monday, July 26. Johnson vetoed it, growling that reporters would only press them more doggedly for clues. Hair-trigger tensions of superpower conflict had intruded upon the serial Vietnam meetings in their sixth consecutive day. Although the North Vietnamese had shot down fifty-five U.S. planes earlier during the Rolling Thunder bombardment, military intelligence officials believed the weekend loss of an American F-4 jet was the first casualty from new surface-to-air missile (SAM) defenses operated by Soviet technicians, some forty miles northeast of Hanoi. "Are you sure they're Russians?" President Johnson asked. Rusk conceded that "killing the first Russians" in Vietnam would be dangerous, but joined McNamara and military commanders in recommending air strikes on the SAM sites themselves. "You cannot order pilots to bomb without helping them get back," he said.

The President declared a recess, admonishing everyone again to absolute secrecy, and called his friend Richard Russell. "We think that the Russians are manning them," he said. "We don't want to say that. We don't want anybody to know that." The new SAM sites were mobile and harder to hit, but to bomb the permanent sites near Hanoi would drive the feuding Chinese and Soviet governments toward unified support of North Vietnam. "You'll have them all in the war in fifteen minutes in my judgment when you go to bombing in Hanoi," said Johnson, wary of North Vietnamese strategy. "I think they're trying to trap us into doing it."

Russell confronted the immediate choice on the mobile sites instead. "Well, I'd say yes, get them tonight if we could," he advised, "but I'd hate like hell to try to get them and miss them." He renewed commiseration with Johnson on the overall war, especially his premonition that "these damn Vietnamese" allies would skulk to the rear and leave the fighting to Americans. "God, that just scared the hell out of me," Russell confessed.

The President reconvened the group in the Cabinet Room late Monday. Arthur Goldberg, hours after being sworn in as U.N. ambassador, asked for assurance that no spasm by hostile superpowers would spoil the chance of diplomatic settlement. CIA Director Raborn reported that Soviet leaders were "expecting us to come" with bombs to counter their missiles, and were likely to remain reserved. Clark Clifford, who had argued the George Ball position to President Johnson at Camp David, urging withdrawal to avoid "catastrophe for my country," reversed counsel in an atmosphere of command decisions under fire. "We are not going to be pushed out of South Vietnam," he said. "We show the enemy our determination by taking out number 6 and number 7." McNamara said the suspect SAM sites designated by these numbers were only "semi-mobile," raising the odds of success. "Take them out," ordered the President. He called the Pentagon Situation Room through the night—at one o'clock, 3:30, and 7:35 Tuesday morning—for mission reports that flattened his hopes. Ground missiles shot down six of the forty-four attacking U.S. aircraft, all F-105s. From postmortem reconnaissance indicating that number 6 was a dummy site, and number 7 vacant, Bundy concluded that the mobile SAMs sighted "may have been a DRV trap," referring to the Democratic Republic of Vietnam, that is, North Vietnam.

Between Tuesday's three secret deliberations, beginning at 8:40 A.M., the President posed for photographs with the Sons of Italy, new HEW Secretary John Gardner, and with a Boy Scout who had bicycled from Idaho on a fitness project, among others, and approved a reply to Martin Luther King's thanks for the appointment of Thurgood Marshall. ("I am convinced that God has sent you to lead us out of this difficult and agonizing wilderness at such a time as this," said King, in a letter dictated from the road.*) Johnson also called Harry Truman, met for two hours with Abe Fortas, and signed into law the Cigarette Labeling Act of 1965, which placed a specified health warning on every pack sold. Despite the mandated labels, consumption would rise toward a record 520 billion cigarettes in 1966, while research sponsored by the American Medical Association, underwritten with nearly $20 million from tobacco sources, corroborated none of the government's alleged ill effects. On the contrary, one newly publicized study team led by a Nobel laureate found that regular smoking fostered higher intelligence. "Let it be clear that we do not intend to create geniuses," microbiologist Daniele Bovet told the *Times,* "but only put the less-endowed individual in a position to reach a satisfactory mental and intellectual development."

On Wednesday, July 28, the President ordered his staff to rustle up cushioning news to surround the Vietnam announcement at noon. Twelve minutes beforehand, Johnson himself called Abe Fortas. "How is your blood pressure?" he asked coyly.

Decades later, Vietnam War historian Stanley Karnow wrote that President Johnson "could not conceal his decision, but he could muffle it." This explained why, agreed biographer Robert Dallek, he "announced the expansion of the war at a press conference rather than in a speech to a joint session of Congress," disclosing only 50,000 of the 100,000 new troops ordered to Vietnam, saying more were likely soon. Still, anticipation made for an electric, somber moment in the packed East Room. No great distance or mitigating hope, the President declared, should "mask the central fact that this is really war." Surveys recorded a daytime television audience of 28 million, with only 4 percent of sets tuned elsewhere. "Once the Communists know, as we know, that a violent solution is impossible," said Johnson, "then a peaceful solution is inevitable." Reporters noted that Lady Bird Johnson covered her face, near tears, as he reprised from his Selma speech—"Let me add now a personal note . . . as I have said before"—a defining purpose since boyhood that he resolved not to see "drowned in the wasteful ravages of

* "As always your eloquent and generous words are a source of strength and comfort," Johnson replied to King. "The struggle to end oppression, and to heal the scars of oppression will not be easy, but it is easier because of your courageous leadership. No cause—no goal of my Presidency—is dearer to my heart or more important to our nation than the achievement of full emancipation in our time."

cruel wars. . . . But I also know, as a realistic public servant, that as long as there are men who hate and destroy, we must have the courage to resist or we'll see it all—all that we have built, all that we hope to build, all our dreams for freedom—all, all, will be swept away on the flood of conquest. So, too, this shall not happen. We will stand in Vietnam."

Defying undertow, President Johnson rose buoyantly to other matters. He introduced his newly appointed director for the Voice of America, NBC News correspondent John Chancellor, "whose face and whose mind is known to this country and to most of the entire world," and presented as a startling surprise, even to himself, the soon-to-be-appointed Justice Fortas.

Not waiting for Johnson to finish questions from the press, Vice President Humphrey called the Oval Office from "a room full of senators over here at the Capitol" to dictate a message of unanimous enthusiasm. "I just couldn't be happier if they'd had Christmas every day," he added, "and every dream I'd ever wanted came true." The President himself rushed back to more congenial tasks with energized relief, pushing Katzenbach at the last hurdle for voting rights, and concurrent victories lifted him to euphoria. "We repealed 14-B today," he crowed to Arthur Goldberg that night, saying he forgave the veteran labor lawyer for telling him once that the anti-union section of the Taft-Hartley Act was forever impregnable. "I put it in the message, and then I backed it up with votes," boasted Johnson. "And we got Social Security passed today."

Thursday's *New York Times* spread war news across three giant tiers, "JOHNSON ORDERS 50,000 MORE MEN/TO VIETNAM AND DOUBLES DRAFT/AGAIN URGES U.N. TO SEEK PEACE." Surrounding front-page stories headlined restraint—"Most in Congress Relieved," said one, alongside "Economic Impact Is Called Slight." The *Times* editorial rested on his "vital" point that the war must be "held down to the absolute minimum necessary to prove to Hanoi and Peking that military aggression is not worthwhile," and the principal news dispatch, "NO RESERVE CALL," recognized that the President avoided congressional scrutiny of a disruptive, costly deployment by declining to activate Reserve forces. He called instead for an extra 18,000 draftees per month.

Draftees would supply politically convenient soldiers only for the moment, as Johnson well knew, but his overriding worry was that candid mobilization would touch off hawkish alarms for unfettered war. "Don't pay any attention to what the little shits on the campuses do," he told George Ball. "The great beast is the reactionary elements in this country." At the same time, Johnson railed that realistic disclosures would backfire to the aid of dovish critics. Public exchanges "just put water on Mansfield's and on Morse's paddle," he fretted to Eisenhower, longing for acquiescence on all sides. "If we could get Morse *and* Ford to quit talking," he opined, "it would be a lot better." To minimize debate, and the need for concurrence, he assumed the burden of war on his own claim of authority. An elastic conscription law allowed him to commandeer manpower for Vietnam by quiet executive decree, at the price of inevitable protest that no such autocratic power should compel young Americans to kill or be killed in the name of free government.

* * *

WHEN EVEN the legendary White House telephone operators failed to locate Martin Luther King, the Attorney General called the FBI at 9:15 that same Wednesday night, July 28. In doing so, Assistant Director DeLoach noted with satisfaction, Katzenbach swallowed his distaste for FBI surveillance methods to the point of admitting he "desperately" needed help to find King about the "damned bill" on voting rights. From tracking agents, DeLoach guided him to call Suite 9-B at the Sheraton after a rally in Cleveland's civic arena, and negotiations went late over the wording of a King statement about the poll tax. The voting rights bill was likely to remain stuck unless key representatives on the House-Senate conference—chiefly Harold Donohue of Massachusetts and Peter Rodino of New Jersey—accepted assurance that civil rights supporters could retreat honorably from a poll tax amendment the House had added July 9 over the Johnson administration's opposition. Katzenbach agreed to substitute an express declaration by Congress that the poll tax abridged the right to vote, plus a directive that the Justice Department "institute forthwith" lawsuits to void the practice, and King agreed before morning that Katzenbach could quote his exact appraisal of the compromise, ending: "I am confident that the poll tax provision of the bill—with vigorous action by the Attorney General—will operate finally to bury this iniquitous device." He agreed also that Katzenbach could call final enactment of the voting rights law his "overriding goal."

Word of the midnight intercession leaked in Washington, where Southerners professed shock that an Attorney General would quote such a person in the official business of the United States, "taking orders" from King. The indignant refrain changed few votes, however, and did not erupt until Katzenbach steered the compromise through Thursday's conference to the floor of the House and Senate.

King, for his part, returned to troubles on the Northern tour. His bronchitis had worsened since Chicago to a fever of 102 degrees. He canceled a New York stop after two warning phone calls from Adam Clayton Powell, and used a day's break to work on several festering issues that menaced the upcoming SCLC convention in Birmingham. He authorized his attorney Chauncey Eskridge to seek collection from a Negro bondsman of misappropriated interest on nearly $400,000 of bail bonds that SCLC had posted in 1963 with borrowed money—the bonds being held at risk because Birmingham still refused to drop more than a thousand criminal cases against young people arrested for protesting segregation. Meanwhile, King mediated a complex pulpit dispute that blocked access to the historic seat of the Birmingham movement at 16th Street Baptist Church. There were fears expressed that the church would be bombed again if he returned, along with quarrels over the allocation of repair funds collected worldwide, plus lingering resentment of high-handed conduct by King's colleague Fred Shuttlesworth. Abernathy had just inflamed the latter situation with a letter banning the celebrated movement choir director at 16th Street Baptist, Carlton Reese, from SCLC events until he apologized satisfactorily for having "disrespected" Shuttlesworth, stressing to Reese that "you and your group must not repent for these acts of insubordination just for the convention, but it must be a move to get right with the movement permanently."

Adam Clayton Powell could not resist tweaking King about why he should stay out of Harlem. "I told him to go to cities where they had no real Negro leadership," he announced to reporters, "like Chicago, Cleveland, and Washington." Powell's colorful disparagement attracted press notice, baiting Negroes who cooperated with King, and the NAACP chapter president in Philadelphia sent up a temperamental flare before the movement tour reached his city. "Moore Assails Two-Day Visit Here of Dr. King," headlined the July 30 *Philadelphia Inquirer,* reporting that Cecil B. Moore denounced King as "an unwitting tool" of manipulations by "appeasers, social climbers, and the egghead white power structure" to degrade what Moore called "my stature in the Negro community." The friction instantly generated a sympathetic FBI report on Moore's confidential plans to harass King as unwelcome. King, still stalled and sick in Cleveland, sent word that he did not want to impose on Philadelphia, which touched off protests against Moore.

With two planeloads of legislators, President Johnson soared over the heartland into Kansas City, Missouri, on Friday afternoon, July 30, then proceeded by motorcade to Independence. Crowds lined the streets. At a ceremony in the auditorium of the Truman Library, the former President spoke only briefly. "I'm glad to have lived this long, and to witness today the signing of the Medicare bill," said Harry Truman, now growing feeble at eighty-one. He first had proposed national health coverage for older Americans in 1945, three months after the end of World War II, and Johnson praised him for inspiring the uphill battle ever since. The new law made 19 million Americans instantly eligible for medical benefits as a supplement to Social Security, which promised over time to lift old age itself above a primordial curse as the most impoverished stage of life. "No longer will older Americans be denied the healing miracle of modern medicine," said Johnson. "No longer will illness crush and destroy the savings that they have so carefully put away over a lifetime. . . . No longer will young families see their own income and their own hopes eaten away simply because they are carrying out their deep moral obligations to their parents and to their uncles and their aunts."

Johnson gave Bess Truman the first pen he used to sign into law the amendment to Social Security known as Medicare. He gave a second to Truman and a third to Vice President Humphrey, who had crafted a number of the arcane provisions necessary to win passage. (A religious exemption excluded the Old Order Amish, who believed health insurance impugned trust in providence.) He gave a fourth pen to Representative Wilbur Mills of Arkansas, who had presided over the graveyard of health legislation until his Ways and Means Committee first broke the lobbying power of organized medicine that spring, during the march from Selma to Montgomery. Doctors would reconcile their duty to the new national commitment, Johnson foresaw, so that in Independence "and a thousand other towns like it, there are men and women in pain who will now find ease." Beaming, grasping hands in jubilation, he said he hoped for no sweeter struggle in public life, "nor any act of leadership that gives greater satisfaction than this."

* * *

CONTINUING VIOLENCE attracted press attention to Americus, Georgia, on Sunday, August 1. Bottles thrown from a car had hospitalized two Negro boys aged three and six, and rumors circulated that Martin Luther King would detour from the North. National newspapers pub-

lished a front-page photograph of church elders lined across the top step
of First Methodist before morning worship, their arms crossed to block
an integrated, kneeling group of six led by SCLC worker Willie Bolden,
and fire chief H. K. Henderson barred a dozen outside First Baptist of
Americus, saying, "You are wasting your time and mine." No reporters
gathered in Selma, Alabama, but an unobserved silence gripped St.
Paul's Episcopal from the moment Jonathan Daniels arrived with Gloria Larry. One of the volunteer ushers trained for integration incidents
went home seething instead, along with several families who left during
the hushed prelude. Larry and Daniels took seats near the middle of the
stone sanctuary. When they stood with the fourth row beckoned for
first-Sunday Communion, all around them stayed seated or sat back
down again in staggered unanimity, and they went forward to the altar
alone.

Rev. Frank Mathews hastened from the service to compose a report
for his bishops, headed "12:30 PM." "This is the *first* time a Negro has attended 11:00 HC [Holy Communion]," he wrote, "so it was definitely a
'crisis situation.' " He would postpone the monthly session of the governing vestry for two weeks to let time "quieten the souls of distraught
men," Mathews confided. He added that the church budget was "beginning to feel the pinch of withheld payment of pledges." Separately, a
member of St. Paul's rushed to the diocese his own description of the
service. Having arrived late, he had noticed heaviness in the air before
he saw "this white man in his near Clerical clothes escorting a negro
woman, standing aside for her to be seated, then sitting down by her and
they both knelt to pray," wrote Garnett Cassell. "It was then that I knew
what was upsetting the congregation enough for me to feel it." Cassell
said Daniels could keep importing Negroes indefinitely. "All of his
many months of activity here in Selma, Ala. has been paid for at the
Spiritual Expense to the Congregation of St. Paul's," he wrote. "Therefore, the time has come when he must be stopped." From Birmingham,
diocesan officials soon prepared replies upholding both the canonical
right to integrated worship and the hope that forbearance would wear
out the "very distasteful" practice. "If he [Daniels] is hanging around
causing trouble," Bishop C. C. J. Carpenter wrote Mathews, "I think I
will just have to write his bishop and tell him to take him on back to
Seminary."

Larry and Daniels continued work in Lowndes County on Monday,
a regular registration day at the old Hayneville jail. Daniels broke away

to accompany a group of parents on the short walk up to the courthouse square, seeking to learn why the school board rejected forty-one of forty-six freedom-of-choice applications for transfer to Hayneville High School. Superintendent Hulda Coleman blocked Daniels at her office door, and received the parents one at a time.

Bernice Johnson went inside alone. Her husband, a part-time preacher, recently consented to open Friendship Baptist for movement activity in Hayneville, but fearful church members had foiled the first meeting by removing the pews. Mrs. Johnson herself filed the applications for their three oldest children, from Malachi down to Samuel, and when Superintendent Coleman said they had tested too poorly for academic work in white schools, she fell back on the reasoning discussed with Hulett, Lillian McGill, and the other parents. "The Lowndes County schools ain't no good," she told Coleman. "That's no secret, they ain't no kind of nothing." The schools turned Negro children out to work in the fields and "passed 'em up" the grades no matter what, Johnson said, which was why the parents wanted the transfer. She tried to hold steady as the superintendent checked names and test scores.

Those outside felt tensions compressed at the color line. Lowndes County people were saying Coleman had closed the Negro schools a week early out of furious embarrassment over the photograph of Rolen School in *The Saturday Evening Post*, illustrating King's passage through Trickem on the Selma march. Now, less than a month before the new fall term, the federal Office of Education still counted Lowndes's among nearly two thousand desegregation plans not yet approved, while local white constituents pushed hard against even minimum concessions. A small group of hostile white people converged upon the waiting parents and demanded to know what a conspicuous outsider was doing in Hayneville.

"I'm with my friends," said Daniels.

1

Two paths to freedom. On the third try, March 21, 1965, Ralph Abernathy, Martin Luther King, Maurice Eisendrath, and Abraham Heschel *(front row, left to right, from nun)* step off from Selma, Alabama, in a nonviolent march to Montgomery for the right to vote.

That same month, Marines lead the first U. S. combat units ashore at Danang to secure a non-Communist South Vietnam.

2

On "Bloody Sunday," March 7, 1965, Alabama State Troopers and a sheriff's posse in clouds of tear gas trample the first attempted voting rights march out of Selma.

Registrar Carl Golson rebukes petitioners led by King, Abernathy *(behind finger)*, and SNCC Chairman John Lewis *(right of King)* in Lowndes County, between Selma and Montgomery, where no black citizen had voted in the twentieth century.

5

Outside Brown Chapel AME Church in Selma, a helmeted sheriff's posse blockades those who have answered King's call to complete the voting rights march.

Behind a "Berlin Wall" imposed by Alabama authorities, marchers sing freedom songs in a round-the-clock vigil.

6

After a week of political upheaval, King watches from Selma as President Lyndon Johnson endorses the voting rights movement in a speech to Congress.

Under court-ordered federal protection, the march covers 54 miles over five days, led here by King *(in white cap)*, Coretta King, James Bevel, John Lewis *(behind and to right)*, and Ivanhoe Donaldson *(below flagpole, in boots)*, with Andrew Young and James Orange *(far left)*.

9

A soldier salutes (*left*) as marchers stretch out from Selma into Lowndes County by day (*below*) and bed down in muddy fields by night (*bottom*).

10

11

12

Jubilant local residents greet the procession along Highway 80 (*above*).
Marchers entering Montgomery on the fifth day wave to observers (*below*).

14

Beneath the dome of Alabama's capitol, where Gov. George Wallace watches behind drawn blinds, a great host completes the march to Montgomery on March 25, 1965.

Rosa Parks speaks to the crowd before King's address on the triumphs and pitfalls of the modern civil rights movement.

15

Viola Liuzzo of Detroit (*right, holding her shoes*) completes the march, but is bushwhacked that night while driving through Lowndes County.

FBI Director J. Edgar Hoover, President Johnson, and Attorney General Nicholas Katzenbach announce four arrests one day after the Liuzzo murder (*below, left to right*), with Hoover concealing that an informant among the suspects had received FBI clearance to join the assault.

17

18

"No section of the country can boast of clean hands in the area of brotherhood," King tells the Massachusetts legislature on April 22, 1965 (*right*), exploring sites for a northern campaign.

Landmarks of 1965 crest with approval ceremonies for Medicare on July 30 (*opposite below, LBJ with Harry Truman*), the Voting Rights Act on August 6 (*above, LBJ with Abernathy and King*), and the Immigration Reform Act on October 3 (*right, at the Statue of Liberty*). By repealing race-based quotas on foreign applicants, President Johnson declares, American law "will never again shadow the gate to the American nation with the twin barriers of prejudice and privilege."

21

Episcopal seminarian Jonathan Daniels (*right, with Bunny West in Selma*), who stayed among civil rights volunteers after the Montgomery march, is arrested at the first Lowndes County demonstration and then murdered by shotgun ambush upon his release from the county jail on August 20, 1965.

22

Witnesses Gloria Larry (*below, left*), Jimmy Rogers (*center, in sweatshirt*), and Willie Vaughn (*behind deputy's baton*), supported by fellow SNCC workers Janet Jemmott (*obscured behind Rogers*) and Courtland Cox (*in straw hat*), approach the Lowndes County courthouse for the Daniels trial, which will result in swift acquittal for a Klansman who admits the shooting.

An emergency "tent city" shelters Lowndes County sharecroppers who have been evicted from plantations after trying to register for the vote.

Mamie Glover peers with son Joe from the flap of their "tent city" home, early in 1966.

On primary day, May 3, 1966, voting for the first time in their lives (*above*), black citizens of Lowndes County choose their own candidates for local office. Seated at one of the outdoor election tables, school teacher Sarah Logan (*in white glasses*) collects ballots bearing a novel black panther as the required election symbol, observed by Jesse "Note" Favors (*far right*), a runner-up for the sheriff's nomination.

Stokely Carmichael, SNCC project director in Lowndes County, hugs a young friend to celebrate the creation of an independent political party under Alabama law.

A pioneer in educa-
tion for civil rights,
Septima Clark (*right*)
teaches literacy and
citizenship to an aspir-
ing voter in Wilcox
County, Alabama.

With his son Marty and daughter Yolanda (*squeezed next to Hosea Williams*), King hur-
ries through a rural Alabama rainstorm in spring 1966 to encourage registration under
the Voting Rights Act.

A large crowd in back-alley Chicago hears King's pitch (*above*) to build a movement against slum conditions in their heartland city.

In January of 1966, King begins the Chicago campaign (*left*) by moving into a freezing, dilapidated tenement on the West Side.

Seminary student Jesse Jackson (*right*) leads marches against segregated Chicago housing and schools in the summer of 1966.

32

Chicago Mayor Richard Daley (*right*) mounts programs to reduce urban poverty and discrimination, then switches to repression when shocking violence against King's integration movement threatens the Democratic power base in white neighborhoods.

33

Summit negotiators Al Raby (*left*), Ross Beatty of the Chicago Real Estate Board (*center*), and Edwin "Bill" Berry of the Chicago Urban League inspect an open-housing agreement in late August 1966. King's Chicago campaign nationalized the issues of poverty and racial injustice but failed to draw a broad response like Selma.

34

A march of 200 miles through Mississippi (*above*) becomes a political and cultural watershed in June of 1966, after integration pioneer James Meredith was shot trying to prove that it was safe for black people to walk in his home state.

The new SNCC chairman Stokely Carmichael (*below, pointing*) proclaims a "black power" slogan at the Meredith March rally in Greenwood on June 16, six weeks after his independent voting effort in Lowndes County was either scorned or ignored.

At a night meeting (*clock-wise from left*), Bernard Lee, Andrew Young, Robert Green, King, Lawrence Guyot, Harry Bowie, and Stokely Carmichael struggle to maintain unity on the Meredith March.

Behind sensational public controversy over black power and Vietnam, the Meredith marchers recruit new voters such as 104-year-old Ed Fondren (*right*), hoisted with his first registration card outside the Panola County, Mississippi, courthouse.

In September 1966, King escorts students with Andrew Young, Joan Baez, and Hosea Williams (*behind, left to right*) past adult mobs that have terrorized black children outside the schools of Grenada, Mississippi.

39

A weary King waits with Andrew Young for a flight out of Mississippi.

40

John Hulett (*right, with balloon*) welcomes the large voter turnout on November 8, 1966, when black citizens of Lowndes County are permitted to cast their first ballots in a general election. School board candidate John Hinson (*below, left, back to camera*) escorts voters to the polls. All seven "black panther" candidates narrowly lose, but Freedom

41

Party founders say they did well for the first try and vow to do better with experience plus future voters such as the young boy (*below, right*) in line with the Mallard family.

42

43

44

Among Vietnam protesters jammed outside the White House gates in May 1967, James Bevel (*above, center, at bars*), Coretta King (*behind Bevel*), and pediatrician Benjamin Spock (*above Coretta King*) stand vigil to deliver a peace petition.

Soldiers in Detroit (*right*) are deployed to suppress one of several large ghetto race riots in the summer of 1967.

45

Early in 1968, President Johnson and Defense Secretary Robert McNamara (*left*) reflect the strain of a governme[nt] and country divided ove[r] the Vietnam War.

46

47

SNCC founder and NAACP counsel Marian Wright (*above*), testifying about acute hunger in Mississippi, urges King to mount a national movement to reduce poverty.

King labors to convince skeptical advisers Andrew Young, Stanley Levison, Clarence Jones, Cleveland Robinson, and James Bevel (*below, clockwise from King*) that an uphill poverty movement offers a more positive emphasis than all-out effort to stop the Vietnam War. Temperamental aide Hosea Williams (*right*) is reconciled to King's choice.

48

On a recruiting drive in March 1968, moved by the extreme hardship of displaced sharecroppers, King pledges to begin a poor people's pilgrimage to Washington from Marks, Mississippi.

A movement for the basic dignity of sanitation workers diverts King to Memphis, where supporters collect donations in symbolic garbage cans.

Memphis, after violence breaks out for the first time in a march led by King, sanitation work-
maintain a picket line alongside National Guard armored vehicles.

April 3, determined to overcome a court injunction and restore nonviolent discipline for a
wed march, King and James Lawson (*in clerical collar*) follow Abernathy into Room 306 at
Lorraine Motel. King will be assassinated on this balcony the next day.

Alabama listeners ponder King's message on his last tour.

CHAPTER 20

Fort Deposit

August 3–14, 1965

THE government of the United States matched King's pace for the last days of his Northern tour. On Tuesday, August 3, while he pushed from street rallies to a speech at the Philadelphia Chamber of Commerce, plus a "unity" photograph with local NAACP president Cecil Moore, then joined five thousand pickets outside segregated Girard College, the House of Representatives passed the voting rights conference report, 328–74. A bomb threat the next day altered King's departing flight for eight speech appearances in Washington, during which the U.S. Senate passed the identical bill, 72–18, to sweep aside the last parliamentary obstacles along with the dominant political reality since the end of Reconstruction. On the White House lawn, President Johnson was greeting ten thousand college interns as "fellow revolutionaries" in the American tradition, exhorting them to surmount "the tyranny of poverty" and the "oppression of bigotry." On Thursday, Katzenbach and John Doar informed Johnson that the Justice Department stood ready to file suit against the Mississippi poll tax by one o'clock Saturday, to deploy federal registrars to at least ten counties on Monday, and to file additional suits on Tuesday against the poll tax laws in Virginia, Alabama, and the President's home state of Texas. Johnson disclosed this breakthrough agenda when King arrived for a small presidential meeting scheduled to discuss conditions in Northern states and the upcoming national conference on race. Thursday night, King returned with several thousand people for an unusual vigil outside the White House gates, rallying for Johnson's "home

rule" bill to let District of Columbia residents elect their own representatives.

At La Guardia Airport in New York, David Dellinger was delighted
to see Bayard Rustin dash aboard his flight early Friday, brimming with
news of an invitation to the President's sudden enactment ceremony for
the Voting Rights Act. "Wonderful," said Dellinger. "Be sure to get one
of the pens he uses to sign it." Dellinger proposed to call Rustin forward
at the Vietnam demonstration to sign the Declaration of Conscience
with the same pen. The idea sorely tempted Rustin with just the sort of
dramatic flair he had pioneered over decades of nonviolent witness.
Like Dellinger, he had gone to prison rather than fight even in the
"good war" against Hitler. Often since, he had warned of nuclear danger by risking jail on this August 6 anniversary of the Hiroshima bomb,
and with Dellinger he had just drafted the Vietnam peace declaration
for their common mentor, A. J. Muste, America's foremost pacifist. Still,
Rustin could not bring himself to celebrate the historic partnership with
President Johnson and protest his new war on the same day. He and
Dellinger separated uncomfortably in Washington.

The President and his Cabinet reached the Capitol by motorcade at
noon. Two sculptures of Abraham Lincoln flanked a special podium in
front of John Trumbull's imposing *Surrender of Cornwallis,* which hung
on the Rotunda wall. "Today is a triumph for freedom as huge as any
victory won on any battlefield," said Johnson. Reviewing the five tumultuous months since the "outrage of Selma" on Edmund Pettus Bridge,
he praised the vote as "the most powerful instrument ever devised by
man for breaking down injustice," and urged every Negro to make use
of it. "You must learn," he said, "so your choices advance your interests
and the interests of our beloved nation." To opponents of the new law,
those reluctant to "bend long years of habit," he advised "simply this: it
must come . . . and when it has you will find a burden has been lifted
from your shoulders, too." He beckoned all sides to treat "the wounds
and the weakness—the outward walls and the inward scars—that diminish achievement."

Led by escorts down a corridor toward the Senate, more than a hundred people jammed into a space twenty feet square, known as the President's Room because Presidents before Franklin Roosevelt had
journeyed there to sign bills into law. Johnson signed the Voting Rights
Act there on a small walnut table he had used as Majority Leader. He
handed signing pens first to Vice President Humphrey and Senator
Dirksen, then to more legislators, to leaders of civil rights groups, and,

as solemn ritual broke into celebration, to invited guests that included Rosa Parks, Rustin, and Vivian Malone, the first black graduate of the University of Alabama. A souvenir pen reached Detective Sergeant Everett Cooper of the protective unit assigned to King.

The President escaped clamor by ducking into the Senate chamber, where the startled presiding officer, Senator Wayne Morse of Oregon, pretended he was still a member. "The chair recognizes the Senator from Texas, the Majority Leader," said Morse in a refrain echoed from the 1950s. Johnson sat briefly at his old desk—front row center, carved of mahogany in 1819 to replace the original burned by British troops—and apologized to its rightful owner for the awkward intrusion. "I'm sorry, I forgot," he told Mike Mansfield, as though he had wandered back in time. Then he recovered his unique, manic perspective to spend the afternoon lashing allies forward by telephone from the White House. "We just got to, you *got* to make it," he told Katzenbach, to stiffen his assurance that immigration reform would pass. With House Majority Leader Carl Albert, Johnson lurched from sentimental congratulation to a sudden announcement that no conference report counted as a significant week's work. "You didn't do a damn thing," he charged. Over Albert's stammering defense—"We're going to pass one of the big ones next week"—Johnson peppered him with tactical comments: "You ought to have told me, you didn't call me. . . . I'll call every human being that you want. . . . I can't get him to pee a drop 'til y'all pee . . ." Desperate to beat a closing window in history, he invoked the late Speaker Sam Rayburn of Texas. "You and John McCormack have got to be Mister Rayburns," needled Johnson. "Now I've been letting you all off. . . . I'll tell you what you've got to do . . ."

Dellinger was among roughly six hundred pickets walking the Pennsylvania Avenue sidewalk in front of the White House. From the vigilant guard of two hundred police and fifteen Secret Service agents, solicitous officers brought out water and a chair to give the eighty-year-old Muste respite from the heat. His fellow marchers carried signs such as "WITHDRAW U.S. TROOPS FROM VIETNAM NOW!" and "JESUS CHRIST DID NOT CARRY A DRAFT CARD." A remnant of twenty-five pickets would lay unmolested all night on the sidewalk, then rejoin the larger group for weekend events called the Assembly of Unrepresented People, featuring workshops by and about Puerto Ricans, migrant laborers, Washingtonians, children, Pacific Islanders, ordinary voters, American Indians, and the poor, among others.

Bob Moses of SNCC, still calling himself Parris, brought to the four-day assembly a delegation of thirty black Mississippians. To memorialize John Shaw, killed weeks earlier in Vietnam—nearly four years after he had followed Moses as a teenager into the first bloody demonstrations for the vote in McComb—several of them had written a "McComb statement" for the Mississippi Freedom Democratic Party newsletter listing five reasons why "Negro boys should not honor the draft here in Mississippi," and hostile reactions were crackling. NAACP field secretary Charles Evers and the Mississippi movement's own lawyer denounced them. John Lewis, though he had signed Muste's antiwar declaration months before, met with President Johnson before attending the Capitol ceremony that day and issued a pained statement dissociating himself from the assembly. MFDP chairman Lawrence Guyot defended the right to dissent but felt obliged to say he would accept military service. On Sunday, the white Mississippi editor most favorable to civil rights would call the McComb statement "close to treason" and flay Guyot for "collaborating in the Communist line." On Monday, August 9—the twentieth anniversary of the second nuclear blast, at Nagasaki—uniformed American Nazis would throw buckets of paint on Moses, Dellinger, and Staughton Lynd as they led the concluding assembly march of eight hundred. A photograph in the next issue of *Life* would present the trio as pariahs branded vividly in red, among three hundred assorted pacifists arrested near the Capitol steps. Dellinger, refusing bond, would serve his full thirty days and hear vaguely in his cell of national upheaval later in August.

Already on Friday afternoon, the assembly's first picket line drew transfixed stares. "Sometimes I wish I had their degree of involvement," one bystander mused, but most reacted viscerally. Xenophobes jeered. Some Negroes and civil rights veterans bristled at the mostly white peace marchers for spurning the hard-won day of jubilee for the Voting Rights Act. Jack Newfield of New York's *Village Voice* disparaged an "incestuous" gathering of "hyper-militants and the authoritarians." Moses, a legend of the black movement in the midst of the peace assembly, floated as usual above crossfires of sentiment. In remarks to a rally of the pickets in Lafayette Park, he analyzed why Americans reacted more intensely to the obscure McComb statement than to the equivalent call for Vietnam war resistance in Muste's Declaration of Conscience, which was signed by five thousand petitioners and handed publicly through the White House gate. He traced much of the disparity to race. Untamed tribal instincts, flushed to the surface, still demanded that minorities submit to prescribed battle lines or be designated enemies themselves. "Negroes better than anyone else are in a position to question the war," Moses said softly through a bullhorn. "Not because they understand the war better, but because they better understand the United States."

* * *

CONFLICTED TRIUMPH scattered to worlds apart on Sunday, August 8. King preached at New York's Riverside Church and addressed a convention of morticians. John Lewis was arrested with SCOPE volunteers at one of two renewed kneel-ins outside the biggest churches in Americus, Georgia, while from deep inside Lowndes County, Stokely Carmichael composed a warning against the illusion of change. "I have my own personal fears about how the Federal Government can swallow us up," he wrote. "Signs of this are appearing in Alabama daily. My own feeling is that SNCC is about to be isolated. If indeed we feel that we should have nothing to do with the 'Establishment,' then it is imperative that we form coalitions of people without power."

Carmichael sent out his proposal for an autumn assembly of unrepresented people from across the South, and presided that night at the first mass meeting yet dared in Fort Deposit. A convoy of thirty cars drove bumper to bumper for nearly twenty miles along remote country roads, southward from Highway 80 into what SNCC records called "the toughest area in Lowndes County." SNCC workers Bob Mants and Jimmy Rogers had been "run out by the Klan" there, Carmichael indicated in reports, but they kept returning until they gathered "forty local kids under a tree." One of them, John McMeans, had prevailed upon his sister-in-law to give Rogers lodging, and Bessie McMeans finally prevailed upon her divided church elders to open a door to the movement itself. Most of the local people arrived on foot to greet the convoy of relative veterans from White Hall, forming together a spirited crowd of some four hundred inside Bethlehem Christian Church, singing hymns, hearing John Hulett and others give testimony as registered voters. Rabbi Saperstein was presented and received as a welcome amazement, but Carmichael seemed too busy to appreciate the freedom message he tried to deliver in the call-and-response of black Christians. There were whispered huddles at the doors, then a supervised evacuation. Just outside, FBI agents held back five carloads of menacing whites until the convoy departed. Carmichael told the Sapersteins to lay across laps to keep their white faces below the window of his back seat, and the cars streamed across the railroad tracks safely out of Fort Deposit.

Early on Tuesday, August 10, crowds of both races were milling tensely around the Lowndes County courthouse when official sedans glided conspicuously into Hayneville, bearing the attorney general of Alabama from Montgomery to investigate radio reports about enforcement of the new national law. Known as a golden orator from Dothan, Richmond Flowers had been elected in 1962 with his friend and schoolmate George Wallace, whom he hoped to succeed as governor, but Flowers had forfeited his history as the more diehard segregationist by announcing that he would tolerate no violence. Since then, rumors encouraged by the Wallace camp marked him as "soft" on race. Meeting only puzzled shrugs on the courthouse lawn, Flowers walked with his aides across the street to the post office.

"Can I help you?" asked the clerk.

"I understand the federal registrars are over here," said Flowers. "Can you tell me where they are?"

Tom Coleman preempted the clerk's reply. "Richmond, we ain't telling you a goddamned thing," he said from behind the counter. Coleman advised leaving the county in a hard voice that made the attorney general feel Coleman's reputation as a lifelong special deputy who had killed more than one alleged troublemaker at the prison farm. His sister Hulda still ran the Lowndes County schools, and he was known to ride with the Klan.

Flowers complied without another word, and learned later that the registrars were discovered far from the normal seat of public business. Local officials, pronouncing themselves "just sick" that their July 6 suspension of literacy tests failed to stave off federal posting—in fact, did not gain a reprieve even from the first South-wide target list of ten counties—had ushered the four freshly trained arrivals to the hometown of Lowndes registrar Carl Golson, touting the benefits of the county's largest and oldest settlement. Fort Deposit had been founded by order of General Andrew Jackson during territorial wars against the Creek Indians in 1813, as a supply depot perched at the highest elevation between Montgomery and New Orleans. This was not very high, nor was the modern population of 1,200 very big. Still, the hamlet offered two traffic lights and the most concentrated minority of white people in a vast Black Belt area staffed by a single public health officer one day a week, lacking ambulance service or a hospital. Three of the county's four doctors and dentists lived there.

Only forty-eight Negroes managed to reach Fort Deposit in time to register. The new era in Lowndes was a mute, constricted version of celebrations in the next county, where applicants outside Selma's courthouse sang the spiritual "Great Day," receiving water and cheers from supporters who passed along their lines in the hot sun. By nightfall in Fort Deposit, resolve took hold among the teenagers who first sneaked to hear SNCC speakers under a tree. Being too young themselves to register, they aimed to lift the blanket of fear from their segregated streets and thereby encourage their elders to journey all the way to the forbidden zone at the southern tip of Lowndes. "There will be demonstrations this Saturday in Ft. Deposit," advised a bulletin disseminated over the SNCC WATS line. The state of Alabama and the Justice Department would be asked to supply protection. "This will be the first demonstration ever held in Ft. Deposit," added the notice. "It is a KKK headquarters . . . THEY ARE REALLY AFRAID OF VIOLENCE."

*   *   *

Jimmy Rogers stayed behind to prepare the young volunteers, and Carmichael drove to Birmingham for the ninth annual convention of King's SCLC, where optimism crested on its theme, "Human Rights— Basic Issues—The Grand Alliance." Some remembered the same event during the siege to integrate Ole Miss in 1962, when they had been confined to Negro venues within the bastion of segregated Birmingham, and a Nazi had slugged King in the face. They could not stop mimicking novel courtesies they received now by contrast in the finest hotels, saying to each other, "Anything else I can do for you, sir?" On Monday, seven hundred registrants fairly promenaded from the Thomas Jefferson to the Redmont for the opening banquet honoring Rosa Parks, featuring an address by NAACP attorney Constance Baker Motley.

On Tuesday, swelling numbers paraded freely to City Hall past blockade spots made landmarks when police dogs and fire hoses had been loosed on marching children in Kelly Ingram Park. They decried the gridlock failure of Birmingham to hire even the first Negro police officer or firefighter, as agreed in the settlement from those 1963 demonstrations and required since by federal law. At the convention, a panoply of speakers represented the movement's cumulative experience along with options for the future. From Washington came Mordecai Johnson, former president of Howard University, a pulpit peer of Howard Thurman and the late Vernon Johns in the front rank of senior orators. He had just resigned from the District of Columbia school board in stinging protest that its appointed members, being accountable to Southerners in Congress rather than to voteless local citizens, were hiring incompetent Negro teachers for patronage. Among speakers from Chicago were the Catholic layman Matthew Ahmann, chief organizer of the 1963 ecumenical conference on religion and race, plus the top union officials of the United Packinghouse Workers, Ralph Helstein and Phil Weightman, who had fought decades to integrate the Midwestern meat plants, then supported the Southern movement since the bus boycott. Joining them among program speakers for one mass meeting, theologian Harvey Cox of Boston questioned his assigned topic, "God's Business," doubting that any movement audience still needed a shove into the pains of the secular world. "You'd be surprised," King replied.

FBI agents reported to headquarters that the chief investigator of the Alabama Ku Klux Klan went unnoticed in the crowd, disguised as a reporter, and wiretaps in New York intercepted a call home from the Jefferson Hotel on Wednesday, August 11. "We are having a good convention," Stanley Levison told his wife, Bea, though he was exhausted and "Martin worked all last night until seven o'clock this morning." The perpetual jostling for King's attention obliged volunteer Wall Street lawyer Harry Wachtel to send in a handwritten note that his legal contact, Carol Agger—"the wife of (newly appointed Justice of the Supreme Court) Abe Fortas"—had secured from the Treasury Department a long-sought tax-exempt status for SCLC's fund-raising arm. Wachtel languished in the background with news of scattered demonstrations, poll tax suits, and Senate confirmation of Thurgood Marshall as Solicitor General. He waited in the hotel lobby to make an appointment as King passed by with Coretta. Later, the frustrated Wachtel wrote a second appeal—"I will need to do this with you, *alone*"—which listed ten pressing questions of finance and Washington strategy.

King remained swamped, largely in preacher politics. The convention did hold a rally led by Fred Shuttlesworth in the bombed 16th Street Baptist Church, but not before its pastor wrung permission from the deacons by threatening to quit. In private, King again faced more than thirty headstrong preachers on his SCLC board, including his father. They frowned over tentative plans to take the movement somewhere north, observing that the first word in SCLC was "Southern," doubting that a Northern movement would "pay its share of the freight," suggesting that big cities take guidance instead from an SCLC brochure, and referring the proposed shift to a committee. Hosea

Williams tried to win board approval for a year-round extension of his SCOPE project, predicting great gains in registration if the board members would lend their presence. His flattery melted no criticism of current results, however, as Williams himself conceded with a revised proposal to terminate SCOPE by the end of the month. King, for his part, ran into trouble with his carefully worded resolution calling for Vietnam peace negotiations. Board members, bridling against intrusion into foreign policy, amended his text to reaffirm that SCLC's "primary function" was to secure the rights of Negroes, in what biographer David Garrow would call an "implicit rebuke" to King. Undercurrents from the leadership disputes seeped into the hotel corridors.

Andrew Young shot high above them in his keynote address at Wednesday's convention midpoint, proclaiming that "the very survival of mankind is at stake in the day-to-day action which grows from this organization." He said the past ten years of the nonviolent movement "have been but our infancy, and like an infant, we have stumbled and stammered," and yet those years had turned a powerless and invisible race into the transforming engine for a great nation. "We are not a rich people," he said. "We are not an especially brilliant people. We are not, God forgive us, even a particularly industrious people. And we are hardly what moralists would call a good people. But somehow, God has chosen us as his people, and called his children from the far corners of the world . . . to gather around us in a glorious procession."

The speech mixed apocalyptic hope with Madisonian balance. The "redistribution of Southern power" was irresistibly in motion, and the Goldwater forces "ran us out of the Republican Party," Young declared, but Negroes "must still find every opportunity to encourage the development of a two-party South." Civil rights had stimulated kindred movements, but he charged that not all of them, specifically the peace movement, understood the value of long-range regard for adversaries. "We have taken power and political reform seriously, while dramatizing an issue," Young boasted, warning that the need for discipline would only grow. "People will not lightly throw off a century of fear and go gaily skipping down to the courthouse to register," he said. "Civics is not taught in the schools." The burden of the nonviolent movement had fallen thus far on the most dispossessed people, he asserted, and they, like others, required constructive coalitions "to insure a balance of power and checks against its abuse."

Young told the Birmingham convention that he felt both exalted and frightened by the awesome power of "that beloved soul force about which Gandhi spoke so much, and which we have only begun to explore." Already, nonviolence was advancing miracles of the deepest, most distinctive patriotism—once again creating ties of democratic strength where hierarchy had reigned. Now he declared from recent experience that the movement could raise a nonviolent army of a hundred thousand or better in almost any large city, "and I tremble to think what might happen if it is not organized and disciplined in the interest of positive social change." So telescoped was movement history that the implications were running decades ahead of adjustment, throwing up new frontiers before most Americans perceived Negroes to be full participants in national politics, let alone modern Founders. "There will not be the same kind of press support or financial support that we have received from the North, as the movement comes closer to home and threatens vested interests," Young predicted. "But if we are true to Gandhi, and seek to attack issues rather than people, we can hope to inspire even our opposition to new moral heights, and thereby overcome."

* * *

ON THAT Wednesday afternoon of Young's speech, Ronald Frye celebrated his discharge from the Air Force by drinking vodka and orange juice with two young ladies and his older brother, Marquette. A California Highway Patrol motorcycle officer followed their weaving 1955 Buick northward on Avalon Boulevard and pulled them over at the corner of 116th, just inside the Los Angeles city limit. Onlookers gathered to watch driver Marquette Frye tightrope-walk a sobriety test in the street, then grandly offer to repeat his performance backward. Raucous laughter prompted a Highway Patrol backup officer to pull out a shotgun, adding taunts and tension to entertainment that built the crowd to some five hundred before a tow truck arrived twelve minutes later, simultaneously with Rena Frye on foot from her home two blocks away. She berated her sons for drinking, then defended them from the officers in caroming rounds of disputed blame and wound up handcuffed herself, thrown into the back of a cruiser. When Marquette Frye refused to follow, shouting, "Go ahead, kill me," police drew revolvers. One officer would testify that he missed Frye's shoulder and inadvertently struck him in the forehead with a nightstick. A witness said Highway Patrol officers drove motorcycles onto sidewalks to push back crowds that saw them as intruders and resented being called "black" instead of

"Negro." Officers waded in to arrest two bystanders for insults, delaying their departure. All three arrested Fryes left the scene with bruises twenty-six minutes after the traffic stop, as crowds now swelled to 1,500 greeted regular Los Angeles police units with jeers and rocks.

A retired man nine blocks from the scene remarked to his wife that such a din of sirens must mean "the King of Siam" was in town. Rushing to find out, he heard feverish rumors that police had manhandled a pregnant Negro woman, and he saw chunks of concrete hurled through car windows. Police commanders, unable to subdue swirling bands by conventional tactics designed for a stationary mass of rioters, evacuated an area east into the section named for Pasadena Realtor and liveryman C. H. Watts. Some Negroes "milled around inside the blocked-off area, protesting police 'brutality' by the officers," reported the *Los Angeles Times,* while others attacked unfamiliar cars, especially if occupied by white people. They burned a television van when reporters fled their approach on foot.

Mayor Sam Yorty first blamed the Highway Patrol for dawdling in city territory. LAPD Chief William Parker appeared on television to defend withdrawal from the riot zone. "What do you want the policemen to do?" he asked brusquely. "Do you want to mass them in there? For what purpose?" His lieutenants had a huge city to protect, said Parker, "and they can't send all the men into Watts and allow . . . open season to every petty criminal and burglar in town." He dodged further scrutiny when violence subsided in the night. The Thursday morning *New York Times* carried a two-inch story on a back page—"Arrest Causes Near Riot in Negro Area of Coast"—next to items about the jailing of fifty SCOPE workers who picketed a segregated gasoline station in Dublin, Georgia, and about the slow progress through the Alabama legislature of a bill "to regulate the sale of dynamite in the wake of recent racial incidents."

In south Los Angeles, crowds returned to Avalon Boulevard as though to work from a night's sleep, and looted a supermarket.

* * *

AT THE Jefferson Hotel in Birmingham, Bayard Rustin opened Thursday's central panel entitled "Visions of Things to Come." Now that President Johnson was fully engaged, "and Congress is turning out decisions like sausages to help us," he prescribed a shift to national economic issues such as jobs and poor schools. Activists must become more pragmatic and yet no less committed to nonviolence, Rustin argued, especially if Vietnam renewed the jingoist climate of the Korean War, "because morally, nothing can move in this country at this moment unless the civil rights movement is moving, and to that extent we have a terrifying responsibility for all of the citizens."

James Bevel shocked the panel audience with a blunt pronouncement: "This year the civil rights movements are out of business." Those who believed otherwise would shrivel into "civil rights shells, making noise," he declared, but Rustin was wrong to suggest that they become lobbyists and administrators. There were dazzling vistas of nonviolence ahead that "Bayard doesn't quite understand," claimed Bevel, beginning to preach. "One day Jesus was talking to some fellows who were in the same dilemma that the American people are in today," he said. "He got them together and said, 'Well, I'll tell you what you do about the whole question of freedom and slavery: know the truth.' " Not truth as dogma from tricky Baptists or bishops, but the healing truth of nonviolence, he quipped, then veered abruptly into his own private life. "I had a girlfriend, I had two," said Bevel. "I used to go see one at seven and the other one at eight. The one I would see at seven . . . she got angry and went outside and tore the windshield wipers off the car . . . in an effort to keep me back." In a flash, he transformed her alleged misconception about how to stop a car into a lesson about where to apply nonviolence. "You've got to know where the pulpit is!" cried Bevel. "Don't preach in the basement!" He said the whole world "disrespects the peasant in Vietnam," just as it disrespected Alabama Negroes until the movement "accepted the role of a peasant in Selma." He wanted to take an international peace army into Vietnam, and also seek the truth of the economy from Harlem to Appalachia. "We must be a nonviolent movement for the world," said Bevel. "The times are pushing us to this."

Ella Baker, the revered senior mentor for SNCC, addressed titters in the audience. "What Bevel has had to say today will be interpreted many ways by many people," she said gently, chiding him for glib provocation. "Some will claim that he, for instance, is a radical. I hope he is, because the word means getting to the root of things. I hope also he is ready to pay the price of being radical." Baker and nonviolent strategist James Lawson closed the panel with pleas for a more thoughtful movement, and for recognition that a minority of demonstrators—and only a tiny fraction of oppressed people—were yet committed to nonviolence ("as exemplified," said Baker, "by the reports coming out of Los Angeles").

At a plenary session in the newly desegregated Civic Auditorium,

King presented the SCLC Freedom Medal to James and Diane Nash Bevel for conceiving what became the 1965 Alabama voting rights campaign. The new landmark law had risen from their anguished response to the Birmingham church bombing, said King, praising them for citizens' initiative unmatched in history. The young couple, still largely unknown, had surmounted the abridgement of their own rights to catalyze a national movement from Selma, where only six months ago Nash had found her husband a comatose prisoner handcuffed to a gurney. There were nods in varying degrees of appreciation and regret among the few who knew that the honorees nevertheless were painfully estranged, and that the wild Bevel who spoke in public about hourly girlfriends was trying only sporadically to reunite with his wife and two young children. Shortly, however, King eclipsed gossip and convention business alike. "Few events in my lifetime have stirred my conscience and pained my heart as the present conflict which is raging in Vietnam," he said from the podium. "The true enemy is war itself." King announced that he intended to appeal for peace negotiations in personal letters to world leaders, including Ho Chi Minh, and reporters bolted for telephones.

A buzz of controversy lingered in an auditorium crowd of 3,500 people by FBI estimate. Some in the party of mortician A. A. "Sam" Rayner felt unsettled or deprived by talk of war politics, and not a few looked forward to an unadulterated dose of movement salvation in the closing programs on Friday, August 13, whispering that Daddy King was the real preacher in the King family. Father Richard Morrisroe, on the other hand, searched out Ivanhoe Donaldson and John Lewis among SNCC workers now dressed uniformly in bib overalls and rural work shirts, many of whom considered the convention a showy distraction. Tales of isolated danger and deprivation had made the distinctive SNCC outfit a newly potent image for movement followers, as it was truthfully said that the mere appearance of telltale dungarees in a Southern vestibule could halt a Negro church service, inspiring the worshippers or putting them to flight. Morrisroe asked Lewis to meet Silas Norman and was introduced instead to Stokely Carmichael, who handed him off during SNCC caucuses to the seminarian Jonathan Daniels. Within hours, Morrisroe decided to retrieve his bag and stay on for a second week of annual vacation. His parishioner Sam Rayner drove back to Chicago an emerging figure in South Side reform politics—destined to be the next alderman elected for the ward around St.

Columbanus Parish on 71st Street—but his wife "nearly choked him" for leaving their young white priest alone in rural Alabama.

Morrisroe absorbed constant wonder. From a convention lecture by economist Leon Keyserling, he drove to Selma and on Friday into Lowndes County for the first time at speeds sometimes above a hundred miles an hour in a Plymouth Fury rented for Daniels by his Episcopal sponsor, ESCRU, after pursuers recently chased him to the Montgomery city limit. At Trickem, Morrisroe separated from Daniels to attend a nonpolitical revival service with the elderly farm couple, Will and Mary Jane Jackson, near the spot where they had been photographed when the great march entered Lowndes. The choir invited him to sing among them on a rough bench, then delivered him to bunk on the porch floor of the SNCC Freedom House. Morrisroe scarcely noticed hardship there because he was smitten by Gloria Larry, whom he pressed for details of her academic work on French literary antecedents in the *Four Quartets* of T. S. Eliot.

Bulletins on gunshot fatalities were spreading nationwide from Los Angeles. After seventy-five people were injured on Thursday, a second lull had convinced authorities again that the riot was spent. Police units withdrew from the emergency perimeter at dawn Friday. Mayor Yorty and Lieutenant Governor Glenn Anderson flew to San Francisco for separate engagements even as angry crowds reconvened near Wednesday's arrest site on Avalon, and an ominous entry appeared in the log at police headquarters: "10:00 A.M. Major looting became general." Marauding bands leapfrogged from the twenty blocks previously sealed toward a peak riot area of 46.5 square miles. Arsonists torched emptied stores. Poet and columnist Langston Hughes reported the sight of a woman stopping obediently at red lights as she rolled a looted sofa down the street. Most of the press retreated because of assaults on white journalists, including a KABC-TV correspondent who was dragged off and was missing for two hours. For information that rioters had invented hand signals to identify and protect residents by neighorhood, office messenger Robert Richardson gained a kind of battlefield promotion as the first Negro reporter ever hired by the *Los Angeles Times*. By midday, California authorities summoned Governor Pat Brown from vacation in Greece, and mobilized 14,000 National Guard troops. Police units, amid rumors that commanders felt slighted by the call for help, moved ahead of them into the riot zone. At 6:30 P.M., LAPD officers shot Leon Posey standing unarmed outside a barber shop, in what would be ruled an accidental homicide. Half a dozen Negro deaths quickly followed this first official casualty—one shot in the back, one firing a gun, one carrying liquor and another shoes. Rioters harassed firefighters called in from a hundred different engine companies.

Shortly before midnight in New York, FBI wiretap monitors came alive to an incoming call from King's secretary, Dora McDonald. "The Negroes have broken into some gun stores," she told Stanley Levison. "They have guns and those big Army knives, and are covering about a 140-block-square area." She said King wanted Levison to draft a telephone statement for him to deliver over Los Angeles radio stations. "Also," said McDonald, "a man from the *New York Times* called and has given me twelve questions that he would like Dr. King to answer." She dictated them to Levison—"what is the text of the letter," the mode of transmission to Ho Chi Minh, the names of intermediaries, the apportionment of blame for the war, and the specifics of King's peace plan? Two questions asked how Bevel's "more militant" stance could be reconciled with nonviolence, and whether King approved.

Levison dictated suggested replies well after midnight to McDonald in Atlanta, for relay to King at his Miami stopover en route to address the Disciples of Christ convention in Puerto Rico. The Vietnam letter was still merely an idea. "Most reporters will try to draw him into going further, until they have a real story," Levison told McDonald. "He hasn't formulated specific proposals for ending the war, and hasn't said he has." The New York FBI office rushed a transcript by encoded Teletype to headquarters at 3:41 A.M. Saturday, and supervisors added to an edited text the sinister preface that a "long-time Communist" was influencing King on Vietnam. The classified report to the White House and Justice Department omitted entirely the intercepted remarks that Levison offered King for broadcast to the rioters in Watts: "I know you have grievances that are hard to live with. I know that any Negro can reach the end of his patience . . . but it is not courage nor militancy to strike out blindly. . . . Tonight the whole world is watching you. If you want all America to respect you, if you want the world to know that you are men, put down your weapons and your rocks. . . . Negroes in the South were not less oppressed than you, and we have run Jim Crow from thousands of places without using a rock or a bullet. . . . Come back to our ranks . . . where real and permanent victories have been won and will be won in the right way."

* * *

FIVE JOURNALISTS found more than twenty teenagers seated around Jimmy Rogers in the shaded area of a church lawn on Pollard Street, taking shelter from heat that already was thick by the appointed hour. The reporters were following a story tip from the SNCC office in Selma, where Silas Norman had supervised advance notice also to federal and state officials: "This Sat. Aug. 14 at 9 A.M. there will be a demonstration in Ft. Deposit, Lowndes Co. Ala. Klan is very active in area. We demand protection of demonstrators." Ominous attention gathered as the young people hand-lettered picket signs such as "No More Back Doors," debating which stores most deserved challenge for cruel habits of segregation aimed at them and their sharecropper parents. A sedan pulled up with two FBI agents to warn of hostile men milling nearby with clubs and shotguns. Cars cruised by slowly with "Open Season" bumper stickers, after a Klan slogan said to be popular locally since the hung jury in the Liuzzo trial. The rented Plymouth Fury arrived bearing Jonathan Daniels, Gloria Larry, Richard Morrisroe, and project director Stokely Carmichael, who conferred while scouts reconnoitered the grim scene only blocks away over the pine hill: a hundred Negroes waiting outside the tiny post office that housed the federal registrars, frozen under the glare of vigilantes who mingled in the street with uniformed officers and deputies. A ninety-three-year-old woman in line allowed that she had not ventured into town for fifty years. Several of the reporters were both shaken and puzzled to be threatened as "Freedom Riders," an anachronism from 1961, by local men apparently enraged at the sight of white people speaking civilly with Negroes.

The teenagers lettered another picket sign: "Wake Up! This Is Not Primitive Time." None flinched when the FBI agents returned to urge cancellation in the face of mob violence or arrest. They grumbled instead against the agents' standard disclaimer—that Bureau personnel were strictly observers, lacking enforcement powers to intervene—and lumped FBI intimidation with others they were itchy to confront. "I don't want to scare the older people away from voter registration," said one, "but we need this." Negroes still had to slink around to back doors, said others, and only something drastic would plant the idea in both races that Fort Deposit was part of America. A spirited local girl added that she "sure would like to get one good whack at the Man," which dissolved peers in howling approval but prompted another huddle among the SNCC staff.

They agreed the demonstration was not their idea—most of them privately opposed it—and first asked Rogers to propose cancellation. When the teenagers demanded to go forward, some veterans favored deferring to local initiative even at the risk of an "open graveyard," while others said they could not dodge responsibility behind a modest ideological pose. They reopened leadership issues that ranged, SNCC-style, as far as Carmichael's reflections on the 1938 humanist novel *Bread and Wine,* by Ignazio Silone, in which he said an educated radical, disguised as a priest, wrestles with the subtle morality of inspiring damaged poor people to risk revolt against Mussolini. The standard for Carmichael was transparently shared risk. He argued that they could and should oppose any demonstration without a pledge of nonviolence, and told the teenagers that smacking the Man gained nothing but cheap regret. Daniels mimicked his extroverted pose of assurance for people in the grip of fear, until young John McMeans insisted that his friends give up commando notions or go home. "If that's what you want to do," said Carmichael, "don't take anything they can call a weapon. Not even a pencil." The teenagers reluctantly surrendered nail files and pocket-knives. Daniels, Larry, Morrisroe, and Ruby Sales stepped forward to round out the escorts called veterans, although only Morrisroe among them had been arrested even once (with Al Raby in Chicago), and kept to himself among strangers. In soothing small talk, Carmichael learned that poet Gwendolyn Brooks was a member of Morrisroe's Chicago parish, and remarked that a good friend at Howard had served as a Carmelite priest in Bolivia. SNCC staff members Jean Wiley and Martha Prescod compiled a family notification roster for bail.

They moved out in three groups of ten at 11:30, more than two hours late, but demonstrations scarcely lasted a minute. Fifty armed men closed on the first signs raised outside McGough's Grocery, and a deputy among them said the pickets were going to jail. "For what?" asked Jimmy Rogers, who briefly considered the halting reply—"for resisting arrest, and picketing to cause blood"—while enveloped in a posse quivering to be a mob, then numbly replied, "All right." As the pickets were marched toward the other groups, clumps of local men fell upon the reporters in two cars nearby, banging, yanking at locked doors while impeding their getaway, and from Golson Motors ran Jack Golson, the county coroner with a shotgun and his brother Carl, the registrar, who smashed a passenger-side window and the windshield with a baseball bat before the car lurched away. A truckload of men chased another car whose driver, panicking when hemmed in, tried a U-turn and bumped into the pursuing truck. Stokely Carmichael, regretting that he had allowed SNCC staff member Chris Wylie to drive, stepped out proposing that gentlemen should let the authorities settle the incident, but both he and Wylie were in handcuffs by the time they reached the miniature Fort Deposit jail.

The car with the shattered windshield drove up like a ghost, the reporters having doubled back in their own variations on the debate they had witnessed all morning—telling one another they could not abandon the story, or were crazy, or must distract the crowd from the young prisoners who bulged from a jail building no more than ten by fifteen feet. On the passenger's side, blood ran from head cuts down the arm of *Life* correspondent Sanford Ungar, who had stared transfixed by the attack and wound up with shards of glass in his mouth. One bystander looking amazed into the car erupted in a convulsive rant about body paint, shaved heads, and "nigger wigs," as ideas occurred to him for completing the reporters' defection from the white race. Shortly afterward, driver David Gordon would record in an interview that he sat frozen with Ungar until the demonstrators were herded onto the rear of a flatbed truck used to collect the city's garbage, and that amid menacing shouts about trash disposal, "I looked directly at Stokely and he had the most serene expression on his face I've ever seen." Prisoners waved to stunned friends in the post office line before the truck pulled away. The reporters, blocked from following, managed to identify one of them as a Bessie Lee Caldwell, holding her new registration slip.

That night SNCC worker Scott B. Smith slipped into the home of a Hayneville contact, and verified from the sound of freedom songs that the prisoners were held in the new county jail there, next door to the old one with the gallows. He crept across Highway 97, through an alley to a hidden observation spot behind the Lowndes County courthouse, drawn by revolving arrivals to a late conference in the sheriff's office. Sporadic gunfire punctuated the night. Fearing that a lynch mob was being gathered, Smith kept watch until forced to retreat before dawn on Sunday. "Because of the dogs in the area [who] were barking," he wrote in his report, "I went back to Mrs. Robinson's house."

CHAPTER 21

Watts and Hayneville

August 14–31, 1965

THE Watts crisis spread improvisation with awe. White House aides shared bulletins late Saturday that Governor Pat Brown had known of many fires and one fatality as he left the Greek islands. "When he got off the airplane, we told him that the death toll was up to seventeen," said Lee White. "Boy, that really sobered him." Jack Valenti interjected that the number went to eighteen minutes later with injuries climbing from 558. Joe Califano said his former colleagues at the Pentagon were virtually headless because Cyrus Vance and other top deputies had taken August leave, Secretary McNamara himself being secluded on Martha's Vineyard along with Attorney General Katzenbach and speechwriter Richard Goodwin, who was sailing, unavailable to draft a presidential statement on the crisis. ("We ought to blow up that goddamned island," growled President Johnson.) Califano, commandeering better space than his rookie office in the basement, retrieved LeRoy Collins from a fishing boat for emergency assignment to the Watts area, where a riot curfew forced Otis Chandler, publisher of the *Los Angeles Times,* to postpone the paper's charity football exhibition between the Dallas Cowboys and Los Angeles Rams. Chandler's newest reporter, his byline slugged "Robert Richardson, 24, a Negro," made the front page with a story headlined " 'Get Whitey,' Scream Blood-Hungry Mobs," followed Sunday by an instant cultural icon: " 'Burn, Baby, Burn' Slogan Used as Firebugs Put Area to Torch." Saturday's front-page editorial denounced the failure of "kid-glove measures." Sunday's mourned "the four ugliest days in our history," with the death toll subsided at thirty-five, and called for universal prayer "to prevent forever the recurrence."

Nationally, battle news from Vietnam echoed Watts, and the Beatles performed hits from their new album *Help!* at New York's Shea Stadium, breaking the attendance record for a pop concert. King aborted a Puerto Rico rest trip but stalled the same Sunday in Miami. Bayard Rustin urged him to avoid the certain embarrassment of a visit to Los Angeles, warning that he would be called an Uncle Tom if he helped quell the riots and a failure or worse if they broke out again. King reproached himself for hiding. "I think I ought to be out there," he told colleagues in the Los Angeles clergy, but they equivocated. The riots were beyond any trauma they had foreseen as hosts of King's rescheduled tour in July, and their ally Governor Brown was lobbying to keep King out of California. King held off until he saw news that Mayor Yorty and a visiting evangelist flew above Watts, with the latter announcing that he perceived the riots as a "dress rehearsal" by "sinister and evil forces . . . whose ultimate objective is the overthrow of the American government." The phone rang again for Rev. Thomas Kilgore, head of SCLC's Los Angeles chapter. "Tom," said King, "if Billy Graham can ride over them in a helicopter, why can't I come out there and talk to those young people?"

King persuaded Bayard Rustin to meet him in Los Angeles Tuesday afternoon, August 17. The rendezvous was personally awkward for Rustin, as Los Angeles had been the site of his arrest in 1953 for "perversion," which led to a break with his fatherly employer in pacifist work, A. J. Muste, and Rev. Kilgore had served as intercessor during Adam Clayton Powell's hushed political threat in 1960, when King banished Rustin to avoid public accusation that he associated with a homosexual. Now Kilgore led a reception committee that included Norman Houston, president of the local NAACP, and Rev. H. H. Brookins, pastor of the huge middle-class congregation at First AME. Rustin joined them as King made a brief statement to reporters at the airport gate, deploring violence, pledging to minister and listen. He ducked questions about Governor Brown's charge that his visit was "untimely," reported the *Los Angeles Times,* "and was hustled off to an undisclosed location," where he and the Californians pondered options on Tuesday night in a climate of poisonous blame.

Republican Jack Shell, who had lost the last gubernatorial nomination to Richard Nixon, announced that the riots carried "amazing political implications" favoring his bid to unseat Governor Brown in 1966, and Brown withdrew most of the riot troops on Tuesday in an assertion of normalcy restored. "I don't know what the governor is doing," snapped Mayor Yorty, a Democratic rival, who denounced as "the big lie" any fault laid to the city. "He's too busy with press relations." Chief Parker, having said Negro leaders gave him the idea to pull out of the riot zone for two days, and then denied that he paid any attention to them, switched to a straightforward cry of victory. "We're on top, and they're on the bottom," he proclaimed, declaring that only fear of police secured order in the riot areas. Parker dismissed critics who perceived racial overtones in his analysis, but he did narrow his postmortem diagnosis of the riot's cause to an Islamic sect among Negroes. From police intelligence reports, he accused "the Black Muslims" of fomenting general insurrection from a spark of disorder.

The smallest Los Angeles crowd since the dawn of professional football turned out Tuesday night for the postponed Rams-Cowboys game, leaving two-thirds of the giant Coliseum empty. With the curfew lifted, members of the Nation of Islam regathered at Muhammad's Mosque of Islam No. 27 on South Broadway, west of Watts, where, shortly after midnight, a surrounding phalanx of one hundred police officers fired by their count one thousand rounds into the structure, shattering every window and splintering doors with shotguns at close range. A coordinated charge turned up three small fires burning inside and "19 men sprawled on the bloodstained floor," according to the *Los Angeles Times,* nine cut by flying glass. Police arrested them for conspiracy to commit arson on their own building and to murder the officers, then arrested forty Muslims for obstruction as they arrived on summons to "defend the Temple." In the aftermath, undercover police took one trusted reporter through the demolished auditorium into a small kitchen where the reporter saw that "tables were broken, utensils lay on the floor, eggs had been splattered, cupboard doors had been ripped from their hinges, apparently in the police search for Muslim gunmen and their weapons." Outside, officers dropped tear gas grenades down storm drains in a last futile effort to locate suspects with guns or riot plans, while from a distance the mosque leader challenged the press to verify official claims of self-defense: "Do you see any bullet marks on this side of the street?"

Correspondents filed dispatches as if from a war zone. One for the *Chicago Tribune* said LAPD officers "stormed the fortified temple of the Negro race extremists," and the *Los Angeles Times* called the raid a "shattering assault" on taboo space. "The fanatical Black Muslims never have permitted a white man to enter their mosque," declared the *Times,* overlooking a more violent police altercation at the same mosque in 1962. Few Negroes in Los Angeles forgot that lethal episode, because Malcolm X had captivated mass meetings from the floor of prestigious Christian churches with electrifying oratory about Chief Parker's force as a daily oppression for Negroes, Mexicans, and other minorities regardless of class or deportment. Even Roy Wilkins of the NAACP for once had made common cause with Malcolm, whose racial separatism he steadfastly deplored, against hard, segregated reality in the shadows of Hollywood. (The LAPD recently had expunged formal rules that barred its few Negroes—none in 1965 above the rank of sergeant—from riding with white partners; the California Highway Patrol claimed three Negroes among three thousand officers.) Malcolm X had commuted cross-country to mesmerize Negro Los Angeles through the 1963 show trial, restraining Muslims from the retaliation Malcolm himself had promised, secretly beginning his fateful break from the sectarian doctrines of the Nation of Islam's founder and leader, Elijah Muhammad.

Three Muslims freed after the 1962 raid were seized again* in Mosque Number 27, as though back from a minor preview, hours after Martin Luther King had arrived from the East. On Wednesday, King pushed through a crowd that engulfed the Westminster Neighborhood Association in the burned-out heart of Watts, and climbed on a small platform with Rustin a step behind, just above heads packed within reach of their chins. A man shouted, "Get out of here, Dr. King! We don't want you." A woman shouted at the man, "Get out, psycho."

Rustin pleaded with the crowd to hear King, who tried several times to begin. "All over America," he said, "Negroes must join hands and—"

"And burn!" shouted a young man near him.

"And work together in a creative way," King persisted.

A young woman called out that "Parker and Yorty" should come themselves to "see how we're living." Another cried, "They'll burn the

---

* Troy X (Augustine), Clarence X (Jingles), and Robert X (Rogers) were arrested both in 1962 and 1965. An account of the April 27, 1962, incident, in which Robert X received four gunshot wounds, forms the first chapter of *Pillar of Fire,* the second volume in this series. Prosecutors dropped charges against these three defendants. Eleven others were convicted in 1963, and remained in prison during the Watts uprising.

most." A third scoffed that big shots never would bring air-conditioned Cadillacs to Watts.

King promised to do "all in my power" to persuade the police chief and mayor to talk with residents. "I know you will be courteous to them," he said with a smile, which brought howls of laughter. He asked about living conditions, police relations, and details of the riots, then shouted out that he believed firmly in nonviolence. "So maybe some of you don't quite agree with that," said King. "I want you to be willing to say that."

"Sure, we like to be nonviolent," called out one man, "but we up here in the Los Angeles area will not turn that other cheek." He denounced local Negro leaders as absentees: "They're selling us again, and we're tired of being sold as slaves!"

Over cheers and cross-talk, another man's voice prevailed. "All we want is jobs," he yelled. "We get jobs, we don't bother nobody. We don't get no jobs, we'll tear up Los Angeles, period."

King continued when the exchanges died down. "I'm here because at bottom we are brothers and sisters," he said. "We all go up together or we go down together. We are not free in the South, and you are not free in the cities of the North."

This time he ignored interruptions. "The crowd hushed, though," observed reporters for the *Los Angeles Times,* "as Dr. King began to speak in an emotion-charged voice." A correspondent for the Negro weekly *Jet* agreed: "The jeering had stopped, and the cynics were drowned out by applause and cheers." King preached on the suffering purpose of the movement to build freedom above hatred. "Don't forget that when we marched from Selma to Montgomery," he intoned, "it was a white woman who died." He called the roll of white martyrs who had joined black ones, crying out that James Reeb had followed Jimmie Lee Jackson in Selma, as Schwerner and Goodman were lynched with James Chaney in Mississippi, the year after Medgar Evers was shot. "Elijah Muhammad is my brother, even though our methods are different," King shouted to a thunderclap of surprise, and his peroration built hope on boundless redemption. "There will be a brighter tomorrow," he cried. "White and black together, we shall overcome."

King moved on to see Governor Brown, who was preoccupied with appointments to a riot inquiry modeled on the Warren Commission. They held a joint press conference of sober but vague cooperation, after which King let slip candor in a personal telegram: "I am very sorry that you see me only as a demonstrator." The governor seemed benign, however, after a sequestered meeting with Mayor Yorty and Chief Parker on Thursday, August 19. King emerged shaken after nearly three hours and managed platitudes for reporters about an "in-depth, frank discussion," conceding that the city leaders "didn't agree with most of the things we said." Pressed for examples, he cited their refusal to let him visit prisoners in the Lincoln Heights jail and their denial that poverty or police conduct contributed to the riots. Because virtually every local Negro had called for Parker's resignation, King said, he had suggested that an independent review board could "do a lot to relieve tension" over specific charges of brutality. It would broaden the scope of judgment beyond police officials who might be partial to their own command.

Mayor Yorty overheard the last of the press exchange. He stepped forward to declare King's visit "a great disservice to the people of Los Angeles and to the nation." To question police conduct after a riot was to "justify lawlessness," he charged, and King "shouldn't have come here." As for reports that his was the only major city not receiving, nor diligently seeking, federal funds in the new War on Poverty, Yorty deflected blame to "changing dictates" from Washington that he said "certainly helped to incite the people in the poverty area." He rejected any notion that Parker should be discharged or even permitted to resign. "Race relations would go to a low ebb," said Yorty, "because the white community would not stand for it."

Reporters jumped to the spilled insults—"King Assailed by Yorty After Stormy Meeting"—and elicited confirming euphemisms on both sides. Yorty's aides said the exchange had been "far from friendly." Rustin told them King had endured "crude" language without losing his temper. Later, Rustin made notes that the session left him and King "completely nonplussed," despite their experience with segregationist officials in the South, because Parker and Yorty steadfastly denied the existence of prejudice anywhere in Los Angeles. When he cited to them the heavy local majority to repeal California's fair housing laws, wrote Rustin, they insisted that Proposition 14 was a nonracial affirmation of personal choice in real estate.

King publicly refined grievance into several levels of confession. "We as Negro leaders—and I include myself—have failed to take the civil rights movement to the masses of the people," he said. He also said, however, that he could not find "any statesmanship and creative leadership" in Los Angeles, and pledged to offer his findings directly to President Johnson.

* * *

JOYCE BAILEY, jailed Saturday on her nineteenth birthday, remained in a Hayneville cell that grew filthy into the week of King's tour of Watts—an exposed, stopped-up toilet close under foot, shrieks for a mop ignored, clean water shut off sporadically from the sink. Her job in the Fort Deposit pajama factory was gone. Her father, a relatively independent railroad worker on the Louisville & Nashville line, brought her mother's home-cooked food until the jailers turned away the bother of all visitors, including John Hulett's intrepid well-wishers and civil rights doctors out of Selma. Her two companions lacked the comfort of home sympathy, and prayed instead that their families would never find out what happened. Gloria Larry knew her stepfather would thunder that he had plotted a whole career of Air Force postings from Bermuda to San Francisco just to keep her *out* of her native South. As the sophisticated elder at twenty-four, Larry struggled to maintain a composed example above primitive ordeals that included tears and frequent screams from the youngest cellmate, Ruby Sales, who lay doubled up from ulcers. Defying Deputy Sheriff Joe "Lux" Jackson, who threatened to have the Negro trusty beat them or worse for the noise, they sang freedom songs to assure the male prisoners on the second floor that their spirits were intact.

Precocious at seventeen, Sales cajoled the trusty to prove a streak of independent humanity by smuggling her notes upstairs to Daniels, with whom she flirted about movement philosophy even though she still mocked his seminarian's collar. Rebellion against middle-class piety had swept Sales from "high" Baptist to skeptic and from head cheerleader now to jail, beginning with the freshman day trip to Montgomery during the Selma march, when she and her Tuskegee professor wound up inside King's former church all night. To her parents, whose ambition for Sales was such that they delivered her all through childhood to separate attendance at the elite First African Baptist of Columbus, Georgia, remaining content themselves in a missionary church, the signal shock of the movement was their daughter's switch from Tuskegee heels and stockings to SNCC overalls. Unable to fathom why anyone would dress like the poorest, most vulnerable people—on purpose—they blamed the young professor, Jean Wiley, who also had joined SNCC. Sales had opposed letting Daniels into the Lowndes County movement, but he proved too charming and too smart about religion for her to maintain the standoffish posture that preachers were opiate-of-the-masses hypocrites above solidarity with black sharecroppers. Daniels had driven with Stokely Carmichael to Columbus to address her family's worries in person, which impressed her father enough to plead with each of them to look out for her. If he learned of the Fort Deposit arrests, Sales feared he would yank her out of Alabama.

Apart from her stomach, the sharpest pain arrived with a note that Carmichael and Chris Wylie posted separate bail on Wednesday, the fifth day, breaking a pact to resist the unjust charges as a united group. No longer could Carmichael be heard calling out for a song, or shouting, "John, it's prayer time now," to prompt a devotional from the devout young McMeans. The female prisoners did not believe a smuggled note that he was needed on the outside to raise money, having heard derisive scoffs at the same bail rationale for King, who at least did raise much of SCLC's budget. To fight nagging suspicion that the SNCC veterans got priority rescue, they were relieved to confirm that Willie Vaughn of the Mississippi movement remained in a cell upstairs. Sales came to attribute the separate bail to the stress she had witnessed in Carmichael from the night she first met him in Montgomery, when she had folded her arms resolutely like his, vowing to resist Martin Luther King's excuses for Bevel and his former trustees who refused to let SNCC run "second front" demonstrations from Dexter Avenue Baptist. In spite of themselves, they both wound up stomping and cheering King's oratory on the larger purpose of the movement, and Sales remembered Carmichael's unsparing description of his convulsive breakdown soon thereafter. Beneath the smooth exterior, she figured, Carmichael must be apprehensive of a second crack-up from his five years exposed on the line.

Opposing pressures grew outside the jail. The SNCC treasury was nearly empty, and just then was collecting a solicited gift of $5,000 from SCLC to meet its subsistence payroll. Silas Norman and Bob Mants, suffering a confused obstruction about bail procedures, had trouble finding lawyers willing to go near Hayneville. Attorney Peter Hall of Birmingham went instead to Montgomery and filed a motion for removal of the Fort Deposit cases into Judge Frank Johnson's federal court. Far greater legal jeopardy hit the Lowndes County courthouse with a triggering letter of intent, as required by the Civil Rights Act of 1964, specifying that the Justice Department was authorized to bring suit on "written complaint alleging a minor child is being deprived by a school board of the equal protection of the laws." Although John Doar mistook the school superintendent for a man, his detailed grievance showed that the rejected Negro schoolchildren had gained hope of redress from Washington, which amplified fears in Alabama. Sheriff Jim Clark already warned by mass circular that the Justice Department would repeat the "criminal assassination" he said it had "planned, encouraged, executed, and helped" perpetrate on nearby Selma,* and Colonel Al Lingo of the state troopers issued a statewide bulletin during the uproar over Watts: "This department is now in receipt of certain reliable information that riots are scheduled for many major cities throughout the nation and in the south particularly." Lingo's alarm, which fell on the August 16 date of Doar's letter to "Mr. Hulda Coleman," urged sheriffs and police chiefs "to begin NOW to form sizeable reserves of auxiliary police, firemen, and deputies." To buy riot gear, Coleman's brother Tom made a trip into Montgomery on Friday morning, August 20.

"Dearest Mum," Daniels had written Tuesday on a scrap, apologizing for a "peculiar birthday card" that was barely legible ("This damned pencil is about an inch and a quarter long"), advising that he had been in jail since Saturday. "The food is vile and we aren't allowed to bathe (whew!)," he added, "but otherwise we are okay. Should be out in 2–3 days and back to work. As you can imagine, I'll have a tale or two to swap over our next martini." Daniels was able to post the scrap homeward to New Hampshire in care of strangers who appealed the visitor ban late Wednesday, enduring a police stop and a traffic fine on the drive into Lowndes, persisting at the courthouse until Sheriff Frank Ryals, trembling with anger, granted permission.

The two Episcopal priests walked into a meal standoff along a fetid corridor of the upstairs cellblock, strewn with tins of pinto beans, fatback, and moldy cornbread that the hungry prisoners refused to eat or the jailers to clear away still untouched. Unnerved themselves, the priests were flummoxed to meet a prisoner as upbeat as his peculiar birthday card. Daniels, alone now that Carmichael and Wylie were gone, called for devotions from an end cell with a verve that was ambiguous to the priests. They could not tell whether he was deliberately or naively mindless of danger. His blithe mood was especially unsettling

---

* "The master of hate, who planned the operation," Clark asserted, "was in the White House."

to Rev. Francis Walter, an Alabama native who had agreed late in July to consider taking up the religious mission in Selma when the seminarian returned to Cambridge. Daniels declined their offer of bail money from ESCRU, the Episcopal civil rights group, because it was insufficient to free all the prisoners.

Richard Morrisroe also declined from two cells over, so weary that he did not pull himself up to confer through the bars. He took shifts sleeping upright on the floor, rotating four bunks between himself, Jimmy Rogers, and six young cousins from Fort Deposit who spent much energy reliving the longest journey of their lives to Birmingham for a performance by soul star James Brown. They reverted to fantasy reruns of their stifled demonstration, speculating that conquest alone could answer the hateful frenzy of the white men they knew, and these conversations engaged even visiting clergy to suggest revised tactics such as surprise, buildup, or more cameras to subpoena the national conscience, until Willie Vaughn erupted from the middle cell. "Reverend, have you ever stood in a picket line and looked into the faces of your adversaries," he yelled, "and watched them soften?" He silenced the cellblock with fierce, hidden desire, as though desperate to recover something pure from Mississippi.

Young John McMeans, who was a welder from the local trade school, told Morrisroe he had aspired to be a preacher. He shared a jail poem written in a small pocket notebook:

> I had a dream just last night,
> Where brave men fought a war for Rights.
> What a war this had to be,
> For blood ran like a raging sea.
> Men yelled out in a painful cry,
> Why do we all have to die?
> Out of the crowd a white man yelled,
> These niggers are giving us hell.
> I rather be buried in my grave,
> Than to be tortured like a slave.

They passed the notebook back and forth so that Morrisroe could record occasional thoughts from his own "Kerry Irish bent," mostly reveries. "My observations seem so to spin around me," he wrote. "I sense little if anything that I have given to these my friends. I sense only what I have received. A year ago I knew a great deal." Again: "Friday morning—a week in jail, a week chosen in a Saturday moment of Ft. Deposit bravado, a week unwanted, a vacation week wasted, spilled out. . . . Its elements will soon blend into a heroic memory. Bravado will return in recollection, in mass meetings and quiet starlit conversation, across pews, over tables, in beds."

Deputies banged open the cell doors with sudden news of freedom early Friday afternoon, August 20, and twenty celebrating prisoners scarcely noticed their crusted bodies as they reunited downstairs to sign their own appearance bonds. It was all Jimmy Rogers could do to hold them briefly at the desk when he realized that bail was not paid but mysteriously waived, and that no lawyer or movement caravan had come for them. Pushed outside, they huddled in the jailhouse yard until ordered to disperse by Deputy Lux Jackson from behind and by Hayneville officers who came along in a patrol car. Willie Vaughn argued for their right to stay by claiming an imaginary federal stake in the property, then vainly pleaded that the group should not "walk uptown integrated," but they vacated under expulsion past the Hayneville cotton gin to the seed warehouse at the corner of Highway 97, a block from the courthouse square. Vaughn ducked off to find a friendly house and notify the Selma SNCC office forty miles away, there being no telephone at the Lowndes County Freedom House. Gathered around a mimosa tree, the remaining nineteen decided against trekking for White Hall or Fort Deposit. Several remarked on eerily deserted streets and wondered why no friends seemed even to know of their discharge. Still, jubilation floated on relief in open sunshine. Parched, eager to taste something cold while awaiting safe transport, clumps of them ventured a block downhill to the clapboard Cash Store, owned by the courteous Virginia Varner, where they had bought snacks on registration days at the Old Jail.

Daniels begged a dime from Ruby Sales on the way. He climbed the two small steps to a narrow porch entrance and froze at a sudden command from inside the screen door: "The store is closed. Get off this property or I'll blow your goddamned heads off!" Daniels retreated a step, leaning to sweep Sales behind with an arm, before Tom Coleman burst forward behind a Savage twelve-gauge barrel fired so close that lead and shell wadding tore a ragged hole only an inch wide from the rib cage downward through liver into spine, hurling Daniels back across the sidewalk to land face-up over the grassy curb. Joyce Bailey was twenty feet away in full flight when a second deafening blast wrenched her hand from Morrisroe's as the priest was swatted down by buckshot spread over his back. Sales crawled madly around the store to hide. Jimmy Rogers and Gloria Larry dived to the ground near Morrisroe, then scrambled behind a hedge when they glanced back to see the man walk toward them from the porch, pointing the shotgun.

Coleman wore a holstered pistol. He stood in survey over each prostrate form, then walked to his car and drove slowly up to the courthouse. From the sheriff's office he called Montgomery, where his state trooper son served as driver and bodyguard to Colonel Al Lingo. "I just shot two preachers," he told them. "You better get on down here."

Joyce Bailey gave way to loud hysteria when Coleman was gone. "You traitors!" she screamed at the empty street. "You just ran off and left!" Heads appeared from scattered places. John McMeans came close and could not shake from his mind the image of blood running as copiously from two people as water when he washed a car. Fort Deposit teenagers banged on the Jackson Beauty Shop and nearby houses, but no one came to the door. Gloria Larry backed away helpless, ears ringing, unable to bear the unworldly moans of Morrisroe begging for water. Spinning around, Rogers locked eyes with several armed men on a path behind the cotton gin. "Nigger, if you don't git, you're gonna be lyin' right down beside 'em," shouted one.

Rogers herded his companions away from the victims and from jail-house reading books abandoned where shock had dropped them in the road—*The Life and Times of Frederick Douglass, Native Son* by Richard Wright, *The Church and the New Latin America.* An hour later, when Dr. William Dinkins arrived from Selma in one of the ambulances used to take James Reeb to Birmingham, he could find no wounded nor anyone who would speak of a shooting. Coroner Jack Golson had hauled the casualties away in the county hearse, Morrisroe barely conscious of Daniels stacked beneath him on a short-legged stretcher.

With both President Johnson and John Doar engaged among featured speakers at the first White House Conference on Equal Employment Opportunity, operators from the SNCC telephone bank left desperate messages for Doar—that Hayneville jailers insisted Peter Hall's clients were still in their cells but refused to let him speak to any as of late Friday, that none of the surrounding hospitals or mortuaries acknowledged arrivals who matched the vanished Hayneville prisoners. Doar broke the wall of silence when an employee of the White Chapel

Funeral Home acknowledged to him possession of a fresh arrival fitting the description for Daniels. He notified the FBI at 6:15 p.m. A Catholic priest, called separately to administer last rites at Baptist Hospital, found a surgeon of war experience he knew to look at the victim without identity papers still breathing on a hallway gurney, and Dr. Charles Cox assembled trauma teams that worked eleven hours to remove his spleen, part of a punctured lung, and buckshot fragments embedded from a shoulder blade to the small intestine. An FBI agent waited outside on promise of immediate word, he assured headquarters, "if Morrisroe should die." Morrisroe would survive.

From the Los Angeles airport, meanwhile, Andrew Young had been trying to arrange an afternoon call with the President, but White House aides notified FBI headquarters that Johnson spurned King's information on Watts. If they meant to placate Hoover with their hostile speculation that King meant only to puff himself up or lay a political trap, they did not go far enough. "The White House makes a great mistake," Hoover wrote on his rush memo, "in even allowing King et al. to get access to it."

* * *

PRESIDENT JOHNSON in fact gathered his advisers for a cross-country telephone summit just before King's homeward flight. Unaware of new trouble—they spoke through the very hour of Doar's inquiries into Alabama—the two principals addressed a history-making civil rights alliance that was menaced already on larger fronts, marked by skewed public attitudes about violence as sickness or cure. Each looked to the other for unlikely rescue, and neither betrayed hostility over rupture near at hand. Their skittish, intimate consultation left few clues that it would seal the last words on record between King and Lyndon Johnson. Unwittingly, they were saying goodbye.

Johnson put Lee White and Harry McPherson on extension telephones to hear him complain to King that he had been swarmed all week by hostile votes in Congress. The Senate had just cut his second-year poverty budget by 13 percent, he said—from $1.89 billion to $1.65 billion—"and now my bill has got to go back to the House, and go through Judge Smith again, go to conference." That setback already stunted the package of new job and education programs, such as Head Start, that Johnson hoped to grow into the range of $10 billion per year. More ominously, the administration had to fight for a 43–43 deadlock on a separate vote to delete another $800 million. The amendment would have "just cut me in half," the President told King, but failed on a tie. "That's how close it was.

"They're determined to destroy it, to scandalize it," Johnson charged. He put King abreast of thorny, nonpartisan obstacles to change within his own government—that Mayor Yorty opposed even limited poverty funds unless he controlled them, for instance, and chairman Franklin Roosevelt, Jr., had taken a long yachting holiday rather than testify before a congressional committee that in his absence halved the Equal Employment Opportunity Commission's first budget. When the President asked about Watts, King spoke frankly about the risk of "full scale race war."

Johnson accepted his prognosis but soon cut it off. "So now what should we *do* about it?" he asked impatiently. "What is your recommendation?"

King hesitated. He had advised already to expect no help from "absolutely insensitive" local politicians such as Chief Parker ("a very rude man, we couldn't get anywhere with him"), which left federal hopes that Johnson had just portrayed under relentless siege. "Well, the problem is, I think," King stammered. "If they can get in the next few days, this poverty program going in Los Angeles," he suggested, "I believe that it would help a great deal."

"We'll get at it," Johnson promised crisply. His aides and his Cabinet would keep working on the mechanics of "crash action," but he prescribed an urgent message for King to shore up the national mandate. "And just say that uh, we, uh, the clock is ticking," the President exhorted, "that, that, uh, that the, the hands are moving, and uh we we just, uh, the good Lord is going to allow us some time, and he's trying to give us some warnings, but the country has just got to stand up and support what I'm doing. And I can't have these poverty things hitting me 43 to 43."

"Yeah, that's right," said King.

Johnson said that King's statements, while already reasonable and just, should reflect more explicitly the language of the Howard University presidential address on poverty. Treating King as a fellow expert on the treachery of speech in a divided society, he warned that the press "might misunderstand" his own attempt that day to discourage racial hatred from any quarter. "I said a man has no more right to destroy property with a Molotov cocktail in Los Angeles than the Ku Klux Klan has to go out and destroy life," Johnson told him, saying he had made that point "to the Equal Employment people today and made it pretty strong." Although the President said he only paraphrased King on the subject, he knew—and he knew King knew—that the filter of race would implicate Negroes broadly while sparing whites except for Klan extremists. Johnson hastened to recall his offsetting plea for understanding. "There's no use giving lectures on the law as long as you've got rats eating on people's uh, uh, children," he told King, quoting himself, "and unemployed, and no roof over their head, no job to go to, and maybe with a dope needle in one side and a cancer in the other."

"Yeah, that's it," said King.

"Because they don't have very good judgment. People don't—that got that kind of condition."

"That's right," said King.

"And we're not doing enough to relieve it," said Johnson, "and we're not doing it quick enough."

"Yes."

The President twice reprised his riot-and-rats refrain, going so far as to preach in rhythm that the neglected of Watts "are all God's children, and we better get at it."

"Yes, yes," King intoned, giving the sort of church response he usually received.

"I want you to know I said that," added Johnson. "Pardon me for interrupting." He used language nearly identical to an earlier, confidential encouragement for John McCone, the former CIA Director, to accept appointment from Governor Brown to lead the Watts riot commission. If anything, the President understated both to King and McCone his lyrical commitment to make civil rights "the most important cause of our time," as proclaimed earlier Friday on the White House lawn. "For our cause is the liberation—the liberation of all of our citizens in all of our sections in all of our nation, through peaceful, nonviolent change," he had declared. "And we shall overcome. And I am enlisted for the duration."

Still, the President anticipated that his once shocking embrace of movement purpose would be lost beneath harsh front-page headlines tomorrow: "Johnson Rebukes Rioters As Destroyers of Rights." He coached King into the bully pulpit as his counterbalance and substitute. "Refer to that Howard University speech," he repeated. "Nobody ever publicized that."

King replied that he had done so already "in almost every speech I've made."

Johnson detected no such message in media coverage and pushed King to shift the focus of the news. "You, you're on television, and you ought to *make* 'em," he pressed. "Hell, have, tell 'em to *read* it, write, and get it, and let's get busy." Flustered, the President longed for him to plow forward ground for another Selma spring. "We've got to keep ahead of it," said Johnson, "and we're not now." He decried instead a landslide slipping away. "They think that I'm getting far away from the election, and that I haven't got the crowds supporting me anymore," he told King, then struck a glancing blow: "They all got the impression too that you're against me in Vietnam."

Johnson pulled back at once. "You don't leave that impression," he assured King, only to writhe for and against violence. "I want peace as much as you do, and *more* so, because I'm the fellow that had to wake up this morning with fifty Marines killed," he groaned, referring to temporarily secret casualty figures from the first American pitched battle, at Chu Lai. "But these folks will *not* come to the conference table, and I'm—"

"I've said that, Mr. President, I *am* concerned about peace," King interjected. "And I have made it very clear, I think, my position is often misinterpreted," he said defensively, alert to Johnson's volatile passion. "Because I've made it very clear that at the present time, two things, first that it is just unreasonable to talk about the United States having a unilateral withdrawal. On the other hand, you have called fourteen or fifteen times for unconditional talks, and it's Hanoi—"

"That's right, that's—"

"—that hasn't responded."

"That's the *perfect* position!" Johnson pounced. "Just exactly the position." He said King should coordinate with Ambassador Goldberg, which prompted King to recall a phone message lost in the chaos of Watts—"I guess two days ago"—about an invitation to visit Goldberg at the United Nations.

"I told him last week to talk to you," the President disclosed. With a burst of restored energy, he said he would have Lee White call King in Atlanta to facilitate not only a Goldberg conference but emergency programs for Los Angeles and plans for the White House conference on race. Johnson thanked King for leadership in Watts—"You did a good job going out there"—and invited suggestions anytime King had money to pay for the phone call. "If you haven't," he said wryly, "why, call collect."

"All right," said King, chuckling.

After Johnson signed off, he and his aides switched briefly to derisive laughter about King's reluctance to salute the battle flag in Vietnam. They mocked him for wobbly judgment and dubious political loyalty, which, together with the fresh ambush from Watts, raised for them a specter of inexplicable, concerted betrayal by Negro allies. Angrily protective of his boss, Harry McPherson had drafted the day's stern language aimed at ingrates who rewarded the administration's historic partnership with riots in California, of all places, and was disappointed that Johnson undercut the message with so many extemporaneous remarks on racial justice. White House aides leaked exaggerated stories about how sharply the President admonished King on Vietnam.

The President squelched the sarcasm with peremptory orders for his staff to mobilize poverty initiatives for Los Angeles by the next morning, Saturday, at ten o'clock. "Let's get up a program," he concluded in a pep talk. "Get everybody that's possible. Let's move in—money, marbles, and chalk." Johnson's manic enthusiasm covered a truce that was inherently unstable. King's oratory could not offset political drift against minority rioters any more than Johnson could maintain the Goldberg initiative as a peaceful approach to Vietnam. Since the President privately entertained faint hope for any Vietnam settlement short of defeat, he seized upon Goldberg as a fig leaf to cover the inescapable hard choice between full-scale war and withdrawal. King, like most leading war opponents then and later, shied from adopting forthright withdrawal as his recommended solution. It is highly doubtful, of course, that he could have preached nonviolence for Vietnam effectively to Johnson on this one chance, even had he known that he would complement informed misgivings shared secretly from George Ball and Richard Russell to the President himself.

President Johnson spoke no more boldly for military force in Vietnam than King did against it. Part of him strongly resisted—even feared—the destructive psychology of war. He still worried that national wrath would steal the remaining energy of his Great Society, and he knew it was far easier to make new enemies than to transcend old ones. George Wallace among many others would rise ardently to cheer combat in Asia. For all Johnson's personal discomfort with King, who to him was no congenial horse trader like Roy Wilkins, he was loath to break from the nonviolent phenomenon that King represented. Johnson's presidential distress sprang from experience that inverted the conventional perspective on violence in politics. He needed military success ahead to govern, but already he knew better than to presume the triumph of superpower might even in obscure Vietnam. Looking back a decade, he appreciated more than anyone the marvel uniquely without arms that had broken the smug, snug world of his U.S. Senate under segregation. "Who of you could have predicted ten years ago," he cried out to five hundred civil rights experts on the White House lawn, "that in this last, sweltering August week, thousands upon thousands of Negro men and women would suddenly take part in self-government? And that thousands more in the same week would strike out in an unparalleled act of violence in this nation?"

* * *

THE HAYNEVILLE shootings made Saturday's front pages nationwide, but nearly all its lasting effects started beneath public view. ESCRU director John B. Morris called the White House apologetically for help with dilemmas that made no sense to most outsiders. Funeral arrangements were stalled, but Lee White could not explain to himself or to President Johnson why local authorities and shippers furtively curtailed the very transactions they yearned for in order to rid Alabama of the controversial corpse. "What does he mean, they're discouraging?" asked Johnson. "The train won't carry it? Or the plane, or what?" White vouched for Morris as troubled but reasonable, and could only guess the Alabama companies were nervous about publicity. Puzzled, and reminded of criticism over the dispatch of a government plane for the body of James Reeb, Johnson told White to let Morris persevere with commercial transport for Daniels to New Hampshire. Unlike the Reeb case, or June of 1964, when Johnson personally had maneuvered J. Edgar Hoover to lead the search for three civil rights workers who disappeared on the first day of Freedom Summer, there was no compelling mystery with national attention foregathered nor any historic legislation in the balance. The President denounced a crime of fleeting priority. In private, when he mentioned "Downs County" as a synonym for injustice, Katzenbach gently corrected his reference to Lowndes.

Colonel Lingo asserted local control of the Hayneville investigation. He first told FBI agents that Tom Coleman was a special deputy sheriff whose actions deserved leeway for his duty under pressure to guard the public, and Sheriff Frank Ryals produced corroborating appointment records going back years. Then the Alabama authorities reversed themselves overnight, most likely on legal advice that any official status for Coleman opened avenues for federal prosecution by the Justice Department, as in the pending triple murder case from Mississippi, using statutes that made it a crime against the United States to deprive anyone of basic civil rights under color of law. Sheriff Ryals recontacted FBI agents with new information that Coleman's identification badge was merely a gun permit. He said he had been aware of a potential false impression from its imprint—"The Bearer Is Appointed and Empowered as a Deputy Sheriff in and for Lowndes County"—and explained that only a lack of clerical help had delayed revision. Carleton Purdue, the county prosecutor, offered a confirming legal opinion that the commonly understood "intent" of the badges was to regulate private firearms.

More important, FBI supervisors accepted the turnabout with transparent relief. By agreeing that Coleman did not function as a deputy—that he was "alone and acted independently"—they found no threshold basis to investigate a host of questions pertinent to federal laws, such as who arranged for the sudden release of the Hayneville prisoners and how Coleman came to be waiting with his shotgun. This preemptive judgment spared agents from sifting through a hostile courthouse, which in turn foreclosed federal indictment not only of Coleman but of any collaborators. Having eschewed jurisdiction, FBI officials resisted Justice Department requests to develop facts that might justify reconsideration. "In order to avoid any possibility of subsequent criticism," their case record shows, they followed orders to pose the few questions Justice Department lawyers took the trouble to spell out for them in writing, but they did so narrowly, without follow-up or initiative, while advertising the Bureau's distaste for the "somewhat nebulous" theory that Coleman may have acted in concert. FBI headquarters pointedly instructed Alabama agents to notify Lowndes County officials and each person interviewed that limited review "is being conducted at the specific request of Mr. John Doar, Assistant Attorney General, Civil Rights Division, U. S. Department of Justice."

* * *

SEPARATELY, CIVIL rights forces set off tremors in American law that rumbled far beyond Alabama race crimes. Charles Eagles, the biographer of Daniels, would discover nearly three decades later that Rev. John Morris sought help from his friend and fellow Episcopalian,

Charles Morgan, Jr., who, since a conversion speech to fellow professionals about collective responsibility for the 1963 church bombing ("We all did it"), had been driven from his Birmingham law practice into ACLU work based in Atlanta. Rushing to Lowndes County, Morgan saw a legal opportunity in the very absence of hope for fair prosecution through the state courts, and within five days he conceived, researched, wrote, and filed a federal lawsuit to strike down the systematic monopoly of white males on Alabama juries. To salvage puckish humor in the face of numb sorrow and rampant fear, Morgan recruited as lead plaintiff one Gardenia White, granddaughter of Rosie Steele, donor of the Lowndes County campsite for the Selma march, and as lead defendant he picked the white jury commissioner Bruce Crook, thus contriving for clerks to name the landmark constitutional case *White v. Crook.* "The jury system stands behind the power to vote," Morgan argued. "How easy is it to cast a ballot when you are afraid someone, from the sheriff on down, might shoot you and no one will do anything about it?"

John Doar soon intervened for the United States on the side of Morgan's clients, spearheading a successful petition that records be opened to document the blanket exclusion of Negroes from Lowndes County juries over the previous fifty years. However, the Justice Department pleadings made no mention of the lawsuit's tandem attack on Alabama statutes that barred female jurors of all races. Theories of sex discrimination remained far-fetched to government lawyers as well as to the mainstream press (a front-page story in the August 20 *New York Times* wondered whether executives must let a "dizzy blonde" drive a tugboat or pitch for the Mets), and the breadth of adverse law magnified risk in Morgan's litigation strategy. While only Mississippi and South Carolina matched Alabama's total prohibition of women from trial juries and grand juries, the laws of thirty states from Massachusetts to Wyoming retained some form of jury restriction by sex. *Hoyt v. Florida,* the most recent U.S. Supreme Court decision in the field, upheld a state law excluding women jurors except those who petitioned a court individually for the chance to serve.

To reinforce his novel case, Morgan brought in the more seasoned legal visionary Pauli Murray, who at fifty-four had just received the first Yale doctorate of law earned by a Negro woman. Murray had experienced formal rejection from the University of North Carolina on one score ("members of your race are not admitted to the University"), and from Harvard on the other ("you are not of the sex entitled to be admitted to Harvard Law School"). More recently in 1963, Murray had upbraided the grand champion of civil rights, A. Philip Randolph, for paradoxical blindness to the rights or contributions of women at his own March on Washington for Jobs and Freedom. In *White v. Crook,* Murray helped Morgan highlight the inconsistent legal status of Annie L. Price, presiding judge of the Alabama Court of Appeals. "She can reverse the verdict of a jury," stated the brief. "She could resign and practice before a jury. But solely because she is a woman she is not eligible to serve on a jury."

*   *   *

POLITICAL EFFECTS, which also would reach the whole country, already churned from the Hayneville crime scene through a traumatized Lowndes County movement. Most of the teenagers had run terrified through woods and brambles halfway to Fort Deposit, and parents smuggled or shooed them out of the county ahead of the expected follow-up murders. Rumors whipped through white areas that Stokely Carmichael was collecting firearms for revenge, while Carmichael warned fearfully of massacre the first night. "Sheriff Clark has deputized over three hundred whites in the past few hours," he told reporters in Selma. In the name of SNCC chairman John Lewis, the Alabama SNCC office issued a public statement that Hayneville survivors "have gone into hiding because they fear for their lives." Panic crackled over one who disappeared somehow past their barricades of protection, and it receded only partly when Gloria Larry turned up safe, having slipped away to the Selma Freedom House desperate for a shower. Colleagues complained of her as a tag-along volunteer still oblivious to SNCC's institutional memory and methods. Recognizing the Hayneville ambush as a "jailhouse giveaway plot," like the one that had delivered Chaney, Goodman, and Schwerner to Mississippi Klansmen, the young movement veterans recoiled from investigating authorities they considered not only hostile but likely conspirators. From SNCC lore about the murders of Herbert Lee and Louis Allen in Mississippi, after cooperating with the pioneer registration work of Bob Moses, they knew that witnesses who dared to tell the FBI about semiofficial crimes had been targeted and killed themselves. Huddled together, meaning to hide the key Hayneville witnesses from FBI agents as well as the Klan, they criticized Larry's trusting autonomy even before learning that she called Rev. Frank Mathews from the Freedom House to tell him what happened to Daniels. They could scarcely imagine her reflex urge to confide at that moment in the white pastor of segregationist St. Paul's.

These tensions flew far from Alabama on Monday, August 23. Rabbi Harold Saperstein found sponsors for Joyce Bailey's first airplane travel to New York, where she and others spent the night with members of the Temple Emanu-El congregation. Stokely Carmichael made the continuing journey to New Hampshire with Rev. Bruce Hanson of the National Council of Churches' Commission on Religion and Race, whom he knew from the commission's sponsorship of Mississippi Freedom Summer. At St. James Episcopal Church, past the casket that John Morris had managed to accompany by charter relay through storms from Montgomery, filed a line of more than a thousand family, childhood friends, seminarians, fellow pilgrims to Selma, and, reported the *New York Times,* "several Negroes who had known Mr. Daniels in the South." Carmichael muttered calming asides on the summer chill of picturesque Keene, near Monadnock Mountain. "Bruce," he said, "now I know why there aren't more black people up here." The *Times* already had published excerpts from one intense seminary essay by Daniels, and in place of the eulogy a professor read another that reflected on Selma as "raw material for living theology."

What undid his colleagues beyond mortality was close awareness of a personal gift in Daniels to bond against type, not only as a civil rights explorer but before that, they knew, as an effete Yankee who chose strangely to test himself at Virginia Military Institute. Isolated there in a martial culture that revered the memory of Stonewall Jackson, cadet Daniels had grown to deliver the valedictory address by election of his senior classmates, before an all-white 1961 VMI graduation audience that included Virginia's "massive resistance" Governor J. Lindsay Almond. He saluted future generals and national leaders—"as well as some magnificent buffoons"—within their ranks. "I wish you new worlds and the vision to see them," said Daniels. "I wish you the decency and the nobility of which you are capable." Only four years later, a new world lingered around his gravesite at Monadnock View Cemetery— Ruby Sales, John Morris, Stokely Carmichael, Harold and Marcia Saperstein, Jimmy Rogers, Francis Walter, Willie Vaughn, Bruce Hanson, Joyce Bailey, Gloria Larry. They joined hands and sang "We Shall Overcome" in tears.

Carmichael and Jimmy Rogers returned to Lowndes County at a turning point. Like Diane Nash in the Freedom Rides, Bob Moses in

Mississippi, and King in Selma, they called on movement witnesses to rally at the site of the most crushing persecution. "We want to show the people that we are not afraid of Lowndes County," Carmichael announced, "and that they can't run us out." Unlike Moses in 1964, however, they did not recruit legions of white volunteers. Moses, responding to virtually unnoticed repression of movement Negroes, had anguished over a Machiavellian calculation that the likely sacrifice of high-profile white students might provoke the federal government at last to intervene. Now, by contrast, whites were sacrificed already and hopes for national politics were jaded, while white volunteers still posed twin burdens as cultural novices and visible targets for violence. Daniels and Morrisroe had set examples of solidarity to the last extreme, refusing bail, and yet the wider public reaction gravitated to their abstract purity rather than the urgent plight of black Alabama. For Carmichael, as for Moses, leadership in cross-racial politics proved almost unbearable close to death. He seldom spoke of Daniels in public, and protectively came to remember that he had opposed whites in Lowndes as being too dangerous for them. "We ain't going to resurrect Jon. We're going to resurrect ourselves," he told a mass meeting. "We're going to tear this county up. We're going to build it back until it's a fit place for human beings."

Carmichael asked SNCC's research director to search Alabama law for footholds that might allow the Lowndes County movement to stand on its own. At thirty-nine, Jack Minnis had come late to civil rights from a rawboned first career as a Louisiana insurance claims adjuster. In 1959, when Tulane University had expelled a fellow graduate student for bringing a Negro into the student lounge, he informed awkward protesters that university officials, while impervious to academic petition, might be sensitive about their application for a large Ford Foundation grant. By 1964, his specialized skill in finding hidden pressure points to attack segregation helped Minnis persuade James Forman to create a fledgling SNCC research department in an abandoned Atlanta cotton warehouse, stocked with Moody's corporate manuals, a *Who's Who*, and used sets of statute books for Southern states. In his 1965 weekly newsletter, *Life with Lyndon in the Great Society,* Minnis chronicled acid disillusionment with liberal democracy. "That Great Medicare Bill that Lyndon flew all the way to Missouri to sign is like a full garbage pail in the sun," he wrote. "Nice and shiny on the outside, but teeming with maggots within." He traced cross-management between companies that received contracts for Vietnam as well as the War on Poverty, and lampooned King, the "Great Philosopher of Non-violence, with his chum Bayard Rustin," for his Watts trip "to do some hand-wringing and soul-searching and whatever else 'leaders' do in such situations." *Life with Lyndon* combed the anemic record of job and school desegregation to prove "just how phony the Civil Rights Act of 1964 is," and ridiculed the Voting Rights Act as another Johnsonian fraud. "And another thing," hedged Minnis, to hint at wounds beneath a cynical veneer. "When we think of all the murders and bombings and beatings and hunger and deprivation during the past five years, we don't give Lyndon any credit at all. It was the Negroes of the South who passed that bill." He scoffed at Johnson's ballyhooed promise* that Negro votes would become real in transforming numbers ("You can believe that if you want to. And you can believe that Lyndon believes it if you want to"), and wondered where a movement burned by misplaced faith "will then turn."

Minnis responded positively to Carmichael's task ten days after the Daniels funeral. "Here's what I've been able to glean from the Alabama Code," he wrote. "Alabama Law says it is possible to bring into existence a totally new political party." Ironically, the obscure provisions were holdovers from late Reconstruction, when white "redeemers" had fashioned laws to facilitate slates of local candidates by county. The statutes spelled out exactly how, where, and when in the election cycle a new organization must meet to organize, Minnis reported, adding that its official symbols "could not resemble, in any way" existing ones such as the emblem (a white rooster) or motto ("White Supremacy for the Right") of the Alabama Democratic Party. "IT IS ABSOLUTELY VITAL" that every participant have valid proof of registration, he stressed, warning that many technical faults would allow a judge to invalidate the entire effort. If the rules were followed scrupulously, however, and if any member won its nomination for county office with at least 20 percent of the total vote in the previous general election, Minnis discerned that the new group "would become a political party, in Lowndes County," local but protected under state law, independent of the courthouse Democrats. "As you can appreciate, Stokely, there's a bit more to it," he wrote. "There are provisions [for] appointment of poll watchers, vote counters, election clerks, etc., that will have to be thoroughly understood by the

* "I was wrong about Johnson on voting," Minnis said thirty-eight years later.

people." Excited, Minnis closed his long letter with a promise to bring law books for the next SNCC staff meeting in Alabama.

*   *   *

THE HAYNEVILLE shootings brushed fault lines that ran deep beneath faith and culture, touching the fundamentals of modern knowledge. By coincidence, Klan Klonsel Matt Murphy died in a highway accident a few hours before Gloria Larry called St. Paul's in Selma, and Rev. Francis Walter happened to be making a courtesy visit at the rector's study when Rev. Frank Mathews received her news about Daniels. The two badly shaken priests masked polar anxieties by sharing liturgical words of peace from the Book of Common Prayer. Walter, apprehensive even beforehand about whether to take the place of the seminarian he met in the Hayneville jail, asked for a memorial service at St. Paul's, which Mathews awkwardly refused on the ground that it would degenerate into "another civil rights demonstration." When an Episcopal priest did preach the funeral for Matt Murphy two days later, at a service dotted with solemn Klan insignia, conflict at the root of church practice again reached Bishop Carpenter of Alabama, the senior Episcopal bishop in the United States. Carpenter defended the local prerogative of both priests. He had long straddled a line between procedure and doctrine—denouncing the Selma marches as meddlesome while endorsing integration as a Christian goal. Rev. John Morris of ESCRU reproached him as one of the leading "chaplains to the dying order of the Confederacy." Yet Carpenter also suffered Klan threats for his statements of brotherhood, and Bishop Will Scarlett of Maine hopefully reminded his friend "that the sight of the great Bishop of Alabama ridden out of his State on a rail . . . would be one of the greatest events of many years. I still think so: I think you have an opportunity of a hundred years."

A dozen years earlier, Bishop Carpenter had helped the aspiring priest Francis Walter secure scholarship money to attend seminary in Sewanee, Tennessee, where a crisis simmered over the all-white student body. Carpenter knew Walter's mother as a prominent Alabama Episcopalian with a rebellious streak, who had dropped out of MIT to compete in a women's boat racing league. One day in the late 1940s, she came upon a solitary "costumed" Negro in the church vestibule and would not rest until, against fervent counsel, she paid a social call and returned home satisfied that the rector's garb and library were genuine, amazed that neighboring Negro Episcopalians had existed all her life in Mobile.

She repeated as epiphany the wife's gracious first words at the rectory door: "May I rest your coat?"

In 1957, her son Francis Walter had secured Bishop Carpenter's permission to serve the missionary Negro parish of Good Shepherd, but family objections centered on the anticipated details of his new wife's social duties at church functions, perhaps alone among Negroes, and Walter painfully withdrew under veiled hints that a distant relative would pull investments ruinously from his father's business. Carpenter, accustomed to such padded turmoil since the *Brown* decision, reassigned Walter quietly to a white Eufaula parish with instructions not to mention civil rights. They came to differ over what compliance meant when anxious parishioners asked how to treat a hypothetical Negro worshipper, and Walter relocated to New Jersey in 1961.

By August of 1965, Walter felt compelled to come home to Alabama at the risk of succeeding Jonathan Daniels. He knew Bishop Carpenter had turned hard against the civil rights movement in the intervening four years of upheaval and recrimination, which were transforming the nation in echoes of the Civil War exactly a century before. Carpenter sanctioned not only the refusal of a Daniels memorial service but also orders to lock St. Paul's and have Wilson Baker arrest anyone with civil rights contacts who approached a worship service. Rector Frank Mathews thanked Carpenter for heading off "spiteful retaliation" by Francis Walter and John Morris, saying they would have used the aura of St. Paul's to praise Daniels as a martyr. "If I antagonize them they'll get vicious," Mathews confided in a sardonic repost, "and then I may have to call on Tom Coleman to get them off my back. . . . Keep the Maalox flowing."

Bishop Carpenter denied Francis Walter even pro forma recognition as unpaid, unattached clergy, like a retiree, so long as ESCRU and the National Council of Churches sponsored his continuation of the Daniels interracial ministry. "I am not able to grant your request to license you to officiate as a Priest of the Church in the Diocese," he wrote after a dismissive audience. This meant Walter could not preach or otherwise hold himself to be an Episcopal priest anywhere in Alabama, including churches of other denominations, on pain of being defrocked under canon law. When Walter appealed to Carpenter's kindly heir for mediation, Bishop Coadjutor George Murray instead closed ranks against his proposed mission as a "direct insult" to all who labored "under proper authorization from their churches." Shifting ground from Christian conscience to the chain of command, he said Walter was not qualified for the task. "One of the heartbreaking things about the kind of undertaking in which you are engaged is that you may well be killed," Murray added, "and the killer will simply feel that he is removing an offending object."

Subsequently, as Walter persisted on his own, both bishops hounded him directly and indirectly to the point of opposing his pending application for parenthood by adoption. They argued that an integrationist couple in Alabama was inherently unstable and bereft of friends, therefore unfit to raise even a white child. Legions of contending psychologists and lawyers would build a massive government file before the Walters adopted a girl four years later.

* * *

FROM LOS ANGELES, King made his way to Montreat, North Carolina, near the home of Billy Graham. His anticipated address there to a church retreat had become newsworthy since the 105th General Assembly of the Southern Presbyterian Church in April, when delegates had debated and voted down a motion to rescind the invitation to him as "unwise under the present circumstances." Running behind as usual, King traded places with another Negro speaker scheduled later on the program, and spoke formally. "The ultimate logic of racism is genocide," he said, "and every Christian must take a stand against it." Preoccupied, King made plans from the road to reevaluate "our whole programmatic thrust" in light of widespread reports that Negroes were turning violent since Watts. "If you don't go North, we're damned," he told Stanley Levison, "but if you do go, we've got some problems." FBI wiretappers soon overheard Levison say goodbye to his son for the last weekend of August. "Martin called a quick meeting," he said.

On Wednesday, August 25, the House of Representatives passed the immigration reform bill by a vote of 318–95, with nays concentrated among subdued Southern members. President Johnson teased Attorney General Katzenbach about whether "you'll ever get that damned immigration bill past the Senate, if you'll ever get Teddy Kennedy to catch up with old man Celler. Here he is seventy years old, and he's already got his bill passed." Exhorting Katzenbach to help the Senate manager match the legislative performance of Judiciary Chairman Emanuel Celler, the President envisioned a wildly grand ceremony to repeal the national quota system among children of immigrants. "And we'll bring Edgar Hoover to scare everybody" like a Halloween mask, he said with a zany chuckle, "and then we'll go up there to Ellis Island with old Manny and get a picture in the paper with him and salute him and click our heels. Does that suit you?"

King's gathering convened Thursday in Atlanta. Northern advisers, including Bayard Rustin, Norman Hill of CORE, and Don Slaiman of the AFL-CIO, caucused separately from the staff for rambling debates on the movement at a crossroads. Most of them emphasized the disadvantages of a move north. They presumed an adverse shift in press coverage once demonstrations hit the home cities of newspapers that crusaded for integration in the South. Levison predicted a decline in fund-raising. Rustin strongly recommended that King not abandon Southern black churches as the proven recruiting base for nonviolence. SCLC should work to consolidate freedoms just beginning to be won under the landmark civil rights laws, he argued, and on Friday harsh news from Natchez, Mississippi, underscored the primitive obstacles still faced by traditional movements. A bomb exploded when the local NAACP chapter president George Metcalfe turned his car key at the end of a work shift in the Armstrong tire plant. Through the previous year of terror across southwest Mississippi, Klansmen had abducted and whipped four of Metcalfe's co-workers, killing Clifton Walker with a shotgun, and they also bombed the popular, arch-segregationist mayor John Nosser, either as a Jew or because he once suggested that Natchez might have to consider the NAACP's mildest demands. Governor Paul Johnson sent the elite Cattle Theft Division of the Mississippi Highway Patrol to investigate the attacks on Nosser. Metcalfe survived with mangled legs and a damaged eye.

King sent staff members to support the Natchez movement. Hosea Williams pushed at the weekend retreat to help across the South with a revamped SCOPE project, conceding that delay in passing the Voting Rights Act had truncated his summer work. Williams was on his best behavior—even praising rival Alabama SNCC workers for superior efforts to develop basic electoral skills among the people—but he could not overcome raw allegations that circulated privately within King's inner circle. "In my candid opinion," wrote SCLC staff director Randolph Blackwell, "the project has degenerated in the main to an experiment in liquor and sex, compounded by criminal conduct, no less than a series of reported rapes."

Drawbacks plagued every option, including the Northern cities King had toured since Selma. He originally preferred familiar Boston, but backed off because he found its Negroes too divided and whites too insulated by patriotic heritage. New York meant subterranean jousts with the master, Adam Clayton Powell, who whispered mischievously that he might fire Wyatt Walker, his assistant minister at Abyssinian Baptist, to sting King a little for thinking he could ever help Harlem. Andrew Young once favored Rochester because of its manageable size and Kodak funding, but decided that a city that lacked a good movement choir must be too small to make an impression. King's Los Angeles base was too middle-class, the city too freighted by colliding images of Hollywood and Watts. Bevel offered at a mass meeting to spare California the expense of its McCone Commission to investigate the Watts riots, with the simple observation that a majority of L.A. Negroes were migrants from Arkansas, Oklahoma, and Texas, unschooled and untrained, dismayed to find conditions too much like home.

King cast his decisive vote for going north. "In the South, we always had segregationists to help make the issues clear," he said. "This ghetto Negro has been invisible so long and has become visible through violence." Unless the movement could establish that the race issue was national—not a deviation peculiar to the Bull Connor stereotype—the promise of nonviolence inevitably would shrivel. King chose Chicago for the music of Mahalia Jackson, the transplanted heartland of Mississippi, and in part because the Al Raby coalition pushed hardest for his help. Among many dissenters, Bevel objected that the Chicago movement lacked strategy beyond the primitive goal of ousting School Superintendent Willis. "In Selma, we didn't organize to get rid of Jim Clark," he said. "We organized for the right to vote." Its Negroes needed to "pick up their souls" to define a movement that could engage the country, he said, and by the end of the meetings on Saturday King assigned Bevel to lead a preliminary staff of twelve to help Chicago do just that.

On Sunday, August 29, King surfaced into the white lights of national television on CBS's *Face the Nation*. The first reporter asked if he worried about charges that his Vietnam "peace initiative" would encourage the enemy, the second why he had not yet sent his letter to Ho Chi Minh, the third whether he intended to undertake negotiations in violation of the Logan Act. A series of Vietnam questions gave way indirectly to Watts. "Have you read the Moynihan Report, so-called?" asked Rowland Evans. King replied that he had read newspaper accounts but not the report itself, which he understood was still confidential. Evans asked, in light of Moynihan's sensitive findings on the illegitimate birth rate among Negroes, whether King favored a new government birth control program. Another reporter asked if such programs should be "addressed specifically to the Negro segment of the population," which led to a series of questions about what city King thought had "the greatest potential to erupt in the manner that Los Angeles has just done." He managed to endorse Johnson's Howard University speech before inquiry shifted to signals of violence beyond Watts, specifically a report from Natchez "the other night where it is alleged that Negroes at a rally shouted 'Kill for Freedom.' " King defended nonviolence. The program closed with "one quick question" on politics: "Do you favor a separate Negro party in the South now that Negroes are registered to vote?"

Public schools opened across the South on Monday, August 30. The U.S. Office of Education announced that nearly two-thirds of the school districts had submitted satisfactory desegregation plans, many admitting Negro students for the first time, and that the extensive breach of segregation was more significant than the small numbers of pioneer students. Nine Negroes safely entered formerly white schools in Philadelphia, Mississippi, near the jail from which Chaney, Goodman, and Schwerner had been lynched in 1964. Peggy Williams, the first Negro admitted to the Gainsboro, Tennessee, elementary school, was elected president of her eighth-grade home room by thirty white classmates. In Atlanta, three Abernathy children joined Yolanda King, nine, and Martin III, seven, to integrate Spring Street School under a "freedom of choice" plan. "Several parents welcomed us and said how happy they were to see us," said Coretta King.

King missed the family drama. Arthur Goldberg had invited him to the United Nations for the promised meeting on Vietnam diplomacy, which fell through. Minor news reached him that four former SCOPE volunteers had been arrested for stealing SCLC's office safe during the Birmingham convention earlier in August, and he learned in New York also on Tuesday that Adam Clayton Powell fired Wyatt Walker, "effective as of this day," sending King a saucy note: "Martin—for your info—Sincerest regards, Adam." In Hayneville, the first four Negro students arrived at the county high school. Hulda Coleman had asked them to stay home Monday so that last-minute security concerns could be resolved. Forty special deputies, a flock of reporters, and assorted adults watched John Hulett's tenth-grade son nervously shine his black shoes with a handkerchief before he went inside. "No one spoke to me the whole day," he said with relief that afternoon. "Some of the white children in the lower grades at Hayneville School wore no shoes at all," reported the *New York Times*.

CHAPTER 22

Fragile Alliance

September 1965

KING prepared diligently to see Ambassador Goldberg at the United Nations on Friday, September 10. His advisers boasted that their New York–based research committee functioned smoothly at last to compile material about Vietnam policy for an important discussion they knew was initiated by President Johnson. Bayard Rustin prepared reports based on sources as diverse as the Buddhist exile Thich Nhat Hanh and the French military scholar Bernard Fall. To broaden perspective, Andrew Young arranged for briefings from foreign reporters who had covered both Vietnam and the American civil rights movement—Sven Oste, a Swede, and the Italian correspondent Furio Colombo. Young also secured research papers from King's neighbor and friend Vincent Harding, a Spelman College professor who had become a Mennonite peace pastor since being drafted into the Korean War. Background themes in Vietnamese history were familiar to King from his absorption with anti-colonial movements in Africa. French rule in Asia, like segregation in America, dated to the late nineteenth century. It made a lasting impression on King that "native" freedom struggles developed similar messages through common sufferings on three continents, and he found an American thread worth sketching to Goldberg.

As a teenage student in 1908, the year of Lyndon Johnson's birth, a Vietnamese of destiny volunteered to translate into French for peasants protesting the colonial *corvée,* or conscription to forced labor, only to be beaten when militia charged the protest with truncheons. He was expelled from his Mandarin academy at the old imperial capital of Hue, then tracked for subversion by the French intelligence service. He fled Vietnam for thirty years, first stowing away on freighters to foreign ports, gaining fluency in seven languages while surviving variously as a cook's helper at the Parker House Hotel in Boston, houseboy in Brooklyn, and assistant pastry chef in Paris. In 1919, under the pseudonym Nguyen Ai Quoc ("Nguyen the Patriot"), the fugitive rented a proper suit and bowler hat to deliver a petition to the assembled peacemakers after World War I on behalf of the Vietnamese people. Though he invoked the right national self-determination from Woodrow Wilson's world-famous Fourteen Points, Nguyen Ai Quoc stopped short of demanding Vietnamese independence and sought merely protection for traditional democratic freedoms such as assembly and speech, plus an end to the despised monopoly sales of alcohol and opium. He received neither satisfaction, reply, nor bare acknowledgment from the Great Powers, but did attract renewed notice from police agents who chased him from France into nomadic years between revolutionary agitation and jail, supported intermittently by the anti-colonial bureaus of the Communist International. Nguyen Ai Quoc's ex-wife was among hundreds executed in a disastrously premature uprising in 1940, when the Japanese invaders swiftly subdued the ruling French. ("Imagine," a Vietnamese peasant later recalled. "France became a colony just like us!") From caves along Vietnam's border with China, Nguyen Ai Quoc built the Vietminh independence party and a small guerrilla army that harassed Japanese occupation forces so effectively as to gain the respectful wartime cooperation of American OSS officers working behind the lines. On the capitulation of Japan after the atomic bombs on Hiroshima and Nagasaki, Quoc entered the capital of Hanoi for the first time in his life, under yet another new name, Ho Chi Minh ("He Who Enlightens"), to proclaim independence on the American model.

It was this historical moment that King emphasized to Goldberg twenty years later. Huge crowds had gathered outside the governor's residence and Hanoi's colonial security garrison on August 19, 1945, ten days after Nagasaki. They carried motives for vengeance far beyond civilian casualties from guns of the occupying armies, as Japanese commanders and Vichy French administrators had requisitioned so much scarce rice, and forced rice farmers to grow so much jute for war matériel, that some 1.5 million Vietnamese had died of starvation within the previous six months in the northern provinces alone—fully

10 percent of the population—with terrible famine of less mortality in the south. The foreign authorities, for their part, still commanded troops and heavy weapons but suffered confusion about the import of the surrender news from distant Tokyo. In the tense standoff, Vietminh leaders persuaded the massed units of both foreign countries to stack arms and withdraw under promise of safety. New Vietminh flags went up. Crowds repeated the transfer of public symbols, buildings, and meager utilities across the country in ten days of nearly bloodless revolution before Ho Chi Minh invited the American OSS commander, Major Archimedes "Al" Patti, to dinner for a last review of his public proclamation. "All men are created equal," Ho began the next day, September 2, speaking in Vietnamese from a wooden platform above a sea of banners, faces, lanterns, and flags. "The Creator has given us certain inviolable Rights." He explained that "these immortal words" came from the American Declaration of 1776, then transposed its bill of grievance against British tyranny to indict the French colonial record. "They have built more prisons than schools," he said. "They have mercilessly slain our patriots. They have . . . fleeced us to the marrow of our bones, reduced our people to darkest misery, and devastated our land." At one point, Ho looked up from his text. "Do you hear me distinctly, fellow countrymen?" he asked, and voices from Ba Dinh Square—some said a million, others 400,000, with like numbers listening by radio hookups in Saigon and elsewhere—cried yes in unison. "For these reasons," Ho concluded, "we . . . solemnly declare to the world that Viet Nam has the right to be a free and independent country, and in fact it is so already."

King summarized the American thread of Vietnamese history with commanding detail. His advisers present—Bayard Rustin, Andrew Young, Bernard Lee, and Harry Wachtel—noted with approval that much of the information seemed new to Goldberg, who broke unaccustomed silence to ask questions. King did not argue, as did some of the former OSS officers recorded in World War II files, that Ho Chi Minh was a Jeffersonian at heart rather than a Communist. He tried to convince Goldberg that Ho was above all a nationalist—potentially a maverick Communist like Marshal Tito of Yugoslavia, amenable to pragmatic reform. Ho had appealed to Wilson's Fourteen Points, FDR's Atlantic Charter, and to America's long anti-colonial heritage because he needed a balance of allies to survive the harsh geopolitics of Asia. China had subjugated Vietnam for a millennium, and Joseph Stalin, Ho's Soviet Communist sponsor, did not bother even to recognize his

1945 government for more than four years. Chinese generals, who marched armies into Vietnam ostensibly to process the Japanese surrender, plundered the feeble new country at leisure—Ho called them "locusts"—and characteristically ordered every clock in Vietnam set back to reflect the hour in Beijing.

Most urgently, Ho Chi Minh had wanted American support to forestall postwar reimposition of colonial rule. In the independence speech of September 2, 1945, he vowed that his people would rise above fear, weakness, and ingrained subservience to former masters: "If the French should invade our country once more, we swear that we will neither serve in their army, work for them, sell them food, nor act as guides for them!" British forces entered southern Vietnam only ten days later, bolstering and rearming French holdovers to assert European control. President Charles de Gaulle, stung that rival allies once again were redressing his nation's military weakness, curtly hastened the expedition of General Jacques-Philippe Leclerc: "Your mission is to reestablish French sovereignty in Hanoi, and I am astonished that you have not yet done so." For more than a year, Ho Chi Minh negotiated defensively for compromise status within the French Union, vainly seeking an agreement that would promise or even mention independence. ("If I listened to such nonsense," de Gaulle cabled Leclerc, "soon France would have no more empire.") Leclerc's successor, General Jean-Etienne Valluy, shelled the port city of Haiphong on the morning of November 23, 1946, causing "no more" than six thousand Vietnamese deaths by the count of a French admiral who went ashore, and the year-old Vietnamese government soon retreated again to jungle caves.

King told Goldberg that the United States wound up financing three-quarters of France's subsequent eight-year war, which killed 74,000 soldiers under the French flag among roughly a million casualties on all sides, including 250,000 civilians, before the underdog Vietnamese won a decisive military victory at the 1954 siege of Dien Bien Phu. Since then, three American Presidents had struggled in place of France to preserve the fallback partition of South Vietnam from what they called Cold War Communist takeover, while Ho's followers struggled to complete what they called a revolutionary war for independence.

King recommended talks to resolve the sharp conflict by negotiation rather than force. Goldberg embraced talks as his specialized talent, and hinted confidentially that he agreed with King's call for a bombing pause to facilitate them. Heartened, King faulted Ho Chi Minh for refusing talks until the United States withdrew its troops. He suggested that Goldberg could encourage Ho to negotiate by ending America's own refusal to talk with Communist organizations, including the Chinese regime of Mao Zedong. Goldberg, seconded by assistants, replied that direct talks were impossible because the United States did not recognize Mao's government, and had blocked China's admission to the United Nations since 1949. King doubted the wisdom of shunning Asia's dominant power, especially since American officials argued that Vietnam took orders from Beijing. "Well, you know," he said, "eight hundred million Chinese won't disappear just because we refuse to admit their existence."

Lawyer Harry Wachtel argued from his research into the 1954 Geneva Accords that the ongoing war to unify the country seemed driven much more by the Vietnamese themselves than by Communist sponsors. For all their vituperation against the capitalist United States, both the Soviet Union and China had pressured Ho to accept far less at Geneva than his armies had won from the disintegrating French colonials. The "temporary" division of Vietnam into a Communist North and non-Communist South had defused confrontation between the nuclear superpowers, said Wachtel, but Cold War arrangements did not explain the allegiance to Ho Chi Minh among peasant farmers. Even Senator Richard Russell, President Johnson's staunch supporter on military issues, had just conceded on national television that Ho was "a very dangerous enemy" because he would win a fair election across both halves of Vietnam. Therefore, Wachtel thought Ho's supporters within South Vietnam should be included in negotiations to protect American interests. "Why can't you talk to the Viet Cong?" he asked.

Goldberg fudged on the delicate issue. "We don't say we won't talk with them," he replied, "but we don't say we will, either." The session lasted seventy minutes before Goldberg withdrew to focus on a crisis over Kashmir, where the Indian and Pakistani armies were clashing. He thanked King for his leadership in the shared cause of civil rights, expressing full confidence in his own capacity for dialogue, and left the visitors with such a positive reception that, after spirited debate among advisers, King decided to outline his "unthinkable" suggestions candidly for the U.N. press corps waiting outside. He mentioned a bombing pause, talks with the Vietcong, and U.N. recognition of China. "In short," he told them, "my plea was that we have a negotiated settlement of this very difficult and agonizing and terrible conflict."

The first sign of seismic reaction was that Goldberg soon rushed out of his Kashmir meeting to address the same television reporters. "We will not be forced out of South Vietnam," he declared. "On the other hand, we do not covet any bases there. We do not seek any territory." He said King's settlement ideas had been received without response. King heard within hours that civil rights colleagues were rebuking his dangerous "intrusion" into foreign affairs, then that Senator Thomas Dodd used similar phrases in Washington to denounce King's "intemperate alignment with the forces of appeasement." Dodd's haste matched his fury. With the Senate already adjourned Friday afternoon, he did not wait for Monday to speak from the floor and instead issued a public statement. Assuming the mantle of racial champion himself—"I was fighting civil rights cases in the South in the 1930s, when Dr. King was still a boy"—Dodd professed an extra measure of sorrow that the Vietnam overture "will make it impossible for me hereafter to regard Dr. Martin Luther King with quite the same respect." King possessed "absolutely no competence to speak about complex matters of foreign policy," Dodd charged. "And it is nothing short of arrogance when Dr. King takes it upon himself to thus undermine the policies of the President."

King convened an emergency conference call that Sunday, September 12. "I want a little advice from all you distinguished wise Americans," he teased, to lighten his introduction.

"Flattery will get you nowhere," quipped Stanley Levison, among the half-dozen scattered advisers coming onto wiretapped phone lines.

King promptly confessed surprise at the spasm of political signals. "I am convinced that Lyndon Johnson got Dodd to say this," he said, beginning painful reinterpretation of his direct presidential conversations that summer. What faded was his wishful hope that Johnson's private anguish about Vietnam meant he was open to settlement ideas. Vividly in its place rose the import of Johnson's sidelong comments that King was perceived to be a public opponent of his war. King now read the U.N. meeting as a trap to draw out his dissent over Vietnam; alternatively, he saw Goldberg as a poor messenger to lay down a blunt demand for political loyalty. Dodd, by contrast, would be a shrewdly effective choice. Many people might read his statement as reasonable, and "say yes, Martin has gone too far," King observed. "Some Negroes would say this." Yet King saw in Dodd the Senate's "strongest supporter of the FBI," which revived the clandestine threat of enforcement by personal attack. Once more, as with J. Edgar Hoover's "notorious liar" outburst before the Nobel Prize, King discussed the chance that the FBI may have acted independently, but this time he sensed politics orchestrated from the White House.

"I really don't have the strength to fight this issue and keep my civil rights fight going," King told the advisers, as the FBI promptly reported back to the White House. He said he would continue "being a minority of one" if his spearhead dissent could be productive, but he believed that none of the warring parties would respond positively to the call for negotiation, including Ho Chi Minh and Zhou Enlai of Communist China. "So I have to find out how I can gracefully pull out," King proposed.

Staff sentiment rallied briefly for a publicity campaign to defend King's stance. Harry Wachtel already had arranged a lunch with the editorial board of the *New York Times*. Andrew Young thought they could generate positive articles from a few senators and prominent religious figures, including Reinhold Niebuhr. Bayard Rustin reported support for King's stand from a broad range of movement leaders including Bob Moses of SNCC. Union leader Cleveland Robinson reported that Whitney Young of the Urban League was telling New Yorkers that he "wouldn't pretend to be as 'godlike' as Martin," and that therefore he refrained from second-guessing President Johnson. "I have no doubt that he has been poked by the Administration," said Robinson, who begged to confront Whitney Young and others for circulating "vicious" innuendo about King's motives. King warned that Senator Robert Kennedy might at most defend his right to speak, far short of endorsing his ideas on Vietnam or China. A close student of journalism, he also cautioned that war criticism was inherently personal, which risked triggering latent condescension toward Negroes. "Once the press takes a negative position to you," he said, "they are very slow to support you." He predicted that character defenses for war dissent "will get very little play."

The advisers agreed that Vietnam negotiations should be promoted by surrogates rather than King himself. Stanley Levison and Clarence Jones, who had not been present for the Goldberg meeting, privately criticized Wachtel and Rustin for letting King add the sensible but politically "insane" proposal to recognize the government of China. This idea displaced Vietnam altogether in headlines—"Dr. King Wants Red China in U.N."—that luckily remained confined to back pages. On the conference call, Levison prevailed with a strategy to reduce King's exposure on Vietnam by starving the publicity. Beginning with the *Times* board, King declined to explain, modify, or revoke his proposals. He stifled questions by repeating woodenly that he had said his piece on Vietnam and was returning to civil rights.

King's regret lingered over the coming weeks. "Should I say in this speech how wrong we are in Vietnam?" he asked on a wiretapped phone line. "I think someone should outline how wrong we are. Uh, I don't know if I'm the person to do this." When Levison reminded him of the considered decision—"Martin, we've just gone over this"—King acceded. On October 5, an opaque public statement quietly withdrew his promise to send peace letters to the major world leaders, including Ho Chi Minh. King declared for the record that "certain factors bearing upon the Vietnamese situation," including the U.N.'s "creative role" to calm the nations fighting over Kashmir, "indicated that at this time it is no longer necessary for me to adopt the course upon which I had decided."

* * *

Two MORE quick storms clouded the political alliance. King inadvertently delayed the lesser one six days by holding off Vice President Humphrey's last-minute dinner invitation until his first opening for travel to Washington. (From wiretaps, FBI executives labeled this date-making exchange a "refusal" by King, which they branded "another example of the high-handed attitude he has taken toward top officials in Government.") In the interim, King attended much of a weeklong SCLC staff retreat at the Quaker Penn Center on St. Helena Island, near Beaufort, South Carolina, shoring up the bedrock commitment to nonviolence. Rev. James Lawson, the roving Gandhian instructor who had prepared Nashville students for the sit-ins, led large interracial workshops. There were spirited arguments about priorities at an odd juncture of giddy triumph and primitive gloom, with laws passed but rights advocates still targeted to a murderous extreme, like Jonathan Daniels and George Metcalfe. They debated the limits of nonviolence for battle-weary practitioners as well as for expanded targets in Northern cities and foreign wars. Singing, gathered in circles on folding chairs, King basked in the inspiration but also mentioned his escape wish to have a simple church outside the movement.

On Tuesday, September 21, heads of the major civil rights groups boarded the presidential yacht *Honey Fitz* for Humphrey's cloistered "stag" dinner cruise. "For the first time in history," integrated leadership had occasion "to enjoy some of the splendor of executive power and

exchange ideas," declared the Negro weekly *Jet,* whose reporters later
ferreted out the menu of roast beef "topped off with peach shortcake."
The cruise began with decorum befitting patriotic scenery down the Potomac River to Mount Vernon and back. King and Whitney Young concealed their tensions over Vietnam. Andrew Young asked discreetly
whether the Goldberg meeting had poisoned Johnson against King, and
was assured to the contrary. When Vice President Humphrey began the
after-dinner discussion with an outline of historic tasks now open to
partnership, CORE director Floyd McKissick complained about slow
enforcement of the big civil rights laws. Debate ensued about whether
the federal registration of 43,000 new voters was a fast start or a minimal
change contained within a dozen counties. The running count of desegregation plans—now submitted by all but a hundred of several thousand school districts across the Southern and border states—was
arguably a breakthrough in principle, as local officials themselves renounced segregation, or mere camouflage for the tiny handful of students thus far able to brave "freedom-of-choice" integration.

McKissick attacked disconnected analysis with a fiery speech about
learning that his own daughter was beaten in a recent demonstration.
Freshly out of a Bogalusa jail himself, he said FBI agents still watched
passively and that not much had changed. Wiley Branton, Humphrey's
aide, retorted that civil rights groups still undercut the urgent need with
press releases trumpeting their own progress, to which John Morsell of
the NAACP objected with vehemence that his colleagues recognized
from a running insiders' feud. Branton, former foundation director at
the Atlanta-based Voter Education Project, had privately accused
Morsell's NAACP of inflating voter registration figures to boost its
share of available funds. Louis Martin, the White House specialist in
minority politics, further inflamed his civil rights cohorts by challenging them to bring solutions into government as well as demands from
outside. He said affected agencies were eager to know what the civil
rights leaders proposed to do about the sensational Moynihan report on
broken Negro families. This topic escalated the dispute about what was
evasion or raw truth.

Clarence Mitchell, the renowned NAACP advocate in Washington,
rose angrily to point a finger at Branton. "You are colored," he said.
"You should be representing us in your job and not opposing us." Branton retorted that Mitchell could no longer hoodwink officials about
what the NAACP actually did. Bystanders traded recriminations over

changing roles close to government. They carried on a verbal brawl laced with the word "traitor," according to one anonymous participant, which "almost turned the boat over."

The next day, President Johnson stripped Humphrey of coordinating responsibility for equal rights. The Vice President returned from the White House mystified and in shock, having been forced to sign a surprise memo in which he recommended his own removal, and Wiley Branton reluctantly accepted a staff transfer to spare Humphrey the embarrassment of his public resignation. Reporters soon questioned the effect of the coup; participants and scholars would remain puzzled over its motive. Some believed the demotion of Humphrey hurt civil rights, while others called it a promotion for the White House to take any issue from the weak office of the vice presidency, especially since Johnson considered Humphrey a bumbler. Still others diagnosed simply a cruel case of Johnson's penchant for dominance. The civil rights leaders, fearing the worst, were consoled by evidence that the move had been planned for weeks. While it afforded some comfort that leadership quarrels seemed inscrutably human and messy at the zenith of white politics, too, the minority mood shifted uneasily into a larger fishbowl. All Humphrey's dinner guests except John Morsell and Clarence Mitchell signed an October truce letter sent to the publisher of *Jet,* minimizing unseemly details that had leaked into the lone published account of the cruise. King and Whitney Young carefully denied any "yacht-wide discussion of Vietnam."

* * *

FAR GREATER trouble erupted from a September 28 news leak that Chicago had a "green light" to receive the first federal money to be appropriated under the new Elementary and Secondary Education Act. The city's initial share of $31 million would supplement the school budget by nearly 10 percent, the *Chicago Tribune* happily declared, triggering panic first in Washington. Officials at the Office of Education, who knew that Chicago had not yet even applied for funds, feared the premature announcement was a ploy by Superintendent Willis to lay claim to the money regardless of legal requirements. Documents already in private circulation suggested, accurately, that Willis had earmarked $2 million to purchase more Willis Wagons, the mobile classrooms used mostly for minority students, which would expose Washington to scandal for subsidizing the most controversial symbol of de facto segregation. Quickly, to forestall inertia, Commissioner Francis Keppel informed Willis and the Illinois school superintendent on September 30 that decisions about new payments for Chicago would be deferred until review of their submitted plans. Keppel did not mention reports that Willis intended to spend the money in two wealthy school districts, which would violate the education law. He did cite the pending complaints, filed by Al Raby and the Chicago movement in July, about acts "of discrimination in the Chicago school system which are in violation of Title VI of the Civil Rights Act." Clearly seeking a defensible settlement of responsibilities under both new laws, Keppel pressed Willis for meetings "to resolve these matters as quickly as possible."

Willis instead convened reporters on October 2 to disclose the "despotic, alarming, and threatening" notice, which he called an illegal punishment before trial. He expressed hope that the Keppel letter "may serve to alert the public to the capricious and autocratic actions emanating from the federal education offices," and political lightning in fact did flash. Chicago Representative Roman Pucinski declared within hours that his education subcommittee would never approve "another nickel" if such "arbitrary and dictatorial" abuse should stand. On October 3, at an otherwise festive occasion in New York, Mayor Daley pulled Lyndon Johnson aside to deliver a sputtering mad tirade against the administration's insult to Chicago. Staff briefings feverishly assured Johnson that the Office of Education had no quarrel with Daley, who "has never liked Willis," but the President judged it foremost a blunder that underlings had pitched Daley and himself into mutual, public embarrassment without prior notice or accommodation, let alone clearance. By the afternoon of October 4, Johnson's special emissary reached agreement in Chicago to "restore" the $31 million while transferring the segregation complaint from Washington back to the local school board itself for evaluation, with predictable results.* Pucinski hailed complete victory as Keppel sank into bureaucratic quarantine. "I was hopeless," he confided. "I was replaced very soon."

Al Raby lapsed from euphoria to despair. Only three days after praising Keppel's deferral letter ("I feel wonderful") as a first miracle step toward creation of "a school system that will make every Chicagoan

---

* In December 1965, Attorney General Katzenbach quietly bemoaned the school board's first self-study as follows: "The report, to say the least, is not very good." A second attempt in January of 1967 backed toward concession that some school policies defied explanation "by factors which do not include race." By then, Keppel's successor, Harold Howe II, said publicly that Northern school segregation fell "beyond the clear purview of the Civil Rights Act."

proud," he decried a "shameless display of naked political power" that had canceled federal leverage in advance. Soberly, he joined King on October 8 at an extended conference of two hundred activists to formulate strategy for a Chicago movement in the new year ahead. Raby had agreed to broaden goals beyond poor schools to include scarce jobs, unfit dwellings, and battered families. James Bevel attacked the complicity of victims in their own stagnation. "If Negroes cannot break up a ghetto in fifteen months," he said, "they will never get out." C. T. Vivian exhorted organizers to spread methods purified with discipline and sacrifice. "Nonviolence is the only honorable way of dealing with social change, because if we are wrong, nobody gets hurt but us," Vivian declared. "And if we are right, more people will participate in determining their own destinies than ever before." King surveyed Chicago obstacles personified in Mayor Daley and Rev. J. H. Jackson, who controlled respectively a massive political machine, built with strong Negro support, and an old-guard clergy that since 1961 had driven King's civil rights upstarts from the dominant organization of Negro Baptists. "I don't consider Mayor Daley as an enemy," King said, renewing the psychological commitment of nonviolence. Once again, as before Selma the previous year, he preached hope by analogy with the intrepid biblical scouts who once found mighty hosts barring the way to Canaan. "There are giants," he cried, "but we can possess the land of freedom."

By November, the combined Chicago staff would initiate hundreds of community rallies and ongoing workshops, plus outreach groups in fifteen categories ranging from Hispanics and gang members to "suburban ladies." Bevel appeared several times a day in a corduroy suit with his trademark yarmulke on a shaved head and a copy of Leo Tolstoy's *What Then Must We Do?* under his arm, to give spitfire lectures on grand themes—what is a slum? how is it organized?—that won applause even from white business leaders, according to grudging reports by police surveillance agents. King addressed doubt that movement tactics could work in Northern cities. He said critics overestimated the alternative capacity of Negro hatred or separatism to mobilize sustained, effective action, as opposed to noise, by riot or otherwise, just as critics still diminished the Southern movement. "In the south, we are taunted, mocked, and abused beyond belief," said King. "A hundred political commentators interred nonviolence into a premature grave."

By December, there would be tensions within the hybrid network of organizers and volunteers. Some Chicagoans believed King's staff too readily downplayed their years of work on local school conditions. Others felt that King and his lieutenants were long on eloquence but short on concrete objectives. Andrew Young invoked historic experience in Birmingham and Selma to counsel patience with tumultuous experimentation, which he called inevitable in a movement gearing up through the Chicago winter. "When the grass turns green," he said, "we've gotta have something in the streets." King promised "something new" in the Northern campaign, but he did not advertise one glaring omission. With national prospects threatened by Vietnam, if not severed by President Johnson's preemptive bond with Mayor Daley, he framed Chicago as a localized struggle aimed at home decision. King set aside his drumbeat call for the whole nation to "rise up and live out the true meaning of its creed." For the first time in his career—or in the tradition stretching back to Frederick Douglass's constitutional arguments against slavery—a campaign for racial justice would aim short of decisive intervention by American citizens as a whole.

CHAPTER 23

Identity

October 1965

FERMENT swirled the notions of group identity that shape politics. Almost daily, stark new dramas shifted meaning back and forth along the broad range of collective disposition toward people—from dear kinfolk all the way to enemy vermin, with intermediate stations including citizen, stranger, and foreigner. President Johnson's private chat with Mayor Daley about Chicago school money took place in Arthur Goldberg's new U.N. apartment at the Waldorf Towers, after ceremonies in New York harbor for the immigration bill. Standing beneath the Statue of Liberty, Johnson looked beyond an era long "twisted and distorted by the harsh injustice of the national quota system." He said most of the world's people had been barred from naturalized citizenship in the United States "because they came from southern or eastern Europe, or from one of the developing continents," while only three countries in Northern Europe received most of the legal entry slots. The law of selective national quotas "violated the basic principle of our democracy," he declared. It was "un-American in the highest sense . . . untrue to the faith that brought thousands to these shores even before we were a country."

"Today, with my signature, this system is abolished," the President announced on October 3. "We can now believe it will never again shadow the gate to the American nation with the twin barriers of prejudice and privilege."

Henceforth, aspiring immigrants from all nations would stand in one line for spaces within an overall yearly limit, which inexorably diversified American culture. The number of formerly proscribed Asian families grew sixteen-fold within the next ten years. Asians joined Latin Americans, Africans, and natives of the Middle East to become the vast majority of new immigrants, taking places formerly reserved for the few nations deemed the most Anglo-Saxon. Admissions from the whole of Europe declined to roughly 15 percent of the annual total. A separate stream of illegal aliens helped swell the nonnative population to 31 million people by the end of the century, but the law ensured a qualified influx from every spot on the globe. Mexico supplied a fifth of the 889,000 new citizens at naturalization ceremonies of 2000, according to Yale scholar Peter Schuck, with its leading share followed by successively smaller portions from Vietnam, China, the Philippines, India, the Dominican Republic, El Salvador, Jamaica, Iran, and on down the list. A school in Falls Church, Virginia, that remained white and Protestant as of 1965—J. E. B. Stuart High, named for the Confederate cavalry general—would draw fully half its 2001 student body of 1,400 from births dispersed among seventy countries.

Johnson embraced this future. "America was built by a nation of strangers," he said on Liberty Island. Its founding ideals, "fed from so many cultures and traditions and peoples," shaped an outlook of unique experience. Americans "feel safer and stronger," he asserted, "in a world as varied as the people who make it up." By its visionary conception, and immense effect, the Immigration Reform Act of 1965 rightfully joined the two great civil rights laws as a third enduring pillar of the freedom movement. Yet these high stakes went strangely unnoticed from the start. Despite Johnson's sweeping rhetoric, leading newspapers characterized the measure as a blow aimed at the Fidel Castro regime—"Johnson Offers Haven to Cuban Refugees"—delivered almost incidentally with a bill that "liberalizes immigration policies." Few outlets went on to describe the law itself, or predict significant change. None detected a purpose akin to civil rights. An inherited belligerence in Cold War politics obscured the welcoming new premise that no foreigner was too foreign to become a fellow citizen.

Plainer news dominated the week. The President stayed in New York to greet Paul VI, the first Pope ever to visit the Western Hemisphere, and Sandy Koufax of the Los Angeles Dodgers refused to pitch the first game of the World Series on Yom Kippur. Months before, the congressional immigration debate had wafted quietly behind the Selma breakthrough. There were no marches or demonstrations to mark a civil rights controversy in black and white. On the House floor, Representative Emanuel Celler denounced the quota system for discriminations within Europe, "because it says, in effect, that an Englishman is better than a Spaniard, that a German is better than a Russian, that an Irishman is better than a Frenchman, that a Swede is better than a Pole." In the Senate, Sam Ervin of North Carolina fell into thickets of antique science when he tried to explain the minuscule quota for Ethiopia. "Anthropologists, historians, and lexicographers assure us that the Abyssinians belong to the Semitic race, which is a branch of the Caucasian race," he ventured. Protesting that he meant no "oblique aspersion upon American Negroes," Ervin bemoaned the charged atmosphere. Comparative discourse on nations and peoples "nowadays arouses great emotions," he warned, "and such emotions magnify the occupational hazards of senators." Later, he candidly allowed that his Senate allies—being committed through the summer in desperate opposition to the voting rights bill—avoided combat on a second front by declining the "forlorn fight to preserve the national origins quota system." Ervin and the once impregnable judiciary chairman, James Eastland of Mississippi, retreated with thanks for the restraint of the opposing floor manager, Edward Kennedy. As a young freshman senator, President Johnson's handpicked choice lacked the seniority customary for the task, but Kennedy marshaled votes to overwhelm the isolated core of Southerners by a tally almost identical to that of the final passage on the Voting Rights Act, 76–18. "It's really amazing," Kennedy told *The Wall Street Journal*. "A year ago, I doubt the bill would have had a chance. This time it was easy."

* * *

THE IMMIGRATION debate, like the Selma movement, tested the most basic assumptions about humanity. What is race? What are its raw ingredients, if any? What is racial identity, and can boundaries or gradations be defined? These questions long had generated novel theories and unstable alliances across the disciplines of religion, science, and law. In early America, a prominent theorist of liberal faith on race was Rev. Charles Colcock Jones of Georgia, who had agonized from Princeton and Andover Seminary over slavery as "a complete annihilation of justice . . . fearful in the extreme." Following the future abolitionist William Lloyd Garrison, young Jones made a special trip in the late 1820s to consult the pioneer pamphleteer of emancipation, Benjamin Lundy, a Quaker harness-maker of Baltimore. Unlike Garrison, who first went to jail under Lundy's spell ("My soul was on fire then"), Jones inherited more than a hundred slaves on three plantations near Savannah. "Could I do more for the ultimate good of the slave population by holding or emancipating what I own?" he asked, and his answer was a lifelong quest to reconcile slavery with the full humanity of Negroes. He baptized and preached among them nearly alone for three decades before the Civil War. Called "Apostle to the Negro Slaves," renowned as an author and national authority on race, Jones rebuked fellow Southern clergy for their indifference to the souls of slaves. "There has been neglect—shall it be said, a *criminal* neglect?" he wrote. "I feel it. . . . The whole country sees it. Can there be no reformation?" He convened planters in Charleston, South Carolina, to resolve that masters could address slaves as brothers or sisters in Christ without endangering the temporal order, but the opposition gentry swiftly imported the eminent Swiss naturalist Louis Agassiz, to deliver a withering counterattack. "The brain of the Negro," Agassiz told the Charleston Literary and Philosophic Society in 1845, "is that of the imperfect brain of a 7 month's infant in the womb of a White."

Agassiz declared as a matter of science that the Negro was an entirely different species, separately created and grossly inferior, which brought enormous relief to slaveholders who denied or feared the implications of common humanity. Horrified, some in the Jones group tried to refute him by arguing that if whites and Negroes were distinct species, mulattoes would be as sterile as mules. The husbandry of mulattoes was an uncomfortable subject for them, however, and many professed with Agassiz that interbreeding was both "abhorrent to our nature" and potentially catastrophic for "the manly population descended from cognate nations." So Jones thundered that slaveholders must stand first on the book of Genesis to proclaim the truth of a single human family sprung from Adam and Eve. "We cannot cry out against the Papists for withholding the Scriptures from the common people," he wrote, "if we withhold the Bible from our servants." Into the ravages of the Civil War and old age, Jones clung steadfastly to his theological truce with slavery, still "certain that the salvation of one soul will more than outweigh all the pain and woe of their capture and transportation, and subsequent residence among us."

The publication of Charles Darwin's *On the Origin of Species* in 1859 eventually finished off Agassiz's theory of polygenism, or multiple creation of distinct human prototypes. By then Agassiz had captured

Boston as the fresh celebrity of globe-trotting science. He drew crowds of five thousand to speeches on biology, paleontology, and his famous discoveries such as the Ice Age, married a Boston Cabot (who became the first president of Radcliffe), and inspired the industrialist Abbott Lawrence to endow for him the Lawrence Scientific School. "His Harvard appointment [in 1848] marked the beginning of the professionalization of American science," observed intellectual historian Louis Menand, and Agassiz gained lasting stature as a founder of both the National Academy of Sciences and the Harvard Museum of Comparative Biology.

Early associates of Agassiz, both Darwinist and anti-Darwinist, labored for the rest of the nineteenth century to classify people by race. Craniologists Samuel Morton of Philadelphia and Josiah Nott of Mobile collected skulls. Phrenologist Peter Camper of Germany measured facial angles, foreheads, and jaws. Thomas Huxley of England (inventor of the term "agnostic") and Paul Broca of the Paris Anthropological Society isolated thirty-four distinct shades of skin color. Robert Bean of Johns Hopkins compared brains by weight, John Fiske of Harvard analyzed wrinkles in brain lobes, and Peter Browne studied hair. An explosion of typologies from these among a host of literal racists—who sought to create a science of human variety—obscured the shortcomings of every effort. Scientists seldom agreed even on the number of categories, as Huxley counted four races, Joseph Deniker seventeen, Ernst Haeckel thirty-six. Proposed systems faltered on skillful demand for verification, often by Franz Boas of Columbia University, because the skulls of Lithuanians unaccountably matched those of Ethiopians. "It is possible that Boas did more to combat race prejudice than any other person in history," race historian Thomas Gossett concluded in 1963.

The failed pretensions of science heaped pressure on judges at the turn of the twentieth century. Always, since the first Naturalization Act of 1790, federal law restricted eligibility for nonnative citizenship to "free white person[s]," and Congress raised the stakes of whiteness in 1907 by mandating that any American woman who married an ineligible alien be stripped of her own citizenship without trial. Courts accepted citizenship applications from some Syrians, Armenians, and Moroccans, but rejected others as nonwhite. A New York judge turned down a decorated U.S. Navy veteran of twenty-five years' service, born at sea to a British father, because his mother was of mixed Oriental descent. When Palestine native George Dow asserted in 1914 that Jesus "cannot be supposed to have clothed His Divinity in the body of one of a race that an American Congress would not admit to citizenship," a South Carolina federal judge dismissed the argument as "purely emotional and without logical sequence," but confessed perplexity over the maze of contending definitions. "What is the white race?" he asked.

The Supreme Court settled the statutory meaning twice within three months, holding first in November of 1922 that "the words 'white person' are synonymous with the words 'a person of the Caucasian race.' " This anthropological standard doomed the citizenship petition of Takao Ozawa, a Japanese immigrant of twenty-eight years' residence, who had submitted evidence of his own white skin along with scholarly opinions that "in Japan the uncovered parts of the body are also white." The test of "mere color," while obvious, had proved "manifestly . . . impracticable," declared a unanimous Court, citing expert accord that skin tone "differs greatly among persons of the same race, even among Anglo-Saxons, ranging by imperceptible gradations from the fair blond to the swarthy brunette, the latter being darker than many of the lighter hued persons of the brown or yellow races."

Only weeks later, the Justices were plainly vexed to hear in arguments for Bhagat Singh Thind that their own experts considered high-caste Punjabi Indians along with certain Polynesians and Hamites to be of Caucasian descent. Even worse, the racial term "Caucasian" appeared to rest on a single specimen in the collection of Johann Friedrich Blumenbach of Göttingen, who in 1795 had conjectured from the resemblance to his German skulls that ancient Europeans may have lived near the specimen's retrieval site in the Caucasus mountains of Russia.* The Justices reversed the *Ozawa* test with howls of newfound contempt for "the speculations of the ethnologist," again unanimously. "What we now hold is that the words 'free white persons' are words of common speech," wrote Justice George Sutherland, "to be interpreted in accordance with the understanding of the common man, synonymous with the word 'Caucasian' only as that word is popularly understood." The *Thind* decision not only threw up expandable barriers to citizenship but also supported a wave of federal denaturalization actions and state laws against land ownership by Asians. "For the Court, science fell from

* Blumenbach, a founder of anthropology, discovered no empirical boundaries to support classification by race. "Innumerable varieties of mankind run into one another by insensible degrees," he wrote.

grace," concluded legal historian Ian Haney Lopez, "when it contradicted popular prejudice."

The global rise of nationalism more than offset all embarrassments to the concept of race. Scholars and politicians alike campaigned for decades to refine a particularly "American race" by carefully limited immigration. Three Harvard graduates formed the Immigration Restriction League in 1894, and in 1910 the Carnegie Institution established a Eugenics Record Office at Cold Spring Harbor on Long Island, where demographers and biologists conducted studies to engineer population quality by eugenics, a term coined by Darwin's cousin Francis Galton. Although eugenics later became stigmatized by association with the Nazis, it "belonged to the political vocabulary of virtually every significant modernizing force between the two world wars," according to historian Frank Dikotter. With Asians blocked by the Chinese Exclusion Act of 1882, as amended, belief in progress within a hierarchy of peoples was so pervasive that the anti-immigration movement looked to measure genetic stratification within whites. "There are certain parts of Europe from which all medical men and all biologists would agree," testified Immigration Restriction League founder Prescott Hall, "that it would be better for the American race if no aliens at all were admitted."

A controversy from the Panama Canal project lifted the Restriction League near victory in 1914, when dark-skinned West Indian diggers sought entry to the United States as an earned reward. "You cannot have free institutions grounded on anything in the world except a homogeneous race," Mississippi Senator John Sharp Williams cried against them, but a comprehensive bill to admit only white people faltered in the mists of science. Williams himself abandoned the legislative term "Caucasian" once a perplexed Henry Cabot Lodge of Massachusetts, grandfather of the future U.S. ambassador to South Vietnam, read from the dictionary on the Senate floor, complaining that it would exclude "very excellent" Finnish constituents assigned to "a branch of the Mongolian race" along with Magyars, Bulgarians, Permians, and Laplanders. Thereafter, Congress managed to restrict legal immigration with an ingenious series of laws culminating in the 1924 National Origins Act, which, according to historian Desmond King, finessed definitions of race by prescribing immigration quotas for individual foreign nations. Henceforth only three countries—England, Germany, and Ireland—were reserved fully 70 percent of the annual 150,000 immigration slots. The remaining quotas heavily favored what Woodrow Wilson had called "sturdy stocks of the north of Europe," over Spain, Italy, Greece, Turkey, Hungary, and eastward rim countries deemed problematic for assimilation. Black Africa received a quota of zero per year, and allotments for all the world's non-European countries added up to 6 percent of the total. Dr. Harry Laughlin of the Cold Spring Harbor laboratory spent eleven years as chief legislative consultant to design and implement the quotas. "National eugenics is the long-term cure for human degeneracy," he said. The *Chicago Tribune* pronounced the National Origins Act "a Declaration of Independence, not less significant and epoch-making for America and the world than the Declaration of 1776."

From 1924, the year J. Edgar Hoover became the first FBI director, immigration policy stayed fixed more than forty years before President Johnson sought to abolish the national quota system in 1965. The restrictive era began about the time the Ivy League heavyweight wrestling champion from Princeton, Charles Colcock Jones Carpenter, battled the professional champion Ed "Strangler" Lewis to a draw in a celebrated exhibition match at the New York Athletic Club. By 1938, when Carpenter was elected Episcopal Bishop of Alabama, the Depression and immigration quotas reduced the American school population by nearly two million children. After 1952, when the McCarran-Walter Act renewed the quota system with minor concessions to the Cold War (token ceilings of one hundred slots for previously excluded Asian and African countries), the national United Church of Christ acquired the dilapidated Old Midway Church property, where Carpenter's great-grandfather C. C. Jones had preached alone among slaves before the Civil War. Church officials restored the site as a rustic retreat center called Dorchester, which Andrew Young rented for Martin Luther King to plan the decisive 1963 Birmingham campaign against segregation. In an abandoned mansion nearby on the Georgia coast, English professor Robert Manson Myers discovered a trunk of musty letters that once maintained communication among the scattered Jones family plantations. Published in 1972 as *The Children of Pride,* the collection would win a National Book Award for the intimate display of far-ranging literary sensibility from the antebellum South. Into the sweet-tempered letters of the patriarch Jones crept bitterness over the collapse of his historic mission to redeem slavery by faith. Denouncing abolitionists as "fanatics of the worst sort, setting at defiance all laws human and divine," Jones hailed Jefferson Davis as the first North American President who "openly professed the orthodox faith of the Gospel," and embraced the Confederate battle cause in his last public sermon.

Like his storied ancestor, the modern Bishop C. C. J. Carpenter soured against events that overtook his lifelong view of progressive race relations. The Episcopal Diocese of Alabama had already named its Gothic stone headquarters in Birmingham permanently for him, but Jonathan Daniels among others had picketed Carpenter House as a "whited sepulchre" of false Christian teaching. Carpenter would be forgotten or forgiven as the principal author of a white clergymen's manifesto against the freedom demonstrations in 1963, which made him the first-named addressee for King's responding "Letter from Birmingham Jail."

The fundamentals of race still were volatile. Equality held sway in public profession, but reputation or actual behavior could skitter for cover beneath popular notions of authority. The geneticists at Cold Spring Harbor regained immense prestige with the discovery of DNA in 1953. The word "Caucasian" still conveyed an air of neutral science. Race kept its childish role as a handy badge to organize conflict, and social scientists rushed into the public clamor for an explanation of Watts.

* * *

THE IMMIGRATION Reform Act of 1965 further established the legal blueprint for a model democracy of citizens drawn from the entire world. Its transforming impact lay dormant, destined to accrue slowly on the far horizons of the twentieth century, and many who celebrated the principle were preoccupied with lingering hatreds very close at home. In Hayneville, an abbreviated trial for the August 20 killing of Jonathan Daniels ended on the morning Congress sent the finished immigration bill to the White House. Alabama Attorney General Richmond Flowers, "shocked and amazed" that a local grand jury indicted Tom Coleman only for manslaughter instead of murder, had assumed control of the prosecution himself, but he failed successively to upgrade the charges, shift the venue from Lowndes County, or postpone the trial until the state's surviving vital witness, Richard Morrisroe, was released from the hospital. Death threats led Flowers to send an aide to court with a last flurry of motions. ("I was afraid," he told reporters.) Judge Werth Thagard briskly denied the motions, reinstated the county prosecutors, and commenced trial all on the same day, before a confident crowd of Klansmen that included Imperial Wizard Robert Shelton, Alabama Grand Dragon Robert Creel, and the three Birmingham defendants due for retrial in the Viola Liuzzo case.

The large national and international press corps scarcely had time to convey the flavor of the proceedings over a trunk of rented phone lines. Reporters noted the old triangular prisoners' cage and the bailiff's quaint method of raising a window to holler down to the yard for witnesses. Young Ruby Sales endured a scathing cross-examination about the nature of her association with the white victim—"a *personal* friend of yours?" Lifelong friends of Tom Coleman testified brazenly that Daniels had seemed to be carrying "something shiny" like a switchblade, and that the wounded Morrisroe had begged not only for water but had cried out, "Where's my gun?" Most telling, according to case historian Charles Eagles the prosecutors incorporated fantastic defense suppositions into their own arguments. The Lowndes County solicitor doubted that a smelly seminarian deserved to be killed for "trying to force his way" into the Cash store, and his assistant suggested a lack of evidence "that Jonathan Daniels was making any attempt to actually cut him [Coleman] with that knife." A defense lawyer in summation, citing chivalric custom that "a man has a right to defend himself and his lady," praised Coleman to the jury as their neighbor and champion: "God give us such men! Men with great hearts, strong minds, pure souls, and ready hands! *Tall men . . ."*

A verdict of acquittal on all charges required ninety-one minutes in deliberation, after which all twelve white men stepped impulsively from the jury box to shake Coleman's hand, one reminding him that they could keep a dove hunting date without further worry. Reactions elsewhere ran toward disbelief and nausea. Commentator Eric Sevareid charged on that night's CBS Evening News that Lowndes County "lives by quite different concepts from the justice that took a thousand years of suffering and martyrdom to establish." Cartoonists lampooned Alabama's Lady Justice variously as sleeping, weeping, stabbed in the back, and a Klansman in disguise. Columnist Max Friedman, who had blistered King as an "intruder" and "self-appointed apostle of peace" for his statements about Vietnam,* predicted that "this contemptible trial" would shame the nation enough to make sure "that equal justice shall

---

* "Since he won the Nobel Peace Prize, something tragic and unexpected has happened to Dr. King," Friedman wrote on August 20, the day of the Daniels murder. "He has become pompous and dull."

never again be so easily mocked." The *Birmingham News* referred to the trial as "an obscene caricature of justice," quoting the National Council of Churches with rare notice and unprecedented approval. "All across the land have come reverberations of shock, even horror, over the outcome," observed the *Atlanta Constitution*. Columnist William S. White confessed on October 4 that the Hayneville courtroom "has broken the heart of Dixie," and raised a native son's conflicted lamentation: "What is left, then, for Southerners who love the South and do not apologize for it and never will?"

King had dispatched aides to shore up two of many hard-pressed movements outside Alabama. In Natchez, Mississippi, site of picturesque antebellum mansions along the famous Natchez Trace, Andrew Young found a powder-keg boycott sustained by nightly mass rallies since the August 27 bombing of George Metcalfe, yet besieged by an all-white detachment of 650 National Guard troops under orders to prevent demonstrations. Local people complained to an SCLC survey team of segregated conditions in blatant violation of civil rights laws, including primitive treatment at federally subsidized Jefferson Davis Hospital: "All Negro patients, irrespective of diagnosis, are packed into one isolated ward in the hospital basement." After Governor Johnson replaced the Guard with Highway Patrol units, and another Negro church burned, long protest lines filed into downtown Natchez over the first weekend of October. Choosing arrest over orders to disperse, five hundred marchers steadily overflowed both the jail and city auditorium until authorities transferred those above twelve years of age to the notorious Parchman prison farm two hundred miles north in the Delta. Prisoners smuggled out word that guards were beating the known leaders, including SCLC's Rev. Al Sampson, and that the 409 Natchez inmates were stripped, force-fed laxatives, and chilled by night fans. "Several people were unable to [bear] the intense cold," wrote Phil Lapansky, a holdover SNCC volunteer from Seattle, "and broke down into intense fits of screaming and crying."

A seesaw crisis also made October 1 headlines from a tiny hamlet known as the home of the Confederate Vice President, Alexander Stephens: "Crawfordville, Ga., Again Denies Buses to Negro Students." Since the school board abruptly had transferred all 165 local white students to schools in surrounding counties, in a unique rebuff to seventy-two freedom-of-choice applications, groups of the Negro applicants tried to board special buses along with the transfer students, only to be repulsed daily by police and Georgia state troopers. Nonviolent vigils supported the young applicants at the bus stops, led by one of the few schoolteachers who pioneered voter registration, Calvin Turner, and opposing crowds of Klansmen cheered the officers. "Kill him!" shouted Herman Jones, a KKK "security squad" lieutenant on October 4, as seventeen-year-old Frank Bates tried to dash around troopers into the bus. Georgia Grand Dragon Calvin Craig gathered waves of out-of-town followers, vowing to force Governor Carl Sanders to suppress the Negroes. SCLC's Hosea Williams exhorted Sanders from the other side while encouraging protests with mixed success. A swim-in succeeded at Stephens State Park, but the town's one restaurant became a private club rather than integrate, and an effort to use the white-only coin laundry merely earned twelve trips to jail.

King himself, back from the planning workshops in Chicago, drove with Coretta a hundred miles east from Atlanta to Crawfordville. "The hardship of the rural South has made it virtually impossible for men and women such as yourselves to engage in the freedom struggle," he told a night rally on October 11. Reviewing the local initiatives—lawsuits over the closed white school, failed petitions for federal registrars, the dismissal of Turner and five colleagues from the Negro school, the shutdown of an early-learning center in the new Head Start program "to kill even this limited opportunity"—King saluted the movement for perseverance. "So you were left with no choice but to demonstrate," he concluded, "and we were left with no choice but to support you."

The next day, as SCLC's Willie Bolden led two hundred marchers back from the courthouse to a church outside Crawfordville, Howard Sims and Cecil Myers broke from a crowd of Klan hecklers past restraints to pummel stragglers. Sims said their "Black Knights" splinter group favored "a little more action" than rival Klans, and papers from the Augusta, Georgia, *Chronicle* to the *New York Times* featured the graphic picture of Myers chasing down SCLC photographer Brig Cabe with a fist raised to strike. The attack made extra news because Sims and Myers were accused in the July 1964 night bushwhacking of Lieutenant Colonel Lemuel Penn on a highway near Athens, Georgia. A local jury had needed only eighty-one minutes to acquit them of murder, despite two confessions from Athens Klan Klavern 244, and the Justice Department was trying to convince the Supreme Court on a separate appeal that Sims and Myers at least should face lesser federal charges for willful violation of protected civil rights. (Hoping so, President Johnson privately opined that Penn had been targeted with two other visibly Negro officers on their drive home from U.S. Army Reserve summer duty: "I think a soldier in uniform ought to have something to do with it, doesn't it?")

In Natchez, 1,200 movement supporters marched downtown on the night of October 6, shortly after a federal judge lifted curfews with an order upholding the right to peaceful protest. Grand Dragon E. L. McDaniel mobilized a counterdemonstration of paramilitary Klan units along the route, and his deputy roamed nearby streets in a sound truck that blared the local theme song, "Move Them Niggers North." Face-offs primed for disaster brought a negotiated settlement within forty-eight hours, but overnight reaction to its most basic concession made city authorities renege. "Never," Mayor John Nosser announced on October 9, could a deal go forward that would "ask city employees to address anyone as Mr., Mrs., or Miss." The mayor's statement, which quieted charges that white leaders had "knuckled under" to the NAACP on courtesy titles, renewed a standoff of marches, boycott, and cross burnings that lasted for weeks, with constant sparks of violence and grim pressure on everyone, including the mayor himself. Born in Lebanon, Nosser had two sons in the Klan. While the boycott of segregated businesses already had forced him to lay off nearly half the 147 employees at his four food stores, renegade Klan units also had bombed his home and two of his Jitney Jungles to underscore warnings against suspected compromise. The vise squeezed Nosser into a wishful escapism, and soon he would claim that Natchez could have prevented the entire racial crisis by offering a police escort at Negro funerals.

Charles Evers mastered his own internecine strife from the day of the George Metcalfe bombing, when he arrived in Natchez to supersede the wounded NAACP leader with a declaration of war. "We're armed, every last one of us!" he shouted at the emergency mass meeting. "And we are not going to take it!" By his startling audacity, Evers once again baited the fury of NAACP superiors in New York. Roy Wilkins had seethed against his maverick presumption since the 1963 funeral of Medgar Evers, when Charles took an unassailable public moment to inform Wilkins that he would assume his martyred brother's job in Mississippi, notwithstanding the lack of an offer or his dubious qualification as a self-described Chicago bootlegger and petty criminal. Wilkins publicized his latest maneuvers to fire Evers in September, only to be checked when Evers invited King's SCLC and other civil rights groups into Natchez with open hints that a hidebound NAACP might fail the challenge of a united movement. A month later, having consolidated a central position in the high-visibility boycott, Evers jettisoned the allied groups. On October 19, his aide privately demanded that King withdraw Rev. Al Sampson "and those individuals who are here with him," charging that criticism of Evers by the SCLC team betrayed an "unwillingness to cooperate." Evers himself disparaged the Natchez SNCC staff as "outside agitators." On December 3, with Metcalfe still in the hospital, he alone would join a dyspeptic Mayor Nosser with news that commanded the front page of the *New York Times:* "Natchez Boycott Ends as Negroes Gain Objectives." The thousand-word agreement called for a biracial commission, the opening of some city jobs to Negroes, integration of public facilities including the library and hospital, and the required use of courtesy titles by city officials and signatory merchants alike, specifically banning the diminutives "boy," "uncle," "auntie," "hoss"—"or any other offensive name." Success made Charles Evers indispensable to Roy Wilkins.

*   *   *

EVERS ECLIPSED a worn, fragmented Natchez SNCC project. A bomb meant for its first Freedom House had destroyed the building next door in August of 1964, after which local sentries posted themselves nightly at the few Negro homes that offered shelter. The acceptance of armed protection, except in avowedly nonviolent demonstrations, was a common adjustment of movement standards to Mississippi gun culture, but the Natchez project gained whispered notoriety when young staff members themselves stockpiled firearms in a shack bought with Freedom Summer donations. Sending notice to the powerful Klan units of Adams County, they deliberately left shotguns and rifles on display for white service workers who installed the telephone. Annie Pearl Avery, a strong-voiced former dishwasher and disciple of Fred Shuttlesworth, who had strained to keep herself nonviolent into jails from Albany to Danville, left Natchez for Alabama with a pistol strapped to the inside of her thigh.

For project director Dorie Ladner, the guns closed off one line of SNCC's competitive distinction from Charles Evers, and compounded divisions that already plagued the interracial cadres thrown together in Mississippi. Bill Ware, a black Mississippian educated in Minnesota, advocated clarifying pan-African doctrines he had encountered in Ghana as a Peace Corps volunteer. Mary King, a white minister's daughter from Virginia, escaped Natchez jointly with Dennis Sweeney into a short-lived marriage in California. Sweeney, a charismatic aspiring political theorist from Stanford, for two years had chosen to test a "naked affirmation of democracy" in the most violently persecuted projects of Natchez and McComb, which freighted him with a brooding edge. Brooding herself, Mary King joined Sandra (Casey) Hayden to circulate that November an influential manifesto aimed in part to heal one rift festering inside the civil rights movement—between its black and white women—with a solidarity based in gender. "There seem to be many parallels that can be drawn between treatment of Negroes and treatment of women in our society," they wrote, proposing to analyze a "caste system" they found pervasive and personal because the sexes, unlike the races, could not find practical respite in isolated communities. "Women can't withdraw from the situation (a la nationalism)," they observed, but the Natchez staff of fifteen dwindled away in separate colors. By October, three of them—Bill Ware, Janet Jemmott of Chicago, and George Greene of Greenwood—migrated to Lowndes County in Alabama.

In the absence of Silas Norman, now conscripted into the Army, the Alabama SNCC staff gathered to confront emergencies such as a cutoff notice for the utility bill of $11.66 at one Freedom House. Martha Prescod, badgering the Atlanta SNCC headquarters for support funds, received mostly evasive requests for cutbacks. Direst scarcity mandated Stokely Carmichael's rule that no county project could spend more than $40 per month, restricted to gasoline, leaflets, and rent. The two stick-shift Plymouths for drop-off and rescue were reserved for Carmichael and George Greene, who enjoyed an admiring debate over their relative skills as chase drivers. Scott B. Smith worked Barbour County mostly alone. Cleophus Hobbs and Annie Pearl Avery covered Hale County on foot. Donald Hughes and Cynthia Washington divided Wilcox. Jimmy Rogers elicited a pledge that fellow fieldworkers, resolving never to pay for food, should canvas long and well enough to gain donated meals at farmhouses.

Throughout the Black Belt, fear since the Jonathan Daniels murder and Coleman trial had dropped the pace of voter registration to a third of the early rush to federal registrars, but cumulative totals for Negroes began to approach white registration: 1,328 to 1,900 in Lowndes. As pressures rose, including threats of eviction against potential voters, SNCC workers joined other civil rights groups on October 9 at the Tuskegee Boy Scout camp to exchange organizing ideas for subsistence, such as food cooperatives and primitive health clinics. Alabama investigators patrolled the camp to take file photographs, refusing to leave. Preachers from Mobile brought a troubled boy disowned by his family for taking part in the movement, and the delicate task of arranging foster care for reenrollment in a school somewhere fell to Rev. Francis Walter, who succeeded Daniels in an ecumenical ministry* sponsored by church groups and the Synagogue Council of America. SCLC representatives, including Albert Turner and Harold Middlebrook, reached agreement with the SNCC project directors to reinforce each other's registration drives in key counties. They mobilized together a trial run for Negroes to vote first in a low-stakes November election of farm councils, administered by the U.S. Department of Agriculture. After lengthy exploration, however, SCLC staff members were undecided about SNCC's proposal to form separate political parties by county.

A lone SCLC emissary turned up to report on October 18 that King's staff in Atlanta found the idea of independent parties legally and politically troublesome, requiring an enormous diversion of energy. Gloria Larry was among observers who heard the SNCC staff members resolve to go forward by themselves. Since the Daniels funeral, she had tried to resume her graduate studies at Berkeley, but soon withdrew with apologies to the department chair for a persistent emptiness toward literature, and made her way back to Selma by bus. Only the day before, Larry had slipped again into St. Paul's Episcopal Church, which precipitated a hushed suspension of worship. An usher had appeared in the painful silence, taking messages quietly back and forth about a woman member's wish not to have a Negro seated in the same pew, then stood exasperated behind Larry to notify the congregation: "She won't move." The three sudden words jolted Larry up and out of the sanctuary. She yearned to join the SNCC staff, but movement friends wondered why Larry still hazarded white churches at all. Almost penniless, she scrounged to the point of coveting the irregular $10 staff stipend, but she found herself slightly apart from a SNCC ethos she called "relational." Young black veterans were turning inward. Emotional exposure at St. Paul's no longer made sense to them, any more than SCLC's

---

* As a white married couple conspicuous in civil rights work, Francis and Elizabeth Walter decided they could not "emotionally take living in Selma." Walter covered his territory from the university town of Tuscaloosa, where his Selma Inter-Religious Project found office space in a black funeral home.

worry that independent county parties would alienate the national Democrats.

No movement worker attended the retrial of Klansman Collie Wilkins for murdering Viola Liuzzo, and the only Negro at the Lowndes County courthouse stayed just long enough to testify on October 20 about surviving the night ambush while helping Liuzzo ferry marchers out of Montgomery. "Leroy," a lawyer called out wryly to Leroy Moton on cross-examination, "was it part of your duties as transportation officer to make love to Mrs. Liuzzo?" Judge Thagard blocked the gratuitous suggestion by defense counsel Arthur Hanes, who had replaced Klan Klonsel Matt Murphy after serving as a pallbearer at his funeral. A hard-line former mayor of Birmingham, who had closed city parks rather than integrate, and refused audiences with Negroes ("I'm not going to meet with 'em," he told the press late in 1961. "I'm not a summertime soldier, I don't give up when the enemy shows up"), Hanes nevertheless was known as a gentleman segregationist of sober deportment befitting a former FBI agent. He presented the case to the jury as a "Parable of the Two Goats," describing his accused client as a Scape Goat for the nation's sins, and the state's chief witness, FBI informant Gary Thomas Rowe, as the Judas Goat who had betrayed his Klan oaths and Southern heritage to a revamped empire of pagan Romans in Washington. "Maybe the murderer is from the Watts area of Los Angeles," Hanes proposed. For the prosecution, Richmond Flowers offered a folksy, derisive rebuttal that the unsupported defense theory—of murder committed by Liuzzo's own civil rights friends—required jurors to believe that phantoms had borrowed, used, and returned a murder weapon owned by the Birmingham Klansmen. "It is absolutely undisputed that this is the gun that killed that woman," he declared, holding the pistol. In a fiery summation on the honor of his Confederate grandfather, and on the dangers of corrupting fact with hatred, Flowers ripped from Black's Law Dictionary the page that defined "true verdict," shredding it before the jurors. "If you do not convict this man," he argued, "you might as well lock up the courthouse, open up the jail, and throw away the keys!" Tempering any hope that his skill or prestige as attorney general might seal victory in the case, which had split 10–2 for conviction in May, Flowers posted a well-known marksman conspicuously in the Hayneville courtroom to cover his back. The jury took ninety-five minutes to acquit the indicted triggerman of all charges on Friday, October 22. By Monday, national reaction spurred the Justice

Department to announce formal support for the ACLU lawsuit against all-white juries in Alabama, and President Johnson received strategy memos on the intractable "chamber of horrors" in racial crimes: an "unbroken chain" of jury verdicts that were unanimous and binding, yet perceived almost everywhere to be grossly unjust.

*   *   *

KING WAS in Europe for a brief speaking tour. He addressed the Free University in Amsterdam, visited the expatriate blues pianist Memphis Slim as well as Queen Juliana of the Netherlands, and was treated with Coretta at the Haynes soul food restaurant in the Montmartre district of Paris. Learning there of the Hayneville verdict, he canceled his British engagements to rush home for protests. The alternative, he told French reporters, was to accept "the beginning of vigilante justice" that could nullify the civil rights laws. New "OPEN SEASON" bumper stickers already proclaimed that integrationists could be killed with impunity in Alabama, and advance news of his return prompted a detailed threat relayed from Lowndes County to the FBI, that attackers waited to kill King "and anyone who is there to protect him."

Andrew Young told Stanley Levison that it was hard to cut short the visit to Europe, where people lined the streets and pressed King for autographs. On his last day, King preached to an interfaith service that overflowed the American Church of Paris, then addressed the topic "The Church in a World in Revolution" before a packed audience of five thousand in the Maison de la Mutualité auditorium, with an estimated ten thousand more listening to loudspeakers outside. Both crowds responded fervently to King's discussion of international crises, such as the holdover colonial secession in Northern Rhodesia (now Zimbabwe), which proved to Young that King did have an audience to speak on Vietnam. An ecumenical spirit waxed through Europe partly because the fourth and last annual plenary of the twentieth century's only Vatican Council was gathered from around the world, with civil rights clergy active in the final struggles to reform Christian doctrines on Judaism.

Unremitting intrigue seeped from the walls of Rome even after a committee of cardinals approved another draft of the *Nostra Aetate* ("In Our Time") declaration on October 15. Rumors predicted that its statement on Jews would be modified or postponed again. Critics took heart from the hesitancy of Pope Paul VI to implement the mandate of his predecessor, John XXIII, for penitent recognition that two millennia of Christian teaching had contributed to the Nazi Holocaust. At a critical moment, the Pope himself had repeated a liturgical broadside about crimes against Jesus by "the Jewish people," who "not only did not recognize Him, but fought Him, slandered and injured Him, and, in the end, killed Him." Reportedly at the Pope's behest, Vatican deputies removed from *Nostra Aetate* a clause that explicitly revoked church portrayals of Jews as a "deicide people" cursed by God. An observer of the warring caucuses wrote that key cardinals "realized fairly late that there were some Catholics, more pious than instructed, whose contempt for Jews was inseparable from their love for Christ." Against them, American cardinals led unsuccessful fights to restore the exculpation clause as the purest antidote to poison within the church. Others objected that the very word "deicide" raised thorny heresies from yesteryear about the dual nature of Jesus, and whether God could be killed; some warned that any positive statement about Judaism risked riots against Christians in Muslim countries. Meanwhile, Rabbi Abraham Heschel had dared to plead secretly in person with Paul VI against a separate new clause seeking final reconciliation with Jews by their mass conversion to Catholicism, saying he would rather "die at Auschwitz" and that what he understood of Christian grace should not countenance a prayer for him to annihilate his faith. Last-minute scandalmongers charged that Vatican reformers were paid agents of a Jewish conspiracy, and a pamphlet proudly claimed that "Christ and the Apostles John and Paul were the first anti-Semites."

On October 28, porters lifted the papal sedan through a sea of spectators into the Basilica of St. Peter, which was decked in full sacred pomp of bishops with miters in long ranks of white and scarlet robes. Votes against *Nostra Aetate* collapsed from the roiling dissent on both sides, leaving an advisory show of consensus—2,221–88—and Paul VI officially promulgated the epochal new teaching on "Non-Christian Relations." In place of "deicide repeal," proponents of reform accepted the qualified statement that treatment of Jesus by Temple authorities "cannot be charged against all the Jews, without distinction, then alive, nor against the Jews of today," along with an edict that "the Church, mindful of the patrimony she shares with the Jews . . . decries hatred, persecutions, displays of anti-Semitism, directed against Jews at any time and by anyone." The declaration commended Paul's scriptural advice to the earliest generation of Jewish and Christian rivals: "So do not become proud, but stand in awe."

Most significantly, *Nostra Aetate* discarded the substitute clause that prescribed ultimate peace only by the conversion of Jews to triumphant Catholicism. In its place, the final version looked to an age when "all peoples will address the Lord in a single voice and 'serve him shoulder to shoulder.' " The three small words—"shoulder to shoulder"— conveyed a breakthrough image of separate identity and common stature. There was equal footing, with no hint of dominant authority. For the Roman Church, which remained vertical in every respect— claiming one truth and superior faith sustained by its steadfastly monarchical organization—a horizontal bond with Jews was revolutionary. It suggested new church governance and belief, comparable in religion to the political shift from a vertical world of rulers and subjects toward horizontal experiments in structured self-government. It introduced a hint of democracy to religion built on hierarchy. In the single month of October, the United States opened citizenship to legal immigrants from the whole world, and the Vatican opened fraternal faith to the remnant people of Jesus.

Among many others, President Morris Abram of the American Jewish Committee hailed *Nostra Aetate* as "a turning point in 1,900 years of Jewish-Christian history." Adherents of both traditions were slow to plumb its meaning, however, in a postwar era marked by the discovery of the Dead Sea Scrolls and enduring stupefaction over the Holocaust. Rabbi Joseph Soloveitchik and other Jewish authorities continued to forbid dialogue with Christians on religious questions as improper, impossible, and impolitic—a proven noose for persecution of Jews. Only gradually, sustained by an explosion of scholarship on the parallel historical development of Christianity and rabbinic Judaism, interfaith pioneers gained confidence that textual exchange and interpretation could enrich understanding without surrendering vital points of difference. In September of 2000, American rabbis and Jewish scholars issued *Dabru Emet* ("Speak Truth"), the first formal response to *Nostra Aetate*. They offered a series of eight elaborated propositions, beginning, "Jews and Christians worship the same God."

*   *   *

JUST WHEN Rome's ecumenical machinery clasped its rough mandate to tame ancient enmities, the psychology of war triggered fresh ones. Among some hundred thousand protesters at scattered Vietnam demonstrations over the weekend of October 16, David Miller, a young Catholic pacifist, lacked confidence in his oratorical ability to communicate urgent shortcomings of "just war theory" to crowds outside an

Army induction center in New York. Nervously, he tried instead to burn his draft card in a gusting wind that blew out his matches. He succeeded with a cigarette lighter. As a registered conscientious objector, legally exempt from military duty in all wars, Miller told reporters that he hoped to commit "a significant political act" by inviting punishment needlessly upon himself, and the October protests exposed raw political nerves long before Miller went to prison for two years.

Overnight, James Reston of the *New York Times* scolded the campus intellectual and "dreaming pacifist" alike for paradoxical stupidity: "They are not promoting peace but postponing it." By Monday, Mike Mansfield told the Senate that he was "shocked at pictures showing some of the demonstrators," and a chorus from both parties seconded his stern reminder that Congress had outlawed the willful defacement of draft cards "within the past month." Senator Russell of Georgia, while confessing his own prior opposition to the war, declared that "the time has passed now to discuss the wisdom of our entrance into Vietnam"—with troop commitments made, the battle flag planted, and American heritage in jeopardy "if we tuck tail and run." Senator Dirksen joined Russell with a call for swift punishment of "the wailing, quailing, protesting young men themselves." From Chicago, Attorney General Katzenbach pledged to investigate peace groups for actions "in the direction of treason." Former Vice President Nixon said that to tolerate comfort for enemies in wartime threatened free speech worldwide. President Johnson, recovering from gall bladder surgery, issued a statement of surprise that anyone "would feel toward his country in a way that is not consistent with the national interest." *Life* magazine disdained the "annoying clamor" of "chronic show-offs" it dubbed "Vietniks." Republican Senator Thomas Kuchel of California branded them "vicious, venomous, and vile." Public animus surged so broadly that defiant SDS leaders Paul Booth and Carl Oglesby called for a modified strategy of "build not burn."

A hundred New York religious leaders signed an emergency appeal for open debate. "It concerns us that the President should be amazed by dissent," explained Lutheran minister Richard J. Neuhaus to an October 25 press conference at the United Nations Church Center. With Rev. William A. Jones of Brooklyn's Bethany Baptist, Neuhaus warned that recent efforts to squelch protest, emanating from "the highest levels of Government," threatened "to subvert the very democracy which loyal Americans seek to protect." Asked whether additional statements could be expected, Rabbi Heschel spontaneously assured reporters that a coalition would organize and function for the duration of the Vietnam War, and afterward defended his promise to startled fellow spokesmen. ("Are we then finished?" he asked. "Do we go home content, and the war goes on?") Heschel spurred new colleagues to prophetic witness against the "evil of indifference," in language reminiscent of his tribute to King before Selma.* "Required is a breakthrough, a leap of action," he said. To accommodate rabbis and women, the ad hoc New York "churchmen" became Clergy Concerned About Vietnam. When superiors promptly ordered two priests to withdraw, and banished the Jesuit co-founder Daniel Berrigan to South America, Heschel joined Neuhaus to protest the Catholic hierarchy's "injury" to ecumenical conscience.

On October 28, a planned anti-conscription ceremony outside New York's Foley Square courthouse degenerated beforehand into an imploded mix of hecklers, reporters, brawlers, angry police officers, and lapsed pacifists—"the most miserable mob scene ever," said Dorothy Day, who had seen plenty of them since founding the Catholic Worker movement in 1934. With A. J. Muste, she called off the demonstration for lack of pacifist discipline, and assorted violence from elsewhere filled the front pages. A Pennsylvania Klan leader committed suicide hours after a Sunday New York Times story exposed his concealed Jewish ancestry. Murky reports from Indonesia suggested purge deaths running into the hundreds of thousands after an army coup, with victims concentrated among Chinese immigrants. U.S. Marines at the Da Nang airbase killed fifty-six Vietnamese guerrillas who mounted a "human wave" attack, including a thirteen-year-old scout they recognized as a Coca-Cola peddler, and captured an eighty-year-old woman with drawings of military installations in her banana basket. Also in Vietnam that Sunday, October 31, transposed numerals on grid coordinates led A1-E Skyraider pilots to drop white phosphorus erroneously on the hamlet of Deduc, killing forty-eight civilians.

Norman Morrison saw a television report about Deduc at home in Baltimore, where he absorbed converging news on his last day,

---

* "Mere knowledge or belief is too feeble to be a cure for man's hostility to man, man's tendency to fratricide," Heschel told a convention of rabbis, introducing King. "The only remedy is *personal sacrifice,* to abandon, to eject what seems dear, even plausible, like prejudice, for the sake of a greater truth, to do more than I am ready to understand for the sake of God."

November 2. A story in *I. F. Stone's Weekly* quoted a French priest from the Catholic refugee village of Duc Co, who said he had watched seven Vietnamese parishioners die of napalm—"always before my eyes were those burned up women and children"—and a letter in the *Baltimore Sun* scolded silent Americans for letting officials believe that "nobody opposes the war in Vietnam except draft-dodgers and addlepates." Morrison chafed gently at his wife's praise for the activist tone of the letter, saying he had already done everything the writer recommended to no avail. Newspapers had published his appeals, and he had petitioned the White House on as many as three consecutive days, sending thoughtful notes to his "fellow" seminarian Bill Moyers (with whom he had overlapped briefly in Edinburgh, Scotland, before switching his ministry from Presbyterian to Quaker), and pleas for peace to Johnson himself ("Every day we sin more against the yellow people of the world!"), closing one "a conscience stricken citizen." When his wife left to pick up Christina, five, and Ben, six, from the Stony Run Friends School, Morrison drove to Washington with their one-year-old daughter, Emily, and mailed a short letter back to "Dearest Anne: For weeks even months I have been praying only that I be shown what I must do. This morning with no warning I was shown as clearly as I was shown that Friday night in August, 1955, that you would be my wife. Know that I love thee but must act for the children of the priest's village."

A traffic policeman recalled a man with a baby walking along the low parapet of a walled garden outside the Potomac River entrance to the Pentagon, then flames shooting fifteen feet high. "He was a torch," said an Army major who was among those who rushed from the parking lot. Near Morrison's corpse they found a Harris tweed coat, a gallon can of kerosene, and a placid, unharmed Emily, whom *Jet* reporters photographed in the arms of rescue nurse Cloretta Jones. Giant headlines spread everywhere—"Baltimore Quaker with Baby Sets Self Afire"—and the *New York Times* devoted two subsequent profiles to the late salaried leader of the venerable Stony Run Meeting of Friends (founded 1782), finding stunned admirers but no background instability and only one prior newsworthy deed, an arrest among nationally prominent clergy at a segregated Baltimore amusement park in 1963. A *Times* editorial recoiled from suicide witness as "alien to the American temper . . . confused and misdirected." *Newsweek* charged that the "macabre act of protest almost included the sacrificial murder of his own baby daughter." The editors of *The Christian Century* preferred "to avert our eyes." In the face of what she called "raspingly discordant" evasions from "many who talk and agitate constantly about religion, politics, race, and peace," a lone Detroit correspondent asserted that Morrison "simply converted his life into a word which would carry. . . . I believe the message, loud and clear, reached the ends of the earth. Who is prepared to say this act was futile?"

Within five days, a composition by North Vietnamese poet laureate To Huu circulated by combat radio among Communist soldiers, mingling shrill propaganda against American leaders—"Johnson! Your crimes multiply . . . McNamara/ Where will you hide?"—with intimate verse imagining Morrison's last thoughts:

> Emily, my child, it's almost dark—
> I can't carry you home
> Once I have turned into a lamp
> Your mother will come looking for you
> You must hold your mother and kiss her for me
> And you must tell your mother
> He died happy. Please don't be sad.
> Washington
> At twilight
> Oh Souls
> Are you hovering or missing?
> I have reached the moment when my heart is brightest!

More than thirty years later, at her first visit to a Peace Park created by war veterans from both sides, retired soldiers in Hanoi would recall for the married and pregnant Emily Morrison their indelible memories of hearing "Emily, My Child" in a particular jungle bunker or tunnel, and Vietnamese half her age recited the poem from school lessons. Her mother, having braced herself for acute discomfort in a strange land, lost protective artifice daily as "many, many Vietnamese men cried in front of us" over a healing image of Americans that survived prolonged slaughter. Robert McNamara, in his eighties, called Anne Morrison Welsh about the disclosure in his troubled memoir that sporadic antiwar protest never "compelled attention" until Norman Morrison "burned himself to death within forty feet of my Pentagon window."* McNamara said he bottled up emotions about Vietnam from that day forward out of "a grave weakness," and she replied that the suicide likewise had been unmentionable in her home. The two discovered in family paralysis a peculiar bonded leeway within the larger trauma of a war then scarcely begun.

The aborted New York draft protest reconvened on Saturday, November 6, this time in Union Square behind police barricades and a cordon of 1,500 supporters wearing "Practice Nonviolence" buttons. Hecklers strained against the perimeter with assorted signs such as "THANKS, PINKOS" and "COWARDS." They shouted down Dorothy Day, quieted through some of A. J. Muste's prayer for illumination of the haunting deed four days earlier at the Pentagon—"Do not weep for Norman Morrison or his family. Let us weep instead for the lethargy of this nation"—then raised a countervailing rhythmic cry of "Give us joy! Bomb Hanoi!" Five pacifists in coats and ties, pelted by missiles and doused by water, managed to ignite their draft cards and sing the "We Shall Overcome" benediction in the midst of another hostile, contagious chant: "Burn yourselves! Not your cards!" Police units escorted the pacifist leaders away for their own protection, but roving bands attacked button-wearing supporters as they dispersed.

Roger LaPorte, clean-cut son of an upstate New York lumberjack, sent off a letter renouncing his divinity school draft deferment. Obsessed by the intensity of the hatred he witnessed at Union Square, he wandered the streets for three nights until the predawn hours of Tuesday, November 9, when he knelt before the United Nations building soaked in gasoline. A Ghanian U.N. guard who tried to beat out the blue flames soon toppled retching, overcome by fumes. "I'm a Catholic Worker," LaPorte gasped to paramedics. "I'm against war, all wars. I did this as a religious action." Horrified, U.N. Ambassador Arthur Goldberg called the immolation "terribly unfortunate and terribly un-

* McNamara, without confirming that he actually saw the immolation, focuses in the memoir on a vivid image: "When he set himself on fire, he was holding his one-year-old daughter in his arms. Bystanders screamed, 'Save the child!' and he flung her out of his arms. She survived without injury." This implausible account contradicts witnesses who said Morrison first set his daughter aside, and disregards uniform reports that she suffered not so much as a scratch or singe mark. McNamara's conflicted portrait recalls empathy for Morrison—"I believed I understood and shared some of his thoughts"—yet bends logic to dehumanize him as fiendishly indifferent toward his own offspring. By contrast, the Vietnamese poem interprets innocent life as the embodiment of Morrison's conscious purpose.

necessary," reiterating his government's "complete commitment to the idea that peace is the only way." Friends of LaPorte said he meant to absorb evil from the world by personal sacrifice, like Jesus, but many pacifists including Muste feared that suicide protest would alienate most Americans instead, and make war seem comparatively normal. The Trappist writer Thomas Merton sensed "something radically wrong somewhere, something that is un-Christian . . . the whole thing gives off a different smell from the Gandhian movement." That afternoon, LaPorte hovered near death at Bellevue Hospital as a massive electric failure paralyzed cities from New York to Boston. He lingered with 25 million people mesmerized through the Great Blackout night of flashlights and candles, then expired after power was restored.

"The people of New York City have never experienced such fellowship, such awareness of being one, as they did last night in the midst of darkness," Rabbi Heschel told his class at Union Seminary. "Indeed, there is a light in the midst of the darkness of this hour. But, alas, most of us have no eyes."

III

Crossroads in Freedom and War

CHAPTER 24

Enemy Politics

November–December 1965

ON the day before the Northeast blackout, King sent a letter of "personal encouragement" to Senator William Fulbright, with whom he had no acquaintance, and also sent a mortified emissary—his father—to fend off a car theft investigation by the FBI. Although Fulbright had not yet broken publicly with the administration on Vietnam, King extrapolated early hints according to his own private readings of President Johnson, and he knew that raging public vitriol against dissent, while the birthright and daily burden of the nonviolent race movement, was a disorienting shock for many newcomers. "I trust that you will not let any pressure silence you," King wrote Fulbright in a guarded note. (Fulbright thanked King with a candid reply that "my influence is not sufficiently strong . . . to do much about the policy which is now being followed.") Daddy King, for his part, walked bravely into Atlanta police headquarters to surrender the purchase documents for a 1965 Chevrolet in SCLC's SCOPE fleet, volunteering that there might be something wrong with the documents. This preemptive move set a tone of forthright cooperation, and covered panic over sudden rumors that Hosea Williams had bought at least four stolen cars from South Carolina thieves cooperating with FBI agents. Williams, sputtering with indignation, avoided contact with King. He stalled surrender of the cars themselves because several had disappeared to scattered projects, and he was determined first to wring a refund out of the suppliers.

On Saturday, November 6, Andrew Young called Levison from At-

lanta with cryptic news that "Hosea has a problem" best not discussed
on the telephone. Half an hour later, word circulated through Stanley
Levison that the SCLC treasury was short $190,000, and that "Martin
acted as if the bottom had fallen out of the world." King sent Young that
same afternoon to New York. Advisers there tied the treasury crisis to a
bookkeeping "goof"—unnoticed checks gone from the theft of SCLC's
safe during the August convention, many of which could be replaced—
but discovered an alarming long-term drop in contributions to a level
roughly one-third of expenditures, so that the current monthly deficit of
$70,000 would bankrupt SCLC by early 1966. Levison, Clarence Jones,
and the others called for drastic spending cuts and fund-raising reforms,
grumbling as usual that King would forgive chronic laxity on the part of
"pompous and ineffective" SCLC treasurer Ralph Abernathy. They
knew that Abernathy recently inveigled Young himself to write an appeal for major SCLC donors to buy Abernathy a new automobile, and
that a chagrined King worked to cover and repay the mistake rather
than openly rebuke his best friend. Even now, out of abiding sympathy
for Abernathy's deep wounds and insecurities, King wrote a detailed
letter to American Express headquarters appealing the recent rejection
of Abernathy's application for credit privileges. (The handy plastic card,
introduced by American Express in 1959, was transforming not only
business travel but much of retail commerce.)

Young and the New York advisers accepted that Hosea Williams
might be in possession of stolen cars, doubted that he had ordered them
stolen, questioned what he knew at the time of sale, and fully expected
his exclamations that he would defy this persecution like all the others.
Combustible, loose with rules, Williams had gone to jail more than anyone on the SCLC staff, and had just committed permanently to the
movement by resigning his vested career as a chemist in the U.S. Department of Agriculture. With Bevel away in Chicago, he was the available choice to mount a protest in remote Alabama, against travesties of
justice in the Liuzzo and Daniels murder trials. Harry Wachtel, the
Wall Street lawyer who had represented King in high-level negotiations
on the Voting Rights Act, discreetly sounded out his contacts at the Justice Department about the likelihood of prosecution. Insiders at SCLC
held their breath and hoped the scandal would fail to explode.

Far from King's sight, the Hosea Williams case boiled in a continuing
dispute that would spill from the secret chambers of government into
the next presidential election. Officials at FBI headquarters ached to an-

nounce an ITSP (Interstate Transportation of Stolen Property) "rackets" case that touched King. "Hosea Williams is the Director of Voter Registration, SCLC," wrote Assistant Director Al Rosen, "and in view of his high position, any prosecutive action taken against him would result in considerable publicity and would focus attention on the activities of the SCLC." However, when FBI agents arrested the first middleman in late October, skeptical federal prosecutors in Atlanta and Washington made sure that the charging documents did not implicate Williams or King on the uncorroborated word of the South Carolina suspect. They asked why a convicted white thief from South Carolina would rent cars under his own name, sell them traceably to Negro middlemen in Atlanta, then confess the whole scheme to an FBI contact from previous arrests. Nevertheless, the neutral arrest statement infuriated Deke DeLoach as a muzzling. By his report he told the Justice Department that "the FBI did not make 'secret arrests' . . . and that we simply would not sit still for this kind of treatment." Alan Belmont, the FBI's third-ranking official, hinted to counterparts at Justice that the Bureau might have corroboration of SCLC's conscious guilt from surveillance intercepts, but this disclosure only ratcheted the matter up to Attorney General Katzenbach. A federal judge quickly sealed the record of the middleman's arrest, which was publicly ignored without a salacious civil rights context. "The Dept Attys may have gotten to the judge," Hoover groused to his inner circle.

FBI officials pushed for broader prosecution while the Justice Department held back for supporting facts, and their standoff intensified because King was the nerve point in a larger struggle over surveillance policy. The FBI scrambled in November to assure Justice that intelligence information would be "compartmentalized" from criminal agents, and therefore would not contaminate the evidence in an active prosecution, but Katzenbach stressed that skilled defense lawyers might win court-ordered discovery of all material about Hosea Williams in the government's possession. Legally, he warned, such discovery could spoil any slim chance of a sustainable conviction, because judges would frown especially upon wiretapped conversations about Hosea's "problem" among at least three SCLC lawyers, Wachtel, Jones, and Levison, as unconstitutional infringements of the right to counsel. Politically, any prosecution of Williams would risk the first public disclosure of the telephone wiretaps on King and his associates, which would bring down seismic repercussions.

For Katzenbach, still more danger lurked in the likely revelation of intercepts also by nonauthorized FBI microphone surveillance—bugs planted in rooms by trespass—at the worst moment. It had taken months of cajolery for him to secure from his nominal subordinates even a bare acknowledgment that the FBI used bugs, then finally a pledge to abandon them, both on the strength of President Johnson's emphatic secret order. "As a consequence, and at your request," Hoover had informed Katzenbach on September 14, "we have discontinued completely the use of microphones." The memo of formal compliance bristled ominously with resentment. Hoover blamed official qualms about bugs on the "unrestrained and injudicious use of special investigative techniques by other agencies." He objected that traditional, accountable FBI methods such as interviews and forensics fell short "in dealing with clandestine operations," and that bugs were vital for the FBI "to assist our makers of international policy" as well as to combat subversion. "To the extent that our knowledge is reduced," Hoover concluded with a royal flourish, "to that extent our productiveness is reduced."

Reluctant submission lasted hardly a month before Hoover rebelled. He chose tactical ground shrewdly, aware that a federal government divided privately over bugs also tottered recently in attitude toward Martin Luther King. When wiretaps next alerted the FBI that King would meet his New York advisers, Hoover knew better than to ask special permission to bug the event. Instead, implying that Katzenbach would have approved if there had been time, he sent notice afterward in an unprecedented sort of post-facto request: "Because of the importance of the meeting, and the urgency of the situation, a microphone surveillance was effected October 14, 1965, on King in Room 345, Astor Hotel. . . . This surveillance involved trespass." Hoover sent Katzenbach two nearly identical notices after King's New York visits in late October and November, which put the Attorney General in a bind. He could ask President Johnson to confront the shaded disobedience, admitting that he could not handle Hoover himself, or he could overlook it. Choosing the latter, Katzenbach entangled himself in a bugging policy contrary to the one Johnson demanded. He became the first Attorney General ever to grant tacit written approval for a specific bug, as opposed to telephone wiretap. The unchallenged memos became leverage for Hoover, and gave Katzenbach still more reason to be wary of a Hosea Williams prosecution. Now he could be implicated as the highest authority for any bugs unearthed by court discovery.

For Hoover, these maneuvers breached the odious prohibition on bugs, and his top officials moved aggressively behind signs of official displeasure toward King. Agents recruited bookkeeper James Harrison as the Bureau's first "penetration" informant inside SCLC. Hoover commended his Atlanta branch on November 10 for "thought and imagination . . . looking toward the possible exploitation of highly sensitive information recently obtained concerning the personal life of subject [King]." DeLoach gave House Speaker John McCormack his acrid confidential version of King's Vietnam dissent, alleged Communist control, and personal faults, reporting afterward that the Speaker "was quite calm. . . . stated that he now recognized the gravity of the situation and that something must be done about it." DeLoach also briefed Fred Buzhardt and Harry Dent, aides to the newly converted Republican Senator Strom Thurmond, but resisted as too dangerous their eagerness to let Thurmond "expose" King publicly with FBI information. Ever careful, Hoover favored confidential weapons that could not embarrass the Bureau, while pushing doggedly for the protected publicity of an authorized indictment against Hosea Williams. "It is disgraceful that we are kept 'under raps' in this case," he scrawled on a memo, and speculated on another memo that even "air tight" evidence for SCLC's complicity would not matter, "as that outfit is above the law in the eyes of the Dept."

King sensed ephemeral new tides against the movement. His friend Morris Abram, a former Atlantan now on temporary Washington assignment away from the American Jewish Committee, solicited his participation in President Johnson's proposed national conference on race, then awkwardly signaled that most of the colleagues King nominated for a November 16 planning session would not be allowed through the White House gates. Inside the administration, Abram and Johnson's civil rights staff remonstrated with security officials not to bar Bayard Rustin on the FBI's renewed allegation that he was a "confirmed Marxist." Lee White reminded the President that Rustin had proved a responsible and insightful ally since the March on Washington, and warned that the proposed FBI blacklist, which extended to Wall Street lawyer Harry Wachtel, among others, would undercut the presidential mandate to insure that civil rights leaders did not "either take away control of the conference from your designated co-chairmen or withdraw their support from it." The blocked invitations vexed King. Andrew Young, while dispatched to lead a march in Selma seeking courtesy titles for Negroes, appealed to Abram and Lee White by telegram on November 13 for reconsideration of "the other names which were submitted by Dr. King." Such consternation within SCLC brought contrasting joy to FBI headquarters when intercepted over the wiretaps and bugs. "We may be overly optimistic, but perhaps this is a favorable trend," wrote a supervisor. "We will continue, as in the past, to furnish the White House derogatory information concerning King's people who indicate possible association with the White House." Hoover approved: "Right."

*   *   *

WITHIN THE broad community of civil rights activists, the November 16 planning session was considered so pivotal that religious leaders in New York convened a conference to prepare for it on November 9, hours before the Northeast blackout. King arrived two days later into the concentrated hum of crosscurrents in the media. Not a single speaker at the religious conference lasted long on the broad promise of Johnson's historic Howard University speech before veering into an electric fixation on the structure of Negro families. Robert Spike, head of the National Council of Churches' Commission on Religion and Race, apologized typically for his extemporaneous remarks on "the damage that is flowing from the Moynihan report." An entire book soon would chronicle the ongoing tar-baby furor over the report's central theory that a "tangle of pathology" infected Negro families, as measured by government statistics. Intellectual arguments cloaked in scientific language resonated through political culture, like Louis Agassiz's theory of the Negro as a separate species. "Because of the newspaper coverage," the book concluded, "the Moynihan Report was taken as the government's explanation for the [Watts] riots."

Nowhere did an author's name appear on the Labor Department report printed in June, but Assistant Secretary Daniel Patrick Moynihan distributed copies avidly to friends and reporters, one of whom, Robert Novak, had surfaced him to fame during the Watts riots of August in a nationally syndicated column—"The Moynihan Report"—calling it a "political atomic bomb" that "exposes the ugly truth about the big city Negro's plight." Novak promoted a forbidden aura about the "much suppressed, much leaked" document, which in fact sold openly in government stores for 45 cents, and diverse commentators helped loose an avalanche of controversy. The *New York Times* reported within ten days that the Johnson administration was studying the report for clues about how to "replace matriarchy," female-headed families, among Negroes. By September, Richard Rovere observed in *The New Yorker* that the upcoming White House conference "aimed at developing a national policy to strengthen the ego of the Negro male in the United States." The *Washington Star* claimed to discern an obstacle looming from the "still secret" Moynihan report: "Negro life is another world as little known to middle class Negroes as middle class whites[,] and not understood at all by leaders such as Martin Luther King."

Race propelled family issues to the forefront of national politics. Gender terms sprang into headlines from Moynihan's opening section that identified matriarchy as the lead indicator of a ghetto deprivation he called pathological. "The very essence of the male animal, from the bantam rooster to the four-star general, is to strut," declared the report. "Indeed, in 19th century America, a particular type of exaggerated male boastfulness became almost a national style. Not for the Negro male. The 'sassy nigger' was lynched."

Pauli Murray of Yale, still working on the federal lawsuit to overturn Alabama's blanket exclusion of women from jury service, raised an isolated howl against suggestions that women were hogging the few positions of relative advantage. It was "bitterly ironic," she wrote *Newsweek,* "that Negro women should be impliedly censured for their efforts to overcome a handicap not of their own making." Those women who did push past double discrimination by race and sex into middle-class prospects faced a chronically severe deficit of comparably situated Negro marriage partners, which to Murray made the female-headed household a desperate, heroic adaptation rather than a preference or sickness. Bayard Rustin objected more generally that for two centuries black families had been denied human status, let alone recognition or protection under state laws, in order to safeguard the property rights and breeding prerogatives of slave owners. "It is amazing to me that Negro families exist at all," he said bluntly. King tried to salvage hope from a past he called too "ghastly" for words. "No one in all history had to fight against so many psychological and physical horrors to have a family life," he said in a New York speech, recalling reproachful questions about why he allowed small children to suffer the trauma of jail-bound demonstrations: "The answer is simple: Our children and our families are maimed a little every day of their lives."

Articles about Moynihan poured that autumn from opinion journals—*Commonweal, The New York Review of Books, The Nation, Chris-*

tianity and Crisis. It made news that many Negroes felt insulted, which itself was new, and news again that Moynihan was nonplussed by the reaction. Few of the contending public voices were Negro or female. Most, including Moynihan, traced the high indices of broken Negro families to historical oppression, but the ambiguous drumbeat of social science spurred inferences of deviant character to run free of analysis: "22.9 per cent of the city-dwelling Negro women who have ever been married are now divorced, separated, or deserted . . . explosive cycle of poverty . . . one Negro family in four is fatherless . . . welfare dependency . . . birth rate for Negroes is 40 per cent higher than for whites." A pathology model subliminally reduced civil rights forces from intrepid agents of change to quarantined patients, while reasserting full diagnostic privilege for mainstream opinion makers. "Moynihan's facts were undisputed," William Manchester later reflected in a survey history that captured an incoming mood, "but such was the Negro agony that year, and so shattering the impact of events on Negro pride, that blacks could not face them."

* * *

FBI BUGS MISSED King in New York on the second weekend of November. John Malone, the New York special agent in charge, advised headquarters that functional devices were planted well ahead in the reserved rooms at the Astor when the target unaccountably checked in elsewhere, too late to plant substitutes. To dodge bureaucratic blame, Malone assured Hoover that he had scolded the New York Hilton for accepting King without a reservation, but the pinched hotel manager chose the government lecture over publicity for turning him away. By "physical surveillance" (snoopers) and subsequent collections, the Bureau sampled the range of worry yanking at the Hilton strategy sessions: King's just published commitment to a Chicago campaign ("Next Stop: The North," *Saturday Review*); orders for the SCLC accountant to cooperate with an FBI audit of car purchases; fantasy speculation that Harry Belafonte might stave off the financial crisis with a benefit gala featuring remarried film stars Elizabeth Taylor and Richard Burton; multiple anxieties for the White House conference beginning Tuesday. "The government thinks the Moynihan report is priceless," Stanley Levison remarked, adding that King must counter its misperceptions. Another wiretap caught the warning synopsis of a new runaway phenomenon. "Malcolm X wrote this book out of compulsion," said Levison.

Consigned to nine months of oblivion in death, Malcolm's name just then achieved sudden and miraculous rebirth. Publisher Nelson Doubleday had pulled the finished autobiography from the presses within days of the grisly February assassination, announcing that he must forgo publication to spare company employees from terror and retribution from the inscrutable Black Muslim factions. A dozen major publishing firms subsequently spurned the orphaned manuscript, just as major organs of American culture buried Malcolm himself with a barbed shortage of funeral charity. The *Washington Post* bid riddance to "the spokesman of bitter racism." *Newsweek* derided him for "blazing racist attacks on the 'white devils' and his calls for an armed American Mau Mau." Columnist Walter Winchell labeled him "a petty punk," and the liberal *Nation* magazine faintly eulogized the "courageous leader of one segment of the Negro lunatic fringe." Such disrepute drove Malcolm's posthumous project at last resort to the feisty Grove Press, known for defying obscenity restrictions to publish works by Henry Miller and the Marquis de Sade. Having survived a "banned in Boston" censorship drive against the 1964 edition of the D. H. Lawrence novel *Lady Chatterley's Lover,* Grove executives prepared *The Autobiography of Malcolm X* for the autumn of 1965 with special security precautions and private trepidation, standing ready to defend First Amendment rights. Editors at *The Saturday Evening Post* introduced their preview excerpt with a memorably backhanded promotion for the late author: "We shall be lucky if Malcolm X is not succeeded by even weirder and more virulent extremists."

Then came the reviews. The *New York Times,* which had appraised Malcolm's "pitifully wasted life" in February—dusting away a "twisted man" marked by "ruthless and fanatical belief in violence"—hailed the autobiography on November 5 as "a brilliant, painful, important book." Eliot Fremont-Smith declared in the bellwether notice that "with his death American Negroes lost their most able, articulate and compelling spokesman," and reviewers elsewhere struck a similar tone of whiplash wonder. "The important word here is conversion," wrote I. F. Stone for the November 11 *New York Review of Books.* Malcolm's unsparing tale of his own serial conversions—"I knew right there in prison that reading had changed forever the course of my life," began one of them—bowled over skeptics into a contagion of sustained sales that approached three million copies by the thirty-third printing of the Ballantine paperback in 1992, with translations into more than a dozen foreign languages. *Time* magazine scorned Malcolm at death as "an unashamed demagogue" whose "gospel was hatred," but came to list his *Autobiography* in 1999 among the ten best nonfiction books of the twentieth century.

Like the Moynihan report, which omitted policy recommendations to concentrate on its thesis of family pathology, the *Autobiography* disregarded goals and ideas for reform. "It tells what happens to an intelligent Negro who discovers that he has, within American society, no future," observed the *Times* review. "And it tells in the most powerful and precise terms what this really means—the systematized destruction of Negro self-esteem as an almost automatic function of white society." Malcolm scorched the promise of American democracy. "I am not interested in becoming American," he said, "because America is not interested in me." Above any political ideology, he clung to the belief that only one force could dissolve racial hatred at the root—purified, nonsectarian Islam—but the *Autobiography* minimized this notion because ghostwriter Alex Haley and the Grove Press editors knew it would leave Americans cold.

The book's spirited struggle with doom seized an audience of classic breadth. Secularist reviewers, wearied by the pious mainstream of the civil rights movement, applauded the unflinching realism. "Here one may read, in the agony of this brilliant Negro's self-creation," wrote I. F. Stone, "the agony of an entire people in their search for identity." Yet theologian James Cone came to adopt Malcolm's honesty as a depth indicator of Christian faith. "As much as I am persuaded by the truth of the gospel of Jesus," resolved Cone, soon to be the first black professor at Union Seminary in New York, "I am equally persuaded that living and preaching Jesus' gospel in America require the exacting test of Malcolm's nationalist critique." Generations of young readers reacted more to the book's raw journey from pimp to martyr, embracing in Malcolm a passage of daring authenticity.

A *Newsweek* poll in the 1990s found that 82 percent of black Americans considered Malcolm X a quintessential "strong black male," lifting him to approval numbers ten times his peak in life, and legions of young whites made him a crossover icon. The *Autobiography* charmed them with humble directness: "I became a bus boy at the Parker House in Boston." White readers and "integration-hungry Negroes" braved merciless, edifying indictments safely on the page. "The white man is in no moral position to accuse anyone else of hate!" Malcolm wrote. "Yes, I will pull off that liberal's halo that he spends such efforts cultivating," he added later. "I know nothing of the South. I am the creation of the northern white man and of his hypocritical attitude toward the Negro." An underlying pleasure in urgent communication, which had driven Malcolm to lecture often at white colleges, softened the raging prose. The book, while contemptuous of nonviolent strategy, presented violence not as an instrument of progress or condition of manhood but as a melancholy fact of life, subordinate to the power of words. "I have never felt that I would live to become an old man," wrote Malcolm. "Even before I was a Muslim—when I was a hustler in the ghetto jungle, then a criminal in prison—it always stayed on my mind that I would die a violent death."

No one could have foreseen that the year of the Voting Rights Act would conclude in lasting effusions over "Negro matriarchy" and Malcolm X. Both aimed to penetrate the broken heart of race without suggesting salves or remedies. Both discarded in passing the nonviolent methods of the civil rights movement. One mingled the wobbliest and sharpest tools of social science to redefine the issue from a presumption that Americans "have gone beyond equal opportunity." The other insisted flatly from the grave that race scarcely had budged, and that the benevolent white liberal was a fraud. "I don't care how nice one is to you," wrote Malcolm X, ". . . almost never does he see you as he sees himself, as he sees his own kind."

* * *

SPLIT IMAGES hovered over a changing landscape. Even sports remained white at Southern colleges until a lone basketball player made the Maryland roster in November. The first two Negro high school students were signing scholarships for Southeastern Conference football at Kentucky, though neither would ever play a game. (One quit after the other died of a broken back suffered in practice, which obliged the university to resolve suspicions of violent discrimination by teammates.) Shortsighted experts debated which Negroes and colleges might dare to step forward, while professional teams rushed ahead into newly integrated markets. By December, hastening to Atlanta behind the Milwaukee Braves, a new football franchise presold its 1966 tickets before receiving any players or even choosing its Falcons nickname. Comedian Danny Thomas helped organize a team called the Miami Dolphins.

Two drama series, *The F.B.I.* and *I Spy,* premiered in the fall television season to long-running popularity. One, under J. Edgar Hoover's detailed supervision, banned a list of unmanly sponsors such as deodor-

ants and cleaning products, and featured agents who were never unbut-
toned, surreptitious, ethnic, wrong, or lethal on the screen, nearly always winging suspects with a clean first shot. The other introduced
young Bill Cosby as the first actor of color ever to star alongside whites,
playing a Rhodes Scholar CIA officer disguised as the tennis trainer for
Robert Culp while both chased down enemy spies. The *Los Angeles
Times* praised Cosby's character as a "non-threatening Negro," and only
a few Southern cities refused the network feed.

Print observers noticed a fundamental shift in attitude toward urban
areas. "No other nation hates its own cities," wrote columnist TRB for
The New Republic. "Only in the USA are suburbs afraid of their parents." The editors of *Life* magazine prepared for December a double
issue called "The U.S. City." Half the spreads displayed dazzling lights,
sophisticated people, and futuristic designs with matching headlines—
"The Proud Shapes," "Trains That Need No Wheels," "Satellites,
Megastructures, Platforms," "Homework Done by Computer." The
other half showcased grim tenements and hungry children—"A Bitter
and Insistent Plague," "Racial Trap," "Torn Family." Scholar Herbert
Gans observed more than a decade later that the *Life* issue marked an
abrupt end to media celebrations of urban vitality, which traditionally
overlooked or romanticized desperado street wars among the poor.
Connotations of the word "city," whose Greek root supplied the ancient
concept and name for politics itself, sagged under impressions suffused
with race.

At the White House, Joe Califano sent the TRB column to Harry
McPherson with a note of worry on November 15. A day before, during
his New York visit, King preached two Sunday services for Adam Clayton Powell on the 157th anniversary of Abyssinian Baptist Church.
Stanley Levison warned that he would suffer more backlash among
contributors for associating with Powell than for his plan to write Ho
Chi Minh. Indeed, mere press notice of the guest sermon provoked
James Phelan, a prominent banker who had stuck with SCLC through
the Vietnam controversy, to send an irate letter canceling his pledge.
Powell, who had tormented King with private blackmail and miscellaneous devilment, was a stylish performer of hybrid personalities—
committee chairman in Congress, scion of a historic pulpit family,
Harlem dandy with skin light enough to pass—who played nimbly in
white and Negro styles all the standout roles from potentate and silver-
tongued crusader to rascal. His mercurial ways irritated many who

agreed with him on specific issues, and enraged those who demanded consistency, but his zest for provoking elite white people delighted multitudes of constituents in Harlem.

King tried to escape his long-standing commitment, then gave in to fear that Powell "would use it against me" if he did. Overriding Levison's protest that middle-class supporters would not understand, King responded also to pleas from Wyatt Walker. He sensed no chance to undo the humiliation of Walker's public dismissal as assistant pastor, but he did hope to dispel malicious rumors from Powell that he, King, despised Walker, never wanted to see him work again, and had insisted that Walker refer to him as America's number one Negro. If Powell declined to appear as host, as appeared likely, King resolved to bring the banished Walker back to Abyssinian on his own guest authority for a farewell "gesture of reconciliation."

Powell swooped into the robing room at the last minute, obliging Walker to wait outside while King pleaded his case alone. Expectant shouts rose from five thousand worshippers before the two Baptist legends appeared together after all on the broad marble platform. Powell, introducing "the greatest living American, black or white," exhorted King with winks and orotund double meaning to expand his work "into the vacuums of leadership" nationwide. He suggested Newark, New Jersey. They hugged and King preached, which earned a front-page headline in the New York Times: "Powell, Denying Rift, Welcomes King to Harlem."

Powell wrote King a note to express satisfaction "that we could present a united front." King did not disclose what transpired to thwart the appearance by Walker, but his signature forbearance slipped with a hint of frustration heavier than all the compressed burdens of the movement. "Adam," he told Walker numbly, "is going to hell."

* * *

IN A syndicated column titled "Power's Long Arm," correspondent Joe Alsop praised spectacular deployment to forge history from the staples of iron and blood. Recalling vivid images of Vietnam's Cam Ranh Bay "as it was in the French time . . . lying blue and empty of all shipping except a few fishing shacks," he described by contrast "the staggering reality" of military engineers "making a sandspit into a port capable of handling 10,000 tons a week": mammoth cranes towed by sea from Okinawa, "bulldozers literally big enough to move mountains . . . landing craft of every sort . . . at every turn there was something to make one's eyes pop out." Alsop flew with General William Westmoreland to An Khe, "a wide green vale among the hills" of central Vietnam. "The great sight here," he wrote, "was the actual delivery halfway round the world of an entire U.S. division in complete fighting trim." Lieutenant Colonel Harold "Hal" Moore, a battalion commander of the new 1st Cavalry Division (Airmobile), explored by jeep along the winding Highway 1 that war historian Bernard Fall memorialized in his book *Street Without Joy,* and located from Fall's book a stone obelisk commemorating French and Vietnamese combatants fallen more than a decade earlier in a remote field still littered with shell casings and fragments of bone. Alsop told American readers that "the key dominant problem"—"grossly insufficient resources"—"no longer exists as it did in the French time." More than 200,000 U.S. soldiers would arrive by Christmas. "The importance of this change that is now going on can hardly be exaggerated," he concluded. "It does not mean, alas, that the war is being won . . . but it does mean that at last there is light at the end of the tunnel, and that is always something."

On November 14, the Sunday when King preached for Adam Clayton Powell in Harlem, Colonel Moore landed at a forest clearing big enough for eight helicopters per drop in the dense Ia (River) Drang Valley, where the Ho Chi Minh Trail turned east from Cambodia through mountainous South Vietnam. His brigade of the 1st AirCav had been awarded a special, honorary designation as the 7th Cavalry, inheriting the spirited "Garry Owen" quick-step that Royal Irish Lancers had brought from Limerick pubs to become the namesake march for the most storied Army unit in the Old West, once commanded by George Armstrong Custer. While Moore claimed a crude field command among brick-hard termite mounds taller than soldiers, 7th Cavalry squads in Operation Silver Bayonet jumped from giant Huey gunships instead of horses, with orders to "search for and destroy the enemy." A popping crescendo greeted skirmishers headed to form a tree-line perimeter, and an experienced captain recognized more regular North Vietnamese Army troops than Vietcong guerrillas. "Every man in the lead squad was shot," recorded Sergeant Steve Hansen of Alpha Company's 3rd Platoon. "From the time we got the order to move to the time where men were dying was only five minutes. The enemy were very close to us and overran some of our dead."

Lieutenant Henry Herrick, son of a UCLA astronomy professor, charged after the Vietnamese up a hill into scrub brush until his second platoon of Bravo Company disappeared even to radio contact beyond surges of sniper bullets, colliding forays, and blind crossfires. Colonel Moore identified three opposing regiments of the People's Army of Vietnam (PAVN), which comprised two thousand troops, and relied heavily on one glaring imbalance to offset the superior numbers commanded by Lieutenant General Nguyen Huu An: "I had major fire support and he didn't." An American artillery base five miles away sent four thousand high-explosive howitzer rounds into the surrounding hillsides the first day. Skyraiders swooped close with napalm and five-hundred-pound bombs. Bullet-riddled Hueys mangled the forest with suppressing fire as they discharged reinforcements. Thirty hours later, a lull in the raging attacks allowed a search party of Bravo Company to find Herrick's lost platoon entirely prostrate. "Even the men who *could* stand up were so traumatized by what happened to them they preferred to lay down," reported a rescuer. One refused to budge until someone moved a transfixing scarlet object a few feet away that proved to be one of many recovered battlefield diaries, with a final entry later translated from Vietnamese: "Oh my dear, when the troops come home after the victory and you do not see me, please look at the proud colors. You will see me there and you will feel warm under the shadow of the bamboo tree." Near the diarist, Lieutenant Dennis Deal studied a North Vietnamese soldier with a severed trunk who had booby-trapped a grenade to his rifle stock while bleeding to death. "If we're up against this," muttered Deal, "it's gonna be a long-ass year."

Two American relief battalions entered the ghastly buzz of landing zone X-Ray on the third morning, November 16, helping first to stack the closest Vietnamese bodies six feet high between persistent assaults. Colonel Moore responded to numbers pressure by lopping off two hundred from his subordinates' estimate of 834 Vietnamese dead from infantry fire, then adding an arbitrarily precise guess of 1,215 killed beyond sight by aerial support, to report a total enemy body count of 1,849. The U.S. casualty list so far was smaller and more reliable—seventy-nine killed, including Lieutenant Herrick, with 121 wounded—concentrated in the units originally enveloped. Charlie Company lost all five officers and more than half its 106 men, many of whom still awaited evacuation in the care of fresh replacements for two slain medics. Army Specialist 4 Hank Thomas of St. Augustine, Florida, lifted each of the lined-up ponchos to collect information for his first twenty-five death tags. He found only two corpses with closed eyes, the others gaping in

arrested stares. Mutilations from the high-powered weapons overwhelmed his training to the point that at first he welcomed cries of
"Medic!" so he could crawl away with bandages and morphine for the
living wounded. Thomas had disclosed to no fellow soldier that he led
the first Freedom Riders into Mississippi jails in 1961, when he was a
cellmate and still nonviolent mentor for Stokely Carmichael, in part because he could not justify the conscription-driven change to himself.
Night volleys rattled him awake from a depleted stupor to a ground's-
eye view along his row of motionless heels.

Americans vacated X-Ray Wednesday morning, November 17, to let
B-52s from Guam drop two hundred tons of ordnance on the mountain
range thought to conceal the withdrawn Vietnamese. Moore's sister outfit of 7th Cavalry, the 2nd Battalion, marched six miles toward a larger
clearing called Albany, where Lieutenant Colonel Robert McDade
gathered his commanders to plan the defense of scheduled helicopter
lifts just before three battalions of North Vietnamese struck the leader-
less companies stretched for five hundred yards along the trail behind,
swarming through defenders who fired in all directions from pockets of
visibility no bigger than kitchens. Those who died seemed to be shot
most often in the midsection. "I don't know why, but when a man is hit
in the belly, he screams an unearthly scream," recorded Army Specialist
4 Jack Smith, son of ABC News anchor Howard K. Smith. "They
didn't ever stop for breath. They kept on until they were hoarse, then
they would bleed through their mouths and pass out. They would wake
up and start screaming again. Then they would die." An hour later, desperate lieutenants averted greater disaster by calling in napalm on their
own positions judged decimated already. Smith's company suffered 93
percent casualties. He and other wounded men survived an endless sixteen hours by playing dead among night stalkers who detected and shot
Americans by listening for their telltale groans. Volunteer retrievers,
heaving survivors toward the rear lines, paused in clouds of smoke as
Captain George Forrest* urged them forward with cries for the safe
entry of friendlies, all radios being disabled. He stood to shine a homing
flashlight on his own dark face—and lived—but one stray soldier in the

---

* Stationed with troops on alert to suppress the riots feared during the 1963 March on Washington, Forrest had been unaware that his own parents were among the marchers. He stood
three months later in the honor guard for President Kennedy's casket at the Capitol Rotunda.
Forrest would return to the Ia Drang Valley for a 1993 reunion of combatants from both
sides, and later became chief administrator for St. Mary's County, Maryland.

chaos mistakenly emptied a full clip into the first movements by return-ing compatriots. Thursday morning, as air strikes hit the Vietnamese reserves massed nearby, the carnage included some hundred PAVN snipers hanging from the ropes that had secured them in the treetops.

At headquarters, the 7th Cavalry brigade commander neglected to mention unsatisfactory and incoherent reports of a second major attack in his personal briefing for General Westmoreland, but journalists reached the Albany landing zone in time to file vivid stories about the combined Ia Drang battles as the first large-scale U.S. engagement in Vietnam, a costly victory by the numbers. The front page of the Novem-ber 19 *New York Times* featured three AP photographs of captioned war drama: "U.S. Casualties Strewn over Vietnamese Valley . . . Wounded American crawls toward medic . . . Dead and injured Americans are il-luminated by flares from U.S. planes that came to aid."

The adrenaline of war stirred martial fervor in both countries, whose leaders praised military performance while masking internal strategic debates. Vietnamese generals credited American soldiers with determi-nation far beyond the effete "paper tigers" scorned in Communist prop-aganda, yet welcomed empirical proof that peasant soldiers would stand up to lethal punishment from advanced weapons and "helicopter cav-alry" tactics. Ho Chi Minh, while favoring remorseless war to drive Americans from Vietnam, conceded doubt about recent orders to initi-ate sustained large-scale engagements in a "heaven-storming" final push. Commanding general Nguyen Chi Thanh and Communist Party first secretary Le Duan, having dared to belittle as a "scared rabbit" even General Vo Nguyen Giap, the legendary architect of Dien Bien Phu, lost momentum to Giap's renewed argument that the huge U.S. buildup recommended more years of patience with hit-and-run guerrilla war-fare.

On the American side, professionals frankly respected the disci-plined motivation of Communist soldiers. CBS News, in a special report that characterized the Ia Drang casualties as "light," aired the straight-forward longing of Special Forces Major Charles Beckwith to have two hundred such adversaries under his command: "They're the best I've ever seen." General Westmoreland focused on attrition ratios rather than long-term commitment to a standoff in valor. With Vietnamese battle deaths reckoned at least ten times the 305 Americans killed in the five-day campaign, he calculated that intensified combat would impose unsustainable losses on the Communist side. Sensing a military advantage to be pressed, he absorbed the painful but instructive ambush as no more threatening to long-term success than Custer's Last Stand of the 7th Cavalry at the Little Big Horn in 1876, which scarcely had destined Sitting Bull to govern the Dakotas. Westmoreland cautioned against "headlines about victory." He warned in a radio interview of danger that Americans "will be overwhelmed by a certain feeling of optimism and may lose sight of what I consider a true appraisal of the situation."

* * *

ON NOVEMBER 16, amid early battle reports from Vietnam, a political crossfire sorely tested the hard-won promise in Washington to eradicate the effects of white supremacy. "I welcome all of you to two days of intense labor for your country," President Johnson told 250 delegates gathered to prepare his spring conference on civil rights. "The tide of change is running with the Negro American on this mid-November evening. Neither the ignorant violence of the Ku Klux Klan nor the despairing violence of Watts can reverse it. For this tide is moved by decency and by love and by justice." To thunderous applause, Johnson saluted the 200,000 Negroes registered in ten weeks since passage of the Voting Rights Act, and he announced that Attorney General Katzenbach would introduce new civil rights legislation to attack discrimination in the justice system. "We intend to make the jury box, in both state and federal courts, the sacred domain of justice under law," he declared. To less enthusiasm, Johnson said he would order the Commission on Civil Rights to give "careful attention to the problems of race and education in all parts of this country."

The President shook hands through the East Room with encouraging words for the assembled scholars, civil servants, activists, and leaders he called "the captains of peaceful armies." Aaron Henry, board chair of the Mississippi NAACP, was one of many sober personalities turned bubbly. "We're eating barbecue at the White House!" he told friends, but working constraints clamped down on the gilded deliberations to follow. White House aides blocked votes on resolutions deemed critical of the administration. In the education workshop, Al Raby argued from his Chicago experience that class sizes in poor Northern schools must be cut in half, that government must eliminate rather than study de facto segregation, and that an essential first step was to reverse October's preemptive assurance of federal funds to Superintendent Willis. Such notions were tabled as premature. Martin Luther King, groping for a productive balance, spent two days in the jobs workshop without making quotable remarks for or against the pace of achievement. Clarence Mitchell of the NAACP urgently pressed a resolution from the justice panel that President Johnson should "speed up the lagging enforcement" of both landmark civil rights acts. "People in the South are in danger of being exterminated," he told a plenary session. "It is a matter of life and death."

Conference co-chair A. Philip Randolph ruled his friend's motion out of order, but White House aides worried that Bayard Rustin and Randolph himself were circulating for spring consideration a supplemental "Freedom Budget" that sought a national investment of $100 billion over ten years in schools, housing, and jobs. The proposals exposed stark gaps between racial reality and the ringing commitment to equal opportunity proclaimed by President Johnson in the War on Poverty as well as his Howard University speech. The sheer scale of accepted tasks made the administration seem overmatched, which threatened its posture of sovereign control. Johnson abhorred intimations of frailty or doubt as the first symptom of failure in national politics. By the same predilection, J. Edgar Hoover's ingrained rejection of the slightest alleged error had doomed White House entreaties for FBI observers at the exploratory, off-the-record workshops. Assistant Director DeLoach refused to supply agents to hear any anticipated "critical or unjustifiable statements concerning the FBI," and suggested instead that if conference participants "didn't know what they were talking about, or falsely accuse the FBI, they should shut up."

White House aides vigorously promoted three alternative workshops on community, welfare, and the family. The panels opened topics not yet digested into budget-busting agendas or daunting politics, with a social science approach that was congenial to the majority of delegates with backgrounds in academics or government. Civil rights veterans resisted these attractions as a diversion or worse that devalued the cumulative experience and purpose of the movement. Of the few delegates who spoke publicly against the shift of focus, Andrew Young defended the Negro family as perhaps unorthodox—often with extra mothers, grandmothers, cousins, "and no father"—yet strong enough to have sustained both the civil rights movement and a vibrant institutional church. "We are not being deprived of family life," he told reporters. "We are being deprived of justice, education, and jobs."

A joke relieved undercurrents of tension among experts trying hard to be polite. "I have been reliably informed," announced a conference moderator, "that no such person as Daniel Patrick Moynihan exists." Peals of laughter confirmed the target of obsessive gossip suffused with race, and Moynihan broke silence the second day to lodge "a point of personal privilege" against one comment that he had undertaken his study of the Negro family in order to explain Watts. Granting that the report had been completed weeks before the riots, Dr. Benjamin Payton of the New York Protestant Council disputed Moynihan's deeper application of cause and effect, and quoted the study's thesis that family deterioration rather than the legacy of discrimination "is the fundamental source of weakness in the Negro community." Heated exchanges receded again into whispered caucuses. In a compounded irony, news outlets made the bow-tied new Wesleyan University professor himself a symbol of civil rights. The *Washington Star* declared Moynihan "The 'Non-Person' at the Rights Parley," and a headline—"Moynihan Conspicuously Ignored"—fashioned for him a white celebrity version of the invisible cage that novelist Ralph Ellison had portrayed at the heart of the black condition.

President Johnson seethed. The deadlocked racial summit annoyed him, as did the publicity about Moynihan, but he resented most the pinch from unruly civil rights leaders he found lacking in political trust for the long haul of a difficult cause. "They come right in and by God take their perch on the White House," Johnson fumed to McGeorge Bundy, "and while they still got their hors d'oeuvres going, and whisky in one hand and a wienie sausage in the other, they're just raisin' unshirted hell and say it's got to be a hundred *billion*." The White House staff spread rumors during the conference that an irate President might abort the event in a fury over leaflets advertising that four delegates, including Martin Luther King, were listed as sponsors of a new march against the Vietnam War. Such warning inhibited use of the White House platform to criticize military priorities, chilling optimism along with dissent, and Johnson's mood darkened with the ensuing news. On Wednesday, November 24, as he released a message of thanks to the armed forces ("A man does not inherit freedom as he inherits the land"), the Pentagon publicly confirmed 240 Americans killed and 470 wounded in the Ia Drang Valley. The understated toll tripled the previous weekly high, and hiked the number of deaths since 1961 to 1,300. Press Secretary Bill Moyers delivered what reporters called "a spontaneous and quite personal description" of Johnson's anguish over the list, which led Thanksgiving Day news along with the miracle story of a lone soldier found wandering with multiple wounds seven days after the battle at Albany clearing. The hometown paper in Coward, South Carolina, retracted its obituary for Toby Braveboy, descended from Creek Indians, who lost most of a hand to gangrene but survived.

* * *

ON SATURDAY, November 27, the rally of thirty thousand at the Washington Monument exposed the hazardous psychology of war protest. From Vietnam, the president of the Communist National Liberation Front (NLF) sent an advance telegram wishing the demonstration "brilliant success," which further guaranteed a lack of mainstream American politicians. Martin Luther King commended the draft of Coretta's address, but canceled plans to speak himself. (She exhorted the crowd never to forget that democratic commitment made America a historic great nation: "This is true in spite of the bombings in Alabama as well as in Vietnam.") Organizers from the Committee for a SANE Nuclear Policy sought to project a moderate image with a dress code and a suggested list of seventeen cautious slogans, such as "Supervised Cease-Fire" and "Stop the Bombing." Although a visible few defied prescription by marching under an NLF banner instead of the American flag, the *New York Times* perceived "more babies than beatniks, more family groups than folksong quartets," and gently mocked a tameness in the mannerly crowd. Norman Thomas, nearly blind in old age, announced from the platform that he wanted to cleanse rather than burn the American flag. "I'd rather see America save her soul than her face," he declared. Baby doctor Benjamin Spock said the war discredited the United States more than it hurt Communism.

Rally organizers vetoed speakers considered too strident or ideological, including Nobel Prize chemist Linus Pauling and Bob Moses of SNCC, which caused infighting among the nascent antiwar groups over alleged "McCarthyite" loyalty tests. Moses, still in transition from his February breakdown, and still answering only to his middle name Parris, spoke privately with movement supporters who would listen. He told one interviewer that some white Southerners justified killing "gooks" in Vietnam for the same reason they condoned the murder of civil rights workers—as a threat to their civilization—yet most Americans justified the war for the very purpose that united them *against* the segregated South, to advance patriotic freedom. He said President Johnson blamed violence on isolated extremists, Klansmen and Com-

munists, while himself defining the Vietnamese as inhuman, robotic infiltrators in their own land, to be met with massive violence. "What do
you do when the whole country has a sickness?" Moses asked, wondering whether anything could "awaken this nation as the South is beginning to be awakened." (The Mississippi Supreme Court, in a stab at
fairness, had just overturned his 1961 criminal conviction from the first
nonviolent march in McComb, when Moses submitted to mob beatings
and then an Orwellian trial on charges of "violent, loud, offensive" conduct.) He sifted cruel paradox with the intensity that had driven him
from New York to become SNCC's solitary pioneer in Mississippi.
"I want this country to be less sure of itself so that it can stop making
war on other countries to export our system," he said. "Another way of
saying the same thing is that I want this country to be *more* sure of itself,
so it can publicly admit it has real problems and must work to solve
them."

At the Washington Monument, one sanctioned speaker wrestled his
thoughts in hypnotic self-examination like Moses, wondering how a
country of consistently progressive government since 1932 could flood
Asia with 200,000 young soldiers to "kill and die in the most dubious of
wars," while straining decades to deploy the first hundred voter registrars in the South. "What do you make of it?" shouted SDS president
Carl Oglesby, a thirty-one-year-old father of three, normally a technical
writer for Bendix appliances in Michigan. Oglesby surveyed the background commitment in Vietnam from Truman and Kennedy to the
current leaders "who study the maps, give the commands, push the buttons, and tally the dead," naming Bundy, Goldberg, McNamara, Rusk,
Lodge, and President Johnson. "They are not moral monsters," he declared. "They are all honorable men. They are all liberals. And so, I'm
sure, are many of us who are here today in protest."

Oglesby groped out loud for a vocabulary of fresh confession to indict
liberalism at its zenith. He traced the fault perhaps to material corruption in a small American populace that consumed half the world's
goods: "How intolerable, to be born moral, but addicted to a stolen and
maybe surplus luxury." He suggested among alternatives a global case
of the stunted perception that comforted the mind of segregation. "We
have become a nation of young, bright-eyed, hard-hearted, slim-
waisted, bullet-headed make-out artists," Oglesby charged. "A nation—may I say it?—of beardless liberals." Calling himself a radical
instead, he acknowledged that bitter apprehensions on the war sounded

"mighty anti-American," then cried out: "Don't blame *me* for that! Blame those who mouthed my liberal values and broke my American heart." Oglesby soon trailed off and stepped politely from the microphone into sustained applause from a dissipating crowd. He looked surprised, then perplexed, when rally coordinator Sanford Gottlieb of SANE lifted his arm like a prizefighter's in spontaneous tribute. Although news accounts overlooked Oglesby as an unknown speaker, activists marked a birth moment for the "New Left" identity associated with young whites moving from civil rights influence to an independent stance on Vietnam.

Two days after the rally, facing a stateside VIP delegation inside a heavily restricted tent at the An Khe redoubt, Lieutenant Colonel Harold Moore bluntly recounted the battle of landing zone X-Ray against an enemy he termed disciplined to the verge of suicidal fanaticism. "Sir, that completes my presentation," he said, and met dead silence instead of examination. Wordlessly, flanked by the Pacific Fleet commander and two of the four Joint Chiefs, Defense Secretary McNamara nodded, shook hands, and exited with confirmation of grit in the backward Vietnamese. General Westmoreland gave him a classified request for another 200,000 troops—to exploit the attrition ratio—beyond the 200,000 already committed but not yet deployed or provided for in the national budget, and McNamara took home what he called a "shattering blow." No character dividend or surprise good fortune yet greeted the can-do American plunge. With the projected numbers now being harvested in flesh, McNamara told President Johnson that exposure to field commanders from the recent combat, "particularly the First Air Cavalry Division," resulted in "my personal judgment that the situation is much more critical than at least I had realized."

In Washington, where partisans of the distant war retained confidence to address collateral issues, Joe Alsop's column on the day of the An Khe briefing detected an "acute and rising anxiety about the next stage of the civil rights movement." He reported that White House officials, shocked by the cold reception for the Moynihan report, "found themselves hardly talking the same language as the movement's leaders." Alsop endorsed their view that Negro delegates had "no practicable program," being mired in protest and unrealistic demands for federal initiative. "Injustice is the theme," he observed, "not what can be done about it." Similarly, columnists Rowland Evans and Robert

Novak charged that "shrill cries of Negro militants" had dominated the workshops, "sweeping the problems posed by the Moynihan report under the table," wasting months that "went into researching the Negro male's loss of manhood, the dominance of the Negro female, the breakdown of family life and the acceleration of illegitimate births." Their column, "Civil Rights Disaster," declared the two-day event the most dismal failure in the "glittering two-year history" of the Johnson administration. "White intellectuals who had come to Washington to discuss Negro social disorganization were stunned by the demagoguery," they concluded. "The question is why? Some disillusioned liberals hint darkly that radical white elements are at work, prodding Negroes to seek the unattainable."

* * *

Lost to obscurity beneath the Ia Drang battles and other national news, the first racially contested elections in modern Alabama selected local farmers to supervise programs for the U.S. Agricultural Stabilization and Conservation Service (ASCS). Movement hopes had dimmed in Greene County when five aspiring black voters were evicted and many received envelopes missing the official mail-in ballots. Only one farmer agreed to run in Hale County, none in Sumter. "Folks there are understandably jumpy," reported a SNCC memo on these pioneer campaigns across five rural counties. Since an unexpected federal edict that any six farmers could put a nominee on the local ballot, which sustained the first Negro candidates, SNCC-sponsored workshops had sparked interest in the practical workings of ASCS crop loans and soil erosion payments. Poor farmers learned how the elected county committees also shaped price supports, distributed vital cotton allotments, and controlled indirect subsidies that could double their money-losing price of two and a half cents per pound for okra. In Lowndes County, where nearly two-thirds of the eligible farmers were black, optimism rose until ballots arrived listing seventy "extra" Negroes nominated by whites. Under deadline, lacking telephones, the unpracticed movement voters failed to sift out the last-minute decoys. The Lowndes County ASCS committee remained white, and a New Deal structure designed to foster citizen participation in governance (like the community agencies newly created for the War on Poverty) devolved again into the hands of the largest landowners. Stokely Carmichael decried the results announced on November 16. "We did it fair and square," he told a mass meeting. "We believed in them, and they cheated us."

Solemn resentment gave way within hours to a sauciness reflected in the circulating SNCC bulletin for the day: "Mr. Stokely Carmichael (star of stage, screen, and television) feels that there is 'something fishy.' " Out of natural verve, protective calm, and hard calculation, he advertised a bigger lesson that movement strategy had the ruling minority of Lowndes County "running scared" already, before the first Negro ever voted in a regular election. The next night, Carmichael drove to a twenty-first birthday party for Sammy Younge, one of the many Tuskegee students who had been drawn into demonstrations since the Selma march. Younge resisted further canvassing for the election workshops. Conflicted, he told Carmichael with droll sarcasm that he needed to "kick Snick" and look out for himself. Younge came from a light-skinned Tuskegee family of relative privilege, having attended boarding school in Massachusetts. The mother of another SNCC worker served as a maid in his household. He had lost a kidney to disease during Navy service, then abandoned schoolwork for the lure of civil rights. When he confided that friends put him down for retreating into a nice car and his favorite Pink Catawba wine, Carmichael soothed familiar movement stress by endorsing the personal retreat. "Makes me no never-mind," he said lightly, adding that he would be glad to share wine with Younge.

With the help of Younge's friend Jimmy Rogers and other Tuskegee students, the Alabama SNCC staff carried roving schools on basic politics especially into Lowndes County, which supplied the bulk of some thirty farm-based activists for a trek to Atlanta at the beginning of December. They gathered at SNCC headquarters for all-day seminars, deciphering Alabama code books with the aid of charts and graphs prepared by the research staff. "The workshop spent one day on the electoral machinery," wrote research director Jack Minnis, "and the rest of the time on the county governmental structure." To nominate candidates for local offices in the 1966 elections, the participants learned strict statutory rules governing the establishment of independent political parties. If even one founding member participated simultaneously in an existing party, for instance, or cast a nominating ballot without verifiable proof of registration, a judge could disqualify the new party and all its nominees from the general election. By Alabama law, a new party also had to gain approval for a visible ballot symbol to aid voters of marginal literacy, meeting specifications of size and distinctiveness. The Lowndes County citizens reacted negatively to several proposed choices, finding a cotton boll sketch too vague, a dove too remote, clasped hands (modeled on SNCC's own logo) too passive, and called instead for an active, farm-based symbol to compete with the Alabama Democratic Party's official logo of a white bantam rooster topped with the motto, "White Supremacy for the Right." Several suggested a cat as the best farm image. "Cats chase chickens," said John Hulett, and Carmichael asked his volunteer artists to draw cats.

The caravan to Atlanta had passed Montgomery, where federal prosecutors weathered secret drama at the third trial of the Klansmen charged with the bushwhack murder of Viola Liuzzo in Lowndes County. Given the two prior failures in state court, their optimism sagged with the notice that star informant Gary Thomas Rowe refused to testify anymore, complaining of stress and isolation as the sequestered target of angry Klan associates. When FBI director Hoover discouraged measures to compel his cooperation, Attorney General Katzenbach himself enticed Rowe with a secret promise of relocation under a new identity. "I am prepared to help you obtain suitable employment either with the federal government or elsewhere," he wrote. "This is not contingent on the performance of any further services or assistance that you may give to the United States at any time in the future." Reluctantly, Katzenbach also sent Assistant Attorney General John Doar to argue the case before U.S. District Judge Frank Johnson—risking a higher government profile for a chance to end the string of abject humiliations in racial hate cases. Doar prepared hastily in the face of restrictions that had chafed Alabama attorney general Richmond Flowers before the state trials. FBI handlers, who never left Rowe's side, severely curtailed acquaintance with the reluctant witness. They instructed Rowe not to answer questions about his background, especially his five previous years as a Klan informant, and forbade inquiry beyond "what happened in the car." Unfamiliarity made for awkward examination, but did limit the scope of a wobbly performance on the stand. Rowe testified that Klan orders for the night of Liuzzo's murder were to preserve white supremacy "by any means necessary, whether bullets or ballots," in an unlikely paraphrase of the late Malcolm X.

FBI director Hoover startled Katzenbach on December 3 with word that the all-white, all-male jury returned verdicts of guilty, and that Judge Johnson promptly sentenced all three Klansmen to the ten-year maximum under a federal civil rights statute. (By coincidence, a second Alabama jury returned a breakthrough verdict almost simultaneously in a trial of less notoriety.*) Katzenbach rejoiced. Congratulating Hoover, he said the prosecution strategy had emphasized the FBI's reputation this time to support the evidence, which he believed swayed the jury. In Montgomery, on his forty-fourth birthday, Doar lapsed briefly from stoic reserve to tell reporters that the case made him proud to be an American. Katzenbach called Texas with news vindicating the arrests announced from the White House on the day after the Selma march. "Really, it was quite a trial," he told Johnson. The President, still recuperating from gall bladder surgery, issued a statement that "the whole nation can take heart" from the outcome.

Barely nodding at the trial news, the Atlanta workshops sank into the mechanics of Alabama government for long hours through the weekend into Monday, December 6. Presenters shared legal research to make plain the duties of elected officers from tax assessor to probate judge. "During the discussions," recorded an internal memo, "it became clear to everyone that the mysterious deaths of Negroes in the South could never have gone uninvestigated and unpunished without the connivance or the collusion of the county coroner." Research director Jack Minnis taught that field organizers and citizens alike could glean a working knowledge of "who's pulling the levers of power." Familiarity reduced exalted positions to specific tasks. "We went into the concept of the *posse comitatus* of the sheriff, quoting statutes all the way," he wrote a friend, "and showing how, theoretically at least, most anything could be done with the other offices if the sheriff chose to enforce what they did." New awareness seeded the first imaginings of actual candidates among the participants themselves, who took home a skeletal plan for legal steps required to field an independent slate drawn from their own first-time voters. "News about the new freedom organization travels fast in Lowndes County," observed SNCC's South-wide circular.

Antagonism spread also, so widely that the National Council of Churches already had asked Rev. Francis Walter to help investigate reprisals. On December 9, having documented twenty of the eighty reported cases in neighboring Wilcox County, the assigned replacement

---

* After twenty ballots, an all-white jury convicted Hubert Strange on December 2 for the random murder of Willie Brewster on the way home from a July 1965 white supremacy rally, at which Connie Lynch and J. B. Stoner had praised the Liuzzo ambush as a model extermination. Stoner, who served as defense counsel for Strange, denounced the jury as "white niggers." Civil rights supporters celebrated in the Anniston courtroom by tearing up leaflets that protested an expected acquittal.

for Jonathan Daniels followed a wilderness road off the map from Possum Bend to a bridge-less dead end at a pig trail near skiffs tied in the Alabama River. He hiked toward bright colors on a distant clothesline, but Ora McDaniels fled her cabin upon sight of an approaching white man. Embarrassed, Walter spent the remainder of Thursday backtracking the river-looped county to find a Negro acquaintance who could mediate an affidavit about her being fired as a maid, and struck with a broom, for registering to vote. The bright colors turned out to be homemade patchwork quilts in distinctive patterns, sold locally at three for $5. Their striking quality inspired Walter to initiate a sustenance project that commanded auction space at New York galleries within six months. William Paley of CBS and Diana Vreeland of *Vogue* bought variations of the 1966 Chestnut Bud quilt. Artist Lee Krasner, widow of Jackson Pollock, would venture into Wilcox County to pick out Crow's Foot originals. Bloomingdale's in 1970 and *Life* magazine in 1972 offered tributes to the Freedom Quilting Bee, sustained more than two decades ahead by Ora McDaniels and her colleagues—among them Lucy Mingo, Polly Bennett, "Mama Willie" Abrams, Mattie Ross, Estelle Witherspoon, and China Grove Myles. Nearly all the folk artisans, who remained in their cabins, dated a new life from the wonder of a courthouse registration march the previous spring.

On Friday, December 10, as Walter began to collect quilts along with affidavits, two public events flashed lingering travail for Alabama. A state trial acquitted the three men charged with the beating death of Rev. James Reeb after the March 9 "turnaround" attempt to cross Selma's Edmund Pettus Bridge. The Dallas County courtroom erupted in applause. Richmond Flowers denounced a trial process epitomized by the blatantly prejudiced all-white jury that included a Klansman who had escorted Nazi leader George Lincoln Rockwell to assault Martin Luther King. "Reeb Verdict Outrages Justice Department / How Hard Did Prosecutors Try?" declared a blunt *Washington Post* headline. Simultaneously *New York Times* reporter Gene Roberts surfaced the first hint of volcanic legend from a scouting visit that found young movement workers at the Atlanta SNCC headquarters crushed by "battle fatigue" and spiraling debt—"the worst in its four and a half year history"—yet still "generating more ideas than money." Courtland Cox described the launch brochure for an Alabama pilot project to "bypass Southern institutions." Ruth Howard and other SNCC artists traced a cat logo from the mascot of Atlanta's Clark College Panthers. "The

Lowndes County Freedom Organization will function as an all-Negro 'third party,' " Roberts disclosed in Friday's *New York Times*. "It will operate in only one county and use a black panther as its party symbol."

* * *

KING CHASED his schedule through the week between Alabama trials, laboring to refine a prophetic message on the relative strengths of violence and nonviolence. He called Stanley Levison with word that rabbis from the Synagogue Council of America were pressing for Vietnam remarks because the American Legion of Boston had just canceled a citizenship award to Rabbi Roland Gittelson over his sponsorship of the Washington peace march. King felt obliged, saying he had preached in Gittelson's synagogue only six months earlier, and called for specific quotations from the Hebrew prophets. Levison dictated paragraphs by relay through Dora McDonald, advising her to keep intact King's favored adaptation of Amos 5:24—"Let justice roll down like waters, and righteousness like a mighty stream"—as an improvement in rhythmic force on the exact biblical translation. King rushed to accept an award at the Waldorf-Astoria hotel in New York. "The stirring lesson of this age is that mass nonviolent direct action is not a peculiar device for Negro agitation," he told the Synagogue Council. "Rather it is an historically validated method for defending freedom and democracy, and for enlarging these values for the benefit of the whole society."

By refusing to give up a bus seat in 1955, King argued, Rosa Parks sparked nonviolent power that opened prospects a decade later for Negro seats in the Alabama legislature. Protests against a constricted economy unleashed reforms that "ultimately will benefit more whites than Negroes," he added, just as the crusade against segregated schools "brought to the fore" a larger realization that the antiquated educational system had been designed for nineteenth-century rural America. "When Negroes by direct action sought to participate in the electoral process," said King, "they awakened the apathetic white who so took his rights for granted that he neglected to use them." But he warned that an undertow of violence against new enemies threatened the bright promise of nonviolence to overcome old ones. "War enlarges itself inexorably," he declared, discounting the repeated official assurance that the military conflict would remain limited. Pointing to "ugly repressive sentiment" against Rabbi Gittelson and others, he asked if dissent were not already "being shot down by bombers in Vietnam," and wondered "whether free speech has not become one of the casualties of the war."

King summoned the bold protest of ancient sources—"Today we particularly need the Hebrew prophets"—whose words had goaded the movement past fear and silence. "They did *not* believe that conscience is a still small voice," he said. "They believed that conscience thunders, or it does not speak at all." He quoted Amos on justice, Micah on beating swords into plowshares, and Isaiah on what King called an "inescapable obligation" to renounce violence of spirit: "Yea, when you make many prayers I will not hear/ Your hands are full of blood/ Wash you, make you clean/ Put away the evil of your doings from before mine eyes."

By the time his repression alert generated a tiny blip on page seventy-three of the morning *New York Times*—"Dr. King Sees Move Against Pacifists"—King was headed to Alabama by way of Atlanta. Documentary filmmaker Arnold Michaelis, in an interview arranged by Stanley Levison, seized a rare opportunity in the cabin of the airplane to film questions on informal background topics. King called plans for professional sports teams in the desegregated South "another very good step forward," but confessed that the move of the baseball Braves from Milwaukee to his hometown would complicate a personal allegiance he traced to 1947, when Branch Rickey had integrated the old Brooklyn Dodgers with King's teenage idol and subsequent friend Jackie Robinson. "And so I have been a Dodger fan," he said, "but I'm gonna get with the Braves now."

Leaving Michaelis temporarily, King disappeared to embattled SCLC projects in rural Alabama, where a mob of nearly two hundred had blocked a Greene County march for school integration led by Hosea Williams. At a mass meeting on Monday, December 6, King and Andrew Young recruited 375 people to continue marches seeking the dispatch of federal registrars into Butler County, adjacent to Lowndes. "This was a heart-melting demonstration," wrote grizzled staff leader Rev. Samuel Wells of Albany, Georgia, who reported that men and women sang in tearful prayer as they "stood toe to toe with the policemen. . . . On Tuesday we marched again. . . . I, for one, was knocked over the head." King by then had hurried toward another rally commitment but was stalled by Alabama state troopers who arrested Young and his passengers alike for speeding, then held them until each paid a fine of $50.

Back at home, King sat on December 9 for a rare filmed interview as his eight-year-old son Marty darted in front of the cameras. Producer Michaelis asked why he had departed from the philosophical acceptance of war expressed on page ninety-five of his first book, *Stride Toward*

Freedom. "There was a time when I felt that war was, or could be, a negative good," King replied. "I never felt that war could be a positive good, but . . . I felt that war could block the spread of some negative evil force like a Hitler, for instance." Subsequent experience in the nonviolent movement had combined with apprehensions about the shrinking world, he explained, to convert him from the Christian pragmatism he once accepted from theologian Reinhold Niebuhr's anguished defense of World War II. "I came to the conclusion that war could no longer serve as a negative good," said King, "because of the potential destructiveness and the actual destructiveness of modern weapons of warfare."

When Michaelis pressed doubts that anyone could claim to oppose Communism in Vietnam without violence, King argued from colonial history that a long struggle for independence was blended into the identity of the Vietnamese Communist Party, while complicity in foreign rule there tainted American definitions of freedom. "There can be no gainsaying of the fact that we have taken a stand against a people seeking self-determination," he said. "If one looks back over the history of this war, there are many things that turn out to be very ugly, and I am absolutely convinced that there is wrong on both sides." King admitted personal indecision. "I don't think President Johnson is a warmonger," he said. "I think he is caught in a very difficult dilemma." He surprised Michaelis by volunteering that he had received this impression in private talks with President Johnson since criticizing the war, "I would say on two different occasions," and that he felt a heavy burden to "do something creative to create the atmosphere for negotiations." King said he approved the dictum* of Mohandas Gandhi that seemingly impossible, saintly missions must be grounded in politics. "I certainly can't claim to be a saint in any sense of the word," he told Michaelis. "I try to emulate all the saints of history . . . and I think it is necessary for anyone who is working in these areas to have a keen sense of political timing."

The atmosphere of war confronted peacemakers with "a very practical problem that runs the gamut of history," said King, "and that is face-saving. . . . If we could get rid of our pride, and this is the word that I think America must hear more and more, that we have got to get rid of our pride. It won't hurt us morally. It isn't going to hurt us from a military point of view to pull out of Vietnam."

---

* Gandhi: "Men say I am a saint losing myself in politics. The fact is that I am a politician trying my hardest to be a saint."

Michaelis raised another awkward subject—"this is a very difficult thing"—about whether King could "see any advantage accruing to the civil rights movement by virtue of your death," and King replied straightforwardly that any impact would depend on the circumstances. He pondered the example of recent suicides by immolation in both Vietnam and the United States. "I must say that I don't think, personally, that this is the highest expression of creative sacrifice," he said, and repeated instead the nonviolent standard of active readiness to die for a cause while refusing to kill. "I wouldn't take my own life, but I would willingly give my life for that which I think is right," King concluded. "And I am convinced that when one does this honestly, that death can have redemptive value."

CHAPTER 25

Inside Out

December 1965–January 1966

THE Watts report posed an alarm starkly in its title, *Violence in the City—An End or a Beginning?,* and responded with words normally shunned as political suicide. "McCone Commission Urges a 'Costly and Extreme' Treatment of Causes," declared the *New York Times* on December 7. Newspaper stories highlighted the call for massive improvements in education, transportation, and employment. The commissioners found that nearly all the 114 Los Angeles elementary schools without cafeterias were located in minority areas, which they correlated with "shockingly lower" test scores. They detected an enormous but immeasurable job shortage for Watts residents—quoting the resigned scoff of a teenage witness, "Go to school for *what?"*—which they associated with a tiny (14 percent) neighborhood ownership of cars to reach jobs elsewhere in the only major American city that did not subsidize public transportation. Their report warned that the August riots would be a mere "curtain-raiser" unless the American public adopted a "revolutionary attitude."

Bayard Rustin pronounced the McCone report a clever but specious bit of fireworks above the color line, in a detailed analysis that began with the commission's baseline characterization of the Watts upheaval: "an insensate rage of destruction . . . not a race riot in the usual sense. What happened was an explosion—a formless, quite senseless, all but hopeless protest—engaged in by a few but bringing great distress to all." Rustin cited McCone's own investigators to counter that the violence had been anything but random. Rioters consistently attacked five types of stores, primarily pawnshops and food markets, made no attempt to steal narcotics from pharmacies, and were more likely to destroy than consume the stocks of liquor stores. He quoted acknowledgment in the report's fine print that "no residences were deliberately burned, that damage to schools, libraries, and public buildings was minimal, and that certain types of business establishments, notably service stations and automobile dealers were for the most part unharmed." For Rustin, steeped in Gandhian discipline, the Watts violence was wrong, mostly self-damaging, and it excused the commissioners to polarize identification with victims by race. The report lumped together thirty-two Negro riot deaths under "justifiable homicide," identified three white deaths (obscuring evidence that two were from friendly fire), and broke down white injuries by occupation or branch of service. "To find out that about 85 per cent of the [1,032 people] injured were Negroes," he observed, "we have to do our own arithmetic."

Violence in Rustin's view gave the McCone Commission cover to finesse the central complaint against a Los Angeles police department personified by Chief William Parker. "Many Negroes feel that he carried a deep hatred of the Negro community," stated the report. "However, Chief Parker's statements to us and collateral evidence such as his record of fairness to Negro officers are inconsistent with his having such an attitude." With that, the commissioners dismissed calls for external checks or civilian review in brutality investigations as a risk to police morale, and Rustin ascribed the brusque evasion to a battlefield mentality that dehumanized Negroes while lionizing the aggressive officer. "Every Negro knows this," he wrote. "There is scarcely any black man, woman or child in the land who at some point or another has not been mistreated by a policeman."

No Negro ranked above sergeant in the Los Angeles police force of roughly eight thousand, although nearly twenty black officers over the past decade managed to attend law school after hours and pass the bar exam while stymied for promotion. Two who once briefly made lieutenant had departed also for law practice—Earl Broady and Tom Bradley, a future mayor of Los Angeles. Broady served with McCone as one of the eight Watts commissioners. He had been elevated to the California bench since being cajoled by Malcolm X to represent those shot and beaten, then jailed, in the sensational 1962 police altercation around and inside the local Muslim temple, and the McCone report bore signs of a truce. There was no mention of the fusillade storming of the same temple toward the end of the Watts violence in a vain search for weapons or riot plans. Judge Broady withheld experienced readings on raw blackjack solidarity in the precincts, perhaps to dampen Chief Parker's countervailing charge that "pagan" conspirators had engineered revolt by contented Negro citizens. Parker, sticking mostly to the compromise thesis of mindless violence, reduced Watts to an image of copycat antics by caged animals: "One person threw a rock and then, like monkeys in a zoo, others started throwing rocks."

Rustin warned of the treacherous ambiguity common to the McCone Commission and the Moynihan study of Negro families. Each document opened freelance controversy "on both sides of the Negro question," he wrote, with a view fixed handily beyond the presumed end of segregated conditions on a ringing but abstract call for wholesale reform. Each mixed encouragement for civil rights with "more sophisticated and compassionate . . . shibboleths about Negroes." Well before Rustin's interpretation reached the small intellectual journal *Commentary,* Moynihan had become an established national oracle on Watts. "Remember that American slavery was the worst slavery the world has ever known," he told a CBS News special about the new McCone report. He sketched the historical pressures on families that "break up when they leave the countrysides, rural peasant life, and sort of dump into slums," where he said Negro women headed a quarter of modern households. The *New York Times* published a December 12 profile, "Moynihan Hopeful U.S. Will Adopt a Policy of Promoting Family Stability," citing his figures that 44 percent of births in parts of Harlem were illegitimate. "I grew up in Hell's Kitchen," he told the *Times.* "My father was a drunk. I know what this life is like."

The same day on NBC's *Meet the Press,* moderator Lawrence Spivak asked how new middle-class Negroes climbed above the report's statistical trend toward family deterioration, and why others could not use the same ladder. "Some people are lucky and some aren't," replied Moynihan. "The world is that way. Some people got out of the South in time, some didn't." *Jet* reporter Simeon Booker protested that Moynihan could have focused on growing divorce in white families "to make it appear that they are the threat to the nation's health." He suggested that racial redress must fall to whites, whereas panelist Robert Novak wondered if Negroes would escape their own responsibility. Moynihan gamely grasped both thorns. "It is an *American* problem," he told NBC viewers, "and any American must commit himself to it." Lightning gathered from his resonant theories already made Moynihan the rarest of public figures—a sociology professor and former civil servant, specializing in urban race relations, with a bright future in national politics.*

* * *

RONALD REAGAN's public career neared the end of its incubation period. The previous March, on the popularity of his nationally televised speech for the losing presidential campaign of Barry Goldwater, the Hollywood actor had begun an active exploration toward a run for governor of California just as students at Berkeley lifted ritual chants of "Fuck" to storm the far ramparts of permitted speech. The wildcat demonstrations, which veered notoriously from a campus movement built to support Mississippi Negroes, gave Reagan cause to join attacks on "filthy" rather than free debate, to disregard the disciplined youth then braving violence at the "Berlin Wall" of Selma, and to sidestep their cresting drive for the whole nation to secure voting rights for the powerless. In an address to California Republicans, Reagan combined spanking disdain for the rowdy Berkeley students with his caustic view of an omnivorous federal government. They were like a newborn baby, he quipped, with "an alimentary canal at one end and no sense of responsibility at the other."

Reagan continued to defend the Goldwater positions against Medicare ("socialized medicine") and the 1964 Civil Rights Act. "I would have voted against it if I had been in Congress," he said, and denounced the 1965 Voting Rights Act by extension as an encroachment on local control, "humiliating to the South." Significantly, however, Reagan hired political advisers to make his test speeches palatable to voters beyond the Goldwater base. Political consultants Stuart Spencer and William Roberts, having managed the California primary campaign against Goldwater by liberal Republican governor Nelson Rockefeller, counseled him to advocate decency and restraint rather than outmoded defiance. Reagan said unruly students could be reclaimed with firm discipline. He avoided talk of civil rights with the nimble evasion of Southern moderates then calling the entire race issue "somewhat passé." He described domestic freedom as a natural possession that was constantly

---

* Moynihan would go on to serve as counselor to President Richard Nixon, 1969–71, ambassador to India, 1973–75, ambassador to the United Nations, 1975–76, and U.S. senator from New York, 1977–2001.

threatened—but never enhanced—by national politics, and therefore he credited no net progress in liberty from the Founding Fathers down through the daunting new commitments to fulfill their national creed. "The original government of this country was set up by conservatives, [and] defined years later by Lincoln," Reagan declared, "as a preference for the old and tried over the new and untried."

By overlooking patriotic wonders in stir from the modern civil rights era, which he recognized as liberal and certainly troublesome, Reagan invited listeners to shed defensive anxiety about racial barriers. He lodged timely charges to degrade the movement's reputation for selfless witness by association with rioters and external enemies, denouncing antiwar demonstrations at Berkeley as "the fruit of appeasement." Reagan called for "a political decision to achieve victory" in Vietnam, and waved off "silly" fears of protracted war. "Why, with our power," he said in October, "we could pave the whole country, put parking strips on it, and be home for Christmas."

Early stories made sport of his film roles and campaign biography— *Where's the Rest of Me?*—but Reagan captured audiences through 150 trial speeches. He called himself a "hemophiliac liberal" converted to citizen-politician, innocent of professional experience or government terminology. Even so, the unannounced candidate distanced himself from the John Birch Society with a strategy fixed on the decisive middle voter. Reagan rebuked founder Robert Welch for "utterly reprehensible" statements that former President Dwight Eisenhower himself was a Communist, but carefully spared the organization and its sympathizers, citing assurance from J. Edgar Hoover that "the FBI has not investigated the Birch Society, because it only investigates subversive organizations." Reagan's pinpoint attack on Welch signaled his refusal to be lumped with "a bunch of kooks," according to his staff, and gained him stature to run on mainstream morality. A *New York Times Magazine* article in November warily recognized his genial appeal: "Tom Sawyer Enters Politics."

* * *

SHORTLY BEFORE Reagan's formal entry into the California governor's race for 1966, Director Hoover confronted a potential scandal from the FBI's unilateral use of spy methods in nearby Las Vegas. A December story in the *Los Angeles Times* disclosed the first public hints of intrigue stewing since the owner of the Fremont Casino Hotel had discovered a microphone bug at his office in 1963. Security technicians traced intercept signals to a dummy business called the Henderson Novelty Company, and officials from the Sands and the Desert Inn soon joined in a lawsuit against eleven FBI employees found monitoring numerous bugs from the Henderson storefront. Publicity spread novel allegations of criminal trespass by law enforcement officers—"FBI Red-Faced on Use of 'Bugs' "—with growing pressure on FBI headquarters either to disown the agents as renegades or show proof of legal authorization for the surveillance. Hoover swiftly dispatched Assistant Director DeLoach to see the Attorney General. "I told Katzenbach that obviously this was no time for feuding in the family," DeLoach reported to FBI headquarters, "and that I wanted to make certain that he fully understood the approval that former Attorney General Kennedy had given with respect to microphones."

Katzenbach tried to calm DeLoach. He predicted that the well-known Washington lawyer Edward Bennett Williams would settle the Las Vegas lawsuit before it generated publicity that his clients were conspiring with organized crime partners to skim profits from their casinos. The greater lesson for Katzenbach was a reminder that surreptitious eavesdropping allowed a shrewd defense attorney like Williams to thwart prosecution by ferreting out government misconduct. (For his track record of stinging discovery motions, Hoover already disparaged Williams as a "shyster.") DeLoach refused to be mollified, and described the threat as more political than legal. Unlike Katzenbach, he knew that Williams was likely to obtain records in a separate criminal appeal that another client, Washington lobbyist Fred Black, had been overheard by coincidence in the bugged executive suite at the Desert Inn. Worse, Black was a business partner of former Senate aide Bobby Baker, the most visible corruption name of the Johnson era, and had been the Johnson family's next-door neighbor until the new President moved into the White House. Still worse, collateral discovery could reveal to Williams that the FBI had bugged Black deliberately in his Washington hotel suite, which was far too political to be excused as a well-intended crusade against gangster influence in Las Vegas casinos.

Undaunted, DeLoach insisted that the real motive behind the bugging story was Senator Robert Kennedy's ambition to ruin President Johnson and the FBI. Williams was a Kennedy friend, he noted darkly, and Kennedy's former press secretary, Ed Guthman, worked for the *Los Angeles Times*. Katzenbach "seemed rather stunned" by the charge, DeLoach later reported. While he tried to assure DeLoach that he did not disclaim involvement with microphone surveillance himself, despite his recent efforts to forbid it, the Attorney General said he did believe private statements from Kennedy himself that he had authorized no bugs during his tenure at Justice. DeLoach warned Katzenbach not to provoke Hoover on this point, then made ready for battle by summoning Kennedy's FBI liaison officer, Courtney Evans. Hoover had fired him after Dallas, exercising sudden freedom to demonstrate disdain for the lame-duck Attorney General, but Evans felt obliged to appear at headquarters for a prolonged inquisition on Christmas Eve.

DeLoach and colleagues knew from the FBI files that they could not confront Evans with Robert Kennedy's signature on a bugging document, or even with evidence that Kennedy ever showed awareness of a bug as opposed to a formally approved telephone wiretap. They coaxed him merely to agree that Kennedy should have perceived the peculiar source of some reports by their nature, without being told, and a miserably conflicted Evans—"upon having his recollection refreshed"—gave ground toward the FBI position. From memos about one lurid intelligence report from Chicago, DeLoach recorded, "he admitted that Kennedy stated that he did not desire to know the location or the source." Evans conceded murkiness in the most sensitive files until DeLoach counted him a vital witness for shared complicity: "He did admit that Kennedy must have known that our information came from microphones." FBI officials seized upon the inference as bedrock. They claimed a general acquiescence from Kennedy in place of verifiable permissions for specific bugs, which they substituted in turn for a gaping void of authority or procedure in law. Without a blush, they transformed the wisp of retrospective accountability into armor for aggressive defense. Katzenbach and Kennedy would " 'leave us to the wolves' if allowed to do so," DeLoach advised Hoover, which made it prudent for the Bureau to put them on notice that "we clearly know the facts and will not hesitate to use them if necessary."

* * *

"THREE DAYS after Christmas," began a SNCC memorandum of record, "Gloria Larry was in the Atlanta SNCC office at 360 Nelson Street looking for help." The document registered shock in two respects. First, the Atlanta office was an unlikely rescue stop because SNCC faced $100,000 in debt, suffered terminations of phone service, and had missed several of its meager subsistence payrolls for staff workers. Jailgoing energy and the treasury were drained so low—"John Robert Lewis is TIRED (me too)," warned an internal notice—that Chairman Lewis issued a melancholy year-end statement pronouncing the miracle achievements of 1965 dimmed "when we have laws that are not being enforced. . . . The scars of racism are so deep that they will take many years to remove." Second, Larry was a surprise choice to speak for Lowndes County on any desperate mission, being a staff new-comer known more for elegance than grit. Larry was already gaunt, however, which reinforced her hammering alarm about the plight of sharecroppers newly registered to vote. Of twenty evicted families that lacked the wherewithal to move, or relatives to pile in with, at least eight wandered helpless outdoors. Larry commandeered $2,000 from SNCC's secret emergency fund and rushed back to Alabama in a loaded caravan. "It has been raining for three weeks in Lowndes County," the office memorandum noted in her wake. "The following supplies have been purchased to protect the evicted families from the elements": ten Army surplus tents, sixty cots, and twelve potbellied stoves.

Carmichael stayed behind to fire a staff worker he caught soliciting and stealing crisis donations from distant white supporters. "Please make sure that they do not send another penny to Eugene," he urged fund-raisers, noting painfully that the scam targets discovered so far in-cluded Rev. Francis Walter, Rabbi Harold Saperstein the summer vol-unteer, and even the mother of Jonathan Daniels. ("I guess you realize this is a very touchy area," Carmichael confided.) He managed also to secure squatter's space for the evicted farmers on land owned by Rosie Steele, who had donated the second night's campsite for the great march toward Montgomery, then rounded up help to dig a latrine, lay plank floors, and pitch the tents. Sammy Younge was a surprise among work-ers who showed up on Thursday, December 30. "I just can't kick it, man," he told Carmichael sheepishly. Having tried hard to stick with his studies, he decided that the movement was "in me," and disclosed his hope to organize an independent "black panther" party for his home county around Tuskegee.

The primitive shelter attracted scattered notice from the outside world. " 'Tent City' Rising In Alabama Field," announced the *New York Times* on New Year's Day. The Negro weekly *Jet* emphasized hard-ship: "Evicted Farmers Wallow in Beds of Mud at Lowndes." These ac-counts noted large cauldrons for water to be hauled from a neighboring well, and ascribed escalating tension to local awareness that some 1,900 new Lowndes County registrants approached parity for Negroes in local voting strength. Jack Crawford had been evicted after his photograph appeared in a magazine article about the federal registrars. Amanda Glover, arriving from the plantation where she had lived since January 20, 1931, said her husband had been too scared of voting "but could have went on and registered for all the good it did him." Annabelle Scott came with her husband, four children, and several grandchildren, one of whom soon contracted hepatitis. Elderly movement stalwarts Will and Mary Jane Jackson occupied cots in the field of tents facing Highway 80, not far from the spot where they had waited all of March 22 to see the distant speck of Martin Luther King approach with flags and soldiers like a biblical mirage. Carmichael said people who registered under such conditions were forever changed, and local leader John Hulett agreed. "People in Lowndes County, whether they live or die, will put up our own candidates," he told reporters. "That's a sure thing."

On Sunday, January 2, Rev. Francis Walter sat on the stage among hometown hosts in Mobile for a historic address by the sitting Attorney General of the United States. Before an overwhelmingly Negro crowd of 4,500, Nicholas Katzenbach marked the 102nd anniversary of slavery's official demise by predicting "a new emancipation" under the Voting Rights Act. Backstage, Walter took his chance to consult briefly about reprisals against new registrants in several counties. Katzenbach renewed a public promise for the Justice Department to initiate lawsuits against voter intimidation, and suggested that affidavits would make stronger evidence if the sharecroppers could brace themselves through formal eviction by sheriffs rather than vacate the plantations on demand. Guardedly, he advised Walter to consider his words mere legal speculation and not a commitment on behalf of the United States. *Jet* magazine noted another nuance of volatile racial politics: Mobile's white newspapers declined to show Katzenbach at the Emancipation Day ceremonies, indicating that racially mixed photographs of a kind once prized to attack white officials might be losing favor because of the offsetting honor implied for Negroes also in the picture, especially now if they had to be identified.

With many Alabama courthouses filled for first Monday registration on January 3, FBI agents arrived in Tuskegee by late afternoon to investigate two complaints relayed from the Atlanta SNCC office. Jimmy Rogers reported first that a registrar had threatened to "spill your guts on the floor" after refusing more than a hundred Negro applicants, evidently nettled beyond endurance that a continued stall would only push the Justice Department to deploy superseding federal registrars to Macon County. Sammy Younge, ducking from his escort post along the line of rattled applicants, added at four o'clock that the local registrar displayed a knife when repeating the same words.

Toward midnight at the local Freedom House, agitated calls about a familiar car sighted near a police commotion at the Tuskegee bus station jolted into panic a vague awareness that Younge had not returned from an errand to buy cigarettes, and Rogers was among those who identified his body. Younge lay face-up next to wide rivulets of blood spreading from his head past his feet, with an arm draped over a golf club. Witnesses said Younge had engaged in what sounded like a running quarrel over the refusal of an elderly attendant to let him use a gasoline station's restroom reserved for whites. He drove off, stopped abruptly, and walked back to renew the argument, but ran across the street into a half filled Greyhound bus once the attendant, Marvin Segrest, waved a pistol. Seizing a golf club from luggage bound for Atlanta, Younge darted in and out of the bus to exchange more shouts. When Segrest fired a shot, the Greyhound sped away and Younge fled exposed on foot until a second bullet struck him in the back of the head. Segrest said he meant "to bluff him." Alarms rousted much of the campus before dawn and collected nearly all the scattered Alabama SNCC staff except Stokely Carmichael, who declared himself immobile. "I just got me three bottles of wine," he told James Forman, "and drank one for me and one for Sammy and one for Jonathan Daniels." More than two thousand students marched Tuesday in small-town Tuskegee. Many returned the next day with a list of eight demands, including prosecution of Segrest and a chance for "more Negroes to be able to work in the downtown area." They rallied around the statue of Robert E. Lee on the courthouse lawn.

In Atlanta, the southwide SNCC staff conducted a marathon debate to frame a response. New marches for more laws were rejected as lame. A proposal to denounce the Younge murder jointly with the Vietnam War met the objection that the connection was strained and that the two issues best be kept separate. A volley of counterarguments recalled Bob Moses on the tendency of race to corrupt democratic values with self-deluded conquest both at home and abroad, which shifted qualms about the statement toward naked practicality. With SNCC nearly bankrupt, leaders warned, an attack on the government's war policy would trigger ferocious opposition, choke off donations from white liberals, and blot out attention to the death of Sammy Younge. Some fretted that they had voted already for SNCC to take a public stand against the war, but had failed timidly to follow through. Others foresaw widespread indifference to any statement about Younge's death *without* the Vietnam linkage, and a majority welcomed Gloria Larry's volunteer effort to distill the prevailing thought into a draft by Thursday, January 6. "We believe the United States government has been deceptive in its claims of concern for the freedom of the Vietnamese people," she began. "The murder of Samuel Younge in Tuskegee, Ala. is no different than the murder of peasants in Vietnam. . . . We ask: where is the draft for the freedom fight in the United States? We, therefore, encourage those Americans who prefer to use their energy in building democratic forms within this country . . . knowing full well that it may cost them their lives—as painfully as in Vietnam."

*　*　*

ON FRIDAY in Chicago, at what the *New York Times* called "a crowded news conference in the garish red-and-gold Gigi Room of the plush Sahara Motel," Martin Luther King released a thirteen-page launch blueprint for "the first significant Northern freedom movement." For the betterment of greater Chicago, whose Negroes had come to outnumber those in all Mississippi, he announced a new campaign aimed at conditions broader than de facto school segregation or the harsh legacy of the rural South. "This economic exploitation is crystallized in the SLUM," said King, which he defined as "an area where free trade and exchange of culture and resources is not allowed to exist . . . a system of internal colonialism not unlike the exploitation of the Congo by Belgium." His Chicago blueprint identified trade unions and welfare boards among twelve institutions that perpetuated slums in an interlocking pattern difficult to understand, he acknowledged, let alone to change. (Five unions shut down final construction on the monumental Gateway Arch project that same day in St. Louis, when a contractor hired the first Negro plumber under sustained pressure from the new U.S. Office of Federal Contract Compliance.) King announced an escalating series of community rallies, organizing drives, and test demonstrations to culminate in May, but he hedged predictions by analogy with the voting rights campaign launched a year earlier. "Just as no one knew on January 2, 1965, that there would be a march from Selma to Montgomery," he announced, "so now we are in no position to know what form massive action might take in Chicago." The uncertainty of future confrontation muted news coverage, but King gained banner headlines in the *Defender* with a promise to move his own family into a freezing local tenement before the end of January: "Dr. King Will Occupy Chicago Slum Flat in New Rights Drive/ He's Out to Close Ghetto."

A series of urgent surprises eclipsed King's announcement inside the White House, conveyed first by four memos about Tuskegee that reached the Oval Office with crisis notations timed to the minute. "The white city officials are frightened," advised one at 10:45 A.M. on Friday, "and some have mentioned that they would like Federal troops or Federal marshals." President Luther Foster of Tuskegee Institute relayed reciprocal fear among Negroes that angry student demonstrations for the first time could endanger Booker T. Washington's fabled Atlanta Compromise of 1895, by which Negroes ceded political control to whites in spite of a local numerical advantage of five to one. A sociology professor hoped to "get by Saturday without bloodshed." John Doar promised to file a Justice Department lawsuit before sundown to address the valid complaints by Foster that segregated Tuskegee restaurants had "turned themselves into sham private clubs in order to avoid Title II of the Civil Rights Act of 1964." President Johnson returned three of the memos with handwritten instructions for aides to call Sammy Younge's father and President Foster on his behalf, and to "support any action we need to take here." Only a minute after he scrawled "4:55 P.M." on his third reply, another inbound memo shifted alarm to the "distressing" new uproar over a "policy statement of the Student Nonviolent Coordinating Committee" about the Younge murder, in which, wrote White House aide Clifford Alexander, "SNCC urged all Americans to seek work in the civil rights movement as a 'valid alternative to the draft.' " Alexander assured President Johnson that White House officials already were mobilizing Negro leaders to "negate the impact of this story" with countervailing expressions of "wholehearted support" for U.S. war policy in Vietnam. "The most difficult part of the equation is what Martin Luther King will do next," he added.

Three words transformed the furor again before it reached King. Asked if he supported his organization's public statement, longtime SNCC communications director Julian Bond told a reporter, "Yes, I do," which ignited a bonfire around him as one of the first eight Negroes elected to the Georgia House since Reconstruction. Both the Younge murder and war issue receded beneath the sudden glare of headlines suggesting treason. "REP. BOND'S LOYALTY FACES CHAL-LENGES," screamed a Southern newspaper. "Georgians Score a Viet-nam Critic/ Negro Elected to Georgia Legislature Faces Expulsion Move," echoed the *New York Times*. In Los Angeles, where he had flown from Chicago, King deflected the first inquiries—"We are in a danger-ous period when we seek to silence dissent"—but later on Saturday was obliged to clear a further statement by telephone for distribution at a full-fledged Atlanta press conference, protesting that segregationists still misread democracy: "It is ironic that some of the prominent persons who now question Mr. Bond's willingness to uphold the Constitution of the U.S. have failed miserably in this regard."

Julian Bond himself withdrew into disbelieving seclusion through the whirling drama over his fate. The lieutenant governor of Georgia announced that Bond's war stance "exactly suits the Kremlin." A vet-eran legislator delivered what passed for friendly appraisal of his slim chance to be seated when the House convened Monday: "This boy has got to come before us humbly, recant, and just plain beg a little." From the Sammy Younge funeral, James Forman barged into all-night At-lanta conclaves to denounce as Uncle Toms all those negotiating a com-promise by which Bond might "clarify" his statement more favorably to the war. Intimidating, in his trademark SNCC coveralls and wild spiky hair, Forman angrily dismissed explanations by overwrought elders that practical Georgia politics was different from civil rights, shouting, "I've been hearing that shit from white folks all my life!" Bond scarcely spoke even in private—while sharing the spotlight of weekend news with the formal debut in California of gubernatorial candidate Ronald Reagan*—except that he did beseech the counsel of Ralph Abernathy at a chance encounter near Paschal's restaurant. "Well," Abernathy replied with a pastoral sigh, "just do something you can live with."

---

* Reagan's January 4 announcement speech set a dual tone. He warned darkly of oppressive liberal government, "neurotic vulgarities" on the college campus, and disorder from thinly disguised minorities—"Our city streets are jungle paths after dark"—balanced by flourishes of hopeful disposition. "Our problems are many," he said, "but our capacity for solving them is limitless." On *Meet the Press*, to a barrage of skeptical questions about how he could hope to escape a landslide defeat running on discredited Goldwater positions, Reagan patiently replied, "I think by simply telling the truth," and he brushed off suggestions of political stigma from his opposition to civil rights: "I am just incapable of prejudice."

On Monday morning, January 10, Bond's face and arms were blotched with bumps when a clerk in the packed House prefaced the swearing-in ceremony with a solemn announcement: "I will ask Representative Bond to step aside." To movement colleagues, chronic hives had been a sign of delicate nerves in Bond since his skin broke out on the picket line and on his one trip to jail in 1960. He had confined himself afterward to full-time publicist's duty behind self-deprecating admissions of acute fear traceable to boyhood relocation in the fearsomely strange white South. "Mother'd ask me to go down to Rich's to get some clothes, and I'd say, 'No, no, I got enough clothes now, don't need any more,' " Bond drolly told friends. "I thought that down here people stopped you on the street and lynched you just for fun." His father, Atlanta University dean Dr. Horace Mann Bond—formerly the first black president of Lincoln University, the oldest institution of higher learning for black males in the Western world—was nearly as mortified that his son had dropped out of college to join SNCC. "My God, I didn't raise my boy to be a Georgia legislator," he moaned in a fretful lapse of reserve during Monday's hasty political trial on whether to seat his son. "I'd hoped he would go into a more academic occupation."

To seal the charges thrown together over a compressed weekend, legislators played a telephone interview surreptitiously recorded and submitted by a reporter:

Reporter: Would you say that again, please?

Bond: I said, "Yes, I do."

Reporter: . . . In other words, you are willing to stand by this as long as it doesn't cost you anything, but if it's going to cost you—you are going to be held in treason—then you can't stand by it?

Bond: Well, I have to think about it again. . . . I'm not taking a stand against stopping World Communism, and I'm not taking a stand in favor of the Viet Cong. What I'm saying is that, first, that I don't believe in that war. That particular war. I'm against all war. I'm against that war in particular, and I don't think people ought to participate in it. Because I'm against war, I'm against the draft. I think that other countries in the world get along without a draft—England is one—and I don't see why we couldn't, too.

Bond's unsuspecting mild voice echoed Monday night in a cavernous House chamber beneath the gold-plated capitol dome, where he reaffirmed his words under oath despite insistent demands to renounce them. Charles Morgan, one of his lawyers, argued that democratic principles should inform an extraordinary moment to "demonstrate to yourselves, demonstrate to the world abroad that there is freedom here in Georgia . . . that we can really exercise those rights here," but a retired legislator thundered back in righteous disbelief: "Is a man qualified to sit in this House who has to think about whether he would commit treason under a given circumstance?" The House voted exclusion by a tidal-wave count that rolled toward front pages nationwide, 187–12. Bond fought back tears, and photographers aimed flashbulbs at his empty seat. James Forman issued a SNCC bulletin after midnight: "Everyone, including Julian, is in a state of shock."

* * *

KING CUT short his Los Angeles trip and flew home to an all-too-familiar overload of trauma. President Johnson sent a telegram of condolence to the family of Vernon Dahmer, whose house in Hattiesburg, Mississippi, was firebombed late Sunday night after Dahmer nnounced on radio that the sheriff agreed to let him collect voter registration forms and supply poll tax loans for fellow Negroes unable to pay. When Dahmer died of seared lungs on the Monday that Bond faced the Georgia House—having held off the gunfire of Klansmen long enough for his wife and daughter to escape the flames—Attorney General Katzenbach released an unusually personal statement from Washington that many Justice Department attorneys had admired Dahmer for exercising "the highest kind of citizenship." Four Dahmer sons converged from active military duty to mourn in uniform over the burned-out hole of their home. Though he had been unknown at large, and was to be obscured on the list of martyrs, Dahmer was revered among civil rights workers as the stalwart host and surrogate father to endangered pioneers since Bob Moses. Especially for veterans of projects in Mississippi, his murder pounded hard upon the Younge and Bond cases to open a public crack in movement philosophy. "I have simply stopped telling people that they should remain nonviolent," Stokely Carmichael told Gene Roberts of the *New York Times*. "This would be tantamount to suicide in Black Belt counties where whites are shooting at Negroes, and it would cost me the respect of the people."

King spoke to the press after a private conference with Julian Bond. "I have a personal concern about the lack of representation in the 136th District because I live there," he said, announcing that he would join Bond as co-plaintiff in a federal lawsuit to overturn the exclusion. (The *New York Times* already reported skepticism among legal experts: "Little Chance Seen for Bond in Court.") On January 14—Bond's twenty-sixth birthday, the day before his own thirty-seventh—King led a protest march through downtown Atlanta to the Georgia capitol. Bond stayed home on the instruction of counsel, but his father walked from Ebenezer among the crowd of 1,500 who heard King speak from the back of a flatbed truck in blustery cold rain. He denounced legislators for blatant hypocrisy in their claim to uphold the Constitution. To support Bond's pacifism, beyond his right to speak, King cited a letter unearthed by historian Arthur Schlesinger among the personal papers of a bitterly war-weary young sailor and future President John F. Kennedy: "War will exist until that distant day when the conscientious objector enjoys the same reputation and prestige that the warrior does today."

King declared a collective purpose "to make it clear that we love America . . . so much that we are going to stand up with all of our might to remind her when she is wrong. We are not newcomers here. We do not have to give our credentials of loyalty. For you see, we worked here and labored for two centuries without wages." He gained preaching rhythm on his themes of black heritage—"Before the pilgrim fathers landed at Plymouth, we were here . . ."—accelerated through perorations to go forward "with this faith . . ." and "let freedom ring . . ." until Isaiah's mountains were laid low and "the wrinkled stomachs of Mississippi will be filled" and "Julian Bond will be back in that state legislature." King closed with the mass chant of a political rally—"We want Julian Bond! We want Julian Bond!"—and left a remnant of marchers to circle the capitol with songs recalling Joshua's trumpet campaign around ancient Jericho.

On the third circuit, Willie Ricks of SNCC exhorted fifty followers to break open a pathway through the guarded capitol doorways, leading a skirmish that drew gleeful publicity about a woman who struck a trooper with her handbag and unruly Negroes eager to fight everywhere but Vietnam. King issued a pained statement against the breach of nonviolence, but did not swerve from public endorsement of SNCC. "I want it heard loud and clear that I believe in the Student Nonviolent

Coordinating Committee," he said, "and I cannot join the chorus of those who are so ready to condemn." The chorus jeered broadly without him. *The Wall Street Journal* branded Bond's position "puerile and repugnant." *Time* magazine pronounced the Vietnam statement "typically intemperate." More sympathetic outlets condemned both Bond and the Georgia House for falling into SNCC's "trap." Prominent Atlanta Negroes called for SNCC members to be jailed or drafted to front lines in Vietnam. Even the author Lillian Smith scolded her SNCC friends famously in print for succumbing to "a mixed up mess of 19th century anarchism and 1930s communism. . . . I've warned them; but they don't listen."* Roy Wilkins rebuked SNCC on behalf of the NAACP, and Jack Greenberg of the NAACP Legal Defense Fund blocked participation in Bond's lawsuit behind a defensive claim that Georgia "would have refused to seat a white person for the same reason."

King knew better—that race powerfully affected standing to criticize war—from the accepted frankness of Senator Richard Russell and others. (Tom Watson, the Populist-turned-Klan-revivalist, had resisted a formally declared World War I as the curse of "our Blood-gorged Capitalists," and yet stood venerated in heroic bronze on Georgia's capitol grounds.) King wrestled with Vietnam's immense gravitational pull on national politics in fitful departures from Sunday's prepared sermon. "Whether people like it or not, some voices must cry out," he told Ebenezer, sketching history at a trot—"Vietnam declared itself independent . . . then came the Geneva Accord . . ."—apologizing for the capsule detours as he warned against following France into "a war that is at bottom perpetuating white colonialism," suddenly decrying violence with Isaiah once more: "Get out of my face—don't pray your long prayers to me—don't come to me with your eloquent speeches—don't talk to me about your patriotism—your hands are full of blood." King begged for citizen education, wisdom, and courage. "Be assured that we will not stop communism with bombs and guns and bullets and napalm," he declared. "We will stop communism by letting the world

* Smith lamented naïveté in SNCC: "Julian Bond (whose parents are wonderful people, one of the finest Negro families in Georgia) is, I fear, pulled this way and that." Conflicted about Vietnam, she sensed that critics were quicker to loathe LBJ and Dean Rusk as Southerners ("I find myself thinking this") than to offer practical plans for peace. "So: I am not agreeing with those who criticize harshly," Smith wrote, "much less those who want to burn their draft cards."

know that democracy is a better government than any other government, and by making justice a reality for all of God's children." Then he snapped back to his text with a quiet apology. "I didn't mean to get off on this," King said, "but every now and then people must hear the truth."

CHAPTER 26

Refugees

January 1966

PRESIDENT Johnson prepared for his State of the Union address that week. "I feel a good deal of the ice cracking under me," he confided to General Maxwell Taylor, "and slipping on the domestic scene." Johnson had extended a one-day Christmas bombing pause over North Vietnam to advertise frenzied overtures for settlement talks with "more than a hundred governments," and he continued the pause past January 9 with a simultaneous U.S. infantry assault launched in strict secrecy from the South Vietnamese government, for the first time, to forestall betrayal by allies only nominally in charge of their cause. With millions of Americans stirring to peace prospects even as others still awakened to serious war in a small country, Johnson elbowed frantically for room on all sides. He told General Taylor that Vietnam costs figured to drive up the next military budget by 40 percent, but he included only a fraction of the realistic $20 billion increase in the January message. "I want a minimum in that defense budget to get by," he instructed McGeorge Bundy. "You're absolutely right," McNamara separately agreed. "You'd just absolutely destroy your Great Society program." Johnson planned to return to Congress for supplemental Vietnam funds only after securing domestic appropriations, and he used the specter of war in turn to stall his fledgling War on Poverty below its second-year peak of $1.7 billion.

Early in January, the President had locked away his top aides to write what became known as the "guns and butter" speech. Charged with an alchemist's task—to amass both without promising new money or favoring one over the other—they cast a wide net for ideas among Johnson's most trusted friends beyond the administration. From the Supreme Court, Abe Fortas boldly proposed to cede the entire Vietnam conflict to the United Nations with a pledge to withdraw American forces in less than three years. By contrast, novelist John Steinbeck recommended massive, erratic bomb strikes based on his experience in the World War II London blitz: "People can get used to anything except what they don't expect." Steinbeck's literary empathy with the Dust Bowl poor still made him a security risk in FBI files, but he forwarded a bellicose mix of strategic advice and amateur designs for unconventional weapons: crop bombs of bright methyl dye, on the theory that Vietnamese would not eat blue rice, plus a "napalm grenade" and spray shotguns for close jungle warfare. "I never knew anyone to hit anything with a .45," he wrote the White House on January 7, "unless he shoves it in his opponent's mouth."

Johnson rejected the final draft at four o'clock on the morning of January 12. Speechwriter Richard Goodwin, recalled again for ad hoc emergency duty, slumped over his typewriter and did not revive until a White House doctor gave him an injection to start over at dawn. Still banished from Johnson's actual presence for suspect loyalty since quitting the staff, Goodwin fell to the margins in a day-long Oval Office flurry of reshuffled sections and shouted orders to ad hoc phrasemakers, including Justice Fortas and Clark Clifford. The State of the Union, as set forth that night before a joint session of Congress, blended raw passions for justice, war, and peace. Johnson pressed the breakthrough in civil rights with proposals that made separate front-page headlines: for new laws to "prohibit racial discrimination in the sale or rental of housing," to integrate juries, and to make it a federal crime to murder or cause malicious injury to civil rights workers. In like spirit, he asked Congress to "prosecute with vigor and determination our war on poverty," to rebuild crumbling cities "on a scale never before attempted," and to begin a historic cleansing of the environment. "Of all the reckless devastation of our natural heritage," said the President, "none is really more shameful than the continued poisoning of our rivers and our air."

He promised to pursue these goals and also stand fast for freedom abroad: "I believe we can continue the Great Society while we fight in Vietnam." Five separate times he raised the "brutal and bitter conflict" where "tonight the cup of peril is full," until Vietnam consumed half the hour-long speech. Johnson called a universal hunger for independence not only "the strongest force in today's world" but freedom's long-range ally to help dissolve Communism, and praised nationalism for "eroding the unity of what was once a Stalinist empire." Military urgency overrode ambivalence on this core issue, however, along with financial realism. Johnson announced that Vietnam costs would increase by only an estimated $5.8 billion in fiscal 1967. Furthermore, he said vigilant pruning would *reduce* the year's overall deficit on the federal budget of $113 billion to $1.8 billion—"one of the lowest in many years"—while wiping out the small international trade deficit. "Time may require further sacrifices," he told the national audience. "And if it does, we will make them." Above qualification and deceit, he smothered doubt with a bared yearning to make his figures come true. "Let us choose peace," he said, "and with it the wondrous works of peace."

A recurring passion in the speech mediated between energized national dreams and his wrenching imperative to let slip the stilled bombers. Johnson pronounced war "a crime against mankind." It is "young men dying in the fullness of their promise," he said. "It is trying to kill a man that you do not even know well enough to hate. Therefore, to know war is to know that there is still madness in this world." The President gained fifty-nine ovations in the House, often with Goodwin's language harking back to the crossroads of Selma. "Finally, I must be the one to order our guns to fire against the—, against all the most inward pulls of my desire," Johnson said with a slight catch. "For we have children to teach, as we have sick to be cured and we have men to be freed. There are poor to be lifted up and there are cities to be built and there's a world to be helped. Yet, we do what we must."

The President stayed up late to savor reviews of a triumphant speech said to have "exhilarated the capital," but he called Press Secretary Bill Moyers long after midnight about an advance news item that Moyers might be longing for his old job at the Peace Corps. "Well, are you happy, or are you unhappy?" Johnson asked in a grave, wounded tone, airing his impression that Moyers "got angry this morning and kind of sulked" through the day, "puffed up like a powder pigeon." The chief aide declared wholehearted support for the speech, but the President probed for discontent until Moyers raised a comment among the customary tirades in which Johnson had chided him for currying favor with reporters by encouraging their suspicions of duplicity in the White House. "Well, that hit me like a ton of bricks," said Moyers. In awkward, glancing protest, he professed a loyalty so resolute that he said it undermined his own reputation and effectiveness as press secretary.

Johnson kept circling the edge of direct accusation. "I don't give a damn a whole lot about the *Washington Post,*" he said softly, "just as long as I understand where I am with you." He pushed the sleep-starved Moyers for more than half an hour to elaborate a grievance or desire. "Do you want to change jobs?" he asked. "Would you prefer to? Are you, did you make a bad deal when you agreed to stay? Would you rather do something else?"

"Uh, no, sir," Moyers answered with repeated sighs. "There's not another job that I believe I should do right now."

"It's coming from within," Johnson warned of destructive news. "There's nothing about it from the outside. The Republicans are not hurtin' us."

* * *

MARTIN LUTHER King sent Johnson a telegram of praise for his commitment to seek peace and his "reassuring" determination not to let Vietnam spoil the hard-won domestic initiatives. "In all of these endeavors," he wrote, "you have both my prayers and my support." King also wired congratulations to Deke DeLoach for a promotion that lifted him among the few FBI executives whispered to be a potential successor to J. Edgar Hoover. Following the considered advice of Negro elders that flattery was the only known solvent for the Bureau's imperious hostility, King slathered on a personal touch: "It makes me doubly proud to know that a fellow Georgian has been elevated to such a key position in the federal government." He reminded DeLoach of discovering a common birth state during their one face-to-face encounter, but of course did not specify that occasion as the scalded truce summit after Hoover had publicly called King "the most notorious liar in the country."

Tremors from the war already swallowed up King's gestures in public anxiety promoted ardently from FBI headquarters. Director Hoover charged that the minuscule American Communist Party played "an ever-increasing role in generating opposition to the United States position in Vietnam," and DeLoach, in a publicized Chicago speech, lumped civil rights clergy and war protesters together with "racketeers, Communists, narcotics peddlers, filth merchants, and others of their ilk" who spread the "malignant disease" of false freedom. "I refer to the arrogant non-conformists, including some educators," he added, "who have mounted the platform at public gatherings to urge 'civil disobedience' and defiance of authority."

On January 14, while King marched for Julian Bond in Atlanta, FBI agents gave Gary Thomas Rowe $10,000 with a carefully scripted message that the payment was a token of gratitude from Director Hoover himself, and should be added to whatever "ultimate settlement" Rowe might receive from the Justice Department for his service as a Klan informant and witness. Rowe "became very emotional," the lead agent reported to Hoover. "[T]ears came to his eyes, and he asked me to personally thank you for your consideration." Rowe signed a release for the FBI and wrote Hoover a devoted farewell the same day, expressing nostalgia over "my last official association with the Bureau." Soon thereafter, his first collect phone call to John Doar's home triggered an inkling of woe for the Justice Department. Based on the Attorney General's written promise before the December Liuzzo trial, Rowe demanded attention to debts, quarrelsome relatives, and real or imagined security threats from vengeful Klansmen, Doar advised Katzenbach, and FBI officials dropped a solid curtain of amnesia to rebuff the Justice Department's plaintive requests for help. "We have no views," Hoover wrote tersely on a memo from DeLoach. "We settled our obligations to Rowe."

Thus the FBI fobbed off Rowe's future as well as his past. Government lawyers inherited a decade of headache over his ensuing performance as a deputy U.S. marshal working under a protective identity in California, where he slugged and threatened to shoot a black doorman, for instance, rather than sign a building register. "Rowe apparently has a super detective complex," concluded one evaluation, "and is prone to display his identification, badge, and weapon to almost anyone who will listen when he is under the influence of alcohol." Years later, during the post-Watergate investigation of intelligence scandals, Rowe's name surfaced in allegations that FBI handlers had received advance notice of Klan violence long before the Liuzzo murder. This news shocked even Katzenbach, who retained an impression that Rowe had turned informant only after he "got scared" during the lethal ambush. In 1979, Attorney General Griffin Bell appointed a task force solely to investigate the FBI's complicity through Rowe in a host of Alabama Klan crimes between 1960 and 1965, both infamous and unknown. Despite stale records and obstruction, task force attorneys concluded that Rowe had warned the FBI days ahead of the Klan-police agreement to beat the 1961 Freedom Riders in Birmingham, for instance, and that Bureau officials had condoned the attack to the point of watching Rowe himself become "one of a handful most intensely involved in the violence." Even so, Justice Department attorneys stoutly defended the FBI against lawsuits for negligent damage. They lost a modest award of $25,000 to Freedom Rider James Peck, whose wounds had required fifty-seven stitches to close, and of $35,000 to the elderly Quaker Walter Bergman, who was confined permanently to a wheelchair since being knocked unconscious in the Birmingham bus station. They won dismissal of a $2 million case when U.S. District Judge Charles Joiner ruled in 1983 that advance approval for Rowe to join the Klan ride that killed Viola Liuzzo "cannot place liability on the government," and it took a shower of adverse publicity to quell as unseemly the Justice Department's subsequent counterclaim to recover all its court costs from the Liuzzo family. Renewed security worries placed Rowe back in Witness Protection until he died obscurely in 1998 under the pseudonym Thomas Moore.

These troubles lay submerged when DeLoach advised Hoover in 1966 that Katzenbach's unguarded letter "gave the FBI an excellent opportunity to divest us of our responsibilities" for the radioactive informant. Among moves to forestall a parallel congressional inquiry into violations of privacy, Hoover sent DeLoach secretly to argue that Senator Edward Long of Missouri should leave the FBI out of contemplated hearings on bugging policy, despite the scandal in Las Vegas. "It seems a little ludicrous to consider the civil rights of such hoodlums have been violated by microphones being placed on them," he advised, by his account, "when these same individuals are dealing in murder, racketeering, and complete sadism." DeLoach returned to headquarters convinced that ulterior motives lay behind claims of congressional duty to learn the facts. "Senator Long thoroughly dislikes Senator [Robert] Kennedy," he reported, "and will use such information against Senator Kennedy." Hoover resisted the temptation to abet an attack on Kennedy, whom he despised, and moved first to neutralize the FBI's vulnerability over its decades of freelance bugging. He sent DeLoach to lobby Katzenbach for three days, playing on his desire to avoid public recriminations, until the Attorney General approved a formal letter to Senator Long late on Thursday, January 20. An investigation not only threatened capabilities essential to national security, he agreed, but would be pointless because bugging practices rested securely on an "understanding" down through the years between the FBI and Attorneys General of both political parties.

An agitated Katzenbach informed DeLoach early Friday that he had lain awake with second thoughts and wanted to revise the letter. He said the understanding provision might infuriate Robert Kennedy, whose support he needed for bills in the Senate, but DeLoach cut short the misgivings. "I told the Attorney General that I was just as sorry as I could be," he reported, "however, this letter had been mailed out last night and no doubt would be in the hands of Senator Long either this morning or early this afternoon." DeLoach also reported, with merciless satisfaction, that Katzenbach instantly declined his offer for the FBI to retrieve the letter from Long with a candid account of his fears about Kennedy. By a combination of bureaucratic skills—patient cultivation of long-range advantage, sealed with masterful control of paperwork—FBI officials fastened Katzenbach to a bugging defense they had constructed from nothing.

Nevertheless, Hoover cautiously placed a moratorium on new bugs "irrespective of what Long does," in order to minimize exposure in the unstable climate since President Johnson's ban on intrusive surveillance. That same Friday, Hoover reacted sharply to notification of hasty installations on King. "Remove this surveillance at once," he ordered. FBI technicians surreptitiously planted no fewer than sixteen bugs anyway, seeking to intercept significant mischief in various rooms occupied for the weekend by King's party at the New York Americana Hotel. This frenzied, unsuccessful attempt remains a mysterious lapse of internal FBI discipline, traceable to mixed signals or perhaps anticipated regret that these would be the last microphone intercepts ever targeted at King. The government's electronic ear would intrude upon the final two years of his life exclusively through the numerous telephone wiretaps authorized by Katzenbach and Robert Kennedy.

*   *   *

KING PREACHED at New York's historic Riverside Church once again that Sunday, January 23, which marked the end of a battle truce for the Vietnamese Tet holiday. "The days that follow may well be decisive," warned an advertisement spread across two pages of the morning *New York Times,* "in determining whether this brutal, bloody war will be ended or escalated." King's name appeared among hundreds of signers drawn from interfaith clergy worldwide, including theologian Karl Barth, rabbis Heschel and Gittelson, Father Daniel Berrigan, Martin Niemoeller of Germany, and bishops from Sweden to Tasmania. Their appeal—headed "they are our brothers whom we kill!"—rebuked both sides for alarming determination to prove sincerity by violence. Thich Nhat Hanh, the monk who had written King about Buddhist theory of nonviolent self-immolation, added the Vietnamese perspective throughout a text circulated by the pacifist Fellowship of Reconciliation: "Helpless villagers in Vietnam, unable either to escape or defend themselves, recoil from the bombing of one side and from the terror of the other." The ad called upon the opposing governments to reinstate the 1954 Geneva Accords under a truce leading to a plebiscite on reunification. Thich Nhat Hanh signed as "A Vietnamese Buddhist . . . whose name is withheld for reasons of prudence." In hiding—soon exiled for the remainder of the century by the diverse autocracies to govern Vietnam—he wrote that foreign military escalation would reinforce Ho Chi Minh's reputation for patriotic resistance and conversely would undermine for Westerners the ultimate goal of forging political allegiance, so that by every boost of violence "the more surely they destroy the very thing they are trying to build." He charged that a million South Vietnamese already lived in refugee camps on whatever portion of the four-cent daily allowance was not stolen in graft.

King flew home to address internal conflicts centered on Hosea Williams, who had been arrested for drunk driving late Saturday night in Birmingham. No sooner did Williams make bail than he scandalized a public meeting on registration goals, exclaiming "You can't Jew us down!" to the few interracial stalwarts of the Alabama Human Relations Council, among them several Jews. SCLC aides labored to curb his outbursts and profligate ways, especially in light of the unresolved FBI car theft investigation. "I think that the root of this problem is that you don't realize the strength of your own personality," Andrew Young counseled privately. "I am sure that you don't mean to abuse and humiliate people, but quite often you do." Still, Williams berated his rival James Bevel for "stealing" King away to Chicago. Determined to recapture the movement spotlight for Alabama by spectacular enrollments of newly registered black Democrats, he excoriated SNCC project directors for what he called their "ignorant, black nationalistic" notion to organize independent parties for selected counties instead. He accused Stokely Carmichael of exploiting sharecroppers with newfangled schemes. "There ain't no Negro in Alabama, including ourselves, that knows one iota about politics!" he shouted. Carmichael retorted that Williams was herding black voters into a party with "White Supremacy" as its official slogan. Francis Walter, who observed several of the tumultuous parleys, found the question of party loyalty "vexing" and Carmichael unpersuasive but game. "I don't blame anyone for resisting Hosea's dogmatic egomania," he recorded in his diary.

Sunday afternoon, Walter drove alone into Alabama's Wilcox County for a mass meeting to map strategy for first-time voters in the May primary. He came upon a visibly charged crowd of Negroes on Highway 41 just outside Camden, held back from an abandoned car by troopers with sawed-off shotguns. Movement supporter David Colson had been poised to turn into the parking lot of Antioch Church when a car behind thumped his bumper. He walked back to investigate, whereupon the driver shot him dead behind the right ear with a .32 caliber pistol and drove away past Mrs. Colson in the car with her small son and three cousins. The crowd calmed slightly when Sheriff P. C. "Lummie" Jenkins announced that J. T. Reaves, a local farmer, had surrendered. Witnesses murmured that Reaves seemed deranged, having bumped into other cars, with Colson the first Negro who dared to inquire like a motorist in an ordinary accident. Reporters arrived from distant cities. "With the pool of blood still fresh outside the windows, the meeting went on after a brief eulogy by [SCLC aide Rev. Daniel] Harrell & Rev. Frank Smith," Walter wrote that night. "There was crying in the church and a great deal of fear. I was afraid." Despite pleas not to let terror achieve its purpose, no one agreed to stand for office in the May primary.

A hundred miles north, King accepted staff advice to avoid contention with SNCC projects over the isolated Black Belt counties plagued with evictions, tent cities, and ingrained fear spiked by the fresh murder in Camden. He confined a hurried visit to Birmingham, where Hosea Williams catapulted Monday morning from the defendant's table to a personal triumph that made national news. He won dismissal of the drunk driving charge in court just before federal officials arrived as a result of his battered month's marches to dramatize the slow pace of Birmingham registration. Twenty-three new registrars—nine of them Negroes—took up stations under superseding authority from the Voting Rights Act. King led a small parade of welcome, and Williams invited white people to make use of the registrars, too. "The more people that register," he grandly declared, "the better government we have." With aides in bemused debate about whether Williams gained his miracle rescues by providence or lunatic boldness, King toured spontaneous voter rallies. He proclaimed a mission to "democratize the total political structure of the state," reported the *New York Times*. The detachment of federal registrars worked well into Monday night to process more than a thousand people the first day. A certifying order from Attorney General Katzenbach made Birmingham the thirty-seventh local jurisdiction served—eleventh in Alabama, first in an urban area.

In Washington that week, also on the legal initiative of John Doar's Civil Rights Division, Katzenbach quietly approved an effort to ban segregation in the 226 state and local jails that held federal prisoners under contract. He recommended that Constance Baker Motley become the first Negro woman to hold a federal judgeship, partly in recognition of her landmark cases to integrate Clemson and Ole Miss, and he joined President Johnson at the White House ceremony to swear in Robert Weaver as the first Negro Cabinet member, heading the new Department of Housing and Urban Development. The President chided Roy Wilkins about Weaver's propensity to travel, which he called "the principal defect of Negroes in government." ("The moment they take an oath, they get an airplane ticket," he teased, and Wilkins agreed, "They do get around.") More seriously, Wilkins, Clarence Mitchell, and Whitney Young complained that White House protocol granted no special reward for political loyalty on Vietnam. Vice President Humphrey took note of their quiet tenacity in a favorable memo, asking "why treat all of the civil rights leaders alike when the SNCC outfit engages in the most outrageous attacks on the President and the Administration."

* * *

JOHNSON AND McNamara had slipped with their wives into the White House theater on Saturday night to watch the James Bond spy fantasy *Thunderball,* then returned to the crucible of inescapable choice over a bombing pause now extended past thirty days. On Monday, January 24, McNamara advised gloomily that he expected a "military stand-off at a much higher level" under troop deployments scheduled for the year, with American casualties to reach a thousand killed per month. He agreed with the CIA assessment that no amount of deliverable ordnance could reduce the flow of soldiers and supplies down the Ho Chi Minh Trail enough to threaten the enemy war effort, and favored renewed bombing because he had exhausted his hope for a diplomatic settlement. Privately, McNamara commended to Johnson a historical explanation for North Vietnam's stunning indifference to peace feelers in the face of pending devastation: they believed they had all but won a terrible long war in 1954, only to negotiate away half their country at Geneva under conciliatory pressure from the world, including their Communist allies, and were steeled never to repeat such a mistake. Monday night in the

White House Cabinet Room, McNamara pressed to restart Rolling Thunder by Friday. "I'd go sooner," he said. "Political delay can be damaging."

Johnson stalled. "I think we'll spend a good deal of political capital in resuming," he countered. War doubters would decry the lapse of restraint. War enthusiasts would claim proof that restraint was dangerous folly.

On Tuesday evening, Johnson gathered twenty congressional leaders from both parties to address the pause under strict pledge of secrecy. Senators Mansfield and Fulbright advocated essentially the *New York Times* peace ad—an international push for plebiscite under a revived Geneva Accord, from a military posture pulled back within "enclaves" to minimize casualties. Everyone else spurned the idea as a passive formula for eventual defeat. Republican leaders Everett Dirksen and Gerald Ford said bombing was the only choice to win. Senator Russell lamented that extra American soldiers inevitably would be killed— "casualties of our care for peace," he called them—by enemy reinforcements moving freely during the pause. "This is the most frustrating experience of my life," he said. "I didn't want to get in there, but we are there." He pleaded for Johnson to bomb with vengeance. "We killed civilians in World War II and nobody opposed," he said. "I'd rather kill them than have American boys die." The only woman among the leaders warned the President that his pause signaled cowardice. "Can't we fight?" asked Frances Bolton of Ohio, the ranking member of the House Foreign Affairs Committee. "Don't let them think we won't fight."

Johnson read out loud from Bruce Catton's Civil War history *Never Call Retreat,* a copy of which he had just received from Senator Robert Kennedy with a handwritten note that "it might give you some comfort to look back at another President, Abraham Lincoln, and some of the identical problems and situations that he faced." When he finished reading the passages Kennedy recommended, about the incomparable loneliness of a war President in the midst of clashing passions and divided counsel, Johnson told the senators he felt the force of Lincoln's reference to himself as "that unhappy wretch called Abraham Lincoln." He called Justice Fortas Wednesday morning to vent against the stubborn pretense that some neglected word or negotiating strategy would unlock a door to sensible compromise. "The problem is not communicating," Johnson fumed. "We understand them, and they understand us." He dashed off mournful descriptions of North Vietnam's one "loud and clear" message, consistent to diplomats "running back and forth to Hanoi and Peking and every other place," which he called the clearly stated purpose "to kill every American soldier in South Vietnam" even if it required "twenty or thirty years," with firm advance notice that Americans "can either leave or get killed."

Johnson's monologue abruptly reversed direction to portray guns aimed also at his back. " 'You can either fight or run,' " he told Fortas, paraphrasing the message from congressional leaders from the night before. " 'And we'll universally condemn you, and history will condemn you, and we'll despise you, if you run.' " He said his generals accused him of tying their hands in order to feed the enemy. "And then you have Eisenhower callin' me yesterday from California, sayin' when are we going to fight?"

Fortas scarcely spoke as the fulmination circled back to the bombing pause in its thirty-third day. "And uh, uh, the, they're going to try and convict and impeach me," Johnson sputtered, "for committing to war two hundred thousand men—"

"Yes."

"And then not supporting, doing this. That's my big problem in the morning. I don't know how much longer I can wait, number one. And number two, what in the hell am I waiting on?"

"Well, that's right," said Fortas.

"They've given me my answer loud and clear."

"Yes."

"What—, I don't—, I just hesitate to mash the button that says to the world, 'He's off again.' "

President Johnson broke away from Fortas to deliver televised remarks for a major initiative long in gestation. "Nineteen sixty-six can be the year of rebirth for American cities," he began. His Model Cities message to Congress proposed to test renovation blueprints for urban systems from parks and schools to sewers across sixty metropolitan areas. "If we become two people, the suburban affluent and urban poor, each filled with mistrust and fear for the other," he warned, "if this is our desire and policy as a people, then we shall effectively cripple each generation to come." News outlets generally praised the comprehensive experiment, because or in spite of its modest cost of $2.6 billion over six years. When the *Washington Post* computed that only $5 million was to be invested in the first budget year, 1967, White House aides would scramble with hopeful bromides to allay an "extremely unfair" but persistent guess that Vietnam already had pinched the bud from Johnson's lofty plan.

* * *

KING BEGAN weekly slum residence that Wednesday afternoon. From the Chicago airport, he was whisked secretly to mediate the lingering frictions over his proposed location. A few leaders from Al Raby's coalition considered it belittling to their hopes that a renowned international figure would advertise black Chicago's most extreme degradation. Some argued that there were plenty of distinguished homes and hovels alike in historic South Side "Bronzeville." Others objected that James Bevel had ignored neighborhood partners in an awkward search for the most symbolic site on the lowly West Side. Word surfaced that traveling aide Bernard Lee had pronounced eight vacancies "unlivable," and landlords recoiled from King's name on the lease, so Lee was obliged to conceal the intended occupant by signing himself. Newspapers discovered the ruse. Their emphasis on last-minute refurbishment by the panicked landlord—"King Picks 'Typical' Flat/8 Men Repair It," reported the *Chicago Tribune*—projected an air of fiasco and false humility for the Chicago campaign.

King appraised the sniping as normal. "I can learn more about the situation by being here with those who live and suffer here," he insisted, then proceeded by caravan into the West Side ghetto of North Lawndale, nicknamed "Slumdale" by residents. A crowd of several hundred waited numbly in the cold to observe the entourage enter a third-floor walk-up at 1550 South Hamlin Avenue. Coretta, looking ahead to the small comfort of promised improvements upstairs, stepped first into the shock of a lock-less ground-floor entry with a bare dirt floor. "The smell of urine was overpowering," she recalled. "We were told that this was because the door was always open, and drunks came in off the street to use the hallway as a toilet." Above, fresh coats of gray and yellow paint did cover the empty apartment of four narrow rooms and "a bath of sorts," lined single-file from the street to overlook a back alley. "You had to go through the bedrooms to get to the kitchen," Coretta noted. They broke away from unpacking for King to deliver an evening speech at Chicago Theological Seminary, where new SCLC staff member Jesse Jackson was a student, then returned to a steady stream of first-night neighbors, including children who darted in to gawk. Bob Black of the *Chicago Defender* photographed eight-year-old Roy Williams sitting shyly on King's lap. Six curious members of the local Vice Lords gang stayed late in discussion with King about their turf battles and his concept of nonviolence.

As he first walked the streets to sample Lawndale and nearby East Garfield, trailing reporters noticed faces peering at the phenomenon from open windows even in zero-degree weather. One old man nearly collapsed when he recognized the famous preacher, and mumbled, "Great God a'mighty, I didn't ever think this day would come." Many in the path remained skeptical about change, however, saying the black people who had made it to Chicago were divided and reluctant to risk what little they had. "It's bad enough to be at the top of nothing," said one mother, "but to be at the *bottom* of nothing?" On Thursday, Al Raby guided King's party from a bustling soul food lunch at Belinda's Pit to a courtesy tour of police headquarters. Press interest fluttered to every hint of future conflict, as when King assured Chief Orlando Wilson that he would give ample notice before marches or civil disobedience. Wilson tried to be gracious by confirming his surprise discovery of some Irish ancestry in King (pretty far back, on Daddy King's side), which he said never hurt in shamrock Chicago.

In another balancing foray to the South Side, King lectured on race and family life that night at the University of Chicago. "Family life not only educates in general," he began, "but its quality ultimately determines the individual's capacity to love." He sketched conditions from the time of his slave great-grandfather on the plantation, when "the institution of legal marriage did not exist." Some Negroes had murdered their own young to spare them, he said bluntly, and "after liberation countless mothers wandered over roadless states looking for the children who had been taken from them and sold." He said city adjustment was often ruinous for ex-slaves, as for other migrant groups of peasant stock. Without mentioning Moynihan by name, he presented alarming statistics from "a recent study" that found 25 percent of Negro women in cities to be divorced. It was triple the rate for white women, said King, though the latter was rising more rapidly, and similar gaps prevailed for illegitimacy, unemployment, and welfare. He warned of the twin danger posed by "historical facts" of stubborn cruelty, seduction, and sorrow. America might mold a new pretext "to justify neglect and rationalize oppression," he said, and Negroes could give in to rage or surrender. King lifted up a narrow alternative for common hope. "What man has torn down," he asserted, "he can rebuild." Negroes in

American cities must seize every opportunity "to grow from within," while others must cooperate "from the outside" to remove invisible barriers of jolting strength. "This is what we intend to fight for in Chicago," he concluded. "A fair chance." In haste, he scrawled an instruction to himself at the end of the surviving text: "Ad lib we shall overcome!"

After a second night on Hamlin Avenue, King left Friday for registration rallies in Birmingham and weekend commitments in New York. His advisers expressed mild optimism about Chicago. Bayard Rustin, who still opposed the Northern campaign, passed along rumors that the city was preparing significant concessions for the spring. Mayor Daley already had beamed back an interview from his Caribbean vacation, promising full repair for every residence classified dilapidated (40 percent of Negro dwellings citywide) within two years. "All of us, like Dr. King, are trying to eliminate slums," Daley announced. As always, King's inner circle salved movement hardship with running tales of mirth. They speculated about the finer appointments Daley might select for King's tenement, and Abernathy, who demanded road perquisites to match his putative co-partner, magnified every palatial detail still lacking from his duplicate apartment one floor below, which retained all its rust and debris without new paint or heat. Blaming his wife's sensitivity, he resolved to bequeath the space to the staff and duck out to a hotel.

King headed back to tenement rounds in a kind of throwback to his quixotic movement years after the bus boycott. He was isolated from a national government rumbling to war. For all the sinews of his experience in heartland Chicago—battling J. H. Jackson there in the stronghold of church culture, addressing its elite Sunday Evening radio forum, sharing Bronzeville galas with Mahalia Jackson and a lawyer with Muhammad Ali—King blew words at a galaxy of strangers. There were fifty square miles of black people concentrated apart from scattered white allies in a vast mosaic of neighborhoods. He began anew as one waif seeking others. Among papers stuffed in his flight bag was a Friday memo urging him to pay a call in Chicago on the parish priest Richard Morrisroe, who was still hospitalized and said to be neglected five months after being shotgunned near the Lowndes County Jail. Stokely Carmichael had been among his few movement visitors.

* * *

SECRETARY OF State Rusk testified before the Senate Foreign Relations Committee that Friday morning, January 27, in an atmosphere of palpable tension. Front-page headlines suggested irresistible war pressures—"A Lonely Johnson Weighs Bombing"—and fifteen senators had released a joint letter pleading with President Johnson to delay. When Rusk explained again the steps necessary to guarantee an independent South Vietnam against Communist aggression, Chairman Fulbright dropped the courtly veneer of Senate discourse to question every premise, especially Rusk's assertion that Congress already had authorized a war of unlimited scale by its 1964 Gulf of Tonkin Resolution. "This was a fire fight, angry, bitter, and hostile," wrote David Halberstam. "Fulbright lost his temper, and he made no attempt to conceal it." He asked whether Rusk believed South Vietnam could be independent "with two hundred or four hundred thousand" American soldiers running its war. Senator Wayne Morse of Oregon brusquely refused to ask questions until the administration agreed to a full inquiry on Vietnam. The normally avuncular Republican George Aiken of Vermont demanded to know if Rusk seriously meant that Ho Chi Minh alone "will determine then whether we send four hundred thousand or two million men into Southeast Asia." Cameras recorded so much sizzling footage that Walter Cronkite would use three full minutes on the half-hour *CBS Evening News*—an eternity by television standards—only to find out that NBC used five full minutes and wanted more. The public sensation touched off heated debate inside the three broadcast networks— consequential for the future of television news—about whether to preempt daytime shows for live coverage of the hearings on the war.

In Vietnam, four thousand U.S. Marines completed the largest amphibious landing since Inchon in the Korean War and pushed south from Quang Nai to trap North Vietnamese regiments against twenty thousand U.S. Army infantry headed north in Operation Masher. While the infantry pushed up the central coastline, repairing all seventy-two bridges destroyed by foes along the forty-five-mile path from An Khe, Lieutenant Colonel Harold Moore landed Friday morning with his 7th Cavalry Battalion in a forward helicopter assault on the target area of Bong Son, and charged first into a thatched hut filled with peasants wounded and terrified from advance artillery fire, including a bloodied six-year-old girl "the same age as my daughter Cecile, back home," he recorded. "I summoned the medics, but I left there heartsick."

In Atlanta, Julian Bond sat quietly that afternoon as three federal judges heard arguments on his lawsuit challenging the refusal to seat him by the Georgia House of Representatives. Lawyers for co-plaintiff King had submitted a brief of unusually petulant fervor, arguing that segregationists still were "cheered" when *they* defied federal policy, and that Bond might have been seated "had he recanted, begged, or crawled. . . . No free man should." Against Bond, Judge Griffin Bell cast the swing vote in a 2–1 ruling "that the judgment of this court is not to be substituted for that of the House." All three judges, citing the acceptance of other newly elected Negroes, agreed from the bench that the evidence excluded race as a motivating factor for the House, which mooted Bond's contention that his civil rights were abridged. On the contrary, their ruling managed torturously to find that Bond himself had introduced improper racial considerations through comments aligned with critics of U.S. war policy "in the Dominican Republic, the Congo, South Africa, Rhodesia," and other foreign nations. The SNCC action he endorsed was "a call to action based on race . . . alien to the pluralistic society which makes this nation," declared the court, ruling that Bond had shifted the "balancing test" against his claim to free speech under the First Amendment.

In Washington, Dean Rusk left the explosive Fulbright hearing for a final war review that included civilians officially labeled "THE WISE MEN" on the confidential White House log. Only one hard-liner now recommended a defensive military posture to encourage the gradualist faction in Hanoi, based on his experience fighting the Chinese Communists. "If you just sit tight there, in six months or a year that will convince them," the Pakistani dictator Ayub Khan predicted by secret cable. "Your enemies expect you to be impatient, to commit more and more forces, and finally to weaken your resolve in the face of unsatisfactory military results and your own democratic pressures." For Americans in the Cabinet Room, however, the most divisive question was whether renewed bombing was a military or political necessity. The Joint Chiefs testily conceded McNamara's evidence that no air campaign could interdict more than half the supplies moving down the Ho Chi Minh Trail—and the Vietnamese would "probably use human backs," he said, if they needed to make up for lost trucks—but they insisted that heavy bombardment must gain some military advantage. To McNamara, bombs in mountainous jungle were largely noise but politically vital nonetheless, because he doubted "the American people will long support a government" that failed to throw every resource behind its soldiers.

Clark Clifford, one of the Wise Men, disputed McNamara's empha-sis on ground forces. "We must fight the war where we are strongest," he said, "and we are strongest in the air." Vice President Humphrey stressed the political dangers of further delay, warning that "Congress will run all over the lot." Johnson closed with a simple three-part con-clusion. He was "not happy with Vietnam." But "we cannot run out." Therefore, the bombing must resume.

*   *   *

THE ALABAMA movements wrestled with fear and political choice over the weekend. In Wilcox County, still traumatized from the Colson murder, Walter Calhoun hinted that he might run against Lummie Jenkins for sheriff—in the Democratic primary. This caused confusion, as many favored an independent county party instead, but Calhoun believed the simplest campaign would be hard enough for first-time voters and a pioneer candidate. (He would be ordered to vacate his grocery store as soon as he filed for office.) Mass meetings in Selma were split between independents who favored Negro candidates and pragmatists who believed their new votes could provide a victory margin for the "decent" segregationist Wilson Baker over Sheriff Jim Clark. Youth organizers in Macon County defied Tuskegee elders to leaflet for a February 6 caucus to begin a "black panther" organization in honor of Sammy Younge. The Greene County movement scraped together a tent city modeled on the one in Lowndes, where SNCC workers continued workshops on the strict legal requirements for a new local party.

In Mississippi, a weekend Poor People's Conference at Mount Beulah emphasized survival more than politics. On Saturday, January 29, seven hundred participants sent a telegram to President Johnson pleading for jobs and emergency housing to relieve conditions of abject peonage worsened by terror. The portion of crops harvested by machine had nearly doubled to 80 percent since 1960. Two sharecroppers had frozen to death Thursday night, and the Klan had burned fifty crosses across the state to continue a January offensive marked by the Dahmer fire-bombing in Hattiesburg. On Sunday, delegates sifted ideas to dramatize their plight, from petitions and a march on Jackson to guerrilla warfare. (The latter notion was floated by fringe rebels called "boppers," mostly young whites who had drifted into the holdover excitement of Freedom Summer with Marxist terminology and trophy guns.) The conference dispatched scouts to the Yazoo National Wildlife Refuge, which they found unsuited to become a squatters' site, but proposals to "occupy" another federal property steadily gained favor.

Only a remnant of the seven hundred volunteered for a bold plan to caravan north one hundred miles through the night to the derelict Greenville Air Base. All admitted new fears about incurring the wrath of the U.S. Air Force. They included Art Thomas, a Methodist preacher and Duke economist who headed the two-year-old Delta Ministry project for the National Council of Churches, plus six members of his staff, a reporter from Copenhagen, and some forty sharecroppers. Many of the latter were recently evicted; some had never ventured beyond their county line. At dawn Monday, January 31, they drove past a startled guard and pried the rusty padlock from a ramshackle barracks, unused since 1960. Once inside with their few blankets and boxes, they elected a governing council led by Unita Blackwell of Issaquena. The council authorized a hand-lettered sign for the door: "This is our home. Please knock before entering."

A sleepless President Johnson called the White House Situation Room at 3:20, and again at 6:06, hoping for reports on the first raids over North Vietnam to end the bombing pause. The front pages of his Monday newspapers featured a large AP photograph of 1st AirCav medic Thomas Cole kneeling half-blind near Bong Son, his own damaged eye wrapped in a bandana as he cradled one wounded soldier with another prostrate just behind. Johnson obtained crisp after-action figures from McNamara after breakfast: 225 sorties aborted by bad weather, seventy-five completed, three aircraft lost, 312 enemy and sixty-eight U.S. killed in Operation Masher. He said the pilots reported heavier antiaircraft fire. Johnson asked, "Did we get much results in your judgment?"

"No," said McNamara. "My judgment is we accomplished practically nothing."

The President talked briefly with Fortas, then announced the renewed bombing on national television from the White House theater at ten o'clock. Eleven hours ahead in Vietnam, dark closed on Monday's battles around the hamlet of Anthai, which Colonel Moore described as "a rat's nest of trenches and bunkers and spider holes" four miles north of Bong Son. One platoon quickly lost twenty-three of forty soldiers on a sand island surrounded by rice paddies, as described by a rare first-person dispatch to the *New York Times*. "I was a passenger on the first of these two choppers," wrote correspondent R. W. Apple. The survivors endured a sudden, prolonged fusillade from the rear, which turned out to be an errant attack by South Vietnamese allies. "We could not move, we could not take cover for there was none," wrote Apple. "We could not shoot back. We could not even tell who was shooting at us."

The President took a call late Monday from his Attorney General. "Mr. President," asked Katzenbach, "have you seen on the ticker about Greenville, Mississippi, this group of Negroes that moved on this abandoned, surplus air base there?"

"No, I haven't," replied Johnson. "No, I haven't."

Katzenbach explained. Fifty squatters refused to move until the Office of Economic Opportunity met demands for job training, relocation, and food assistance. Local officials refused to help.

"Did they do any damage?"

"Well, they've broken in, and the danger mainly is fire," the Attorney General replied. "You see, there's no plumbing in there, uh, it's cold." The occupants were lighting fires in little potbellied stoves, and Katzenbach worried also about the precedent: "My concern with this group is that if they stay on there, we'll have more."

When Johnson asked about getting a court order if negotiation failed, Katzenbach advised against it. "In fact, I'm not even sure we can get one," he said. "I didn't want to bring charges against them." He said Cyrus Vance and the Pentagon were preparing to move them on military authority.

The President suggested that perhaps Roy Wilkins and Martin Luther King could help explain history's proven snare whenever Negroes relied on the U.S. military to settle political questions in the South. "If you go to moving in," he prompted, "we go back to Reconstruction days, and we have a lot of unshirted hell, and they better move off."

A television crew landed in a Learjet to film the awkward standoff at Greenville Air Base. Federal negotiators offered freedom; occupants said they had no place to go. Negotiators said they should move for their own good, lacking heat and basic sanitation; occupants said they had never had any. "If that's all you got to say," Unita Blackwell told Major General R. W. Puryear, "I guess we'll stay right here." Puryear's air police unit broke into the barracks with billy clubs Tuesday morning, February 1. About half Blackwell's group consented to retreat under escort, while the others went limp and were dragged beyond the gates of federal property. Federal officials recommended a crash poverty program to alleviate suffering among "many thousands" of sharecroppers losing what little livelihood and shelter they had. "If we do not do this,"

Katzenbach wrote Johnson, "there is a real possibility that Mississippi will be the Selma, Alabama of 1966."

In Vietnam, an intensified U.S. air campaign more than made up for the long January pause. Bombing runs over North Vietnam in 1966 tripled the heavy numbers of the sustained 1965 campaign, to 79,000 sorties. Southward infiltration of Ho Chi Minh's soldiers increased substantially anyway, as McNamara and the CIA expected. For all the concussion to fall on North Vietnam, American pilots dropped more than triple that ordnance in air support for ground troops south of the border—eventually some four million tons, according to historian Christian Appy—to make South Vietnam the most bombed country since the invention of war.

The President somberly anticipated the devastation if not the result. Joe Califano noticed that he gave up alcohol from the moment he unleashed the bombers again. Johnson also severely curtailed the use of his clandestine telephone recording system, as though he had preserved all the history he wanted to make.

CHAPTER 27

Break Points

February–April 1966

THE Alabama State Democratic Committee revised the official party emblem by striking the words "White Supremacy" from the banner above the crowing white rooster that had identified Democratic candidates on every ballot since 1904. One official emerged from Birmingham's Tutwiler Hotel to denounce the reform as nothing short of blasphemy. "The white race is supreme in this world by the mandate of God Almighty," Henry Sweet of Bessemer told reporters as he bemoaned the sight of "beautiful white ladies" cheering civic progress in the hotel lobby. "What we're fighting for is womanhood," Sweet ruefully explained. Another committee member, Sidney Smyer of Birmingham, excoriated all sides for concealing their intrigues behind unrecorded votes in a cowardly secret session. Moderates, including supporters of Attorney General Richmond Flowers, labored to appease some 100,000 newly registered Negroes while minimizing the wrath of white voters, and observers aired theories about why Governor Wallace allowed dominant segregationists to acquiesce behind closed doors.

Wallace disdained any political threat from Flowers in the May primary. While barred from succeeding himself, he had arranged confidently to run his wife, Lurleen, for surrogate governor even though she was a shy political novice freshly diagnosed with terminal cancer of the uterus. Wallace himself already looked to the 1968 presidential race, and rumors flew of a tacit understanding with President Johnson. If Wallace quietly retired the "White Supremacy" banner, thereby making Alabama more palatable to national Democrats, Johnson might relax loyalty rules to accommodate a fellow Democrat's run on a third-party ticket in 1968. The likely Wallace sweep of Deep South states would console Johnson by denying to any Republican nominee all the electoral votes Barry Goldwater had won outside his home in Arizona.

On February 7, a panel of three federal judges ruled unanimously for Gardenia White and her fellow Lowndes County plaintiffs in *White v. Crook,* the lawsuit contesting "old-boy" juries as evidenced by the Liuzzo and Daniels murder trials. The judges ordered county officials to add registered Negro voters to jury selection panels. They also voided as unconstitutional the state law that excluded females of every race, and declared jury service "a responsibility and a right that should be shared by all citizens, regardless of sex." The victorious plaintiffs' legal team included seventy-eight-year-old Dorothy Kenyon, who had entered law practice from the suffrage movement in 1919. Her colleagues Charles Morgan and Pauli Murray anticipated leverage from *White v. Crook* to put women on juries far beyond Alabama. "The principle announced seems so obvious today," Murray would write in a 1987 memoir, "that it is difficult to remember the dramatic break the court was making with scores of previous judicial decisions."

Analysts at the time widely discounted the impact. The lawyers had challenged the Alabama statute banning women jurors for tactical reasons—to get *White v. Crook* quickly into federal court, explained the *New York Times*—when their main goal was to attack the exclusion of Negroes by arbitrary practice rather than law. *White v. Crook* gave women "another windfall from the civil rights movement," wrote legal correspondent Fred Graham, recalling that the amendment to outlaw employment discrimination by sex had been "received politely, but not seriously, on Capitol Hill" until Southerners embraced chivalry in a desperate ploy to kill the Civil Rights Act of 1964. Graham advised *Times* readers that enforcement of the new jury standard would nullify exclusion laws in South Carolina and Mississippi, and could oblige twenty-six other states to discard lesser restrictions on women. In Montgomery, where *White v. Crook* was announced, a newspaper survey found local leaders bemused by the sudden prospect of female jurors. "My first reaction to the ruling was laughter," confessed a League of Women Voters president who said her chapter had been promoting other goals. The head of a Republican ladies club reflected gamely that while "women at times become a little emotional, they can *learn* to serve on juries." The district attorney worried that "some of the language in court can be pretty rough." The *Montgomery Advertiser* wondered whether Alabama could adopt limits practiced elsewhere: "Can pregnant women be exempted from jury service? Can school teachers be excused? Nurses?"

Such dilemmas were remote to SNCC fieldworkers, who felt little assurance in mixed juries or reformed slogans. The judges delayed the effective date of their jury order, anyway, and movement veterans fully expected resourceful segregationists to strike Negroes from actual juries if the courts managed to get them on the selection panels. Few would be surprised ten months later when a jury of white men acquitted Marvin Segrest for the murder of Sammy Younge, causing student riots in Tuskegee. Judge Frank Johnson, protector of the Selma march and a member of the *White v. Crook* panel, issued a strong decision on February 11—"Lowndes Schools Ordered to End All Segregation"—but the resulting hardship was clearer than the benefit. Twenty-four of the twenty-seven dilapidated Negro schools were closed forthwith, which obliged the families to relocate, but freedom-of-choice integration remained too daunting for nearly everyone. Also in February, Judge Johnson dismissed the Justice Department's lawsuit on persecution of sharecroppers for lack of proof that evictions were motivated specifically to punish voter registration. The available evidence showed that Cato Lee's landlord had evicted him instead for his stated desire to send his children to white schools, Johnson ruled.

Hard experience left young movement veterans doubtful that democratic norms would reach Lowndes County, where local officials blatantly adjusted the election process to maintain control. They hiked filing fees tenfold in February—from $50 to $500 to run for sheriff as a Democrat in the May primary—which added a crushing disincentive for any aspiring Negro candidate. They reduced the number of polling places for the vast area to eight, which discouraged voters who lacked cars, and put all but the courthouse location in white businesses or homes. Organizers and friends of the Lowndes County movement expected little countervailing fairness from state or federal government, and had grown jaundiced even about the bedrock contribution of the Voting Rights Act. It was part of the "fraud and deceit behind which the Lyndon gang operates its Empire," wrote SNCC research director Jack Minnis in the final issue of *Life with Lyndon in the Great Society*. Through the tumultuous peak year of domestic suffering and achievement, the tone of his weekly newsletter had sunk from skeptical satire on LBJ's jumbo persona into cheerless hostility, corroded by Vietnam. With optimism for national politics all but expired, SNCC leaders declined to spend any more precious mimeograph paper on the President.

From Atlanta, Minnis supported the Alabama staff in wide-ranging research after the daylight canvassing hours. Bob Moses, back in Birmingham from a trip to Africa, circulated study material for an informal New Orleans "roots" conference to strengthen awareness of black heritage. Tina Harris wrote a paper on the Bible and anthropologist Louis Leakey. ("So whether you believe that Man descended from the Ape, or that God created Man, the fact is that Adam was born in Africa.") With Harris and Bob Mants, Stokely Carmichael analyzed General William T. Sherman's ill-fated Field Order No. 15 on land distribution, which had resulted from a Civil War press scandal during Sherman's March to the Sea through Georgia. After a subordinate Union commander pulled up pontoon bridges from Ebenezer Creek to rid his army of black fugitives teeming along behind, leaving them to drown or be reenslaved by pursuing Confederate cavalry, Sherman, instructed to make amends, grumpily consulted twenty slave preachers in Savannah on January 12, 1865. "The way we can best take care of ourselves is to have land, and turn in and till it by our labor," Rev. Garrison Frazier advised, by the War Department's record of the "colloquy." Sherman's ensuing special order distributed a mule and forty acres per family of new Freedmen, but President Andrew Johnson rescinded it shortly after the Lincoln assassination in order to restore confiscated and abandoned plantations to former Confederate owners.

For Carmichael, the "far-reaching step" of Field Order No. 15 all too briefly had matched a national will for restitution with skills of the oppressed, and the swift reversal set a pattern for blasted hopes. Still, Carmichael applied for a "self-help housing grant" to finance a "Poor People's Land Corporation" in Lowndes County. He received promises of "triple-A priority" consideration by the new Office of Economic Opportunity poverty agency in Washington. The proposal might be a century late, Carmichael recognized in the study paper on Sherman, because harsh agricultural economics made homestead designs a "Pandora's Box" for the Black Belt. "But somehow," he wrote, "the plantation to Ghettoes treadmill has got to be stopped."

The Lowndes County movement invested greater hope locally to transform the landscape for politics and business alike. By Alabama law, a newly organized county party could set filing fees as low as zero to attract candidates. While no one yet agreed to stand for office—not even the intrepid John Hulett—Lowndes County drew crowds well into the hundreds each Sunday night to promote an independent "black panther" ticket, whereas similar rallies were lucky to attract twenty people in Wilcox, Sumter, or Greene. On February 19, scouring for stories to raise money from distant contributors, SNCC's James Forman recorded an interview about how the project had survived the notorious fear in Lowndes County. Carmichael traced its spark to the impulsive display of suicidal contempt outside the Negro high school after Viola Liuzzo's murder. "Whenever we went canvassing," he said, "people would always say, 'Are you those civil rights fighters that cussed the cops out?' " SNCC worker George Greene, remarking that primitive conditions demanded constant choice between stoicism and daredevil risk, said there were now only four staff cars for all of rural Alabama. "I spent a couple of nights in the tents," he told Forman. "I found it to be a very trying experience."

*   *   *

KING ROSE early in Atlanta on Wednesday, February 23, for the special election to fill his home district's vacated seat in the Georgia House, and bumped into the leading candidate at his polling place. "I'm voting for you," he assured Julian Bond, but playfully refused to show his marked paper ballot before he and Bond dropped theirs ceremoniously together in the box. Bond won election a second time, receiving all but thirteen votes. "If they bar me again, I'll sue them again," he told reporters. The House Rules Committee promptly did so, unanimously, and Governor Sanders ordered a third vote while the Supreme Court considered the standoff.

King had left the polls quickly for Chicago. After changing into work clothes that afternoon at his Hamlin Avenue apartment, he led a procession of two hundred people through bitter cold to a six-unit tenement house, where he announced from the steps that the Chicago Freedom Movement was assuming "trusteeship" on behalf of tenants who had begged for help. He said the building had no heat, was unfit for habitation, and the $400 per month aggregate rent would be appropriated for vital repairs. King invoked "supralegal" authority. "The moral question is far more important than the legal one," he said, then trooped inside with a work party to clean ashes from the furnace. Changing clothes again, he addressed a Wednesday night education rally at Jenner School before keeping a late engagement at the South Chicago home of

Elijah Muhammad. The Nation of Islam leader had sought an introduction through intermediaries for years, never harder than now, across
awkward gaps of custom and public dispute. Coretta was asked to sit
separately with the Muslim women. King and Muhammad found chatting ground as fellow preacher's kids from Georgia, the former Elijah
Poole having grown up a "whooping" Baptist in his native Cordele.
King readily agreed that he found the struggle of nonviolence "not always easy," but he could not coax from Muhammad even a wink of pulpit guile about his sectarian doctrine that all white people were created
devils. The old man rigidly scolded Al Raby for having married a white
woman, and smiled only when King said he doubted they could reach a
productive understanding. "All we have to do is drink a cup of coffee,"
Muhammad responded. That week, for their annual Savior's Day Convention, Nation of Islam house organs trumpeted the King summit as
another symbolic wonder from the one they venerated as Holy Apostle
of Islam.

Public attention fastened upon a clash of race and real estate, leaving
the Muslim audience only squib notice outside the Negro press. "Dr.
King Seizes a Slum Building," announced the February 24 *New York
Times,* which covered the escalating conflict the next day: "Dr. King Assailed for Slum Tactic." From New York, Stanley Levison called on his
wiretapped phone line to criticize the surrender of the legal high
ground in Chicago, but Andrew Young said they could not afford the
numb delay of a lawsuit. Unforgettably, he had seen a shivering baby
wrapped in newspapers. "We *wanted* to do it illegally," he told Levison.
"We want to be put in jail for furnishing heat and health requirements
to people with children in the winter." Levison approved of his courage
but not the result. A prominent black federal judge denounced the
takeover as theft. Mayor Daley, while reprimanding the use of "illegal
ways" to improve slums, refused to prosecute or jail King, charged the
landlord with code violations, and announced a crash city program to
inspect 15,000 buildings on the West Side. The slum owner turned out
to be an eighty-one-year-old invalid instead of a sleek profiteer. "I think
King is right," John Bender told reporters, offering his property to anyone who would assume the mortgage.

Staff effort salvaged a remarkable mass meeting at which two owners
of more substantial slum investment faced grievances under King's protection, flanking him on the platform of the movement's citywide headquarters, Warren Avenue Congregational in East Garfield. One by one,

tenants came forward hesitantly with church-style "testimony" about rats and rotted floors. "Don't be afraid," the evening's pulpit mistress cajoled. "Your *landlord* wasn't afraid to come here." John Condor, given the chance to respond, introduced himself and partner Lou Costalis as residents of the neighborhood before and since the massive white flight of the 1950s. "We're with you, believe it or not," he announced.

"No, you ain't!" shouted a voice. Occasional catcalls escaped a generally hushed crowd as the white landlords pleaded helplessness, arguing that "the big boys" in the downtown business Loop constricted slums with "red-line" bank restrictions to favor concentrated public housing and marginal ghetto business over home ownership. "Don't fight the wrong fight," pleaded Condor.

King closed with thanks to the landlords for putting a human face on complex injustice, then lifted the crowd from a queasy, anticlimactic mood by preaching on familiar themes. "We are somebody because we are God's children," cried King. ("That's right!" answered voices from the pews.) "You don't need to hate anybody," he said—violence would only meet greater force, but nonviolence could march into the hearts of opponents and bystanders alike. He exhorted them to organize by door-to-door canvass across Chicago. "We are going to change the whole Jericho road!" shouted King, and the landlords themselves joined in the applause.

Recruitment percolated beneath overt challenge to Chicago's political machine. King confided to Stanley Levison that audiences already booed mention of courtesy telegrams from Mayor Daley's black aldermen, and speculated that Al Raby might be able to topple U.S. Representative William Dawson, dean of Chicago's black politicians. King worried, however, that a partisan campaign would stigmatize the movement for shortsighted ambition, and he cultivated a series of contacts to radiate broader influence, such as Catholic archbishop John Cody.* Testing teams of middle-class Negroes fanned out to shop for homes in white suburbs, almost invariably to be turned away by real estate agents. King accepted limits from sympathizers who were vulnerable and conflicted in raw local politics. Adlai Stevenson III, son of the

---

* FBI director Hoover sent agents to warn Cody that King was "influenced by communist-oriented thinking," and received assurance that the archbishop found King too "glib." Cody, who had presided over the integration of parochial schools in New Orleans, may have devised this improbable reading of King to placate Hoover. His actions would remain cautious but friendly to the Chicago movement.

late governor and U.N. ambassador, painfully withdrew as host of a private reception in light of Mayor Daley's arbitrary power to strike him from the Democratic slate in an upcoming race for Illinois treasurer. Rev. Clay Evans convened a local chapter of SCLC's job integration program, Operation Breadbasket, as a buffered outlet for black clergy too fearful of retribution to join King at public rallies. Construction of the new sanctuary at Evans's Missionary Baptist Church was halted, its city permits abruptly canceled, and the exposed steel girders would rust over the next seven years. Evans recruited to Breadbasket an irrepressible seminary dropout he had found only the previous year in his charity line for a food basket to feed his young family. On meteoric energy, Jesse Jackson quickly had become assistant pastor at Missionary Baptist, a volunteer driver for King and James Bevel, founder of the Kenwood-Oakland organization near Hyde Park (the newest neighborhood group in the Chicago protest coalition), and finally the local staff director for Operation Breadbasket. By February, *Jet* magazine called the twenty-four-year-old Jackson a fresh "luminary" in the Chicago movement.

Stanley Levison urgently recommended program cutbacks in either Chicago or the South to reduce SCLC's burgeoning debt, but grumbled that King "mopped the floor" with his unwelcome advice at an emergency conference in Atlanta, resolving instead to intensify fund-raising between weekly circuits into Chicago. To entice potential contributors there, the SCLC movement staff carefully scheduled a promotional gala after Mayor Daley's March 10 slate-making summit at the Sherman Hotel, when the machine's ticket for the 1966 elections would be finalized. King stopped in New York on March 11 for a private dinner speech at the home of Israeli financier Meshulem Riklis, whose lawyer, King's adviser Harry Wachtel, expected a "minimum take" of $25,000 for SCLC from guests, including conductor Leonard Bernstein* and violinist Isaac Stern. The next night, Saturday, March 12, Harry Belafonte welcomed a sellout crowd of 12,000 to the Freedom Festival benefit at the Chicago International Amphitheater, where King described Chicago as the giant of migrant black communities stretching from Watts and Blackbottom Detroit to Harlem and Roxbury Boston. Northern

* The FBI wiretap on Levison, who was not invited to the Riklis dinner, later picked up Wachtel's gossipy report that Bernstein promised Coretta a concert solo and diva Maria Callas flirted with King.

ghettos had locked down bodies and hopes "even unto the third and fourth generation," he said, and the sixty thousand chronically unemployed Negroes of Chicago would be called "a staggering depression" in white society. With a voice that conveyed anguished hope like fire from a well-sealed wood stove, he exhorted his audience to "plunge deeper into the philosophy of nonviolence" as they fought to spread the "new democracy" bursting from the South.

"Never before in the history of the civil rights movement," King declared from the Chicago stage, "has an action campaign been launched in such splendor." The event netted $80,000. Stanley Levison called home to pronounce his weekend visit "terribly exciting" in spite of prior misgivings about a Northern campaign: "You could see that this was an audience with spirit, a fighting audience." He said King had to hide from a crush of visitors to his slum apartment. "When they start mass action in the spring," Levison predicted, "that is when everyone will start paying attention."

Mayor Daley trumped King with a volley of bigger numbers. He announced from City Hall that his progress teams had visited 96,761 poor families and exterminated 1,675,941 rats in poor neighborhoods. He set a public goal to eradicate slum conditions for all of Chicago by December 31, 1967, then led seventy thousand marchers down State Street past half a million spectators in the grand Saint Patrick's parade on March 17, and invited King to visit him the next day.

King declined but could not disclose the reason: President Johnson had summoned him on strict pledge of secrecy. Eleven national civil rights leaders agreed not to boast of their appointment on pain of suffering the President's fury. For King, the mantle of Washington remained irresistible—both tempting and essential. Ever since the bus boycott, he had extolled an alliance between national politics and the nonviolent movement, first as a patriotic dream "deeply rooted" in the democratic heritage and finally in the historic consequences from Birmingham to Selma. If the pattern held true, the best hopes for the Chicago movement required validating engagement on the larger stage, with Johnson drawn in—preferably also with Congress and the courts—to clarify principles at stake in the competitive dialogue with Mayor Daley.

Everything and nothing had changed in the nine months since President Johnson had declared a national goal at Howard University to make equal opportunity real by confronting both the cycle of poverty and the legacy of segregation. The next morning, before he could see

President Johnson, King confronted another flare-up in the FBI car theft investigation. A front-page story in the *Atlanta Constitution* alleged that the Justice Department had seized control from the local U.S. attorney in order to keep Hosea Williams out of a freshly announced racketeering indictment. It also revealed the mortifying detail that Daddy King himself had surrendered a stolen car from the SCLC fleet, and quoted a charge by Georgia's lieutenant governor that favoritism for Williams proved the "glaring humbuggery of the Great Society." FBI wiretaps intercepted King's emergency conference call with his advisers on March 18. Andrew Young wanted to decry the leak as blatantly political; others worried about the risk of pushing the administration to close ranks behind Georgia. King broke away from his hotel to the White House Cabinet Room, arriving twenty minutes late. He heard part of Johnson's downbeat preview of legislation—chances were poor of passing protection for civil rights workers, reported Katzenbach, and "particularly difficult" if not impossible on housing discrimination— then raised eyebrows still higher by excusing himself forty-five minutes early. King said he had to catch a plane, which was true, but he first rushed back to his conference call and approved a low-key statement: SCLC had bought cars only from salesmen "we felt to be reputable . . . and we received documents of title." Separately, once a skeletal news release lifted secrecy about the civil rights briefing, King felt free to joke with a *Jet* reporter about Johnson's exacting specifications that he approach the White House by "irregular routes" to a secluded south gate, laughing that he had to sneak in the back door.

*   *   *

DAILY HEADLINES since the renewed bombing of January 31 heated a war climate of enemies and divisions, which submerged the reconciling platform of civil rights. From his White House bedroom, on the afternoon of the first televised Senate hearings about Vietnam, President Johnson ordered Secretary of State Rusk to yank the South Vietnamese allies to a mid-Pacific heads-of-state summit without acknowledging its sudden origin—"I don't want any other human to know this." He roared off two days later for a Honolulu rendezvous modeled on FDR's famous sessions with Stalin and Churchill, which upstaged public examination of the war with bugle-cry coverage of military statesmanship, as Johnson plainly intended. Yet the Senate hearings continued through February. In private, Johnson called them a "very, very disastrous break . . . they pour the stuff out of the filth on television." He howled against public exposure on both political flanks, from Chairman Fulbright's professorial doubt about the whole war to ferocious cries for a military showdown throughout Asia. Johnson referred to the latter danger in shorthand as [Mississippi Senator John] "Stennis bombing China." He wondered plaintively at a congressional reception why "Americans who dissent can't do their dissenting in private."

Parallel conflict tore at television executives by the half-hour. The competing networks sacrificed revenue programs for much of February 8 to broadcast the Senate testimony of Lieutenant General James Gavin, a Korean War hero and Vietnam critic, along with President Johnson's return from Honolulu. NBC broadcast the complete Fulbright hearings two days later, but CBS stuck with the scheduled morning reruns of *I Love Lucy* at ten o'clock, followed by *The Real McCoys* and *The Andy Griffith Show*. Leaders of the CBS News Division, humiliated by NBC's contrasting choice, pleaded with superiors to switch to the dramatic Senate testimony by Ambassador George Kennan, widely considered the father of Cold War "containment" policy. Kennan was admitting that Vietnam would unite swiftly under Communism without full-scale American military intervention, and that any such consolidation "would be exploited mercilessly by the Chinese and North Vietnamese . . . in world opinion, as a means of humiliating us." Even so, he presented that sad prospect as a lesser evil than the war being launched, but no one saw Kennan's argument on CBS. Network president Frank Stanton, in communication with the White House, held firm for the daytime comedies and on February 15 forced the resignation of his protesting chief of CBS News, Fred Friendly. The departure itself generated controversy because of Friendly's reputation as a champion of journalistic duty to foster debate on great public issues. In 1954, he had produced a watershed CBS broadcast by Edward R. Murrow that helped puncture the intimidating spell of Senator Joe McCarthy. Now Friendly's own downfall marked resurgent conflict over loyalty and dissent in a war crisis.

President Johnson ventured a confidential call to *Time* founder Henry R. Luce for media support across partisan lines. Luce, born in 1898 to missionary parents at Tengchow, China, was a lifelong Republican and fierce opponent of the New Deal. He had conceived the "American Century" slogan that his magazine empire popularized into common usage for the era, and while Luce doubted that any Democrat could be a worthy steward of its leadership mission, especially in Asia, he gave Johnson a gruff blessing for the war measures thus far. "I got no bellyache," said Luce. He expressed sympathy for Johnson's tale of command woes to the point of sharing at length a theory from childhood experience that racial prejudice worked against the call to military sacrifice across the Pacific. Luce said Americans considered Asia "a bunch of yellow men and Chinamen and God knows who, who are not any part of our Western civilization. Do you follow me?" He postulated that a contempt for Oriental people lay "psychologically at the bottom" of Johnson's troubles, driving an unspoken but pervasive reluctance to send "men and treasure" to Vietnam. Luce sensed it deep within Fulbright and other members of Congress. "I don't think they know they feel it," he told Johnson.

The President endorsed Luce's rare view of missionary brotherhood as the test of just war and even a crusade for civil rights. "I don't see the difference," he said, "between doing it for a white man in Europe or a brown man in Asia."

"You made a very good point, and I think it cuts straight," Luce replied, as though Johnson had originated the idea. "I think that's the psychological trigger." Luce called Johnson shortly afterward to commend a special section in the forthcoming *Life* magazine as a rejoinder to the Fulbright hearings. The lead editorial, "Vietnam: The War Is Worth Winning," presumed that the outcome would turn on whether Americans bothered to apply themselves, and Luce forewarned Johnson about one line of friendly criticism: "It is deplorable that such a courageous and far-sighted policy should be so badly explained." What he wanted was more grand vision and less harping about the need to prevent catastrophe, he said, in line with his war advice to "really go at it instead of fiddling around." The President grasped Luce as bosom adviser, asking how then he could send the next 50,000 or 100,000 troops without a crippling national debate. "What does a man do that doesn't want to be a dictator," he pressed intensely, "that just wants to do what's right?" Luce sidestepped the political question, saying he would no more instruct the master of consensus than "tell my late grandmother to suck eggs."

Senator Robert Kennedy stepped briefly into the politics, alarmed by the gulf between architects and critics of the war whom he had observed intermittently from the back of Fulbright's hearing room. At the last of the televised sessions, Secretary Rusk insisted that Vietnam was a proxy contest to ward off global conquest by the major Communist powers—"If we don't make clear where we stand, then the prospect for peace disappears"—and Kennedy called a press conference for the next morning, February 19. To stimulate meaning for the vaguely defined alternative of "negotiations," he suggested that neither side could expect surrender and that the United States should entertain talks with South Vietnamese Communists toward granting them "a share of power and responsibility." Kennedy went skiing that afternoon, reportedly expecting little reaction to such a tentative idea, but lightning struck. "The uproar was general," wrote Arthur Schlesinger. *Newsweek* said he "jolted the Administration like a Claymore mine." Kennedy's friends George Ball and McGeorge Bundy went on national television to denounce his idea as naive, quoting Kennedy's late brother the President against him on the folly of trusting Communists. The *New York Daily News* and the *Chicago Tribune* called him "Ho Chi Kennedy." Vice President Humphrey spouted quotable metaphors to ridicule a coalition with the Vietcong variously as arsenic in the medicine chest, an arsonist in the fire department, and, most famously, "letting the fox into the chicken coop." Kennedy swiftly qualified his statement by declaring firm opposition to Communist takeover in South Vietnam.

On February 23, he and President Johnson maintained the awkward truce of professionals. They flew together in the presidential cabin to New York and shared a limousine with Chief Justice Earl Warren to the Waldorf-Astoria, where some five thousand antiwar pickets protested Johnson's receipt of the Freedom House Award. On the hotel sidewalk, pacifist A. J. Muste presented a "people's" freedom award in absentia to Julian Bond of Georgia, who was rerunning that day for his vacated House seat. In the Grand Ballroom, Freedom Rider James Peck leapt to his feet among the black-tie guests just as Johnson began his acceptance speech, shouting, "Peace in Vietnam! Peace in Vietnam!" only twice before a hand clapped over his mouth and agents dragged him off to serve sixty days.

Kennedy's friends rallied comfort in a siege. "The reason it is going to cause you such public pain," Burke Marshall wrote of the Vietcong statement, "is that it has substance in it." A political strategist advised him to keep future comments about Vietnam "on a high, solid level . . . with a little more patriotic rhetoric," thereby to regain an independent stance between the nagging impotence of the Fulbright camp and the "emotional and psychological box" of Kennedy's friend McNamara, who had been urging him to visit the troops. The senator avoided provocative Vietnam statements for the next year, brooding, and sought out instead the most daunting leadership issues outside the military arena. He gave a series of speeches on poverty. He arranged to visit South Africa, having consulted Robert Spike, leader of the church council on civil rights, about the delicate liaison with banned democratic activists inside the bastion of apartheid. He accepted invitations from two states where he said people "hate my guts," which touched off death threats and a parallel flurry of secret memos inside the Justice Department over Hoover's adamant refusal to provide FBI protection or even observers.

On March 18, while King navigated irregular routes to and from the White House, Kennedy spoke first to public controversy about his day-trip across Alabama and Mississippi. "Somebody down here suggested it was like putting a fox in the chicken house," he quipped at the new Ole Miss Rebel Dome. "And some of my friends said it was like putting a chicken in a fox house." His self-deprecating humor disarmed the crowd of 8,500 for a straightforward speech about patriotic renewal he called barely begun. The Ole Miss student body counted thirteen Negroes in the fourth year since the lurching mess of stagecraft to enroll James Meredith. "We must create a society in which Negroes will be as free as other Americans," said Kennedy. "Free to vote and to earn their way, and to share in the decisions which affect their lives." He quoted Emerson that every citizen must choose either truth or repose. The students gave him three standing ovations, partly for pluck alone.

*   *   *

KENTUCKY DEFEATED Duke that night in the Final Four of the NCAA college basketball tournament, 83–79. The March 19 championship game was all but conceded to powerhouse Kentucky before the shocking cultural upset by a little-known team from El Paso. Coach Don Haskins received forty thousand hostile letters afterward. His own university president had implored him all season to observe common etiquette and play no more than three black players at a time. Years later, basketball historian Frank Fitzpatrick reviewed films of the timepiece black-and-white broadcast, which preserved an awed hush when Haskins actually sent out five black starters to contest the five white Kentucky Wildcats, with scattered Confederate flags and few discernible dark faces at the new Cole Field House in Maryland. The workmanlike 72–65 victory by Texas Western turned pitiful mismatch into churning reappraisal. Kentucky coach Adolph Rupp privately complained of in-

cessant calls from his university president. "That son of a bitch wants me
to get some niggers in here," he said. "What am I gonna do?"

Rupp, the legendary "Baron of the Bluegrass," was strong enough to
resist. The Kentucky legislature had flown the capitol flag at half mast
to mourn his loss to integrated City College of New York in 1950, when
even the professional NBA was still segregated, and his last team would
be all white when he retired in 1972 with the most career wins of any
college coach. However, Vanderbilt offered Perry Wallace a scholarship
two months after "the game that changed American sports," breaking
the Southeastern Conference color line. By 1968, when Auburn made
Henry Harris a second breakthrough for basketball, black students held
a paltry eleven of 2,236 SEC scholarships in all sports combined. Every
pioneer suffered ostracism and stress. (Harris jumped to his death from
a building.) Only inexorable transformation over decades led to a more
comfortable era when Kentucky would win the 1998 national basketball championship with a black coach, let alone black players. Intervening tragedy and embarrassment were dampened in public memory. Ole
Miss simply abolished its track team for the 1970s rather than surrender
or defend segregation in a nakedly quantifiable sport. The NCAA rules
committee banished the flamboyant, intimidating "dunk" shot from all
college basketball games (including warm-up drills) for eight years between 1968 and 1976, which somehow cushioned the influx of black
players.

* * *

PRESIDENT JOHNSON's frustration seeped into a national mood made
irascible by Vietnam. Questioning his lifelong gift as a judge of character, he sent Bill Moyers to verify by soul-searching conversation that
Senator Fulbright remained both privately and publicly against military withdrawal. "He admitted to no solutions and accepted the thesis
that we cannot pull out," reported Moyers, who concluded that Fulbright was "basically defeatist in nature toward any Western White involvement in Asia . . . irretrievably committed to doubts which put him
beyond the pale of reasoning." Fulbright's dissent rubbed a blister in
Johnson. How could the senator conceal his fundamental agreement
that the "loss" of South Vietnam must be avoided? Like every elected
national leader, Fulbright skirted the risk by implying vaguely that
Vietnam negotiations could avoid disaster—knowing better, in
Johnson's view—and aimed all his skeptical realism at the war policy instead. The Senate inquiry amounted to a public flogging, the President

seethed, because Fulbright knew that administration witnesses could not acknowledge ambivalence once troops were committed.

The dissenters unhinged Johnson. To him, they undermined the tenuous hopes for military success without offering an honest alternative, which made them disloyal, impractical, and unprincipled all at once. The President railed against conduct so alien to his code of politics that he explored like a palm reader for eccentric motivations. On Fulbright alone, he ordered a compilation of every personal contact during his presidency—which ran four full pages, broken down into luncheons, meetings, receptions, and so on—to study whether some overlooked social slight might have provoked a peevish tantrum on Vietnam. He accused Senator Mansfield of poisoning Fulbright "because of your goddam trip," recalling that Mansfield once pulled rank on Fulbright's plans to borrow a coveted presidential jet for a flight to Europe. On March 2, the day Fulbright voted with only four senators to repeal the Gulf of Tonkin Resolution, losing 92–5, Johnson said he heard from one mutual friend that Fulbright was "going through a menopause" and from another that he was "off his rocker because of Mrs. Fulbright being sick." That night, Vice President Humphrey whispered to Johnson that Fulbright had accosted him "with this look in his eyes that was most unusual" and demanded that Humphrey find a way out of Vietnam, saying, "That's what we pay you for . . . I'm not joking. . . . This is the goddamdest war. Just get busy and settle it."

"I just looked at him," Humphrey reported. "I said, 'Bill, you—what's *wrong* with you?' He really was quite angry! I just sort of think . . . he talks about it and thinks about it so much that he's lost his sense of judgment, Mr. President."

In April, Fulbright began to warn in lectures that the United States "was succumbing to the arrogance of power." He said the U.S. military presence was turning Saigon into "an American brothel." President Johnson retorted publicly that power in Vietnam brought "not arrogance but agony."

In May, he would decry "nervous Nellies" who quaked from the fight, and mock Fulbright in person before a dinner audience of fellow Democrats. White House aide Harry McPherson dared to scold his boss in a memo the next morning for unbecoming sarcasm "trying to beat down Fulbright's ears." Buried in the senator's "sophomoric bitching," he added, were questions that "cannot be shouted out of existence." The

President tolerated the rare staff rebuke and punished McPherson merely with weeks of sulking disregard.

He obsessed into knots over Robert Kennedy, egged on by a press theme of Shakespearean enmity between rival usurpers for the White House. "Bobby is behind this revolt up there on Vietnam," Johnson complained to Katzenbach, coaching him to intercede for a truce. The President recited his own record of loyalty to Kennedy from disasters like the Bay of Pigs—"I didn't run or shimmy or bellyache or cry"—down through a list of presidential appointments and pardons and favors for the whole family—"I've done every damn thing they asked"—and perceived a gratuitous plague of "Kennedy infiltration" as his sour, Job-like reward. To Deke DeLoach, Johnson listed senators who attended Russian cocktail parties, plus Joe Alsop and other Kennedy friends, among dissenters he fearfully pressed the FBI to sift for subversive "sons-of-bitches boring from within." To Dean Rusk, he whispered runaway suspicions that Kennedy's influence was driving the strongest holdovers within the administration into pessimism at the verge of heresy—most critically, Robert McNamara. "When he [McNamara] said the other day that we only have one chance out of three of winning, it just shocked me," Johnson lamented, "and furthermore it shocked everybody at the table."

* * *

BATTLEFIELD NEWS hardened politics. An April edition of the *New York Times* reported 1,361 American soldiers killed over the first ninety-nine days of 1966, matching the cumulative toll over the five previous years. Six died in a three-minute ambush on the second or third mission to retake the Bong Son area, during which 1st AirCav medic Hank Thomas discovered his own arm shaking because a bullet had splintered open the hand bones. "Oh shit, I'm going home," he said, and soon returned for six months of surgical reconstruction at Army hospitals, observing a nation bizarrely changed. Concentrated hostility he had endured as a Freedom Rider seemed to spill from civil rights into the broader culture. In a Mississippi cemetery, standing red-faced with a posse of flashlights over the exhumed remains of a humble farmer, Sheriff Earl Fisher of Washington County blamed itinerant Klansmen for the rampant false belief that Negroes had stockpiled a fiendish arsenal in their coffins. On a sidewalk in Bogalusa, Lousiana, enraged by the look of another presumed civil rights outsider, three white women pummeled an Italian violinist touring with the San Pietro Chamber Orchestra of Naples. Nationally, "The Ballad of the Green Berets" by Staff Sergeant Barry Sadler overtook Simon & Garfunkel's "The Sounds of Silence" as the number one song played on the airwaves, and Sadler's album of death-defying war choruses displaced the Beatles' *Rubber Soul* atop sales charts for thirteen weeks. (The latter recording suffered sporadic radio boycotts and bonfire incineration over comments by John Lennon that his band was more popular "right now" than the namesake of Christianity. "Jesus was all right," Lennon remarked in a London newspaper interview published on March 4, "but his disciples were thick and ordinary.")

Rancorous trends surfaced elsewhere in the arts. *The Sound of Music* maintained box office supremacy for an astonishing seven months through the end of 1965—Martin Luther King's favorite film, reported his traveling aide Bernard Lee, the one he ducked away to see again on harried speech trips. By April 18, 1966, when the film won Best Picture at the first Academy Awards ceremony ever broadcast in color, Best Director Robert Wise noted a strong undercurrent against his theme of romantic escape from ugly war, and wryly invited critics to "see my new film, *The Sand Pebbles,* where people get sliced to pieces with bayonets." By 1967, signature characters in cinema shifted from the Trapp family singers to the Depression-era gangsters Bonnie and Clyde, as boldly promoted in studio ads: "They're young, they're in love, and they kill people." *Newsweek*'s movie reviewer Joseph Morgenstern soon retracted his scruples about the spellbinding gore of its slow-motion shoot-out scenes.

Book critics wrangled over the January 1966 publication of *In Cold Blood,* which the *New York Times* praised as a "remarkable, tensely exciting, moving, superbly written 'true account'—the undeserved, unforeseen, hideous slaughter of an ideal American family," while doubting author Truman Capote's boast to have invented the "nonfiction novel." A British writer called the book immoral for its exploitive sympathy with the real-life killers all the way to the bottom of their drop from the Kansas gallows. For Capote, controversy accented a year of transcendent fame he parlayed into a Thanksgiving "Party of the Century" at New York's Plaza Hotel, featuring an eclectic guest list of masked celebrities who attracted more press coverage than a White House state dinner. Before that, far below on the scale of literary events, James Meredith advertised his spring memoir of integration, *Three Years in Mississippi,* with pithy attacks on the civil rights movement.

"Nonviolence has no meaning," he told reporters in April. "This is a rough, tough country and always has been. . . . I admire Dr. King as an individual, but his philosophy just doesn't square with the American way of life. He's never been in the military. He's a professional preacher."

CHAPTER 28

Panther Ladies

April–June 1966

TREMORS from the larger world shook the laboratories of new democracy in Alabama. On Sunday afternoon, March 27, five hundred Lowndes County citizens and nearly a hundred SNCC workers gathered "far out in the rurals" to mark a year's passage since the first stir against terror, with schoolteacher Sarah Logan presiding. She called for the invocation by Rev. R. U. Harrison, whose son had been chased from his pulpit and the county for daring even to mention the vote. She brought on John Hulett to review their birth pains after his caravan flight from the Klan, beginning with the first attempt to register the next day, when Martin Luther King himself had appeared at the courthouse, and the first political meeting in the back of Haralson's store at night before any church would open to them, when twenty-eight people had dared to form the Lowndes County Christian Movement for Human Rights with the strangely miraculous encouragement of white preachers visiting from a pilgrimage trapped behind the "Berlin Wall" in nearby Selma.

"We had to stand for hours in the sun, rain, and the cold" for months after the great march to Montgomery, said Hulett, describing the quest to register. "We had only one attempt to demonstrate. It ended in a tragedy with our losing Jonathan Myrick Daniels of Keene, New Hampshire. We tried to get our people out of jail, but we did not have the money." After Hulett, and movement songs by youth leaders Timothy Mays and Clara Maul, Logan introduced a small woman billed as the "mother of the civil rights movement" on hand-lettered programs for a "first anniversary" service entitled "No More Chains and Sorrow." Rosa Parks, having braved the trip from her Detroit home to the backwoods church in Lowndes, praised a political awakening among the most oppressed people of her former state.

Loudspeakers transmitted her words to an overflow crowd outside, where anxious sentries eyeing distant surveillance cars also waited to serve hot food from the back of a station wagon. After Parks came young Julian Bond of Atlanta as living proof that they could aspire not only to vote for the first time but also to be elected. Bond quoted poet Sterling Brown on the passing of the hangman's era and Frederick Douglass on the need for constant agitation—as in his case pending before the Supreme Court. "I'm not sure of the future," said Bond, "but the people in Lowndes County realize that the way we've done things in the past has been a mistake." Stokely Carmichael followed with a fiery reprise on his year among them. Declaring the recent repeal of the "White Supremacy" slogan nothing more than a cosmetic change for the Alabama Democratic Party, he strongly urged that new Lowndes voters use the May 3 primary day to select their own slate for local offices. No one yet volunteered to be the first Negro candidate, but many of the crowd returned on Saturday, April 2, to take preliminary steps. They voted to create an "independent structure" called the Lowndes County Freedom Organization, adopting bylaws, a symbol, and other formalities required to begin a county-wide political party under Title 17, Section 337 of the Alabama Code. They elected six officers, including financial secretary Ruthie Mae Jones and vice chairman R. S. Strickland. "Once you get power," said chairman Hulett, "you don't have to beg."

Alabama native John Lewis had been agitating separately toward the black vote—for South Africans—and was arrested with colleagues James Forman, Bill Hall, Cleveland Sellers, and Willie Ricks in South Africa's imposing consulate on Madison Avenue. Their vanguard sit-in remained obscure, being some twenty years before mass demonstrations stirred popular hope for imprisoned Nelson Mandela against apartheid itself, but Harry Belafonte paid bail for the five SNCC pioneers only days before he toured Europe. French actors Yves Montand and Simone Signoret hosted Belafonte and Martin Luther King on March 28 at a sold-out festival of music and speech in Paris. Swedish scholar Gunnar Myrdal, author of the authoritative 1940s study on race, *An American Dilemma,* presented them in Stockholm to King Gustav VI, who welcomed their joint program at the Royal Opera House as a national honor. Tickets for March 31 had vanished within a half-hour in February, and they agreed to a repeat performance on April 3. An ad hoc network relayed television broadcasts throughout Northern Europe, including Finland. The post office of Sweden established a unified mailing address for SCLC. The Bank of Sweden publicized an ongoing special account for civil rights contributions, and transferred initial proceeds of at least $100,000.

Spectacular success in Europe muffled tensions across the Atlantic Ocean all the way back into Alabama. King's original church sponsors in Paris had canceled less than two weeks before the engagement under a cloud of government displeasure, and a last-minute appeal had yielded the emergency rescue led by artists. Actors Peter O'Toole of England and Melina Mercouri of Greece joined the French stars to commandeer a substitute venue ten times larger. Secretary of State Rusk ordered Ambassador Charles "Chip" Bohlen not to attend the reconstituted King-Belafonte event in Paris, and, as a precaution against Vietnam controversy, Ambassador Graham Parsons canceled plans to greet King at the airport in Stockholm. A soothing report from the U.S. embassy later found that the high-profile visit "did not create any difficulties for the American image here," because King was "quite explicit" to say he opposed Vietnam as a matter of individual conscience rather than as a political priority for the civil rights movement. His conflicted restraint satisfied nervous sponsors of the Swedish gala, diplomats added, at the cost of press criticism that "King wears a muzzle" on the war in Vietnam.

* * *

KING RETURNED home April 10 buoyed by the dramatic rally of support overseas and determined to break through hesitancy that had been eating at him since the debates at SCLC's convention in August. He pressed his SCLC executive board to take an official stance on Vietnam at the semiannual meeting in Miami, and announced the favorable result there on April 13. "It is imperative to end a war that has played havoc with our domestic destinies," King told reporters. The approved resolution committed SCLC on nonviolent principle. "If we are true to our own ideals," it stated, "we have no choice but to abandon the military junta under such manifestly vigorous popular opposition. We believe the moment is now opportune, and the need urgent, to reassess our position and seriously examine the wisdom of prompt withdrawal."

The words "abandon" and "withdrawal" vaulted past Robert Kennedy's explosive call for negotiations, and landed King on the front pages without quite the voltage of a potential contender for the White House. The initial *New York Times* story noted that Vietnam dissent had nearly bankrupted SNCC, and cited a national poll in which 41 percent of Americans said dissent from that quarter made them feel "less in favor of civil rights for Negroes." Several of King's allies dismissed him archly to the *Times* for making "the greatest of mistakes to mix domestic civil rights and foreign policy."

FBI wiretaps picked up Stanley Levison's pragmatic assessment of infighting between and within civil rights groups. He observed that King's peers were delighted to see him "sticking his neck out" on Vietnam. "Roy [Wilkins] and Whitney [Young] have snuggled up to Johnson," he told Clarence Jones. "Martin is now in a different relationship to the White House than he used to be. They are on the inside, and I think they love it." To Levison, this much was normal politics. He aimed for a long-range view of movement progress, and indeed wanted King to compliment the FBI for arresting thirteen Mississippi Klansmen recently to break open the Vernon Dahmer firebomb murder case. ("J. Edgar Hoover may dislike Martin intensely," Levison said on the tapped line, "but his men are now doing the job in the field.") What disturbed Levison was an internal breach with Bayard Rustin, who was "sore" at King for pushing the Vietnam resolution. The friction exceeded prior jockeying among advisers who shared bruises and miracles alike from service close to King. Rustin had grounded his idealism and tactical genius in nonviolence for more than thirty years, choosing prison over service in World War II, and it seemed inexplicable that he of all people would change his compass during an epochal surge of vindication and promise. Levison thought Rustin accommodated the war to protect his new stature in mainstream politics. Rustin said mature democracy demanded compromise at home and abroad.

King primed a new movement campaign while laboring to harvest practical results from the one just behind. Several trips after a perfunctory introduction to Mayor Daley, he left Chicago again on April 28 for what turned out to be his final meeting at the White House—a pep talk from President Johnson on the formal civil rights message to Congress, which received there a tepid response—then scurried south to give four speeches late into the same night on a get-out-the-vote push for the May 3 Alabama primary. From Montgomery at breakneck speed, he covered

825 miles to give nine speeches in scattered rural churches on Friday, April 29. At the second stop, in Wilcox County, 1,500 newly registered voters waited under a scorching sun outside Antioch Baptist Church, where movement supporter David Colson had been shot dead in January. "If they aren't afraid to come to hear Dr. King," SCLC organizer Dan Harrell told reporters, "they won't be afraid to vote." An afternoon rainstorm caught King far behind schedule as always, trotting across a field toward a Marengo County church between his two oldest children, Yolanda and Marty, flanked by Fred Shuttlesworth and Hosea Williams.

Opposing forces scrambled to master a new electorate. No fewer than nine white men ran for governor against George Wallace's "stand-in" wife, Lurleen, with black registration already doubled to 240,000 under the Voting Rights Act. Attorney General Richmond Flowers, publicly recognized as "the first major white candidate in modern times to campaign directly among the Negro people in a Deep South state," pledged to haul down the Confederate Battle Flag as a symbol of defiance rather than progress. SCLC ran workshops on rudimentary politics for the first fifty-four Negroes to qualify as candidates in a Democratic primary. A movement journal published a signal photograph of one kissing a baby. A grizzled out-of-state incumbent advised them to expect no quarter and accept only cash contributions. Church women taught new voters how to mark ballots. Newspapers erratically scolded Negroes as foolish rookies when two of them ran for the same office, as craven supplicants when a Tuskegee group endorsed the white sheriff over a Negro, and as sinister robots when reporters detected a potential "Negro voting bloc."

Hosea Williams had assumed the role of slate-maker. "We must let the Negro vote hang there like a ripe fruit," he told one crowd, his arms raised to mime the caress of a vineyard inspector, "and whoever is willing to give the Negro the most freedom can pluck it." As King's deputy for Alabama, he asserted primacy over traditional Negro leaders in deciding whether to broker deals with white moderates or push selected Negro candidates. "We've got the Black Belt sewed up," he said, declaring unabashedly that whoever registered voters should control them. Editors at *The Southern Courier,* a small newspaper formed by Freedom Summer volunteers, chided his overbearing ways in an editorial: "Have a Seat, Hosea . . . but give him a hand as he goes, folks." They reminded readers that each voter was "the anvil" of democratic trust and responsibility. "Remember that the choice in the end is yours," they wrote, "and you do not have to vote the way you have said you were going to vote. No one can control your vote if you make up your own mind." King echoed their advice with pleas above all for a large turnout. He avoided Lowndes County, and did not join the vituperation by Williams and others against its resolve to work outside the Democratic primary.

Sadly, the *New York Times* out-bossed even Hosea Williams. Fixed upon the "exciting, precedent-breaking" opportunity to defeat "old-line segregationists" behind Lurleen Wallace, the paper called late in April for Negroes to "fuse their strength with liberal white voters" in the Democratic primary race for governor, and aimed a laser of rebuke at Negroes who adopted a different political strategy. A lead editorial branded the Lowndes County plan to run an independent slate of local candidates a pointless "boycott," as though the sharecroppers and canvassers risking their lives to vote for the first time, under conditions scarcely imaginable in New York, were madly possessed to throw away the ballot itself. The article, "Sabotage in Alabama," perceived in SNCC workers only "destructive mischief-making . . . a rule-or-ruin attitude . . . extremism for the sake of extremism . . . a revolutionary posture toward all of society and Government." The editors might well have paid tribute to a year of miraculous new citizenship in the county that killed Viola Liuzzo and Jonathan Daniels. Instead, America's best newspaper—long a voice of authority sympathetic to civil rights—recognized no competing priorities or capacity for basic self-government. To portray the Lowndes County movement as frivolous vandals against the right to vote, the *Times* blotted out yearnings and exertions toward freedom seldom matched since Valley Forge. Such dismissal helped provoke black power conflict and rebellion soon to grip the whole country.

* * *

THE MAY 3 primary races showcased colorful politics at the historic divide. Lurleen Wallace, Alabama's first female candidate for governor, sought to become only the third woman to hold that office in the United States. Her husband, George, pledged daily to "tote the wood and draw the water at the governor's mansion," quoting Governor Edward "Pa" Ferguson's successful 1924 campaign for Miriam "Ma" Ferguson in Texas. Wallace had picked up Ferguson yarns from President Johnson at a governors' briefing on Vietnam. He now omitted the word "segregation" from stump speeches, reporters noted, but pointedly renounced an agreement to integrate mental hospitals. Wallace said Washington's "dictatorial" conditions for federal support insulted all Alabama, and so did Richard Nixon's barb that the state was running "a dime-store girl for governor." (The former Vice President demeaned the candidate's only former employment in the hope that a Wallace family failure would forestall a third-party presidential bid for 1968, which third-party failure would help Republicans retain the Deep South Goldwater states.) Other public voices complained that federal "occupation" under the Voting Rights Act treated Alabama like "some kind of banana republic." Attorney General Katzenbach did his best to hide civil servants being trained to safeguard new Negro voters at the polls—"I am attempting to do the least that I can safely do without upsetting the civil rights groups," he assured President Johnson—and he quietly concentrated observers in Selma for the high-visibility showdown between challenger Wilson Baker and incumbent Sheriff Jim Clark.

John Doar diverted Justice Department lawyer Charles Nesson into last-minute negotiations over the Lowndes County nominating convention. "If we do not hear from you, or if the US Government does not find itself able to protect the participants," Stokely Carmichael petitioned Doar, "we shall be forced to look to such resources as we can muster on our own." On April 26, Sheriff Frank Ryals had forbidden access to the Hayneville courthouse, but Carmichael, citing Alabama law that founders of a local party must convene "in or around a public polling place on the day of the primary," pressed a right to use the county's only qualifying site. Ryals bluntly informed Nesson that it would be more than dangerous enough in Lowndes County for the first ordinary black voters, and any convention of Negroes on the courthouse lawn would become a "turkey shoot." John Hulett insisted they had no choice. Rattled, Nesson dashed between Selma and Montgomery for ideas to avert a disaster.

The freedom organization meanwhile continued nightly mass meetings, and SNCC research director Jack Minnis finished local workshops on practical government. He used illustrated booklets to explore simple questions—"How does voting work?" "What is politics?"—plus primers and statute books for leadership seminars. New rivals for a "freedom nomination" addressed the packed candidates' forum at Mr. Moriah Church. "Vote for me and I'll stand up for fair treatment," declared Jesse "Note" Favors, whose opponent, Sidney Logan, vowed to wipe out the ingrained fear of the sheriff's uniform. The children of bricklayer John Hinson, who was running for a seat on the board of education, handed out paper cutouts of a schoolhouse marked "Vote for Hinson." Some speakers wrestled regrets about missing their first vote for governor to nominate local candidates instead. Others jumped up to testify when Hulett relayed official warnings that a party convention meant suicide. "We been walkin' with dropped down heads, a scrunched up heart, and a timid body in the bushes, but we ain't scared anymore!" cried an old farmer who urged the crowd not to meddle or pick a fight, but to stand. "If you have to die, die for something," he said, "and take somebody before you."

Nesson returned on Sunday, May 1 with a proposal to relocate from the courthouse to a black church near Hayneville, where the convention, though still unguarded, would be less inflammatory to white voters on primary day. An emergency movement caucus rejected his verbal assurance that the change would be legal. Any judge who disagreed could strike their slate from the November ballot, Hulett replied, and his people would take their chances at the courthouse unless Alabama authorities specified in writing that the church met the statutory requirement to be "in or around a public polling place." The renewed standoff obliged Nesson and cohorts to chase down Attorney General Richmond Flowers in the final sprint of his own campaign. To sign the proposed legal finding would encourage withdrawal from the Democratic primary, which would cost him votes for governor, and any accommodation to Negroes would further alienate white voters. On the other hand, Flowers knew from the Liuzzo and Daniels trials that he may not have a single white supporter in Lowndes County anyway, and his own fearful experience had kindled nagging admiration for the besieged movement. Flowers signed, and Nesson rushed the legal opinion back for posting at the Hayneville courthouse by three o'clock on Monday afternoon, May 2. Joyful news for Hulett reverted instantly to pressure. Less than a day remained to spread notice of the site switch across seven hundred square miles of plantations with few cars and virtually no telephones.

* * *

ON THE climactic primary morning, John Doar supervised five hundred federal observers in Dallas County. From Selma, where lines stretched back from the courthouse to Brown Chapel before the polls opened, he drove eighteen miles to find the tiny hamlet of Orville flooded with rural Negroes waiting to cast their first votes. The turnout jumped above 17,000, nearly triple the county norm, and voters across the state surmounted hardships in combustible crowds. Parents carried "Stand Up for Alabama" pamphlets that Governor Wallace had distributed through the students at every white school. An election official blamed the Negroes for delays, charging that one confused voter lingered in a booth for twenty-eight minutes. Negroes in Wilcox County complained that false information about a polling place ended only when voting equipment was spotted at Harvey's Fish Camp, a bait shop decidedly unfriendly to them, but local women soon passed out fried chicken to boost morale along the line. In Birmingham, an old man who fainted in the hot sun refused an ambulance until he could "pull that lever" on what might be his last chance, and others waiting late into the night built fires to keep warm. A woman with a "Vote Wallace" sign stood hours behind a man wearing a "Grow with Flowers" button.

Nerves started tight at First Baptist Church in Hayneville, half a mile from the courthouse. A farmer fidgeted with three shotgun shells in his overalls. FBI agents took photographs, and reporters interviewed SNCC leaders from Atlanta and Mississippi. At three o'clock, having received final instructions, supporters of the Lowndes County Freedom Organization spilled outside the church into a roped-off area where movement clerks verified names against the county's list of registered voters with poll taxes paid to date. "We wanted to make it all legal," Carmichael announced. Those approved filed past seven stations to vote separately for each local office. For voters who wanted to match names with faces, the competing candidates themselves smiled from designated spots nearby. Voices on a bullhorn kept repeating the most important legal notice: no one should vote who intended to participate also in the Democratic primary, as overlaps could invalidate the entire freedom ticket. Groans answered reports that more than a hundred Negroes were voting at the courthouse. Volunteers collected the completed ballots—each one headed with the official black panther emblem and creed, "One Man, One Vote"—and placed them into cardboard boxes on the seven wooden tables. Worry turned slowly to relief among voters milling in the churchyard to await the count, mostly sharecropper men in Sunday hats and women in earrings and print dresses. Scattered SNCC workers sang freedom songs. "We're making history, that's right," an old woman repeated to herself. Jumping to the church steps, Willie Ricks praised the "bad niggers" of Lowndes County in a comically triumphant speech before Hulett called everyone back inside to announce the nominees. John Hinson defeated Mrs. Virginia White for the school board 511–327. Mrs. Alice Moore received 852 votes running unopposed for tax assessor ("Tax the rich to feed the poor, that's my slogan"). Sidney Logan, having defeated Note Favors 492–381, accepted the nomination with brief remarks that he had wanted to run for sheriff since Deputy Lux Jackson and his gun had shooed them away from their first attempt to register.

A bigger story obliterated the Lowndes County initiative before the polls closed. "It's a Lurleen Landslide!" declared an early edition of the *Montgomery Advertiser* dotted with cutlines of shock: "Exuberant Wallace . . . Ecstatic . . . Smiles, Hugs . . . No Runoff." From the Jefferson Davis ballroom, Governor Wallace hailed a mandate "to return constitutional government to this country." By contrast, Martin Luther King glumly observed from Birmingham's Thomas Jefferson Hotel that "white Alabamians are desperately grasping for a way to return to the old days of white supremacy." The editor of the *Advertiser* expressed amazement that *"literally,* most all white Alabamians voted for [Lurleen] Wallace." Her vote far exceeded that of the nine male contenders combined, and nearly tripled that of second-place Richmond Flowers. With his heavy black support, the Attorney General had calculated that he could become governor with only 21 percent of the white vote, but so crushing was his loss that the *New York Times* said "it may be many years . . . before any serious Alabama politician will risk a close political identification with the Negro." Stung by the results, *Times* editors wisely took solace in the huge biracial turnout: "The fact of overwhelming importance about Alabama's primary was its peacefulness."

Only a student newspaper and one small socialist journal reported a tiny gush of black optimism for November's general election. "We're going to take power in Lowndes County and rule," an ebullient Stokely Carmichael predicted on primary night. "We don't even want to integrate. . . . Integration is a subterfuge for white supremacy." Farmers in tent cities were pulling off a miracle of civic organization to put their candidates on the ballot, argued Courtland Cox, and the *Times* "has a hell of a lot of nerve" to excoriate them for sacrificing a handful of anti-Wallace votes in the Democratic primary. "It's not our job to get Wallace out of the party," added Carmichael. "Did they ask the Jews to reform the Nazi Party?" He said the four-to-one black majority in Lowndes opened a new political phase of the movement. "Nonviolence is irrelevant," he declared. "What King has working for him is a moral force, but we're building a force to take power. We're not a protest movement."

Alabama's primary day raised three distinct waves of euphoria. The broad civil rights coalition celebrated one cliffhanger victory only after Justice Department lawyers beat back weeks of courthouse attempts to steal, impound, and disqualify ballot boxes from six minority precincts in the Dallas County sheriff's race. To John Doar, the final, supervised count was the culmination of a career struggle in public service to establish voting rights and law in mutual support above the long, hard disillusionment of race—in this case by securing for Wilson Baker his fair margin of victory over the virulent segregationist Jim Clark. Separately, on the center stage of Alabama politics, Governor Wallace asserted his full hegemony by summoning both U.S. senators and all eight representatives to stand mute while he read a proclamation pledged to defy freedom-of-choice desegregation guidelines for the 1966–67 school year as a "totalitarian" blueprint "devised by socialists" in Washington, "which has as its objectives the capture and regimentation of our children and the destruction of our public education system." Almost simultaneously, SNCC staff members rolled from Hayneville into Tennessee with a notion to treat all of America like Lowndes County.

Jack Minnis lobbied quietly for Stokely Carmichael to unseat John Lewis as national chairman during SNCC's annual meeting at a wooded church camp in Kingston Springs, near Nashville. Carmichael agreed to run, furious that Lewis had campaigned for Richmond Flowers without once coming to support the unique Lowndes gamble sanctioned by his own organization, but a powerful ethos of shared risk and camaraderie discouraged personal ambition. Leadership in SNCC was considered an accident or distraction never to be sought, and no one spoke openly of the contest. Instead, all through the second week in May, young movement veterans buried internal politics within their marathon strategy debates. They labored to remember and revise the founding assumptions of college students caught up in six years of upheaval since the 1960 sit-ins. "We assumed that we could forget history," one confessed, "because we were different." Charlie Cobb recalled a shared sense of responsibility to bring injustice into the healing light of government attention. As late as 1963, a mission "to free men's minds" for equality had been accepted across the SNCC's broad spectrum of personality, from skeptical power analyst Courtland Cox to Christian mystic Charles Sherrod. "We assumed that this country is really a democracy, which just isn't working," said Carmichael. "We had no concept of how brutal it could be if we started messing it up."

Ivanhoe Donaldson argued that "interracial democracy" had become too vague a purpose now that the whole country gave it lip service, and pushed for organizing targeted "pockets of power" like the Bond campaign in Atlanta. James Forman advocated a world perspective on colonialism. Ardent racialists objected that SNCC had nothing to learn from white men like Karl Marx. Shrewd dialecticians explored worlds of meaning inside the word "vote," from the structure and process of raw politics to bonds of "consciousness" between citizens. Attacks on the forthcoming White House Conference indirectly struck at Lewis, who had attended the planning sessions, but Lewis had proved himself no stooge of President Johnson by his vehement opposition to the war in Vietnam. Conflict tore at Bob Mants among many others. He could not reconcile the Carmichael who "talked black" in Lowndes County with the loyalist who defended some forty white staff members from proposals to make SNCC an all-black vanguard. Mants pleaded with Carmichael not to abandon him for the tinsel glory of a national office. While angry with Lewis for ignoring their work in Lowndes, Mants still took comfort behind Lewis's steadfast courage on Pettus Bridge. With talks exhausted toward midnight on May 13, Carmichael supporters made perfunctory, half-joking nomination speeches in the face of the chair's heartfelt desire to stay on, and Lewis won reelection to a fourth term 60–22. Carmichael himself voted for the incumbent with a shrug.

Worth Long of Arkansas, having arrived late from Mississippi with Julius Lester, a quick-witted SNCC worker from Fisk University, gained the floor to ask what just happened, and his awed response silenced the hall. "John Lewis?" Long frowned. "How'd y'all do *that*? You can't do that." Jack Minnis, who seldom spoke in meetings, vented his frustration that the candid objection came too late to do any good. "Sorry 'bout that, white boss," retorted Long, who jumped from exposed personal ground to a procedural outburst: "I challenge this election!" He accused Forman of allowing the vote to proceed on sentimental regard for Lewis once half the staff members had slipped off to bed. In pandemonium, while some rushed to summon absentees and others fumbled for the bylaws, Minnis quickly devised a plan to revive Carmichael by turning SNCC culture in his favor. Accordingly, Cleveland Sellers resigned as national program secretary to make way for a clarifying revote, and Ruby Doris Robinson likewise relinquished her fresh mandate to replace Forman as executive secretary. When

Lewis adamantly rejected pressure to follow suit, he broke the spell of deference. Previously sheepish voices said he hungered too much for office. Some confessed a tacit consensus that he had not represented SNCC's evolving independence for at least two years. Wounded, Lewis soon lashed out at unjust conspirators, then pleaded that Carmichael was not a Southerner. Several articulate Northerners retorted that Lewis was a copy of his hero Martin Luther King, and wincing admirers wished he did not invite the comparison. Worth Long later asserted that Lewis "was finished" when he fell back on his commitment to nonviolence.

By dawn on Saturday, May 14, Lewis stood painfully isolated among those who stripped him of reelection. Julian Bond, who avoided the endless staff sessions whenever possible, publicly announced the result from Atlanta as "just a normal organizational change," and the shift in student leadership attracted modest press notice. One story found Lewis to be "obviously shaken by his defeat" at the hands of those who favored "third-party politics for Southern Negroes." The *National Guardian* disclosed that Stokely Carmichael had acquired the nickname "Delta Devil" for his fast-driving getaways in Mississippi. A *New York Times* profile identified the new chairman as a twenty-four-year-old "organizer of Alabama's all-Negro 'Black Panther' political party," and characterized his philosophy on a spectrum reserved for civil rights figures: "Mr. Carmichael does not advocate violence, but neither does he believe in turning the other cheek."

*   *   *

MARTIN LUTHER King contained troubles through the week of the SNCC elections. Rivals from the Blackstone Rangers and East Side Disciples exchanged gunfire inside a Chicago YMCA just before he arrived for a speech on May 13. King defended as a setback what critics took as definitive proof of lunacy in James Bevel's effort to convert the notorious street gangs into nonviolent brigades. Stanley Levison, visiting from New York, privately admired "the instinctive drama" of SCLC staff members who ran the gang workshops, and predicted that James Orange, the fearsome-looking teenager recruited from the 1963 Birmingham demonstrations, would become "a living legend" for his work in Chicago. Orange had taken nine beatings to prove his nonviolent discipline to gang members who respected his hulking three-hundred-pound frame and convincing street wisdom. "The people in the North are more beaten down," Orange observed.

Levison huddled in King's Hamlin Avenue tenement rooms over launch delays for the Chicago demonstrations. King had abandoned the slum "trusteeship" under legal pressure, in part because his Chicago lawyer, Chauncey Eskridge, turned out to own substandard ghetto property himself. Levison pushed for consolidation of SCLC to avert a deficit he projected at $450,000 for 1966 in spite of the windfall from Europe. This was five times his most recent estimate and nearly half SCLC's annual budget. Levison detected a sudden adverse shift in the country. "The Vietnamese War is increasingly seizing the emotions of people," he advised. "The impression that people gained [is] that the civil rights struggle is over. . . . Finally, the recent stock market decline has an effect." (The Dow Jones Industrial Average would not recover its April 1966 peak of 995.15 for sixteen years, until 1982.) His warning of massive layoffs or swift bankruptcy was firm—"Dear Martin. . . . The publicity that would ensue would be a disaster for both the organization and you personally"—and King resolved to take drastic action by the end of the month. King said other groups fared even worse, confiding that CORE had just begged him for a $28,000 loan to forestall government seizure of its office furniture for delinquent payroll taxes. Publicly, King renewed his commitment to begin a new march soon. "If anywhere," he declared, "it is in Chicago that the grapes of wrath are stored."

The new SNCC chairman, Stokely Carmichael, presented a novel guest speaker in Berkeley on May 21, then again in Los Angeles the next day. John Hulett, on his first trip west, took it as a calming sign that the sun poked through dark clouds the moment he faced a giant rally of the Vietnam Day Committee. "There was something in Alabama a few months ago they called fear," he said. He introduced Lowndes County in simple sentences, ending with a detailed story of the May 3 primary. To answer curiosity about the local party emblem, he described the black panther as a creature who retreats "backwards, backwards, and backwards into his corner, and then he comes out to destroy everything that's before him. Negroes in Lowndes County have been pushed back through the years," said Hulett. "We have been deprived of our rights to speak, to move, and to do whatever we want to do at all times. And now we are going to start moving."

Hulett's panther speeches created a stir within California movement circles, but Ruby Doris Robinson made national news from Atlanta by rejecting President Johnson's invitation to Washington for June 1. Her press statement on May 23 called the grand White House Conference on civil rights a "useless endeavor" and pronounced the federal government "not serious about insuring constitutional rights to black Americans," then stated that SNCC invitees "cannot in good conscience meet with the chief policy maker of the Vietnam War to discuss human rights in this country when he flagrantly violates the human rights of colored people in Vietnam." Asked whether the snub of Johnson meant desegregation was no longer a goal, Robinson replied that white people must initiate integration from now on. "We been head-lifted and upstarted into white societies all our lives, and we're tired of that," she said. "And what we need is black power." She presented Lowndes County as the model of an independent black movement. (In her crossfire with scandalized reporters, the unfamiliar name came out variously as "Loudon" and "Lawson.") Columnists Evans and Novak cut through press interpretations with a May 25 attack on "the extreme black racists" led by Carmichael.

Questions about SNCC's attitude chased King to Chicago, overwhelming his formal announcement on May 27 that a protest coalition of some 163 organizations had agreed to begin the "action phase" of the movement against slums, "which we hope will dramatize the problems and call forth a solution." He tried to buffer any threatened turn from integration as the inevitable sign of "discontent and even despair," and patiently explained that separatist strategies never had attracted more than token support among the mass of American Negroes. King outlined the schedule for a "mammoth" first march down State Street on June 26 to present goals and demands whether Mayor Daley accepted them or not, "if I have to tack them on the door."

King shuttled between Chicago and Washington. "I always hate to talk about violence," he said on the May 29 broadcast of *Face the Nation* as reporters pressed him exclusively on that subject. Did he accept predictions of summer riots worse than Watts, "and what do you intend to do about it?" Did he agree with "the most militant of the civil rights organizations" that "integration is irrelevant," or feel eclipsed by SNCC's intention to "take the battle for civil rights into the streets" and "be a lot more militant than leaders like you wish to be?" Did he still believe in the face of widespread criticism "that your position on our getting out of Vietnam is necessary for you to take?" King resisted on all fronts the implication that "militancy" carried stronger conviction or a more powerful effect than nonviolence: "Well, I hate to put it like that. . . . We must be militantly nonviolent." He repeated his opposition to war as an engine of hatred: "I know that where your heart is there your money will go, and the heart of many people in the Administration and others happens to be in Vietnam."

King rushed back to Chicago for two days of movement sessions interrupted by an audience that consumed much of May 31. Pacifist leader A. J. Muste had arranged for him to meet the Vietnamese monk Thich Nhat Hanh, who had written King a year earlier about the Buddhist concept of nonviolent self-immolation. They conferred privately on religion and the latest crises in South Vietnam. (Five more monks burned themselves in protest of lethal raids on Buddhist pagodas by the military government, and angry students were destroying the American consulate in Hue.) Afterward, they held an impromptu press conference at the Sheraton-Chicago Hotel that attracted perplexed notice in the *Tribune:* "King Equates Rights Fight with Monks." The two men flew to Washington on separate missions—King for the White House Conference and Thich Nhat Hanh for a tour of witness against war.

The new Vietnamese exile fasted with Rabbi Abraham Heschel and Father Daniel Berrigan. He meditated with the Trappist author Thomas Merton, who became convinced that the Buddhist was "more my brother than many who are nearer to me by race and nationality, because he and I see things exactly the same way." He met privately with Secretary McNamara for thirty-three minutes, generating a small *Washington Post* story that began as follows: "The purple-robed Buddhist monk, a small, delicate Vietnamese poet, faced a group of American reporters dressed in gray and brown business suits at the Mayflower yesterday." Thich Nhat Hanh identified himself as an anti-Communist who mourned destruction by 300,000 "dollar-making people" at war in his country of peasants, 80 percent of them Buddhist. "Now the U.S. has become too afraid of the communists to allow a peaceful confrontation with them to take place," he wrote, "and when you are afraid, you cannot win."

* * *

THE WHITE House Conference, "To Fulfill These Rights," was born a living anachronism on the first two days in June. A year's gestation made it too awkward to celebrate and too big to hide, full of new burdens turned heavy while ancient ones retained stubborn vigor. Many of the 2,400 delegates arrived at Washington's Sheraton-Park Hotel touched by the apt parable of a Vietnam casualty just refused burial in his home state. "My son was not a shoeshine boy like his father," nurse Annie Mae Williams had complained. "He was a soldier, a paratrooper in the Green Berets." Neither the Justice Department nor the Third Army's funeral assistance unit could secure a plot in the hometown cemetery of Wetumpka, Alabama, where Mayor Demp Thrash said the Negro section was full, and the flag-draped coffin sat for a week in limbo until federal authorities made space for Private First Class Jimmy Williams far across the Georgia line on May 30, among Union graves at the notorious Confederate prison in Andersonville. "Negro G.I.'s Burial Placates Mother," noted the *Times*. Elsewhere, the Mississippi Senate narrowly defeated a bill to disperse Negroes into other states, and Virginia's Supreme Court unanimously upheld the criminal sentence of Mildred and Richard Loving for marital "corruption of the blood." The latter decision opened to federal appeal the statutes in sixteen states that flatly outlawed interracial marriage, along with subtler "family purity" laws in several others.*

Outside the Sheraton-Park, SNCC supporters and New York activists carried protest signs—"Save Us from Our Negro Leaders," "Uncle Toms!" Derisive cries of "Black Jesus!" singled out King in the throng of entering delegates, and several white students who tried to join the all-black picket line told reporters they were not offended to be turned away. White House aides exchanged calls and messages about the dangers of revolt, updating Harry McPherson's memo of worry that "the conference might be demoralized by dissent, by angry radical factions, or by a sense of futility on the part of the Negro participants." On calmer soundings, a motorcade ventured from the White House at 9:40 P.M. on the night of June 1. First sight of the unscheduled entrance brought the guests to their feet in a continuous shout of "LBJ! LBJ!" as the President shook hands in the great banquet hall, lingering briefly with King, A. Philip Randolph, Roy Wilkins, and conference chairman Ben Heineman, a railroad executive from Chicago.

The President's short speech set a tone of humble realism. He said the struggle for full equality "does not require that righteous anger be silenced." He said no one should "expect us, even together, to put right in

* A 1913 Massachusetts law, for example, voided marriages between persons not eligible to be wedded in their home states. That obscure statute would be reapplied from race to gender in 2004 as a legal impediment to the recognition of same-sex marriage. Some states banned miscegnation only if a white person was involved, to prevent what Virginia judges called "the obliteration of racial pride."

one year or four all that took centuries to make wrong." Then he declared himself in one sentence: "I do pledge this—to give my days, and such talents as I have been given, to the pursuit of justice and opportunity for those so long denied them." A standing tribute began a barrage of seventeen ovations that punctuated his recital of enduring goals since Selma. To close, Johnson deliberately broke status protocol that made it taboo for any speaker to follow a sitting President. He honored the pioneers of civil rights by introducing to the podium one of their own, his new Solicitor General of the United States, Thurgood Marshall, and the motorcade returned from thundering acclaim to the White House by 10:32 P.M. "In the light of his car, his eyes were large and his face almost incandescent with the pleasure of an unexpected and flawless triumph," wrote McPherson. "It was about the last one he would have."

Johnson had engineered a wondrous truce. Louis Martin, the shrewd minority aide he inherited from Truman and Kennedy, packed the conference rooms with security monitors and sprinkled the corridors with attractive female college students who dispensed goodwill Hawaiian leis. A loose debate structure fostered short, disconnected statements about race from the massive array of delegates. There were Rockefellers from three states alongside hundreds of jail veterans and movement workers. James Meredith shared the floor with the segregationist Governor Paul Johnson, who had barred him from Ole Miss. *Jet* magazine marveled to see "towering" Bill Russell of the Boston Celtics sitting beside Rev. J. H. Jackson, King's pulpit nemesis in Chicago. ("Why don't you picket *him?*" Chauncey Eskridge quipped to students of Jackson.) One delegate proposed a racism inquest on "America's number one untouchable sacred cow," J. Edgar Hoover. Another disavowed hope so long as the cost of war was headed up from $14 billion in Vietnam and down from $1.4 billion on poverty. The conference staff steered the action agenda away from tripwire controversy over budgets or the Negro family, which left Daniel Moynihan "a silent, unnoticed delegate" in the *Times* account. Delegates sustained Deputy U.N. Ambassador James Nabrit by a ten-to-one margin when he declared a rump motion on Vietnam to be out of order, which provided the closing banner headline atop the June 3 *Washington Post:* "Rights Session Rejects a Viet Pullout."

Reporters noticed that King was "conspicuously missing" from photograph sessions to begin the second day. He remained in his hotel room, hurt by Thurgood Marshall's victory speech that championed law to the exclusion of nonviolent movements past or future: "I submit that the history of the Negro demonstrates the importance of getting rid of hostile laws, and seeking the security of new, friendly laws." Though accustomed to much saltier private criticism from Marshall, who once called him "a boy on a man's errand," and who still disparaged his "missionary" marches as a nuisance, King sagged under the cumulative evidence that he was being smothered to safeguard an official definition of freedom. He resisted staff entreaties to leave Washington early, fearing that segregationists would seize upon any whisper of disaffection, and regained composure to be "totally ignored" among the delegates. "Indeed," wrote biographer David L. Lewis, "his wife came nearer to making a contribution to the proceedings when she was asked to sing."

King returned home to preach from Isaiah 61 about religion's core mission "to heal the broken-hearted." ("You see, broken-heartedness is not a physical condition," he told the Ebenezer congregation. "It's the condition of spiritual exhaustion.") He ordered all but a remnant of the Alabama SCLC staff to be dismantled by Tuesday, one week after the runoff primary confirmed only a seed of promise within the Wallace landslide. Lucius Amerson of Tuskegee won the Democratic nomination and presumptive election in November to become Alabama's first Negro sheriff since Reconstruction—and vowed exuberantly to integrate his deputies "if I can find qualified white people who are willing to serve"—but other Negro candidates fell to fear and inexperience. A rarely subdued Hosea Williams, loath to be consolidated into Chicago under a cloud of failure, improvised a bittersweet parting hymn with seventy paid workers: "No more Alabama, over me . . ."

On Saturday, June 4, King and Coretta visited the prestigious Cathedral of St. Philip in Atlanta, center of protest since an affiliated Episcopal school rejected young Marty King's application to third grade in 1963, citing his race. No one yet knew that the segregation policy would give way for September of 1967. The Kings comforted two priests finishing a week-long protest vigil inside the doorway.

* * *

ROBERT KENNEDY landed that Saturday night in Johannesburg with a traveling party reduced to two aides. To quiet his anticipated "publicity stunt" against apartheid, South Africa had revoked entry visas for forty American journalists who booked the flight, and a government spokesman announced that no officials would meet the senator at the airport or anywhere else in the country. Still, 1,500 people broke through glass doors to surround the airplane. Hecklers shouting "Chuck him out!" engaged in sporadic fistfights with surging admirers whose handshakes tore away Kennedy's cuff links. He climbed on a car roof to make a rattled arrival statement about the common heritage of frontier settlers in the Transvaal and in his state of New York, including "those of Dutch descent like my wife."

When swirling, destitute people shouted "master, master" in the Bantu areas, an embarrassed Kennedy pleaded with them not to use the word. An explosion of defensive public comment about his tour forced the government to let him see Chief Albert Luthuli, who had lived since 1959 under a formal ban that sealed him away without movement or communication. Apartheid law mandated a long prison term for anyone who quoted him. At a barren farm near Durban, Kennedy presented Luthuli with a battery-operated tape recorder and a cassette of President Kennedy's June 11, 1963, address calling segregation a moral issue "as old as the Scriptures and . . . as clear as the Constitution." Both the visit and the gift were suggested by Allard Lowenstein, the Democratic activist who had sought out Bob Moses with ideas from his own formative travels in southern Africa, and had recruited hundreds of student volunteers to Mississippi for the 1964 Freedom Summer.

Lowenstein knew what the recording would mean to Luthuli in his forced vacuum of news, and reciprocal exposure to South Africa proved captivating in part through the stubborn grace of the only black Nobel Peace Prize winner before Martin Luther King. Kennedy had begun the trip largely on an impulsive dare, like carrying a flag to the summit of a mountain named for his late brother, but he wrote more personally in his journal that Luthuli's eyes could turn "intense and hard and hurt, all at once," and came to treasure indelible faces that emerged from the starkest confinements of race. At Natal University, Kennedy absorbed questions from twenty thousand white students about the biblical authority for apartheid, then blurted out, "What if God is black?" Challenged to name the U.S. President who had proclaimed an everlasting gulf between the races in 1885, he shrugged with a combative grin, "the one who was beaten in 1888."

On Monday, June 6, Kennedy flew over the political prison at Robben Island to Cape Town. An empty chair on a university stage there marked a place for the national student leader who had invited him to South Africa and had since been banned for five years. "We stand here in the name of freedom," Kennedy told a crowd of 15,000 white people on their annual Day of Affirmation. His address placed "the racial in-equality of apartheid" on a broad footing with hatred and suffering from New York to India—"These are differing evils, but they are the common works of man"—then confronted above all the "danger of fu-tility, the belief there is nothing one man or one woman can do against the enormous array of the world's ills." He invoked nonviolent witness against the stronghold of South Africa. "It is from numberless diverse acts of courage and belief that human history is shaped," said Kennedy. "Each time a man stands up for an ideal, or acts to improve the lot of others, or strikes out against injustice, he sends forth a tiny ripple of hope, and . . . those ripples build a current which can sweep down the mightiest walls of oppression and resistance."

The Cape Town speech stirred imagination worldwide. "This little snip thinks he can tell us what to do," protested a South African minis-ter. Theologian Reinhold Niebuhr cabled "enthusiastic appreciation" from New York. The *Washington Post* likened his "political safari" to Attila the Hun's descent upon Rome. Hostile American journals chas-tised Kennedy for sharpening racial divisions, and for "attempting to shake hands with every black African he could reach." From his car roof, above a sea of outstretched hands, he joined spontaneous rendi-tions of "We Shall Overcome."

* * *

JAMES MEREDITH's maverick announcement had made no news from the White House Conference, where a wag hung a sign in the Sheraton-Park press room that the "March Against Fear" would be sponsored by an imaginary "World Committee for the Preservation of James Mere-dith." A friend worried that Meredith was obsessed by the negligible re-sponse to his published memoir; others thought he resented gossip about poor spring grades in Columbia Law School. When he did pro-ceed to Memphis, and set out as promised from the Peabody Hotel, re-ports noted eccentricities in keeping with his determination to walk 220 miles back into his home state without the marshals or U.S. Army brigades that guarded him at Ole Miss, proving that Negroes could ex-ercise freedom now even in Mississippi. Meredith wore a yellow pith helmet, carried an ivory-tipped walking stick, and displayed a white horse's tail among gifts from a Sudanese chief. He covered the twelve miles to the Tennessee line on Sunday, June 5, and another fourteen miles on Monday before a voice called his name from the wooded shoul-der near Hernando, Mississippi. "I only want James Meredith!" shouted

Aubrey Norvell, scattering reporters and a small entourage that included a white Episcopal priest and a volunteer publicist from New York. Norvell, a forty-year-old hardware contractor, fired his 16-gauge automatic shotgun three times and surrendered, still smoking his pipe, to a dozen assorted escort officers who jumped from their cars. The sheriff of DeSoto County said the suspect appeared to be intoxicated. An Associated Press bulletin flashed news of Meredith's death at 6:33 P.M., in time for many evening broadcasts. A correction at 7:08 P.M. said he was in surgery.

President Johnson denounced "an awful act of violence" within the hour from his ranch in Texas. Attorney General Katzenbach, acknowledging the presence of FBI agents at the scene, convened an evening press conference to address the chances for federal prosecution under the Voting Rights Act. "James Meredith is not only a friend," he said, "but also a brave man." Robert Kennedy reacted from Stellenbosch, South Africa, wishing Meredith a full recovery, and CORE that night became the first civil rights organization vowing publicly to take up the "March Against Fear" at the spot of his ambush on Highway 51. In Atlanta, debating whether to join, Andrew Young argued that King's staff was stretched far too thin already, "running back and forth to Chicago." Hosea William said Young was scared of Mississippi. "He was furious with me because he thought I wasn't angry enough over the shooting of Meredith," Young recalled. "We almost came to blows right then and there."

Young refused to join the early-morning flight to Memphis on Tuesday, June 7. Rev. James Lawson, the Gandhian mentor to the early Nashville student movement, escorted his SCLC colleagues through crowds of reporters and converging pilgrims into the hospital, past police cordons and anxious medical personnel into Meredith's room. Surgeons by then had removed some seventy shotgun pellets from his back to his scalp. King, combining pastoral and political roles delicately, emerged with permission from the groggy but still temperamental Meredith to begin a march of tribute in his name, and Lawson's station wagon, stocked with fried chicken for lunch in transit, led a caravan down into Mississippi. Twenty-one marchers, observed by at least that many reporters, resumed the walk from the point of the previous day's bloodstains in the quiet afternoon heat. King locked arms with Floyd McKissick and Stokely Carmichael, the two new leaders of CORE and SNCC respectively, before a line of Mississippi state troopers confronted them at the top of the first gentle hill with orders to get off the pavement. King blinked with surprise, and called for protection instead, but the troopers resolutely shoved him aside with the others. "We walked from Selma to Montgomery in the middle of the road," he protested to no avail, stumbling backward. Troopers knocked Cleveland Sellers to the ground. Carmichael lunged toward the most aggressive one, but King kept his arm crooked tightly with an elbow and called out for help.

The swirling scuffle would highlight the next day's front pages, but the marchers quickly recovered and walked six miles on the dirt shoulder under the frowning gaze of the troopers. Lawson and Hosea Williams led closing prayers in a pasture before banter resumed over the incident. Carmichael said it was hard to fight while square-dancing with King, who mimicked his own profound sermon tones with a smile, "I restrained Stokely, *nonviolently.*" Carmichael apologized for his breach of discipline, reminding King that in six years "on the front lines" he had been beaten unconscious and arrested many times without a hint of retaliation. While mindful of demonstration protocol, and acutely conscious that King had congratulated him for the SNCC leadership with a friendly reminder of magnified danger in every public gesture, Carmichael insisted that the purpose for any joint march was not yet defined. This much became clear that night at a rally of a thousand people in Lawson's Centenary Methodist Church back in Memphis. Roy Wilkins of the NAACP and Whitney Young of the Urban League proposed to unite behind President Johnson's civil rights bill of 1966, but McKissick swept away the crowd by scoffing at new laws, Johnson's White House conference—"I *still* say it was rigged"—and even the Statue of Liberty: "They ought to break that young lady's legs and throw her into the Mississippi!" Carmichael said he refused to beg for undelivered rights and protections, to great applause, and Charles Evers brought down the house with a pledge to avenge Meredith with an armed black host "like Buck Jones and Tim McCoy," two Hollywood cowboys famous for gunplay. King managed to recapture movement themes with a closing reminiscence about Birmingham, saying Bull Connor was always happy to see a few Negroes throw rocks: "He was an expert in that. He had maps of the heart of violence."

Raw leadership debate shifted to the Lorraine Motel. By midnight, Roy Wilkins lost any small inclination to march himself, in part because he could not bear to hear the President scorned as "that cat Johnson" in youth jive. "Dr. King, I'm really sorry for you," he said on departing for the airport, and Whitney Young soon followed. All night, stripped down to an old-fashioned strap undershirt, King presided over a room jammed with movement veterans from Fannie Lou Hamer to the lawyer Charles Morgan. Hosea Williams and Ernest Thomas, founder of the Deacons for Defense, set a daunting tone with their loud argument—"Shut up, chubby," said Thomas—about whether nonviolence took more guts or brains than armed protection.

By Wednesday morning, when King took a compromise agenda to Bowld Hospital in Memphis, Meredith remained too weak to sit but was feisty enough to reject the chain of command. He believed in only one general, and it was still his march. Roles crazily reversed when an administrator interrupted their long remonstrations with an agitated demand for Meredith to vacate the hospital within five minutes because of Klan threats. King objected loudly to the cowardly nonmedical "eviction," but Meredith called for a wheelchair and rolled out to face a bank of television lights. Incoherently, he said he was embarrassed to have been bushwhacked by an amateur marksman, and would have dispatched Norvell himself if he had brought his gun as planned instead of his Bible, which for some reason he had given to a photographer during a rainstorm. Then Meredith fainted. Reporters saw tears running down his cheeks while doctors tried feverishly to revive him, and "three friends rolled him away from the tumultuous scene" for a flight home to New York.

The march resumed on a tenuous mandate, covering only three miles that afternoon. "It'll build up," said Stanley Levison, predicting a "junior Selma" in spite of crippling handicaps: no logistical preparation, federal protection, or compelling reason for volunteers to walk four times the Selma distance. The lines grew to 208 people on Thursday, and finished nine miles. King paused on the road to announce the death by heart attack of a local sharecropper who had joined them. He flew away to Chicago meetings and returned in time to preach the funeral of Armistead Phipps in Enid, Mississippi, apologizing that he had never before stood in a pulpit without "proper ministerial attire," telling mourners they had identified Phipps's body by his poll tax receipt and his membership card in the Mississippi Freedom Democratic Party. "This was a man who was not afraid," he said.

King, Carmichael, and the other SNCC workers enjoyed their first prolonged company on the road. They detoured past country courthouses to register bystanders who gathered, and celebrated a 104-year-old farmer named Ed Fondren who came out on the shoulders of neighbors with his first voter's card. King complained of private frictions only with Charles Evers, over his popular roadside speeches professing eagerness to shoot it out with the Klan. Such bravado had built a political base for Evers in Natchez, but King finally boiled over about hypocrisy rather than the politics. "If you really believed that sort of thing," he said sharply, "you'd start by shooting 'Delay' Beckwith." He reminded Evers that the Klansman who had killed his brother Medgar "is walking around Mississippi today," not far from the line of march.

One of several opportunistic Klan plots to assassinate King played out in Natchez on Friday, June 10. Claude Fuller, James Jones, and Ernest Avants of the Cottonmouth Moccasin Gang picked up at random a sixty-five-year-old farm caretaker named Ben Chester White on the pretext of hiring him to do some chores. They nicknamed him "Pop" as a kind of sedative on their drive to a creek bridge out of town, where they pulled out a pistol, a carbine, and a shotgun. The plan was to lure King from his march in northern Mississippi down to Natchez with a spectacular lynching. "Oh, Lord," pleaded White. "What have I done to deserve this?"

CHAPTER 29

Meredith March

June 1966

SYMBOLS of liberty began to change hands during the Meredith march. From California, Robert Kennedy's political counselor Fred Dutton warned that novice candidate Ronald Reagan was discovering a talent to communicate both martial fervor for Vietnam and revolt against the liberal era within a sensibility of freedom. Nationwide application of that compound message "would result in '66 and '68 in the worst setback for the Democratic party since 1920," Dutton wrote prophetically to President Johnson. The Reagan style mixed nostalgia with dogged optimism. At a primary debate before an assembly of California's Negro Republicans in March, he had bristled when asked how he could oppose the new civil rights laws and still ask for black votes. "I resent the implication that there is any bigotry in my nature," Reagan exploded, and flung a balled-up piece of paper at the audience as he stalked out. "Don't let anyone ever imply that I lack integrity!" The incident raised doubts about the candidate's composure until Reagan pressed reporters to make up their minds whether he was a "square" or a wild-eyed kook. "Fellows," he said jovially, "you can't have it both ways." It became a smaller story when he erupted again on June 1. "I resent that," he told the Negro Men of Tomorrow Club, dismissing a member who had questioned his breezy claim to be for equal rights and against the Voting Rights Act. "I answered fully. I gave a pretty sincere answer."

Reagan rose above stigma with tangled but forceful professions. "If I didn't know personally that Barry Goldwater was not the very opposite of a racist," he declared, "I could not have supported him." His display of innocent sensitivity insulated him from discomforts widely shared. Reagan's rebuttal to civil rights philosophy never called for the repeal of the laws, nor cultivated active resistance, and he generally avoided controversy over enforcement. While disputing Martin Luther King's prescription for the body politic, he consoled the fearful and guilty with anesthesia potent enough to numb whole decades of adaptation to the broadening thrust of equal rights. Pat Brown, the incumbent Democratic governor, considered Reagan so naive, extremist, and "beatable" that he foolishly hired operatives to smear Reagan's opponent in the Republican primary. When Reagan won by 800,000 votes on June 7, editors at the *New York Times* scolded the electorate with barely restrained shock: "The Republicans, against all counsels of common sense and political prudence, insisted upon nominating actor Ronald Reagan for Governor."

Former Vice President Richard Nixon nurtured the South's fledgling Republican Party with a more calibrated version of the Reagan formula. He carefully supported the civil rights laws, and explained in private that the national party could not win by fighting them like Goldwater, nor compete with sectional demagogues like George Wallace. Nixon instead promoted two-party government by attacking national Democrats for domestic turmoil and foreign appeasement. In May, he told a full-throated rally of Birmingham Republicans that "thousands of American boys wouldn't be dead today" if President Johnson had bombed Vietnam more and relied less on ground troops. In South Carolina, he absolved the Deep South's pioneer Republican and foremost segregationist. "Strom is no racist," Nixon declared of the manifestly grateful Senator Thurmond. "Strom is a man of courage and integrity." In Mississippi, Nixon advised Republicans to neutralize civil rights by tucking the burden away as a settled embarrassment. "There is no future in the race issue for the South," he told a fund-raiser in Jackson. "There is no future in the race issue for the Republican Party. There is no future in the race issue for the Democratic Party. This issue has hurt the South, as it has hurt the nation. And now it is time to go forward to the other great issues."

Travis Buckley failed to heed Nixon's counsel for an election that coincided with Reagan's victory on June 7, when Mississippi joined the last Southern states to organize a Republican primary. The new party was still fighting a century of anti-Lincoln culture across Dixie, not long after Senator John Tower of Texas lamented that "you practically had to hold a gun on somebody to get him to run as a Republican." Against GOP rivals, who mustered for the debut contest in only one of Mississippi's five congressional districts, Buckley campaigned on his notoriety as the Klan lawyer for eleven White Knights arrested so far in the firebomb murder of voter registration leader Vernon Dahmer. He lost the nomination to a candidate of more sober demeanor, who would lose in turn to the well-established segregationist Democrat G. V. "Sonny" Montgomery. "We're not ever going to beat Sonny," a Republican leader conceded, but he predicted accurately that his party would "get the district when he retires." Incumbents and courthouse ties stretched out through the next political generation a wholesale partisan realignment of Southern white voters, marked from the Goldwater-Johnson divide of 1964. By 1996, when Charles "Chip" Pickering succeeded Montgomery, Southern Republicans not only supplanted the "solid" Democrats of the segregation era but also supplied most of the leaders for a national party molded after Ronald Reagan.

Buckley handled juries better than voters. He successfully represented Ernest Avants, one of three Klansmen arrested in Natchez, days after the random execution of Ben Chester White on June 10, 1966. In spite of grisly physical evidence from the murder vehicle, and the haunted confession of driver James Jones that two jumpy accomplices had fired nineteen shots into the victim before he could move from the back seat, Buckley won acquittal with white supremacy rhetoric and the brazen claim that White must have been dead already from carbine bullets when Buckley's client partially decapitated him with a shotgun. Jones and carbine shooter Claude Fuller handily evaded conviction for their lifetimes, but Avants survived long enough in a parallel evolution of the political climate to meet extraordinary justice. On proof from tenacious prosecutors that the killing site at Pretty Creek fell just inside Homochitto National Forest, the courts in 2003 allowed a federal trial for the separate charge of murder on U.S. property, and a Mississippi jury found Avants guilty almost thirty-seven years after his crime.

Only a quarter of registered Negroes voted in Mississippi's June 1966 primary elections. The low turnout disappointed movement leaders, but the legislature nevertheless continued frenzied special sessions through the Meredith march, galvanized by 100,000 black registrations that had raised the total fivefold since 1964, from a paltry 6.7 percent of eligible Negroes to better than a third. The all-white politicians passed thirteen major laws to dilute the potential effect. They redrew boundaries, raised filing fees, attached Negro districts to white ones, and mandated at-large elections where they could submerge local black majorities. They muffled racial terms in floor debate to conceal their purpose, until the coded manipulation of population statistics provoked legislators from white areas to warn plainly of obsession. "We get so concerned because some Negroes are voting in a few counties," protested Senator Ben Hilbun of Oktibbeha County, "we are going to disrupt our entire institutions of government."

* * *

THE MEREDITH marchers approached Grenada on national Flag Day, June 14, over crude KKK notices painted on the surface of Highway 51: "Red [sic] nigger and run. If you can't red run anyway." Through rainstorms, confusion, blisters, and petty harassment, assorted volunteers had covered roughly half the planned 200-mile route to the Mississippi capital in Jackson. Vincent Young, a bus driver from Brooklyn, used his annual vacation to wear out a pair of shoes while he carried a hand-lettered sign: "No Viet Cong Ever Called Me Nigger." A seventy-one-year-old white sharecropper's daughter from Georgia wore a quaint sunbonnet as she helped a young black nurse from Belzoni hand out salt tablets, and the morning *New York Times* chronicled roadside debates over a pistol sighted at the previous campsite. "The movement is no place for guns," said an "astounded" Methodist minister from New Jersey, but AME Bishop Charles Tucker suggested that anyone who failed to protect himself with arms "ought to take off his pants and wear skirts." Ernest Thomas defended a compromise that allowed his Deacons to patrol after the march hours reserved for nonviolent discipline, and the *Times* mischievously quoted a staff marshal pleading for discretion: "If you want to discuss violence and nonviolence, don't talk around the press." Rev. Edwin King, the civil rights veteran from Tougaloo College, complained privately that most reporters had turned hostile "even to Martin." Journalist Paul Good noted that only the *Times* showed interest in the primitive conditions among sharecroppers encountered along the way, and cited an explicitly jaundiced dispatch from the bellwether UPI newswire: "This march has become part movement, part circus. Among the 350-odd marchers . . . are about 50 white youths who wear T-shirts and denims, sandals and weird cowboy hats adorned with Freedom buttons. . . . 'This is a great assembly of kooks,' said a Mississippi Highway Patrolman. Most newsmen agreed."

Marchers broke into a spirited, hand-clapping dance over the Yalobusha River Bridge, singing, "Walk for your children, brother, make them free!" Crowds of Negro residents watched the first living presence of the civil rights movement ever to reach Grenada—"Population 12,000, and Still Growing"—a town tightly segregated from schoolhouses to the library. Many stared or waved. Some made half-hearted promises to join, and more than a few could not resist. "I was just looking," said Tessie McCain, "and all of a sudden I was marching." Several dropped out again before local white people could recognize them, but one Highway Patrolman estimated "about a mile of niggers" behind the parade downtown along Pearl Street. Robert Green interrupted his speech at the Confederate Memorial to wedge a small American flag behind the medallion of Jefferson Davis. "We're tired of Confederate flags," he shouted to audible gasps. "Give me the flag of the United States, the flag of freedom!" Andrew Young recorded a stab of worry that his friend Green, a Michigan State professor on loan to SCLC, was suffering a fit of suicidal bravado to live down his staid academic persona.

Cheers grew slowly with relief that Highway Patrol officers seemed resigned to prevent rather than lead hothead retribution. Floyd McKissick of CORE tested the meaning of strange new signs that changed the dual public restrooms for both sexes from "white" and "colored" to "No. 1" and "No. 2." Pointing to the Grenada County courthouse, he cried, "We're going over to the toilets marked 'No. 1,' and see if it ain't a little better." Long lines quickly spilled across the lawn unmolested. With festive spontaneity, extra lines made sure the "No. 2" facilities were not reserved for white people, and new lines formed outside the registrar's office. Nearly two hundred registered to vote before a celebration packed New Hope Missionary Baptist Church that night. "You've never had this town before, and now you've taken it over in a day," shouted a warm-up speaker. "That's freedom. So sing about it." Fannie Lou Hamer led freedom songs. Martin Luther King returned from negotiations with a stunning announcement that Grenada County officials agreed to deputize six respected Negro teachers as registrars. "This, my friends, is our great opportunity," he said, and began to preach: *"Now* is the time to make real the promises of democracy." Overnight, the county's Negro registration doubled from 697 in a miracle of punctured fear. By contrast, wrote Paul Good, federal registrars in adjacent Carroll County waited "four straight days without a single Negro applicant appearing."

Euphoria was brief. Leaving staff members in Grenada to help a local movement, the strategy committee turned the march west into the Mississippi Delta, off Meredith's planned route, hoping to dramatize feudal oppression in the plantation region. King drove to registration rallies at Charleston in Tallahatchie County, and Winona in Montgomery, then broke away on June 15 to tend the Chicago campaign for two days. By the time he left, reports from Grenada soured official Mississippi on the experiment to minimize embarrassing incidents with a show of tolerance. The march was "turning into a voter registration campaign," Governor Paul Johnson told a hurried news conference. He reduced the Highway Patrol protection detail from twenty cruisers to four, and instructed local jurisdictions to take charge: "We aren't going to wet-nurse a bunch of showmen all over the country." That afternoon, Grenada police arrested the first volunteers who tried to integrate a movie theater, and civilians beat movement workers on the street without interference. A Confederate flag replaced Green's radioactive symbol of the Union. To a catalogue of flagrant exhibits for segregation, Justice Department lawyers in town added shattered windows and four slashed tires on their own rented car.

From Grenada, John Doar managed to file a U.S. lawsuit charging that officials had repulsed Negro voters illegally on June 7 at the polls in nearby Greenwood. The march columns were headed there, and Carmichael continued to receive favorable scouting reports on the two-day, thirty-mile trek down Highway 7. "They're going wild for it," said Willie Ricks, of the calculated message Carmichael used to win over his own central committee. Against strong SNCC sentiment to shun the Meredith march as another celebrity-driven "big show," he proposed to make Mississippi's poor black enclaves into a showcase for independent politics on the Lowndes County model, which he called "people relating to the concept of Black Power." Hoping to borrow rather than fight or deny King's mass appeal this time, Carmichael had persuaded a June 10 emergency session of the central committee to keep Forman in Atlanta, and he cross-examined colleagues nightly about their field tests of a new SNCC slogan, still doubting he could count on the response Ricks claimed for crowd-building speeches in familiar cotton fields and churches ahead. Greenwood had been a movement foothold since Bob Moses dared to enter the Delta in 1962. Carmichael himself had lived and gone to jail there as regional director for the 1964 Freedom Summer project. He knew the police chief, "Buff" Hammond, as a relative moderate, but their schoolyard encounter swiftly deteriorated on Thursday afternoon, June 16. Carmichael said police must be blocking the advance tent crews by mistake, as weary marchers had to camp at the only public space available to Negroes; Hammond said any assembly on the grounds of Stone Street Negro School required a permit from the all-white school board, which was closed. "We'll put them up anyway," Carmichael protested. Officers handcuffed him and two others.

A historical moment teetered for six hours. By supper, King issued a statement from Chicago on the Mississippi crackdown. FBI wiretappers forwarded from New York to Washington Stanley Levison's judgment that political pressure was hardening Governor Johnson, along with King's comment that he "had expected something like this" because the "the police were too polite" and the march "just did not feel like Mississippi." In Greenwood, where the morning *Commonwealth* warned against King as a hate-monger "who can be compared to Josef Stalin and Mao Tze Tung," local officials thought better of dispersing his hordes. They reversed themselves to allow the school campsite, which added jolts of vindication to the mass meeting that night. Willie Ricks guided Carmichael to the speaker's platform when he made bail, saying most of the locals remembered him fondly. "Drop it now!" he urged. "The people are ready."

Carmichael faced an agitated crowd of six hundred. "This is the 27th time I have been arrested," he began, "and I ain't going to jail no more!" He said Negroes should stay home from Vietnam and fight for black power in Greenwood. "We want black power!" he shouted five times, jabbing his forefinger downward in the air. "That's right. That's what we want, black power. We don't have to be ashamed of it. We have stayed here. We have begged the president. We've begged the federal government—that's all we've been doing, begging and begging. It's time we stand up and take over. Every courthouse in Mississippi ought to be burned down tomorrow to get rid of the dirt and the mess. From now on, when they ask you what you want, you know what to tell 'em. What do you want?"

The crowd shouted, "Black power!" Willie Ricks sprang up to help lead thunderous rounds of call and response: "What do you want?" "Black power!"

*   *   *

KING RETURNED to a movement flickering starkly in its public face. At the mass meeting on Friday, June 17, after a tense march to the Leflore County courthouse, Willie Ricks dueled Hosea Williams in alternate chants of "Black Power!" versus "Freedom!" On Saturday's march past the tiny hamlet of Itta Bena—James Bevel's hometown, three years after sharecroppers there had braved their first civil rights ceremony to mourn the assassination of Medgar Evers, only to be hauled from church by way of Greenwood jail to Parchman Penitentiary, where some were suspended by handcuffs from cell bars in the death house—King and Carmichael faced persistent interviews in motion down Highway 7 toward Belzoni. "What do you mean," asked a broadcast reporter, "when you shout black power to these people back here?"

"I mean," Carmichael replied, "that the only way that black people in Mississippi will create an attitude where they will not be shot down like pigs, where they will not be shot down like dogs, is when they get the power where they constitute a majority in counties to institute justice."

"I feel, however," King interjected, "that while believing firmly that power is necessary, that it would be difficult for me to use the phrase black power because of the connotative meaning that it has for many people." Carmichael walked alongside, hands clasped behind his back with beguiling pleasantry. Both wore sunglasses.

A small story the same day from southern Mississippi revealed a first hint of Klan conspiracy attached to the corpse fished out of Pretty Creek, quoting the police statement by James Jones that deafening shots had blasted the head of Ben Chester White and left "parts of it all over my new car." King left to raise funds for the Meredith campaign at a rally of 12,000 on Sunday in Detroit's Cobo Hall, sponsored by Walter Reuther of the United Auto Workers. The FBI received death threats against King from a Klan unit among Reuther's members at Cadillac Assembly Plant Number 1, which they didn't disclose, but inquiries about black power generated headlines along his trail back to Mississippi: "Supremacy by Either Race Would Be Evil, He Says." On Tuesday, June 21, King and Ralph Abernathy detoured by car with twenty volunteers from the main column to commemorate three victims of Klan murder exactly two years earlier, on the first night of Freedom Summer. Several hundred local people joined a rattled walk from Mt. Nebo Baptist Church to the Neshoba County courthouse in Philadelphia, Mississippi. Shocked employers along the sidewalk pointed out their family maids. ("Yes, it's me," the matronly Mary Batts called out to acknowledge a stare, "and I've kept your children.") Hostile drivers buzzed the lines at high speed, and one young woman shouted from the back seat of a blue convertible that swerved to a stop: "I wouldn't dirty my goddamned car with you black bastards!" When a line of officers blocked access to the courthouse lawn, Deputy Sheriff Cecil Price, face-to-face with King, granted respite for public prayer among the by-standers closing in from both sides of the narrow street, scores of them armed with pistols, clubs, and at least one garden hoe.

King turned to raise his voice above the lines kneeling back along the pavement. "In this county, Andrew Goodman, James Chaney, and Mickey Schwerner were brutally murdered," he cried. "I believe in my heart that the murderers are somewhere around me at this moment." Reporters heard "right behind you" and "you're damn right" among grunts and chuckles in response. One wrote, "King appeared to be shaken." King knew Deputy Price himself was among eighteen defendants in the pending federal conspiracy indictment, which had been filed in the absence of a state response to the murders and remained stalled in pretrial legal maneuvers.

"They ought to search their hearts," he continued out loud. "I want them to know that we are not afraid. If they kill three of us, they will have to kill all of us. I am not afraid of any man, whether he is in Michigan or Mississippi, whether he is in Birmingham or Boston." Jeers soon drowned out the closing chorus of "We Shall Overcome." Only darting blows struck the return march until someone toppled newsmen carrying heavy network cameras. "Some 25 white men surged over the television men, swinging, and then flailed into the line of march, their eyes wide with anger," observed *New York Times* correspondent Roy Reed. "The Negroes screamed." Attackers "hurled stones, bottles, clubs, fire-crackers and shouts of obscenity," he added, and police did not intervene "until half a dozen Negroes began to fight back." That night, careening automobile posses sprayed Philadelphia's black neighborhood with gunfire. Riders in the fourth wave narrowly missed a startled FBI agent posted near the mass meeting at Mt. Nebo. Return shots from one targeted house wounded a passing vigilante, and this noisy postlude attracted a misleading headline for Reed's dramatic front-page account of the courthouse standoff: "Whites and Negroes Trade Shots."

The Philadelphia trauma intensified conflict within the movement over strategy. King, lamenting "a complete breakdown of law and order," requested federal protection in a telegram to President Johnson, and rejoined the main march in Yazoo City during a fierce debate that erupted during the Tuesday night mass meeting. Ernest Thomas of the Louisiana Deacons for Defense and Justice ridiculed hope for safety in the hands of federal agents he said were always "smiling, writing a lot of papers, sending it back to Washington, D.C." He advocated vigilante committees to meet lawless repression. "If I must die, then I have to die the way that I feel," Thomas shouted to a chorus of cheers.

King came on late with an impassioned rebuttal. "Somebody said tonight that we are in a majority," he said. "Don't fool yourself. We are not a majority in a single state. . . . We are ten percent of the population of this nation, and it would be foolish of me to stand up and tell you we are going to get our freedom by ourselves." He challenged boasts of armed promise in the isolated black-majority counties: "Who runs the National Guard of Mississippi? How many Negroes do you have in it? Who runs the State Patrol of Mississippi?" Any vigilante campaign would backfire "the minute we started," he argued, not only in military result but also in public opinion—"And I tell you, nothing would please our oppressors more"—so that "it is impractical even to think about it." King won back the crowd with a sermon against violence. "I am not going to allow anybody to pull me so low as to use the very methods that perpetuated evil throughout our civilization," he said. "I'm sick and tired of violence. I'm tired of the war in Vietnam. I'm tired of war and conflict in the world. I'm tired of shooting. I'm tired of hatred. I'm tired of selfishness. I'm tired of evil. I'm not going to use violence no matter who says it!" Then he retired to internal debates through the night and most of Wednesday. Carmichael rejected "black equality" as an alternative to black power, insisting there was nothing inherently violent in the word "power." King vowed to leave the march if the inflammatory rhetoric continued. The leaders compromised on a pledge to avoid the overtly competitive sloganeering, which advertised divisions at the core of a small movement based within an impoverished racial minority.

President Johnson deflected King's request for federal protection by relaying assurances from Governor Paul Johnson "that all necessary protection can and will be provided." Additional units of the Mississippi Highway Patrol "were promptly dispatched," he advised from Washington, urging King to "maintain the closest liaison with Assistant Attorney General John Doar, who will remain in Mississippi until the end of the march." Johnson's reply telegram reached King late June 23 on a long day's walk through rainstorms into Canton. Latecomers were building numbers toward the finale set for Jackson, twenty miles ahead, and local supporters swelled the crowd above two thousand for a night rally on the grounds of McNeal Elementary School for Negroes, where

Hosea Williams was arrested in a new dispute over permits. As tent workers rushed to put up shelter, a Highway Patrol commander announced over a megaphone: "You will not be allowed to erect the tents. If you do, you will be removed."

Hushed disbelief spread with the realization that the Highway Patrol phalanx was turning inward. "I don't know what they plan for us," King called out from the back of a flatbed truck, "but we aren't going to fight any state troopers." Giving the microphone to Carmichael, he ran his right hand nervously over his head as armed officers spread along the perimeter. Carmichael chopped the air again with his finger. "The time for running has come to an end!" he shouted, soaked in perspiration, his eyes and teeth gleaming against the dark night. "You tell them white folks in Mississippi that all the scared niggers are dead!" Cheers covered an interlude just long enough for newsmen to count sixty-one helmeted officers fastening gas masks in unison. John Doar helplessly parried a cry for intervention: "What can I do? Neither side will give an inch."

When the first loud pops sounded, King called out above the squeals that it was tear gas. "Nobody leave," he shouted. "Nobody fight back. We're going to stand our ground." The speakers' truck disappeared beneath thick white clouds, however, as guttural screams drowned out his attempt to sing "We Shall Overcome." Choking, vomiting people ran blindly or dived to the muddy ground where fumes were thinner, but charging officers kicked and clubbed them to flight with the stocks of the tear gas guns. Within half an hour, the Highway Patrol units impounded the tents and dragged from the cleared field a dozen unconscious stragglers. They revived a three-year-old boy from Toronto, Canada. Hysteria lingered in the haze. Observers called the violence "worse than Selma," and Episcopal priest Robert Castle of New Jersey wondered out loud "if democracy in Mississippi and perhaps in the United States was dead." Two friends held up Carmichael, who had collapsed and kept repeating incoherently, "They're gonna shoot again!" Andrew Young, having leapt from the speakers' truck in panic, bent at the waist to stagger through the streets, shouting hoarsely: "We're going to the *church!* We gotta worry about the *people* now!" Reporters followed King as he retreated, wiping his eyes. "In light of this, Dr. King" asked CBS News correspondent John Hart, "have you rethought any of the philosophy of nonviolence?"

"Oh, not at all," King replied. "I still feel that we've got to be nonviolent. How could we be violent in the midst of a police force like that?" To the battered remnant that night in a rendezvous church, his remarks brushed with bitterness over the "ironic" assurances received only hours before from President Johnson. "And the very same men that tear gassed us tonight," said King, "are the men that we are told will be our protectors." Catching himself, he veered into a strangely subdued reverie: "You know, the one thing I have learned . . . on this march is that it is a shame before almighty God that people earn as little money as the Negro people of Mississippi. You know the story." He spoke of the humbling, bonding effect of seeing faces in desperation so closely.

* * *

REFUGEES SCATTERED for the night, many to sleep on the floor of a Catholic school gym. While the marchers regrouped in Canton on Friday, June 24, some two thousand white Mississippians converged on Philadelphia to see if any Negroes dared to reappear as promised at the courthouse scene of Tuesday's mayhem. "We were brutalized here the other day," King declared over a megaphone in their midst, "and I guess someone felt that this would stop us and that we wouldn't come back. But we are right here today standing firm, saying we are gonna have our freedom." Catcalls and shouts of "nigger" drowned out most of his remarks. A few bottles and eggs landed among the three hundred exposed volunteers who pushed with King back to Mt. Nebo Baptist Church, none too trusting of their Highway Patrol escort.

The glum but dutiful line of officers was a visible result of the latest private tussle between Washington and Governor Johnson along the razor's edge of Mississippi politics. (John Doar was filing a new federal lawsuit against Neshoba County authorities for failure to provide basic law enforcement.) On the movement side, relations were equally charged but more fraternal than supposed. In Philadelphia, Carmichael, Floyd McKissick, and Willie Ricks stood with King once again to face the quivering hostility of armed civilians and officers alike. Ricks had pulled King to safety through the tear gas in Canton, and King knew Carmichael and Ricks had endured many of the toughest movement projects for years, each suffering the death of more than one young friend. In private, King conceded to his advisers that the Meredith march had been a "terrible mistake," but he insisted that its troubles lay beyond the publicized internal squabbles. While he tolerated the loyal exuberance of subalterns like Hosea Williams, who contested SNCC rivals in everything from card games and water pistol ambushes to shoving matches, King respected SNCC's earned right to an independent voice. "Listen, Andy," he told Young, "if Stokely is saying the same thing I am saying, he becomes like my assistant." He teased Ricks over his new nickname, "Black Power," in a way that Ricks prized as collegial recognition from a lifelong master of striking fire in an audience. When King said he lacked only clothes to make a fine minister, Ricks boldly asked to borrow some, and King surprised him with an invitation to take freely from his closet in Atlanta. When Carmichael confessed that he had used King's fame as a platform to test the black power slogan, King shrugged, "I have been used before." For all their strategic arguments, which outsiders fanned into a presumption of deep enmity, King and Carmichael discovered a common sense of fun to relieve tedium and tension on the exposed hike through Mississippi. On the last night, King bolted from interminable disputes about overdue bills and the rally program. "I'm sorry, y'all," he told the collected leadership. "James Brown is on. I'm gone."

Carmichael hurried with King from a dean's house to musical bedlam on the Tougaloo College football field, where the soul star Brown writhed in French cuffs and a pompadour through a freedom concert arranged by Harry Belafonte. For want of a piano, Sammy Davis, Jr., performed scat songs a cappella. At the microphone, actor Marlon Brando playfully slapped to his sweaty forehead one of the bumper stickers Willie Ricks had been plastering surreptitiously on police cars: a black panther emblem with words adapted from Muhammad Ali, "We're the Greatest." Brando said he felt "wholly inappropriate," and fumbled for words: "You can't imagine how I feel, because I haven't really participated in this movement, not in the way my conscience gnaws at me that I should." He paid tribute to the estimated ten thousand Mississippians who had walked part of the way from Memphis, and to the array of visiting marchers. Ann Barth, granddaughter of Swiss theologian Karl Barth, joined Allard Lowenstein and numerous veterans of Selma, including one-legged Jim Leatherer and Henry Smith of Mississippi, who wore the orange vest given those who had made the whole trip to Montgomery on foot. Unable to push through the crowd, the thirty-year pacifist Jim Peck sent King a note about an early staff purge against white people: "I wanted to assure you that, despite the dirty deal I have received from CORE, I am still with The Movement and shall be as long as I live."

On Sunday, June 26—three weeks after Meredith left Memphis—

the marchers swelled to 15,000 over the final eight miles from Tougaloo into Jackson. Newcomers included Walter Reuther of the autoworkers and Al Raby with ten busloads from Chicago, plus both King's "twin" white lawyers from New York, Harry Wachtel and Stanley Levison. Film crews from the television networks gathered reactions from the bystanders along the way. "I don't like the niggers," said a typically blunt man. "They stink." A reporter quoted seventy-eight-year-old Monroe Williams as he hobbled on a cane in his first demonstration: "If my daddy had done this, it would have been a lot better for me." Investigators recorded feverish anxiety over social norms in flux. A waitress on North Mill Street, confronting integrated customers from Texas, summoned a Negro cook to take the order while she telephoned a gang of segregationists to intervene. The latter arrived almost simultaneously with the Deacons for Defense and agents from the new Jackson FBI office, both called by the Texans, and the FBI agents in turn called local police officers, who resolved the standoff by shutting down the restaurant.

The closing rally gathered at the "rear" plaza of the state capitol, because Highway Patrol officers in gas masks, backed by National Guard with bayoneted M-1 rifles, sternly blocked the southern front where Mississippi governors traditionally took office near a goddess statue to Confederate womanhood. Disjointed speeches wilted in the heat. King preached from Luke on the parable of Lazarus and Dives, then improvised on his dream oratory "that one day the empty stomachs of Mississippi will be filled, that the idle industries of Appalachia will be revitalized." James Meredith, healed enough to make cantankerous public comments about the reshaped march ("The whole damn thing smells to me"), mis-introduced "Michael" Carmichael, who called upon black soldiers to resist "mercenary" service in Vietnam and declared, "Number one, we have to stop being ashamed of being black." Short prayers between speeches provided respites of inspiration. "We thank Thee, O God, that Thou hast given us the courage to march these past days," said Robert Green. Reverend Allen Johnson of Jackson prayed from the thirteenth chapter of Hebrews: "Be not forgetful to entertain strangers, for thereby some have entertained angels unaware. Remember them that are in bonds as though bound with them, and them which suffer adversity, as being yourselves also in body."

Gnomish Harold DeWolf, King's theology professor from Boston University, had collapsed of heatstroke near Tougaloo. Negro rescuers urged him to disregard occasional taunts of "We don't need whitey" from black power advocates along roads to the hospital. Finally released, DeWolf heard Andrew Young call his name on the public address system as he approached the capitol, and soon was drafted to give the last prayer captured for the hour-long CBS television special that night. "O God, father of all mankind," he said, "we see spread out before Thee the red and black soil of Mississippi, an altar on which a great burnt offering has been laid."

A *New York Times* retrospective said the Meredith march "made it clear that a new philosophy is sweeping the civil rights movement. . . . It had Mr. Carmichael as its leader and the late Malcolm X as its prophet. It also had a battle cry, 'Black Power,' and a slogan directed at whites, 'Move on Over, or We'll Move on Over YOU.' . . . Reporters and cameramen drawn to a demonstration by the magic of Dr. King's name stay to write about and photograph Mr. Carmichael." Primal signals compelled action in distant quarters. Within a month, religious thinkers bought space in the *Times* to interpret "the crisis brought upon our country by historic distortions of important human realities." Their joint composition—"BLACK POWER: Statement by National Committee of Negro Churchmen"—rode the conceptual mix of theology and blackness like a fresh rodeo bull, using the noun "power" fifty-five times. "We are faced now with a situation where conscience-less power meets powerless conscience," declared the consortium of bishops and pastors, "threatening the very foundation of our nation."

Stanley Levison downgraded the contagion with a jeweler's eye for politics. To him, the cry of black power disguised a lack of broad support for SNCC and CORE with cultural fireworks that amounted to an extravagant death rattle. "They're just going to die of attrition," he predicted when King called after midnight on July 1, "and as they die they're going to be noisier and more militant in their expression. . . . Because they're weak, they're making a lot of noise, and we don't want to fall into that trap." Levison, perceiving a larger obstacle than the demise of two civil rights groups, worried that the movement's historic achievements were not consolidated enough to resist or reverse what King called a "mood of violence" throughout the country. He deflected King's instinctive response to formulate a warning about the spillover dangers of "defensive violence," an understandable and prevalent doctrine. When King pressed to "clarify many misconceptions" and to refine nonviolence as "a social strategy for change" in the democratic tradition,

Levison gently but firmly said he and literary agent Joan Daves had unearthed no interest. New York publishers and magazine editors considered King's position "well-known and obvious." They wanted something novel and strong. Black power was hot, whether or not it would last. King was too Sunday School, and he no longer commanded attention at the White House.

"I've heard nothing from President Johnson," King admitted to reporters in Mississippi. "It's terribly frustrating and disappointing. I don't know what I'm going to do." Attorney General Katzenbach had delivered the administration's only public comment on the egregious persecutions inflicted along the march, saying he regretted the Canton attack because tear gas "always makes the situation more difficult." A deputy White House press secretary said the President himself had "no specific reaction." King had learned from sit-in students six years earlier that the most eloquent sermons alone could not move entrenched habits of subjugation, and that oratory must be amplified by disciplined nonviolent witness. That lesson helped ignite since Birmingham and Selma a chain reaction locked within many meanings of the word "movement," from small personal inspiration to historic national change. "In the past, he had been able to deliver the power of response in Washington," wrote Paul Good. "Not now. . . . The silent rebuff made the Nobel Prize winner just one more put-down Negro."

* * *

THE PSYCHOLOGY of war consumed President Johnson throughout June, when perplexity and frustration over the Vietnam death toll registered in public support numbers declining steadily from 46 percent to 40. The Joint Chiefs long had proposed to bomb petroleum storage facilities near the principal North Vietnamese cities, but Johnson withheld approval, weighing the risks of hitting Soviet ships in Haiphong harbor or diplomats in the capital of Hanoi. Military and intelligence analysts, who doubted that success would reduce supplies significantly to the battlefields in South Vietnam, gave way in policy debates to the charged image of any gallon of fuel spared for the transport of foe or matériel to kill an American soldier. Not to bomb "is to pay a higher price in U.S. casualties," Johnson told the National Security Council on June 17. "The choice is one of military lives versus escalation." By June 28, wrestling with final approval for bombers poised to strike, he looked again for positive assurance that "we get enough out of this for the price we pay," but McNamara confirmed instead the relentlessly circular claims of force. "I don't see how you can go on fighting out there, Mr. President, *without* doing it, to be frank with you," he said. "I don't see how you can keep the morale of your troops up. I don't see how you can keep the morale of the people in the country who support you up, without doing it."

"Okay, Bob, go ahead," ordered the President. That night, he violated a security pact with McNamara not to divulge the imminent attacks to his lone dinner guest. Richard Russell of Georgia threatened "a lot of trouble to us," Johnson had warned, because the Senate's champion of military strength still grumbled against the war as folly. Russell once proposed covert schemes to install a South Vietnamese government that would invite American defenders to leave, for instance, and had startled television viewers with his pronouncement that free elections would unify Vietnam under Ho Chi Minh. He made headlines that spring by denying the strategic value in Southeast Asia, scoffing at the fabled "domino theory," and calling for withdrawal unless a Vietnamese survey or plebiscite legitimized an invitation to foreign troops. All Russell's peace flares vanished quickly for lack of interest. War critics showed no inclination to make common cause with the venerable segregationist, even to follow his political lead out of Vietnam, but President Johnson courted him ardently to go in deeper—flattered him, patted his head like a country granddad, assured him yet again that their bosom intimacy from the Senate survived what Russell called "the vast chasm between our views on the misnamed civil rights issue." At dinner, Johnson described the Meredith march as a kind of penance for his domestic break with Russell. He praised Mississippi authorities for preventing greater violence and claimed to have dispatched Martin Luther King to counteract firebrands such as Stokely Carmichael, for whom the President predicted death by assassination within ninety days.

"He was obviously in high good humor," Russell wrote that night in a diary memo, "and from my acquaintance with him, I decided that some policy had suddenly resolved itself favorably or that he had finally arrived at a decision on something that had been troubling him. It was the latter." Russell realized the stakes when Johnson rolled out target maps and confided that bombers were about to take off. As the senator left, resolved to endorse a decisive commitment to arms, the President asked his converted daughter, Luci, whether any Catholic sanctuary would receive him that night. "The monks live in the church," she replied of a parish order she knew, and called ahead to have St.

Dominic's opened to receive a stealthy prayer motorcade. Returning to the White House, Johnson stayed awake to receive ten flash relays before dawn on June 29. Walt Rostow, who had replaced McGeorge Bundy as National Security Adviser, reported black clouds spread over fifty square miles at twenty thousand feet above Haiphong. "So it looks like we burned up quite a bit of oil," he said. From the Pentagon, Cyrus Vance advised skepticism toward the preliminary estimate of 80 percent damage to Hanoi targets. The President, braced to hear otherwise, cross-examined him about the safe return of all pilots and the strange absence of antiaircraft fire. "Thank you," he said finally. "Let's go to bed."

Four of five Americans consulted in polls believed the drastic new bombing campaign would end the war soon, and majority approval rebounded for the balance of the year. Meanwhile, military analysts confirmed secret projections that the actual flow of war matériel would recover in spite of the bombing, as the North Vietnamese dispersed not only oil supplies and transportation lines but urban families into the countryside. (The population of Hanoi dropped by December from 800,000 to 200,000.) Knowing that the Vietnamese could replace their losses indefinitely, and were doing so, American war planners counted on the psychological wear of modern airpower upon a land-bound adversary. McNamara pictured enemy soldiers under combined assault in the South, utterly devoid of flying machines for mobility or retaliation in the sky. "They also know that nobody is protecting North Vietnam," he told Johnson, "and we have a free rein." The mismatched punishment lured McNamara to defy his own numbers that pointed stubbornly to a savage stalemate. "The only thing that will prevent it, Mr. President, is their morale breaking," he said. More than faith in the cause, or the steely will to marshal sacrifice, a strange identification across the line of slaughter consoled American leaders through their own dire apprehensions. "And if we hurt them enough, it isn't so much that they don't have more men as it is that they can't get the men to fight," McNamara anticipated. "I myself believe that's the only chance we have of winning this thing . . . because we're just not killing enough of them to make it impossible for the North to continue to fight. But we are killing enough to destroy the morale of those people down there, if they think this is gonna have to go on forever."

Ho Chi Minh responded with a national appeal on July 17, warning that "the Johnson 'clique' " may send a million men into a war that could last twenty more years. "Hanoi, Haiphong and other cities and enterprises may be destroyed," he said, "but the Vietnamese people will not be intimidated." Ho advised Washington by indirect channels that much of his population had never known anything but war. Weakened by lung disease at age seventy-six, he called for mobilization of reserves in words that soon would be carved on his mausoleum: "Nothing is more important than independence and freedom."

Beyond males of every age, some 1.5 million North Vietnamese women formed combat and support brigades that included air defense units. By 1967, seven thousand antiaircraft batteries, two hundred missile sites, and a meager hundred airplanes would oppose U.S. bombers overhead. The government already celebrated as a patriotic heroine twenty-year-old Ngo Thi Tuyen, who would defend and repair the Dragon's Jaw Bridge under perpetual bombardment until laser-guided American bombs wiped out the vulnerable link of Highway 1 in 1972. *Nhan Dan,* the Communist newspaper, acknowledged "feudal" resistance to the policy of equal advancement: "Many Party members do not wish to admit women because although they think that they are courageous and diligent, they also believe that 'women cannot lead but must be led.' "

Ho Chi Minh's call generated 170,000 emergency youth troops, nearly all girls, who marched south with knapsacks, cooking pots, and shovels to maintain the heavily bombed Ho Chi Minh Trail. Vu Thi Vinh said she defied her parents, lied about her age to join at fifteen, and wrote competitive essays to be selected for "dare to die" teams that defused unexploded ordnance. A cohort volunteered even though she loathed socialism and the "peasants" running the government. "Many of us temporarily lost our hair from malaria," recalled Nguyen Thi Kim, "and living in the jungle for so many years made us look terrible." By 1975, the emergency troops had shepherded war matériel south and an estimated 700,000 wounded soldiers back to North Vietnam, while helping air defenders bring down some of the 8,558 U.S. aircraft lost in Southeast Asia. Women survivors, who often would be left sterile, disfigured, and bitterly alone in a society that treasured the extended family, adapted to unspeakable carnage in war. "It was terrible," said volunteer Le Minh Khue, "but we were young and we made jokes." They arranged work choruses according to a proverb that songs are louder than bombs, and made up nicknames for dreaded jets such as the "genie of thunder" F-105. "When the helicopters dropped soldiers," a female veteran observed of American deployments, "they looked like dragonflies laying eggs."

* * *

AMERICAN WOMEN stirred politically on the day U.S. bombers first struck Hanoi and Haiphong. A small caucus convened over a seminal speech that accused the Equal Employment Opportunity Commission of trivializing the legal rights accorded women two years earlier by the Civil Rights Act of 1964. Rep. Martha Griffiths of Michigan said the EEOC had reduced thousands of sex discrimination complaints to amusing asides, wondering in its newsletter whether punishment could reach employers who refused to hire "a woman as a dog warden or a man as a 'house mother' for a college sorority house." She cited two exceptions to prove the rule of heedless condescension. First, the EEOC had just allowed "Help Wanted Male" and "Help Wanted Female" advertising sections to continue in newspapers nationwide, with a declaration that the separation rested on a lawful intent to "obtain a maximum reader response and not on a desire to exclude applicants of a particular sex." Griffiths called this precedent a capitulation to the newspaper lobby as well as a transparent contradiction of the EEOC's moves to abolish separate job listings by race, and she denounced no less sharply a second sex discrimination case in which the EEOC reserved BFOQ (bona fide occupational qualification) status for the airline industry's policy of firing any stewardess who married or reached the age of thirty-three. "Is it because the Commission does not want to recognize that women's rights are human rights?" she asked on the House floor. "Or is it an unconscious desire to alienate women from the Negroes' civil rights movement? Human rights cannot be divided into competitive pieces."

Tempers flared in the June 29 caucus at the Washington Hilton Hotel. Legal strategist Pauli Murray among others proposed a new organization modeled on the NAACP to push for gender equity in the enforcement of Title VII, but some dissenters felt the parallel would diminish women. Several women with influential positions believed they could seek parity more effectively within regular channels, and others argued that a self-proclaimed women's lobby would be perceived as arrogant and unprofessional. The last point was too much for Betty Friedan, author of *The Feminine Mystique,* who had been recruited as an independent voice. "Get out! Get out!" Friedan cried. "This is my room and my liquor!" The quarreling confederates fell back on plans to petition the state and federal agencies represented at the Third National Conference of Commissions on the Status of Women, but overtures were rebuffed the next morning as improper for advisory bodies and government employees.

By noon on June 30, Dr. Kay Clarenbach of Wisconsin led a handful of well-tailored but chagrinned moderates to concede that the activists may have been correct, and Friedan made up for shortcomings in collaborative tact with her facile pen, sketching on a lunch napkin the consensus brief for an ad hoc civil rights group ". . . to take the actions needed to bring women into the mainstream of American society, now, full equality for women, in fully equal partnership with men. NOW. The National Organization for Women." Twenty-eight charter members contributed $5 toward the initial expenses. The founding announcement in October drew no major press notice until November 22, when the *New York Times* covered a repeat performance by Friedan on the fashion page beneath Thanksgiving recipes: "Speaking in a gravelly alto from the depths of the large fur collar that trimmed her neat black suit, the ebullient author suggested that women today were 'in relatively little position to influence or control major decisions. But,' she added, leaning forward in the lilac velvet Victorian chair and punching the air as if it were something palpable, 'what women do have is the vote.' "

To protest government inaction, NOW members first carried giant balls of red tape on thin picket lines. Martha Griffiths, their forerunner and inspiration, spoke sometimes as brashly as Diane Nash or Stokely Carmichael on the Freedom Rides. "If you are trying to run a whorehouse in the sky," she told airline executives at a congressional hearing, "then get a license." Too slowly for participants, but swiftly relative to the antecedent momentum in race relations, a new women's movement coalesced to transform daily life through politics.

CHAPTER 30

Chicago

July–August 1966

BLACK power followed the civil rights movement up the Mississippi River heartland, from the Delta's primitive soil to Chicago's granite expanse. Hosea Williams stayed behind in Grenada, where police outside the jail clubbed three hundred people to break up a sympathy vigil for forty-three others arrested earlier, and King charged publicly that local officials had reneged on "every promise made" during the Meredith march. Headlines favored the new national controversy—"CORE Hears Cries of 'Black Power,' " "Black Nationalists Gain More Attention in Harlem," "NAACP Head Warns 'Black Power' Means 'Black Death' "—which framed the front-page coverage even for Chicago's grand kickoff rally on July 10: "Dr. King and CORE Chief Act to Heal Rights Breach." Floyd McKissick trimmed his speech at Soldier Field to fit a movement trumpeted with warm-up music that ranged from the Singing Nuns of Mundelein College to blues legend B. B. King. Reporters chased a roving band of the Blackstone Rangers gang to photograph their black power banner. A white limousine delivered Martin Luther King, who spoke under a parasol in clammy 98 degree heat. His children begged to see the headquarters of the famous Mayor Daley, but three-year-old Bunny collapsed on Andrew Young's shoulders before the baked remnant of five thousand walked three miles downtown. She slept while King ceremoniously taped the parchment of fourteen demands to a locked door at City Hall.

Mayor Richard Daley once again bracketed the challenge with official events. He announced one day before the rally that Chicago had moved to repair 102,847 apartments in 9,226 substandard buildings so far, with housing fines double those of the previous year, then hosted preliminary negotiations two days later on July 11. King conceded Daley's evasive points that slum conditions existed in every major city and had preceded his administration, but declined entreaties to join or critique the local abatement drive. Likewise, Daley endorsed King's goal but avoided comment on his "Open City" demands for integrated housing and employment. With each side firmly refusing to be drawn into the other's agenda, the mayor complained of nonconstructive pressure and emerged ever the booster for Chicago—"We will expand our programs"—while King called for nonviolent direct action to reveal "the depth and dimensions of the problem." James Bevel and Bernard Lafayette were leading drills for five hundred nonviolent volunteers to be deployed the next day, but a pothole intervened on the Near West Side corner of Roosevelt and Throop.

While calling for roadside assistance, the driver of an ice cream truck saw children dart from his paralyzed vehicle with purloined treats, and he told the first arriving police that the culprits were playing in the spray from nearby fire hydrants. Officers shut them off, drawing protest from adults who cited long-standing tradition and pointed to gushing hydrants only three blocks north. Beneath a crossfire of shouts—that the Italian neighborhood was in a different police precinct, with no reported ice cream thieves, versus complaints that three of the four closest swimming pools were off-limits to black residents—a sporadic duel of wrenches turned the hydrants on and off until officers arrested Donald Henry, who appealed to the gathering crowd: "Why don't you do something about it?" A cascade of curses, splashes, and rocks brought thirty backup police cruisers. Broken windows radiated from street reports of black children whacked with truncheons for trying to cool themselves.

King and Coretta, on their way to a mass meeting, detoured around jolting sights of zigzag marauders and a crescendo of sirens. Confused reports filtered into Shiloh Baptist Church about the terms set by gang leaders to parley about the ongoing violence—expulsion of white people from the church and/or proof that prisoners were alive. Responding to the latter, King made his way with gospel singer Mahalia Jackson to the 12th District police station and negotiated the release of six battered teenagers who presented their own grievances to a tumultuous Shiloh crowd, chiefly police brutality and the lack of playgrounds or swimming pools. King preached against riots and halfhearted reform. "It's like improving the food in a prison," he said. "One day that man wants to get *out* of prison." He invoked President Kennedy on the urgency of the movement—"those who will make this peaceful revolution impossible will make a violent revolution inevitable"—and confessed his own anguish: "We have stood up for nonviolence with all our hearts. . . . I need help. I need some victories. I need some concessions." For once he could not hold an audience against hecklers inside and the noise of urban chaos beyond the walls. Hundreds of young people stalked out. At a roadblock of garbage cans on Ashland Avenue, gang members shattered windows on a car and surrounded the occupants until Bill Clark of the West Side Organization jumped among them, pointing to familiar faces and shouting, "You gotta beat me if you're going to beat these guys." Rev. Archie Hargraves and Al Sampson of SCLC joined Clark in a human shield around three terrified Puerto Rican men. Nearly all night, leaders from the Chicago movement coalition roamed at their own peril with pleas for angry people to go home.

Violence subsided until late Wednesday, July 13, when crews from the water department began to refit the water hydrants with tamper-proof locks. Bricks flew through windows again, then at firefighters who answered alarms to burning, looted stores. Vandalism and the first sniper shots jumped a mile to housing projects on West Madison Avenue. Thursday night, on his continuous rounds of mediation, King received notice that more serious riots were spreading miles west into Lawndale and Garfield Park. His children at the Hamlin Avenue apartment rushed impulsively to see what caused the sudden bangs and crashes of glass below, which prompted Coretta to shriek, "Get away from that window or you'll get your heads blown off!" Her quotation spiced a scoop for an encamped British reporter.

By Friday morning, when King briefly returned home, the riots had claimed two fatalities nearby: a pregnant fourteen-year-old killed while walking with friends and a twenty-eight-year-old black man from Mississippi, shot in the back. Mayor Daley, who until then had minimized the disturbance as "juvenile incidents," appealed publicly for National Guard troops to quell a situation he said outsiders had incited beyond his control. He blamed King's staff—"people that came in here have been talking for the last year of violence, and showing pictures and instructing people in how to conduct violence"—and his leading Negro ally indicted the movement at a tandem press conference. "I believe our young people are not vicious enough to attack a whole city," declared Rev. J. H. Jackson. "Some other forces are using these young people."

King and Raby reacted within hours by leading what amounted to a sit-in at City Hall, protesting "unfortunate" distortions of their struggle to prevent rather than start violence. When Catholic Archbishop James Cody himself joined them, Daley received the group with conciliatory effusion. "Doctor King, I want to make one thing clear," he said. "We know that you did nothing to cause the disorders, and that you are a man of peace and love." King reciprocated with a pared-down list of four suggestions, one of which sealed a heavily satirized truce. "Now there was a program, and Daley liked it," wrote Mike Royko in the *Chicago Daily News*. "Give them water. He had a whole lake of it right outside the door." City workers would distribute ten portable swimming pools and refit the hydrants yet again with spray nozzles instead of locks. "We don't need sprinklers," grumbled a dissenter. "We need jobs." Attorney General Katzenbach, with White House approval, dispatched two top assistants to Chicago as four thousand National Guard troops rolled in to restore order late Friday, July 15. The riots were a miniature Watts, with the two fatalities and eighty serious injuries, including six police officers wounded by gunfire, plus $2 million in property damage and some five hundred arrests.

John Doar and Roger Wilkins of the Justice Department knocked unannounced at Hamlin Avenue before midnight. For Doar, who had been diverted from a canoe vacation in his native Wisconsin, the big city was unsettling after six years of civil rights field trips to the rural South. A bottle shattered against his car en route from appointments with Chicago officials. Wilkins, nephew of NAACP leader Roy Wilkins, expected King to have slipped after hours to the hotel comforts cherished by his peers, and was surprised to find him in a ghetto "showplace" rattier than advertised. Scores of Vice Lords and Cobras were crammed into chairs and floor spots, questioning King intensely. Some vented hardships and toughness blankly to King as a stranger, saying Molotov cocktails got attention, while others knowingly articulated their gang culture to one of the most famous people in the world. King engaged them one by one, sometimes turning to Abernathy to share their own war stories from jail or the relief of a joke about black preachers. The Washington men waited four hours—"four *hot* hours, four sweaty hours," Wilkins recalled—mesmerized by an unrecorded seminar on pain and respect that preempted their exalted rank. For Andrew Young, the turning point was a perceptive, heartfelt speech on distinctions between the tactics and philosophy of nonviolence by Richard "Peanut" Tidwell, leader of the Roman Saints, who engineered a pact to give movement methods a try. When the gangs left, consultations between the Justice Department men and King commenced and continued into dawn on Saturday, July 16.

Internal deliberations reeled from a disastrous beginning. The gang summit was regarded as a crucial but tentative step toward recovery, neutralizing a random force prone to sabotage. Stanley Levison thought most Americans would not blame King for the riots but might believe he could have stopped them. He said Daley's cleverly mixed signals would turn the riots against the movement unless the movement turned them against Daley. To retreat now would suggest failure. To go forward meant trying to revive nonviolence from the lingering smoke of a riot. King bemoaned the prior delays, and confessed that an earlier launch for the action campaign might have averted this setback. The sprawling coalition had nothing to show for nearly a year's preparation beyond its own urgent warnings and postponements into a record-breaking siege of heat. (In New York City alone, an extra 650 deaths for the week spiked the mortality rate 40 percent above normal.) Woes had piled up like biblical pestilence with discovery on Thursday of eight student nurses systematically bound, raped, strangled, and stabbed in their South Chicago dormitory. Horror over an unfathomable mass murder sapped low reserves of public trust. Even so, movement leaders mounted rebuilding demonstrations Sunday in Gage Park, then Monday in the Belmont Cragin neighborhood. "We must move on with our positive program to make Chicago an open city," King declared.

* * *

MAYOR DALEY hacked at the movement's weakened lines of appeal to the national government. "King's rally on a week from Sunday was fifty percent Johnson—'Johnson's a killer, Johnson's a destroyer of human life, Johnson is a killer in Vietnam,' " he told the President privately on July 19. "He [King] is not your friend. He's against you on Vietnam. He's a goddam faker." Daley portrayed the riots as a result of sinister and mystifying ingratitude toward Northern benefactors. His monologue skewed the movement's demands, some of which duplicated Johnson's own legislation in Congress.

The President squeezed in a word to seek an end point. "What shape have you got King in?" he asked. "Is he about ready to get out?"

"I don't think so," Daley replied. He spilled plans to overwhelm the movement with patronage and the poverty programs—"We got rodent control, we got insects, we destroyed a thousand slum buildings in six months"—while branding King a defector in the great quest for fairness. "What the hell, that's the main thing you've been fighting for," the mayor exclaimed, "and then to see them run on the goddam foreign question!

"You don't run from people who have been your friends," Daley continued emphatically. "You stick with them." Like Richard Russell, he opposed the war but subordinated his opinion in national crisis. Pointedly, Daley pledged Chicago's entire machine to Johnson's Vietnam course by their two-way code of political loyalty. "That's what I've been talking about with our leaders tonight," he declared. "Eighty of them in the convention, and I told 'em the same thing. I told 'em, 'We don't run. We might be defeated, but we stand with Johnson on Vietnam. We stand for justice for all our people, and we also stand for law and order, and I'll be damned if we let anyone take over themselves the running of the city.' "

"You're just as right as you can be, Dick," said the President, who signed off succinctly: "And I'll support you."

* * *

On Thursday, July 28, King called for an all-night vigil Friday outside a real estate office that consistently refused to serve black customers. Earlier in the day, several clergy on the agenda committee had argued for a respite instead, to calm potential allies already strained by the daily actions such as integrated shopping trips and "friendship" basketball games on white playgrounds. Others still resisted the movement's emphasis on residence—"All housing should be available to all people"—as a misguided, elitist approach to the goal of ending slums. The heated tactical debates essentially deferred to James Bevel, who in turn relied on his Nashville seminary friend and Freedom Ride cellmate Bernard Lafayette. After Lafayette and his young wife, Colia, created SNCC's first Selma project in 1963, the American Friends Service Committee had hired them on the recommendation of James Lawson to test nonviolent methods in Chicago, where they found comparative weakness in the popular drives for open schools and open employment. The school struggle proved tired after a decade, with its target, Superintendent

Benjamin Willis, set to retire late in August, and a diffuse jobs campaign yielded piecemeal results.* Housing showed contrasting potential, even though relatively few black people wanted or could afford to live in white neighborhoods. Lafayette called the inner boundaries of Northern cities an invisible indicator of Jim Crow that was anything but subtle—"segregation without signs." Studies by his American Friends Service Committee colleagues estimated that only one percent of residential listings was open to black applicants, with restrictions traceable from the formal policy of 1917 to a blunt contemporary statement by the Illinois Association of Real Estate Boards: "All we are asking is that the brokers and salesmen have the same right to discriminate as the owners who engage their services." By harrowing tests from working-class Belmont Cragin to upscale Oak Park, Lafayette's action groups sampled the latent capacity of housing demonstrations to expose human forces that locked people into slums.

To begin the new stage of nonviolent witness, fifty volunteers set up Friday outside F. H. Halvorsen Realty at the corner of Kedzie Avenue and South 63rd Street, but hecklers ten times their number gathered with such menace that Bevel aborted the vigil before midnight. He accepted an offer to leave in police vans, which touched off marathon debates with Al Raby about whether the ground for nonviolent witness had been abandoned or insufficiently prepared. Some workers stayed up to paint signs such as "All God's Children Need a Place to Live," making sure their message would reach adversaries and the public alike, while others summoned reinforcements with extra warnings that this was no training exercise.

A column of 250 left New Friendship Baptist Church at ten o'clock on Saturday morning, July 30. They walked west from Halsted Avenue for twenty-four blocks along South 71st Street, turned north at Kedzie through a golf course, and emerged from pastoral Marquette Park at 67th Street, where several hundred angry white residents chanted, "Nigger go home!" Chicago police officers with nightsticks cordoned the route toward 63rd Street, but eggs, bottles, and rocks flew over them to strike the marchers with such force that Bevel and Raby turned back in pell-mell retreat without reaching Halvorsen Realty, one of twenty-

* In the fifth Chicago settlement for SCLC's Operation Breadbasket, Jesse Jackson reached agreement with the Bowman Dairy on July 22 to hire forty-five black workers in previously white positions.

three firms in the area that had refused to show properties to black or integrated test groups. New leadership arguments complicated the aftermath. Should the movement complain about lax police protection, at the risk of diluting its witness, or steel supporters to "receive" blows that dramatized the depth of hatred at the color line? Organizers mobilized to try again rather than surrender to violence.

Sunday afternoon, a caravan of automobiles parked under police guard at the foot of Marquette Park to facilitate the return trip. An escort of some two hundred officers in riot helmets guided 550 people up Kedzie into a waiting crescendo of neighborhood fury. The previous day's rocks escalated to cherry bombs and bricks. Some errant missiles went through store windows, but others felled victims. Sister Mary Angelica, a first-grade teacher at Sacred Heart School, went down unconscious and bleeding to cheers of "We got another one," as movement marshals pushed through with her to a police cruiser bound for Holy Cross Hospital. Older residents aimed special venom at "white niggers"—roughly half the marchers—and pelted the police escorts as traitors. Chants of "white power" gave way to mob cries of "Burn them like Jews!" When a captain persuaded Raby to turn west for the shelter of a narrow tree-lined street, teenagers dashed through alleys for flank attacks, opened fire hydrants to drench the confined lines, and swarmed ahead to mass four thousand strong. A radio alarm from the Eighth District rallied police units citywide, but forty marchers and two officers had been carried off to the hospital when the besieged lines recrossed Marquette Park. Before Bevel and Raby could decide whether to risk dispersing to the parked cars, teenagers fanned out to slit tires, smash windows, and roll over vehicles bearing the telltale "End Slums" stickers. Dodging officers in pursuit, they set a dozen cars ablaze with Molotov cocktails and pushed two others into a pond on the golf course. Andrew Young saw the taillights of his rented Ford at the water line. Jesse Jackson said he had been hit three times but waved off questions about what happened. "I don't know," he told reporters blankly on the forced return walk. Some of the dazed and weary joined a chorus of "We Shall Overcome" raised by supporters waiting at the Ashland Avenue color line.

The shock of Southern-style hate images, which made front pages everywhere, put Chicago's leaders under severe stress. Rabbi Robert J. Marx regretted his role as a community observer for the Chicago Federation of thirty-three Reform Jewish congregations, saying he had seen

in the raging fears of ordinary parents and children "how the concentration camp could have occurred and how man's hatred could lead them
to kill." Marx wrote a pained confession about the difficulty of being a
prophet close to home. "I was on the wrong side of the street. I should
have been with the marchers." The august *Chicago Tribune,* on the other
hand, identified with the rampage of those "baited into a near-riot last
weekend," and drew battle lines against "the imported prophets of
'nonviolence' who are seeking to incite trouble with marches into white
neighborhoods." Mayor Daley, caught in the middle, told neighborhood
representatives from Chicago Lawn and Gage Park that community violence would only backfire against their worthy goal to end the unrest.
His pleas for restraint—to let the marchers deplete their energy and go
away—struck local leaders as mealy-mouthed bunk unworthy of
America's strongest mayor. Many of them found it especially galling
that Daley's police officers, widely known to them by their first names,
were arresting the young white defenders rather than the uninvited
strangers.

The mayor sent his black alderman to meet with Raby and King for
the first time, creating a muffled fanfare that he was probing toward a
settlement. Within the movement, daily housing tests in other areas
stoked expectations that peaked Thursday night in a mass meeting of
1,700 people. "If there is any doubt in anybody's mind concerning
whether we have a movement here in Chicago," King told a live radio
audience from New Friendship, "you ought to be in this church
tonight!" Announcing that he would lead the next day's showdown personally—"My place is in Gage Park"—King addressed ethnic friction
within the movement. Even if Jews or Catholics should reject his help,
he pledged, "I would still take a stand against bigotry." By the same
token, he urged new white allies to uphold their principles in spite of
distrust from unfamiliar, frustrated black people. "You ought to stand
up and say, 'I'm free and this is a free country and I believe in justice,' "
King urged, " 'and I'm gonna be in the movement whether you want
me or not.' " He acknowledged fatigue with a watchword of tenacity. "I
still have faith in the future," he said. "My brothers and sisters, I *still* can
sing 'We Shall Overcome.' "

On Friday afternoon, August 5, specially trained vanguards of
twenty went ahead to establish picket lines outside Halvorsen and three
other real estate companies along Kedzie. A huge body of 960 Chicago
police deployed in riot helmets between the assembling march lines and

some five thousand residents who had descended in advance to the northern edge of Marquette Park. Young men carried Confederate flags or crude handmade signs such as, "The Only Way to End Niggers Is Exterminate." Noise built impatiently for the arrival of King, who was late as usual. No sooner did he emerge from a car at five o'clock than a perversely hostile chant broke out, "We want King! We want King!" Officers held the crowd back beyond the range of bricks but not rocks or cherry bombs, and screams answered the first explosions. Densely packed marchers moved forward awkwardly, some with bent arms shielding their heads. A palm-sized rock soon staggered King to the pavement, his chin propped on his left knee, which raised both shrieks of triumph and cries of fear. Pulled up to his feet, he flinched from a bang above the roar of voices. Officers and aides asked if he was all right. "I think so," said King, swaying slightly just before the gunlike report of another cherry bomb made him duck again. He straightened up with a glazed stare, a lump swelling behind his right ear.

As the embattled columns moved slowly through Chicago Lawn toward Gage Park, families of mostly Italian, Lithuanian, and Polish origin emerged on bungalow porches to aim special abuse at vested Catholic clergy. One middle-aged woman ran alongside the black cleric George Clements until she collapsed, screaming, "You dirty nigger priest!" Marshals secluded Clements in one of the escort cars, which became a prime target for rocks. Back in the ranks, Rabbi Marx was struck by a rock as he kept his pledge to join some six hundred marchers. Up front, blood streamed from the broken nose of a volunteer bodyguard who shielded King with Raby, Lafayette, and Jesse Jackson. Ahead, a phalanx of seventy-five officers cleared a path through teenagers, one of whom retreated with the sign, "King Would Look Good with a Knife in His Back." A knife that fell short pierced the shoulder of a heckler, who was hauled away among thirty casualties. King paused only briefly to salute and absorb steadfast pickets at the four real estate offices, curtailing ceremonies because of intensified bombardment in the commercial district.

By seven o'clock, when the three-mile march reentered Marquette Park under remorseless pursuit, Deputy Police Chief Robert Lynskey waited with a fleet of transit buses to speed evacuation and extra police to meet a new threat. "There are at least twenty-five hundred people up there," he said, pointing to a knoll in the open park space. While nimble teenagers chased the buses—an undercover officer in one reported broken windows and injuries from flying glass—angry adults just home from work ran down to attack through gaps in the police line. Women poured sugar into gas tanks. Men set more vehicles on fire. A small group wrenched Father George Clements from his escort car and beat him until police intervened. A larger group of one hundred surrounded and pummeled six isolated officers until emergency help arrived. "The reinforcements came running, firing pistols in the air," observed *New York Times* correspondent Gene Roberts, "and pummeling and clubbing whites with their nightsticks. 'You nigger-loving S.O.B.'s,' said a middle-aged man in a green Ivy League style suit. 'I'll never vote for Mayor Daley again.' "

Deprived of marchers, swirling bands stoned police cars until midnight while King consoled a stunned and disoriented crowd that filled New Friendship. He said it was a sad day for Chicago when people called nuns bitches. He explained again how he believed disciplined courage could bring social sickness into healing light, earned cheers with drumbeat vows that violence would not stop the movement, and endorsed plans to march in twenty neighborhoods like Gage Park. Dripping with perspiration, King left the church to face news cameras about the day of mayhem. "I have never in my life seen such hate," he said. "Not in Mississippi or Alabama. This is a terrible thing."

* * *

KING PREACHED at Ebenezer on his way to the tenth annual convention of SCLC. One year after the triumphant celebration in Birmingham, when the Selma movement had melted national indecision about voting rights, a pervasive climate of violence paralyzed and even hardened the response to the Chicago marches. He marveled that gang marshals had batted down incoming missiles and insults on the marches with a uniform forbearance conceded by astonished police officers who despised them as thugs. "I saw their noses being broken and blood flowing from their wounds," King remarked, "and I saw them continue and not retaliate—not one of them—with violence." He hesitated to publicize the miracle reform, however, because the gang pact was unstable at best. A Vice Lord nicknamed "Duck" already threatened to shoot Bevel for over-praising his commitment to nonviolence. Tempers sizzled in church between rivals who had fortified themselves with alcohol to endure white attackers, and multiple strains closed New Friendship Baptist to future use by the civil rights coalition.

Lurid details of extraneous horror seeped from the arraignment of

Richard Speck for the July 14 serial murder of eight nurses. In hiding, the twenty-four-year-old Dallas drifter had tried to commit suicide at a Chicago Loop flophouse that rented "fireproof" cubicles covered with chicken wire for ninety cents a night. Conflicted nurses at Cook County Hospital helped save his life for trial, but the first court appearance on August 1 eerily overlapped a landmark of terror on live television. From the high observation deck of a university tower in Austin, Texas, barricaded sniper Charles Whitman killed fourteen and wounded thirty-one random pedestrians before officers killed him. Stupefied viewers learned that the young ex-Marine left frank notes—"I don't really understand myself these days"—about murdering his wife and mother just beforehand to spare them the embarrassment of his plans. Four days later, a teenager said he shot a night watchman "to have fun like the guys in Chicago and Austin." White Americans recoiled from a monstrous contagion among themselves. Crime statisticians soon added a new category for mass murder, and police departments invented SWAT teams. The news from Texas eclipsed Speck's "crime of the century" as well as the first White House family wedding since the era of Theodore Roosevelt.

On Monday, August 8, two days after Luci Johnson's marriage, King answered questions at an airport press conference about why his convention was in Mississippi if racial hatred was worse in Chicago. He described regional differences as subtle but important, arguing that Southern brutality "came in many instances from the policemen themselves," whereas the Chicago police "are doing a good job of seeking to restrain the violence." It was a relief in some respects for him to return to the clarity of outspoken segregationists. By tradition, Mississippi politicians had just launched the election season at the Neshoba County Fair in Philadelphia, where Deputy Cecil Price remained indicted, with every candidate jockeying to impress outdoor crowds. Governor Paul Johnson inveighed against "a dark and ominous cloud" unlike any normal political slogan—"Don't be fooled!"—calling black power "a storm that contains the thunder of terror . . . and harbors the seeds of a hurricane of hate and hostility that can sweep sanity aside." State Auditor Hamp King welcomed a pendulum of change "back our way, away from the colored madness." U.S. Senator James Eastland quoted J. Edgar Hoover that civil rights groups were "nothing but a hatchery for Communists," heaped wry praise on the Yankee mayor of Chicago—"He said no, we're not gonna give you nothin'!"—and won his usual prize for foot-stomping laughter and acclaim with a caricature of the Meredith march. "I flew over the scene at 3,500 feet," Eastland shouted, "and the marchers smelled up that high."

With Coretta, King returned Monday night to Rankin County Airport. He went personally to draw along his Jackson police escort and provide what assurance he could for the keynote speaker, Edward Kennedy. The three of them drove back through hate leaflets and nails strewn on the roadway, declining to stop when flat tires stranded two police cruisers and several reporters from their convoy. (FBI agents estimated three hundred pounds of "what appeared to be 1¾" roofing nails," and advised headquarters that Kennedy arrived safely at the King Edward Hotel despite nails in all four tires.) King tinkered hurriedly with his introduction of "a young man on the way up," though Kennedy at thirty-four was only three years his junior. He praised his precocious legislative skill, noting how "this freshman senator earned the respect of his colleagues," then presented Kennedy like a baptismal candidate as "the ninth child, the fourth and youngest son of proud parents." Nearly a thousand SCLC delegates in the emotion-charged banquet hall erupted for one who dared to come among them looking so much like the revered, assassinated President. They stood to cheer when Kennedy asked why the nation would spend upward of $2 billion per month to make war in South Vietnam and not make "the same kind of effort for the twenty million people of the Negro race right here in America, whose freedom and future are also at stake?" They stood again when he cautioned against separatism: "If you isolate yourselves, you will be crippling your effectiveness in what is basically not a white or Negro cause, but an American cause." The Kings rushed Kennedy back for a late-night departure that minimized the risk of his first visit to Mississippi.

A high fever sent King to bed for most of the convention with what Abernathy called "his virus, the one he always got during the tensest moment in a campaign." He complained of depletion until Stanley Levison mollified him with rosy predictions for mail solicitations and a new book contract. ("We're at a real turn in the movement," Levison said on a wiretapped line. "A lot of people are confused . . . this is the time when a book can be useful.") King sent Andrew Young in his stead to deliver a downbeat president's address, which acknowledged a broad shift of interest from race to Vietnam and claimed grim success already for one of the prime objectives of a Northern movement: to break down persistent illusions that race was a regional rather than national issue. "Chicago has proven that not long can one section of this nation wallow in pious condemnation of another," Young declared, "while it practices worse atrocities against its black citizens."

In King's absence, the delegates passed a resolution to support a guaranteed income base for all Americans. They ratified Al Lowenstein and Charles Morgan as the first two white board members, and bid farewell to staff members departing from movement fatigue. Among them, King apologized to the fastidious program director Randy Blackwell for SCLC's "non-existent structural and organizational foundations" to manage the avalanche of daily crises across the South. A youth group in Jackson was petitioning SCLC for help with city swimming pools still closed to evade the civil rights law, and Hosea Williams, who risked his life to integrate Grenada's public library, left Blackwell a trail of browbeaten colleagues, bail bills, and complaints from rental companies about cars he had lost, wrecked, or abandoned.* King nearly always tolerated backwash from his quarrelsome, headstrong lieutenants as the price of creative tension essential to a movement—and teased Andrew Young for being so "normal" that he would teach people to adjust to segregation—but the unruly competition exacted a toll. On his sickbed, King learned that his latest staff prodigy had committed him impulsively to a suicidal march.

Jesse Jackson idolized, imitated, and almost literally absorbed King. On his first staff trip to Atlanta, lodged in King's home for lack of money, he had explored tirelessly the nexus between theology and movement politics, nearly always answering his own questions before the nonplussed host could reply. Andrew Young among others resented but admired his urge to take charge, which was vital and irrepressible like a wonder of nature. Jackson churned out sermons and strategy papers for the Chicago movement framed in King's grand language, and he synthesized the tactical flair of nonviolent mentors Lafayette and Bevel, especially Bevel's gift for poetic flights of imagination. In the af-

---

* The New York counsel for Avis Corporation described one of the rented vehicles for which Williams demanded an emergency replacement: "A subsequent close examination of the Ford indicated, in addition to extensive rear-end damage, that the front door locks had been jimmied, the glove compartment lock had been almost completely removed, the radio antenna had been removed, the radio was disconnected and was almost wholly removed from its place, the spare tire and jack were missing, the upholstery was extensively soiled and stained, and the interior filled with debris, papers, old clothes, and empty liquor bottles."

tershock of Gage Park, Jackson cut through backroom disagreements about whether to continue or suspend the marches. He plumbed layers of historical degradation before a mass meeting at Warren Avenue Congregational Church. "I have counted up the cost," Jackson solemnly concluded. "My life. Bevel's life. Even Dr. King's life. Over and against the generation and the continuation of a kind of sin that's going to internally disrupt this country and possibly the world." He spread his arms in surrender. "I counted the cost!" Jackson shouted. "I'm going to Cicero!"

Apoplexy flashed through Chicago. Cook County Sheriff Richard Ogilvie announced that the response of his suburban jurisdiction "would make Gage Park look like a tea party." In May, teenager Jerome Huey had been beaten to death on a Cicero street when his job interviews extended past dusk. While movement leaders gritted their teeth over the freelance outburst, Bevel gamely supported Jackson in public. "They can buy tanks and they can arm every child," he declared, "but we are going to Cicero."

* * *

HOWLS AGAINST the daily vigils put Cicero in abeyance, and a month's upheaval since the Soldier Field rally buckled major figures on all sides. On August 10, "with a heavy heart," Archbishop Cody of Chicago called for a moratorium on demonstrations to prevent loss of life. His edict exonerated the marchers—"They have not been guilty of violence and lawlessness, others have"—repeated his seminal blessing for their "Open City" principles, and went so far as to confess a contravention of moral order. "It is truly sad, indeed deplorable, that the citizens should ever have to be asked to suspend the exercise of their rights because of the evil doing of others," the archbishop declared. "However, in my opinion and in the opinion of many men of goodwill, such is the situation in which we now find ourselves."

Chicagoans debated whether Cody had defected from the movement, come to his senses, or succumbed to a runaway revolt in his diocese. Intermediaries crisscrossed the city with feelers toward settlement. Walter Reuther among others relayed proposals to King and Al Raby in Mississippi. Mayor Daley welcomed Cody's stand but pursued multiple avenues toward relief. With every neighborhood march, his subordinates were reporting wholesale erosion of support for the fall reelection of Illinois Senator Paul Douglas, a prominent supporter of President Johnson's open housing bill. Challenger Charles Percy had safely endorsed one item from the list King taped to City Hall—replacement of the "absentee" Democratic precinct captains assigned to black neighborhoods—which infuriated the mayor as cross-party tampering by a Republican. Beyond the Douglas-Percy contest, continued marches so threatened his political base that Daley himself initiated peace talks. When the president of the Chicago Real Estate Board stalled a request to convene them, fearing correctly that the mayor sought to sidestep the public spotlight, Daley enlisted the prestigious Chicago Conference on Religion and Race. Named for the ecumenical assembly in January of 1963, at which King met Rabbi Abraham Heschel, the CCRR was the home chapter of the commission formed since by the National Council of Churches. Rev. Robert Spike, ex-director of the parent group, had relocated from New York just in time to be drafted with pillars of the local clergy.

Paradoxically, the prospect of talks heightened tension. The American Nazi Party warned of race betrayal at a Chicago rally, spawning a mob that attacked police officers. Newspapers and some marchers bridled at continued demonstrations now that civilized compromise lay within reach, while others discerned plots to puncture the movement with false hope. Seven hundred people with eight hundred police guards entered the Bogan neighborhood on August 12, when, by coincidence, John Lennon was apologizing downtown for long-ago remarks about Jesus before an evening concert to begin the Beatles' last American tour.* Twelve hundred people survived simultaneous marches two days later into three different neighborhoods, led by Raby, Bevel, and Jesse Jackson. On Tuesday, August 16, vigils drew hostile crowds to six real estate offices in Jefferson Park, and pickets formed at selected sites throughout the Chicago Loop. "We are here," read signs outside an imposing structure at Dearborn and Madison, "because the Savings and Loan Associations refuse to loan money to Negroes who wish to buy beyond the ghetto." Most bystanders shunned, but some spontaneously joined, the teaching demonstrations about broad institutional resistance.

Summit negotiators filed Wednesday morning into the Cathedral House of St. James Church, Chicago's oldest Episcopal congregation (1857). Sealed from the press, forged by public crisis, the biracial mix of

---

* The Vatican newspaper accepted Lennon's apology in the simmering scandal, but apartheid South Africa banned Beatles music for blasphemy. In New York, police arrested two young women for threatening to jump from the twenty-second floor of the Americana Hotel unless granted a personal audience with their idols.

potentates, Quakers, and shop stewards was scarcely imaginable before nor likely ever again. Men occupied all fifty-six seats around a giant horseshoe of tables. Ben Heineman of the Chicago North West Railroad, who had chaired the White House Conference in June, presided by request of the CCRR clergy. Clark Stayman, president of the Chicago Mortgage Bankers Association, said his members accepted the movement's guidelines for equal housing loans. Mayor Daley agreed to each of the six demands that required city action, centering on enforcement of the dead-letter fair housing ordinance of 1963.

Soaring hope collided with the Chicago Real Estate Board, whose executives said their members acted merely as agents for property owners, and could no more betray their clients by showing listings to black people than Martin Luther King could endorse segregation. "You can accuse us as though we created that bigotry until the end of the world," said Arthur Mohl, "but we are not the creators. We are the mirror." King objected that the real estate industry had spent $5 million to repeal California's fair housing law by Proposition 14. Only the day before, he added, Attorney General Katzenbach had told him that lobbying expenditures to kill the federal housing bill could cure the slums of a major city. "Now don't tell me you're neutral," King said sharply. "Leadership has got to say that the time for change has come."

Industry spokesmen deflected pressure by casting doubt on Mayor Daley's promise that the Chicago Housing Authority would disperse public housing units outside the ghetto. CHA director Charles Swibel, while emphasizing his loyal commitment to initiate the process, described so many obstacles to the necessary site approvals that he foresaw a need for more ghetto high-rises in the meantime. His equivocation prompted Al Raby to move for summary dismissal, but Daley secured a recess. Aides leaked to reporters a terse sentence from his ensuing phone call to president Ross Beatty of the Chicago Real Estate Board: "In the interest of the City of Chicago, you cannot come back here this afternoon with a negative answer."

When they reconvened, Beatty's discourse turned hushed expectation to puzzlement. "We've heard your statement," Raby responded, "but we're not sure what you're saying." On cross-examination, Beatty clarified that his board refused to modify established positions, such as the Real Estate Board's legal attack on the 1963 ordinance, but indicated a willingness to "withdraw all opposition to the philosophy of open occupancy at the state level—provided it is applicable to owners as well as to brokers." Bevel dismissed the maze of qualification. "The question is whether Negroes are going to be served in your office tomorrow morning," he said. Arguments shifted erratically. Jesse Jackson pressed the real estate executives to seek King's "theological level." Mayor Daley asked again why the movement picked Chicago. Rev. Spike complimented the "profound" change in Beatty's stance. Charles Hayes of the United Packinghouse Workers cautioned Spike: "If I as a union negotiator ever came back to my men and said to them, 'I got the company to agree that philosophically they were in support of seniority,' I'd be laughed out of court."

By evening, King implored exhausted negotiators to let a delegated subcommittee advance the day's "constructive and creative" start, understanding that marches would continue. "Let me say that if you are tired of demonstrations, I am tired of demonstrating," he asserted. "I am tired of the threat of death. I want to live." He said marches no more created the problem than a doctor caused a cancer by finding it. "I hope we are here to discuss how to make Chicago a great open city, and not how to end marches," he continued. "We've got to have massive changes. Now, gentlemen, you know we don't have much. We don't have much money." He reviewed the grim shortages of training and advantage among movement people. "We have only our bodies," said King, "and you are asking us to give up the one thing we have when you say, 'Don't march.' We want to be visible. . . . If we hadn't marched, I don't think we'd be here today. No one here has talked about the beauty of our marches, the love of our marches, the hatred we're absorbing." A skeptical delegate asked how more talks could resolve the impasse, and Chairman Heineman gaveled adjournment with stolid ambiguity. "The purpose of the subcommittee," he declared, "is to come back with proposals designed to provide an open city."

News outlets considered the summit a failure, quoting Mayor Daley's bitter regret that "there does not seem to be a cessation of the marches." In seclusion, King appraised Daley as a decent man, fixated on control, "about my son's age in understanding the race problem." Thursday night, he exhorted a mass meeting at Mount Hope Baptist Church to prepare overnight for marches and reprisals. Bevel tweaked the mayor by vowing to keep up the neighborhood demonstrations "until every white person out there joins the Republican Party." On Friday, August 19, as movement teams tested racial barriers at one hundred real estate offices, including several in Daley's home area of Bridgeport, the mayor sent lawyers to Chancery Court Judge Cornelius J. Harrington, a political vassal, and obtained within two hours a sweeping injunction to ban more than one demonstration per day, strictly confined between the daylight rush hours. News of the court order interrupted the first session of the summit subcommittee, and prompted an outraged Robert Spike to suggest aborting the talks for breach of faith. Bevel and Raby restrained him with the argument that dramatic action by either side raised the crisis toward resolution. In Birmingham and Selma, crippling injunctions had preceded historic national breakthroughs. In Chicago, announced Raby, "The issue is still justice in housing."

* * *

SUNDAY, ON a ninety-minute edition of *Meet the Press,* King revealed a temporary decision not to defy the injunction. Questioners passed lightly over Chicago to focus on a general theme that black initiatives had turned noxious across the country. "Isn't it time to stop demonstrations that create violence and discord?" moderator Lawrence Spivak asked a panel of guests. King insisted that nonviolent demonstrations neither caused nor cured anything in themselves, and were designed to bring hidden conditions into conscious public responsibility. Floyd McKissick of CORE said King's process was endangered for the simple reason that "nonviolence is something of the past." Prompted on this point, James Meredith endorsed black vigilante groups while Stokely Carmichael distinguished between vigilantes and self-defense. Carmichael, in a business suit, refused invitations to rescue his black power doctrine from a storm of alleged press distortions, saying SNCC had just banned further attempts to clarify the term. He did acknowledge defining any black soldier in Vietnam as a mercenary, which provoked a surge of comment. "I personally think that one of the greatest things happening in America today is the war in Vietnam," said Meredith, "because for the first time black men, Negroes, are fighting [without unit restrictions] in a war." Carmichael sheepishly denied reports that he had called King and Roy Wilkins "Uncle Toms" in recent speeches—"I couldn't have possibly said that"—citing a SNCC policy that forbade speaking ill of any black leader. Wilkins claimed a larger unity in the historic purpose of civil rights, and tried to make light of the nationally televised bickering that so "terribly distressed" fellow panelist Whitney Young. It was a kind of promotion, Wilkins observed with his laconic smile, for young radicals to call him a tool of the black power structure instead of the white one.

King had cut short his appearance and slipped out of Chicago's NBC affiliate less than halfway through the contentious broadcast. Aides said only his presence could contain the fierce yearning to break the injunction. ("Get your grandmother up from the South!" Bevel cried. "So she can keep the kids while we're in jail.") At Liberty Baptist Church, the new march headquarters for the South Side, King defended the chosen course. Exactly five hundred volunteers—the maximum number permitted—filled an eighty-six-car caravan that arrived punctually for once at the lone demonstration site for the afternoon. In a steady rain, King led a march five miles through East Side neighborhoods near the city steelworks and Trumbull Park, where novelist Alan Paton had recorded a year-long siege against the last pioneer black family in 1954. "About 2,000 residents lined the route despite the downpour," observed one correspondent, hurling jeers and projectiles over a buffer of four hundred officers. Some held signs denouncing "Archbishop Cody and His Commie Coons." King detoured with his nervous escort toward one clump of angry teenagers. "You are all good looking and intelligent," he said, as they backed away. "Where did all that hate come from?"

Sunday's East Side march, which made front pages in distant cities, fueled only one of several burners underneath local politics. In Marquette Park, American Nazi commander George Lincoln Rockwell invited four robed Klansmen and the anti-Jewish polemicist Connie Lynch to share a swastika-draped spectacle that mortified Chicago's civic dignity. At a rally on the North Side, Republican senatorial candidate Charles Percy denounced the "failed" Democratic machine. In suburban Evergreen Park and Chicago Heights, Bevel, Jesse Jackson, and American Friends Service Committee activist Jerry Davis led satellite marches in two areas not covered by Judge Harrington's injunction. Such deployments, as an alternative to jail-going defiance in the city, revealed a calculation that dispersal into Cook County suburbs would intensify rather than relieve pressure on Mayor Daley. King himself announced preparations to take three thousand marchers the following Sunday into Cicero.

Instantly, Jesse Jackson's prior outburst about Cicero was reborn a strategic thunderclap. Mayor Daley showed hints of panic at a press conference: "We've got commies, we've got Nazis, and everybody else you can name showing up. I wish they'd go home!" Sheriff Ogilvie declared marching in Cicero "awfully close to a suicidal act," and Governor Otto Kerner dispatched National Guard units in advance. While daily marches ventured into new areas such as West Elsdon, the *Chicago Daily News* denounced King's Cicero plan as blackmail by threat of martyrdom. On Thursday, when the *New York Times* pleaded for a moratorium on Chicago demonstrations to avoid "the present downhill course to nowhere," all seven black aldermen joined a 45–1 solidarity vote for Daley and rejected a consolation motion simply to disapprove of segregated housing. Still, votes of every color were leaking beyond the chamber, and all sides seized a last chance for reprieve.

Summit negotiators reconvened at the Palmer House hotel on Friday, August 26, with television cameras posted outside the stately Walnut Room. Thomas G. Ayers, president of both the Commonwealth Edison power company and the Association of Commerce and Industry, delivered subcommittee recommendations that strengthened the August 17 commitments in minor respects. The parties accepted a modest goal of at least one percent black occupancy in all seventy-five Chicago neighborhoods within a year, but they omitted the figure from the written document to avoid specific quotas or ceilings, and also to minimize potential ridicule for the great furor and effort over such nominal stakes. Mayor Daley moved immediately to approve the report, but Raby asked first to hear the assembled leaders embrace steps to reach the one percent goal. Archbishop Cody rose for the first time to say that the Roman Catholic association of Rogers Park already had resolved to accept Negro residents, and that priests in all 454 parishes would pursue the seven-step campaign outlined for religious groups. "We are like a little United Nations," he said, "and we will commit our moral, financial, and religious resources to the fulfillment of this agreement." Rabbi Marx said likewise for the Reform Jewish congregations. Heads of labor, business, and civic groups followed suit until Ross Beatty wavered on behalf of the Chicago Real Estate Board. King interrupted to ask whether Beatty could reconcile support with his complaints on radio that real estate companies would go out of business if forced to sell or rent to Negroes. Beatty filibustered. "We'll do all we can, but I don't know how we can do it," he replied. "Frankly, I'm confused."

Daley fidgeted and scowled through a miserable soliloquy from the refined Princeton graduate. (Beatty said, "I hope everyone will understand that we are not all bums.") He moved again for a vote, and glowered impatiently when the rattled parties secured a recess instead. Staff members stalled the waiting reporters. Bevel and Jesse Jackson urged the movement caucus to demand more guarantees, but others predicted that Daley would walk out and leave them to face jail or Cicero. Back in plenary session, King declared a willingness to vote despite misgivings on his side, especially about the surviving injunction. Rev. Donald Zimmerman, chairman of the Church Federation of Greater Chicago, benignly suggested that a court review of the injunction would set fair limits for protest, and King, taken aback, asked if he knew that the appeals would consume several hundred thousand dollars of scarce civil rights money over at least three years. Raby also bristled at the casually academic idea, and charged the city with bad faith for seeking to cripple the movement only two days after forming the Ayers subcommittee.

The mayor stood up. People could make any statement about bad faith, he shrugged, then offered a testimonial. "I was raised in a workingman's community in a workingman's home," he said. "My father was a union organizer, and we did not like injunctions. I know the injustice of injunctions. But I faced the decision of what to do with three and a half million people." His police force was battered, said Daley. Violence was draining protection from much of the city, and he had resisted advice to shut down the marches altogether. King thanked the mayor for his candor and confessed a reciprocal dilemma. "If that injunction stands," he said, "somewhere along the way we are going to have to break it." Chairman Heineman, seizing a moment of favorable chemistry, brokered a compromise with a proposal to keep the ban only for marches in residential areas, reflecting the agreement, and to restore protest rights elsewhere for the movement agenda on schools and employment. Daley agreed—"we can amend our injunction"—and King adjusted a few words to fit his constitutional position. "I don't think that we can accept a conference 'to modify the injunction,' " he said, "because we are opposed to the injunction totally, but we can accept 'a separate negotiation through the continuing body on that issue.' " With that final nuance, the ten-point Open Housing Summit Agreement passed unanimously.

"This is a great day for Chicago," Heineman told the press.

CHAPTER 31

Valley Moments

September 1966

CHICAGO nationalized race, comple-
menting the impact of Watts. Without it King would be confined to
posterity more as a regional figure. The violence against Northern
demonstrations cracked a beguiling, cultivated conceit that bigotry was
the province of backward Southerners, treatable by enlightened but
firm instruction. Already the campaign has "shown Chicago what it has
known in its secret heart, that it has a terrifying and terrible race problem," wrote a Chicagoan for the *Washington Post*. Editors at *The Saturday Evening Post* confessed starkly for Americans at large: "We are all,
let us face it, Mississippians."

Since King's first scouting trip to Boston, Northern expansion had
aimed to promote awareness for the nationwide challenge of equal citizenship, and Chicago advanced this understated purpose perhaps too
well. Its realism eroded sectional support when a fresh mandate to overcome segregation was still sinking in. With King himself expressing dismay over the severity of Northern resistance, diverse public voices
embraced reasons to stand aside. *The New Republic* magazine held out
for a suitable start, saying, "King has hardly begun to do the work which
could force necessary basic changes." Columnists Evans and Novak allowed that "fanatical, indefensible violence" had precipitated "major
concessions for open housing, even from the Chicago realty board, long
a champion of existing segregated housing patterns," but they discounted the "pillow" settlement because "King has not and will not
come to terms with the basic problem of slumism," and pronounced

him "in a state of decline with the young Negro leadership class." A *Chicago Daily News* reporter called the agreement "only a paper victory." Angry white residents picketed City Hall with charges of treachery ("Daley Sold Out Chicago") and surrender ("Summit Another Munich").

Catcalls of "black power!" drowned out the presentation of terms at Liberty Baptist Church, moving King to invite a dissenter into the pulpit. SNCC's Monroe Sharp declared that black people should tend to their own problems without supplication to Mayor Daley or hostile white neighbors, but he also scolded King for giving up the supreme test of Cicero. Like James Forman through the agonizing attempts to cross Pettus Bridge, Sharp blew hot and cold on the efforts to balance sacrificial zeal with long-range purpose. His rump coalition vowed to march regardless of the settlement, without Raby or King, jettisoning the commitment to nonviolence. The *New York Times* profiled allied CORE leader Robert Lucas: "Prefers Action to Talk." Early on Sunday, September 4, King surprised Lucas with good wishes for the ordeal, setting aside the implicit rebuke. ("I was pleased but also shocked to think," Lucas recalled, "that Martin would call a little old guy like myself.") An anxious few gathered in Franklin Park to hear leaders with bullhorns assert an inner defiance apart from political demands. "We are *not* marching into Cicero to appeal to the white conscience," shouted Chester Robinson of the West Side Organization. "We do *not* come hat in hand, scratching our heads, shuffling our feet to beg for a few concessions."

A column of 250, including fifty white people, crossed the Belt Line Railroad into Cicero, engulfed within a protective brigade of two thousand National Guardsmen and five hundred helmeted Cook County officers. Three thousand residents shrieked and hurled rocks with a savagery that earned the anticipated raw headlines—"Guards Bayonet Hecklers in Cicero's Rights March." Some demonstrators used baseball mitts to catch and fling back missiles, fulfilling their vow to fight.

* * *

ON SEPTEMBER 6, two days after Cicero, most of SNCC's national steering committee asked for an impromptu appointment in the Atlanta City Hall. Stokely Carmichael offended the courtly mayor, Ivan Allen, by declining to shake his hand, and petitioned directly for release of twelve SNCC workers who had been arrested three weeks earlier at an anti-Vietnam picketing vigil outside the main induction center for

Army draftees. To the mayor's reply that such a case was a federal matter beyond his power, Carmichael insisted that the city should do something. He did not reveal his group's distress over its inability to raise the collective bond of some $30,000, but he did express outrage that one of the protesters had been charged with capital insurrection, like the celebrated Depression-era black defendant Angelo Herndon. Mayor Allen herded the disruptive group from the building with polite but pointed suggestions to become registered Atlanta voters.

That same afternoon, the strained introduction affected Atlanta's worst riot in sixty years. Allen waded into Summerhill residents enraged over a car theft suspect who had been shot twice by police as he fled on foot. The mayor dodged flying rocks and bottles, pleading for people to go home, and tried unsuccessfully to borrow a cigarette to keep his hands from trembling with the realization that he had underestimated the hostility of the crowd. When he climbed on a police car to be heard, its roof buckled. Hosea Williams, arriving at the scene, saw the silver-haired mayor in a sea of black faces with Stokely Carmichael among SNCC colleagues on the fringe. He credited Allen with "the guts of a lion" but no street sense—saying Carmichael "would have *paid* Ivan Allen to jump up on that car"—and assumed that his SNCC rivals from the Meredith march had whipped up another fever. Angry people rocked the exposed target until Allen tumbled down among them, then the crowd backed away and set off marauding. A thousand officers and tear gas restored order by midnight, leaving sixteen people hospitalized and seventy-five jailed. No fatalities and only one burned building softened the blow to Atlanta's progressive image, and Allen's staff recovered their boss shaken but unharmed, wearing heavy leg pads under his suit. They suspected an uncanny premonition of violence on his part until the mayor sheepishly disclosed that he had blistered his shins in a leaf-burning accident on his forested city property.

A biracial commission soon hedged reports of riot conspiracy, citing numerous warnings of unrest in Summerhill since Atlanta had condemned the overcrowded acres there to build the major league baseball stadium. "SNCC members are not responsible for parking space for four thousand cars in the middle of an area which has no parks for children to play in," declared the civic panel. (With the taxpayers too strapped to develop replacement housing, Allen had financed stopgap projects such as swing sets and paved alleys by dunning Coca-Cola magnate Robert Woodruff to match contributions from his own pocket.)

Also, the mayor knew the neighborhood smoldered against retrograde police conduct, if only from the hushed August scandal over an officer demoted for arresting and pointing his gun at Barbara Aaron, wife of Atlanta Braves star outfielder Henry, when she questioned an instruction that no nigger women belonged at the players' entrance. On the other hand, Carmichael had summoned protesters to the shooting scene over radio station WAOK, and the first two people arrested had been SNCC staff members Bill Ware and Robert Walton for inviting bystanders to broadcast inflammatory accounts of the original shooting from a sound truck. This was more than enough for Allen to blame Carmichael's black power doctrine. "S.N.C.C. Assailed on Atlanta Riot," announced the *New York Times* front page. Eugene Patterson, the normally tempered editor of the *Atlanta Constitution,* diagnosed robotic mayhem from his office. "Negroes didn't have any clear idea of what had hold of them Tuesday," he wrote. "Demagogues had hold of them; SNCC was in charge."

The *Times* reported that rioters spat on its correspondent Roy Reed. On September 8, Reed withheld from his dispatch a far more unnerving encounter with a friendly news source after Atlanta police arrested Carmichael on charges of incitement to riot. "I think it's only fair to warn you," said Willie Ricks, "that when the revolution starts, if I ever see you in the sights of my gun, I'll kill you." The incident put a lasting chill on Reed just as renewed unrest gripped the Boulevard section over the shooting death of a black teenager on his own doorstep by a passing motorist. (The suspect, a white parolee, would be sentenced to life in a precedent-breaking 1967 case.) Crazily, with Carmichael in jail, Hosea Williams declared his intention to lead properly disciplined marches for justice in the Boulevard case, only to be arrested himself, reportedly with the connivance of SCLC board members. Rev. Sam Williams scolded Hosea Williams as "a hired hand" who had forgotten Martin Luther King's promise not to mount demonstrations in his hometown.

* * *

KING WAS in Memphis for a confidential retreat about staff morale, hosted by James Lawson. One by one, nearly forty young workers outlined depression and conflict. Many said Hosea Williams berated them beyond endurance. Williams had countered with his own personal crisis over the plight of "Big Lester" Hankerson, the Savannah seaport gangster converted to nonviolence but left dysfunctional by a beating in Grenada, Mississippi. He demanded to know if it was right to expose his friend to such damage for nothing. "We screamed for help and there was no help," said Williams. "Is this in keeping with nonviolence?" The Grenada staff had revolted against his solution: schemes to induce more newsworthy violence upon white volunteers. They said violence was a hazard, not a purpose. Andrew Young said nonviolent risk should be shared, never imposed, but he fared no better at supervision than the departed Randy Blackwell. Williams often reduced SCLC executives to tears, and King finessed the conflict with sermons on love. Privately, he recruited Lawson to intensify his counseling of young workers who suffered battle fatigue and personal dissipation. In Chicago, Bevel avoided visits from his Nashville mentor like a scourge.

From Memphis, King called Stanley Levison over the wiretapped line to report euphemistically that SCLC was improving its "administrative controls." When he asked about attention to the Atlanta riots, Levison said they were on the front page of the *Times* every day, with the latest editions noting Julian Bond's departure from SNCC, following an earlier resignation by John Lewis. King said Bond was a good man struggling to avoid the impression of deserting his colleagues. He thought black power would wane within the movement as its strategic pitfalls became clear, but "the press is keeping it alive." Cringing in anticipation of pressure for public comment, King said, "Stokely may do time for the riot."

Schools opened in Grenada a few days later. Officials had postponed enrollment for more than a week to wrestle with the twin dilemma of a freedom-of-choice integration order combined with a flood of three hundred transfer applications from black parents recruited by the local SCLC project. Many citizens figured stern admonitions would reduce the number close to zero before classes finally convened on Monday, September 12, but 150 black students entered John Rundle High and the adjacent Lizzie Horn Elementary. As disappointed white people gathered outside, irate men pushed two latecomers to the ground. They repulsed thirty more—shouting, "Nigger, you better turn around"— then roused neighbors to protest the breach of segregation. Virtually every local officeholder and constable swelled the crowd to four hundred before the schools dismissed their white students at midday. Half an hour later, black students emerged separately into a wall of menacing stares. Once the head of their line departed behind two Highway Patrol cars, taunts escalated to blows and general assault on those behind. High school students Dorothy Allen and Poindexter Harbie crawled screaming through a gauntlet, struck by a man with a tree limb and kicked bloody in the face. A woman tripped twelve-year-old Richard Sigh with her umbrella, whereupon men with pipes broke Sigh's leg near the hip and chased him away in a frantic hop. Others mauled polio victim Emerald Cunningham. Memphis reporter Charles Goodman noticed a woman draw back, cover her mouth, and repeat to no one as she watched a swirling clump of men whip a pigtailed girl: "How can they laugh when they are doing it?" Three reporters were beaten themselves.

Opposing forces responded within hours to mob brutality that injured thirty children. Governor Johnson dispatched reinforcements, prompting nearly five hundred white citizens to denounce him that night in Grenada's City Hall. "You get the Highway Patrol out of here," declared one speaker, "and in twenty-four hours there won't be a nigger left." The city manager, who admitted calling the state for help, resigned his office to vengeful cheers. Andrew Young flew in to lead a remnant of thirty black students to school on Tuesday, while John Doar filed for a permanent injunction in Oxford. Hosea Williams bailed out from Atlanta to march with Young Tuesday night, but retreated from the Grenada town square in a hail of rocks. Still, project workers mustered eighty-seven black children for Wednesday's march to class. On Thursday, September 15, having closed Grenada's schools until Monday, U.S. District Judge Claude Clayton ruled that local officials had "virtually abdicated their responsibility." He enjoined them by name to protect all students and assigned superseding command to the Highway Patrol. FBI agents arrested thirteen men on Friday, including a justice of the peace, for Monday's violence outside the schools.

Segregationists mounted a short-lived drive to impeach Governor Johnson for complicity in the "federal intervention." White moderates in Grenada, finding no support for cross-racial dialogue, circulated a generic petition for calm. On Sunday, in a widely anticipated sermon of catharsis, Rev. C. B. Burt of First Methodist Church asked forgiveness for the "bestiality" he had witnessed in familiar faces, which reminded him of his stunned entry to the Nazi death camp at Buchenwald as a World War II chaplain. "I can tell you my heart was not filled with compassion for the German people," he confessed, "but I never saw an American soldier mistreat a German child." Many wept, and rumors flew. Rev. Burt denied any hidden agenda to make his congregation "ready" for black worshippers.

Folksinger Joan Baez arrived in Grenada that weekend with fellow pacifist Ira Sandperl, and children beseeched them to intercede with fearful families to obtain consent for integration, saying their parents would listen to white people. These requests introduced them firsthand to the strain within the mixed SCLC staff over imbalances of racial risk and authority. On Monday, September 19, carrying schoolbooks, Baez and Sandperl joined escorts for the mile-long walk through a corridor of Highway Patrol officers and sullen bystanders to the two white schools, where the 160 black students comprised 10 percent of the overall enrollment. Young Richard Sigh would wear a leg cast until January. (Over the Christmas holidays, fourteen volunteer tutors from UCLA and Georgetown would offer supplemental lessons to relieve deficiencies and grinding ostracism in regular class.) On that Monday night, Martin Luther King arrived to salute the battered pioneers at a tumultuous mass meeting of a thousand people. "His speech was fiery in tone but moderate in content," reported the *New York Times*.

Andrew Young summoned Baez early the next morning to a local minister's home. He said King refused to get out of bed, and asked her to sing. Extreme rousting measures for exhaustion had failed, which meant King was despondent beyond tired, and Young pushed Baez past an anxious household to be a siren of revival. She sang "Pilgrim of Sorrow" in a cappella soprano until King smiled faintly by the second or third verse. Rising to touch off the usual late scramble, he escorted two young girls from the movement center at Bell Flower Baptist Church to Lizzie Horn Elementary, his hands lightly on their shoulders. Young carried a child just behind. Baez, admiring the jive gaits of energetic girls who seemed oblivious to danger, moved forward to ask King half in jest, "Why are we doing this? In the white school they'll lose all this spirit." King shushed her and pointed to photographers. "Not while the cameras are running," he said with a smile. Later he said the girls must take their spirit into a tough world, but he relapsed into depression himself. King skipped his own scheduled news conference, irritating stranded reporters so much they wrote about the insult, and slipped away to catch a plane from Memphis.

* * *

GRENADA MARKED a convergence of what King called "valley moments." On September 19, the day he arrived there, the Civil Rights Act of 1966 failed in the U.S. Senate when a 52–41 vote fell short of the margin required to shut off a Southern filibuster. Defeat was hardly a surprise, as pessimism had circulated for months. (Bracing for the vote ten days earlier, White House Press Secretary Bill Moyers announced, "We have received no word that the bill is dead.") Still, finality was a compound blow. Lost were mandates for diversified juries and courthouses, plus federal protections for civil rights work. Without the latter, given the refusal by some states to prosecute crimes of racial persecution, the Justice Department possessed only the poor remedy of an outmoded 1870 Reconstruction statute under which the thirteen men in Grenada had just been arrested. King knew the chances of conviction were slim, even for unprovoked public violence against children. All eight Grenada defendants who went to trial would be acquitted the next June, despite fair instructions from Judge Clayton and consistent testimony from eyewitnesses, including a courageous police captain. (Diana Freelon, one of the teenagers beaten on the first day of school, would be elected mayor of Grenada 38 years later, in 2004.)

Almost plaintively, editors of the *New York Times* had tried to salvage the 1966 bill by stressing a comfortable preoccupation with the South: "The Senate has an obligation today to do justice for the Southern Negro. . . . The pending bill, like its four predecessor measures dating back to 1957, is essentially a bill for the relief of the Southern Negro." In sharp contrast, the Senate filibuster focused on the national implications of the open housing section, and Sam Ervin of North Carolina gleefully noted a shift in discomfort "now that others' oxen are being gored." Minority Leader Everett Dirksen of Illinois doomed the bill by rising on his crutches to call the housing provisions "a package of mischief for the country."

The defeat was a stinging referendum on King's open housing campaign in Dirksen's home state. More broadly, it neutralized his dream formula of patriotic appeals for the whole nation to "rise up and live out the true meaning of its creed." No longer did calculated sacrifice from Birmingham or Selma catapult issues to a transforming national stage. With attitudes hardening for Vietnam, vanguard movements receded to local stature. For all its faults, the voluntary agreement in Chicago was stronger than federal fair housing laws. For all its grit and tribulation, the Grenada, Mississippi movement created no resonant symbols like Rosa Parks or the four martyred Birmingham schoolgirls, and aroused no groundswell for federal protection. Those themes lost public traction.

Always before, King had beacons in reality to buttress his slave-grounded oratorical conviction that a morning star would rise from bleakest despair: the *Brown* decision, anti-colonial triumphs across Africa, a generally favorable press. Now he learned that the Supreme Court, sick of demonstrations, might reimprison him for the Birmingham jail campaign of 1963. Some liberation heroes in Africa already had turned tyrant, and King had just submitted to questions for a CBS television special on black power. "Don't you find," asked correspondent Mike Wallace, "that the American people are getting a little bit tired, truly, of the whole civil rights struggle?" News of Grenada and the Senate failure overlapped an influential front-page series in the *New York Times,* "Civil Rights: A Turning Point," with a subtitle pointed downward, "Support for Negro and His Problems Found to Wane." The first installment explored a central question: "How deep does white disengagement go, and where does it leave the Negro?" A second article— "Housing Equality Hits a Raw Nerve . . . Idea of a Negro Neighbor Stirs Anxiety"—prompted Stanley Levison to decry an exposed point of view. "We are witnessing almost a propaganda drive to drive away white liberals," he complained on his wiretapped line. The September 21 conclusion surveyed predictions of backlash across the political spectrum. "It's fear," said Chicago Representative Roman Pucinski, who offered a bill to limit racial demonstrations. House Republican leader Gerald Ford called Democrats "the party with the big riots in the streets," and unnamed representatives said Congress considered Stokely Carmichael an anarchist. Harlem's Adam Clayton Powell relished his claim of expertise about the scary side of black power. "These are a new breed of cats," he told the *Times.* "They hiss A. Philip Randolph. They boo Martin Luther King. They even picket my church."

Racial anxiety paralyzed the upper reaches of the administration. Attorney General Katzenbach blocked a proposed White House summit on civil rights strategy, forecasting disaster at every turn. He said concrete progress in jobs and education had come too slowly to help, especially with the Vietnam budget constraints, while President Johnson's notice would magnify debilitating controversy whether or not he excluded the proponents of black power. "The President does not strengthen the leadership of Roy Wilkins or Martin Luther King," Katzenbach asserted, "when they are made to appear to be his lieutenants or apologists." White House aide Harry McPherson chafed against Katzenbach's prevailing logic, grumbling that President Johnson "has not (to my knowledge) talked to any Negro at all" through the death throes of his civil rights bill. Something must be wrong, he fumed, when most Americans still identified race as the nation's chief domestic problem, and trusted Johnson's leadership, yet somehow the President felt hamstrung by minuscule public support for a youth doctrine. "Surely, the next generation of Negro leadership does not have to be dominated by Stokely Carmichael and Willie Ricks," McPherson wrote Katzenbach on September 20, and he warned the President not to shirk his historic mantle. "You are stuck with it, in sickness as in health," McPherson advised. "The very fact that you have led the way toward first-class citizenship for the Negro, that you are identified with his cause, means that to some extent your stock rises and falls with the movement."

Carmichael himself made bail after a week in Atlanta's lockup. (The judge drastically reduced his bond after a grand jury, lacking testimony that he had advocated or practiced violence, returned a weak indictment for misdemeanor riot.) He resumed a travel schedule that matched King's, fueled by publicity so intense that SNCC's New York office compiled by mid-September an encyclopedia of journalism about black power. "It shows how the press cultivated a rising hysteria among whites," wrote staff member Elizabeth Sutherland. Four months of stories conveyed chills and thrills like a blockbuster horror movie, obsessing critics and fans alike. "Everything seemed to go on fast forward," Carmichael said later. "His style dazzles," wrote *New York Times* correspondent Bernard Weinraub, who followed as "Stokely Carmichael rushes from ghetto to ghetto with the drive of a political candidate. . . . He sleeps just a few hours a night. He eats on the run and drinks milk to keep up his energy." Carmichael popped out of cars to gasps of recognition, and delivered impromptu speeches: "This country don't run on love, brothers. It's run on power, and we ain't got none!" Weinraub's profile for *Esquire* magazine, "The Brilliancy of Black," called him "the most charismatic figure in the Negro movement." For *Ebony* magazine, historian Lerone Bennett accompanied him from a childhood block in the Bronx, where his family still occupied the only black household, down to South Georgia and across into Lowndes County, Alabama. "A shiver of nervous exhilaration ran through Carmichael's body," Bennett concluded. "He pushed the accelerator to the floor, took both hands off the wheel and shouted: 'I don't care what white folks say, we are home, baby. Baby! We're *home!*' "

Carmichael would remember black power as a ride on the tail of a comet. "Who could have thought it? I mean two simple, clear, very commonly used English words," he wrote, granting that King had been right to worry about cross-racial connotations. Almost daily in speeches, SNCC's new chairman recited a passage from *Alice in Wonderland:*

> "When I use a word," Humpty Dumpty said in rather a scornful tone, "it means just what I choose it to mean, neither more nor less."
>
> "The question is," said Alice, "whether you *can* make words mean so many different things."
>
> "The question is," said Humpty Dumpty, "who is to be master, that's all."

Carmichael's claim to master his own words clashed with the dominant culture's inclination to hear what it pleased. He tried to carve out meaning for black power with stabs at mainstream civil rights. "He says that LBJ killed the civil rights movement the moment he stood before nationwide TV and said, 'We shall overcome,' " wrote Eldridge Cleaver, who chaired a Malcolm X Afro-American Society in California. " 'But he will never,' Carmichael says, 'stand before the nation and say, 'We want Black Power.' " For SNCC, Carmichael had opposed the Civil Rights Act of 1966 as "a fraudulent bunch of words" and "hypocrisy which attempts to delude the black people of America." When King joined an intra-movement plea to suspend picket lines during the White House wedding, Carmichael called him a lackey in a public telegram: "You have displayed more backbone in defending Luci than you have shown for the colored people of Vietnam being napalmed by Luci's father." He proclaimed alienation from white sympathizers—"All those people who are calling us friends are nothing but treacherous enemies"—and when a professed colleague at a forum nearly begged him to recognize the potential for exceptional white allies, Carmichael refused with unflinching directness like the late Malcolm X: "No, not one." Prestigious journals invited him to define black power by personal confrontation. "We cannot be expected any longer to march and have our heads broken in order to say to whites: come on, you're nice guys," he wrote in the September 22 issue of *The New York Review of Books.* "For you are not nice guys. We have found you out."

* * *

TWICE IN Chicago, obscured by publicized summer meetings with King and Nation of Islam leader Elijah Muhammad, Carmichael encountered his Alabama jail mate, Richard Morrisroe. At the intensive care unit in Montgomery, Morrisroe had been haunted by skin privilege from what he learned of emergency kindness and medical exertions to prolong his life, whispering to Carmichael that a similarly mangled black victim would have died many times over. Now, still feeble and unsteady in physical therapy, Morrisroe suffered reverse disorientation. He said his wounds still hurt too much to shift easily into a movement with no place for white people. "You're different," Carmichael replied. Warmly but awkwardly, he urged Morrisroe to look past political tactics in steadfast witness for inclusion.

Richmond Flowers, the lame-duck attorney general of Alabama, had waited more than a year for Chicago doctors to approve a day trip south for Morrisroe. On September 13, 1966, he met Morrisroe at the Montgomery airport and drove in mutual trepidation past a quiet Hayneville crime scene to the Lowndes County courthouse. Once Morrisroe managed his first sworn testimony, recalling details from the fetid week in jail until the second shotgun roar and his weak cries for water, Flowers asked him delicately by pre-agreement to show the grand jury his wounds. Morrisroe stood to remove a clerical collar and shirt, revealing bright sunken scars massed entirely along the back, indicating that he had been shot in retreat, and the attorney general noted the absence of "even one BB pellet" on the stomach. By exhibiting a priest on the witness stand in dramatically torn flesh, Flowers intended to shame Tom Coleman's claim of self-defense.

A grand juror broke the charged silence. "Father, may I ask a question?" he said. When Flowers nodded approval, he continued abruptly, "Did you kiss that nigger girl in the mouth?"

Morrisroe shuddered. "Sir, I've never embraced a woman in my life," he said. Scattered giggles punctuated further speculations of prurient interest in Ruby Sales and Gloria Larry, ignoring testimony that they had turned to flee with Jonathan Daniels the instant Coleman surprised them. For Flowers, the crude rebuff mocked his last effort to salvage any justice in the Hayneville shootings or revive his political career. He descended into disgrace, soon imprisoned on three politicized counts of neglecting petty corruption and reduced to a footnote in sports-mad Alabama. His namesake son, perhaps the state's most celebrated young athlete, had given up a dream invitation to play college football for coach Bear Bryant because he could not stand hearing his father booed at home events, and fans across Alabama would curse Flowers again when Junior scored the winning touchdown for archrival Tennessee in

1968, the year Tennessee fielded its first black player. The Alabama team remained white into the next decade.

Pride and denial rendered glacial transformations almost invisible. The precious ballot, seldom so studied and treasured for its promise of democracy, still had not yet been cast by any black citizen of Lowndes County in a general election on September 19, when Gloria Larry reported a rash of drive-by shootings into the tent city encampment on Highway 80 amid Klan warnings to vacate before the November vote. Morrisroe had hastened back to Chicago by then, striving to put prayerful distance between him and Alabama. His disappointment festered instead against the home diocese, where supervising bishops blocked his return to active service at St. Columbanus or any other black parish. They said Morrisroe was too enmeshed in politics for his own good, endangering the mission of the church, and only reluctantly approved a compromise assignment to St. Sylvester, a parish of mostly Puerto Rican congregants. Morrisroe stayed in the priesthood long enough to learn Spanish on visits to the island, where he appreciated cultural subtleties among his dark-skinned parishioners, and he recovered personal balance with a Chicago legal career after his 1973 marriage in San Juan. The bride's four-year-old nephew, Bernabe Williams, who served as ring bearer, grew up to play center field for the New York Yankees.

*   *   *

ON MONDAY, September 26, Judge Werth Thagard dismissed all charges in the Morrisroe case with prejudice, freeing Tom Coleman from further risk of trial. Tuesday night, CBS aired its television special *Black Power, White Backlash,* sandwiching King's defense of nonviolence between Stokely Carmichael on Malcolm X tactics ("by any means necessary") and interviews with Cicero children about what would happen if any Negroes moved in ("they'd be killed"). Adam Clayton Powell tartly asserted that King did not yet understand black power and therefore was in "agonizing reappraisal" to avoid falling among "the decadent aristocratic colonials of the civil rights movement." CBS correspondent Mike Wallace concluded the broadcast: "There can be no doubt that at the end of summer, 1966, the white man and the black man in the North eye each other with more suspicion and hostility than they ever have before."

On Wednesday, in a runoff election called "a stunning upset," Georgia's Democratic nomination for governor was won by Lester Maddox, the entrepreneur who famously had chased away black customers with a pistol, distributed ax handles to patrons as anti-integration tools, and closed his fried chicken restaurant in Atlanta rather than comply with the Civil Rights Act of 1964. Mayor Ivan Allen registered numb embarrassment over the success of a caricature segregationist—"The seal of the great state of Georgia lies tarnished"—which only sweetened Maddox's claim to represent the unrepentant common citizen. "Georgians are determined to turn back the trend of socialism," he declared in victory, accusing high-toned Democrats of complicity with President Johnson to betray God and private property.

King absorbed the Maddox blow at home between speaking trips to Dallas and Chicago. He told reporters only that "Georgia is a sick state." The next night, he confided to Stanley Levison a sense of confusion. He said Whitney Young had called so disconsolate that he discussed resigning from the movement to shock white America, and confessed he might do the same. Levison gently cautioned that King's resignation "wouldn't be shocking enough." They took comfort in fund-raising details and plans to keep going. On September 30 in Chicago, King buckled under press questions about the last few months. "I do think we stand in one of those valley moments, rather than at the peak of united activity and at the peak of noble achievement that we've seen over the last few years," he said, "in civil rights, and in our nation, and [in] the whole thrust towards a more democratic society."

CHAPTER 32

Backlash

October–November 1966

THE fall political campaigns showcased an unstable clash of moods over Vietnam and civil rights. Ray Bliss, the Republican national chairman, said his candidates would stress race issues because polls showed that 58 percent of party supporters made urban disorder a top priority. The next day, October 4, Republican mayor Theodore McKeldin publicly begged the tavern keepers of Baltimore to serve Negro customers during the baseball World Series against the Los Angeles Dodgers, calling their stubborn resistance "a distasteful irony" given that the local Orioles probably owed their first championship berth to the newly arrived black star, Frank Robinson. A few days later in Alabama, four members of the Diocesan Council of Catholic Women were turned away from formal tea at the governor's mansion, igniting controversies about who had known the guest list would be integrated. At a rare White House press conference, describing his plans to tour Asia before November, President Johnson tried gamely to smile when asked about Senator Strom Thurmond's bellicose charge that "we could win the war in Vietnam in 90 days if we wanted to." He said he always welcomed the views of senators.

The President scheduled the trip abroad in part to escape frustration. Many Democratic candidates already considered him an albatross rather than an asset for the off-year elections, in spite of his historic record. "FDR passed five major bills the first one hundred days," Johnson fumed to his aides. "We passed two hundred in the past two years. It is unbelievable." War measures gave him political boosts that seemed to wear off more quickly as the public impression of Vietnam changed from pesky to serious. Nicholas Katzenbach had just left the Justice Department for voluntary reassignment to the surpassing foreign challenge, and Johnson sent the new undersecretary of state ahead with McNamara to evaluate the course yet again. The President, meanwhile, tried to curb a growing testiness. His recent complaints to Jewish War Veterans, wondering mordantly why rabbis were so prominent in Vietnam dissent, caused speculation about a conditional link between American military commitments to South Vietnam and Israel. Anxiety over global strong-arming led to summit meetings and more head-lines—"Goldberg Mollifies Jews on President"—but some rabbis felt compelled to deny suggestions of a security deal that stifled conscience. "If Abraham had no hesitation about challenging the judgment of God over Sodom and Gomorrah, lest it should sweep away the innocent with the guilty," said Abraham Heschel, "should not an American have the right to challenge the judgment of our President when horrified by the war in Vietnam?"

King did not speak out directly, though he had collaborated with Heschel for nearly a year in an ecumenical group of antiwar clergy. His pressures during the fall campaigns mirrored Johnson's. He received invitations to visit Israel and Jordan, each beckoning with a polar view of the conflicted Holy Land, and pragmatists within the national civil rights movement pushed him to accommodate Johnson toward a broad political realignment, looking beyond Vietnam. Bayard Rustin first sought approval for a public letter he drafted in King's name to the Negro youth of America, gently rebuking black power: "I implore all of you to remember that Molotov cocktails, and looting, and hatred, cannot, and will not, solve the problems we really care about." King's most trusted labor supporters joined a conference call to obtain his signature. "Tell them that they can't solve problems with rocks," suggested Ralph Helstein of the meatpackers union, "any more than nations can solve them with bombs." When King resisted, saying any letter should address all practitioners of violence, not just black ones, Rustin drafted instead a newspaper advertisement. To accommodate King, he addressed a general audience with a text that affirmed "racial justice by democratic process" and condemned only "strategies of violence, reprisal or vigilantism."

Still, King resisted entreaties to sponsor the advertisement jointly with traditional allies led by Roy Wilkins and A. Philip Randolph. On

October 10, two days before he had Rustin and other advisers debate the question in Atlanta, a front-page leak to the *New York Times* underscored his worries: "Dr. King Weighing Plan to Repudiate 'Black Power' Bloc." Tricks of racial perception gnarled a complex decision. King applauded the efforts of Rustin's broad coalition to gain a favorable reception for a ten-year national freedom budget, treating seriously the White House position that America could afford "guns and butter" to fight poverty as well as the Vietnamese, but he sensed a hidden bargain to blame the black fringes for shortcomings on both fronts. This made bad politics for an exposed racial minority, and he bridled at an implicit endorsement for the wars as a package. On nonviolent principle, King fought the impulse to repudiate. Like fear, that impulse slid toward enemy-thinking, hierarchy, and pride—the chief barriers to interracial democracy.

So King refused to join the advertisement, "Crisis and Commitment," which appeared in the October 14 *New York Times* along with a news story about its provenance: "7 Negro Leaders Issue a Statement of Principles Repudiating 'Black Power' Concepts." Instead, he held a press conference in Atlanta to outline his ideas for the future, including generous praise for the freedom budget. He carefully reprised his written critiques of black power as an invitation to a mutual standoff. Black people were overwhelmingly victims even in their own riots, King wrote for the current issue of *Ebony* magazine, pointing out that Charles Whitman alone, "the young demented white student at the University of Texas . . . killed more people in one day than all the Negroes have killed in all the riots in all the cities since the Harlem riots of 1964. This must raise a serious question about the violent intent of the Negro." Militant talk defined make-believe battle lines for the negative instrument of force, King maintained, adding, "Violence as a strategy for social change in America is nonexistent." By contrast, no one had ever been killed in a nonviolent demonstration, and when Negroes marched in a well-defined democratic movement, "so did the nation."

Reporters in Atlanta passed over all arguments consigned to *Ebony,* asking why King withheld his name from the ad. They pressed him to specify an objection to the joint statement, which did not explicitly mention black power. King emphasized choices of tone and tactics, but finally conceded that he could have supported the overall message. From this alone jumped news. Many stories took their cue from the *Times* headline: "King Endorses Racial Statement / Backs Negro Repudiation of Black Power Concept," and King biographer David Garrow later judged the incidental consent "a serious misstep." It threw away the hard calculations based on experience "at tiptoe stance," raising new controversy over King's change of mind. Wiretapped phone lines buzzed with recrimination. Rustin called Stanley Levison on October 15 to say King had brought trouble on himself by not signing the ad in the first place. Levison called a nonplussed Andrew Young, who said, "Bayard did this to us." King told Levison apologetically that he had been backed into tacit support for the ad because Rustin had forecast disaster if he attacked it. Even more than feared, the substance of King's position was subordinate to appetites for projected remorse over black power, which in turn delivered to the White House the useful image of a self-tamed ally. "What bothers me is that when I make these tactical errors," said King, "it's usually when I'm trying to deal with Bayard."

* * *

McNAMARA AND Katzenbach wrote reports in a windowless KC-135 transport on the day-long fight from Vietnam, while Bill Moyers and Harry McPherson returned from a parallel scouting tour of Asian capitals. After only thirty-six hours home, their combined missions melded into a gigantic presidential entourage that recrossed the Pacific Ocean for state visits to seven nations. "I know that I can wave no wand," President Johnson declared at his send-off on Monday, October 17. Behind measured confidence and displays of pomp, he sagged under troubled assessments. McNamara was "a little less pessimistic militarily than the previous year, because the huge buildup was inflicting casualties at the annual rate of sixty thousand dead, blunting the earlier projections of imminent defeat. On the other hand, he "saw no reasonable way to bring the war to an end soon," because the Vietnamese Communists had adapted through 1966 to a war of attrition, with morale intact and infiltration up threefold in spite of 84,000 U.S. bombing sorties. McNamara also wrote Johnson that "the important war," for political allegiance, "has if anything gone backward."

That failure was the topic Johnson assigned to Katzenbach, whose inspections in the Vietnamese countryside compelled a rare top secret memo of lyrical focus on "the unceasing, backbreaking toil of the peasant population . . . it is not so much water that their rice grows in; it is sweat." He described for the President a political chasm between the rice paddies and American officials who discussed pacification "in a strange language of abbreviation and acronym. For example: 'If we can get MACV, USAID and JUSPAO to prod the GVN, then maybe ARVN—working with the PF, RF, PFF, CIDG and the PAT cadres—can get RD off the ground.' " Back in Washington, Katzenbach formed a high-level "non-group" to brainstorm outside bureaucratic channels about connecting policy more effectively with the neglected outlook of ordinary Vietnamese. There was a surreal quality to the exercise, echoing the best experts. Bernard Fall, the French military historian who respected Ho Chi Minh's cause but patrolled with U.S. soldiers, said the growing deployment of 325,000 American troops already formed a distinct culture. They made Vietnam the first war zone of cheap transistor radios, blaring escapist pop songs with lyrics like "What a day for a daydream," and invented a "Batman" vocabulary of minimalist slang, as in "Charlie zapped a slick," meaning South Vietnamese Communists destroyed an unarmed transport helicopter.

Shock pierced the civil rights community before Air Force One reached the first stop in Honolulu. That same Monday, a custodian found Rev. Robert Spike bludgeoned to death in a guestroom of the new Christian Center at Ohio State University, where he had preached the night before. Three Protestant denominations issued tributes while detectives swarmed, and the family received telegrams of condolence from dignitaries including King, Vice President Humphrey, and Stokely Carmichael ("Our heartfelt sympathy in your loss which is a loss for all of us"). News stories reviewed the breadth of Spike's influence: praise from Bob Moses for marshaling the unlikely church support essential to Mississippi Freedom Summer, honor from President Johnson with a seat next to Lady Bird for the "We Shall Overcome" address to Congress, and a recent appointment to the National Council on the Humanities. Edwin "Bill" Berry of the Chicago Urban League called Spike "one of the best thinkers who ever lived." With no reported progress in the criminal investigation, Spike's peers mobilized from his former office at the New York headquarters of the National Council of Churches on Riverside Drive. NCC officials prepared to hire private detectives and offer a reward.

Secret fears and hatreds abruptly stifled grief. Jack Pratt, the general counsel hired by Spike in 1963 for the NCC's Commission on Religion and Race, warned that public resolution was "the last thing" his colleagues should seek. He disclosed from a trip to Ohio that the body had been clad only in a raincoat, with homosexual literature nearby. To NCC General Secretary Edwin Espy, among others who knew Spike as a starched theologian with a picturebook family, these alien clues suggested an unspeakable plot to smear the victim, until Pratt made clear that any trial would unearth a forbidden world along with a few witting clergy who had shared, restrained, or protected Spike's furtive liaisons with men. Hushed National Council of Churches representatives miserably tested clues on his family. "This staggers my mother," recalled Paul Spike, then a student at Columbia University. "In fact, it comes close to shattering her." Mother and son fought an undertow of memories that seemed freighted with alibi or glancing confession, and would cling to disbelief when unnerved church officials shut down inquiry for damage control by triage. The family half-mourned a national church so terrified of truth.

Willful avoidance sealed Spike in mystery, opening doors to conspiracy theories. (Andrew Young always feared his friend had been killed for agitation against the Vietnam War; others suspected the shadowy FBI, working perhaps even with Spike's internecine rivals in the civil rights field.) Publicly, the murder case shriveled to a news squib that an itinerant man in custody probably would not be tried because prosecutors considered him insane. Newspapers still shunned this form of scandal because they could not bear to print the necessary words. A harbinger series in the *Atlanta Constitution* had just noted the appearance of startling picket signs outside the United Nations—"U.S. Claims No Second Class Citizens / What About Homosexuals?"—but profiled skulking, Jekyll-and-Hyde creatures of severely retarded emotions, who "would cut off their left arms to be cured." Within decades, human energies founded on the civil rights movement would obliterate much of this lethal stigma and lift nearly all the closeted silence. The transformation, which lay just beyond the imagination of visionaries like Robert Spike, would be a swift one for history but too late for him.

* * *

RICHARD NIXON captured the central glare of public attention by predicting for Republicans "the greatest political comeback of any political party in this century." On the October 23 broadcast of *Meet the Press,* he sparred with correspondents about which party was "playing the backlash issue," pointing to Lester Maddox and George Wallace as proof that Democrats would remain "the party of racism in the South." ("I don't know one Republican candidate who is riding the backlash," he claimed.) Asserting that neither party in the South actually favored integration, Nixon pointed to Republican unity on Vietnam as the pivotal divide. The election of forty or more new Republicans to the House "will serve notice to the enemy in Vietnam," he declared, "that the United States is not going to do what the French did ten years ago: cut and run." Nixon branded Lyndon Johnson the first American President who had failed to unite his own party behind a war. "The division in the United States on Vietnam is primarily within the Democratic Party," he told viewers.

A new liability of war dissent ripened that same week when the FBI arrested Ken Kesey, author of *One Flew Over the Cuckoo's Nest* and *Sometimes a Great Notion,* shortly after he announced his intention to defy drug charges "as a fugitive and as salt in J. Edgar Hoover's wounds." Kesey had outraged some young protesters, and captivated others, by telling antiwar rallies that it was foolish to oppose Vietnam with the politicians' tools of ballyhoo and speeches—"that's what *they* do"—breaking instead into a harmonica rendition of "Home on the Range." With his cult following of Merry Pranksters, Kesey expressed disdain for the trapdoor psychology of war debate by beatific withdrawal and absurd theatrics. Shortly before the October arrest, he appeared at a flamboyant "Love Festival" to disregard the effective date of a new California statute that outlawed the psychedelic drug LSD. After making bail, he renewed a sporadic cross-country association with renegade Harvard professor Timothy Leary, who in September had proclaimed himself founder of a religion based on spiritual discovery through the use of LSD, marijuana, and peyote, with the signature mantra, "turn on, tune in, and drop out." In New York, loosely affiliated groups brought a Yellow Submarine prop to a demonstration before the November elections. Others scheduled a "Human Be-In" for January in San Francisco, featuring the new rock groups Grateful Dead and Jefferson Airplane, where the former teach-in activist Jerry Rubin promoted countercultural politics "in the Marxist tradition of Groucho, Chico, Harpo, and Karl."

The hippie phenomenon, modifying the "hip" beatnik rebellion of the 1950s, caught on more slowly than black power in the press. Among politicians, Ronald Reagan recognized it early in the development of counterpoint for his California gubernatorial campaign, which one opposing consultant already called "a major cultural-political watershed." Reagan framed his call to old-fashioned morality against a blended specter of Watts and Berkeley. He proposed to bypass court review of Proposition 14 with legislation to repeal the state's fair housing law outright, and narrated television ads over ominous film of riots: "Every day the jungle draws a little closer. . . . Our city streets are jungle paths after dark." Denouncing Berkeley for "orgies so vile I cannot describe them," he promised to recruit ex-CIA Director John McCone for a repeat of his Watts commission assignment, this time targeting the incumbent governor and university chancellor for what Reagan termed their "appeasement of campus malcontents and filthy speech advocates." To take the edge off his attacks, Reagan quipped that a male hippie "dresses like Tarzan, has hair like Jane, and smells like Cheetah." Ten days before the election, he released a telegram to Stokely Carmichael suggesting firmly that he cancel all speech dates in California, and challenged Governor Pat Brown to send one like it. Much to the satisfaction of the Reagan campaign, the ploy heightened news coverage of Carmichael's October 29 address exhorting Berkeley students to say "hell, no" to the Vietnam draft.

Lyndon Johnson landed triumphant on November 2 after seventeen days and 31,500 miles abroad, the longest presidential trip in history, laden with gifts, including two white kangaroos from Australia. At the palace in Thailand, he had drawn his bath from a silver spigot in the shape of a water buffalo, and his unscheduled detour to South Vietnam's Cam Ranh Bay on October 26 made him the first Commander-in-Chief to salute U.S. troops in an active war zone since FDR at Casablanca in 1943. The pageantry of resolve at Asian war councils spiked his favorable rating on Vietnam to 63 percent, provoking Richard Nixon to attack a long-haul strategy he said "resigns" America to war that "could last five years and cost more casualties than Korea." Nixon proposed vigorous bipartisan action to win the war by 1968, and the President responded with unusual public venom. (Nixon's barbs cut close to the grim secret forecasts that he and Johnson would fulfill nearly in lockstep despite all their enmity.) At a homecoming press conference, Johnson denounced the "chronic campaigner" whose habit was "to find fault with his country and his government" every other October. He said Nixon "never did really recognize and realize what was going on when he had an official position in the government," and icily reminded reporters that President Eisenhower once asked them for a week to think of any contribution from his two-term Vice President.

Johnson canceled plans to barnstorm for Democrats. Disappointing polls showed that a commander's glow from overseas could not swing local races, and that ineffective appeals for Pat Brown among many doomed candidates more likely would injure his own standing. He went home to Texas instead. On Monday, November 7, beneath attention fixed on the last campaign rallies nationwide, Johnson visited the Welhausen School at Cotulla. "I was the song leader," he told a group of parents in the room where he once taught jumbled classes. "You would not believe that, but I tried to be, anyway." He said the school had not changed much since 1928, and that nearly three-quarters of Mexican-American students still left school before the eighth grade. "Right here I had my first lessons in poverty," he recalled. Those vivid memories still shaped all he sought to accomplish in politics, declared Johnson, "for the conscience of America has slept long enough while the children of Mexican-Americans have been taught that the end of life is a beet row, a spinach field, or a cotton patch."

* * *

WITH SIDNEY Logan, the freedom organization candidate for sheriff, John Hulett walked into the Lowndes County courthouse early on November 7 to obtain from Probate Judge Harrell Hammonds a certified copy of the final voter list guaranteed to a new sponsoring group that appeared on the official ballot by meticulous observance of state law. There were 5,806 names in all. "We have enough registered people in Lowndes County to win," Logan told reporters. Hulett expressed caution, knowing his first-time voters must perform under the harsh scrutiny of election authorities whose presence they were conditioned to avoid. "We have never tried to get out the vote," he admitted, "so we don't know exactly what we can do." Later that morning, as never in living memory, officially designated black and white poll watchers mingled at the courthouse to hear the mandatory explanation of rules. When reporters asked what role Stokely Carmichael would play, Hulett tactfully replied that Carmichael no longer lived in Lowndes County and that SNCC workers deferred to local citizens. "The help they have given us is in courage," said John Hinson, county school board candidate, "letting you know you are an American."

Carmichael was finishing his third day in jail. Keeping to Selma, he had refrained from public statements about the Lowndes County election, observing a SNCC policy designed to avoid the extra tension of his black power notoriety, but Mayor Joe Smitherman ordered him arrested with Stuart House and Thomas Taylor, who had been urging people to vote from a sound truck. ("I saw some Negroes aroused," a Selma police officer testified, "who wouldn't usually get aroused on Saturday.") Only by frantic exertion did Carmichael make bail in time to reach the final mass meeting Monday night near Hayneville, where 650 people packed Mt. Moriah Baptist Church. Divided by residence into the eight voting precincts, they questioned lawyer Morton Stavis about election law—disputed ballots, counting procedure, how to challenge a "graveyard" voter—and watched SNCC's Courtland Cox demonstrate how to use a voting machine. They had posted highway signs with their emblem and safety instructions—"PULL THE LEVER for the BLACK PANTHER and go on HOME!"—but stalwarts who learned what pressures awaited poll watchers at the white-owned ballot sites decided to linger after they voted to show support, keeping the legally required distance of thirty feet.

Carmichael's entrance in the midst of preparations electrified the church. "We have worked so hard for this moment," he said, reviewing the twenty months since people had been afraid even to mention the voting rights movement in nearby Selma. His speech ranged from naked sentiment—"It is the will, the courage, and the love in our hearts"—to rhythmic thunder: "We will pull that lever to stop the beating of Negroes by whites! We will pull that lever for all the black people who have been killed! We are going to resurrect them tomorrow! We will pull that lever so that our children will never go through what we have gone through. . . . We are pulling the lever so people can live in some fine brick homes! We are going to say good-bye to shacks! Dirt roads! Poor schools!" After swaying choruses of "We Shall Overcome," Hulett dismissed the crowd with pleas to come early and look nice, as Carmichael hugged people at the door.

On election day in Lowndes, cool and sunny, clumps of voters held up pieces of white paper to beckon the few roving poll drivers who circled rural highways. They ate premade sandwiches dispensed outside the Benton precinct, where large morning numbers allowed fellowship to the point of comforting banter. They held steady in Hayneville, where Tom Coleman and other Klansmen stalked alongside evenly divided lines. For poll watcher Eddie Mae Hulett, wife of the movement leader, the first worrisome sign at Benton was a truckload of sharecroppers who refused to look at her when she asked if they needed help, going meekly into the voting booth with a white official suggested by their plantation owner. The Justice Department observer found no basis to intervene. Driver Andrew Jones, after a long day under siege in Fort Deposit, saw the lights go out suddenly at the City Hall polling station.

He told voices accosting him in the dark that he was waiting to take the poll watchers home, then grabbed a striking hand and hung on until something hard from behind "cracked the hide on my head." Jones fell under blows as two of his daughters jumped from the station wagon and ran screaming for help. They managed to get him into Selma's Good Samaritan Hospital by way of the Lowndes freedom headquarters at Mt. Gillard Baptist Church, where the bloody sight of him superseded a climactic election night. Carmichael and John Hulett activated their emergency vow that attackers would get only "the first shot" for free, and armed black posses scrambled across the county like Minute Men, fanning out to ward off follow-up attacks. SNCC's Jennifer Lawson wielded the Jackson family rifle to protect the Lowndes County Freedom House near White Hall. In a yard near Fort Deposit, guarding Andrew Jones's wife and nine children, Scott B. Smith wore military fatigues and brandished his shotgun until dawn.

All seven nominees from the freedom organization lost fairly close races, and the three who worked for white employers also lost their jobs. Fort Deposit poll watcher Clara McMeans promptly got fired from a maid's livelihood because the boss said her activity "was reflecting on him and his friends." The Andrew Jones family was evicted before he was released from the hospital. Since encountering Carmichael in Montgomery on the last day of the Selma march, Jones had become Fort Deposit's first registered black citizen, watched the first local demonstrators go to jail on a garbage truck with Jonathan Daniels, and forfeited both paying jobs as a lumber worker and janitor for the Alabama power company. Now he remained in Fort Deposit to build a home on land donated by a movement farmer, with grit that inspired outsiders who witnessed the 1966 election. Months later, volunteer Mark Comfort would lead a truck convoy back from California with food and supplies for evictees still holding out in the tent city. "Even though we lost, the people have strong confidence," John Hulett said on the day after the vote. Alice Moore took a politic line about her defeat for tax assessor, saying she always expected to lose by a few hundred intimidated no-shows and plantation voters but had not wanted to discourage anyone by letting on. Charles Smith, president of the Lowndes County Christian Movement for Human Rights, noted philosophically that half the county's eligible black voters still had not registered. "I think the cat did well for the first time out," he announced.

Democratic principle inched forward in Lowndes County. A movement that had shaped national commitments from Alabama and Mississippi returned there to begin everyday politics based on a common right to vote. The fledgling local group, having attracted more than twice the required 20 percent of total election turnout, gained official recognition under Alabama law as the Lowndes County Freedom Party. "We have a party now," declared Stokely Carmichael. "Black people aren't discouraged. We're on the move." He said so from Boston, however, and the party to acquire fame with him was about guns instead of the vote or Alabama, where he now planned for SNCC to maintain no more than a token presence.* A phenomenon took root from reports that went home to Oakland, California, with Mark Comfort—of armed defenders springing up election night in the dark countryside to win "The Battle of Fort Deposit" without firing a shot, preserved in a trophy photograph of one rifled warrior next to the highway signboard image of a black panther.

Notions to adapt the striking ballot symbol had circulated in the wake of Carmichael's speeches since May. J. Edgar Hoover secretly alerted FBI offices to talk of forming a New York black panthers outfit among activists with a "propensity toward violence" and no "actual connection" to the "legitimate political party" in Alabama, but Huey P. Newton and Bobby Seale quickly preempted all contenders. Beginning that fall from Oakland, their Black Panther Party for Self-Defense flashed lightning with military poses of black separatist rebellion from the heart of big cities. The sensation all but expunged real antecedents that were sound and contrary in every respect—ballot struggles by patriot sharecroppers, quilting women, and priestly martyrs—just as fascination with black power eclipsed Stokely Carmichael's six prior years in the nonviolent movement.

*　*　*

"A POST-ELECTION silence settled today on the LBJ ranch," reported the *New York Times* on November 10. In seclusion, the President groaned, "I don't think I lost that election. I think the Negroes lost it."

---

* Carmichael expected H. Rap Brown to be SNCC's only Alabama fieldworker after the 1966 election. Silas Norman had been drafted into the Army. Bob Moses, though nine years beyond draft age, fled conscription in August, and his future wife, Janet Jemmott, left Lowndes County eventually to join him for a decade of exile in Tanzania. Bob Mants also left, though he later settled in Lowndes. Newlywed Gloria Larry House went to Detroit with co-worker Stuart House on medical advice that their unborn baby would not survive her meager diet at the SNCC Freedom House. She became a Wayne State University professor.

He emerged for a press conference several days later to address the dismal 1966 tally of net loss to Republicans: forty-seven House members, three senators, eight governors, and 677 seats in state legislatures. Johnson first took ten questions about war matters, especially U.S. nuclear missile capabilities versus the China and Soviet Union, then put the best face he could on the results. He said Democrats still controlled both chambers of Congress—the House by 248–187, the Senate by 64–36—with roughly the same margin he enjoyed before the 1964 landslide. Asked directly about the influence of "white backlash," the President dodged. "I just don't have the answer to it," he replied. "I don't know." He said the abnormally large shift could be traced to three popular Republican governors in big states: George Romney of Michigan, James Rhodes of Ohio, and Ronald Reagan of California. Privately, however, Johnson saw an adverse trend instead of a fluke. He predicted that most of the new Republicans in Congress would vote with the Southern Democrats while seeking colleagues to replace them. This was the backlash he feared. "It'll move beyond George Wallace and become respectable," he told Bill Moyers.

Wallace, for his part, bristled at suggestions that Ronald Reagan surpassed him overnight in presidential stature. "He *used* to be a liberal," Wallace warned reporters at a victory celebration. "Now he's a conservative, and he might change back again." Wallace claimed to have orchestrated the nation's most impressive win against the Republican trend despite the handicap of a stand-in novice candidate, his wife, Lurleen, who won 63 percent of the Alabama vote but sat quietly through a press conference devoted mostly to his larger ambitions for 1968. The outgoing governor indignantly rejected any backlash label— "I never made a statement in my political career that reflects on a man's race"—and presented himself as a crusader for constitutional states' rights. Wallace said, "My only interest is the restoration of local government."

In California, Governor-elect Reagan deflected instant clamor that he was destined for the White House, calling it "very flattering that anyone would even suggest such a thing." His contest drew a record 79 percent of registered Californians to the polls, and he won by 993,739 votes out of 6.5 million, carrying all but three of fifty-eight counties. Reagan acknowledged a groundswell. "It seems to be all over the country," he said. "The people seem to have shown that maybe we have moved too fast." He discounted white backlash as a benefit to him or other Republicans, emphasizing his personal abhorrence of bigotry and contrasting the new Negro Republican senator Edward Brooke of Massachusetts with segregationist Democrats Lester Maddox and George Wallace. "For me," said Reagan, "the vote reflects the great concern of the people with the size and cost of government." His dubious but genial disclaimer of racial politics in California was more attractive than the bitter view of his vanquished opponent, who grumbled that Reagan won a 57 percent landslide with only 5 percent of the black vote and a quarter of Hispanics. "Whether we like it or not," said the two-term incumbent Pat Brown, "the people want separation of the races."

Political analysts found backlash effects central to the success of Republican challenger Charles Percy over three-term Senator Paul Douglas of Illinois, who maintained his "unequivocal stand in favor of open-occupancy legislation." All the muscle of Democratic precinct captains barely carried the city of Chicago itself for Douglas, and Republican Sheriff Richard Ogilvie, who had been so visible against the fair housing marches into his suburbs, wrested from the Daley machine 18,000 patronage jobs under partisan control of the Cook County Board. This political feat established Ogilvie to become the next governor of Illinois, and Mayor Daley, according to biographers Adam Cohen and Elizabeth Taylor, perceived a grave threat to his own reelection in April of 1967. He criticized Martin Luther King early in November as a troublemaker bent on creating backlash votes for Republicans. One day after the election, Daley had his chief negotiator deny any binding responsibility under the Open Housing Summit Agreement of August 26. "There were only certain suggestions put down and goals to be sought," Thomas Keane told the Chicago City Council. An uproar ensued. "Any attempt to destroy that hope is an act of cruelty," said King, but the mayor moved decisively to shore up the white ethnic wards, relegating integration to a charitable zone at the margin of politics. His press secretary later confided that Daley's "idea of affirmative action was nine Irishmen and a Swede."

* * *

PRESIDENT JOHNSON underwent surgery after the election to remove a throat polyp and repair the scar from his gall bladder operation, while submitting also to political pain he could defer no longer. Announcements dribbled out that the ceiling for the ongoing Vietnam buildup would rise from 400,000 to 470,000 troops, and Defense Secretary McNamara, who had lopped 50,000 soldiers from the request by the Joint

Chiefs, presented the figure as a "leveling off" in future military effort. Still, journalists anticipated a bloody future from combat deployments in 1967 that projected roughly twice the average for 1966, when 30,000 Americans were wounded and 5,000 of the 6,644 cumulative U.S. fatalities occurred. To pay unbudgeted war expenses being filched from other Pentagon accounts, McNamara soon asked Congress for a supplemental appropriation of $12.4 billion, which more than doubled the admitted Vietnam estimate and pushed annual costs toward 20 percent of the overall national budget. Such sums threatened to deform the tiny South Vietnamese economy, whose prices had jumped 125 percent to absorb the flood of American war dollars. ("Runaway inflation can undo what our military operations can accomplish," McNamara secretly observed.) To curb inflationary pressures from the Vietnam deficit at home, the President unhappily asked for an income tax surcharge.

Johnson prepared to strike a tone of gallant realism in his 1967 State of the Union address. Vowing to "stand firm" in Vietnam, he quoted Thomas Jefferson's "melancholy law of human societies to be compelled sometimes to choose a great evil in order to ward off a greater." He reintroduced the failed omnibus civil rights bill of 1966, and promised to "intensify our efforts" in the War on Poverty. Anticipating a political crossfire, Johnson ordered archivists to retrieve every word the late President Kennedy said about helping the poor, and his economists compiled impressive statistics showing that 8.4 million new jobs since 1960 had reduced the poverty rate from 22 to 17 percent of the population. Still, Johnson's own anti-poverty director denounced pressures to keep the third Office of Economic Opportunity budget stalled at roughly $1.5 billion, dwarfed by—and sacrificed to—the escalating price for Vietnam. "The poor will feel that democracy is only for the rich," Sargent Shriver told reporters. Rustin's freedom budget, launched to headlines on October 26, fell dormant with its plan to rescue the remaining 34 million poor Americans, of whom three in four were white, and Martin Luther King discreetly complained to the White House staff of domestic "retreat." At the same time, countervailing forces sought to eliminate the anti-poverty campaign entirely. "Our work was just beginning," Johnson recalled balefully in his memoir, "but there were some who felt that even this beginning was too much." Elements of reaction in both political parties worried Johnson more than his liberal critics. They pressed for all-out war in Vietnam and attacked the anti-poverty agency as a utopian dream tinged with black power subversion.

A political strategist admonished President Johnson that "the best minds are now in this game" against him, determined to exploit his association "with eliminating ghettos and generally pouring vast sums into the renovation of the poor and the Negro. The average American is tired of it." A White House counselor advised less bluntly that government leaders were wearing down under conflict between Vietnam and the Great Society. "You have a tired cabinet," wrote Harry McPherson. "They are good men, but they are beyond asking the hard questions now." Johnson privately confronted Democratic governors who blamed the midterm losses on poor communication, especially his cornpone television persona and the vexing school desegregation guidelines. "I think it is unfair to take your leader and publicly say that it is his image that has caused all the problems," he asserted in full pique, and the governors returned equally wounded complaints. "All of us want to help you," insisted John Connally of Texas. "All of us want to look forward to 1968. We are all now on the defensive." Seeping doubt plagued Johnson's efforts to protect his mandate from 1964. "Now is indeed 'The Valley of the Black Pig,' " Lady Bird Johnson told her diary, recalling an apocalyptic poem by William Butler Yeats. "A miasma of trouble hangs over everything."

* * *

FIVE DAYS after the election, King convened the far-flung SCLC staff of seventy-five for a stabilizing retreat on the coastal island of St. Helena, South Carolina, near the town of Frogmore, where the Penn Community Center inherited the rustic grounds of an old Quaker school for freed slaves. James Lawson and Ira Sandperl conducted joint seminars on the philosophy of nonviolence. Joan Baez performed solos between rousing group songfests that relieved strife brimming from the campaigns in Grenada and Chicago. Workshops vented fatigue, doubt, and abandonment. "The only time I have ever been hit is by a staff member," said one overwrought worker. Rival factions loyal to Bevel and Hosea Williams blamed each other for division, sabotage, unnecessary suffering, and the disillusionment of vulnerable followers. Williams fiercely resisted suggestions that he shift his operations into black Chicago for a winter registration drive to offset Mayor Daley's push in the white wards, until a threat of open revolt silenced the commotion. "Dr. King, we love you," Willie Bolden announced, "but I'm gonna be frank. Hosea Williams is our leader."

Williams made choking gestures toward Bolden, knowing the loyal outburst would only feed rumors that he was plotting a "coup" against King. Williams nurtured reciprocal suspicions against Bevel and his mercurial new protégé, Jesse Jackson. The Williams camp presented themselves as workhorses in the Selma tradition against dilettante theorists who seldom went to jail and had lured King to grief in Chicago. The Bevel camp disparaged Williams as a domineering crew boss for reformed seaport gangsters, incapable of grasping a national movement or the self-sustaining potential of Operation Breadbasket, spearheaded by Jackson. King himself, when present, tolerated the clash of headstrong lieutenants as a necessary by-product of frontier hardship and conviction. He ignored the scathing duels over his leadership, and seldom restrained the combatants. ("Remember, we are a nonviolent organization," he placidly interjected.) Only in the end, when Williams growled at his hint that temporary consolidation in Chicago might be best, did King exhibit his will. "All right, forget it," he told Williams. "Just forget it."

Williams stopped short to gauge the intensity of King's remark, then folded. "Doc, you know I'll go," he said, and with the notable exception of Willie Bolden, most of his staff soon packed off sullenly into the Chicago winter. Privately, King rebuked Andrew Young for allowing Bevel and Jackson to combine so heavily against Williams, sapping resilience, and distress over the criticism snapped Young's exhausted nerves. Leaving the retreat early for another assignment, he fell unconscious in the Savannah airport. One of the doctors who helped revive him sent Young straight on to Tel Aviv, reasoning that negotiations abroad would amount to prescribed rest.

Battered emotions long had been a staple of the movement, testing King far past his trained experience at funerals. On Monday evening, November 14, he suspended the turmoil at Penn Center to explore thoughts out loud. "Whether I have anything to say or not," he said, "I want you to try desperately to listen." He honored the assembled SCLC workers and guests. "I found myself shedding a few tears this afternoon when I listened to Lester [Hankerson] talk about what he had gone through in Mississippi," King confessed. "And many of our staff members go through experiences not quite as bad as Lester that we often know nothing about. And I want to thank you, because you have done this out of loyalty to a cause." He acknowledged "a great deal of confusion in the air," and professed no certainty or answers—"I am still searching myself"—to begin what he called "my informal statement" on the past, present, and future of the movement. In its surviving rough outline, biographer David Garrow later identified the skeletal structure of King's next and final book, *Where Do We Go from Here: Chaos or Community?*

Reviewing the movement decade, King concluded that change from its great mandates for equal citizenship was broad but neither swift nor deep. "While this period represented a frontal assault on the doctrine and practice of white supremacy," he said, "it did not defeat the monster of racism. . . . And we must never forget that the roots of racism are very deep in America." King defined the obstacle on a philosophical plane, distinguishing between the "empirical" statement that black people lagged behind and a stubborn "ontological" disposition to divide races for battle. He saw both. "And the fact is that the ultimate logic of racism is genocide," he asserted. "If you say that I am not good enough to live next door to you . . . because of the color of my skin or my ethnic origins, then you are saying in substance that I do not deserve to exist. And this is what we see when we see that [form of] racism still hovering over our nation."

King used the premise of latent combat identity to analyze the twin obsessions of the political year. He presented black power and the white backlash as independent phenomena, rejecting common theories that one justified or propped up the other. He said backlash was nothing new. It was a vocabulary of denial like the idealized Ku Klux Klan stories that had numbed and distorted the aftermath of the Civil War. He described backlash as coded resistance to structural changes beyond free access to a bus or library. Like the original segregation laws, it served notice that white men were determined to retain tangible privilege from jobs to neighborhoods. By contrast, King defined black power as a cry of pain. "It is in fact a reaction to the failure of white power to deliver the promises and to do it in a hurry," he said. "Once we recognize this we begin to understand what is happening in this revolution."

He explored the nature of revolution, speaking from his outline. "Now first, when you look at a revolution," King ventured, "you must always realize that the line of progress is never a straight line." There were inevitable counterrevolutions, splits, and convolutions "when you feel like you are going backwards," he said. "Virtually all revolutions in the past have been based on hope and hate." Conflict made for tumbling factions even when the revolutionaries were fellow aristocrats like Thomas Jefferson and John Adams, and King admitted taking extra risks from a submerged minority base. "To fire people and motivate them, get them moving," he said, civil rights leaders had shouted "All, Here, Now!" for democratic rights long abridged. "We knew that we morally deserved our freedom, and we should have had it now," he declared, "but deep down within we knew it couldn't come now."

On top of unmet expectations, the movement carried extra burdens from a nonviolent discipline that embraced punishment without the outlet of rage. "We transform the hate element of the traditional revolution into positive nonviolent power," King asserted, "and it was precisely this hope and nonviolent power that guided the psychological turning point through all of the victories that we achieved." Yet these achievements were strained by the very tactics that created them. "The minute hopes were blasted," he said, "the minute people realized that in spite of all these gains their conditions were still terrible, then violence became a part of the terminology of the movement in some segments. It is in this context that we must see what is happening now." King called it a harsh truth that it was easier to feed the frustrations of violence with more violence than to soothe the frustrations of nonviolence with more sacrifice and hope. "Interestingly enough, in a revolution when hope diminishes," he said, "bitter hatred develops toward the very people who build up the hope, because in building up the hope they were not able to deliver the promises."

His meditation came to a bleak turn. King said the nonviolent movement was menaced on both flanks by the violent tones of white backlash and black power. Then, far from advising a respite to let historic adjustments settle, he pressed the full three-part credo of his Nobel Prize address: "All that I have said boils down to the conclusion that man's survival is dependent upon man's ability to solve the problems of racial injustice, poverty, and war." At Penn Center, he called them "the inseparable triplets." No longer could the movement expect to make progress on race in Grenada or Chicago while avoiding the violent propensity of "a sick nation that will brutalize unjustifiably millions of boys and girls, men and women, in Vietnam," King told the assembly. "And the two issues cannot be separated. They are inextricably bound together." They were chambers of collateral refuge for hostility. So was poverty. He said violence of spirit infected the economic system.

King smiled at Williams: "Now, Hosea, I want you to hear this because you are a capitalist." Just as they must "not be intimidated" to speak out against the war in Vietnam, he said, they could not let charges of Communism silence misgivings about the capitalist distribution of wealth. "Maybe America must move toward a democratic socialism," King bluntly suggested, and the movement must consider economic critiques by taboo thinkers such as Karl Marx. "If you read him, you can see that this man had a great passion for social justice," he said. "You know Karl Marx was born a Jew, had a rabbinic background." The early Marx was clearly influenced by Amos and other Hebrew prophets, King asserted, but fell prey to economic determinism that justified "cutting off individual liberties" in a proletarian dictatorship. "The great weakness of Karl Marx is right here," he said, "that he did not recognize that the means and ends must cohere. . . . Now this is where I leave brother Marx and move on toward the kingdom."

To do so, King said they must set aside the triumphant celebrations of 1965, regird themselves for protracted labor, and deepen their commitment to nonviolence. "We have a method," he declared, "and we must develop it." Their method may be only an experiment, but war-hungry critics must understand that violence was uncertain, too. "Violence may murder the liar," said King, "but it doesn't murder the lie. It doesn't establish truth. . . . Violence may go to the point of murdering the hater, but it doesn't murder hate. It may increase hate." The reflex to violence divided mankind into warring tribes, subverting the essential promise of democracy and religion alike. "I still want SCLC to be that lamp of hope, that light in a very dark situation," he said. "We must still believe that we are going to deal with this problem by enlisting consciences" rather than particular racial groups. "For there is no salvation through isolation."

King closed with meditations on history. His small band of cohorts, many of them barely calmed from their internal feuds, absorbed a call to take on nothing less than the global cousins of segregation. He presented a radical leap in the language of steadfast commitment. Far from a plan, it was a raw summons to witness, and King broke off with an awkward new metaphor instead of his polished oratory. The landmarks of 1964 and 1965 had advanced "the football of civil rights" to "about the 50-yard line," he declared. Now they faced diehard resistance in opposition territory. "As we move on, sometimes we may even fumble the ball," said King, "but for God's sake, recover it. And then we will move on down the field."

* * *

ANDREW YOUNG returned on November 30 from his twelve-day mission to Jordan and Israel. The foreign ministries of both countries eagerly sought an ecumenical pilgrimage, he reported, and were making arrangements for King to preach to as many as five thousand travelers from a boat just offshore on the Sea of Galilee. Young hoped to create a peace headquarters at either Hadassah Hospital or the old Hebrew University, which still sat vacant in Jordanian territory, but cooperating officials were "scared to death" that hostilities would shut off desperately needed foreign revenue. The Young visit coincided with riots over Operation Shredder, a quick predawn raid on Palestinian militia near Hebron that turned into a pitched battle with the unexpected arrival of a Jordanian army patrol. The Israeli commander and fifteen Jordanian legionnaires were killed, with many soldiers wounded and more than a hundred homes destroyed. Undersecretary of State Katzenbach scolded Israeli Foreign Minister Abba Eban for a bungled cross-border provocation against the most moderate Arab head of state, King Hussein, who had kept his Patton tanks east of the Jordan River to assuage Israeli security concerns but now felt compelled by military leaders to move some of them toward Jerusalem.

King said regretfully that the threat of general war might force him to cancel his visit to the region in 1967. One host government or both would react viscerally to any statement approaching peace politics, and Young's fallback idea to emphasize religious reconciliation seemed lamely unpromising. (Hardly anyone noticed King's public appeals for the relief of Jews persecuted in the Soviet Union.) Stanley Levison thought it would take genius for any outsider to find a constructive position in the cauldron of Middle East politics. He agreed with Young that any trip should be confined to sightseeing, which would put King in the untenable position of ducking urgent problems at home to lead tourists through a war zone.

Levison fretted separately about newly transcribed copies of King's rambling self-examination at Penn Center. King himself worried from hard experience about the passages of internal criticism, and restricted distribution to avoid another round of negative news stories "hammering at black power" on his authority. That would only discredit the civil rights movement again, he figured, advertising divisions against his purpose to shape a positive alternative and let the weaknesses of black power run their natural course. Levison, the chief SCLC fund-raiser and FBI target, highlighted reservations about the transcript's pulpit style and its colloquial reference to the father of Communism. "Martin disagrees with Marx but calls him 'brother Marx,' " Levison said on his wiretapped phone line. "I don't think that would be good for the contributors."

* * *

IN AN early appraisal of the 1966 Chicago civil rights movement. Bernard Lafayette told veterans they already had met key goals. Their campaign disproved theories that racial grievance in northern cities was "too subtle to dramatize," he said, and refuted the widespread doubt that fragmented city people could be "mobilized for nonviolent direct action in the face of mass violence." Scholars who specialized in Chicago history concluded accurately that the open housing settlement, though it put only a small dent in residential segregation, "was certainly far stronger than the settlements that had brought SCLC's Birmingham and St. Augustine campaigns to a close." The Metropolitan Chicago Leadership Council for Open Housing, created by the agreement, remained over decades a respected coalition for stable neighborhood integration, carrying two of its many lawsuits into the U.S. Supreme Court. Chicago politicians renounced local commitments, just as Birmingham leaders had reneged on promises to integrate department store bathrooms and the police force. What sharply distinguished the movements was the disparity in their wider impact. The weaknesses of the Birmingham settlement disappeared in a rippling tide that dissolved formal segregation by comprehensive national law. The Selma campaign itself never defeated or converted Sheriff Jim Clark, but the nation democratized voting rights to make segregationists such as him relics of the past. No corresponding shift enhanced the Chicago settlement in outcome or reputation, and all its shortcomings remained an eyesore.

To cushion their loss, some movement leaders adopted the conceit that they had once bowled over opposing forces by themselves. "We should have known better," wrote Ralph Abernathy, "than to believe that we could come to Chicago and right its wrongs with the same tactics we had used in Montgomery, Birmingham, and Selma." Bayard Rustin, narrowing his framework to excuse himself along with the rest of the country, turned a jaundiced eye on his bosom friend. "I knew he had to fall on his face," said Rustin. "Daley cut Martin Luther King's ass off."

By the cycles of history, a period of letdown and division was perhaps inevitable to let the country absorb enormous changes mandated by the letter and spirit of equal citizenship. Cruel flukes compounded this letdown. The quest for interracial justice came of age just as the national climate turned hostile over the Vietnam War, and the movement's most distinctive tenet—nonviolent witness for democracy—nearly vanished simultaneously from public discourse. Nonviolence became passé across the spectrum. Black people discarded it like training wheels to claim the full belligerent status of regular Americans. Even stalwart practitioners like Diane Nash yearned for something stronger, doubting its reward. White people were eager to dismiss nonviolence as a church notion misplaced in national politics. Hippies made it look selfish. Many thinkers ignored what they considered an outmoded handicap suited to a phase of the race problem. Almost no one honored or analyzed the broader legacy of nonviolent citizens, and King would grow ever more lonely in his conviction that the movement offered superior leadership discipline for the whole country. To him, the decline of nonviolence magnified compound dangers inherited from "enemy thinking"—the tendency to wall off groups of people by category. In religion, enemy psychology could invert the entire moral code to make violence a holy cause. In politics, enemy psychology could subvert the promise of democracy with a hierarchy of fear, secrecy, and arbitrary command for war.

The realignment of 1966 was at once blatant and subliminal, symbolic and momentous. Its backlash feature first appeared to be no more than a balancing correction for the near extinction since 1964 of the Goldwater Republicans, the last defenders of legal segregation outside the South, but observers in subsequent decades looked on the normally obscure midterm year as a fulcrum of more lasting change toward political dominance by the heirs of Goldwater. Political scientists Earl and Merle Black traced a "Great White Switch" in partisan voting patterns across the South. Nicholas Lemann, a student of the black exodus from the South into Chicago, identified a larger reaction of potent, cumulative effect. "The beginning of the modern rise of conservatism coincided exactly with the country's beginning to realize the true magnitude and consequences of the black migration," he wrote in 1991, adding that the influential neo-conservative movement was founded then "by former liberals who lost faith in large part over the issue of race in the North; in Irving Kristol's famous apothegm, 'a neo-conservative is a liberal who has been mugged by reality,' it's not difficult to guess what color the mugger was." In a mirror thesis, Matthew Dallek concluded his book about the rise of Ronald Reagan with a terse review of his opponent's "one crippling defect" in the 1966 election: "He was a liberal. And when Pat Brown went down, so did the philosophy that he had clung to throughout his adult life. It has never really recovered."

IV

Passion

CHAPTER 33

Spy Visions

December 1966–February 1967

POLITICAL passions tested democ-
racy's institutional core. In *Bond v. Floyd,* the Supreme Court weighed
the argument by Georgia that criticisms of the Vietnam War, rather
than Julian Bond's color per se, left the state representative-elect short
on the sincere character required to take his oath of office. "We are not
persuaded," Chief Justice Warren wrote tartly, "by the state's attempt to
distinguish between an exclusion alleged to be on racial grounds and
one alleged to violate the First Amendment." A unanimous ruling on
December 5 ordered Georgia's House to admit Bond, the twenty-six-
year-old former SNCC publicist who had been elected three times but
not yet seated. "We're all disappointed," said one state official, "that the
Georgia legislature will apparently not be allowed to make its own decisions." Such grumbling marked what might have seemed a remedial
lesson for the South, but just then a movement erupted in Washington
to expel Representative Adam Clayton Powell. "Fight in Congress to
Bar Powell Planned by California Democrat," announced the *New York
Times.* "Powell's Just Too Blatant," a *Washington Post* headline proclaimed. The powerful chairman of the House Education and Labor
Committee, while duly elected twelve times from Harlem, had infuriated colleagues with flamboyant displays of "the freeloading available to
all and practiced more quietly by many," reported the *Post.* "Powell's
creed has been that he can do anything a white man can do."

By uncanny coincidence, the prolonged feud over FBI surveillance
emerged garishly that same week. Thurgood Marshall, Solicitor Gen-

eral of the United States, asked the Supreme Court to vacate the freshly upheld conviction of Joe Schipani of Brooklyn, noting with apology that prosecutors had failed to inform either defense lawyers or judges of evidence obtained from devices installed "by means of trespass," namely microphone bugs. Because this was the third such case recently discovered, Marshall further advised, the Justice Department would examine past and present federal prosecutions for the taint of undisclosed eavesdropping. "U.S. Reviews Cases in Bugging Quest," declared the lead front-page story in the *Times*.

Publicity ruptured the fragile truce covering eighteen months of subterranean maneuver. When outsiders had unearthed FBI bugs, disputes within the government over responsibility had drawn the unusually blunt presidential order to forbid all surreptitious microphones, and compliance became what Katzenbach called "an issue of great emotion" between the FBI and Justice Department: "There was very nearly a threat on the part of the FBI to stop organized crime investigations if they couldn't have this technique." FBI Director Hoover claimed broad but vague legal authority. Senator Robert Kennedy reacted viscerally, being vulnerable already because his signature lurked on hundreds of formal requests for less intrusive wiretap surveillances on telephone lines, which did not require break-ins to install. Kennedy insisted that he had not even known of FBI bugs when he was Attorney General, let alone approved them, and warring charges of secret misconduct culminated in a cryptic appeal to his successor and former deputy. "As you know, this is a damn important matter for me," Kennedy wrote Katzenbach by hand-delivered courier. "I just don't want to receive a shaft—it's not deserved—and anyway I don't like them deserved or not. . . . I can't write you as many memos as J. Edgar Hoover. And there is no sense in our talking about it by phone. I feel strongly about it—and I write you (just that as there's) not much else to say."

By July of 1966, Katzenbach had managed to trace and shut down not only shadowy bugs but also many wiretaps. The President demanded more restrictions than Katzenbach himself thought justified, and in particular prodded him to confirm the removal of the sensitive installations on Martin Luther King. ("You got that little situation prohibited?" Johnson asked carefully by telephone. "It's gone," the Attorney General replied. "It better be," said the President.) Katzenbach, having employed cajolery, including legal predictions that the King wiretap would surface ruinously if the government indicted Hosea Williams for car theft, had transferred to the State Department in part because his relations with Hoover were frayed beyond civil respect.

The FBI Director reduced his bureaucratic risk, and, over the pained objection of intelligence deputy William Sullivan, suspended parallel operations to gather data by investigative burglary. "We do not obtain authorization for 'black bag' jobs outside the Bureau," Sullivan acknowledged in a plea for reconsideration. "Such a technique involves trespass and is clearly illegal; therefore, it would be impossible to obtain any legal sanction for it." Nevertheless, Sullivan defended the FBI position that burglary had proved "an invaluable technique" of "wide-range effectiveness," gleaning information otherwise off-limits, and Hoover would be obliged to repeat his protective ban when Thurgood Marshall ignited the public controversy over bugs. "I note that requests are still being made by Bureau officials for the use of 'black bag' techniques," Hoover informed his top executives. "This practice, which includes also surreptitious entrance upon premises of any kind, will not meet with my approval in the future."

After more than four decades in office, Hoover much preferred the authoritarian cloak of political spy work to accountable duty in law enforcement, but he channeled the FBI's clandestine activity away from the forbidden zone of trespass. When FBI sources learned that Martin Luther King, desperately low on SCLC funds, planned to ask Teamsters president Jimmy Hoffa for a donation like the $25,000 bestowed long ago at the Liuzzo funeral, Hoover authorized Deke DeLoach to launch preemptive sabotage. Agents discreetly monitored results over the consolation wiretaps on Stanley Levison, which Katzenbach had left in place, and preserved Levison's shocked recounting to Clarence Jones of a planted New York Daily News story that Hoffa hoped to buy friends like King because he faced thirty-five years of federal jail sentences under appeal. ("Yike, does it really say that?" exclaimed Jones, prompting Levison's miserable retort: "What, do you think I made it up?") Informants soon told FBI agents that an embarrassed Hoffa was calling King "a faker." With the rendezvous aborted, and the FBI role safely concealed, Hoover scrawled "Excellent" on a report that "our counterintelligence aim to thwart King in receiving money from the Teamsters has been quite successful to date."

The Levison wiretap alerted Hoover also to a budding association between King and former White House adviser McGeorge Bundy, who, as president of America's largest private philanthropy, had announced on consecutive days two Ford Foundation initiatives tinged with penance. First Bundy proposed to harness satellite communications technology toward what would become the first public broadcast network, in a project developed purposefully with television executive Fred Friendly. Across deep lines of dissent, Bundy the Vietnam architect shared an overriding conviction with war critic Friendly, who had been forced out of CBS over the Fulbright hearings, that commitments of national will demanded unfettered debate and straightforward constitutional decisions. Bundy next catapulted race relations high onto the Ford Foundation agenda, proclaiming that "full equality for all American Negroes is now the most urgent domestic concern in this country." FBI agents already knew of the intended shift, being privy to surprise among King's advisers when Bundy quietly hired two of their contacts to make up for his admitted lack of prior interest in civil rights. Eavesdroppers overheard doubt that staid foundations really meant to fund SCLC citizenship programs, no matter how much they professed to admire nonviolent workshops with Chicago youth gangs, but grant negotiations progressed into meetings between Bundy and King. After the 1966 elections, Bundy allowed his two new race specialists virtually to join the SCLC staff, preparing King's forty-four-page testimony for a U.S. Senate hearing on the challenge of poverty. Levison, the skeptical idealist, vacillated between worry and giddy hope to rescue the movement's financial base. "I don't want five million dollars," he told Andrew Young. "I want less. Five million dollars could destroy us."

DeLoach recruited an intermediary to poison the foundation against King, but John Bugas, vice president of the parent Ford Motor Company, ran into Bundy's steely refusal to hear derogatory secrets from an anonymous source. When Bugas, a former FBI agent, said the source preferred not to be divulged, Bundy guessed FBI and offered to listen if its officials would speak openly for themselves, which set off boiling evasion at headquarters. "I personally feel that Bundy is of the pseudo-intellectual, Ivy League group that has little respect for the FBI," DeLoach concluded. He despaired of the direct approach, and Hoover concurred: "We would get nowhere with Bundy."

* * *

HOOVER COULD and did mount fierce political attacks against a rare public challenge, such as the Supreme Court's reproach for cases corrupted with bugs. To circumvent his own secrecy restrictions, he sent a scripted letter of inquiry to himself on a confidential mission with

DeLoach, who induced Iowa Republican Representative H. R. Gross to sign, and Gross compliantly released Hoover's ad hominem reply for the front pages of Sunday, December 11. "Hoover Asserts Robert Kennedy Aided Buggings," declared the *Times*. Kennedy offered a statement of rebuttal—"Apparently, Mr. Hoover has been misinformed"—together with a letter from his former FBI liaison stating that Kennedy had processed many wiretap applications but never a bug. From headquarters, the FBI sprang an overwhelming counterattack at precisely 2:25 P.M. the same Sunday, built on a declaration from Hoover that Kennedy's position was "absolutely inconceivable." DeLoach's aides sent copies, buttressed with sample documents from "the official records of the FBI," to every satellite office "for the use and assistance of reliable news contacts." They assured superiors that while they obeyed fine points of the FBI image code—declining news requests to read material on camera, for instance, lest film footage preserve self-declarations on unsavory topics—Hoover's blistering words led most Sunday evening newscasts, followed by Kennedy's besieged reaction that he had been unaware of bugs nonetheless.

Issues of democratic norms and constitutional balance gave way to sensational headlines across the country: "RFK and JEH" (Little Rock), "Bugs and Justice" (New York), "Which Do You Believe?" (Chattanooga), "Bugging Furor Bad Business" (Sacramento). *The Christian Science Monitor* called the personality clash a "donnybrook" suited to Washington, "a town which relishes a good fight between public officials almost better than anything else." Stories from the capital—"President Aloof in Bugging Feud"—suggested accurately that President Johnson was bombarded with FBI allegations against Kennedy. (Hoover went so far as to have DeLoach brief Justice Fortas on indiscretions he said "could destroy Kennedy," and Ramsey Clark, Katzenbach's successor at Justice, advised Johnson that Hoover had lined up affidavits from witnesses, "forty or fifty of them," to say Kennedy was complicit in bugs.) On December 14, James Reston of the *New York Times* reported that suspicions of officials were so widespread that "nobody in Washington could be sure his telephones were private." His column surfaced the rumor that "the Government, beginning with the Kennedy Administration, listened in on the telephone conversations of Martin Luther King, the Negro leader, during the racial disorders. . . . Who authorized the taps? We do not know."

Billowing paranoia overshadowed the next day's Senate hearings on poverty, in which King cited a multibillion-dollar adjustment in the war budget to indict misguided national priorities. "The error alone is more than five times the amount committed to antipoverty programs," he said. "The bombs in Vietnam explode at home—they destroy the hopes and possibilities for a decent America." Using the black quarter of the poverty population as a barometer, he charged that "the attainment of security and equality for Negroes has not yet become a serious and irrevocable national purpose." Robert Kennedy, one of only two senators present, engaged King in a forlornly inquisitive dialogue about why nonviolence seemed to have yielded hope so far only in the South.

Afterward, reporters who pressed King about the Reston story obtained a dampening reaction: "Dr. King 'Assumes' Phone Is Tapped / But Says He Doesn't Know Why / Embassies Calm." FBI officials refused comment, but their New York wiretap units, in a compounded irony, monitored the chilled discussions among King's lawyers about the wiretap news. Stanley Levison said President Kennedy himself had warned King about FBI surveillance in 1963. Harry Wachtel thought King should display less forbearance and more outrage. "When you have a guy doing an illegal act," he told Levison, "you should not be so sweet about it."

*   *   *

HOOVER ESCAPED in melodramas over lost American innocence, including what NBC News anchor David Brinkley drolly branded "the biggest publishing story since the New Testament." Jacqueline Kennedy, the widowed First Lady, sued on December 16 to block a forthcoming book on the Kennedy assassination because it reopened too many raw wounds. William Manchester, her chosen author, agreed to remove his opening chapter about Kennedy's earlier trip to Texas, cast as an allegory on frontier manhood, in which Lyndon Johnson inveigled an elegantly squeamish President-elect to kill a deer on his ranch. Otherwise Manchester defended his manuscript and confessed to the widow an abject failure "to suppress my bias against a certain eminent statesman [LBJ] who always reminded me of somebody in a Grade D movie on the late show." Gossip oozed into the press about whether, why, and how hard Robert Kennedy pressed for revisions. By Christmas, President Johnson fulminated to Fortas and other confidants that leaks from the book mocked him all through the bloodstained transfer of power. "I don't think I called Mrs. Kennedy 'honey,' " he told Bill Moyers. "I think that's their idea of 'you all' and 'comin'"—C-O-M-I-N—and this stuff they write about Texas." Moyers warned of press rumors that Johnson had compiled notes from his White House phone calls to rebut Manchester. "Well, that's wrong," Moyers briskly assured the President, "because there are no verbatim transcripts."

"Well, no, there are," Johnson countered. "There are a good many."

Moyers stopped short. "I thought—"

"They don't think so, but there are a good many," the President whispered.

Moyers backtracked. "I thought that Juanita [presidential secretary Juanita Roberts] had said that we didn't have the equipment in those days," he said.

"Well, there are a good many," Johnson insisted.

"But he's talking here about, about," Moyers stammered, "between *you* and other people."

"Well, there are," the President solemnly admonished. "There are a good many." Hidden telephone recorders captured Johnson's cautionary signal that not even his closest aide knew all his defenses.

Moyers had just resigned from the White House. The President chided him for cooperating with Manchester's slanted account, and he fretted privately that Vietnam would push Moyers closer to Robert Kennedy as war debate surged Christmas Day in reaction to the first American news dispatch out of North Vietnam. For the next three weeks, Harrison Salisbury of the *New York Times* surveyed bomb damage to civilian areas of Hanoi, toured school ruins, and described residential sections of Nam Dinh where the Pentagon alleged no military targets: "The cathedral tower looks out on block after block of utter desolation." Secretary McNamara's spokesman spasmodically denounced the reports and then conceded a small error rate quantified at 1.5 civilian deaths per sortie. The *Time's* military correspondent defended the bombing as accurate, while the rival *Washington Post* impugned Salisbury's integrity: "Ho Tries New Propaganda Weapon . . . Harrison Salisbury of *The New York Times* is Ho's chosen instrument."

Streams of vitriol and patriotic zeal sloshed together in January. Published excerpts from the Manchester book relived the national trauma of Dallas just as Jack Ruby, owner of the Carousel strip club, died of cancer while awaiting retrial for the murder of presidential assassin Lee Harvey Oswald. In a void of dignified or satisfying answers, maverick prosecutor Jim Garrison of New Orleans prepared the first conspiracy indictment of shadow devils to feed cynicism for decades. Beginning

January 8 in Binh Duong Province, a systematic assault of B-52s, sixty-ton bulldozers, defoliants, and thirty thousand soldiers burned four villages and flattened forty square miles north of Saigon. Operation Cedar Falls, which defied Senator Russell's maxim on the political folly of detaching the Vietnamese from their land, aimed to move all ten thousand inhabitants to relocation camps in a bold tactical reversal of the search-and-destroy sequence. American casualties set a weekly record at 1,194, including a death toll near the peak of 240 from the 1965 Ia Drang battles. Salisbury's twentieth dispatch, "North Vietnam Spirit Found High," reported that popular street songs in Hanoi paid tribute to the obscure war protester Norman Morrison, who had immolated himself outside the Pentagon late in 1965.

FBI Director Hoover slipped up to Capitol Hill when the 90th Congress convened on January 10. On the House side, away from ceremonial pomp, war frictions, and the tumult of California Democrat Lionel Van Deerlin's successful drive to bar Adam Clayton Powell from taking the oath, Hoover briefed loyal supporters about the Kennedy dispute. He "pointed out we had many other documents proving Bobby was lying," according to his aide's notes, and rejected the idea of court-approved surveillance because "there are many untrustworthy Federal judges, including some in the District of Columbia, whom we would not want to have knowledge of particular installations." Before a closed Senate committee, Hoover testified formally on the eavesdropping leaks. "*None* of this misinformation has emanated from the FBI," he lied. He reviewed eavesdropping since Prohibition, illustrating the meticulous wiretap process with a pregnant reminder that Robert Kennedy had signed the secret order on Martin Luther King, stating falsely that the initiative had been Kennedy's. He conflated wiretaps with bugs to disguise the fact that he alone had controlled the latter without a speck of due process. He argued at length that Kennedy had seen material he knew came from bugs, or so should have inferred, and on this presumption Hoover spun an invisible tradition of authority stretching back to the early Eisenhower administration. Quoting only a small portion of his private lodestar, a May 20, 1954, memo from Attorney General Herbert Brownell, Hoover concealed the memo's dissenting purpose and never let on that it plainly skirted adverse law. ("It is quite clear that in the *Irvine* case the Justices of the Supreme Court were outraged by what they regarded as the indecency of installing a microphone in a bedroom," Brownell wrote. "It may appear, however, that important intelligence . . . can only be obtained . . . in such a location. . . . It is my opinion that under such circumstances the installation is . . . not prohibited by the Supreme Court's decision.")

This tortured rationale for an era of bugs would embarrass free government in future years, with Hoover safely dead, but the living Director silenced Congress and the press alike. His towering image as chief protector from domestic fears was at once too formidable and too fragile for public discussion. William Manchester scarcely mentioned FBI performance in his account of the Kennedy assassination, except to note Hoover's fury that the Warren Commission dared criticize his Bureau at all. Behind assertions of spotless rectitude, buttressed by the intimidating secret files, Hoover's fits of eccentric hysteria were so jarring that outsiders kept their rare glimpses to themselves. When Manchester, for instance, asked in a book interview about Oswald's brief expatriation to Moscow, Hoover launched an oddly defensive tirade against Soviet Premier Nikita Khrushchev. "The Director told Manchester that he had always felt it better to kick individuals like Khrushchev in the shins once in a while rather than to boot-lick them," recorded DeLoach. "The Director explained that Khrushchev was basically an oriental and that individuals opposing orientals usually lost face in the oriental's opinion when fear or trepidation was shown."

*   *   *

FOR ROBERT Kennedy, fortunes fluctuated amid talk of a 1968 bid to unseat President Johnson. The bugging scandal and Manchester book turned January straw polls from a 53–47 percent Kennedy lead into a 39–61 percent deficit, but the uproar over Salisbury's bombing series renewed pressure for him to oppose the carnage. Columnist Walter Lippmann asked whether Kennedy could live with a failure to provide a moral alternative. When the senator tried to downplay talk of political insurrection, by referring to Johnson as "a man of compassion," rival partisans debated which champion better served the poor. In England, where he retreated from the crossfire, Oxford University students who pressed Kennedy to denounce Vietnam extracted no more than an expression of "grave reservations" about the bombing within an overall endorsement for Johnson's war goal to preserve South Vietnam, but stories emphasized his frank rapport with antiwar students. In Paris, President Charles de Gaulle warned anew that the United States could not prevail against the tide of Vietnamese politics, but he coldly advised Kennedy not to ruin a bright future by contesting a disaster in progress.

Columnist Joe Alsop, writing as an "affectionate, admiring, and deeply concerned uncle," offered identical advice from the opposite pole, and begged Kennedy to avoid involvement in protests that could turn military victory into stalemate. "Anyone who is in any degree implicated in the latter result will never be forgiven," he warned. Back home, Kennedy confronted a tempest over reports that he brought a North Vietnamese "peace feeler" from Paris. Nonplussed, summoned to the Oval Office on February 6, he guessed that Johnson's State Department must have leaked a grossly inflated detail from his routine debriefing, about a minor French official who thought an American bombing halt would induce North Vietnam to negotiate. "It's not *my* State Department, goddam it!" the President erupted. "It's *your* State Department!" The two men called each other names.

Undersecretary of State Katzenbach witnessed the personal duel, which he later called "a perfectly ridiculous episode." His frantic search had failed to locate the Kennedy debriefing in State Department records of highly classified peace initiatives, including a current overture from President Johnson to Ho Chi Minh himself, because it had been widely dispersed with other ordinary messages. The President saw conspirators within his government magnifying an illusion that Kennedy could settle Vietnam on nearly painless terms, evading the brutal choice between defeat and war. Kennedy saw an unstable warmonger scheming to make him a scapegoat, and Katzenbach resumed his role from the triangular bugging feud as a battered second for each contender. ("I succeeded in getting both Hoover and Kennedy mad at me," he recalled.) Hard questions of substance all but vanished once again—first the constitutional standards for surveillance, now the uncertain capacity of American arms to establish political allegiance among the Vietnamese. Director Hoover, having incited the personality diversion, disappeared in a Kennedy-Johnson rift that lasted far beyond their lives. Projections of animus between the two icons became a political language in itself, subsuming relatively small differences on issues. It would symbolize their era's demise, and substitute for lessons that fell between them.

The play *MacBird!*, which opened a hit Off-Broadway that February, previewed an extreme polarization of public debate. Long spurned by publishers, with one reading for investors marred by scuffles and cries of treason, the script presented Johnson as mastermind not only of the Kennedy assassination but also of misfortunes like Adlai Stevenson's fatal heart attack and Edward Kennedy's 1964 plane crash. In a burlesque of Shakespeare, the usurper MacBird cavorted on stage with jangling spurs, a feathered scepter, and ludicrous armor borrowed from a baseball catcher's gear, while the Robert Kennedy character vowed cold-blooded restoration like ancient MacDuff: "At each male birth, my father in his wisdom/Prepared his sons for their envisaged greatness . . . /Our pulpy human hearts were cut away/And in their place precision apparatus/Of steel and plastic tubing was inserted." Playwright Barbara Garson, a veteran of student protest at Berkeley, dismissed the visible structure of American politics as a facade to cover a throwback to dynastic powers. Critics and audiences divided over her portrayal of barons turning state crimes and even wars into props for rivalries plotted in frothy speeches of royal entitlement. "Two opposing Americas were rubbing sleeves," observed *The New Republic*. *Newsweek* hailed in *MacBird!* "the total catharsis of satire." The *New York Times* scorned "a crackpot consensus" against responsible government, blended from political left and right. "The cruelty and vulgarity are almost beyond description," wrote Edith Oliver in *The New Yorker*, which refused a theater advertisement for the first time in the magazine's history. "We deemed the whole thing in bad taste," an executive said to explain the ban, "what with Vietnam and all."

* * *

SNCC CONTINUED its disintegration behind the fame of black power. A December conference in upstate New York stalled for three rancorous days on a motion from the all-black Atlanta SNCC project to expel the last seven white staff members. Combatants tangled from definitions to dialectics, not excluding the thorny classification of Hispanics and Native Americans. Where established SNCC leaders saw petty distraction, Bill Ware of Atlanta argued tirelessly that revolutionaries against white racism must "cut the umbilical cord" of dependence. Stokely Carmichael and James Forman fought the motion on tactical points, having explained awkwardly to their caucus that it would be unwise to contest black solidarity in principle. Doing so would repeat Martin Luther King's fundamental error, argued Carmichael, objecting that King stood inflexibly for nonviolence in a violent world. Ruby Doris Robinson supported black nationalism but railed against the separatists for chattering about white people instead of doing any work. Forman, bridling at suggestions of sentimental favoritism for longtime SNCC workers, or his white wife, raged that the historic brotherhood of sit-ins had degenerated into pot-smoking pretenders, and offered a substitute motion to disband SNCC entirely. Nearly half the members left in fatigue or disgust before the anti-white initiative passed by a single vote, 19–18, with twenty-four abstentions. Bob Zellner retreated silently to check out of the Peg Leg Bates Country Club with Jack Minnis, who called himself "a tough old bastard" but went years unable to speak of the scalding result. Clayton "Peg Leg" Bates, the strangely ecumenical host for a racial purge, had survived a childhood sharecropper accident to become the one-legged tap dancer for vaudeville's Harlem Blackbirds and big bands from Duke Ellington to Jimmy Dorsey, a star on *The Ed Sullivan Show,* command performer at the British royal court, and hotel owner among the Jewish resorts in the Catskill Mountains. Back inside, motions to reconsider the vote trailed off in a fog of irritation, with the blunt Ivanhoe Donaldson muttering vacantly, "If it was so damned painful, why the hell did we have it?"

Many founders of SNCC had dispersed widely after seven years in the crucible of nonviolence. Two days after Christmas, Diane Nash was the youngest of four American women herded suddenly to a concrete bunker below one of Hanoi's French hotels, thrown together in an air raid with foreign guests, including by chance correspondent Harrison Salisbury. They watched waitresses put on tin helmets to shoot rifles at American bombers with only the most remote chance of hitting one and marveled at war details so vivid they sowed controversy within the small delegation sponsored by peace groups, which had ventured far across cultures to experience fire from their own country. "There are no innocent civilians in North Vietnam," one of them provocatively asserted after two weeks' exposure to total war mobilization in a peasant society—riveted but troubled, with a tinge of admiration. Nash agreed with companion Barbara Deming that Americans must understand the Vietnamese resistance, which was unified even in the face of extermination from the sky. Deming, a journalist for a pacifist magazine, had met Nash less than four years earlier at the height of the Birmingham children's marches against segregation. Now their delegation met Ho Chi Minh for an hour in the palace of the former French governor, and the venerable pacifist A. J. Muste talked separately with Ho a few days later. The North Vietnamese leader professed admiration for the American people as distinct from their government. "President Ho did not ask us to convey what he had said," Muste wrote President Johnson, cautioning that Ho's offer to receive Johnson hospitably for talks did not seem to indicate any weakening of military resolve. Muste and three of the women came home to have their passports seized for illegal travel. Their public comments gained little reaction. Nash delayed her return to the United States, laboring separately to sort out her immense arc since Selma—from the epitome of nonviolent discipline and vision into grudging respect for war, clarity adrift. She refused to speak with white reporters, finding them oblivious to the racial complexities of Vietnam.

Thoughts of Asia also tormented SNCC pioneer James Bevel. He stalled overtures from Muste to lead an antiwar mobilization planned for spring, and Nash, his estranged wife, broke off attempts to reconcile in the midst of serial philandering that he rationalized with bold incantations about truth experiments in nonpossessive love. Instead, she had stretched the concept of movement responsibility once again, as in the Freedom Rides, this time to a continent without black people, leaving him behind in Chicago with a moribund anti-slum campaign and rare domestic care of their two small children. Bevel's agitation intensified until one day, watching a load of diapers wash in the basement, he surrendered to a mysterious gale of voices from the doorway. Recruiting emergency baby-sitters, he told Muste's colleagues of a peculiar sign favoring the protest job and commandeered enough travel funds to reach Atlanta in search of Martin Luther King.

King had fled the country to escape daily intruders such as Bevel. Facing a draconian two-month deadline to produce a book manuscript, he managed to compose nearly three thousand words a day between speech trips into January, when the first showdown over Adam Clayton Powell demanded a response. "From my personal relationships with him, I really don't care what happens," King confided, "but I have to look beyond that." Stanley Levison advised that, "unpalatable as it is," King must defend Powell from an unconstitutional stampede to take his seat in Congress. King temporized with a telegram of personal sympathy, which Powell promptly released as a blanket endorsement. Meanwhile, from California, King agreed with Levison that any credible book must address Vietnam, but he dodged pleas to meet in New York with Al Lowenstein, Benjamin Spock, and Yale chaplain William Sloane Coffin. This would be about politics, he anticipated, because Lowenstein already had told him that "a group of people" thought King should run as the antiwar candidate for President in 1968. January inaugurations added pressure for King to interpret the new wave of anti–civil rights governors: Lester Maddox in Georgia, Ronald Reagan in California, and Lurleen Wallace in Alabama. (The *Times* noted signs of moderation in Governor Maddox, who dropped the word segregation from his address and shook hands with Negroes, telling Julian Bond, "I see you finally got your seat.") From Bimini, Powell brashly predicted triumph despite the January 10 House vote to bar him pending investigation, and claimed political strength to dominate even " 'Weak-kneed' Wilkins and Martin 'Loser' King."

Bayard Rustin warned a civil rights leadership summit on January 14 that Powell's repellent arrogance could split the movement, while A. Philip Randolph decried irrationality for and against Powell, and King advised the group to be philosophical about joint efforts to uphold impartial standards. "Because Adam will turn right around next week and blast every one of us," he said. "This is the way he operates." Telling colleagues he must seal himself off to write, King flew to secluded rooms at Ocho Rios on the coast of Jamaica, beyond telephones and most newspapers but not an alarming story in which the SCLC staff vented its distaste for the Northern registration drive. "I don't like Chicago," Hosea Williams told the *New York Times* of January 16. Lester Hankerson underscored his vivid picture of frostbite and apathy with a quote explaining why he would rather get beaten again in Grenada: "The people here are not interested in first-class citizenship." The story made King break isolation to call the mainland, where an infuriated Levison urged summary dismissals long overdue—"I mean the movement is entitled to that"—and Andrew Young was predicting that Williams would cry his way to forgiveness as always. King instructed them to postpone drastic punishment until his return. "I got so upset about it I could not write a line," he said. "And I was doing well, too."

Under the circumstances, Young swallowed notice that a possessed visitor had just bowled him over for a plane ticket and directions to the hideaway. Traveling aide Bernard Lee soon banged on King's door, bracing the surprise with SCLC formality. "Mr. President," he announced, "Bevel is here." In rushed Bevel with his bizarre tale of tumbling diapers and noises that first had sounded like a host of familiar cousins but crystallized into one strange voice: "Why are you teaching nonviolence to Negroes in Mississippi but not to Lyndon Johnson in Vietnam?" Bevel recounted the questions that swirled around the basement and left him astonished, ending, "Are the Vietnamese not your brothers and sisters, like those you thought you heard at the door?" King, nervously adjusting his necktie, deflected any summons abroad as an abdication of his civil rights mandate from the SCLC board—"Ben

Hooks and Joe Lowery wouldn't stand for it"—and on January 19 managed to hustle Bevel out of Jamaica with temporary leave to join Muste's staff. He called his top aides in distress, asking why Young had not noticed something badly wrong. "Bevel sounds like he's off his rocker and needs a psychiatrist," he said, recounting Bevel's visionary instructions for King to take an open boat "peace shield" across the Pacific Ocean into the rivers of Vietnam, "preaching all the way that the war must end."

Not for the first time, King dismissed theatrics from Bevel only to have them linger stubbornly in his mind. He kept turning to one item packed with his book research, transfixed by a twenty-four-page photo essay in the January *Ramparts* magazine of young Vietnamese with stump limbs, shrapnel scars, and faces melted by napalm, its text introduced by the pediatrician Spock: "A million children have been killed or wounded or burned . . ." It gnawed at King whether Bevel was crazier than the prevailing reasons for such carnage. He acknowledged that Bevel boasted of steering him with wild inspirations in Birmingham and Selma, but he also recognized a fine line between lunacy and wisdom in prophetic movements. No food would taste good, King told Bernard Lee, until he discovered his part to end the war. While cut off four more weeks in Jamaica, laboring feverishly every day for words to reinvigorate civil rights, he started with a January 25 letter to the Nobel Peace Prize committee in Norway nominating the exiled Vietnamese monk for the 1967 award: "Thich Nhat Hanh offers a way out of this nightmare . . ."

* * *

IN KING's absence, Al Lowinstein pursued many avenues to harness an antiwar coalition. The whirling law professor and citizenship activist orchestrated an open letter from fifty Rhodes Scholars questioning Vietnam policy, which made front pages on January 27, then escorted forty of the one hundred student body presidents who had just issued a similar appeal ("Student Leaders Warn President of Doubts on War") into an audience with Secretary of State Rusk on January 31. They emerged in numb dismay over Rusk's stolid reply to a question about what would happen if Vietnam escalated into nuclear war among the superpowers: "Well, somebody's going to get hurt." Lowenstein, working separately with chaplain Coffin of Yale ("462 on Yale Faculty Urge Halt in Bombing"), encouraged the ailing theologian Reinhold Niebuhr to make a declaration for peace, and helped Stanford theologian Robert McAfee

Brown write a statement of conscience for more than two thousand religious leaders gathering January 31 in Washington. None of the nation's 250 Catholic bishops attended, but Senator Eugene McCarthy, badgered by seminary constituents for his previous silence, concluded before a mass meeting that Vietnam policy failed Catholic doctrines of justifiable war. Rabbi Abraham Heschel exhorted the assembly to make witness through the corridors against complacency about violence: "In a free society, some are guilty but all are responsible." After two days of vigils, Heschel calmed six fellow sponsors from CALCAV (Clergy and Laity Concerned About Vietnam) on their way to the Pentagon, designating Coffin their spokesman with instructions to control his emotions. When Secretary McNamara parried them with an opening aside that religious leaders should have been more involved in civil rights, Coffin explained that most of those present had marched or been jailed like McAfee Brown and himself with the Freedom Riders. He and John Bennett, president of Union Theological Seminary, outlined Brown's statement circumspectly until Heschel interrupted with a passionate jeremiad about the blasphemy of war upon the face and children of God. Tension spiked, but McNamara engaged in the moral dialogue to the point of missing appointments. He described religious dissent as legitimate and perhaps even a welcome balance, hinting at a far greater burden of political pressure to escalate the war. The delegation absorbed twin jolts in the cockpit of so much harm: Heschel's spontaneous outburst and McNamara's transparent regret.

Arriving in Jamaica on February 3, Andrew Young relieved Bernard Lee in the marathon flurry of dictation and handwritten changes for King's book. He brought stateside reports on the antiwar fervor along with an "explosive" cover story in *Commentary* magazine, "The President & the Negro: The Moment Lost." Levison warned King of its sweeping thesis by Daniel Moynihan that President Johnson was abandoning civil rights because movement leaders—"unable to comprehend their opportunity . . . [and] caught up in a frenzy of arrogance and nihilism," had shunned the Moynihan report's recommended focus on matriarchal pathology in the Negro family. "An era of bad manners," Moynihan concluded, "is almost certainly begun."

On February 13, King transferred his book operation to a Miami hotel for five days, exchanging draft chapters and revisions with an editorial team. He learned there of the heart attack in New York that abruptly felled A. J. Muste, without whom, King once said, "the Amer-

ican Negro might never have caught the meaning of nonviolence."
Commemorative speakers for the eighty-two-year-old scion of pacifism
included Norman Thomas, Bayard Rustin, and James Bevel, the new
coordinator of Muste's antiwar mobilization set for April. They recalled
his faith motto from the Book of Job—"Though he slay me, yet will I
trust him"—which anchored the pacifist discipline Muste believed essential to progress. "If it does not have the spiritual connection," he
wrote in 1941, "I am sure that it will go wrong," either by erosion of
hope "or by going off the deep end on the use of violence."

From Miami, King initiated a conference call about his desire to be
more active for peace. He described the goading impact of the *Ramparts*
photographs, but advisers split over participation with Bevel in a giant
march to the United Nations. Union leader Cleveland Robinson was
strongly in favor, citing the "naked reality" that the war had crippled
their domestic work. Andrew Young wanted first to round up other
black ministers to cushion the leap. Stanley Levison confessed his fear
that clashes between civil rights and peace would neutralize King on
both fronts, reducing him to "a small-time peace leader." He urged an
antiwar strategy of recruiting key political figures such as UAW president Walter Reuther, but King stressed the movement's bottom-up experience in reaching the national leader who mattered most. "You have
to have the masses behind you before you can go to the president," he argued. Still, King shrank from more splits in the movement or damage to
its economic base—"We would probably lose the Ford Foundation"—
and Levison persuaded him to nestle his antiwar mission in respectable
company.

On February 25, three days after the New York premiere of
MacBird!, King joined four U.S. senators in California to address a Vietnam conference at the Beverly Hilton Hotel. The American war effort
was pronounced unconstitutional by Ernest Gruening of Alaska, wrong
by George McGovern of South Dakota, and misguided by Mark Hat-
field of Oregon. Eugene McCarthy of Minnesota raised doubts: "We
should hesitate to waste our strength . . . in so highly questionable a
cause." King struck intimate tones in the keynote speech to an overflow
crowd of 1,500 "Americans and lovers of democracy," sketching recent
history to lament cultural blinders on a heartfelt national purpose to establish freedom. "For nine years we vigorously supported the French in
their abortive effort to re-colonize Vietnam," he said, and his vision of
the war echoed Thomas Jefferson's haunted premonition of justice

awakened for slaves. "When I see our country today intervening in what is basically a civil war," said King, "destroying hundreds of thousands of Vietnamese children with napalm, leaving broken bodies in countless fields and sending home half-men, mutilated mentally and physically . . . and all this in the name of pursuing the goal of peace, I tremble for our world." He likened America in Vietnam to the prodigal son of Christian scripture, "strayed to the far country," and exhorted his audience to reclaim the prodigal like anguished parents. "I speak out against this war because I am disappointed in America," he cried. "There can be no great disappointment where there is no great love." The speech did make scattered front-page headlines—"Dr. King Advocates Quitting Vietnam"—but muted response thereafter signaled a passing nod for the fringe piety of harsh times.

CHAPTER 34

Riverside

March–April 1967

TREPIDATION and infighting over Vietnam shaped King's decisive next step to Riverside Church, while ugly racial transitions nagged for attention. In Natchez, Mississippi, Wharlest Jackson punched off-duty from Armstrong Tire and Rubber at 8:01 P.M. on Monday, February 27, ending his first shift on a cement-mixer job previously restricted to white workers, which earned a raise of 17 cents per hour, but an explosion nine minutes later hurled his mangled corpse fifty yards. Investigators said a heat-fuse bomb under Jackson's pickup resembled one that nearly killed George Metcalfe, Jackson's fellow NAACP officer and carpool rider from the Armstrong plant. That night at Mississippi State's Old Maroon Gym, Perry Wallace of Vanderbilt broke the state's color line for Southeastern Conference sports. (Rival Ole Miss had dodged the hurdle by canceling its home game with Vanderbilt's freshman basketball team.) Spectators waving a noose rained down betrayal coins, calls of "nigger!" and bone-rattling choruses of "Dixie." Elsewhere, a bomb ruined the new Head Start pre-school of Liberty, Mississippi, while arson fires in Lowndes County, Alabama, destroyed a black church and the makeshift anti-poverty office.

Wharlest Jackson's murder would remain unsolved, like the Metcalfe bombing, and a local trial with spectacular revelations soon freed a defendant who confessed the random murder of Ben Chester White during the previous summer's Meredith march ("Jury Told of Plot to Slay Dr. King / Killing of a Negro Intended as Lure, Sheriff Testifies"). By contrast, Justice Department prosecutors advanced tenaciously against the Mississippi Klan, winning reindictment that same February 27 of thirty-one conspirators in two landmark cases: the 1966 firebomb murder of Vernon Dahmer and the 1964 triple lynching of James Chaney, Andrew Goodman, and Michael Schwerner. Not a few politicians bemoaned the federal effort more than the crimes themselves. Clark Reed, head of Mississippi's renascent Republican Party, complained on statewide television that the Wharlest Jackson murder "has done more toward destruction of states' rights than the liberal extremists could have brought about on their own."

In Washington, one political drama climaxed on March 1 with House rebellion against a select investigating committee and the leadership of both political parties, which proposed formally that Adam Clayton Powell be admitted once he paid a fine of $40,000 for misuse of funds, surrendered all seniority, accepted garnishment of his congressional salary to pay a court judgment from the Esther James libel case, and stood mute under custody for censure in the well of the House. A few defenders objected that miscreants had retained House standing even in prison without such chastisement, but an opposing groundswell sought riddance of Powell altogether. Republican leader Gerald Ford coyly observed that although the Constitution required a two-thirds vote to expel a seated member, the House could exclude anyone in Powell's un-sworn limbo status by simple majority without stating a cause. Democrat Emanuel Celler, floor manager for the major civil rights bills, threatened to impeach any Supreme Court Justice who ruled differently. "Mr. Speaker, I have a reasonably strong stomach," announced Representative H. R. Gross, "but it will revolt at the aroma that will arise if today Adam Clayton Powell is offered a seat in this chamber."

Only Drew Pearson, the muckraking columnist, questioned the central complaint that scofflaw Powell refused to pay the libel judgment due a constituent whose integrity he maligned, pointing out in one column that Esther James had a record of gangster arrests back to 1933. Neither Pearson nor the select committee mentioned the libel's origin in ten extraordinary House speeches that listed her among hundreds of names on "police pads" for the Harlem underworld. Ignored, Powell had repeated his radioactive charges publicly in 1960, arguably losing constitutional immunity, and while his lawyers produced ample testimony that criminals gave regular payoffs to Esther James, it would take wrenching scandals well after Powell's death to prove completed transfers into the chain of police command. Silence smothered his cries against the protected scourge of numbers and narcotics rackets ("All pads are due on the first of the month"), especially since the impish crusader himself sometimes claimed to seek only a fair share for black officers in the corruption dominated by New York City's all-white corps of 212 police captains. Prevailing fiction suggested that Powell gratuitously insulted a lowly "bag woman" on the streets. The *New York Times,* which argued that hesitancy to punish Powell marked him the beneficiary rather than the victim of prejudice, nurtured a sympathetic widow's image for Esther James: "a 66-year-old domestic who lives on her earnings as a servant and her late husband's railroad pension." When reporters encamped near his Bimini island hideaway relayed the 307–116 House vote for permanent exclusion, Powell shrugged with affected nonchalance from his boat *Adam's Fancy.*

The next afternoon, March 2, Robert Kennedy proposed to suspend the bombing of North Vietnam. After weeks of fitful preparation, Kennedy carefully chose words from divided contributors, including Richard Goodwin. He opposed military withdrawal, affirming "determination and intention to remain in Vietnam until we have fulfilled our commitments," but he urged risks to end the horror he confessed helping to create there under President Kennedy. "It is we who live in abundance and send our young men out to die," he said. "It is our chemicals that scorch the children and our bombs that level the villages. We are all participants." If a bombing halt did not succeed, he argued, it would shift the onus for war more clearly upon North Vietnam. While Kennedy addressed a packed Senate gallery, the President tried vainly to overshadow him in the news—visiting Howard University by surprise to reiterate his goal of redress for segregation, holding a spontaneous press conference, disclosing an expected first grandchild. More successfully, Johnson arranged instant rebuttals and prodded senators from both parties to cross-examine Kennedy before he left the Senate floor about bombing halts already tried and failed. ("All right," Richard Russell promised. "I have some misgivings about getting into a debate with the little piss-ant, but I'll see about it.") More ominously, having ordered a compilation of FBI secrets two weeks earlier, Johnson signaled grave political retribution at stake. Headlines about Kennedy's Vietnam speech coincided with the next day's first corrosive story alleging his secret involvement in CIA assassination plots against Fidel Castro, which may have "backfired against his late brother." ("President Johnson is sitting on an H-bomb," wrote Drew Pearson.) Republican presidential contender Richard Nixon needed no cue to denounce Kennedy for "prolonging the war by encouraging the enemy."

King followed the uproar into New York for a March 6 consultation at Harry Wachtel's law office on Madison Avenue. The scheduled agenda—last-minute revisions for King's book, chronic money trouble, and deferred crisis over Hosea Williams—gave way to a renewed deadlock on the April 15 antiwar march to United Nations Plaza. All senior advisers strenuously opposed King's participation. Bayard Rustin said it would ruin any hope of future cooperation with President Johnson. Historian Lawrence Reddick among others said the march would be sectarian and ineffective because the organizers welcomed all voices, including partisans of the Vietcong. Andrew Young joked that a Communist was said to be the most rational voice in the protest coalition. King first rescued the subject from swift oblivion with comments of critical sympathy. His recurring doubts extended debate past mild surprise into vexation, provoking wary looks at James Bevel as the sole advocate for the march. Stanley Levison, who rarely repeated what his unique access allowed him to tell King alone, stressed that the absence of elected officials on the platform would leave King foolishly weakened among a "squabbling pacifist, socialist, hippie collection," and Cleveland Robinson agreed even though he was a march sponsor himself. Concerted objections wore down but failed to break King's refrain that it would be cowardly to shun a just cause for fear of isolation. Agreeing only to postpone his decision a few days, he rushed an hour late to an evening fund-raiser hosted by wealthy New Yorkers. After a distracted presentation there on civil rights history since Rosa Parks, King hinted privately at his dilemma. William vanden Heuvel, a Kennedy adviser who had accompanied Edward to Mississippi and Robert to South Africa, told him to expect a vale of woe for any public break on Vietnam.

King flew home to manage a daring internal counteroffensive by Hosea Williams, who lodged a manifesto blaming Bevel for personal dissolution and leadership failures throughout SCLC: "Our staff problems are unbelievable." His travels had him return through Washington on March 13, but King abruptly canceled an appointment he had secured with the President for that day. From his close reading of Johnson—a volatile mix of regret and determination being dragged from civil rights to Vietnam—King mingled distress about how to approach him with stewing delay over his own protest stance. The latest weekly report of 1,617 American war casualties—232 killed, 1,381 wounded, four missing—broke the January record by four hundred. In the wake of Robert Kennedy's Vietnam speech, headlines tracked extraordinary press competition to unearth details of the Oval Office encounter a month earlier. The *New York Times* borrowed news from *Time* magazine's current issue: "Discussion with Johnson Bitter, a *Time* Article Says." Anonymous sources said the two men had accused each other of spilling innocent blood, with Kennedy calling Johnson a son of a bitch and Johnson vowing "all you doves will be destroyed" within six months. A historian of the feud later catalogued the excited phrases by political reporters who "raided their arsenals of hackneyed military metaphors" about throwing down gauntlets and crossing the Rubicon.

In New York, King's advisers frantically canvassed potential antiwar leadership. Their ostensible mission was to broaden the April 15 mobilization rally, but their real hope was to break the spell of King's compulsion to be there. They offered pained reminders of Bevel's unstable history, including his latest "visit from Jesus," and gathered new evidence to reinforce their argument that King should not fall sway to a lunatic "over-simplifier." As march coordinator, Bevel did compensate for his mercurial style by hiring Bernard Lafayette and Paul Brooks, a biracial team of Freedom Riders steeped in nonviolent diplomacy from James Lawson's Nashville workshops. Co-workers complimented Bevel's "way of shaking cobwebs from the mind," and he gained publicity with a colorful vow that a peace movement "must take the position of the folks whose kids were burned up this morning." On the other hand, he flummoxed Mobilization headquarters with strange edicts—"What this demonstration needs is some Indians!"—and unsettled activists who had expected a civil rights figurehead of reverent appeal. The local chapter of Women Strike for Peace complained to Bevel of his "emphasis on 'mass murder' and talk of sending a ship of volunteers to North Vietnam." He fared worse with novel shock theater, barging in on the CALCAV founders with plaintive cries that his brother had died that day in Vietnam, cultivating shared personal grief until he unveiled a trick lesson that the movement should treat *every* soldier and victim as family. "Jim Bevel has scared the daylights out of John Bennett and Abraham Heschel," a CALCAV letter confided. Not even these committed religious leaders would go near the Mobilization protest, reported Levison, Rustin, and Wachtel, strengthening their unified insistence that King must find another venue, and word of his contrary resolve on March 14 pitched them into disbelief bordering on rebellion. "I'm gonna march," said King. "I promised Bevel."

* * *

ANDREW YOUNG sent out a resigned note that King "feels conscience-bound to participate," then scrambled with colleagues to limit the damage. Their first move was a tactical demand that King speak first and leave early, lest his usual closing slot trap him on the platform through inflammatory speeches by Stokely Carmichael and others. Young also solicited from John Bennett an invitation for King to lecture in the chapel of Union Theological Seminary a few days beforehand, hoping to cushion the anticipated hostile reception with a controlled presentation of his Vietnam message.

Bennett assigned arrangements to CALCAV's executive secretary Richard Fernandez, which became a mixed blessing for King's advisers. Fernandez was an awkward career misfit among Congregationalist clergy—son of a Boston oil executive, not quite accepted to lead any congregation because he carried a Hispanic surname but spoke no Spanish. He had hitchhiked to interview King and Abernathy for a term paper on the bus boycott, gone to jail with fellow New England seminarians in North Carolina, and ventured on his spring leave as a campus chaplain into Birmingham's nonviolent youth workshops just before the seminal marches of 1963. When interviewed in 1966 for the CALCAV position, Fernandez brashly informed Bennett, Heschel, and Coffin that they would never turn public opinion against the war with theological pedigrees and sermons. Within a year, he raised the number of active CALCAV chapters from eight to sixty-eight by goading clergy into systematic outreach beyond the comfort of friends. Within a week of the King assignment, Fernandez informed Bennett and Young of three requirements to build effective "cover" for the intended march with Bevel. First, they should transfer the preview lecture into the immense Riverside Church, which CALCAV secured for the evening of April 4. Second, they should engage a professional publicist, Fred Sontag, who would donate his services on a final condition: King must agree for once to submit a speech text at least five days in advance. *"This would give us a maximum amount of time,"* Fernandez wrote with demanding emphasis on March 21, *"to reproduce it for the press."*

Stanley Levison flew to Atlanta with an appeal to reconsider the Vietnam thrust altogether. ("I lost," he reported home over his wiretapped phone line, "and we'll just have to live with the consequences.") King departed for Chicago behind schedule on March 24, leaving Young only a four-part outline of the Riverside Church address. For an orator trained in synthetic improvisation, who often conceived speeches on a last-minute briefing, the imminent deadline would have been a shock even without extra handicaps. Trusted assistants stalled the project, which obliged Young to farm out the drafting assignment to scattered volunteers, including professors Vincent Harding of Spelman and John Maguire of Wesleyan. King tried to relay comments from the maw of a floundering movement in Chicago, where he apologized for his three-month absence at a rally packed into Liberty Baptist Church. A press conference followed with volleys of skeptical questions about the stalled summit agreement, a "miserably failed" registration drive, the chance of riots, and Mayor Daley's public charges that King's return was a "politically inspired" trespass into the mayoral campaign. "I have made it clear over and over again that the issue in Chicago is injustice," King replied. "It was injustice before Mayor Daley was elected. If he is re-elected, it will be injustice then." He punctuated a blur of private councils with a March 25 speech at the Chicago Theological Seminary, praising stand-out progress in the drive to integrate the workforces of all-white companies under Jesse Jackson, the precocious director of SCLC's local Operation Breadbasket. At noon, King and Dr. Benjamin Spock led five thousand supporters in a Chicago Area Peace Parade from Wacker Drive along State Street through the downtown Loop. A few hecklers seized passing placards—"Draft Beer, Not Boys," "Would Napalm Convert You to Democracy?"—and threw them in the Chicago River. At the Coliseum on South Wabash, King earned standing ovations with a reprise of his Beverly Hills speech on Vietnam. "This war is a blasphemy against all that America stands for!" he cried.

White House officials noticed the reemergence. "He's canceled two meetings with me, and I don't understand it," dictated President Johnson, wondering in the midst of greater war travails why his aide Louis Martin did not bring King to see him. The latest Pentagon figures of March 23 put the week's American casualties above two thousand for the first time at 2,092, with 211 killed. Famed British historian Arnold Toynbee declared victory in Vietnam an illusion "unless the American army is prepared to stay there forever." North Vietnam released worldwide the recent exchange of secret letters in which Johnson's offer of peace talks and a bombing halt, on condition of a military freeze, met plainspoken rejection "Vietnam is thousands of miles from the United

States," wrote Ho Chi Minh. "The Vietnamese people have never done any harm to the United States. . . . They will never accept talks under the threat of bombs." Worst for Johnson, General Westmoreland had just contradicted the administration's public assurance of military headway with a classified request for another 200,000 soldiers, which would raise the authorized troop ceiling to 670,000.

Levison, far from reconciled to King's plans, called Chicago after midnight with a new battery of arguments. Contributors would feel betrayed because SCLC's fund-raising letters had never solicited for protest against the war, he said, and King's civil rights currency was so weak that literary agent Joan Daves could not find even a small magazine to publish a promotional excerpt from the new book. Most harshly, Levison reported an angry aside from *Saturday Review* editor Norman Cousins that wrongheadedness on Vietnam would reduce King's reputation to mud. "I anticipated some of this," King replied, "and it doesn't bother me at all." He tried to mollify Levison on March 27 with a cheerful report that at least a thousand Negroes joined the Chicago march, easing fears that King would become a token leader for white ideologues. Levison vacillated between approval and despair over King's public emphasis that he was protesting out of love for America. That positive message was a weak candle, Levison feared, against a Vietnam storm darkening right over the stubborn end of segregation, causing anger in young people so intense that it "does boil down" to alienation from the entire country. "You can't be identified with that," Levison pleaded. "I'm not just talking opportunistically. It's not sound thinking." He declined King's urging to pursue the issue among the long-winded SCLC preachers assembling in Kentucky.

Muhammad Ali, with improbable assistance from Hosea Williams, had his hometown brewing over race and Vietnam before King reached Louisville late on March 28. In the ninth defense of his heavyweight championship, a frustrated, vengeful Ali toyed with Ernie Terrell through six rounds once the challenger stood woozy and aimless, with Ali shouting "What's my name?" over jabs, punishing the scornful denial of his right to name himself. Purple headlines detected fiendish cruelty in the ring: "Cassius Reveals His Wickedness." Jimmy Cannon of the *New York World-Journal & Telegram* acidly concluded that "Cassius Clay had a good time beating up another Negro"; Arthur Daley of the *Times* called him "a mean and malicious man." Ali compounded the press furor by announcing that he would defy on religious grounds his conscription order to report for Army duty in April, and King escaped the tempestuous SCLC board for two hours on March 29 to meet privately with Ali about the likely repercussions—being deprived of his boxing title and sent to prison. Chafing that the sectarian Nation of Islam forbade participation in America's "slavemaster" politics, including war protest, Ali whispered that he might disobey Elijah Muhammad and appear at the April 15 Mobilization. When they emerged, King deflected personal questions into more general controversy. "My position on the draft is very clear," he said. "I'm against it."

Irrepressible Ali chided the jostling reporters for getting "shook up" that such diverse black men could talk civilly, "like Kennedy and Khrushchev," but he revealed one sharp disagreement: he had spurned SCLC's local campaign to break out of segregated neighborhoods. "Black people should seek dignity and self-respect before they seek open housing," Ali said, and dismissed journalists with Elijah Muhammad's separatist gibe that Negroes still "lost" to self-hatred could turn mansions into slums within a day.

Offsetting Ali's scorn, the local integration drive received a boost in publicity from Hosea Williams, who with a dozen staff aides had mounted a shrewd retreat from Chicago ahead of the SCLC board meeting. Williams vowed in the midst of the demonstrations that unless Louisville broke the racial confinement into city areas called Parkland, Smoketown, and Little Africa, where black families still raised hogs and chickens, SCLC would send pickets and protest dashers into the manicured glory of the May 6 Kentucky Derby. The very thought scandalized Kentuckians, including many civil rights leaders, but it won surprise endorsement from Rev. A. D. King. "We can start by planning to disrupt the horses," he said, "since white folks think more of horses than of Negroes."

The younger King, who was hosting the SCLC board sessions at his Zion Baptist Church, carefully picked another moment to extricate his brother for a scripted personal word with Georgia Davis, the candidate soon to be elected Kentucky's only black state senator. "Martin has been thinking about you since you last met," he told her. "After the meeting tonight, ride with me to the Rodeway Inn and meet him there."

The stark proposition froze Davis. The elder King studied her and said only, "Yes, I'd like for you to come," before hurrying on. Davis, who had been on the charter flight that picked up King in Atlanta for the final leg of the Selma march, contemplated her choice with starstruck savvy about the terms of discretion available to black females. Toward midnight, she cringed inwardly as A. D. King vouched for her past a posted police guard she knew by name, and King soon arrived with apologies for the precautionary approach through his brother. "I had no choice," he said with a sigh, beginning a furtive, occasional affair.

The next day, March 30, some SCLC board members accused King of trying to impose his Vietnam resolution like a bishop. "This is no Methodist Church!" shouted Rev. Roland Smith, proclaiming himself a staunch supporter of his government's anti-Communist crusade. Parliamentarians stalled with quibbles about the composition and voting status of the fifty-seven-member board. Someone complained that lunch was getting cold. Hosea Williams would recall that Daddy King himself helped vote down a resolution that approved SCLC resistance to the war, but a weaker version passed amid calls not to embarrass SCLC's president. King, breaking away for an interview with *New York Times* correspondent John Herbers, confirmed plans to give "a major policy paper" about Vietnam the next Tuesday at Riverside Church.

On April 2, when his interview appeared on the front page of the Sunday *Times,* King preached at Ebenezer while cobbling together speech changes past the deadline crunch. Andrew Young telephoned revisions for three sections submitted from Atlanta, but Al Lowenstein delivered his negotiated draft of a fourth part straight to CALCAV headquarters in New York. Richard Fernandez rushed assembled copies to Rabbi Heschel and Union Seminary president John Bennett, who had agreed to close the eight o'clock Riverside program with commentary on King's speech. A third responder, historian Henry Steele Commager, received his copy on arrival from Cambridge, England. By Tuesday morning, promotional releases drew a full turnout for King's preview reception at New York's Overseas Press Club, where publicist Fred Sontag distributed embargoed speeches and promised "live and remote pickups" for broadcasts.

While busloads of CALCAV supporters converged from Connecticut, Pennsylvania, and other neighboring states, advisers in King's suite at the Americana Hotel fretted all afternoon over their paradoxical success. Their intended buffer of a seminary lecture loomed instead with consequence, and the rumbling signs of a big political event magnified sudden alarm over the neglected speech. Levison and Harry Wachtel, who seldom agreed on political language or style, huddled in the bedroom to draft an emergency substitute for dissent they found too personal and raw. Realizing that noticeable deviation from the press text would be criticized, they collaborated in a futile effort to compress King's Vietnam stance into a poetic but impregnable new introduction. King used the same charged moments to absorb by remarkable short-hand memory an orator's rhythm for words he already found comfortable. He discarded the preface as they rushed uptown to Riverside Church, where a processional march of one hundred clergy gathered in the narthex. All 2,700 pew spaces and 1,200 portable seats were filled, and an overflow line stretched toward 120th Street as in the halcyon 1930s when King's idol Harry Emerson Fosdick first preached at the Gothic cathedral financed by John D. Rockefeller, Jr. Wachtel squeezed into a VIP room in the Riverside library, but acute foreboding sent Levison straight home to bed.

* * *

A STANDING ovation died down to cavernous tension before King imposed deeper quiet with a meditation on hesitant voices. "I come to this magnificent house of worship tonight because my conscience leaves me no other choice," he said. Paying tribute to the first line of Robert McAfee Brown's CALCAV statement on Vietnam—"A time comes when silence is betrayal"—King confessed that the emotional vortex of war left doubters "mesmerized by uncertainty" and had made his pulpit "a vocation of agony" for the previous two years "as I have moved to break the betrayal of my own silences and to speak from the burnings of my own heart." He still felt the forceful admonishment to leave Vietnam policy alone, King allowed, but it left him "nevertheless greatly saddened" that so many people considered the topic a senseless and disconnected shift from civil rights. That presumption fitted those who "have not really known me" or understood the movement, he lamented. "Indeed," said King, "their questions suggest that they do not know the world in which they live."

He undertook to explain "why I believe that the path from Dexter Avenue Baptist Church . . . leads clearly to this sanctuary tonight." Seven reasons began with two lesser ones confined to race. Vietnam had "broken and eviscerated" the historic momentum for justice since the bus boycott, he asserted. Moreover, circumstance compelled poor black soldiers to kill and die at nearly twice their proportion for a stated purpose to guarantee liberties in Southeast Asia that remained myths at home, fighting "in brutal solidarity" with white soldiers "for a nation that has been unable to seat them together in the same schools." King derived a third theme from young rioters who had countered his pleas for nonviolence with quips that the nation itself relied on "massive doses of violence" to solve social problems. "Their questions hit home," he intoned, "and I knew that I could never again raise my voice against the violence of the oppressed in the ghettos without having first spoken clearly to the greatest purveyor of violence in the world today—my own government."

This naked pronouncement further hushed Riverside as King moved through reasons centered in patriotism, his Nobel Prize commission, and religious imperative. Just as the movement always had adopted America's larger, defining goal of a more perfect democratic union—helping to spread concentric ripples of freedom behind rights for black people, liberating white Southerners themselves from segregation—so King argued by reverse synergy that a hardening climate of war could implode toward fearful subjugation at home. "If America's soul becomes totally poisoned," he warned, "part of the autopsy must read 'Vietnam.' " He marveled that religious leaders so readily evaded their core convictions to excuse violence. "Have they forgotten that my ministry is in obedience to the one who loved his enemies so fully that he died for them?" he asked. "What then can I say to the Vietcong, or to Castro, or to Mao, as a faithful minister of this one? Can I threaten them with death, or must I not share with them my life?" Finally, he declared for Vietnam an impetus broader than American ideals but short of religious apocalypse or perfection. "We are called upon to speak for the weak, for the voiceless, for the victims of our nation, for those it calls enemies," he said. "No document from human hands can make these humans any less our brothers."

King quickened his pace to describe decades of nearly continuous war from the viewpoint of ordinary Vietnamese. "They must see Americans as strange liberators," he said. His historical sketch grew relentlessly more intimate past the "tragic decision" of 1945 to revoke independence with a nine-year attempt to reestablish French colonial control. "Now they languish under our bombs," said King, "and consider us, not their fellow Vietnamese, their real enemies." He filtered out geopolitical labels to highlight personal realities on the ground. "They move sadly and apathetically as we herd them off the land of their fathers into concentration camps," said King. "They watch as we kill a million acres of their crops. . . . They wander into town and see thousands of the children homeless, without clothes, running in packs on the streets like animals." Villagers and soldiers degraded each other as Americans subjected their own troops to inner scars beyond the hazards of war. "We are adding cynicism to the process of death," he charged, "for they must know after a short period . . . that their government has sent them into a struggle among the Vietnamese. . . .

"Somehow this madness must cease," King declared, but he predicted no peace initiatives to match the appetite for war: "The world now demands a maturity of America that we may not be able to achieve." His audience stirred as from shock when he presented five proposals drawn from Lowenstein's draft, including a permanent bombing halt and a unilateral cease-fire. Applause first greeted the final brisk point: "Five, set a date that we will remove all foreign troops from Vietnam in accordance with the 1954 Geneva Agreement." A renewed wave of approval swept over his immediate call for a national effort to "grant asylum to any Vietnamese who fears for his life under a new regime." King did not hide from the stigma of military defeat by Communists, nor quibble about negotiating terms. Yet neither did he discount anyone's yearning for democracy, whether a faceless peasant's or Lyndon Johnson's. Instead he offered bare, conflicted remorse for "sins and errors in Vietnam" that had neglected, spoiled, and trampled essential bonds of solidarity in freedom. By treating the Vietnamese more as subject "natives" than citizens, the American example long since undermined a democratic road to independence.

The Riverside crowd embraced King's message as though relieved to hear biting reflection sustained with nuance so devoid of malice, and perhaps also because his candid doubts of practical impact rang humbly true. They clapped for his endorsement of draft resistance and again for his praise of seventy declared conscientious objectors thus far from his Morehouse alma mater alone. He said each listener should weigh methods by individual conscience and collective promise—"But we must all protest." Witness to belief was more important than immediate results, he told them to more applause, "and if we ignore this sobering reality, we will find ourselves organizing Clergymen and Laymen Concerned committees for the next generation." The crowd stayed with King through skeins from his speeches since the Nobel Prize lecture. He called Vietnam symptomatic of a tragic impulse to meet rising hope in the world's "barefoot and shirtless people" with military force disguised as American values. "Communism is a judgment against our failure to make democracy real and follow through on the revolution that we initiated," he declared. Summoning a renewed freedom movement "out into a sometimes hostile world," seeking to overcome poverty, racism, and war, King's peroration ran past his text to extol again the biblical vision of the prophet Amos—"when justice will roll down like waters and righteousness like a mighty stream."

A second standing ovation gave way to hurried comments by the sponsors. "There is no one who can speak to the conscience of the American people as powerfully as Martin Luther King," said John Bennett. "I hope that he will make us see the monstrous evil of what we are doing in Vietnam." Reporters converged afterward to grill King about the chances for nuclear escalation, Communist exploitation, or antiwar sabotage, and one asked how a rabbi could condone any comparison of American policy to Hitler. "I am not aware that Dr. King made such an analogy," replied Heschel. "He only made reference to concentration camps, which apparently in the mind of this listener conjured up such an analogy." Among surprise well-wishers pushing through the throng came Morehouse schoolmate and Juilliard musician Robert Williams, who had composed his first published choral work, "I Can't Turn Back," one traumatized night during the bus boycott. From Riverside back to the Americana Hotel, Williams reclaimed his old Montgomery role as volunteer escort for a friend now euphoric with relief. Whatever happened, said King, the manifest attention to his speech meant that at least he was making plain to the world his brief for peace in Vietnam.

*   *   *

KING FIRST blamed distorted news coverage for a rude shock, which one historian called "almost universal condemnation" beyond the walls of Riverside. When he beseeched advisers to defend his real position, Harry Wachtel recruited Rabbi Heschel—and reported back his gratifying pledge that "any attack on you is an attack on him"—to answer Jewish war veterans who branded King's Vietnam dissent a slander on their resistance to the Nazi Holocaust. When Reinhold Niebuhr, the aged and impaired theologian, managed to write an introduction for CALCAV's pamphlet of the collected Riverside addresses, King fervently hoped over wiretapped phone lines that "it would help to clarify things" if newspapers would publish excerpts, or even his own statements of correction, but Stanley Levison considered the speech itself an obstacle to public understanding. "I do not think it was a good expression of you," he bluntly advised, "but apparently you think it was." With his trademark directness, Levison called it unwise to focus on Vietnamese peasants rather than average American voters. "The speech was not so balanced," he told King. It was too "advanced" to rally his constituency, and covered so many angles that reporters sidestepped his message by caricature and label. "What on earth can Dr. King be talking about?" wrote a Washington columnist on April 5, wondering how any civil rights leader could overlook the benefits of integrated combat. "If there hadn't been a war, it would have served the Negro cause well to start one."

White House aides reacted strongly to King. Trusted counsel Harry McPherson warned President Johnson an hour before the Riverside event: "Martin Luther King has become the crown prince of the Vietniks." John Roche of Brandeis, who had succeeded Eric Goldman as Johnson's academic liaison, far outstripped McPherson's rare agitation the next day with a shrill judgment that King "has thrown in with the commies." In an "EYES ONLY" report to the President, Roche claimed inside knowledge that King, "who is inordinately ambitious and quite stupid (a bad combination) . . . is painting himself into a corner with a bunch of losers." White House aide Clifford Alexander more diplomatically called King to argue in detail that the administration was maintaining budgetary commitments to equal rights despite soaring Vietnam costs. Alexander and others mobilized civil rights leaders to isolate King's threat to their White House alliance. Former ambassador Carl Rowan angrily told King that millions of their fellow black people would suffer for his insults against the greatest civil rights President in American history. He ascribed sinister motives to King in a syndicated column later expanded for *Reader's Digest,* and King's folly became a front-page theme within a week of Riverside. "N.A.A.C.P. Decries Stand of Dr. King on Vietnam / Calls It a 'Serious Tactical Mistake' to Merge Rights and Peace Drives," announced the April 11 *New York Times,* which followed two days later with a headline about United Nations undersecretary Ralph Bunche, the only other black American Nobel Peace laureate: "Bunche Disputes Dr. King on Peace." When President Johnson pressed to find out what King actually said at Riverside, he had to wait for a text supplied by J. Edgar Hoover.

King launched crisis consultations on his way to California. Stanley Levison set aside his reservations about the Riverside address to dictate a vigorous defense statement for an overflow press conference at the Biltmore Hotel in Los Angeles, calling it a myth that King advocated a merger of organizations or goals, challenging critics to take a "forthright stand" on the war. Pressed for an admission that his peace talk did harm to Negroes, King lapsed into testiness that went unreported: "The war in Vietnam is a much graver injustice to Negroes than anything I could say against that war." After a speech at Occidental College, he kept telling advisers that the phalanx of rejection left him "temporarily at a loss." When he called Bunche, King reported, the diplomat had dissembled so miserably that "I felt sorry for him," Bunche claiming to have misunderstood Riverside as a mandate to "fuse" civil rights with peace groups, promising to make clear now how much he agreed with King on the war itself. "He wasn't telling the truth and he was trembling and all," said King. "So I just got off him." He said even the White House aides half-apologized for their political offensive, complaining of war hawks on the other side. The only consolation King wrung from his plight was a dawning reminder of similar distress "in every movement we have started," and a night's reflection clarified the pattern. "This was very true in Birmingham," he told Levison. From President Kennedy on down, even nonsegregationists had opposed the disruption and protest, and no one had conceded any chance of a positive outcome. "The press was against me," said King. "The middle-class Negro community was against me, and finally they came around." The antiwar movement needed to fashion a breakthrough, like the children's marches or the confrontations on Pettus Bridge.

Levison cautioned against dangerous hopes. "It will be harder than Birmingham," he told King, which was disheartening indeed. Levison already conceded that the burden went deeper than specific words of the Riverside address or his own vanity as a speechwriter. American public discourse broadly denied King the standing to be heard on Vietnam at all. It invested mountains of calculation into military prospects but recoiled from any thought of withdrawal, especially on the recommendation of a civil rights preacher, and future generations would remain locked in what Andrew Young called debilitating paralysis between "those who are ashamed that we lost the war and those who are ashamed that we fought it." King offered a precarious narrow course that demonized neither side, restrained by a nonviolent imperative to find slivers of humanity in the obscene polar conflict. While upholding for his own country, personified by Lyndon Johnson, a supreme but imperfect commitment to democratic norms, he granted the Vietnamese Communists a supreme but imperfect resolve to be free of external domination. On balance among Vietnamese, war by foreigners entrapped the complicit United States in a colonial past that forfeited liberating status. To curtail unspeakable cruelty and waste, Americans must refine their cherished idea of freedom by accepting that they could support but not impose it in Vietnam. To honor sacrifice with understanding, Americans must grant the Vietnamese people the elementary respect of citizens in disagreement. The lesson was at once wrenching and obvious, in the way modern people might be chastened by the centuries it took to establish that the Inquisition's bloody enforcement profaned rather than championed Christian belief.

King flew north to San Francisco, still stung. He complained most of featured editorials in two nationally respected newspapers, the *Washington Post* and the *New York Times,* respectively a supporter and a critic of the war. While neither paper engaged the substance of his Riverside argument, both archly told him to leave Vietnam alone for his own sake. "Many who have listened to him with respect will never again accord him the same confidence," declared the *Post*. "He has diminished his usefulness to his cause, to his country, and to his people." Editors at the *Times* pronounced race relations difficult enough without his "wasteful and self-defeating" diversions into foreign affairs. In "Dr. King's Error," they summarized the Riverside speech as "a fusing of two public problems that are distinct and separate," and predicted that his initiative "could very well be disastrous for both causes."

The call for segregated silence on Vietnam dashed any expectation that King's freedom movement had validated the citizenship credentials of blacks by historic mediation between the powerful and dispossessed. It relegated him again to the back of the bus, conspicuous yet invisible. King felt cut off even from disagreement, in a void worse than his accustomed fare of veneration or disfiguring hostility, and he broke down more than once into tears.

* * *

A JOURNEY of parallel emotion swallowed up Robert Kennedy. At the Jackson airport, a waiting bodyguard of a dozen U.S. marshals escorted him on April 9 through Klan flags, epithets, and hostile picket signs: "Send Bobby to Hanoi," "Race Mixers Go Home." Nearly a thousand people crowded into the ballroom of the Hotel Heidelburg for an unprecedented drama the next day, when Mississippi's most widely honored politician—whose youthful courage in the Senate had helped puncture the paranoid hysteria from Joseph McCarthy, and whose long service would gain recognition in the namesake aircraft carrier USS

John C. Stennis—appeared before a subcommittee of peers to duel unlettered witnesses from the civil rights movement, including Amzie Moore and Fannie Lou Hamer. Stennis renewed his campaign against a "national scandal" of new poverty programs, chiefly Head Start for preschool children, testifying that grant recipients were "throwing money away" on lavish expenses and indirect support for racial agitation. Unita Blackwell of Issaquena County chided Stennis for glossing over the poverty itself. "We have children who have never had a glass of milk," she said. NAACP counsel Marian Wright rebutted Stennis on charges of fraud. "He is wrong," she testified, to gasps in the ballroom, citing audits that contradicted the investigators Stennis had sent to scrutinize and shut down the fledgling county efforts run by the poor. Wright challenged the subcommittee to examine people instead of numbers. "Starvation is a major, major problem now," she testified.

A few subcommittee members ventured the next day by chartered airplane into the Mississippi Delta, where more than three-quarters of black adults had not finished elementary school. In Greenville, they visited new adult literacy classes sponsored by the federal anti-poverty agency, the Office of Economic Opportunity, under the aegis of the Roman Catholic diocese. They accompanied some parents home to the Delta Ministry's Freedom City, an encampment maintained more than a year now for refugees who had tried to occupy the old Greenville Air Base. Ida Mae Lawrence told senators she had been stripped of her midwife's license for registering to vote. Mothers said they could not afford the $2 per month charge to obtain Food Stamps. "What did you have for breakfast?" Robert Kennedy asked a boy. "Molasses." "For supper?" "Molasses." "For lunch?" "Don't have no lunch." For Marian Wright, who had assumed the senators were jockeying for headlines on the hunger issue, most of the skeptical distance natural to a SNCC founder and Yale lawyer collapsed as Kennedy pushed into places she would never go herself. He sat on primitive cots and dirt floors that smelled of urine, holding nearly naked children with distended bellies and open sores. Badly shaken, he would call the day an epiphany that turned stale all prior achievements of a lifetime, but he recovered enough steely reserve to tell reporters only that he was not sure the poverty programs "have been implemented in the best way." Republican Senator George Murphy of California said Americans who really saw Mississippi would declare a national emergency. All nine members of the subcommittee signed a letter to President Johnson reporting personal and scientific evidence of famine, and Kennedy was moved to appeal separately across the gap of their contentious personal history. "I cannot agree with you more that something must be done," he wrote Martin Luther King. "If you have any suggestions, I would appreciate hearing from you."

* * *

KING REMAINED in California for a final bombardment of cross-country advice. Rabbi Heschel, still worried that Bevel would degrade the cause with his marching delegation of Sioux Indians billed to represent the "first victims" of genocide by the United States, sent word that it was not too late for King to pull out of the antiwar Mobilization in New York. King qualified the underlying dispute. "I don't want to be up on that stage debating Bevel," he told Harry Wachtel, fretting that he "would have to say too much" to distinguish between Bevel's intemperate tone and his racial interpretation of Vietnam. King said he frankly agreed that future wars were likely to target nonwhite people in formerly colonized areas of the world, but he thought Stokely Carmichael's high media profile made him a much bigger tactical liability than Bevel. Andrew Young concurred. NBC News had just broadcast four minutes of the SNCC chairman exhorting black people to resist the "racist war" in Vietnam by any means necessary, he observed on a conference call, "and I know that scared the hell out of white folks." Harry Belafonte volunteered to host a truce meeting with Carmichael and other fractious civil rights leaders. King predicted that protest numbers would determine the impact more than message—ten thousand or less would be ruinous, a hundred thousand or more would force attention. If there were few black people among them, he expected critics to say he was losing his constituency. If many, it would amplify charges that he was merging incompatible movements. These political landmines helped Stanley Levison persuade King to adjust his Riverside call for unilateral withdrawal. Levison argued that a straightforward campaign to leave Vietnam, no matter how carefully explored or mournfully presented, would make King an "easy mark" for the combined furies of war, defeat, and surrender. His revision sheltered the central message instead among public figures advocating a negotiated settlement.

King flew overnight from a speech at Stanford University to join the April 15 Mobilization in New York's Central Park. As crowds gathered through the morning, a rump group of about seventy Cornell students burned their Selective Service cards in the first large ceremony of its kind, attesting in signed pledges to resist conscription even into prison if their collective number reached five hundred, and onlookers added a hundred more cards to the tiny pyre in a Maxwell House coffee can. FBI surveillance units hovered to record evidence of the federal crime, while police commanders relayed to King intelligence reports of a sniper plot to kill him. SNCC's Ivanhoe Donaldson, repeating the haphazard precautions from Selma two years earlier, helped arrange peace marshals loosely ahead of front ranks that stepped off shortly after noon with Dave Dellinger, Belafonte, Bevel, King, Benjamin Spock, Stokely Carmichael, and student mobilization leader Linda Dannenberg among notables linked arm in arm. A street-wide swath of marchers spilled behind them steadily for four hours, turning south on Madison Avenue and east again on 47th Street into United Nations Plaza. Scattered hecklers threw red paint; a few workers pelted marchers with nails from a construction site on Lexington Avenue. The security threat made it easier for King to stay off the platform except for his own speech, which repeated much of Riverside with a tamer refrain: "Stop the bombing! Stop the bombing!" He remarked privately that the magnitude of the rally exceeded the March on Washington, then navigated a tempestuous summit at Belafonte's apartment late into the night. In the quiet afterward, the singer's assistant expressed chagrin that Carmichael "talked down" to King with measured approval for shifts toward his own "radical" peace position. Levison replied over a wire-tapped line that King had calmed him on the same subject with a reminder to look beneath personality fireworks, observing that Belafonte was drawn to the intensity and flair of SNCC protest but would stick with King on the integrity of nonviolence.

Opening words fixed the tone for the next morning's live telecast of *Face the Nation:* "Dr. King, yesterday you led a demonstration here which visibly featured the carrying of Viet Cong flags, a mass burning of draft cards, and one American flag was burned. . . . How far should this go?" King fended off the half-hour barrage. No, he did not consider Secretary McNamara a racist. Yes, he did think racial factors excluded Adam Clayton Powell from Congress. No, he "would never call the President a fool," and he had never promised to shun Stokely Carmichael or anyone else. Press disputes clouded the number and character of the April 15 demonstrators. The *New York Times* counted 100,000, which was 25,000 fewer than the police estimate and a fraction of King's insistence on "fully 300,000 and perhaps 400,000 people." Andrew Young thought there were more than a million. The *Daily News* expressed relief: "CITY SURVIVES PEACE MARCH." *Time* magazine perceived a motley host: "anarchists under black flags; Vassar girls proving that they are, too, socially conscious; boys wearing beads and old Army jackets; girls in ponchos and serapes, some with babes on their shoulders . . . many of them carrying posters, all of them out for a spring housecleaning of their passions." Social critic Marya Mannes of the *Times* considered the protesters strong on courage but short on dignity. One study found that nearly half the 531 people aboard a ten-car train delegation from Cleveland were attending their first demonstration. A high school teacher from Indiana was fired for "bad judgment" when he wrote the *Bloomington Tribune* about why Korean War service compelled him to attend the rally in New York.

President Johnson chose Mobilization Day to announce that FBI director Hoover was sending him regular reports on the antiwar movement. It was a subtle but powerful signal. Johnson stopped short of bellicose language or the full war mobilization urged by hawkish advisers, because he remained worried that uncontrollable national fury could obliterate Vietnam without achieving the political goal of stable free government. Still, his timing alone generated headlines of suspicion—"F.B.I. Is Watching 'Antiwar' Effort President Says"—that offered more than enough encouragement for Hoover to step up propaganda. The Director had just approved leaks to friendly news sources that "would cause extreme embarrassment to King," and stories reached even the prestige newspapers. In "The Struggle to Sway King," the *Washington Post* unearthed internal deliberations from 1965 to Riverside in considerable detail ("Ranged against Bevel and Young on that point were most of Dr. King's older advisers"), and reported the conclusion of "high Administration officials" that King had "leaped headlong into peace campaigns partly in search of money and headlines" and also because "he is just terribly naive." On April 19, Hoover sent DeLoach to the White House with a top secret summary that collapsed the FBI's own wiretap evidence into stark falsehood about a maleable King pushed into war protest by his inner circle, telling President Johnson that he "is an instrument in the hands of subversive forces seeking to undermine our Nation." War hardened the FBI stereotype of King as a minstrel stooge for evil masters. In his 1995 memoir, written two decades after pained revelations had discredited the FBI's vendetta,

DeLoach managed only a barbed concession that King "operated with far less discipline and far less cunning than seasoned communists," and still blandly alleged that conspirators like Levison "aimed him and pulled his trigger with apparent ease."

* * *

KING TESTED new protest vehicles to escape the polarized rancor. On April 23, he appeared with a youth coalition at Christ Church of Cambridge, Massachusetts, to announce Vietnam Summer, modeled consciously on the Mississippi Freedom Summer of 1964, in which students and other volunteers would knock on doors for peace. "I think the war in Vietnam has strengthened the forces of reaction in our country," King lamented, "and has excited violence and bigotry." On April 24, he joined veteran political activists in New York for the founding of Negotiation Now. Civil rights lawyer Joe Rauh, who had criticized King's Riverside speech for fear that its frontal attack would only elect Richard Nixon in 1968, outlined plans to gather a million signatures on peace petitions, but reporters besieged King about news leaks out of Cambridge that he planned to run for President himself. King denied the reports while fuming privately that overbearing peace intellectuals simply publicized as fact what they wanted him to do. ("I begin to see why Spock has difficulty with these people," Levison told King.)

The next day in Washington, war critics took the Senate floor with arguments for peace negotiations on a fine line between escalation and withdrawal. "No senator is suggesting that we pull out of Vietnam," stated the forthright dove George McGovern of South Dakota. "Not a single senator has suggested that." Two days later, in the first address to Congress by a wartime field commander, General William Westmoreland denounced passivity in Vietnam as a formula for retreat. His report stirred ovations with praise for the soldiers. "They believe in what they are doing," said Westmoreland. "They are determined to provide the shield of security . . . for the future and freedom of all Southeast Asia." That same week, George Wallace declared that he would run for President in 1968 as the candidate of victory in Vietnam and backlash at home—not white backlash, he insisted, but "backlash against big government in this country."

In Cleveland, where King rushed on April 25 to lay ground for a voter registration campaign, Rev. O. M. Hoover regaled a preachers' dinner with stories of the group journey to Oslo for the Nobel Prize, and colleagues leavened apprehension of riot or failure with rounds of fraternal jokes. Reporter David Halberstam preserved a punch line about an old minister wrestling with temptation to seek a new forty-year-old wife: "Lord, would two twenties be all right?" King left for a speech at Berkeley, after which a graduate student blocked his way with a grandiose but piercing request not to dismiss so easily a run for president. "You're the most important man we've got," the student pleaded on behalf of draft resisters. "So please weigh our jail sentences in the balance when you make your decision." The appeal flustered King, who composed himself to compliment "a moving and persuasive statement" before flying on to Minnesota and Wisconsin for various engagements. In Chicago, he announced agreement with Jewel food stores to open 512 jobs for black applicants. To mark the promotion of Jesse Jackson into Bevel's vacant post as Chicago director of SCLC, King agreed to a three-hour stopover in Greenville, South Carolina, for a program at the city auditorium after a thorough bomb search, followed by hurried professional photographs at Jackson's family home. Back in Louisville for renewed brinkmanship that spared Proud Clarion to win the Kentucky Derby, he read out loud from the proofs of *Where Do We Go from Here* and took solace in an unguarded remark to Georgia Davis, "I really am a writer." Both King and his brother A.D. would be hit by rocks during sporadic demonstrations that overlapped the drama about the native celebrity who, accompanied by King's Chicago lawyer, Chauncey Eskridge, quietly fulfilled his public vow to refuse Army induction in Houston on April 28. The boxing world stripped Muhammad Ali of his title and license within an hour, well before indictment or trial, as the cover story in *Sports Illustrated* went from "Champ in the Jug?" to "Taps for the Champ."

In Atlanta King ran into his neighbor Vincent Harding, the Spelman professor who had drafted most of the Riverside speech, and teased him for causing a month of ceaseless trouble. He complained of having to fight suggestions at every stop that his Vietnam stance merely echoed the vanguard buzz of Stokely Carmichael. Harding sensed Carmichael was swept up by a peculiarly American phenomenon in the mold of Malcolm X, built on the sensational illusion that violence alone measures power and that menacing language accordingly registers heroic strength rather than noise. Having devoted himself to Mennonite peace theology since his own military service in Korea, Harding still believed as a mentor that Carmichael and peers had been not only stronger through SNCC's formative era but also more "radical" in the true sense of going to root causes and solutions for injustice. King kept trying to reach SNCC veterans on precisely this point, stressing the bonds of common experience in the South. He startled Carmichael with a personal call near midnight on April 29, fairly begging him to attend church for once at Ebenezer the next morning.

With Carmichael seated in a front pew, King apologized for the rare use of a manuscript. His sermon embellished recent Vietnam speeches with confessions on the cumulative burden of nonviolence. He acknowledged resentment that history's victims remained so accountable for the overall state of race relations, still obliged to catalyze progress by further suffering and improvisation, and he bridled like Malcolm X that America admired nonviolence mostly when practiced by blacks for the comfort of whites. "They applauded us on the freedom rides when we accepted blows without retaliation," King declared with an edge of sarcasm. "They praised us in Albany and Birmingham and Selma, Alabama. Oh, the press was so noble in its applause and so noble in its praise that I was saying be nonviolent toward Bull Connor." His trademark passion, while quivering to defend a steady course, let slip rage at being patronized and misunderstood: "There is something strangely inconsistent about a nation and a press that will praise you when you say be nonviolent toward Jim Clark, but will curse you and damn you when you say be nonviolent toward little brown Vietnamese children!" The congregation broke into applause. "There is something wrong with that!"

CHAPTER 35

Splinters

May–June 1967

CLEVELAND Sellers intercepted King in Atlanta for emergency counseling. He was twenty-two, polite and sturdy by nature. His parents, a schoolteacher and a rural entrepreneur, had implored him in 1962 not to risk their hard-earned tuition to diversions at a college outside South Carolina—only to watch him disappear from Howard University into a maelstrom of protest and jail they preferred not to hear about. Now Sellers recalled late-night debates on the Meredith march to tell King he could no longer raise a spiritual objection to violence and was resolved instead to take a political stand against the draft. Such a defense would only weaken bleak prospects in court, King replied, but he advised Sellers to make sure he could look at himself and others with belief to last beyond a maximum five-year prison sentence. Satisfied, he offered prayer for strength, and Carmichael provided escort to the showdown on Monday, May 1, whispering, "Don't let them get to you." Like Ali, Sellers made national news—"Rights Leader Refuses to Be Inducted into Army"—by ignoring the ritual order to step forward. A *New York Times* account of the tense ceremony stressed fashion details: "He showed up at the induction center at 7 A.M. wearing a mustache, sunglasses, a green turtleneck sweater and a brown collarless jacket. He wore brown shoes but no socks, and his brown and white checkered trousers came to about six inches above his ankles." Carmichael told reporters that sixteen SNCC colleagues had been drafted so far by a Selective Service system just now accepting its first black officials—one of 161 board members in South Carolina, five of 509 in Georgia—to offset charges of biased conscription for a racist war.

Sellers attracted notice as program secretary for a national organization of greatly magnified public presence since its black power doctrine and sharp attacks on American purpose in Vietnam, but zestful alarm in the press masked organizational disintegration already far advanced. Only about seventy SNCC staff members remained. With the ranks thinned of extraordinary figures such as Bob Moses, Diane Nash, and John Lewis, those who still endured persecution and fatigue joked that every word in SNCC's storied name was now a misnomer. They were no longer students or nonviolent. They no longer coordinated sacrifice beyond the wisdom and courage of the nation's elders, nor operated by egalitarian grassroots committee. Instead, they competed for celebrity attention while reverting to youthful disputes as tawdry as snipes at their clothes.

One feud snapped over car keys, as Carmichael battled Bill Ware and separatist colleagues who had spearheaded votes to expel white staff members at December's Peg Leg Bates conference. When Ware's Atlanta project refused to surrender a Plymouth from the tiny SNCC fleet, Sellers tracked down and hot-wired the car for a trip to Mississippi, but Carmichael had a flat tire on the way, and, lacking a trunk key to reach the spare, had to flag down a passing motorist to borrow a jack so he could hitchhike with the damaged tire in search of repair. When Sellers filed a police report to recover a commandeered station wagon, Ware denounced him for stooping to "a racist henchman cop of the white master Allen of Atlanta to settle an internal dispute between the supposedly black people of SNCC." Ware's telegram to James Forman threatened retribution for "calculated conspiracy to destroy the black ideology": "We have tapes and other information that could fall into black people's hands across the country." Carmichael sent the Atlanta project a one-sentence reply: "You have been fired from the Student Nonviolent Coordinating Committee." Elsewhere, he suspended the North Carolina project, closed dysfunctional support groups in Chicago, Los Angeles, and San Francisco, and confided that staff members were dodging eviction in Washington, where "most of the equipment has been stolen from the office."

Other strains snapped when the program secretary caught his live-in girlfriend repeatedly in trysts with staff member Hubert G. Brown. Sellers cursed and beat her in a savage outburst—for which he would offer public contrition—shrieking that such betrayals tore apart SNCC's already frayed network of trust. Brown, who had met with President Johnson as a student leader during the Selma crisis, supervised Alabama registration projects since Carmichael left to become SNCC chairman. Late in March, he addressed the second anniversary meeting of the Lowndes County Christian Movement for Human Rights. Brown somberly discussed the two recent arsons at movement churches, but he brightened with sly speculation about a subsequent arson of white property. "Lightning hit over here at Good Hope Presbyterian," he cried, relishing hope above murmurs and laughter that the amazing coincidence "straightened things out in white folks' minds." SNCC worker Scott B. Smith took the floor to make a blunt speech. "I have learned how to hate," he said. "I know how to hate." An old man waved his cane to object that their mission was to make everybody "be better people, both white and colored." Black Panther leaders John Hulett and Sidney Logan already had rolled a trailer onto the ashes of the anti-poverty site to rebuild homemade furniture for job classes, but vigilante mystery stirred. Logan's baby bull was found shot in the head. Twenty cattle owned by Probate Judge Harrell Hammonds were poisoned, prompting hushed debate about whether it was Klan punishment for letting Panther candidates on the 1966 ballot or a black warning not to trust white moderates. When gifts of fresh beef arrived for the refugees still living in the tent city on Highway 80, Scott B. Smith hinted that African butchers had been recruited in the night from Tuskegee's veterinary school, and there were rumors of bull genitals hung from Klan mailboxes. "Burning churches and killing cows ain't going to do it," Panther candidate Robert Logan told a mass meeting. "Our movement is stronger than ever." Still, upstarts adopted a refrain of sarcastic swagger: "Yeah, lightning."

Stokely Carmichael issued a statement on the church burnings— "Black people are now serving notice that we will fight back"—and ended public remarks about arson with a vow: "We'll all worship in one church or we'll all worship outside." These cryptic references, like Carmichael's mixed reception on black campuses, failed to make news. Some students at Miles College in Birmingham called him a reverse supremacist and a "damned fool" for advocating an all-black faculty, while Carmichael scolded them for accepting a lame curriculum— "You are all a bunch of parrots"—and needled them for bourgeois self-absorption. ("Why are you here?" he asked females enrolled at Morgan

State. "So you can kick down a door in the middle of the night to look for a pair of shoes?") What registered beyond the halls was his daredevil cry against white America. At Tougaloo, reported the *Baltimore Afro-American,* "Carmichael's strong anti-Vietnam statements set off almost five minutes of chanting, 'We ain't going, hell no!' " At Miles, reported the *New York Times,* he exhorted students to repudiate American law. Quoting Frederick Douglass, that there could be no freedom while slaves obeyed their masters, he won thunderous acclaim for his updated maxim: "If you want to be free, you've got to say, 'To hell with the laws of the United States!' " The *Nashville Banner* vainly urged Vanderbilt to forestall a riot by barring Carmichael, and on the night after his departure, an unruly customer at Fisk's dinner club sparked three days of altercation that left ninety students arrested and fifty injured, three of them shot by the five hundred anti-riot police still massed on high alert. The Tennessee House of Representatives passed a resolution that Carmichael should be deported regardless of his U.S. citizenship. Shouts of vindicated alarm from all sides prompted a *New York Times* editorial, " 'Black Power' in Nashville," cautioning that "it is not easy to determine if these disturbances were touched off by Mr. Carmichael's fiery words or by the preceding effort to silence him." This aura enveloped SNCC's chairman through the Mobilization rally down into federal court later in April, accompanied by Hubert Brown, to appeal his far-fetched conviction for inciting Selma's black voters to riot before the November election.

* * *

DISTANT ADMIRERS of the Lowndes County movement launched a spectacular debut on May 2, one day after Cleveland Sellers refused Army service. They created an icon for the era, offered in tribute, but they could scarcely have imagined better images to conceal their inspiration from rural Alabama. Commotion riveted the California Assembly when a wall of reporters and photographers banged backward through the doors, facing the bearers of shotguns and rifles who had asked directions to the second-floor chamber in Sacramento. Legislators gasped in mid-debate. Many of them scattered as two dozen young black men pressed forward with guns pointed toward the ceiling, several in leather jackets and black berets, accompanied by six unarmed black women. One intruder loudly proclaimed citizens' protest of a gun control bill endorsed by "the racist Oakland police" as officers converged into standoff. Defenders risked grabbing some but not all the stone-faced men, and discovered their weapons to be fully loaded, before a deal permitted Bobby Seale to read aloud a founding manifesto that denounced "the racist power structure of America" for historical repression of nonwhite people from native Indians to the Vietnamese: "The Black Panther Party for Self-Defense believes that the time has come for Black people to arm themselves against this terror before it is too late." Seale's group then withdrew under an exit truce across the capitol lawn, past news cameras and gaping tourists, including an eighth-grade social studies class on a field trip with chaperones. A huge cruiser posse arrested twenty-six of the retreating demonstrators near a gas station four blocks away.

Such was the "colossal event" conceived by manifesto author Huey P. Newton, a twenty-five-year-old emigrant from Louisiana named for its late flamboyant governor Huey P. "Kingfish" Long. To defend followers in their showcase criminal trial, Newton invested his first Black Panther speaking fee in a pound of marijuana, which he cut into "nickel bags" for sale from the back of his roving Volkswagen. Issuing strict orders for his small, militarized command to resist targeted stops by Oakland police—"We don't give up our guns, we don't give up our dope"—he set a pattern for clashes until his own murder for drug debts outside a crack cocaine house in 1989. By contrast, Newton's instant fame spread romantic theories about revolutionary violence. One *New York Times* profile—"A Gun Is Power, Black Panther Says"—explained his rationale for storming the Assembly. A longer article, which introduced the poster photograph of Newton staring with scepter and carbine from a flared cane-back throne, explored his debt to the writings of Du Bois, Marcus Garvey, Malcolm X, and Mao Zedong. A front-page survey on May 7—"The New Left Turns to Mood of Violence in Place of Protest"—observed that the Argentine guerrilla Che Guevara gave burgeoning white activists across the country their own ethnic model in the mold of Malcolm X and Huey Newton. "When we have organized the white radicals, we can link up with the Negro radicals," said Students for a Democratic Society leader Greg Calvert, who announced an active campaign to foment urban sedition. "We aren't a bunch of liberal do-gooders," claimed William Pepper of the more moderate Vietnam Summer coalition. "We are revolutionary." The *Times* reporter noted parenthetically that New Leftists rejected liberal as "a dirty word."

The birth of Oakland's Black Panthers resonated also in mainstream politics. It guaranteed passage of the bill Bobby Seale denounced before

the Assembly, as Governor Reagan soon would sign new firearm restrictions with an extra provision banning weapons in public places, but
Pyrrhic victory for gun control already had backfired on a grander scale.
Less than a week after the sensational scare in California, officers of the
National Rifle Association made front-page headlines—"Rifle Club
Sees Guns As Riot Curb"—with a counterpoint study showing Negro
involvement in nine of eleven selected mob actions, arguing without
historical precedent that armed private citizens "could prove essential"
to maintain public order. The NRA harvested fear across the color line
while crusading for unfettered weaponry as vociferously as the Black
Panthers, and Governor Reagan gained political stature from the
specter of Huey Newton's guns. Appearing on the traumatized capitol
grounds just as Bobby Seale drove away, he reassured voters by keeping
a picnic date with the social studies class. Poise in crisis elevated a battered new governor who was roiling his political base with the largest
state tax increase in history and the first major law to permit "therapeutic" abortion. ("I had been led to believe there was a honeymoon period,"
Reagan quipped, "but evidently I lost the license on the way to the
church.") Now he renewed attacks on "central casting anarchists" with
the authority of a candidate who had vowed to clamp down on unruli-
ness from Watts to Berkeley. On May 15, debating Robert Kennedy in a
town forum televised from London, Reagan said protest undermined
domestic hope and prolonged war abroad. While Kennedy defended
difficult ground—disputing students who called U.S. intervention immoral, groping for peace talks and elections ("Can you deliver the
North Vietnamese?"), confronting urgent complexity from "a heritage
of 150 years we've been unjust to our minority groups"—Reagan said
the problem "lies in the hearts of men," and pictured welcome change
since his early years in radio when "the rulebook called baseball 'a game
for Caucasian gentlemen.' " He imagined a bright future "if the Berlin
Wall should disappear." Surprised reviewers thought the disparaged
rookie governor held his own with his simple story lines.

* * *

ON MAY 12, at Paschal's Motor Hotel in Atlanta, some colleagues rolled
their eyes when Stokely Carmichael told a crowded press conference he
was "stepping down" from tedious administrative duty to resume his
preferred post as a grassroots field organizer. In truth he enjoyed little
support for reelection to head SNCC, even from those who valued his
charisma and agreed with his black power stand. Many thought he had

subverted their brotherhood collective with showmanship, popularizing the derisive term "honky" for white people and mocking the politic piety that good Negroes looked to them only for friendship: "The white woman's not queen of the world—she can be made like anything else." SNCC women in particular thought Carmichael succumbed to shooting-star celebrity that mistook headlines and saucy clichés for a political program. Executive Secretary Ruby Doris Smith had upbraided him most directly, and was dearly missed at the gloomy Atlanta elections because she was dying swiftly at twenty-five of virulent lymphosarcoma. The new chairman, who emerged from the compromise between urban separatists and those who still pushed for electoral black power in the tattered rural projects, was introduced to the press as H. Rap Brown, having dampened the given name Hubert in favor of a movement nickname earned with rare talent to "rap" poetic in assorted dialects. (His spontaneous routines had supplied free entertainment for the Alabama wedding reception of Gloria Larry and Stuart House.) A first intelligence report on the new SNCC officers gleaned no prior FBI information about Brown. Reporters asked if the new chairman would generate publicity like Carmichael. "Hopefully not," he replied.

Rap Brown presided over a review of personnel that consumed two more days. The central committee sifted the status of dissenters, casualties, and slackers ("It was difficult to get her out of bed"), along with faint hopes to harness Carmichael's world travel now that he dwarfed SNCC itself in the media. Late on May 14, when tension finally wore down avoidance, Bob Zellner was admitted to address the troublesome petition for him and his wife, Dorothy, to work in the white community under SNCC sponsorship. The question was whether a project of arm's-length cooperation would accommodate the white exclusion policy set at the Peg Leg Bates conference. "I think I have gotten over the emotional stage," Zellner nervously told a dozen peers seated before him. "I am not completely tied up emotionally, but I do want some things to be settled."

Disputes surfaced about whether the central committee possessed authority to revise what had been decided by the hazy votes in New York. Some questioned Zellner about the evolution of SNCC's purpose, and most who favored the project itself wobbled on his incorporated request to affirm SNCC membership. When Bill Hall of Tuskegee tried to separate the issues, wondering if white workers might be retained on the staff but excluded from policy meetings, Zellner asked to speak before being excused for the vote. "We don't have to go into the history of my relationship," he said, boiling down a statement his wife had submitted for them, "but I feel and have always felt that SNCC was as much a part of me as anybody else, and that I was SNCC and will always be SNCC. . . . I will not accept any sort of restrictions or special categories because of race. We do not expect other people to do that in this country, and I will not accept it for myself."

With Zellner waiting again outside, Rap Brown opened debate "in the light of our hope to become a revolutionary force and also in light of the fact that this may occur again and again." Tortured clashes echoed segregationist dynamics. While defending the exclusion policy as necessary, one speaker criticized implementation thus far as "very sloppy and kind of barbaric." Bill Hall, drawing analogies to the anti-colonial war in Algeria, said the question was not Zellner's race but whether he could subordinate his identity to be used "as a technician" in the event of armed black struggle. Fay Bellamy considered it "very unfair of Bob Zellner" to bring sentiment and personal history into a political question, saying he should recognize the public disadvantage of having even one white person on a committee devoted to black power. "Now it shouldn't make any difference," she conceded, "but it does." Ralph Featherstone, newly elected to replace Cleveland Sellers, agreed with Hall but cautioned that Zellner had more than nostalgia on his side. "In principle, Bob is right," he said. "When we say that whites should not make policy about black communities, that is a two-way street." Stanley Wise, newly elected to replace Ruby Doris Smith, quoted Frederick Douglass on gaining the upper hand—"it is absolutely crucial that we strike the first blow"—proposing to look past unfortunate regrets to build the capacity for all-black decisions, "but, as Fay said, understanding that there is no racism involved."

James Forman, visibly agitated, said, "I think we are confusing some things. Bob is my best friend." When a voice above the hubbub taunted, "You said the same thing about Fay the other day," Forman's explosion silenced the room: "That is right, goddammit! I have *two* best friends!" He thundered that Zellner had every right to be emotional, evoking his long service since police in the primitive McComb of 1961 had beaten Zellner into jail with Bob Moses and SNCC chairman Charles McDew, but Forman calmed to recommend that the membership question be deferred until the next meeting of the full staff. Bill Ware moved instead to offer everything except a staff vote, but others denounced another "shucking and jiving proposal" they felt would expose SNCC to Zellner's rejection of second-class citizenship. Speakers wrestled with contradictions until they collapsed behind a countermotion to sever membership entirely. Before Zellner was resummoned, Forman browbeat his colleagues to clarify that the vote applied to all white people and not merely the one "who had the guts to come before this body." Rap Brown prefaced a terse verdict by quoting to Zellner his own promise that SNCC bonds could not be broken, then added: "The only thing that is being cut is your privilege as a staff member."

"I think it is a mistake, but that is among us," Zellner replied. Promising silence to the press, he asked only for the recorded transcript of his words to assure his wife that he had stood firm through what she would call the worst experience of her life. SNCC's leaders veered from searing fatigue with their original principles toward uncertain new revolution, and soon would lose the remaining black members, too.

* * *

A RAW egg splattered Dr. Benjamin Spock outside the White House on May 17. Police hauled away one counterdemonstrator who called him a traitor, and Spock kept vigil for three days among two hundred Mobilization supporters. James Bevel and Coretta King stood with him jammed against locked gates, trying to deliver an unanswered appeal for President Johnson to meet with the leadership of the April 15 protests. Coretta represented her husband, who was promoting the voter registration drive in Cleveland. Bevel had talked his way into Washington's St. Mark's Episcopal Church, Secret Service officials privately advised, where undercover agents observed that a rector favored for worship services by President Johnson "actively participated" in strategy sessions as "Bevel made numerous inflammatory remarks." The Mobilization leaders scheduled a follow-up national protest for October 21, centered in Washington. On May 19, a polling analysis assured the President that 70 percent of Americans and nearly half of Negroes disagreed with King on Vietnam. The study issued a caveat, however, based on "sketchy data" about his brief antiwar push since April: "Dr. King may well have within his power a capability of influencing between a third to one half of all Negro voters behind a candidate he might endorse for President in 1968."

President Johnson had summoned Senator Russell the previous week about a pending order to bomb the power station near Ho Chi Minh's headquarters, which McNamara advocated and Rusk opposed. Russell counseled that all such bomb targets were incidental now, as he believed only a full invasion of North Vietnam would be decisive. Harry McPherson, the sole aide present at the somber consultation, volunteered to inspect the southern war zone as a fresh if amateur set of eyes for his vexed President. He was making notes to himself about the immense scale of the military effort from a Huey helicopter on the way to Da Nang—"an air strike in progress . . . a division camp here, a battalion forward area there . . . great areas have been scraped off the hilltops . . . we have just about paved the road-side for a hundred miles"—when U.S. jets first raided within the city limits of Hanoi to bomb the power plant. North Vietnam scrambled thirty fighters to meet them on May 19, Ho Chi Minh's seventy-seventh birthday, and Luu Huy Chao would recall antiaircraft ground fire so thick that it downed several fellow MiG pilots along with five Americans.

That same day in Washington, Secretary McNamara showed the President his draft response to Westmoreland's request for 200,000 more soldiers. Its central conclusion marked a wrenching turn for McNamara and deeper crisis for Johnson: "The war in Vietnam is acquiring a momentum of its own that must be stopped." Although McNamara amassed details behind one consoling achievement—"there is consensus that we are no longer in danger of losing this war militarily"—he could see no constructive end. The CIA supported him with maddening new conclusions that nearly total destruction (85 percent) of power plants and petroleum storage had failed to diminish the opposing flow of manpower—and worse, that both major alternatives, more bombs *and* fewer bombs, would only harden North Vietnam's popular will to persevere. "Twenty-seven months of U.S. bombing of North Vietnam have had remarkably little effect on Hanoi's strategy," McNamara wrote. As for American troops in South Vietnam, he found that massive exertion and heroism generated greater than proportional opposition, while nominal allies from the South Vietnamese army grew "tired, passive, and accommodation-prone." McNamara stressed that even Westmoreland's plan for 670,000 soldiers, which would require national mobilization of the Reserves, predicted no North Vietnamese willingness to negotiate until well after the 1968 U.S. elections. He recommended against the additional troops because he foresaw no gain to offset a bloodier stalemate, and warned of pitfalls instead. "There may be a limit beyond which many Americans and much of the world will not permit the United States to go," McNamara wrote. "The picture of the world's greatest superpower killing or seriously injuring 1,000 non-combatants a week, while trying to pound a tiny backward nation into submission on an issue whose merits are hotly disputed, is not a pretty one."

These haunted words might have made McNamara welcome in the Mobilization vigil outside the White House fence, which was dispersing from its final day. For President Johnson, who had backed into Vietnam with Cold War inertia bottomed on his naked political fear of being called a coward, apprehensions long shared with his advisers ran into a number more real than any of McNamara's famous calculations. "I've lost ten thousand boys out there," Johnson kept saying. His war would become "increasingly hostage to the dead," author Thomas Powers later observed.

* * *

A SUPERSEDING crisis struck before Johnson could devise a course between McNamara and Westmoreland. On Monday, May 22, President Gamal Abdel Nasser of Egypt closed the Strait of Tiran, which cut off Israel's shipping lifeline from the Red Sea into its sole southern port at Eilat. On Tuesday, Secretary-General U Thant complied with Nasser's legal notice evicting United Nations peacekeepers from the Sinai Peninsula, where the Egyptian army now marched. Arab forces instantly mobilized from Kuwait and Saudi Arabia to Libya, and Iraqi units convoyed to support Jordan and Syria. In a single day, wrote historian Arthur Hertzberg, "the mood of the American Jewish community underwent an abrupt, radical, and possibly permanent change." Outcries went up for U.S. intervention to save Israel. President Johnson, worried that Soviet reaction on the Arab side might draw the superpowers into a world war, appealed publicly for restraint on Wednesday while Israeli Foreign Minister Abba Eban pleaded to the United Nations. The forces encircling Israel were openly bent upon her annihilation, he said, with a twenty-five-to-one advantage in population plus a three-to-one superiority in war planes and tanks. On Thursday, urging Eban to hold tight for diplomacy, Defense Secretary McNamara offered his confidential military judgment that Israel could defeat the Arab nations on all fronts within a week, despite the numerical odds.

These war spasms caught Martin Luther King on his way to a peace conference in Switzerland. He was just leaving a retreat at the Frogmore Center in South Carolina, already swamped by fiscal and political demands. Some seventy staff members complained of abandonment by

SCLC's senior executives. Jesse Jackson's office telephones in Chicago were about to be cut off for unpaid bills. Workers still assigned to beleaguered Grenada, Mississippi, confessed a worn-down commitment to nonviolence even among themselves. "We control ourselves in public," said one, "and then come home and attack each other viciously or in petty ways." King listened, then tried to rally spirits grown weary as the movement stretched to encompass Northern projects along with Southern holdovers and broader initiatives to stop war. He preached again on the connection between civil rights and Vietnam, adding for these colleagues a candid confession that he once succumbed to official blandishments about an imminent peace. "I backed up a little when I came out in 1965," he said. "My name then wouldn't have been written in any book called *Profiles in Courage*. But now I have decided. I will not be intimidated." From stops in Chicago and New York, King flew to Geneva for the *Pacem in Terris* convocation sponsored by the Center for the Study of Democratic Institutions. Soviet delegates suddenly canceled along with Ambassador Goldberg and most American government representatives. King drew large crowds, but James Reston told *Times* readers that the threat of Middle East war reduced the novel concept of hybrid peace exploration to a "prayer meeting." Back in New York, FBI wiretappers picked up Stanley Levison's May 31 lament that Vietnam politics "is suffering badly because half the peace movement is Jewish, and the Jews have all become hawks."

Harry McPherson gamely continued westward from South Vietnam across India into Tel Aviv airport before dawn on Monday, June 5. An Israeli general in escort told him after breakfast to ignore air raid sirens and radio warnings of Egyptian bombardment massed from Sinai, which was McPherson's first hint that preemptive Israeli strikes had just destroyed nearly all Nasser's war planes on the ground. From the United Nations in New York, Middle East envoy Ralph Bunche woke the Secretary-General at home: "War has broken out!" The Moscow–Washington hotline jangled alive at 7:47 A.M.—in McNamara's office because the equipment was not yet rigged to the White House. By afternoon, incoming Jordanian artillery opened a second front to a crippling counterattack from the air, and Israeli soldiers swiftly captured all of Jerusalem for the first time in 1,900 years. At 2:30 P.M. on Wednesday, according to war historian Michael Oren, the chief rabbi of the Israeli Defense Forces climbed the Temple Mount inside the walled Old City and emotionally proposed to blow up both

Muslim structures built there in the long Jewish exile: Al Aksa Mosque and the Dome of the Rock. Generals Moshe Dayan and Yitzhak Rabin overruled him, but to secure military possession in the ongoing battle they ignored instructions to surrender holy sites to the control of civilian clergy from the three Abrahamic religions. World powers and the belligerents needed three more chaotic days to implement a cease-fire, during which time Israel drove Syria from the Golan Heights on a third front. McPherson returned home Sunday from immersion in two successive wars—one endless, one lightning—amazed by solidarity in Israel. "The spirit of the army, indeed of all the people, has to be experienced to be believed," he told President Johnson.

*   *   *

THE SIX DAY WAR spawned lasting shock in world politics. Egyptian citizens heard bulletins of glorious success toward liquidating "the Zionist entity" only hours before bloody remnants of their army retreated pell-mell across the Nile, leaving 15,000 dead and five thousand prisoner. Ho Chi Minh, who once gratified patriarch David Ben-Gurion with the offer of sanctuary in Hanoi for an Israeli government-in-waiting—back when the Vietnamese independence movement of 1946 was briefly more established than Jewish guerrillas trying to create Israel—proved no more accurate than Radio Cairo with his first-day proclamation that Israelis were "doomed to ignominious defeat" as "agents of the United States and British imperialists." The ideological force of Pan-Arab nationalism all but evaporated. For the Soviet Union, which had switched its support abruptly from Israel to the Arab nations in 1954, the disaster wasted massive military aid and deflated claims of invincible Communist sponsorship.

Miracle reprieve shifted Jewish identity. "The whole world fell in love with us," said Orthodox theologian David Hartman. "To be Israeli was really sexy." Jews prayed again at the Western Wall of Herod's Temple as biblical places reentered everyday life. Rabbi Heschel rushed to Jerusalem among pilgrims. "There is great astonishment in the souls," he wrote. "It is as if the prophets had risen from their graves." In New York, at a nationwide celebration only two days after the war, the traditional prayer of thanksgiving for another day of life dissolved into waves of nearly universal weeping that Arthur Hertzberg said swept up assimilated Jews previously "remote to the synagogue" and indifferent to Israel. Outdoors in Washington, manning one of the emergency tables that collected an astonishing $100 million, Office of Economic Opportunity official Hyman Bookbinder was struck by a modest woman who donated her savings of $1,700. Bookbinder, a secular Jew born to Polish Bundists during World War I, soon quit government to work for the American Jewish Committee and would join his first synagogue after the Yom Kippur War of 1973.

A warrior's exultation hardened the awakening of Jewish spirit. "We grew so fast into a visible central power that the seeds of arrogance as well came in," observed David Hartman. First news of Israel's deliverance prompted a vulgar outburst from Abe Fortas in his Supreme Court chambers: "I'm going to decorate my office with Arab foreskins." The implications of the war were so fantastic as to be hushed in numb realization that tiny Israel not only thrashed the surrounding Arab hosts single-handed, against restraining counsel from Washington, but also administered a sting to her aloof benefactor. For three hours on Day Four, Israeli war planes strafed and torpedoed the plainly marked U.S.S. *Liberty* spy ship in international waters off the coast of Egypt, killing thirty-four American sailors, wounding 170. Official statements of regret would leave the origin and anatomy of the attack shrouded in secrecy, as if both sides needed to muffle the repercussions. Writer Jonathan Kaufman later analyzed a new strain of "muscular Judaism" that sprouted beside cultured moralism built through many centuries of Diaspora, when scattered communities had relied on Jewish teaching to promote tolerance and social justice in host countries. Immediately after the Six Day War, the American gadfly I. F. Stone charged that the intoxicating rebirth of mighty Samson actually reduced Israel into the clench of her enemies. "Both Israelis and Arabs in other words feel that only force can assure justice," he wrote. "A certain moral imbecility marks all ethnocentric movements. The Others are always either less than human, and thus their interests may be ignored, or more than human, and therefore so dangerous that it is right to destroy them."

In America, the Six Day War crystallized two historic transformations of Jewish political culture—both stoked for a century in the cauldron of ideological ferment that had arrived with destitute immigrant families. Much of the evolving debate applied arcane Marxist vocabulary to competitive polemics over which factions invented, rescued, or betrayed the best comprehensive plan to uplift oppressed people everywhere. Countless theories adapted to the onslaught of the Depression and Holocaust into the Cold War, but few experts or ideologues had expected a significant mass movement to rise from the black South. While

Jewish activists participated heavily in the strange inner workings of church-based nonviolent politics, leading writers held back in guarded approval. A seminal essay of estrangement appeared just before Birmingham in 1963, when *Commentary* editor Norman Podhoretz wrote that although he had grown up paying lip service to civil rights, "I was still afraid of Negroes. And I still hated them with all my heart." Dismissing integration and democracy as false hopes for "the Negro problem in this country," Podhoretz saw no solution until "skin color does in *fact* disappear," and confessed a desperate fantasy: "it means—let the brutal word come out—miscegenation." In early 1967, the *New York Times Magazine* published debate from the premise of a broad divergence in nature. To a screed from James Baldwin, "Negroes Are Anti-Semitic Because They're Anti-White," Robert Gordis of the Jewish Theological Seminary replied, "Negroes Are Anti-Semitic Because They Want a Scapegoat." The Six Day War accelerated an ideology of progress projected through rather than against the established power of the United States, allied with Israel as the strong model democracy of the Middle East. Black power served as a foil of squandered potential. Sudden prosperity in arms made ideas more martial, as did fading concern with minorities and the poor, but the pioneer intellectuals still aspired to a visionary outlook. In *Neoconservatism: The Autobiography of an Idea,* Irving Kristol traced idealistic political philosophy from his Trotskyite youth to the commanding center of 1980s Washington, with no mention at all of the nonviolent civil rights era.

A parallel line of influential Jewish thought followed the extraordinary arc of Max Shactman, the Polish-born party leader who on a starry-eyed 1925 delegation to Moscow had hailed the Communist International as "a brilliant red light in the darkness of capitalistic gloom." From firsthand knowledge, Shactman broke first with Stalin, then with Leon Trotsky for underestimating Stalin's monstrous perversion of workers' opportunity, then also with Norman Thomas and A. J. Muste among many "second-rate" anti-Soviet rivals, and finally with the idea of an independent socialist presence in American politics. In 1965, as the spellbinding luminary of backroom New York dialectics, Shactman stunned the regulars in "our socialist loft on 14th Street" with an offhand comment that American stooges running South Vietnam "may be no worse than the thugs in Hanoi." Bayard Rustin, among many protégés then building a "Shactmanite base" within the American labor movement, chafed under demands from new union employers to support the Lyndon Johnson Vietnam policy. In 1967, *Dissent* magazine founder Irving Howe made notes on Rustin's misery under group pressure not only to compromise his lifelong pacifist stance but speak favorably of the American war cause. Rustin pleaded for leeway to salvage his ties within the civil rights movement, where very young leaders like Courtland Cox and Stokely Carmichael, who had idolized Rustin for years, blamed him for the betrayal that spurred their revolt against nonviolence. Unlike Rustin, socialist leader Michael Harrington split with Shactman over Vietnam, and he coined the word "neoconservative" for Shactman's coalition thrust. As the term gained currency in the intellectual beehive of Manhattan, it suggested strong military purpose with a utopian residue focused on Israel. The powerful neoconservative school in American politics would grow from a merger of labor-wing Shactmanites into the larger movement associated with Irving Kristol.

Instantly, by contrast, the outbreak of the Middle East war threw the Vietnam peace movement into a political crossfire. Martin Luther King, back from Geneva, smarted from criticism that he had abandoned nonviolence by lending his name with Reinhold Niebuhr and other religious leaders to a prewar *New York Times* ad that sounded alarm over the hostile Arab encirclement. As he hopscotched between Cleveland and Chicago, King complained that "the *Times* played it up as a total endorsement of Israel." On Day Two, Stanley Levison told King that people were too emotional to see that war "settles nothing" beyond survival. On Day Five, J. Edgar Hoover rushed to the White House a report suggesting that King's subversive advisers would risk Israel to undercut President Johnson in Vietnam. Meanwhile, Rabbi Heschel endured mounting criticism on the same point. Israeli emissaries warned that his Vietnam protest threatened vital American protection, and colleagues at the Jewish Theological Seminary further ostracized Heschel in their zeal for both wars. Movement leaders compressed decades of agonizing reappraisal into the short week of battle. Andrew Young told King he feared Israel would not compromise on its conquest of Jerusalem. Levison and Harry Wachtel said the great powers should impose a comprehensive peace—but would not do so. By June 11, one day after the cease-fire, King complained to advisers that he had interpreted his nonviolence to support Israel's right to exist, "and now Israel faces the danger of being smug and unyielding."

Doubts about consistency so plagued the antiwar clergy that several times they gathered secretly at the Union Theological Seminary office of John Bennett, chief organizer of the prewar ad in the *Times*. Could they oppose one war and praise the other in good faith, and exactly how should they draw the distinction? Rabbi Heschel, who was pouring forth a book of joyful meditation on Israel, fared badly with his first efforts to justify the Israeli war by character as well as circumstance, stating almost giddily that the Jewish soldiers were reluctant and hardly meant to hurt anyone. Harry Wachtel would recall that Heschel was "roughly handled" for such effusions by colleagues who normally deferred to him. Heschel and the priest Daniel Berrigan fell into temperamental strain. King mostly listened. Rabbi Balfour Brickner said the CALCAV group should pursue settlements for Vietnam *and* the Middle East, arguing that immediate peace advocacy was the surest way to keep legitimate self-defense from becoming a loophole for violence. Most participants thought the combination would make two difficult tasks impossible. Heschel, from his delicate experience as a Jewish contact inside the Vatican Council, said a religious peace campaign for Israel would provoke anti-Semitism. John Bennett sent Al Lowenstein and others a running tally of the contrasts between the two wars, but pragmatism recommended separate treatment. Heschel preserved his ecumenical wonder in his new book—"All men are created equal, yet no two faces are alike"—which would include a stern rebuke from the Talmud: "When the Egyptians who had enslaved the children of Israel were sinking in the Red Sea, the angels were jubilant and wanted to sing a song of praise and triumph. But God, the Father of all men, said to the angels, 'My creatures are drowning—and you sing!' "

King regretted the immobilizing effect of Middle East passions on Vietnam protest. "It has given Johnson the little respite he wanted from Vietnam," he told Levison. To King, Vietnam was the ongoing war for which Americans must assume civic responsibility, and he had no way of knowing about doubts within the government. On June 13, Harry McPherson gave President Johnson his raw impressions of Vietnam, stressing the blatant corruption among the South Vietnamese and the candor of American soldiers. He quoted a lieutenant general: "Before I came out here a year and a half ago, I thought we were at zero. I was wrong. We were at minus fifty. *Now* we are at zero." McPherson's report strained to understand the baffling ferocity of the enemy without demonizing the Vietnamese. If he were a young peasant in the hamlets he saw, McPherson bluntly conjectured, and were offered the chance of "striking back at my Frenchified oppressors and their American allies, and of rising to a position of leadership in the VC, I would join up." Yet he cast his lot loyally in battle. "Every aspect of our national life and our role in the world is involved in Vietnam," McPherson assured Johnson. "I feel that I am only another of those many men who have a part of their souls at stake there."

*   *   *

THE FABLED summer of 1967 jumbled extremes of hope and horror, many of which penetrated King's life with special force. On Monday, June 12, the U.S. Supreme Court struck down laws against interracial marriage in sixteen states through the landmark case *Loving et Ux. v. Virginia,* which grew from a bedroom police raid and the subsequent conviction of Richard and Mildred Loving for cohabitation under pretense of wedlock. Until then, Virginia declared void any marriage with only one partner classified white by its written legal standard: "such person as has no trace whatever of any blood other than Caucasian." Mildred Loving's ancestry blended Europe, Africa, and Cherokee Indian. Against Virginia's appellate courts, which found in the anti-miscegenation statute a legitimate state purpose to prevent "the corruption of blood," "a mongrel breed of citizens," and "the obliteration of racial pride," the Justices ruled that a racial definition of crime violated Fourteenth Amendment guarantees of equal protection under law. Their decision confronted sexual taboos long at the heart of violent white supremacy. Most Americans within a generation would find it quaint or fantastic that three-quarters of citizens in 1967 opposed interracial marriage, and not even the wildest imagination on record from the 1960s predicted that turn-of-the-century politics would divide closely on the rights of same-sex couples.

That same Monday, ending their annual term, the Justices narrowly sided with a legal quest from Alabama to reimprison King and seven fellow ministers for violating a court injunction against protest. The 5–4 decision in *Walker v. City of Birmingham* grew from the pivotal Good Friday decision early in the 1963 Birmingham campaign, and carried implications far graver than the remaining contempt sentence of only five days. Andrew Young noted on the first shocked conference call that much longer sentences trailed in cases on appeal. Stanley Levison said the ruling could cripple any movement. In vigorous dissent, Chief Justice Earl Warren scolded colleagues for holding that although the Birmingham injunction did unlawfully abridge the right of protest, it should have been obeyed through the four years of litigation on its validity, remaining "entirely superior in the meantime even to the United States Constitution."

"Now even the Supreme Court has turned against us," King lamented in private. A *New York Times* editorial, while opining that retroactive jail for King "is profoundly embarrassing to the good name of the United States," rejected Chief Justice Warren's dissent: "The majority held—we think rightly—that obedience to the law and to the normal procedures set forth in the law has to be paramount."

News coverage of demonstrations heightened weariness and fear of disorder. Stokely Carmichael, who no longer bothered to declare that he had submitted to nonviolence for five harrowing years, learned of Monday's Supreme Court decisions in the Prattville, Alabama, jail, under arrest for incitement to riot. Police officers confiscated a news photographer's film showing that he had addressed a Sunday afternoon workshop of twenty young women on folding chairs in the shade outside a Baptist church. His sharp remarks about persistent surveillance—shouting "black power" at police patrols, demanding to be called "Mr. Carmichael"—led to his arrest followed by a night of marauding gunshots in and out of the black neighborhood and rumors that he had been lynched. John Hulett arrived from adjacent Lowndes County to investigate, only to be beaten early Monday near the Autauga County courthouse. SNCC chairman Rap Brown issued a press statement from Atlanta: "We feel that this is a part of America's Gestapo tactics to destroy SNCC and to commit genocide against black people. We are calling for full retaliation from the black community across America. We blame Lyndon Johnson." By Monday afternoon, when Brown posted bond for Carmichael, they walked from jail through two platoons of young Alabama National Guardsmen lined stiffly with fixed bayonets. Federal Judge Frank Johnson would sort through competing charges for the balance of the year to conclude, "Fault is on both sides."

On Tuesday, June 13, President Johnson informed his black assistants Louis Martin and Clifford Alexander that he was about to integrate the Supreme Court. "You know, this is not going to do me a bit of good politically," he told them, grousing for effect with a host of reasons. When Solicitor General Thurgood Marshall arrived, concealed from the press by elaborate stealth, the President fretted in jest that he was fated to ruin a good friendship just as President Truman had broken with the retiring Justice Tom Clark over an adverse legal opinion. Marshall said the President might be correct if he expected a yes-man on the Court, which made Johnson·beam that he was appointing a man of common sense much like himself. "He doesn't have a Harvard degree like you, Cliff," he told Alexander in a customary dig. Johnson announced Marshall from the Rose Garden at noon;·and news stories flashed about jubilation among civil rights leaders that the great-grandson of a slave would become the first of any minority to occupy a top rank in one of the three constitutional branches of government. Nearly all the other questions were about world stability after the Six Day War.

King appeared for a relatively evenhanded interview on the nationwide Sunday broadcast *Issues and Answers* about race relations in the midst of two difficult wars. On the Middle East, King thought a complex peace required security for Israel and development for the Arab nations. "The whole world and all people of good will must respect the territorial integrity of Israel," he said, listing the vital ports and trade routes. He proposed also a "Marshall Plan" to relieve desperate poverty among the mass of Arab citizens and refugees. "So long as they find themselves on the outskirts of hope," he said, "they are going to make intemperate remarks. They are going to keep the war psychosis alive." King sparred with the correspondents over assertions that civil rights leaders cared mostly for black soldiers in Vietnam, and bristled at charges that he foolishly targeted President Johnson for insult. "I have never called President Johnson's name in dissenting on the war in Vietnam," King said firmly. He insisted on collective error through four Presidents, beginning with Harry Truman's decision not to recognize Vietnamese independence in 1945. This was a point of common emphasis with Coretta, who had drawn a mixed response at a San Francisco Mobilization rally by calling Johnson an "uncertain president" torn over conflicting advice.

President Johnson sent again for Senator Russell on Monday evening, June 19. He sought advice about whether to pursue a summit meeting when Soviet Premier Alexei Kosygin visited the United Nations, but Russell, "knowing his abhorrence for being alone," confided to his diary that he thought the President simply needed company. The Georgia senator took the chance to bemoan the choice of Thurgood Marshall without expecting to derail his Senate confirmation, pining for a Supreme Court Justice who could quote something "other than the 14th Amendment, which is used solely now to excuse striking down the rest of the Constitution." Russell thought he made some small impression with his proverb that a loss of tradition kills "at least one half of patriotism." The President maneuvered afterward to meet the Soviet Premier for three days at Glassboro, New Jersey, halfway between Washington and the United Nations, on a calculated hunch that the Soviet disaster in the Middle East might induce the colorless Soviet bureaucrat to engineer a settlement with North Vietnam. Kosygin, however, talked secretly to Johnson like an exasperated uncle. He said he knew from direct reports that American soldiers were fighting well—in fact, as bravely as he could wish for his own soldiers—but he could not understand what Johnson hoped to accomplish except to maim young Americans for a decade or more. U.S. battle deaths exceeded 1,000 for June and averaged 770 per month throughout 1967, up from 412 in 1966. The joint statement from Glassboro reported frank discussion and little progress.

* * *

ON JUNE 24, during the Johnson-Kosygin talks, King called Stanley Levison from California about the poor reception for his new book, *Where Do We Go from Here, Chaos or Community?* Levison offered a practical suggestion to boost sales by sending a promotional copy to all 18,000 SCLC contributors of $20 or more, but King was more distressed about the slight interest he encountered while "running all over the country, Cleveland and Chicago, back and forth." The *New York Times Magazine* had published an excerpt about the Meredith march and black power, which proved to be a stale controversy. Harry Belafonte added star power by joining King for a network television interview about the book, but the material was inherently difficult. "I am opposed to violence," Belafonte told viewers. "I really am, whether it is in the black hand or in the white hand." He said he believed that although a significant percentage of black people would endure committed nonviolent struggle against the most intractable problems, "it is the resistance on the part of the white community to respond that is indeed the Achilles heel of the democratic process in America." King argued from the book that white supremacy was an ever-present force in history, making it a cause rather than a result of black frustration and violence. On the other hand, he warned that courageous all-black politics in isolated Lowndes County "cannot be made a measuring rod for the whole of America." He challenged violence across the board. A member of the television audience sharply objected that Communists were a national enemy and therefore anyone who shirked the fight in Vietnam was a traitor. "And what would you say to that, sir?" he asked King.

Reviews of the book were slow to come and tepid at best. Eliot Fremont-Smith of the *Times* said a "return to nonviolence" was no more wistful than other miracles King had championed, and "perhaps one shouldn't despair until he does." Several critics thought the author seemed bewildered by the range of attack since the triumphs of a simpler time. One said his method was being treated "like a pre-historic relic," and another gave faint credit for "standing up strongly now in opposition to the use of riots and violence in pursuit of racial change." Nearly all reviewers assessed King's argument for nonviolent politics by its suitability to others, especially to black people in cities. "The Negro male, too, is now bent upon proving his manhood," observed a New York reviewer, "and many—particularly the young—appear to see violence as a more valid sort of proof than nonviolence." The most scathing white critics rebuked King for "irrelevancy" to black people. "It is as if he is misdefining black power in order to make it easier to reject," wrote David Steinberg for *Commonweal*. "He had simply, and disastrously, arrived at the wrong conclusions about the world," charged Andrew Kopkind in *The New York Review of Books*. "Whites have ceased to believe him, or really to care; the blacks hardly listen." Kopkind listed many insights King "could have seen" or "might have understood" had he not been so credulous, ending with a bedrock assertion—"Morality, like politics, starts at the barrel of a gun"—on which he dismissed King's promise from the left before anyone condescended so boldly from the right. Vietnam and black rebellion "have contrived this summer to murder liberalism—in its official robes," Kopkind concluded. "There are few mourners."

Young people dominated mass culture in the crossover summer when baby boom Americans under eighteen peaked at seventy million. On June 25, the first full television program ever beamed by satellite to most of the world featured the Beatles from London with a new song, "All You Need Is Love." A music festival from Monterey, California, flashed into icon status along with its pop discoveries from Janis Joplin to Jimi Hendrix, and the show trials of June showcased young defendants. A jury convicted Richard Speck in the mass murder of eight Chicago nurses. A court-martial sentenced Captain Howard Levy to three years at hard labor, rejecting his defense that medical duty in Vietnam would implicate him in atrocities suggested by the casually graphic testimony of *Green Berets* author Robin Moore about bounties paid for severed ears ("Brutality is a way of life over there"). Attorney Charles Morgan represented Levy as well as Muhammad Ali, who on June 20 received the maximum sentence of five years for draft evasion. Two years later, Morgan's questions of an FBI witness would elicit the first official revelation of government surveillance directed at civil rights leaders, when Special Agent R. R. Nichols acknowledged in appeals court that he once overheard Ali over a wiretapped phone line, talking with Martin Luther King, in his capacity as manager of the King wiretap unit in Atlanta. Director Hoover banished Nichols to Oklahoma City for a candor that began to pry open the FBI's clandestine political machinery.

Hoover stood unchallenged through King's lifetime. A *Life* magazine story aborted the fitful, anemic Senate investigation into wiretap and bugging practices by charging that corrupt senators only sought to weaken the FBI in order to protect Teamster boss James Hoffa. Hoover's letter of congratulation to committee chairman Edward Long goaded the *New York Times* into a plaintive editorial: "There is—or should be—something extraordinary about a career civil servant like Mr. Hoover patting a member of the United States Senate on the head in this fashion." The result hovered in the news background with stodgy adult politics. A Mississippi jury acquitted the eight defendants charged with beating Grenada children on the first day of school. Of the major religious denominations in convention that June, Southern Baptists reserved judgment on any withdrawal from Vietnam "apart from an honorable and just peace," and Southern Presbyterians voted to end separate racial jurisdictions despite objections from Mississippi and Alabama. In Portland, Oregon, Northern Presbyterians completed an eight-year saga to adopt the first belief statement since the Westminster Confession of 1647, narrowly defeating an overture from Washington, D.C., and elder Robert McNamara, to delete a phrase some feared would bar Presbyterians from sensitive positions in government: "The church, in its own life, is called to practice the forgiveness of enemies and to commend to the nations as practical politics the search for cooperation and peace. This search requires that the nations pursue fresh and responsible relations across every line of conflict, *even at risk to national security.*"

A. D. King, who was among the eight preachers ordered back to jail in Birmingham, tracked down his brother while in the grip of chronic alcoholic depression, threatening again to kill himself. King roused friends by telephone to intervene in Louisville until A.D. calmed down, and he preached a sermon called "Ingratitude" at Ebenezer on the third

Sunday of June. Decrying an "acid," universal affliction, he told of a wealthy black man in Chicago who had just touted his own model achievements before an audience without ever acknowledging his parents. He repeated a homily that most people were "dependent on more than half of the world" before breakfast every morning—soap from France, sponge from a Pacific Islander, coffee from South America. He said millions absorbed blessings without a thought that "we wouldn't have a civil rights bill today if some three thousand children hadn't packed up the jails in Birmingham, Alabama." He called ingratitude a sin that overlooks both common bonds and the accumulated hurts still dividing humanity. "And finally ingratitude is a sin, because it causes one to fail to realize his dependence on God," King preached. "I don't mind what you call him, but there is a creative power in this universe." He cited miracles of relief and refreshment. "How is it that you can close your eyes and somehow fade away as far as your conscious mind is concerned?" he asked the congregation. "And processes begin to take place. You dream, and you dream about things and you see things and you are away from everything. But then early in the morning you wake up. That's a miracle to me. And this morning I want to thank God for sleep."

CHAPTER 36

King's Choice

July–November 1967

J. Edgar Hoover sent his liaison to the White House on July 10 with a secret report that King and Stokely Carmichael opposed the Vietnam War in order "to replenish their empty larders" among other nefarious motives. "It was indicated," Deke DeLoach reported back to headquarters, "that the general public is gradually beginning to realize that the civil rights activities of these men have been phoney since their start." In response, President Johnson urged DeLoach to arrange leaks against Carmichael but not King. His careful evasion was a double letdown for Hoover, because Johnson still shielded King and declined to undertake leaks himself. "I assume we have to do it," Hoover grumbled, "but I don't like it." He knew that only a President had the stature to generate derogatory King stories without implicating the FBI as his source.

Two days later, Johnson imposed a Vietnam policy truce in the Cabinet Room. "There is not a military stalemate," Secretary McNamara agreed from his latest inspection trip to Vietnam. General Earle Wheeler echoed the desired words—"There is no stalemate"—for the Joint Chiefs, who trimmed the pending troop request by 100,000. McNamara insisted they could make do with less, but he declared for the first time in council that the prescribed steady course would win the war. He and Wheeler thought American war reporters were "in a very bad mood," which obscured progress, and President Johnson recessed negotiations on a note of grim consolation. He said constant reminders of ten thousand war dead since 1965 left him certain

North Vietnam must feel the loss of that many in the past sixty days alone.

That night, taxi driver John Smith was reported tailgating a police cruiser in Newark, New Jersey, which would have been strange behavior even if Smith's driver's license had not been revoked for a series of eight minor accidents. Shortly after 9:30, taxi dispatchers relayed word that Smith was seen dragged prostrate into the Fourth District police station behind his passenger. Upward of two hundred people gathered, and several Molotov cocktails smashed against the station's exterior wall, before a joint delegation of citizens and police commanders refuted rumors of lynching but confirmed Smith's transfer to a hospital. When the community leaders tried to channel the hostility into a midnight march, broken store windows littered the route.

Mayor Hugh Addonizio declared early on Thursday, July 13, that the isolated trouble was over, and a front-page *New York Times* story— "Racial Violence Erupts in Newark"—outlined local controversies preceding the Smith incident. The mayor had just appointed a white precinct worker with a high school education to become superintendent of a school system abruptly turned 70 percent black. (Since 1960, seventy thousand white residents had left the city of 400,000.) Eighty percent of crime took place in a dilapidated ghetto where officials proposed to condemn 150 acres for a medical school. By afternoon, picketers outside City Hall were demanding housing instead, and cries of "Black Power!" scorned news that the city agreed to hire its first Negro police captain. A distant glow of store fires scattered police officers and reporters along with the crowd.

In a sitting room of the White House residence, President Johnson had summoned news photographers to display what he called "a meeting of the minds." One by one, he polled McNamara and the Joint Chiefs about whether an unspecified number of reinforcements would meet all military requirements for Vietnam, and cameras recorded each emphatic assent. Through a night of escalating riot bulletins, Johnson agreed with New Jersey Governor Richard J. Hughes, a staunch political ally, that state forces could handle Newark without emergency federal assistance. State troopers entered the central ghetto at dawn Friday, and National Guard soldiers threw up 137 roadblocks by afternoon. Sporadic gunshots punctuated fires and generalized looting. Newark Police Commissioner Dominick Spina would testify that much of the alleged sniper fire was stray shots from police officers, troopers, and

Guardsmen, whose separate radio frequencies did not allow them to communicate. A small girl lost an eye and her hearing to a bullet that penetrated her bedroom wall. When Spina ducked into the Hayes Housing Project, a resident told him teenagers on the fourth floor were dropping cherry bombs, but massive retaliation from the street killed two mothers and a grandmother on the tenth floor, where an orphaned son vacantly collected a dozen spent bullets in a coffee can. When violence subsided on Monday, Newark counted 1,200 people jailed, six hundred injured, and twenty-three dead, including two white officers and two small children. Images flashed around the world of soldiers standing over prostrate looters outside the burned shells of ghetto stores. A leading newspaper in Johannesburg archly observed that stubborn Yanks should understand at last the moral necessity of South African apartheid. "America's obsession with integration only causes chaos, strife and destruction," argued *Die Vaderland*.

Detroit police raided five "blind pigs," or unlicensed speakeasies, toward dawn the next Sunday. Four raids netted the usual handful of inebriated gamblers, but the fifth ran into eighty-two people celebrating the safe return of two black veterans from "the ultimate riot," as some soldiers called Vietnam duty. Scuffles, sirens, and accelerated calls for backup marked protracted efforts to haul away all the prisoners, and some 540 police officers responded by 8:30 that morning to showers of rocks and pockets of looting. U.S. Representative John Conyers appealed for calm but was hooted down and his district office ransacked. Looters beat to death a black man who tried to protect his store. A rioter ripped open his shirt before a cowed reporter and said of an ugly scar, "I got that in Germany. I was in Korea, too. I'm 42, and I can't get a job." Governor George Romney, flying over in a helicopter, ordered seven thousand Michigan National Guard troops into what he said looked like a bombed city. Attorney General Ramsey Clark woke President Johnson at 2:45 A.M. on Monday, July 24, with word that Romney was inquiring about federal troops. Johnson yanked Cyrus Vance from his fresh retirement into Detroit as an ad hoc emissary, and McNamara rushed two airborne brigades into Selfridge Air Force Base outside the city.

"There were dark days before," King told a conference call of advisers that night, "but this is the darkest." He approved Stanley Levison's doleful statement warning that any nation failing to provide jobs ultimately cannot govern. He would remind people that a prostrate, Depression-era America had treated employment conditions no worse than those in black Newark and Detroit as a national emergency, but he knew most Americans heard him only when he dutifully denounced violent crime and supported federal intervention to restore order. By coincidence, the deadline to abort his trip to the Middle East fell just when responsibility seemed urgent at home and his nonviolent message most awkward for triumphant Israel. A visit centered in annexed Jerusalem would provoke antagonisms, King said, "and any way you say it they don't plan to give it up." So he canceled.

President Johnson anguished late Monday over a final decision to deploy the airborne brigades. "Well, I guess it's just a matter of minutes before federal troops start shooting women and children," he said morosely. Vance reported fires raging out of control, 1,200 arrests, and a disorganized, ill-trained Michigan Guard. Justice Fortas was drafting legal proclamations based on President Franklin Roosevelt's precedent in the 1943 Detroit race riots. Some hesitation was political, as Governor Romney, a Republican presidential contender for 1968, was loath to declare the situation beyond state control. Democrats jockeyed with Republicans over shadings of blame and intrusion. When Vance urged that the Guard be federalized to gain experienced command, Johnson worried out loud that critics would say, "We cannot kill enough people in Vietnam, so we go out and shoot civilians in Detroit." General John Throckmorton said his men would fire only upon life-threatening provocation. J. Edgar Hoover rushed into the Oval Office with ominous intelligence that Detroit was lost and Harlem would be "torn to pieces" in half an hour. The President went on national television just before midnight to explain his dispatch of troops.

Two thousand Army paratroopers proved decisive while firing a minuscule total of 205 bullets over five days. The sole military fatality died in crossfire between Michigan National Guard units at a poorly marked roadblock, as inexperienced Guard troops ignored Throckmorton's orders to unload weapons. One unit fired several thousand rounds into a single house, then delivered three occupants to an "alley court" of police officers who tried to extract confessions that they were the riot masterminds. The result was concussion for absentee landlords trying to safeguard their property, but an immediate wire service account folded the mistake into sensational coverage: "Two National Guard tanks ripped a sniper's haven with machine guns Wednesday night and flushed out three shaggy-haired white youths. . . . Detroit's racial riot set a modern record for bloodshed." Press reports of $500 million in property damage exaggerated by a factor of twenty, according to the subsequent national inquiry on civil disorders. "We deplore the few who rely upon words and works of terror," President Johnson declared on Thursday, July 27, announcing the bipartisan study commission to be headed by Illinois Governor Otto Kerner. Forty-three people were killed in downtown Detroit. Groping for perspective, a shell-shocked *New York Times* editorial observed that the cumulative toll from Newark and Detroit fell far beneath the Pentagon's latest casualty report in Vietnam, which was the lowest weekly total for 1967: 164 Americans killed and 1,442 wounded. Selective panic hushed savagery but magnified suspicion. John Hersey, author of *Hiroshima,* was asked to investigate riot mysteries for the Kerner Commission and became transfixed by the case of police officers who had rounded up ten unarmed black men and two young white prostitutes for interrogation in a motel, after which all suspects emerged beaten, unclothed, and terrified except for three found executed on the floor.

In California, Governor Reagan denounced "mad dogs against the people," and a hundred Los Angeles police stormed the Muslim mosque again on a false tip about concealed arms. President Johnson called J. Edgar Hoover about stories that former President Eisenhower accused him of failing to see or control a "pattern of insurrection." Hoover called Johnson with electrifying reports that Martin Luther King himself was implicated in plans to destroy the Chicago Loop. This absurd contention receded when Chicago stayed quiet, but Johnson clung to notions that his torment was plotted and artificial. "I don't want to foreclose the conspiracy theory now," he instructed his Cabinet.

Black power enthusiasts fed speculation with competitive rhetoric. From Bimini, Adam Clayton Powell predicted riots for thirteen new cities in "a necessary phase of the black revolution." (He praised rioters for attacking John Conyers, who had served on the House committee that investigated him, and quipped, "No wonder he was hit by a rock.") Rap Brown became famous between Newark and Detroit, beginning with a news squib that it might be time for "guerilla war on the honkie white man." President Johnson called Hoover about a remark quoted from Washington's Episcopal Church of the Incarnation—"If you give me a gun and tell me to shoot my enemy, I might shoot Lady Bird"— and Brown coined in the same pulpit speech an epigram that gripped the country as truism or demonic slander: "Violence is necessary. It is as American as cherry pie." Some fourteen charges of incitement had already been lodged when a manhunt located the SNCC chairman in a Virginia airport on July 26, during the Detroit riots. (Hoover's success bulletin to the White House preserved a whisper of FBI reform: "I took occasion to have a Negro Agent participate in the arrest.") Ex-chairman Stokely Carmichael released a statement the next day on arrival in Havana as a guest of Cuban Premier Fidel Castro: "We are preparing groups of urban guerillas for our defense in the cities." Roy Wilkins, newly appointed to the Kerner Commission, all but shuddered on a televised news panel. King, asked if he wished to interpret for viewers Carmichael's uncanny timing or purpose, said, "No."

President Johnson allowed an interval of recovery before making harsh summer news on August 3. To curb inflation, and reduce a budget deficit projected to exceed $28 billion, he called for a 10 percent income tax surcharge. He also announced his decision to send another 55,000 soldiers to Vietnam, toward a new ceiling of 525,000 by mid-1968. The Pentagon request for 200,000 reinforcements remained officially secret, but a seminal *New York Times* story debunked the labored claim of slow victory only days later. It provoked Johnson enough to call the military press office in Saigon and denounce Communist influence behind the radioactive thesis, "Vietnam: The Signs of Stalemate." The President demanded action to root out commanders who disclosed to reporter R. W. Apple that they expected years more combat because enemy troop strength actually had increased despite thirty months of rising carnage: an estimated 200,000 enemy dead with 12,269 Americans killed and 74,818 wounded. On *Meet the Press,* meanwhile, correspondents pressed King to choose whether he would seek to revive nonviolent demonstrations against Vietnam or the race riots. They said colliding passions weakened either course. "The tragedy is that we are today engaged in two wars and we are losing both," King replied. "We are losing the war against poverty here at home. We are losing the war in Vietnam morally and politically."

*   *   *

KING HAD promised to clarify a new strategic role at his annual SCLC convention. He flew to San Francisco, where he spoke privately of ambitious hopes and then addressed an association of black real estate agents on their obligation to "the least of these." Back east the next day, he paid tribute to high-spirited radio pioneers such as Purvis Spann, the Magnificent Montague, and Georgia Wood of Philadelphia before an audience of minority disc jockeys. "No one knows the importance of

'Taul Paul' White in the massive nonviolent demonstrations of the youth of Birmingham in 1963," said King, adding with levity that it was a miracle to hear "joyful rhythms" from the cocoon of his own youth flung all around the globe and now "coming back across the Atlantic with an English accent." He praised the radio crowd for using the vitality of black music to build crossover bridges on the strength of nonviolence. "Yes, you have taken the power which Old Sam had buried deep in his soul!" King cried, soaring on hyperbole above laughter and applause. "And through amazing technology performed a cultural conquest that surpasses even Alexander the Great and the culture of classical Greece." Yet he said they had barely begun the larger quest for freedom. He exhorted them to nourish comfort in being black—"We're gonna start with ourselves by freeing our own psyche"—and move resolutely against the evil triumvirate of poverty, racism, and war.

From a brisk overnight trip for *Meet the Press,* King returned home for the opening SCLC banquet on August 14. Mayor Ivan Allen welcomed 1,400 guests to the ballroom of Atlanta's new Hyatt Regency Hotel. Aretha Franklin performed her hit songs "Respect" and "Baby I Love You," which shared the top of the current music charts with the Beatles' *Sgt. Pepper* album and Scott McKenzie's rhapsody on a flowering San Francisco youth movement. Actor Sidney Poitier described his pioneer screen roles since being stranded years ago on the "colored" side of the Atlanta bus station, and proclaimed King "a new man in an old world." Over three more days, Benjamin Spock addressed an overflow session on peace in Vietnam, and King explained to a heritage workshop that the convention's "Black Is Beautiful" posters signaled a drive to upgrade negative connotations buried deep in the English language.* "They even tell us that a white lie is better than a black one," he said. Delivering the annual president's report from his own pulpit, King recalled that when a handful of black preachers had gathered there at Ebenezer to form the Southern Christian Leadership Conference, just after the Montgomery bus boycott, such a glamorous banquet with three hundred white participants was scarcely conceivable. Libraries, white-collar jobs, and "the fresh air of public parks" had been off-limits to black people. Even casual association between races, when not illegal, was suffused with danger. "A decade ago, not a single Negro entered

* The *New York Times* account conveyed skepticism about King's linguistic goal: "He offered no explanation as to how this could be done."

the legislative chambers of the South except as a porter or chauffeur," he said. To confront poverty and war above the stupendous legal achievements taking hold on the civil rights front, King called for renewed dedication to nonviolence. He waxed philosophical about a narrow path between anemic love and abusive power, preaching as though to himself on the trials of ministry in public service. "What I am trying to get you to see this morning is that a man may be self-centered in his self-denial and self-righteous in his self-sacrifice," King declared. "His generosity may feed his ego and his piety may feed his pride. So, without love, benevolence becomes egotism and martyrdom becomes spiritual pride."

King connected these difficult ideas with inspirational oratory on freedom, but his themes lacked practical direction. Priorities scattered under the compound trauma of hardship, fatigue, riots, and foreign war. A delegate from Birmingham complained that he could not understand a word of the seminar on poverty. Former SNCC chairman John Lewis stayed up all night arguing against "the politics of alienation" with Stanley Wise and Willie Ricks, who said black militants should jettison deadweight liberals in favor of political alliances overseas. Personal disputes and alcohol plagued leaders behind the scenes. When Bayard Rustin and Kenneth Clark did not appear for their panel on the urban crisis, King filled in alone. He attacked Congress in unusually strong language for hooting down President Johnson's modest rat-control bill that aimed to reduce the 14,000 bites reported per year, mostly of children: "The tragic truth is that Congress, more than the American people, is now running wild with racism." Of ghetto conditions, King said it was "purposeless to tell Negroes not to be enraged when they should be," and he sketched a plan to channel grievances into organized nonviolence. "Mass civil disobedience can use rage as a constructive and creative force," he asserted. Demonstrations could curtail violence "if we set to the task."

These remarks received an unfriendly reception on front pages everywhere. "Dr. King Planning Protests to 'Dislocate' Large Cities," headlined the August 16 *New York Times*. In "Formula for Discord," an editorial the next day said King courted disaster "in the present overheated atmosphere." The announcement alone had damaged his cause "whether or not Dr. King goes ahead with his perilous project," the *Times* added, because it strengthened "powerful Congressional elements already convinced that the answer to urban unrest lies in repression." Similar reactions followed, and King's own staff confessed shock that he laid out such an undigested plan. If the goal of the Chicago movement had to be scaled back from ending slums to denting residential segregation, how could a national drive on cities lead to better results? In the wake of the SCLC convention, Stanley Levison guessed King must see opportunity in a surprisingly mild public reaction to the riots—measured by low constituent mail to Congress and a national poll showing that two-thirds of Americans still favored aggressive steps to eliminate ghettoes. Some aides thought King was laying ground to shift the venue from Northern cities back to Southern ones, or the method from protest to political action, or the issue from poverty to Vietnam. To sort through the options, King scheduled a retreat with key advisers after a Labor Day conference in Chicago.

* * *

LEVISON URGED King not to attend the National Conference for New Politics at all. Two years in the making, the event brought together nearly three thousand delegates from 372 political reform groups, but ethnic and ideological splits already paralyzed the sponsors. One board member resigned to protest the excesses of black power, and another proposed an internal truce committee to deal with "the ancient corruptions of populism": white racism and anti-Semitism. Harvard instructor Martin Peretz, the NCNP's principal architect, had expelled young activists from his home for singing anti-Israeli songs about the Six Day War. Peretz wanted King to develop a Vietnam peace constituency for the 1968 presidential election, but others either manipulated King to run himself or called him an Uncle Tom. "What rubs off on you," Levison warned, "is that you are dealing with people who do not know their politics." King said it was too late to abandon Spock and William Sloane Coffin, especially since they supported his notion of civil disobedience in distressed cities. Hoping for the best, he gave the kickoff speech on August 31.

Bongo drummers mocked his arrival outside the Chicago Coliseum with a rhythmic chant, "Kill whitey, kill whitey," and Ralph Abernathy confided that King hesitated to speak because of threats from delegates inside. Pre-set groups heckled King from the perimeter as he presented a new line of advocacy for Vietnam peace. He argued plainly for U.S. military withdrawal, having resolved that calls for negotiations, bombing halts, and deescalation only evaded the necessary hard decisions. To make his case, King wrestled the most compelling justification for the war—democratic solidarity with anti-Communist Vietnamese. ("I do not want to be on any 'hate Johnson' thing," he had insisted on a wire-tapped phone line.) His restrained political stance only inflamed the confrontational moods in the Coliseum. Pickets carried banners such as "Down with Non-Violence," and decoys distracted the crowd with shouts of "Make way for Rap Brown!" It was "awful," King told Levision after woodenly completing the address. "The black nationalists gave me trouble. They kept interrupting me, kept yelling things at me." A police surveillance report noted that King looked "afraid, worried and tired" as he left the Coliseum. He ducked out of Chicago early the next morning. Foreboding and clashes in the hallways made Julian Bond abandon the conference, too, even though he was its national co-chair.

Chaos reigned for the five-day conference beneath ballroom chandeliers at the Palmer House Hotel, where the Chicago housing summit had concluded the previous summer. Some three hundred black delegates withdrew to the Hyde Park Methodist Church, which they threatened to burn down until the host clergy and all white visitors departed. One speaker proposed to burn the many black churches whose pastors still refused them space. Others suggested thirteen disparate resolutions—"Condemn the imperialistic Israeli government," and "Demand the immediate re-seating of Adam C. Powell"—that were dispatched to the Palmer House as a nonnegotiable condition for black delegates to rejoin the main conference. A tumultuous vote there to acquiesce prompted a minority lament from NCNP founder Arthur Waskow that "a thousand liberals thought they could become radicals by castrating themselves." Next the black caucus forwarded a new ultimatum that it would stay in Hyde Park unless granted half the ballots on every formal vote—to redress the legacy of racism—and a Michigan State professor helped persuade the main body to accept the heavily weighted formula. "We are just a little tail on the end of a very powerful black panther," he said. By then the Palmer House was a maze of caucuses and manifestos. Burly guards admitted only black delegates to Rap Brown's rambling speech: "The only difference between Lyndon Johnson and George Wallace is that one of their wives got cancer. . . . We should take lessons in violence from the honkies. Lee Harvey Oswald is white. This honky who killed the eight nurses is white. . . . You see, it's better to be born handicapped in America than to be born black." In the ballroom, James Forman rammed through resolutions about Africa without bothering to call for the "nays." When two women moved that half the delegates should be female, men drove them from the microphone with catcalls and wolf whistles. Charles Sherrod, then in his sixth year of SNCC fieldwork in Albany, Georgia, pleaded against posturing games: "I am here to remind you that there are still people in the South fighting to be free." James Bevel, who later branded the delegates "masochistic fascists," said he believed the angry men who promised to kill him if he opposed the anti-Israel resolution.

Of the nonsectarian press, only *The New York Review of Books* claimed for the NCNP deliberations a shining political discovery. "The organizers *are* 'the movement,' " wrote Andrew Kopkind. Everyone else saw fiasco and folly. *New Yorker* correspondent Renata Adler, who had been bemused at times but captivated by the long trek from Selma to Montgomery, ridiculed the self-absorption of organizers as a fantasy detachment from the citizenry at large. "Throughout the convention," she wrote, "delegates seemed constantly to emerge, wet-lipped and trembling, from some crowded elevator, some torrent of abuse, some marathon misrepresentation of fact, some pointless totalitarian maneuver, or some terminal sophistry, to pronounce themselves 'radicalized.' " Most participants lapsed into delusion or searing regret. "I am afraid that many of our friends are so flipped out that they think events in Chicago were just marvelous," Martin Peretz wrote Andrew Young. NCNP executive director William Pepper went so far as to extol the convention as "the most significant gathering of Americans since the Declaration of Independence."

To answer a volley of protest from Jewish political leaders, and at least thirty letters from rabbis, King busily disclaimed the NCNP's unbalanced resolution against Israel.* Diminishing press coverage relieved the larger embarrassment, as mainstream reporters rapidly lost interest in the squabbling caucuses once delegates dropped any pretext of concerted action on Vietnam or their stated agenda—especially the newsworthy goal to unite behind a presidential candidate or third party for the 1968 election. Still, the unseemly disintegration of a citizens' mass movement was a blow for King. It raised the odds against both alternative new campaigns. It hardened prior resistance to his Riverside speech on Vietnam and his call for nonviolent protest in riot-torn cities. Far more openly than Mississippi Freedom Summer, it revealed the

* "Israel's right to exist as a state in security is incontestable," King wrote Morris Abram, president of the American Jewish Committee. "At the same time the great powers have the obligation to recognize that the Arab world is in a state of imposed poverty and backwardness that must threaten peace and harmony."

strain of fresh cross-cultural alliances besieged by old habits of race and war. "Coalitions are virtually impossible in this reactionary climate," Andrew Young wrote the Singer heiress Anne Farnsworth, a large contributor to SCLC with her husband, Martin Peretz. Depression left him on the verge of giving up, Young added on September 6—"about three steps away from 'the Hippy solution' "—but he recalled the Selma breakthrough and said maybe they could find another one.

*   *   *

KING'S FIRST attempt to set a course for nonviolent struggle collided with his headstrong inner circle. On Wednesday, September 12, when SCLC's executive staff gathered at the Airlie House conference center in rural Virginia, James Bevel enjoyed a prodigal's welcome south after two years in Chicago and the peace movement, but celebrations turned into a strategic dispute. Folksinger Joan Baez favored a coordinated offensive to resist the war in Vietnam. She outlined her own preparations for pacifist demonstrations at military posts and conscription centers, protesting the coercion of young Americans to kill and be killed. In sharp contrast, the young lawyer Marian Wright maintained a priority to uplift the invisible poor. She said that whereas the antiwar movement already had legions of recruits, national attention was turning away from people like her clients in Mississippi. She proposed to transport into Washington a representative host of faces from every region and race—men who never worked, women who could not read, children who seldom ate—for educational witness until Congress provided jobs or income. Wright modeled her notion on the Bonus Army of World War I veterans, who had occupied the capital to seek relief from the Great Depression.

Hosea Williams attacked both ideas. Civil rights had stalled over black power and urban riots beyond its Southern turf, he said, while even Willie Bolden's mother complained that "Dr. King went too far" to question foreign policy in wartime. Williams favored training new voters from the last great success at Selma, and still resented the reduction of his own South-wide staff from 180 fieldworkers to roughly a dozen. Bevel eloquently rebutted Williams, as usual. He argued that peace must be the first priority for any vanguard, prophetic movement, because Vietnam was devouring the spirit and treasure for any other national purpose. Jesse Jackson, Bevel's protégé, opposed either national drive before a catalyzing local success like Birmingham. For him, a move from weakness only invited humiliation. Jackson wanted first to rebuild SCLC's movement in heartland Chicago, where he said abundant numbers could be mobilized either for peace marches or the destitute poor.

King mostly listened. Abernathy and Young occasionally made favorable comments about a poverty caravan, but they reflected King's guarded wish rather than their own conviction. In fact, King alone had received Marian Wright's proposal like an answered prayer. Its focus on abject poverty opened an important but neglected dimension in human rights, where there was ample space for democratizing nonviolence outside the factional glare of the peace movement. Also, having been stumped about how to dramatize poverty from remote Mississippi or Alabama, King welcomed the inspiration to bring its faces and stories into the capital instead. Wright got the gist of her idea from Robert Kennedy, who told her after the hearings in Mississippi that Congress would address such misery only if someone made it more uncomfortable not to.

Warring critiques elevated tension at Airlie House for five days. Historian Lawrence Reddick, King's first biographer, stalked out with a prickly declaration that he would hear no more grandiose plans while SCLC remained functionally incompetent and nearly bankrupt. When King tried a musical metaphor, imagining poverty harmonized in diverse strains from black and native Indian to Appalachian white, Joan Baez tartly questioned all that effort tuning an orchestra for slaughter in Vietnam. When Wall Street lawyer Harry Wachtel asked whether Operation Breadbasket really hoped for more than token jobs and corporate write-offs, Jesse Jackson bristled against doubt from "a slavemaster." King rebuked Jackson, then invited him to preach reconciling devotionals, and Jackson dazzled his detractors with eloquence on Ezekiel's vision of new life from dry bones. To counter King's worry about surging hostilities that fragmented and discredited the Vietnam protest, Bevel belittled the poverty campaign as bus fare next to the crisis of a misguided war. He said the first duty of nonviolence was to resist organized brutality. If Washington and Jefferson risked "crucifixion" by kings to establish democracy, he preached, the lowliest American should do no less to refine the spirit and practice of equal citizenship. Late one night, King literally howled against the paralyzed debate. "I don't want to do this any more!" he shouted alone. "I want to go back to my little church!" He banged around and yelled, which summoned anxious friends outside his room until Young and Abernathy gently removed his whiskey and talked him to bed.

King greeted colleagues sheepishly the next day. "Well, now it's established that I ain't a saint," he told newcomers before the retreat ended on Sunday, September 17.

Back on the road, King renewed a determined search for executive staff to help resolve the strategic impasse. In Cleveland and San Francisco, pressed for comment about the interracial marriage of Secretary of State Dean Rusk's daughter, he called the ceremony at Stanford "a mighty fine thing." The cover story of *Time* magazine recorded President Johnson's emphatic assurance that the Secretary of State need not resign, and emerging private details included the formal stipulation by Rusk of disregard for a deeded covenant still prohibiting the resale of his Washington home to any descendant of Africa, Asia, or "a denizen of the Ottoman Empire." The *New York Times* described several pioneer weddings made possible by the Supreme Court's *Loving* decision— "Negro and White Wed in Nashville"—and other scattered events marked lighter anxiety after the grim summer of riots and war. FBI agents in the Grand Bahamas tracked a ring of pranksters who skillfully covered George Washington's portrait on dollar bills with an image of King. Republican U.S. Representative George Bush pronounced himself satisfied that seven new microscopes in his Houston district were academic and benign, not rifle scopes secretly retooled for insurrection as he had suggested in a speech about miscellaneous purchases under the federal anti-poverty program. Governor Lurleen Wallace, though gravely ill, pushed through an amended resolution for the song "Dixie" and a presentation of Confederate colors to precede every football game at a public school or site in Alabama—not just the homecoming game, as legislators had proposed.

King worked to convince the mild-mannered Bernard Lafayette, who had shifted from SNCC to Quaker-sponsored slum projects in Chicago, that he was fierce enough in nonviolence to supervise the combative energies of Bevel, Jesse Jackson, and Hosea Williams. In public, meanwhile, King and Harry Belafonte launched an eight-city fundraising tour that sorely disappointed their hopes to replenish the SCLC treasury. Audiences fell short, and performers even quarreled on stage. At the Oakland Coliseum, singer Sammy Davis warned a meager first-night crowd not to stray from traditional civil rights issues, and promoted his goodwill trip to entertain U.S. troops in Vietnam. Joan Baez promptly challenged Davis to beckon the soldiers home instead, winning mixed applause for her resolve to blockade the Army induction center nonviolently at dawn. As Baez stayed behind to serve ten days in jail with 123 fellow resisters, a bomb-threat evacuation delayed another small concert the next evening in Los Angeles.

*   *   *

AUDIENCE APPEAL for King dipped into a kind of public relations trough, obscured between dramatic youth clashes over Vietnam and nostalgia for simpler racial heroes and villains. Early in October, a showcase federal trial finally commenced in the lynch-murder of three civil rights workers more than three years earlier on the first night of Mississippi Freedom Summer. With an all-white jury impaneled, a jovial mood prevailed when one of the first prosecution witnesses was asked if the murder victims really had recruited "young male Negroes to sign a pledge to rape a white woman once a week during the hot summer of 1964." On objection, asked to supply legal ground for the lewd inquiry, the defense lawyer disclosed that the handwritten speculation had just been passed to him from defendant Edgar Ray "Preacher" Killen. U.S. District Judge Harold Cox banged his gavel to silence laughter in the Meridian courtroom. "I'm not going to allow a farce to be made of this trial," he declared. Cox, though himself an ardent segregationist, fixed a tone of decorum for proceedings marked by jolting surprise. FBI Inspector Joseph Sullivan delivered witnesses who elicited gasps by revealing that they had worked for the FBI from inside the local White Knights of the Ku Klux Klan. A local police officer identified prominent fellow Klansmen, including several mortified defense lawyers. Rev. Delmar Dennis said he had turned against the White Knights because of sickening violence and the chronic refusal of rowdies to pay fines levied by the Klan chaplain for vulgar language. He described firsthand an elaborate plot consummated with orders for Deputy Sheriff Cecil Price to hold the civil rights workers in jail while a lynch party was assembled, quoting boastful but inaccurate congratulations from White Knights founder Sam Bowers: "It was the first time that Christians planned and carried out the execution of a Jew." After the trial, Dennis would remain besieged under threat, abandoned by his family and ambushed more than once as a turncoat to the Klan. Almost daily, the trial revealed bombshell witnesses who had confessed their part in the systematic murder of James Chaney, Andrew Goodman, and Michael Schwerner. James Jordan, pale with heart trouble and remorse, petrified of Klan retribution, recounted details of the night's frantic coordination to bury the three bodies fifteen feet deep in a fresh earthen dam.

Courtroom drama from Mississippi shared headlines with National Draft Resistance Week. On Monday, October 16, hours after the Joan Baez group was arrested in California, one hundred clergy led four thousand people from the Boston Common to historic Arlington Street Unitarian, which rested on 999 pilings sunk in Old Back Bay. Bells tolled "We Shall Overcome" while police lines restrained crowds of hecklers, and nearly three hundred prescreened volunteers filed solemnly into the last home church of the Selma martyr James Reeb. Sixty-seven of them burned their draft cards with a church candle in front of whirring cameras from the television networks. Another 214 surrendered cards to Yale chaplain William Sloane Coffin, who announced that senior counselors would share the risk of punishment by presenting the cards to Washington authorities on Friday in ritual defiance of conscription laws. "Are we to raise conscientious men," Coffin cried from the pulpit, "and then not stand by them in their hour of conscience?"

Across the country in Oakland, a coalition of militant student groups took their turn trying to shut down the Army induction center by more aggressive tactics than the previous day's pacifists, whom they derided as "jailbirds." A series of blockades, feints, and rolling jeers led to a police countercharge that cleared entrances quickly at the cost of some fifty arrested or wounded students. The incident, dubbed "Bloody Tuesday," attracted thousands from Berkeley and San Francisco, some with makeshift helmets and shields behind street barricades, to harass the induction center in "urban guerrilla" fights modeled on the 1871 Paris Commune.

On Wednesday, a demonstration in Wisconsin telescoped protest moods from the entire decade. University students jammed Commerce Hall to block job interviews on the Madison campus with representatives of Dow Chemical Company, which manufactured napalm. Nearly all were inexperienced and curious, with vague anticipations of a sit-in, while a few activists circulated leaflets calling for decisive physical resistance. When police officers pushed through to clear access to the interview room, students prevented removal of those arrested by locking arms around their ankles. When the police chief sought a path in close quarters to retreat back outside, students suggested he jump out the window. Claustrophobia bred skittering fear. Trapped females heard ominous advice to remove earrings, and police reinforcements covered badges before they barged inside after their comrades. Some officers were struck with their own nightsticks, but most clubbed through flailing arms and flying objects. Forty-seven students and nineteen officers left by ambulance, many bleeding profusely from head wounds, in mayhem that stunned the several thousand bystanders. Clumps of enraged students shouted "Sieg heil!" at officials and called uniformed officers "pigs," adopting hostile slang from the black power rebellion. It took the first tear gas ever fired in the academic enclave to disperse them, and author David Maraniss, who later reconstructed the clash from all sides, traced a sharp transformation in most participants. Casual protest vanished quickly, along with any hopes to emulate the nonviolent discipline of the civil rights era, and a typical student proposed drastic measures to the first strategy meeting in the aftermath. "I'm a radical!" she declared. "I don't know what it means, but will someone please explain it to me? I've just become a radical."

FBI wiretappers overheard Stanley Levison relay assurance that his son Andrew, a freshman at Wisconsin, was not beaten or arrested—"only gassed"—during Wednesday's upheaval. "It was a brutal business," said Levison. The younger Levison wanted to "stand up" by renouncing a draft card before he was old enough to have one, but his father advised against rashly forfeiting his freedom. Levison also tried to steady King, who called from Houston in acute distress about a third failure on the Belafonte tour. When King complained of a "vicious" editorial, which urged Negroes to boycott the local concert because his Vietnam stance "borders on treason," his intercepted words rocketed to FBI headquarters with a proposal to distribute the editorial clandestinely among "friendly news media sources," especially in the last five cities on the concert schedule. Hoover secretly approved the dual scheme to suppress SCLC's revenue with attack material shown to be "extremely irritating" for King.

That same Wednesday, Inspector Sullivan embodied the FBI's public mission during summations in the Mississippi Klan case. John Doar confessed to the Meridian jury that this was only the second trial he ever handled personally. Representing the United States, he acknowledged in open court the gaps and limits of the extraordinary investigation. "Midnight murder in the rural area of Neshoba County provides few witnesses," he explained. His spare, motionless oration broke only with a raised finger at Deputy Sheriff Cecil Price to illustrate broad stains from the crime. "Price used the machinery of law—his office, his power, his authority, his badge, his uniform, his jail, his police car, his police gun," Doar said slowly. "He used them all to take, to hold, to capture and kill." The assistant attorney general from small-town Wisconsin stressed that judgment rested entirely with citizens of Mississippi, and he could devise no better conclusion than a paraphrase of Lincoln at Gettysburg. "What I say, what the other lawyers say here today . . . will soon be forgotten," Doar told the jury, "but what you twelve people do here today will long be remembered."

In Washington, government officials braced for the weekend National Mobilization to End the War in Vietnam. To discourage attendance, they publicized fear of Communist saboteurs and refused to supply portable toilets or water fountains. To reinforce two thousand police, they nationalized 1,800 National Guard troops, imported four battalions of military police plus units of the 82nd Airborne, and concealed reserves in the basement of the Commerce Department. McNamara warned President Johnson that the jails available would not hold mass arrests that could stretch into thousands. Johnson discarded advice to be elsewhere, vowing that demonstrators "are not going to run me out of town," but then flummoxed his national security advisers by asking what would happen if he refused to seek reelection in 1968. ("You must not go down," pleaded Rusk.) In a pensive interview on Thursday, October 19, the President brazenly denied that he ever questioned or regretted the basic decisions to intervene and bomb in Vietnam. More candidly, he complained of sour results from his decision to present the war as a measured cause rather than a crusade against demons. "If history indicts us for Vietnam," Johnson predicted with a sigh, "it will be for fighting a war without trying to stir up patriotism."

On Friday, a day ahead of the Mobilization protests, William Sloane Coffin joined Dr. Spock and nine anxious peace counselors at the Justice Department. They presented statements of their complicity in breaches of the Selective Service Act, along with a briefcase containing 994 draft cards surrendered in ceremonies nationwide—all those from Boston plus 298 from California Resistance, forty-five from Chicago Resistance, and so on. "Dr. Coffin, am I being tendered something?" John McDonough asked blankly. The assistant deputy attorney general recoiled each time the Yale chaplain handed him the briefcase. Coffin tried to make light of the macabre standoff in their attempted surrender for multiple felonies, but Arthur Waskow, who had prepared himself for a life-changing arrest, exclaimed archly that McDonough was abusing his childhood respect for the law. "And you, sir, refuse the evidence?" he cried. "Where, man, is your oath of office?" The counselors left the briefcase untouched.

While demonstrators poured into Washington, the *Meridian Star* perceived a new curse attached to "the Friday after Friday the 13th." In the first civil rights convictions ever rendered by and against white Mississippians, jurors that morning reached guilty verdicts on seven of eighteen Klansmen, including Deputy Price and Imperial Wizard Sam Bowers. John Doar gave thanks and soon retired from eight arduous years in the Justice Department. King, heading for a Chicago concert with Belafonte, was "pleasantly surprised" by what he called "a first step in a thousand-mile journey."

Defiantly, the White Knights had intensified terror attacks in the face of the criminal charges. Just before the trial, they destroyed Temple Beth Israel in Jackson and the home of a Tougaloo College dean; afterward, they bombed the homes of a black minister, a rabbi, and a Polish family mistakenly believed to be Jewish. While free pending sentence, Bowers himself turned up once in action when a traffic constable stumbled on him with a .45-caliber submachine gun and a young passenger who later confessed a dozen Klan bombings. Bowers served six years under the weak federal statute that protected the exercise of civil rights, then resumed on parole in 1976 a professed calling as "preacher of Jesus the Galilean." (His Christian Identity sect held that Jesus was not a Jew but the incarnation of "lost" Aryan tribes.) It would be another twenty-two years before local officials tried and convicted him under state law for ordering the 1966 firebomb murder of Vernon Dahmer. And not until 2005 would the climate and conscience of Mississippi produce the first landmark of local jurisprudence in Neshoba County, with a jury verdict against seventy-nine-year-old Edgar Ray Killen for the three murders more than four decades earlier.

In Washington, during Saturday's speeches at the Lincoln Memorial, reporters observed a "sprinkling of Negroes" reach informal consensus not to join the ensuing confrontation. "We don't want to play Indian outside the white man's fort," John Lewis informed Mobilization leader David Dellinger, who led nearly fifty thousand remaining marchers across the Potomac to besiege the Pentagon with vigils, skirmishes, and bonfires for thirty-three hours. Demonstrators dropped flowers into the gun barrels of blockading soldiers, and fierce or stealthy forays sometimes breached one of the Pentagon entrances. Abbie Hoffman's hippie troupe failed to "exorcise" the gargantuan building by levitation, as merrily advertised, but they did urinate along its outer walls. Protest factions, though suffering volleys of tear gas and countercharges by club-wielding U.S. marshals, drew attention to themselves rather than government policy in Vietnam. Norman Mailer declared a new literary species for his quick book about the spirited joust, subtitled "History As a Novel, the Novel as History." Mailer was one of nearly seven hundred arrested, but none of the two hundred Wisconsin students was among them. Freshly traumatized by the bloody shock on their campus, many scorned the constraining faith of "liberals" that they could and should stop the war without violent systemic change, yet could not quite attack "enemy" soldiers so close across the lines. Some shared a premonition with *Times* columnist James Reston that obscene chants and banners vilifying President Johnson—"LBJ the Butcher"—would backfire "almost enough to retrieve his declining fortunes at the polls." At home in Madison, opposing students flocked to job interviews with Dow Chemical.

*   *   *

ALMOST UNNOTICED, King slipped into the aftershock of the Pentagon siege on Monday, October 23. His testimony before the Kerner Commission remained confidential, but it groped for anti-poverty tactics of "escalating nonviolence" somewhere between timid supplication and destructive riots. "Well," he told reporters outside, "I think that the time has come, if we can't get anything done otherwise, to camp right here in Washington just as they did with the Bonus March—just camp here and stay here by the thousands and thousands." These remarks, which the *Washington Post* called an "appeal to anarchy," earned no better public reception than his Washington concert with Belafonte and Aretha Franklin. During final stops that week in Philadelphia and Boston, secretary Dora McDonald asked Levison to console King through a worrisome despondence over the paltry crowds, and lawyer Chauncey Eskridge warned that the entire series "will be lucky to break even." In Boston, King discovered Bernard Lafayette in the process of taking another job because of SCLC's paperwork delays. "I thought you were coming to Atlanta," he pleaded, pausing to repair one of several logistical tangles. Helpers feverishly solicited a donated private plane to meet King in rural Iowa so he could honor a promise to address Sunday's fall convocation at tiny Grinnell College, where his mentor Benjamin Mays received an honorary degree, without flouting, hedging, or seeking even routine delay of the final court orders to surrender for jail on Monday.

He rushed home long enough to change into dungarees and return with three fellow defendants for an airport ceremony, on legal advice that they would become muted prisoners the moment they landed on Alabama soil. King told Atlanta reporters the sentence was "a small price to pay for the historic achievement" initiated in 1963 when "thousands of Negro citizens, facing dogs, fire hoses, mass arrests, and other outrages against human dignity, bore dramatic witness to the evils which pervaded in the most segregated city in our nation." At the same time, he cited the four dissenting Supreme Court Justices to excoriate the majority decision as churlish, vindictive, and dangerous. It was worse than jailing Boston patriots retroactively for dumping tea from Britain, because no theft or vandalism was at issue from the freedom marches. "As we leave for a Birmingham jail today," said King, "we call out to America: 'Take heed. Do not allow the Bill of Rights to become a prisoner of war.' " Armed Alabama deputies, who boarded the departing flight with King's party, asserted control on arrival to wave wide-eyed regular passengers out of the airplane through a double line of officers forming in the rain. A hundred movement supporters waited in the Birmingham terminal to greet the four prisoners, only to watch them hauled off by police cars that darted onto the runway. Photographers captured King carrying three books to jail under his arm: the Bible, an economics text, and *The Confessions of Nat Turner*. A rare, two-part review in the *New York Times* had just praised William Styron's historical novel for bringing "coherent voice to a catastrophe we hardly knew had happened," but black critics faulted the author for projecting too glibly a writer's hold on inner thoughts from the bloody 1831 slave rebellion. "I absorbed by osmosis," Styron maintained, "a knowledge of what it is to be a Negro."

Alarm radiated from an empty Birmingham jail Monday night, attracting an agitated crowd of five hundred until Sheriff Melvin Bailey acknowledged that he had diverted King to a facility eighteen miles away. No visitors were permitted there, but Tuesday's vigil outside a county jail in Bessemer featured a man praying as if possessed through a downpour, and by Wednesday the four prisoners were transferred secretly back downtown. With a smuggled camera, cellmate Wyatt Walker took a photograph of King staring through the bars. King complained of flu, and did not fulfill a notion to write a sequel for his Letter from Birmingham Jail. He made only tactical notes—including one for Harry Wachtel to reconvene at Union Seminary the fractious talks comparing Vietnam with the Six Day War in the Middle East—and he sketched a proposed "Bill of Rights for the Disadvantaged." His model was the 1944 GI Bill of Rights, and to a lesser degree the Bonus Act of 1936. The latter had passed over President Franklin Roosevelt's veto, reversing more than three years of sporadic government action to rout impoverished World War I veterans encamped in Washington. The GI Bill, which FDR passively and unhappily approved, helped transform the American economy with the offer of college tuition grants for 11 million World War II veterans. In jail, King began an opinion piece for the *New York Times,* arguing by analogy that the nation must take another leap of faith toward redress and opportunity.

Otherwise he sifted prison gossip about Birmingham authorities who, while interpreting the Supreme Court victory to mean that Negroes themselves were to blame for the lingering stigma of dogs and fire hoses, suffered with protesters actually in custody again. Deputies fretted over a prediction by one fortune-teller that buildings would be leveled after King's assassination on their watch. When a local judge obligingly cut short the sentence, a spontaneous Friday night mass meeting celebrated the freed prisoners at Tabernacle Baptist. "This looks like '63!" Rev. Ed Gardner shouted above the music. King's brother A.D. told cellblock stories. Abernathy roasted his lawyers for letting preachers go to jail, joking that he was "off the hook" on a reciprocal pledge to keep the lawyers out of hell. He claimed prison converts for the movement and regaled the crowd with his hardship pitch to white jailers: "Think what we live on—white potatoes, neck bones, pig feet, and hog snoots!" Abernathy's yarns coaxed mirth from King, who covered his mouth behind the pulpit and agreed to speak briefly despite the flu. "Our movement isn't over," he said. "Some of us are going to have to pack our little [jail] bags and make our way to Washington."

King returned to Cleveland for the off-year elections. A dozen SCLC staff members had been deployed there since the summer, when King himself averaged roughly two days per week dashing through registration rallies. On election night, November 7, candidate Carl Stokes left King and Abernathy in a hotel suite with a promise to summon them downstairs if he should become the first black mayor of a major city, the nation's seventh largest. They watched late returns gain what reporters called a narrow wonder—"Stokes, the great-grandson of a slave, defeated Seth Taft, the grandson of the 27th President of the United States"—but King slowly deflated when no signal came for him to join the televised victory statements. Andrew Young interpreted the rebuff as cold politics. Having imported allies to turn out an astonishing 75 percent of the isolated black wards, Stokes avoided association with controversial figures who might offend broader support. Stung, King asked Levison to meet him for consultation in Chicago, where he spoke over Veterans Day weekend. Levison had welcomed prior success in the Cleveland primary as a boost for King's public standing, saying progress there might answer critics who "tried to pronounce you dead in Chicago," just as Birmingham once rebutted claims that segregation had crushed him in Albany. Now Levison was obliged to shore up King's commitment to the role of prophet above politician.

In colonial Williamsburg, ending a 5,100-mile speaking tour on Vietnam, President Johnson was shown on November 12 to George Washington's front pew at the historic Bruton Parish Episcopal Church—organized 1633, completed 1715 in cruciform brick. Rev. Cotesworth Pinckney Lewis, descended from two signers of the Constitution, interrupted an orthodox sermon to address Johnson directly. "I feel presumptuous even in asking questions," he said. "But since there is a rather general consensus that something is wrong in Vietnam . . . we wonder if some logical, straightforward explanation might be given without endangering whatever military or political advantages we now enjoy." Lady Bird Johnson "turned to stone on the outside and boiled on the inside," she recalled, as Lewis expressed his plainspoken bafflement. He said most of the world considered the American role in distant Vietnam a neocolonial blunder of "appalling" civilian casualties, triple the military toll, while brave commanders felt "inhibited" by constraints they thought prolonged the conflict. "While pledging our loyalty," Lewis concluded, "we ask respectfully, why?" The Johnsons managed smiles as they shook hands from the postlude into a tempest. Virginia's governor called the sermon an unpardonable lapse of courtesy. Bruton's vestry rebuked its rector, who refused further comment, and members of Congress roundly denounced him for effrontery. Beneath command levels, an avalanche of citizen mail thanked Lewis for his candor, and almost 90 percent of Virginia correspondents scolded their governor for putting social deference above the stakes of war.

King departed for northern England to accept an honorary degree from the University of Newcastle Upon Tyne, known for Roman antiquities at the far outpost of Emperor Hadrian's stone border. He left his country stirred senseless by upheavals from silly to profound. The *New*

York State Journal of Medicine released a scientific study of young people who smoked dried banana peels, finding their craze entirely a "psychologic elaboration" because the chemicals were inert. The editors of *Newsweek,* openly proclaiming an advocacy stance for the first time, published a special issue on the crisis of race—"What Must Be Done"— with stories dissecting massive barriers to keep black people poor and invisible: "The Cold Fact Is That the Negro in America Is Not Really in America." *Newsweek's* task force recognized that the most immediate obstacle to its uphill agenda "is obviously Vietnam," but nothing made the war an exclusive or supreme priority. Indeed, for King, the cognitive force of *Newsweek* solidified two reasons behind his instinctive preference for a poor people's campaign. Whereas Vietnam protest strongly implied a negative or limited purpose to desist from war, the poverty crusade sought constructive change grounded in civil rights exhortations for America to "rise up and live out the true meaning of its creed." Tactically, antiwar protests already teemed with chaotic energy, including groups intoxicated by violence themselves, but the anti-poverty field remained fallow and fertile for movement discipline. King let Stanley Levison draft arguments why black people remained the vanguard of nonviolence, and dropped any pretense of neutrality about his next passion.

*   *   *

HE VOWED to lead a "camp-in" of poor people to Washington. "I'm on fire about the thing," King told seventy SCLC staff members at the Penn Conference Center in Frogmore, South Carolina. He said reflection and prayer made him wish they had extended their 1966 anti-slum campaign into Cicero, so that, by enduring the brutality that loomed there, they could have raised a hopeful standard of urban witness before the riots of 1967. King said they must rise above violent symptoms spreading from foreign war and domestic despair. At the week-long retreat, beginning on November 26, he warned that only hysteria looked for rage to sustain idealism. "Violence has been the inseparable twin of materialism, the hallmark of its grandeur," he said. "This is the one thing about modern civilization that I do not want to imitate." He confided that he had just met with Olympic athletes trying to craft a protest of racism for the Mexico City Summer Games, only to find them disillusioned and abused by a black power conference at which delegates threatened to beat each other. Their ordeal underscored a lesson for King that "hate has no limits." He said, "I refuse to hate. Many of our inner conflicts are rooted in hate." King declared a moral imperative to dispel national hostility now clouding miracles from the civil rights movement. If resistance in Washington exceeded the travail of Birmingham or Selma, he pledged to intensify sacrifice accordingly. "So I say to you tonight that I have taken a vow," he announced at the retreat. "I, Martin Luther King, take thee, nonviolence, to be my wedded wife."

Bevel objected that no dramatic plunge could rescue a misguided strategy. Predicting that Americans would ignore the "camp-in," he argued that Vietnam rightly demanded the focused energy of a movement devoted to democratic values. Bevel disputed King's constitutional basis for a campaign to raise the standard of living, and preached so vigorously that FBI intelligence reports of leadership friction reached President Johnson within days: "[Bevel] addressed the retreat at great length opposing King's plans. . . . King was visibly angry at Bevel for opposing him in this regard." Jesse Jackson criticized King more subtly. He said the plan rested too narrowly on demonstrations and support from the poor, then broke away to meet top investment bankers in New York. An Episcopal bishop had interceded by telephone and letter for King to excuse Jackson from South Carolina in light of his precocious skill with important donors—"his ability to confront without repelling." Hosea Williams, meanwhile, opened a third line of attack. While reserving judgment on the Washington campaign itself, he alone rebelled when King went around the room for endorsement of the new SCLC executive director, William Rutherford, lately of Zurich, Switzerland. "I can't support you," said Williams. He exploded against every credential King cited for Rutherford as the proven administrator SCLC grievously had lacked—his management companies, his roots in Southside Chicago, his doctorate from the Sorbonne. Williams bridled against supervision by a bigshot virtual foreigner without a day's experience in civil rights. Privately, he answered King's wounded appeals with a raw howl against Rutherford: "That nigger don't know nothin' about niggers!"

Andrew Young settled the retreat with an analysis of civil disobedience that might arise in Washington. More than Birmingham's blatant color line, or Selma's biased voting standards, Young said the staff should prepare for actions to explain and carry out "noncooperation" with otherwise just laws—targeted demonstrations to dramatize smothered rights and misplaced priorities, general ones to impede normal life in the capital. When staff members examined Young about philosophical distinctions, or questioned the value of blocking access to the Agriculture Department, King urged them to work through their misgivings. "The great burden of this will be on you," he said. "I can't do it by myself. Andy can't do it by himself." He said he would try to neutralize rivals and doubters in advance by letting them "curse me out about the ineffectiveness of this." No one yet could show that nonviolence was unsuited to intractable economic issues, he argued, any more than a single bucket on a burning house proved water could not quench fire. King pictured starting with one delegation of unemployed people to present demands for jobs or income at the Labor Department, then spread out to lobby Congress while other poor groups made their way to Washington from ghettoes and Indian reservations and white Appalachia and rural plantations, some walking or riding mules "through the tough areas, that's drama right there." They could invite allies to join nonviolent witness in the capital—clergy, college students, President Johnson's poverty experts, *Newsweek* readers, the peace movement. "Now they may not respond," said King. "I can't promise that, but I do think we've got to go for broke this time." The alternative was surrender or riots. "I figure our riots last about four days," he said forlornly, "and then you see these helpless mothers standing in line trying to get some milk for their children."

King and Young stepped aside beneath the Penn Center pine trees to check for culture shock in Rutherford, who had expatriated to Europe in 1949 with a steamer trunk and a one-way boat ticket, pulled apart by race. (His sister worked as a maid; his parents rebuffed white friends he brought home as one of only seven black students at the University of Chicago.) Eighteen years later in Geneva, when Rutherford translated spontaneously for French and German reporters who surrounded King at the *Pacem in Terris* convention, the chance introduction turned into a swift agreement for him to sell or license his businesses, resign the publicity chairmanship of the Swiss-American Chamber of Commerce, and leap home into the revolution he had missed. The new partners exchanged confidences. King brushed aside Rutherford's cautionary disclosure of car theft buried in his childhood past as a Chicago gang apprentice called "Wild Bill." When Rutherford confessed discomfort to see his revered chief executive sit through blistering criticism from subordinates, King replied that movements ran on tempered lunacy, which demanded respect for anyone who inspired others to risk nonviolence. Bevel should be accepted as a free spirit, King advised, but he greeted Rutherford with two secret assignments steeped in suspicion.

First, he asked how Hosea Williams and SCLC comptroller James Harrison managed to keep an extra apartment on their meager salaries, and whether Williams was involved in any embezzlement to pay the rent. "I want you to find out," King said. Second, he charged Rutherford to determine whether Jesse Jackson's vexing independence sprang from breakaway ambition. "I either want him in SCLC or out," he ordered bluntly. "You go whichever way you want." Rutherford promised to hone SCLC for King's purpose so long as he kept the one chisel he had demanded: the unfettered authority to fire staff. "Even Lillian?" asked King, of the indispensable office manager Lillian Hunter, then numbly confirmed his assent.

The poverty campaign stagnated all week in the Frogmore workshops. Only Bernard Lafayette, SCLC's new program director, pitched himself into the operational plans for his mandate, and Rutherford, the enthusiastic technician, found the mood of his native country distinctly unfavorable. ("Public preoccupation with Vietnam is stunning," he told Young.) King worked from a blackboard, batting down objections. "The day of the demonstration isn't over," he said. "And I say to you that many of our confusions are dissolved—they are distilled in demonstrations." He denied that the campaign slogan, "Jobs or Income," was indecisive or inadequate. Their public goals had been simple in Birmingham and Selma, King insisted, and the program of Jesus himself boiled down to the word repent. "You see, I don't care if we don't name the demand," King declared. "Just *go* to Washington!" He said more than once that this might be the last campaign, because poverty was bigger than race. One of King's remarks—"the victory we seek, we'll never win"—provoked an eruption from Hosea Williams that it was wrong to stir up vulnerable people for a losing battle. ("I got really upset," Williams recalled. "I just get cooking.") King pleaded with the staff not to shrink from lost causes or association with outcasts—"I would hope that we in SCLC are the custodians of hope"—in exhortations that rambled at times into distracted theology. "I'm not talking about some kind of superficial optimism which is little more than magic," said King. "I'm talking about that kind of hope that has an 'in spite of' quality." A distinctive rendition of one Bible verse bubbled up: "There is something in the book of Revelation which says, 'Make an end on what you have left, even if it's near nothing.' "

King overrode doubt and dissent. He went straight home to a press conference on Monday, December 4—exactly eight months since taking on the furors of Vietnam at Riverside Church, one day before the twelfth anniversary of his debut speech for the bus boycott. Unlike the reluctant spokesman whose thunderclap oratory first caught up with Montgomery's local protest, now he conjured up a resurgence by sheer force of will. "The Southern Christian Leadership Conference will lead waves of the nation's poor and disinherited to Washington, DC next spring," King announced. The campaign would begin with three thousand pilgrims "trained in the discipline of nonviolence," and last until the country responded. "We don't know what will happen," he declared. "They may try to run us out. They did it with the Bonus Marches years ago, you remember." Fielding questions about potential clashes, he vowed to desist only if the protesters themselves indulged in violence. "The Negro leader's mood seemed deeply pessimistic," reported the *New York Times,* and the front page heralded trouble: "Dr. King Planning to Disrupt Capital in Drive for Jobs."

CHAPTER 37

New Year Trials

December 1967–January 1968

LEADERSHIP conflict seized the country while King labored to galvanize his small staff. On November 26, far from the obscure retreat at Frogmore, Senator Robert Kennedy vacillated openly between apology and disgust. "We're killing innocent people because we don't want to have the war fought on American soil," he told television viewers, "or because they're 12,000 miles away and they might get 11,000 miles away. Do we have that right?" When journalists pressed him to reconcile his scathing reproach over Vietnam with his public support for President Johnson's reelection, Kennedy shrugged. "I don't know what I can do to prevent that, or what I should do that is anything different," he said, "other than try to get off the earth in some way." His morbid candor silenced the CBS broadcast of *Face the Nation* until its moderator found a soothing comment: "Senator, nobody wants you to get off the earth, obviously."

Kennedy said personal history made him reject overtures to run in 1968 against his late brother's successor. "It would immediately become a personality struggle," he declared, and paint him "an overly ambitious figure trying to take the nomination away from President Johnson, who deserves it." He welcomed a potential quest by Senator Eugene McCarthy, however, to provide a healthy political choice for millions of people who opposed the war, and "Dump Johnson" activist Allard Lowenstein celebrated McCarthy's agreement to run on *Meet the Press* the following Sunday, December 3. "Aren't you still waiting for Bobby?" a panelist objected, alluding to Lowenstein's chronic solicitation of Kennedy. "In fact, isn't Senator McCarthy still waiting for Bobby?" Lowenstein gamely insisted that no citizens' challenge to an incumbent wartime President could afford hesitation. The previous night, before the insurgent Conference of Concerned Democrats at Chicago's Sheraton-Blackstone Hotel, Lowenstein had lifted 12,000 delegates repeatedly to their feet with his firebrand eloquence on bedrock democracy—blasting Vietnam as stealthy moral corruption by executive tyranny—while the candidate-in-waiting seethed offstage. Senator McCarthy, unhappy to be eclipsed by his own introduction, followed with learned but meandering remarks on the folly of war and the peril of dissent. His announcement projected a whimsical reserve, suggesting that Johnson's hunger for power was itself a root cause of woe in Vietnam. Intense public scrutiny generated both admirers and detractors for McCarthy's poetic detachment, which seemed either a fresh virtue or quixotic flaw. Circumstance sparked friction between him and Kennedy as reluctant, rival puritans—one barely in the race, the other still out.

Quite apart from electoral revolt, Lady Bird Johnson bemoaned a pall of loss that descended with the final month of strain for Robert McNamara. On two successive days, he came alone to Johnson with appeals for reduced military action in Vietnam. The President withheld McNamara's stark shift from all national security officials, including the Wise Men consultants who ratified the escalation strategy unaware. For McNamara, the suppression of his views breached confidence and raised tension "to the breaking point." For Johnson, signs of emotional distress in McNamara led to whispers that "we could even have another Forrestal on our hands," in an ominous reference to the breakdown and suicide of the first Defense Secretary, James Forrestal. Johnson ordered National Security Adviser Walt Rostow to collect evaluations of McNamara's written dissent without disclosing his authorship, and the Wise Men rejected it almost uniformly. "I can think of nothing *worse* than the suggested program—stating that we are going to 'stabilize' our level of military effort and halting the bombing," wrote Justice Abe Fortas. "This is an invitation to slaughter. *It will, indeed, produce demands in this country to withdraw*—and in fact, it must be appraised for what it is: *a step in the process of withdrawal.*" President Johnson, buttressed anew with secret consensus, let slip to reporters that the Defense Secretary was off to head the World Bank. This amounted to deft political euthanasia for Vietnam's chief architect, and McNamara's puzzlement would survive in a stricken memoir nearly three decades later: "I do not know to this day whether I quit or was fired."

The President retained the haunted skepticism he had expressed privately for years, especially about the recurrent promise of victory by more and bigger bombs. "I am beginning to agree with Bob McNamara," he told military commanders, "that it does not appear the targets are worth the loss in planes." Having ruled out both withdrawal and stalemate, Johnson simply demanded what McNamara no longer could sustain: public faith that battle was securing control of Vietnam. Officials followed the prime recommendation of his Wise Men to "show some progress." They emphasized themes to supplant what McGeorge Bundy called a negative drone of "deaths and dangers to the sons of mothers and fathers with no picture of a result in sight." General Westmoreland publicly predicted troops could start home within two years. Ellsworth Bunker, the new U.S. ambassador in South Vietnam, announced momentum to "accelerate the rate of progress," and seldom did military judgment strike a clanging note. Colonel John Paul Vann, a legendary warrior who had spent five years developing counterguerrilla strategy in Vietnam, was feted during home leave until the National Security Adviser asked for private assurance that the worst fighting could be over in six months. "Oh, hell no, Mister Rostow," Vann replied on December 8. "I'm a born optimist. I think we can hold out longer than that." His plucky gloom stung Walt Rostow, who remarked curtly that such an iconoclast did not belong in government service. (Vann returned to Vietnam duty, and would be killed there in 1972.)

President Johnson restrained an impulse to brand the war critics unpatriotic, but he did prod his government to harass them in private. He reacted viscerally to King's first fund-raising appeal for the anti-poverty drive on Washington, for instance, which framed SCLC's campaign in language drafted by Stanley Levison: "Nonviolence can be adapted to militant forms of protest that embody creative disruption while avoiding physical or moral destruction. . . . The riots and the cancer of war can destroy the democratic core of American life. However, there are constructive forces that can be organized." On this letter, the President himself scrawled specific instructions to investigate retaliation through the tax code. Sheldon Cohen, Commissioner of the Internal Revenue Service, replied on blank stationery that his agents had audited King and his SCLC foundation "for the last three or four years" but found no legal leverage. Justice Fortas and his wife, tax lawyer Carol Agger, secretly concurred that King's conduct would not sustain fraud charges or revocation of the tax-exempt status they helped secure in happier times. Almost simultaneously, Johnson received a classified FBI report that the Ford Foundation soon would announce a grant of $230,000 to King for leadership training of minority preachers in scattered cities. When the President asked Hoover for an explanation, being unwilling to inquire directly, Hoover concealed the painful truth that McGeorge Bundy at Ford had rebuffed FBI maneuvers to scuttle the grant. Instead, DeLoach fed Johnson a bald tale that the softhearted Bundy had earmarked no less than $4 million for King until the FBI silently intervened.

A recompense to Hoover was the signal of the President's controlled fury, despite King's vital support for his Great Society agenda, which added a margin of safety for the FBI's intensified clandestine attacks. Hoover listed King and SCLC prominently among targets in a formal directive for all FBI offices "to expose, disrupt, misdirect, discredit, or otherwise neutralize the activities of black nationalist hate-type organizations." This was the third full-scale COINTELPRO (Hoover's acronym for "counterintelligence program") in FBI history. Already agents were leaking propaganda to favored journalists—"FBI's Report on King Ready"—and supplying grist for a lengthy congressional speech by Representative John Ashbrook that portrayed King as a "power-hungry tyrant." In December, Hoover explored ways to revive the King wiretaps shut down on Johnson's orders.

* * *

ON SUNDAY, December 10, King drew an overflow crowd in Montgomery for a ninetieth anniversary service at his first church. "Even some of the members are here for the first time," joked the current pastor, Murray Branch. From the pulpit, King introduced his diagnosis of a nation sick with racism, "obsessive materialism," and militarism— "headed toward its spiritual doom"—then preached on the meaning of hope. Focusing on the middle word from Paul's biblical litany of faith, hope, and love, he distinguished hope from desire along a social dimension, and argued that real hope could not be selfish. "You may desire a new beautiful house, but you hope for freedom," said King. "That has a 'we' quality. You may desire sex, but you hope for peace." He parsed hope from optimism and magical expectation by invoking internal commitment. "Genuine hope involves the recognition that what is hoped for is in some sense already present," said King. He tried several illustrations and quoted Jesus: "The kingdom of God is in you." He recalled discussions with "some of my nationalist friends" in which King claimed to pinpoint at hope's swinging gate the fateful divide between doctrines of violence and nonviolence. Finally, he appealed to history's foremost specialists in hope. "They were our slave fore-parents," he said. "Think about it." He contrasted the brutal slave centuries with the miraculous vitality born in spirituals. "Every now and then, I feel discouraged living every day under the threat of death," said King, opening his peroration on a balm of hope in Gilead. After the somber address, he followed the congregation from Dexter Avenue Baptist into close view of a Ku Klux Klan rally just outside at the foot of Alabama's capitol. Grand Dragon James Spears denounced draft dodgers, gun control laws, and "Martin Lucifer King," plus Dean Rusk for permitting an interracial marriage. A wiry Klansman in hooded regalia paraded grimly with a misspelled placard: "Our Forefathers Got Us the Rights to Bare Arms."

King rushed to Chicago for another speech that evening, then made his way back home. At a Wednesday press conference in Atlanta, he introduced SCLC program director Bernard Lafayette with the mandate to coordinate a spring "Poor People's Campaign for Jobs or Income." News stories emphasized that Lafayette, twenty-seven, was a SNCC founder and Freedom Rider who had "left the student committee before it embraced the black power doctrine." King also presented William Rutherford, his new executive director for internal administration, and an FBI wiretap in New York picked up ripples of impact. "He's done in a week what hasn't been done in two or three years," King told Stanley Levison that afternoon. "He's really working hard." Staff workers went through mail stacked away randomly in boxes, finding contributions unopened for months and a yellowed letter of introduction from Rutherford himself. Tracers discovered stray rental cars in Virginia and Kentucky. Rutherford dismissed the daughter of an SCLC board member for running up huge entertainment bills during the Belafonte concert tour. He confronted Atlanta's only black financial broker over his discretionary investment of SCLC funds in gold Krugerrands from apartheid South Africa, and when the broker contrarily observed that no one ever questioned the dividend checks, fired him, too.

"Hosea offered his resignation again," King told Levison. Williams hotly defended his stance with an uncharacteristic flurry of memos, including three long ones on December 15 alone. "I would also like to register my indignation and displeasure at your attempt to evaluate my character," he advised Rutherford. That same week, when Jesse Jackson skipped the first executive staff meeting on the poverty campaign, Rutherford imposed a system of fines for unexcused absence and tardiness. "You promised me your full cooperation," he complained in a letter of notice, which, while conceding that fines "appear a bit juvenile," asked how they could organize all America if SCLC could not assemble its own staff. With Andrew Young, Rutherford flew to parley with Jackson in Chicago, leaving behind a positive report on his second confidential assignment from King. Locks now secured James Harrison's finance office, and a new transaction window allowed SCLC employees to conduct business without wandering among desks stacked with money. Discreet audits balanced the daily cash flow, satisfying Rutherford that no movement funds were being siphoned into the hideaway apartment for Harrison and Hosea Williams. Thus reassured, King lost interest in the mysterious luxury. Neither he nor anyone else at SCLC suspected that Harrison had been a government spy for two years—meeting agents furtively with tips and purloined reports, more than doubling his salary from King with FBI payments to his informant account coded AT-1387-R.

* * *

ON FRIDAY night, December 15, core issues of violence and power attracted unusual press interest to a forum of one hundred intellectuals in New York's Greenwich Village. "Generally speaking, violence always arises out of impotence," declared Hannah Arendt, author of *The Human Condition* and *Eichmann in Jerusalem*. She disputed the close association of power with violence, as in the common definition of government itself as a monopoly of legitimate physical force. ("All politics is a struggle for power; the ultimate kind of power is violence," wrote sociologist C. Wright Mills.) She also doubted classical doctrines that put violence at the heart of natural processes, such as Karl Marx's vital birth pangs of history and Georges Sorel's essential shock for social innovation. "And now we hear from Sartre that not labor but violence creates man," Arendt caustically observed. She argued against "mirages of violence," and invoked a surprise warning from Frantz Fanon, the African voice for anti-colonial warfare, that brutality most often churned into cycles of revenge. Fellow panelists praised Arendt but qualified her sensibility with slivers of justification for the sword. Author Conor Cruise

O'Brien wryly quoted an Irish agitator that "violence is the best way of insuring a hearing for moderation." Linguist Noam Chomsky said he could point easily to circumstances "in which violence does eliminate a greater evil."

Writer Susan Sontag objected from the floor that theoretical gymnastics dodged the burning issue of their time: "whether we in this room, and the people we know, are going to be engaged in violence." Chomsky responded with three cogent reasons why protesters should remain nonviolent: practical futility against superior government force, political recognition that "violence antagonizes the uncommitted," and understanding that "immense harm is done to the individual who participates in violent action." Against Chomsky, dissenters cited undercurrents of rebellion gaining strength since Watts. Indeed, the *New York Times* published front-page survey results that same weekend— "A White Liberal Shift on Integration"—indicating that black power doctrines were becoming fashionable. Intellectuals warmed to rationales that riot and separate development could relieve humiliation. Thomas Pettigrew of Harvard sighed that academic supporters were turning against integration just when opponents began to give ground. The *Times* quoted Daniel Moynihan mimicking professorial barbs across the color line: "Well, you just won Newark, so we'll take Princeton." Norman Mailer expressed consoling gusto that "war may be the last of the tonics." Bayard Rustin bemoaned a precedent for smoke screen disengagement, asserting that when Reconstruction had exposed the urgent need to include four million ex-slaves in the nation's homestead offer of forty acres and a mule, "that was difficult to bring about, so people turned their interest away from the Negro."

Tom Hayden challenged Hannah Arendt at the Greenwich Village forum. "You may put me in the position of a leper," he said, "but I say a case can be made for violence in the peace movement." Still youthful at twenty-seven, Hayden had gone to jail in the civil rights movement before helping create SDS in 1962, and, from rare experience as a white poverty worker based in Newark, he also defended the violence of rioters "getting mattresses and clothes and a supply of liquor for the winter." Pointing to historical examples in Spain and Cuba, he insisted that if dissidents laid a strong political foundation, violence could be legitimate and positive. Besides, he argued, American protesters had exhausted peaceful democratic channels. "It seems to me," Hayden told Arendt, "that until you can begin to show—not in language and not in theory, but in action—that you can put an end to the war in Vietnam, and an end to American racism, you can't condemn the violence of others who can't wait for you." Like Stokely Carmichael, he won much of the crowd with his upstart passion, and the eminent philosopher struggled to articulate her point that history's forward push on the strength of nonviolence was sadly overlooked. "And if we look at the revolutions that have taken place," Arendt added, "I'm not at all sure that the success has been based on the violence."

Over the next year, spurred by wars and nearly worldwide political crisis, Arendt would rethink her positions, finding it "insufficient to say that power and violence are not the same." In her book, *On Violence,* she framed an original thesis against assumptions ingrained from high theory down to common instincts in everyday life. "Power and violence are opposites," she asserted. "Where the one rules absolutely, the other is absent. . . . Violence can destroy power; it is utterly incapable of creating it." Arendt debunked violence. She omitted the ritual draping of force with noble ambition and moral regret, to proclaim instead a dawning historical reality of impotent destruction. She defined violence as the negation of consent, which is the constructive material of modern politics, and branded as "philosophical prejudice" the belief that violence by armies and movie heroes is a necessary evil toward greater good. "Such time-honored opinions have become dangerous," Arendt wrote, "for the simple reason that they inspire hope and dispel fear—a treacherous hope used to dispel legitimate fear."

* * *

A WEEK before Christmas, President Johnson composed a unique "Memorandum for the File" on McNamara's written defection from the administration's Vietnam strategy. "I have read it, and studied it, with utmost care," he wrote, then set forth why he believed the stabilization plan "would be read in both Hanoi and the United States as a sign of weakening will." Johnson treated his memo like a final testament—isolated from staff review, preserved with a note tasking National Security Adviser Walt Rostow to "read the attached *very carefully*"—and left the next day for an odyssey abroad. From funeral services for the late Australian prime minister Harold Holt, and war talks in Melbourne with Asian leaders, he veered north for a ten-hour flight to Khorat Air Base in Thailand, where he saluted hastily assembled American pilots at midnight: "A mere handful of you men are pinning down several hundred thousand North Vietnamese." After a similar speech to enlisted air mechanics before dawn, Johnson flew on to review troops in South Vietnam by mid-morning that Saturday, December 23—"We're not going to yield, and we're not going to shimmy!"—then headed west by surprise, dragging a planeload of reporters infuriated over the blind itinerary. A one-hour runway summit in Pakistan interrupted airborne logistical snarls radioed back secretly from Rome. To avoid Italian war protesters, massed already on rumors of an impromptu visit, Johnson transferred into a helicopter Saturday night for an unrehearsed garden landing inside the walls of Vatican City. He hurried with a lone aide to meet Paul VI in the papal library.

For seventy-five minutes, Johnson described a war policy aimed toward peace so that the United States could return to human priorities in education, health, and justice. "My right hand keeps the pressure steady," he told the Pope, "and with my left hand we seek negotiations." On the premise that "Hanoi is simply not going to the conference table," the President mounted a sensitive request for the Vatican to convince South Vietnam's minority Catholic rulers, including the new President Nguyen Van Thieu and most of Thieu's fellow military officers, that they must initiate their own secret accommodations with the Vietcong. While Johnson pressed the perilous scheme to split the Vietnamese Communists politically, North from South, Paul VI noticed one sentence in the joint statement predrafted for reporters: "We will never surrender South Vietnam to aggression or attack." He objected gently. "I very clearly understand your good intentions and good hopes," said the Pope, "but you must understand I can never agree to war." On the contrary, he suggested a halt in American bombs—"to make it a more defensive war instead of an offensive war. It will strengthen your moral position in the world." Johnson refused the Pope's plea to extend the upcoming holiday truce, citing the unified contention of his military leaders that Ho Chi Minh would exploit any chance to move reinforcements safely in "trucks lined up bumper-to-bumper." During a thirty-seven-day bombing pause, the President charged, the Vietnamese Communists had amassed a seven-month supply of equipment to kill American soldiers.

Paul VI indirectly questioned the vise grip of war logic. "Where do they get their men, their means, their matériel?" he asked.

Johnson dodged the hint of popular cooperation against him. "By terror they are recruiting in the South," he replied, "and they are now down to fourteen-year-old boys." The President, insisting that his enemy was militarily desperate, nevertheless pushed his politically desperate idea for the Pope to induce settlement talks by South Vietnamese Catholic allies, "in their own way." The Pontiff said that he would do anything possible. They both knew that the South Vietnamese leaders, viewing contact with Communists as suicidal treason, preferred to rely on American arms. Johnson secured permission to release their joint statement "with the one sentence removed," and rushed back to Air Force One. It was still Saturday of the longest presidential day on record, which one bleary-eyed White House assistant later called "a Phineas Fogg adventure." The homeward flight again chased the spin of the earth to reach Washington early December 24, bearing a Christmas Eve message centered on President Johnson's inexhaustible desire to resolve the Vietnam conflict. He soon exploded with rage, however, over news reports from Vatican sources that the Pope questioned his commitment to peace.

* * *

New Year celebrations displayed a culture of youthful exuberance shadowed by anxiety. The national census meter clicked proudly past two hundred million citizens heading into 1968, which would be the first year in history without a legal execution anywhere in the United States, state or federal. The price of a first-class postage stamp rose on January 7 from 5 to 6 cents. Measured from its first official casualty, the American military effort in Vietnam became six years old, and within months would pass the Revolution of 1775–81 to become the nation's longest war, but the murky status of earlier deaths in Asia left the starting point shrouded in dispute. Appropriately, Vietnam struck many Americans as a terrible undertow from the distant haze. Year-end reviews put the cumulative toll at 15,900 U.S. soldiers killed and 99,000 wounded. While few anticipated that 1968 alone would approach those totals, or would become the watershed of political assassination and upheaval at home, apprehensions pointed to a bloody year. General Westmoreland sent six thousand Marines to hold the isolated mountain fortress of Khe Sanh from forty thousand North Vietnamese, touching off jittery analogies with the decisive French surrender at nearby Dien Bien Phu.

Domestic advisers inside the White House debated whether the President's January message on civil rights should state forthrightly that "full non-discrimination may take as long as a generation to achieve." Opponents feared such a slow timetable "gives ammunition to the Black

Power types," who considered the Great Society a fraud. Proponents favored realism over Pollyanna dreams, hoping to cultivate patience for long-haul progress despite setbacks and scars. In Mississippi, Robert G. Clark of Holmes County persevered that month to become the twentieth century's first black member of the legislature. He skipped the inaugural banquets for lack of an invitation, borrowed a car to trail the official parade, stood alone beneath those seated for the platform ceremonies, and followed his elected peers inside to take the oath from an isolated desk—all without being addressed—then survived decades of adjustment to become speaker pro tempore in 1992.

In New York, the U.S. Equal Employment Opportunity Commission opened 1968 with hearings on a void of minority faces in television, newspaper, subway, and billboard advertisements. Media executives, pleading helplessness to affect images projected by their sponsors, stressed their internal commitments to diversify. "Immediately following World War II we determined to search actively for non-white employees," testified CBS vice president William Fitts, but he conceded meager results above the mailroom, and CBS hired its first black on-camera correspondent, Hal Walker, nine days after the hearing. John Mortimer, personnel director for the *New York Times,* suffered withering questions about the contrast between his paper's workforce and its crusading editorials. "I don't believe so," he replied, when asked if the *Times* ever had employed a Puerto Rican reporter. Clifford Alexander, the newly appointed EEOC chairman, confirmed reports that investment firms had just broken a color bar against sending black clerks or messengers onto the traders' floor. "My understanding," said a vice president of Bache & Company, "was that we were the first company to do so." Witnesses established that sixty of ninety-one New York City employment agencies still accepted test job orders for a "white Gentile secretary," and some prominent advertisers confined their goals well short of hiring any minority professionals. "We have no segregated facilities," testified Frederick Moseley of the Morgan Guaranty Trust. Before 1970, when the New York Stock Exchange accredited its first black member,* leaders in Congress would secure Alexander's early res-

---

* Joseph L. Searles. King's lawyer Clarence Jones was an allied member through his partnership in a NYSE firm. Muriel Siebert became the first female member in 1967. Beneath the ownership level, Merrill Lynch had hired three black men in 1965 to integrate its sales force of 2,250 stockbrokers.

ignation from the EEOC for badgering employers beyond their pace of comfort.

In Washington, J. Edgar Hoover announced that Communist leaders "can look back on 1967 with a degree of satisfaction." News analysts observed that his yearly report, which consolidated fearful threats from subversion, antiwar protest, and racial agitation, converted the acknowledged scarcity of real Communists into a more sophisticated danger. Nothing would please national enemies more, he warned, "than to witness a continuation of widespread opposition, especially non-Communist opposition, to the Government's policy in Vietnam." He said the parallel surge of black power "has created a climate of unrest, and has come to mean to many Negroes the 'power' to riot, burn, loot, and kill." Privately, Hoover launched a coordinated alarm. On January 2, he formally requested new wiretaps on King. The next day he sent President Johnson a classified blueprint based on informant reports from James Harrison, listing the fifteen cities and five rural areas from which King sought volunteers for civil disobedience in Washington that spring, together with the intended distribution of forty-six recruiters chosen thus far. On January 4, without notifying the White House, Hoover ordered FBI field offices to develop files on each staff member and volunteer for a new clandestine operation coded POCAM (for "poverty campaign"), designed to stop King in a specialized thrust of the FBI's COINTELPRO against "Black Nationalist/Hate Groups."

Government pressure struck from another quarter on January 5, when the Justice Department filed criminal charges against five of the adults who had facilitated the surrender of nearly a thousand draft cards the previous fall. King addressed blaring headlines—"SPOCK IN-DICTED"—with a wistful air for the clear-cut moral choice. "I wish I did not have my ministerial exemption," he declared in his Sunday sermon. "And I say to the federal government, or anybody else, they can do to me what they did to Dr. Spock, and William Sloane Coffin, my good friend the chaplain of Yale. They can just as well get ready to convict me." All the next week, through speeches from Minnesota into North Dakota, King resisted overtures to join new Vietnam rallies with Spock because of his lingering sponsorship by National Conference for New Politics groups that had organized the venomous Labor Day fiasco in Chicago. More uncomfortably, King refused to ask the defendants to accept prison rather than contest the prosecution, but he did permit an accompanying legal adviser to do so at a January 11 caucus in New York.

Harry Wachtel said standard defense strategy would collapse a drama of conscience into protracted litigation about the technical limits of dissent, forfeiting a rare chance to magnify the impact of antiwar sentiment. Coffin at least initially agreed, having aimed the draft card ceremonies toward being imprisoned with otherwise obscure young draft resisters. However, newly retained defense lawyers were scandalized by the notion of surrendering to the government's draconian conspiracy indictment, and their professional zeal—to fight, win, and keep clients out of prison—bowled over the traumatized, conflicted defendants. King expressed only general support, and justified his reticence to Wachtel. "I can't tell another man when to go to jail," he said.

At a press conference the next morning in the Belmont Plaza Hotel, reporters lost interest when Coffin declared his resolve "to confront the government in the courts of the United States in the traditional American way." King salvaged news—"Dr. King Calls for Antiwar Rally in Capital"—by announcing a second pilgrimage of CALCAV clergy in February. "Either we will end the war in Vietnam," King said, "or many of our most sensitive citizens must be sent to jail." In the Spock-Coffin case, celebrity lawyers would dominate the summer conspiracy trial in Boston by presenting the defendants as strangers to protest and each other. James St. Clair, counsel for Coffin, offered testimony that the collected draft cards actually expedited conscription by pre-identifying miscreants. The radical attorney Leonard Boudin disputed every action charged to Spock, who recorded surprise that "somebody brought up as goody-goody as I was could go to sleep at my own trial for a federal crime." When Telford Taylor, the former chief prosecutor at Nuremberg, won a jury verdict of acquittal, his client Marcus Raskin collapsed in tearful regret while the four co-defendants welcomed convictions that would be overturned later on appeal. In the end, legal tactics sacrificed civil disobedience to vindicate the First Amendment. By contrast, seminarian Barry Johnson of CALCAV's New York staff would answer his summer draft notice chained to eight adult supporters, including Rabbi Balfour Brickner and the mother of a soldier killed in Vietnam, praying for the Army to choose: arrest them together, or cut Johnson away from his "co-conspirators." Officials at the Whitehall Induction Center ignored the tangled implications and never prosecuted Johnson, as government lawyers avoided controversy that would advertise military coercion for an unpopular war.

* * *

KING FLEW to San Francisco for weekend speeches. On Sunday, January 14, he and Andrew Young drove to the Santa Rita Rehabilitation Center in Oakland, where nonviolent teams were incarcerated again for anti-draft sit-ins—their sentences bumped up this time from ten days to three months. The visitors caused a commotion on the female cellblock that housed Joan Baez with her mother, and King hardly exchanged greetings before a regular inmate bounded around the corner with a scrap of paper and a pencil stub. Guards quickly took her away to lockdown penalties without the autograph, but the inmate broke into dance with ecstatic cries that she did not care because she met King and shook his hand. Her shouts spurred a chorus from other cells imploring King to right wrongs, improve the food, bring a good lawyer, and check on neglected children.

The noise did not die down until he reached an isolated cell in the men's wing. From solitary, Ira Sandperl interrupted a report on the outside world to suggest a wholly restructured anti-poverty campaign. "Don't go to Washington," he advised with customary fervor, warning of centralized corruption there, urging demonstrations instead where poor people lived. As King tried to justify the capital as a proper fulcrum for response, Sandperl felt a silencing contrast between the well-tailored figure in starched cuffs and the face of weary depression. King asked a favor. "When I'm in jail in Washington," he said, "come visit me there." Sight of him on departure prompted a round of shouts from the male inmates, including one jaunty plea that stuck in King's memory: "Doctor, you all be sure to fix it up now so I can get me a job when I get out of here." Emerging from Santa Rita into foggy rain and startling applause, King managed a short pep talk on Vietnam and poverty. "I might say that I see these two struggles as one struggle," he said, and closed by asking the informal street vigil to "join in the old Negro spiritual, 'I ain't gonna study war no more.'" With Young, King took a midnight flight through Dallas and reached home early on January 15.

They arrived late and exhausted for King's morning presentation at Ebenezer. Some sixty members of the SCLC staff were gathered from scattered posts with their travel possessions, ready to disperse straight from Atlanta to recruiting assignments for the poverty campaign. Bill Rutherford's summons had described a mandatory workshop of crisp final instructions—"it is imperative"—but King labored more broadly to overcome festering doubt and confusion about why they must go to Washington. He thanked Daddy King and others for fill-in speeches to cover his tardiness. He made a faltering joke about the tepid response of friends with their coats still on—"they act like it's cold in my church"—and betrayed rare unease in a defensive speech.

Unemployment statistics could not capture the plight of poor people, he argued, nor did the popular lure of riots and black power supersede SCLC methods. "Riots just don't pay off," said King. He pronounced them an objective failure beyond morals or faith. "For if we say that power is the ability to effect change, or the ability to achieve purpose," he said, "then it is not powerful to engage in an act that does not do that—no matter how loud you are, and no matter how much you burn." Likewise, he exhorted the staff to combat the "romantic illusion" of guerrilla warfare in the style of Che Guevara. No "black" version of the Cuban revolution could succeed without widespread political sympathy, he asserted, and only a handful of the black minority itself favored insurrection. King extolled the discipline of civil disobedience instead, which he defined not as a right but a personal homage to untapped democratic energy. They must "bring to bear all of the power of nonviolence on the economic problem," he urged, even though nothing in the Constitution promised a roof or a meal. "I say all of these things because I want us to know the hardness of the task," King concluded, breaking off with his most basic plea: "We must not be intimidated by those who are laughing at nonviolence now."

By tradition, workshops closed Monday night on a plenary round of music. "Talk about Peter, talk about Paul!" they sang in jubilant harmony, stomping their feet ahead of claps on the back beat. "Talk about Doctor King, you can talk about 'em all! Long as I know I'm gonna get my freedom, it's all right, whoa, it's all right!" A shout from Andrew Young blocked King at the door—"Don't let him out of here!"—and hands pulled him into a sudden chorus of "Happy Birthday." King wore a sheepish, captured look, recorded by one home movie camera, when pioneer Coca-Cola executive Xernona Clayton came forward to toast his turning thirty-nine. "We know you really don't need much," allowed Clayton, a former SCLC employee, but she recalled complaints about food and the shoestring policy in prison. "So when you go to jail, here's some shoestring potatoes," she said. Laughter spread while King solemnly examined the canned snack, his necktie slightly askew. "Then we know how fond you are of our President and Mrs. Johnson," Clayton added, holding up an illustrated novelty mug, stifling giggles to read the inscription: "We are cooperating with Lyndon Johnson's War on Poverty/Drop coins and bills in the cup."

Contention returned on Tuesday with a vengeance. King coaxed

Hosea Williams to stand beside him at an interim press conference, silent and fuming, while he sketched a poverty campaign "patterned after the bonus marches back in the '30s," with encampments and disciplined petitions to dramatize hardship. "I guess the only difference is that we aren't going to be run out of Washington," vowed King. Reporters sought confrontational details such as predicted jail numbers or an early threat to tie up street traffic and sabotage power grids. Some made news from King's forthright agreement that he could be indicted like Dr. Spock—"I heard a rumor that they are going to indict ninety more"—and his pledge to keep Ebenezer a sanctuary for draft resisters. "We don't have a bit of business in Vietnam fighting today," he said. "That is a civil war."

King retreated to the poverty workshops, which he conceded were "rather stormy." James Bevel and Jesse Jackson maintained strategic objections to the entire Washington plan. Hosea Williams, who filed a written protest that his once formidable Selma department "at this time consists of one person, the Director," sulked openly about being stripped of staff and budget. "I couldn't hardly get gas money down the street," he recalled. Fieldworkers complained directly to King that their leaders drifted away from the sessions, undercutting morale. "Who ain't here?" asked one. "I don't see Hosea." Organizers also confessed practical troubles. They found poverty an abstraction, unlike skin color or the ballot, and complained that potential recruits did not want to think of themselves as poor. Should the staff look for degraded human exhibits or articulate witnesses? They found uprooted people nevertheless resistant to change—homeless but reluctant to leave hometowns, filled with unanswerable questions about what to expect. Some SCLC workers shared Jesse Jackson's qualm that President Johnson could foil the drama simply by endorsing their poverty agenda. Others fretted that alluring competitors would brand their nonviolent approach old-fashioned and pious. "What's gonna happen when we bring these people to Washington," a staff member asked King, "and Stokely's gonna be there?"

King remonstrated almost until the moment on Wednesday, January 17, when Bernard Lafayette sent staff members to recruiting destinations with knapsacks and bus tickets, mostly in pairs. "I don't want to psychoanalyze anybody but myself," King said, admitting that he straddled love and hate, hope and despair. He speculated that similar frustration afflicted the whole country, including war hawks and segregationists with their own "haunting doubts," then encouraged his colleagues to look past conflicting goals and unfinished plans. "Just go to Washington," he urged. If a Rosa Parks committee had waited months to refine its blueprint in 1955, King warned, "we never would have had the Montgomery bus boycott." He said movements had a way of distilling choices, and perhaps a committed poverty campaign would decide to "call the peace movement and let them go on the other side of the Potomac." First, he said, "we got to be fired up ourselves." To illustrate the contagious power in nonviolence, King recalled the sight of the ferocious Blackstone Rangers absorbing blows in Chicago. He encouraged his staff relentlessly, calling hope a "final refusal to give up." The sick world needed a jolt of conscience, he said, and this might be their last movement. He preached like a salmon fighting upstream.

*   *   *

IN WASHINGTON, when five thousand women of the Jeannette Rankin Brigade marched through snow for the January 15 opening of Congress, rows of police blocked them on the authority of Vice President Humphrey. Senator Ernest Gruening, whose wife, Dorothy, was among the marchers, mustered only three votes against a hasty ruling that no visitors or petitions should be received before Wednesday's State of the Union address, out of courtesy to President Johnson. A standoff ensued with the women massed at the foot of Capitol Hill, dressed in mourning black. Singer Judy Collins led choruses of "We Shall Overcome." Coretta King, missing the birthday celebration in Atlanta, joined leaders, including Ella Baker, Fannie Lou Hamer, and the brigade's namesake, eighty-seven-year-old Jeannette Rankin—a suffragette and pacifist from Montana, the first female ever to serve in the U.S. House and the only representative to vote against American entry into both world wars. Lively internal debates posed a linkage between violence and patriarchy. A caucus from Chicago resolved that full citizenship required women to go "beyond justifying themselves in terms of their wombs and breasts and housekeeping abilities." One feminist troupe improvised a "Liturgy for the Burial of Traditional Womanhood." A critic from *Ramparts* magazine derided "narrow-minded bitches" for dividing the antiwar movement, but brigade leaders held the factions together in broad protest—"because," declared Jeannette Rankin, "you can't have war without women." Congressional leaders ended the snow vigil by allowing a small delegation inside to deliver the brigade's consensus petition, which called for legislators to stop the war and "make reparation for the ravaged land we leave behind in Vietnam." House Speaker John McCormack emphasized his distaste for both measures.

Safely in their wake, President Johnson entered the House chamber on the evening of January 17. Resting his short, sobering State of the Union address on a theme of perseverance, he said the American people "have the will to meet the trials that these times impose." Johnson omitted the annual Vietnam review and prognosis from early speech drafts. "The enemy has been defeated in battle after battle," he declared simply, adding that Americans were equally steadfast on the conditions for peace. Johnson surveyed a vast array of new freedom and prosperity at home, then paused. "Yet there is in the land a certain restlessness, a questioning," he said. As though in disbelief, he reviewed seven years of unparalleled economic growth, with seventy million television sets and legions of parents "who never finished grammar school" but would see their children finish college. "Why?" he asked again. "Why then this restlessness?"

"Because," Johnson answered rhetorically, "when a great ship cuts through the sea, the waters are always stirred and troubled." His nautical metaphor for the era dominated reviews. In the *Times,* James Reston faulted the President for a deaf ear to the "mutinous cries below decks." The speech received only one thunderous ovation from Congress—for a statement that Americans "have had enough of rising crime and lawlessness"—and many observers said Johnson missed his own signals to slow down the ship of state. Others criticized his focus on speed rather than the compass, saying the President evaded moral choice and the clash of democratic values by pushing hard in every direction. King lamented in a sermon what he called "a spiritless message."

Johnson insisted that the nation must not wait for peace to enact his stalled Great Society agenda. "Especially the civil rights measures," he told Congress. "Fair jury trials, protection of federal rights, enforcement of equal employment opportunity, and fair housing." Beyond these, he proposed significant new initiatives, including tripled construction of low-income housing and a $2.1 billion subsidy for business "to train and to hire the hard-core unemployed." His speech confronted cost implications for a national treasury that had just suffered by far the largest annual deficit since World War II—running at $25 billion, or nearly the whole war bill in Vietnam, fully one-sixth of the national budget. Johnson pleaded again for a temporary surtax to cover half the shortfall, and he vowed economies to attack the rest. Few believed him, but the task came to possess Lyndon Johnson. The weaker his presidency, the more determined he grew to prove—at least by the budget—that a battered, polarized nation could afford both his military and social commitments. While pushing through token initiatives for the Great Society, he pared federal expenditures with a vengeance to eliminate the annual deficit. Almost unnoticed in 1968, Johnson engineered a landmark feat despite the bloodiest, costliest year of foreign war and domestic disorder. His final budget cycle left national accounts $3.242 billion ahead, posting the last surplus for the next twenty-nine years and six Presidents.

Another fiscal trend percolated from the states. In congressional hearings, House Banking Committee chairman Wright Patman berated Governor Nelson Rockefeller for "claims that New York must have a lottery so that its children may go to school." The New York legislature, by repealing an 1833 statute against "radically vicious" games of chance, had just legalized the twentieth century's second state-sponsored lottery for public revenue. While far less swaddled by inhibition than the pioneer 1964 sweepstakes in New Hampshire—which allowed only two drawings per year, and required customers to fill out forms in triplicate—New York did steer ticket sales for its monthly lottery to the teller windows of duly licensed banks. This arrangement lent an air of respectability to transactions ordinarily associated with bookies, but it ran into Representative Patman's jurisdiction over federally chartered and insured financial institutions. "It seems incomprehensible," he declared, "that New York State—a fabulously rich area—could not finance education without resorting to gambling."

For Wright Patman, the collision with Rockefeller echoed a formative struggle when he entered Congress in 1929 from the poorest region of East Texas. Into the maw of the Depression, he had become chief sponsor of the bonus bill to relieve destitute fellow veterans of World War I, who issued him membership card number one for their "Bonus Expeditionary Force." Patman's cause won by losing. He failed in a daring bid to impeach Treasury Secretary Andrew Mellon, but publicity about the wealthy banker's lavish art purchases amplified charges of contrasting disregard for the veterans. In 1932, President Herbert Hoover sent regular Army troops under General Douglas MacArthur to rout the unresisting veterans by force, burning their shantytown encampments, but revulsion against the violence built public sympathy for the marchers, who kept returning until the bonus bill passed over FDR's veto in 1936. Now, decades later, Patman lost by winning. In February of 1968, when his anti-gambling bill outlawed lottery sales from banks, New York lawmakers blamed "hillbilly morals" for obliging them to throw open vendor licenses to convenience stores. Soon a Princeton-based consulting firm would recommend simple games modeled on the illicit numbers racket, plus an Italian fantasy contest called lotto. To spread beyond the Northeast, lotteries won exemption from federal laws that ban gambling notices on commercial airwaves, and the interval between drawings shrank from weeks to minutes. Early promises to restrain a dominant new voice of state governments dissolved slowly with promotional bonanzas like "The De Ville Made Me Do It" in New Hampshire. "The way to sell lottery tickets," said New York's director of advertising, "is by appealing to people's greed."

In Vietnam, the first artillery of a full-scale siege struck Khe Sanh before dawn on Sunday, January 21. For the next eleven weeks, commanders made good on the military judgment that air support would keep the Marine outpost from succumbing like the French army at Dien Bien Phu. American bombers concentrated 1,300 tons of explosives daily on North Vietnamese units trying to charge or claw their way up the hilltop redoubts. The concussion of incoming shells left more nerve damage and grime than bloodshed, as the garrison, having stockpiled two tons of body bags, used only three on an average day to evacuate corpses along with a dozen wounded and constant military bulletins. A special medics' bunker on the exposed Khe Sanh runway facilitated treatment for those injured during vulnerable takeoffs and landings. President Johnson tracked the siege on a topographical replica of Khe Sanh in the White House basement. First he grilled the National Security Council and secured assurances from the Joint Chiefs—in writing—that they lacked no provision for military success. Then he ordered confident public statements to reinforce a recent tide of "unusually good press from South Vietnam." The Associated Press quoted General Westmoreland's assessment that countrywide enemy forces "seem to have run temporarily out of steam." The New York Times reported that a two-year drive by local allies had achieved a "dramatic decline" in Vietcong sabotage. On January 25, news dispatches carried an announcement from White House pacification chief Robert Komer that two-thirds of South Vietnam's eighteen million people now lived in areas made secure from attack.

*   *   *

THE ADMINISTRATIVE mission to rescue SCLC pitched Bill Rutherford into turmoil deeper than chaos and rebellion. Late in January, he fined three workers for chronic absence and fired a staff preacher, "effective immediately," for billing prostitutes to the Chicago voter registration project. He managed younger people with personalities marked by varying mixes of combat fatigue, kamikaze idealism, dissipation, and premature nostalgia. A few already were lifelong casualties, but none would regret enlistment in the nonviolent wars for which Rutherford deeply admired them. His control of the budget and the schedule thrust him also into tensions within the King family. Coretta called frequently to track King's prolonged absences, and the occasional flubbed alibi led to awkward silence. A search for King once sent Rutherford knocking at Coretta's door when King had told each he was with the other. Like advisers before him, Rutherford learned quickly not to pass along even the most indirect suggestion that she join a road engagement, because King instinctively detected and rebuffed her desire to go along. King bristled against tampering with his marital arrangements. He stoutly upheld a mother's duty to stay home with their four young children, and barred joint travel in order to guarantee a surviving parent. Coretta complained that his family concerns did not extend to an education fund for the children or a personal will in the face of the constant death threats. King made it a principle that theirs should be an unprivileged household, forswearing maids or a second car, but she felt the dogged austerity as a penalty from his consuming guilt. In his absence, she transferred her grievances in part to SCLC with daily hardship appeals, and Rutherford, squeezed between the couple and his own work standards, quietly diverted staff members willing to serve as temporary chauffeurs and home attendants. He hoped to make small amends for Coretta's cruel isolation, but her lasting agitation over slights and displays earned her the office nickname, "Queen."

As a newcomer, Rutherford stood at the periphery of SCLC's most private drama. He saw the swirling, teasing flirtations of its inner circle, and he discouraged prurient speculation about the link between Coretta's regal suffering and King's pursuits elsewhere. Rutherford could only guess about what he called "a double life," marveling at burdens King must carry beyond the superhuman pressures and expectations of the movement. He was not privy to the raw candor among the preachers. James Bevel, for instance, had stunned them with a radical new stance that they must "confess all our stuff to our wives." King first said he would rather die, that they did not even know a chaste colleague in the pulpit except perhaps James Lawson, who was a United Method-ist, and that disclosure would do nothing except rupture families. Bevel persisted with typically elaborate theories drawn from two disparate books: *The Kingdom of God Is Within You,* by Leo Tolstoy, and *The Function of the Orgasm,* by the unorthodox psycho-biologist Wilhelm Reich. By opening his mind, Bevel said, they allowed him to realize that he had been closest to Diane Nash during the Freedom Rides, before their ro-mance or marriage, and had experienced the purest creation when ac-cessing the hearts of Birmingham's teenagers for witness in jail. Bevel thought King could apply nonviolence to every stubborn harm between people, "just like you did for segregation," but must build from truth in-stead of lies. When King asked why the confessional approach had not reconciled Nash to him after three years of tumultuous separation, Bevel somehow blamed Nash for abandoning his new "scientific part-nership" to eradicate the causes of lust.

Ordinarily, Ralph Abernathy would have counseled earthy skepti-cism toward such advice, especially since Bevel ingeniously spun his pu-rity experiments themselves into enticements for guilt-free seduction, but Abernathy was gone for most of January on a pilgrimage to India and South Vietnam.* King's formidable armor wore down in midlife, draining assurance from his glib mantra as a young scholar that many great men of religion had been obsessed with sex—St. Augustine, St. Paul, Martin Luther, Kierkegaard, Tillich—and his self-reproach spilled over when Coretta underwent surgery for an abdominal tumor on January 24. He disclosed to her the one mistress who meant most to him since 1963—with intensity almost like a second family even though she lived in Los Angeles—a married alumna of Fisk, of dignified bear-ing like Coretta, but different. The result was painful disaster. Juanita Abernathy exploded with the fury of a trusted second that King picked Coretta's most vulnerable moment, just as she recovered from her hys-terectomy, to ambush her sanctuary of willful, silent discretion. If he was truly desperate to be honest, she said, King should purge himself privately to God or a psychiatrist. Abernathy, back from Asia, grew so

---

*Abernathy wrote King on January 18 from Saigon's Hotel Caravelle, "I feel so empty away from you and our struggle for the freedom of our people," adding a self-conscious superscript to his letter: "Please keep for the sake of history."

alarmed that he canvassed the regular mistresses for hidden fits of jealousy or romantic blackmail strong enough to break down the careful habit of secret, nonpossessive affairs, but he found no conventional clues to explain the rash new fatalism in King.

The attack of penitent melancholy coincided with a ferocious push for public sacrifice through the movement, as before with King in Birmingham and Selma. On January 29, he exhorted his New York advisers to design lobbying strategies for the campaign against poverty, but he faced a new spearhead of resistance. Bayard Rustin submitted a memo warning that Washington demonstrations "can only lead to further backlash and repression," and he added sharply in person that King should forget any "mystical bullshit" about success. It was fatuous to hope for a shantytown occupation to help poor people more than the established power of trade unions, said Rustin. He predicted countermovements far stronger than black power or white backlash, saying King could not hold discipline in the unruly national mood. His critique was biting and witty. Afterward, Stanley Levison told Rutherford on his wiretapped line that Rustin "showed his true colors by opposing civil disobedience," and Rustin would be sensitive for the rest of his life to implications that new union employers had compromised his lifelong distinction in pacifist witness. In 1995, when information from the secret wiretaps seeped into public view, he wrote the *New York Times* to rebut an impression "that in 1968 I rejected the philosophy of nonviolence as espoused by Dr. King." Harry Wachtel, who had shared the doubts about a favorable outcome in Washington, insisted privately to Rustin that what wounded King was Rustin's scorn for the effort itself. "He felt let down, because he held you up so high," Wachtel recalled in an old man's accounting. At the time, King had nodded, winced, and smiled through the steady barrage of negative advice in Wachtel's law office, then appealed for help anyway. With disarming aplomb, he asked a recognized expert to craft a statement on the primary goal to dramatize the hidden faces of American poverty. "We didn't know we were poor until we read your book," King teased the author Michael Harrington, who could not resist the assignment even though he had just seconded most of Rustin's dissent.

* * *

IT RAINED early in Memphis on Tuesday, January 30. The river city was not on King's recruiting list, and his campaign would visit there only by detour, but many faces of poverty assembled at its sewer and drains division to hear the arbitrary "cutting down" announcements. A foreman sent home twenty-one low-level black workers without pay an hour before sunshine suddenly reappeared, leaving white crews with good weather but few men to supervise. T. O. Jones, a former employee fired for trying to organize a labor union, reported the fluke hardship to the incoming director of public works, who agreed to meet Jones on Thursday about the plaintive hope of powerless sewer workers for a rainy day grievance procedure.

Also on Tuesday morning, Robert Kennedy told reporters he had decided not to contest President Johnson for the Democratic nomination "under any conceivable circumstances." Several disappointed aides resigned to work elsewhere against the Vietnam War. Allard Lowenstein reportedly accosted Kennedy within hours to exchange emotional tirades of regret. A last-second substitution in the official news release changed the word "conceivable" to "foreseeable," which added grist for lampoons as well as anguish about Kennedy's tilting indecision. "Besides the columnists and cartoonists, you have really been getting it the last several days from the mass TV shows like the Smothers Brothers, the new Martin and Rowan *Laugh-In* and others," confided counselor Fred Dutton. To speed political recovery, Dutton prescribed an attractive family vacation at the Winter Olympics with a side visit to the Pope, which he thought would "demonstrate that you are relaxed and enjoying things (in contrast to most of the rest of the country)."

The Kennedy announcement relieved political worries for President Johnson, who swamped the declared rival Eugene McCarthy in voter polls. Johnson met Tuesday with top national security officials. The siege at Khe Sanh, while suspended for the three-day Buddhist celebrations called Tet, had acquired the worldwide media drama of a tense duel. Military leaders considered the natural mountain fortress secure against anything except full-scale invasion from North Vietnam, a remote contingency that might require tactical nuclear weapons or chemical agents as "active candidates for employment." Johnson reviewed battle statistics from Khe Sanh and updates from the galling January 23 capture by North Korea of the spy ship *Pueblo* with all her crew, which would remain a hostage crisis for the year. At 2:35 in the afternoon, Walt Rostow returned from an emergency call to announce that "we are being heavily mortared in Saigon." He said the enemy had broken the holiday truce with daredevil attacks on the presidential palace and the U.S. embassy compound, plus scattered targets elsewhere.

"This could be very bad," Johnson groaned. He said it reminded him of the February 1965 barracks assault in Pleiku, which had prompted the first air strikes on North Vietnam. "What comes to mind in the way of retaliation?" he asked. Chairman Wheeler of the Joint Chiefs said the Vietcong infrastructure made guerrilla attacks difficult to repulse, and the only suggestions came from McNamara, whose successor was being confirmed that day in the Senate. They must counter the psychological effect by publicizing military success at Khe Sanh, he urged, and retain General Nguyen Ngoc Loan as national police chief despite the State Department's efforts to remove him for brutal corruption. Rusk grumbled that Loan was "rather uncooperative." McNamara called him indispensable in crisis, and CIA director Richard Helms concurred.

Investigators later concluded that a part-time Vietnamese chauffeur nicknamed Satchmo had guided nineteen Vietcong sappers into the U.S. diplomatic compound in Saigon through an eight-foot hole blown in the wall. News film from the Tet offensive's most symbolic pitched battle reached New York too late for some network broadcasts Tuesday night—CBS showed instead a rocket attack that shut down the Da Nang airbase—but Wednesday's *New York Times* carried three stories of vivid description: "In one of the strangest scenes of the Vietnam War, helmeted American troops ran crouching across broad Thong Nhat Boulevard to assault the gate of their own embassy at dawn today." A front-page photograph in the *Washington Post* showed a Vietcong corpse on the embassy lawn. Satchmo's body lay next to a Soviet machine gun. His entire assault team was killed along with seven embassy guards.

Seventy thousand guerrillas launched similar attacks of coordinated surprise in thirty-six of South Vietnam's forty-four provincial capitals. In Saigon alone, assault teams used prearranged codes to pick up weapons that had been hidden in more than four hundred homes by the Vietcong political director, who lived next door to Deputy U.S. Ambassador William Porter. Top analysts in Washington instantly acknowledged the absence of warning as a calamitous intelligence failure, while their counterparts in Hanoi suffered dashed hopes to touch off a general uprising. "Saigon's 4 million people had barricaded themselves inside their houses," wrote war historian A. J. Langguth, "and refused to obey when the Vietcong banged on their doors and told them to come out." Few Vietnamese civilians believed it was yet safe to flout either side.

The plans left massive carnage. Battles from the offensive would stretch well past Tet—killing nearly four thousand American and six thousand South Vietnamese soldiers, plus an estimated 58,000 Communist soldiers and 14,000 civilians. General Westmoreland insisted that Ho Chi Minh counted on weak knees in the United States to offset a crushing military defeat, and war critics asked how the Communists so quickly replaced enormous losses. The American public first rallied angrily for retaliation, but one small event pushed above the contending claims of momentum, credibility, and might. A South Vietnamese patrol was marching through Saigon's Cholon district when the national police chief stopped his passing motorcade and spontaneously took custody of its lone Vietcong prisoner. Without a word, General Loan marched him into a quiet square outside the An Quang temple, paused long enough for news cameras to focus on a slight man in a checkered shirt, squinting with his hands bound behind, then pulled out a pistol and shot him point-blank in the head. After photographs and film of the random street execution circled the world on Thursday, the third day of the Tet offensive, poll measurements recorded the most decisive single drop in American support for the Vietnam War. As King's movement believed, lasting power rose against the tide of violence.

CHAPTER 38

Memphis

February–April 1968

GULLY-WASHER storms plagued Elvis Presley's escape on February 1. In poor visibility, the decoy limousine roared out of his Graceland mansion too fast to draw pursuit, but fans and reporters on stakeout scrambled in time to follow a crowded blue Cadillac that hid the singer and expectant Priscilla within his rowdy entourage called the Guys. Conflicting shouts urged driver Charlie Hodge to outrun labor pains and the chase caravan but not to risk the baby on slick roads. By afternoon, word of the impending delivery drew a hundred Elvis calls per hour through the switchboard at Baptist Hospital, some noting with delight that it was precisely nine months since the Las Vegas wedding. The Guys took over the physicians' lounge to wait, and Assistant Police Chief Henry Lux announced that Elvis would be billed for two officers guarding a maternity suite on the fifth floor. One reporter found a patient who vacated the room next door to give the Presley clan extra space. "Tell him I moved for him," said the mother of newborn Deena Castinelli, "and I wouldn't mind him stopping by and saying hello before I leave."

Elsewhere in Memphis, three men opened talks on the trouble in the city's sewer and drains division. When P. J. Ciampa flew in for a stopover, T. O. Jones introduced himself with a retinue of union supporters, then escorted Ciampa downtown to show that a fired trash man could produce the national field director of the fast-growing American Federation of State, County and Municipal Employees (AFSCME). Charles Blackburn explained to Ciampa that he had been director of public works less than two weeks after a career in the insurance business, but he thought there was a fair way to distribute the rainy day layoffs. Blackburn politely withheld from his job briefing a hard-nosed assessment that of several hundred trash collectors Jones claimed would support a union, only about thirty paid regular dues, and that the city would refuse to recognize a sanitation union regardless. He did say that overall labor policy was reserved for his friend, Mayor Henry Loeb, who preferred to handle such matters personally in open forum every Thursday. (Loeb answered all fifty-four citizens in line that afternoon, telling one delegation that the city garage could not afford to repair vehicles for the Shelby County Rescue Squad.) Ciampa offered to compose a letter about how other cities had established more efficient personnel agreements with AFSCME locals, which Blackburn agreed to receive, then excused himself. On the drive to catch a flight back to Washington, Ciampa confided to Jones why he thought this was enough for a first session. Moments later, two Public Works vans startled Jones by barreling across his path well above ambulance speed, their emergency flashers engaged. He tore after them to a scene of wailing disaster near the corner of Colonial and Quince.

Foreman Willie Crain's five-man crew had headed for the dump in one of the early pushbutton compressor trucks that replaced the old flatbeds starting in 1957. Only two of the four collectors could squeeze into the driver's cab after hauling their tubs on foot, and the two junior men normally jockeyed from handholds and footrests on the outside. They faced a hard choice in bad weather because city rules barred shelter stops in residential neighborhoods—after citizen complaints about unsightly "picnics" by the Negro sanitation workers—and torrential cloudbursts late Thursday drove them through side-loading slits into the huge storage cylinder itself, where a tight mound of garbage left only a small gap behind the pistonlike compacting plate. When Crain heard screams, he could not slam on the brakes, jump out, and disengage the pushbutton compressor fast enough. Investigators would conclude that a freak shift by an onboard shovel may have shorted wet wires to the separate motor. A witness looking through her kitchen window said she saw one man struggle almost out before his raincoat or something grabbed and pulled him back down head first, leaving parts of both legs exposed.

It was a gruesome chore to retrieve the two crushed bodies from the garbage packer and pronounce them dead at John Gaston Hospital.

Echol Cole and Robert Walker soon became the anonymous cause that diverted Martin Luther King to Memphis for his last march. City flags flew at half-mast for them, but they never were public figures like Lisa Marie Presley, whose birth at 5:01 P.M. was being announced by her grandparents Gladys and Vernon. Cole and Walker would not be listed among civil rights martyrs, nor studied like Rosa Parks as the catalyst for a new movement. Their fate was perhaps too lowly and pathetic. Television newscasts ignored them, and the local black newspaper tried to ignite a more dignified scandal by branding the Memphis post office a "fortress of discrimination" that kept Negro employees beneath clerk posts in which they would handle money. Across town, the leading white newspaper emphasized technical efforts to prevent another truck malfunction. Its popular feature about the human dimensions of race— "Hambone's Meditations"—remained a sore point with the NAACP but was widely defended as harmless and folk-wise. On February 2, the *Commercial Appeal* offered a minstrel cartoon with Hambone's daily proverb: "Tom's boy mus' be one dem *brain* workers—he stan' roun' wid he han's in he pocket all de time!!" Privately, T. O. Jones reminded his stunned members that city policy left the families of "unclassified workers" with no death or survivors' benefits. Mayor Loeb bestowed $500 by special decree, but the pregnant widow Earline Walker made her mark to sign over one of Robert's last two paychecks for cheap burial across the Mississippi line in Tallahatchie County, where they had been sharecroppers.

* * *

KING PREACHED "The Drum Major Instinct" at Ebenezer that Sunday, February 4. He freely adapted a sermon published under that title during his seminary years by evangelist Wallace Hamilton, based on the biblical story of two disciples who beseech Jesus for the most prominent eternal seats in heaven. Their desire springs from a universal impulse for distinction, said King—"this quest for recognition . . . this drum major instinct." He pictured an itch to lead parades in everything from Freud's ego theories to modern ads for whiskey and perfume. An extreme drum major "ends by trying to push others down to push himself up," he warned, driving racism in culture and arrogance in nations. Yet Jesus in the Bible account does not rebuke James and John for their ambition itself, but teaches instead that true reward follows humble service. Here King's message turned. "And the great issue of life," he declared, "is to harness the drum major instinct." He sketched the biog-

raphy of supreme Christian sacrifice with clear echoes of his own turmoil, noting that "the tide of public opinion turned" against Jesus when
he was still young. "They said he was an agitator," said King. "He practiced civil disobedience. He broke injunctions." Jesus was betrayed by
friends, cursed, killed, and buried penniless in a borrowed tomb—but
now after nineteen centuries "stands as the most influential figure that
ever entered human history." For all the worldly gloss about a "lord of
lords," King found nothing royal about Jesus: "He just went around
serving."

This was hardly the first time King flirted with martyrdom in a
speech. One of the first profiles written about him during the bus boycott noted "a conspicuous thread of thanatopsis" in his private conversation as well. What emerged this Sunday was a brooding reverie on
external and internal burdens from the drum major instinct. "And
every now and then I think about my own death," he told his congregation. He gave fitful instructions for the service—"tell them not to talk
too long"—hoping someone would mention "that Martin Luther King,
Jr. tried to give his life serving others." The eulogist should omit all his
honors and attainments simply to testify perhaps that King tried to love
enemies, comfort prisoners, "be right on the war question," and feed the
hungry. "Yes, if you want to say that I was a drum major," he cried, "say
that I was a drum for justice! Say that I was a drum major for peace—I
was a drum major for righteousness—and all of the other shallow
things will not matter." In thunderclap rhythm, with his distinctive
voice blending ecstasy and despair, King finished the oration soon to become famous by the disembodied recording played at his funeral.

For the moment, King labored at close quarters to harness drum
major instincts. He sent Ralph Abernathy, who was back from Asia, on
a mission with his gift for blandishment. Abernathy pretended to confide in Hosea Williams that he had convinced King the only way to pull
off the Washington poverty campaign was to "bring back Hosea
Williams." They collaborated on a new master plan for leadership in
staggered phases, designating Williams the high-energy recruitment
chief for rural areas, which eventually placated the first of SCLC's three
disaffected staff lieutenants.

King himself flew north on February 5 to parlay for support, but ran
into what his hosts consciously prepared as "a grand piece of psychological warfare." Thirty welfare mothers waited in the Chicago YMCA
behind name placards that isolated King next to a woman with a grand-

child in her lap. Beulah Sanders of New York interrupted King's appeal by asking where he stood on the Kennedy amendments to H.R. 12080, and his mumbled responses brought specialized questions about welfare issues until King agreed meekly to listen. From one far corner, Andrew Young winced as the women "jumped on Martin like no one ever had before," with lectures of extra impact, Young thought, because King was always subject to his mother's natural authority more than the bluster of Daddy King. From another far corner, Bernard Lafayette rebelled to ask how anyone could accuse King of shirking the struggle of a group less than six months old. George Wiley, founder and executive director of the National Welfare Rights Organization, was the first black scholar to earn an Ivy League doctorate in chemistry. Squeezed out of CORE, he had considered a position with SCLC before launching NWRO with foundation grants, and Lafayette knew Wiley orchestrated this confrontation to promote his grassroots constituency of welfare recipients. Lafayette accosted each woman who scolded King, demanding to know where she had been when his home was bombed in Montgomery or his marches stoned there in Chicago. King kept quiet, but later teased the angel of mercy who had curtailed his whipping, and Wiley soon wrote Young with bargaining terms for a few NWRO women to join the camp-in against poverty.

King's party flew into overlapping crises the same night in Washington, where the second nationwide mobilization of clergy gathered to oppose the war in Vietnam. A newly released CALCAV-sponsored book, *In the Name of America,* analyzed more than a thousand news reports indicating that U.S. war practice routinely violated international law in sixteen areas, including defoliation, aerial bombardment of civilians, and forced relocation of villagers. Its allegations of war crimes, which the State Department branded "absolutely unsupportable," made front-page news against the shock from the continuing bloodshed of the Tet offensive. On sidewalks three blocks from the White House, a pro-war religious group protested the CALCAV mass meeting at New York Avenue Presbyterian Church, and a minister among the hundred pickets said nuclear weapons would be justified "to preserve freedom and lessen the loss of lives." Inside, by contrast, Rabbi Abraham Heschel asserted that "hardening of the heart is the suspension of freedom." There would be greatness in common confession that Vietnam was wrong, Heschel pleaded, as "God Himself admitted that He made a mistake." Last among the speakers, Andrew Young lamented a permeating mood of violence. "Guerilla warfare in the ghettos is a day-to-day conversation," he said. Young urged the CALCAV audience not to blame circumstances or Lyndon Johnson for the poison of Vietnam. "Why is it that we want to lay it all on one poor Texas school teacher?" he asked. Every citizen has an ownership share in democracy, and must emulate the marching children who acted to redress its faults in Birmingham and Selma even as underage victims of segregation. "Ours has been the mildest and most respectable dissent," said Young. "When are we really going to stand up and challenge the values of this country?"

Legal maneuvers intensified through the night over CALCAV's plan to conduct a one-hour service for war dead at Arlington National Cemetery the next morning, February 6. Moments before the scheduled start, an emergency injunction from the U.S. Court of Appeals sustained a government petition to ban such "partisan" use of patriotic ground. Two rabbis rushed off to find a ceremonial Torah while Richard Fernandez and others gave modified instructions to 2,500 CALCAV members willing to cross the Potomac River on buses at noon. The rabbis joined the head of a wordless procession of eight abreast, hoisting their Torah scroll despite Jewish custom against bearing scripture into graveyards. When they halted before the Tomb of the Unknown Soldier, King shouted: "In this period of absolute silence, let us pray." Reporters measured ensuing stillness in suspense to learn how far the clergy would push their risk of contempt of court; one described an eerie clicking of heels as soldiers changed the honor guard nearby. After six minutes, Heschel called out—*"Eloi, eloi, lama sabachthani?"*— and a Catholic bishop gave a terse benediction for silent departure: "Let us go in peace. Amen." News stories translated Heschel into English— "My God, my God, why have you forsaken me?"—pointing out that the Aramaic cry of Jesus in Mark's Crucifixion story was in turn a quote from King David's Book of Psalms.

King shuttled between the mobilization and the Presbyterian Church of the Redeemer, where his SCLC board was debating approval for the poverty campaign. In the car, he scanned last-minute dictation from Stanford theologian Robert McAfee Brown, then laid aside the drafted speech already released to the press. "I have to give it my own way," he said, and he told CALCAV's final plenary that the Vietnam intervention "has played havoc with the destiny of the whole world." King spoke extemporaneously to returned marchers who overflowed New York Avenue Presbyterian: "I said some time ago—and the press jumped on me about it, but I want to say it today one more time, and I am sad to say it—we live in a nation that is the greatest purveyor of violence in the world today." His speech drifted into underlying unity between causes of peace and humanity—"When I say poor people, I am not only talking about black people"—then stopped abruptly. *Newsweek* said King "seemed preoccupied with plans for his 'poor people's mobilization.' " William Sloane Coffin closed the CALCAV protest with a sermon from Ezekiel: "You corrupted your wisdom for the sake of your splendor."

The evening recess for SCLC's board spared a convoy to negotiate privately with Washington's Black United Front, a pilot group just created by Stokely Carmichael after his five-month tour of Third World countries. (U.S. intelligence agencies sent the White House a digest of his strident comments from Algeria to North Vietnam; the FBI compiled an alarmist secret dossier called "SNCC/Black Power"; lawyers wrangled over his confiscated passport.) Public silence since his return in December gave Carmichael an aura of mystery like Malcolm X, magnified by the spread of black power culture. Members of King's entourage met hostile passage at the perimeter of the church summit, which one aide called "commandos occupying the place with walkie-talkies and bodyguards." A white SCLC worker was rudely expelled along with reporters. Preachers were harassed as Uncle Toms, and Rutherford's secretary left in tears from more personal disparagement. Seconds jousted informally. Hosea Williams renewed antagonisms from the Meredith march, saying SNCC leaders had accomplished nothing with black power except to feed off King's reputation. A female SNCC veteran accused King of selling out the Selma movement when he turned around the second attempt to march beyond Pettus Bridge, which King hotly denied. He and Carmichael occupied a goodwill zone where they shrugged off the trappings of competition to reminisce about the movement. When King pitched the spring campaign, Carmichael applauded its focus on grassroots poverty but detected "serious tactical error." By his analysis, the proposed multi-racial coalition missed a correct move toward black solidarity. Also, camp-in boldness risked trapping the poor without honorable retreat, and the underlying hope for national politics was misguided within a system he called fixed upon exploitation. After some debate, King appealed for a benevolent truce. "Well, if you are against this," he said, "will you let us try?"

Carmichael postponed judgment while King wrestled his peers. A few SCLC board members worried that the poverty campaign would fail if perceived as an antidote to black power. Walter Fauntroy, the local SCLC representative, was himself a leader in Carmichael's Black United Front. Rev. Jefferson Rogers, who hosted the board meeting, reconciled new trends of militant thought with his lifelong devotion to the mystical theologian Howard Thurman, and King's approach seemed dated when the *Amsterdam News* of Harlem had just banished the word "Negro" for "black." Other board members supported the Rustin position that demonstrations in Washington would only exacerbate public backlash and enrage the best civil rights President in history. The crossfire left King raw by the time Carmichael came to declare neutrality on Wednesday, February 7. The Black United Front would neither support nor oppose the Poor People's Campaign, he said, and Carmichael vowed on principle not to criticize fellow black leaders in public. This was the best outcome King's staff had hoped for, and they were nonplussed when he erupted against their satisfaction.

King berated them for agreeing glibly that Carmichael could ridicule nonviolence so long as he did not attack King. He said the priority should be to protect nonviolence—not him—with a vehemence that shook Bill Rutherford enough to seek advice. "Martin got very upset with me," he complained over Stanley Levison's wiretapped phone line, "and started shouting and cussing me out." Rutherford fumbled to discern what made King so unhappy. "He said to me, 'the enemy is violence, violence begets violence,'" Rutherford told Levison, "and he went into one of these preaching things. I didn't react at all. I'm really pretty quiet." He found the sudden fury both unnerving and peculiar, because to him the American Revolution and other wars so clearly proved good, and Levison offered comforting reasons why King was wrong. "The enemy are the forces keeping us from getting rights, and violence is one of their methods," he explained. "So we try to develop a counterpoint to violence. But violence is not the enemy. What if they could keep everybody in servitude without using violence? Would Martin be for servitude?"

These were shadings of conviction at the heart of politics. Consensus among his bosom advisers left King isolated with his obsessive belief that nonviolence remained a force for freedom stronger than all the powers of subjugation. Late Wednesday, to a mass meeting of civil rights dignitaries at the Vermont Avenue Baptist Church, he preached against the grip of despair. "And if I can leave you with any message tonight," said King, "I would say don't lose hope. . . . It may look like we can't get out of this thing now. It may appear that nonviolence has failed, and the nation will not respond to it. But don't give up yet. Wait until the next morning." He stayed overnight to address Washington's Chamber of Commerce, arguing that the self-interest of wealthy Americans required opportunity among the poor, and fell so far behind schedule to New York that he nearly missed his national appearance on NBC's *Tonight Show*. Harry Belafonte extended the film session at Rockefeller Center to include King in a broadcast that marked sensitive transitions in media history. King mixed small talk about his family and frantic schedule with frank thoughts on martyrdom and Vietnam. Belafonte, while holding superior ratings through the week as the spotlighted black substitute for entertainment icon Johnny Carson, survived a primitive scandal elsewhere in network television. When British singer Petula Clark placed a hand on Belafonte's wrist to close a duet, representatives of the sponsoring Chrysler Corporation mounted a hushed campaign to snip her interracial touch from the finished broadcast.

King's *Tonight Show* moment coincided with a signal tragedy in Orangeburg, South Carolina. All Star Bowling Lanes, a prime recreational facility for the rural town of twenty thousand, still maintained strict segregation despite the Civil Rights Act of 1964, and when students from Orangeburg's two black colleges belatedly demanded service—eight years after the sit-ins of 1960—owner Harry Floyd successfully appealed for some five hundred troopers and National Guard soldiers to help police defend his property rights under state law. They repulsed would-be bowlers with some violence on February 6, then deployed two nights later to seal off the South Carolina State campus as students rallied outside behind a bonfire—some singing "We Shall Overcome," others chanting "Your mama is a whore," a few throwing projectiles. Loud volleys killed three students and sent twenty-seven others into the segregated emergency ward of Orangeburg Hospital, but public reaction stayed mute from the first AP bulletins that students had been hit "during a heavy exchange of gunfire." The AP wire omitted subsequent corrections that no students fired weapons, and that nearly half the victims were shot in the back or the soles of their feet. Two reporters would write a haunted book about why the massacre story disappeared for lack of interest—or never registered—without even a mention in *Time* magazine. Quietly, Justice Department lawyers intervened to end the laggard segregation at the hospital, and they secured an order that made protest survivors the first black customers at All Star Bowling Lanes. Meanwhile, news followed a melodramatic theme of riot and retribution to South Carolina's death row, where SNCC leader Cleveland Sellers was transferred with a bullet wound in the left shoulder. The governor's spokesman pronounced him the outside agitator behind a black power insurrection in Orangeburg—"the biggest nigger in the crowd"—even though Sellers had retreated to his parents' nearby home before his federal trial, becoming a peripheral adviser in the student bowling crisis, which he found anachronistic. In March, Sellers would draw the five-year maximum sentence for draft resistance, with another year added on state conviction for unspecified criminal activity at Orangeburg. By his final release in September of 1974, he had a new family, a Harvard master's degree, and a laconic sense of recovery. "Being locked up for something I hadn't done when my first child was born was frustrating," he recalled in a 1990 memoir.

King sent a lonely Orangeburg appeal to U.S. Attorney General Ramsey Clark: "We demand that you act now to bring to justice the perpetrators of the largest armed assault undertaken under color of law in recent Southern history." He relied on private reports from college administrators who had opposed the student demonstrations, but three FBI agents hamstrung any federal investigation with false statements that they did not witness the incident personally. King moved on to recruit poverty volunteers Saturday in Philadelphia, Pennsylvania, where he fell briefly ill from exhaustion, and summoned seventeen top staff people to Atlanta for a rare Sunday showdown on February 11, one week after his "Drum Major" sermon. He listed the blunt failures of preparation: lackadaisical staff work, negligible progress, weak recruits. He wanted a legion of hard-core poor for Washington, but saw only a few half-committed middle-class young people. "I throw this out to get us shocked enough to start doing the job," King said, adding that he would rather cancel the April campaign than launch a halfhearted effort. Staff members vowed to do better. Bernard Lafayette raised the fallback option of delay.

In Memphis, public works director Charles Blackburn promised to review a $6.97 payroll deduction for the replacement rain gear of sanitation worker Gene Falkner, but he saw no room to bargain on the larger items, including pay raises, union recognition, safety equipment, rainy days, or health benefits. "Well, the men want an answer," said a union steward who invited city officials along to explain their stance to the men. This gave Blackburn his first inkling that sanitation workers were assembled and waiting on a Sunday night. He saw no reason to repeat himself, nor any pressing danger, but the stewards' report touched off floor speeches about the lessons of Echol Cole and Robert Walker. "This was a strike that *we* called," a veteran trash collector would remember. "Labor didn't call it. *We* called it." On Monday morning, 930 of the 1,100 sanitation workers walked off the job with 214 of the 230 affiliated men in the sewer and drains division. From AFSCME headquarters in Washington, P. J. Ciampa dampened the euphoria of local leader T. O. Jones by chewing him out for basic errors: a wildcat action without a treasury or plan, begun in winter when garbage does not stink, against a mayor too new to have many enemies. Still, Ciampa flew in with union supporters by afternoon, when Mayor Loeb pronounced the strike illegal and vowed to hire replacements if necessary. "Let no one make a mistake about it," Loeb declared. "The garbage is going to be picked up in Memphis."

* * *

PRESIDENT JOHNSON convened his own Sunday night council in the White House residence. Like most Americans, his advisers scarcely noticed news squibs about Orangeburg or Memphis labor trouble, but the second week of Tet rattled experts no less than average citizens— perhaps more so—beneath a careful public posture of control. Officials of divergent views swayed daily to the point of vertigo inside a shifting government. Senator Robert Byrd, a staunch supporter, had alarmed the White House with forceful reasons why Tet proved everything in Vietnam was wrong. "I do not want to argue with the president," Byrd privately told Johnson, "but I am going to stick with my convictions." On Friday, when General Westmoreland had cabled secretly for "reinforcements at any time they can be made available," Clark Clifford, the incoming Secretary of Defense, questioned the "strange contradiction" of sending more troops to answer an enemy offensive already pronounced a catastrophic failure. The Sunday war council puzzled over the wording of Westmoreland's cable that he would "welcome" reinforcements. How badly did he need them?

On Monday morning, February 12, after back-channel exchanges with the Pentagon, Westmoreland declared his need "desperate" and the time window small. "We are now in a new ball game," he cabled Washington, "where we face a determined, highly disciplined enemy, fully mobilized to achieve a quick victory." President Johnson regathered his advisers to ask what could have changed so drastically since Friday. He said the two Westmoreland cables did not seem written by the same person. Some military leaders supported Johnson's nagging worry that Tet was a diversion for the real target at Khe Sanh. Others thought the enemy was prolonging suicidal losses to cripple the "badly mauled" South Vietnamese army, which made White House advisers fret more about Americanized war. But they approved the immediate call for six new battalions, and Johnson sent his top general to assess Westmoreland's further requests in person. News of the surprise escalation paralleled the renewal of the siege at Khe Sanh. "More exploding rockets sent showers of hot fragments zinging," said the AP dispatch. "The Americans dove for cover. . . . One prayed, a few cried, some were unconscious." General Earle Wheeler, chairman of the Joint Chiefs, generated more front-page headlines before leaving for Vietnam: "Wheeler Doubts Khesanh Will Need Atom Weapons." Johnson himself sought counsel from former President Eisenhower, who urged deference to Westmoreland as the general carrying the gravest responsibility in American history. Johnson asked how that could be, given that Eisenhower once commanded ten times as many soldiers, and Eisenhower replied that World War II was different. "Westmoreland doesn't know who the enemy is," he said, "and there is not any clearly defined front." The President also toured military installations in that third week of the Tet offensive, when American casualties set a new weekly high of 543 killed and 2,547 wounded. He reported back to his foreign policy team that talks with departing paratroopers in North Carolina "really melted me and brought me to my knees." He described a miserable Saturday night of insomnia aboard a Vietnam-bound troopship off California. "About three o'clock, and every hour after, I went to the door and saw this big hulk of a Marine," said Johnson. "I kept telling him, 'I am freezing.' He kept saying, 'Yes, sir,' but he never moved."

While Johnson toured, Hosea Williams barnstormed the South in a twin-engine Cessna 406, whose pilots were most unsettled to see that Martin Luther King was an unnamed passenger on the charter contract fobbed off by another company. A writer for the *New York Times Magazine* probed King in transit on press themes. Had he abandoned moral issues for class struggle? Did he know black militants were scoffing at nonviolence? Landing in Jackson on February 15, they drove to the first mass meeting at the Mt. Beulah Center of Edwards, Mississippi. FBI agents and state "sovereignty" investigators followed as King detoured past an all-black junior high school where squealing students waited outside to see him. Williams and Andrew Young sometimes fanned out to separate caucuses of poor people undecided about the new campaign. The Cessna reached Birmingham Thursday night for King to salute veterans from the breakthrough freedom marches of 1963. "I'm here to solicit your support!" he cried. "I want to know if you're going to Washington." The next morning, King told a packed house at Selma's Tabernacle Baptist what a blessing it was to be met at the tiny airport by a black deputy sheriff instead of Jim Clark's posse. He greeted Amelia Boynton, "mother" of the local voting rights movement, and Marie Foster, who still taught literacy for citizenship—also Rev. Lorenzo Harrison, who had fled the Lowndes County Klan into Brown Chapel a week before Bloody Sunday. "Believe in your heart that you are God's children," King told the crowd. "And if you are a child of God, you aren't supposed to live in any shack." Offstage, Rev. M. C. Cleveland discreetly presented a bill for three-year-old damages to First Baptist Church, including windows smashed by the posse and eight chairs ($36) broken by the voting rights pilgrims.

Young pulled at King to leave, and they flew over the Highway 80 march route from Selma to Montgomery. From the pulpit of Maggie Street Baptist Church, King introduced Mrs. Johnnie Carr, who headed the improvement association formed during the bus boycott, and acknowledged Rev. A. W. Wilson of Holt Street Baptist, "who pastors the church where we had our first big mass meeting," said King, "and I see Brother Marlow and Brother James and Brother Tom . . ." He reviewed a dozen years from the stirring of Rosa Parks through the glory of civil rights into riot and war. "I've agonized over it, and I'm trying to save America," he said. "And that's what you're trying to do if you will join this movement." He exhorted the middle-class crowd to organize contributions through their churches, which added a tone of reproach to his favorite ecumenical parable from Luke. "Dives didn't go to hell because he was rich," said King. "Dives went to hell because he passed by [the beggar] Lazarus every day but never really saw him. Dives went to hell because he allowed Lazarus to become invisible. . . . And I'll tell you, if America doesn't use its vast resources and wealth to bridge the gap between the rich and the poor nations, and between the rich and poor in this nation, it too is going to hell."

He lingered briefly with deacon R. D. Nesbitt, who had hired him for

Dexter Avenue Baptist in 1954. During the Cessna flight home, when the magazine writer asked on camera about the constant threats of jail and ambush, King described his two scariest memories—one from the march "through that narrow street" in Chicago as thousands of screaming people threw rocks even from the trees, when his police guards themselves ducked at once, the other from the commemorative march to the Neshoba County courthouse in Mississippi, when voices growled that the killers of the three young civil rights workers were standing close behind. "I just gave up," said King, but his talk of surrender to death turned playful. "Well, it came time to pray," he intoned, "and I sure did not want to close my eyes. Ralph said he prayed with his eyes open." In Atlanta, King switched to commercial flights for hurried engagements in Detroit before preaching at Ebenezer February 18 on a theme for the poverty campaign—the familiar parable of the Good Samaritan. King confessed that fear had made him bypass needy strangers on dangerous roads in modern Atlanta, falling short of the Samaritan's example. "And until mankind rises above race and class and nations," he told the congregation, "we will destroy ourselves by the misuse of our own power and instruments." Observers noted an air of frantic melancholy about King, who rushed on to Miami Sunday night.

J. Edgar Hoover secretly notified the White House that King was hosting black preachers from major cities at Miami's "plush new Sheraton-Four Ambassadors Hotel," courtesy of the Ford Foundation. Prompted by President Johnson, National Security Adviser Walt Rostow asked McGeorge Bundy if he realized he was sponsoring a week-long event likely to promote attacks on Vietnam policy along with "massive civil disobedience" in Washington. By coincidence, the front page of Sunday's *New York Times* broke news of a major shift by the Ford Foundation to fund programs on race. "The first conclusion I offer is that the most deep-seated and destructive of all the causes of the Negro problem is still the prejudice of the white man," wrote Bundy in a lofty but introspective president's report. "Prejudice is a subtle and insidious vice. It can consume those who think themselves immune to it. It can masquerade as kindness, sympathy, and even support." The *Times* story did not mention specific initiatives such as the leadership conference in Miami, where King somberly welcomed 150 ministers on Monday, February 19. "The problem is that the rising expectations for freedom and democracy have not been met," he said. "And interestingly enough, in a revolution when hope diminishes, the bitterness is often turned toward those who originally built up the hope." Death threats were so specific—a bomb warning into the Miami FBI office, a sniper boast from a caller who asked the hotel for King's room number—that police security officers convinced King to miss two days of the proceedings under guard.

*   *   *

JAMES LAWSON declined the trip to Miami, leaving him and King mildly disappointed in each other. King had hoped the preachers gathered by the Ford Foundation would take workshops from the movement's most gifted teacher of nonviolent theory and tactics, and he still wanted to pursue with Lawson a job to rebuild the SCLC staff. Lawson, for his part, doubted from prior assignments that King really could bring himself to address battle fatigue and dissipation among his young aides, or correct the bullying of underlings by Hosea Williams. He remained a loner within SCLC's prevailing Baptist culture, whose freelance pastors lacked patience for Lawson's delicate side negotiations with the United Methodist bishop in charge of his job placement. So Lawson stayed home to monitor the sanitation strike in Memphis.

The aspiring union workers had suffered badly in public relations. Local editorials rallied behind the city government against the effrontery of the strikers and the health hazard of garbage piles on the streets. News broadcasts made permanent replacement collectors seem swift and inevitable: "The city hired 47 new sanitation workers today, turned down an estimated 30 other applicants, and is expecting 'many, many more' to apply tomorrow." Bumper stickers appeared on Memphis cars—"CIAMPA GO HOME"—after AFSCME's site representative spoke sharply in televised negotiations. ("Oh, put your halo in your pocket and let's get realistic!" he told Mayor Loeb.) Union officials made an emergency decision that the gruff son of a Pennsylvania coal miner was culturally unsuited to a Southern campaign, and Jerry Wurf, AFSCME's international president, assumed command in the strike's second week. Mayor Loeb promptly escorted Wurf to the annual Memphis banquet for the National Conference of Christians and Jews, where Loeb drew thunderous ovations above barely polite reception for the union executive. To Wurf, Loeb's intended lesson was to demonstrate that he had no exploitable weakness among prominent citizens as a converted Jew, recently confirmed into the Episcopal Church, and that Wurf of New York could expect little rebound sympathy from fellow Jews in Memphis. At six feet five inches, Loeb stood a head taller than

Wurf. A graduate of elite schools—Andover Academy and Brown University—Loeb had commanded a PT boat in the Navy, then inherited a chain of businesses from a father he said would turn over in his grave if he recognized a union. When Wurf asked in private what made sanitation workers different from bus drivers, teachers, and police officers with local unions, Loeb vowed to protect his workers from outside exploitation. When Wurf offered to donate the first year's dues to Loeb's favorite charity, the mayor replied that the strike was illegal and defeated already. He would discuss issues only after the men went back to work.

Lawson met Wurf at the first public forum, on Thursday, February 22. Prodded by intermediaries from all sides, City Council members sought a face-saving compromise between Loeb's demand for surrender and the union's package of reforms, but their hearing stalled over recognition to speak. One by one, striking workers deferred to union officials, each of whom was gaveled to silence. "We insist on hearing from the men themselves!" said the chairman, and the standoff grew raucous until the union side pretended to capitulate. From their daily rally at the United Rubber Workers Hall, more than seven hundred strikers soon entered the ornate council chamber of rosewood panel and scarlet carpet. They shouted assent when leaders asked if they wanted the union. From the floor, Lawson and other local preachers sparred with council members about whether they could hear the men now. "I have to walk both sides of the street," declared the exasperated committee chairman, Fred Davis, one of three black members on the City Council of thirteen, hinting plaintively that he must lean far toward Mayor Loeb's requirements to get votes for any resolution. Davis tried vainly to thin the crowd by half to meet fire codes, then to adjourn the deadlocked hearing, but the strikers broke defiantly into the movement song: "We shall not be moved!" They sang "God Bless America," and preachers interspersed prayers with impromptu sermons all afternoon in what became a mass meeting of occupation. A white man from the Tennessee Council on Human Relations sent out for a hundred loaves of bread and thirty pounds of bologna. Rev. Ezekiel Bell, the only black pastor in the Memphis Presbytery, called his church kitchen for mustard and utensils. Eight women used the city attorney's table to make sandwiches they wrapped ceremoniously in paper napkins for dispersal by hand. "We cast our bread upon the water!" called out William Lucy, a black deputy to Wurf.

Some 150 officers surrounded the muffled noise of City Hall in police cruisers, waiting for orders as messengers shuttled between caucuses and the Davis committee, which remained besieged on the council platform. Ten days into the strike, only twenty of two hundred sanitation trucks were in service. Replacement workers were proving difficult to find or keep, despite the city's influx of sharecroppers displaced by the nearly total mechanization of cotton farms. Boy Scout troops spearheaded civic drives of curbside cooperation to help the overmatched replacement crews, but they stopped short of removing trash themselves. With backlogged piles in front of some downtown businesses, voices at the Memphis Country Club were muttering that public unions were a minor cost of business, and the embattled Public Works Committee resolved to propose its bare-bones settlement without a hearing. Chairman Davis completed less than two sentences of the announcement at 5:38 P.M.

"The men were on their feet cheering," wrote Memphis historian Joan Beifuss. "Jubilantly they thronged the aisles." Leaders handed out chunks of leftover food as mementos, and cleanup crews busily swept up crumbs behind a happy departure. On Friday, overflow crowds forced a shift into Ellis Auditorium for a vote by the full City Council, and more than a thousand sanitation workers arrived in their best clothes—suits and baseball hats, starched shirts and fedoras, Sunday shoes and tan raincoats. Dignitaries and curious newcomers came, too, but the prospects for a settlement had chilled overnight. The front page of the *Memphis Commercial Appeal* emblazoned incendiary headlines: "Committee Surrenders but Loeb Holds Firm/ Strike Boosters Hold Picnic in Chambers of City Council." Stories described the event "as if it were a raid by barbaric Visigoths," a critic would write. The editorial cartoon presented a fat Sambo caricature of T. O. Jones perched on a garbage can labeled "City Hall Sit-In," with fumes curling upward to spell a message: "Threat of Anarchy."

Council members entered long enough to pass a resolution delegating "sole authority" in sanitation matters to Mayor Loeb, then filed out by a rear exit under police escort. They left a stunned silence behind, followed by puzzled questions and scattered boos. Wurf came forward with groping explanations that the promised settlement vote must have been aborted, but the public address system went dead before he or local leaders could respond. In confusion, James Lawson noticed white councilman Jerred Blanchard peek back into the auditorium. "Jerry," he pleaded, "could you give us a microphone?" Blanchard had voted for the substitute resolution, angry over yesterday's abuse of Fred Davis, but he regretted skulking out the back door. From a law student's memory of one courtroom argument in the 1940s by the legendary NAACP attorney Charles Houston, Blanchard retained a stab of conscience about the attitudes toward nearly half the city population. Now he rushed off to say the public address system should be restored, if only to prevent pandemonium. (For such gestures, Blanchard said, he became known as the council's "fourth nigger.") Loeb refused on the ground that the sanitation workers should leave, not talk. A white lawyer bolted in to warn that it was going too far for police units to attack the workers in retreat. When Loeb denied any such plan, the lawyer cited his own eyes— "Well, the police have their gas masks on"—and the mayor confirmed quickly by radio that masked units indeed had formed several rows deep across Main Street, linked arm-in-arm. Lawson and Jerry Wurf were imploring the police commanders to let the angry, devastated men walk together to a church.

New police instructions allowed the marchers to move out four abreast in the right lane. Cruisers rolled slowly beside the front ranks to make sure no strays crossed the center line, while foot patrols stretched parallel to the marchers behind. The police formation, which magnified the tension, conflicted with the stated goal to keep northbound Main Street open for traffic. Toward Gayoso Avenue, two blocks before a turn into Beale Street's famous blues corridor, cruisers angled rightward to pinch marchers toward the curb, and a piercing shriek emitted from Gladys Carpenter, a City Council employee known for her journeys to march in Selma and Mississippi. When sanitation workers jumped to lift a car tire off her foot, officers jumped from the rocking cruiser to spray incapacitating Mace. Within seconds, radio reports triggered general mayhem from an order to disperse the procession. Seventy-two-year-old O. B. Hicks crumpled to the sidewalk from a "blinding chemical." Jacques Wilmore, who begged an officer to stop hitting the bloodied Hicks, flashed credentials as regional director for the U.S. Civil Rights Commission, only to be Maced himself, and Hicks would be hospitalized under arrest for night-riding. Hundreds of strikers fled in panic, but some were dragged toward jail on their bellies. James Lawson looked back in time to see a solid line of officers charging behind truncheons and spray cans of Mace, then choked from several doses at close range. He recovered enough to lead a remnant of the marchers nearly three miles to safety in the [Bishop Charles] Mason Temple, the mother congregation for the Pentecostal Church of God in Christ.

P. J. Ciampa came there late. After stragglers pulled him semiconscious from the sidewalk gutter, they found water to rinse Mace from his eyes, then flagged down a passing sedan. Hustled into the back seat, Ciampa blinked at the strange sight of polished spats on an imposing black preacher who moaned in the throes of conversion. For Rev. H. Ralph Jackson, it became his mantra that a lifetime of dutiful trust "went down the drain" the instant police officers gassed him like others in clerical garb. He had avoided "race trouble" always to climb the hierarchy of the AME church. No fewer than nine AME bishops had just witnessed Mayor Henry Loeb dedicate the grand new headquarters building for the AME Minimum Salary Division to support needy ministers, with effusive praise for its national director, and Jackson burst into Mason Temple to say Memphis police *never* would attack white preachers like that, without even speaking. "This happened to me because I was black," he proclaimed. Astonished wags quipped that the foremost Uncle Tom of Memphis was reborn a lion of protest. He joined leaders Ezekiel Bell and James Lawson to tell counterparts in the white clergy that the labor struggle was now a test of civil rights. A lone white minister was whisked forward to read scripture when he ventured by surprise into the next mass meeting. Inspired by the martyred German theologian Dietrich Bonhoeffer, Rev. Bill Aldridge tried to articulate why Christian obligation must override passions of race or class, but exposure first made him shiver in every culture. ("Goodness knows why I was there," he recalled.) Distressed members of his prestigious Presbyterian congregation circulated letters stipulating that their assistant pastor's sojourn among the garbage workers "does not represent the majority of people at Idlewild Church."

* * *

In Miami, a Ford Foundation observer reported confidentially to McGeorge Bundy that SCLC's conference on urban ministry subsided from chaos into lessons led by the spirit. He said young James Bevel, "who breathes fire and smoke," preached early in the week on the structure of slums "like a man unprepared to accept any shred of the present American system," and Daniel Moynihan had the misfortune to follow "in an atmosphere of almost total hostility" toward his famous report on pathology in Negro families. Moynihan became "unusually timid," added the observer, taking refuge in abstractions that worsened his reception, "but he did make a speech before a group of black ministers and got out alive."* Subsequent presentations—notably by Alvin Pitcher of Chicago and Virgil Wood of Boston—challenged the preachers with rare models of church-based mobilization for education and employment. Rev. C. T. Vivian quoted one voice from a survey of attitudes toward the evangelical slum church: "I have shouted until my garter-holders have come loose . . . but it didn't change the conditions under which I live, so I don't shout no more." On Friday, February 23, King reprised his determination late in 1964 to leave the Nobel Prize mountaintop for the valley of Selma. "And the valley calls us," he said. "We will be returning to valleys filled with men and women who know the ache and anguish of poverty . . . filled with thousands and thousands of young people who've lost faith in America." He preached again on Lazarus and Dives. ("Hell is the pain you inflict upon yourself for refusing God's grace.") "I want you to go back and tell our brothers and sisters to wait until the next morning—don't give up too early," he said. "Tell the black nationalists, who want to give up on nonviolence, don't give up yet." He exhorted the preachers "as we leave Miami to go out and prophesy," then ducked away to New York for an evening speech.

Managers at the Four Ambassadors advanced numerous polite reasons to head off a songfest of farewell hymns by their SCLC guests, but skeptics sensed corporate nerves badly frayed by the thought of black preachers massed in the new cathedral lobby. During delicate negotiations, a check-in telephone call brought emergency news of the Mace riot on Main Street—"Oh Lord, all hell's broke out here"—which caused ministers Samuel "Billy" Kyles and Benjamin Hooks of Memphis to cancel family trips and book the next flight home. They had time to join about fifty remaining colleagues around the Sheraton's piano for movement songs and spirituals in harmony, closing with "We Shall Overcome," and tension dissipated to the point that one hotel patron inquired about hiring the ensemble to sing on the beach.

King reached Carnegie Hall to address a hundredth-birthday celebration for the late scholar W. E. B. Du Bois. Ossie Davis presided. Pete Seeger sang in appreciation, and King sketched a life that had spanned nearly a century of upheaval, starting in 1868 just as Congress im-

* Moynihan complained to Bundy of "near demented Black militants," who dominated a conference "so suffused with near madness as to begin to wonder whether I had not slipped my own moorings as well."

peached Abraham Lincoln's successor, Andrew Johnson. Among luminous books by DuBois, King cited *Black Reconstruction in America* for puncturing the hoary myth that "civilization virtually collapsed" while ex-slaves could vote and hold office, by chronicling the introduction of public schools among many institutions sturdy enough to survive white supremacy's restoration by force. DuBois proved, he said, "that far from being the tragic era white historians described, it was the only period in which democracy existed in the South." King's tribute covered DuBois the NAACP founder and early crusader against segregation, down to the defiant expatriate whose death was announced during the 1963 March on Washington. "We cannot talk of Dr. DuBois without recognizing that he was a radical all of his life," said King. "Some people would like to ignore the fact that he was a Communist in his later years."

Stanley Levison candidly bemoaned King's Carnegie Hall performance. "I've never heard Martin read anything as badly," he told friends over his wiretapped phone. He said King had used a prepared text, strayed from proven oratorical themes, and matched rather than elevated the tone of "the deadest meeting I've ever seen." For Levison, the DuBois event was emblematic of despair in progressive circles. "The people are depressed," he said. "They feel that nobody has answers to riots in the streets. They feel frustrated about Vietnam." Levison thought the depression was unwarranted but real, like the paradox of DuBois, who could be recognized either for a long arc of achievement or his bitter, halfhearted flight into Communist ideology.

Levison groped for bearings when radicals and rulers alike boiled over in every direction about race, violence, and democracy. In Oakland, California, Stokely Carmichael, after a sensational "Free Huey" speech on the birthday of Huey Newton, had just been named "Prime Minister of the Black Nation" in a fantasy merger between remnants of SNCC and the Black Panther Party. Carmichael had turned hard against his own years of creative privation in the voting rights movement. "The vote in this country is, has been, and always will be irrelevant to the lives of black people!" he told the Oakland rally for Newton. He posed for photographs with sunglasses and a rifle, calling for solidarity with Cuba and North Vietnam, but he turned also against any "white" Marxist anchor for political thought, in part because Fidel Castro and Ho Chi Minh had rejected his request for separate black leadership. "Communism is not an ideology suited for black people, period, period, period," Carmichael declared. "Socialism is not an ideology fitted for black people." He embraced color—"Black nationalism must be our ideology"—with little but militant rhetoric to govern internecine competition. His SNCC rival James Forman became "Foreign Minister" by vowing personal retribution against whites on an enormous scale—"The sky is the limit if you kill Huey Newton!"—but soon wound up menaced himself by Black Panthers with pistols. From jail, after a gun battle with police, Newton wanted Carmichael to wear Panther leather instead of African robes, and Eldridge Cleaver sneered at Carmichael as a pretender with a "suitcase full of African souvenirs." Willie Ricks sighed: "SNCC people were the bad niggers in town, and then the Panthers jumped up and started saying, 'We are badding you out.'"

In Washington, the nation's leaders fragmented over real violence. On Tuesday, February 27, they gathered secretly in shock over a cable from Vietnam requesting 205,179 more U.S. soldiers above the current ceiling of 535,000. "This is unbelievable and futile," numbly observed White House counselor Harry McPherson, who rarely spoke in military meetings. New Defense Secretary Clifford feared popular revolt against pouring troops down a rat hole. That same evening, CBS News televised the respected anchor Walter Cronkite from the rubble of the formerly serene Vietnamese imperial capital of Hue, which Tet attackers had held for twenty-six days under massive U.S. bombardment. "What about those fourteen Vietcong we found in the courtyard behind the post office?" Cronkite asked his viewers, doubting that civilian or military casualties could ever be tabulated. "They certainly hadn't been buried," he said. Cronkite glumly announced a "speculative, personal, subjective" judgment from his inspection tour of the war zone: "To say that we are mired in stalemate seems the only realistic, if unsatisfactory, conclusion."

President Johnson returned from his Texas ranch after midnight, doubly shaken. Cronkite's broadcast assured a drop in war support among moderate Americans, and the giant troop request risked defection even by war hawks in Congress. Early Wednesday morning, General Wheeler of the Joint Chiefs rushed straight from his transpacific flight to the White House, where he told Johnson's war cabinet that the battle initiative was conceded to the enemy in the Vietnamese countryside, and that Westmoreland lacked the reserves to hold cities unless he abandoned several provinces. Wheeler's manner was graver still than the cable he had sent ahead from Vietnam, which drove the President to exaggerated caution. "Buzz, we are very thankful that you are back," he said gently. Johnson commanded strict secrecy while he thrashed for options, but the search for new solutions collided with war weariness. Mendel Rivers, chairman of the House Armed Services Committee, irascibly said the administration should authorize nuclear weapons or withdraw. Among key senators, Henry "Scoop" Jackson warned that he would balk at any troop shipment big enough to require new taxes or a call-up of the Reserves, and the President stooped to subtle provocation with his powerful friend Richard Russell of Georgia—saying war critic William Fulbright now put Russell among his converted Vietnam doves.

"Well, did he call my name?" asked the prickly Russell, who denounced the war in private but scarcely spoke to Fulbright, whom he regarded as a prima donna.

"It was just enough, like an old cow if you ever milked in the country days," Johnson coyly replied. "Just as you get the bucket full, she dragged her tail through the top of it and leaves a little streak. That is the way he dragged your name through it."

Hard upon Cronkite and the Wheeler crisis came the report of the Kerner Commission on riots, which paralyzed even Johnson's guile. He seethed first that news outlets jumped the release date with feverish headlines on March 1: "Panel on Civil Disorders Calls for Drastic Action to Avoid 2-Society Nation/ Whites Criticized/ Vast Aid to Negroes Urged, with New Taxes if Needed." The President steadfastly ignored an avalanche of publicity about the Kerner Commission, which found no political conspiracy behind the urban riots of 1967, and traced them primarily to racial deprivation. "What white Americans have never fully understood—but what the Negro can never forget—is that white society is deeply implicated in the ghetto," declared the report. "White institutions created it, white institutions maintain it, and white society condones it. . . . White racism is essentially responsible for the explosive mixture which has been accumulating in our cities since the end of World War II." Aides bravely warned the President that refusal to acknowledge his own commission was a publicity blunder, especially since the Kerner recommendations so closely paralleled his "racial redress" speech at Howard University in 1965. But it was too painful for Johnson to rationalize or deny that his domestic agenda was lost to a Vietnam budget more than three times what his commission urged for investment in cities. Instead, he escaped Washington with a stealthy new travel regimen to avoid hordes of antiwar protesters—no advance schedule for reporters, short notice to intended hosts—and turned away from questions about the riots.

The Kerner Commission enjoyed a record burst of popular interest—with 740,000 paperback copies sold in the first eleven days of March—then vanished without official notice. Potentates in Congress dismissed the idea of helping cities when they could not even pass a small surtax to pay for Vietnam, and one television network soon broadcast a prime-time news special, *What Happened to the Riot Report?* From the opening fanfare, what galled President Johnson most was the Kerner report's signature sentence: "Our nation is moving toward two societies, one black, one white—separate and unequal." History had reversed course! The report baldly stated that American race relations were growing more segregated and stratified, which to Johnson was catchy but insidious slander. If the civil rights era was counterproductive, then historic commitments since *Brown v. Board of Education* were empty and liberal democracy itself futile. Together with Tet, the report left in near ruins both his war and his peace paths to advance freedom. Johnson's fury was so strong that he could not bring himself to sign routine thank-you letters for the eleven Kerner Commission members, including stalwart friends Roy Wilkins and I. W. Abel, president of the United Steelworkers. "I'd be a hypocrite," said Johnson. He ordered his staff to hide or destroy the unsigned drafts.

* * *

JAMES LAWSON made King laugh with calculations that Roy Wilkins's ego would not allow him to follow King into Memphis, because the inevitable fall-off in audience would reflect poorly on him, but Lawson thought he could persuade Wilkins to be the first national speaker. Memphis was an NAACP town, and the local NAACP leaders had endorsed the fundamental cause of the garbage strikers before the Mace attacks of February 23. For ten days since, more than a hundred local black preachers organized to join strikers in protest marches to City Hall every morning and afternoon, with nightly mass meetings in churches across the city. It was the broadest coalition ever in Memphis, Lawson reported by telephone, with the energy of movements they had experienced together from Nashville and Albany to Selma, but all he wanted now was permission to say he had *invited* King. This would help lure Wilkins.

King seized the reprieve, pleading exhaustion from his own labors.

Only a handful of reporters turned out in Atlanta on Monday, March 4, to hear him postpone the starting date for SCLC's "nonviolent poor people's march on Washington." Leaders would begin "a lobby-in against Congress" on April 22, King disclosed, when a simultaneous "mule train" of three thousand pilgrims would set out from Mississippi to reinforce them. Details remained vague, as there might be more than one mule train, and King promised only that the legislative agenda would resemble the new Kerner Commission proposals. "It may be," he said, "that in one or two instances we are stronger than they are." King seemed unfazed by reports that federal authorities were mobilizing a backup force of ten thousand MPs to contain him, but he escaped to Mexico on Tuesday for a rest. In Memphis, that afternoon's march to City Hall ended with the first planned sit-in against the suspended negotiations. Fearing Mace, first-time demonstrators weakly chanted, "We want arrest," and managed to sing "Leaning on the Everlasting Arms." Officers hauled off NAACP leader Maxine Smith, possessor of degrees from Spelman and Middlebury colleges, along with several preachers and more than a hundred sanitation workers. On the way to jail, Lawson told reporters he had invited King to Memphis.

King's gloomy distraction pushed friends to the brink of alarm. He preached at Ebenezer on "Unfulfilled Dreams," clinging to the Bible's message of consolation when King David of Israel realized he would never live to see a temple built in Jerusalem: "You did well that it was in your heart." King identified with crushed hopes. Bullets had ended Gandhi's hope to witness independent India, he said, and "Paul never got to Spain." People constantly fell short both on great dreams for the world and intimate promises to redeem their character. "You don't need to go out this morning saying that Martin Luther King is a saint," he cried. "Oh, no. I want you to know this morning that I am a sinner like all of God's children." He longed from the pulpit to hear the comfort of David: "It is well that it is within thine heart. It's well that you are trying. You may not see it. The dream may not be fulfilled, but . . . thank God this morning that we do have hearts to put something meaningful in."

The flight to Acapulco was so sudden that no hotel could be reserved, and King complained oddly and persistently that he did not get into the Las Brisas resort where Luci Johnson had spent her honeymoon. Ralph Abernathy soon wangled rooms there by invoking King's Nobel celebrity, whereupon King refused to leave El Presidente because the staff workers had made such a fuss over him. Abernathy kept rooms in both hotels, but King slept little in either. He stared alone from a high balcony until nearly dawn and evaded Abernathy's questions about what was wrong—pointing enigmatically to a rock in Acapulco harbor, then singing "Rock of Ages." His conduct alarmed Abernathy enough to make discreet inquiries about whether the FBI may have threatened King directly again, but he found no such reports.

In Washington, Director Hoover clamped down when a single hint of FBI surveillance surfaced publicly. Late in February, five days after Hoover circulated another secret report within the government, Richard Harwood disclosed in the *Washington Post* that FBI officials had offered to reporters tape-recorded evidence of "moral turpitude" on King's part. No other news outlet would touch the cryptic revelation, which Harwood buried among equally sensitive suggestions that Hoover had become a pampered tyrant with homosexual leanings. Over the next decade, a few journalists would regret their failure to expose firsthand evidence of Hoover's penchant for spy vendettas above public service. ("I didn't do my job," recalled David Kraslow of the *Los Angeles Times*. "I should have blown the thing sky high, but I didn't.") At the other extreme, the editors of *Parade* magazine asked permission to print the following answer to a fake question about the extent of the FBI's sex dossier: "Not a complete file, but it has a great deal of titillating information about his sexual activities." When Bureau officials sternly refused, "because it clearly intimates that the FBI is furnishing information to the public concerning Martin Luther King," the editors canceled the item. Publications avoided the controversy to preserve the prime FBI news source.

Internally, Hoover emphasized his supreme rule that operations must carry "no possibility of embarrassment to the Bureau." While demanding an invisible hand, he expanded covert, extralegal assignments on March 4 by adding eighteen new FBI field offices to the twenty-three largest ones already tasked for the COINTELPRO campaign against black groups. Two days later, Hoover approved parallel instructions against the SCLC poverty campaign in Washington, declaring it "a grave threat to peace and order in this city." The goals were to discredit black groups and "prevent the rise of a 'messiah' who could unify, and electrify, the militant black nationalist movement." Hoover targeted King, Stokely Carmichael, and Muslim leader Elijah Muhammad as potential messiahs, twisting the religious word into something alien and violent. "King would be a very real contender for his position," he wrote, "should he abandon his supposed 'obedience' to 'white liberal doctrines' (nonviolence) and embrace black nationalism." There were grumbles in the field about the draconian schedule for submission of counterintelligence ideas "to pinpoint potential troublemakers and neutralize them before they exercise their potential for violence." What did Hoover's nobly dramatic words really mean? Most offices lacked a dark face to help infiltrate civil rights groups, as the integrated FBI still employed only forty black rookies among six thousand agents. Some veterans considered political chores inherently childish, or thought militants needed no help to discredit themselves.

The approved COINTELPRO actions ran heavily to propaganda and petty sabotage. Detroit was the first office to volunteer nonexistent transportation and lodging for SCLC's anti-poverty volunteers. Miami recruited and paid the producer for a local NBC television special on young black leaders made to appear especially fearful, angry, and incoherent on screen. (Hoover himself praised the skillful use of hard chairs, lights, and slow camera techniques showing "each movement as they squirmed about in their chairs, resembling rats trapped under scientific observation.") Savannah said Hosea Williams lost two hundred poverty recruits because of planted news stories that he would strand them sick and penniless in Washington. Several offices sowed bitter discord with forged tips that black leaders were spies for the CIA or the Bureau itself—a tactic borrowed from the wars against the Communist Party. New York falsely warned May Charles Carmichael that the Black Panthers were on the way to shoot her son, which would cause him to leave for Africa the next day. ("Mrs. Carmichael appeared shocked upon hearing the news," reported the FBI supervisor, "and stated she would tell Stokely when he came home.") The Jackson, Mississippi, office pioneered leaflets to peddle rumors that King wanted the poverty campaign for money and aggrandizement. Headquarters updated a secret, twenty-page monograph on King, which appended to the usual sinister interpretation of his career a partial list of recent SCLC contributors: New York governor Nelson Rockefeller ($25,000), Harry Belafonte ($10,000), Anne Farnsworth ($150,000), the Ford Foundation ($230,000), Merrill Lynch ($15,000), and the U.S. Department of Labor ($61,000 for job training). The last figure caused President Johnson to scribble a note: "Show this to [Labor Secretary] Bill Wirtz."

A grim omen transformed official Washington. On Saturday night of the Gridiron Club's satirical revue, shock passed visibly through the ballroom behind whispers and advance copies of a headline in the March 10 *New York Times:* "Westmoreland Requests 206,000 More Men, Stirring Debate in Administration." Reporters ambushed White House press secretary George Christian at his table, and speechless senators excused themselves. The next day, President Johnson issued a furious but technical denial, which served to confirm the hotly debated secret while eroding his credibility. On Monday, television entertainer Jack Paar endorsed Eugene McCarthy in a network interview that broke his career pattern of lampooning all politicians and the vote itself; Paar told viewers he had been converted by his college daughter in "this children's crusade" for McCarthy. On Tuesday, McCarthy confounded political observers by winning 42 percent of the vote against an incumbent President in New Hampshire's first primary test, despite a late blitz of LBJ ads calling McCarthy the champion of draft dodgers and surrender. On Wednesday, ABC News anchor Howard K. Smith broadcast a passionate editorial for war mobilization "on an overwhelming scale," far beyond the pending troop request. On Thursday, Pentagon officials said the week's 509 combat deaths pushed the running total to 139,801 American casualties (19,670 killed and 120,131 wounded), which surpassed Korea to make Vietnam the fourth bloodiest war in American history. That afternoon, with President Johnson listening on a telephone extension, intermediaries deadlocked over Robert Kennedy's tormented new offer to stay out of the presidential race in exchange for public steps to change Vietnam policy. By Saturday, March 16, when Kennedy formally challenged both Johnson and McCarthy for the Democratic nomination, political warriors from the White House scrambled to lock down "blood oath" commitments.

The President took soundings among bellwether politicians such as Senator Russell and Mayor Daley of Chicago, who knew how to shift ground skillfully. Russell already was touting more bombs instead of soldiers, though doubting victory through airpower. "I can't afford to lose Russell," Johnson confided. "Now if I lose him, we've got nothing." Johnson feared that approving the latest troop escalation would isolate him as the candidate of all-out war. "We can't take it and hold," he warned Defense Secretary Clifford, "because people like Daley and them are not going to hold."

"They won't hold," Clifford repeated. Following the President's lead, he suggested a slogan that would stall disengagement politics for seven more years: "We are not out to win the war—we are out to win the peace."

"That is right," Johnson replied. Through Clifford, he embraced an offer from McGeorge Bundy to reconvene the bipartisan advisers called the Wise Men, who had approved the course of the war as recently as November of 1967. Now the President hoped to regain political and military initiative short of Westmoreland's escalation. "We're not going to get these doves," he told Clifford, "but we can neutralize the country to where it won't follow them, if we can come up with something."

* * *

THE GLARE of Vietnam overshadowed contemporary landmarks. Even as their rivalry boiled into open warfare for the presidency, Johnson and Robert Kennedy collaborated to gain a Senate vote at last on the civil rights bill from 1966. The lynch-murders of Freedom Summer had inspired its federal protections for the exercise of basic political rights, while Alabama's travesty trials for the killers of Viola Liuzzo and Jonathan Daniels generated the provisions for integrated juries. Despite two intervening years of backlash and division, the civil rights coalition pushed tenaciously on fundamental points to invoke cloture for the eighth time in history. Republican leader Everett Dirksen of Illinois once again claimed credit for "pulling it out of the fire," with timely compromise on the historic open housing provisions. Only three Republican senators joined the old segregationist core of seventeen Southern Democrats to oppose final passage, 71–20, nearly duplicating the tally on the Voting Rights Act of 1965. Celebrations were subdued because prospects remained uncertain in the House.

Empirical results from the freedom movement advanced quietly by inertia. On March 11, in *Washington v. Lee,* the U.S. Supreme Court overturned the wholesale segregation of state prisons and local jails by race. The Equal Employment Opportunity Commission resolved after two years to challenge industry rules requiring flight attendants to be single young women, but it would take another five months to ban the separate "Girl Friday" want-ad sections. In Memphis, where the sanitation strike entered its second month, more than a thousand black students now integrated Memphis State University, but school officials, still worried that Tiger fans would not accept any change in their Saturday spectacle, pressured the athletic department to defend the all-white football team on competitive grounds. "We would like to recruit Negro players in Memphis, if they can play," the head coach announced before spring practice. Such contortion seemed antiquated already, which united all sides in belittlement of strained or outdated racial news. White students made front pages with a hippie "be-in" at New York's Grand Central Station in March, but it was a tiny squib that the South African government introduced three measures to "complete" the apartheid system, including abolition of the four seats in the National Assembly for which mixed-race Coloreds had been allowed to elect white representatives. Only a small movement journal recorded the brazen clash at Tuskegee Institute when student followers of Stokely Carmichael pelted four State Department visitors with eggs, calling themselves a simulated "Vietcong air force" to show the panel of experts what it felt like to be bombed in their own country. The same journal headlined the plea from a rural rally outside Tuskegee, where no utility service reached farmhouses or the Negro school: " 'A Phone Before I Die.' "

On March 15, a dozen white men returned a guilty verdict for the 1966 firebomb attack on Vernon Dahmer. "It was the first time a state jury in the South has convicted anyone for murder in a civil rights case," reported the *Los Angeles Times*. Judge Stanton Hall, who whittled on the bench with a confiscated razor, sentenced Klansman Cecil Sessum to life. District Attorney James Finch, always proclaiming that he never voted for LBJ but considered the Negro victim one of the hardest-working farmers in Hattiesburg, prosecuted and convicted three more Klansmen with an emotional summary: "You twelve men represent Forrest County to the world when it comes to justice." Star witness Billy Roy Pitts testified each time that he had dropped his gun in the Klan posse's wild flight after their bullets pinned Dahmer in the firebombed home to suffer mortal burns, and had confessed since "because I done what I done and the Lord wouldn't let me go on livin' that kind of life." The four trials exhausted the pioneer courage in the local courts, leaving eleven indictments unresolved, and the story lapsed nearly thirty years before reporter Jerry Mitchell noticed that Mississippi had neglected to have Billy Roy Pitts serve even a day of his life sentence. This invisible dereliction—a wonder in the annals of jurisprudence—made news until Pitts surrendered from Louisiana. His testimony then buttressed one of the atonement prosecutions revived by a new generation of elected Southerners, aimed at surviving figures long admired, forgotten, or excused. On August 21, 1998, Mississippi peers convicted Sam Bowers of ordering the Dahmer murder, among others, and sent the former Imperial Wizard to prison at seventy-three.

* * *

BLIND VIOLENCE alone could seal a more dogmatic estrangement than race. Earlier in March, toward the end of the Tet offensive, one wounded medic from the 101st Airborne Division whispered a prayer from the evacuation helicopter: "God help you guys for what you did." His elite Tiger Force platoon had been detached into central Vietnam with orders to drive the inhabitants of selected villages into refugee camps, thereby depriving enemy soldiers of food and shelter. Isolated, victimized by snipers and booby traps on patrol, platoon leaders surrendered the unit to sporadic but indiscriminate revenge. Twenty-seven of its forty-five soldiers later told Army investigators that it was routine to wear shoelace necklaces of human ears. Private Sam Ybarra, who had joined the Army on the day of his release from an Arizona jail, pushed ahead in pathological displays. He scalped "gooks," shot a boy for his shoes, and decapitated a Vietnamese infant to remove the "Buddha band" from its neck. At least one fellow soldier pondered killing Ybarra, but pulled back to "creepy" fatalism. "The way to live is to kill," said Sergeant William Doyle, "because you don't have to worry about anybody who's dead." Ybarra stood three courts-martial in Vietnam for drug abuse, and would drink himself to death from nightmares on his mother's couch. So many soldiers filed complaints, and even confessions, that the Pentagon's longest war crimes investigation waited years at the threshold of White House authority to prosecute, until the cases were dropped with quiet relief at the war's end. Official aversion to the anticipated publicity proved stronger than distaste for the alleged crimes, and the Tiger Force history would not surface until a 2003 newspaper series in the Toledo, Ohio, *Blade,* full of haunted, cathartic recollections from aging veterans.

On March 16, while Robert Kennedy's campaign announcement jolted American politics from the room where his late brother had announced for President in 1960, a fresh unit of the Army's Americal Division raided a remote cluster of hamlets in Quang Nai Province, which was base area also for the Tiger Force. Since arriving in February, soldiers from Charlie Company of the 1st Battalion, 11th Brigade, had endured losses without seeing an enemy to fight—six killed and twelve wounded in a minefield, a sergeant killed two days previously when he picked up a disguised bomb that cost others an arm, two legs, and an eye. On their traumatized march back to camp, the head of the column had come across a lone farmer in a rice field. "They shot and wounded her," Private Greg Olson wrote home just before the raid. "Then they kicked her to death and emptied their magazines in her head. They slugged every little kid they came across. Why in God's name does this have to happen? . . . This isn't the first time, Dad. . . . I don't know why I'm telling you all this; I guess I just wanted to get it off my chest." Olson, a Mormon from Oregon, rushed early into the reported enemy stronghold of My Lai, with commanders from other outfits poised to reinforce the only major thrust in the region.

From above, pilot Hugh Thompson of Georgia first puzzled that his three-man scout helicopter drew no fire for the hovering big gunships to suppress. Not a hostile shot was reported, nor a weapon captured all day. He dropped green (meaning safe) smoke flares near an alarming number of killed and wounded civilians around the village perimeter, marking them for assistance by the ground troops—only to fly over again and find the wounded all dead. Mounting horror drove Thompson to land three times. At a drainage ditch filled with casualties, a Charlie Company sergeant said the only way to help was to put them out of their misery. Back in the air, Thompson's crew frantically debated whether an artillery accident, enemy atrocity, or any logical military action could explain the methodical rifle fire into stacks of bodies. Groups of soldiers across the scattered hamlets pushed families and isolated peasants into dugout cellars or water wells, then dropped grenades in after them. Several groups of sixty or more were herded into open spaces and mowed down. Some soldiers balked. Some made light of it and paused for lunch. Some sobbed and shot at the same time. Thompson next landed ahead of a pursuit squad from Charlie Company, shouting orders for eighteen-year-old gunner Larry Colburn to shoot his fellow Americans if they fired at him or the ten villagers huddled ahead. Colburn was as stunned as Private Olson, who, from the refuge of his nearby machine gun post, watched the strange pilot interpose himself on the verge of an enraged fight with the 2nd platoon's lieutenant, until unprecedented SOS landings by two gunships evacuated the Vietnamese to safety. Thompson flew back to the drainage ditch to check for survivors and his own sanity. His crew chief waded hip-deep in the carnage to pry from a mother's corpse one silent but squirming small boy, so covered in blood and filth that they were well into the escape flight before they decided he was not hit.

At brigade headquarters, the three helicopter soldiers filed complaints about a massacre of civilians, and South Vietnamese district officials compiled a secret burial list of some five hundred My Lai villagers, including more than a hundred children younger than six. However, only the authorized account of My Lai reached front pages like Sunday's *New York Times:* "American troops caught a North Vietnamese force in a pincer movement on the central coastal plain yesterday, killing 128 enemy soldiers in day-long fighting." This version remained intact until a young draftee returned home in 1969 with notes of terrible witness unburdened on him by training buddies assigned to Charlie Company. Ron Ridenhour, who inspired confidence in his citizen's gumption, sent thirty registered letters to generals, Cabinet officers, members of Congress, and the new President, Richard Nixon. Eight months later, news tips about a simmering military investigation led to publication in *Life* magazine of graphic My Lai photographs taken by an Army photographer, which triggered a national scandal of colliding emotions: denial, outrage, dogged pride, and wrath against war or disclosure. Nixon freed the one lieutenant convicted by court-martial, of twenty-two My Lai murders, and it took decades to open perspective across enemy lines. In 1998, the Army gave the Soldier's Medal for Gallantry to former pilot Thompson, gunner Colburn, and posthumously to the crew chief, Glenn Andreotta, long since killed in combat. In 2001, returning to Vietnam for dedication of My Lai Peace Park, Colburn was dumbfounded to compare life stories with forty-one-year-old Do Hao, who remembered vividly the day he was yanked into the sky from a ditch full of silent relatives.

*   *   *

IN TUMULTUOUS mid-March 1968, Martin Luther King quietly tested strategies to overcome social barriers by nonviolence, being far from sure they would work. He closed to reporters his anxious summit meeting with seventy-eight "non-black" minority leaders on Thursday, March 14. Mostly unknown to each other, let alone to King, they ventured by invitation from across the United States to Paschal's Motor Lodge in the heart of black Atlanta. Wallace Mad Bear Anderson spoke for a poor Iroquois confederation of upstate New York. A deputy came from the bedside of César Chávez, who had barely survived a twenty-five-day fast in penance for violent lapses by striking California farmworkers. Tillie Walker and Rose Crow Flies High represented plains tribes from North Dakota, while Dennis Banks led a delegation of Anishinabes. During introductions, Bernard Lafayette whispered to King what he had gleaned about basic differences among Puerto Ricans, as distinct from Mexicans (Chicanos), or the defining cause of the Assiniboin/Lakota leader Hank Adams, who spearheaded a drive for Northwestern salmon fishing rights under the 1854 Treaty of Medicine Creek. Lafayette had checked repeatedly to make sure King wanted the hardscrabble white groups, and the answer was always simple: "Are they poor?" Paschal's was dotted with coal miners, some of whom braved fierce criticism from Appalachian rivals, and Peggy Terry admitted being raised in a Kentucky Klan family. After moving to Montgomery during the bus boycott, she had gone once on a lark to see "that smart aleck nigger come out of jail," and the actual sight of King buffeted by a mob churned into her independent nature. Now Terry kept a few black friends in the Jobs Or Income Now (JOIN) group from uptown Chicago's poor white district, and she wowed movement crowds by asking where else a hillbilly housewife could trade ideas or jail cells with a Nobel Prize winner.

Hosea Williams made no secret of his wish for the nonblack summit to fail. With several other SCLC staff leaders, he mercilessly ribbed young Tom Houck, who had come into the St. Augustine movement as an orphaned high school dropout from Massachusetts, then stayed on to chauffeur the Kings, and since had developed enough grit to scour the country for nonblack leaders under tutelage from Lafayette and Bill Rutherford. "First he was Coretta's boy," groused Williams. "Now he's taking our money and giving it to Indians." Internal staff resistance complained that these strangers would slow them down, ruin cohesion, and make it even tougher to compete with the black power trend. Lafayette fretted constantly over the risk of insult to, from, and between the guests. Leaders did rise from the floor to complain of exclusion, but they also acknowledged initiatives adapted from the black movement. Since the bus boycott, said several Native Americans, the model tribal leader no longer was an "Uncle Tomahawk" angling for token promotion. Others questioned nonviolence with doubtful respect. Vincent Harding, who had drafted most of the Riverside Vietnam speech, came late to observe and made note of hushed deliberation on assorted faces contemplating whether to recommend the experimental coalition under King.

In an aside, King first asked, "Tijerina who?" He absorbed a fiery speech about regaining communal lands stolen by noncompliance with the Treaty of Guadalupe Hidalgo, in which the United States had acquired the territory that became seven Southwestern states to end the Mexican-American War of 1848. Lafayette cautioned that Reies López

Tijerina was a charismatic, chronic fugitive—hailed as a Chicano Malcolm X, disparaged as a "wetback" Don Quixote—best known for leading an armed protest posse that briefly occupied a New Mexico courthouse on June 5, 1967. At Paschal's, Tijerina asked what mention of land issues would be offered in return for nonviolent discipline, and King said the answer flowed from the movement's nature: a common willingness to sacrifice put all their grievances on equal footing. On reflection, Tijerina proposed that particular stories from Native American groups be dramatized first in Washington, followed by black people second and his own Spanish-speaking groups last. His offer, which deferred both to historical order and the spirit of King's presentation, received acclamation that extended to Chicano leaders sometimes at odds with Tijerina, such as Corky González of Denver. The summit closed on a wave of immense relief. Myles Horton, who helped recruit the white Appalachians, expressed euphoria after nearly four decades of cross-cultural isolation at his Highlander Center. "I believe we caught a glimpse of the future," he told Andrew Young.

King broke away to give a Thursday evening speech to nearly three thousand cheering supporters in the wealthy Detroit suburb of Grosse Pointe. Some of the two hundred pickets on the sidewalk crashed inside with shouts of "Commie!" and "Traitor!" until officers ejected them to end heckling that King called the most intense yet during a speech, and tremors from national politics followed him. Robert Kennedy left a message for King at the SCLC office. Burke Marshall persisted until he reached King late Friday, saying Kennedy knew the California Democratic Council endorsed Senator McCarthy that night—amid rumors that King would do the same when he addressed the group at noon—and he hoped King at least could refrain from political commitments until they talked. King did stay noncommittal to reporters who intercepted him at the Disneyland Hotel in Anaheim, where his speech earned cheers without preferring a candidate or attacking President Johnson by name. "The government is emotionally committed to the war," King charged that Saturday, March 16. "It is emotionally hostile to the needs of the poor." Kennedy's delayed entry and McCarthy's shortcomings roiled voter loyalties from the first weekend of a bitter three-way contest, when the President issued his most bellicose call for "total national effort" to win in Vietnam. "We love nothing more than peace," Johnson told the National Farmers Union, "but we hate nothing worse than surrender and cowardice."

King withdrew in Los Angeles to manage the aftermath of his non-black summit. He sent a telegram to César Chávez ("We are together with you"), knowing Robert Kennedy had just visited Chávez dramatically at the end of his fast. He resolved to change Michael Harrington's draft call to Washington with broader emphasis on all the invisible sub-nations of American poverty. He promised to squeeze in personal visits to Indian reservations and migrant labor camps from California and Appalachia to Massachusetts. With his schedule already jammed, and the start date looming in April, these extra commitments sorely distressed King's aides even before James Lawson tracked him down by telephone in Los Angeles through the leaders of Holman United Methodist Church—where King would preach the first of several sermons on Sunday, and where Lawson already had designs to become pastor. Lawson could hear Andrew Young and Bernard Lee remonstrating in the background. Any thought of going to Memphis was preposterous, they said, because King would get snared and bogged down as always, then have to postpone Washington again. To counter, Lawson told King why he would find no more potent juncture of poverty and race than the month-long garbage strike. He played to an orator's vanity with glowing accounts that Wilkins and Bayard Rustin had just drawn upward of seven thousand people, then closed with a practical argument that King's upcoming poverty tour of Mississippi could begin from Memphis, like the Meredith march.

A flurry of logistical changes began with flight detours out of New Orleans from Los Angeles on Monday, March 18. Lawson met King's plane that evening with Jesse Epps, an AFSCME representative known for volunteer work in SCLC's Grenada, Mississippi, movement. When Epps apologized that the crowd waiting was not the ten thousand Lawson had promised, King looked so crestfallen that Lawson quickly waved off the ruse. "Jim was wrong," Epps corrected, beaming. There were *fifteen* thousand at least, he said. "No one else can get in the house."

It took a flying wedge of preachers and sanitation workers to guide King's party into the cavernous Mason Temple through crowded aisles and a pulsing crescendo of cheers. Against all fire codes, some spectators climbed high into rafters that suspended a giant white banner with a Bible quote from Zechariah: "NOT BY MIGHT, NOT BY POWER, SAITH THE LORD OF HOSTS, BUT BY MY SPIRIT." The platform below teemed with dignitaries, from AFSCME president Jerry Wurf to Rev. H. Ralph Jackson in his spats, plus three stately new garbage cans filled with donations. When King in his blue suit reached the bank of microphones, the noise receded no lower than a constant hum, and applause erupted again each time he paid tribute to their unity and purpose. "You are demanding that this city will respect the dignity of labor," he said.

They clapped when he asked if they knew most poor people worked every day, and even cheered most sentences of his exegesis on the parable of Lazarus and Dives. "You are here to demand that Memphis will see the poor," King cried. Energy in the hall brimmed so close to the surface that he backed off to summarize the previous decade. "Now our struggle is for genuine equality, which means economic equality," he resumed. There was no need to build or persuade by the rules of oratory, as a feeder line in rhythm easily rekindled the crowd. "We are tired," said King. "We are tired of being at the bottom. ["Yes!"] We are tired. . . . We are tired of our men being emasculated so that our wives and our daughters have to go out and work in the white lady's kitchen." He used old riffs—"Now is the time . . ."—and improvised new ones on staying together and the nature of power. "Power is the ability to achieve purpose," said King, to applause. "Power is the ability to effect change . . . and I want you to stick it out so that you will be able to make Mayor Loeb and others say 'Yes' even when they want to say 'No.'" He paused through the next ovations with a quizzical look.

"Now you know what?" he asked. "You may have to escalate the struggle a bit." His conversational tone for once hushed the crowd. "If they keep refusing, and they will not recognize the union," said King, "I tell you what you ought to do. And you are together here enough to do it. In a few days you ought to get together and just have a general work stoppage in the city of Memphis."

This time cheers rose into sustained, foot-stomping bedlam, which drowned out further words, and King stepped back into the embrace of colleagues already in furious consultation. With Lawson, Andrew Young passed King a note that perhaps he could swing back through Memphis. Temporarily at least, the rejuvenating clamor made the garbage strike seem the heart of a poverty movement instead of a foolish diversion from the Washington goal. Abernathy tried to hold the departing crowd until King returned to the podium. "I want to tell you that I am coming back to Memphis on Friday," he said, "to lead you in a march through the center of Memphis."

Walter Bailey welcomed his guests when the excitement was over.

He had bought the old Melba Inn in 1945, when he could still raise turkeys in the back, and meant to name it for his wife, Lorene, before the sign came out Lorraine Motel "some kinda way." Bailey enjoyed the SCLC preachers above Count Basie and many celebrities, because King was approachable enough to let people slap him on the back. "You could touch him," said Bailey, who remembered the thick shoulders. "He was hard as a brick."

Into the night, King coldly appraised the strike with his friends Benjamin Hooks and Billy Kyles. A shopping boycott hurt downtown merchants, but AFSCME sustenance for families ran low. Garbage piles grew slowly because the city found emergency crews for nearly half its trucks. Mayor Loeb's majority held solid. Later, eager students in bathrobes and slippers intruded with a command invitation to the Lorraine conference room, where the traveling women's choir from a Texas college serenaded King with a midnight medley on the theme "Hallelujah."

* * *

KING'S BARNSTORMING caravan descended from Memphis into the wonder and strain of Mississippi. With Bevel and Dorothy Cotton, he appealed for poverty recruits Tuesday morning in Batesville, then pushed west into Marks, where a small crowd waited in a flimsy board church with old funeral parlor calendars for interior walls. "Statistics reveal that you live in the poorest county in the United States," King told them. "Now this isn't right." He was describing the "great movement" ahead in Washington when a white man wobbled through the door and reached furtively in his pocket. The man pulled out a hundred-dollar bill for the collection plate, turning panic to awe, then introduced himself as a Mr. Mobley with a slurred speech to the effect that they were all going to the same place and should mind their own business. "But let me say this," he added. "There ain't nobody hungry here in Mississippi. Old Kennedy got up here the other day and said folks are starving to death."

"All right, all right," King said carefully. "Thank you so much, brother Mobley. Thank you."

"Wait a minute here," said Mobley. "I ain't just exactly through." In fits and starts, he said an old colored preacher was supposed to come with him but could not make it. That was all.

"Well, we want to thank you so much, brother Mobley," King said, beckoning Abernathy and Hosea Williams to escort the troubled donor outside, and there was no way to tell how much the odd exchange put

King off balance for the subsequent presentations. On invitation, local residents came forward in a stream. One mother said her children ate pinto beans "morning noon and night." Another said hers stayed home from school because they had no clothes. Both Abernathy and Andrew Young were surprised to see tears roll down King's face from the plain-spoken eloquence about hurt and disease. He wiped his eyes with the back of his hand. "I've listened to your problems, and it is—it has touched me," said King. As he fumbled for words, Nina Evans walked up to say she had no food and no way to get any. King asked Hosea Williams to take down her name.

Right then, on the drive to Clarksdale, King resolved that the mule train for Washington would leave from Marks. He delivered an inspired pitch for volunteers to six hundred people waiting in Chapel Hill Baptist Church, but only two tentative hands went up to show interest in the long journey. They moved on to Greenwood two hours behind schedule, touching off shouts of joy—"He's here! He's here!"—as two local ministers virtually lifted King through the crowd at Jennings Temple Church. Praising Greenwood as "a real movement town," he spoke nakedly of the testimony about Delta conditions in nearby Marks. "I wept with them as I heard numerous women stand up on their feet," said King. "I heard them talking about the fact that they didn't even have any blankets to cover their children up on a cold night. And I said to myself, 'God doesn't like this.' And we are going to say in no uncertain terms that we aren't going to accept it any longer. We've got to go to Washington in big numbers."

He pleaded for lone grandparents or whole families alike, saying food and shelter would be provided. "Now we just want you to sign up and go," King exhorted. "Don't have to worry about anything. Just have the will to go to Washington." He promised freedom schools and music festivals along with demonstrations every day. He said they were going to put real sharecropper huts on trucks and present them to the Smithsonian as relics of modern poverty. "We're not playing about this thing," cried King. "We're going to have a time in Washington. We're going to make this nation move again, and we're going to make America see poor people."

Once again, King's call for volunteers turned cheers into fearful silence. Switching to the chartered Cessna, he flew to the same result at packed churches in Grenada and Laurel. Nearly eight hundred people still waited at St. Paul Methodist when the Cessna landed after midnight in Hattiesburg—four hours late—and the Mississippi marathon ended toward dawn in a Jackson motel. Though back up early, they were still six hours late to the last stop Wednesday night in Bessemer, Alabama, outside Birmingham. Crowds waited endlessly to press around King. Pleading hoarseness, he left most of the speaking to Hosea Williams, who announced another delay until April 27 on the start date for the mule train to Washington. Behind the scenes, recruitment troubles in rural areas stiffened resentment of Indian and Hispanic groups scheduled to join the Southeastern pilgrimage in Jackson. One of Williams's deputies grumbled that the newcomers failed to understand they were mere children within the freedom movement. In public, Williams pointed to three white observers with tape recorders in the balcony. "You can pass all the riot laws you want," he shouted, "but you cannot suppress the dignity of man!" Bad weather mercifully allowed King to cancel several Alabama stops on Thursday, March 21, for sleep at home before the flight back to Memphis.

Crises converged for nonviolence and violence alike. In Washington, J. Edgar Hoover reported secretly to President Johnson that King had raised only $1,000 from eight Mississippi rallies and was discouraged by a lack of response to his anti-poverty drive. The President was consumed by his forthcoming speech on the big Vietnam troop request. To clear the way, he decided to relieve General Westmoreland from battlefield command with a promotion to Army chief of staff. He complained to Senator Russell that Robert Kennedy already was "storming these states and those governors and switching the bosses all over the country." Of the Wise Men summoned for final advice the next Monday, only Justice Fortas of Memphis pushed in advance to send all the soldiers, telling Johnson that anything less would advertise weakness with "our own sensitivity to criticism, our own dislike of bloodshed."

From Memphis, an amazed James Lawson called King before dawn on Friday, March 22. A rare dusting of snow in the Mississippi Delta had become a freak blizzard of sixteen inches on the first day of spring. The march would have to wait a few days, Lawson said wryly, but King could claim delivery of a work stoppage beyond dreams. Nothing moved at all, and interpretations of providential wonder circulated through silent, blanketed Memphis. "Well, the Lord has done it again," H. Ralph Jackson mordantly declared. "It's a white world." A church woman in white Memphis claimed to receive a sobering command for charity toward the strike: "The Lord sent the snow to give us another chance."

CHAPTER 39

Requiem

March 23–April 4, 1968

FINAL choices pressed hard upon the leaders of refined democracy. Uncannily for King, they tested nonviolent commitments widely deemed foolhardy or weak. When a prominent black editor scolded him for traveling through Klan countryside without bodyguards, King rejected armed security as an uncomfortable illusion. "I'd feel like a bird in a cage," he said. His two sons, but not their sisters, crisscrossed rural Georgia in the chartered Cessna on a rare family trip, landing with extra relief after one of the twin engines stalled both in Macon and Waycross. "Now Marty and Dexter have been to Albany before," King told a church crowd, recalling the 1961–62 struggle when toddler Dexter "came to visit daddy in the city jail." He apologized for being late, but extolled again his summons to join poor people across cultural lines. "There is a day when the bones get back together," said King. Like Ezekiel's biblical vision of dry bones, mule trains from the Black Belt would connect with caravans from barrios and coalfields and Indian reservations, springing to life in Washington. "Finally, this is a nonviolent movement," he said. "I don't apologize for nonviolence. I have no apology to make."

The next morning, March 24, King preached the Sunday installation service for Rev. Wyatt Tee Walker at a newly organized church in Harlem. Not by coincidence, Adam Clayton Powell marched outside the converted theater on 116th Street with a thousand followers, shouting "Judas!" to accuse Walker of poaching from his immense congregation nearby. This display of shrill pulpit politics was lost in spectacular news from Powell's fugitive return to the United States. With the lawsuit to overturn his expulsion from the House still headed for the U.S. Supreme Court, Powell had slipped from Bimini into momentary custody of the New York county sheriff, then to a judge's apartment for arranged parole on various contempt judgments—all to reclaim pastoral and political supremacy after eighteen months in exile. Newspapers, including the *New York Times,* covered on their front pages his dramatic appearance in Abyssinian Baptist's platform pulpit of semicircular marble, with a dozen somber bodyguards he called "the wave of the future." Led by Charles 37X Kenyatta of the Harlem Mau Mau Society, "Adam's Commandos" embraced Powell when he denounced a light-skinned portrait of Jesus—"Get that out of here!"—and ordered black replacements throughout the church. One commando lifted a Bible impaled on the tip of his machete. "The audience reaction was mixed," reported the *Times.*

"The man hanging on that cross might be me," Powell cried in his sermon, "but Jesus had one Judas and I have about 5,000!" Predicting worldwide revolution by autumn, he implored the congregation not to "die like hogs in some inglorious spot." He promised to crush incipient church revolt, and scoffed that he could win absentee reelection to Congress with Mickey Mouse as his campaign manager. "I'm here to preach black leadership for you white people," Powell told two hundred reporters, many of whom rushed to Walker's new church for reaction to Powell's acid declarations that nonviolent protest was dead. On the contrary, replied King, "I think it is just arriving." He refused comment otherwise, which earned a small news item beneath Powell's apocalyptic convulsions: "Nonviolence Tactic Defended by King."

King's advisers gathered Monday in New York for a contentious review of the poverty campaign. Every aspect of the preparations struggled uphill, especially fund-raising, and several advisers remained wary at best of King's commitment to detour again into Memphis on Thursday, now that the snow had melted. To shore up one avenue of recent promise—for logistical support in Washington from religious groups and civic coalitions—Harry Wachtel broke away to a private airport with a small group. Only King, Andrew Young, and the pilot would fit with him in a single-engine charter that King beheld with dismay, saying he much preferred at least two engines. They survived an argument and a hurried evening flight into the Catskills, where conservative rabbis from the 68th Rabbinical Assembly waited for an introduction.

"Where in America today do we hear a voice like the voice of the prophets of Israel?" asked Abraham Heschel. "Martin Luther King is a sign that God has not forsaken the United States of America. . . . The situation of the poor in America is our plight, our sickness. To be deaf to their cry is to condemn ourselves."

King returned Heschel's salute by describing their first encounter more than five years earlier in Chicago, when Heschel's exhortation before the Birmingham movement had "inspired clergymen of all the religious faiths of our country . . . to do something that they had not done before." In lieu of a speech, King responded to an inquiry moderated by Rabbi Everett Gendler, and the rabbis submitted a host of questions about separatism, "anti-Israel Negroes," and practical politics. "Have your contributions from Jews fallen off considerably?" asked one. Another sought behavioral tips "if we are on a committee and there is a Negro militant and a Negro moderate." A third questioned the huge disparity in social energy for war over justice. King's replies followed nonviolence as the plumb line of engagement. He said Israel needed security for the outpost of vibrant democracy, just as displaced Arabs needed a foothold for opportunity, and that violence would secure neither. He said militancy was a term of persistence, and therefore balance, rather than violence. He mused that segregation once looked impregnable in Birmingham, and that President Johnson called a voting rights bill impossible until Selma unlocked hidden powers of freedom. Now King asked the rabbis to take a new leap of faith in Washington. "We need bodies to bring about the pressure that I have mentioned to get Congress and the nation moving in the right direction." As Young moved around the convention to secure pledges, King thanked Rabbi Gendler for answering his call to jail witness long ago in Albany, Georgia, on devotion alone, before there was a glimmer of success. They sang "We Shall Overcome" for him in Hebrew.

Back in Manhattan that night, King jumped from a car to walk the last crosstown block over the objections of Wachtel, who said it would be safer to circle the one-way streets. "Harry," said King, "if they couldn't protect Kennedy, how can anything protect me?" He soon knocked unannounced to resume a running debate. Arthur Logan was an uptown physician to celebrities from Duke Ellington to Governor Nelson Rockefeller, and a source for sleeping pills that King often fussed were no match for his insomnia. His son-in-law Clifford Alexander, a Harvard protégé of McGeorge Bundy, had become a pioneer

black executive in the Johnson administration. Logan's skin was so fair
that he and Adam Clayton Powell greeted each other with chortling
irony—"Us black folks got to stick together!"—but Logan agreed that
Powell's desperate street rebellion had gone too far. King was glad to
hear of delicate maneuvers to terminate Powell's career while vindicating his rights in Congress, but the immediate quarrel lay with Logan's
wife, Marian—cousin of NAACP leader Walter White, and former
club singer at Café Society and the Blue Angel. Nicknamed "Madame
Board," the only female on SCLC's governing body had channeled all
her stage pluck into a six-page memo arguing that King should abort
the anti-poverty mobilization to Washington. Her opposition pained
King, and he asked why she was circulating the private memo to all the
other SCLC board members. Any leak would be trumpeted as internal
rebellion, King groaned, which made him feel stabbed in the back. He
suspected collusion with Bayard Rustin, who had not been "right" since
he went to work for labor unions supporting the Vietnam War.

"Martin, I did it because lots of times you don't listen to me," Marian
Logan replied. She accused him of preaching to her instead, and she
cried into the night as he preached again that she should reconsider.
Arthur Logan refereed the prolonged tussle with reminders of shared
ordeals and a steady supply of vodka and orange juice. To his plea for a
respite, when Logan said anxiety had injured his wife's health already,
King paused to agree she did look poorly, then lurched off again on reasons why she could support his cause and thereby look better as well. He
said the flaws predicted in her memo had been attributed to each movement since the bus boycott—it would raise tensions, invite repression,
expose disunity, and make things worse. "We'd never have *had* a movement, Marian," King declared. "Of *all* people, I never thought I'd have
to *explain* this to you." He protested most bitterly her written charge that
he was "prepared to court violence as a last resort." Never, he said.
Demonstrations would accept punishment, as always, and nonviolence
helped each movement look for ways to break through political indifference and disdain. King conceded that the poverty campaign might
fail, but he begged her not to foreclose the effort.

Arthur Logan called a truce near dawn. They agreed for the moment
that while every movement was daunting, an economic campaign
across barriers of culture and class seemed more so. King retreated from
his favorite sofa in a living room that held three hundred for receptions
at the elegant Logan brownstone. Exhausted, he canceled early recruit-

ment events Tuesday morning, March 26, then rallied to visit a selected tenement family in Harlem. "I am still so excited," sputtered Mrs. Bennie Fowler, mother of eight, who served King a home-cooked lunch under her kitchen clothesline.

* * *

A DOZEN members of the Senior Advisory Group—the Wise Men— crowded into the family dining room of the White House residence to hear General Earle Wheeler, chairman of the Joint Chiefs, and General Creighton Abrams, who would succeed Westmoreland in the Vietnam field command. Wheeler backed off the pressure for all or most of the 205,000 additional troops, saying, "We do not fear a general defeat with the forces we now have." Abrams predicted a year of hard fighting and attrition. After the Tuesday lunch, President Johnson invited the generals to walk over to the West Wing for consultations with these Wise Men—looking toward war decisions to be announced Sunday night in a televised presidential speech.

McGeorge Bundy chilled the Cabinet Room with his opening words. "Mr. President, there is a very significant shift in most of our positions since we last met." He reported gravely that last November's unanimity for slow but steady war progress had given way to a reverse majority: "We must begin the steps to disengage." One by one, the eminent guests tersely confirmed Bundy's summary of their individual opinions— World War II general Omar Bradley, Korean War general Matthew Ridgway, McNamara deputy Cyrus Vance, Republican treasury secretary Douglas Dillon—and not until Maxwell Taylor, the Army general and former ambassador to South Vietnam, did a steadfast hawk register shock. "Well, I have been somewhat amazed, Mr. President, by the views expressed here by some of my friends," he said.

The President seemed numb. He stirred to rumors that the classified war briefings for the Wise Men must have been skewed. "The first thing I am going to do when you all leave here is to get those briefers [from] last night," he joked wanly, but the repeat performances would demonstrate consistency and balance across the top agencies. They agreed that U.S. allies had inflicted enormous military casualties on a Communist force structure of 230,000 before Tet: eighty thousand killed, with an estimated three soldiers wounded for every death. By elementary math, U.N. ambassador Arthur Goldberg had asked an instantly famous question the previous night during the Pentagon presentation by Major General William DePuy: "Who the hell is there left for us to be fighting?" The troublesome answer was North Vietnamese infiltration plus South Vietnamese recruitment spurred by hostility to foreign troops. Analysts agreed that the latter phenomenon was political and intractable.

In the Cabinet Room, war loyalists stifled alarm. Walt Rostow later said he "smelled a rat" among the Wise Men. General Taylor decided Pentagon dissenters must have "impregnated them with their doubts." Out loud, several voices recommended a more defensive military strategy to make up for broad withdrawals from the South Vietnamese countryside since Tet. Former ambassador Henry Cabot Lodge proposed to abandon search-and-destroy missions in favor of a "shield" posture in populated areas. Rusk thought U.S. forces still could "deny military victory to the Vietcong and North Vietnamese." Both Fortas and Wheeler asserted that the American goal always was to force a settlement—never to achieve a military solution.

Dean Acheson erupted at General Wheeler. "Then what in the name of God are five hundred thousand men out there doing?" he demanded. "Chasing girls? This is not a semantic game, general. If the deployment of all those men is not an effort to gain a military solution, then words have lost all meaning."

Acheson, notoriously imperious, had championed the Vietnam War with his prestige as a principal architect of the Cold War and President Truman's Secretary of State for Asian crises up through the war in Korea. His emphatic defection lit a smoldering new stalemate among the Wise Men, which Johnson tried to control with gratitude. "What we want to do is take what you have said," he concluded, "and what Congress may be able to approve, what we may need to do, and try to make our course here as effective as possible." That evening, General Abrams took the President aside to offer strained comfort about assuming a stalemated command. "I know there is a lot of dying men out there, but you should know about me," said Abrams. "I had made up my mind several years ago whether I would continue serving in the Army with all this business, and I decided there was something worse than being dead. I thought I would put up with it. I don't like it, but it's worth it."

To answer military valor with proper judgment nearly crushed Johnson. He decided that no peace initiative would produce a response from Hanoi worth the risk in lives, but he informed Wheeler and Abrams that they could expect only a small fraction of the 205,000 additional soldiers—roughly 14,000, toward a peak of 549,000. For both these reasons, he called for ringing war themes in the latest drafts of his Sunday Vietnam speech: "We have set our face against the enemy, and he will fail."

Johnson knew, however, that this posture would expose the secret flaw that had haunted him and close advisers since the escalations more than three years ago. He was fighting not to lose. The United States had no political bonds with the South Vietnamese people anywhere near as strong as the Communist movement to expel foreigners, and still fell woefully short of the cultural appreciation or contact skills to nourish them. Military power could stave off defeat, but the domestic cost had skyrocketed since 1965, when few Americans knew of Vietnam. Public opinion polls had shifted nearly 20 percent against the war since Tet. Political director Lawrence O'Brien pleaded for drastic action to address "deepening disenchantment" among LBJ supporters, then warned bluntly that Johnson would lose to Eugene McCarthy in the April 2 Wisconsin primary less than a week away, which posed a dangerous humiliation for a sitting President. Johnson moaned that he was throwing away every sane advantage of incumbency by demanding both new taxes and huge domestic cuts in an election year. "I don't give a damn about the election," Johnson told Wheeler and Abrams, with unhappiness more convincing than his literal statement. "I will go down the drain."

* * *

STANLEY LEVISON reached King by telephone during Tuesday's stops in Harlem, Queens, and Rockville Centre, Long Island. His mission, relayed from Atlanta, gave FBI wiretappers access to candid talk about partisan politics, as King readily approved a letter requesting media outlets to remove his name from presidential straw polls, including *Time* magazine's survey of college students. King told Levison he did not want to diminish antiwar opinion already split between McCarthy and Kennedy, and that while he had endorsed no candidate, "we have to be realistic enough to see that if there's any possibility of stopping Lyndon, it's going to be Kennedy." (Hoover rushed the inflammatory intercept to the White House, leaving out King's qualified public comment that Johnson might win back his alienated voters if he settled the Vietnam War.) On the phone, King said McCarthy fell far short of Kennedy's strength among white working-class voters as well as minorities, and Levison agreed that the choice should not rest narrowly on McCarthy's "Galahad" courage to challenge Johnson first.

"We'll make him Secretary of State," King quipped. He let Andrew

Young accompany Levison on a side trip to Boston, seeking another financial contribution from Anne Farnsworth, provided they returned in time for King's detour on Thursday. "We rescheduled that march," King told Levison. "I've never seen a community as together as Memphis, and it hasn't had much coverage." One story deep in Sunday's *Times*—"Memphis Protest Avoids Violence"—noted an interim study of the sanitation workers' strike by Atlanta's Southern Regional Council, which found that the daily marches sustained over six weeks had acquired "the tone and much of the spirit" from civil rights movements earlier in the decade.

With Levison, Young returned to New York for a Wednesday night fund-raiser at the apartment of Harry and Julie Belafonte. They were pleased to see some donors drifting back after several years, perhaps convinced on reflection that King was less upstaged by black power or misguided on Vietnam. Very late, after Levison and the guests had gone home, King paced back and forth in his socks, drinking sherry from a personal bottle of Harveys Bristol Cream on which for years he had denoted authorized withdrawals with mock fanfare. He talked of the day's breakneck antipoverty rallies across northern New Jersey—in Paterson, Orange, Jersey City, and especially Newark, where he had visited churches, riot-torn ruins, upscale telephone executives, two welfare families, and the angry black playwright LeRoi Jones. King rambled about the poverty campaign as a monster more complex than race, which could bring new hope into view only if they made headway also against Vietnam and the great divisions of class. He quoted Bevel's line that there was nothing unconstitutional about starving. His nearly incoherent fatigue put King increasingly at loggerheads with Young, who said they must not let all the world's burdens drive them into the ground. Young wanted to postpone the Washington campaign until June. He said they had no business going back to a Memphis struggle that would only drain limited energy. His soothing insistence irritated and frustrated King until he slammed his palm on the Belafontes' sitting room bar, rattling glasses, and said he felt closer to the rage of Newark than to Young's calm priorities. "We may be integrating into a burning house," said King. They had no choice but to push forward, he fumed, in a state of temper that silenced his friends.

Only traveling aide Bernard Lee accompanied King back to Memphis the next morning, March 28. Because of flight delays out of Atlanta, they did not land in Memphis until 10:30—half an hour after the scheduled start for the march—and by then impatience rustled through crowds outside Clayborn Temple AME. Early arrivals had cheered an unexpected delegation of black schoolteachers, who risked their jobs to be there, then welcomed scores of white trade union supporters alongside forty priests and nuns who marched with the blessing of Tennessee's Catholic bishop, Joseph Durick. Nearly all the thousand striking sanitation workers stood near the front, many with assorted relatives, including children. A preacher on the garbage force had suggested the new slogan to honor their crushed co-workers Cole and Walker—I AM A MAN—which William Lucy of AFSCME had printed on masses of placards to supplement regular themes such as WE ARE TOGETHER and MACE WON'T STOP TRUTH. Bored, unruly teenagers darted about with hand-lettered rebel messages on the reverse side: DAMN LOEB / BLACK POWER IS HERE and LOEB EAT SHIT. At 10:15, James Lawson ran about fifty feet to confront a group of students trying to shoulder their way into a closed liquor store, remonstrating in his clerical collar until he drove them away, then returning agitated to the starter's post. A young man back in the crowd paraded with a noose hung from a tree branch, shouting about a big day for nonviolence with sarcasm that frightened or puzzled adults but vastly amused his peers.

Pandemonium greeted King at 10:56. Young people engulfed his borrowed white Lincoln, and Ralph Abernathy pretended to apologize for the enthusiastic crowd. "It's my fault," he told King inside the car. "My speech last night was too inspiring and arousing." King laughed. The assembled march, which Abernathy had arrived Wednesday to promote, was numbered anywhere between six thousand and twenty thousand, with estimates clouded by spectators teeming the sidewalks along Hernando Street. At the eye of a demonstration, King and Bernard Lee recognized the first hints of abnormal tension in faces that pressed against the car's glass, making it impossible to get out. Lawson pushed through, leaned inside a passenger window, and said the crowd was compressed with pent-up energy. He and Lee managed to agree above the noise that they should move out right away, dispensing with preliminary speeches. Still, it took nine minutes to extricate King and wedge him into the head of a march line across both lanes, locked arms between Abernathy and H. Ralph Jackson. Police motorcycles roared ahead of a flatbed press truck loaded with cameras facing backward, and the huge throng began to stretch out north along a long block of

Hernando to famous Beale Street, turning left by the park named for
W. C. Handy, pioneer of the blues.

Next to the statue holding a trumpet, a wreath of fresh flowers
marked the tenth anniversary of Handy's death in 1958. Above, officers
in police helicopter 201 sighted a clump of thirty students with rocks
and clubs trotting west along Beale Street to merge at the turn, then radioed a frantic complaint that one of the television news helicopters
"came within a hundred feet of us." Young people pushed among the
sanitation workers, shouting, "Let me get by," and one college student
watched high school students dismantle an old bed frame into metal
bars. As the march swung right into Main Street for the last ten blocks to
City Hall, a surge pushed the front ranks into an uncomfortable speed,
nearly a trot, jostled and patted from behind. Abernathy sensed an
overly familiar, hostile edge in the cries of tribute—"We're glad you
came to Memphis"—not long before loud pops turned anxious heads to
listen for gunshots. Crashes after the bangs signaled instead the unmistakable sound of storefront windows being smashed along Beale and
Main. Moans went up that something was wrong. Young marauders
ran through overmatched marshals to attack storefronts ahead of the
march—Shainberg's department store, York Arms Company, Perel
and Lowenstein's—sometimes needing multiple blows to break the
heavy plate glass. A helicopter bulletin at 11:24 reported fifteen young
people destroying a parked car a few hundred yards to the side, and
marshals relayed shouted commands to halt the line of march. "It had
come seven blocks," wrote Memphis historian Joan Beifuss, "and lasted
about twenty-five minutes."

Assistant Police Chief Henry Lux, marching within twenty feet of
King, lent his bullhorn in the emergency. "This is Reverend Lawson
speaking!" shouted the voice above chaos. "I want everybody who's in
the march, in the Movement, to turn around and go back to the church."
Lawson joined a heated debate in the middle of Main Street, surrounded by pleas for calm as well as battle cries of "Black Power!" and
"Burn it down, baby!" King was torn between pledges to shun violence
but never the movement faithful. Most others yelled to evacuate him as
a target of opportunity, and Bernard Lee pulled King and Abernathy
among swirling followers down McCall Avenue toward the Mississippi
River. Lee bulled and dodged interference until he flagged down two
astonished women in a Pontiac, then a police motorcycle. Lieutenant
M. E. Nichols, appraising danger by radio, avoided roadblocks already

sealing off routes to the Lorraine Motel, and escorted the Pontiac under siren to the uptown Rivermont Holiday Inn.

Trouble radiated from wild looting on both flanks of the regular sanitation marchers, who were fighting panic to double back in good order. Four minutes after King's departure, radio orders to disperse the march brought a convergence of new tactical police units that scattered rampaging young people behind them in every direction. Nine officers would be injured, including one beaten by five teenagers with the flat sticks that held the placards. Two hundred eighty black people would be arrested and more than sixty hospitalized for emergency treatment—mostly teenaged males, but also females younger than twelve and as old as seventy-five. One patrolman cornered a sixteen-year-old suspected looter in a stairwell and shot him point-blank with a sawed-off shotgun. (Twenty witnesses claimed the riot's lone fatality died with his hands raised, but city officials pronounced it self-defense the same day and then disposed of all physical evidence for lack of a pending investigation.) Fleet young rioters threw rocks or bricks and then ducked back among neighborhood buildings for cover. At Clayborn Temple, where nearly two thousand marchers had taken refuge, officers lobbed tear gas canisters inside to flush out vandals, and one intrepid reporter found Lawson trembling in failed efforts to establish police communication under siege. That same afternoon, the Tennessee legislature swiftly proposed and enacted the first state of emergency since the 1866 Reconstruction riot against black soldiers stationed in Memphis, when forty-eight people had died over three days of rape and pillage. Now before dark, mobilized by Governor Buford Ellington, the first armored personnel carriers rolled into the city with 3,800 National Guard soldiers to enforce the seven o'clock curfew proclaimed by Mayor Loeb.

Trapped at the Rivermont, King watched nonstop television news lift Memphis before the whole nation. Officials of the Illinois Central Railroad announced that the *Panama Limited* would skip the Memphis stop between New Orleans and Chicago. Local news outlets praised a few embattled peacemakers of both races, and a reporter for the NBC affiliate told viewers that he was "accidentally exposed to Mace today for the second time." Nearly all stories marshaled politicians to praise police conduct in a senseless and shameful crisis. Some civic leaders blamed media exaggeration for defaming the "City of Good Abode," while others said the riot erased forty years of progress: "You can't take these Negro people and make the citizens out of them you want." For King, the dominant attitudes were familiar and immaterial next to the recycled images of bleeding officers, shattered windows, and jubilant black people hauling liquor from ransacked stores. He sank beneath the bedcovers in his underwear, transfixed by the news, smoking cigarettes.

The telephone rang incessantly. From the Atlanta SCLC office, a confidential buzz reached Andrew Young in Washington, where King's schedule for Friday was canceled already. Young called Stanley Levison. Given his own recent frictions over the Memphis trip, he sought more soothing counsel for King's disaster, and Levison got through to Suite 801 at 9:15 P.M. Thursday night by the FBI wiretapper's log in New York. King confessed despair. Young black militants seemed to have provoked the riot, he told Levison, which ignited police and black bystanders against each other. He blamed everybody including himself for lack of foresight. He said his depression made him think of calling off the poor people's march.

Levison groped for triage with four succinct points. First, acute fatigue made King's depression unduly grim. Second, King should stay positive about nonviolence and maintain that the riot came from interlopers. Third, the Washington campaign would be different because of direct training and supervision by the SCLC staff. Fourth, King should postpone an emergency conclave until Saturday in Atlanta, so he could recuperate.

King approved the delay and the evaluation, but they brought no sleep. He howled at Abernathy and Lee until nearly dawn. "Maybe we just have to admit that the day of violence is here," said King. "And maybe we just have to give up and let violence take its course."

*　　*　　*

"THE VIOLENCE in Memphis was a godsend to the FBI," wrote King scholar Adam Fairclough. Until then, under intense pressure from headquarters, the field offices churned out operations against King mostly aimed for harassment or sabotage. When SCLC sent out fundraising letters to seventy thousand supporters late in March, headquarters approved a fictitious news leak to Northern newspapers that King did not need contributions because Washington churches and synagogues already had agreed to support the poverty marchers. Headquarters simultaneously authorized anonymous letters to selected black outlets in the South stating just the opposite—there was "no provision to house or feed marchers" in a Washington campaign geared for "King's personal aggrandizement." (Director Hoover issued the usual security instructions: "Prepare the letters on commercially purchased stationery and take all necessary precautions to insure they cannot be traced to the Bureau.") Otherwise, the schemes ran to lame propaganda. Headquarters subsidized the lecture tour of a cranky black woman from the early HUAC era, who said she had infiltrated civil rights groups for the FBI and found them subversive. Marlin Johnson, head of the Chicago FBI office, bravely cautioned against one plan to embarrass King as a hate partner of the "anti-white" Nation of Islam. The target black audience knew better, he objected, and the parallel idea to smear King as an associate of Muslim boxer Muhammad Ali might backfire, because Ali was widely considered "a black folk hero." Nevertheless, Hoover ordered Chicago to implement the attack.

FBI headquarters seized upon the Memphis upheaval within hours. Top officials disseminated to "cooperative news sources" a blind memorandum stating that "the result of King's famous espousal of nonviolence was vandalism, looting, and riot." The lapse from nonviolent discipline freed the FBI from inhibitions due to public respect for King's conduct, if not his message, which opened character assassination on all fronts, and by the next day, March 29, Hoover approved a second effort "to publicize hypocrisy on the part of Martin Luther King." The document whiplashed him as cowardly and violent, servile and uppity. "Like Judas leading lambs to slaughter," Hoover confidentially advised news contacts, "King led the marchers to violence, and when the violence broke out, King disappeared." A gossipy addition highlighted the place of refuge. "The fine Hotel Lorraine in Memphis is owned and patronized exclusively by Negroes," stated the propaganda sheet, but King had chosen instead "the plush Holiday Inn Motel, white owned, operated, and almost exclusively white patronized." This petty account twisted every motive and circumstance to release torrents of FBI contempt. By April 2, Hoover formally requested permission to reinstall wiretaps at SCLC. Two days later, the Mississippi FBI office sent headquarters a two-pronged COINTELPRO proposal, first, to breed confusion and resentment on King's poverty tours by spreading false information about whether he or surrogates would appear at scheduled rallies, and second, to distribute leaflets skewering King as a fancy dresser who deserted his people. The combination would "discredit King and his aides with poor Negroes who he is seeking support from," argued Mississippi, but the Bureau would not have time to act on the plan. At a far pole from accountable public trust, or constitutional duty, Hoover corrupted the FBI to wage political war.

At the White House, by contrast, President Johnson wrenched

slowly from the grip of enemies. On Wednesday, one day after the stunning shift by the Wise Men, he asked who would get the Democratic nomination if he decided not to run for another term. One aide said Kennedy, and braced for a Johnsonian tirade against the Harvard tormentor and sniveling runt, or worse, but the President asked benignly instead, "What's wrong with Bobby?" A new President Kennedy would have a grace period with Congress to work on his major liability, Johnson observed. "He doesn't know how to deal with people on the Hill, and a lot of them don't like him, but he'll try."

Such dispassion baffled wary aides. They had no way to guess how the storied Kennedy-Johnson animus might fare if detached from the rivalry for the White House, nor could they picture Johnson relinquishing power. Defense Secretary Clifford scowled down one whisper about possible abdication as juvenile lunacy. Still, the President received a private tabulation that Kennedy had voted with him on three-quarters of key Senate decisions, and he wrestled alone with contingent issues of political survival, honor, and Vietnam.

On Thursday morning of the ill-fated Memphis march, top foreign policy officials reviewed the presidential address for Sunday evening. Secretary Clifford roundly criticized an eighth draft presented by counselor Harry McPherson, which announced a modest troop increase with resolve. Clifford said it was all war, therefore out of step with the mood of the country, and the administration's Vietnam policy softly collapsed. Secretary of State Rusk, the war's steadiest defender, conceded without objections on precedent or authority, and National Security Adviser Rostow, the war's most unshakable optimist, gave no rebuttal. Instead, the three-hour meeting simply drifted into preparations for a unilateral bombing halt above North Vietnam's 20th parallel. The watershed was tacit—without calculations of battlefield attrition, political settlement, or personal consequence—and floated on an unspoken amazement that survived into memoirs by McPherson and Clifford. Rusk would remember suggesting that the President deserved an alternative, and McPherson delivered to the White House residence before midnight a companion draft with a new tone from its first sentence: "Tonight I want to speak to you of the prospects for peace in Vietnam and Southeast Asia."

Johnson decried the Memphis riot in two speeches and a statement on Friday, pledging to "stand behind local law enforcement agencies to the full extent of our Constitutional authority." He called the events a reminder that "violence and repression can only divide our people." In the Rose Garden that morning, the President spoke to young people from the Philadelphia Police Athletic League about vital civic lessons—respect for others, the rules of fair play—and quoted Lincoln that no grievance was fit for "redress by mob law." He broke away at ten o'clock to dictate changes by telephone for Sunday's Vietnam speech. Again, perhaps inevitably, not a word acknowledged painful and momentous choice. McPherson scribbled notes blindly until he realized Johnson was working from the peace draft.

* * *

KING WOKE groggy for the aftermath. Memphis television showed littered but deserted streets patrolled by National Guard vehicles with mounted machine guns, and Hambone's cartoon meditation in the Friday morning *Commercial Appeal* offered dubious cheer: "Don' mak no diff'unce whut kin' o' face you's got, hit look mo' bettuh *smilin'!!*" At ten o'clock, Abernathy answered sharp knocks at the Rivermont suite to find three young men from the local Black Organizing Project, closely watched by an encamped white reporter. When he ducked back into King's bedroom to say strangers had come with apologies—apologies for all the rumors that they had started yesterday's riot through their affiliated youth gang called the Invaders—King asked Abernathy to receive them because he was already late for a press conference. While getting dressed, he heard introductory disputes over basic terms. Rather than a gang, insisted the Black Organizing Project leaders, the Invaders was a political awareness and fitness group for students, modeled on Elijah Muhammad's Fruit of Islam.

"We aren't saying that you caused the trouble," Abernathy conceded. "But everybody else is saying so. If you didn't do it, who did?"

"The people," replied one of the BOP leaders. He said local preachers had led the march into a trap by concealing the leadership struggles within the black community, and that King would fare worse next time if he blamed the Invaders. King emerged just then buttoning his shirt. He exchanged pleasant greetings that briefly stilled the room, and returned fully dressed to lament that he had not known of such friction. "Cabbage, why didn't you tell me?" he asked spokesman Charles Cabbage, "if for no other reason than you're a Morehouse man. We are brothers." He flattered the new graduate of his alma mater partly for exceptional height—a foot taller than he—and recalled him as a campus activist who had applied for an SCLC job under Hosea Williams.

Cabbage brightened. "Dr. King, I tried to get to you to tell you, but they wouldn't let me," he replied, adding that Lawson in particular had belittled and excluded the youth representatives on the strike council. King said this was news to him. Abernathy said he had heard from the other side that the Invaders had scattered through the pre-march crowd to make incendiary speeches before melting away on King's approach. The Invaders hotly rebutted him with professions of good faith.

Yesterday's violence was gone, King interrupted quietly, and blame mattered less than preventing another riot. Extraneously, as though puzzled, he asked why any leader would resort to violence anyway, since riots never lasted more than two or three days of destruction that fell heavily on bystanders and other black people. When he asked what the BOP leaders could do to ensure a badly needed peaceful march now, Cabbage ran down a list of transportation needs and unmet budgets for up to two thousand members from local colleges and high schools. King carefully replied that his staff would review the list to put them in touch with potential supporters, and he made only one comment. You can't hold yourself out as leaders of these young people and then hide behind random violence, he warned. You have influence—that's why you are in this room.

On their way out, the BOP trio soared with relief. "We are going to get our program going," Cabbage confided, "because that man is good for his word." One of his colleagues was elated but dazed, sensing that King saw through their contrivance with a strange absence of reproach. "Nobody could be as peaceful as that man," he would recall. "It was one of the few times in my life when I wasn't actually fighting something." King, for his part, sent Abernathy and Lee downstairs to the press conference while he composed himself, and his resilient bravado startled them a few minutes later. Without waiting for an introduction, King told assembled reporters that yesterday's violence was at least partly planned. He said greater preparation was required to safeguard peaceful protest with the sanitation strikers, but it could and should be done. "Nonviolence can be as contagious as violence," he declared, and dismissed suggestions that failure obliged him to cancel the larger anti-poverty campaign. "We are fully determined to go to Washington," said King. Violence permeated American society, he declared, and he could not promise a summer free of riots. "I can only guarantee that our demonstrations will not be violent."

Back upstairs, King called Stanley Levison with thanks for encouragement on points that had sustained him through the press conference,
then relapsed into fears of ruin. He said influential black critics scented
his weakness over this—Roy Wilkins, Bayard Rustin, Adam Clayton
Powell—and would reinforce the public damage. "You know, their
point is, 'Martin Luther King is dead, he's finished,' " King complained.
" 'His nonviolence is nothing. No one is listening to it.' Let's face it. We
do have a great public relations setback."

"That is only if you accept their definition," Levison replied, "and
this, I think, is a profound error you are making."

No, King insisted. The problem was widespread eagerness to see
things that way. "I talked to the fellows who organized the violence
business this morning in my room," he said. "They came to me. I didn't
even call for them. They came up here—they love me. They were fighting the leadership of Memphis. They were fighting Jim Lawson. . . .
They were too sick to see that what they were doing yesterday was hurting me much more than it could hurt the local preachers. But it is out
now. What do we do?" He said he was thinking of extremes such as one
of Gandhi's long fasts for penance.

"Martin, I'm not just talking about this march," Levison persisted.
"I'm talking in general about what seems to me the box or the trap that
you are placing nonviolence in. The other side can always find a few
provocateurs to start violence no matter what you do." King would be
paralyzed unless he could "hypnotize every single Negro alive," said
Levison. "That's too much to ask."

King, like James Lawson, said the movement was distorted by unstable myths in the press. For years, stories suggested that most American
black people accepted nonviolence, when in fact only a tiny fraction
practiced its severe leadership discipline. Then stories perceived a massive shift from the presumed weakness of "Negro nonviolence" to the
projected virility of black power, although even tinier numbers accepted
political violence. Still, King told Levison he was in no position to correct false impressions now that a riot "broke out right in the ranks of our
march." He could not go to Washington promising only one percent violence, and therefore he must seek rehabilitation in Memphis. "So I've
got to do something that becomes a kind of powerful act," he said. Until
then, he would be dismissed.

"This is what I am not so sure about," said Levison.

"Well, you watch your newspapers," said King. "Watch the *New York*

Times editorials. . . . I think it will be the most negative thing about Martin Luther King that you have ever seen."

"For a time, yes," admitted Levison, unable to check King's mood.

"There will not be even one sympathetic—even with our friends, it won't be there."

King broke away to catch an afternoon flight home. AFSCME president Jerry Wurf escorted him to the airport so they could exchange crisis strategy in person, and they agreed the sanitation strike had very little time to mount a comeback. Wurf admitted a negotiating error in his early offer to defer all economic demands, including a 10 cent hourly raise, which left no room for compromise once Mayor Loeb publicly rejected bargaining rights for the union as immoral. Wurf had just squeezed a $20,000 sustenance donation from AFL-CIO leader George Meany, but strike support was costing $50,000 per week. Impoverished strikers already were suffering evictions and repossessions of scarce property. For Wurf, the desperate challenge was to find reinforcements among distant white trade unions that were tepid at best about civil rights or critics of the Vietnam War, and thereby raise bargaining leverage decisively above the uncollected garbage and daily marches. Doggedly at that moment, Lawson was leading sanitation men back to City Hall under a precarious truce, secured by intermediaries, that police would attack only if they saw young people in the line. ("We never had any problem with what we called the 'tub-toter,' " said assistant chief Lux.) With their placards now hung from strings instead of sticks, as a nonviolent precaution, marchers stepped gingerly over riot debris between boarded windows and National Guard formations of bayoneted rifles, past piles of garbage starting to cook in 82 degree weather.

This was plainly not enough to secure a settlement. For King, Memphis prefigured the huge dilemma of Washington. How could he mobilize a large coalition in the face of a hostile consensus that nonviolence would not work? His internal opposition now included young factions maneuvering a treacherous line between competitive hustle and sincere belief that guerrilla methods superseded "old-time" civil rights. "The young people here have reached a political consciousness that those ministers do not understand or control," one Invader told a movement journal. "As for nonviolence, that died in Newark and Detroit." Another proclaimed the end of marches in an interview featured among world events on NBC's *Nightly News.* "I think my answer is 'by any means necessary,' " Coby Smith told viewers, echoing Malcolm X. "If the community can only respond to force and burning and shooting and looting, then we'll do it."

*   *   *

KING ASKED Abernathy to drop him off straight from the Atlanta airport at the downtown Butler Street YMCA, where he hoped a steam bath and rubdown from his blind masseur would revive him for a promised Friday night out with Coretta and the Abernathys. Shortly, however, he called Juanita Abernathy from the gym to say he did not feel like going to a restaurant or movie. "If I get some fish, will you cook it?" he asked. "Corrie will help you." She readily agreed, in part because he sounded so needy, and saved for a surprise her annual casserole of leftover pig dishes that he and Abernathy considered a sublime delicacy. That night, after the casserole and fish, the other three instinctively tried to divert King with light memories from Montgomery before the bus boycott, about church gossip and eager young couples. Although vacant and depressed, he seemed vaguely entertained and refused to go home. He fell asleep in his clothes on a love seat, grumbling that it was too small. Abernathy dozed nearby. Coretta, still tender from surgery, lay across a bed, and Juanita Abernathy slumped over a kitchen counter.

They woke late for the emergency meeting about Thursday's riot. Lawyer Chauncey Eskridge had arrived from Chicago along with Stanley Levison from New York, Walter Fauntroy from Washington, and Joseph Lowery from Mobile. Jesse Epps came from Memphis with a mandate from AFSCME and James Lawson to ensure King's return for a "redemption" march, but the top SCLC staff members lodged dozens of complaints by the time Abernathy and King trudged up to the third-floor conference room at Ebenezer. Some said trade unions always shortchanged partnership with black groups. Several grilled Bernard Lee about Memphis. Who trained the marshals? Did Lawson collect weapons in advance, or conduct workshops on nonviolence with the participants? Did the marshals even try to keep bystanders separate from the lines? Why did King and Abernathy start the march if they felt ominous stirrings all around them? Not a few critics recalled their predictions that King would get bogged down in this backwater movement. Bernard Lafayette objected that Memphis would mean more strain and distraction for a Washington crusade they had postponed twice already. "Why take us to Memphis, broke as we are?" he asked.

King absorbed the raw speeches mildly, as was his custom, then rose from a wooden Sunday School table to argue that they all underestimated their problem. "We are in serious trouble," he said. The Memphis riot had discredited nonviolent tenets at the heart of their movement. If they simply abandoned the garbage strike, a presumption of violence would follow them to the national stage with greatly magnified risk and opposition. Therefore, said King, he felt by no means committed to either Memphis *or* Washington—regardless of what he told the press—unless first convinced that they could restore the integrity of nonviolent protest. This was a staff decision, because he could not do it alone. "Memphis is the Washington campaign in miniature," he said.

His appeal backfired by reopening dissent against the Washington campaign itself. Andrew Young warned that the whole plan might be moot for the year, anyway, as the tangled logistics could well push the start back into June, when the summer recess of Congress would deprive them of "Pharaoh" rulers to plague. Young proposed to make constructive use of delay, and questioned the enormous effort to assemble and maintain a novel protest army of polyglot poor people in Washington. He doubted Stanley Levison's analogy with the Bonus Marchers of 1932–34, whose suffering and rejection had kindled delayed support for New Deal initiatives, and James Bevel renewed his attack on the entire calculation. "Aw, that's just a bunch of bullshit," he declared. "We don't need to be hanging around Washington. We need to stop this war." Bevel described Vietnam as a political sickness more deeply rooted than poverty, and his rhetoric bristled with street militancy poised ingeniously at the limit of nonviolence. Jesse Jackson, like Bevel, excelled in slashing vocabulary that suggested a competitive preacher's "chops" better suited to the new moods than King's ecumenical language. Jackson called Memphis too small and Washington too unformed. Nobody could tell him how long they might be in Washington, where they would be suspended on nothing more than political supplication tied to the lowest strand of the economy. How could he justify breaking off commitments to Operation Breadbasket, which forged real power out of settlements ranging from neighborhoods and youth gangs to big corporations?

This time King stood seething. "Ralph, give me my car keys," he said quietly. Abernathy surrendered them with a stricken, quizzical look as King said they could go on without him. "He did something I've never heard him do before," Levison confided afterward on his wiretapped phone. "He criticized three members of the staff with his eloquence. And believe me, that's murder. And was very negative." King said

Young had given in to doubt, Bevel to brains, and Jackson to ambition. He said they had forgotten the simple truths of witness. He said the movement had made them, and now they were using the movement to promote themselves. He confronted Bevel, who had been a mentor to Jackson and Young, as a genius who flummoxed his own heart. "You don't like to work on anything that isn't your own idea," said King. "Bevel, I think you owe *me* one."

Abernathy, Jackson, and Young rushed after King. "Doc, doc, don't worry!" called Jackson in the stairwell. "Everything's going to be all right."

King whirled on a landing and pointed up to shout. "Jesse, everything's *not* going to be all right!" he cried. "If things keep going the way they're going now, it's not SCLC but the whole country that's in trouble. I'm not asking, 'Support me.' I don't need this. But if you're so interested in doing your own thing that you can't do what this organization's structured to do, if you want to carve out your own niche in society, go ahead. But for God's sake, don't bother me!" His fury echoed in the conference room.

Abernathy returned alone, helpless. He said King left instructions to put his schedule on hold, beginning with tomorrow's sermon in Washington to defend the poverty campaign. Recriminations wore on for eight hours. Hosea Williams accused Bevel and Jackson of scheming to topple King. Jesse Epps said King would be scorned as a coward unless the staff facilitated a successful return to Memphis. Staff members flayed Epps and Lawson for causing the crisis, and arguments for contending options flew apart without King at the hub. William Rutherford said neither Memphis nor Washington made much sense to him, because they defied the stable plans and budgets dear to a professional manager, but he conceded that irrational inspiration from the movement was precisely what had lured him home from decades in exile. Stanley Levison criticized King in absentia for presenting their challenge as nothing less than making nonviolence popular, saying the goal was merely to keep a bunch of kids from ruining their protest method. If they did that, Levison argued, focus could be restored for projects on poverty and racism. On his reduced scope, Lafayette and Rutherford circulated with a pragmatic message that there would be support funds in the Washington campaign for Breadbasket and Vietnam protest, with an implicit message that Jackson and Bevel would be pinched otherwise through the SCLC budget. Andrew Young allowed that a corrective march would be quicker and surer if they all worked together. "All right," he bargained with Epps. "For this one time."

Gestures of accommodation ended with a mystical pronouncement from Joseph Lowery. "He said very quietly, 'The Lord has been in this room this afternoon,' " Levison told a friend. " 'I know he's been here because we could not have deliberated the way we did without the Holy Spirit being here. And the Holy Spirit is going to be with us in Memphis and Washington, and I know we're going to win.' And then," Levison continued, "because he was a little embarrassed at giving a little sermon, he ends up giving kind of an Indian war whoop. At which point Andy got up and started to do a little dance. And then somehow all of us were standing up shaking hands with each other." Many of those present guessed—from alarmingly indiscreet movements in the wings—that King had arranged a rendezvous with his respected Atlanta mistress of many years, but only Abernathy knew how to track them down. King returned to learn of the battered reconciliation: they would go to Washington through Memphis. Bevel, Jackson, Williams, and James Orange agreed jointly to organize nonviolent workshops, as with the Chicago gangs. Lafayette would recruit poverty volunteers from one extra city, and Rutherford said he could run the next staff meeting from the Lorraine Motel.

* * *

KING KEPT the next morning's engagement in Washington after all. He found the public mood broadly shuttered against him, as sympathetic voices saw in the Memphis "mini-riot" a harbinger of national calamity. "How do you keep the looters out?" asked Edward Brooke on the Senate floor. The *New York Times* warned against "emotional demonstrations in this time of civic unrest." Its editors reminded King that Gandhi once "had made a 'Himalayan miscalculation' by asking his people to adopt civil disobedience before they understood or were ready for it." The Memphis march served only "to solidify white sentiment against the strikers," said the *Times,* and "Dr. King must by now realize that his descent on Washington is likely to prove even more counterproductive." The *Washington Post* brooded in plaintive apprehension. "Let us have a march, by all means," an editorial soon suggested in feinted support. "But why not turn it around and have its route run from Washington to where the poverty is, instead of from where the poverty is to Washington?"

Overtly hostile opinion took up the FBI's dual themes. Tennessee representative Robert Everett told the U.S. House that King "ran like a scared rabbit," while John Stennis of Mississippi led senators demanding that the administration blockade the anti-poverty hordes preemptively at the D.C. city limits. In a Saturday editorial, "King's Credibility Gap," the *Memphis Commercial Appeal* argued that "King's pose as the leader of a non-violent movement has been shattered." On Sunday, the *Commercial Appeal* headlined its attack, "Chicken a la King," while the *St. Louis Globe-Democrat* branded "The Real Martin Luther King . . . one of the most menacing men in America today." The accompanying cartoon in St. Louis presented a grotesque zombie labeled King aiming a huge pistol from clouds of gun smoke and bullets with the caption: "I'm Not Firing It—I'm Only Pulling the Trigger." Congressional investigators would discover a decade later that the *Globe-Democrat* was among the FBI's regular outlets, and that the editorial borrowed wholesale from Hoover's clandestine propaganda: "Memphis could be only the prelude to a massive bloodbath in the national's [sic] capital in several weeks."

King climbed into the high white pulpit of Washington's National Cathedral during the eleven o'clock service on Sunday, March 31. Three thousand people filled the sanctuary, and another thousand listened over loudspeakers outside or by remote feed to the adjacent parish church of St. Alban's. Having apologized privately that he lacked time to prepare a special address, King began with an awkward mis-citation of the biblical text ("Behold, I make all things new") for one of his standard sermons: "Remaining Awake Through a Great Revolution." He recited an allegory derived from Washington Irving's early American tale of Rip van Winkle, who awoke from a twenty-year sleep into a world filled with strange customs and clothes, new vocabulary, and a mystifying preoccupation with the commoner George Washington instead of King George III. Just as Rip van Winkle had missed the American Revolution, King argued, people remained deaf to the day's ongoing cries for freedom.

He spoke grandly of new technology and interdependence on a shrinking globe. Not until halfway through the sermon did King veer off personally into the underlying cause. "I have literally found myself crying," he said. "I was in Marks, Mississippi the other day, which is in Quitman County, the poorest county in the United States." He described malnourished children of illiterate parents, adding stories from his visits to tenements in Harlem and Newark. He sketched again

Luke's parable of Dives and the beggar Lazarus, saying that while there was nothing wrong with wealth or new about poverty, there was hellish shame in subjugation blind to common humanity or citizenship. "We are coming to Washington in a 'poor people's campaign,' " he said. They would not settle for a "histrionic gesture," nor seek "to tear up Washington," but they would "engage in traumatic nonviolent action." King grounded his purpose in nonviolence despite Levison's quibbles, because it unified the method with the necessary twin goal, to end the Vietnam War. He said those who still believed in war to solve the social and political problems of mankind were sleeping through the revolution, too.

"In summary," King declared, "nothing will be done 'til people of good will put their hearts and souls in motion." He told the congregation that the odds were stacked heavily against the Washington campaign, but they should reject despair. "I say to you that our goal is freedom," he cried. "And I believe we're going to get there, because however much she strays from it, the goal of America is freedom." Press outlets filtered King's sermon into news stories built around confrontation. "Oh, we're always willing to negotiate," he replied at a press conference, which generated the headline: "Dr. King Hints He'd Cancel March if Aid Is Offered." Another story focused on speculation about where the poverty encampment might pursue legislators if Congress adjourned for the election season: "King Threatens Demonstration at Conventions." For those interested but not present at Sunday's cathedral service, the gist of King's message lay dormant in a composition already sent to the printer. "I'm committed to non-violence absolutely," he wrote. "I'm just not going to kill anybody, whether it's in Vietnam or here." His article, published as "Showdown for Non-Violence," would emerge a posthumous testament in the April 16 issue of *Look* magazine. "The American people are infected with racism—that is the peril," King concluded. "Paradoxically, they are also infected with democratic ideals—that is the hope."

* * *

PRESIDENT JOHNSON also set his course in storms of colliding emotion. Early Sunday morning, March 31, he and Lady Bird trundled outside in pajamas to greet their daughter Lynda on the White House South Grounds after her sleepless return flight from California. Pale and haggard, she vented angrily at the President about sending her newlywed Marine Captain Chuck Robb off to war duty in Vietnam. "Daddy, I want to ask you a question," she said. "Why do we have to fight over there when so many people are opposed to the war?" Lady Bird pulled her away, and Lynda Robb confessed upstairs that her steely composure was dissolving. Yesterday's farewell moments at Norton Air Force Base had turned into a chaotic media scrum, after which she sobbed uncontrollably through actor Dustin Hoffman's hit film about youth rebellion, *The Graduate*. Many Marine families from Robb's company had done their best to leave progeny in case the husbands did not come home, but she did not yet know she was pregnant. Her mother ordered a sedative to make her sleep.

The President met secretly after breakfast with a trusted former speechwriter, Horace Busby, who waited in turmoil with the advance draft for Johnson's address on Vietnam. Busby was elated to read of the bombing halt and invitation for peace talks, but utterly nonplussed to learn that they were a blind leap. "No, we have heard nothing from Hanoi," the President said brusquely. "Not a whisper, not a wink." Johnson waved all that aside to ask for Busby's judgment about a more personal matter. If he closed that night's speech with a second bombshell announcement, that he would not seek reelection, would he lose authority for the remaining ten months of his term? "Point Two," said the President. "Will this hurt or help in getting peace? Will Hanoi or Moscow or Peking—or Saigon, for that matter—think we are collapsing over here?" Would American soldiers think Johnson reneged on his duty to protect them? Did he have a better chance to pass the tax increase as a candidate or noncandidate? To a host of related questions, Busby hazarded a consistent reply that the dramatic surrender of power would enhance Johnson's stature. Otherwise, for instance, he thought the peace initiatives would be discounted as election year subterfuge. These answers earned him the commission to refine an alternative "peroration," and the President secluded Busby with a writing pad in the second-floor Treaty Room of the White House residence. "Don't let a soul know you're over here," he instructed.

Shortly before King began his sermon at the Episcopal Cathedral, Johnson went to Catholic mass with his daughter Luci, then detoured his motorcade for a surprise visit to the home of Hubert Humphrey. He told the thunderstruck Vice President not to inform even his wife, Muriel, that there was a one-in-four chance he would withdraw. Back in the White House, Johnson met the four top managers of his reelection effort, including Lawrence O'Brien, who coupled bad news of the latest bottom in his Gallup approval rating (36 percent) with confident predictions that he already had enough delegates to win the Democratic nomination. The President said nothing to them of his withdrawal from the race, knowing any hint would deflate his campaign, but the electric tension later in the small dining room made clear that the option had let slip among the family and houseguests. Plates went untouched. After lunch, while Johnson practiced the body of the speech in the Oval Office, his tearful daughter Luci woke her sister to tell her the news. "Chuck will hear this on his way to Vietnam," Lynda Robb cried, and Busby cringed in the Treaty Room away from their wailing fits of disbelief.

The President warned selected friends late Sunday. When he told the principal speech author there might be a special ending tacked on, Harry McPherson said he was pretty sure what it was. "I'm very sorry, Mr. President," he sadly observed. McPherson's shorthand perception relieved Johnson from any need to explain his political logic that no President could survive ambivalence in war.

Johnson was equally spare. "Well, I think it's best," he said. "So long, podner."

Less than an hour before the nine o'clock address, Johnson sent Busby's final peroration ahead to the TelePrompTer unit being set up with television cameras in the Oval Office. Glum aides and technicians transmitted the words. When Defense Secretary Clifford and his wife, Marny, arrived at 8:25, bringing confirmation that formal orders already had stopped all bombing north of 20 degrees latitude, the President showed him the speech coda as he dressed for television. "Nothing in my career ever surprised me so much," Clifford recorded. A distraught family friend emerged to tell the others that Johnson wanted no more emergency appeals for reconsideration or delay: "He said that the decision has been made." Newcomers to the small audience of dignitaries stared in puzzlement at anguished faces.

Thirty-five minutes into the historic address, which went so far as to designate Averell Harriman the U.S. representative for nonexistent peace talks, Johnson abruptly turned personal: "Finally, my fellow Americans, let me say this. Of those to whom much is given, much is asked." He professed a philosophy he said sustained him since the "tragedy and trauma" of the Kennedy assassination "fifty-two months and ten days ago . . . binding up our wounds, healing our history, moving forward in new unity to clear the American agenda and to keep the

American commitment for all of our people." Now, faced with crippling divisions at home and abroad, Johnson declared his resolve not to "devote an hour or a day of my time to any personal partisan causes" in the election year. "Accordingly," he announced, "I shall not seek, and I will not accept, the nomination of my party for another term as your President."

Lady Bird Johnson waded into the aftershock. "Nobly done, darling," she said, but the staggering finality of the speech left a mood of resignation around her. "Can I go to England now?" asked Lynda Robb with a mordant smile. Mayor Daley of Chicago led an avalanche of callers suspended between protest and congratulations. The President alone, relishing the bewildered commentary on the television networks, claimed ebullient release that it was over. "I never felt so right about any decision in my life," he kept saying.

President Johnson's twin jolt lifted the whole country into euphoria. Commentators praised his statesmanship in the cause of peace, and his poll ratings reversed symmetrically from stark disapproval to approval. Cheering crowds instead of pickets mobbed him on a speech trip to Chicago on Monday, when securities on the New York Stock Exchange gained more percentage value than in any previous session. The markets also broke a long-standing record for most shares traded, which had stood nearly four decades since the "Black Tuesday" crash of 1929, but this new mark lasted only two days. Early on Wednesday, April 3, when news flashed of North Vietnam's agreement to enter talks with the United States, peace buyers so overwhelmed the Big Board that its ticker lagged nearly an hour behind trades.

Hopes for early peace proved false. Johnson changed only one political fact about Vietnam with his magnanimous abdication: he turned the country away from military escalation as a viable option to resolve the conflict. Major candidates from both parties henceforth would run on troop reductions and slogans of peace with honor, but Johnson escaped rather than solved the dilemma that broke him. He offered no convincing narrative to reconcile the concrete experience of Vietnam with American character and purpose. Even freed from the cares of reelection, he recommended no such story to compete with the North Vietnamese claim on history. Fifteen of sixteen paragraphs in Hanoi's response insisted that Johnson's speech was merely a stopgap toward inevitable failure. "This is a defeat," said Radio Hanoi, "and at the same time a perfidious trick of the U.S. Government to appease public opinion." One grudging paragraph accepted talks only to ratify Hanoi's constant prescription: "The United States must bring its aggressive war in Vietnam to an end, withdraw all U.S. and satellite troops from South Vietnam and let the Vietnamese people settle the internal affairs of Vietnam themselves."

No American leaders wanted to dignify North Vietnam's terms, and public esteem toward Johnson spiked high on the wish that the political sacrifice by the war's sponsoring embodiment might open some more palatable way to peace. "Your speech was magnificent," Robert Kennedy told Johnson Wednesday morning. The President had just walked into the Cabinet Room to share with Kennedy the Hanoi dispatch received only twelve minutes earlier. Kennedy said he appreciated the heavy burdens on Johnson, and regretted letting their differences leave him out of touch. A lot of it, Kennedy said tactfully of the feud, "was my fault." The President said the press had exaggerated their differences, and, turning to Theodore Sorensen, Kennedy's counselor and family friend, opined that the rift might never have developed if Sorensen had stayed on in the White House. Sorensen said they must not let the press divide them. He embraced consultation on common issues, and observed as a former speechwriter that Johnson's Vietnam address had the ring of a man searching for peace. Johnson said he felt no belligerence toward any of his critics: "I want everybody to get together to find a way to stop the killing."

They achieved an intimate but guarded understanding on the new political landscape. Kennedy had requested the private talk when, after a weekend spent investigating extraordinary poverty among the White Mountain Apaches of Arizona, he landed Sunday night in a New York media blitz. "You're kidding," he reacted to the first couriers who pushed through the passengers into his plane. Suddenly, Kennedy no longer was running to unseat his late brother's former Vice President. "Can I ask about the political situation?" he asked Johnson. "Where do I stand in the campaign?" Would the President marshal forces against him?

He intended to honor his neutrality pledge, Johnson replied, but he also did not wish to mislead Kennedy. He said he felt much closer to Vice President Humphrey, who might run, and was about to hold the same meeting with him. "If he asks my advice," Johnson told Kennedy, "I won't give it." (Humphrey, in fact, would be wounded to receive no mandate from Johnson.) While reserving his options, the President said he would try to stay out of the race not because he was so pure but because he was scared. "If I thought I could get into the campaign and hold the country together," he declared, "I would have run myself."

Kennedy and Sorensen pressed Johnson on political details. Would he allow Cabinet members to take sides in the Democratic primaries? (Postmaster General Lawrence O'Brien was eager to go back to the Kennedys once released from loyal campaign duty for LBJ.) Would Johnson give courtesy warning of any adverse stands he felt compelled to take? The President hesitated, then agreed, and the horse trading provoked a maudlin speech. Johnson acknowledged the torture of being Vice President—"and you wouldn't have liked it either," he told Kennedy in a pointed aside—and complained that his surviving devotion to President Kennedy was not fully appreciated. He had never fired a Kennedy appointee, the President whispered, and had asked many like Sorensen not to leave. He regarded all he had done as a continuation of the Kennedy-Johnson program. He believed President Kennedy could look down to this day and agree Johnson had kept faith in education, poverty, and civil rights even while repaid with disaffection by Negroes and young people. "The next man who sits in this chair," he managed to say, "will have to do better."

"You are a brave and dedicated man," Robert Kennedy responded, so softly he cleared his throat and said so again.

Had Vietnam yielded magically to symbols, the dynastic saga of Johnson and Kennedy might have been celebrated for the glorious triumph of opposites over tragedy. As it was, however, an assassin would take Kennedy in two months, and the war would drag on toward North Vietnam's victory through two more Presidents until 1975, two years past Johnson's death. What would outlast even the war was a legend of personal enmity between him and Kennedy so strong that it swallowed up the lessons of Vietnam along with many lingering issues of substance, thus helping to introduce a cynical era of spitball politics. Meanwhile, the Kennedy-Johnson program maintained inertia beneath the April 3 summit. A federal court ruled that Alabama could not maintain single-race sports conferences for high schools. By a vote of 2,033 to 792, the Missouri Athletic Club eliminated the word "white" from its by-laws, on promise from club officers that the change would affect guest restrictions but not new memberships for the near future. Headlines revealed a drive to raise tenfold the percentage of black recruits accepted into National Guard units nationwide, which ranged by state from none to negligible, and the Pentagon also announced an odd mix in weekly American casualties from Vietnam: a record number of wounded (3,886) but the lowest total killed (330) since the beginning of January's Tet offensive.

* * *

A BOMB scare stalled Eastern Air Lines Flight 381 more than an hour on the Atlanta runway, which made King's return trip to Memphis coincide almost exactly with the White House parley between Kennedy and President Johnson. The pilot announced belated clearance for take-off with an upbeat apology that threats to King had generated a precautionary overnight guard for the aircraft, plus an extra hand search of the baggage compartment. Like the strangers exposed, King could only guess the level of danger. He had received no briefing, because of J. Edgar Hoover's spiteful edict that excluded him from the kind of notice other threat targets received, and the FBI confined warning to police agencies, the Secret Service, and the Federal Aviation Administration of one local phone threat recorded Monday in particularly clear diction: "Your airline brought Martin Luther King to Memphis, and when he comes again a bomb will go off, and he will be assassinated."

SCLC comptroller James Harrison endured frayed nerves on King's flight to preserve his secret status as the prized FBI informant. Harrison would obey risky orders to call the Memphis FBI office with inside reports on the transplanted staff meetings, but he had compromised his Atlanta handlers by embezzling funds from the SCLC treasury. The FBI indulged the crime (which in turn eroded its control of Harrison by common complicity), partly because Hoover's white agents had trouble replacing human sources within the civil rights movement. The Memphis police force, by contrast, had integrated its force of 850 officers with roughly one hundred black recruits, nearly all of whom drew hazardous political assignments. They escorted garbage trucks with replacement workers, for instance, and many courted fury by infiltrating strike supporters and black power groups on undercover duty. ("Had one in our meetin'," recalled a striker. "The only way we knowed he was police, his radio went off while he was there.") On this fifty-second consecutive day of the City Hall vigils and uncollected garbage, King's chief of staff William Rutherford made note of the suspicion between black people and police units through the city, beginning at the airport. A woman from James Lawson's greeting party accosted a plainclothes black detective in the crowd as a turncoat spy. Lawson himself told police inspector Don Smith that King could not cooperate with the uniformed security detail because of his nonviolent objection to firearms. He also defended a recommendation for King not to submit his schedule in advance, or accept security officers into private events, arguing bluntly that the two Mace attacks revealed the intention of the police to repress legitimate protest more than to apprehend criminals such as window-breakers. During this dispute, Robert Lewis stepped from a hearse through the surrounding reporters to beseech Lawson for the honor of an introduction to King, and Abernathy joked on the way into town that their morning already sandwiched a bomb search with the hungry-looking welcome from Lewis, the richest black undertaker in Memphis.

Detective Ed Redditt shrugged off being publicly exposed again at the airport. As a community relations officer for the police department, he had been an unlikely choice for undercover duty, but the commanders of the new anti-riot squads needed operatives familiar with black Memphis. Redditt and his partner followed King's party to the Lorraine Motel, then followed them again at noon to James Lawson's Centenary Methodist Church. Radio orders split them up temporarily from there, with the partner remaining on stakeout. While unable to enter the church, he had no trouble learning that Jesse Jackson gave a rousing speech to the strike committee on the potential for boycott techniques from Operation Breadbasket to help sanitation workers. King emerged to address the latest crisis: a federal court order secured by Mayor Loeb against the "redemption" march set for Monday, April 8. He told reporters he would ask the district judge to modify or vacate the order, but that he would march in defiance of the court order if necessary. "We are not going to be stopped by Mace or injunctions," King declared. His group departed so quickly that the partner lost them. He rushed north to Clayborn Temple on a hunch that they might be joining the daily pilgrimage to City Hall, only to hear by police radio that Redditt spotted King returning to the Lorraine with Lawson at 2:15. Redditt by then had selected a makeshift surveillance post among lockers on the rear wall of Fire Station Number 2. By taping a newspaper over the window, with two holes cut to match his binoculars, he had a clear view over the motel parking lot to King's Room 306, on an open balcony. Redditt and his partner took the first shift transmitting a log: 2:30, U.S. marshals serve the federal injunction on King, who poses with them outside for photographers. At 3:00, local ACLU lawyers enter 306, presumably about the next day's emergency hearing in court, and by 4:00, King receives known members of the Invaders youth gang.

The large Invaders delegation included the police department's most valued undercover officer, known as "Agent 500." A native of Mississippi, Marrell McCullough had distinguished himself since being hired upon Army discharge the previous year. He agreed to grow one of the early Afro hairdos in Memphis, and mastered black power rhetoric with paramilitary swagger so convincing, boasted the special unit commander, that half his fellow police officers "would have given their eye teeth to have locked him up." Held forth as the Invaders' "Minister of Transportation," McCullough added presence to the student leaders, while his firsthand bulletins as Agent 500 complemented James Harrison's FBI spy work on the inner deliberations at the Lorraine. When Charles Cabbage requested some $200,000 to start a "Liberation School," King's top aides acknowledged from contacts since Monday that the Invaders could turn out young people in large numbers, but found them fixated on ambition to purge James Lawson while committed to teach guerrilla warfare and martial arts. They said the Invaders had painted the windows of their storefront black except for small sentry slits, and that guards stood armed during negotiations. Cabbage and his cohorts hotly replied that there was a time to pray and a time to fight, but Abernathy and Bernard Lee waved aside their stories of arrest and persecution, saying true or not, they were no excuse to extort money from King. Andrew Young entered the fierce standoff with a gambit developed since the Meredith march. "How many people did you kill last year?" he asked the Invaders. Last week? What are you waiting for? Why not try something real in the meantime? He offered to help them translate militancy into a funding proposal that King could endorse, without violence, and the meeting stumbled to uneasy recess.

In police jargon, Detective Redditt recorded the movement of the Invaders from King's room back to their own: "4:50. About nine male coloreds and one female colored entered Room 316." He noticed quite a bit of activity to secure Coca-Colas and ice. "View from Fire Station window is very good," Redditt wrote. The four-officer security detail left the motel permanently a few minutes later, on orders from downtown that they were no longer to stand unwanted outside King's door. Tom Offenburger, SCLC's press secretary, emerged briefly from the nonstop staff meeting to tell reporters before their Thursday deadlines that the start of the poverty campaign in Washington would be delayed once again, until April 29. Two senior police lieutenants, including the founder of the Domestic Intelligence Unit, appeared at 6:35 to assume personal command of the fire station surveillance post for the night. They ordered Redditt and his partner to cover King's evening speech, where black officers would be less conspicuous than whites, but Redditt had scarcely entered the Mason Temple after supper when a preacher advised him to leave. Word was out that Redditt was peeping at Dr. King through binoculars from a fire station, he warned, and there was too much stress among the garbage workers to guarantee his safety. Redditt fled, keeping his panic in check while planning his revenge against those who exposed him. He remembered only two men likely to have recognized him, or to have passed word so quickly to strike sympathizers, and he resolved to find out if his superiors valued his work enough to use their clout on behalf of a black officer. They did, and before midnight both black firefighters from Station Number 2 would receive peremptory transfer orders to report elsewhere in the morning.

* * *

TORNADO WARNINGS made King fret about his crowd, as ominous streaks of gray and purple crossed the sky from the west. Radio bulletins told of a seven o'clock twister that picked up and dumped a stretch of asphalt on cars near Star City, Arkansas, killing seven people, and the first squalls hit Memphis half an hour later in slanted sheets of rain. Phone calls from the Lorraine to Lawson in Mason Temple verified that the crowd indeed was thin—perhaps fewer than two thousand in the huge hall that had packed seven times that many for King's visit on March 18. He feared the sharp drop-off would invite belittling stories of a downward trend for him, along with the riot and new federal injunction. "Ralph," said King, "I want you to go speak for me tonight."

Abernathy balked, and suggested sending Jesse Jackson, but King insisted. He was still testy about Jackson from Atlanta. Abernathy asked if he could take Jackson along. "Yes," said King, "but you do the speaking."

Song leaders and speakers filled the time in Mason Temple while Abernathy drove through the rain. James Lawson emphasized that Monday's big march would go forward regardless of the outcome in federal court, because the day's injunction applied only to King and a handful of associated "non-residents of the state of Tennessee." He said they could survive this injunction like the earlier one secured by Mayor Loeb against Jerry Wurf and the AFSCME leadership, which had called forth unprecedented unity among local black churches behind the strike. Lawson rallied spirits, and murmurs of anticipation ran through the hall when Abernathy, Jackson, and Young were sighted— only to hush when King's absence registered. For Abernathy, a keen reader of crowds, the palpable disappointment was worse than he feared. He went to a vestibule telephone instead of the podium and marshaled enticements for King—mentioning news cameras, the big spray of microphones, and Lawson's point that the movement seldom gathered so many people in the South. Most of all, Abernathy told King this was a core crowd of sanitation workers who had braved a night of hellfire to hear him, and they would feel cut off from a lifeline if he let them down. When King gave in, Abernathy pressed for assurance. "Don't fool me now," he said, and King promised to hurry.

His entrance caused an eerie bedlam of communion under shelter. Cheers from the floor echoed around the thousands of empty seats above, and the whole structure rattled from the pounding elements of wind, thunder, and rain. Two giant exhaust fans in the ceiling leaked and creaked so badly they had to be shut down. Abernathy seized the spotlight to introduce King with a saucy, tongue-in-cheek imitation of his "Drum Major" sermon, detailing a lineage of preachers. "His daddy is a preacher. His granddaddy was a preacher. His uncle was a preacher. His brother is a preacher, and of course," Abernathy cried, pointing to himself, "his dearest friend and other brother is one of the world's greatest preachers!" For half an hour, he reviewed the honors and attainments of King's life as though appropriating each one into a family arsenal for the sanitation workers. King had not yet decided whether to become President of the United States, Abernathy teased, "but he is the one who tells the president what to do."

King came smiling to the microphones about 9:30, just as the storms crested. (Tornadoes killed five more people. One at ten o'clock demolished forty trailer homes just north of Memphis, where the only serious injury was a man struck by a flying television.) He strung together several of his speech themes aimed toward the shared moment, beginning with a poetical tour of history. "If I were standing at the beginning of time," and could choose any lifetime, he would "take my mental flight" past the glories of ancient Egypt, Greece, and Rome—"But I wouldn't stop there," he kept saying—down past scenes from the Renaissance and Martin Luther and Abraham Lincoln until he could say, "If you allow me to live just a few years in the second half of the twentieth century, I will be happy." It might seem strange with the world so messed up, King said, but he chose above all to see the stirrings of a human rights revolution for freedom worldwide. "I can remember when Negroes were just going around as Ralph has said, so often scratching where they didn't itch and laughing when they were not tickled." He smiled. "But that day is all over. We mean business now, and we are determined to gain our rightful place in God's world."

He saluted every aspect of the Memphis movement, beginning with the families of sanitation workers. "I call upon you to be with us Monday," King said. "We need all of you." Overlooking the intramural controversies, he praised Lawson for his vanguard career in nonviolence, and he turned once in mid-speech to ask Jesse Jackson for a reminder about local tactics. Then he meandered into another speech theme to recap the parable of the Good Samaritan. "If I do not stop to help the sanitation workers," he concluded, "what will happen to *them*. That's the question. . . . We have an opportunity to make America a better nation. And I want to thank God, once more, for allowing me to be here with you."

Abruptly King swerved into a third oratorical run, retelling of his brush with death when a demented woman stabbed him at a Harlem bookstore in 1958—how a doctor told the *New York Times* that the blade would have severed his aorta if he so much as sneezed, and how a little girl wrote a simple letter of thanks that he did not sneeze. "I want to say that I am happy that I didn't sneeze," said King, "because if I had sneezed, I wouldn't have been around here in 1960 when students all over the South started sitting in at lunch counters. And I knew that as they were sitting in, they were really standing up for the best in the American dream, and taking the whole nation back to those great wells of democracy. . . ." His voice climbed again in rhythm and fervor, using survival as a melodramatic device to relive the civil rights movement. "If I had sneezed," he cried near the end, "I wouldn't have been down in Selma."

Experienced preachers behind him felt fleeting anxiety that King might miss his landing, because he was in full passion on a peroration unsuited to close. The "sneeze" run always came earlier in his speeches, being informal and thin. King sputtered at the podium, then slipped a gear. "And they were telling me—now it doesn't matter now," he said. "It really doesn't matter. I left Atlanta this morning. . . ." He told briskly of the pilot's bomb search announcement. "And then I got into Memphis." He frowned. "And some began to say the threats—or talk about the threats—that were out, what would happen to me from some of our sick white brothers. Well, I don't *know* what will happen now. We've got some difficult days ahead. But it doesn't matter with me now."

King paused. "Because I've been to the mountaintop," he declared in a trembling voice. Cheers and applause erupted. Some people jerked involuntarily to their feet, and others rose slowly like a choir. "And I don't mind," he said, trailing off beneath the second and third waves of response. "Like anybody I would like to live—a long life—longevity has its place." The whole building suddenly hushed, which let sounds of thunder and rain fall from the roof. "But I'm not concerned about that now," said King. "I just want to do God's will." There was a subdued call of "Yes!" in the crowd. "And he's allowed me to go up the mountain," King cried, building intensity. "And I've looked over. And I have s-e-e-e-e-n, the promised land." His voice searched a long peak over the word "seen," then hesitated and landed with quick relief on "the promised land," as though discovering a friend. He stared out over the microphones with brimming eyes and the trace of a smile. "And I may not get there with you," he shouted, "but I want you to *know, tonight* ["Yes!"] that we as a people will get to the promised land!" He stared again over the claps and cries, while the preachers closed toward him from behind. "So I'm happy tonight!" rushed King. "I'm not worried about *any*thing! I'm not fearing *any* man! Mine eyes have seen the *glo*-ry of the coming of the Lord!" He broke off the quotation and stumbled sideways into a hug from Abernathy. The preachers helped him to a chair, some crying, and tumult washed through the Mason Temple.

King sat spent, drenched in perspiration. Friends gathered around with congratulations and wonder for his thunderclap ending of little more than one hundred words. They said he transcended death while capturing freedom, gazing forward and backward on both. They compared details from the biblical story of Moses, who was permitted to see Canaan across the Jordan River from atop Mount Nebo, but died there for transgressions before his people entered the Promised Land. King revived in preacher talk with peers, and lingered eagerly to greet the sanitation workers. Notwithstanding an endless day since the airport bomb search, in fact, he hummed with incandescent stamina and disappeared with Abernathy and Bernard Lee for a long night on the town. When they returned by taxi to the Lorraine Motel after four o'clock the next morning, King saw a car with Kentucky license plates outside a room with the lights still burning. "Where's the Senator?" he called in booming welcome for Georgia Davis, who had just completed her first legislative session as the only black or female member of the Kentucky Senate. She was vacationing with her best friend, a mistress to King's younger brother, A.D., when they persuaded A.D. King to fly down from Louisville to Florida for a drive up through the Alabama and Mississippi storms into Tennessee, arriving too late at the Mason Temple. The brothers caught up on family talk and the Memphis crisis before King followed Davis to her Room 201 for the short remainder of night. Only then, after an abbreviated morning huddle to send Andrew Young into federal court as his designated witness, did he collapse for a nap.

* * *

IN A jammed U.S. Court for the Western District of Tennessee, Mayor Loeb watched his attorneys defend the injunction to exclude SCLC from any march in downtown Memphis. Frank Holloman, director of the combined fire and police divisions, testified that neither the city nor King would be safe. "The white citizens of Memphis, in letters to me and telephone calls to me, are greatly agitated at the present time," he told the court. "There was a theft from a sporting goods store last evening of guns and ammunition." Citing numerous threats that King would not survive, Holloman also listed fourteen reasons why the march would endanger the half-million citizens in his charge. "Number one," he testified, "I am convinced that Dr. Martin Luther King, his leaders, or others, cannot control a massive march of this kind in this city or elsewhere." Judge Bailey Brown qualified Holloman to give expert opinion based on his distinguished career in the FBI, where he had served as chief inspector, but the judge asked pointedly for evidence that King's influence in a constitutional demonstration would be a net plus for violence. "I would rather local people lead the march," replied one of Holloman's subordinates.

Back at the Lorraine Motel, Chicago lawyer Chauncey Eskridge reported to Room 306 about eleven o'clock Thursday morning. "Chauncey," said King, "drop your bags right here and get down to court." He hurried Eskridge to fortify the ACLU lawyers on his position crafted from the Selma march, which was to assert the right of protest while accepting reasonable conditions to promote safety and nonviolence. Eskridge left before Charles Cabbage and three other Invaders intruded on King's revolving staff session to declare a more aggressive posture. They demanded specific commitments to their budget, and, in exchange for accepting tactical nonviolence along with temporary positions on his staff, they wanted equal respect for their doctrine of "tactical violence." King rejected them firmly in his way. "I don't negotiate with brothers," he said—brothers only look for ways to help each other in good conscience. When the Invaders stormed off, King turned on Hosea Williams for letting the Invaders hoodwink him. He had wanted Williams to seek common ground with them, he said, but never to compromise the core principle of nonviolence on the SCLC staff. Pacing the room, he worked himself into a sermon much like the scolding he had inflicted on Bill Rutherford in Washington. Williams went away fuming. He believed King had sent mixed signals. He thought Bevel and James Orange deserved King's wrath more than he did, and grumbled that they were off joyriding with other Invaders.

Abernathy sent down to the motel kitchen for two orders of fried Mississippi River catfish. King dispatched some staff members back to Atlanta, and he sent Bernard Lafayette to Washington for Friday's opening press conference at the national headquarters of the Poor People's Campaign. Instead of postponing the event because of Memphis, Lafayette would substitute for King, and they went over what he should say. King instructed Lafayette to keep his room at the Lorraine and come right back to help train marshals over the weekend. "In the next campaign," he remarked, "we'll have to institutionalize nonviolence and take it international." Lafayette blinked in disbelief. Before he could ask about this flash of optimism, so high above the tribulations of Memphis and Washington, King only smiled as he turned back inside, where Abernathy was having communication trouble with the motel waitress. She kept bringing two of the wrong side items but only one lunch dish. This vexed co-owner Lorene Bailey, who lionized King, long after he and Abernathy amiably decided to share catfish off the one plate.

In the afternoon court session, lawyers for Memphis grilled James Lawson about how any assurances of nonviolence could be credible in light of his failures as chief marshal to keep peace in the march a week ago. "Are you telling the Court that unless there is a march that there will be violence," asked one, "and people will disobey the laws, have looting, fires, Molotov cocktails, et cetera?" Lawson sparred with the lawyers, arguing that the best way to avoid a riot was to have a creative protest against injustice. Another line of cross-examination asked how the sanitation workers could have any grievance to justify protest, since they could make up to $3,700 per year, or nearly twice the average family income for Negroes in Memphis. Flustered, Lawson said even that dubious comfort made sanitation workers eligible for Food Stamps. Judge Brown interceded to ask whether the defense would accept a restriction against sticks used to carry placards. "There will be no sticks in any march, or any other potential weapons or weapon," Lawson agreed, and he confessed regret from the stand: "That, that was a major error to even have such signs."

In Room 306, Abernathy had fallen asleep shortly after finishing his catfish, but King, still restless after a series of business calls, went downstairs to meet his brother and the two Kentucky women in Room 201. They caught up on Louisville politics and gossip. A.D. worried about where to get a pair of pants pressed. King admitted severe anxiety that he might have to defy a federal rather than a state injunction on Monday, because this would tarnish the movement's anchor hope for vindication through the national compact, and he complained intermittently about hearing nothing all day from Andrew Young about how he fared in court. For relief, he and A.D. placed a call to Mama King in Atlanta. They talked with her for nearly an hour, pretending at first to be each other and often laughing uproariously at her tales of life with Daddy King, who came on the line, too. Afterward, the two brothers merrily sifted for ways in which their father might be considered modern even though it choked him to pay his maid a measly $25 a week. King called upstairs to wake Abernathy, who soon heard a buoyant replay of the phone call home. "She's always happy when A.D.'s with me," said King. "She doesn't often have a chance to talk to us both together."

He reminded Abernathy that Billy Kyles expected them at five o'clock for an early supper before the mass meeting. They certainly would arrive late, with extra guests such as Eskridge and the Kentucky group, but King claimed to worry most about the menu. He wanted to make sure they would get real soul food rather than some dainty starvation of asparagus and greens. "Call her," he prodded Abernathy with an insistent undercurrent of mirth, until the exasperated sidekick called Gwen Kyles. She said there was plenty of food and the dinner was at six o'clock, not five. (By disclosing the actual time, she inadvertently spoiled her husband's trick to combat King's chronic tardiness.) As for the puzzling question about the menu, she mentioned a few dishes hesitantly until excitement spread through her household that Abernathy was repeating each item to King—roast beef, sweetbreads, chitterlings, pork chops, neck bones, fried chicken, and ham in the meat line, plus six kinds of salad, featured turnip greens and candied sweet potatoes, a bread table of hot rolls, corn bread, corn muffins, biscuits, and corn pones, and pretty much the works for dessert. Kyles had recruited the best cooks from her church, along with many helpers, favored daughters, and hostesses in finest clothes to spread forth a feast. ("They were really laying for that dinner," she recalled.) Her menu, greatly embellished in Abernathy's relayed account, more than satisfied King, but A.D. still preferred supper at the motel. He often shied from social events that invited comparison to his world-famous older brother, while hating also to embarrass him with his binge weakness for alcohol.

By mid-afternoon, as the last major witness in the federal hearing, Andrew Young withstood withering cross-examination on "the so-called doctrine of nonviolence," which lawyers for Memphis treated like a crackpot myth. "Now the nonviolent school is to be distinguished from the so-called passive school?" asked one, who wondered how meek notions could be squared with militant words. Young managed to parry a question about how the movement had "plagued" Birmingham in 1963. "Really, by marching down to City Hall every day for about forty-five days," he said, "and having a prayer meeting." He did concede that he had never seen King so depressed by the difficulty of maintaining nonviolent discipline and spirit. "I think history shows that most of the riots that have occurred in America have occurred during or just after wartime," Young testified, "when the whole country is attuned to violence." He bristled when asked why prominent Negroes like Roy Wilkins said King could not control demonstrations. Because the NAACP "has almost no history of mass action," Young replied, "and I think of Mr. Wilkins very much like my father."

The cross-examiner pounced on the witness to explain the implied criticism of his own father. Young replied bluntly that his father, as a comfortable member of the New Orleans establishment, would feel no urgency about the plight of 1,300 garbagemen who were not eating very well. The need for change was urgent and real, he added, quickly recovering. "I would like to remind you that there is almost no place else in the world where people even assume that this kind of change should come about nonviolently except Martin Luther King and the Southern Leadership Conference. There is no tradition of nonviolence anywhere else in the world, in labor, and even in most areas of our own government," Young testified in a rush. "And certainly when America felt oppressed by Britain, they didn't seek nonviolence to seek redress of grievance. So I say we do have probably the only vested interest in nonviolence in this society, and we intend to make it work, and we would not want to run any unnecessary risks, because it jeopardizes what Dr. King has made a way of life for him."

The lawyer for Memphis suffered the outburst. "Are you through?" he asked.

"Yes, sir," said Young.

At four o'clock, a bungled intelligence crisis led to the removal of Detective Redditt from the surveillance post at Fire Station Number 2. His superiors downtown discussed the threats against Redditt with a visiting investigator for U.S. senator John McClellan, who was in town to see whether the dangers of Memphis could justify federal action to curtail King's Washington campaign. The investigator marveled that he had just received parallel reports of a plot to kill a black officer in Memphis. In fact, as he soon discovered to his chagrin in the files, the alleged plot was directed toward Knoxville, not Memphis, on the shaky word of an informant from Mississippi. Still, the prospect of a double-jointed conspiracy within the black community tended to overstimulate intelligence officers hostile to civil rights, and the seeming confirmation of a "hit contract" rocketed up to fire and police director Holloman on his return from federal court. He ordered a police guard to hide Redditt and his family in a motel under assumed names. Redditt's partner, officer Willie Richmond, took over the surveillance post alone. He let a fireman or two peep through the binoculars when they came by to use the lockers and vending machines.

Also at four o'clock, an escaped convict bought a pair of Bushnell binoculars just up Main Street at York Arms Company, one of the businesses whose windows were smashed on March 28. He drove back to finish setting up a surveillance post more or less by the method Redditt had used the day before. The convict had driven from Atlanta, where the newspapers said King was leaving for a march in Memphis, arriving late the previous night. This day, reading front-page news that King was staying at the Lorraine, and perhaps hearing radio reports that specified Room 306, he had located and studied the motel until an hour ago, when he rented a room for $8.50 per week in Bessie Brewer's flophouse next door to Fire Station Number 2. With the seven-power Bushnells, he could read room numbers on the motel doors seventy yards distant, and the same strength on his Redfield scope would make human figures seem only thirty feet away. The scope was mounted on a .30-06 Remington Gamemaster, which was engineered so that its 150-grain slug would lose less than .01 inch in altitude and reach the motel balcony with 2,370 pounds of knockdown power—enough to drop a rhinoceros. However, the odd angle of an occluding building next door meant the convict could fire the long rifle only by leaning out his window. To avoid that, he must wait until he sighted his target from the room, then run with the rifle down the hallway to the common bathroom, find it unoccupied, and hope King stayed long enough on the balcony to get a clear shot from a rear window above the bathtub.

About five o'clock, when Andrew Young returned from court to find a general bull session in Georgia Davis's Room 201, King greeted him with playful fury by wrestling him to the floor between the two beds. Abernathy, Hosea Williams, Bernard Lee, and A.D. King joined in a wild tickling punishment of Young for failure to keep "our Leader" informed all day, which turned into a free-for-all pillow fight, with King sometimes squaring off against A.D. as in childhood. Once the hysteria subsided, Young said he thought the hearing went pretty well. Chauncey Eskridge walked in from a lawyers' conference with Judge Brown just as the motel television shifted from local news centered on last night's tornadoes ("death and destruction . . . over the mid-South last night") to the network broadcast. King joked that his esteemed lawyer was more reliable even than Walter Cronkite, and Eskridge said Judge Brown would permit SCLC to lead Monday's march under the restrictions King and Lawson desired: a prescribed route, no weapons, and narrow ranks to give the marshals wide space on the flanks to keep the spectators away. This relief started a fresh buzz of determination for weekend preparations. Young claimed vindication. King watched only part of the national news, which featured a rare, standing ovation in New York's St. Patrick's Cathedral when President Johnson entered for the installation of Terence Cardinal Cooke as archbishop. They should all get ready for dinner, King said, and Officer Richmond noted through binoculars at 5:40 his brisk walk with Abernathy upstairs to their Room 306.

While dressing, Abernathy disclosed sheepishly to King that he could not join him in Washington for the preliminary lobbying in the Poor People's Campaign, because the new start date of April 29 conflicted with his long-scheduled spring revival in Atlanta. King said this would never do. West Hunter Street Baptist was a magnificent congregation, he purred, claiming that he would have gone there himself if Daddy King had not invited him to Ebenezer, and surely the deacons would understand that Abernathy had to revive the soul of a whole nation instead. Abernathy weakened, but did not give in until King promised to help secure a substitute revival leader of stature. He placed a call to a New Orleans revivalist. In the esoteric bargaining, King and Abernathy used the little-known childhood first names they reserved for each other in private—Michael and David, respectively—and they ignored the commotion outside. Upstairs, Hosea Williams loudly evicted the last of the Invaders from two rooms provided during negotiations, after discovering to his outrage that fifteen of them had crammed inside to live on meals charged to the SCLC account. Downstairs, Jesse Jackson rehearsed an Operation Breadbasket ensemble, and bystanders crowded into the room to belt out extra hymns such as "Yield Not to Temptation" and "I'm So Glad Trouble Don't Last Always."

Rev. Billy Kyles left Jackson's songfest and knocked at Room 306 to hurry King along. Abernathy played him for a sign of deliverance. "Why don't you do my revival?" he asked Kyles, who adroitly dodged, saying he thought he was scheduled to preach in Columbus, Ohio. King chimed in to needle Kyles about the relative status of his invitations. "Anybody'd rather come to Atlanta than go to Columbus," he said. He shifted tone to inquire how Memphis churches achieved such unity behind the sanitation workers, who were not members of the prestige congregations, but Abernathy reopened preachers' banter on the subject of food. "All right now Billy, I don't want you fooling me," he said, warning that if he went all the way to the Kyleses' home for T-bone steaks or filet mignons, which he pronounced "FEEL-ay MEEN-yuns," then, "you're gonna flunk." King shuddered at the memory of a preacher in Atlanta whose house was so big that he could afford to serve only cold ham bone, cold potatoes, cold bread, and Kool-Aid. Abernathy said the Kool-Aid wasn't even sweet.

"Now Billy," said King, "if you've bought this big new house and can't afford to feed us, I'm gonna tell everybody in the country."

Kyles rejoined that there would be more soul food than King's waistline needed.

"Your wife can't cook, anyway," King teased. "She's too good-looking." He fell into a chauvinist bromide about the value of plain wives, and Abernathy took up the flip side with remarks on the beauty of Gwen Kyles. He retreated to the bathroom with a flirtatious grin that he must splash on Aramis cologne just for her.

King walked ahead of Kyles to look over the handrail outside, down on a bustling scene in the parking lot. Police undercover agent Marrell McCullough parked almost directly below, returning with James Orange and James Bevel from a shopping trip to buy overalls. Orange unfolded his massive frame from McCullough's little blue Volkswagen, tussling with Bevel, and Andrew Young stepped up to rescue Bevel by shadow-boxing at a distance. King called down benignly from the floor above for Orange to be careful with preachers half his size. McCullough and Orange walked back to talk with two female college students who pulled in just behind them. Jesse Jackson emerged from the rehearsal room, which reminded King to extend his rapprochement. "Jesse, I want you to come to dinner with me," he said.

Kyles, overhearing on his way down the balcony stairs, told King not to worry because Jackson already had secured his own invitation. Abernathy shouted from Room 306 for King to make sure Jackson did not try to bring his whole Breadbasket band, while Chauncey Eskridge was telling Jackson he should upgrade from turtleneck to necktie for dinner. Jackson called up to King: "Doc, you remember Ben Branch?" He said Breadbasket's lead saxophonist and song leader was a native of Memphis.

"Oh yes, he's my man," said King. "How are you, Ben?" Branch waved. King recalled his signature number from Chicago. "Ben, make sure you play 'Precious Lord, Take My Hand,' in the meeting tonight," he called down. "Play it real pretty."

"Okay, Doc, I will."

Solomon Jones, the volunteer chauffeur, called up to bring coats for a chilly night. There was no reply. Time on the balcony had turned lethal, which left hanging the last words fixed on a gospel song of refuge. King stood still for once, and his sojourn on earth went blank.

POLICE undercover agent Marrell Mc-
Cullough first reached the victim and grabbed a cleaning-cart towel to
stanch blood loss from a massive wound opened downward through the
jaw. The knot from King's necktie was blown off the balcony. Frantic
telephone calls for help went nowhere because Lorene Bailey kept slap-
ping her head oddly to mutter nonsense instead of working the motel
switchboard, saying, "Somebody done hit that old white truck." She
went to the hospital, too, with a fatal cerebral hemorrhage. Someone
whisked A. D. King from the trauma of sirens to the Kyles home, where
the evening's banquet was spread untouched. "They got my brother," he
said vacantly. Gwen Kyles said Negroes were "born to truth," compelled to face hard realities in a white world, and she supported a remarkable civic commitment across racial lines to gather every scrap of
memory or fact that might shed light on the world-shaking local
tragedy.

Volunteers from the Memphis Search for Meaning Committee managed to secure even the unused news footage normally discarded by
local television stations. In a segment filmed outside the emergency
room at St. Joseph's, one young reporter failed to elicit any response
from a catatonic Ralph Abernathy about the crime scene or how King
had been pronounced dead, but a throwaway question on personal history brought forth a reverie about the cold January morning in 1954
when a friend-to-be turned up at the Montgomery parsonage in the
company of a pulpit legend, and Abernathy launched into yarns about
the irascible genius Vernon Johns, oblivious to the reporter's desperate
pleas for comment on bulletins of looting in Washington and fires in
Chicago. Riots erupted in 110 American cities. A remorseful Congress
passed the nondiscrimination bill for housing transactions one day after
what amounted to a state funeral in Atlanta, with the casket wagon
drawn by mules. On orders from President Johnson, federal mediators

settled the Memphis strike with a 10 cents-per-hour raise and Mayor Loeb's face-saving claim of helplessness to stop a sanitation union imposed by the City Council. The probate court in Atlanta established that King died intestate, leaving no will and a net worth less than $6,000—his estate's largest asset being a disputed bequest of $12,351.36 from the eccentric poet and essayist Dorothy Parker.

In 1970, Alabama voters elected to countywide office three founding members of the Lowndes County Freedom Organization, which by then had merged into affiliation with the statewide Democratic Party. The new sheriff, John Hulett, served continuously for twenty-two years and then won three terms as county probate judge before retiring in 2001. Lowndes County remained conspicuously poor, owing in part to the scarcity of larger vision, but the climate of racial terror and subjugation long since had dissipated from the courthouse in Hayneville.

On December 12, 1972, a ripple of surprise passed through surviving luminaries of the civil rights era—including Roy Wilkins, Clarence Mitchell, Whitney Young, and Justice Thurgood Marshall—when ex-President Lyndon Johnson slowly entered the dedication ceremony for the LBJ Library. He rose to commend a speech by State Representative Julian Bond of Georgia—"whom I don't know so well but admire a great deal"—in remarks about why the presidential papers on equal rights held the "most intimate meanings" for him on the nature of government. Johnson warned of complacency that could visit storms upon future generations. Afterward, short of breath and gobbling blood pressure pills, he sought out an awed Bond to offer private encouragement with a heartfelt note of thanks for his independent convictions on freedom, overlooking Bond's signal dissent against a Vietnam War that still raged more than four years after it broke Johnson's presidency. Six days later, President Nixon ordered 36,000 tons of ordnance dropped on Hanoi and Haiphong. Although the "Christmas bombing" killed some 2,196 North Vietnamese civilians at a cost of ninety-three more U.S. airmen lost from twenty-six aircraft, its true purpose was to force South Vietnamese allies to pretend that American withdrawal was a victory. Johnson died a month later, just before the Vietnam settlement signed on January 27, 1973.

In July of 1974, lawyer Pauli Murray knelt trembling in Philadelphia, Pennsylvania's, Church of the Advocate to receive a blessing from the newly priested Jeannette Piccard, a seventy-nine-year-old chemist and pioneer of high-altitude balloon flight. Male priests shouted in the background that female clergy were a grave sin against the peace of Christ. "God here and now as father and judge sees you trying to make stones into bread," cried one, and the Episcopal House of Bishops quickly pronounced the ordination of Piccard's maverick group "invalid" by emergency decree. Murray herself persevered with her seminary education through the upheaval over the sanctity of male-only clergy, and on January 8, 1977, at the age of sixty-six, she became the only black pioneer among the first female priests ordained by official sanction of the Episcopal Church, at a ceremony in the Washington Cathedral. It was a decade since her Lowndes County lawsuit with Charles Morgan had opened jury service to women in many states.

The church struggles of the 1970s coincided with special investigations of corrupt government secrets in the Cold War era—political manipulations, assassination plots, spy games, and petty tyranny from high officials. News of the FBI wiretaps, which had emerged from the Muhammad Ali draft trial in 1969, led to muffled allegations about King's extramarital affairs. A comprehensive review of the murder investigation showed FBI agents capable of disciplined public duty alongside a numbing array of extra-constitutional bugs, vendettas, and crimes. Within days, they had traced the mark in a T-shirt abandoned with the assassination rifle to the Home Service Laundry in Los Angeles, while following a service sticker from the suspected getaway car in Atlanta to a Los Angeles address listed in the same phony name as the bundle of clothes. Neighbors remembered a loner who attended bartender school. The Birmingham clerk who sold the murder weapon identified his customer among bartenders in a graduation photograph, and fingerprints from the weapon led to a matching photograph of the escaped convict James Earl Ray, who evaded capture through two months of clumsy stickups and street-savvy acquisition of false identities. Meanwhile, the political side of the FBI brazenly suggested to President Johnson that Stokely Carmichael or Rap Brown ordered King killed, and high FBI officials planted a malicious story that the family of King's Los Angeles mistress had arranged the murder—going so far as to arrange a confrontation with the couple by columnist Jack Anderson.

Shortly after the assassination, a grief-stricken Stanley Levison complained that most Americans already distorted the loss of "their plaster saint who was going to protect them from angry Negroes." Pride and fear subverted King's legacy from all sides. James Bevel, ignoring the frailty of life, promptly declared James Earl Ray a mere pawn, because "there is no way a ten-cent white boy could develop a plan to kill a million-dollar black man." In 1978, Bevel stood witness at an eerie wedding ceremony conducted in prison by James Lawson, helping inmate Ray begin his short-lived marriage to a courtroom artist. More than forgiveness, the motive of Bevel and Lawson was to assert that some evil greater than Ray must account for all the pain, and some casualties from the movement gave way to the undertow of many conspiracies. Dennis Sweeney, who suffered greatly in Mississippi demonstrations, was committed to an asylum for the unhinged murder of his mentor Allard Lowenstein in 1980. Rap Brown, as the sectarian Muslim leader Jamil Al-Amin, was sentenced to life for the baffling murder of a sheriff's deputy. Dexter King publicly proclaimed James Earl Ray innocent of his father's murder in 1997—"in a strange sort of way, we're both victims"—citing fantastic theories grounded in dogma that the federal government was guilty instead.

Critics of the movement made political history from a mirror distrust. In 1983, President Ronald Reagan announced his belief that secret FBI files one day would establish whether King was a loyal American or a Communist sympathizer. "But since they seem bent on making it [King's birthday] a national holiday," he added, "I believe the symbolism of that day is important enough that I will sign that legislation when it reaches my desk." Reagan's sunny disposition tempered his political platform that government was bad—proven despotic, incompetent, and wasteful—at least when aimed toward the purposes of the civil rights era. This became the dominant idea in American politics, as a cyclical adjustment in history shifted the emphasis of patriotic language from citizenship to command, shrinking the public space.

A paradox remains. Statecraft is still preoccupied with the levers of spies and force, even though two centuries of increasingly lethal "total warfare" since Napoleon suggest a diminishing power of violence to sustain governance in the modern world. Military leaders themselves often stress the political limits of warfare, but politics is slow to recognize the glaring impact of nonviolent power. In 1987, students spilling into the streets of South Korea compelled a dictator to respect a permanent structure for elections. In 1989, the Soviet empire suddenly dissolved in a velvet revolution of dockworkers' strikes and choruses of "We Shall Overcome" at the dismantled Berlin Wall. There was no warning from experts, nor any hint of the nuclear cataclysm long prepared for and dreaded. That same year, Chinese students inspired the world from Tiananmen Square with nonviolent demonstrations modeled on the sit-ins, planting seeds of democracy in the authoritarian shell of Communist control. In 1990, Nelson Mandela emerged from twenty-seven years in prison to a Cape Town balcony, where he destroyed the iron rule of apartheid not with Armageddon's revenge but a plea for hopeful consent: "Universal suffrage on a common voters' roll in a united, democratic, and non-racial South Africa is the only way to peace and racial harmony."

Like America's original Founders, those who marched for civil rights reduced power to human scale. They invested enormous hope in the capacity of ordinary people to create bonds of citizenship based on simple ideals—"We the people"—and in a sturdy design to balance self-government with public trust. They projected freedom as America's only story in a harsh world. "The arc of the moral universe is long," King often said, quoting the abolitionist Theodore Parker, "but it bends toward justice." His oratory mined twin doctrines of equal souls and equal votes in the common ground of nonviolence, and justice refined history until its fires dimmed for a time.

King himself upheld nonviolence until he was nearly alone among colleagues weary of sacrifice. To the end, he resisted incitements to violence, cynicism, and tribal retreat. He grasped freedom seen and unseen, rooted in ecumenical faith, sustaining patriotism to brighten the heritage of his country for all people. These treasures abide with lasting promise from America in the King years.

ACKNOWLEDGMENTS

IN August of 1983, completing the first year's run of archival work on a book project contractually designed for three years, I stayed a week at the Lorraine Motel in Memphis. The assassination site, which is now the widely acclaimed National Civil Rights Museum, was then more or less a flophouse. Guests were obliged to knock at the office to be let in each time they returned, as the room keys had been stolen. One moment from that research trip struck me with particular force: a television news outtake of one young white reporter struggling to coax any word from Ralph Abernathy on the night of the murder, then giving up, unexpectedly jumpstarting him with a question about the past, and finally struggling just as hard to interrupt nonstop reveries about an unknown man. Something about the memory of Vernon Johns revived Abernathy from mortal shock into mirth and wonder.

Homework on Johns, King's predecessor at his first pulpit, did far more than enliven my own interviews with Abernathy, which had been wooden at best. Almost any mention of Johns started an engine of candor in many preachers of their generation, and the lively character who emerged suggested a way out of my first paralysis: how to begin without an essay on Southern black churches, which would violate a cardinal rule that storytelling narrative offers the most durable path for historical work across racial barriers. Vernon Johns seemed human and authentic enough to bring alive the culture of American black churches in the age of segregation.

Alice Mayhew is one of the few editors who would support a first chapter for *Parting the Waters* that set aside historical interest in King to introduce a predecessor drawn from folk sources. Her confidence has sustained this trilogy for two extra decades. We share devotion to the material, and I will always treasure her friendship. Many of her colleagues at Simon & Schuster have carried heavy loads gracefully again through the production for this volume, especially our skillful coordinator, Roger Labrie, along with Karolina Harris, Irene Kheradi, Ted Landry, Victoria Meyer, Allison Murray, Jackie Seow, Gypsy da Silva, and John Wahler. Carolyn Reidy and David Rosenthal kept faith from the top. Elisa Rivlin provided able counsel. Copy editor Fred Chase patiently cleaned the words, and Kevin Kwan tracked down the illustrations. Elizabeth Hayes fostered promotion, Sonny Luo solved technical problems, and I wish to thank the many publishing professionals who tended this book beyond my sight.

By gathering the television outtakes with a host of oral histories and artifacts from 1968, eighty citizens from an ad hoc Memphis Search for Meaning Committee created the most unique of many special archives indispensable to research in the civil rights era. Eleanor McKay, John Terreo, David and Carol Yellin, and author Joan Turner Beifuss guided me through the resulting Mississippi Valley Collection at Memphis State University. To study the Jonathan Daniels Collection at the library of Episcopal Divinity School in Cambridge, I relied on Barbara Bishop, Esther Griswold, and David Siegenthaler. Wendy Chmielewski steered me through the vast holdings of the Swarthmore College Peace Collection at the McCabe Library in Swarthmore, Pennsylvania.

This work rests on documentary sources from many institutions acknowledged in the two previous volumes, but several of new or continuing value merit special notice. Coretta Scott King kindly encouraged me to continue work in the central repository of primary documents at the King Library and Archives in Atlanta, where archivist Cynthia P. Lewis offered knowledgeable help. Among the employees of libraries and archives cited here, I am especially indebted to the following: Claudia Anderson, Barbara Constable, Regina Greenwell, Tina Houston, Harry Middleton, Rebekah Ross, E. Philip Scott, and Linda Sulkey of the Lyndon B. Johnson Library in Austin, Texas; David Coleman, Taylor Fain, Kent Germany, Max Holland, Ken Hughes, Frederik Lovevall, Timothy Naftali, Jon Rosenberg, Lorraine Settimo, David Shreve, and Philip Zelikow of the Presidential Recordings Project at the University of Virginia's Miller Center of Public Affairs, where I have benefited greatly from an advisory role in the transcription and interpretation of the newly released Lyndon Johnson tape recordings; Debbie Beatty, David M. Hardy, John Kelso, Linda Kloss, Helen Ann Near, and Tamara Lingham of the FBI's Records Management Division; Linda Evans, Archie Motley, Ralph Pugh, and Corey Seeman of the Chicago Historical Society; Judy Edelhoff, Katherine King, Mary Roonan, and Steve Tilly of the National Archives; James H. Hutson of the Manuscripts Division of the Library of Congress; Mark J. Duffy and Jennifer Peters of the Archives of the Episcopal Church in Austin, Texas; Melissa Bush and George King of the Richard B. Russell Library at the University of Georgia in Athens; Kristin Gleeson, Sarah Vilan Kuhn, Peggy Lou Shriver, and Margaret Sly of the Presbyterian Historical Society in Philadelphia, Pennsylvania; Ann L. Koch and Deborah Slinghuff of the Sheridan Libraries at the Johns Hopkins University in Baltimore; and Carla Hayden of the Enoch Pratt Free Library in Baltimore.

For the FRUS series of official government documents essential to passages on the Vietnam War, I am grateful to editorial teams led by Glenn W. LaFantasie, David C. Humphrey, Edward C. Keefer, Ronald D. Landa, David S. Patterson, Kent Sieg, and Louis J. Smith. For reciprocal study in Vietnam, I am grateful above all for the courtesy of Lady Borton, along with Christian G. Appy, Murray Hiebert, and Nguyen Qui Duc, who suggested or arranged the following contacts for an all-too-brief research visit in Hanoi: Nguyen Thi Ngoc Toan, David Elder, Vo Dien Bien, Col. Chuck Searcy, Dinh Xuan Lam, Ngo van Hoa, David Thomas, David Lamb, Sandy Northrop, Duong Hanh, Nguyen Hoang van Khoan, Hoang Cong Thuy, and Dang Hoang Tinh, director of the Ho Chi Minh Museum.

This work relies heavily on oral history to retrieve firsthand memories. Those who provided interviews are listed throughout the notes in numbers far too great to repeat here, but I want to emphasize my gratitude to them. In this volume, for their generous help in locating witnesses in Lowndes County, Alabama, I am indebted to Catherine Coleman Flowers, Hasan Kwame Jeffries, and the late Timothy Mays.

At my alma mater, the University of North Carolina at Chapel Hill, Jacquelyn Hall offered cooperation and advice in the general discipline of oral history, along with her associates Johanna Clark-Sayer, Melynn Glusman, and Beth Millwood. Timothy D. Pyatt, Rachel Canada, Richard A. Shrader, and Anne Skilton provided archival advice along with primary information from the Southern Historical Collection. Its curator, Timothy West, has agreed to catalogue and preserve all my cumulative source material, including recorded interviews, for the use of future researchers.

For advice and help beyond contributions cited in the notes, the following people more than deserve public thanks: Roland M. Baumann, Bill Baxter, Agieb Bilal, Philathia Bolton, Franklin Branch, Rosann Catalano, Robin Coblentz, Andrew Foster Connors, Connie Curry, Richard Deats, Jack D. Ellis, Ray English, Dorothy and Nicole Fall, Jo

Freeman, Roger and Frances Gench, Lex Gillespie, Lawrence and Monica Guyot, Seymour Hersh, Tom Houck, Martha Hunt Huie, Maurice Hundley, Robert H. Janover, Teresa Johanson, Loch Johnson, Janice Kaguyutan, Laurel Kamen, Randy Kryn, Christopher Leighton, Willy Leventhal, Mary Lilliboe, Jerry Mitchell, Charles F. Newman, Gustav Niebuhr, Jan Nunley, Peggy Obrecht, David Person, Frank Madison Reid, Judy Richardson, Guido van Rijn, John Roberts, Betty Garman Robinson, Howard Romaine, John Rothchild, Lisa Rzepka, Yusuf Salaam, Rose and Hank Sanders, Nuvolina Sherlock, Maria Varela, Levi Watkins, Penny and Kendall Weaver, Susan Weld, George B. Wiley, Curtis Wilkie, Mary Jane Wilkinson, Lawrence Wofford, and Edwin M. Yoder; plus Paola di Floria, Alice Rubin, and Jay Leavy of CounterPoint Films; Mary Ellen Gale, Michael Lottman, Jim Peppler, and Robert Ellis Smith, formerly of the *Southern Courier;* Bruce Hartford and colleagues at the Veterans of the Civil Rights Movement website; and Sara Rostolder Mandell and Jane Ramsey of the Jewish Council on Urban Affairs in Chicago.

Harry Belafonte, who once stalled me for years as a most reticent interview subject, has become a stalwart partner and friend in ongoing efforts to translate the civil rights era into film. Associates on this path of heartbreak and hope have included Jon Avnet, Jonathan Demme, Jed Dietz, Tom Fontana, Susan Lyne, Paul Nagle, Anna Hamilton Phelan, Arnold Rifkin, Carol Schreder, Helen Verno, Paula Weinstein, and Winifred White-Neisser.

Martha Healy diligently carried out the primary transcription for the Johnson telephone recordings. Dan Hartman of Discount Computer Service kept the machines running, and Jennifer Helfrich of Iseeman, Inc. showed me how to navigate data programs.

More personally, I want to thank Julian Bond, Pam Horowitz, and Kent Germany for insightful critiques of the early manuscript. They may try to blame me for errors they should have caught, but discerning readers now know better. Examples from the movement always refilled the well of inspiration. My literary agent, Liz Darhansoff, helped keep our family solvent and cheerful through many contract extensions. Through the hardships and joys of her own career, Christy has built our partnership of the heart. Our daughter, Macy, has grown to zestful independence. Our son, Franklin, who was born weeks before my first trip to the Lorraine Motel, finished college in time to help me with final research. I give thanks to my mother, the dear memory of my father, and many loved ones for sustaining me in the blessing of a life's work.

NOTES

ABBREVIATIONS USED

AAP	Private Papers of Archie E. Allen, Santa Barbara, California
AC	*Atlanta Constitution*
ADAH	Alabama Department of Archives and History, Montgomery, Alabama
ADW	*Atlanta Daily World*
AEC	Archives of the Episcopal Church, Austin, Texas
AFF	Ford Foundation Archives, New York
AJ	*Atlanta Journal*
AJA	American Jewish Archives, Cincinnati, Ohio
AJC	Archives of the American Jewish Committee, New York
AMC	Arnold Michaelis Collection, Hargett Library, University of Georgia
ANP	Associated Negro Press, Claude A. Barnett Papers, Chicago Historical Society
APR	Papers of A. Philip Randolph, Library of Congress
A/AR	Anne Romaine Oral History Collection, King Library and Archives, the Martin Luther King, Jr., Center for Nonviolent Social Change, Inc., Atlanta, Georgia
A/AT	Papers of Arthur Thomas, King Library and Archives
A/CS	Papers of Charles Sherrod, King Library and Archives
A/JF	Papers of James Forman, King Library and Archives
A/KP	Papers of Dr. Martin Luther King, Jr., King Library and Archives
A/KS	Speeches of Dr. Martin Luther King, Jr., King Library and Archives
A/MFDP	Papers of the Mississippi Freedom Democratic Party, King Library and Archives
A/OH	Oral History Collection, King Library and Archives
A/RM	Papers of Robert Mants, King Library and Archives
A/SC	Southern Christian Leadership Conference Records, King Library and Archives
A/SN	Papers of the Student Nonviolent Coordinating Committee, King Library and Archives
BAA	*Baltimore Afro-American*
BIR	Archives Division, Birmingham Public Library, Birmingham, Alabama
BIR/AB	Papers of Albert E. Boutwell, Birmingham Public Library
BIR/BC	Papers of Eugene T. "Bull" Connor, Birmingham Public Library
BIR/C	Papers of Bishop C. C. J. Carpenter, Birmingham Public Library
BIR/FW	Papers of Francis X. Walter, Birmingham Public Library

BN	*Birmingham News*
BUK	Papers of Martin Luther King, Jr., Special Collections Department, Mugar Library, Boston University
BW	*Birmingham World*
CALCAV	Clergy and Laity Concerned About Vietnam
CD	Chicago *Defender*
CDD	Chicago *Daily Defender*
CHS	Archives and Manuscripts Division, Chicago Historical Society
CORE	Papers of the Congress of Racial Equality, Library of Congress
CU/OH	Oral History Collection, Columbia University Library
DDE	Dwight D. Eisenhower Library, Abilene, Kansas
EU	Robert W. Woodruff Library, Emory University
FAC	FBI File No. 77-59135 (Archibald James Carey, Jr.)
FACP	FBI File No. 100-51230 (Adam Clayton Powell, Jr.)
FAL	FBI File No. 105-10368 (Allard K. Lowenstein)
FAR	FBI File No. 62-110365 (Albert Anderson Raby)
FBNH	FBI File No. 100-448006 (COINTELPRO, Black Nationalist/Hate Groups)
FBPA	FBI File No. 157-4825 (Black Panther Party, Alabama)
FCLCV	FBI File No. 105-170160 (Clergy and Laity Concerned About Vietnam)
FCNL	FBI File No. 100-449698 (COINTELPRO, New Left)
FCT	FBI File No. 67-9524 (Clyde Tolson Office Files)
FDCA	FBI File No. 44-12831 (Election Laws, Dallas County, Alabama)
FEM	FBI File No. 105-24822 (Elijah Muhammad)
FGTR	Gary Thomas Rowe, Jr. Headquarters Informant File, FBI
FHHH	FBI File No. 62-77485 (Hubert H. Humphrey)
FHOC	FBI J. Edgar Hoover Official and Confidential File
FJ	FBI File No. 100-407018 (Clarence Jones)
FJMD	FBI File No. 44-30271 (Jonathan Myrick Daniels)
FJNY	FBI File No. 100-73250 (Clarence Jones, New York Office)
FK	FBI File No. 100-106670 (Martin Luther King, Jr.)
FL	FBI File No. 100-392452 (Stanley Levison)
FLNY	FBI File No. 100-111180 (Stanley Levison, New York Office)
FLP	FBI File No. 44-25873 (PENVIC, Lemuel Penn Murder Case)
FMB	FBI File No. 44-25706 (MIBURN, Chaney-Goodman-Schwerner Murder Case)
FMX	FBI File No. 100-399321 (Malcolm X)
FMXNY	FBI File No. 105-8999 (Malcolm X, New York Office)
FNR	FBI File No. 62-78270 (Nelson Rockefeller)
FR	FBI File No. 100-158790 (Bayard Rustin)
FRFK	FBI File No. 77-51387 (Robert F. Kennedy)
FRUS	U.S. Department of State, *Foreign Relations of the United States,* U.S. Government Printing Office
FRW	FBI File No. 62-78270 (Roy Wilkins)
FSC	FBI File No. 100-438794 (Southern Christian Leadership Conference)
FSMM	FBI File No. 44-28544 (Selma to Montgomery March)
FSN	FBI File No. 100-439190 (Student Nonviolent Coordinating Committee)
FVL	FBI File No. 44-28601 (Viola Liuzzo Murder Case)
HOH	Oral History Collection, Harry Lasker Library, Highlander Research and Education Center, New Market, Tennessee

JDC	Jonathan Daniels Collection, Episcopal Divinity School, Cambridge, Massachusetts
JFK	John F. Kennedy Library, Boston, Massachusetts
JMP	Private Papers of Jack Minnis, New Orleans, Louisiana
LBJ	Lyndon Baines Johnson Library, Austin, Texas
LAHD	*Los Angeles Herald-Dispatch*
LAHE	*Los Angeles Herald-Examiner*
LAT	*Los Angeles Times*
LHM	Letterhead Memorandum (FBI term designating reports for external distribution)
LOC	Library of Congress
MA	*Montgomery Advertiser*
MCA	Memphis *Commercial Appeal*
MDAH	Mississippi Department of Archives and History, Jackson, Mississippi
MS	*Muhammad Speaks*
MOB	Museum of Broadcasting, New York
MSSC	Records of the Mississippi State Sovereignty Commission, University of Southern Mississippi, Hattiesburg
MVC	Mississippi Valley Collection, Memphis State University
NA	National Archives, Washington, DC
NAACP	Papers of the National Association for the Advancement of Colored People, Library of Congress
NCC	National Council of Churches, New York
NCCIJ	Papers of the National Catholic Conference for Interracial Justice, Marquette University Archives, Milwaukee, Wisconsin
NR	Not Recorded (for unrecorded serials in FBI files)
NT	*Nashville Tennessean*
NYAN	*New York Amsterdam News*
NYT	*New York Times*
OFMS	Office Files of Mildred Stegall, LBJ Library, Austin, Texas
OH	Oral History
PC	*Pittsburgh Courier*
PDD	President's Daily Diary, LBJ Library, Austin, Texas
PEA	Film Collection, Peabody Awards Committee, University of Georgia
POH	Presbyterian Office of History, Philadelphia, Pennsylvania
PPP	Public Papers of the Presidents
RJB	Ralph Johnson Bunche Oral History Collection (formerly Civil Rights Documentation Project), Moorland-Spingarn Research Center, Howard University
RN	Papers of Reinhold Niebuhr, Library of Congress
RR	Papers of Richard Russell, Richard B. Russell Memorial Library, University of Georgia
RS	Files of the Chicago Police Department "Red Squad," Chicago, Illinois
RSP	Ralph Smeltzer Papers, Lamont Library, Harvard University
SAC	Special Agent in Charge (FBI term for the head of an FBI office)
SC	*Southern Courier*
SCPC	Swarthmore College Peace Collection, McCabe Library, Swarthmore, Pennsylvania
SCRBC	Schomburg Center for Research in Black Culture, New York
SHSW	State Historical Society of Wisconsin, Madison, Wisconsin

SKP	Martin Luther King, Jr., Papers Project, Stanford University
STJ	*Selma Times-Journal*
TOU	Lillian Pierce Benbow Special Collections, Tougaloo University, Tougaloo, Mississippi
UAB	University of Alabama in Birmingham, Oral History Research Office
UF	University of Florida
UGA	University of Georgia
UNC	Southern Historical Collection, William Round Wilson Library, University of North Carolina at Chapel Hill
WP	*Washington Post*
WS	*Washington Star*

INTRODUCTION

PAGE

xi   "every votary of freedom": Federalist No. 39, in Rossiter, ed., *Federalist,* p. 240.

xii   "virtue in the people": Wood, *Radicalism,* pp. 234–35; Ketcham, *Madison,* p. 262.

xii   "Sir, I know just how": Branch, *Pillar,* p. 509.

xii   "rise up and live out": Washington, ed., *Testament,* p. 219.

xii   "as old as the Scriptures": Branch, *Parting,* pp. 823–24.

xii   "I believe that unarmed truth": Branch, *Pillar,* p. 541.

xii   "But what is government": Federalist No. 51, in Rossiter, ed., *Federalist,* p. 322.

1: WARNING

PAGE

5   Haynes spread word: Int. Lorenzo Harrison, Sept. 8, 2000.

5   hens would not lay eggs properly: Int. Mary Lee King, June 28, 2000.

5   plainspoken Hulda Coleman: Eagles, *Outside Agitator,* pp. 185–89.

5   Haynes had confided to Coleman: Int. Uralee Haynes, Sept. 8, 2000; Couto, *Ain't Gonna,* pp. 89–90.

6   last attempt to register: Eagles, *Outside Agitator,* pp. 120–21.

6   Mt. Carmel Baptist on February 28, 1965: Int. Lorenzo Harrison, Sept. 8, 2000; int. Uralee Haynes, Sept. 8, 2000; int. John Hulett, Sept. 8, 2000.

6   shotguns and rifles: SAC, Mobile, to Director, March 1, 1965, FDCA-442.

6   said he had been braced: Int. Lorenzo Harrison, Sept. 8, 2000.

6   recognized among the Klansmen: Int. Bernice Johnson, Feb. 16, 2001.

6   dumped the body of Bud Rudolph: Int. Uralee Haynes, Sept. 8, 2000.

6   There was Tom Coleman: Int. Lorenzo Harrison, Sept. 8, 2000; int. Uralee Haynes, Sept. 8, 2000; int. John Hulett, Sept. 8, 2000; Eagles, *Outside Agitator,* pp. 187–91.

7   Sheriff Jesse Coleman: Eagles, *Outside Agitator,* pp. 100–101, 186.

7   barely a fifth of the county's households had telephone service: Ibid., p. 109.

7   the only armed pickup sighted: Int. John Hulett, Sept. 8, 2000.

7   fell to deacon John Hulett: Eagles, *Outside Agitator,* pp. 122–23; Couto, *Ain't Gonna,* pp. 84, 94–96.

7   slave ancestor was said to have founded Mt. Carmel Baptist: Int. John Hulett, Sept. 8, 2000. A plaque outside Mt. Carmel Baptist Church, Gordonville, Alabama, reads, "Founded 1819—Rev. J. Hullett."

7   led a close convoy: Ibid.

7   "If I have to leave, you take it": Int. Lorenzo Harrison, Sept. 8, 2000.

7   never again in the twentieth century: Ibid.

2: SCOUTS

PAGE

8   James Bevel was preaching: Fager, *Selma, 1965,* pp. 82–83.

8   twelfth chapter of Acts: Acts 12:2–3.

8   walked with them from this same church in a night vigil: Branch, *Pillar,* pp. 592–94.

8   "a nightmare of State Police stupidity and brutality": Garrow, *Protest,* p. 62.

8   "Negroes could be heard screaming": NYT, Feb. 20, 1965, p. 1.

9   "is falling kind of hard on me": Int. James Bevel, Nov. 23, 1997, Dec. 10, 1998; int. Bernard Lafayette, May 28, 1990.

9   "go unto the king": Esther 4:8.

9   "We must go to Montgomery and see the king!": Fager, *Selma, 1965,* p. 83; Branch, *Pillar,* p. 599.

9   Rev. Lorenzo Harrison burst through the doors: NYT, March 1, 1965, p. 17; SAC, Mobile, to Director, Feb. 28, 1965, FDCA-450.

9   "I said you ought not to be crying": *Jet,* March 11, 1965, p. 4.

9   Then Harrison himself broke down: Int. Lorenzo Harrison, Sept. 8, 2000.

10   open Tabernacle Baptist for the first church meeting: Branch, *Pillar,* pp. 81–84.

10   "inasmuch as Harris [sic] could furnish": SAC, Mobile, to Director, March 1, 1965, FDCA-442.

10   scouted into Lowndes County along Highway 80: Int. James Bevel, Sept. 6, 2000; "Great Day at Trickem Fork," *Saturday Evening Post,* May 22, 1965, p. 94.

10   "Dr. King asked us to come down here": Alvin Adams, "SCLC Organizing in Lowndes County, Alabama," JMP.

10   no church yet dared to open its doors: SAC, Mobile, to Director, Feb. 16, 1965, FDCA-345.

10   others warily had gauged: STJ, Feb. 26, 1965, p. 1.

10   "My few days here are a refreshing": LAHE, Feb. 26, 1965, p. B-1.

10   death threats from callers: Ibid. Also SAC, Los Angeles, to Director, Feb. 23, 1965, FK-914; SAC, Los Angeles, to Director, Feb. 24, 1965, FK-980; Los Angeles LHM dated Feb. 26, 1965, FK-NR.

11   News stories tracked a manhunt: LAT, Feb. 27, 1965; BAA, March 6, 1965, p. 1.

11   Reporters pressed King: Transcript of MLK press conference at L.A. Airport, Feb. 24, 1965, A/KS.

11   In his sermon at Victory Baptist: CDD, March 1, 1965, pp. 1, 10.

11   "the biggest hypocrite alive": Branch, *Pillar,* p. 598.

11   "pitifully wasted": NYT, Feb. 22, 1965, p. 20.

11   "I flunked on you, Sully": Int. Jean Jackson, May 27, 1990.

11   one of Coretta King's music teachers: Ibid.

12   Bevel himself claimed to hear voices: Int. James Bevel, Dec. 19, 1998.

12   denounced Bevel to King as unstable: Int. Hosea Williams, Oct. 29, 1991; int. Willie Bolden, May 14, 1992.

12   King refused his insistent demands: Branch, *Pillar,* pp. 76, 196–97.

12   King had indulged Bevel: Branch, *Parting,* pp. 753–54; int. Andrew Young, Oct. 26, 1991.

12   King was in Selma largely on a quixotic leap: Branch, *Pillar,* pp. 138–40, 165, 524.

12   discovered wandering Selma's streets: Ibid., pp. 598–99; Fager, *Selma, 1965,* p. 81.

12   Hotspur and Joan of Arc: Branch, *Parting,* pp. 424–25, 559; Branch, *Pillar,* pp. 54–57.

13   "How dare you, lie to me": Int. James Bevel, Nov. 23, 1997; int. Diane Nash, Dec. 8, 1998.

14   "rise up and live out the true meaning": Washington, ed., *Testament,* p. 219.

14   "how worthy I'm going to try to be": LBJ phone call with MLK, 9:20 P.M., Nov. 25, 1963 (the day of President Kennedy's funeral), Beschloss, *Taking,* p. 39.

14   Then Johnson had turned suddenly coy and insecure: Branch, *Pillar,* pp. 452–54.

14   "That will answer seventy percent of your problems": LBJ phone call with MLK, 12:06 P.M., Jan. 15, 1965, Cit. 6736-37, Audiotape WH6501.04, LBJ.

14   "That'll get you a message that all the eloquence": Ibid.

15   When a haggard King placed an ad: Branch, *Pillar,* pp. 580–84.

15   FBI agents overheard his call: Branigan to W. C. Sullivan, Feb. 28, 1965, FK-983.

15   "a return to Reconstruction": Horace Busby to Bill Moyers and Lee White, "The Voting Rights Message," Feb. 27, 1965, Legislative Background, Voting Rights Act of 1965, Box 1, LBJ.

15   Katzenbach himself strongly opposed: Int. Nicholas Katzenbach, June 14, 1991.

16   "leave control of voting machinery": Katzenbach to Moyers and White, March 1, 1965, Moyers Papers, Box 6, LBJ.

16   "The game now is in the fourth quarter": LBJ phone call with Robert McNamara, 9:10 A.M., Feb. 26, 1965, Cit. 6887, Audiotape WH6502.06, LBJ.

16   bleak reality that guerrilla armies were defeating: Cf. Bundy to LBJ, Feb. 7, 1965 (" . . . defeat appears inevitable . . . prospect in Vietnam is grim. . . .") in FRUS, Vol. 2, pp. 174–81; Logevall, *Choosing,* pp. 330–32; Branch, *Pillar,* pp. 306–10.

16   "forgive you for anything except being weak": LBJ phone call with Richard Russell, June 11, 1964, Cit. 3680-81, Audiotape WH6406.05, LBJ.

16   "this is a terrible thing": LBJ phone call with McGeorge Bundy, 11:24 A.M., May 27, 1964, Cit. 3522, Audiotape WH6405.10, LBJ.

16   "makes the chills run up my back": LBJ phone call with Richard Russell, 10:55 A.M., May 27, 1964, Cit. 3519a, Audiotape WH6405.10, LBJ.

17   approved secretly on February 13: Logevall, *Choosing,* pp. 343–44.

17   another military coup by South Vietnamese allies: NYT, Feb. 19, 1965, pp. 1, 10; Karnow, *Vietnam,* pp. 392–402.

17   six chronically unstable governments: Ibid. The nature of South Vietnamese politics made regimes difficult for Americans to count, and the *Times* put the number at nine. NYT, March 3, 1965, p. 10.

17   "Now we're off to bombing those people": LBJ phone call with Robert McNamara, 9:10 A.M., Feb. 26, 1965, Cit. 6887, Audiotape WH6502.06, LBJ.

17   President transfixed by a report: Robert Kleiman, "U.S. Said to Plan Limited Air War as Lever on Hanoi," NYT, March 1, 1965, p. 1. Datelined Saigon, the story reported that the "highest American and South Vietnamese officials" were "virtually certain" of Johnson's approval for a sustained air war that would be "neither announced nor officially admitted." The story quoted a high official that the goal of the new campaign was not to bomb North Vietnam into submission but to "do something we could stop doing to them, in return for equivalent concessions."

17   "Am I wrong in saying": LBJ phone call with Robert McNamara, 10:46 A.M., March 1, 1965, Cit. 7002-03, Audiotape WH6503.01, LBJ.

17   mountainous doubt and brutally frank pessimism: Ambassador Maxwell Taylor to the Department of State, 11:00 A.M., Jan. 6, 1965, FRUS, Vol. 2, pp. 12–19. On February 22, 1965, opposing General William Westmoreland's request that same day for Marine combat units in Vietnam, Ambassador Taylor cabled Washington as follows: "White-faced soldier, armed, equipped and trained as he is not suitable guerrilla fighter for Asian forests and jungles. French tried to adapt their forces to this mission and failed; I doubt that US forces could do much better." Gravel, ed., *Pentagon Papers,* pp. 418–19. See also McNamara, *In Retrospect,* pp. 146–74; Langguth, *Our Vietnam,* pp. 333–48.

17   "Somebody ought to be removed, Bob": LBJ phone call with Robert McNamara, 10:46 A.M., March 1, 1965, Cit. 7002-03, Audiotape WH6503.01, LBJ.

17   "We are going to bring": NYT, March 2, 1965, pp. 1, 10.

18   one surprise dispersal: Branch, *Pillar,* p. 586.

18   around the Lowndes County courthouse: Eagles, *Outside Agitator,* pp. 120–21; "Great Day at Trickem Fork," *Saturday Evening Post,* May 22, 1965, p. 94.

18   "Who is that little fella": Int. John Hulett, Sept. 8, 2000.

18   "refused to know their own selves": Int. Elzie McGill by Robert Wright, Aug. 4, 1968, RJBOH.

18   spoke with an odd accent: Int. Rocena Haralson, Feb. 16, 2001.

19   Emma and Matthew Jackson: Int. Matthew Jackson and int. Emma (Mrs. Matthew) Jackson by Robert Wright, Aug. 4, 1968, RJBOH.

19   "In the name of humanity": NYT, March 2, 1965, p. 1.

19   266 people managed to finish: Ibid.

19   Wilcox County seat of Camden: McCarty, *Reins,* p. 20.

20   "too small to be a republic": Applebome, *Dixie,* p. 103.

20   "2,250 whites registered": McCarty, *Reins,* p. 137.

20   no electric lights: Ibid., p. 97.

20   Ben Miller took a cow: Ibid., p. 104.

20   sixty-eight families of Negro sharecroppers: Callahan, *Quilting Bee,* pp. 35–36.

20   never had seen a water faucet: Ibid., p. 74.

20   "Well, how about you acting": McCarty, *Reins,* p. 144.

21   "Don't even carry a hair clamp": Callahan, *Quilting Bee,* p. 166.

21   fifty wet Alabama state troopers: Fager, *Selma, 1965,* p. 84.

21   two riflemen intended to shoot him: Branch, *Pillar,* pp. 591–97.

21   "This is a magnificent thing": NYT, March 2, 1965, p. 19.

21   named for Robert Y. Hayne: Eagles, *Outside Agitator,* p. 90.

21   William Lowndes Yancey: McCarty, *Reins,* pp. 34–35.

21   sell Marlboro cigarettes or Falstaff beer: Eagles, *Outside Agitator,* p. 113.

21   refused to give his name or title: NYT, March 2, 1965, pp. 1, 19.

22   "You are damned dumb": Fager, *Selma, 1965,* p. 84; Eagles, *Outside Agitator,* pp. 120–21.

22   Photographers snapped a picture: WP, March 2, 1965, p. 8.

22   fired from his regular job: Int. Lorenzo Harrison, Sept. 8, 2000; Rev. Maurice McCrackin pamphlet, "Operation Freedom Helps in Selma," April 1965, RSP1.

22   "revealed no incidents throughout": Teletype, Mobile office to Director, March 1, 1965, FDCA-453.

22   he hesitated for six minutes: Teletype, Mobile office to Director, March 1, 1965, FDCA-454.

3: DISSENT

PAGE

23   In full academic regalia: CDD, March 3, 1965, p. 1.

23   reprise on his Nobel Peace Prize lecture: Branch, *Pillar,* pp. 542–43.

23   "The war in Vietnam is accomplishing nothing": Garrow, *Bearing,* p. 394; "MLK on Vietnam/Washington, DC," misdated March 6, 1965, A/KS.

23   brought the number of Americans killed: NYT, March 7, 1965, p. 3.

23   no formal announcement of the new bombing policy: FRUS, Vol. 2, p. 390.

23   104 Air Force jets, six of which were lost: Ibid.; Logevall, *Choosing,* p. 363.

24   forty policemen who stood guard: Garrow, *Bearing,* p. 394.

24   seeking counsel about his dilemma: Hoover to Marvin Watson, March 9, 1965, FK-971.

24   Bad weather delayed: Teletype, Mobile office to Director, March 3, 1965, FDCA-460.

24   two thousand mourners filed past: Fager, *Selma, 1965,* p. 85.

24   the afternoon funeral procession: BAA, March 13, 1965, p. 13; Mendelsohn, *Martyrs,* pp. 148–49.

24   "a tear glistened": NYT, March 4, 1965, p. 23.

24   Recycling the text: Ibid. Also Branch, *Pillar,* p. 600; Fager, *Selma, 1965,* pp. 85–86.

25   "What time they be marchin'?": Webb and Nelson, *Selma, Lord, Selma,* p. 71.

25   rain rinsed its blue dye: Ibid., p. 81.

25   He set the starting date for Sunday, March 7: NYT, March 4, 1965, p. 23.

25   To give himself some wiggle room: STJ, March 4, 1965, p. 1.

25   At a crisis staff meeting: Int. Fay Bellamy, Oct. 29, 1991; int. Frank Soracco, Sept. 12–14, 1990; int. Silas Norman, June 28, 2000.

26   Bellamy had introduced herself to Malcolm X: Branch, *Pillar,* pp. 578–79.

26   an opposing war council: Lesher, *George Wallace,* p. 319; Carter, *Politics,* pp. 246–47.

26   "laughingstock of the nation": Jones, *Wallace Story,* pp. 355–56.

27   Stanley Levison rode an elevator: Hoover to Marvin Watson, March 9, 1965, FK-971.

27   "We cannot afford to lose him": SAC, New York, Teletype to Director, March 4, 1965, FK-963.

27   warning to President Johnson: Hoover to Marvin Watson, March 5, 1965, FK-931.

27   information that Levison had been a Communist: Garrow, *FBI and King,* pp. 42–46; Branch, *Parting,* pp. 516–17, 835–36.

27   preserved secretly as the official predicate: Ibid. Also Branch, *Pillar,* pp. 153–54.

27   "on a highly confidential basis": Baumgardner to Sullivan, March 2, 1965, FK-938.

27   insisted that the advisers "clear" Levison: Int. Harry Wachtel, Nov. 29, 1983.

28   "Escalation in the manner recently conducted": Stanley D. Levison to LBJ, "Dear Mr. President," Feb. 14, 1965, Name File, LBJ.

28   "to express my vigorous dissent": Clarence B. Jones to LBJ, March 4, 1965, Name File, LBJ.

28   upbringing in a chauffeur's household: Branch, *Parting,* pp. 317–18; Branch, *Pillar,* pp. 41–47.

28   Assuming that Wallace would stop Sunday's march: SAC, New York, Teletype to Director, March 6, 1965, FK-969; Abernathy, *Walls,* p. 326.

28   a side dispute that awkwardly followed: Garrow, *Bearing,* pp. 394–95; int. Harry Wachtel, Nov. 29, 1983.

29   He took Walter Fauntroy with him: Handwritten note that King was received in the Fish Room with Fauntroy, Bernard Lee, and Andrew Young on March 5, attached to briefing memo from Lee White to LBJ, March 4, 1965, EX HU2/ST 24, Box 26, LBJ.

29   past a line of uniformed American Nazis: Washington, D.C., LHM, March 8, 1965, "American Nazi Party/Racial Matters," FK-NR.

29   close to a common agenda: BAA, March 13, 1965, p. 1; notes on King meeting with LBJ, 6:17–7:35 P.M., PDD, March 5, 1965, LBJ.

29   "The President told me": NYT, March 6, 1965, p. 9.

29   Airline sources told FBI agents: SAC, Atlanta, to Director, March 5, 1965, FK-964.

29   basement of Frazier's soul food café: Minutes, SNCC executive committee meeting, 9:45 P.M., March 5, 1965, A/SN6; Carson, *Struggle*, p. 158; Lewis, *Walking*, p. 319.

29   rules of procedure: Ibid. Also three-page, eleven-point rules of procedure "Adopted by the Executive Committee March 5, 1965, Atlanta, Georgia," Reel 1, SNCC.

29   "Who the hell is Robert": Int. Martha Prescod Norman, June 29, 2000.

30   Disagreements festered: Carson, *Struggle*, pp. 123–52; Branch, *Pillar*, pp. 479–82, 506–9.

30   Nearly a hundred of the summer volunteers: Forman, *Making*, pp. 414–22; Sellers, *River*, p. 130.

30   addressed internal racial hostilities: Branch, *Pillar*, pp. 223–24, 295–96.

30   withdrawal announcement at the previous meeting: Ibid., pp. 588–90.

30   A ruling from the chair suspended: Minutes, SNCC executive committee meeting, 9:45 P.M., March 5, 1965, A/SN6.

30   Silas Norman had left Wisconsin: Int. Silas Norman, June 28, 2000.

31   the Selma project had opposed Bevel's plan: "A Short Summary of the Executive Committee Meeting, March 5 and 6, 1965 in Atlanta, Ga.," A/SN6.

31   to ask why SNCC should participate: Minutes, SNCC executive committee meeting, 9:45 P.M., March 5, 1965, A/SN6.

31   drafting a letter to Martin Luther King: Ibid. Also int. Silas Norman, June 28, 2000; int. Ivanhoe Donaldson, Nov. 30, 2000.

4: BOXED IN

32   "Good God, I'd rather hear": LBJ phone call with Richard Russell, 12:05 P.M., March 6, 1965, Cit. 7026-27, Audiotape WH6503.03, LBJ.

32   Russell had been breathing: Fite, *Richard Russell*, pp. 426–27.

33   morose stall on the Marine orders: Preparations to send the Marines were underway, but Johnson told National Security Adviser McGeorge Bundy that he had not made the decision, saying, "I'm still worried about it." LBJ phone call with McGeorge Bundy, 10:30 A.M., March 5, 1965, Cit. 7022, Audiotape WH6503.02, LBJ.

33   languished in controversy for as long as forty years: NYT editorial, "The Education Bill Advances," March 3, 1965, p. 40.

33   "If we don't pass anything but education": LBJ phone call with Vice President Hubert Humphrey, 11:25 A.M., March 6, 1965, Cit. 7024, Audiotape WH6503.02, LBJ.

34   a million votes per month: Oral History with Commissioner of Education Francis Keppel, July 18, 1968, LBJ; int. Jack Valenti, Feb. 25, 1991.

34   "before the vicious forces concentrate": LBJ phone call with Martin Luther King, 12:06 P.M., Jan. 15, 1965, Cit. 6736-37, Audiotape WH6501.04, LBJ.

34   "We're smarter than they are": LBJ phone call with Vice President Hubert Humphrey, 11:25 A.M., March 6, 1965, Cit. 7024, Audiotape WH6503.02, LBJ.

34   surprise intervention by white people: Fager, *Selma, 1965*, pp. 87–89; Friedland, *Lift Up*, pp. 120–21; Mobile LHM, March 12, 1965, FDC-565, pp. 3–5.

34   mission congregation established for Negroes: Chestnut and Cass, *Black*, p. 40.

34   "We did not interfere in your problems": STJ, March 7, 1965, p. 1.

35   The clear message to Ellwanger: Int. Joseph Ellwanger, June 12, 2001.

35   Marjorie Linn walked beside him: Ibid.

35   "take some warm white bodies down there": Oral history of Eileen Walbert, Helen Baer, and Mary Young Gonzalez, interviewed by Maurice Baer, Oct. 27, 1975, UAB.

35   several dozen Unitarians: Presentation by Gordon D. Gibson to the General Assembly of the Unitarian Universalist Association, June 23, 2000, www.uua.org/uuhs/Gibson .html.

35   Ellwanger himself never had joined a racial demonstration: Int. Joseph Ellwanger, June 12, 2001.

35   "most of them sturdily built and roughly dressed": NYT, March 7, 1965, p. 1.

35   One minute later, as recorded by FBI agents: SAC, Mobile, Teletype to Director, March 6, 1965, FDCA-477.

36   "in no way does Rev. Ellwanger represent the church": STJ, March 7, 1965, pp. 1, 2.

36   previous edicts from Homrighausen: Int. Joseph Ellwanger, June 12, 2001; *Jet*, March 25, 1965, p. 41. Ellwanger's parishioner was Chris McNair, father of bomb victim Denise McNair.

36   "there are white people in Alabama who will speak out": Joseph Ellwanger, "Statement of Purpose," for "Demonstration by 72 Alabama Whites in Selma," March 7, 1965, BIR/C10f49.

36   "the whites hooted and yelled": SAC, Mobile, Teletype to Director, March 6, 1965, FDCA-477.

37   "Tears trickled down the cheeks": NYT, March 8, 1965, p. 20.

37   return by way of Church Street: Int. Joseph Ellwanger, June 12, 2001; Fager, *Selma, 1965*, p. 88.

37   since slugging Martin Luther King: Branch, *Pillar*, p. 561.

37   rocking the car to turn it over: SAC, Mobile, Teletype to Director, March 6, 1965, FDCA-477.

37   lose her job as well as a car: Oral history of Eileen Walbert, Helen Baer, and Mary Young Gonzalez, interviewed by Maurice Baer, Oct. 27, 1975, UAB.

37   James Bevel's sermon of praise: Fager, *Selma, 1965*, p. 89.

37   Joyce Ellwanger, pregnant with her first child: Int. Joseph Ellwanger, June 12, 2001; NYT, March 7, 1965, p. 46.

38   Baker fulminated, threatening to resign: Garrow, *Protest*, pp. 72–73; Fager, *Selma, 1965*, pp. 89–90.

38   "Captain Baker": Fager, *Selma, 1965*, pp. 5–6; int. W. D. "Cotton" Nichols, May 28, 1990.

38   A parallel debate raged privately at the governor's mansion: Garrow, *Protest*, pp. 72–73; Jones, *Wallace Story*, pp. 357–59.

38   "lie down in the road": SAC, Mobile, Teletype to Director, March 6, 1965, FDCA-477, p. 5.

38   four o'clock news conference: Ibid.

39   "Negroes should not be permitted": STJ, March 7, 1965, p. 2.

39 "The answer is yes": LBJ phone call with Secretary of Defense Robert McNamara, 2:32 P.M., March 6, 1965, Cit. 7028, Audiotape WH6503.03, LBJ.

40 pre-mobilized shipments of Marines: State Department cables mentioned the ongoing mobilization of the Marine deployments as early as February 26, 1965. See Gravel, ed., *Pentagon Papers,* p. 420.

40 held back the Pentagon news release until nightfall: NYT, March 7, 1965, p. 1.

40 SNCC debate about Selma lasted: Carson, *Struggle,* p. 58; Sellers, *River,* p. 119; int. Betty Garman Robinson, Jan. 29, 1991; int. Charles Cobb, Aug. 20, 1991; int. Fay Bellamy, Oct. 29, 1991; int. Silas Norman, June 28, 2000; int. Ivanhoe Donaldson, Nov. 30, 2000; int. James Forman, Feb. 13, 2001; int. Jack Minnis, April 8, 2001.

40 Julian Bond proposed: Ibid. Also Minutes, SNCC executive committee meeting, March 6, 1965, A/SN6, p. 5.

41 proposed for disenfranchised Negroes to submit: Silas Norman and John Love report, "Selma, Alabama," March 1965, Reel 37, SNCC. The report lists three other disagreements with King and his SCLC organization: (1) that SCLC was not pushing hard yet for elimination of the literacy requirement for voters; (2) that SCLC opposed SNCC's plan to create a Freedom Democratic Party in Alabama, similar to the Mississippi Freedom Democratic Party begun in 1964; and (3) that "SCLC pushes the idea that local people need leaders like Martin Luther King and Rev. Abernathy, and others, while SNCC says that local people build their own leaders, out of their own communities."

41 Bob Moses himself had opposed the Mississippi congressional challenge: Int. Bob Moses, July 31, 1984; Feb. 15, 1991; int. Lawrence Guyot, Feb. 1, 1991; int. Worth Long, Sept. 12, 1983.

41 migrating to other states: "SNCC Workers Expand into Ala. Black Belt," *Student Voice,* March 5, 1965, p. 1; int. Lawrence Guyot, Feb. 1, 1991; int. Mary Lane by Robert Wright, July 12, 1969, RJBOH. Lane was recruited into SNCC from her home in Greenwood by Bob Moses in December of 1961. She recalls "a lot of staff meetings that were held after the summer of '64, but there was really never any home work done afterwards." Lane states that many workers were called away to work in other states, and that her project director in Greenwood, Stokely Carmichael, left for Alabama.

41 disappearing into Alabama: Branch, *Pillar,* pp. 588–90, 611; int. Silas Norman, Aug. 25, 2000. Moses arrived in Birmingham from Mississippi on March 7, 1965, the day of the big march in Selma: int. Bob Moses by Joe Sinsheimer, Feb. 13, 1985.

41 "roughly handled the white workers": WATS report, March 1, 1965, Reel 15, SNCC.

41 "If these people want to march": Lewis, *Walking,* pp. 318–20.

42 melt back among the people as organizers: Int. Jack Minnis, April 8, 2001.

42 "a house on a hill and two Cadillacs": Judy Richardson to Jack Minnis, March 9, 1965, JMP.

42 "why we bother with the vote at all": Ibid.

42 "sets the stage": Jack Minnis to Courtland Cox, March 4, 1965, responding to Courtland Cox to SNCC Staff and Others, Re: "Student Involvement in the Challenge," March 4, 1965, JMP.

42 "I think it illusory": Ibid.

42 voted toward midnight to disapprove: John P. Lewis and Silas Norman, Jr., to MLK, March 7, 1965, A/KP23f17. King's office received the letter on Monday, March 8. Someone signed for Lewis, who had already departed for Selma when it was completed on Sunday.

43 Mants seized the chance: Int. Bob Mants, Sept. 8, 2000.

5: OVER THE BRIDGE

PAGE

44   A chorus of automobile horns: Webb and Nelson, *Selma, Lord, Selma,* p. 87.

44   "Quiet Please, We Are Trying": Warren Hinckle and David Walsh, "Five Battles of Selma," *Ramparts,* June 1965, p. 24.

44   "There's three more cars": Ibid.

44   Young quickly sought out Hosea Williams: Young, *Burden,* p. 354; int. Andrew Young, Oct. 26, 1991; int. Hosea Williams, Oct. 29, 1991.

45   "Hosea, you're not with me": Int. Hosea Williams, Oct. 29, 1991.

45   "how well I got this thing organized": Ibid.

45   Bevel just as openly denigrated Williams: Young, *Burden,* pp. 382–84; int. Hosea Williams, Oct. 29, 1991; int. James Bevel, Dec. 10, 1998; int. Andrew Young, Oct. 26, 1991.

45   Young wound up arrested: Branch, *Pillar,* pp. 123–27.

45   "the prettiest girl in the church": Ibid., pp. 322–25, 332–35; Young, *Burden,* pp. 290–93.

45   Albert Turner, a bricklayer: Raines, *Soul,* pp. 204–7, 212–14; Webb and Nelson, *Selma, Lord, Selma,* p. 92.

45   Rev. John B. Morris by coincidence: "The Saga of Selma: A Tape Recording by ESCRU," transcript, p. 1, JDC; ESCRU newsletter, March 14, 1965, p. 5; Morris to Andrew Young, April 2, 1965, A/SC44f12.

46   founder of the Episcopal Society for Cultural and Racial Unity: Shattuck, *Episcopalians,* pp. 97–107. Morris knew Andrew Young and other civil rights activists from his work with ESCRU in numerous protests, including an effort to desegregate Atlanta's Lovett School, an institution of Episcopalian ties that rejected King's son Martin III in 1963: Ibid, pp. 135–37; Branch, *Pillar,* p. 110.

46   alongside stories about the upcoming Marine deployment: "White Alabamians Stage Selma March to Support Negroes," and "3,500 Marines Going to Vietnam to Bolster Base," NYT, March 7, 1965, p. 1. The military story reflects the Johnson administration's effort to minimize the significance of the deployment, as well as press skepticism: "The Pentagon said that the marines would have a limited mission. . . . It appeared evident that the marines would do more than act as military policemen."

46   a photograph of Sheriff Jim Clark: NYT Magazine, March 7, 1965, p. 37.

46   "I am sure he loves his wife": Ibid., p. 33.

46   "to satisfy his revenge against me": Sheriff Jim Clark on ABC's *Issues and Answers,* March 7, 1965, Tape 243, A/JF; Rosen to Belmont, "Appearance of Sheriff James G. Clark, Dallas County, Alabama, on ABC Television Program, 'Issues and Answers,' 3/7/65," March 8, 1965, FK-NR.

46   his voice urged citizens: Lesher, *George Wallace,* p. 324.

46   Clark in person: Fager, *Selma, 1965,* pp. 91–93; Warren Hinckle and David Walsh, "Five Battles of Selma," *Ramparts,* June 1965, p. 25.

47   try to elude the troopers: Garrow, *Bearing,* p. 397.

47   "It is not a dangerous gas, usually": Lesher, *George Wallace,* p. 322; NYT, March 8, 1965, p. 20.

47   Frank Soracco: Branch, *Pillar,* pp. 559, 576–77; int. Frank Soracco, Sept. 12–14, 1990.

47   added a roving speech for nonviolent discipline: Lesher, *George Wallace,* p. 322.

47   John Lewis arrived at Brown Chapel: Lewis, *Walking,* pp. 323–24.

47   "could have kissed him": Int. Hosea Williams, Oct. 29, 1991.

47 they debated whether to confirm the change: Ibid. Also int. Ralph Abernathy, May 31, 1984; int. Andrew Young, Oct. 26, 1991; int. James Bevel, Dec. 10, 1998; Abernathy, *Walls,* pp. 327–28; Young, *Burden,* p. 355.

48 If stopped, they would sit in prayer: WATS report, Selma, Alabama, March 7, 1965, Reel 15, SNCC.

48 a backpack stocked haphazardly: Lewis, *Walking,* p. 320; Lesher, *George Wallace,* p. 324.

48 "God Will Take Care of You": Fager, *Selma, 1965,* p. 93.

48 run into a glowering Wilson Baker: SAC, Mobile, Teletype to Director, March 7, 1965, FDCA-476; Raines, *Soul,* pp. 220–21.

48 stepped off again two abreast at 2:18 P.M.: SAC, Mobile, Teletype to Director, March 11, 1965, FDCA-502; Warren Hinckle and David Walsh, "Five Battles of Selma," *Ramparts,* June 1965, p. 26.

48 followed by a vehicular train: Lesher, *George Wallace,* p. 322.

49 Police officers held up the ambulances and hearses: NYT, March 8, 1965, p. 20; BAA, March 20, 1965, p. 2; int. Diane Nash, Oct. 26, 1997.

49 opened a vista of forbidding reception: NYT, March 8, 1965, pp. 1, 20; Garrow, *Protest,* pp. 73–74; SAC, Mobile, to Director, March 7, 1965, FDCA-476.

49 "Chicken Treat, Home of the Mickey Burger": Lesher, *George Wallace,* p. 324.

49 FBI communications were sifting: SAC, Chicago, Teletype to Director, March 6, 1965, FK-950; McGowan to Rosen, March 6, 1965, FK-970; Branigan to Sullivan, March 7, 1965, FK-1011.

49 "some sort of power struggle": Raines, *Soul,* pp. 423–25.

50 wore a new athletic supporter: Ibid., pp. 416–17.

50 lifting some details into lore: Fager, *Selma, 1965,* pp. 93, 241; Lewis, *Walking,* p. 326; int. Bob Mants, Sept. 8, 2000.

50 unnerving new sights and sounds: STJ, March 8, 1965, p. 2; Webb and Nelson, *Selma, Lord, Selma,* p. 94; int. Bob Mants, Sept. 8, 2000.

50 "It would be detrimental to your safety": Part 1, Episode 6 of the PBS documentary *Eyes on the Prize,* produced by Blackside Productions, Inc.

51 "high-water pants": Int. Bob Mants, Sept. 8, 2000.

51 With nightsticks held chest high: Part 1, Episode 6 of the PBS documentary *Eyes on the Prize,* produced by Blackside Productions, Inc.; NYT, March 8, 1965, p. 1; Fager, *Selma, 1965,* pp. 93–94; Lewis, *Walking,* pp. 326–28.

51 fired by Sheriff Clark himself: Raines, *Soul,* p. 221.

51 the cloud of tear gas from canister and spray: Part 1, Episode 6 of the PBS documentary *Eyes on the Prize,* produced by Blackside Productions, Inc.

51 Lafayette Surney was describing the departure: WATS report, "Selma, March 7, 1965," Reel 15, SNCC.

52 Diane Nash's efforts to extricate the blockaded medical teams: "The Saga of Selma: A Tape Recording by ESCRU," transcript, p. 1, JDC; ESCRU newsletter, March 14, 1965, p. 5; int. James Bevel, Dec. 10, 1998; int. Diane Nash, Oct. 26, 1997; Andrew Young remarks on Volume I, Segment 6 of the PBS documentary *Eyes on the Prize,* produced by Blackside Productions, Inc.

52 around the wide-area telephone service phone receiver: Int. Fay Bellamy, Oct. 29, 1991; int. Ivanhoe Donaldson, Oct. 30, 2000; int. James Forman, Feb. 13, 2001.

52 Many clung to the bridge railing: Int. Frank Soracco, Sept. 12–14, 1990; int. Bob Mants, Sept. 8, 2000; int. Cleophus Hobbs, Sept. 6, 2000.

52   hollered for Hosea Williams: Webb and Nelson, *Selma, Lord, Selma,* p. 97.

52   Surney, a young movement veteran from Ruleville, Mississippi: Dittmer, *Local People,* p. 137; Payne, *Light,* p. 169.

52   Dr. Moldovan and two nurses broke away: NYT, March 8, 1965, p. 20.

52   The heavy gas curled thickly: Warren Hinckle and David Walsh, "Five Battles of Selma," *Ramparts,* June 1965, pp. 27–28.

53   Moore and Boynton rode into Selma: Robinson, *Bridge,* pp. 254–56; Silora, *Judge,* pp. 204–5; int. Bernard Lafayette, May 29, 1990.

53   By 3:30 P.M.: SAC, Mobile, Teletype to Director, March 7, 1965, FDCA-502, p. 4.

53   attacked stragglers in a frenzy: Fager, *Selma, 1965,* pp. 94–95; Garrow, *Bearing,* p. 399.

53   troopers threw one teenager: Garrow, *Protest,* p. 76.

53   John Webb cried with his shotgun: Webb and Nelson, *Selma, Lord, Selma,* p. 98.

53   Frank Soracco did not stop running: Ibid., pp. 100–101; int. Frank Soracco, Sept. 12–14, 1990.

53   confronted the sheriff in front of reporters: Raines, *Soul,* pp. 221–22.

53   "I've already waited a month": STJ, March 8, 1965, p. 2.

53   "I've never seen anything like it": WATS report, "Selma, March 7, 1965," Reel 15, SNCC, p. 2.

53   "We have a problem": Ibid. The SNCC worker reporting from Selma was Willie Emma Scott.

53   Leaders ventured outside: Raines, *Soul,* p. 222; Horne, *Fire,* pp. 356–57; Young and Bevel remarks on Part 1, Episode 6 of the PBS documentary *Eyes on the Prize,* produced by Blackside Productions, Inc.

54   "Johnson Asks Congress": STJ, March 8, 1965, p. 1.

54   "Members of the posse beat": Ibid., p. 2.

54   "Negroes lay on the floors": NYT, March 8, 1965, p. 20.

54   fifty-eight of them occupied every surface: SAC, Mobile, Teletype to Director, March 7, 1965, FDCA-480; Warren Hinckle and David Walsh, "Five Battles of Selma," *Ramparts,* June 1965, p. 28.

54   Burwell Infirmary: Report on Burwell Infirmary, Selma, Alabama, by Margaret Hatch, May 11, 1965, RSP1.

54   lacerations and broken bones: SAC, Mobile, Teletype to Director, March 7, 1965, FDCA-480.

55   more suffering from tear gas: Lewis, *Walking,* p. 331.

55   "Tear gas—that's the baddest thing": WATS report, "Selma, March 7, 1965," Reel 15, SNCC, p. 2.

55   SNCC headquarters swarmed: "Report on Selma 3/7/65," Reel 5, SNCC, pp. 1–6.

55   two bulletins by 5:30 P.M.: Press release 5:30 P.M. EST and "Information on Today's Brutality in Selma, Alabama," 6:30 P.M. EST, March 7, 1965, Reel 37, SNCC.

55   Forman hired a second emergency charter flight: Int. Kwame Ture (Stokely Carmichael), Jan. 31, 1984; int. Ivanhoe Donaldson, Nov. 30, 2000.

55   "misstatements and distortions": "Report on Selma 3/7/65," Reel 5, SNCC, p. 6.

55   "I'm just curious": Dialogue from MGM film *Judgment at Nuremberg* (1961), directed by Stanley Kramer, written by Abby Mann, starring Spencer Tracy, Burt Lancaster, Richard Widmark, Judy Garland, Maximilian Schell, Montgomery Clift, and Marlene Dietrich.

56   Frank Reynolds broke in upon this film conversation: Carter, *Politics,* p. 248; Garrow, *Bearing,* p. 399.

56   shortly after nine o'clock: Garrow, *Protest,* p. 78.

56   social dinner at the White House: PDD, March 7, 1965, LBJ. Dinner guests were Mr. and Mrs. William S. White, Congressman and Mrs. Jack Brooks, Congressman J. J. Pickle, Clark Clifford, and Mr. and Mrs. Jack Valenti.

56   "the cauldron is boiling": Johnson, *Diary,* p. 248.

56   touched Red Beach 2 at 9:03 P.M.: Shulimson and Shulimson, *Marines,* p. 12.

56   Squad leader Garry Parsons: AP story on Marine landing, STJ, March 8, 1965, p. 2.

57   "a renewed march from Selma to Montgomery": MLK press release 8:30 P.M., March 7, 1965, A/KS8.

57   "Mr. President, I understand": Rev. F. D. Reese int. by Larry D. Vasser, March 13, 1978, for the Alabama Historical Commission, BIR.

57   preaching perseverance to a mass meeting of 450: Mobile LHM, March 12, 1965, FDCA-565, pp. 7–8; Webb and Nelson, *Selma, Lord, Selma,* pp. 105–7.

6: THE CALL

PAGE

58   "He Reveals Plans": NYT, March 8, 1965, p. 1.

58   "King Calls for Another Try": WP, March 8, 1965, p. 1.

58   President Johnson made his first call: PDD, March 8, 1965, LBJ.

58   "I didn't give the arrests any publicity": LBJ phone call with Attorney General Nicholas Katzenbach, 8:10 A.M., March 8, 1965, Cit. 7029-30, Audiotape WH6503.03, LBJ.

58   "the most notorious liar": Garrow, *FBI,* pp. 121–22; Branch, *Pillar,* p. 526.

59   mistaken FBI agent Dan Doyle: STJ, March 8, 1965, p. 2.

59   considered Hoover to be actively senile: Int. Nicholas Katzenbach, June 14, 1991.

59   Picket lines sprang up: NYT, March 9, 1965, p. 1.

59   their leader emerged to tell reporters: STJ, March 9, 1965, p. 2; int. Rev. Jefferson Rogers, July 17, 2001.

59   "It did not take the Attorney General long": Ibid.

59   "Our basic difficulty is we have no communication": LBJ phone call with Senator Lister Hill, 4:24 P.M., March 8, 1965, Cit. 7039, Audiotape WH6503.04, LBJ.

59   "You can't trust him": LBJ phone call with Buford Ellington, 8:29 A.M., March 8, 1965, Cit. 7031-32, Audiotape WH6503.03, LBJ.

60   "This fella's sent out wires all over the United States": LBJ phone call with Senator Lister Hill, 4:24 P.M., March 8, 1965, Cit. 7039, Audiotape WH6503.04, LBJ.

60   "ministers' march to Montgomery": ESCRU newsletter, March 14, 1965, p. 5. Text of telegram cf. MLK to Rev. Arthur Walmsley, March 8, 1965, RSP2.

60   ten church executives vowed: NYT, March 9, 1965, p. 1.

60   with its own press release: NCC, Commission on Religion and Race, press release, March 8, 1965, RSP2.

61   astonished Catholics rushed: Int. Matthew Ahmann, Feb. 12, 1991.

61   "Sister Cecilia, do you want": Warren Hinckle and David Walsh, "Five Battles of Selma," *Ramparts,* June 1965, pp. 36–37.

61   "recognized ecumenical activity": Memo from the Presiding Bishop, "Re: Executive Council involvement in the Selma-Montgomery March," RSP2.

61   "a foolish business and a sad waste of time": Shattuck, *Episcopalians,* p. 154.

61   made room on the floor for Harris Wofford: Wofford, *Kennedys and Kings,* pp. 178–79.

61   revolving picket line of outside clergy: Int. Robert Stone, June 3, 1993; int. Metz Rollins, Dec. 13, 1991; Branch, *Pillar,* pp. 214–24.

61   Robert McAfee Brown hastily arranged: Friedland, *Lift Up,* p. 122; int. Robert McAfee Brown, July 17, 1991.

62   ran into an AME Zion minister: Int. Israel Seymour Dresner, July 31, 1991.

62   handfuls of pioneer clergy: Branch, *Parting,* pp. 630–31, 785; Branch, *Pillar,* pp. 340, 354–56.

62   Scattered veterans of the movement: Int. Virgil Wood, Aug. 2, 1994.

62   "Pack your bags": Frady, *Jesse,* p. 189.

62   soon said goodbye to her husband: Statement of Barbara Krasner, March 18, 1965, A/SN94.

62   More than a hundred Unitarian leaders: Howlett, *Greater,* p. 199.

62   modified his prior interpretation: Eagles, *Outside Agitator,* pp. 26–27.

62   "He hath scattered the proud": Luke 1:51–52.

62   "decisive, luminous, Spirit-filled": Untitled student paper by Jonathan Daniels, handed in June 22, 1965, at the Episcopal Theological School, Cambridge, Massachusetts, JDC, p. 2.

63   "pressure is mounting": DeLoach to Mohr, March 9, 1965, FK-1070.

63   block an honorary degree: Ibid.; Branch, *Pillar,* p. 246.

63   "I told him that King was a phony": DeLoach to Mohr, March 9, 1965, FK-1070.

63   "burrhead": Garrow, *FBI,* p. 106.

63   one via the Secret Service: SAC, Detroit, to Director, March 9, 1965, FK-982.

63   killing squad from the Coushatta, Louisiana, Ku Klux Klan: Belmont to Tolson, March 9, 1965, FDCA-521.

63   "No," Hoover scrawled: Ibid.

63   "not to tell King anything": SAC, Mobile, to Director, March 9, 1965, FDCA-487.

63   previous order to exclude King: Branch, *Parting,* p. 692; Branch, *Pillar,* pp. 196–98.

64   FBI agents recorded that at 10:30 P.M.: Mobile LHM dated March 12, 1965, FDCA-565, p. 8.

64   "Any man who has the urge": STJ, March 9, 1965, p. 2.

64   breakout rendition of "Battle Hymn of the Republic": Webb and Nelson, *Selma, Lord, Selma,* pp. 108–9.

64   "Life for me ain't been no crystal stair": Andrew Kopkind, "Selma," *New Republic,* March 20, 1965, p. 7.

64   "If a man is 36 years old": King address of March 8, 1965, A/KS8.

64   "We must let them know that if they beat one Negro": Ibid. Also STJ, March 9, 1965, p. 2.

64   first fifty traveling clergy: Norman Kilpatrick, "The Selma Nobody Knows," BAA, March 20, 1965, p. 5.

64   "I hear that Dr. Martin Luther King": STJ, March 9, 1965, p. 2.

65   "The Negroes are still meeting": LBJ phone call with Bill Moyers, March 8, 1965, Cit. 7044, Audiotape WH6503.04, LBJ.

65   Katzenbach kneeling in shirtsleeves: NYT, March 9, 1965, p. 24; Fager, *Selma, 1965,* p. 100.

65   "I think it's outrageous what's on TV": LBJ phone call with Bill Moyers, March 8, 1965, Cit. 7044, Audiotape WH6503.04, LBJ.

65   For the remainder of a long hard night: Garrow, *Protest,* pp. 85–86; Garrow, *Bearing,* pp. 400–403; Forman, *Sammy Younge,* pp. 77–78; Young, *Burden,* pp. 359–60; Abernathy, *Walls,* pp. 335–37.

65   "too deeply committed": Louis Martin to Marvin Watson, March 8, 1965, Ex HU2/ST1, FG135, LBJ.

65   About two o'clock Tuesday morning: SAC, Mobile, to Director, 2:51 A.M., CST, March 9, 1965, FDCA-479.

65   "have his heart": Int. Harry Wachtel, Nov. 29, 1983.

66   tenderfoot church elders could not walk far: New York LHM dated March 11, 1965, FK-NR.

66   agents gleaned from wiretapped conference calls: Rosen to Belmont, March 9, 1965, FDCA-491.

66   coming to rest in King's own private office: Judy Upham oral history dated January 6, 1966, pp. 15–16, JDC.

66   dozed in the Hertz rental office: Howlett, *Greater,* p. 200.

66   "What happened with Martin Luther King?": LBJ phone call with Bill Moyers, 7:33 A.M., March 9, 1965, Cit. 7045, Audiotape WH6503.04, LBJ.

67   Collins landed at Craig Air Force Base: Wagy, *Governor,* p. 183.

67   "a man from the President": Int. Jean Jackson, May 27, 1990.

7: DEVIL'S CHOICE

PAGE

68   the bed collapsed under a conclave: Int. Jean Jackson, May 27, 1990.

68   King sat at the dining room table: Ibid. Also Abernathy, *Walls,* pp. 336–39; Garrow, *Protest,* pp. 85–86.

69   Like Katzenbach, Doar privately agreed with King's lawyers: Int. Nicholas Katzenbach, June 14, 1991; int. John Doar, May 12, 1986.

69   "This is a *federal* order": Westin and Mahoney, *Trial,* p. 172.

69   Doar was a pioneer of tenacity: Branch, *Parting,* pp. 331–35, 647–72, 825–27.

70   discomfited government lawyers as overwrought: Sikora, *Judge,* p. 196; int. Nicholas Katzenbach, June 14, 1991.

70   "But Mr. Attorney General": Garrow, *Bearing,* p. 402.

70   "You're talking to the wrong people": Int. Fred Shuttlesworth, March 9, 1999.

71   worse than improper for Collins to tinker: Int. Nicholas Katzenbach, June 14, 1991; int. John Doar, May 12, 1986.

71   "I don't believe you can get": Garrow, *Bearing,* p. 402.

71   "ominously quiet, oppressively tense": Martin E. Marty, "Selma: Sustaining the Momentum," *Christian Century,* March 24, 1965, p. 358.

71   floor of the maternity ward: Friedland, *Lift Up,* p. 124.

72   asking for autographs: Statement of Barbara Krasner, March 18, 1965, A/SN94.

72   "coolest cats in town": Andrew Kopkind, "Selma," *New Republic,* March 20, 1965, p. 7.

72   "it ain't gonna be our women": Howlett, *Greater,* p. 201.

72   cushion the expected licks: Int. Willie (Ricks) Mukasa, May 14, 1992.

72   fanned out to search for Hosea Williams: STJ, March 9, 1965, p. 1.

72   Judge Johnson signed just before ten o'clock: Johnson signed the restraining order at 9:46 A.M., March 9. Mobile LHM dated March 12, 1965, FDCA-565, p. 8.

72   "numbering between two thousand": SAC, Mobile, to Director, March 9, 1965, FDCA-504.

72   "Injunctions aren't legal": STJ, March 9, 1965, p. 1.

72   "As far as I'm concerned": Wofford, *Kennedys and Kings,* p. 181.

72   "heavy responsibility deliberately to break the law": Howlett, *Greater,* p. 204.

72   Willie Ricks of SNCC climbed the steps: Int. Ivanhoe Donaldson, Nov. 30, 2000; int. Willie (Ricks) Mukasa, May 14, 1992; Sellers, *River,* p. 123.

73   "Do you think people really would?": Wofford, *Kennedys and Kings,* p. 181.

73   estimated eight hundred travelers: *Jet,* March 25, 1965, p. 23.

73   a SNCC delegation that pressed arguments: Int. Fay Bellamy, Oct. 29, 1991; int. Cleveland Sellers, Dec. 14, 1983; int. James Forman, Feb. 13, 2001.

73   discharged passengers at an open field: Judy Upham oral history dated January 6, 1966, p. 17, JDC.

74   advice not to hamper his defense by specifying his intentions: New York LHM dated March 11, 1965, FK-NR; Greenberg, *Crusaders,* p. 357; Westin, *Trial,* pp. 57–59, 173; int. Harry Wachtel, Nov. 29, 1983.

74   "an unruly mob": NYT, March 10, 1965, p. 22.

74   five times around the Detroit federal building: NYT, March 10, 1965, p. 1; Fager, *Selma, 1965,* p. 106.

74   picketed a New York City FBI office: STJ, March 10, 1965, p. 2.

74   "Johnson Is Goldwater in Disguise": NYT, March 10, 1965, p. 22.

74   strategy talks on education: PDD, March 9, 1965, pp. 1–2, LBJ.

74   "Good Lord, Mr. President": Richard B. Stolley, "The Nation Surges to Join the Negro on His March," *Life,* March 26, 1965, p. 34.

74   wandered off in search of a candy bar: Judy Upham oral history dated January 6, 1966, p. 18, JDC.

74   "Almighty God, thou has called us": MLK prayer of March 9, 1965, transcribed by "SJE," A/KS.

74   "a great rustling": NYT, March 10, 1965, p. 22.

75   At 2:17 P.M., as recorded by FBI observers: SAC, Mobile, to Director, March 9, 1965, FDCA-504.

75   "You son of a bitch!": NYT, March 10, 1965, p. 22.

75   crudely drawn street map he handed to King: King, "Behind the Selma March," *Saturday Review,* April 3, 1965, p. 57.

75   "I'll do my best": Wagy, *Governor,* p. 186; Abernathy, *Walls,* p. 339.

75   "This cause is now submitted": NYT, March 10, 1965, p. 22.

76   "I am aware of the order": Fager, *Selma, 1965,* p. 103; STJ, March 10, 1965, p. 2.

76   "ignored" the court order: SAC, Mobile, to Director, March 9, 1965, FDCA-504.

76   five hundred Alabama troopers: STJ, March 9, 1965, p. 2.

76   six ambulances poised in the rear: *Jet,* March 25, 1965, p. 24.

76   A few skeptics stood on lookout near the front: Int. Fay Bellamy, Oct. 29, 1991.

76   "We're at the critical moment": Wagy, *Governor,* p. 187.

76   "What's that applause?": STJ, March 10, 1965, p. 1.

76   on the arm of Rev. Farley Wheelwright: NYT, March 10, 1965, p. 22.

77   psychiatrist Belinda Strait: NYT, March 8, 1965, p. 20; BAA, March 20, 1965, p. 3; *Jet,* March 25, 1965, p. 48.

77   open line to Governor Wallace: Garrow, *Bearing,* p. 404.

77   the way to Montgomery lay open: Fager, *Selma, 1965,* p. 104.

77   "We will go back to the church now!": Int. Fay Bellamy, Oct. 29, 1991; Wofford, *Kennedys and Kings,* p. 183.

77   Governor Collins remained petrified: ("I was standing right there, and I didn't know who was going to double cross me.") LeRoy Collins int. by Joe B. Frantz, Nov. 15, 1972, p. 32, LBJ.

77   "Now I'm sure": STJ, March 10, 1965, p. 1.

77   Katzenbach called the White House: Wagy, *Governor,* p. 188.

77   King retreated at 3:09 P.M.: SAC, Mobile, to Director, March 9, 1965, FDCA-504, p. 3.

77   "If I hadn't done anything else": LeRoy Collins interview by Jack Bass and Walter De Vries, May 19, 1975, Series A-49, Collection 4007, UNC.

78   "Now I want to think": STJ, March 10, 1965, p. 1.

78   "Thank you, Lord": Wofford, *Kennedys and Kings,* p. 183.

78   cried fitfully over a U-turn: Int. Edwin King, June 26, 1992.

78   fretted about treachery and betrayal: Int. Cleveland Sellers, Dec. 14, 1983; int. Willie (Ricks) Mukasa, May 14, 1992; int. Fay Bellamy, Oct. 29, 1991; int. Silas Norman, June 28, 2000; int. Ivanhoe Donaldson, Nov. 30, 2000; int. James Forman, Feb. 13, 2001; Fager, *Selma, 1965,* p. 105; Lewis, *Walls,* p. 334.

78   Ricks and others launched: Ibid. Also Webb and Nelson, *Selma, Lord, Selma,* p. 110.

78   "Well, crud": Judy Upham oral history dated January 6, 1966, pp. 19–20, JDC.

78   first Episcopal bishop, James Pike of California: Ibid. Also transcript of John B. Morris tape, "The Saga of Selma," p. 3, JDC.

78   two new planeloads of clergy: Mobile LHM dated March 12, 1965, FDCA-565, p. 12.

78   "the greatest demonstration for freedom": "Selma: 'Ain't Gonnas Let Nobody Turn Me 'Round,' " *New Republic,* March 20, 1965, p. 7.

78   "Why didn't we just sit down": Wofford, *Kennedys and Kings,* pp. 184–85.

79   "I've paid my dues in Selma": Ibid. Also statement of Barbara Krasner, March 18, 1965, A/SN94.

79   senior seminarians caught rides: Judy Upham oral history dated January 6, 1966, p. 21, JDC.

79   upward of fifty Unitarians: Mendelsohn, *Martyrs,* p. 167.

79   "Do you prefer to eat": Howlett, *Greater,* p. 208.

79   "Imagine a Harvard theologian": *Jet,* March 25, 1965, pp. 26–29.

80   much relieved about Selma: Johnson, *Diary,* p. 250.

80   Metropolitan Club was strictly segregated: Jack Valenti to LBJ, March 9, 1965, WHCF, Box 56, LBJ.

80   ninth of ten war briefings: PDD, March 9, 1965, LBJ.

80   "there are no tricks in it": Transcript of recorded congressional reception, March 9, 1965, Congressional Briefings on Vietnam, Box 1, LBJ, p. 1.

80   "about 150 have proven to be Vietcong": Ibid., p. 16.

80   "you just got one President": Ibid., p. 19.

80   Unitarian ministers emerged from Walker's Café: Mendelsohn, *Martyrs,* pp. 168–70; Howlett, *Greater,* pp. 210–13; *Jet,* March 25, 1965, pp. 26–29; Clark Olsen, "The Longest March," *UU World,* May–June 2001.

81   Diane Nash called a doctor: Ibid.

81   Reeb spoiled X-rays: Margaret Hatch, "Report on Burwell Infirmary, Selma, Alabama," May 11, 1965, p. 2, RSP1.

81   Reeb vomited and lapsed into unconsciousness: Ibid. Also Mendelsohn, *Martyrs,* p. 170.

81   his own Piper Cub: Chestnut and Cass, *Black,* pp. 139–41.

81   "They came here from other sections": MLK statement of March 9, 1965 [mislabeled March 10, 1965], "Brutal Beating of Three White Ministers," A/KS.

82   he surrendered the pulpit at 10:30 P.M.: Mobile LHM dated March 12, 1965, FDCA-565, p. 12.

82   Judith Upham and Jonathan Daniels: Judy Upham oral history dated January 6, 1966, pp. 21–22, JDC.

8: THE GHOST OF LINCOLN

PAGE

83   "a squat figure in blue jeans": "Nuns at Selma," *America,* April 3, 1965, p. 455.

83   "We are testifying": NYT, March 11, 1965, p. 21.

83   "If nonviolence can work in Alabama": "What Lies Beyond Selma," WS, March 16, 1965, cited in *Congressional Record,* March 17, 1965, p. H-5304.

83   At 12:47 P.M., Rev. L. L. Anderson led: Mobile LHM dated March 12, 1965, FDCA-565, p. 13.

83   "You can make all the statements you want": Int. L. L. Anderson, May 27, 1990; Warren Hinckle and David Welsh, "Five Battles of Selma," *Ramparts,* June 1965, p. 32.

84   more than thirty speakers stepped forward: "Nuns at Selma," *America,* April 3, 1965, pp. 454–56.

84   radio station KMOX: Ibid. Also *America,* March 27, 1965, p. 411.

84   Ralph Abernathy announced at dusk: Mobile LHM dated March 12, 1965, FDCA-565, p. 14; WATS report, March 10, 1965, Reel 15, SNCC.

84   "What do you want *my people* to do?": Frady, *Jesse,* p. 191.

84   Wilson Baker strung a clothesline: Fager, *Selma, 1965,* p. 116.

84   silhouetted them behind the long clothesline: Warren Hinckle and David Welsh, "Five Battles of Selma," *Ramparts,* June 1965, p. 36.

84   radioed ahead for a Birmingham taxi: Howlett, *Greater,* p. 215.

84   "I told the children this morning": Ibid., p. 219.

85   a day trip to Camp David: PDD, March 10, 1965, LBJ.

85   "This minister's gonna die, isn't he?": LBJ phone call with Nicholas Katzenbach and Bill Moyers, 9:32 P.M. [?], March 10, 1965, Cit. 7054, Audiotape WH6503.05, LBJ.

85   having apologized profusely for recommending: LBJ phone call with Nicholas Katzenbach, 9:00 A.M., March 10, 1965, Cit. 7048, Audiotape WH6503.04, LBJ.

85   "It just doesn't sing yet" *to* "keep the rowdies down": LBJ phone call with Nicholas Katzenbach and Bill Moyers, 9:32 P.M. [?], March 10, 1965, Cit. 7054, Audiotape WH6503.05, LBJ.

85   Democratic Majority Leader threatened revolt: Ibid. The next morning, LBJ told Katzenbach that Mansfield had sent a "mean note" insisting that he would submit his own voting rights bill out of anger that Katzenbach was working through Dirksen. (LBJ: "Mansfield is huffy and mad and grumpy.") LBJ phone call with Nicholas Katzenbach, 10:35 A.M., March 11, 1965, Cit. 7059–60, Audiotape WH6503.06, LBJ.

85   supervised field trip shifted within hours: Forman, *Sammy Younge,* pp. 79–109; Sellers, *River,* pp. 125–26; int. Gwen Patton, April 15, 2000; int. Jimmy Rogers, March 7, 2000; int. James Forman, Feb. 13, 2001.

85   a convoy of cars and chartered buses: STJ, March 10, 1965, p. 2.

86   "no different from other black people": Forman, *Sammy Younge,* p. 103.

86   clashes with the constricting rings of police: WATS report, March 10, 1965, Montgomery, Alabama, Reel 15, SNCC.

86   breaking into the nearby First Baptist Church: Ibid., p. 92; int. Willie (Ricks) Mukasa, May 14, 1992.

86   "open contempt": "Dr. King Says He Did Not Intend March to Montgomery Tuesday," NYT, March 12, 1965, p. 1.

86   King testified as the first witness: Ibid.

86   "even after a marshal read you the order": Sikora, *Judge*, pp. 194–202.

86   "between this court and the alleged contemptors": Ibid., p. 193.

87   Rufus Youngblood rushed: PDD, March 11, 1965, pp. 1–8, LBJ.

87   two diagrams on the front page: NYT, March 12, 1965, p. 1.

87   allowed the peek she desired: Johnson, *Diary*, p. 250.

87   maids could serve coffee: WP, March 12, 1965, pp. 1, 10.

88   "Bevel and Forman almost came to blows": WATS report, March 11, 1965, Montgomery, Alabama, Reel 15, SNCC.

88   join students newly recruited: Int. Willie (Ricks) Mukasa, May 14, 1992.

88   "What did you set out to do?": Int. James Bevel, Dec. 10, 1998.

88   "I decided to stop trying to talk": Forman, *Sammy Younge*, p. 93; int. James Forman, Feb. 13, 2001.

88   "Anybody who wants to come with me: WATS report, March 11, 1965, Montgomery, Alabama, Reel 15, SNCC.

88   Forman and Bevel wound up: Ibid.; Forman, *Sammy Younge*, pp. 93–94.

88   only two of twelve demonstrators: WP, March 12, 1965, p. 1.

89   detailed instructions for removing the intruders: PDD, March 11, 1965, p. 8, LBJ.

89   different precinct stations in unmarked cars: WP, March 12, 1965, p. 1.

89   "The ghost of Lincoln": NYT, March 13, 1965, p. 12.

89   initiated and scripted by Johnson: LBJ phone call with Nicholas Katzenbach, 10:35 A.M., March 11, 1965, Cit. 7059–60, Audiotape WH6503.06, LBJ.

89   "totally unreasonable force": Ibid.; NYT, March 12, 1965, p. 1.

89   pronounced dead at 6:55 P.M.: Mobile LHM dated March 12, 1965, FDCA-565, p. 15.

89   presidential C-140 airplane take the widow: Howlett, *Greater*, p. 223; NYT, March 13, 1965, p. 10.

89   "But what is there to say?": Johnson, *Diary*, p. 251.

90   "Racism Killed Our Brother": WP, March 13, 1965, p. 8.

90   struck a demonstrator from Wisconsin: Mobile LHM dated March 12, 1965, FDCA-565, p. 17.

90   "I'm a segregationist": NYT, March 10, 1965, p. 21.

90   He pledged solemnly to the crowd: Fager, *Selma, 1965*, p. 117.

90   as he had promised the Justice Department already: Nicholas Katzenbach ("I've arranged with them down there that . . . when the minister dies, they'll file first-degree murder charges within an hour") in phone call with LBJ and Bill Moyers, 9:32 P.M. [?], March 10, 1965, Cit. 7054, Audiotape WH6503.05, LBJ. See also Belmont to Rosen, March 10, 1965, FDCA-526, which reflects that FBI officials encouraged Baker to file murder charges to *supersede* federal ones.

90   Lola Bell Tate: *Jet*, April 1, 1965, p. 53; WATS report, Selma, March 12, 1965, Montgomery, Alabama, Reel 15, SNCC.

90   Collins made his way back outside: LeRoy Collins interview by Jack Bass and Walter De Vries, May 19, 1975, Series A-49, Collection 4007, SOHP, UNC, pp. 25–26.

90   to seek a negotiated truce: Mobile LHM dated March 12, 1965, FDCA-565, p. 18.

90   "They attempted to drive it": NYT, March 13, 1965, p. 10.

91   DeLoach fended off the courtesy duty: DeLoach to Mohr, March 10, 1965, FDCA-

570. DeLoach identified the Justice Department aide who suggested the idea as James Flug. "What do we know of Flug?" Hoover wrote on the memo.

91   "numbers game": Rosen to Belmont, March 11, 1965, FDCA-581.

91   "any information whatsoever": Rosen to Belmont, March 11, 1965, FDCA-669.

91   removed him by morning: Belmont to Tolson, March 12, 1965, FDCA-603. At 10:10 A.M., headquarters called Inspector Joe Sullivan in Meridian, Mississippi, where he headed the ongoing investigation of the June 1964 murders of civil rights workers James Chaney, Andrew Goodman, and Michael Schwerner, and ordered Sullivan "to proceed immediately to Selma, Alabama for the purpose of taking charge of the investigations of civil rights matters there."

91   rain fell so hard that only eighty: WATS report, Selma, March 12, 1965, Reel 15, SNCC.

91   Jesse Jackson with a mild case of pneumonia: Frady, *Jesse,* pp. 193–94.

91   Seventy Catholics arrived: NYT, March 14, 1965, p. 63.

91   adjourned en masse to Selma: Presentation by Gordon D. Gibson to the General Assembly of the Unitarian Universalist Association, June 23, 2000, www.uua.org/uuhs/Gibson.html.

91   symphony honored Reeb: Howlett, *Greater,* p. 225.

91   Wilson Baker could not keep his agreement: WATS report, March 12, 1965, Selma, Reel 15, SNCC. Mayor Smitherman and Sheriff Clark issued a joint public statement the next day that was published on the front page of the local newspaper: "We say to all of these outside agitators, both white and Negro, you are not needed or wanted in our city. Your presence is incendiary and can only cause racial strife. . . . The false issue of voting rights has been repeatedly raised. . . . We are therefore convinced first that our entire community must stand firmly where we are today and that we must not yield to or compromise with unlawful pressure or unruly demonstrations. Local government must not prostitute itself before the mob." STJ, March 14, 1965, p. 1.

91   Baker did cut down: NYT, March 13, 1965, p. 1; Fager, *Selma, 1965,* p. 123.

92   a large truck pulled up outside: Sellers, *River,* p. 127.

92   Silas Norman berated Forman: Int. Silas Norman, June 28, 2000; int. Martha Prescod Norman, June 29, 2000.

92   many thousands of scarce SNCC dollars: The figure cited is $5,000 in Carson, *Struggle,* p. 160. Cleveland Sellers remembers the figure at $25,000: int. Cleveland Sellers, April 15, 2000.

92   Cleveland Sellers was stunned: "Forman went crazy in Montgomery—bought all those tents, spent money. We were frustrated over the fact that SCLC had kind of taken over." Int. Cleveland Sellers, Dec. 14, 1983.

92   abandoned the occupation of Dexter Avenue Baptist: Forman, *Sammy Younge,* pp. 95–96.

92   "plainly astonished": NYT, March 13, 1965, p. 10.

92   corrective discipline straight from Hoover's office: Cf. McGowan to Rosen, March 12, 1965, FDCA-556; Morrell to DeLoach, March 18, 1965, FDCA-709.

92   three-minute news film: Garrow, *Protest,* p. 99.

92   Judge Johnson, visibly affected: Lewis, *Walking,* p. 337.

92   confirmed instincts within Governor Wallace's inner circle: Lesher, *George Wallace,* p. 330.

92   "The niggers are like cats": NYT, March 10, 1965, p. 22.

92   yearning to regain public initiative: Carter, *Politics,* p. 252.

92   "some of the greatest internal problems": Jones, *Wallace Story,* pp. 375–76.

92   Undercover agents scattered: "Sit-ins Averted at the White House," NYT, March 13, 1965, p. 1.

92   President Johnson sat in the Cabinet Room: PDD, March 12, 1965, LBJ; Howlett, *Greater,* p. 224; int. Joseph Ellwanger, June 12, 2001; int. Jefferson Rogers, July 17, 2001. Humphrey briefed LBJ for the meeting in a memo dated March 12, 1965, Legislative Background, Voting Rights Act of 1965, Box 2, LBJ.

93   a mammoth ecumenical assembly: NYT, March 13, 1965, p. 1; program, "Interreligious Witness for Voter Registration," sponsored by NCC Commission on Religion and Race, National Catholic Welfare Conference, and Union of American Hebrew Congregations, March 12, 1965, BIR/C11f5.

93   "Why has it taken so long": Richard B. Stolley, "The Nation Surges to Join the Negro on His March," *Life,* March 26, 1965, p. 34; Warren Hinckle and David Welsh, "Five Battles of Selma," *Ramparts,* June 1965, p. 51.

93   three thousand clergy itself made front-page news: "Clergy Irate at Response of Johnson to Rights Plea," NYT, March 13, 1965, p. 1.

93   called for his dog Blanco: PDD, March 12, 1965, LBJ.

93   lie facedown on the White House driveway: Ibid. Also WATS report, March 13, 1965, Washington, D.C., Reel 15, SNCC.

93   his staff arranged and announced a summit conference: NYT, March 13, 1965, p. 10; Carter, *Politics,* p. 252.

9: WALLACE AND THE ARCHBISHOP

PAGE

94   "They all say, 'we want troops' ": LBJ phone call with Robert McNamara, 9:22 A.M., March 13, 1965, Cit. 7064-65, Audiotape WH6503.04, LBJ.

95   Attorney General Katzenbach alone into his private bathroom: Int. Nicholas Katzenbach, June 14, 1991.

95   submission drill for squeamish aides: Cf. Goodwin, *Remembering,* pp. 256–57.

95   "Write down six things for me": Int. Nicholas Katzenbach, June 14, 1991.

96   one thing in common with Martin Luther King: Jones, *Wallace Story,* p. 178.

96   King had done on leaving the Selma jail: Branch, *Pillar,* pp. 580–81.

96   "Lem, I want to introduce you": PDD, March 13, 1965, p. 2, LBJ.

96   "Well, governor": Mann, *Walls,* p. 456.

96   "You cannot deal with street revolutionaries": Carter, *Politics,* p. 252.

96   "Finally, Mr. President": Goodwin, *Remembering,* p. 321.

96   Johnson never took his eye off Wallace: Johnson, *Vantage,* p. 163.

96   "Those goddam nigras": Lesher, *George Wallace,* p. 332.

97   "I know you're like me": Dallek, *Flawed,* p. 216.

97   "Why are you off on this black thing?": Comments of Horace Busby in "The Great Society Remembered," Guggenheim Productions, Inc., 1985, quoted in Carter, *Politics,* p. 253.

97   stop harkening back to 1865: Jones, *Wallace Story,* p. 381.

97   "looked at me like I was some kind of dog mess": Carter, *Politics,* p. 253.

98   "Don't you shit me": Int. Nicholas Katzenbach, June 14, 1991; Ashmore, *Hearts,* p. 379; Carter, *Politics,* p. 253.

98   "a great gentleman, as always": NYT, March 14, 1965, pp. 1, 62.

98   "when the President works on you": Carter, *Politics,* p. 110.

98   "the meeting has gone badly": Lee White to LBJ, "Points to Consider in Connection with the Wallace Meeting," March 13, 1965, Legislative Background, Voting Rights Act 1965, Box 2, LBJ.

98   "sort of cowed and pliable": Int. Jack Valenti, Feb. 25, 1991; Burke Marshall oral history by T. H. Baker, Oct. 28, 1968, p. 32, LBJ. Marshall, John Doar's predecessor as assistant attorney general for the Civil Rights Division at the Justice Department, was present as a special consultant for most of President Johnson's meeting with Governor Wallace.

98   gobbled a bowl of soup: PDD, March 13, 1965, p. 3, LBJ.

98   "First, I urged": "The President's News Conference of March 13, 1965," PPP 1965, pp. 274–81.

98   "an unemployed agitator ceases to agitate": Mobile LHM dated March 19, 1965, FDCA-693, p. 5.

99   a few commanders reportedly asked: Fager, *Selma, 1965,* pp. 126–29.

99   meet at the doorstep of First Presbyterian: Mobile LHM dated March 19, 1965, FDCA-693, pp. 9–10.

99   At St. Paul's Episcopal: Ibid. Also Malcolm E. Peabody, Jr., to Bishop C. C. J. Carpenter, March 18, 1965, BIR/C15f28; John B. Morris "To All Bishops," March 27, 1965, BIR/C11f5; Shattuck, *Episcopalians,* p. 155; Judy Upham oral history dated January 6, 1966, pp. 10–12, JDC.

99   raised Anglican in Jamaica: Int. Ivanhoe Donaldson, Nov. 30, 2000.

100   observances spilled widely to mark the week: NYT, March 16, 1965, pp. 1, 22, 23.

100   From All Souls Unitarian Church: Howlett, *Greater,* p. 228.

100   "Her plump face shining in the sun": NYT, March 16, 1965, p. 22.

100   President Johnson convened seven congressional leaders: Senate Majority Leader Mike Mansfield, Senate Minority Leader Everett Dirksen, Senator Thomas Kuchel, House Speaker John McCormack, House Majority Leader Carl Albert, Representative Hale Boggs, and Representative William McCulloch, 5:00–6:30 P.M., March 14, 1965, PDD, LBJ.

100   "You made the White House fireproof": "Mr. Valenti's Notes, March 14, 1965," Legislative Background, Voting Rights Act of 1965, Box 1, LBJ.

100   more would die like Reeb: Richard B. Stolley, "The Nation Surges to Join the Negro on His March," *Life,* March 26, 1965, p. 35.

100   "This is a deliberate government": "Mr. Valenti's Notes, March 14, 1965," Legislative Background, Voting Rights Act of 1965, Box 1, LBJ.

100   Attorney General Katzenbach allowed: Garrow, *Protest,* p. 104.

101   advance the date to Monday: NYT, March 15, 1965, p. 1.

101   Bill Moyers called in emergency help: Spike, *Photographs,* pp. 108–9; *Jet,* April 1, 1965, p. 10.

101   civil rights speech at Gettysburg: Branch, *Pillar,* pp. 91–92.

101   Busby dismissed the Justice Department draft: Miller, *Lyndon,* p. 525.

101   yanked in a startled new speechwriter: Goodwin, *Remembering,* pp. 325–26.

101   At the Lowndes County seat: Eagles, *Outside Agitator,* p. 122.

101   neighboring counties such as Wilcox: Wilcox County report of Gerald Olivari, May 18, 1965, Folder 25, Reel 37, SNCC.

101   had ever been inside the long-abandoned relic: Int. John Hulett, by Stanley Smith,

101   May 30, 1968, RJBOH; int. Elzie McGill by Robert Wright, Aug. 4, 1968, RJBOH; int. John Hulett, Sept. 8, 2000; Hampton and Fayer, *Voices,* p. 272.

101   "I wonder if that old thing still works": *Saturday Evening Post,* May 22, 1965, p. 94.

101   Mattie Lee Moorer noticed items: Int. Mattie Lee Moorer, March 10, 2000.

101   A news photographer later captured the registrar: *Saturday Evening Post,* May 22, 1965, p. 94.

102   ventured alone on Tuesday to witness: Presentation by Sidney Logan and John Hulett at Mt. Gillard Baptist Church, Trickem, Alabama, March 7, 2000.

102   President Johnson convened the Joint Chiefs: FRUS, Vol. 2, pp. 395–96; McNamara, *In Retrospect,* pp. 176–77.

102   "arrest the deterioration": Johnson Report outline dated March 14, 1965, FRUS, Vol. 2, pp. 438–39.

102   "current expectation of early victory": Bundy, "Memorandum for Discussion," March 16, 1965, FRUS, Vol. 2, pp. 446–49.

102   "70% to avoid a humiliating defeat": McNaughton memo of March 10, 1965, FRUS, Vol. 2, pp. 427–32; also in amended form dated March 24, 1965, in Gravel, ed., *Pentagon Papers,* pp. 694–702.

102   The report stunned the assembled commanders: McNamara, *In Retrospect,* pp. 176–77.

102   "Kill more Vietcong": Logevall, *Choosing,* p. 370.

103   appointment with columnist Walter Lippmann: PDD, March 15, 1965, LBJ; Johnson, *Diary,* p. 251.

103   "The reappraisal of our present policy": Lippmann, "Vietnam Policy Reexamined," March 18, 1965, in *Congressional Record,* March 18, 1965, p. 5452.

103   "Your policy is all stick": Steel, *Walter Lippmann,* pp. 560–61; Bird, *Color,* p. 314.

103   "He doesn't understand that I'm debatin' ": LBJ phone call with Bill Moyers, 9:40 A.M., March 10, 1965, Cit. 7051, Audiotape WH6503.05, LBJ.

103   "Mac, I've got Walter Lippmann": Steel, *Walter Lippmann,* p. 561.

104   relieved his anxiety about being ostracized: Ibid. See also Busby to LBJ, "About: Walter Lippmann," March 9, 1965, Box 52, Horace Busby Papers, LBJ.

104   Somewhat to their chagrin: Valenti, *Human,* pp. 64–66; int. Horace Busby, Feb. 3, 1992.

104   "I just wanted to remind you": Goodwin, *Remembering,* p. 329.

104   "A liberal Jew": Ibid., p. 326.

104   weekend speeches in Chicago: "5,000 Hear King at Liberty Baptist Church," CDD, March 15, 1965, p. 1; Rev. A. P. Jackson to MLK, March 16, 1965, A/KP5f24; Joseph D. Hanson to MLK, March 16, 1965, A/KP5f24. On Sunday, March 14, Chicago FBI agents monitored King's travel, his press conference in the VIP Room of O'Hare Airport, and his televised address from the Chicago Sunday Evening Club, then reported by coded Teletype to headquarters: "Primarily religious sermon, no reference Bureau or government, and only passing reference racial matters. Military and Secret Service advised." SAC, Chicago, to Director, Atlanta, and Mobile, March 15, 1965, FK-996.

104   President Johnson's personal invitation: Johnson's diary shows that he called King "in Chicago" at 10:48 P.M. Sunday night, and King told reporters that he and the President discussed the voting rights bill. Johnson did not record the call. PDD, March 14, 1965, LBJ; NYT, March 17, 1965, p. 27.

104   "I never saw any violence": Sikora, *Judge,* p. 215.

104   two of those charged in the Reeb murder: WP, March 16, 1965, p. 12.

105   "tiptoe stance": Cf. "Letter from Birmingham Jail" in Washington, ed., *Testament,* p. 293.

105   "in some quarters": Clarence Jones telegram to MLK, March 15, 1965, A/KS.

105   intensified King's vulnerability: Cf. "Administration Trying Feverishly to Prevent New Clash in Selma/ Some Vow to March No Matter What," WP, March 16, 1965, p. 1. "Some Negroes in Selma have rejected Dr. King's leadership because they feel he 'sold out' in the arranged confrontation last Tuesday."

105   he declined the President's invitation: MLK telegram to LBJ, March 15, 1965 ("I just talked with Mr. Valenti stating that complications in my schedule will make it impossible. . . . I had looked forward to being there with you."), A/KP13f7.

105   secured an excused absence from Judge Johnson: ("King will attempt to be excused from appearance in federal court, Montgomery."), SAC, Mobile, to Director, March 15, 1965, FDCA-611.

105   "got tired and even a little hostile": Fager, *Selma, 1965,* p. 133.

105   futile attempts since dawn to circumvent: FBI agents reported a march briefing by Hosea Williams at 6:58 A.M., nonviolent instruction by Rev. Charles King of Evanston, Indiana, at 8:00 A.M., and a large march led by SCLC's Rev. C. T. Vivian at 9:24 A.M., blocked by Sheriff Clark. Mobile LHM dated March 19, 1965, FDCA-693, p. 12.

105   brink of open fisticuffs: Garrow, *Protest,* p. 105.

105   swelling bank of dignitaries: NYT, March 16, 1965, pp. 1, 31.

106   first direct Vatican contact in nine hundred years: Poulos, *Breath,* p. 105.

106   alone in a Charleston hotel room: Int. Archbishop Iakovos, Jan. 24, 2002.

106   seven of eighteen bare bulbs: WP, March 16, 1965, p. 12.

106   "I found myself greatly agitated": Richard D. Leonard, "Selma65: A View from the Balcony," *UU World,* May–June 2001.

106   "James Reeb was martyred" *to* "We thank God for his goodness": MLK eulogy for James Reeb, Selma, Alabama, March 15, 1965, *UU World,* May–June 2001.

107   "At times, life is hard": Branch, *Parting,* p. 892.

107   "the most sacred values in our Judeo-Christian heritage": Branch, *Pillar,* pp. 47–48.

108   "the shirtless and barefoot people" *and* "not yet discouraged about the future": Ibid., pp. 542–43.

108   Clark received mortifying news: Mobile LHM dated March 19, 1965, FDCA-693, p. 12.

108   Four minutes later: Ibid., p. 13.

108   "Grown men wept": Fager, *Selma, 1965,* p. 134.

108   met briefly in Geneva after the bus boycott: Int. Archbishop Iakovos, Jan. 24, 2002; Branch, *Parting,* p. 214.

108   A march of some 3,500 people: WP, March 16, 1965, p. 1.

108   this hard-won release more impressive: Judy Upham oral history dated June 6, 1966, p. 13, JDC.

108   his five children watched: NYT, March 16, 1965, p. 1.

108   A photographer captured the extraordinary assembly: Friedland, *Lift Up,* pp. 129–30; *Life,* March 26, 1965.

108   to remove a mourning wreath: NYT, March 16, 1965, p. 31.

10: AND WE SHALL OVERCOME

109   Stokely Carmichael reported: WATS report, March 15, 1965, Reel 15, SNCC.

109   Carmichael saw police units: Int. Kwame Ture (Stokely Carmichael), Jan. 31, 1984.

109   SNCC colleagues came upon Carmichael: Ibid. Also Sellers, *River,* p. 127; int. Cleveland Sellers, Dec. 14, 1983. (Dates adjusted to fit the record.)

110   a standoff that lasted into Monday evening: Forman, *Sammy Younge,* p. 98; Carson, *Struggle,* p. 160; Fager, *Selma, 1965,* pp. 138–39.

110   "Melzetta Poole, 19, Alabama State": WATS report, "Montgomery, Ala., March 15, 1965, People injured in march," Reel 15, SNCC.

110   "300 Negro demonstrators blocking an ambulance": WP, March 16, 1965, p. 1. A small story in the same day's *New York Times* presented a toned-down police version as "one unconfirmed report," and noted a conflicting statement from SNCC headquarters in Atlanta that "there was no ambulance involved and that the mounted deputies charged into the crowd without provocation." NYT, March 16, 1965, p. 31.

110   the contrast of bustling normalcy at an airport concourse: Int. Willie (Ricks) Mukasa, May 14, 1992.

110   Carmichael collapsed on the floor: Int. Kwame Ture (Stokely Carmichael), Jan. 31, 1984.

110   Lady Bird Johnson stoically watched: Johnson, *Diary,* p. 252.

110   "fourteen goddam wooden fingers": Rowan, *Breaking,* p. 250.

111   heard no sound from the arriving sphinx: Goodwin, *Remembering,* p. 330.

111   script changes that lengthened Goodwin's draft: "President's Remarks to Accompany Voting Message, Draft 1 Goodwin, 3/15/65," as compared with "Remarks of the President to a Joint Session of Congress, March 15, 1965 (As Actually Delivered) (9:02 P.M. EST)," Moyers Papers, Box 6, LBJ.

111   Where Goodwin exhorted: Ibid.

111   a boycott by the entire Mississippi and Virginia delegations: Mann, *Walls,* p. 461.

112   his largest television audience—some seventy million viewers: Garrow, *Bearing,* p. 408.

112   "I speak tonight for the dignity of man": "Remarks of the President to a Joint Session of Congress, March 15, 1965 (As Actually Delivered) (9:02 P.M. EST)," Moyers Papers, Box 6, LBJ.

112   chamber that seemed stunned and on edge: Goldman, *Tragedy,* pp. 378–79.

113   a first lone clap: Richard B. Stolley, "The Nation Surges to Join the Negro on His March," *Life,* March 26, 1965, p. 35; Goodwin, *Remembering,* p. 332.

113   quotation from St. Mark: Mark 8:36.

114   a standing ovation spread in waves: WP, March 16, 1965, p. 1.

114   "remarkable views of the reaction of Congress": NYT, March 16, 1965, p. 31.

114   one of two threats of searing disgrace: Richard B. Stolley, "The Nation Surges to Join the Negro on His March," *Life,* March 26, 1965, p. 35; *Newsweek,* March 29, 1965; Mann, *Walls,* p. 461. There is conflict in these accounts about whether it was the first or last half of the printed speech that wound up on the TelePrompTer. The latter is more consistent with details in common. Mann quotes Valenti's comment to the TelePrompTer operator: "I almost died a thousand deaths getting it here in time."

114   quietly muttered, "Goddam": Mann, *Walls,* p. 463; int. Harry McPherson, Sept. 24, 1991, and Nov. 15, 2001.

114   "a turncoat": Kotz, *Judgment Days,* p. 319.

114   "a dagger in your heart": Remarks of Joseph Smitherman in *Eyes on the Prize,* Part 1, Episode 6, "Bridge to Freedom (1965)," Blackside, Inc., 1986.

114   "Can you believe he said that?": Int. Jean Jackson, May 27, 1990.

115   A tear rolled down King's cheek: Remarks of C. T. Vivian in *Eyes on the Prize,* Part 1, Episode 6, "Bridge to Freedom (1965)," Blackside, Inc., 1986; Lewis, *Walking,* pp. 339–40.

115   A second standing ovation: WP, March 16, 1965, p. 1.

115   "Manny, I want you to start hearings tonight": *Newsweek,* March 29, 1965.

115   "Jack, how did I do?": Goodwin, *Remembering,* p. 336.

11: HALF-INCH HAILSTONES

PAGE

116   "There cannot be anyone alive": Editors' News Service Dispatch 311, "President's Address Draws Strong Support from Morning Newspapers and Columnists," March 17, 1965, Legislative Background, Voting Rights Act of 1965, Box 1, LBJ.

116   Chicago mayor Richard Daley called to praise: LBJ phone call with Richard Daley, 10:03 A.M., March 16, 1965, Cit. 7069, Audiotape WH6503.07, LBJ.

117   "That was a terrific speech": LBJ phone call with Thomas Watson, 4:19 P.M., March 16, 1965, Cit. 7071, Audiotape WH6503.07, LBJ.

117   all eighteen assistant majority whips: PDD, March 16, 1965, LBJ.

118   pass these four above all others: Ibid., note, p. 5.

118   Seminarians Judith Upham and Jonathan Daniels suffered an acute letdown: Judy Upham oral history dated June 6, 1966, pp. 14–15, JDC.

118   James Bevel told morning crowds: Mobile to Director, March 16, 1965, FDCA-624; Mobile LHM dated March 19, 1965, FDCA-693, pp. 14–16.

118   they could not bring themselves to wrap up: Morris Samuel int. by John B. Morris, Feb. 1966, pp. 19–20, JDC.

118   "The imperative was too clear": Eagles, *Outside Agitator,* p. 38.

118   drop seminary for the term and pack Upham's Volkswagen: Ibid., p. 40.

118   James Forman led a crisis march of some six hundred students: Forman, *Sammy Younge,* pp. 99–100. Forman puts the number at more than a thousand. Other sources cited below vary the estimates between six hundred and a thousand.

119   "wearing a cowboy hat": Fager, *Selma, 1965,* p. 139.

119   spun from a yard with a lit cigar: *Eyes on the Prize,* Part 1, Episode 6, "Bridge to Freedom (1965)," Blackside, Inc., 1986.

119   "the sound of the nightstick carried": NYT, March 17, 1965, pp. 1, 26.

119   "That cracker was just talkin' shit": Int. James Bevel, Dec. 10, 1998; int. James Forman, Feb. 13, 2001.

119   They muted their ongoing dispute: WATS report, March 16, 1965, Reel 15, SNCC.

119   signs from nineteen scattered schools: Ibid.

120   "We are deeply astonished": Dr. Erno Ottlyk to MLK, March 22, 1965, A/KP21f12.

120   another 250 Wayne State University students: Stanton, *From Selma,* p. 138.

120   "Prior to today I felt": Ibid., p. 139.

120   the daughter of a Tennessee coal miner: Ibid., pp. 83–91, 154.

120   Alice Herz realized: Int. Helga Herz, Dec. 3, 2001.

120   She had joined the first giant march: Shibata, ed., *Phoenix,* pp. 158–59.

120   poured two cans of Energine dry cleaning fluid: Ibid., p. 153.

121   "GOD IS NOT MOCKED": Ibid., p. 3.

121   Alice Herz struggled ten days: Robinson, *Abraham,* p. 202.

121   She had confided nothing: Int. Helga Herz, Dec. 3, 2001.

121   "When you understand why": Shibata, ed., *Phoenix,* p. 157; Zaroulis and Sullivan, *Who Spoke Up?,* p. 3.

121   "A holy courage must animate": Alice Herz to Shingo Shibata, May 1, 1952, in Shibata, ed., *Phoenix,* pp. 35–37.

121   first Vietnam peace casualty: DeBenedetti, *Ordeal,* p. 107.

121   the late mass meeting in Montgomery: Fager, *Selma, 1965,* p. 140.

121   "There's only one man in this country": *Eyes on the Prize,* Part 1, Episode 6, "Bridge to Freedom (1965)," Blackside, Inc., 1986.

122   "the last time I wanted to participate": Forman, *Sammy Younge,* p. 99.

122   King came behind him with a fiery speech: Fager, *Selma, 1965,* p. 140.

122   "The cup of endurance": Arlie Schardt, "Tension, Not Split, in the Negro Ranks," *Christian Century,* May 12, 1965, pp. 614–16.

122   "It won't be forthcoming": Sikora, *Judge,* pp. 222–23.

122   nearly two thousand people on a mile-long walk: NYT, March 18, 1965, p. 1; Fager, *Selma, 1965,* pp. 140–41.

122   a spasm of national publicity: Garrow, *Protest,* pp. 108–10.

123   Other photographs on an inside page: NYT, March 17, 1965, p. 26.

123   National Press Club banned females: WP, March 17, 1965, p. 1.

123   "We are sorry there was a mix-up": NYT, March 17, 1965, p. 1.

123   "Police protection was thoroughly organized": Benjamin R. Epstein, "Notes on a Visit to Selma," RSP1.

123   Half-inch hailstones fell: SAC, Mobile, to Director, 2:03 A.M. CST, March 18, 1965, FDCA-656; Mobile LHM dated March 19, 1965, FDCA-693, pp. 17–18.

123   emerging at 5:15 P.M.: NYT, March 18, 1965, pp. 1, 21.

123   "There are points that we agree on": *Eyes on the Prize,* Part 1, Episode 6, "Bridge to Freedom (1965)," Blackside, Inc., 1986.

12: NEUTRALIZE THEIR ANXIETIES

PAGE

124   they could catch a plane to New Orleans: Sikora, *Judge,* p. 226.

124   "I am opposed to every word": *Congressional Record,* March 18, 1965, p. 5388.

124   "As American citizens, they have faith in America": Ibid., p. 5402.

124   opposed sending the bill to committee: Garrow, *Protest,* p. 113.

125   "I didn't experience fear": Associated Press, *World in 1965,* p. 60.

125   With Deputy Defense Secretary Cyrus Vance: Before taking the arranged call from Governor Wallace, President Johnson met for half an hour with Katzenbach, Ellington, Vance, Bill Moyers, Jack Valenti, and Lee White. PDD, March 18, 1965, LBJ.

125   "pourin' in from all over the country": LBJ phone call with Governor George Wallace, 4:33 P.M., March 18, 1965, Cit. 7094-96, Audiotape WH6503.09, LBJ.

126   on cue for live statewide television: Jones, *Wallace Story,* p. 403.

127   "And it is upon these people": STJ, March 21, 1965, p. 5; FBI transcript dated March 20, 1965, FSMM-NR.

127   Thunderous cheers answered his concluding appeal: Carter, *Politics,* p. 256.

127   "I've been leavin' since 3:30": LBJ phone call with Buford Ellington, 9:13 P.M., March 18, 1965, Cit. 7124, Audiotape WH6503.10, LBJ.

127   "in comes this goddam wire": LBJ phone call with Nicholas Katzenbach, 10:00 P.M., March 18, 1965, Cit. 7129-30, Audiotape WH6503.10, LBJ.

128   "in a highly agitated condition": Hoover to Tolson et al., 1:41 P.M., March 19, 1965, FCT-NR.

128   reached the LBJ Ranch before two o'clock: PDD, March 18, 1965, pp. 8–9, LBJ.

128   Anderson Watts was merely his sharecropper: BAA, March 27, 1965, p. 2.

129   When police arrested eighty-four of the students: WATS report, March 18, 1965, Reel 15, SNCC.

129   At midnight, the most persistent thirty-six: WATS report, March 19, 1965, Reel 15, SNCC.

129   "Willie Ricks told you to say that": Int. Willie (Ricks) Mukasa, May 14, 1992.

129   "Come here, son": Ibid. Also Sellers, *River,* p. 124; int. Cleveland Sellers, Dec. 14, 1983. Sellers places this incident a few days earlier in Selma, but Mukasa remembers Montgomery and details consistent with the later date.

129   "I've known people who sold out": Int. Robert Castle, March 3, 1993.

130   He offered more than once to bounce them: Int. Richmond Smiley, Dec. 28, 1983; int. Richmond Smiley by Judy Barton, Jan. 27, 1972, A/OH.

130   "I'll be just like Rockefeller's wife": Int. Metz Rollins, Dec. 13, 1991.

130   Bayard Rustin urge King to renounce: FBI LHM dated March 20, 1965, FSMM-162, p. 2.

130   "the Reverend's show": SAC, Jackson, to Director and Mobile, March 19, 1965, FSMM-91, p. 2.

130   "Everybody's entitled to one": Int. Ivanhoe Donaldson, Nov. 30, 2000.

130   littered church basements: BAA, March 27, 1965, p. 2.

130   outdoor soundstage out of stacked coffin crates: Int. Ivanhoe Donaldson, Nov. 30, 2000; NYT, March 25, 1965, p. 27; Lewis, *Walking,* p. 345.

130   Donaldson and SNCC's Frank Soracco undertook the delicate assignment: Int. Frank Soracco, Sept. 13, 1990; int. Ivanhoe Donaldson, Nov. 30, 2000; Fager, *Selma, 1965,* pp. 145–46.

131   They selected Rev. F. Goldthwaite Sherrill: Shattuck, *Episcopalians,* p. 155.

131   "Arguments take place in any family": *Christian Century,* May 12, 1965, pp. 614–16.

131   "two hotheaded extremists": "Inside Report: Danger from the Left," WP, March 18, 1965, p. 25.

131   "political timing": Branch, *Pillar,* p. 587.

131   "get a martyr": SAC, Mobile, to Director, March 19, 1965, FSMM-249.

131   "sufficiently to neutralize their anxieties": FBI LHM dated March 20, 1965, FSMM-162, p. 2.

132   Forman . . . agreed to suspend demonstrations: Rosen to Belmont, March 20, 1965, FSMM-23.

132   "two-day nervous breakdown": *Esquire,* Jan. 1967, p. 135.

132   His experimental motto was "use King": Int. Kwame Ture (Stokely Carmichael), Jan. 30, 1984.

132   he drove into the wilds with a stack of leaflets: Greenberg, ed., *Circle,* pp. 98–99; int. Bob Mants, Sept. 8, 2000. SNCC workers Judy Richardson and Willie Vaughn also were present.

132   John Jackson: John Jackson int. by Robert Wright, Aug. 3, 1968, RJBOH; int. John Jackson, March 25, 2005.

133   for the county's first political meeting of Negroes: Eagles, *Outside Agitator,* pp. 122–26; Matthew Jackson int. by Robert Wright, Aug. 4, 1968, RJBOH; Emma Jackson int. by Robert Wright, Aug. 4, 1968, RJBOH; int. John Hulett, Sept. 8, 2000; int. Rocena Haralson, Feb. 16, 2001; int. Charles Smith, Feb. 16, 2001.

133   "almost began to feel up to my ears": Recorded memoir by Atkins Preston, Medical Committee for Human Rights, courtesy of Meredith Kopald, Albuquerque, New Mexico.

133   "This is stupid": Fager, *Selma, 1965,* p. 144.

133   "at least we had good music": NYT, March 20, 1965, p. 13.

133   "No white churchman is going to be free": Transcript, "The Saga of Selma: A Tape Recording by ESCRU," JDC, p. 3.

134   "with good hearts, good feet": Ibid., p. 7.

134   James Bevel followed with a featured address: "The Saga of Selma: A Tape Recording by ESCRU," AEC.

134   soul tune by Garnet Mimms & the Enchanters: "Quiet Place," as identified courtesy of blues scholar Guido van Rijn of the Netherlands.

134   "Call your missionaries from Africa": Ibid.

135   "but I have a problem with shabbat": Int. Isreal Dresner, July 31, 1991.

135   had found seeds of a surprising bond: Branch, *Pillar,* pp. 21–32.

135   Heschel consulted fellow authorities: Int. Sylvia Heschel, Feb. 4, 1991.

135   visit friends at five different ranches: PDD, March 19, 1965, LBJ.

135   "likely to leak some time": Moyers to LBJ, with 7:00 P.M. cover note, March 19, 1965, Legislative Background, VRA '65, Box 1, LBJ.

135   "Cy Vance strongly": Ibid.

135   suppression of the Whiskey Rebellion: NYT, March 21, 1965, p. 71.

135   Sixty-eight of them landed: Ibid. Also SAC, San Antonio, to Director, 9:09 P.M., March 19, 1965, FSMM-12; BAA, March 27, 1965, p. 1.

136   retired at three o'clock: PDD, March 19, 1965, LBJ.

136   Lady Bird sitting nearby under a shawl: NYT, March 21, 1965, p. 1.

136   "Over the next several days": "The President's News Conference at the LBJ Ranch," 11:00 A.M., March 20, 1965, PPP, pp. 299–307.

136   "somewhat of a family quarrel": Transcript, "The Saga of Selma: A Tape Recording by ESCRU," JDC, pp. 5–9.

136   the bishops conducted Communion services: Shattuck, *Episcopalians,* p. 155.

136   homemade sausages and fifty more sandwiches were ready: Charles V. Willie, "Reflections on a Saturday in Selma," RSP2, BIR/C15f30.

136   Viola Liuzzo processed newcomers at one of the welcome tables: Stanton, *From Selma,* p. 155.

136   Hank Thomas wandered carefully: Int. Hank Thomas, March 14, 1991.

137   "By late Saturday": Fager, *Selma, 1965,* p. 149.

137   "not particularly tense": NYT, March 21, 1965, p. 76.

137   FBI agents reported the Leo Haley incident: Mobile LHM dated March 22, 1965, FDCA-721; NYT, March 21, 1965, p. 76.

137   "get that damn nigger Martin Luther King": McGowan to Rosen, March 20, 1965, FSMM-118.

137   immensely relieved that military units: Hoover first resisted the idea that FBI agents

would have any contact at all with the politically dangerous Alabama authorities, scrawling on a memo, "I thought the military (Federal) was in control." However, Inspector Joseph Sullivan bravely argued that the Bureau must have contact with both warring sides in Alabama in order to fulfill its duties as observers, in case there were violations of the federal court order. Hoover, under pressure from LBJ, permitted carefully limited contact behind a great show of FBI presence. See Belmont to Tolson, March 19, 1965, FSMM-177; Rosen to Belmont, March 20, 1965, FDCA-759.

137 "Immediately contact airlines": Director to "All SACs, Continental Offices," March 19, 1965, FSMM-45.

137 "a total of 1,856 persons are already in Selma": Rosen to Belmont, March 20, 1965, FSMM-179.

137 priests from Connecticut: SAC, Mobile, to Director, March 20, 1965, FSMM-105.

137 Greyhound bus from Dallas: SAC, Jackson, to Director, March 19, 1965, FSMM-91.

137 Assistant Director DeLoach summarized: DeLoach to Hoover, March 20, 1965, FRW-NR; M. A. Jones to DeLoach, March 16, 1965, FRW-NR.

138 "the best truck farmers in America": M. A. Jones to Nichols, Aug. 30, 1956, FRW-NR.

138 They joined Vice President Humphrey: WS, March 21, 1965, p. 1.

138 had contrived his Texas retreat: NYT, March 20, 1965, p. 13.

138 "We're havin' a small war": WS, March 21, 1965, p. 15.

139 *Atlanta Journal and Constitution* resolved to boycott: Comments of Bill Shipp, "Covering the South: A National Symposium on the Media and the Civil Rights Movement," Center for the Study of Southern Culture, University of Mississippi, 1987.

139 "Gene, let's go over and catch the bus": Int. Eugene Patterson, April 6, 1991.

139 had wrestled with the race issue in prize-winning columns: Egerton, *Speak*, pp. 256–58, 331–34.

139 "the most melancholy aspect": Shattuck, *Episcopalians*, p. 118.

139 "Damn, it would be fun": Int. Eugene Patterson, April 6, 1991.

13: TO MONTGOMERY

PAGE

140 Our Lady of the Universe: Moyers to LBJ, March 21, 1965, Box 56, WH Confidential, LBJ.

140 demolition team arrived from the Third Army's 142nd Ordnance Detachment: Mayor Albert Boutwell to LBJ, March 23, 1965, Ex HU2/ST1, Box 24, LBJ.

140 "dashed up the hill to Mr. Shores's house": NYT, March 22, 1965, pp. 1, 27.

140 over special hotlines: "Field Commanders in Alabama Linked by 'Hot Line' to Pentagon," NYT, March 22, 1965, p. 1.

141 turning out specialized breakfasts: Int. Jean Jackson, May 29, 1990.

141 FBI agents recorded: FBI Selma to Director, March 21, 1965, FSMM-83.

141 doctors completed medical exams: McGowan to Rosen, March 21, 1965, FSMM-154, p. 2.

141 Heschel from the Hebrew scriptures: Benjamin R. Epstein, "Notes on a Visit to Selma," RSP1, p. 3.

141 A high delegation of Episcopalians returned from St. Paul's: Transcript, "The Saga of Selma: A Tape Recording by ESCRU," JDC, p. 10.

141 "Hawaii Knows Integration Works": WP, March 22, 1965, p. 10.

141   King wore one around his neck: Ibid. Also Webb and Nelson, *Selma, Lord, Selma,* p. 124.

141   Attorney General Katzenbach funneled to the White House: Katzenbach memo un-headed, closed "3-21-65, 12:15 P.M.," HU/ST1, FG/35, Box 28, LBJ.

141   would take longer: McGowan to Rosen, March 21, 1965, FSMM-154, p. 3.

142   "C. P. T., Colored People Time": Renata Adler, "Letter from Selma," *New Yorker,* April 10, 1965, p. 121.

142   lurched forward at 12:46 P.M.: FBI Selma to Director, March 21, 1965, FSMM-48. The *New York Times* put the start time a minute later at 12:47, NYT, March 21, 1965, p. 26.

142   the networks would fire anyone who missed impact footage: Int. Frank Soracco, Sept. 12–14, 1990; Young, *Burden,* p. 364.

142   a moving shield of volunteer marshals: Int. Ivanhoe Donaldson, Nov. 30, 2000; Fager, *Selma, 1965,* pp. 150–51.

142   with nineteen jeeps and four military trucks: FBI Selma to Director, March 21, 1965, FSMM-48.

142   a red roadster played "Dixie": WP, March 22, 1965, p. 10.

142   Demonstrative females seemed comparatively undaunted: "Great Day at Trickem Fork," *Saturday Evening Post,* May 22, 1965, p. 89.

142   A well-dressed woman got out of her Chrysler: Renata Adler, "Letter from Selma," *New Yorker,* April 10, 1965, p. 124.

142   Silas Norman shellacked the floor: Int. Silas Norman, June 28, 2000; int. Ivanhoe Donaldson, Nov. 30, 2000.

143   "The federal government has given them everything": NYT, March 22, 1965, p. 26; WP, March 22, 1965, p. 10.

143   Brigadier General Henry Graham: Ibid. Also Branch, *Parting,* pp. 463–65, 471.

143   Jonathan Daniels and Judith Upham approached Selma: Judy Upham oral history dated June 6, 1966, p. 19, JDC.

143   "another mood—jubilation": Adler, "Letter from Selma," *New Yorker,* April 10, 1965, p. 124.

143   Harris Wofford trotted among latecomers: Wofford, *Kennedys and Kings,* p. 187.

143   "felt my legs were praying": Int. Sylvia Heschel, Feb. 4, 1991; Neusner, *Grow,* p. 206.

143   the youngest participant in a stroller: Lisa Maria Stone of Pasadena, California, age fifteen months, as identified in WP, March 22, 1965, p. 10.

143   FBI agents photographed seventeen cars: FBI Selma to Director, March 21, 1965, FSMM-48.

143   "Coonsville, USA": *Jet,* April 8, 1965, p. 8.

144   galloped wildly toward the march: Wofford, *Kennedys and Kings,* p. 189.

144   "I'm going out of service!": NYT, March 22, 1965, p. 26.

144   multitude ate bologna sandwiches: WP, March 22, 1965, p. 10.

144   John Doar argued: Int. John Doar, May 12, 1986.

144   halted the run fifteen miles outside Montgomery: McGowan to Rosen, March 21, 1965, FSMM-154; Hoover to Katzenbach, March 22, 1965, FSMM-3.

144   David Hall's field at 5:07 P.M.: FBI Selma to Director, March 21, 1965, FSMM-48, p. 5.

144   donated by the International Ladies Garment Workers Union: McGowan to Rosen, March 21, 1965, FSMM-154, p. 6.

144   three tons of supper: Fager, *Selma, 1965,* p. 151; WP, March 22, 1965, p. 10.

144   nine-car train special loaded a thousand people: Mobile LHM dated March 26, 1965, FSMM-374, p. 14; NYT, March 22, 1965, p. 26.

145 Bill Moyers notified President Johnson: Moyers to LBJ, "Bombing Devices Found in Birmingham," 10:45 P.M., March 21, 1965, WH Confidential, Box 56, LBJ.

145 a penniless rebellion trip at the age of seventeen: Caro, *Path,* pp. 123–29.

145 "we ate pork and beans three times a day": PDD, March 22, 1965, p. 2, LBJ.

145 his foreman about a newborn goat kid: PDD, March 21, 1965, p. 2, LBJ.

145 cans of oatmeal before six o'clock: FBI Selma to Director, March 22, 1965, FSMM-157; Fager, *Selma, 1965,* p. 153.

145 some walked barefoot: Associated Press, *Year in 1965,* pp. 52–53, WP, March 22, 1965, p. 1.

145 "There are about 392 people": Joseph A. Califano, Jr., the Special Assistant, to McNamara et al., "Report as of 1200," March 22, 1965, Ex HU2/ST1, Box 24, LBJ.

145 a lone Piper Cub: Rosen to Belmont, March 22, 1965, FSMM-226. "This is the same leaflet that was dropped on demonstrators in Selma on March 13, 1965," Rosen noted.

145 "noticeably increased": WP, March 22, 1965, p. 1.

146 A demolition team took lead position: FBI Selma to Director, March 22, 1965, FSMM-200.

146 Major General Carl Turner: Ibid.

146 Andrew Young's announcement: Ibid., p. 3; Wofford, *Kennedys and Kings,* p. 189.

146 157 from Dallas: FBI Selma to Director, March 22, 1965, FSMM-135, p. 2.

146 "Dr. King's Special Guests": Wofford, *Kennedys and Kings,* p. 189; Mobile LHM dated March 26, 1965, FSMM-374, p. 18. The FBI compiled a partial list of the "notables": George Fowler, chairman, New York State Commission on Human Rights; Theodore Gill, San Francisco Theological Seminary; Dr. J. Alfred Cannon, professor of psychology, UCLA Medical School; Robert Gist, Screen Directors Guild; Jeremiah Gutman, Lawyers Constitutional Defense Committee; Reverend Rodney Shaw, Christian Social Conference, Methodist Church; Henry D. Ginigini, assistant to Senator Dan Inonyi [sic]. FBI documents from the previous day's march called Rabbi Heschel "Abraham Hersch."

146 "Pick it up, now!": WP, March 22, 1965, p. 1.

146 FBI agents counted 308 marchers: Mobile LHM dated March 26, 1965, FSMM-374, p. 19.

146 "Report No. 2 as of 1400": Califano to McNamara et al., "Report No. 2 as of 1400," March 22, 1965, Ex HU2/ST1, Box 24, LBJ. Califano's military sources put the number of whites on the march at thirty-seven. There is a discrepancy of fifteen from the preceding FBI count at approximately the same time, due to error, the continuous flux of arrivals, and perhaps confusion over marchers versus staff.

146 "opaque waters dotted with lily pads": Fager, *Selma, 1965,* p. 154.

146 250 of the marchers needed medical treatment: Mobile LHM dated March 26, 1965, FSMM-374, p. 18.

146 King removed his green marching hat: Int. John Lewis by Archie E. Allen, Jan. 20, 1979, AAP.

146 Negro teenagers wrote "VOTE": Kasher, *Movement,* p. 187; Moore, *Powerful,* p. 188.

146 Sister Mary Leoline of Kansas City: *Jet,* April 8, 1965, pp. 11–12; WP, March 22, 1965, p. 1.

147 hopped on one leg with crutches: Adler, "Letter from Selma," *New Yorker,* April 10, 1965, p. 131; Moore, *Powerful,* pp. 192–93; Associated Press, *Year in 1965,* p. 51.

147 causing Worth Long of SNCC to howl: Int. Ivanhoe Donaldson, Nov. 30, 2000; int. Frank Soracco, Sept. 12–14, 1990.

147 · Bevel and others coerced: Ibid.

147 Soracco chased weary dawdlers: *Saturday Evening Post,* May 22, 1965, p. 92.

147 "I'm used to walking": *Jet,* April 8, 1965, p. 11.

147 he had stood numb near the courthouse lawn: Int. Mary Lee (Jackson) King, June 28, 2000.

147 "Lordy!": "Great Day at Trickem Fork," *Saturday Evening Post,* May 22, 1965, p. 90.

147 Mattie Lee Moorer threw her arms: Eagles, *Outside Agitator,* p. 126.

147 "the ladies took Dr. King away from me": Int. Mattie Lee Moorer, March 10, 2000.

148 "I done kissed him!": *Saturday Evening Post,* May 22, 1965, p. 90.

148 "Lord, I Cannot Stay": Int. Mattie Lee Moorer, March 10, 2000.

148 Rolen Elementary: Adler, "Letter from Selma," *New Yorker,* April 10, 1965, p. 132; Fager, *Selma, 1965,* p. 155.

148 Coretta King joined the march: King, *My Life,* p. 268; Wofford, *Kennedys and Kings,* pp. 190–91.

148 joined the ranks with a small flock of nieces: Int. Timothy Mays, March 9, 2000.

148 "Well, you're shaking hands with him now": *Saturday Evening Post,* May 22, 1965, p. 92.

148 "I'll walk one step, anyway": Adler, "Letter from Selma," *New Yorker,* April 10, 1965, p. 135.

148 an imperfectly healed broken leg: Int. Rocena Haralson, Feb. 16, 2001.

148 camp in a cow pasture infested with red ants: FBI Selma to Director, March 22, 1965, FSMM-200, p. 4.

149 "when prices was up": BAA, April 3, 1965, p. 13.

149 a teenager sneaked under a tent flap: Adler, "Letter from Selma," *New Yorker,* April 10, 1965, p. 138.

149 "Well, actually, ma'am": Ibid.

149 soaked blistered feet in a tub: Int. Jean Jackson, May 27, 1990.

149 returning to overnight at Steele's campsite: Rosen to Belmont, March 23, 1965, FSMM-239, p. 2.

149 "Mr. Young is in charge": Califano to McNamara et al., "Report No. 6 as of 1000," March 23, 1965, Ex HU2/ST1, Box 24, LBJ.

149 space launch of Gemini 3: PDD, March 23, 1965, LBJ; Associated Press, *Year in 1965,* pp. 60–62.

149 Team Alpha to Team Bravo: Califano to McNamara et al., "Report No. 3 as of 1600," March 22, 1965, Ex HU2/ST1, Box 24, LBJ.

149 "It hit with drops as big as quarters": *Saturday Evening Post,* May 22, 1965, p. 92.

150 "a nigger won't stay out in the rain": Adler, "Letter from Selma," *New Yorker,* April 10, 1965, p. 144.

150 "A few youngsters put on cornflakes boxes for hats": "Alabama March Passes Midpoint," NYT, March 24, 1965, p. 1.

150 "Reverend Abernickel": Wofford, *Kennedys and Kings,* pp. 192–93.

150 obediently turned outward: Ibid.; Fager, *Selma, 1965,* pp. 156–57.

150 "Just tell him no": LBJ phone call with Drew Pearson, 11:35 A.M., March 23, 1965, Cit. 7139–40, Audiotape WH6503.11, LBJ.

150 Johnson continued seamlessly: PDD, March 23, 1965, LBJ, p. 2.

150 "Sometimes I just get all hunkered up": Diary of Ambassador David K. E. Bruce, in FRUS, Vol. 2, pp. 471–72.

151 "It is still raining": Califano to McNamara et al., "Report No. 7 as of 1300," March 23, 1965, Ex HU2/ST1, Box 24, LBJ.

151   congratulate Gemini 3 astronauts: PDD, March 23, 1965, p. 4, LBJ.

151   "I think we've got you something": LBJ phone call with John McCormack, Wilbur Mills, Wilbur Cohen, and Carl Albert, 4:54 P.M., March 23, 1965, Cit. 7141–42, Audiotape WH6503.11, LBJ.

152   "a sea of mud": FBI Selma to Director, March 23, 1965, FSMM-201.

152   bales of hay and straw: Ibid., p. 3; NYT, March 24, 1965, p. 1.

152   "community sing": Mobile LHM dated March 26, 1965, FSMM-374, p. 20.

152   Odetta found Pete Seeger: Adler, "Letter from Selma," *New Yorker,* April 10, 1965, pp. 146–48.

152   recruited seminarian Jonathan Daniels: Eagles, *Outside Agitator,* p. 41.

152   broke down into shouts and seizures: FBI Selma to Director, March 23, 1965, FSMM-215; Rosen to Belmont, March 23, 1965, FSMM-239.

152   extra creosote cleaner in a rented water truck: FBI LHM dated March 24, 1965, FSMM-258, p. 2; FBI Selma to Director, March 24, 1965, FSMM-188; McGowan to Rosen, March 24, 1965, FSMM-218.

152   Wet Guardsmen on perimeter duty broke discipline: NYT, March 24, 1965, p. 33.

152   "You goddam kids": Wofford, *Kennedys and Kings,* pp. 193–94.

152   Two photographers scuffled: Fager, *Selma, 1965,* p. 157.

152   arrested one of twenty-eight pickets at the Hotel Sheraton: NYT, March 24, 1965, p. 32.

152   William Walker, whose family in Selma: Cleveland LHM dated March 24, 1965, FK-1097.

153   made room for two Ohio priests: Rev. Edward J. Griffin and Rev. Thomas J. Gallagher, per SAC, Cleveland to Director, March 24, 1965, FSMM-317.

153   before seven o'clock Wednesday morning: Hoover to Katzenbach, March 25, 1965, FSMM-214.

153   Jonathan Daniels hitched a ride back: Judy Upham tape 2, oral history dated June 6, 1966, p. 20, JDC.

153   "All those who wish to take hot baths": Adler, "Letter from Selma," *New Yorker,* April 10, 1965, p. 144.

153   The march doubled to 675 people: Hoover to Katzenbach, March 25, 1965, FSMM-214.

153   crash impact on the moon crater Alphonsus: Associated Press, *Year in 1965,* p. 65.

153   WHHY broadcast news: Adler, "Letter from Selma," *New Yorker,* April 10, 1965, p. 148; NYT, March 24, 1965, p. 33; Wofford, *Kennedys and Kings,* pp. 194–95.

153   King rejoined the columns: Mobile LHM dated March 26, 1965, FSMM-374, pp. 24–25.

153   delegation from the Anti-Defamation League: Epstein, "Notes on a Visit to Selma," p. 4, RSP1.

154   thunderstorms at 1:30: Mobile LHM dated March 26, 1965, FSMM-374, p. 23; *Saturday Evening Post,* May 22, 1965, p. 93.

154   officials processed a rash of unseen threats: FBI HQ LHM dated March 24, 1965, FSMM-258; Hoover to Katzenbach, March 25, 1965, FSMM-214.

154   "The latest estimates ran": Califano to McNamara et al., "Report No. 11 as of 1630," March 24, 1965, Ex HU2/ST1, Box 24, LBJ.

154   twenty prominent historians: NYT, March 23, 1965, p. 28.

154   stranded all night by balky crews: FBI HQ LHM dated March 24, 1965, FSMM-258, p. 2; BAA, April 3, 1965, p. 12.

154   Two hundred students came straight from Kilbey State Prison: NYT, March 24, 1965, p. 33; int. Charles Strain, DePaul University, Feb. 21, 2002.

154   "a grandeur that was almost biblical": NYT, March 25, 1965, p. 1, cited in Garrow, *Protest,* p. 116.

154   Hands passed food: Wofford, *Kennedys and Kings,* p. 196; Fager, *Selma, 1965,* p. 158.

154   Poles snapped on two of the field tents: FBI Mobile to Director, March 24, 1965, FSMM-320.

14: THE STAKES OF HISTORY

PAGE

155   "sit on your tail up there in Boston": LBJ conversation with Henry Cabot Lodge, 3:35 P.M., March 24, 1965, Cit. 7145-46, Audiotape WH6503.12, LBJ.

156   flayed Lodge to confidants: Cf. Dictabelt of LBJ conversation with McGeorge Bundy, 5:55 P.M., Dec. 9, 1963, LBJ.

156   "ain't worth a damn": Branch, *Pillar,* pp. 308–9.

156   "things screwed up good": Dictabelt of LBJ conversation with William Fulbright, 7:01 P.M., December 2, 1963, LBJ.

156   Johnson blamed Lodge for conniving: Branch, *Pillar,* pp. 176–77.

156   McNamara considered him: McNamara, *In Retrospect,* p. 106.

156   "thinks he's emperor out there": LBJ conversation with Richard Russell, 10:55 A.M., May 27, 1964, Cit. 3519a, Audiotape WH6405.10, LBJ.

156   "crossed the Rubicon": Taylor, *Swords,* p. 341.

156   "The Vietnamese have no tradition": McGeorge Bundy to LBJ, March 8, 1965, with attached "Memorandum by the Presidential Consultant on Vietnam (Lodge)," March 8, 1965, in FRUS, Vol. 2, pp. 414–20. Johnson referred to the March 8 memo in his March 25 conversation with Lodge, Cit. 7147-49. The White House diary states that he and Lodge took an eleven-minute walk on March 9, shortly before the second attempted march from Selma to Montgomery. "No other record of their conversation has been found," noted the official FRUS historians who published the declassified papers in 1996.

156   Ambassador Taylor consistently opposed: Cf. McNamara, *In Retrospect,* p. 174; Logevall, *Choosing,* pp. 295, 362, 369; FRUS, Vol. 2, pp. 12–19, 347–49, 408–11, 554–55.

156   "sap the already flaccid purpose": FRUS, Vol. 2, pp. 486–90.

156   "white-faced soldier, armed, equipped": Taylor, top secret telegram to Rusk, Feb. 22, 1965, in FRUS, Vol. 2, pp. 347–49, cited in Langguth, *Vietnam,* p. 348.

156   "Don't you mention this other thing": LBJ conversation with Henry Cabot Lodge, 3:35 P.M., March 24, 1965, Cit. 7145–46, Audiotape WH6503.12, LBJ.

157   "work moratorium": Menashe and Radosh, *Teach-Ins,* pp. 4–16.

157   "we have not yet learned": Ibid., pp. 59–64.

157   confusion on the verge of panic: Fager, *Selma, 1965,* pp. 158–59; Wofford, *Kennedys and Kings,* pp. 195–96; Adler, "Letter from Selma," *New Yorker,* April 10, 1965, pp. 150–51.

157   Equipment failure left the St. Jude campsite: FBI Selma to Director, March 25, 1965, FSMM-314.

157   ten thousand close to thirty thousand: Mobile LHM dated March 26, 1965, FSMM-374, p. 31; Hoover to Katzenbach, March 26, 1965, FSMM-214, p. 3.

157   fifty-seven people collapsed: NYT, March 25, 1965, p. 27.

157   Coretta King read: Wofford, *Kennedys and Kings,* p. 196; King, *My Life,* p. 269.

157   "I was born and reared just eighty miles from here": "The Saga of Selma: A Tape Recording by ESCRU," AEC.

158   Viola Liuzzo of Detroit slept in her car: Stanton, *From Selma,* p. 164.

158   another contentious late staff meeting: Int. Richmond Smiley, Dec. 28, 1983; int. Jack Pratt, March 25, 1991.

158   a delegation of 293 landing at 4:45 A.M. from Burbank: Rabbi Jacob Pressman, "March on Montgomery," March 27, 1965, A/KP21f12.

158   four hundred people from New York City: NYT, March 25, 1965, p. 27.

158   a long line of rumbling buses: Epstein, "Notes on a Visit to Selma," RSP1, p. 4.

158   the university tower struck eight o'clock: Menashe and Radosh, *Teach-Ins,* p. 7.

158   the conscious model of SNCC's Freedom Schools: Ibid., p. 9; Cagin and Dray, *Not Afraid,* pp. 173–74. William Gamson, chair of the University of Michigan Sociology Department, suggested the Vietnam civic action at an informal meeting of faculty on March 11.

158   The "teach-in" phenomenon: Viorst, *Fire,* p. 398; Wells, *War Within,* p. 24; Powers, *War,* pp. 55–56.

158   "Good morning, sir, how did you sleep?": LBJ conversation with Henry Cabot Lodge, 8:52 A.M., March 25, 1965, Cit. 7147-49, Audiotape WH6503.12, LBJ.

158   "I am smoking too many of them": LBJ conversation with Nicholas Katzenbach, 9:35 A.M., March 25, 1965, Cit. 7150, Audiotape WH6503.12, LBJ.

159   "an acre of English ground": Associated Press, *World in 1965,* pp. 94–95.

159   planted three PT-109 tie clasps: Ibid., pp. 58–59; Thomas, *Robert Kennedy,* pp. 306–7.

159   "Where is my immigration bill": LBJ conversation with Edward Kennedy, 12:44 P.M., March 25, 1965, Cit. 7156, Audiotape WH6503.13, LBJ.

159   "The tents have been taken down": Califano to McNamara et al., "Report No. 12 as of 1000," March 25, 1965, Ex HU2/ST1, Box 24, LBJ.

159   he scrawled a hasty addendum: Califano, "Memorandum for the President, SUB-JECT: Montgomery Situation Report as of 1100 EST," March 25, 1965, Ex HU2/ST1, Box 24, LBJ.

159   "I'm Dr. Bunche": Int. Jack Pratt, March 25, 1991. Pratt, a lawyer on the staff of the Commission on Religion and Race, from the National Council of Churches, was serving as chauffeur for the King party.

160   "Make way for the originals": Adler, "Letter from Selma," *New Yorker,* April 10, 1965, p. 153.

160   Newcomers surged around them: Fager, *Selma, 1965,* p. 159.

160   "our president told us Dr. King": "50-Mile Marchers Irked," *Washington Evening Star,* March 26, 1965, p. 5.

160   "All you dignitaries": Ibid.

160   "You fellows deserve to go first": Wofford, *Kennedys and Kings,* p. 197.

160   to serve summons on several legal actions: FBI Selma to Director, March 25, 1965, FSMM-314; Rosen to Belmont, March 25, 1965, FSMM-339.

161   a host of clergy including Orloff Miller: Adler, "Letter from Selma," *New Yorker,* April 10, 1965, p. 153; Johnson and Adelman, *Photobiography,* pp. 198–99.

161   Rosa Parks found herself shoved: Brinkley, *Rosa Parks,* pp. 198–99.

161   "I *was* in it, but they put me out": Orson, *Freedom's Daughters,* pp. 343–44.

161   Viola Liuzzo asked a priest: Fager, *Selma, 1965,* p. 160.

161   carrying her purse and shoes: Stanton, *From Selma,* pp. 164–65.

161   "It required one hour": Mobile LHM dated March 26, 1965, FSMM-374, p. 31.

161   104 road-blocked intersections: WS, March 25, 1965, p. 1.

161   touched depths of an odyssey come home: Abernathy, *Walls*, p. 357; King, *My Life*, p. 270.

161   St. Jude hospital where Coretta had given birth: King, *My Life*, p. 268.

161   down Oak Street past Holt Street Baptist Church: Miller, *Martin*, p. 230.

161   "Many cried": WS, March 25, 1965, p. 1.

161   "This is it": BAA, April 3, 1965, p. 2.

161   business district that was eerily deserted: Harrington, *Fragments*, p. 127.

161   Governor Wallace had proclaimed: Fager, *Selma, 1965*, p. 161; Carter, *Politics*, p. 256; Lesher, *George Wallace*, p. 337.

162   showered with leaflets: FBI Selma to Director, March 25, 1965, FSMM-314, pp. 6–7.

162   twenty-fifth anniversary of Highlander: Garrow, *Bearing*, p. 98. Speech text from tape recording, MVC.

162   Tennessee had persecuted: Branch, *Parting*, pp. 121–22, 289–90, 825–26.

162   centerpiece of an attack campaign: Ibid., pp. 853–54; Branch, *Pillar*, pp. 189–90.

162   John Doar had watched mobs beat: Branch, *Parting*, p. 447.

162   Judge Johnson bristled against all street politics: Sikora, *Judge*, pp. 147–48.

162   "something special about democracy": Ibid., p. 231; Bass, *Unlikely*, p. 262.

162   Soldiers stood behind wooden barricades: NYT, March 26, 1965, p. 22. The *Times* reported the soldiers stationed "about every 25 feet." CBS News said ten feet apart.

162   "I believe in you": Lewis, *Walking*, pp. 343–45.

162   he shook a crutch defiantly: Wofford, *Kennedys and Kings*, p. 197.

162   "You're only likely to see": Adler, "Letter from Selma," *New Yorker*, April 10, 1965, p. 154.

163   Harwell Mason slave pen: Branch, *Parting*, p. 2.

163   "Segregation After Death": Ibid., p. 12.

163   along with Coretta's parents: King, *My Life*, p. 270.

163   Negroes and integrationists, plywood temporarily covered: *Washington Evening Star*, March 25, 1965, p. 1.

163   "This is a revolution": Wofford, *Kennedys and Kings*, p. 198.

163   a black mourning banner would fly: Jones, *Wallace Story*, p. 429.

163   "to show that socialism has taken over": DeLoach to Mohr, March 22, 1965, FSMM-237.

163   "Let's teach 'em the words!": Epstein, "Notes on a Visit to Selma," p. 4, RSP1.

163   singers grouped around the cluster of microphones: Johnson and Adelman, *Photobiography*, p. 201.

163   "Great day!": CBS News Special Report: *Civil Rights March on Montgomery*, March 25, 1965, Tape T79:0049051, MOB.

164   "makes a Southerner's blood run hot": Jones, *Wallace Story*, p. 429.

164   threatened CBS News president Fred Friendly: Friendly, *Circumstances*, p. 171.

164   "I look worse than anybody else": Adler, "Letter from Selma," *New Yorker*, April 10, 1965, p. 156.

164   Some prostrate orange vests could not be roused: Int. Frank Soracco, Sept. 13, 1990; int. Ivanhoe Donaldson, Nov. 30, 2000.

164   extra speakers into the all-male procession: Program list provided by Andrew Young; FBI Selma to Director, March 25, 1965, FSMM-314, pp. 4–6.

164   Amelia Boynton of Selma read a petition: Text of petition "read by Mrs. Amelia Boynton," in SAC, Mobile, to Director, March 27, 1965, FSMM-362.

164   "My family was deprived": *Civil Rights March on Montgomery,* March 25, 1965, Tape T79:0049051, MOB.

164   Faltering, she said others could put it all better into words: Wofford, *Kennedys and Kings,* p. 199.

164   "They told us we wouldn't get here": Transcript of address labeled "Steps of the Capitol, Montgomery, Alabama, 'How Long? Not Long,' " March 25, 1965, A/KS, reconciled with John B. Morris recording in "The Saga of Selma: A Tape Recording by ESCRU," AEC.

164   Already he strayed from lyrical prepared remarks: "Address by Dr. Martin Luther King, Jr.," March 25, 1965, A/KS.

164   King looked over heads: Johnson and Adelman, *Photobiography,* pp. 200–201.

164   cameras from every network: Garrow, *Protest,* p. 117; Friendly, *Circumstances,* p. 171.

165   King had refined with fellow preachers since graduate school: Branch, *Parting,* p. 93.

165   Southern states had permitted biracial voting: Woodward, *Jim Crow,* p. 54.

165   white supremacists themselves had ridiculed the crippling inconvenience: Ibid., pp. 67–69.

167   banish any fraternal organization: Ibid., p. 100.

167   "The river was dyed red": Wood, *Radicalism,* p. 175.

167   "as though their marriages were legal": Ibid., pp. 176–77.

169   Governor Wallace watched three television sets: Jones, *Wallace Story,* p. 432.

169   What lasted in print: NYT, March 26, 1965, p. 22; Washington, ed., *Testament,* pp. 227–30.

170   "I come to say to you this afternoon": Transcript of address labeled, "Steps of the Capitol, Montgomery, Alabama, 'How Long? Not Long,' " March 25, 1965, A/KS, reconciled with John B. Morris recording in "The Saga of Selma: A Tape Recording by ESCRU," AEC; NYT, March 26, 1965, p. 22.

170   "Because truth crushed to earth": Quotation from William Cullen Bryant (1794–1878), "The Battle-Field"; cf. Carson and Holloran, eds., *Knock,* p. 14.

170   "Because no lie can live forever": Quotation from Thomas Carlyle (1795–1881).

170   "Because you shall reap what you sow": Paraphrase of Galatians 6:7.

170   " 'Truth forever on the scaffold' ": Quotation from James Russell Lowell (1819–91), *The Present Crisis.*

170   "Because the arc of the moral universe": Quotation from Rev. Theodore Parker (1810–60).

15: AFTERSHOCKS

PAGE

171   "Who is our leader?": "The Saga of Selma: A Tape Recording by ESCRU," AEC.

171   "I know of no other woman": CBS News Special Report: *Civil Rights March on Montgomery,* March 25, 1965, Tape T79:0049051, MOB.

171   Abernathy dismissed the crowd with reminders: SAC, Mobile, to Director, March 25, 1965, FSMM-313; Rabbi Jacob Pressman, "March on Montgomery," March 27, 1965, A/KP21f12.

171   "Stragglers must not remain": Leaflet instructions headed, "Welcome to the March on Montgomery," A/KP21f12.

171   "Within ten minutes": Adler, "Letter from Selma," *New Yorker,* April 10, 1965, p. 157.

171   "two or three places": "President Turns Cabinet Meeting into Impromptu News Conference," WP, March 26, 1965, p. 1.

171   "God have mercy on your souls": NYT, March 26, 1965, p. 23.

171   "heavy budget of news": Horace Busby to LBJ, March 26, 1965, Box 52, Horace Busby Papers, LBJ.

171   This was a mild version: LBJ to Collins, March 25, 1965, and Collins to LBJ, March 24, 1965, Ex FG/ST1, Box 229, LBJ.

172   Jonathan Daniels knelt quietly on the pavement: Eagles, *Outside Agitator,* p. 42.

172   loaded Upham's Volkswagen: Judy Upham oral history dated June 6, 1966, pp. 21–22, JDC.

172   recognized Viola Liuzzo: FBI interview with Samuel Edmondson, Saginaw, Michigan, April 1, 1965, in Mobile report dated April 2, 1965, FVL-128; FBI interview with Louis Miller in SAC, Memphis, to Director, April 2, 1965, FVL-125.

172   nineteen-year-old volunteer Leroy Moton: Stanton, *From Selma,* p. 169; FBI interview with Leroy Moton, March 26, 1965, FVL-11.

172   Liuzzo tried to calm her passengers: FBI interviews with passengers Clarissa Brown, Carla Austin, Lizbeth Stewart, and Clarence Smith, Jr., March 26, 1965, in Mobile report dated April 12, 1965, FVL-295.

172   of four Birmingham Klansmen: Stanton, *From Selma,* pp. 46–50; Sikora, *Judge,* pp. 244–49; Rowe, *Undercover,* pp. 165–71; deposition of Gary Thomas Rowe, Jr., April 27, 1965, in *Beulah Mae Donald et al. v. United Klans of America,* Civil Action 84-0725-C-S, U.S. District Court for the Southern District of Alabama.

173   Eugene Thomas had been obliged to display: Ibid. When arrested the next morning, Thomas possessed a "Special Police Badge" from Fairfield, Alabama, with his name engraved, plus special deputy commissions from the city of Bessemer, Alabama, and from Jefferson County (Birmingham). Mobile FBI report dated March 30, 1965, pp. 23–24, FVL-NR.

173   The Klansmen followed Liuzzo: Stanton, *From Selma,* pp. 50–51; Sikora, *Judge,* pp. 250–53.

174   Leroy Moton was absorbed with the radio dial: Sikora, *Judge,* pp. 257–58.

174   Moton managed to turn off the engine: Ibid. Also NYT, March 27, 1965, pp. 1, 10; BAA, April 3, 1965, p. 1, April 10, 1965, p. 17; Chaves, *Ordaining,* pp. 193–94.

174   driven by a Disciples of Christ minister: Mendelsohn, *Martyrs,* pp. 185–86; FBI Selma to Director, 4:37 A.M., March 26, 1965, FVL-99.

174   let two nieces of Napoleon Mays: Int. Timothy Mays, March 9, 2000.

174   "The woman is from Michigan?": LBJ phone call with Nicholas Katzenbach, 11:25 P.M., March 25, 1965, Cit. 7160, Audiotape WH6503.13, LBJ.

174   Just before one o'clock: LBJ called to "FBI Duty Officer, Agent Herbert," 12:55 A.M., March 26, 1965, PDD, LBJ; Rosen to Belmont, March 26, 1965, FVL-156.

174   FBI inspector Joe Sullivan: On his way to the scene, Sullivan called the FBI with the first word of the Liuzzo shooting at 10:30 P.M. Washington time, about ninety minutes after the crime. Rosen to Belmont, March 25, 1965, FSMM-315; Rosen to Belmont, March 25, 1965, FVL-3.

175   At 1:49 A.M., Diane Nash: Rosen to Belmont, March 26, 1965, FVL-NR.

175   "The president just called me": Int. Joseph Sullivan, March 3, 1991.

175   enabled Sullivan to sense something extraordinary: Ibid.

175   "one of our men *in* the car": LBJ phone call with J. Edgar Hoover, 8:10 A.M., March 26, 1965, Cit. 7162, Audiotape WH6503.13, LBJ.

176   "Do you know Hoover had a guy": Int. Jack Valenti, Feb. 25, 1991.

176   "Looks like we'll be pretty much": LBJ phone call with Nicholas Katzenbach, 8:20 A.M., March 26, 1965, Cit. 7163, Audiotape WH6503.13, LBJ.

176   remain sealed from its background: Int. Nicholas Katzenbach, June 14, 1991.

176   He tasked White House lawyer Lee White: LBJ phone call with Lee White, 8:40 A.M., March 26, 1965, Cit. 7164, Audiotape WH6503.13, LBJ.

176   "much in control of himself": LBJ phone call with Lee White, 9:27 A.M., March 26, 1965, Cit. 7165–66, Audiotape WH6503.13, LBJ.

177   "the appearance of a necking party": Hoover to Tolson et al., 9:32 A.M., March 26, 1965, FVL-16.

177   slanderous Klan fantasy dressed as evidence: Selma to Director, March 26, 1965, FVL-19; Detroit FBI report dated April 1, 1965, FVL-117, p. 89; Rosen to Belmont, April 5, 1965, FVL-162; Stanton, *From Selma,* pp. 52–53; O'Reilly *"Racial,"* pp. 216–17; Sikora, *Judge,* p. 256.

177   "Yes, he's a Teamster man": LBJ phone call with J. Edgar Hoover, 9:36 A.M., March 26, 1965, Cit. 7167, Audiotape WH6503.13, LBJ.

178   "hold off until after the case is broken": Addendum marked "9:45 A.M.," Hoover to Tolson et al., 9:32 A.M., March 26, 1965, FVL-16.

178   "paternalistic at best": Powers, *Secrecy,* pp. 410–11.

178   potentially ruinous secrets: The career of Gary Thomas Rowe as an FBI informant is presented officially in the Headquarters Informant File for informant BH 248-PCI (RAC). His most notorious Klan activity was a central role in the May 14, 1961, beating of Freedom Riders at the Birmingham Trailways terminal, with prior sanction from both the Birmingham police and the FBI, as first detailed in 1975 by the U.S. Senate Select Committee to Study Governmental Operations with Respect to Intelligence Activities (known as the Church Committee), headed by Senator Frank Church of Idaho. See U.S. Department of Justice Task Force Report entitled *The FBI, the Department of Justice, and Gary Thomas Rowe, Jr.,* Washington, D.C.; Branch, *Parting,* pp. 420–22; Stanton, *From Selma,* pp. 208–10. For sketches of Rowe's involvement in many acts of Klan violence while an informant, see McWhorter, *Carry,* pp. 177–78, 192–93, 204–9, 212–13, 256, 434–37, 500–501.

178   prior FBI approval to ride: Sikora, *Judge,* p. 243.

178   "Hoover panicked": Stanton, *From Selma,* p. 52.

178   in unmailed letters recovered from her car: Rosen to Belmont, April 5, 1965, FVL-162.

179   a record White House news day: Brink, *Black and White,* p. 212; PDD, March 26, 1965, LBJ.

179   "So when the House acts": Miller, *Lyndon,* p. 500.

179   not to bump *Search for Tomorrow:* Friendly, *Circumstances,* pp. 172–74.

179   Johnson called the Liuzzo house at 12:30: NYT, March 27, 1965, p. 10.

179   "the terrorists of the Ku Klux Klan": "Televised Remarks Announcing the Arrest of Members of the Ku Klux Klan," March 26, 1965, PPP, pp. 332–33; statement, Office of the White House Press Secretary, preserved in King's files at A/KP13f7.

180   triumph gave way to renewed crisis: Belmont to Tolson, March 26, 1965, FVL-154.

180   had returned secretly to the crime scene: FBI Birmingham to Director and Mobile (Selma), March 26, 1965, FVL-9.

180   arraignment in full Klan character: Rowe, *Undercover,* pp. 180–85.

180   "an unexplained four-hour delay": NYT, March 26, 1965, p. 10.

180   "all agents must keep their mouths shut": Belmont to Hoover, March 26, 1965, FVL-33.

180   "I want no comments nor amplifications": Hoover addendum on Belmont to Tolson, March 26, 1965, FVL-154. Headquarters relayed these instructions by telephone in advance of regular channels, as reported in McGowan to Rosen, March 29, 1965, FVL-173.

180   his decision to call King the nation's most notorious liar: Jones to DeLoach, "Representative Wendell Wyatt (R.-Oregon), Meeting with Director, March 25, 1965, FK-NR.

181   "blinded by prejudice": Baumgardner to Sullivan, March 23, 1965, "Subject: Communism and the Negro Movement—A Current Analysis," FK-NR.

181   refused to cut his hair: Johnson, *Diary,* p. 254.

181   UPI national ticker at 2:26 P.M.: Tavel to Mohr, March 30, 1965, FVL-NR.

181   "The FBI had that car": NYT, March 28, 1965, p. 58.

181   "a malicious lie": Ibid.

181   "I had to blast the story": Hoover to Tolson et al., 1:38 P.M., March 29, 1965, FCT-NR.

181   DeLoach wisely advised colleagues: DeLoach to Mohr, March 28, 1965, FVL-NR.

182   explain why it took seven hours: Tavel to Mohr, March 30, 1965, FVL-NR.

182   one unfortunate assistant admitted leaving: Ibid.

182   "another vindication of the propriety": Jones to DeLoach, March 29, 1965, FVL-NR.

182   "an authentic American folk hero": "Durable F.B.I. Chief: John Edgar Hoover," NYT, March 27, 1965, p. 11.

182   "an impressive monument to efficiency and integrity": Ibid.

182   Martin Luther King sent Hoover a telegram of thanks: Garrow, *Bearing,* p. 413.

183   "would only help build up this character": DeLoach to Mohr, March 28, 1965, FVL-NR.

183   Producers had agreed to film him: Spivak to MLK, March 27, 1965, A/KP17f17; Garrow, *Bearing,* p. 414.

183   "I would say that the march was not silly at all": Transcript, *Meet the Press,* March 28, 1965, A/SC4f42.

184   Bishop Carpenter of Alabama had brokered: Carpenter to "The Congregation of St. Paul's Church, Selma, Alabama," March 25, 1965, BIR/C8f24; John B. Morris, "To All Bishops," March 27, 1965, BIR/C11f5; STJ, March 28, 1965, p. 1; Bishop George Murray to Rt. Rev. John E. Hines, March 25, 1965, BIR/C11f5.

184   Wilson Baker arrested an armed member of Sheriff Clark's posse: Mobile LHM dated April 2, 1965, FDCA-771, pp. 4–5.

184   two anguished pastoral letters that week: Rev. T. Frank Mathews to "My dear Fellow Churchmen," March 23, 1965, BIR/C10f50; Rev. T. Frank Mathews to "My dear Fellow Churchmen," March 25, 1965, BIR/C8f24. Excerpts from the second letter: "It may be of some help to all of us to visualize the consequences had not this resolution-of-compliance-with-the-Canons been adopted. As a priest of the Episcopal Church, it is clear that I would have to resign as your rector. You would not be able to replace me with another Episcopal priest, since this congregation would have to dissolve its communion with the Protestant Episcopal Church in the U.S.A. As individuals and as a group you would no longer be Episcopalians and the Book of Common Prayer would no longer be yours. . . . I know all of you are 'Big' people who love your church with a big love. As an Episcopal Church, we must abide by the Canons. . . . Unless the group

is disorderly and creating a disturbance (in which case it is the canonical responsibility of the ushers to refuse them admittance), it is not for us to judge any man's motives for attending church. Perhaps *our* motives are not always as pure as they should be; I know *mine* are not. But I do know that our Vestry has seen its duty and it has done it— and I am proud of them."

184   "That was as bad as my senior sermon": NYT, March 29, 1965, p. 29.

184   "the first breakthrough in Selma": ESCRU newsletter, Selma Supplement, April 4, 1965, p. 1.

184   "Glory to God in the highest!": Eagles, *Outside Agitator,* pp. 47–51.

184   "Selma Protestant Church Integrated for First Time": NYT, March 29, 1965, p. 1.

184   Morris complained: Rev. John B. Morris to Andrew Young, April 2, 1965, A/SC44f12.

184   *"now,* while people are still in motion": Minutes, "12:30 A.M., Friday," March 26, 1965, Reel 37, SNCC.

185   Sunday afternoon stringing power cords: W. C. Heinz and Bard Lindeman, "Great Day at Trickem Fork," *Saturday Evening Post,* May 22, 1965, p. 94.

185   Storekeeper William Cosby presided: Mobile LHM dated April 2, 1965, FDCA-771, p. 5.

185   the featured speaker at Mt. Gillard: Ibid.

185   Lafayette had ventured into Selma: Branch, *Pillar,* pp. 63–66, 81–85.

185   "too much leadership concentrated": Int. Bernard Lafayette, May 28, 1990.

185   "An immediate result of Mrs. Liuzzo's death": NYT, March 28, 1965, p. 58.

185   "suggested to you that you tap a line": LBJ phone call with Nicholas Katzenbach, 6:42 P.M., March 29, 1965, Cit. 7179–80, Audiotape WH6503.14, LBJ.

186   another visit to the White House: Alsop had visited the White House for the same purpose on March 4, 1965. See Moyers to LBJ, "(One Copy Only)," March 4, 1965, Office of the President, Moyers, Box 8, LBJ.

187   Alsop, ironically, was both the conduit and the victim: Branch, *Pillar,* pp. 293–95.

188   Alsop biographer Edwin Yoder would unearth documents: Yoder, *Joe Alsop's,* pp. 152–56.

188   "but I like him, and I'm his friend": LBJ phone call with Nicholas Katzenbach, 6:42 P.M., March 29, 1965, Cit. 7179–80, Audiotape WH6503.14, LBJ.

188   Philip Graham . . . committed suicide: Graham, *Personal,* p. 331.

188   Katzenbach formally ordered: Powers, *Secrecy,* p. 402; Gentry, *Hoover,* p. 583.

188   Only the President's surprise initiative: Int. Nicholas Katzenbach, June 14, 1991.

188   memorial service that Liuzzo's: NYT, March 30, 1965, p. 30.

189   privately reproached both Myers and Sayers: Stanton, *From Selma,* pp. 176–77; Emrich to Carpenter, April 1, 1965, BIR/C15f29.

189   "what a bitter pill it was": George M. Murray to Mathews, March 25, 1965, BIR/C10f50.

189   a bargain for their departure: Judy Upham oral history dated June 9, 1966, pp. 1–2, JDC.

189   Church lawyers picked at Carpenter's interpretation: Eagles, *Outside Agitator,* p. 51.

189   "Losing this family would be a terrific financial blow": Mathews handwritten response on Murray to Mathews, June 18, 1965, BIR/C10f53. The exchange comments on the resignation of St. Paul's vestryman David McCullough, as recorded in McCullough to Mathews and Carpenter, April 10, 1965, and Mrs. D. N. (Annette) McCullough to Carpenter, April 17, 1965, both BIR/C8f24. Mrs. McCullough's handwritten letter to Bishop Carpenter is typical of the dissent: "I cannot understand the change in

our Episcopal Churches, ministers & Bishops. Some of the ministers are actually being made hypocrites, because they do not believe in all these canon changes & integration in our churches. These are *man made laws not God's laws.* Can't any of you see all this forcing of the negro race in everything we do is the Communistic plan? The fact is that all this is leading up to one thing, negroes and whites marrying & to me that's the most sinful thing that our churches & mainly Episcopal ones are doing. . . . I have worked with the altar guild & taken care of the altar linen for years, but I cannot do it now or go to church. This has just about broken our hearts."

189   "If she is cured": Mathews to "Germy," July 27, 1965, commenting on the "idiotic letter" of Mrs. Hugh Underwood, BIR/C10f54.

189   Bishop Carpenter curdled against the movement: Branch, *Parting,* pp. 737–45.

190   "having the limb cut out from under me": Carpenter to Bishop Reuben H. Mueller, March 30, 1965, BIR/C11f5. The reply for the National Council of Churches is Edwin Espy to Carpenter, April 14, 1965, BIR/C15f29.

190   "After the nail has been driven": Carpenter to C. Kilmer Myers, March 19, 1965, BIR/C15f28. Another rebuke over Selma is Carpenter to Myers, March 24, 1965, BIR/C15f28.

190   "rude and inexcusable": Carpenter to Rt. Rev. Richard S. Emrich ("Dear Joe"), April 6, 1965, BIR/C15f29.

190   "I have not answered him at all": Ibid.

190   "When we answer somebody": Emrich to Carpenter, April 1, 1965, BIR/C15f29.

190   a red leather saddle and a model village: PDD, March 29, 1965, pp. 6–7, LBJ.

190   sedan stalled by the riverfront hotel: FRUS, Vol. 2, p. 494; Langguth, *Vietnam,* pp. 351–52; Sheehan, *Bright,* pp. 463–64; NYT, March 30, 1965, p. 1; STJ, March 30, 1965, p. 1.

191   "we're not sure if it's male or female": LBJ phone call with Situation Room duty officer, 8:10 A.M., March 30, 1965, Cit. 7181, Audiotape WH6503.16, LBJ.

191   "cleared up the policy on taps": LBJ phone call with Robert McNamara, 8:14 A.M., March 30, 1965, Cit. 7182, Audiotape WH6503.16, LBJ.

191   the White House was preparing a statement: "Statement by the President on the Bombing of the U.S. Embassy in Saigon, March 30, 1965," PPP, 1965, p. 347.

191   "with a high wall around it": LBJ phone call with McGeorge Bundy, 9:12 A.M., March 30, 1965, Cit. 7183–84, Audiotape WH6503.16, LBJ.

191   fellow New England aristocrat: Bird, *Color,* pp. 15, 32; Yoder, *Joe Alsop's,* pp. 33–39.

191   an ambulance, a truck, twenty-six cars: WATS report, Selma, March 29, 1965, March 30, 1965, 12:45 P.M. and 1:30 A.M., Reel 15, SNCC; Mobile LHM dated April 2, 1965, p. 6, FDCA-771.

192   longshoreman and hotel bellhop: Branch, *Pillar,* pp. 125–27.

192   had defied his own deacons to open Tabernacle Baptist: Ibid., pp. 64–65, 81–84.

192   "hasten the day when every man": NYT, March 31, 1965, p. 16.

192   assigning Lowndes among new trial projects: Int. Silas Norman, June 28, 2000; int. Bob Mants, Sept. 8, 2000; int. Timothy Mays, March 9, 2000.

192   "Don't go to Greene County": Int. Mattie Lee Moorer, March 10, 2000.

192   Golden Frinks of North Carolina: Mobile LHM dated April 2, 1965, p. 6, FDCA-771, p. 7; Branch, *Pillar,* pp. 139–41.

192   "I pay traffic fines here": *Chicago Tribune,* March 31, 1965, p. 14.

193   an anticlimactic freedom petition to the governor: "Wallace Meets Biracial Group," NYT, March 31, 1965, p. 1; SAC, Mobile, to Director, March 27, 1965, FSMM-362.

16: BEARINGS IN A WHIRLWIND

PAGE

194   by way of Los Angeles: SAC, Los Angeles, to Director, March 29, 1965, FK-1076.

194   to record him among the dignitaries: *Jet,* April 22, 1965, pp. 28–29; Stanton, *From Selma,* p. 178.

194   "soon died out because few knew the words": NYT, March 31, 1965, p. 22.

194   Observed from the gate by FBI surveillance agents: FBI New York to Director, March 31, 1965, FK-1148.

194   King suffered a letdown from Selma: Int. Harry Wachtel, Nov. 29, 1983; int. Clarence Jones, Jan. 16, 1984; int. Bayard Rustin, Sept. 24, 1984; int. Andrew Young, Oct. 26, 1991.

194   a windfall gift of $25,000 for SCLC: Hoffa to King, March 29, 1965, A/KP12f44; King to Hoffa, April 12, 1965, A/KP12f44.

195   Wachtel forwarded the papers to Anthony Liuzzo: Wachtel to Anthony Liuzzo, March 31, 1965, A/KP25f29.

195   he privately called "stupid": Hoover to Katzenbach, April 2, 1965, FSC-279; FBI HQ LHM dated April 2, 1965, FK-2831.

195   announcing in King's name: NYT, March 28, 1965, p. 1.

195   "we want the federal government to come in here": Fairclough, *Redeem,* p. 258.

195   "are of course admirable": NYT, March 30, 1965, p. 46.

195   Other newspapers decried the notion: BAA, April 3, 1965, p. 24.

195   SCLC board met through the week: Garrow, *Bearing,* pp. 415–17.

195   "throw thousands of Negroes in Alabama": NYT, April 2, 1965, p. 24.

195   "with a fifty-dollar hat": Garrow, *Bearing,* p. 415.

195   into the cities of the North: Minutes, SCLC board meeting, April 1–2, 1965, p. 1, A/KP29f5.

195   Bevel wondered what could trouble city Negroes: Int. Bernard Lafayette, May 28, 1990.

196   Rustin, who favored attention to issues of economic justice: NYT, March 12, 1965, p. 17.

196   "We must not split what we have": Minutes, SCLC board meeting, April 1–2, 1965, A/KP29f5.

196   Bevel campaigned to undermine him with King's executive staff: Int. Hosea Williams, Oct. 29, 1991.

196   somewhere at the Atlanta airport: FBI Baltimore to Director, April 1, 1965, FVL-75.

196   "and I am busier than Hoover": SAC, Atlanta, to Director, April 14, 1965, FSC-NR.

196   Pressures of the world stage: Minutes, SCLC board meeting, April 1–2, 1965, pp. 1–16, A/KP29f5; Jesse L. Douglas to MLK, April 7, 1965, A/SC144f17; C. T. Vivian to MLK, April 9, 1965, A/KP28f2; Chauncey Eskridge to Andrew Young, April 13, 1965, A/SC39.

197   "I know of no one that articulates my ideas": Minutes, SCLC board meeting, April 1–2, 1965, p. 7, A/KP29f5.

197   Board members first recoiled in shock: Garrow, *Bearing,* p. 417.

197   depressed before Selma: Ibid. Branch, *Pillar,* pp. 530–33, 540–43.

197   a new black mistress of stylish discretion: Int. Clarence Jones, Jan. 16, 1984; int. John Lewis, May 31, 1984; confidential interviews; Garrow, *Bearing,* p. 421.

198   Settlement was imminent: Garrow, *Bearing,* p. 421.

198   house of $10,000 was a haunting luxury: Ibid. Also Stein, *Journey,* pp. 108–9.

198   "conscience fairly devoured him": King, *My Life,* pp. 75, 179.

198   *Afro-American* devoted an issue: BAA, April 3, 1965, pp. 1, 27–28.

198   fraud arrests at a local barber school: *Baltimore Sun,* April 1, 1965, p. 54.

198   Rev. C. K. Steele admonished King: Garrow, *Bearing,* p. 417.

198   Rustin disparaged Abernathy: Int. Bayard Rustin, Sept. 24, 1984.

199   "Who are we": Int. Clarence Jones, Jan. 16, 1984; int. Harry Wachtel, Nov. 29, 1983; int. Bayard Rustin, Sept. 24, 1984; int. Andrew Young, Oct. 26, 1991.

199   "We must by all means protect his symbolism": Minutes, SCLC board meeting, April 1–2, 1965, p. 11, A/KP29f5.

199   King sought out Stanley Levison: Hoover to Katzenbach, April 15, 1965, FK-1212; Fairclough, *Redeem,* p. 257.

199   "Dear Martin": Levison to MLK, April 7, 1965, A/KP14f40.

199   Wachtel and others slowly accommodated: Int. Harry Wachtel, Nov. 29, 1983.

199   scour future SCOPE workers: Hoover to SAC, Albany, "Summer Community Organization and Political Education (SCOPE) Program, Information Concerning (Internal Security)," n.d. (April 1965, based on Baumgardner to Sullivan, April 8, 1965), FSC-NR. Hoover's instructions concluded: "All offices are cautioned to conduct no inquiry which might give the impression that the FBI is investigating the legitimate activities of the SCLC."

199   "If we can obtain information disproving": Hoover to SACs, Atlanta, Knoxville, April 6, 1965, FK-1154.

199   Levison had read to fill hours: Int. Beatrice Levison, Jan. 3, 1984; int. Andrew Levison, Aug. 6, 1999.

199   "Selma was bigger than Birmingham": Levison to MLK, April 7, 1965, A/KP14f40.

200   King was "too humble": Int. Beatrice Levison, Jan. 3, 1984.

201   electing a broomstick: Wood, *Radicalism,* p. 366.

201   ordained the first female rabbi: Nadell, *Women,* pp. 168–69. Recent scholarship suggests that Regina Jonas of Offenbach, Germany, may have become history's first female rabbi in 1935, but Jonas and most records of the era were lost in the Holocaust. Cf. Elisa Klapheck, *Fräulein Rabbiner Jonas: The Story of the First Female Rabbi.* Wiley, 2004.

202   "a natural inclination in mankind": Wood, *Radicalism,* p. 28.

17: TEN FEET TALL

PAGE

205   Sculptress Jimilu Mason: PDD, April 6, 1965, p. 3, LBJ.

205   "I'm going to hold out that carrot": Steel, *Walter Lippmann,* pp. 562–63; Bird, *Color,* p. 316.

205   "The vast Mekong River": PPP, 1965, pp. 394–99.

205   Johnson mentioned a dream to end war itself: LBJ sent a succinct note of credo and congratulations to his confidante on issues of world peace and economics, British economist Barbara Ward: "My dear Barbara: Much of what you have written and what you have said and what you inspired was in that Baltimore speech. I have said that we must understand the world as it is if ever we want it to be as we wish. The Baltimore speech says exactly what I believe and what I hope." LBJ to "Lady [Barbara Ward] Jackson, April 15, 1965, Name File, Barbara Jackson, LBJ.

206   "I call heaven and earth to record": Deuteronomy 30:19.

206   "master stroke": Max Ascoli in *The Reporter,* April 22, 1965, p. 8. "His speech on Viet-

nam, which was called definitive by the newspapers even before it was delivered, is the supreme evidence of the President's capacity for arousing consent among men of hitherto different opinions," wrote Ascoli.

206 "a very timely and fine move": LBJ phone call with Dwight D. Eisenhower, 5:58 P.M., April 8, 1965, Cit. 7330, Audiotape WH6504.03, LBJ.

206 mail to the White House shifted overnight: Logevall, *Choosing,* p. 371; FRUS, Vol. 2, p. 544.

206 Goldschmidt had collaborated: Oral history int. of Arthur E. Goldschmidt and Elizabeth Wickenden, June 3, 1969, LBJ.

206 never negotiate if the positions were reversed: Dallek, *Flawed,* p. 261.

207 social policy advocate since the New Deal: Ibid. Oral history int. of Elizabeth Wickenden, Nov. 6, 1974, LBJ; Caro, *Path,* pp. 451–54.

207 "Yeah, we're gonna pass it tonight": LBJ phone call with Arthur "Tex" Goldschmidt, 10:27 A.M., April 8, 1965, Cit. 7329, Audiotape WH6504.03, LBJ.

207 Medicare did pass: Dallek, *Flawed,* p. 208.

207 Both education and voting rights cleared Senate hurdles: Associated Press, *World in 1965,* p. 259; Mann, *Walls,* p. 467.

207 Air Force jet fighter that was missing and presumed shot down: LBJ phone call with General James M. Fogel and Assistant Secretary of Defense Cyrus Vance, 12:05 A.M., April 9, 1965, Cit. 7331, Audiotape WH6504.03, LBJ; FRUS, Vol. 2, p. 535.

207 "I believe you can go": LBJ phone call with McGeorge Bundy, 11:00 A.M., April 8, 1965, Cit. 7339, Audiotape WH6504.04, LBJ.

207 the first Major League baseball game ever played indoors: Associated Press, *World in 1965,* p. 78.

207 home run to right-center: NYT, April 10, 1965, p. 1.

208 Milwaukee Braves and Detroit Tigers played: NYT, March 28, 1965, p. F-15.

208 "on ground we didn't own": Pomerantz, *Peachtree,* p. 381.

208 fifth year of a nationwide boom economy: NYT, March 28, 1965, p. F-14.

208 "I am not a prophet": "Remarks at the Dedication of the Gary Job Corps Center, San Marcos, Texas, April 10, 1965," PPP, 1965, pp. 408–12.

208 "Come over here, Miss Katie": "Remarks in Johnson City, Tex., Upon Signing the Elementary and Secondary Education Bill," April 11, 1965, PPP, 1965, pp. 412–14.

208 $1.3 billion, which covered only 6 percent: Dallek, *Flawed,* pp. 196–203; Goldman, *Tragedy,* pp. 350–63.

208 "Poverty has many roots": Associated Press, *World in 1965,* pp. 76–77.

208 Johnson waxed euphoric: Goldman, *Tragedy,* pp. 363–65.

208 He mingled at the ceremony: PDD, April 11, 1965, pp. 5–6, LBJ.

208 mimicking his awkward gringo gait: Caro, *Path,* pp. 167–71; Adler, *Johnson Humor,* p. 91.

209 Quoting Thomas Jefferson's admonition: Dallek, *Flawed,* p. 201.

209 On Palm Sunday in Selma: Eagles, *Outside Agitator,* p. 51.

209 "The bishop says": Judy Upham oral history dated June 9, 1966, p. 24, JDC.

209 pull on dress gloves: Jonathan Daniels, "A Burning Bush," *New Hampshire Churchman,* June 1965.

209 "You goddam scum": Upham and Daniels, "To Whom It May Concern," May 12, 1965, BIR/C8f24; Judy Upham oral history dated June 9, 1966, p. 25, JDC.

209 Daniels and Upham stifled rage: Daniels and Upham, "Report from Selma—April, 1965," in *Episcopal Theological School Journal,* January 1966, p. 6, JDC.

209   "There are still moments": Daniels to Mary Elizabeth Macnaughtan, April 12, 1965, in Schneider, *Martyr,* p. 72.

209   Viola Liuzzo had naively endangered herself: Judy Upham oral history dated June 6, 1966, p. 22, JDC; Morris Samuel oral history by John B. Morris, Feb. 1966, JDC.

210   a large crowd being tear-gassed in Camden: WATS report, "Camden via Selma," April 9, 1965, Reel 16, SNCC; BAA, April 17, 1965, p. 2; Judy Upham oral history, dated June 9, 1966, p. 13, JDC; Gerald Olivari, "Wilcox County," May 18, 1965, Reel 37, SNCC.

210   "a kind of grim affection": Daniels to Molly D. Thoron, April 15, 1965, in Schneider, *Martyr,* pp. 72–73.

210   Young pianist Quentin Lane: Judy Upham oral history dated June 9, 1966, p. 10, dated July 26, 1966, p. 9, JDC.

210   a breather from the stress of integration: Daniels to Mary Elizabeth Macnaughtan, April 12, 1965, in Schneider, *Martyr,* pp. 70–72.

210   "We are trying to live the Gospel": Judy Upham oral history dated July 26, 1966, p. 8, JDC.

210   "Preach it, brother": Ibid., pp. 9–16.

210   a formal letter of inquiry: Daniels and Upham to Rt. Rev. C. C. J. Carpenter, April 21, 1965, BIR/C8f24.

211   "I pray he doesn't get bumped off": Daniels to Mary Elizabeth Macnaughtan, April 12, 1965, in Schneider, *Martyr,* pp. 70–72.

211   SNCC disorganization bordering on anarchy: Carson, *Struggle,* pp. 154–57; Fleming, *Soon,* pp. 158–59.

211   "How do you deal with people": Minutes, executive committee meeting, April 12–14, 1965, Holly Springs, Miss., p. 2, SNCC Records, 1964–65, SC659, SHSW.

211   "I will not look for them": Ibid., p. 11.

211   first major rally against the Vietnam War: Cagin and Dray, *Not Afraid,* p. 438ff; Dellinger, *From Yale,* pp. 198–201; Longenecker, *Peacemaker,* p. 295; Zaroulis and Sullivan, *Who Spoke Up?,* p. 40; DeBenedetti, *Ordeal,* pp. 111–12.

211   Moses had presided: Carson, *Struggle,* pp. 111–14, 142–48; Branch, *Pillar,* pp. 193–94, 222–24.

211   left Mississippi for Selma: Minutes, executive committee meeting, April 12–14, 1965, Holly Springs, Miss., pp. 10–11, SNCC Records, 1964–65, SC659, SHSW.

211   "How many of us are willing": Minutes, SNCC meeting of "12:30 AM Friday," March 26, 1965, Folder 15-20, Reel 37, SNCC.

212   "completely fraudulent": "Special Report: The New Voting Bill," March 23, 1965, JMP.

212   "Lyndon and Hubert": *Life with Lyndon in the Great Society,* April 15, 1965, Vol. 1, No. 12, JMP.

212   "since the power structure is so immoral": Barbara Brandt, "Why People Become Corrupt," March 28, 1965, JMP.

212   "What in the hell is going on?": Penny Patch, Chris Williams, Elaine LeLott, Lewis Grant, and Ed Brown to "Sncc folk," March 19, 1965, JMP; Curry et al., *Deep,* pp. 153–65.

212   "We destroy each other": Journal of Elaine DeLott (Baker), March 16, 1965, cited in Curry et al., *Deep,* p. 278.

212   Silas Norman chastised Ivanhoe Donaldson: Minutes, executive committee meeting,

April 12–14, 1965, Holly Springs, Miss., p. 16, SNCC Records, 1964–65, SC659, SHSW.

212   "What will Julian do": Ibid., p. 27.

213   triple the personal reach of the campaign: Charles Cobb, "Atlanta, The Bond Campaign," Reel 20, SNCC; int. Frank Soracco, Sept. 13, 1990; int. Charles Cobb, Aug. 20, 1991; int. Ivanhoe Donaldson and Charles Cobb, Nov. 30, 2000.

213   "If the direction really comes": Minutes of Alabama staff meeting, April 21–22, 1965, p. 7, ASN94.

213   "People get strength from each other": Minutes of Alabama staff meeting, April 23, 1965, p. 2, ASN94.

213   lacked indoor plumbing: Int. Gloria Larry House, June 29, 2000.

213   "My head done blossomed": Int. Bob Mants, Sept. 8, 2000.

213   "I seed y'all up there": Ibid.

213   he recruited Scott B. Smith: Carson, *Struggle,* p. 163; minutes, executive committee meeting, April 12–14, 1965, Holly Springs, Miss., p. 11, SNCC Records, 1964–65, SC659, SHSW.

214   cultivated a backwoods aura: Int. Jimmy Rogers, March 7, 2000; int. Silas Norman, June 28, 2000; int. Scott B. Smith, April 11, 2003.

214   "powder keg": Minutes of Alabama staff meeting, April 23, 1965, p. 3, A/SN94.

214   "The people didn't know": Carson, *Struggle,* p. 164.

214   "go through the SNCC workers": Ibid., p. 1.

214   "Milestones on the Road to Freedom": *Boston Globe,* April 23, 1965, p. 1.

214   "For one who has been barricaded": MLK speech of April 22, 1965, Massachusetts House Document 4155, located in RFK Papers, JFK.

214   "He never mentioned Boston": "Dr. King Enthralls Legislature," *Boston Globe,* April 23, 1965, p. 19.

215   1965 Kiernan Report on Education: NYT, April 23, 1965, p. 15.

215   "Every Negro must prepare": *Boston Globe,* April 23, 1965, p. 19.

215   a weak case for a Boston movement: Int. Virgil Wood, Aug. 2, 1994; int. Paul Chapman, Nov. 4, 1994; int. Bernard Lafayette, May 28, 1990; Rev. Gilbert Caldwell to the author, Feb. 10, 1998; Boston LHM dated April 16, 1965, FK-NR.

215   "horribly divided along class lines": Archie C. Epps to MLK, April 19, 1965, A/KP33f4.

215   Elliot Richardson a sporting nickname: Int. Virgil Wood, Aug. 2, 1984; int. Hosea Williams, Oct. 29, 1991; *New York Herald Tribune,* April 24, 1965, p. 1.

215   indeed went to Selma: Kabaservice, *Guardians,* pp. 229–30.

215   The voting rights bill still faced crippling amendments: NYT, April 22, 1965, p. 21.

215   mere 1.18 percent of Negro students: MLK speech to NYC Bar Association, April 21, 1965, A/KS8, p. 11.

216   rally on Boston Common: "Dr. King, in Boston Common Rally, Warns Against Nation of Onlookers," NYT, April 24, 1965, p. 1.

216   Within sight of gravestones: NYT, March 19, 1965, p. 21.

216   "King's New Tack": *New York Herald Tribune,* April 24, 1965, p. 1.

216   Muste and Benjamin Spock: A. J. Muste to MLK, April 25, 1965, A/SC4:44; Benjamin Spock to MLK, April 30, 1965, A/KP23f4.

216   a motion to rescind an invitation to King: NYT, April 23, 1965, p. 14; NYT, April 24, 1965, p. 39; NYT, April 25, 1965, p. 56.

216   St. John's Episcopal of Savannah: NYT, April 25, 1965, p. 79; NYT, April 30, 1965, p. 13.

216   First Baptist of Houston: NYT, April 25, 1965, p. 74.

216   his sleeping pills no longer worked: Int. Harry Wachtel, May 17, 1990.

216   "not using those words, of course": Wachtel and Rustin conversation, April 21, 1965, FK-NR.

216   "Normally they're tellin' you": LBJ phone call with Lee White, 7:54 A.M., April 20, 1965, Cit. 7353-54, Audiotape WH6504.05, LBJ.

216   "None of them want to do it": LBJ phone call with Clarence Mitchell, 8:45 P.M., May 6, 1965, Cit. 7580, Audiotape WH6505.05, LBJ.

216   to picket the Bishop of Alabama: Eagles, Outside Agitator, p. 56.

216   She took off her shoes: Judy Upham oral history dated July 26, 1966, pp. 47–52, JDC.

217   leaflet of grievance against Bishop Carpenter: ESCRU statement of April 29, 1965, signed by Jonathan Daniels, Judith Upham, Rev. Albert Dreisbach, Rev. Henri Stines, and Rev. John B. Morris, BIR/C8f24. ("The Carpenter of Birmingham must not be allowed to forever deny the Carpenter of Nazareth . . .")

217   "I cannot imagine the good people": Carpenter to Daniels and Upham, April 23, 1965, BIR/C8f24.

217   When the seminarians reluctantly complied: Upham and Daniels, "To Whom It May Concern," May 12, 1965, BIR/C8f24.

217   "go to church with eyes closed": Daniels and Upham to Carpenter, April 28, 1965, in Schneider, Martyr, p. 76.

217   "There is a difference between humility": Ibid.

217   conduct involuntarily repelled Upham: Judy Upham oral history dated July 26, 1966, pp. 54–55, JDC.

217   tracked the arrival of Clarence Jones: SAC, Atlanta, to Director, April 30, 1965, FSN-NR.

217   two sides vented familiar disputes: Garrow, Bearing, pp. 423–24; Branch, Parting, pp. 578–79.

217   "more dramatic": Int. Harry Belafonte, March 6, 1985.

217   cooperative statement between King and Lewis: Joint statement, April 30, 1965, A/SC27f55.

217   "these things could not be allowed to fester": NYT, May 1, 1965, p. 9; CD, May 5, 1965, p. 4.

217   "I think the cats are honest": Minutes of Alabama staff meeting, April 21–22, 1965, p. 2, A/SN94.

217   Carmichael and Scott B. Smith ran into the seminarians again Sunday night: Judy Upham oral history, dated July 26, 1966, pp. 28, 57, JDC.

217   Daniels and Upham managed: Ibid., pp. 58–60.

218   Armed registrars processed sixty of 150 applicants: Garrow, Protest, p. 127; Eagles, Outside Agitator, p. 131.

218   week-long trial in Hayneville: Stanton, From Selma, pp. 111–23; Mendelsohn, Martyrs, pp. 191–93.

218   Inspector Joe Sullivan: Rosen to Belmont, May 4, 1965, FVL-291; Rosen to Belmont, May 6, 1965, FVL-325.

218   Klan Klonsel Matt Murphy: NYT, May 7, 1965, p. 25.

218   "treacherous as a rattlesnake": Associated Press, World in 1965, p. 198.

218   "a traitor and a pimp and an agent of Castro": NYT, May 6, 1965, p. 24.

218   "No one, prosecutor or defense lawyer": NYT, May 7, 1965, p. 25.

219   "sees you driving your Negro maid home": Ibid.

219   Katzenbach privately braced: Hoover to Tolson et al., May 7, 1965, FVL-302.

219   the jury made front-page news: "Liuzzo Case Jury Retires for Night Without a Verdict," NYT, May 7, 1965, p. 1.

219   Farmer Edmund Sallee said: NYT, May 8, 1965, p. 15.

219   "should have stayed home": "Murder in Alabama: American Wives Think Viola Liuzzo Should Have Stayed Home," Ladies' Home Journal, July 1965, pp. 42–44; Stanton, From Selma, pp. 170–72.

219   they could have won over the two holdouts: NYT, May 8, 1965, p. 15; St. Petersburg Times, May 8, 1965, p. 1, FVL-331.

219   vowing to flush him from hiding: SAC, Mobile, to Director, May 5, 1965, FVL-332.

219   Katzenbach prevailed upon Paul Johnston: NYT, May 30, 1965, p. 1; New York Herald Tribune, June 6, 1965.

220   "You presently refuse to abide": Cabaniss, Johnston, Gardner & Clark to Paul Johnston, May 24, 1965, Box 3, BIR/PJ.

220   Nationally prominent lawyers and judges: Cf. Charles Alan Wright to Johnston, May 28, 1965, Box 3, BIR/PJ; J. Skelly Wright to Johnston, June 2, 1965, Box 1, BIR/PJ; Bernard G. Segal to Johnston w/ encl. Maxwell M. Rabb to Johnston, June 3, 1965, Box 1, BIR/PJ.

220   U.S. Justice Department task force: Ralph S. Hornblower III to Michael E. Shaheen, Jr., "Synopsis of Task Force Report on Gary Thomas Rowe, Jr.," Dec. 4, 1979, DOJ, pp. 1–9.

220   detailed mass of Rowe's FBI record: McWhorter, Carry, pp. 192–213, 434–36, 542.

220   claim to have killed a black man: Ibid., pp. 500–502.

220   "What sorely troubles me": Inez Robb, "Some Disturbing Questions," Washington Daily News, May 17, 1965, p. 27, cited in Stanton, From Selma, p. 52.

220   "Back in the '30s or '40s": Handwritten note ("This is absolutely untrue . . .") on Jones to DeLoach, May 19, 1965, FVL-NR.

221   "No," Hoover scrawled: Handwritten note on Jones to DeLoach, May 25, 1965, FVL-NR.

221   "Bundy Is Unable to Appear": NYT, May 16, 1965, p. 1.

221   the principal debater's late scratch: White House memos on Bundy's planned debate include James C. Thomson to Bundy, May 14, 1965; Chester L. Cooper to Bundy, May 14, 1965; and Chester L. Cooper to Bundy, May 15, 1965, all in McGeorge Bundy Office Files, Box 18-19, LBJ. Cooper assured Bundy that he had "underplayed the nature and extent of our advance preparations" to inquiring reporters. Walt Rostow, who would succeed Bundy as National Security Adviser, represented the State Department at the teach-in and confided afterward in a classified memo that the critics "represent in academic life a minority of no great distinction." Rostow to Rusk ("Hold for Bundy"), May 17, 1965, McGeorge Bundy Office Files, Box 18–19, LBJ.

221   negotiations in the Dominican Republic: Szulc, Diary, pp. 4–11; Dallek, Flawed, pp. 262–63; Associated Press, World in 1965, pp. 88–93; Draper, Abuse, pp. 9–14.

221   patched radio feed to 100,000 listeners: DeBenedetti, Ordeal, p. 115; Powers, War, p. 61.

221   "We are here to serve notice": Menashe and Radosh, eds., Teach-Ins, pp. 156–58.

221   "the very sure and very terrible consequences": Ibid., pp. 165–71.

221   Famously, he observed: NYT, May 16, 1965, pp. 1, 62; Bird, *Color,* p. 319; Powers, *War,* p. 62.

222   parallel campus debates: Cf. Menashe and Radosh, eds., *Teach-Ins,* pp. 23–29, for an account of the teach-in at Washington University of St. Louis, which stretched over thirteen hours into the early morning of May 16.

222   limiting speakers to professors and government officials: Joan Wallach Scott, "The Teach-In: A National Movement or the End of an Affair?," in Menashe and Radosh, eds., *Teach-Ins,* pp. 190–93.

222   "battle of the eggheads": Bird, *Color,* p. 318. Journalist Meg Greenfield found the panel of war critics to be imbalanced with physical scientists and psychologists over political scientists, which she thought contributed to an overall "diffusiveness, pointlessness, and the final lack of any coherent and identifiable argument." *Reporter,* June 3, 1965, pp. 16–19.

222   Daniel Ellsberg: NYT, May 16, 1965, p. 62.

222   "from the standpoint of maximizing": NYT, May 17, 1965, pp. 30–31.

222   a more raucous panoply of speakers: Robert Randolph, "2,000 at Berkeley Teach-In on Vietnam," *National Guardian,* May 29, 1965, in Menashe and Radosh, eds., *Teach-Ins,* pp. 32–36.

222   "should be repudiated by all true scholars": Menashe and Radosh, eds., *Teach-Ins,* p. 29.

222   Staughton Lynd of Yale: Ibid., pp. 54–59.

222   expounded on the threat of nuclear annihilation: Petras, ed., *We Accuse,* pp. 73–82.

222   "Jefferson for me is an ultimate": Ibid., pp. 83–98.

222   "out of the pusillanimities": Ibid., pp. 6–22.

222   Julian Bond's unheralded victory: "Bond Wins Ga. House Primary," SNCC newsletter *The Student Voice,* April 30, 1965, p. 2, in Carson, Ed., *Student,* p. 216; Neary, *Julian Bond,* p. 82.

222   long poem he had written for a girlfriend: Int. Charles Cobb, Aug. 29, 1991.

223   So cry not just for Jackson: Petras, ed., *We Accuse,* pp. 135–41. The poem appears elsewhere in slightly different form: "Charlie's poem," *The Student Voice,* June 6, 1965, reprinted in Carson, ed., *Student,* pp. 221–22; Untitled in ten-folio manuscript, "i want to say/about all," JMP.

223   "their familiar role of opposing all wars": Friedland, *Lift Up,* p. 144.

223   "California ain't nothing but Mississippi": Petras, ed., *We Accuse,* pp. 118–35.

223   "among the greatest human beings": Ibid., p. 149.

223   "I saw a picture in an AP release": Ibid., pp. 149–53.

224   Sunday's *San Francisco Examiner* ignored: Menashe and Radosh, eds., *Teach-Ins,* p. 36.

224   "a bleary-eyed, bearded young man": NYT, May 23, 1965, p. 26.

224   "Fuck Defense Fund": Heirich, *Beginning,* pp. 256–58.

224   "moral spastics": Ibid., p. 264.

224   Jesse Unruh initiated: Ibid., p. 275.

224   A bomb threat: [Name deleted] to W. C. Sullivan, May 20, 1965, FHHH-NR.

224   He met privately with Vice President Hubert Humphrey: Ibid. Also Garrow, *Bearing,* p. 426.

225   Among King's worries: Two separate New York LHMs dated May 25, 1965, FK-NR.

225   believing Levison would regain unfair access: Int. Harry Wachtel, May 17, 1990.

225   he had prevailed upon Archibald Carey: Church, Supplementary Detailed, p. 171; Garrow, *Bearing,* p. 425.

225   "I interrupted Dr. Carey": DeLoach to Mohr, May 19, 1965, FAC-30.

225   Carey had cured: Branch, *Pillar,* pp. 533–34.

225   authorized the leak of confidential bug and wiretap information: Church, Supplementary Detailed, p. 175; Garrow, *FBI and King,* pp. 170, 275.

226   "It is an axiom of nonviolent action": King address to the American Jewish Congress, May 20, 1965, A/KS.

226   enigmatic notice on back pages: NYT, May 21, 1965, p. 36.

226   filed a cloture petition: *Congressional Record,* May 21, 1965, p. S-11188; NYT, May 22, 1965, p. 1.

226   "Disappointment is a hallmark": King sermon, "How to Deal with Grief," May 23, 1965, A/KS4.

226   repeating his text from Jeremiah: Jeremiah 10:19.

226   another trademark sermon: Cf. "Why Could We Not Cast Him Out?," Branch, *Parting,* pp. 700–702.

226   "I've been to the mountaintop": King sermon, "How to Deal with Grief," May 23, 1965, A/KS4.

226   cloture tally of 70–30: NYT, May 26, 1965, p. 1.

227   "Fake! Fake! Fake!": Ibid.

227   a clash of iconic images: Remnick, *King,* pp. 252, 258; Associated Press, *World in 1965,* pp. 96–97. Author Remnick found Neil Leifer's photograph perhaps "the most lasting image of Ali in the ring, period."

227   "strategy adviser": *Jet,* June 10, 1965, pp. 52–55.

227   "Uncle Tom was not an inferior Negro": Remnick, *King,* p. 246.

227   Hollywood films since 1927: Watkins, *Real Side,* pp. 200–202, 226–8, 247–62. Born on May 30, 1902, in Key West, Florida, Lincoln Theodore Monroe Andrew Perry (named by his father for four U.S. Presidents) had been half a World War I vaudeville act first called Skeeter and Rastus, then Step 'n Fetchit. Perry kept the stage name when his partner quit, and made his debut as Stepin Fetchit in silent films of the 1920s.

227   McGeorge Bundy returned: Szulc, *Diary,* p. 285.

227   "use of citizen-owned television airways": NYT, May 27, 1965, p. 1.

227   one of only two Republican votes: Ibid., p. 24.

227   "final resting place of the Constitution": *Congressional Record,* May 26, 1965, p. S-11732.

227   Defeated Southern Democrats foresaw: Ibid., passim, pp. S-11715–11752.

227   "garden variety": Branch, *Pillar,* p. 334.

227   Russell was one of the few: Ibid., p. 258.

227   disdained both the Lewiston fight and Ali himself: NYT, May 27, 1965, p. 1; Remnick, *King,* p. 247; *Sports Illustrated,* June 7, 1965, pp. 12, 22–25.

228   "on behalf of a heartened nation": NYT, May 27, 1965, p. 1.

228   "another pygmy at his feet": Tom Wicker, "Lyndon Johnson Is 10 Feet Tall," NYT Magazine, May 23, 1965, p. 23ff.

18: LEAPS OF FAITH

PAGE

229   to stampede the sleepiest bureaucracy in Washington: Francis Keppel oral history by John Singerhoff, July 18, 1968, LBJ, p. 15.

229   "We believe we are entitled": Orfield, *Reconstruction,* p. 88.

229   "screaming and hollering revolution": LBJ phone call with Carl Sanders, 8:35 P.M., May 13, 1965, Cit. 7656-58, Audiotape WH6505.11, LBJ.

230   delivery to Sanders of a mounted deer head: Ibid.

230   "I've got my back to the wall": LBJ phone call with Carl Sanders, 11:46 A.M., May 18, 1965, Cit. 7752, Audiotape WH6505.22, LBJ.

230   "Virtually all place the burden": Roy Wilkins to Francis Keppel, May 13, 1965, private papers of Robert H. Janover, Bloomfield Hills, Michigan. Janover was a member of the consulting task force on school desegregation for the U.S. Office of Education, 1965–66.

230   complained of nitpicking: William Mills, counsel for a North Carolina school board, wrote that "every time the Board whatever it is told is lacking or needs to be done in order to comply, some other 'bureaucrat' gets hold of the plan and makes an additional demand." William L. Mills, Jr., to Senator B. Everett Jordan (D.-N.C.), June 5, 1965, private papers of Robert H. Janover.

230   "It is most disturbing to me": Sam J. Ervin, Jr., to [HEW Secretary] Anthony J. Celebrezze, June 10, 1965, private papers of Robert H. Janover.

230   Pandemonium reigned: Orfield, *Reconstruction,* pp. 78–80; Marion S. Barry and Betty Garman, "SNCC: A Special Report on Southern School Desegregation," Sept. 1965, pp. 1–8 (courtesy of Betty Garman Robinson).

230   mostly second-career school administrators: Orfield, *Reconstruction,* p. 52.

230   Temporary S: Ibid., p. 102; Janover to U.S. Circuit Judge Damon J. Keith et al., January 30, 1997, private papers of Robert H. Janover.

231   Johnson swore Nabrit to silence: James M. Nabrit oral history by Stephen Goodell, March 28, 1969, LBJ.

231   lawyers addressed intergovernmental disputes: Cf. Alan G. Marer to Stephen Pollack, June 11, 1965, Administrative History/Department of Justice, Vol. 7, Part 10, a[1], LBJ. Also Pollack to Katzenbach, June 11, 1965, St. John Barrett to Pollack, June 15, 1965, and John Doar to S. A. Andretta, July 9, 1965, all in Legislative Background, VRA '65, Box 1, LBJ.

231   The guiding strategy, announced in advance: NYT, June 20, 1965, p. 1.

231   *"The courts acting alone have failed": United States v. Jefferson County Board of Education,* 372 F.2d 836 (1966), at 847, italics in original.

231   thirty front-line civil rights lawyers: John Doar, "The Work of the Civil Rights Division in Enforcing Voting Rights Under the Civil Rights Acts of 1957 and 1960," 1989, courtesy of John Doar.

231   seventy Negroes tried to walk: WATS report, June 3, 1965, Reel 16, SNCC; NYT, June 4, 1965, p. 17; *Jet,* June 24, 1965, pp. 14–17.

231   violence struck Bogalusa, Louisiana: NYT, June 4, 1965, p. 17; Meier, *CORE,* pp. 345–50.

232   "face up to the sixty-four-dollar question": FRUS, Vol. 2, p. 709; PDD, June 3, 1965, p. 1.

232   "off the streets": PPP 1965, Vol. 2, pp. 627–30.

232   intended agenda on race: Goodwin, *Remembering,* pp. 342–45; James M. Nabrit oral history by Stephen Goodell, March 28, 1969, LBJ.

232   "But freedom is not enough": NYT, June 5, 1965, p. 14; "Remarks of the President at Howard University, Washington, D.C., 'To Fulfill These Rights,' June 4, 1965," LBJ.

233   Johnson confessed a national legacy: Wood, *Radicalism,* pp. 144–45.

233   Like Lincoln, who quoted Psalm 19: Ibid., pp. 155–59.

234   "remarkable in the history": NYT, June 5, 1965, pp. 1, 14.

234   "for your magnificent speech": MLK telegram to LBJ, June 7, 1965, A/KP13f8.

234   "seem incredibly puny": NYT, June 6, 1965, p. IV-10.

234   "the failure of Negro family life": Mary McGrory, "President Talks Frankly to Negroes," WS, June 6, 1965.

234   inklings of political mayhem: Melman, *America*, pp. 133–35.

234   "half-witted white kids": NYT, June 6, 1965, p. 53.

235   investigation to be reopened: *Baltimore Sun*, Dec. 20, 1998, p. C-1.

235   "Flight Out of Egypt": Ottley, *Lonely*, pp. 159–72.

235   not yet established its first public high school for Negroes: Orfield, *Reconstruction*, p. 13.

235   two thousand reaching the Illinois Central Terminal: Lemann, *Promised*, pp. 15–17, 43.

235   "HALF A MILLION DARKIES": Ottley, *Lonely*, p. 171; Joravsky, *Race*, p. 8.

235   "shall be filled solidly": Anderson and Pickering, *Confronting*, p. 46.

235   Eugene Williams floated across an imaginary line: Tuttle, *Riot*, pp. 3–10; Waskow, *Race Riot*, pp. 38–59; Ottley, *Lonely*, p. 184; Joravsky, *Race*, p. 7.

236   Al Capone's headquarters: Pacyga, *Chicago*, p. 301.

236   Café de Champion: Travis, *Black Chicago*, p. 40.

236   "I saw Duke Ellington": Ibid., p. 78.

236   Singer Cab Calloway enjoyed: Ibid., p. 40.

236   the largest Protestant congregation: Tuttle, *Riot*, p. 98; Pacyga, *Chicago*, p. 328; Branch, *Parting*, pp. 55–56; Branch, *Pillar*, pp. 28–29.

236   Greater Bethel AME bought the Jewish Lakeside Club: *Esquire*, May 1989, p. 94.

236   Chicago's oldest synagogue: Pacyga, *Chicago*, pp. 312–13, 326.

236   "Each machine did the work": Lemann, *Promised*, pp. 3–5.

236   average of five hundred Negroes: Ibid., p. 70.

236   this time into West Chicago: *Esquire*, May 1989, pp. 94, 96.

236   lumped together as the "German Jews": Ibid; also, Hertzberg, *Jews in America*, pp. 177–88; Johnson, *History of the Jews*, pp. 369–75.

237   Marshall Field retail stores at last modified company rules: Ralph, *Northern*, p. 11; Cohen, *Pharaoh*, p. 58.

237   Elizabeth Wood: Joravsky, *Race*, pp. 21–24; Cohen, *Pharaoh*, pp. 70–73.

237   besieged new apartments near Midway Airport: Lemann, *Promised*, p. 71.

237   Trumbull Park Homes: Cohen, *Pharaoh*, pp. 101–4.

237   "My people will be in the streets": Joravsky, *Race*, p. 25.

237   victory margin of 125,000 votes: Cohen, *Pharaoh*, pp. 137–41; Anderson and Pickering, *Confronting*, p. 53.

237   Robert Taylor Homes: Pacyga, *Chicago*, pp. 352–55.

237   two of the three poorest census tracts: Hodgson, *Islam*, p. 295.

238   Negro ward bosses simply bought enough memberships: Cohen, *Pharaoh*, pp. 205–7; Orfield, *Reconstruction*, p. 155.

238   claiming 50,000 members: Travis, *Black Chicago*, p. 143. Author Travis was elected president of the Chicago NAACP chapter in 1959.

238   "De Facto Segregation in the Chicago Public Schools": *Crisis*, February 1958, pp. 87–127; Ralph, *Northern*, p. 15.

238   School Superintendent Benjamin Willis: Ralph, *Northern*, p. 20; Anderson and Pickering, *Confronting*, p. 77.

238   When a small group of parents sued in 1961: *Webb v. The Board of Education of the City of Chicago,* Civ. No. 61C1569 D.C., N.D., Ill.; Anderson and Pickering, *Confronting,* pp. 85–86.

238   150,000 "extra" students: Cohen, *Pharaoh,* p. 283.

238   "Big Ben the Builder" *and* "an administrative cyclone": Orfield, *Reconstruction,* p. 161.

238   corroborate allegations of managed disparity: Ibid., pp. 156–58; Anderson and Pickering, *Confronting,* pp. 95–96; Cohen, *Pharaoh,* p. 284.

238   To settle the 1961 *Webb* case: Anderson and Pickering, *Confronting,* pp. 116–18: Cohen, *Pharaoh,* p. 308; Orfield, *Reconstruction,* p. 162.

239   "Then came Birmingham": Anderson and Pickering, *Confronting,* p. 107.

239   Mayor Daley instructed Democratic precinct captains: Cohen, *Pharaoh,* pp. 308–9.

239   "Willis—Wallace": Anderson and Pickering, *Confronting,* pp. 118–20.

239   Nearly a quarter of a million students boycotted classrooms: Ibid.; *Jet,* Nov. 7, 1963, pp. 48–55; Ralph, *Northern,* p. 21.

239   "Negroes are still a minority": *Chicago Tribune,* Oct. 24, 1963, cited in Anderson and Pickering, *Confronting,* pp. 119–20.

239   were divided in the giddy aftermath: Int. Lawrence Landry, April 30, 1991; int. Donald Rose, Feb. 21, 1985.

239   the Daley organization actively opposed: Cohen, *Pharaoh,* p. 313.

239   the turnout of roughly 150,000: Ibid.; Anderson and Pickering, *Confronting,* p. 133; Ralph, *Northern,* p. 22.

239   "Many Negroes have improved": *Business Week,* Feb. 1, 1964, p. 38, cited in Lemann, *Promised,* p. 112.

240   "alternately frightened or bored much": *Chicago Daily News,* Feb. 20, 1965, cited in Anderson and Pickering, *Confronting,* p. 151.

240   switched votes to grant Willis: Cohen, *Pharoah,* p. 328. The three swing votes on the eleven-member board had been reported to be against Willis, and their private correspondence reflected such sentiment. "I can't vouch for the other two but my guess is that all three of us would be 'con' on another four year term," wrote Cyrus Adams to board president Frank Whiston. "Marge [Wilde] gets madder at Ben than I do." Adams to Whiston, Jan. 18, 1965, Box 9, Cyrus Adams Papers, CHS.

240   Dissenters instantly faulted them: Anderson and Pickering, *Confronting,* pp. 153–54.

240   "the usually legalistic Chicago NAACP": *Jet,* June 24, 1965, p. 20.

240   King's aide James Bevel: Garrow, *Bearing,* p. 432.

240   "Civil rights forces of Chicago": Anderson and Pickering, *Confronting,* p. 155.

240   his first trip to jail: Albert Anderson Raby file, RS, CHS; Anderson and Pickering, *Confronting,* p. 156.

240   When students organized their own walkout: *Jet,* June 24, 1965, p. 20; Cohen, *Pharaoh,* p. 328; Orfield, *Reconstruction,* p. 164.

240   determined remnant of 252 people: Anderson and Pickering, *Confronting,* p. 157; Associated Press, *World in 1965,* p. 260.

240   "one of the largest mass arrests": Ralph, *Northern,* p. 25.

241   "Who is this man Al Raby?": Cohen, *Pharaoh,* p. 328.

241   press inquiries and an FBI investigation: *Chicago Daily News,* June 14, 1965, p. 8; Chicago LHM dated July 30, 1965, FAR-1.

241   five years of night classes: Robert McClory, "The Activist," *Chicago Tribune Sunday Magazine,* April 17, 1983, p. 27ff.

241   Teachers for Integrated Schools: Anderson and Pickering, *Confronting,* p. 87.

241   "You don't think these children": *Jet,* July 15, 1965, p. 48.

241   he joined 196 people handcuffed the next day: Ralph, *Northern,* p. 26; Anderson and Pickering, *Confronting,* pp. 157–58.

241   Raby, like Morrisroe: Int. Al Raby, Feb. 20, 1985; int. Richard Morrisroe, Feb. 20, 2002.

241   reciprocal entreaties for King: Ibid.; New York LHM dated June 14, 1965, FSC-NR; int. Bernard Lafayette, May 28, 1990; *Chicago Sun Times,* April 2, 1965, p. 1; *Chicago Tribune,* April 6, 1965, p. 1.

241   King promised a reply: Garrow, *Bearing,* p. 428.

241   a graduation address at Wilberforce College: *Jet,* June 24, 1965, p. 27.

241   press inquiries about Communism: UPI dispatch of June 16, 1965, which quotes King: "I'm just not going to keep answering these charges against me," in FK-NR; "Martin Luther King: Eye of Civil Rights Storm," in *Baltimore Evening Sun,* June 20, 1965, p. D-3.

241   more complaints about his staff: Cf. Randolph T. Blackwell to MLK, June 10, 1965, A/KP28f21.

241   Mary probably was not a virgin: Rev. Matthew E. Neil to MLK, June 3, 1965, with attached draft reply to Rev. Alexander Shaw and handwritten notes by Andrew Young, A/KP34f5.

241   distraught Hofstra University officials: Wiretap conversation of Clarence Jones with Harry Wachtel, cited in New York LHM dated June 16, 1965, FK-NR.

241   oversleeping, hurrying into robes: *Elyria Chronicle-Telegram,* Jan. 14, 1999.

241   King's previous visit there: *Elyria Chronicle-Telegram,* Oct. 24, 1964; *Oberlin News-Tribune,* Oct. 29, 1964.

242   "It is not enough to say": Oberlin alumni magazine, August, 1965, pp. 4–6.

242   at Antioch College: "Negotiate Vietnam Peace Doctor King Says at Antioch," *Dayton Daily News,* June 20, 1965, re MLK address at 10:00 A.M., June 19, 1965, cited in Cincinnati LHM dated June 22, 1965, FK-1510.

242   Hosea Williams introduced Bayard Rustin: SCOPE orientation June 15, 1965, Hosea Williams, Tape 29, King Archives.

242   "Negroes have seen what white America": SCOPE orientation, June 15, 1965, Hosea Williams, Tape 155, King Archives.

242   King took a mixed tactical line: Garrow, *Bearing,* p. 428.

242   "Greetings from the Chicago movement": WATS report, June 15, 1965, Reel 16, SNCC.

242   John Lewis and two hundred new prisoners: Dittmer, *Local People,* p. 345; *Light,* p. 161.

242   The Mississippi dragnets made front-page news: NYT, June 15, 1965, p. 1; NYT, June 16, 1965, p. 1.

242   "We just been doing it": NYT, June 16, 1965, p. 21.

243   find out what happened to her mother: Int. June Johnson, April 9, 1992.

243   they lied miserably to their friends: Curry et al., *Deep,* p. 205.

243   "COME TO JACKSON": MFDP to MLK (in Jamaica), June 22, 1965, A/KP16f6; int. Lawrence Guyot, Feb. 1, 1991.

243   A pastor from Huntsville, Alabama: Press release, Commission on Religion and Race, National Council of Churches, June 22, 1965, regarding an inspection report filed by Rev. W. Raymond Berry, United Church of Huntsville, Alabama, Rev. Ian J. McCrae of Indianapolis, and John M. Pratt, counsel for the CORR, in RG5, Box 16f10, NCC, POH.

243   "We inspected what we can only describe": Statement by The Rev. Ian McCrae, The Rev. W. Raymond Berry, and John M. Pratt, June 22, 1965, Folder 125, Reel 43, SNCC.

243   fell on June 12 to a military junta: Karnow, *Vietnam,* p. 427; FRUS, Vol. 2, pp. 761–62.

243   "absolutely the bottom": McNamara, *In Retrospect,* p. 186.

243   "thus, we are approaching the kind of warfare": Westmoreland to Admiral Ulysses Sharp, June 13, 1965, in FRUS, Vol. 2, p. 1.

243   Westmoreland's new "bombshell" appeal: Westmoreland to Admiral Ulysses Sharp, June 7, 1965, in FRUS, Vol. 2, p. 733ff; McNamara, *In Retrospect,* pp. 187–93.

243   still being shipped: McNamara, *In Retrospect,* p. 183; FRUS, Vol. 2, pp. 736–41; LBJ phone call with Robert McNamara, 12:05 P.M., June 21, 1965, Cit. 8167, Audiotape WH6506.05, LBJ.

243   "to protect us against catastrophe": LBJ phone call with Robert McNamara, 7:15 P.M., April 20, 1965, Cit. 7356, Audiotape WH6504.05, LBJ. McNamara used variants of the word "catastrophe" four times in his brief conversation with President Johnson from a conference in Honolulu. He reported success in persuading departing ambassador Maxwell Taylor to accept "in good humor" the unavoidable use of American troops, which Taylor had opposed.

244   "the North Vietnamese just said": LBJ phone call with Senator Birch Bayh, 1:20 P.M., June 15, 1965, Cit. 8135, Audiotape WH6506.03, LBJ.

244   "except just praying and gasping": LBJ phone call with Robert McNamara, 12:15 P.M., June 21, 1965, Cit. 8168–69, Audiotape WH6506.05, LBJ.

244   McGeorge Bundy debated the Vietnam War: NYT, June 22, 1965, p. 1; CBS News Special Report, *Vietnam Dialogue,* T77:0571, MOB.

244   stopped short of an argument: Powers, *War,* pp. 67–69; Wells, *War Within,* p. 33.

244   "I may have been dead wrong": Bird, *Color,* p. 321.

244   furious with Bundy for disregarding direct and indirect warnings: LBJ phone call with Bill Moyers, 9:15 P.M., May 13, 1965, Cit. 7659, Audiotape WH6505.11, LBJ; LBJ phone call with Abe Fortas ("Mr. Davidson"), 8:45 P.M., May 14, 1965, Cit. 7684–87, Audiotape WH6505.13, LBJ.

244   "I'm just against the White House debating": LBJ phone call with McGeorge Bundy, 12:45 P.M., May 31, 1965, Cit. 7852, Audiotape WH6505.34, LBJ.

244   "Did we use conventional uh, weapons?": LBJ phone call with Gerald R. Ford, 7:50 P.M., June 17, 1965, Cit. 8154–55, Audiotape WH6506.05, LBJ.

245   "There are some things": LBJ phone call with McGeorge Bundy, 12:45 P.M., May 31, 1965, Cit. 7852, Audiotape WH6505.34, LBJ.

245   "The president sent me down": Langguth, *Our Vietnam,* pp. 367–69; Bird, *Color,* pp. 321–23.

245   "I am pretty depressed": LBJ phone call with Robert McNamara, 8:41 A.M., July 2, 1965, Cit. 8302, Audiotape WH6507.01, LBJ, cited in Beschloss, *Reaching,* p. 381.

245   "If we succeed": CIA memorandum to McNamara, June 30, 1965, in FRUS, Vol. 3, p. 86.

245   "last clear chance": George Ball, "Cutting Our Losses in South Viet-Nam," undated (circa June 28, 1965), ibid., pp. 62–66.

245   "drifting toward a major war": Ball to LBJ, June 18, 1965, in FRUS, Vol. 3, pp. 16–21.

245   "No one can assure you": George Ball, "A Compromise Solution for South Viet-Nam," undated (circa July 1, 1965), ibid., pp. 106–9 (italics in original).

245   "a small state of personal crisis": Bird, *Color,* pp. 332–35.

245   a "middle way" proposal: William Bundy, "A 'Middle Way' Course of Action in South-Vietnam," July 1, 1965, in FRUS, Vol. 3, pp. 113–15.

245   rushed to the White House a note of distress: McNamara, *In Retrospect,* pp. 192–95; Rusk, *As I Saw It,* p. 450.

245   "would lead to our ruin": Rusk to LBJ, "Viet-Nam," July 1, 1965, in FRUS, Vol. 3, pp. 104–6.

245   Rusk pushed to restrict: McGeorge Bundy to LBJ, 5:50 P.M., July 1, 1965, in FRUS, Vol. 3, pp. 115–16. ("I find that both Rusk and McNamara feel strongly that the George Ball paper should not be argued with you in front of any audience larger than yourself, Rusk, McNamara, Ball, and me. They feel that it is exceedingly dangerous to have this possibility reported in a wider circle.")

245   Harold G. Bennett: Ibid., p. 46; Langguth, *Our Vietnam,* p. 369.

246   thought he was deceitfully pro-war: Steel, *Walter Lippmann,* pp. 574–75.

246   "any area where blood could be spilled": LBJ phone call with McGeorge Bundy, 12:45 P.M., May 31, 1965, Cit. 7852, Audiotape WH6505.34, LBJ.

246   McNamara winced: McNamara, *In Retrospect,* pp. 193–94.

246   "rash to the point of folly": Bundy to LBJ, June 30, 1965, in FRUS, Vol. 3, pp. 90–91; Karnow, *Vietnam,* pp. 439–40.

246   "What are the chances": Bundy to LBJ, July 1, 1965, ibid., pp. 117–18.

246   "Still more brutally": Bundy to LBJ, June 30, 1965, FRUS, Vol. 3, pp. 90–91.

246   "You think that we can really beat": LBJ phone call with Dwight D. Eisenhower, 11:02 A.M., July 2, 1965, Cit. 8303, Audiotape WH6507.01, LBJ, in Beschloss, *Reaching,* pp. 383–84.

246   seemed to Eisenhower a plaintive tone: "Memorandum of Telephone Conversation: 10:55 A.M., July 2, 1965," Papers 1961–69, Box 10, DDE.

246   for a cross-examination that ran nearly two hours: FRUS, Vol. 3, pp. 118–19; McNamara, *In Retrospect,* pp. 195–96; Bird, *Color,* pp. 335–36; Langguth, *Our Vietnam,* pp. 372–73.

246   caught the press by surprise: NYT, July 3, 1965, p. 1; PDD, July 2, 1965, p. 1, LBJ.

246   "I could not help but think": Johnson, *Diary,* pp. 293–94.

246   on her eighteenth birthday: Ibid.; Caro, *Means,* p. 138.

247   476 discrimination complaints: Greenberg, *Crusaders,* p. 413.

247   EEOC mediators settled 110 of those complaints: Graham, *Civil Rights Era,* pp. 234–37.

247   fifteen to the Justice Department for litigation over such issues: Ibid., p. 248; Greenberg, *Crusaders,* pp. 414–29.

247   *Quarles v. Philip Morris:* 279 F. Supp. 505 (1968); NYT, May 3, 1967, p. 35.

247   "What about sex?": Graham, *Civil Rights,* p. 211.

247   "Executive training programs": NYT, Sept. 13, 1964, p. 47.

248   "a mischievous joke perpetrated": Harrison, *Sex,* p. 188.

248   Southerners had introduced sex equality: Carl M. Brauer, "Women Activists, Southern Conservatives, and the Prohibition of Sex Discrimination in Title VII of the 1964 Civil Rights Act," *Journal of Southern History,* Vol. 49, No. 1, Feb. 1983; Jo Freeman, "How 'Sex' Got into Title VII: Persistent Opportunism As a Maker of Public Policy," *Law and Inequality,* Vol. 9, No. 2, 1991; Branch, *Pillar,* pp. 231–34. Brauer notes (p. 53) that the Johnson administration supported the sex provision in order to keep the civil rights bill intact on its treacherous course through both houses of Congress, and that Johnson himself endorsed it in an April 1964 letter to Mrs. Modell

Scruggs. Freeman emphasizes the lobbying role played by the National Women's Party and others, which mitigates the "fluke" interpretation of the sex amendment. All studies emphasize the leadership of Rep. Martha Griffiths (D.-Mich), who rose on the House floor on February 8, 1964, amid titters over the surprise amendment, to begin a scolding, stirring argument for the provision on its own merits. Had there been any doubt that "women were a second-class sex," she declared, "the laughter would have proved it."

248 still divided the want-ads by gender: Graham, *Civil Rights Era,* p. 214. Cf. NYT, July 2, 1965, p. 56; WP, July 2, 1965, p. C-9.

248 "bunny problem": Graham, *Civil Rights Era,* p. 211.

248 "a shapeless, knobby-kneed male 'bunny' ": Harrison, *Sex,* p. 189.

248 "Amelia Jenks Bloomer": NYT, Jan. 15, 1965, p. 17.

248 "just abolish sex itself": Graham, *Civil Rights Era,* p. 211.

248 "There are some people": Ibid., p. 217.

19: GULPS OF FREEDOM

PAGE

249 the last of the Mississippi demonstrators: John Doar to John Lewis, Aug. 17, 1965, Reel 1, SNCC.

249 "A 'whitewash' if there ever was one": Hoover handwritten comment on UPI release by Al Kuettner dated June 16, 1965, FSC-NR.

249 "dingy green walls and a bare floor": "King Spurns Lure of Wealth, Lives Modestly in Atlanta," AP release by Don McKee dated June 20, 1965, FK-1513. Hoover wrote on the FBI file copy: "Even this obvious 'whitewash' doesn't clean him up."

249 might have concealed in Swiss bank accounts: Church, Supplementary Detailed Staff Reports, pp. 145–47; Baumgardner to Sullivan, Dec. 10, 1965, FK-2143.

249 Ralph Abernathy's Atlanta press conference: Abernathy press statement, July 1, 1965, A/SC59f10.

249 "We will check with FBI men": Baumgardner to Sullivan, July 1, 1965, FSC-408.

250 "if I find anyone furnishing information": Hoover handwritten note, ibid.

250 "so as to give the lie": DeLoach to Mohr, July 1, 1965, FSC-391.

250 top FBI officials received notice: Handwritten notes on Baumgardner to Sullivan, July 1, 1965, FSC-408.

250 "Fast Refutation by FBI": *Atlanta Times,* July 13, 1965, p. 8; "FBI and King's Group Clash over File Check," *Washington Daily News,* July 2, 1965, news clip, FSC-A.

250 One Illinois paper conflated: "King Calls Red Infiltration Charge a Red Herring," *Royal Oak Daily Tribune,* July 3, 1965, news clip, FSC-564.

250 fresh outburst from Mayor Daley: NYT, July 1, 1965, p. 27.

250 "The actual work to redeem the soul": King address to United Church of Christ, General Synod, Palmer House, Chicago, July 6, 1965, File 951, RS, CHS.

250 "take over": *Chicago Tribune,* July 7, 1965, p. 3.

250 King parried both questions, then withdrew: "Investigator's Report/Intelligence Division/Chicago Police Department," July 7, 1965, File 951, RS, CHS.

251 "deprived of any and all Federal assistance": CCCO complaint dated July 4, 1965, cited in Cohen and Taylor, *Pharaoh,* p. 334; Orfield, *Reconstruction,* p. 165.

251 why the national CORE delegates: Meier, CORE, p. 404; NYT, July 6, 1965, p. 1.

251 picked up comments on Vietnam: Allan Jones, "Dr. King Calls for End to War in Viet

Nam," *Richmond Times-Dispatch,* July 3, 1965, p. 1; UPI dispatch, "Dr. King Declares U.S. Must Negotiate in Asia," NYT, July 3, 1965, p. 6. The FBI caught up late with the Vietnam controversy. The Richmond office forwarded the July 3 *Times-Dispatch* story to headquarters after Katzenbach's July 6 call alerted Hoover, in LHM dated July 7, 1965, FSC-NR.

251   but an incoming emergency call: "Investigator's Report/Intelligence Division/Chicago Police Department," July 7, 1965, File 951, RS, CHS.

251   Wilson Baker had arrested Rev. F. D. Reese: Ibid. Also NYT, July 7, 1965, p. 1; Fager, *Selma, 1965,* pp. 196–99.

251   J. Edgar Hoover was alerted to sensitivities: Hoover memorandum for Tolson et al., 5:53 P.M., July 6, 1965, FK-1551. This document was declassified beginning in 1975, but not fully released until 1999.

252   "King's injection into the Vietnam situation": Baumgardner to Sullivan, July 7, 1965, FK-1555; Hoover to Marvin Watson, and Watson to LBJ, with attached FBI LHM "The Position of Martin Luther King, Jr. and the Communist Party, USA, on Vietnam," July 7, 1965, OFMS, LBJ.

252   King announced that morning: "Statement of Rev. Dr. Martin Luther King, Jr., to the Press, July 7, 1965," File 951, RS, CHS; "Chicago press conference on Chicago movement, July 7, 1965," A/KS; NYT, July 8, 1965, p. 36; Anderson and Pickering, *Confronting,* p. 160.

252   "During entire press conference": SAC, Chicago, to Director, July 7, 1965, FK-1547.

252   Leaving Andrew Young with Bevel: "Investigator's Report/Intelligence Division/Chicago Police Department," July 7, 1965, p. 3, File 951, RS, CHS.

252   first phone conversation initiated by King: "Contacts with Civil Rights Leaders, 1963–68," Legislative Background, VRA '65, Box 1, LBJ.

252   "This is Martin King": LBJ phone call with MLK, 8:05 P.M., July 7, 1965, Cit. 8311-14, Audiotape WH6507.02, LBJ.

255   Jonathan Daniels reached Selma for a third stay: Judy Upham oral history, dated July 26, 1966, p. 80, JDC; Eagles, *Outside Agitator,* pp. 80–81.

256   "I wanted to shout to them": Daniels class paper submitted at the Episcopal Theological School, June 22, 1965, JDC.

256   Daniels carried a secret intention: Marc Oliver int. by Rev. John B. Morris, Feb. 1966, JDC; Maurice Ouellet int. by P. Selby, June 1966, JDC.

256   "It meant absorbing their guilt as well": Daniels class paper submitted at the Episcopal Theological School, June 22, 1965, JDC.

256   Lonzy and Alice West drove Daniels: Webb and Nelson, *Selma, Lord, Selma,* pp. 12, 51, 131–32.

256   Daniels retained an open bond: Ibid. Also Eagles, *Outside Agitator,* pp. 76–78.

256   edict that made national news: NYT, June 26, 1965, p. 13; "Selma Aftermath," *Jubilee,* August, 1965, pp. 16–23.

256   Wests of their family priest: Maurice Ouellet int. by P. Selby, June 1966, JDC; Eagles, *Outside Agitator,* pp. 75–76.

256   first meeting with Negroes on freedom-of-choice integration: Ernest Bradford, "Report by the Committee for the Improvement of Educational Opportunities," July 2, 1965, RSP2.

257   Mayor Joseph Smitherman stalled the downtown boycott: Fager, *Selma, 1965,* pp. 188–95.

257   A close observer of the emergency perceived him: Dave Smith to Ralph Smeltzer, June 28, July 7, and August 1, 1965, all in RSP2.

257   Ralph Abernathy flew in with an earthy appeal: *Jet,* July 22, 1965, p. 7; Fager, *Selma, 1965,* pp. 196–200.

257   "The SNCC people here": Charles Fager to Randolph Blackwell, July 31, 1965, A/SC146f10.

257   Selma Free College: Letitia (Tish) Fager to Randolph Blackwell, June 26, 1965, RSP2; Letitia (Tish) Fager to Randolph Blackwell, Sept. 8, 1965, A/SC146f12; "On the Freedom Trail in Alabama," Sept. 10, 1965, private papers of Rabbi Harold Saperstein; int. Gloria Larry House, June 29, 2000.

258   canvassed the poorest sections: Eagles, *Outside Agitator,* pp. 81–85.

258   shocked the volunteers: Int. Marc Oliver by Rev. John B. Morris, Feb. 1966, JDC.

258   Ouellet had feared: Maurice Ouellet int. by P. Selby, June 1966, JDC.

258   white side of the laundromat: Int. Marc Oliver by Rev. John B. Morris, Feb. 1966, JDC.

259   mentor also to a middle-aged couple: Harold and Marcia Saperstein, of Temple Emanu-El, Lynbrook, N.Y. "On the Freedom Trail in Alabama," Sept. 10, 1965, private papers of Rabbi Harold Saperstein.

259   "I think it's all right for you": Int. Harold and Marcia Saperstein, Dec. 12, 1991.

259   cabin since July 6: WATS reports for Selma (July 6, 1965), Lowndes County (July 7 and 9, 1965), Reel 16, SNCC; Selma SNCC daily report, July 6, 1965, Reel 18, SNCC; Eagles, *Outside Agitator,* p. 132.

259   Lillian McGill quit her federal job: Jeffries, "Freedom Politics," p. 72.

259   SNCC workers mobilized outside reinforcements: Int. Harold and Marcia Saperstein, Dec. 12, 1991; int. Gloria Larry House, June 29, 2000; int. Jimmy Rogers, March 7, 2000; int. Ruby Sales, March 22, 2003.

260   "We've fought for the removal": Eagles, *Outside Agitator,* p. 132.

260   visionary text of Ezekiel: Ezekiel 37:1–14; int. Gloria Larry House, June 29, 2000.

260   Lowndes County was taking applications: Jeffries, "Freedom Politics," pp. 144–45.

260   families of nearly fifty children: Bob Mants/Lowndes County, WATS report, July 25, 1965, Reel 16, SNCC; Eagles, *Outside Agitator,* p. 139; Jeffries, "Freedom Politics," p. 146.

260   Daniels accompanied several to the courthouse: Int. Bernice Johnson, Feb. 16, 2001.

260   punctuated by nearby Klan rallies: Eagles, *Outside Agitator,* p. 144; Stanton, *From Selma,* p. 123; Dave Smith, "Selma—July 17, 1965," eyewitness report, with attached STJ advertisement for July 16 Klan rally on "Hiway 22 South," RSP1.

260   "Buster Haigler sent for me": Affidavit of Cato Lee, Lowndesboro, Alabama, witnessed by Robert Mants, July 1965, Reel 18, SNCC.

260   county's largest private financier: Jeffries, "Freedom Politics," p. 147.

260   "the Ku Klux Klan would be through here": Affidavit of Eli Logan, White Hall, Alabama, July 1965, Reel 18, SNCC.

260   "the same man who measured my land": Affidavit of Martha Johnson, Hayneville, Alabama, July 1965, Reel 18, SNCC.

260   "Then he said, 'We didn't bother y'all' ": Affidavit of Jordan Gully, Hayneville, Alabama, July 1965, Reel 18, SNCC.

261   Henry Cabot Lodge to return: Associated Press, *World in 1965,* p. 261; Karnow, *Vietnam,* p. 440; NYT, July 10, 1965, p. 3; LBJ phone calls with Juanita Roberts, 8:56 A.M. and 10:00 A.M., July 9, 1965, Cit. 8320–21, Audiotape WH6507.02, LBJ.

261   Bill Moyers to White House Press Secretary: NYT, July 9, 1965, p. 1; Evans and Novak, *Lyndon B. Johnson,* p. 533; LBJ phone call with Robert McNamara, 1:19 P.M., July 8, 1965, Cit. 8311–13, Audiotape WH6507.02, LBJ.

261   Moyers dazzled reporters: Deakin, *Straight Stuff,* p. 247.

261   Joseph Califano from the Pentagon: NYT, July 25, 1965, p. 51.

261   He ordered a verbatim transcript: Califano, *Triumph,* p. 70.

261   "Get 'em! Get 'em!": Francis Keppel oral history by David G. McComb, April 21, 1969, LBJ, p. 19.

261   less than a quarter of three thousand Southern districts: Orfield, *Reconstruction,* pp. 108–9; Marion S. Barry and Betty Garman, "SNCC: A Special Report on Southern School Desegregation," Sept. 1965, p. 9, courtesy of Betty Garman Robinson.

261   Lowndes County among a majority: Jeffries, "Freedom Politics," pp. 144–55. On June 2, 1965, school superintendent Hulda Coleman notified the U.S. Office of Education that Lowndes County would desegregate first the four grades of high school by free-dom-of-choice application for the fall term. Commissioner Keppel formally notified Coleman that the plan was insufficient on September 20, 1965.

261   break the psychological barrier: Orfield, *Reconstruction,* pp. 148–49.

261   orders to install a telephone: Califano, *Triumph,* pp. 25–26.

261   Thurgood Marshall with an offer: Williams, *Thurgood Marshall,* p. 314.

261   "They won't have *any*": LBJ phone call with J. William Fulbright, 1:00 P.M., July 9, 1965, Cit. 8324–25, Audiotape WH6507.02, LBJ. Johnson reminded Fulbright that Carl Rowan, the most prominent Negro official in the State Department, had just re-signed as director of the U.S. Information Agency.

262   drinks on the Truman balcony: Johnson, *Diary,* p. 299.

262   Johnson completed one phase: Marie Fehmer, "Summary of Conversation with Arthur Goldberg," June 24, 1968, and Juanita Roberts to LBJ, July 13, 1968, Office of the President, Box 5, LBJ; LBJ phone call with Dean Rusk, 8:45 P.M., July 19, 1965, Cit. 8357–58, Audiotape WH6507.05, LBJ; LBJ phone call with Arthur Goldberg, 9:00 P.M., July 19, 1965, Cit. 8359–60, Audiotape WH6507.05, LBJ; LBJ phone call with Abe Fortas, 4:31 P.M., July 21, 1965, Cit. 8370, Audiotape WH6507.06, LBJ; LBJ phone call with Arthur Goldberg, 8:28 P.M., July 19, 1965, Cit. 8355, Audiotape WH6507.05, LBJ.

262   day after Stevenson's burial: NYT, July 20, 1965, p. 20.

262   he told Galbraith flatly: LBJ phone call with John Kenneth Galbraith, 12:06 P.M., July 20, 1965, Cit. 8362, Audiotape WH6507.05, LBJ.

262   "If you want a movement to move": Anderson and Pickering, *Confronting,* p. 161.

262   220 clergy: Chicago police surveillance report dated July 26, 1965, File 940, RS, p. 126447, CHS.

262   in 1961 had branded King an apostate: Branch, *Parting,* pp. 500–507.

263   "sacrifice body and soul": NYT, July 25, 1965, p. 39.

263   three-car motorcade: "Schedule of Martin Luther King's Visit to Chicago, July 23–26, 1965," A/SC150f4.

263   On through eight speech stops in the lead car: Ibid.

263   covering 186 miles of city streets: NYT, July 25, 1965, p. 39.

263   driven off King's advisory staff: Branch, *Parting,* pp. 328–29.

263   "Let me commend you": ". . . and the noble citizens of our nation accompanying you for your all-important mission to Vietnam. The war in Vietnam must be stopped. America must be willing to negotiate with all involved parties. While we are all con-cerned about Communist invasion, we must instill in the mind of our nation that the way to fight communism is not through bombs, guns and gases. It is through economic and political programs that will convince the people of the world that only in demo-cratic society can man prosper and develop to his full potential." MLK, "Cablegram

Message sent to Alfred Hassler in Saigon," July 5, 1965, Jacob Weinstein Papers, Box 15, Folder 1, CHS.

263   Pastor Martin Niemoeller: Aside from Niemoeller, Jacob Weinstein, James Lawson, and Alfred Hassler, executive director of the Fellowship of Reconciliation, the delegation consisted of Dr. Harold A. Bosley, Rt. Rev. William Crittenden, Dr. Edwin T. Dahlberg, Dr. Dana McLean Greeley, Elmira Kendrick, Rt. Rev. Edward Murray, Dr. Howard Schomer, Elsie Schomer, Rev. Annalee Stewart, and Andre Trocme of Geneva. "A Report from Vietnam," July 11, 1965, Jacob Weinstein Papers, Box 15, Folder 1, CHS. The text of this report would appear as a paid appeal in the *New York Times* on the Sunday following President Johnson's July 28 announcement of troop escalation in Vietnam, NYT, Aug. 1, 1965, p. IV-5.

263   the only black person among the fourteen delegates: James Lawson oral history by David Yellin and Bill Thomas, Sept. 23, 1969, MVC.

263   "gave us great prestige": Jacob Weinstein, Office of the President, Central Conference of American Rabbis, "Dear Colleagues," July 30, 1965, Jacob Weinstein Papers, Box 15, Folder 1, CHS.

264   "To say something while experiencing": Letter to MLK, June 1, 1965, in Thich Nhat Hanh, *Lotus,* pp. 106–8; "A Letter to Martin Luther King from a Buddhist Monk," *Liberation,* December 1965, pp. 18–19.

264   Thich Nhat Hanh challenged Americans: "He recognized that Communism was an evil, but war was even a greater evil and he could not understand how justice could be established on the dead body of peace." Jacob Weinstein, Office of the President, Central Conference of American Rabbis, "Dear Colleagues," July 30, 1965, Jacob Weinstein Papers, Box 15, Folder 1, CHS.

264   ended late Saturday at Friendship Baptist: Pacyga, *Chicago,* pp. 210, 296.

264   complained of exhaustion after preaching: Chicago police surveillance report dated July 26, 1965, File 940, RS, p. 126448, CHS.

264   six afternoon stops: Ibid.; "Schedule of Martin Luther King's Visit to Chicago, July 23–26, 1965," A/SC150f4.

264   urged large middle-class crowds: NYT, July 26, 1965, p. 12.

264   "Dives didn't go to hell": "17,000 Hear Dr. King at Six Chicago Rallies," *Minneapolis Tribune,* July 26, 1965.

264   "Take a day off on Monday": NYT, July 25, 1965, p. 39.

265   "You don't think I know": Int. C. T. Vivian, May 26, 1990.

265   "Johns died?": Ibid.

265   his demise weeks earlier: Evans, ed., *Dexter Avenue,* p. 68; *Jet,* July 22, 1965, p. 47.

265   "The Romance of Death": "A Sermon Delivered May 16, 1965," published by the Howard University School of Religion, March 1966, courtesy of Jeanne Johns Adkins; Branch, *Parting,* p. 902.

265   "Segregation After Death": Branch, *Parting,* pp. 12, 705.

266   "I need to rest": Garrow, *Bearing,* p. 434.

266   reviewing the half-century of exodus: Chicago police surveillance report dated July 28, 1965, File 940, RS, pp. 138187–88, CHS.

266   "Chicago did not turn out to be a New Jerusalem": *Jet,* Aug. 12, 1965, pp. 6–7; Ralph, *Northern,* p. 35.

266   King led a walking mass: NYT, July 27, 1965, p. 18; Anderson and Pickering, *Confronting,* p. 161.

266   "a greater vision of our task": "A Prayer for Chicago," SCLC newsletter, Jan.–Feb. 1966, p. 2.

266   "There can be no disagreement": Cohen and Taylor, *Pharaoh,* p. 340.

266   permission to release simply the names: Valenti, notes of meeting, 12:30–3:15 P.M., July 26, 1965, in FRUS, Vol. 3, pp. 240–47. Those present with LBJ were Vice President Humphrey, McNamara, Rusk, Arthur Goldberg, Bundy, Lodge, General Wheeler, George Ball, Clark Clifford, Richard Helms, William Raborn, and LBJ aides Moyers, Valenti, and Horace Busby.

266   shot down fifty-five U.S. planes: Wheeler to McNamara, July 14, 1965, in FRUS, Vol. 3, p. 144.

266   "Are you sure they're Russians?": Valenti, notes of meeting, 12:30–3:15 P.M., July 26, 1965, in FRUS, Vol. 3, p. 241.

266   "We think that the Russians": LBJ phone call with Richard Russell, 5:46 P.M., July 26, 1965, Cit. 8399-8400, Audiotape WH6507.08, LBJ.

267   The President reconvened the group in the Cabinet Room: Valenti, notes of meeting, 6:10–6:55 P.M., July 26, 1965, in FRUS, Vol. 3, pp. 253–56.

267   hours after being sworn in: Goldberg was sworn in earlier on July 26, at 11:40 A.M., in the White House Rose Garden. Department of State *Bulletin,* August 16, 1965, pp. 265–67; PPP, July 26, 1965, pp. 786–87.

267   Clark Clifford, who had argued the George Ball position: Clifford, *Counsel,* pp. 418–21. In his memoir, Clifford says that Ball gave him a note of gratitude for supporting his lonely position: "I'm glad to have such an eloquent and persuasive comrade bleeding on the same barricade."

267   "catastrophe for my country": Valenti, "Notes of a Meeting, Camp David, Maryland, July 25, 1965, 5 P.M.," in FRUS, Vol. 3, p. 238. Clifford advised LBJ to get out of Vietnam, though not until after holding on through the monsoon season. Valenti's notes on what Clifford told LBJ make him largely prophetic on the war ahead: "Don't believe we can win in SVN [South Vietnam]. If we send in 100,000, the NVN [North Vietnamese] will meet us. If the North Vietnamese run out of men, the Chinese will send in volunteers. Russia and China don't intend for us to win the war. If we don't win, it is a catastrophe. If we lose 50,000+ it will ruin us. Five years, billions of dollars, 50,000 men, it is not for us."

267   "We are not going to be pushed out": FRUS, Vol. 3, p. 256.

267   He called the Pentagon Situation Room through the night: PDD, July 27, 1965, p. 1, LBJ.

267   "may have been a DRV trap": FRUS, Vol. 3, p. 257.

267   three secret deliberations: PDD, July 27, 1965, LBJ.

267   approved a reply to Martin Luther King's thanks: LBJ to MLK, July 27, 1965, Name File, Box 144, LBJ.

267   "I am convinced that God": MLK to LBJ, July 16, 1965, A/KP13f8.

268   Cigarette Labeling Act: Associated Press, *World in 1965,* pp. 134, 261.

268   a record 520 billion cigarettes: "Smoking Scare? What's Happened to It," *U.S. News & World Report,* Jan. 11, 1965, p. 38ff; NYT, Jan. 2, 1966, p. IV-7; *Business Week,* Dec. 3, 1966, pp. 143–47.

268   corroborated none of the government's alleged ill effects: NYT, June 19, 1968, p. 18.

268   "Let it be clear": "Tobacco Called Help in Learning," NYT, April 18, 1965, p. 31.

268   the President ordered his staff to rustle up cushioning news: Califano, *Triumph,* p. 47.

268   "How is your blood pressure?": LBJ phone call with Abe Fortas, 11:48 A.M., July 28, 1965, Cit. 8406, Audiotape WH6507.09, LBJ.

268   "could not conceal his decision": Karnow, *Vietnam,* p. 441.

268   "announced the expansion of the war": Dallek, *Flawed,* pp. 276–77.

268   "mask the central fact that this is really war": NYT, July 29, 1965, p. 12.

268   Lady Bird Johnson covered her face: Ibid.

268   as he reprised from his Selma speech: LBJ's first call that morning, at 6:55 A.M., and his last outgoing call before the press conference, after the one to Fortas, were to speech-writer Richard Goodwin, who crafted both the March 15 "We Shall Overcome" speech and the July 28 Vietnam announcement around lyrical passages uniting Johnson's boyhood formation with American purpose. PDD, July 28, 1965, pp. 1, 4.

269   "I just couldn't be happier": Hubert Humphrey phone call with Juanita Roberts (over LBJ taping system), 1:05 P.M., July 28, 1965, Cit. 8408, Audiotape WH6507.09, LBJ.

269   "We repealed 14-B today": LBJ phone call with Arthur Goldberg, 7:20 P.M., July 28, 1965, Cit. 8412, Audiotape WH6507.09, LBJ.

269   "JOHNSON ORDERS 50,000 MORE MEN": NYT, July 29, 1965, p. 1.

269   "held down to the absolute minimum": Ibid., p. 26.

269   "Don't pay any attention": Clifford, *Counsel,* p. 417.

270   "just put water on Mansfield's and on Morse's paddle": LBJ phone call with Dwight D. Eisenhower, 11:45 A.M., July 23, 1965, Cit. 8371, Audiotape WH6507.05, LBJ.

270   DeLoach noted with satisfaction: DeLoach to Mohr, July 29, 1965, FK-1662.

270   the House had added July 9: *Congressional Record,* July 9, 1965, pp. H16207–86.

270   "I am confident that the poll tax provision": MLK quoted in Katzenbach letter of July 29, 1965, cited by Rep. William Cramer of Florida, *Congressional Record,* August 4, 1965.

270   Southerners professed shock: Ibid.

271   Katzenbach steered the compromise through Thursday's conference: NYT, July 30, 1965, p. 1.

271   His bronchitis had worsened since Chicago: Garrow, *Bearing,* pp. 434–35.

271   calls from Adam Clayton Powell: Powell phone calls to MLK July 4 and July 20, over-heard on the MLK wiretap, cited in FACP-293.

271   Chauncey Eskridge to seek collection: Fred Wallace to Jack Greenberg, July 1965, and Chauncey Eskridge to Maurice Ryles, Reliable Bond Company, July 29, 1965, both A/KP10fl. The Eskridge letter begins: "When Dr. King was here in Chicago the other day, we discussed the enclosed memorandum prepared at my request by Attorney Fred L. Wallace of the NAACP Legal Fund." The dispute would be settled at a meeting of bankers, lawyers, Shuttlesworth, the bondsman Ryles, and others in December of 1965. See Eskridge to Orzell Billingsley, Jr., Sept. 14, 1965, A/SC3:38; Eskridge to Erskine Smith, Nov. 16, 1965, A/SC10f2; Eskridge to A. G. Gaston and Eskridge to Fred Shuttlesworth, Dec. 21, 1965, A/SC10f2.

271   King mediated a complex pulpit dispute: Int. Andrew Young, Oct. 26, 1991; *Jet,* Aug. 12, 1965, p. 48.

271   "you and your group must not repent": Abernathy to Carlton Reese, July 15, 1965, A/KP31f9.

271   Adam Clayton Powell could not resist: NYT, July 29, 1965, p. 58.

271   "I told him to go to cities": Ralph, *Northern,* p. 35.

271   "Moore Assails Two-Day Visit": *Philadelphia Inquirer,* July 30, 1965, p. 10.

271   a sympathetic FBI report: Philadelphia LHM dated July 30, 1965, FSC-NR.

271   protests against Moore: Ralph, *Northern,* p. 36.

272   with two planeloads of legislators: PDD, July 30, 1965, LBJ.

272   "I'm glad to have lived this long": NYT, July 31, 1965, pp. 1, 8.

272   excluded the Old Order Amish: Associated Press, *World in 1965,* pp. 128–29.

272   "gives greater satisfaction than this": NYT, July 31, 1965, p. 9.

273   front-page photograph of church elders: NYT, Aug. 2, 1965, p. 1.

273   Larry and Daniels took seats: Eagles, *Outside Agitator,* pp. 58–59.

273   went forward to the altar alone: Int. Gloria Larry House, June 29, 2000.

273   "This is the *first* time a Negro": Mathews to "Bishops Carpenter and Murray," Aug. 1, 1965, BIR/C8f25.

273   "this white man in his near Clerical clothes": Mortimer Garnett Cassell to Suffragan Bishop George M. Murray, Aug. 3, 1965, BIR/C10f55.

273   "very distasteful": Murray to Cassell, Aug. 5, 1965, BIR/C10f55.

273   "If he is hanging around causing trouble": Carpenter to Mathews, Aug. 12, 1965, BIR/C8f25.

274   seeking to learn why the school board rejected: Eagles, *Outside Agitator,* p. 139; Jeffries, "Freedom Politics," pp. 146–48.

274   Bernice Johnson went inside alone: Int. Bernice Johnson, Feb. 16, 2001.

274   Coleman closed the Negro schools a week early: Lowndes County WATS report, June 5, 1965, Reel 16, SNCC; "Great Day at Trickem Fork," *Saturday Evening Post,* May 22, 1965, pp. 89–93. The WATS report noted that Superintendent Coleman was the sister of Tom Coleman, "a known Klansman."

274   less than a month before the new fall term: Orfield, *Reconstruction,* p. 109.

274   "I'm with my friends": Int. Bernice Johnson, Feb. 16, 2001.

20: FORT DEPOSIT

PAGE

275   pickets outside segregated Girard College: Garrow, *Bearing,* p. 436; Philadelphia LHM dated August 3, 1965, FSC-NR; Hoover to SAC, Philadelphia, Aug. 11, 1965, FK-1706.

275   House of Representatives passed: *Congressional Record,* Aug. 3, 1965, p. 19191; Garrow, *Protest,* p. 132.

275   A bomb threat the next day: NYT, Aug. 5, 1965, p. 12.

275   Senate passed the identical bill, 72–18: *Congressional Record,* Aug. 4, 1965, p. 19378. Forty-nine Democrats and thirty Republicans voted for the final bill. The supporting Democrats included three Southerners: Albert Gore of Tennessee, George Smathers of Florida, and Ralph Yarborough of Texas. The only Republican to vote nay was Strom Thurmond of South Carolina, who had switched parties ten months earlier to become the first of the Deep South's new "Goldwater Republicans" in the Senate. The only other Southern Republican, John Tower of Texas, had voted against the voting rights bill on first passage, but was absent for the decisive vote on the conference report.

275   "fellow revolutionaries": NYT, Aug. 5, 1965, p. 13.

275   Justice Department stood ready to file: "Outline of Proposed Implementation of Voting Rights Act of 1965," attachment for Doar to Califano, Aug. 5, 1965, Legislative Background, VRA '65, Box 1, LBJ.

275   Johnson disclosed this breakthrough agenda: MLK press statement after White House meeting, Aug. 5, 1965, A/KS; Hoover to SAC, Atlanta, Aug. 6, 1965, FK-1688.

275   meeting scheduled to discuss conditions: Lee White to LBJ, July 23, 1965, Name File, Box 144, LBJ; Lee White to LBJ, Aug. 4, 1965, Diary Back-up, Box 20, LBJ. Johnson's

diary shows that the meeting included Ralph Abernathy and Walter Fauntroy with King, and aides Lee White and Major Hugh Robinson with LBJ, lasting from 4:17 to 5:55 P.M., and that Juanita Abernathy joined the group afterward for photographs: PDD, Aug. 5, 1965, p. 5, LBJ.

275   Thursday night, King returned: NYT, Aug. 6, 1965, p. 12.

276   "Be sure to get one of the pens": Dellinger, *From Yale,* pp. 220–21.

276   He and Dellinger separated: Ibid.; Longenecker, *Peacemaker,* pp. 291–92.

276   "Today is a triumph": NYT, Aug. 7, 1965, pp. 1, 8.

277   "The chair recognizes the Senator": WP, Aug. 7, 1965, p. 4.

277   carved of mahogany in 1819: Caro, *Master,* pp. 4, 581.

277   "We just got to": LBJ phone call with Nicholas Katzenbach, 6:10 P.M., Aug. 6, 1965, Cit. 8514, Audiotape WH6508.02, LBJ.

277   "You didn't do a damn thing": LBJ phone call with Carl Albert, 6:16 P.M., Aug. 6, 1965, Cit. 8515-16, Audiotape WH6508.02, LBJ. LBJ immediately called Speaker Mc-Cormack with congratulations that also jumped quickly into battering pressure: "Now, will you help us work on higher education and immigration, and get a bill quickly on those two?"

277   Dellinger was among roughly six hundred pickets: Dellinger, "We Seek No Wider War," *Liberation,* Sept. 1965, pp. 4–6; Zaroulis and Sullivan, *Who Spoke Up?,* pp. 20–21, 50–53; Dellinger, *From Yale,* pp. 208–15.

277   guard of two hundred police: NYT, Aug. 7, 1965, p. 3.

277   Bob Moses of SNCC: A. J. Muste, "Assembly of Unrepresented People: The Weekend That Was," *Liberation,* Sept. 1965, pp. 28–29.

278   followed Moses as a teenager: On McComb in 1961, see Dittmer, *Local People,* pp. 99–115; Branch, *Parting,* pp. 492–523.

278   "Negro boys should not honor the draft": Dittmer, *Local People,* pp. 349–51; Lawson, *Pursuit,* pp. 96–97.

278   John Lewis, though he had signed: Muste to Lewis, March 29, 1965, Reel 1, SNCC.

278   issued a pained statement: NYT, Aug. 7, 1965, p. 3; John Lewis, oral history by Archie Allen, pp. 213–14, AAP. Marion Barry reported that he and Cleveland Sellers of SNCC joined Lewis for the meeting with LBJ. White House records show that only James Farmer of CORE and Lewis were present as guests. Lewis hand-delivered a letter to the President. See Barry, WATS report, Aug. 6, 1965, Reel 16, SNCC; PDD, Aug. 6, 1965, p. 1, LBJ; Lewis to LBJ, Aug. 6, 1965, and Lee White to Lewis, Aug. 9, 1965, Legislative Background, VRA '65, Box 1, LBJ.

278   photograph in the next issue of *Life*: "Pacifist Protests," *Life,* Aug. 20, 1965, p. 31.

278   "Sometimes I wish": WP, Aug. 7, 1965, pp. 1, 14.

278   "hyper-militants and the authoritarians": DeBenedetti, *Ordeal,* pp. 120–21.

278   Muste's Declaration of Conscience: Powers, *War,* p. 192; Zaroulis and Sullivan, *Who Spoke Up?,* p. 20. Muste had been trying to get King to sign the declaration for months. Cf. Muste to MLK, April 23 and July 11, 1965, both A/SC4f44.

279   "Negroes better than anyone else": A. J. Muste, "Assembly of Unrepresented People: The Weekend That Was," *Liberation,* Sept. 1965, pp. 28–29; Robinson, *Abraham,* p. 132.

279   King preached at New York's Riverside Church: Log, Aug. 8, 1965, A/SC29; speech to National Funeral Directors, Aug. 8, 1965, A/KS9.

279   John Lewis was arrested: Americus, Georgia, WATS report, Aug. 8, 1965, Reel 16, SNCC.

279 "I have my own personal fears": Stokely Carmichael, "A Working Paper on a South-Wide People's Conference," Aug. 8, 1965, Reel 16, SNCC.

279 at the first mass meeting yet dared in Fort Deposit: "via Selma," Fort Deposit WATS report, August 9, 1965, Reel 16, SNCC; Eagles, *Outside Agitator*, p. 167.

279 "the toughest area in Lowndes County": "Lowndes County Weekly Report," Aug. 5, 1965, Reel 18, SNCC.

279 "run out by the Klan": Jeffries, "Freedom Politics," pp. 79–81.

279 crowd of some four hundred: Ibid. Also int. Jimmy Rogers, March 7, 2000; int. Bob Mants, Sept. 8, 2000.

279 Carmichael told the Sapersteins to lay across laps: Int. Harold and Marcia Saperstein, Dec. 12, 1991.

280 golden orator from Dothan: Carter, *Politics*, pp. 232, 275–76; Lesher, *George Wallace*, pp. 172–75; Jones, *Wallace Story*, pp. 54–55.

280 "Richmond, we ain't telling you": Int. Richmond Flowers, Aug. 9, 1990; "Flowers Puts Klan Issue in Lowndes County Case," MA, Aug. 22, 1965, p. 1, cited in Mobile FBI report dated Aug. 25, 1965, FJMD-32, pp. 121–22.

280 "just sick": Eagles, *Outside Agitator*, p. 164.

280 by order of General Andrew Jackson: Ibid., pp. 109–10; town of Fort Deposit, official Web site, 2002.

280 Three of the county's four doctors and dentists: Ibid.

280 Only forty-eight Negroes: Alabama Voting Rights report, Aug. 13, 1965, Reel 16, SNCC.

281 applicants outside Selma's courthouse: Int. Harold and Marcia Saperstein, Dec. 12, 1991.

281 resolve took hold among the teenagers: Int. Jimmy Rogers, March 7, 2000; int. Bob Mants, Sept. 8, 2000.

281 "There will be demonstrations": Jimmy Rogers, "Lowndes County Ala." WATS report, Aug. 11, 1965, Reel 16, SNCC.

281 "Human Rights—Basic Issues—The Grand Alliance": Program, Ninth Annual Convention, Southern Christian Leadership Conference, August 9–13, 1965, King Archives.

281 the same event during the siege: Branch, *Parting*, pp. 642–46, 653–56.

281 "Anything else I can do for you, sir?": Int. Harvey Cox, May 3, 1991.

281 swelling numbers paraded freely to City Hall: SAC, Birmingham, to Director, Aug. 10, 1965, FSC-497.

281 They decried the gridlock failure: Sermon, "Selma Insights," attached to a letter from John Ruskin Clark to Francis X. Walter, Dec. 16, 1965, BIR/FW2f5, p. 3.

281 came Mordecai Johnson: Mays, *Born*, pp. 39, 148; Reddick, *Crusader*, p. 80; King, *My Life*, p. 71; Wofford, *Kennedys and Kings*, p. 117.

281 school board in stinging protest: *Jet*, July 8, 1965, p. 26.

282 ecumenical conference on religion and race: Branch, *Pillar*, pp. 21–32.

282 integrate the Midwestern meat plants: Halpern, *Meatpackers*, pp. 33–42, 110–12, 127–44.

282 "You'd be surprised": Int. Harvey Cox, May 3, 1991.

282 FBI agents reported to headquarters: SAC, Birmingham, to Director, Aug. 10, 1965, FSC-497.

282 "We are having a good convention": Wiretap transcript of telephone conversation between Stanley Levison and Bea Levison, Aug. 11, 1965, FLNY-9-663a.

282 send in a handwritten note: Wachtel note headed, "Martin—," Aug. 11, 1965, A/KP25f31. Wachtel included a draft thank-you note to Agger, which would be sent out, "Dictated by Dr. King, but signed in his absence," while King was in Los Angeles for the Watts riots. MLK to Miss Carol Agger, Aug. 19, 1965, A/KP25f31. The formal approval from the IRS arrived in a letter written to the Gandhi Society for Human Rights, Inc., care of Harry Wachtel, dated Aug. 10, 1965, A/KP25f31.

282 Senate confirmation of Thurgood Marshall: Fenderson, *Thurgood,* p. 114.

282 He waited in the hotel lobby: Birmingham LHM dated Aug. 17, 1965, FK-NR, p. 3.

282 Wachtel wrote a second appeal: Wachtel to MLK, handwritten, Aug. 13, 1965, A/KP25f31.

282 pastor wrung permission from the deacons: *Jet,* Aug. 12, 1965, p. 48; Rev. John Cross oral history, A/OH, pp. 52–57. Cross recalled that his church member Maxine McNair, mother of Denise McNair, one of the four girls killed by the church bomb, helped sway the congregation with an appeal that she and her husband, Chris, did not lose their only child in order to give up.

282 King again faced more than thirty: Minutes, SCLC board meeting, Aug. 9–10, 1965, A/KP29f5.

283 Williams himself conceded: Ibid., pp. 5–6, 12–13.

283 resolution calling for Vietnam peace negotiations: Wachtel sent an early draft to MLK attached to a letter of July 26, 1965, A/KP25f31. FBI wiretappers overheard King's conversations about the Vietnam resolution with Wachtel, Rustin, and Andrew Young. Cf. SAC, New York, to Director, Aug. 4, 1965, FK-1693; NY LHM dated Aug. 10, 1965, FK-NR.

283 David Garrow would call an "implicit rebuke": Garrow, *Bearing,* p. 438.

283 "the very survival of mankind": Andrew J. Young, "An Experiment in Power," Keynote Address, Ninth Annual Convention, Aug. 11, 1965, A/SC131f1.

284 Ronald Frye celebrated his discharge: Horne, *Fire,* pp. 53–56; *Jet,* Sept. 2, 1965, pp. 4–22; *Jet,* Sept. 9, 1965, pp. 14–18.

284 One officer would testify: Governor's Commission, *Violence in the City,* pp. 10–12.

285 C. H. Watts: Horne, *Fire,* p. 26.

285 "milled around inside the blocked-off area": LAT, Aug. 12, 1965, p. 1.

285 "What do you want": CBS Reports, *Watts: Riot or Revolt?,* broadcast of Dec. 7, 1965, T77:0395, MOB.

285 "Arrest Causes Near Riot": NYT, Aug. 12, 1965, p. 15.

285 crowds returned to Avalon Boulevard: Horne, *Fire,* pp. 57–59.

285 "and Congress is turning out decisions like sausages": Transcript of recording, " 'Visions of Things to Come,' A Panel of the SCLC Convention, Birmingham, Ala., Thursday, Aug. 12, 1965," JMP.

286 "One day Jesus was talking": Ibid.

286 an international peace army into Vietnam: SC, Aug. 20, 1965, p. 1.

287 King presented the SCLC Freedom Medal: Program, Ninth Annual Convention, Southern Christian Leadership Conference, Aug. 9–13, 1965, King Archives, Atlanta, Ga.; int. Diane Nash, Oct. 26, 1997; int. James Bevel, Nov. 23, 1997; and Dec. 10, 1998.

287 citizens' initiative unmatched: Branch, *Pillar,* pp. 75–77, 139–41, 245–46, 524.

287 the honorees nevertheless were painfully estranged: Ibid., pp. 587–88.

287 "Few events in my lifetime": King statement, Aug. 12, 1965, A/SC28f7.

287 including Ho Chi Minh: "Dr. King to Send Appeal to Hanoi," NYT, Aug. 13, 1965, p. 1; " 'I'll Contact Reds': King," *Chicago Tribune,* Aug. 13, 1965, p. 1.

287   3,500 people by FBI estimate: Birmingham LHM dated Aug. 17, 1965, FK-NR, p. 1.

287   mortician A. A. "Sam" Rayner: Int. Richard Morrisroe, Feb. 20–21, 2002.

287   Daddy King was the real preacher: Int. Harold and Marcia Saperstein, Dec. 12, 1991.

287   Father Richard Morrisroe: Int. Richard Morrisroe by John Morris, Feb. 1966, JDC; Eagles, *Outside Agitator,* pp. 166–67.

287   the next alderman: Anderson and Pickering, *Confronting,* pp. 316, 326.

288   "nearly choked him": Int. Richard Morrisroe, Feb. 20–21, 2002.

288   delivered him to bunk on the porch floor: Ibid.; Mendelsohn, *Martyrs,* pp. 204–5.

288   *Four Quartets* of T. S. Eliot: Int. Richard Morrisroe, Feb. 20–21, 2002.

288   After seventy-five people were injured: LAT, Aug. 13, 1965, p. 1; NYT, Aug. 13, 1965, p. 1.

288   a second lull had convinced authorities: Governor's Commission, *Violence in the City,* pp. 15–16; Horne, *Fire,* p. 69.

288   "10:00 A.M. Major looting became general": Transcript, CBS Reports, *Watts: Riot or Revolt?,* broadcast of Dec. 7, 1965, p. 13, T77:0395, MOB.

288   Langston Hughes reported: Bayard Rustin, "The Watts 'Manifesto' and the McCone Report," *Commentary,* March 1966, p. 30.

288   assaults on white journalists: Horne, *Fire,* pp. 59–60, 323; LAT, Aug. 14, 1965, pp. 1, 12.

288   first Negro reporter ever hired by the *Los Angeles Times:* Ibid., pp. 66–67, 103; transcript, CBS Reports, *Watts: Riot or Revolt?,* broadcast of Dec. 7, 1965, T77:0395, MOB, p. 24.

288   California authorities summoned Governor Pat Brown: "Eight Men Slain; Guard Moves In," LAT, Aug. 14, 1965, p. 1, reprinted in Library of America Anthology, *Reporting Civil Rights,* pp. 414–20.

288   mobilized 14,000 National Guard troops: Governor's Commission, *Violence in the City,* pp. 16–18.

288   moved ahead of them into the riot zone: Ibid., p. 19; Horne, *Fire,* pp. 70–75.

289   "The Negroes have broken into some gun stores": Wiretap transcript of telephone conversation between Stanley Levison and Dora McDonald, 11:30 P.M., Aug. 13, 1965, FLNY-9-665a, p. 6. In previous conversations that day under the same intercept number, Levison and Andrew Young had discussed the wording of closing statements for the Birmingham SCLC convention.

289   Levison dictated suggested replies: Wiretap transcript of telephone call from Stanley Levison to "Dora," 1:05 A.M., Aug. 14, 1965, FLNY-9-666.

289   Miami stopover en route: Garrow, *Bearing,* p. 439.

289   rushed a transcript by encoded Teletype: SAC, New York, to Director, 3:41 A.M., Aug. 14, 1965, FK-1727.

289   "long-time Communist": Blind LHM dated Aug. 16, 1965, marked "Original to the White House and xerox copies to Secretary of State Rusk, the Attorney General, Deputy Attorney General, and Assistant Attorneys General Yeagley and Doar," FK-1768.

289   "I know you have grievances": Ibid.; wiretap transcript of telephone call from Stanley Levison to "Dora," 1:05 A.M., Aug. 14, 1965, FLNY-9-666, pp. 2–3.

290   shaded area of a church lawn: Mendelsohn, *Martyrs,* pp. 205–7; Eagles, *Outside Agitator,* pp. 169–71; int. Jimmy Rogers, March 7, 2000, March 12, 2003; int. Gloria Larry House, June 29, 2000; int. Ruby Sales, March 22, 2003; int. Joyce Bailey, April 11, 2003; int. Geraldine Logan (Gamble), April 11, 2003.

290 a story tip from the SNCC office: Patricia Brooks to John Lewis, July 25, 1965, Reel 1, SNCC; WATS report on phone calls to John Doar and a Lewis telegram to George Wallace, Aug. 12, 1965, Reel 16, SNCC.

290 "I don't want to scare": Patricia Brooks, "Lowndes County: Prelude to Murder," *National Guardian,* Aug. 28, 1965, p. 8.

290 "one good whack at the Man": Ibid.

291 They reopened leadership issues: Int. Jimmy Rogers, March 7, 2000; int. Richard Morrisroe, Feb. 20–21, 2002; int. Ruby Sales, March 22, 2003.

291 "If that's what you want to do": Int. John McMeans, April 12, 2003.

291 demonstrations scarcely lasted a minute: Ibid.; WATS report by Shirley Walker and Jean Wiley, Aug. 14, 1965, Reel 16, SNCC; Richard Morrisroe int. by John B. Morris, played at the Pick Congress Hotel dinner, Chicago, Feb. 20, 1966, JDC.

292 The car with the shattered windshield: "48 Picketers Arrested in First Fort Deposit March," SC, Aug. 20, 1965, p. 6.

292 shards of glass in his mouth: Int. Sanford J. Ungar, May 27, 2003.

292 "I looked directly at Stokely": Oral history int. by David Gordon, Oct. 5, 1965, JDC.

292 "Because of the dogs": Scott B. Smith, "Report of Incident," dated Aug. 16, 1965, A/SN94; int. Scott B. Smith, April 12, 2003.

21: WATTS AND HAYNEVILLE

PAGE

293 "When he got off the airplane": Transcript of White House phone call among Jack Valenti, Lee White, and Joseph Califano, 6:25 P.M., Aug. 14, 1965, Cit. 8536-37, Audiotape WH6508.04, LBJ.

293 secluded on Martha's Vineyard: Ibid. Lee White recalled later that Califano took charge in the Watts crisis on the strength of his contacts at the Pentagon, more than making up for his lack of seniority. (White had served as White House counselor since 1961, and before then had worked for LBJ in the Senate. By contrast, Califano started work at the White House about two weeks before the riot.) "And before I knew it, Joe was kind of on the telephone with the President much more than I was," White stated, "which didn't really disturb me very much." Califano reached LBJ that Saturday night with a proposal on the vacation problem: "I think, sir, that what we need is a memorandum that says that the head of an agency and the deputy head of an agency cannot be out of town at the same time without permission from the White House, which is the same kind of memorandum that Bob has out in the Defense Department." LBJ phone call with Joseph Califano, 8:09 P.M., Aug. 14, 1965, Cit. 8538-39, Audiotape WH6508.04, LBJ.

293 "We ought to blow up": Califano, *Triumph,* p. 60.

293 retrieved LeRoy Collins: Lee White oral history by Joe B. Frantz, March 2, 1971, pp. 17–18; NYT, Aug. 15, 1965, p. 77; Califano, *Triumph,* p. 63; Horne, *Fire,* p. 284.

293 curfew forced Otis Chandler: LAT, Aug. 14, 1965, p. 1.

293 " 'Burn, Baby, Burn' ": LAT, Aug. 15, 1965, p. 1; Horne, *Fire,* pp. 326–27. The phrase originated with disc jockey Nathaniel "Magnificent" Montague, who before August had opened his KGFJ radio broadcast shouting "Burn with Montague!" Watts historian Gerald Horne found the term "a reference to music and musicians and to a style of life, not necessarily a call to arson," but the arson connotation took hold during the riots. Outraged authorities obtained Montague's agreement to desist.

294   attendance record for a pop concert: *Rolling Stone Rock Almanac,* p. 105.

294   stalled the same Sunday in Miami: Garrow, *Bearing,* p. 439.

294   Bayard Rustin urged him to avoid: Branigan to Sullivan, Aug. 14, 1965, FK-1720; SAC, New York to Director, 1:09 A.M., Aug. 15, 1965, FK-NR.

294   "I think I ought to be out there": Int. Thomas Kilgore, Nov. 8, 1983.

294   King's rescheduled tour in July: King had completed a tour of Los Angeles as a possible site for a "Northern" movement, a few days after a postponement on July 6 to confer with LBJ about Vietnam. Cf. Transcript of King appearance on Channel 2, KNXT-TV, program *Newsmakers,* July 10, 1965, FK-1614.

294   "dress rehearsal": NYT, Aug. 16, 1965, p. 18.

294   "sinister and evil forces": LAT, Aug. 15, 1965, p. C; *Jet,* Sept. 2, 1965, p. 27.

294   "if Billy Graham can ride": Int. Thomas Kilgore, Nov. 8, 1983.

294   King persuaded Bayard Rustin: NY LHM dated Aug. 18, 1965, FK-NR; SAC, Los Angeles, to Director and Atlanta, Aug. 17, 1965, FK-1726. The wiretap intercepted Rustin's draft of a press statement, which King delivered in modified form on arrival in Los Angeles.

294   the site of his arrest in 1953: Longenecker, *Peacemaker,* pp. 153–65.

294   Rev. Kilgore had served as intercessor: Branch, *Parting,* pp. 314–16, 328–29, 860–62.

294   King made a brief statement: "Statement by Dr. Martin Luther King, Jr. on Arrival in Los Angeles, August 17, 1965," A/KS.

294   "and was hustled off": LAT, Aug. 18, 1965, pp. 3, 15; WP, Aug. 17, 1965, pp. 1, 4.

294   "amazing political implications": NYT, Aug. 16, 1965, pp. 1, 17.

295   "I don't know what the governor is doing": LAT, Aug. 19, 1965, p. 1.

295   Negro leaders gave him the idea: NYT, Aug. 15, 1965, p. 76.

295   "We're on top": *Jet,* Sept. 9, 1965, p. 8; Bayard Rustin, "The Watts 'Manifesto' and the McCone Report," *Commentary,* March 1966, p. 29; NYT, Aug. 18, 1965, p. 20; Horne, *Fire,* p. 138.

295   he accused "the Black Muslims": "Parker Hints Muslims Took Part in Rioting, Believes Members of Group Moved in on What Otherwise Was Unorganized Action," LAT, Aug. 17, 1965.

295   postponed Rams-Cowboys game: LAT, Aug. 19, 1965, p. 3; Horne, *Fire,* p. 332.

295   "19 men sprawled": LAT, Aug. 19, 1965, p. 1; LAT, Aug. 20, 1965, p. 17; Horne, *Fire,* pp. 126–28.

295   "tables were broken": LAT, Aug. 19, 1965, p. 24.

295   tear gas grenades down storm drains: NYT, Aug. 19, 1965, p. 16.

295   "Do you see any bullet marks": *Jet,* Sept. 2, 1965, pp. 28–29.

295   "stormed the fortified temple": *Chicago Tribune,* Aug. 19, 1965, p. 1, newsclip, RS, File 589, CHS.

296   "shattering assault": LAT, Aug. 19, 1965, p. 1.

296   "The fanatical Black Muslims": "Police Break Muslim Taboo, Enter Temple," Ibid., p. 24.

296   altercation at the same mosque in 1962: Branch, *Pillar,* pp. 3–10.

296   Malcolm X had captivated mass meetings: Ibid., pp. 10–20.

296   expunged formal rules that barred: Ibid.; Horne, *Fire,* pp. 145, 156.

296   Three Muslims freed after the 1962 raid were seized again: CD, Aug. 23, 1965, newsclip, RS, File 589, CHS.

296   "Get out of here, Dr. King!": NYT, Aug. 19, 1965, p. 16. King's interactions at the

Westminster center drawn also from "Dr. King Hears Watts Protest over Heckling," LAT, Aug. 19, 1965, p. 3; "King Did Overcome Hostility to Reason with L.A. Youths," *Jet,* Sept. 2, 1965, pp. 24–26; transcript, CBS broadcast of December 7, 1965, p. 15, T77:0395, MOB; Horne, *Fire,* pp. 182–83, 219.

297   King moved on to see Governor Brown: Garrow, *Bearing,* p. 439; LAT, Aug. 20, 1965, p. 1.

297   "I am very sorry that you see me": MLK to Edmund G. Brown, Aug. 19, 1965, A/KP5f1.

298   "in-depth, frank discussion": LAT, Aug. 20, 1965, pp. 1, 3, 26.

298   "King Assailed by Yorty": Ibid.; NYY, Sept. 20, 1965, p. 16.

298   "completely nonplussed": Bayard Rustin, "The Watts 'Manifesto' and the McCone Report," *Commentary,* March 1966, p. 32.

298   "We as Negro leaders": LAT, Aug. 19, 1965, p. 26.

298   "any statesmanship and creative leadership": LAT, Aug. 21, 1965, p. 4; MLK interview in Los Angeles, Aug. 20, 1965, ABC-20030, A/KS.

299   offer his findings directly to President Johnson: Ibid.; Los Angeles LHM dated Aug. 23, 1965, FK-NR.

299   Joyce Bailey, jailed Saturday: Transcript, joint interview of Jimmy Rogers, Ruby Sales, Gloria Larry, Willie Vaughn, Shirley Walker, and Joyce Bailey at the Episcopal Theological School, following a memorial service for Jonathan Daniels, Aug. 25, 1965, JDC; Eagles, *Outside Agitator,* pp. 172–74, 227–28.

299   Gloria Larry knew: Ibid.; int. Gloria Larry House, June 29, 2000.

299   Sales cajoled the trusty: Eagles, *Outside Agitator,* p. 231; int. Ruby Sales, March 22, 2003.

299   Sales had opposed letting Daniels: Ibid.; int. Ruby Sales by Daniel Zwerdling, *Weekend All Things Considered,* National Public Radio, Aug. 23, 1997, JDC.

300   "John, it's prayer time now": Int. John McMeans, April 12, 2003.

300   The SNCC treasury was nearly empty: John Lewis to MLK, July 22, 1965, Reel 1, SNCC. Lewis asked King for a "gift or loan of $10,000 so we can meet our payroll and cover pressing bills."

300   gift of $5,000 from SCLC: Ralph Abernathy to John Lewis, Aug. 19, 1965, enclosing SCLC's check of $5,000 as a gift, A/SC44f10. Abernathy sent a separate gift of $7,000 the same day to Victoria Gray in the Washington office of the Mississippi Freedom Democratic Party, which was challenging Mississippi's members in the House of Representatives on the ground that their elections unconstitutionally limited black voters.

300   obstruction about bail procedures: Int. Silas Norman, June 28, 2000; int. Martha Prescod Norman, June 29, 2000; int. Bob Mants, Sept. 8, 2000.

300   motion for the removal of the Fort Deposit cases: Eagles, *Outside Agitator,* p. 177.

300   "written complaint alleging a minor child": John Doar to Mr. [sic] Hulda Coleman, Aug. 16, 1965, ADAH, Alabama Governors' Legal Advisors' Files, School Files D-W, 1963–67, SG 20061, Folder 22, cited in Jeffries, "Freedom Politics," p. 154.

301   "criminal assassination": James G. Clark, sheriff of Dallas County, open letter dated June 28, 1965, BIR/C10f56. "This is about a murder," wrote Clark in a four-page letter he asked recipients to pass along to friends. "You might say it is a lynching. It is about the assassination of a peaceful town, Selma, Alabama, racially undisturbed in September, 1963. . . . The President directed this train of venom at the deep South states in a revengeful plan—the victims were the states that refused to vote for him, especially Alabama. . . . How the dirtiest, filthiest, slimiest, most unwashed, along with some

genuinely concerned people, carried this out in detail is history. . . . Is this too shocking for you to believe? Even citizens in Selma who have lived through this horror are
still experiencing it and wonder how it came about. . . . God help you if these bunch of
race baiters and criminals, with the blessings of the Federal government, descend
upon you, your family, your block, or your city. It will be an experience that you can
never erase from your mind."

301 "This department is now in receipt": Colonel Albert J. Lingo to "All Sheriffs and Po-
     lice Chiefs, All Counties and Municipalities, State of Alabama," Aug. 16, 1965,
     BIR/FW2f8.

301 Coleman's brother Tom made a trip into Montgomery: Eagles, *Outside Agitator,* p. 220.

301 "Dearest Mum": Jonathan Daniels to Constance Daniels, Aug. 17, 1965, cited in
     Schneider, *Martyr,* p. 83.

301 enduring a police stop: Eagles, *Outside Agitator,* pp. 174–75.

301 jailers to clear away untouched: Int. Francis Walter, Sept. 7, 2000; int. Richard Morris-
     roe, Feb. 20–21, 2002; int. Jimmy Rogers, March 7, 2000.

302 Rev. Francis Walter: Francis X. Walter oral history by Stanley Smith, Aug. 1968, RJB,
     pp. 7–8; Callahan, *Quilting Bee,* p. 6.

302 He took shifts sleeping upright on the floor: Richard Morrisroe int. by Rev. John B.
     Morris, presented at Chicago ESCRU dinner, Feb. 20, 1966, pp. 9–11; int. Jimmy
     Rogers, March 7, 2000; int. Richard Morrisroe, Feb. 20–21, 2003; int. Jimmy Rogers,
     March 12, 2003; int. Sammy Bailey, April 11, 2003; int. John McMeans, April 12, 2003.

302 "Reverend, have you ever stood": Sermon, "Selma Insights," attached to a letter from
     John Ruskin Clark to Francis X. Walter, Dec. 16, 1965, BIR/FW2f5, p. 6.

302 I had a dream just last night: Quotation from "a small, 3 x 5 notebook," in "A Letter to
     the Catholic Community of Saint Columbanus and to Our Park Manor Neighbors,"
     Feb. 18, 1980, courtesy of Richard Morrisroe.

302 "Kerry Irish bent": Ibid.

303 Deputies banged open the cell doors: NYT, Aug. 21, 1965, p. 1; transcript, interviews
     of cellmates by John B. Tillson following the Jonathan Daniels memorial service in
     Cambridge, Massachusetts, Aug. 25, 1965, JDC; Richard Morrisroe int. by John B.
     Morris, played at the Pick Congress Hotel dinner, Chicago, Feb. 20, 1966, JDC;
     Mendelsohn, *Martyrs,* pp. 209–10; Eagles, *Outside Agitator,* pp. 177–79.

303 "The store is closed": Ibid.; Ruby Sales handwritten statement headed "On Friday,
     August 20," Reel 18, SNCC; int. Jimmy Rogers, March 7, 2000; int. Gloria Larry
     House, June 29, 2000; int. Ruby Sales, March 22, 2003; Hampton and Fayer, *Voices,* pp.
     274–75.

303 Savage twelve-gauge barrel: Mobile report dated Jan. 20, 1967, FJMD-65, p. 2. The
     FBI identified the weapon used by Coleman as a "Savage, Model 775-A, twelve gauge,
     semi-automatic, with variable choke, bearing serial number 287076."

303 Shell wadding tore a ragged hole: Eagles, *Outside Agitator,* p. 221.

303 Joyce Bailey was twenty feet away in full flight: Int. Richard Morrisroe, Feb. 20–21,
     2002; int. Joyce Bailey, April 11, 2003; Mobile FBI report dated Oct. 7, 1965, FJMD-49,
     p. 2.

304 "I just shot two preachers": Mendelsohn, *Martyrs,* p. 210.

304 "You traitors!": Int. Joyce Bailey, April 11, 2003; int. John McMeans, April 12, 2003;
     int. Gloria Larry House, June 29, 2000; int. Sammy Bailey, April 11, 2003; int. Ruby
     Sales, March 22, 2003.

304 jailhouse reading books abandoned: Eagles, *Outside Agitator,* p. 229.

304	he could find no wounded: Int. Shirley Walker by John B. Tillson, Aug. 25, 1965, JDC, pp. 6–7.
304	Morrisroe barely conscious of Daniels: Int. Richard Morrisroe, Feb. 20–21, 2002.
304	first White House Conference on Equal Employment Opportunity: *Report of the White House Conference on Equal Employment Opportunity, August 19, 20, 1965,* GPO 66-60299; NYT, Aug. 21, 1965, p. 1.
304	left desperate messages: Int. Shirley Walker by John B. Tillson, Aug. 25, 1965, JDC, pp. 6–7.
304	insisted Peter Hall's clients were still in their cells: Willie Emma Scott, WATS report of 7:30 P.M., Aug. 20, 1965, Reel 18, SNCC.
304	Doar broke the wall of silence: Int. Shirley Walker by John B. Tillson, Aug. 25, 1965, JDC, p. 7.
305	He notified the FBI: McGowan to Rosen, Aug. 20, 1965, FJMD-15.
305	to administer last rites: Int. Richard Morrisroe, Feb. 20–21, 2002.
305	Dr. Charles Cox assembled trauma teams: Ibid.; Mendelsohn, *Martyrs,* p. 211; Eagles, *Outside Agitator,* pp. 180–82.
305	"if Morrisroe should die": Mobile office report dated Sept. 10, 1965, FJMD-38, p. 3.
305	"The White House makes a great mistake": Hoover note on DeLoach to Mohr, Aug. 20, 1965, FK-1783.
305	cut his second-year poverty budget: NYT, Aug. 20, 1965, p. 1.
306	"just cut me in half": LBJ phone call with MLK, 5:10 P.M., Aug. 20, 1965, Cit. 8578, Audiotape WH6508.07, LBJ.
306	had taken a long yachting holiday: NYT, Aug. 13, 1965, p. 14; NYT, Aug. 18, 1965, p. 10.
307	"rats eating on people's uh, uh, children": LBJ phone call with MLK, 5:10 P.M., Aug. 20, 1965, Cit. 8578, Audiotape WH6508.07, LBJ.
307	He used language nearly identical: LBJ phone call with John McCone, 12:10 P.M., Aug. 18, 1965, Cit. 8550, Audiotape WH6508.05. After teasing McCone about making "filthy gold" in retirement from government, Johnson advised him to take the commission assignment in order to help the country understand the nation's "powder kegs" in places like Watts: "They've got really absolutely nothing to live for, 40 percent of them are unemployed, these youngsters, and they live with rats and they've got no place to sleep and they start, they're all, uh broken homes and illegitimate families, and all. Narcotics are circulating around them, and we've isolated them, and they're all in one area, and when they move in, why, we move out."
307	"Johnson Rebukes Rioters": NYT, Aug. 21, 1965, p. 1.
307	"Refer to that Howard University speech": LBJ phone call with MLK, 5:10 P.M., Aug. 20, 1965, Cit. 8578, Audiotape WH6508.07, LBJ.
308	pitched battle, at Chu Lai: NYT, Aug. 22, 1965, p. IV-1.
308	"I've said that, Mr. President": LBJ phone call with MLK, 5:10 P.M., Aug. 20, 1965, Cit. 8578, Audiotape WH6508.07, LBJ.
309	switched briefly to derisive laughter: Office conversation after LBJ phone call with MLK, with voices, including LBJ, Harry McPherson, Lee White, and perhaps Jack Valenti, 5:24 P.M., Aug. 20, 1965, Cit. 8579–80, Audiotape WH6508.07, LBJ.
309	Harry McPherson had drafted: McPherson remarks in PBS documentary, *The Great Society Remembered,* Guggenheim Productions, Inc., 1985.
309	The President admonished King on Vietnam: Garrow, *Bearing,* p. 440.
309	"Let's get up a program": Office conversation after LBJ phone call with MLK, with

voices, including LBJ, Harry McPherson, Lee White, and perhaps Jack Valenti, 5:24 P.M., Aug. 20, 1965, Cit. 8579–80, Audiotape WH6508.07, LBJ.

310   "Who of you could have predicted": NYT, Aug. 21, 1965, pp. 1, 8.

310   "What does he mean": LBJ phone call with Lee White, 7:40 P.M., Aug. 21, 1965, Cit. 8608, Audiotape WH6508.09, LBJ.

310   had maneuvered J. Edgar Hoover: Branch, *Pillar,* pp. 365–74.

310   Katzenbach gently corrected: In a phone call six days after the Daniels murder, LBJ exhorted Attorney General Katzenbach to push a home rule bill with the argument that it was harder to gain the vote for Washington, D.C., than for "Downs County" or Mississippi. LBJ: "Where is Downs County?" Katzenbach: "Lowndes." LBJ: "Alabama? Lowndes." Katzenbach: "Lowndes is in Alabama." LBJ: "Now. A man's got a whole lot better chance of getting the vote in Lowndes, a nigra has, in Lowndes County, Alabama, than he has of getting the vote in the District of Columbia Committee in the House of Representatives." LBJ phone call with Nicholas Katzenbach, 2:50 P.M., Aug. 26, 1965, Cit. 8639, Audiotape WH6508.11, LBJ.

310   He first told FBI agents: Teletype, Mobile Office, to Director, 1:36 A.M., Aug. 21, 1965, FJMD-2.

311   Alabama authorities reversed themselves: Eagles, *Outside Agitator,* pp. 195, 201.

311   identification badge was merely a gun permit: Teletype, Office, Mobile to Director, 2:31 P.M., Aug. 24, 1965, FJMD-22; Director to FBI Mobile, Aug. 26, 1965, FJMD-26.

311   "alone and acted independently": Rosen to Belmont, Nov. 2, 1965, FJMD-53.

311   "is being conducted at the specific request": Ibid.

311   Rev. John Morris sought help from his friend: Eagles, *Outside Agitator,* pp. 199–200.

312   "We all did it": Branch, *Parting,* p. 891.

312   Gardenia White, granddaughter of Rosie Steele: Int. Gardenia White, March 10, 2000; int. Timothy Mays, March 9, 2000.

312   petition that records be opened: Eagles, *Outside Agitator,* p. 253; NYT, Oct. 26, 1965, p. 28.

312   pitch for the Mets: "For Instance, Can She Pitch for Mets?," NYT, Aug. 20, 1965, p. 1.

312   laws of thirty states from Massachusetts to Wyoming: Table 8, "State Laws with Respect to Jury Service by Women, as of January 1965," in Plaintiffs' Brief, Vol. 1, by Charles Morgan, Jr., Orzell Billingsley, Jr., Judge Dorothy Kenyon, Dr. Pauli Murray, and Melvin L. Wulf, *White v. Crook,* Civil Action No. 2263-N.

312   upheld a state law: *Hoyt v. Florida,* 368 U.S. 57 (1961), cited in Pauli Murray and Mary O. Eastwood, "Jane Crow and the Law: Sex Discrimination and Title VII," *George Washington Law Review,* December 1965, p. 237.

312   Pauli Murray: Murray, *Song,* pp. 115, 239, 359–64; Olson, *Daughters,* pp. 285–90.

313   "She can reverse the verdict": Plaintiffs' Brief, Vol. 1, by Charles Morgan, Jr., Orzell Billingsley, Jr., Judge Dorothy Kenyon, Dr. Pauli Murray, and Melvin L. Wulf, *White v. Crook,* Civil Action No. 2263-N, p. 61.

313   parents smuggled or shooed them: Int. Sammy Bailey, April 11, 2003.

313   Stokely Carmichael was collecting firearms: McGowan to Rosen, Aug. 20, 1965, FJMD-15.

313   "Sheriff Clark has deputized": SC, Aug. 28–29, 1965, p. 1; SNCC press release dated Aug. 20, 1965, Reel 16, SNCC.

313   "have gone into hiding": Ibid.

313   Gloria Larry turned up safe: Int. Gloria Larry House, June 29, 2000.

313   "jailhouse giveaway plot": Int. Martha Prescod Norman, June 29, 2000; int. Silas Nor-

man, June 28 and Aug. 25, 2000; int. Jimmy Rogers, March 12, 2003; int. Ruby Sales, March 22, 2003.

313   murders of Herbert Lee and Louis Allen: Branch, *Parting,* pp. 509–22; Branch, *Pillar,* pp. 222–23.

313   hide the key Hayneville witnesses from FBI agents: FBI Mobile to Director, 1:36 A.M., Aug. 21, 1965, FJMD-2; FBI Mobile to Director, 6:57 P.M., Aug. 21, 1965, FJMD-3; Rosen to Belmont, Aug. 21, 1965, FJMD-16. The investigating FBI agents complained to headquarters that SNCC witnesses talked to reporters but not to them, and that SNCC leaders in Selma refused to make the witnesses available unless conditions were negotiated to guarantee their safety. Director J. Edgar Hoover approved instructions that no interviews were to be conducted in the SNCC office, and that "the Student Non-Violent Coordinating Committee should not dictate the terms under which our interviews would be conducted."

313   she called Rev. Frank Mathews: Int. Gloria Larry House, June 29, 2000; Mendelsohn, *Martyrs,* p. 218.

314   Rabbi Harold Saperstein found sponsors: Int. Harold and Marcia Saperstein, Dec. 12, 1991; int. Gloria Larry House, June 29, 2000.

314   with Rev. Bruce Hanson: Int. Bruce Hanson, Feb. 22, 1991; int. David Saperstein and Al Vorspan, May 23, 1991.

314   to accompany by charter relay: Eagles, *Outside Agitator,* p. 182; Charles H. Douglass to C. C. J. Carpenter, Aug. 26, 1965, BIR/C8f25. Rev. Douglass, then rector of St. John's Episcopal Church in Montgomery, reported to Bishop Carpenter that after the first radio reports of a shooting in Hayneville, he had learned from a funeral contact at White Chapel that a body had been delivered there with no identification except a 1961 Virginia Military Institute class ring. From its engraved hometown of Keene, New Hampshire, Douglass had located the Daniels parish and home through Episcopal channels, notified Mrs. Constance Daniels of the murder, and suggested that she remove her son's body "directly" to New Hampshire. "I told her I felt this was best for her and certainly for our situation in Alabama," Douglass wrote Carpenter. As an aside, Douglass advised the bishop of inside information from Lowndes authorities that the Daniels prisoners had "made a shambles of the jail" and then provoked Deputy Sheriff Coleman with "a considerable amount of verbal taunting." The general reaction to the shooting in Montgomery, he wrote, was "about what you would expect with a mixture of regret but an overtone of 'they had it coming to them.'"

314   "several Negroes who had known": NYT, Aug. 25, 1965, p. 24.

314   The *Times* already had published: NYT, Aug. 21, 1965, p. 9.

314   "raw material for living theology": Eagles, *Outside Agitator,* p. 183.

314   an effete Yankee who chose strangely: Josiah Bunting int. by Daniel Zwerdling, *Weekend All Things Considered,* National Public Radio, Aug. 23, 1997, JDC; Eagles, *Outside Agitator,* pp. 11–18; int. William Braithwaite, Feb. 9, 2001.

314   "as well as some magnificent buffoons": Daniels valedictory address, 1961, courtesy of William Braithwaite.

314   sang "We Shall Overcome": Eagles, *Outside Agitator,* pp. 182–84.

315   "We want to show the people": NYT, Aug. 23, 1965, p. 19.

315   He seldom spoke of Daniels: Int. Jimmy Rogers, March 12, 2003; int. Francis Walter, Sept. 7, 2000; int. Bob Mants, Sept. 8, 2000; int. Gloria Larry House, June 29, 2000.

315 came to remember that he had opposed: Int. Kwame Ture (Stokely Carmichael), Jan. 31, 1984.

315 "We ain't going to resurrect Jon": Eagles, *Outside Agitator,* p. 181.

315 Carmichael asked SNCC's research director: Carson, *Struggle,* p. 165; Jeffries, "Freedom Politics," p. 89.

315 Jack Minnis had come late to civil rights: Int. Jack Minnis, April 7–8, 2001.

315 "That Great Medicare Bill": Minnis, *Life with Lyndon in the Great Society,* Vol. 1, No. 27, Aug. 5, 1965, JMP.

316 "Great Philosopher of Non-violence": Ibid., Vol. 1, No. 29, Aug. 19, 1965, JMP.

316 "just how phony the Civil Rights Act": Ibid., Vol. 1, No. 30, Aug. 26, 1965, JMP.

316 "When we think of all the murders": Ibid., Vol. 1, No. 28, Aug. 12, 1965, JMP.

316 He scoffed at Johnson's ballyhooed promise: Int. Jack Minnis, April 8, 2001.

316 "Here's what I've been able to glean": Minnis to SNCC staff in Alabama, Sept. 4, 1965, A/SN94.

317 Matt Murphy died in a highway accident: *Jet,* Sept. 9, 1965, p. 9; SC, Aug. 28–29, 1965, p. 1; Stanton, *From Selma,* p. 123.

317 Rev. Francis Walter happened to be making a courtesy visit: Int. Francis Walter, Sept. 7, 2000; John Ruskin sermon, "A New Understanding of the White Problem," attached to Ruskin to Francis Walter, Dec. 16, 1965, BIR/FW2f5. Ruskin, a Unitarian minister from San Diego, had met Rev. Walter on a pilgrimage to Selma. He recalled in his sermon that Rev. Mathews of St. Paul's was explaining to them his reservations about the civil rights movement, largely by recounting the troubles Daniels had caused at his worship services: "When the telephone rang and the rector answered it and was informed that Jonathan Daniels had just been shot and killed over at Hayneville, in Lowndes County. This shook us all up very badly and, after a few important telephone calls, we had a moment of memorial prayers for Jonathan Daniels. Then Father Walters asked his colleague in the ministry for permission to have a memorial service for Jonathan Daniels at St. Paul's Episcopal Church. The rector refused and stuck to his refusal because, as he said, 'A memorial service for Jonathan Daniels would just turn into a demonstration.' The real irony of this became apparent the following Monday when a newspaper carried the picture of a funeral service for the late Mr. Matt Murphy, the notorious Klan leader."

317 "another civil rights demonstration": "Statement by the Rev. T. Frank Mathews, Rector of St. Paul's Church, Selma, Alabama, in Reply to a request from *The Living Church* for a Comment Regarding the Death of Jonathan Daniels," Aug. 24, 1965. "It is my understanding that a Memorial Service is being planned for Brown's Chapel," the statement concluded. "Any additional service in St. Paul's would appear to the community of Selma to be another civil rights demonstration for which we do not feel this church building should be used or the liturgy of the Church employed. I do not feel that Rev. John Morris understands the situation here in Selma, or he would not have been critical of a decision that is calculated to avoid further discord and to support the efforts of thinking and concerned persons toward the restoring of a spirit of good will among both races in this community where Jonathan Daniels lived and worked the last five months of his life."

317 funeral for Matt Murphy two days later: Ibid.; Peter L. Albrecht to Rt. Rev. Anson P. Stokes of Boston, Aug. 27, 1965, JDC.

317 "chaplains to the dying order": NYT, April 11, 1960, p. 25.

317 Yet Carpenter also suffered Klan threats: Int. George Murray, July 16, 1987. Murray,

who succeeded Carpenter as bishop, recalls that Carpenter defied one direct death threat on the telephone. Many Alabamians rebuked Carpenter for his public criticism of Governor George Wallace's "segregation forever" speech. Cf. Maurice Rogers to Carpenter ("Your disgusting, cowardly statement of January 16, 1963. . . .), Jan. 16, 1963, BIR/C12f29.

317   "that the sight of the great Bishop": Will Scarlett to "Chuck" [Carpenter], July 22, 1960, BIR/C15f16.

318   "May I rest your coat?": Int. Francis Walter, Sept. 7, 2000.

318   Walter relocated to New Jersey: Int. Francis Walter, Sept. 7, 2000. Callahan, *Quilting Bee,* pp. 7–8; Shattuck, *Episcopalians,* pp. 119, 198.

318   orders to lock St. Paul's: Frank Mathews to The Rt. Rev. C. C. J. Carpenter, Aug. 24, 1965, BIR/C8f25.

318   "If I antagonize them they'll get vicious": Frank Mathews to George [Murray], Oct. 14, 1965, BIR/C10f57.

318   "I am not able to grant": Carpenter to Francis X. Walter, Oct. 5, 1965, BIR/C10f57.

318   When Walter appealed to Carpenter's kindly heir: Walter to The Right Rev. George Murray, Oct. 4, 1965, BIR/C10f57.

319   "One of the heartbreaking things": George Murray to Francis X. Walter, Oct. 12, 1965, BIR/C10f57.

319   Walter persisted on his own: "Meeting of a Steering Committee of the Selma Interreligious Project, September 23, 1965, Episcopal Church Center, New York City," Rev. Francis Walter, Rev. Arthur Walmsley, Rev. Homer Jack, Rabbi Balfour Brickner, Rev. Bruce Hanson, BIR/FW2f8; Francis Walter to George Murray, Oct. 14, 1965, BIR/C10f57. "I was saddened by the letter you sent October 12," Walter replied to Bishop Murray, "but more distressed by the apparent vacuum it creates between the diocese and the [Selma Inter-Religious] Project. It is the last thing I intend to embarrass or insult you or the Diocese of Alabama. Given this feeling of mine and your position of being unable to cooperate or ask others to do so, I am not going to ask for an appointment with anyone at Diocesan House, nor will I embarrass you by dropping by. Though my thinking is not settled on what my relations should now be with clergy in the towns I will be visiting, I think I'll adopt the same general policy. . . . I'm assuming that my staying away from Episcopalians is roughly what you want."

319   pending application for parenthood by adoption: Walter to Bishop Leland Stark, Jan. 30, 1967, BIR/FW1f24; int. Francis Walter, Sept. 7, 2000; Callahan, *Quilting Bee,* pp. 9–10.

319   105th General Assembly: NYT, April 23, 1965, p. 14; NYT, April 25, 1965, p. 56.

319   King traded places with another Negro speaker: Int. Gayraud Wilmore, May 14, 1992.

319   "The ultimate logic of racism": MLK address, "The Church and the Frontier," Aug. 21, 1965, A/KS9.

319   "our whole programmatic thrust": Wiretap transcript of MLK phone call with Stanley Levison, Aug. 25, 1965, FLNY-9-677.

319   "Martin called a quick meeting": Wiretap transcript of Stanley Levison phone call with Andrew Levison, Aug. 25, 1965, FLNY-9-677a.

319   passed the immigration reform bill: *Congressional Record,* Aug. 25, 1965, pp. 21820–21; NYT, Aug. 26, 1965, p. 1.

319   "And we'll bring Edgar Hoover": LBJ phone call with Nicholas Katzenbach, 2:50 P.M., Aug. 26, 1965, Cit. 8639, Audiotape WH6508.11, LBJ.

320   King's gathering convened: Garrow, *Bearing,* pp. 441–43; Longenecker, *Peacemaker,* pp. 304–5.

320   George Metcalfe turned his car key: Dittmer, *Local People,* pp. 353–54; Davis, *Race,* pp. 180–83; Associated Press, *World in 1965,* p. 152.

320   previous year of intensified terror: Dittmer, *Local People,* pp. 304–8; Branch, *Pillar,* pp. 495–97.

320   "In my candid opinion": R. T. [Randy] Blackwell to MLK and RDA, Aug. 25, 1965, A/KP28f23.

320   Drawbacks plagued every option: Int. Bernard Lafayette, May 28, 1990.

321   Bevel offered at a mass meeting: Sermon, "A New Understanding of the White Problem," attached to a letter from John Ruskin Clark to Francis X. Walter, Dec. 16, 1965, BIR/FW2f5, p. 3.

321   "In the South, we always had segregationists": Minutes, SCLC executive staff meeting, Aug. 26–28, 1965, A/KP32f9.

321   King chose Chicago: Ibid.; Anderson and Pickering, *Confronting,* pp. 174–77; Ralph, *Northern,* p. 42.

321   "In Selma, we didn't organize": Int. Bernard Lafayette, May 28, 1990; Ralph, *Northern,* p. 51.

321   "Have you read the Moynihan Report": Transcript, CBS, *Face the Nation,* Aug. 29, 1965.

322   Public schools opened across the South: NYT, Aug. 31, 1965, p. 1.

322   Peggy Williams: NYT, Sept. 1, 1965, p. 21.

322   "Several parents welcomed us": NYT, Aug. 31, 1965, p. 42.

322   Arthur Goldberg had invited him: NYT, Aug. 25, 1965, p. 3, Sept. 1, 1965, p. 12; Harry Wachtel to MLK, Sept. 2, 1965, A/KP25f32.

322   arrested for stealing SCLC's office safe: AC, Sept. 1, 1965, p. 1; wiretap transcript of MLK phone call with Stanley Levison, Sept. 6, 1965, FLNY-9-689a.

322   "Martin—for your info—Sincerest regards, Adam": Powell note on copy of letter to "My dear Wyatt," Aug. 31, 1965, A/KP19f45.

323   "No one spoke to me": SC, Sept. 4–5, 1965, p. 1.

323   "Some of the white children": NYT, Sept. 1, 1965, p. 20.

22: FRAGILE ALLIANCE

PAGE

324   King prepared diligently to see Ambassador Goldberg: Harry Wachtel to MLK, Sept. 2, 1965, A/KP25f32; int. Harry Wachtel, Nov. 29, 1983; int. Bayard Rustin, Sept. 24, 1984; int. Andrew Young, Oct. 26, 1991.

324   Young arranged for briefings: Young, *Burden,* pp. 430–31.

324   research papers from King's neighbor: Int. Vincent Harding, Dec. 30, 2004.

324   a Vietnamese of destiny volunteered to translate: Ho Chi Minh background from Fall, *Viet Nams,* pp. 81–102; Shaplen, *Lost,* pp. 35–46; Duiker, *Ho,* pp. 36–51; Karnow, *Vietnam,* pp. 130–38.

325   a disastrously premature uprising in 1940: Duiker, *Ho,* pp. 242–48.

325   "France became a colony just like us!": Borton, *Sorrow,* p. 52.

325   cooperation of American OSS officers: Patti, *Why,* passim; Duiker, *Ho,* pp. 282ff; Appy, *Patriots,* pp. 38–41; Karnow, *Vietnam,* pp. 146–63.

325   this historical moment that King emphasized: Int. Harry Wachtel, Nov. 29, 1983.

325   Huge crowds had gathered outside: Patti, *Why,* pp. 163–65.

325 1.5 million Vietnamese had died of starvation: Duiker, *Ho,* p. 330; Shaplen, *Lost,* p. 46; Karnow, *Vietnam,* p. 160; Borton, *Sorrow,* p. 63.

326 ten days of nearly bloodless revolution: Duiker, *Ho,* pp. 310–20; Karnow, *Vietnam,* pp. 160–63; Patti, *Why,* pp. 165–68.

326 Ho Chi Minh invited the American OSS commander: Patti, *Why,* pp. 220–24, 243–47.

326 "All men are created equal": Ibid., pp. 250–53; Duiker, *Ho,* pp. 322–23.

326 Joseph Stalin: Duiker, *Ho,* pp. 420–25.

327 plundered the feeble new country: Patti, *Why,* pp. 284–93; Karnow, *Vietnam,* p. 167.

327 ordered every clock in Vietnam set back: Patti, *Why,* p. 293.

327 "If the French should invade": Giap, *Unforgettable,* p. 31.

327 British forces entered southern Vietnam: Patti, *Why,* pp. 297–99; Duiker, *Ho,* pp. 332–37.

327 "Your mission is to reestablish": De Gaulle to Leclerc, Sept. 25, 1945, cited in Duiker, *Ho,* p. 353.

327 "If I listened to such nonsense": Ibid., p. 355.

327 shelled the port city of Haiphong: Ibid., pp. 388–97; Patti, *Why,* pp. 382–83.

327 King told Goldberg: Int. Harry Wachtel, Nov. 29, 1983; int. Bayard Rustin, Sept. 24, 1984; int. Andrew Young, Oct. 26, 1991.

327 France's subsequent eight-year war: Shaplen, *Lost,* p. xi; Fall, *Viet Nams,* p. 129; Appy, *Patriots,* pp. 44–47.

328 "Well, you know": Int. Andrew Young, Oct. 26, 1991.

328 had pressured Ho to accept far less at Geneva: Karnow, *Vietnam,* pp. 215–21; Duiker, *Ho,* pp. 457–61; Langguth, *Our Vietnam,* pp. 78–80.

328 "a very dangerous enemy": Richard Russell interviewed on CBS, *Face the Nation,* Aug. 1, 1965.

328 The session lasted seventy minutes: NYT, Sept. 11, 1965, p. 9; *Jet,* Sept. 30, 1965, p. 7.

328 "In short," he told them: MLK and Goldberg press conferences at the U.N., Sept. 10, 1965, A/KS.

329 "We will not be forced out": Ibid.

329 "intemperate alignment with the forces of appeasement": Senator Thomas J. Dodd statement, "Dr. Martin Luther King's Activities in Connection with U.S. Foreign Policy," reprinted in *Congressional Record,* Sept. 15, 1965, p. S-23908.

329 King convened an emergency conference call: Garrow, *Bearing,* p. 445.

329 "I want a little advice": Wiretap transcript of MLK conference phone call with Stanley Levison, Andrew Young, Clarence Jones, Harry Wachtel, Cleveland Robinson, Wyatt Tee Walker, and Walter Fauntroy, Sept. 12, 1965, FLNY-9-695a.

330 the FBI promptly reported back to the White House: FBI HQ LHM dated Sept. 15, 1965, FK-1866; Marvin Watson to LBJ, 8:20 P.M., Sept. 15, 1965, Box 32, OFMS, LBJ.

330 politically "insane" proposal: Wiretap transcript of phone call between Stanley Levison and Clarence Jones, Sept. 13, 1965, FLNY-9-696a.

330 "Dr. King Wants Red China in U.N.": WP, Sept. 11, 1965, p. 7.

331 "Should I say in this speech": Wiretap transcript of MLK conference phone call with Stanley Levison, Bayard Rustin, Andrew Young, Harry Wachtel, and John Barber, Sept. 28, 1965, FLNY-9-711a, cited in Garrow, *Bearing,* pp. 697–98.

331 "certain factors bearing": Untitled MLK statement, Oct. 5, 1965, A/KS.

331 "another example of the high-handed attitude": Baumgardner to Sullivan, Sept. 10, 1965, FK-1861.

331   SCLC staff retreat at the Quaker Penn Center: Garrow, *Bearing,* p. 446.

331   mentioned his escape wish: Power, *I Will,* p. 9.

331   boarded the presidential yacht *Honey Fitz:* The Sept. 21 date comes from King's "Schedule for the Month of September 1965," A/SC1f30, and from Whitney M. Young, Jr., et al. to John H. Johnson, Oct. 4, 1965, A/KP13f4.

331   "For the first time in history": *Jet,* Oct. 7, 1965, pp. 8–10.

332   The cruise began with decorum: Ibid.; Garrow, *Bearing,* p. 447.

332   The running count of desegregation plans: WP, Sept. 12, 1965, p. 6.

332   escalated dispute about what was evasion or raw truth: Int. Wiley Branton, Sept. 28, 1983; Rainwater and Yancey, *Moynihan Report,* pp. 195–96.

333   "almost turned the boat over": Herbers, *Priority,* pp. 126–28.

333   President Johnson stripped Humphrey: Califano, *Triumph,* pp. 64–69; Califano to Katzenbach, Sept. 1, 1965, WHCF, Box 56, LBJ; Humphrey, *Education,* pp. 408–9; Graham, *Civil Rights Era,* pp. 184–86; Mann, *Walls,* pp. 484–87.

333   Wiley Branton reluctantly accepted: Int. Wiley Branton, Sept. 28, 1983.

333   Reporters soon questioned the effect: John Herbers, "Rights Blocs Fear Easing of Enforcement by U.S.," NYT, Oct. 17, 1965, p. 1.

333   "yacht-wide discussion of Vietnam": Whitney M. Young, Jr., et al. to John H. Johnson, Oct. 4, 1965, A/KP13f4.

333   Far greater trouble erupted: Orfield, *Reconstruction,* pp. 181–202; Herbers, *Priority,* pp. 139–41; Fairclough, *Redeem,* p. 283; *Jet,* Oct. 21, 1965, pp. 22–24; Harold M. Baron to Edwin C. Berry, "Title VI of the U.S. Civil Rights Act of 1964 and the Federal Aid Controversy in Chicago," Nov. 5, 1965, A/SC150f26.

333   Commissioner Francis Keppel informed: Keppel to Benjamin C. Willis, Sept. 30, 1965, and Keppel to Ray Page, Sept. 30, 1965, Cyrus Adams Papers, Box 13, CHS.

334   "despotic, alarming, and threatening": Willis press release, Oct. 2, 1965, in ibid.

334   political lightning in fact did flash: Orfield, *Reconstruction,* pp. 191–92; Cohen and Taylor, *Pharaoh,* pp. 350–51; WP, Oct. 3, 1965, p. 5.

334   Mayor Daley pulled Lyndon Johnson aside: Dallek, *Flawed,* p. 324; Cohen and Taylor, *Pharaoh,* p. 352.

334   Staff briefings feverishly assured him: Douglas Cater to LBJ, 10:45 P.M., Oct. 3, 1965, and Douglas Cater to LBJ, Oct. 5, 1965, EX HU 2-5/ST13, Box 54, LBJ.

334   Johnson's special emissary reached agreement: Orfield, *Reconstruction,* p. 195.

334   with predictable results: Katzenbach to Lee White and Douglas Cater, Dec. 17, 1965, EX HU 2-5/ST13, Box 54, LBJ; Orfield, *Reconstruction,* p. 202.

334   Keppel sank into bureaucratic quarantine: Douglas Cater oral history by David G. McComb, April 29, 1969, pp. 21–22, LBJ.

334   "I was hopeless": In a confidential oral history nearly three years later, Keppel recalled the Chicago incident as a "colossal defeat" that "will probably be put on my gravestone." Francis Keppel oral history by John Singerhoff, July 18, 1968, LBJ, pp. 21–23. Also, Francis Keppel oral history by David G. McComb, April 21, 1969, LBJ, pp. 25–26; Cohen and Taylor, *Pharaoh,* p. 353.

334   "I feel wonderful": Orfield, *Reconstruction,* p. 189.

335   "shameless display of naked political power": CDD, Oct. 7, 1965, p. 1.

335   an extended conference of two hundred activists: Anderson and Pickering, *Confronting,* p. 182ff; Cohen and Taylor, *Pharaoh,* pp. 355–56.

335   "If Negroes cannot break up a ghetto": Garrow, *Bearing,* p. 448. Similarly, Bevel

wrote: "Our task is not to patch up the ghetto, but to abolish it." James Bevel, "SCLC—Chicago Report," Oct. 26, 1965, A/KP5f26.

335   "Nonviolence is the only honorable way": Anderson and Pickering, *Confronting*, p. 185.

335   dominant organization of Negro Baptists: Branch, *Parting*, pp. 500–507.

335   "I don't consider Mayor Daley": Garrow, *Bearing*, p. 448.

335   he preached hope by analogy: Branch, *Pillar*, pp. 487–89.

335   "There are giants": Deuteronomy 1; Joshua 1–2.

335   outreach groups in fifteen categories: James Bevel, "SCLC—Chicago Report," Nov. 8, 1965, A/SC150f22.

335   shaved head and a copy of Leo Tolstoy's *What Then Must We Do?*: Ralph, *Northern*, pp. 49–50.

335   reports by police surveillance agents: Investigator's report/Intelligence Division, Chicago police department, Oct. 20, 1965, File 951-B, RS, CHS: investigator's reports, Nov. 4 and Dec. 21, 1965, File 940, RS, CHS.

335   "In the south, we are taunted": King, "Next Stop: The North," *Saturday Review*, Nov. 13, 1965, p. 105.

335   tensions within the hybrid network: Ralph, *Northern*, pp. 51–55.

336   "When the grass turns green": Anderson and Pickering, *Confronting*, pp. 186–87.

336   "something new": Ibid., p. 188.

23: IDENTITY

PAGE

337   Goldberg's new U.N. apartment: Cohen and Taylor, *Pharaoh*, p. 351. While finalizing plans to host the Johnsons for dinner on Sunday, October 3, Goldberg asked to meet LBJ at the airport and fly with him by helicopter to Liberty Island. "Because I'm an immigrant," Goldberg told Johnson, "and I'd love to see you sign that bill." (LBJ phone call with Arthur Goldberg, 7:02 P.M., Oct. 1, 1965, Cit. 9006, Audiotape WH6510.01, LBJ.)

337   "twisted and distorted by the harsh injustice": WP, Oct. 4, 1965, p. 7.

337   inexorably diversified American culture: Schuck, *Diversity*, pp. 87–99.

338   A school in Falls Church: Joel Swerdlow, "Changing America," *National Geographic*, Sept. 2001, pp. 42–61.

338   "America was built by a nation of strangers": WP, Oct. 4, 1965, p. 7.

338   joined the two great civil rights laws: King, *Making*, pp. 243–53.

338   Yet these high stakes went strangely unnoticed: Schuck, *Diversity*, p. 87.

338   "Johnson Offers Haven": WP, Oct. 4, 1965, p. 1.

338   "liberalizes immigration policies": NYT, Oct. 4, 1965, pp. 1, 4.

338   Few outlets went on to describe the law: "Congress Sends Immigration Bill to White House," NYT, Oct. 1, 1965, p. 1; editorial, "Nation of Strangers," WP, Oct. 5, 1965, p. 16; "Immigration Change, Papal Visit Mesh," *Christian Science Monitor*, Oct. 5, 1965, p. 1.

339   "an Englishman is better than a Spaniard": Celler remarks, *Congressional Record*, Aug. 25, 1965, p. 21755.

339   "Anthropologists, historians, and lexicographers": Ervin remarks, *Congressional Record*, March 4, 1965, p. 4145.

339   "forlorn fight to preserve": Ervin remarks, *Congressional Record,* Sept. 17, 1965, p. 24232.

339   "It's really amazing": WSJ, Oct. 4, 1965, p. 16.

339   "a complete annihilation of justice": Clarke, *Wrestlin',* p. 162.

339   Jones made a special trip: Ibid., p. 24.

340   "My soul was on fire then": Mayer, *All on Fire,* pp. 51–56.

340   "Could I do more for the ultimate good": Clarke, *Wrestlin',* p. 14.

340   "Apostle to the Negro Slaves": Ibid., p. xxi.

340   "There has been neglect": Jones, *Religious,* p. 276.

340   masters could address slaves as brothers or sisters: Clarke, *Wrestlin',* p. 107.

340   "The brain of the Negro": Menand, *Metaphysical,* p. 109.

340   Agassiz declared as a matter of science: Ibid., pp. 97–116; Gossett, *Race,* pp. 59–61; Clarke, *Wrestlin',* pp. 108–12.

340   "abhorrent to our nature": Menand, *Metaphysical,* p. 115.

340   "the manly population descended": Ibid.

340   "We cannot cry out against the Papists": Jones, *Religious,* p. 167.

340   "certain that the salvation of one soul": Clarke, *Wrestlin',* p. 27.

340   Agassiz had captured Boston: Menand, *Metaphysical,* pp. 97–101.

341   Craniologists Samuel Morton and Josiah Nott: Ibid., pp. 102–12; Gossett, *Race,* pp. 58–66.

341   An explosion of typologies: Gossett, *Race,* pp. 69–83.

341   "It is possible that Boas": Ibid., pp. 418, 429–30; King, *Making,* p. 70.

341   first Naturalization Act of 1790: Lopez, *White,* pp. 1–3, 42–43.

341   Congress raised the stakes of whiteness: Ibid., pp. 46–47.

341   Syrians, Armenians, and Moroccans: Ibid., p. 67.

341   turned down a decorated Navy veteran: *In re Knight,* 171 F. 299,300 (E.D.N.Y. 1909), cited in ibid., p. 59.

342   "cannot be supposed to have clothed His Divinity": *In re Dow,* 213 F. 355, at 364, cited in ibid., pp. 74–75.

342   "What is the white race?": Ibid.

342   "the words 'white person' ": *Ozawa v. United States,* 260 U.S. 178, 197 (1922).

342   citizenship petition of Takao Ozawa: Lopez, *White,* pp. 79–86.

342   the Justices were plainly vexed: Ibid., pp. 70–72, 86–92.

342   racial term "Caucasian" appeared to rest: Gossett, *Race,* pp. 37–39.

342   "What we now hold": *U.S. v. Thind,* 261 U.S. 204 (1923), cited in Gossett, *Race,* pp. 86–92.

342   "For the Court, science fell from grace": Gossett, *Race,* p. 94.

343   "American race": King, *Making,* p. 131.

343   Immigration Restriction League: Ibid., p. 52.

343   Eugenics Record Office at Cold Spring Harbor: Ibid., pp. 166–75; Gossett, *Race,* pp. 401–6.

343   eugenics, a term coined by Darwin's cousin: Gossett, *Race,* p. 155.

343   eugenics later became stigmatized by association with the Nazis: Ibid., pp. 427–29, 445. Two generations before Hitler, eugenics was popular in progressive American magazines and scholarly journals. Gossett (pp. 306–7) quotes an 1895 article in *Political Science Quarterly* by Columbia University professor John W. Burgess: "We must preserve our Aryan nationality in the state, and admit to its membership only such non-Aryan race-elements as shall have become Aryanized in spirit and in genius by

contact with it, if we would build the superstructure of the ideal American commonwealth."

343   "belonged to the political vocabulary": King, *Making,* p. 168.

343   "There are certain parts of Europe": Ibid., p. 75.

343   "You cannot have free institutions": Ibid., pp. 153–55.

343   "a branch of the Mongolian race": *Congressional Record,* Dec. 31, 1914, pp. 804–5.

343   1924 National Origins Act: King, *Making,* pp. 199–228.

344   "sturdy stocks of the north of Europe": Ibid., p. 51.

344   "National eugenics is the long-term cure": Ibid., p. 185.

344   The *Chicago Tribune* pronounced: Gossett, *Race,* p. 407.

344   Ed "Strangler" Lewis to a draw: Int. George Murray, July 16, 1987; int. Douglas Carpenter (son), July 1, 1987. Biographical material also drawn from the Carpenter Papers collection at the Birmingham Public Library.

344   reduced the American school population: Felix X. Cohen, "Immigration and National Welfare," a pamphlet of the League for Industrial Democracy, 1940, p. 4.

344   the McCarran-Walter Act renewed: King, *Making,* pp. 224, 238, 244–46.

344   The Old Midway Church property: Branch, *Parting,* p. 689.

344   "fanatics of the worst sort": Myers, *Children,* Vol. 1, p. 23.

345   "openly professed the orthodox faith": Ibid., Vol. 4, pp. 49–51. "And moreover, under the old Constitution of the United States, we never had a *Christian president,*" Rev. Jones wrote to his son on March 7, 1862. "General Washington was a communing member of the Episcopal Church; and while it is hoped and believed that he was a true Christian, yet the evidence is not so clear and satisfactory as we could wish. Our first President [Confederate Jefferson Davis] is accredited a *Christian man....* His proclamation is Christian throughout in language and spirit; and the close of his inaugural address, in prayer to God as the Head of a great nation in such a time as the present, melts into tenderness under a consciousness of weakness and imperfection, and yet rises into the sublimity of faith—the sublimity of an unshaken faith. Oh, for pious rulers and officers!"

345   his last public sermon: Myers, *Children,* Vol. 3, pp. 306–9; Clarke, *Wrestlin',* p. 172. "Our meeting of our new General Assemble, independent of the old, was fully, every presbytery in the Confederate States being represented," Jones wrote his son on December 20, 1861. "By request of the assembly I delivered an address before that body, the Tuesday evening after it commenced its sessions, on the religious instruction of the Negroes—one of the rare opportunities granted me of doing good."

345   first-named addressee: Branch, *Parting,* pp. 741–42.

345   Hayneville, an abbreviated trial: Summary in Mobile FBI report dated Oct. 7, 1965, FJMD-49, pp. 1–3.

345   "shocked and amazed": Eagles, *Outside Agitator,* pp. 202–3.

345   "I was afraid": Ibid., p. 215.

345   commenced trial all on the same day: Eagles, *Outside Agitator,* pp. 206–16.

346   holler down to the yard for witnesses: NYT, Oct. 1, 1965, pp. 1, 3; Robert E. Smith, "Coleman Tried Among Friends," SC, Oct. 3–4, 1965, p. 1.

346   according to case historian Charles Eagles: Eagles, *Outside Agitator,* pp. 218–42.

346   keep a dove hunting date: Ibid., p. 244.

346   "lives by quite different concepts": Eric Sevareid remarks, *CBS Evening News with Walter Cronkite,* Sept. 30, 1965, transcript in JDC.

346   Columnist Max Friedman: Friedman, "Verdict in Hayneville Outrages Jonathan

Daniels' Home Town," undated, copy in JDC; Friedman, "Martin Luther King Could Share Bertrand Russell's Pitiable Fate," LAT, Aug. 20, 1965, p. II-5.

347   "an obscene caricature of justice": BN, Oct. 3, 1965.

347   "All across the land": AC, Oct. 7, 1965, p. 4.

347   has "broken the heart of Dixie": "Verdict in Hayneville," WP, Oct. 4, 1965, p. 22.

347   In Natchez, Mississippi: SCLC Press Release, "In response to an invitation from Charles Evers," Sept. 2, 1965, A/KS; Hoover memo for Tolson et al., 10:45 A.M., Sept. 2, 1965, FCT-NR; NYT, Sept. 3, 1965, p. 1; NYT, Sept. 4, 1965, p. 22; MLK column re Natchez, "Special to the Amsterdam News," Sept. 17, 1965, A/KP17f10; William H. Booth, president, Jamaica, NY, NAACP, to MLK, Sept. 23, 1965, A/KP17f10; Garrow, Bearing, p. 446.

347   "All Negro patients": Junius Griffin, Ed Clayton, and Robert Green to MLK, "Re: On Site Visitation to Natchez, Mississippi," Sept. 27, 1965, A/SC146f24.

347   long protest lines filed into downtown Natchez: Dittmer, Local People, pp. 357–58; Davis, Race, pp. 185–86; Baltimore Evening Sun, Oct. 4, 1965, p. 1.

347   transferred those above twelve years of age: Ibid.; Dorie Ladner and Charlie Horowitz, WATS report from Natchez, Oct. 4, 1965, Reel 16, SNCC; SC, Aug. 30–31, 1965, p. 2.

347   "Several people were unable": Phil Lapansky and Charlie Horowitz, WATS report from Natchez, Oct. 5, 1965, Reel 16, SNCC.

347   "Crawfordville, Ga.": NYT, Oct. 1, 1965, p. 1.

348   "Kill him!": Baltimore Evening Sun, Oct. 4, 1965, p. 2.

348   protests with mixed success: MS, Oct. 22, 1965, p. 21.

348   back from the planning workshops in Chicago: "Dr. King 'Marching' on Crawfordville," CDD, Oct. 11, 1965, p. 3.

348   "The hardship of the rural South": MLK speech at Crawfordville, Georgia, Oct. 11, 1965, A/KS; Garrow, Bearing, p. 450.

348   night rally on October 11: SC, Oct. 23–24, 1965, p. 4.

348   dismissal of Turner and five colleagues: NYT, July 7, 1965, p. 22.

348   Willie Bolden led two hundred: Athens Daily News, Oct. 13, 1965, p. 1; Augusta Chronicle, Oct. 13, 1965, p. 2.

348   graphic picture of Myers: NYT, Oct. 13, 1965, p. 1.

348   bushwhacking of Lieutenant Colonel Lemuel Penn: Branch, Pillar, pp. 398–99, 427–29.

348   eighty-one minutes to acquit: Ibid., pp. 477–78.

348   the Justice Department was trying to convince: Ibid., pp. 608–9; Rosen to DeLoach, March 30, 1968, FLP-399; "Interesting Case Memorandum," Nov. 1, 1968, FLP-NR.

349   "I think a soldier in uniform": Branch, Pillar, pp. 437–38. LBJ erred in suggesting that Penn was shot wearing his uniform. Lt. Col. Penn and his companions, having completed their two weeks of summer training at Fort Benning, were off-duty in civilian clothes. Their uniforms did hang in the back seat, but did not figure in the Supreme Court's March 28, 1966, decision to reinstate the federal indictment.

349   a federal judge lifted curfews: Dittmer, Local People, p. 358.

349   "Move Them Niggers North": Davis, Race, p. 186.

349   "Never," Mayor John Nosser announced: Ibid., p. 189.

349   Born in Lebanon: Dittmer, Local People, pp. 358–59.

349   lay off nearly half: Davis, Race, pp. 173, 185.

349   offering police escort at Negro funerals: Ibid., p. 172.

349   "We're armed": Dittmer, *Local People,* p. 354.

349   Roy Wilkins had seethed: Ibid., pp. 177–78, 355; Davis, *Race,* pp. 183–84.

349   Chicago bootlegger and petty criminal: Ibid.; Berry, *Amazing Grace,* p. 17.

349   Wilkins publicized: "NAACP May Oust Evers As Aide in Mississippi," NYT, Sept. 10, 1965, p. 22.

350   demanded that King withdraw Rev. Al Sampson: Archie Jones, acting president of the Natchez NAACP branch, to MLK, Oct. 19, 1965, A/SC4f12.

350   "Natchez Boycott Ends": NYT, Dec. 4, 1965, p. 1.

350   Success made Charles Evers indispensable: Dittmer, *Local People,* pp. 356–62; Davis, *Race,* pp. 187–92.

350   destroyed the building next door: Davis, *Race,* p. 168; Dittmer, *Local People,* p. 353.

350   local sentries posted themselves: King, *Freedom Song,* p. 512.

350   staff members themselves stockpiled firearms: Annie Pearl Avery, "There Are No Cowards in My Family," unpublished interview with Dorothy Zellner, 1997, courtesy of Judy Richardson.

350   Annie Pearl Avery: Ibid.; int. Scott B. Smith, April 12, 2003; Carmichael, *Ready,* p. 465.

350   Bill Ware: Carson, *Struggle,* pp. 192–95.

351   with Dennis Sweeney into a short-lived marriage: King, *Freedom Song,* pp. 510–16; Chafe, *Never,* pp. 450–53.

351   "There seem to be many parallels": Casey Hayden and Mary King, "A Kind of Memo," dated November 18, 1965, published as "Sex and Caste," in *Liberation,* April 1966, pp. 35–36; King, *Freedom Song,* pp. 437–67; Curry et al., *Deep,* pp. 371–72.

351   staff of fifteen dwindled away: Dittmer, *Local People,* p. 361.

351   three of them: Notes, staff meeting, Nov. 2, 1965, Reel 37, SNCC.

351   In the absence of Silas Norman: Int. Silas Norman, June 28, 2000.

351   Alabama SNCC staff gathered to confront: Notes, staff meeting, Nov. 2, 1965, Reel 37, SNCC.

351   their relative skills as chase drivers: Int. Bob Mants, Sept. 8, 2000.

351   began to approach white registration: Eagles, *Outside Agitator,* p. 197.

351   Tuskegee Boy Scout camp: Diary of Francis Walter, Oct. 9, 1965, courtesy of Francis Walter; int. Martha Prescod Norman, June 29, 2000.

352   Rev. Francis Walter, succeeded Daniels: Francis Walter, "Report by the Director, Selma Inter-Religious Project, October 25, 1965," BIR/FW2f5; Callahan, *Quilting Bee,* p. 10; int. Francis X. Walter by Stanley Smith, August 1968, RJB; int. Francis Walter, Sept. 7, 2000. In addition to the Synagogue Council of America, the Selma Inter-Religious Project was sponsored by the National Council of Churches of Christ, the National Catholic Conference for Interracial Justice, and the Unitarian-Universalist Association.

352   November election of farm councils: Eagles, *Outside Agitator,* pp. 134–36; Cleophus Hobbs and Terry Shaw, "Report: Hale County," Aug. 26, 1965, Reel 18, SNCC; Tina Harris, "Money Spent for ASCS Workshop, Sept. 17–18, 1965," with undated "MEMO" on the workshop from "Janet, Tina" to "Silas, Muriel, Staff," Reel 37, SNCC. The farm council elections were held by the Agriculture Department's Agricultural Stabilization and Conservation Service (ASCS), which had been formed in 1961.

352   A lone SCLC emissary turned up: Diary of Francis Walter, Oct. 18, 1965, courtesy of Francis Walter.

352   she had tried to resume her graduate studies: Int. Gloria Larry House, June 29, 2000.

352   "She won't move": Diary of Francis Walter, Oct. 18, 1965, courtesy of Francis Walter.

352   She yearned to join the SNCC staff: Int. Gloria Larry House, June 29, 2000; int. Francis X. Walter by Stanley Smith, August 1968, RJB, pp. 15–16; Diary of Francis Walter, Oct. 18, 1965, courtesy of Francis Walter. Walter encountered Larry at both the Oct. 9 and Oct. 18 meetings.

353   stayed just long enough to testify: SAC, Mobile, to Director, Oct. 12, 1965, FVL-492. The frightened witness Leroy Moton, who had been riding with Viola Liuzzo when Klansmen shot her on March 25, 1965, was secluded before the Liuzzo trial as a volunteer teacher at the SCLC Freedom School in Crawfordville, Georgia, where KKK violence followed him.

353   "was it part of your duties": NYT, Oct. 21, 1965, pp. 1, 28.

353   serving as a pallbearer at his funeral: Jones to DeLoach, Aug. 24, 1965, FVL-449.

353   "I'm not going to meet with 'em": McWhorter, Carry, pp. 251–53.

353   gentleman segregationist: Ibid., pp. 180–81, 190–92.

353   befitting a former FBI agent: Ibid. Hanes remained on the FBI Special Correspondents' List in 1965, and had exchanged complimentary notes with J. Edgar Hoover during the "notorious liar" controversy with Martin Luther King, urging the Director "not to succumb to leftist pressure groups and resign or retire." Jones to DeLoach, Aug. 24, 1965, FVL-449.

353   "Parable of the Two Goats": SAC, Mobile, to Director, Oct. 22, 1965, FVL-523.

353   "Maybe the murderer": Stanton, From Selma, pp. 127–28.

353   "It is absolutely undisputed": NYT, Oct. 23, 1965, p. 1.

353   Flowers posted a well-known marksman: Int. Richmond Flowers, Aug. 9, 1990. "When I stood up inside the rail," Flowers recalled, "he [state trooper bodyguard Harvey Wilson] stood up and faced the courtroom, and always had his coat kicked back with his pistol [showing]. He was an excellent marksman, and everybody knew it."

354   support for the ACLU: NYT, Oct. 26, 1965, p. 28.

354   "chamber of horrors": Joe Califano to LBJ, Oct. 25, 1965, WHCF, Box 56, LBJ. Califano attached for LBJ recent memos by Lee White (October 13) and George Reedy (October 2) on the same subject, growing out of the Tom Coleman trial.

354   King was in Europe: Garrow, Bearing, p. 451; MLK, schedule for October 1965, A/KP1f30.

354   blues pianist Memphis Slim: Jet, Nov. 11, 1965, pp. 50–52.

354   "the beginning of vigilante justice": NYT, Oct. 24, 1965, pp. 1, 78.

354   "OPEN SEASON" bumper stickers: Stanton, From Selma, p. 128.

354   threat relayed from Lowndes County: Mobile Office LHM, "Unknown Subject; Threat to Kill Martin Luther King, Jr.—Victim," Oct. 28, 1965, FK-[serial number illegible].

354   Andrew Young told Stanley Levison: Wiretap transcript of telephone conversation between Stanley Levison and Clarence Jones, Oct. 26, 1965, FLNY-9-739a; FBI Headquarters LHM dated Oct. 26, 1965, FK-[serial number illegible].

354   Unremitting intrigue seeped: Cf. NYT, March 14, 1965, p. 33; NYT, June 20, 1965, p. 28; NYT, June 23, 1965, p. 23; int. Marc Tanenbaum, Feb. 5, 1991; int. Frank Murphy, March 8, 1991; int. John Oesterreicher, May 24, 1991; int. Thomas Stransky, Feb. 27, 1992.

355   "not only did not recognize Him": NYT, April 11, 1965, p. IV-4.

355   Vatican deputies removed from Nostra Aetate: NYT, Sept. 11, 1965, p. 1.

355 "realized fairly late": Joseph Roddy, "How the Jews Changed Catholic Thinking," *Look,* Jan. 25, 1966, p. 23.

355 American cardinals led unsuccessful fights: Vorgimler, ed., *Commentary,* pp. 108–21; Yzermans, ed., *Participation,* pp. 581–85.

355 word "deicide" raised thorny heresies: Remarks to the council by Augustin Cardinal Bea, Oct. 14, 1965, in Bea, *Church,* pp. 169–72; Vorgimler, ed., *Commentary,* pp. 106–7.

355 Rabbi Abraham Heschel had dared to plead: Branch, *Pillar,* pp. 167–69, 482–85.

355 Last-minute scandalmongers: Vorgimler, ed., *Commentary,* p. 122.

355 porters lifted the papal sedan: Associated Press, *World in 1965,* pp. 232–36.

355 Votes against *Nostra Aetate* collapsed: Bea, *Church,* pp. 24–27; NYT, Oct. 29, 1965, p. 1.

355 "So do not become proud": Romans 11:20, cited in *Nostra Aetate,* footnote 12.

356 "a turning point in 1,900 years": NYT, Oct. 29, 1965, p. 24.

356 Rabbi Joseph Soloveitchik: "Scholar Delimits Interfaith Talks: Rabbi Says Theology Should Not Be Discussed," NYT, Jan. 30, 1966, p. 75; "Rabbi Says Faiths Are Not Related," NYT, Aug. 16, 1964, p. 7; Gilbert, *Vatican,* pp. 292–301; Branch, *Pillar,* p. 484.

356 issued *Dabru Emet:* "Dabru Emet," NYT, Sept. 10, 2000, p. 23.

356 series of eight elaborated propositions: Frymer-Kensky et al., eds., *Christianity, passim;* Institute for Christian and Jewish Studies, Baltimore, www.icjs.org/what/njsp/index.html.

356 demonstrations over the weekend of October 16: Wells, *War Within,* pp. 56–57.

356 David Miller, a young Catholic Worker pacifist: Powers, *War,* pp. 86–87.

357 "a significant political act": NYT, Oct. 16, 1965, pp. 1–2.

357 "They are not promoting peace": Reston, "Washington: The Stupidity of Intelligence," NYT, Oct. 16, 1965.

357 "shocked at pictures": *Congressional Record,* Oct. 18, 1965, p. S-27251.

357 Congress had outlawed the willful defacement: Friedland, *Lift Up,* p. 158; Powers, *War,* p. 86.

357 "if we tuck tail and run now": *Congressional Record,* Oct. 18, 1965, pp. S-27253–54.

357 "the wailing, quailing": Ibid., p. 27254.

357 Katzenbach pledged to investigate: NYT, Oct. 18, 1965, p. 1.

357 "in the direction of treason": Wells, *War,* p. 58.

357 Nixon said that to tolerate comfort: Menashe and Radosh, eds., *Teach-Ins,* p. 233.

357 "would feel toward his country": NYT, Oct. 26, 1965, p. 4.

357 "annoying clamor": John K. Jessup, "The Answer to What VIETNIKS Call a Moral Issue," *Life,* Oct. 29, 1965, p. 40-D.

357 "vicious, venomous, and vile": *Congressional Record,* Oct. 18, 1965, p. S-27252.

357 Public animus surged so broadly: "Church Assails Draft Dodgers," NYT, Oct. 20, 1965, pp. 1, 2.

357 "build not burn": Zaroulis and Sullivan, *Who Spoke Up?,* p. 60.

357 "It concerns us": NYT, Oct. 26, 1965, p. 4.

358 Rabbi Heschel spontaneously assured reporters: Hall, *Because,* p. 14.

358 "Are we then finished?": Friedland, *Lift Up,* p. 159.

358 "evil of indifference": Branch, *Pillar,* pp. 167–68.

358 Heschel joined Neuhaus: Hall, *Because,* p. 15; Friedland, *Lift Up,* pp. 161–63.

358 "the most miserable mob scene ever": DeBenedetti, *Ordeal,* pp. 128–29.

358 A Pennsylvania Klan leader committed suicide: NYT, Oct. 31, 1965, p. 1; NYT, Nov. 1, 1965, p. 1.

358 Murky reports from Indonesia: Ibid.

358   a "human wave" attack: NYT, Oct. 31, 1965, p. 1.

358   hamlet of Deduc: NYT, Oct. 31, 1965, p. 1; NYT, Nov. 1, 1965, p. 1.

358   Norman Morrison saw: NYT, Nov. 7, 1965, p. 2; Zaroulis and Sullivan, *Who Spoke Up?*, pp. 1–3; DeBenedetti, *Ordeal,* p. 129.

359   "always before my eyes": *Baltimore Evening Sun,* Nov. 25, 1965, p. B-1.

359   "nobody opposes the war in Vietnam": *Baltimore Sun,* Nov. 2, 1965, p. 10.

359   Morrison chafed gently: *Baltimore Evening Sun,* Nov. 25, 1965, p. B-1.

359   Newspapers had published: *Baltimore Sun,* Aug. 3, 1965, republished Nov. 4, 1965, p. 18.

359   petitioned the White House: Morrison to "Mr. President," April 14, 15, and 16, 1965, WHCF, Name File, LBJ.

359   notes to his "fellow" seminarian Bill Moyers: Morrison to Moyers, Feb. 15, 1964, and July 24, 1965, WHCF, Name File, LBJ. In the first letter, Morrison offered encouragement to the early Johnson administration, including a long-range appraisal of the Cold War: "Our governmental system is not nearly as easily transportable as the Russian one, but it has stood longer and is universally recognized as more idealistic, based as it is on the dignity of man as created in the image of justice and goodness for all. Our main disadvantage is that we are too far ahead to identify with the have-nots. The world is already fearful and jealous of our power. We are muscle-bound in foreign affairs with little in the way of practical and consistent alternatives to offer to revolutionary minded have-nots. Our prime exportable gift has so far been to assure protection with massive, essentially irrelevant, military strength. . . . China is determined to identify herself with the revolutions of the world even if it means breaking her ties with Russia. The country that can best fit itself to identify with the revolutions of the future will have gained the world by 2000. This will certainly not be Russia." Morrison's second letter to Moyers, just before LBJ announced the major troop commitment to Vietnam, pleaded: "Many of us had begun to feel that it wasn't worth writing any more as things went from bad to worse. If the right decision is made it will have to be great and probably not helpful politically. . . . We pray that you and your boss will have the courage to replace patriotism with a true God."

359   "Every day we sin more": Morrison to LBJ, Feb. 17, 1965, WHCF, Name File, LBJ.

359   "Dearest Anne": *Baltimore Evening Sun,* Nov. 25, 1965, p. B-1.

359   "He was a torch": NYT, Nov. 3, 1965, pp. 1, 8.

359   rescue nurse Cloretta Jones: *Jet,* Nov. 25, 1965, pp. 22–23.

359   "Baltimore Quaker with Baby": *Baltimore Sun,* Nov. 3, 1965, p. 1.

359   devoted two subsequent profiles: "Colleagues Stunned by Quaker's Self-Immolation," NYT, Nov. 4, 1965, p. 5; "Death of a Quaker: His Friends See a Lesson," NYT, Nov. 7, 1965, p. 2.

359   "alien to the American temper": NYT, Nov. 11, 1965, p. 46.

359   "macabre act of protest": *Newsweek,* Nov. 15, 1965.

360   "to avert our eyes": *Christian Century,* Nov. 17, 1965, p. 1404.

360   "raspingly discordant": Mrs. R. W. Barney in *Christian Century,* Jan. 12, 1966, p. 84.

360   poet laureate To Huu: NYT, Dec. 11, 2002, p. 30; Appy, *Patriots,* p. 155.

360   "Emily, my child, it's almost dark": "Emily, My Child," by To Huu, Nov. 1965, translation from Vietnamese courtesy of Lady Borton.

360   married and pregnant Emily Morrison: Anne Morrison Welsh letter to "Dear Friends," May 1999, courtesy of Margot Watson.

360   "many, many Vietnamese men cried": Appy, *Patriots,* pp. 150–55, 228–31.

360   Robert McNamara, in his eighties: Ibid., p. 153.

360   "within forty feet of my Pentagon window": McNamara, *In Retrospect,* pp. 216–17. Although witnesses put the site at least 150 feet from his third-floor office at the Pentagon, McNamara brings it much closer in his 1995 memoir.

361   this time in Union Square: DeBenedetti, *Ordeal,* p. 129.

361   "Do not weep for Norman Morrison": Zaroulis and Sullivan, *Who Spoke Up?,* pp. 61–62.

361   "I'm a Catholic Worker": NYT, Nov. 10, 1965, pp. 1, 5.

361   "terribly unfortunate": Ibid.

362   Friends of LaPorte said: NYT, Nov. 11, 1965, p. 4; DeBenedetti, *Ordeal,* p. 130.

362   feared that suicide protest would alienate: Robinson, *Abraham,* p. 202.

362   "something radically wrong somewhere": Friedland, *Lift Up,* pp. 160–61.

362   expired after power was restored: NYT, Nov. 11, 1965, p. 4; Associated Press, *World in 1965,* pp. 208–13; NYT, Aug. 15, 2003, p. 22.

362   "The people of New York City": Heschel, "No Religion Is an Island," Union Seminary *Quarterly Review,* Vol. 21, No. 2, Part 1, Jan. 1966, p. 118.

24: ENEMY POLITICS

PAGE

365   "I trust that you will not": MLK to J. William Fulbright, Nov. 8, 1965, A/KP24f49.

365   "my influence is not sufficiently strong": Fulbright to MLK, Dec. 13, 1965, A/KP24f50.

365   surrender the purchase documents for a 1965 Chevrolet: Rosen to Belmont, Nov. 8, 1965, FK-NR. The Hosea Williams case, which never became public, began in mid-October and is covered by a host of documents in the FBI's file on SCLC, beginning Rosen to Belmont, Oct. 18, 1965, headed "Unknown Subjects Morris Findlay, Hosea Williams, Harold Belton Andrews, Interstate Transportation of Stolen Motor Vehicle," FSC-NR.

365   he was determined first to wring a refund: SAC, New York, to Hoover, Nov. 10, 1965, FSC-893. A copy of this wiretap report on Stanley Levison's conversations about the car investigation made its way into the King section of Hoover's Official and Confidential Files.

366   "Hosea has a problem": Wiretap transcript of telephone conversation between Andrew Young and Stanley Levison, 11:30 A.M., Nov. 6, 1965, FLNY-9-750.

366   "Martin acted as if the bottom": Wiretap transcript of telephone conversation between Stanley Levison and Clarence Jones, 12:04 P.M., Nov. 6, 1965, FLNY-9-750a.

366   advisers analyzed the treasury crisis: New York LHM dated Nov. 8, 1965, FSC-886; Baumgardner to Sullivan, Nov. 10, 1965, FSC-880.

366   to buy Abernathy a new automobile: Wiretap transcript of telephone conversation between MLK and Stanley Levison, Oct. 1, 1965, FLNY-9-750a; New York LHM dated Oct. 4, 1965, FSC-717. King reported to Levison that only one of fifty solicited donors had responded, but that Abernathy had obtained a $3,000 car. To avert potential embarrassment, King wanted to reimburse SCLC, and Levison, though sharply critical of Abernathy, agreed to contribute half the money himself.

366   King wrote a detailed letter to American Express: MLK to Carl W. Volckmann, American Express Company, Nov. 15, 1965, A/KP2f26; Carl W. Volckmann to Abernathy, Sept. 13, 1965, A/KP2f26.

366   introduced by American Express in 1959: Laurel Kamen to the author, Sept. 5, 2003.

366   Young and the New York advisers: Int. Harry Wachtel, Nov. 29, 1983.

366   resigning his vested career as a chemist: Hosea L. Williams telegram to William M. Seabron in the Office of the Secretary, U.S. Department of Agriculture, Oct. 12, 1965, A/KP35f17.

367   "Hosea Williams is the Director": Rosen to Belmont, Oct. 22, 1965, "Harold Belton Andrews/Interstate Transportation of a Stolen Motor Vehicle," FSC-NR.

367   skeptical federal prosecutors: R. I. Shroder to Rosen, Oct. 28, 1965, FSC-NR; Rosen to Belmont, Nov. 1, 1965, FSC-NR.

367   infuriated Deke DeLoach: DeLoach to Mohr, Oct. 29, 1965, FSC-NR.

367   Alan Belmont: Belmont to Tolson, Oct. 29, 1965, FK-NR.

367   "The Dept Attys may have gotten": Hoover note on DeLoach to Mohr, Oct. 29, 1965, FSC-NR.

367   The FBI scrambled in November: Cf. Rosen to Belmont, Nov. 10, 1965, FSC-894.

367   Katzenbach stressed that skilled defense lawyers: Katzenbach oral history by Paige E. Mulhollan, Nov. 12, 1968, p. 33ff., LBJ; int. Nicholas Katzenbach, June 14, 1991.

368   months of cajolery: Ibid.; see above, pp. 187–89.

368   "As a consequence": Hoover to "THE ATTORNEY GENERAL," Sept. 14, 1965, untitled, Section 114, FHOC.

368   "Because of the importance": Hoover, "MEMORANDUM FOR THE ATTORNEY GENERAL RE: MARTIN LUTHER KING, JR.," Oct. 19, 1965, FK-1990; Sullivan to Belmont, Oct. 14, 1995, FK-1981.

368   Hoover sent Katzenbach two nearly identical notices: Baumgardner to Sullivan, Oct. 29, 1965, FK-2021; Hoover, "MEMORANDUM FOR THE ATTORNEY GENERAL RE: MARTIN LUTHER KING, JR.," Dec. 1, 1965, FK-2183.

369   Agents recruited bookkeeper James Harrison: Garrow, *FBI and King,* p. 178.

369   "thought and imagination": Director to SAC, Atlanta, Nov. 10, 1965, FK-2025. For other examples of FBI communications aimed to infiltrate SCLC, and learn more of internal dissension or bickering "which might be exploited under the counterintelligence program," see Director to SAC, Atlanta, Sept. 27, 1965, FSC-657; SAC, Atlanta, to Director, Nov. 2, 1965, FSC-838; SAC, New York, to Director, Nov. 8, 1965, FSC-856.

369   "was quite calm": DeLoach to Mohr, Aug. 14, 1965, FK-1782.

369   DeLoach also briefed Fred Buzhardt and Harry Dent: DeLoach to Mohr, Sept. 15, 1965, FK-1881.

369   "It is disgraceful": Hoover comment on Rosen to Belmont, Nov. 8, 1965, FSC-887. Hoover probably meant "under wraps" instead of "under raps."

369   "as that outfit is above the law": Hoover comment on Rosen to Belmont, Oct. 30, 1965, "Harold Belton Andrews, et al.," FSC-NR.

369   solicited his participation: Morris B. Abram, co-chairman, White House Conference to Fulfill These Rights, telegram to MLK, Oct. 27, 1965, A/KP26f10; MLK reply to Abram "c/o Mrs. Thornell the White House," Oct. 29, 1965, A/KP26f10. King, just back from Europe, declined the urgent summons to a preliminary meeting on October 30, citing his daughter Yoki's piano recital, and sent Ralph Abernathy and Walter Fauntroy in his place.

369   most of the colleagues King nominated: MLK telegram to Lee White, Nov. 2, 1965, A/KP26f10, nominating as SCLC delegates himself, James Bevel, Ralph Abernathy, Septima Clark, Robert Green, Lawrence Reddick, C. T. Vivian, Dorothy Cotton, An-

drew Young, Hosea Williams, Harry Wachtel, Randolph Blackwell, and Walter Fauntroy.

369   remonstrated with security officials: Lee White to Marvin Watson, Nov. 12, 1965, HU2, MC, HU6, WHCF Box 56, LBJ.

369   Lee White reminded the President: Lee White to LBJ, Nov. 2, 1965, Name File, "Bayard Rustin," LBJ.

369   dispatched to lead a march: Martha Prescod, Selma WATS report, Nov. 15, 1965, Reel 16, SNCC.

370   "the other names which were submitted": Andrew Young telegram to Lee White, Nov. 13, 1965, A/KP26f10.

370   "We may be overly optimistic": Baumgardner to Sullivan, Nov. 18, 1965, FSC-NR.

370   religious leaders in New York convened: Rainwater and Yancey, *Moynihan Report,* pp. 211–14.

370   King arrived two days later: Levison phone call to Clarence Jones, 2:45 P.M., Nov. 11, 1965, FLNY-9-755a; SAC, New York, to Director, Nov. 19, 1965, FK-2069.

370   "the damage that is flowing": Tape transcript, "Planning Meeting for Metropolitan New York Pre–White House Conference on Civil Rights," Nov. 9, 1965, NCC, RG 6, Box 48, File 7, POH.

370   "Because of the newspaper coverage": Rainwater and Yancey, *Moynihan Report,* p. 192.

370   distributed copies avidly: Robert D. Novak, "Washington's Truth Teller," WP, March 31, 2003, p. 13; int. Harry McPherson, Sept. 24, 1991.

370   "political atomic bomb": Rowland Evans and Robert Novak, "Inside Report: The Moynihan Report," WP, Aug. 18, 1965, cited in Rainwater and Yancey, *Moynihan Report,* pp. 375–76.

370   sold openly in government stores: Ibid., p. 151.

371   "replace matriarchy": John Herbers, "Report Focuses on Negro Family: Aid to Replace Matriarchy Asked by Johnson Panel," NYT, Aug. 27, 1965, p. 13.

371   "aimed at developing a national policy": "Letter from Washington, September 2," *New Yorker,* Sept. 2, 1965, p. 116ff.

371   "Negro life is another world": Richard Wilson, "Gloomy Study Faces Parley on Negro," WS, Sept. 24, 1965, cited in Rainwater and Yancey, *Moynihan Report,* p. 152.

371   Gender terms sprang into headlines: "Drive for Negro Family Stability Spurred by White House Panel," NYT, July 19, 1965, p. 1; "Behind the Riots: Family Life Breakdown in Negro Slums Sows Seeds of Race Violence/ Husbandless Homes Spawn Young Hoodlums, Impede Reforms, Sociologists Say," WSJ, Aug. 16, 1965, p. 1.

371   "The very essence of the male animal": Office of Policy Planning and Research, United States Department of Labor, *The Negro Family: The Case for National Action,* March 1965, U.S. Government Printing Office No. 1965 O-794-628, p. 16.

371   "bitterly ironic": Pauli Murray letter cited in Rainwater and Yancey, *Moynihan Report,* p. 185.

371   "It is amazing to me": Ibid., p. 200.

371   "No one in all history": MLK speech at Abbott House, Westchester County, New York, Oct. 29, 1965, cited in ibid., pp. 402–9.

371   Articles about Moynihan poured: Christopher Jencks, "The Moynihan Report," *New York Review of Books,* Oct. 14, 1965, pp. 39–40; Herbert J. Gans, "The Negro Family: Reflections on the Moynihan Report," *Commonweal,* Oct. 15, 1965, pp. 47–51; William F. Ryan, "Savage Discovery: The Moynihan Report," *Nation,* Nov. 22, 1965; Benjamin

F. Payton, "New Trends in Civil Rights," *Christianity and Crisis,* Dec. 13, 1965. The Rainwater and Yancey book dissects these commentaries, pp. 216–45.

372   "explosive cycle of poverty": *Newsweek,* Aug. 9, 1965, pp. 32–36.

372   "Moynihan's facts were undisputed": Manchester, *Glory,* pp. 1296–97. Others offered sharply different assessments of the uproar. "Today the Moynihan Report stands as probably the most refuted document in American history (though of course its dire predictions about the poor black family all came true)," wrote Nicholas Lemann in 1991. "Attacks on it are still being published." Lemann, *Promised,* p. 177.

372   Malone assured Hoover: SAC, New York, to Director, Nov. 19, 1965, FK-2069.

372   King's just published commitment: MLK, "Next Stop: The North," *Saturday Review,* Nov. 13, 1965, p. 33ff.

372   orders for the SCLC accountant: MLK telegram to Jesse Blayton, Nov. 17, 1965, A/KP22f16.

372   Harry Belafonte might stave off: New York LHM dated Nov. 15, 1965, FSC-888; New York LHM dated Nov. 22, 1965, FK-NR.

372   "The government thinks": Wiretap transcript of Levison conversation with Gloria Cantor, Nov. 14, 1965, FLNY-9-758a.

372   "Malcolm X wrote this book": Wiretap transcript of Levison conversation with King's literary agent, Joan Daves, Dec. 3, 1965, FLNY-9-777a.

373   Publisher Nelson Doubleday had pulled: Tim Warren, "The Rocky Road to Publication of Book on Malcolm X," *Baltimore Sun,* Nov. 16, 1992, p. D-1.

373   major organs of American culture buried Malcolm: Cone, *Martin,* p. 39.

373   "We shall be lucky": Ibid.

373   "twisted man": Branch, *Pillar,* p. 598.

373   "American Negroes lost their most able": Eliot Fremont-Smith, "An Eloquent Testament," NYT, Nov. 5, 1965, p. 35.

373   "The important word here": I. F. Stone, "The Pilgrimage of Malcolm X," *New York Review of Books,* Nov. 11, 1965, p. 3ff.

373   "I knew right there in prison": Malcolm X, *Autobiography,* p. 179.

374   ten best nonfiction books: "Malcolm X Project," The Institute for Research in African-American Studies, Columbia University, www.columbia.edu/cu/iraas/index.html.

374   omitted recommendations: Rainwater and Yancey, *Moynihan Report,* pp. 8, 28; U.S. Department of Labor, *The Negro Family: The Case for National Action* (1965), p. 93.

374   "I am not interested in becoming American": Cone, *Martin,* p. 38.

374   knew it would leave Americans cold: Int. Alex Haley, Dec. 4, 1990; Tim Warren, "The Rocky Road to Publication of Book on Malcolm X," *Baltimore Sun,* Nov. 16, 1992, p. D-3.

374   "Here one may read": *New York Review of Books,* Nov. 11, 1965, p. 4.

374   "As much as I am persuaded": Cone, *Martin,* p. 153.

374   "strong black male": "Malcolm X Project," www.columbia.edu/cu/iraas/index.html.

374   "I became a bus boy": Malcolm X, *Autobiography,* p. 69.

374   "The white man is in no moral": Ibid., p. 241.

374   "Yes, I will pull off": Ibid., p. 271.

375   "I have never felt": Ibid., p. 378.

375   "I don't care how nice": Ibid., p. 27.

375   sports remained white: Fitzpatrick, *Walls,* p. 64.

375   students were signing scholarships: *Jet,* Jan. 6, 1966, p. 57.

375   died of a broken back: Fitzpatrick, *Walls,* p. 142.

375   presold its 1966 tickets: NYT, June 8, 1965, p. 52; NYT, Dec. 23, 1965, p. 34.

375   Comedian Danny Thomas: NYT, Aug. 17, 1965, p. 26.

375   under J. Edgar Hoover's detailed supervision: Powers, *Secrecy,* pp. 435–36; Branch, *Pillar,* p. 544; Brooks and Marsh, *Directory,* p. 236.

376   Bill Cosby as the first actor: " 'I Spy' with Negro Is Widely Booked," NYT, Sept. 10, 1965, p. 71; NYT, Sept. 16, 1965, p. 93; Dates and Barlow, eds., *Split Image,* pp. 280–84; Brooks and Marsh, *Directory,* p. 354. NBC outlets initially refused the show in Birmingham, Savannah, Daytona Beach, Albany (Georgia), and Alexandria, Louisiana.

376   "No other nation hates": *New Republic,* TRB, "Cities in Straitjackets," *New Republic,* Nov. 13, 1965, p. 6.

376   "The Proud Shapes": *Life* Special Double Issue, "The U.S. City: Its Greatness Is at Stake," Vol. 59, No. 26, Dec. 24, 1965.

376   an abrupt end for media celebrations: Gans, *Deciding,* p. 48.

376   Califano sent the TRB column: Califano to McPherson, Nov. 15, 1965, WHCF, Ex LG, Box 1, LBJ; int. Harry McPherson, Oct. 10, 1991.

376   157th anniversary of Abyssinian Baptist Church: NYT, Nov. 9, 1965, p. 75.

376   Stanley Levison warned: Levison phone call with Dora McDonald, Nov. 24, 1965, FLNY-9-768a.

376   provoked James Phelan: Ibid.; MLK to James Phelan, Dec. 6, 1965, A/KP18f45. "While Congressman Powell has criticised me on numerous occasions, I have always followed my consistent philosophy of not retaliating with criticisms, but trying to do the job of brotherly reconciliation," King wrote Phelan at Chase Manhattan Bank. His five-page apologia insisted that Powell was "not the incarnation of evil so much of the press has painted," and placed him instead in a long tradition of flamboyant ethnic pioneers such as New York mayor James J. Walker: "When the Irish, Italian, Jewish and other minorities were struggling for equal access to American society, each produced leaders with conflicting and confusing tendencies."

377   "would use it against me": New York FBI report dated Feb. 9, 1966, FJ-89, p. 2A.

377   pleas from Wyatt Walker: Ibid.; Walker to MLK, Sept. 9, 1965, and Walker to MLK, Oct. 6, 1965, A/KP36f2. At Walker's request, to rehabilitate his job prospects, King wrote promotional letters recommending him for honorary degrees.

377   did hope to dispel malicious rumors: Ibid.; David Boyers to DeLoach, Sept. 29, 1965, FK-NR; SA [deleted] to SAC, New York, Oct. 6, 1965, FJNY-902.

377   "gesture of reconciliation": NY LHM "Re: Martin Luther King, Jr./Security Matter," dated Nov. 15, 1965, FK-[illegible].

377   "the greatest living American": NYT, Nov. 15, 1965, p. 1.

377   "that we could present a united front": Powell to MLK, Nov. 23, 1965, responding to MLK's letter of Nov. 16, 1965, A/KP18f45.

377   "Adam is going to hell": Int. Wyatt Walker, Aug. 20, 1984.

377   "Power's Long Arm": WP, Sept. 17, 1965, p. 21.

378   Fall memorialized in his book *Street Without Joy:* Moore, *Soldiers,* p. 43.

378   light at the end of the tunnel: Alsop, "The Brand-New War," WP, Sept. 13, 1965, p. 21.

378   Colonel Moore landed: Langguth, *Our Vietnam,* pp. 395–96.

378   "search for and destroy the enemy": Moore, *Soldiers,* pp. 15, 24–25, 57.

378   "Every man in the lead squad was shot": Ibid., p. 78.

378   charged after Vietnamese up a hill: Ibid., pp. 65–70.

379   "I had major fire support": Ibid., p. 104.

379   "Even the men who *could* stand up: Appy, *Patriots,* pp. 128–35.

379   "If we're up against this": Ibid., p. 135; Moore, *Soldiers,* pp. 175–77.

379   on the third morning, November 16: Langguth, *Our Vietnam,* p. 401; Library of America Anthology, *Reporting Vietnam,* p. 208; Moore, *Soldiers,* pp. 158–65.

379   his first twenty-five death tags: Int. Hank Thomas, March 14, 1991.

380   he led the first Freedom Riders: Branch, *Parting,* pp. 412–18, 482–84; Branch, *Pillar,* pp. 36–37.

380   still nonviolent mentor for Stokely Carmichael: Int. Hank Thomas, Dec. 17, 2003; Carmichael, *Ready,* pp. 150, 156–57, 165, 181–84, 195–98.

380   dropped two hundred tons of ordnance: Moore, *Soldiers,* p. 215.

380   three battalions of North Vietnamese struck: Ibid., pp. 223–28, 234–35; Langguth, *Our Vietnam,* pp. 402–5.

380   "I don't know why": Library of America Anthology, *Reporting Vietnam,* p. 215.

380   calling in napalm on their own positions: Moore, *Soldiers,* pp. 258–59.

380   93 percent casualties: Library of America Anthology, *Reporting Vietnam,* p. 222.

380   Captain George Forrest: Moore, *Soldiers,* pp. 207, 226–27, 297; *Baltimore Sun,* Nov. 11, 2003, p. 1.

381   brigade commander neglected: Moore, *Soldiers,* p. 306.

381   a costly victory by the numbers: "U.S. Units Pull Out After Killing 637," NYT, Nov. 17, 1965, p. 1.

381   three AP photographs: Neil Sheehan, "Battalion of G.I.'s Battered in Trap; Casualties High," NYT, Nov. 19, 1965, p. 1.

381   praised military performance: Cf. McNamara to LBJ, Nov. 30, 1965, in FRUS, Vol. 3, p. 591ff; Moore, *Soldiers,* pp. 46–51.

381   "heaven-storming" final push: Duiker, *Ho,* pp. 548–52; Moore, *Soldiers,* p. 12.

381   "They're the best I've ever seen": CBS News, "The Battle of Ia Drang Valley," Nov. 30, 1965, T79:0238, MOB; Moore, *Soldiers,* p. 32.

381   General Westmoreland focused on attrition ratios: Langguth, *Our Vietnam,* p. 407; Moore, *Soldiers,* p. 339.

382   "headlines about victory": NYT, Nov. 25, 1965, pp. 1, 2.

382   "I welcome all of you": LBJ remarks, Nov. 16, 1965, PPP, pp. 1113–15.

382   "the captains of peaceful armies": Ibid., p. 1114; NYT, Nov. 17, 1965, p. 1.

382   "We're eating barbecue": Harrington, *Fragments,* p. 128.

382   working constraints clamped down: WP, Nov. 19, 1965, p. 1; *Jet,* Dec. 2, 1965, pp. 14–17; *Jet,* Jan. 6, 1966, pp. 3–4.

382   class sizes in poor Northern schools: Al Raby statement at Chicago Board of Education budget hearing, Dec. 13, 1965, A/SC149f13, p. 3.

383   "People in the South": NYT, Nov. 19, 1965, p. 1.

383   A. Philip Randolph ruled his friend's motion out of order: Rainwater and Yancey, *Moynihan Report,* pp. 254–56.

383   "critical or unjustifiable statements": DeLoach to Mohr, "White House Meeting Entitled 'To Fulfill These Rights,' " Nov. 10, 1965, FK-NR.

383   White House aides vigorously promoted: McPherson, *Political,* pp. 340–42; Rainwater and Yancey, *Moynihan Report,* pp. 246–51.

383   "We are not being deprived": WS, Nov. 19, 1965, p. 2.

384   "I have been reliably informed": Rainwater and Yancey, *Moynihan Report,* p. 248.

384   "a point of personal privilege": Ibid., p. 253.

384   "is the fundamental source of weakness": Office of Policy Planning and Research, United States Department of Labor, *The Negro Family: The Case for National Action,* March 1965, U.S. GPO No. 1965 O-794-628, p. 5.

384   "Moynihan Conspicuously Ignored": WS, Nov. 19, 1965, p. 2.

384   publicity about Moynihan: LBJ's irritation with Moynihan was evident in phone conversations and notes, such as his comment scrawled on a January 1967 *Chicago Daily News* story about an automobile insurance commission: "Ask [White House aide Douglass] Cater who the hell appointed Moynihan. I want to get him out now." WHCF, Name File, Daniel Patrick Moynihan, LBJ.

384   "They come right in": LBJ phone call with McGeorge Bundy, 9:31 A.M., Dec. 3, 1965, Cit. 9306, Audiotape WH6512.01, LBJ.

384   The White House staff spread rumors: Harrington, *Fragments,* p. 128.

384   240 Americans killed: NYT, Nov. 25, 1965, pp. 1–2.

385   retracted its obituary for Toby Braveboy: Ibid., p. 3; Moore, *Soldiers,* pp. 274–76.

385   "brilliant success": "Asian Communists Sure Public Opinion in U.S. Will Force War's End," NYT, Nov. 28, 1965, p. 1.

385   commended the draft of Coretta's address: Transcript of MLK interview by Arnold Michaelis, Dec. 9, 1965, p. 13, MS 2952, b7f5, AMC; King, *My Life,* p. 295.

385   "This is true in spite of the bombings": Transcript, Arnold Michaelis filmed interview with MLK, Dec. 9, 1965, "Section on Vietnam," p. 6, Arnold Michaelis Collection, MS2952, b7f5, AMC.

385   sought to project a moderate image: Dellinger, *From Yale,* pp. 204–8.

385   "more babies than beatniks": "Thousands Walk in Capital to Protest War in Vietnam: Demonstrators Decorous," NYT, Nov. 28, 1965, p. 1.

385   "I'd rather see America save her soul": Ibid., p. 86.

385   Rally organizers vetoed speakers: Zaroulis and Sullivan, *Who Spoke Up?,* pp. 63–65.

385   infighting among the nascent antiwar groups: Halstead, *Out Now!,* pp. 93–112.

386   "What do you do when the whole country": "A Talk with Bob Parris," *Southern Patriot,* Oct. 1965, p. 3.

386   "violent, loud, offensive": NYT, Oct. 12, 1965, p. 34; Branch, *Parting,* pp. 492–523.

386   "What do you make of it?": Carl Oglesby address, "Let Us Shape the Future," Nov. 27, 1965, *Liberation,* Jan. 1966, pp. 11–14.

386   SDS president Carl Oglesby: Sale, *SDS,* p. 195.

387   lifted his arm like a prizefighter's: Powers, *War,* pp. 92–94; Halstead, *Out Now!,* p. 113.

387   birth moment for the "New Left" identity: Ibid.; Harrington, *Fragments,* p. 159; DeBenedetti, *Ordeal,* pp. 132–34; Sale, *SDS,* pp. 242–45.

387   "Sir, that completes my presentation": Moore, *Soldiers,* pp. 319, 339.

387   classified request for another 200,000 troops: McNamara to LBJ, Nov. 30, 1965, in FRUS, Vol. 3, pp. 591–94.

387   "shattering blow": McNamara, *In Retrospect,* pp. 221–22.

387   "particularly the First Air Cavalry Division": LBJ phone call with Robert McNamara, 9:09 P.M., Nov. 30, 1965, Cit. 9200, Audiotape WH6511.09, LBJ.

387   "acute and rising anxiety": Alsop, "Protesting or Being Practical," WP, Nov. 29, 1965, p. 17.

388   "shrill cries of Negro militants": Evans and Novak, "Inside Report: Civil Rights Disaster," WP, Nov. 24, 1965, p. 17.

388   five aspiring black voters were evicted: Selma WATS report, Nov. 11, 1965, Reel 16, SNCC.

388   "Folks there are understandably jumpy": Undated memo from "Janet, Tina," regarding the ASCS workshops, Reel 37, SNCC.

388   interest in the practical workings of ASCS crop loans: Eagles, *Outside Agitator,* pp. 134–36.

388   nearly two-thirds of the eligible farmers were black: Ibid., p. 198.

388   "We did it fair and square": "New Political Group in Lowndes to Name Own Negro Candidates," SC, Jan. 1–2, 1966, p. 1.

389   "star of stage, screen, and television": Selma WATS report, Nov. 16, 1965, Reel 16, SNCC.

389   "running scared": Diary of Francis Walter, Dec. 17, 1965, p. 77, courtesy of Francis Walter.

389   birthday party for Sammy Younge: Forman, *Sammy Younge,* p. 181.

389   Tuskegee students who had been drawn into demonstrations: Cf. SC, July 30, 1965, p. 1.

389   a light-skinned Tuskegee family: Forman, *Sammy Younge,* pp. 31–33, 56, 70–71, 139, 154–59, 174–79.

389   served as a maid in his household: Int. Cleveland Sellers and Gwendolyn Patton, April 15, 2000.

389   farm-based activists for a trek to Atlanta: Atlanta WATS report, Dec. 6, 1965, Reel 16, SNCC; Jeffries, "Freedom Politics," pp. 95–98; Hampton and Fayer, *Voices,* pp. 276–77.

389   "The workshop spent one day": Jack Minnis to Jack O'Dell, Dec. 18, 1965, JMP.

389   reacted negatively to several proposed choices: Jeffries, "Freedom Politics," pp. 95–98.

390   the third trial of the Klansmen: Stanton, *From Selma,* pp. 128–30; NYT, Nov. 30, 1965, p. 33.

390   Gary Thomas Rowe refused to testify: Hoover to Tolson et al., Nov. 24, 1965, FVL-635.

390   "I am prepared to help you obtain": Katzenbach to Gary Thomas Rowe, Nov. 27, 1965, attachment to Document 40, Gary Thomas Rowe, Jr., Headquarters Informant File, FBI.

390   restrictions that had chafed: Int. Richmond Flowers, Aug. 9, 1990.

390   "by any means necessary": NYT, Dec. 1, 1965, p. 32.

390   Hoover startled Katzenbach: Hoover to Tolson et al., 3:13 P.M., Dec. 3, 1965, FVL-611; Hoover to Tolson et al., 3:18 P.M., Dec. 3, 1965, FCT-NR; Stanton, *From Selma,* p. 128; Sikora, *Judge,* p. 262.

390   a second Alabama jury: NYT, Dec. 1, 1965, p. 32; NYT, Dec. 2, 1965, p. 37; Dec. 3, 1965, p. 1; *Jet,* Dec. 9, 1965, p. 9; Mendelsohn, *Martyrs,* p. 194; SC, July 23, 1965, p. 1.

391   Doar lapsed briefly: NYT, Dec. 4, 1965, p. 35; Bass, *Taming,* p. 256ff.

391   "Really, it was quite a trial": LBJ phone call with Nicholas Katzenbach, 4:10 P.M., Dec. 3, 1965, Cit. 9311, Audiotape WH6512.02, LBJ.

391   "the whole nation can take heart": NYT, Dec. 4, 1965, p. 1.

391   Atlanta workshops sank into the mechanics: Jeffries, "Freedom Politics," pp. 93–97.

391   Presenters shared legal research: Cf. William Kunstler to Stokely Carmichael, with attachments, Dec. 10 [1965], Reel 37, SNCC.

391   "During the discussions": SNCC research, "Background on the Development of Political Strategy and Political Leadership in Lowndes County, Alabama," July 1966, p. 7, Reel 18, SNCC.

391   "who's pulling the levers of power": Int. Jack Minnis, April 7–8, 2001.

391   "We went into the concept of": Jack Minnis to Jack O'Dell, Dec. 18, 1965, JMP.

391   "News about the new freedom organization": Atlanta WATS report, Dec. 6, 1965, Reel 16, SNCC.

391   asked Rev. Francis Walter to help investigate reprisals: Nov. 21 entry regarding call from Rev. Bruce Hanson, "Selma Inter-religious Project, Calendar of Wilcox County Events," BIR/FW2f15.

392   followed a wilderness road: Diary of Francis Walter, Dec. 9, 1965, p. 68, courtesy of Francis Walter.

392   backtracking the river-looped county: Int. Francis Walter, Sept. 7, 2000.

392   Freedom Quilting Bee: Callahan, *Quilting Bee,* passim, especially pp. 3–4, 13–18, 57–67.

392   Nearly all the folk artisans: Ibid., pp. 143–241.

392   acquitted the three men charged with the beating death: NYT, Dec. 11, 1965, p. 1; Stanton, *From Selma,* p. 48.

392   Richmond Flowers denounced: NYT, Dec. 18, 1965, p. 17.

392   "Reeb Verdict Outrages Justice Department": WP, Dec. 13, 1965, p. 3. The jury foreman, William Vaughan, had resigned from St. Paul's Episcopal Church to protest its token integration the previous spring. Another juror, Harry Vardaman, was the brother of defense alibi witness Ben Vardaman, who was implicated in the Reeb attack by federal investigators.

392   Gene Roberts surfaced the first hint: "Student Rights Group Lacks Money and Help but Not Projects," NYT, Dec. 10, 1965, p. 37.

392   Ruth Howard and other SNCC artists: Int. Bob Mants, Sept. 8, 2000; int. Gloria Larry House, June 29, 2000. The history of the panther logo was recalled in e-mail exchanges over the Ole Miss–based SNCC mailing list, including notes posted as follows: Bob Zellner, March 3, 2002; Margaret Herring, March 5, 2002; Charlie Cobb, March 5, 2002; Dorothy Zellner, March 5, 2002; Judy Richardson, March 5, 2002; Jack Minnis, March 5, 2002; Patrick Jones, March 5, 2002; Scott B. Smith, March 15, 2002.

393   He called Stanley Levison: Wiretap transcript of telephone conversation between Stanley Levison and MLK, 12:40 P.M., Dec. 2, 1965, FLNY-9-776a.

393   he had preached in Gittelson's synagogue: Wiretap transcript of telephone conversation between Stanley Levison and MLK, 11:40 A.M., Dec. 4, 1965, FLNY-9-778.

393   Levison dictated paragraphs by relay: Wiretap transcript of telephone conversation between Stanley Levison and Dora McDonald, 1:20 P.M., Nov. 24, 1965, FLNY-9-768a.

393   "The stirring lesson of this age": MLK address, Dec. 5, 1965, A/KS.

394   Micah on beating swords into plowshares: Micah 4:3.

394   "Yea, when you make many prayers": Isaiah 1:15–16.

394   "Dr. King Sees Move Against Pacifists": NYT, Dec. 6, 1965, p. 73; New York LHM dated Dec. 7, 1965, FK-2137.

394   an interview arranged by Stanley Levison: Wiretap transcript of telephone conversation between Stanley Levison and Clarence Jones, 9:32 P.M., Oct. 25, 1965, FLNY-9-738a; New York LHM dated Oct. 28, 1965, FK-NR.

394   "And so I have been a Dodger fan": Transcript, "Martin Luther King, Jr.: A Personal Portrait, in Conversation with Arnold Michaelis," WOR-TV, April 3, 1973, MS 2952, b7f6, AMS, p. 3.

394   a mob of nearly two hundred had blocked: SCLC Alabama press release dated Dec. 1, 1965, A/KP28f6.

394   "This was a heart-melting demonstration": Rev. Samuel B. Wells, "Report from But-
        ler County, Alabama," A/SC165f12; Branch, *Parting,* pp. 612–14, 867–68.

394   arrested Young and his passengers alike: FBI, Mobile, to Director, urgent Teletype
        dated Dec. 7, 1965, FK-2119.

395   "I never felt that war could be a positive good": Undated transcript, [Dec. 9, 1965],
        "Dr. Martin Luther King, Jr. in Conversation with Arnold Michaelis," MS 2952, b7f5,
        AMS, pp. 6–10. A portion of the Michaelis-King interview was broadcast by WNET
        Channel 13 in New York on March 8, 1966, as noted in New York LHM dated March
        9, 1966, FK-NR.

395   "There can be no gainsaying": Ibid., p. 7.

395   "I don't think President Johnson is a warmonger": Ibid., p. 19.

395   "I certainly can't claim to be a saint": Ibid., p. 46.

395   "a very practical problem that runs the gamut of history": Ibid., p. 21.

396   "I wouldn't take my own life": Ibid., pp. 50–53.

25: INSIDE OUT

PAGE

397   "McCone Commission Urges": NYT, Dec. 7, 1965, pp. 1, 26.

397   nearly all the 114 Los Angeles elementary schools without cafeterias: Governor's
        Commission, *Violence in the City,* pp. 53–55.

397   "shockingly lower": Ibid., p. 50.

397   "Go to school for *what?*": Ibid., p. 39.

397   ownership of cars to reach jobs: Ibid., pp. 65–67.

397   "curtain-raiser": "McCone Commission Urges": NYT, Dec. 7, 1965, p. 1.

397   "an insensate rage of destruction": Governor's Commission, *Violence in the City,* pp. 1,
        4–5.

397   Rustin cited McCone's own investigators: Bayard Rustin, "The Watts 'Manifesto' and
        the McCone Report," *Commentary,* March 1966, pp. 29–35. See also "An Analysis of
        the McCone Commission Report" by the California Advisory Committee to the U.S.
        Commission on Civil Rights, reprinted as Exhibit 89, in Hearings of the U.S. Senate
        Committee on Labor and Public Welfare, "Federal Role in Urban Affairs, 89th Con-
        gress [1966], pp. 802–12.

398   "To find out that about 85 per cent": Ibid., p. 31.

398   "Every Negro knows this": Ibid., p. 32.

398   No Negro ranked above sergeant: Broome, *LAPD's Black History,* pp. 116–18.

398   being cajoled by Malcolm X: Branch, *Pillar,* pp. 3–20, 78–81; int. Earl Broady, March
        25, 1991.

399   Chief Parker's countervailing charge: "Parker Hints Muslims Took Part in Rioting,"
        LAT, Aug. 17, 1965, p. 1; NYT, Sept. 14, 1965, p. 22.

399   "One person threw a rock": Dallek, *Right Moment,* p. 142.

399   "on both sides of the Negro question": Bayard Rustin, "The Watts 'Manifesto' and the
        McCone Report," *Commentary,* March 1966, p. 29.

399   Moynihan had become an established national oracle: Moynihan, "Behind Los Ange-
        les: Jobless Negroes and the Boom," *Reporter,* Sept. 9, 1965, p. 31.

399   "Remember that American slavery": CBS Reports, *Watts: Riot or Revolt?,* Dec. 7, 1965,
        Tape T77:0395, MOB.

399   "I grew up in Hell's Kitchen": NYT, Dec. 12, 1965, p. 74.

399 "Some people are lucky": Transcript, guest Daniel P. Moynihan, *Meet the Press,* Dec. 12, 1965, Vol. 9, No. 44.

400 "an alimentary canal at one end": Dallek, *Right Moment,* pp. 100–103.

400 Reagan continued to defend the Goldwater positions: "The Real Ronald Reagan Stands Up," *Life,* Jan. 21, 1966.

400 "I would have voted against it": LAT, Jan. 22, 1965; Dallek, *Right Moment,* p. 188; Dugger, *On Reagan,* pp. 197–98.

400 Stuart Spencer and William Roberts: Edwards, *Reagan,* pp. 83–90; Boyarsky, *Rise,* pp. 106–11.

400 "somewhat passé": Governor Carl Sanders of Georgia, quoted in NYT, Sept. 13, 1965, p. 23.

401 "The original government": NYT Magazine, Nov. 14, 1965, p. 175.

401 "the fruit of appeasement": Dallek, *Right Moment,* p. 190.

401 "a political decision to achieve victory": NYT Magazine, Nov. 14, 1965, p. 184.

401 "we could pave the whole country": LAT, Oct. 21, 1965.

401 150 trial speeches: Edwards, *Reagan,* p. 101.

401 "hemophiliac liberal": NYT Magazine, Nov. 14, 1965, p. 46.

401 citizen-politician: Boyarsky, *Rise,* pp. 137–38.

401 "utterly reprehensible": Dallek, *Right Moment,* pp. 124–27.

401 "the FBI has not investigated": Edwards, *Reagan,* p. 94.

401 "a bunch of kooks": Dallek, *Right Moment,* pp. 103–11.

401 "Tom Sawyer Enters Politics": Leo E. Litwak, "The Ronald Reagan Story; Or, Tom Sawyer Enters Politics," NYT Magazine, Nov. 14, 1965, p. 46ff.

401 first public hints of intrigue: LAT, Dec. 19, 1965, p. 1; WP, Dec. 20, 1965, p. 1.

402 Henderson Novelty Company: "FBI Use of Listening Devices Prompts Charges and Inquiries," NYT, July 3, 1966, p. 25.

402 "I told Katzenbach": DeLoach to Tolson, Dec. 20, 1965, FRK-1800.

402 surreptitious eavesdropping allowed a shrewd defense attorney: "High Court Asked to Hear Tax Case," NYT, May 28, 1966, p. 24; int. Ed Weisl, Jr., May 23, 1991.

402 Hoover already disparaged Williams: Thomas, *Man to See,* pp. 199–203, 499–501; Branch, *Pillar,* p. 181.

402 Washington lobbyist Fred Black: Cf. "Baker's Partner Fought U.S. Claim," NYT, April 22, 1964, p. 32; "Associate of Baker Guilty in Tax Trial," NYT, May 6, 1964, p. 1; "Black Gets up to Four Years for Tax Evasion," NYT, June 20, 1964, p. 9; "Associate of Baker Loses Tax Appeal," NYT, Nov. 11, 1965, p. 7.

402 the Johnson family's next-door neighbor: "FBI Had Sanction in Eavesdropping," NYT, July 14, 1966, p. 1.

403 believe private statements from Kennedy himself: Nicholas Katzenbach oral history by Paige E. Mulhollan, Nov. 12, 1968, p. 33ff, LBJ; Katzenbach oral history by Larry J. Hackman, Oct. 8, 1969, p. 47ff, JFJ; int. Nicholas Katzenbach, June 14, 1991.

403 Kennedy's FBI liaison officer, Courtney Evans: Schlesinger, *Robert Kennedy,* pp. 293–96, 678; Powers, *Secrecy,* pp. 391, 397; Branch, *Parting,* pp. 907–11; Branch, *Pillar,* p. 250.

403 "upon having his recollection refreshed": DeLoach to Tolson, Dec. 24, 1965, FRK-1804.

403 "He did admit that Kennedy must have known": Ibid.; Gale to DeLoach [with handwritten notes by Hoover], Dec. 30, 1965, Section 129, FHOC. DeLoach held a similar session on December 30, 1965, with senior Justice Department prosecutor William

Hundley, and reported that Hundley also considered it "obvious" that certain intelligence "was obtained as a result of microphone coverage." Gale to DeLoach, Dec. 30, 1965, Section 129, FHOC.

403   " 'leave us to the wolves' ": DeLoach to Tolson, Dec. 20, 1965, FRK-1800, p. 3; Shesol, *Contempt,* p. 350.

403   "Three days after Christmas": "Background Information," Dec. 28, 1965, Reel 18, SNCC.

403   SNCC faced $100,000 in debt: "Fund Lag Plagues Rights Movement," NYT, Jan. 19, 1966, p. 1.

404   "John Robert Lewis is TIRED": Penny Patch memo to "Jim, Nancy, Jimmy," et al., Dec. 11, 1965, Reel 1, SNCC.

404   a melancholy year-end statement: "Statement on 1966 by John Lewis, Chairman," Dec. 30, 1965, Reel 20, SNCC.

404   Of twenty evicted families: Lowndes County WATS report, Jan. 4, 1965, Reel 16, SNCC; "Background Information on Lowndes County Tent City," Feb. 28, 1966, Box 1, A/RM.

404   "It has been raining": Background Information," Dec. 28, 1965, Reel 18, SNCC.

404   "Please make sure": Carmichael to Muriel Tillinghast, 1:00 A.M., Dec. 26, 1965, JMP. "The rest of the staff feels that we should not call the police," Carmichael added. "I agree. His system is very simple[—]he calls up these people and tells them that there is an emergency please wire him some money." On a separate matter, Carmichael asked Tillinghast to remove fieldworker Cleophus Hobbs from the payroll because he had been drafted into the Army: "Please STOP his check immediately."

404   Rabbi Harold Saperstein: Fraud warnings evidently reached Saperstein in time. He and his wife sent $50 to the Atlanta SNCC office instead of the suspected embezzler. "I would appreciate it if you would inform Stokely Carmichael of this donation," Saperstein wrote Tillinghast from Temple Emanu-El of Lynbrook, New York, "and give him our personal greetings." Saperstein to Tillinghast, Jan. 3, 1966, Reel 18, SNCC.

404   "I just can't kick it, man": Forman, *Sammy Younge,* pp. 183–84.

404   attracted scattered notice: "Freedom City, Alabama," SC, Jan. 8–9, 1966, p. 1; "Alabama Negroes Evicted from Homes for Political Views," *Jet,* Jan. 13, 1966, p. 4.

404   " 'Tent City' Rising": NYT, Jan. 1, 1966, p. 15.

405   "Evicted Farmers Wallow": *Jet,* March 10, 1966, pp. 14–19.

405   soon contracted hepatitis: Friends of SNCC memo, "Tent Cities," March 18, 1966, Box 1, A/RM.

405   Carmichael said people who registered: Carmichael, *Black Power,* p. 104.

405   "People in Lowndes County": Edward M. Rudd, "New Political Group in Lowndes to Name Own Negro Candidates," SC, Jan. 1–2, 1966, p. 2.

405   Historic address by the sitting Attorney General: *Mobile Register,* Jan. 2, 1966, p. 1; *Mobile Register,* Jan. 3, 1966, p. 1; *Jet,* Jan. 13, 1966, p. 4.

405   Walter took his chance: Diary of Francis Walter, Dec. 17, 1965, p. 77, courtesy of Francis Walter.

405   Mobile's white newspapers: *Jet,* Jan. 20, 1966, pp. 14–17.

405   "spill your guts on the floor": WATS report, Mahoney and Zellner to Elizabeth, 3:30 P.M., Jan. 4, 1966, Reel 16, SNCC; WP, Jan. 7, 1966, p. 2.

406   Witnesses said Younge: NYT, Jan. 5, 1966, p. 12; Forman, *Sammy Younge,* pp. 185–95; Carson, *Struggle,* p. 188.

406   "to bluff him": NYT, Dec. 9, 1966, p. 38; NYT, Dec. 10, 1966, p. 1; "Anatomy of a Murder Trial," SC, Dec. 24–25, 1966, p. 4.

406   "I just got me three bottles of wine": Forman, *Sammy Younge,* p. 184.

406   two thousand students marched Tuesday: NYY, Jan. 5, 1966, p. 12; Forman, *Sammy Younge,* pp. 197–98.

406   "more Negroes to be able to work": WATS report, Jan. 6, 1966, Tuskegee, Reel 16, SNCC.

406   a marathon debate to frame a response: Int. Gloria Larry House, June 29, 2000, and Dec. 18, 2003.

407   for SNCC to take a public stand: John Lewis to SNCC staff, Dec. 7, 1965, Reel 1, SNCC.

407   Gloria Larry's volunteer effort: Int. Gloria Larry House, Dec. 18, 2003; int. Martha Norman, Dec. 20, 2003; int. Julian Bond, Jan. 10, 2004; handwritten fragments of Jan. 6, 1966, SNCC statement, courtesy of Gloria Larry House.

407   "We believe the United States government": Forman, *Making,* pp. 445–46; NYT, Jan. 7, 1966, p. 2.

407   "a crowded news conference": NYT, Jan. 8, 1966, p. 22.

407   a thirteen-page launch blueprint: "A Proposal by the Southern Christian Leadership Conference for the Development of a Nonviolent Action Movement for the Greater Chicago Area," A/KP5f27; Garrow, *Bearing,* pp. 457–58; Anderson and Pickering, *Confronting,* p. 188; Cohen and Taylor, *Pharaoh,* p. 356.

407   Negroes had come to outnumber: Margaret Long, "The Movement," *New South,* Vol. 21, No. 1, Winter 1966, p. 98; WP, Jan. 8, 1966, p. 6.

407   "This economic exploitation": "Statement by Dr. Martin Luther King, Jr.," for release at 11:00 A.M., Jan. 7, 1966, File 940, RS, CHS. The statement includes nearly all the written proposal cited above.

407   Five unions shut down: Graham, *Civil Rights Era,* pp. 285–86.

408   "Dr. King Will Occupy": CD, Jan. 8–14, 1966, p. 1.

408   four memos about Tuskegee: Clifford L. Alexander, Jr., to LBJ, 4:10 P.M., Jan. 6, 1966; Alexander to LBJ, 10:45 A.M., Jan. 7, 1966; Alexander to LBJ, 1:00 P.M., Jan. 7, 1966; Alexander to LBJ, 4:22 P.M., Jan. 7, 1966—all in EX HU2/ST1, Box 25, LBJ.

408   "get by Saturday without bloodshed": NYT, Jan. 8, 1965, p. 22.

408   "support any action we need to take here": LBJ handwritten note, "Cliff—4:55 P.M.— Ask Doar to follow this & support any action we need to take here—L," on Alexander to LBJ, 4:22 P.M., Jan. 7, 1966, EX HU2/ST1, Box 25, LBJ.

408   "negate the impact of this story": Clifford L. Alexander, Jr., to LBJ, 4:56 P.M., Jan. 7, 1966, EX ND9-4, MLK Name File, Box 144, LBJ.

408   "Yes, I do": Neary, *Julian Bond,* p. 93.

409   sudden glare of headlines: Ibid., p. 108; Williams, *Bonds,* p. 223; "Defiance of Draft Call Urged by SNCC Leader," AC, Jan. 7, 1966, p. 1; "Rep.-Elect Bond Facing an Ouster Fight After Urging Draft Dodging," AC, Jan. 8, 1966, p. 1.

409   "Georgians Score a Vietnam Critic": NYT, Jan. 8, 1966, p. 3.

409   "We are in a dangerous period": Garrow, *Bearing,* p. 458; NYT, Jan. 9, 1966, p. 4.

409   "It is ironic that some": Transcript of press conference, Jan. 8, 1966, "Julius Griffin reads Dr. King's Statement, John Lewis reads 'Statement on Georgia Attack on SNCC,' and 'Statement of SNCC supporting Julian Bond,' " Reel 20, SNCC, pp. 0959–0963.

409   withdrew into disbelieving seclusion: Int. Julian Bond, Jan. 10, 2004.

409   "exactly suits the Kremlin": Neary, *Julian Bond,* p. 108.

409   "This boy has got to come": Williams, *Bonds,* p. 224.

409   "I've been hearing": Frady, *Southerners,* pp. 174–75; "Report from James Forman,"
       Jan. 10, 1966, Reel 20, SNCC.

409   gubernatorial candidate Ronald Reagan: Edwards, *Reagan,* pp. 101–2; Boyarsky, *Rise,*
       pp. 139–40; WP, Jan. 5, 1966, p. 1; transcript, guest Ronald Reagan, *Meet the Press,* Jan.
       9, 1966, Vol. 10, No. 2.

409   beseech the counsel of Ralph Abernathy: Neary, *Julian Bond,* p. 107.

410   "I will ask Representative Bond": Ibid., p. 109; Morgan, *One Man,* pp. 150–61.

410   chronic hives had been a sign: Williams, *Bonds,* pp. 206, 214.

410   "Mother'd ask me to go down": Frady, *Southerners,* p. 171.

410   first black president of Lincoln University: Williams, *Bonds,* pp. 83–87, 144ff.

410   "My God, I didn't raise": Frady, *Southerners,* p. 171.

410   legislators played a telephone interview: Neary, *Julian Bond,* pp. 93–97, 118–19.

411   "demonstrate to yourselves": Ibid., p. 121.

411   The House voted exclusion: NYT, Jan. 11, 1966, p. 1.

411   Bond fought back tears: Neary, *Julian Bond,* p. 124.

411   "Everyone, including Julian": "Jan. 10, 1965 [sic—1966]—2 A.M.—Forman/Atlanta to
       [Elizabeth] Sutherland/N.Y., Details on Julian Bond situation," Reel 16, SNCC.

411   King cut short: Garrow, *Bearing,* p. 458.

411   condolence to the family of Vernon Dahmer: President Johnson took reports from his
       aide Clifford Alexander at 7:34 and 8:23 on Monday, within hours of the death in Hat-
       tiesburg, and approved a telegram to Mrs. Dahmer in a call the next morning with
       Katzenbach, PDD, LBJ.

411   "the highest kind of citizenship": Branch, *Pillar,* pp. 606–7.

411   Four Dahmer sons converged: Ibid. A photograph of the four Dahmer sons in mourn-
       ing appears in *Pillar of Fire.*

411   Dahmer was revered: Ibid., pp. 50–63, 224, 392.

411   "I have simply stopped telling people": NYT, Jan. 10, 1966, p. 11.

412   "I have a personal concern": MLK statement dated Jan. 12, 1965 [sic—1966], A/KS10.

412   "Little Chance Seen for Bond": Sidney E. Zion, "Little Chance Seen for Bond in
       Court," NYT, Jan. 12, 1966; AC, Jan. 12, 1966, p. 1.

412   King led a protest march: AC, Jan. 15, 1966, p. 1; int. Julian Bond, Jan. 10, 2004.

412   King speak from the back of a flatbed truck: Ibid.; "Address by Dr. Martin Luther
       King, Jr. at the State Capitol," Jan. 14, 1966, A/KS10.

412   "War will exist until that distant day": Ibid.; Schlesinger, *Thousand Days,* p. 89.

412   Willie Ricks of SNCC exhorted: NYT, Jan. 15, 1966, p. 1; Williams, *Bonds,* p. 230.

412   struck a trooper with her handbag: AC, Jan. 15, 1966, p. 1; Margaret Long, "The
       Movement," *New South,* Winter 1966, p. 95.

412   King issued a pained statement: Garrow, *Bearing,* p. 458.

413   The chorus jeered broadly without him: "Rights Group Widely Criticized for Attack-
       ing Vietnam Policy," NYT, Jan. 16, 1966, p. 60; Neary, *Julian Bond,* pp. 125–27; Good,
       Trouble, pp. 253–54.

413   Prominent Atlanta Negroes called: AC, Jan. 8, 1966, p. 1; Septima Clark oral history
       by Judy Barton, Nov. 9, 1971, A/OH.

413   Lillian Smith scolded: AC, Jan. 14, 1966; "Miss Smith on SNCC," *New South,* Winter
       1966, pp. 64–66; Carson, *Struggle,* p. 189. The *Constitution* introduced Smith's letter

with a heartfelt editorial: "On this page today one of the most distinguished women of American letters presents the most eloquent, and we believe the most accurate, analysis of the Julian Bond incident that will be written. . . . She has devoted much of her life to social protest against injustice to Negroes, and the ostracism and agony she has endured as a result are a more reliable credential than the scars of the Student Nonviolent Coordinating Committee, because she has stood by her convictions a good deal longer. Her literary works, from *Strange Fruit* to *Killers of the Dream,* speak for her integrity."

413   Roy Wilkins rebuked: NYT, Jan. 9, 1966, p. 4; Wilkins, "SNCC Does Not Speak for Whole Movement," LAT, Jan. 17, 1966.

413   "would have refused to seat": Greenberg, *Crusaders,* p. 409.

413   "our Blood-gorged Capitalists": Woodward, *Tom Watson,* pp. 451–58; Williams, *Bonds,* p. 225. "His first reaction was one of amazement at the universality of the war madness," Woodward wrote of Watson, adding, "It was Watson's idea that '*big armaments, instead of ensuring* PEACE, *insure* WAR.' " Watson denounced World War I to fellow Georgians as a cynical venture driven by the investments of bankers such as J. P. Morgan: "Where Morgan's money went, your boy's blood must go, ELSE MORGAN WILL LOSE HIS MONEY! That's all there is to it."

413   "Whether people like it or not": MLK sermon, "Transformed Nonconformist," Jan. 16, 1966, the prepared text filed in A/SC28f20 as compared with transcript of delivered sermon in A/KS10.

26: REFUGEES

415   "I feel a good deal of the ice": LBJ phone call with Maxwell Taylor, 8:56 P.M., Dec. 27, 1965, Cit. 9339, Audiotape WH6512.05, LBJ.

415   Christmas bombing pause: FRUS, Vol. 4, pp. 1–192; Clifford, *Counsel,* pp. 433–37; McNamara, *In Retrospect,* pp. 225–29.

415   frenzied overtures for settlement talks: Cf. LBJ phone call with Averell Harriman, 10:36 A.M., Dec. 28, 1965, Cit. 9344, Audiotape WH6512.05, LBJ.

415   infantry assault launched in strict secrecy: "8,000 G.I.'s Open Biggest Attack of Vietnam War/ Start of Operation Withheld from South Vietnamese to Bar a Leak to Foe," NYT, Jan. 9, 1966, p. 1.

415   "I want a minimum in that defense budget": LBJ; LBJ phone call with McGeorge Bundy, 9:31 A.M., Dec. 3, 1965, Cit. 9306, Audiotape WH6512.01, LBJ.

415   "You're absolutely right": LBJ phone call with Robert McNamara, 10:10 A.M., Dec. 22, 1965, Cit. 9327, Audiotape WH6512.04, LBJ. Johnson had often discussed plans to defer anticipated Vietnam budget requests for political reasons. Cf. LBJ phone call with McNamara, 12:15 P.M., Dec. 2, 1965, Cit. 9305, Audiotape WH6512.01.

415   "guns and butter": "LBJ's Decision: Guns and Butter," *U.S. News & World Report,* Jan. 24, 1966, pp. 27–28, 62.

416   cast a wide net for ideas: Valenti to LBJ, Dec. 9, 1965, Name File, Barbara Jackson, LBJ.

416   Abe Fortas boldly proposed: Fortas to LBJ, Jan. 7, 1966, in FRUS, Vol. 4, p. 32; Kalman, *Abe,* p. 297.

416   "People can get used to anything": John Steinbeck to Valenti, with suggestions for LBJ

and "thanks for the President's warm and loving message," Jan. 7, 1966, Valenti Papers, AC84-57, LBJ.

416   security risk in FBI files: Cf. Jones to DeLoach, "John Ernst Steinbeck," July 20, 1965, Steinbeck FBI File 100-106224-13.

416   amateur designs for unconventional weapons: Cf. Valenti to LBJ, April 28, 1965, quoting a letter from Steinbeck ("The Vietnam War is troublesome. . . . What is needed is a counter Cong."); Steinbeck to Valenti, July 22, 1965; Steinbeck to Robert McNamara, Oct. 8, 1965, all in Valenti Papers, AC84-57, LBJ.

416   "I never knew anyone to hit anything": Steinbeck to Valenti, Jan. 7, 1966, Valenti Papers, AC84-57, LBJ.

416   Johnson rejected the final draft at four o'clock: Califano, *Triumph,* pp. 117–18; Goodwin, *Remembering,* pp. 423–24; FRUS, Vol. 4, pp. 56–57.

416   Goodwin fell to the margins: Ibid. The President's diary records that Goodwin entered the Oval Office for nine minutes during the afternoon revisions, and that Clifford and Fortas stayed for three hours after he left. PDD, Jan. 12, 1966, pp. 1–4, LBJ.

416   The State of the Union: NYT, Jan. 13, 1966, pp. 1, 14; *Vital Speeches of the Day,* Vol. 32, pp. 226–30; Dallek, *Flawed,* pp. 299–302.

416   proposals that made separate front-page headlines: "Ban on Color Line in Housing Asked/ President Also Seeks Law for Federal Penalties in Civil Rights Murders," NYT, Jan. 13, 1966, p. 1.

417   "exhilarated the capital": Califano, *Triumph,* p. 302.

417   "Well, are you happy": LBJ phone call with Bill Moyers, 1:27 A.M., Jan. 13, 1966, Cit. 9488-89, Audiotape WH6601.07, LBJ.

418   "It's coming from within": LBJ phone call with Bill Moyers, 1:27 A.M., Jan. 13, 1966, Cit. 9488-89, Audiotape WH6601.07, LBJ.

418   "In all of these endeavors": MLK telegram to "The President," 10:35 P.M., Jan. 13, 1966, Name File, Box 144, LBJ.

418   Deke DeLoach for a promotion: O'Reilly, *"Racial,"* p. 211.

418   advice of Negro elders that flattery: Branch, *Pillar,* pp. 533–34.

418   "It makes me doubly proud": MLK telegram to DeLoach, Dec. 6, 1965, A/KP10f12.

418   Hoover had publicly called: Branch, *Pillar,* pp. 526–37.

418   "an ever-increasing role": NYT, Jan. 7, 1966, p. 3.

418   "I refer to the arrogant non-conformists": NYT, Dec. 15, 1965, p. 14.

419   FBI agents gave Gary Thomas Rowe $10,000: SAC, San Diego, to Director, Jan. 6, 1971, FVL-NR; J. G. Deegan to W. R. Wannall, Aug. 18, 1975, Document 74, FGTR.

419   Rowe "became very emotional": Curtis Lynum, SAC, San Francisco, letter to Hoover, Jan. 17, 1966, FVL-704.

419   "my last official association": Rowe to J. Edgar Hoover, Jan. 14, 1966, FVL-705.

419   Doar advised Katzenbach: Doar, "Memorandum to the Attorney General," Feb. 9, 1966, attachment to Document 52, FGTR.

419   "We have no views": Hoover's handwritten notation on DeLoach to Tolson, "Gary Thomas Rowe/Former Bureau Informant," Feb. 10, 1966, Document 52, FGTR.

419   slugged and threatened to shoot a black doorman: SAC, San Diego, to Director, Oct. 13, 1967, Document 61, FGTR.

419   "Rowe apparently has a super detective complex": SAC, San Diego, to Director, Nov. 3, 1966, Document 60, FGTR.

419   Rowe's name surfaced: O'Reilly, *"Racial,"* p. 251.

419   This news shocked even Katzenbach: Int. Nicholas Katzenbach, June 14, 1991.

419   Griffin Bell appointed a task force: Ralph Hornblower, III to Michael E. Shaheen, Jr., Office of Professional Responsibility, "Synopsis of Task Force Report on Gary Thomas Rowe, Jr.," Dec. 4, 1979, p. 1.

419   "one of a handful": Ibid., p. 3.

420   Justice Department attorneys stoutly defended the FBI: Stanton, *From Selma,* pp. 202–10.

420   "cannot place liability on the government": Ibid., p. 207.

420   Rowe back in Witness Protection: McWhorter, *Carry,* pp. 572–73.

420   "gave the FBI an excellent opportunity": DeLoach to Tolson, Dec. 28, 1965, FVL-677, filed also as an attachment to Document 42, FGTR.

420   "It seems a little ludicrous": DeLoach to Tolson, Jan. 17, 1966, FRK-1802.

420   desire to avoid public recriminations: Katzenbach to Hoover, Jan. 13, 1966, Section 114, FHOC. Katzenbach suggested to Hoover then that delving into prior "misunderstandings" about the legality of microphone surveillance policy "would seem to be academic."

420   Katzenbach informed DeLoach early Friday: DeLoach to Tolson, Jan. 21, 1966, FRK-1810.

421   "irrespective of what Long does": Hoover's handwritten instruction on Hoover to Katzenbach, "FBI Use of Microphone Coverage," Jan. 17, 1966, Section 129, FHOC.

421   "Remove this surveillance at once": Hoover's handwritten instruction on Sullivan to DeLoach, Jan. 21, 1966, FK-2224.

421   no fewer than sixteen bugs: Hoover LHM for Katzenbach, Jan 21, 1966, Section 129, FHOC.

421   would intrude upon the final two years: Garrow, *FBI and King,* p. 150.

421   King preached at New York's historic Riverside Church: Garrow, *Bearing,* p. 459.

421   "The days that follow": NYT, Jan. 23, 1966, pp. E6–7.

422   added the Vietnamese perspective: Friedland, *Lift Up,* pp. 154–56, 170; Thich Nhat Hanh, *Lotus,* pp. 97–98.

422   "the more surely they destroy": Thich Nhat Hahn, *Lotus,* p. 68.

422   lived in refugee camps: Ibid., p. 75.

422   arrested for drunk driving: MA, Jan. 24, 1966, p. 1; NYT, Jan. 24, 1966, p. 16.

422   "You can't Jew us down": SCLC memo, Jan. 23, 1966, A/KP34f7; Irving M. Engel to Hosea Williams, Jan. 26, 1966, A/KP34f7; Irving M. Engel to MLK, Feb. 14, 1966, A/KP34f7.

422   SCLC aides labored to curb: Abernathy to MLK, "January 21, 1966, Executive Staff Meeting," A/SC62f21.

422   "I think that the root": Andrew Young to Hosea Williams, Dec. 31, 1965, A/KP28f6.

422   Williams berated his rival James Bevel: Int. Hosea Williams, Oct. 29, 1991.

422   "ignorant, black nationalistic notion": R. T. Blackwell to Andrew Young, Jan. 28, 1966, A/SC47f11.

422   "There ain't no Negro in Alabama": SC, Jan. 22–23, 1966, p. 1; Jeffries, "Freedom Politics," pp. 100–101.

422   "I don't blame anyone": Entries for Oct. 29, 1965, and Jan. 7, 1966, diary of Francis Walter, courtesy of Francis Walter.

423   Reporters arrived from distant cities: "Farmer Kills Negro After Cars Collide," AC, Jan. 24, 1966, p. 1; "White Man Charged in Killing," MA, Jan. 24, 1966, p. 1; Edward

M. Rudd, "All Quiet in Camden After Negro Killed, White Man Arrested," SC, Jan. 29–30, 1965, p. 1.

423   "With the pool of blood still fresh": Entry for Jan. 23, 1966, pp. 90–92, diary of Francis Walter, courtesy of Francis Walter.

423   King accepted staff advice: R. T. Blackwell to Andrew Young, Jan. 28, 1966, A/SC47f11.

423   counties plagued with evictions: *Jet,* March 10, 1966, pp. 14–19.

423   dismissal of the drunk driving charge: NYT, Jan. 25, 1966, p. 35.

423   battered month's marches: NYT, Jan. 12, 1966, p. 19; NYT, Jan. 21, 1966, p. 27; Lawson, *Pursuit,* p. 33.

423   "The more people that register": NYT, Jan. 23, 1966, p. 72.

423   "democratize the total political structure": BN, Jan. 24, 1966, p. 4; NYT, Jan. 25, 1966, p. 35.

424   Katzenbach quietly approved: King, *Separate,* pp. 168–69. In 1968, a unanimous U.S. Supreme Court would overturn the Alabama law requiring jail and prison segregation by race: *Lee v. Washington* 390 U.S. 333 (1968).

424   Constance Baker Motley: WP, Jan. 26, 1966, p. 2.

424   swear in Robert Weaver: NYT, Jan. 19, 1966, p. 1; PDD, Jan. 18, 1966, LBJ; Johnson, *Diary,* pp. 352–53.

424   "The moment they take an oath": LBJ phone call with Roy Wilkins, 10:50 A.M., Nov. 4, 1965, Cit. 9105-07, Audiotape WH6511.01, LBJ.

424   "why treat all of the civil rights leaders alike": Humphrey to Califano, Jan. 22, 1966, EX HU2, FG 440, Box 4, LBJ.

424   James Bond spy fantasy *Thunderball:* PDD, Jan. 22, 1966, LBJ.

424   a thousand killed per month: McNamara to LBJ, Jan. 24, 1966, in FRUS, Vol. 4, p. 116.

424   no amount of deliverable ordnance: Statement of CIA deputy director Richard Helms at White House meeting of Jan. 22, 1966, 12:00–2:12 P.M., in FRUS, Vol. 4, p. 105ff; McNamara, *In Retrospect,* p. 228.

424   North Vietnam's stunning indifference: LBJ phone call with Robert McNamara, 9:15 A.M., Jan. 17, 1966, Cit. 9502-03, Audiotape WH6601.08, LBJ.

425   "I'd go sooner": Jack Valenti notes, "Meeting in Cabinet Room," Jan. 24, 1966, Office of the President, Valenti Papers, Box 13, LBJ.

425   Johnson gathered twenty congressional leaders: PDD, Jan. 25, 1966, pp. 6–7, LBJ.

425   "This is the most frustrating experience": Jack Valenti notes, "Meeting in Cabinet Room, 5:30 P.M.–7:40 P.M.," Jan. 25, 1966, Office of the President, Valenti Papers, Box 13, LBJ.

425   "Can't we fight?": Ibid. Bolton was then eighty years old, having served in Congress since 1939. A pioneer advocate of training and education for modern nurses, she helped establish the Army School of Nursing during World War I, and she founded a college-level nursing school that was renamed for her in 1935 at Western Reserve University in her native Cleveland.

425   Johnson read out loud: "Johnson Stimulated by Lincoln in Agony of Decision Making," WP, Jan. 27, 1966, p. 14.

425   received from Senator Robert Kennedy: Karnow, *Vietnam,* p. 499.

425   "it might give you some comfort": Schlesinger, *Robert Kennedy,* p. 792.

425   "The problem is not communicating": LBJ phone call with Abe Fortas, 9:54 A.M., Jan. 26, 1966, Cit. 9535-36, Audiotape WH6601.11, LBJ.

426   "Nineteen sixty-six can be": LBJ remarks from the Cabinet Room, 11:53 A.M., with a message to the Congress on American cities, Jan. 26, 1966, EX SP 2-3/1966/LG, LBJ.

426   *Washington Post* computed: WP, Jan. 27, 1966, pp. 1, 20.

427   scramble with hopeful bromides: Cf. Califano to LBJ, 4:35 P.M., Jan. 27, 1966, EX SP 2-3/1966/LG; Harry McPherson to LBJ, 5:10 P.M., Jan. 27, 1966, LG, Model Cities '66, Box 2, LBJ. Califano advised LBJ of eight specific steps already taken "after the *Washington Post* editorial today (which is extremely unfair)."

427   King began weekly slum residence: NYT, Jan. 21, 1966, p. 27; CD, Jan. 22–28, 1966, p. 1; *Chicago Tribune,* Jan. 27, 1966; "Showdown Looms: Moral Power Against Poverty Profiteers," *Jet,* Feb. 10, 1966, pp. 14–20.

427   reported the *Chicago Tribune: Chicago Tribune,* Jan. 23, 1966, p. 3.

427   "I can learn more about the situation": Ralph, *Northern,* p. 55.

427   A crowd of several hundred waited: NYT, Jan. 27, 1966, p. 37; Ralph, *Northern,* p. 55; Cohen and Taylor, *Pharaoh,* pp. 360–61.

427   "The smell of urine was overpowering": King, *My Life,* pp. 278–79.

427   Speech at Chicago Theological Seminary: MLK log, January 1966, A/SC131f9.

428   Vice Lords gang stayed: CD, Jan. 29–Feb. 3, 1966, p. 1.

428   "Great God a'mighty": Ibid.

428   on Daddy King's side: Ibid.; Reddick, *Crusader,* p. 42.

428   "Family life not only educates": Address, University of Chicago, Jan. 27, 1966, A/SC28f22.

429   he scrawled an instruction to himself: Ibid.

429   His advisers expressed mild optimism: Garrow, *Bearing,* p. 460.

429   "All of us, like Dr. King": Cohen and Taylor, *Pharaoh,* pp. 362–63.

429   lacking from his duplicate apartment: Abernathy, *Walls,* p. 371; CD, Feb. 12–18, 1966, p. 1.

429   a call in Chicago on the priest Richard Morrisroe: Junius Griffin to MLK, Jan. 28, 1966, A/KP34f18.

429   hospitalized and said to be neglected: *Jet,* Jan. 27, 1966, pp. 50–52.

429   Stokely Carmichael had been among his few movement visitors: Int. Richard Morrisroe, May 22, 2003, Feb. 7, 2004. Carmichael had visited Morrisroe in Montgomery the previous September, before his condition was stable enough for transfer to Oak Park Hospital just outside Chicago.

430   "A Lonely Johnson Weighs Bombing": NYT, Jan. 28, 1966, p. 1.

430   fifteen senators had released a joint letter: "15 in Senate Urge President Extend Pause in Bombing," ibid.; PDD, Jan. 27, 1966, p. 3, LBJ.

430   "This was a fire fight": Halberstam, *Powers,* pp. 503–4.

430   "with two hundred or four hundred thousand": Fulbright, *Vietnam Hearings,* p. 13.

430   George Aiken of Vermont demanded: Ibid., pp. 29–30.

430   Walter Cronkite would use a full three minutes: Friendly, *Circumstances,* pp. 219–20.

430   Operation Masher: NYT, Jan. 28, 1966, p. 12; *Life,* Feb. 11, 1966, p. 21; FRUS, Vol. 4, p. 187, footnote 3. The maneuver was retitled "Operation White Wing," evidently to make it sound more attractive.

430   "the same age as my daughter Cecile": Moore, *Soldiers,* p. 342.

430   Julian Bond sat quietly that afternoon: LAT, Jan. 29, 1966, p. 1.

431   "had he recanted, begged, or crawled": Neary, *Julian Bond,* pp. 127–29.

431   "a call to action based on race": Ibid.; Morgan, *One Man,* pp. 159–60.

431   "THE WISE MEN": PDD, Jan. 28, 1966, p. 3, LBJ.

431   "If you just sit tight there": "Text of Message from Ambassador McConaughy—Karachi 1510, Washington, Jan. 27, 1966," in FRUS, Vol. 4, pp. 160–63.

431   no air campaign could interdict more than half: Cf. comments during the 556th meeting of the National Security Council, Jan. 29, 1966, in FRUS, Vol. 4, p. 186.

431   "probably use human backs": Jack Valenti notes, "Meeting in Cabinet Room," Jan. 28, 1966, Office of the President, Valenti Papers, Box 13, LBJ.

432   run against Lummie Jenkins: NYT, Feb. 20, 1966, p. 68.

432   This caused confusion: WATS report, Feb. 13, 1966, Reel 16, SNCC; "2 Rights Groups Promote All-Negro Slates for Local Elections in the South," NYT, Jan. 23, 1966, p. 73.

432   a February 6 caucus to begin: SAC, Mobile, to Director, Feb. 21, 1966, FBPA-2.

432   scraped together a tent city: "Background Information on Lowndes County Tent City," Feb. 28, 1966, Box 1, A/RM.

432   Conference at Mount Beulah: Dittmer, *Local People,* pp. 366–67.

432   doubled to 80 percent: Hilton, *Delta,* p. 78.

432   delegates sifted ideas: Ibid., pp. 82–88.

433   Art Thomas: Findlay, *Church People,* pp. 116–17.

433   President Johnson called: PDD, Jan. 31, 1966, p. 1, LBJ.

433   medic Thomas Cole: NYT, Jan. 31, 1966, p. 1; *Life,* Feb. 11, 1966, cover, p. 24D.

433   "Did we get much results": LBJ phone call with Robert McNamara, 9:20 A.M., Jan. 31, 1966, Cit. 9543, Audiotape WH6601.11, LBJ.

433   announced the renewed bombing: "Johnson Asks U.N. to Summon Vietnam Peace Conference/ Bombing in North Resumes," NYT, Feb. 1, 1966, p. 1.

433   "a rat's nest of trenches": NYT, Jan. 31, 1966, p. 8.

433   "I was a passenger": R. W. Apple, ".50-Caliber Ordeal on a Vietnam Field," NYT, Feb. 1, 1966, p. 1.

434   "have you seen on the ticker": LBJ phone call with Nicholas Katzenbach, 4:26 P.M., Jan. 31, 1966, Cit. 9544, Audiotape WH6601.11, LBJ.

434   "If that's all you got to say": Hilton, *Delta,* p. 101.

434   dragged beyond the gates of federal property: Ibid., pp. 102–3; MA, Feb. 2, 1966, p. 5.

434   "If we do not do this": Katzenbach to LBJ, "Subject: Civil Rights—Mississippi," Feb. 14, 1966, EX HU, Box 27, LBJ. Those evicted from the Greenville airbase would live for the remainder of 1966 at a church-aided tent city in Washington County, Mississippi. Cf. MLK to LBJ (sixteen-page telegram), Aug. 16, 1966, with attached McPherson to LBJ, Aug. 16, 1966, Harry McPherson Papers, Box 14, LBJ.

435   Bombing runs over North Vietnam: McNamara, *In Retrospect,* p. 244.

435   some four million tons: Appy, *Patriots,* pp. 200–201.

435   Joe Califano noticed: Califano, *Triumph,* p. 121.

27: BREAK POINTS

436   "The white race is supreme": NYT, Jan. 23, 1966, p. 1.

436   run his wife, Lurleen: Lesher, *George Wallace,* pp. 356–58; Carter, *Politics,* pp. 278–81.

436   rumors flew of a tacit understanding: Morgan, *One Man,* pp. 93–95.

437   ruled unanimously for Gardenia White: "U.S. Judges Overturn State Law, Women Eligible for Jury Service," MA, Feb. 8, 1966, p. 1; "Woman Juror Ban Upset in Alabama," NYT, Feb. 8, 1966, p. 25.

437   "a responsibility and a right": Ibid.; *White v. Crook,* 251 F. Supp. 401, 408–09.

437   Charles Morgan and Pauli Murray anticipated: Morgan, *One Man,* pp. 46–47.

437   "The principle announced seems so obvious today": Murray, *Song,* pp. 363–64.

437   "another windfall from the civil rights movement": Fred Graham, "The Law: Rights Case Yields Dividend for Women," NYT, Feb. 13, 1966, p. IV-8.

437   "My first reaction to the ruling": MA, Feb. 12, 1966, p. 1.

438   white men acquitted Marvin: NYT, Dec. 9, 1966, p. 38; NYT, Dec. 10, 1966, p. 1; "Anatomy of a Murder Trial," SC, Dec. 24–25, 1966, p. 4.

438   "Lowndes Schools Ordered": MA, Feb. 12, 1966, p. 1; SC, Feb. 19–20, 1966, p. 1.

438   dismissed the Justice Department's lawsuit: Eagles, *Outside Agitator,* p. 255; SC, June 18–19, 1966, p. 1.

438    $50 to $500 to run for sheriff: Ibid.; WP, March 3, 1966.

438   "fraud and deceit": *Life with Lyndon in the Great Society,* Vol. 1, No. 44, Dec. 2, 1965, JMP; Jack O'Dell to Jack Minnis, Dec. 8, 1965, JMP.

439   Bob Moses, back in Birmingham: Int. Bob Moses, July 30, 1984; int. Bob Moses, Feb. 15, 1991; Carson, *Struggle,* p. 201.

439   "So whether you believe": Tina [Harris] to Janet [Jemott], Bob [Moses], Dona [Richards], "The First Two Sessions of the Discussion Groups," Spring 1966, Reel 18, SNCC.

439   ill-fated Field Order No. 15: Litwack, *Storm,* p. 400ff; Foner, *Reconstruction,* pp. 70–71, 158–60; Davis, *Sherman's March,* pp. 90–94, 130–40; Branch, *Parting,* p. 689.

439   "The way we can best take care": "Colloquy with Colored Ministers," Jan. 12, 1865, transcript in *Journal of Negro History,* Jan. 1931, pp. 88–94.

439   "far-reaching step": Stokely Carmichael, Bob Mants, Tina Harris, "Proposal for a 'Poor Peoples Land Corporation,' " ca. Feb. 1966, A/RM1.

439   "triple-A priority": Transcript, "Riding in the car from Atlanta," Feb. 19, 1966, A/SN94, p. 5.

440   no one yet agreed to stand for office: Alabama, "News of the Week #4," March 16, 1966, Reel 16, SNCC.

440   lucky to attract twenty people: "Stu House reports from Selma," WATS report, Feb. 13, 1966, Reel 16, SNCC; Tina Harris to Bill Mahoney, Cleve Seller[s], Jim Forman, "Freedom Organizations in Alabama," Reel 18, SNCC.

440   "Whenever we went canvassing": Transcript, "Riding in the car from Atlanta," Feb. 19, 1966, A/SN94.

440   "I'm voting for you": Int. Julian Bond, Jan. 10, 2004.

440   "If they bar me again": NYT, Feb. 24, 1966, p. 75.

440   The House Rules Committee promptly did so: NYT, May 24, 1966, p. 27.

440   "The moral question is far more important": NYT, Feb. 24, 1966, p. 75.

440   rally at Jenner School: Anderson and Pickering, *Confronting,* p. 190.

441   King and Muhammad found chatting ground: *Jet,* March 10, 1966, pp. 6–9; CD, Feb. 26–March 4, 1966, p. 1; int. Bennett Johnson. Johnson, a publicist and founder of a Negro Voters League in Chicago, had made several trips to Atlanta for Muhammad to arrange an audience with King.

441   "All we have to do is drink": Int. Bennett Johnson, April 26, 1990.

441   house organs trumpeted the King summit: "Muhammad, King Meet on Eve of Savior's Day," MS, March 4, 1966, pp. 1, 3.

441   "Dr. King Seizes": NYT, Feb. 24, 1966, p. 75.

441   "Dr. King Assailed": NYT, Feb. 25, 1966, p. 18.

441   he had seen a shivering baby: Young, *Burden,* p. 388.

441   "We *wanted* to do it illegally": Wiretap transcript of telephone conversation between Stanley Levison and Andrew Young, March 1, 1966, FLNY-9-865a, p. 5.

441 judge denounced the takeover: Cohen and Taylor, *Pharaoh,* pp. 363–64.

441 Mayor Daley: Anderson and Pickering, *Confronting,* p. 191; NYT, March 10, 1966, p. 36.

441 "I think King is right": Ralph, *Northern,* pp. 56–57, 78.

441 remarkable mass meeting: Ibid., p. 63.

442 "Don't be afraid": "What's Next for the Civil Rights Movement: Requiem or Revival?" *Look,* June 14, 1966, pp. 70–80.

442 "We are going to change the whole Jericho road": Ibid.

442 Al Raby might be able to topple: Wiretap transcript of telephone conversation between Stanley Levison and Andrew Young, March 1, 1966, FLNY-9-865a, p. 5.

442 archbishop John Cody: Garrow, *Bearing,* pp. 460–61; Garrow, *FBI and King,* p. 176; Ralph, *Northern,* p. 75.

442 fanned out to shop for homes: AFSC, "A Prospectus for a non-violent project to achieve open occupancy through the Chicago area," ca. March 1966, LCMOC folder, West Side Christian Parish papers, CHS, p. 2.

442 Adlai Stevenson III: Jonathan Alter to the author, Feb. 20, 2002, with attached diary entry for March 2, 1966.

443 Rev. Clay Evans convened: Frady, *Jesse,* pp. 196–98; Ralph, *Northern,* pp. 68–70, 85; Garrow, *Bearing,* p. 462; int. Clay Evans, Feb. 21, 1985; Clay Evans remarks at Chicago Divinity School, April 24, 1995.

443 founder of the Kenwood-Oakland organization: "Dr. King Launches Attack on Chicago School Setup," CD, Feb. 5–11, 1966, p. 2.

443 fresh "luminary": *Jet,* Feb. 10, 1966, p. 18.

443 Stanley Levison urgently recommended: Garrow, *Bearing,* p. 462; wiretap transcript of telephone conversation between Stanley Levison and MLK, Feb. 8, 1966, FLNY-9-844a.

443 "mopped the floor": Wiretap transcript of telephone conversation between Stanley Levison and Adele Cantor, Feb. 14, 1966, FLNY-9-850a.

443 slate-making summit: Cohen and Taylor, *Pharaoh,* p. 367.

443 "minimum take": Wachtel to MLK, Feb. 18, 1966; MLK to Wachtel, March 21, 1966, thanking Wachtel and his wife, Lucy, for an evening that "will live in my memory eternally;" Wachtel to MLK, May 11, 1966, reporting on contributions received from March 11 pledges, A/KP25f35.

443 conductor Leonard Bernstein: Wiretap transcript of telephone conversation between Stanley Levison and Harry Wachtel, April 6, 1966, FLNY-9-901.

443 Harry Belafonte welcomed a sellout crowd: Ralph, *Northern,* p. 75.

444 "even unto the third and fourth generation": *Chicago Sun-Times,* March 13, 1966, pp. 2–3.

444 "Never before in the history": Ibid.

444 Stanley Levison called home: Wiretap transcript of telephone conversation between Stanley Levison and [name deleted], 12:43 P.M., March 14, 1966, FLNY-9-NS.

444 Mayor Daley trumped King: Cohen and Taylor, *Pharaoh,* pp. 368–69.

444 King declined: NYT, March 17, 1966, p. 31.

444 strict pledge of secrecy: Califano to LBJ, March 16, 1966, MLK Name File, Box 144, LBJ.

445 "glaring humbuggery": AC, March 18, 1966, p. 1.

445 FBI wiretaps intercepted: Baumgardner to Sullivan, March 18, 1966, FSC-1266.

445 arriving twenty minutes late: PDD, March 18, 1966, LBJ. LBJ entered the scheduled

1:00 meeting at 1:14. King arrived at 1:24 and left at 2:35, saying "had to leave town on a plane," according to LBJ's office diarist. The meeting continued until 3:11 P.M.

445   "particularly difficult": Garrow, *Bearing,* p. 467. One of LBJ's legislative aides used the word "impossible" three times on the first page of a memo about prospects for the 1966 civil rights package: Henry Wilson to LBJ, March 11, 1966, Henry Wilson Papers, Box 11, LBJ.

445   "we felt to be reputable": Junius Griffin telegram to MLK at the Washington Hilton Hotel, March 18, 1966, A/KP22f16. The statement hedged for King on what Williams might have known: "The whole matter of purchasing cars was turned over to one of my assistants, Hosea Williams, in whom I have the highest confidence and respect."

445   skeletal news release: NYT, March 19, 1966, p. 17.

445   "irregular routes": *Jet,* April 7, 1966, p. 42.

445   "I don't want any other human": LBJ phone call with Dean Rusk, 4:25 P.M., Feb. 3, 1966, in FRUS, Vol. 4, p. 203.

445   upstaged public examination of the war: Wallace, *"Hear,"* p. 352; Langguth, *Our Vietnam,* p. 420.

445   "pour the stuff out of the filth on television": LBJ phone call with Lawrence O'Brien, 8:27 A.M., Feb. 5, 1966, Cit. 9623, Audiotape WH6602.02, LBJ.

446   "Americans who dissent can't do": Meeting in the Cabinet Room, Feb. 24, 1966, Office of the President, Valenti Notes, Box 13, LBJ.

446   NBC broadcast the complete Fulbright hearings: Friendly, *Circumstances,* pp. 221–33; Halberstam, *Powers,* pp. 504–5.

446   "would be exploited mercilessly": Fulbright, *Vietnam Hearings,* p. 107ff.

446   communication with the White House: Cf. Bill Moyers to Frank Stanton, Feb. 14, 1966, WHCF, Name File, LBJ; Halberstam, *Powers,* pp. 438–42.

446   held firm for the daytime comedies: Friendly, *Circumstances,* pp. 235–54; Halberstam, *Powers,* pp. 505–7.

446   The departure itself: NYT, Feb. 16, 1966, p. 1.

446   he had produced a watershed CBS broadcast: Friendly, *Circumstances,* pp. 23–67.

447   "I got no bellyache": LBJ phone call with Henry R. Luce, 9:35 A.M., Feb. 21, 1966, Cit. 9650-51, Audiotape WH6602.06, LBJ.

447   a special section in the forthcoming *Life:* "Special Section on Vietnam, A Searching Assessment," *Life,* Feb. 25, 1966.

447   "It is deplorable": Ibid., p. 29.

447   "What does a man do": LBJ phone call with Henry R. Luce, 11:56 A.M., Feb. 21, 1966, Cit. 9653, Audiotape WH6602.06, LBJ.

447   "If we don't make clear": NYT, Feb. 19, 1966, p. 1.

448   Kennedy called a press conference: Shesol, *Contempt,* pp. 288–90.

448   "a share of power and responsibility": "Kennedy Bids U.S. Offer Vietcong a Role In Saigon/ Suggests Sharing of Power in South Vietnam Presents Best Hope for an Accord/ Breaks with Johnson/ Senator Says Neither Side 'Can Have Complete Surrender,' " NYT, Feb. 20, 1966, p. 1.

448   lightning struck: Shesol, *Contempt,* p. 290; Stein, *Journey,* p. 212; NYT, Feb. 21, 1966, p. 20.

448   "The uproar was general": Schlesinger, *Robert Kennedy,* p. 794.

448   They flew together in the presidential cabin: PDD, Feb. 23, 1966, pp. 6–8, LBJ.

448   five thousand antiwar pickets: Robinson, *Abraham,* p. 205; DeBenedetti, *Ordeal,* pp. 148–49.

448   A. J. Muste presented: Zaroulis and Sullivan, *Who Spoke Up?,* p. 78.

448   twice before a hand clapped: PDD, Feb. 23, 1966, p. 9, LBJ.

448   to serve sixty days: NYT, May 10, 1966

448   "The reason it is going to cause":
        Senate Correspondence, personal

448   "on a high, solid level": Fred Du
        Statements," Feb. 23, 1966, RFK
        ton, F., '65–'66, Box 3, JFK.

448   "emotional and psychological box"
        Papers, Senate Correspondence, p

448   avoided provocative Vietnam state
        Kennedy, p. 797; Collier, *Kennedys,*

449   series of speeches on poverty: Thon

449   having consulted Robert Spike: Ro
        1965 [with handwritten notes abou
        Africa Correspondence, Box 13, JFI

449   "hate my guts": Schlesinger, *Robert .*

449   flurry of secret memos: Cf. Katzenl
        Jackson, to Director, March 9, 196(
        1966, FRK-1818; DeLoach to Tolsor
        bach, March 15, 1966, FRK-1825; H(
        17, 1966, FRK-833.

449   "Somebody down here": WLBT news film 0173/D39, March 18, 1966, MDAH.

449   "We must create a society": RFK address, University of Mississippi Law School
        forum, 2:30 P.M., March 18, 1966, and RFK address, University of Alabama, 8:30 P.M.,
        March 18, 1966, RFK Papers, Senate Speeches and Press Releases, March 11–20, 1966,
        Box 2, JFK.

449   three standing ovations: Jack Nelson, "Ole Miss Students Laugh at Kennedy's Quips
        on Barnett," LAT, March 19, 1966, p. 1.

449   Coach Don Haskins received: Fitzpatrick, *Walls,* p. 228.

449   Frank Fitzpatrick reviewed films: Ibid., p. 24.

450   "That son of a bitch": *Sports Illustrated,* April 4, 1991, p. 70ff.

450   flown the capitol flag at half mast: Fitzpatrick, *Walls,* p. 57.

450   Vanderbilt offered Perry Wallace: Charles H. Martin, "Jim Crow in the Gymnasium:
        The Integration of College Basketball in the American South," *International Journal of
        the History of Sport,* 1993, pp. 80–81.

450   eleven of 2,236 SEC scholarships: *Sports Illustrated,* Feb. 19, 1968, p. 10.

450   Harris jumped to his death: Fitzpatrick, *Walls,* p. 238.

450   when Kentucky would win: Tubby Smith, who grew up in segregated Maryland,
        coached Kentucky to its seventh NCCA basketball championship in 1998. Cf. "His-
        tory in Black, White—And Gray," *Baltimore Sun,* Dec. 10, 1969, p. D-1.

450   abolished its track team for the 1970s: Joan Paul, Richard V. McGhee, and Helen Fant,
        "The Arrival and Ascendence of Black Athletes in the Southeastern Conference,
        1966–1980," *Phylon,* Vol. 45, No. 4, 1984, p. 286.

450   intimidating "dunk" shot: Fitzpatrick, *Walls,* pp. 239–41.

450   "He admitted to no solutions": Moyers to LBJ, Feb. 21, 1966, Office of the President,
        Box 4, LBJ.

451   he ordered a compilation of every personal contact: "Mr. President, Official Times you

saw Sen. Fulbright—39, Unofficial times—17, TOTAL—46 [sic]," Juanita Roberts to LBJ, Jan. 7, 1966, with attached note from LBJ instructing her to "get me that list separated." Office of the President, Box 4, LBJ.

451   "because of your goddam trip": LBJ phone call with Lawrence O'Brien, 8:27 A.M., Feb. 5, 1966, Cit. 9623, Audiotape WH6602.02, LBJ.

451   voted with only four senators: Evans, *Lyndon B. Johnson,* p. 597.

451   "going through a menopause": LBJ phone call with Hubert Humphrey, 6:05 P.M., March 2, 1966, Cit. 9812-13, Audiotape WH6603.01, LBJ.

451   "I just looked at him": Ibid.

451   Fulbright began to warn: "Fulbright Warns of Peril in Power," NYT, April 22, 1966, p. 16; "Fulbright Warns of 'Fatal' Course by U.S. in Vietnam," NYT, April 29, 1966, p. 1; "Hyperbole on Vietnam," editorial, NYT, May 1, 1966, p. IV-10.

451   "not arrogance but agony": WS, May 18, 1966; NYT, May 18, 1966, pp. 1, 8; Zaroulis and Sullivan, *Who Spoke Up?,* pp. 82–83.

451   "nervous Nellies": NYT, May 18, 1966, p. 1.

451   mocked Fulbright in person: Evans, *Lyndon B. Johnson,* p. 599; Dallek, *Flawed,* p. 367.

451   "trying to beat down Fulbright's ears": McPherson to LBJ, May 13, 1966, McPherson Papers, Box 7, LBJ.

452   sulking disregard: Int. Harry McPherson, Sept. 24, 1991.

452   "Bobby is behind this revolt": LBJ phone call with Nicholas Katzenbach, 10:02 P.M., March 17, 1966, Cit. 9895-96, Audiotape WH6603.09, LBJ.

452   "I didn't run or shimmy": Ibid.

452   "Kennedy infiltration": LBJ phone call with Dean Rusk, 10:10 A.M.[?], Feb. 20, 1966, Cit. 9649, Audiotape WH6602.05, LBJ, in FRUS, Vol. 4, pp. 241–44.

452   "sons-of-bitches boring from within": LBJ phone call with Deke DeLoach, 7:49 P.M., March 14, 1966, Cit. 9887-89, Audiotape WH6603.07, LBJ; Theoharis and Cox, *Boss,* p. 398.

452   "When he said the other day": LBJ phone call with Dean Rusk, 10:10 A.M.[?], Feb. 20, 1966, Cit. 9649, Audiotape WH6602.05, LBJ, in FRUS, Vol. 4, pp. 241–44.

452   1,361 American soldiers killed: NYT, April 16, 1966, p. 1; Zaroulis and Sullivan, *Who Spoke Up?,* p. 82.

452   mission to retake the Bong Son area: Moore, *Soldiers,* p. 343.

452   discovered his own arm shaking: Ints. Hank Thomas, March 14, 1991, Dec. 17, 2003.

452   exhumed remains of a humble farmer: *Jet,* Dec. 2, 1965, pp. 6–8.

452   three white women pummeled: NYT, Dec. 5, 1965, p. 74.

453   "The Ballad of the Green Berets": *Rolling Stone Rock Almanac,* p. 113; *Life,* March 4, 1966, p. 93ff; DeBenedetti, *Ordeal,* p. 151.

453   comments by John Lennon: *Rolling Stone Rock Almanac,* pp. 112–14; NYT, Aug. 5, 1966, p. 20.

453   *The Sound of Music:* "Biggest Money-Making Movie of All Time—How Come?" NYT Magazine, Nov. 20, 1966, p. 45ff; NYT, April 19, 1966, p. 34; NYT, May 14, 1966, p. 19.

453   Martin Luther King's favorite film: Int. Bernard Lee, June 19, 1985.

453   Bonnie and Clyde: Vincent Canby, NYT, Sept. 17, 1967, p. II-21; Roger Ebert, "Great Movies: 'Bonnie and Clyde,' " www.suntimes.com/ebert/greatmovies/bonnie_clyde .html.

453   publication of *In Cold Blood:* Eliot Fremont-Smith, "The Killed, the Killers," NYT, Jan. 10, 1966, p. 23; "British Acclaim 'In Cold Blood,' " NYT, March 15, 1966, p. 36.

453   "Party of the Century": NYT, Nov. 29, 1966, p. 53; *Jet,* Dec. 15, 1966, pp. 40–43.

454   "Nonviolence has no meaning": Bob Considine, "Meredith of Ole Miss: 'Fear Grips Every Negro,' " syndicated column of April 3, 1966, in FK-NR.

28: PANTHER LADIES

PAGE

455   far out in the rurals: Undated description, "Lowndes County, Alabama. The tone of the meeting was set . . . ," Reel 18, SNCC.

455   schoolteacher Sarah Logan presiding: Program, "No More Chains and Sorrow," Mount Moriah Number 1 Church in Beechwood, Lowndes County, 2:30 P.M., March 27, 1966, Reel 18, SNCC.

455   "We had to stand for hours": "Lowndes Marks a Year Full of Historic Change," SC, April 2–3, 1966, p. 3.

456   Lowndes County Freedom Organization: Eagles, *Outside Agitator,* p. 255; Jeffries, "Freedom Politics," pp. 105–10.

456   "Once you get power": "Lowndes Party Elects Officers," SC, April 9–10, 1966, p. 1.

456   South Africa's imposing consulate: unidentified newspaper story dated March 22, 1966, in John Lewis chronology file 5, AAP; int. James Forman, Feb. 13, 2001.

456   twenty years before mass demonstrations: Julian Bond speech to the fortieth anniversary of SNCC, April 15, 2000, at Shaw University in Raleigh, North Carolina. Bond had been present for the New York sit-in at the South African consulate.

456   Yves Montand and Simone Signoret hosted: *Jet,* April 7, 1966, p. 58; *Jet,* April 14, 1966, pp. 62–63.

456   to King Gustav VI: "Dr. King in Stockholm," one-inch squib, NYT, April 1, 1966, p. 14.

457   proceeds of at least $100,000: Garrow, *Bearing,* p. 490. Harry Belafonte remembers the figure as $300,000: int. Harry Belafonte, April 7, 2004. According to FBI wiretaps on Clarence Jones, Belafonte's secretary was overheard to say on April 6, 1966, that there was "a possibility of another $200,000" from Sweden: New York LHM dated April 8, 1966, FSC-1316. Stanley Levison later advised King by letter that the foreign receipts had fallen $100,000 short of a projected $200,000: Levison to MLK, May 20, 1966, A/KP14f41.

457   church sponsors in Paris had canceled: Int. Harry Belafonte, April 7, 2004.

457   Secretary of State Rusk ordered: NYT, March 29, 1966, p. 15.

457   Ambassador Graham Parsons canceled: William Gordon confidential report dated April 4, 1966, United States Information Service/Stockholm, Department of State, A/SC2f6.

457   "King wears a muzzle": Ibid.

457   He pressed his SCLC executive board: Garrow, *Bearing,* pp. 469–70; Miami LHM dated April 19, 1966, FK-NR.

457   "It is imperative": NYT, April 14, 1966, p. 6.

457   "If we are true to our own ideals": Ibid., p. 1.

458   "sticking his neck out": Wiretap transcript of telephone conversation between Stanley Levison and Clarence Jones, April 23, 1966, FLNY-9-918a.

458   arresting thirteen Mississippi Klansmen: NYT, March 29, 1966, p. 1.

458   "J. Edgar Hoover may dislike": Wiretap transcript of telephone conversation between

Stanley Levison and Bill Stein, March 29, 1966, FLNY-9-893a; SAC, New York, to Director, March 30, 1966, FK-2425.

458   introduction to Mayor Daley: Cohen and Taylor, *Pharaoh,* p. 371.

458   he left Chicago again on April 28: Garrow, *Bearing,* p. 470.

458   final meeting at the White House: Ibid.; "To the Cabinet Room for Signing of Civil Rights Message, 2:35–4:15 P.M., April 28, 1966, PDD, LBJ; Dallek, *Flawed,* p. 325; Ralph, *Northern,* pp. 173, 301.

458   four speeches late into the same night: "People to People, Dr. King's Itinerary," April 28–30, A/KP-NA.

459   825 miles to give nine speeches: NYT, April 30, 1966, p. 1.

459   An afternoon rainstorm caught King: SC, May 7–8, 1966, p. 2.

459   nine white men ran for governor: "It All Comes Down to This—Tomorrow Climaxes Long, Bitter Campaign," MA, May 2, 1966, p. 1.

459   "the first major white candidate": Baldwin, *Balm,* p. 82, citing NYT, April 14, 1966, p. 27.

459   pledged to haul down the Confederate Battle Flag: MA, Feb. 26, 1966, p. 1; Flowers campaign ad, MA, May 1, 1966, p. 7-B.

459   SCLC ran workshops: SC, March 26–27, 1966, p. 1; wiretap transcript of telephone conversation between Stanley Levison and Clarence Jones, April 5, 1966, FLNY-9-900. Levison told Jones he "flipped" over the workshops as "the best fundraising thing I ever saw. . . . SCLC *must* set up an Academy of Political Science and Government, and train all candidates for office. We want trained men."

459   first fifty-four Negroes to qualify: NYT, May 4, 1966, p. 1. Other sources put the number of Negro candidates for state or local office in the Alabama primary as high as eighty.

459   photograph of one kissing a baby: SC, April 30–May 1, 1966, p. 1.

459   Newspapers erratically scolded Negroes: NYT, April 21, 1966, p. 30; SC, March 26–27, 1966, p. 5; NYT, April 30, 1966, p. 1.

459   "We must let the Negro vote hang": SC, March 5–6, 1966, p. 6.

459   *The Southern Courier:* R. Jefferson Norrell, "Reporters and Reformers: The Story of the *Southern Courier,*" *South Atlantic Quarterly,* Vol. 79, Winter 1980, pp. 93–104.

459   "Have a Seat, Hosea": SC, April 16–17, 1966, p. 2.

459   "the anvil": SC, April 23–24, p. 2.

460   *New York Times* out-bossed: "Sabotage in Alabama," April 21, 1966, p. 38; "S.N.C.C. Defends Vote Stand in Alabama," James Forman letter to the editor, NYT, May 3, 1966, p. 46.

460   Alabama's first female candidate: NYT, May 5, 1966, p. 1.

460   "tote the wood and draw the water": Lesher, *George Wallace,* pp. 358–64; Carter, *Politics,* pp. 272–73. Nellie Ross succeeded her late husband as governor of Wyoming, also in 1924.

461   "a dime-store girl for governor": Lesher, *George Wallace,* p. 367; Carter, *Politics,* p. 283.

461   "some kind of banana republic": Carter, *Politics,* p. 287.

461   civil servants being trained: MA, May 2, 1966, p. 3.

461   "I am attempting to do the least": Garrow, *Bearing,* p. 471.

461   Charles Nesson into last-minute negotiations: Jeffries, "Freedom Politics," pp. 112–14; Mobile LHM dated May 18, 1966, FBPA-7; int. Charles Nesson, Nov. 9, 2005.

461   Frank Ryals had forbidden access: Selma office to Bill Mahoney et al., re "Freedom Organizations," n.d., April 1966, Reel 18, SNCC.

461   "in or around a public polling place": Eagles, *Outside Agitator,* p. 256.

461   Jack Minnis finished local workshops: "Political workshops are being held nightly in Lowndes . . .": "Daily Reports" from Selma Office, n.d., April 1966, Reel 18, SNCC; int. Jack Minnis, April 8, 2001.

461   He used illustrated booklets: Pamphlet of the Lowndes County Freedom Organization, file attachment in SAC, Mobile, to Director, Feb. 21, 1966, FBPA-2.

461   "Vote for me and I'll stand up": SC, April 30–May 1, 1955, p. 1; Stokely Carmichael to "Mr. Hewlett" [sic], "List of Lowndes County People Who Are Scheduled to Speak on 'Freedom Day,' " n.d., April 1966, Reel 18, SNCC.

462   "We been walkin' ": Eagles, *Outside Agitator,* p. 255.

462   Nesson returned on Sunday: John Hulett, Los Angeles speech of May 22, 1966, in *The Black Panther Party,* a Merit Publishers pamphlet, June 1966, pp. 11–13.

462   chase down Attorney General Richmond Flowers: "News of the Field #3," May 6, 1966, Reel 17, SNCC; "Lowndes County Report," May 2, 1966, Reel 18, SNCC.

462   John Doar supervised five hundred: John Doar, "The Work of the Civil Rights Division in Enforcing Voting Rights," speech at the U.S. Department of Justice, ca. 1989, courtesy of John Doar.

463   "Stand Up for Alabama": Carter, *Politics,* p. 287.

463   Harvey's Fish Camp: SC, May 7–8, 1966, p. 1.

463   "Grow with Flowers": Ibid.

463   First Baptist Church in Hayneville: Mobile LHM dated May 6, 1966, FBPA-6; "News of the Field #11," Reel 17, SNCC; NYT, May 4, 1966, p. 28; MS, July 22, 1966, p. 8; Lawson, *Pursuit,* p. 108; Jeffries, "Freedom Politics," p. 118.

463   "We wanted to make it all legal": MA, May 4, 1966, p. 2.

463   Voices on a bullhorn: SC, May 7–8, 1966, p. 6.

464   "It's a Lurleen Landslide": MA, May 4, 1966, p. 1.

464   "white Alabamians are desperately grasping": NYT, May 5, 1966, p. 35; *Jet,* May 19, 1966, pp. 14–17.

464   *"literally,* most all white": Carter, *Politics,* p. 287.

464   the Attorney General had calculated: Int. Richmond Flowers, Aug. 9, 1990.

464   "it may be many years": NYT, May 5, 1966, p. 35.

464   "The fact of overwhelming importance": NYT, May 5, 1966, p. 46.

464   "We're going to take power": Carmichael interview for *The Militant* by John Benson, May 3, 1966, reprinted in *The Black Panther Party,* a Merit Publishers pamphlet, June 1966, pp. 24–29.

464   "has a hell of a lot of nerve": Courtland Cox interview, Black Panther Party, in *The Free Student,* May–June 1966, copy in FBPA-NR.

465   ballot boxes from six minority precincts: MA, May 6, 1966, p. 1; *Jet,* May 26, 1966, p. 8.

465   the final, supervised count: John Doar, "The Work of the Civil Rights Division in Enforcing Voting Rights," speech at the U.S. Department of Justice, ca. 1989, courtesy of John Doar. In his remarks, Doar described the end of the contested vote count as follows: "The result in the six boxes: Baker, 1,412, Clark, 92, enough votes to determine the result of the election. However the Dallas County Democratic Executive Committee immediately rejected all the votes in the six boxes. This was done by a majority of the forty men on the self-perpetuating, lily-white Democratic Executive Committee. The [Civil Rights] Division was determined that the black citizens of Dallas County not be disillusioned with their first experience in actual participation in a local elec-

tion. . . . From that time until the federal court decided the contest twenty days later, federal observers guarded the boxes."

465   Wallace asserted his full hegemony: Lesher, *George Wallace*, p. 366; Orfield, *Reconstruction*, pp. 266–68.

465   SNCC's annual meeting: Accounts of the May 8–14, 1966 SNCC staff meeting at Kingston Springs, Tennessee, include Forman, *Making*, pp. 447–56; Carson, *Struggle*, pp. 200–204; Sellers, *River*, pp. 155–59; Lewis, *Walking*, pp. 364–69; Fleming, *Soon*, pp. 160–62; Carmichael, *Ready*, pp. 479–83. More specific sources cited below.

465   Carmichael agreed to run: Viorst, *Fire*, pp. 368–70; int. Kwame Ture (Stokely Carmichael), Jan. 31, 1984; int. Jack Minnis, April 8, 2001.

465   "We assumed that we could forget history": "Assumptions Made by SNCC," SNCC staff conference, May 11, 1966, Box 7, A/SN.

466   "pockets of power": Ibid; Carson, *Struggle*, p. 201; Julian Bond speech to the fortieth anniversary of SNCC, April 15, 2000, at Shaw University in Raleigh, North Carolina.

466   Conflict tore at Bob Mants: Int. Bob Mants, Sept. 8, 2000.

466   Lewis won reelection: Ed Hamlett int. by Archie E. Allen, Nov. 5, 1968, AAP; John Lewis int. by Archie E. Allen, Jan. 28, 1979, AAP.

466   Carmichael himself voted: Ibid.

466   Worth Long of Arkansas: Int. Worth Long, Sept. 12, 1983; int. Julius Lester by Archie Allen, Nov. 7, 1968, AAP.

466   In pandemonium: Int. Kwame Ture (Stokely Carmichael), Jan. 30, 1984; int. Fay Bellamy, Oct. 29, 1991; int. Jack Minnis, April 8, 2001; Sellers, *River*, pp. 158–59.

467   "just a normal organizational change": *Nashville Tennessean* news clip, n.d., AAP; *Jet*, June 2, 1966, pp. 6–9.

467   attracted modest press notice: Jack Nelson, "2 Veteran Rights Leaders Ousted by SNCC," LAT, May 17, 1966, in Library of America Anthology, *Reporting Civil Rights*, pp. 491–94; "New SNCC Leader Aims for Rural Negro Power," SC, May 21–22, 1966, p. 1.

467   "obviously shaken by his defeat": NYT, May 17, 1966, p. 22.

467   "Delta Devil": William A. Price, "SNCC Charts a Course," *National Guardian*, June 4, 1966, p. 1, Folder 21, Reel 53, SNCC.

467   identified the new chairman: Gene Roberts, "New Leaders and New Course for 'Snick,' " NYT, May 22, 1966, p. 4-E.

467   exchanged gunfire inside a Chicago YMCA: Ralph, *Northern*, pp. 94–95; Garrow, *Bearing*, p. 471; Cohen and Taylor, *Pharaoh*, pp. 378–79; Chicago LHM dated May 23, 1966, FK-2541.

467   "the instinctive drama": Wiretap transcript of telephone conversation between Stanley Levison and an unknown male, May 13, 1966, FLNY-9-938a.

467   "The people in the North": SC, May 28–29, 1966, p. 6.

468   Levison huddled in King's Hamlin Avenue tenement: Wiretap transcript of telephone conversation between Stanley Levison and Marilyn Hanesworth (for Clarence Jones), May 11, 1966, FLNY-9-936a; New York LHMs dated May 10 and May 18, 1966, FK-NR.

468   abandoned the slum "trusteeship": NYT, April 6, 1966, p. 28; NYT, April 7, 1966, p. 25; "King Done with Slum Building," *Chicago Daily News*, April 15, 1966; "Find King Attorney Owns Flats in Probe of Slum Properties," *Chicago Sun-Times*, April 24, 1966; "Legislation Urged to Protect Tenants' Protest Rights," *Chicago Sun-Times*, April 25, 1966; "Report from Bob Johnson, *Jet* Magazine, Re *Chicago Sun-Times* article concerning Chauncey Eskridge, April 25, 1966," A/KP10f3.

468 deficit he projected: Levison to MLK, May 20, 1966, A/KP14f41; wiretap transcript of telephone conversation between Stanley Levison and Clarence Jones, June 10, 1966, FLNY-9-966a.

468 the Dow Jones Industrial Average: John Rothchild to the author, May 10, 2004.

468 begged him for a $28,000 loan: Wiretap transcript of telephone conversation between Stanley Levison and Adele Kanter, May 16, 1966, FLNY-9-941a.

468 "grapes of wrath are stored": Philip Dripps, "The Northern Offensive: King in Chicago," *Christian Advocate,* June 2, 1966.

468 Berkeley on May 21: SAC, Mobile, to Director, July 12, 1966, FBPA-8.

468 took it as a calming sign: Int. John Hulett, Sept. 8, 2000.

468 "There was something in Alabama": John Hulett, Los Angeles speech of May 22, 1966 in *The Black Panther Party,* a Merit Publishers pamphlet, June 1966, pp. 11–13.

469 "useless endeavor": "Rights Unit Quits Parley in Capital," NYT, May 24, 1966, p. 28; "SNCC Statement on the White House Conference," May 23, 1966, with attached transcript of press questions, BIR/FW1f45. The statement was signed by all then members of SNCC's new central committee: James Forman, Charles Cobb, Fred Meely, Robert Mants, Ralph Featherstone, John Lewis, Ivanhoe Donaldson, Courtland Cox, Robert Smith, and Jack Minnis, plus Stokely Carmichael as chairman.

469 "the extreme black racists": WP, May 25, 1966, p. 25.

469 "which we hope will dramatize": Anderson and Pickering, *Confronting,* pp. 193–94.

469 "if I have to tack them on the door": Garrow, *Bearing,* p. 472.

469 King shuttled between Chicago and Washington: Wiretap transcript of telephone conference call among MLK, Stanley Levison, Clarence Jones, and Walter Fauntroy, May 28, 1966, FLNY-9-953a.

469 "I always hate to talk": Transcript, *Face the Nation,* Vol. 9, Program 22, May 29, 1966, pp. 143–47.

470 A. J. Muste had arranged: Robinson, *Abraham,* p. 133; Thich Nhat Hahn, *Lotus,* p. 88.

470 latest crises in South Vietnam: Cf. "Buddhists Charge Betrayal in Junta's Move on Danang," NYT, May 19, 1966, p. 1; "Ky Denounces Thich Tri Quang, Top Buddhist Leader, as a Red," NYT, May 22, 1966, p. 6; "Johnson Appeals for Unity in War/ Ky's Forces Gain/ Unrest Deplored," NYT, May 22, 1966, p. 1; "Buddhist Students Wreck American Center in Hue," May 27, 1966, p. 1; "Student Mob in Hue Burns American Consular Office," June 1, 1966, p. 1.

470 "King Equates Rights Fight": *Chicago Tribune,* June 1, 1963, p. B-3.

470 Thich Nhat Hanh for a tour of witness: "A Proposal for Peace," Statement read by Thich Nhat Hanh in Washington, D.C., June 1, 1966, in Thich Nhat Hahn, *Love,* p. 49ff.

470 "more my brother than many": Friedland, *Lift Up,* pp. 170–71; "3 Clergymen Here Begin Protest Fast," NYT, July 4, 1966, p. 2.

470 "The purple-robed Buddhist monk": WP, June 6, 1966, p. 9.

470 "Now the U.S. has become": Thich Nhat Hanh, "Our Green Garden," *New York Review of Books,* June 9, 1966, in Thich Nhat Hahn, *Love,* p. 57ff.

470 refused burial in his home state: "Slain Negro G.I.'s Mother Charges Cemetery Bias," NYT, May 27, 1966, p. 32; "Viet Nam Not Segregated," SC, May 28–29, 1966, p. 1.

471 "My son was not a shoeshine boy": "No Room in the Cemetery," BAA, June 4, 1966, in Library of America Anthology, *Reporting Vietnam,* pp. 259–61.

471 "Negro G.I.'s Burial": NYT, May 28, 1966, p. 28; "Military Burial for PFC Williams/

145 Miles from His Home," SC, June 4–5, 1966, p. 1; "Negro G.I. Is Buried at Andersonville," NYT, May 31, 1966, p. 24.

471 defeated a bill to disperse: *Chicago Tribune,* May 31, 1966, p. 11.

471 Mildred and Richard Loving: WP, March 8, 1966, p. 1; 206 Va. 924, 147 S.E. 2d 78 (1966).

471 subtler "family purity" laws: "Race, Sex, and Forbidden Unions," NYT, Dec. 14, 2003, p. WK-4; "Bans on Interracial Unions Offer Perspective on Gay Ones," NYT, March 17, 2004, p. 16; *Loving v. Virginia* 388 U.S. 1 (1967), at 7, 11.

471 Outside the Sheraton-Park: "Militants Fail to Sway Delegates," WP, June 2, 1966, p. 1; "Picketers, Conferees Swap Jests," WP, June 2, 1966, p. 4; SC, June 4–5, 1966, p. 1.

471 "Black Jesus!": NYT, June 2, 1966, p. 21.

471 "the conference might be demoralized": Harry McPherson memo of June 2, 1966, attached to PDD, June 2, 1966, LBJ; Robert E. Kintner, "Appearance at the Civil Rights Conference, Sheraton Park Hotel," 3:00 P.M., June 1, 1966, White House Conference, Box 56, LBJ.

471 a motorcade ventured from the White House: PDD, June 1, 1966, LBJ; int. Harry McPherson, Oct. 10, 1991.

471 "does not require that righteous anger be silenced": NYT, June 2, 1966, p. 1.

472 seventeen ovations: *Jet,* June 16, 1966, pp. 16–20.

472 "In the light of his car": McPherson, *Political,* pp. 347–48.

472 Johnson had engineered a wondrous truce: Rainwater and Yancey, *Moynihan Report,* pp. 271–91; Anderson and Pickering, *Confronting,* pp. 194–95; Garrow, *Bearing,* p. 473.

472 attractive female college students: Int. Harry McPherson, Oct. 10, 1991; *Jet,* June 16, 1966, p. 31.

472 "a silent, unnoticed delegate": NYT, June 4, 1966, p. 12.

472 "Rights Session Rejects": WP, June 3, 1966, p. 1.

472 "conspicuously missing": Ibid.

473 "I submit that the history": WP, June 2, 1966, p. 4.

473 "a boy on a man's errand": Williams, *Thurgood Marshall,* pp. 252, 341.

473 "his wife came nearer": Lewis, *King,* p. 312.

473 "to heal the broken-hearted": MLK sermon, "Guidelines for a Constructive Church," Ebenezer Baptist Church, June 5, 1966, Tape 59, A/KS; Carson and Holloran, eds., *Knock,* pp. 101–15.

473 staff to be dismantled by Tuesday: "SCLC Moves Out of Ala.," SC, June 4–5, 1966, p. 1.

473 Lucius Amerson of Tuskegee: Jack Nelson, "Negro Wins Ala. Sheriff Nomination," WP, June 1, 1966, p. 4; *Jet,* June 16, 1966, pp. 8–11.

473 "if I can find qualified white people": *Jet,* June 16, 1966, p. 30.

473 Negro candidates fell to fear and inexperience: "Kirksey Is Only Negro to Win Outside Macon [County]," SC, June 4–5, 1966, p. 1.

473 King and Coretta visited: AC, Sept. 12, 1966; ESCRU newsletter, Sept. 29, 1966, courtesy of John B. Morris.

473 Robert Kennedy landed: Schlesinger, *Robert Kennedy,* pp. 800–808; Thomas, *Robert Kennedy,* pp. 321–23.

474 "those of Dutch descent": Arriving statement, Johannesburg, South Africa, June 4, 1966, 11:40 P.M., Adam Walinsky Papers, Box 14, JFK.

474   a battery-operated tape recorder: Frank Taylor, "In South Africa," *National Observer,* June 13, 1966, pp. 1, 17.

474   suggested by Allard Lowenstein: Chafe, *Never,* pp. 282–84; Allard K. Lowenstein, oral history by Larry J. Hackman, April 23, 1969, and Dec. 2, 1969, JFK.

474   had sought out Bob Moses: Branch, *Pillar,* pp. 118–23.

474   largely on an impulsive dare: Thomas, *Robert Kennedy,* p. 321.

474   "What if God is black?": Senator Robert Kennedy, "Suppose God Is Black," *Look,* Aug. 23, 1966, p. 44ff.

474   "the one who was beaten in 1888": Frank Taylor, "In South Africa," *National Observer,* June 13, 1966, p. 1.

474   "We stand here in the name of freedom": Schlesinger, *Robert Kennedy,* pp. 803–4; address of Senator Robert F. Kennedy, June 6, 1966, RFK Senate Papers, Box 17, JFK.

475   The Cape Town speech stirred imagination: "Kennedy Denounces Apartheid as Evil," NYT, June 7, 1966, p. 1.

475   "enthusiastic appreciation": Edwin Espy, General Secretary, National Council of Churches, to RFK ("Reinhold Niebuhr joins me . . ."), June 7, 1966, RFK Senate Papers, Box 13, JFK.

475   "political safari": WP, June 5, 1966, p. 1.

475   "attempting to shake hands": "With Robert Kennedy in White Africa," *U.S. News & World Report,* June 20, 1966, p. 46.

475   wag hung a sign: *Jet,* June 23, 1966, pp. 26–27.

475   negligible response to his published memoir: Williams, *King God Didn't Save,* pp. 92–94.

475   he resented gossip about poor spring grades: NYT, June 5, 1966, p. 78.

475   reports noted eccentricities: Ibid.; NYT, June 6, 1966, pp. 1, 27.

475   "I only want James Meredith": NYT, June 7, 1966, p. 1; James H. Meredith, "Big Changes Are Coming," *Saturday Evening Post,* Aug. 13, 1966, in Library of America Anthology, *Reporting Civil Rights,* pp. 520–24; *Jet,* June 23, 1966, pp. 14–21; *U.S. News & World Report,* June 20, 1966, pp. 36–38; Dittmer, *Local People,* p. 392.

476   flashed news of Meredith's death: "Meredith Death Reported on TV in Error," NYT, June 7, 1966, p. 29.

476   "He was furious with me": Young, *Burden,* pp. 393–94.

476   Twenty-one marchers: Garrow, *Bearing,* pp. 475–76; int. James Lawson, Nov. 14, 1983.

477   Troopers knocked Cleveland Sellers to the ground: Sellers, *River,* p. 161.

477   highlight the next day's front pages: "Troopers Shove Group Resuming Meredith March," NYT, June 8, 1966, p. 1.

477   closing prayers in a pasture: SC, June 10–11, 1966, pp. 1, 6; Garrow, *Bearing,* p. 476.

477   Carmichael apologized: Carmichael, *Ready,* p. 503.

477   rally of a thousand people: NYT, June 8, 1966, p. 1; *Jet,* June 23, 1966, pp. 16–20; Lewis, *King,* pp. 319–20.

477   "He was an expert in that": King speech at Meredith rally, June 7, 1966, A/KS.

477   debate shifted to the Lorraine Motel: Dittmer, *Local People,* pp. 392–93; Viorst, *Fire,* pp. 371–73; Stokely Carmichael and James Forman conversation, Tape 229, A/JF.

477   Roy Wilkins lost any small inclination: Wilkins, *Standing,* pp. 315–16; Carson, *Struggle,* pp. 207–8.

477 "Dr. King, I'm really sorry for you": Int. Kwame Ture (Stokely Carmichael), Jan. 31, 1984.

478 old-fashioned strap undershirt: Morgan, *One Man,* pp. 71–74.

478 feisty enough to reject: Garrow, *Bearing,* p. 478; James H. Meredith, "Big Changes Are Coming," *Saturday Evening Post,* Aug. 13, 1966, in Library of America Anthology, *Reporting Civil Rights,* pp. 525–32; Williams, *King God Didn't Save,* p. 95.

478 Roles crazily reversed: "Meredith Regrets He Was Not Armed," NYT, June 8, 1966, p. 1; "March's Leaders Demand Action," NYT, June 9, 1966, p. 1.

478 "three friends rolled him away": "Meredith Flies Home After Fainting in Hospital," NYT, June 9, 1966, p. 32.

478 "It'll build up": Wiretap transcript of telephone conversation between Stanley Levison and Joe Filner, 1:48 P.M., June 8, 1966, FLNY-9-964a.

478 "junior Selma": Wiretap transcript of telephone conversation between Stanley Levison and Joe Filner, 11:54 A.M., June 8, 1966, FLNY-9-964; wiretap transcript of telephone conversation between Stanley Levison and Adele Kantor, 1:27 P.M., June 9, 1966, FLNY-9-965a.

478 The lines grew to 208 people: "Mississippi March Gains Momentum," NYT, June 10, 1966, p. 1.

478 funeral of Armistead Phipps: Ibid., p. 35; Garrow, *Bearing,* p. 479.

478 "proper ministerial attire": MLK funeral speech marked "Eighth Day Meredith March," June 12, 1966, A/KS.

478 enjoyed their first prolonged company: Sellers, *River,* pp. 163–65; int. Kwame Ture (Stokely Carmichael), Jan. 31, 1984.

478 celebrated a 104-year-old farmer: Dittmer, *Local People,* p. 395.

479 "If you really believed": Wiretap transcript of telephone conference call among MLK, Stanley Levison, Bayard Rustin, and Walter Fauntroy, 9:00 A.M., June 12, 1966, FLNY-9-968.

479 Ben Chester White: "3 Whites Arrested in Death of Negro Outside of Natchez," NYT, June 15, 1966, p. 27; " '66 Killing Goes to Trial Monday," *Jackson Clarion-Ledger,* Feb. 23, 2003.

479 The plan was to lure King: *Jet,* April 27, 1967, p. 6; Jerry Mitchell, "The Last Days of Ben Chester White," *Jackson Clarion-Ledger,* Feb. 23, 2003.

479 "Oh, Lord," pleaded White: Jerry Mitchell, "Avants Found Guilty in '66 Klan Killing," *Jackson Clarion-Ledger,* March 1, 2003.

29: MEREDITH MARCH

PAGE

480 "would result in '66 and '68": Frederick G. Dutton to Bill Moyers, June 10, 1966, Name File, Ronald Reagan, WHCF, LBJ.

480 "I resent the implication": Edwards, *Reagan,* pp. 116–17; Dallek, *Right Moment,* pp. 199–202.

480 "you can't have it both ways": Boyarsky, *Rise,* pp. 148–50.

480 "I resent that": "Angry Reagan Fires Back at Negro Questioner," WP, June 2, 1966, p. 6.

481 hired operatives to smear: Cannon, *President Reagan,* p. 44.

481 "The Republicans, against all counsels of common sense": NYT, June 9, 1966, p. 46,

cited in Dallek, *Right Moment,* p. 210. "He is innocent of experience in government, and his speeches suggest he is equally innocent of knowledge."

481   "thousands of American boys": Carter, *Politics,* pp. 327–29.

481   "Strom is no racist": Bass, *Strom,* pp. 223–24.

481   "There is no future in the race issue": WLBT news film of Nixon appearance in Jackson, May 6, 1966, Tape 0176/D42, MDAH.

481   organize a Republican primary: "GOP's Mississippi Primary Is a First," WP, June 5, 1966, p. 2; NYT, June 5, 1966, p. 78.

482   "you practically had to hold a gun": Black and Black, *Rise,* p. 90.

482   "We're not ever going to beat Sonny": Ibid., p. 353.

482   realignment of Southern white voters: Ibid., pp. 1–5, 211–21, 395.

482   one of three Klansmen arrested in Natchez: "3 Men Held in Mississippi on Charge of Killing Negro," NYT, July 8, 1966, p. 13; *Jet,* July 7, 1966, p. 14.

482   haunted confession of driver James Jones: "His brains, his brains," Jones blurted to Highway Patrolman Donald Butler, after failing a lie-detector test. "When we shot him his brains went all over." Jones said, "Fuller shot him with a machine gun, and Avants blowed his head off." Jerry Mitchell, "The Last Days of Ben Chester White," *Jackson Clarion-Ledger,* Feb. 23, 2003, p. 1.

482   Buckley won acquittal: Bullard, *Free,* p. 92.

482   evaded conviction for their lifetimes: "Confession Never Used in '66 Slaying," AC, Jan. 19, 2000, p. 14.

482   guilty almost thirty-seven years after his crime: Jerry Mitchell, "Avants Found Guilty in '66 Klan Killing," *Jackson Clarion-Ledger,* March 1, 2003, p. 1.

482   Only a quarter of registered Negroes: Dittmer, *Local People,* p. 394.

482   had raised the total fivefold since 1964: Lawson, *Pursuit,* p. 297.

483   thirteen major laws to dilute: Parker, *Black Votes,* pp. 34–37.

483   "We get so concerned": Ibid., p. 59. Parker argues that the Mississippi Constitution helped the legislature conceal its purpose by forbidding the use of specific county names in state statutes. A provision to change from an elected school superintendent to an appointed one in the heavily Negro area of Belzoni, for instance, applied formally in the law to "any county created after 1916 through which the Yazoo River flows."

483   The Meredith marchers approached Grenada: "Marchers Upset by Negro Apathy," NYT, June 14, 1966, p. 19; Lawson, *Pursuit,* p. 56; Paul Good, "The Meredith March," *New South,* Summer 1966, pp. 2–5; "Grenada, Mississippi, 1966/Chronology of a Movement," www.ctmvet.org/info/grenada.html.

483   Rev. Edwin King: Int. Edwin King, June 26, 1992.

484   "Walk for your children": Gene Roberts, "Negroes Win Voting Gains on Stop in Grenada, Miss.", NYT, June 15, 1966, p. 1.

484   "about a mile of niggers": Paul Good, "The Meredith March," *New South,* Summer 1966, p. 6.

484   "We're tired of Confederate flags": NYT, June 15, 1966, p. 26.

484   Andrew Young recorded: Young, *Burden,* p. 396.

484   "You've never had this town before": "March Doubles Vote Registration Along Route Through Mississippi," SC, June 18–19, p. 1.

484   "This, my friends, is our great opportunity": MLK remarks, Grenada, Mississippi, misdated June 16, 1966, A/KS.

484   Negro registration doubled from 697: Dittmer, *Local People,* p. 395.

484   "four straight days": Paul Good, "The Meredith March," *New South,* Summer 1966, p. 7.

485   broke away on June 15: Garrow, *Bearing,* p. 481.

485   soured official Mississippi on the experiment: "Mississippi Shuns March Incidents," NYT, June 16, 1966, p. 35. On June 7, Governor Johnson had pledged to provide "sufficient policemen and any other state forces to see that these demonstrators get all the marching they want provided they behave themselves, commit no acts of violence nor take a position of provocative defiance." NYT, June 8, 1966, p. 1.

485   "turning into a voter registration campaign": "Mississippi Reduces Police Protection for Marchers," NYT, June 17, 1966, p. 1.

485   Grenada police arrested: Paul Good, "The Meredith March," *New South,* Summer 1966, p. 7.

485   repulsed Negro voters illegally: NYT, June 17, 1966, p. 33.

485   "They're going wild for it": Int. Willie (Ricks) Mukasa, May 14, 1992.

485   "people relating to the concept of Black Power": Minutes, central committee meeting, June 10–12, 1966, A/SN6.

485   June 10 emergency session: Ibid.; Sellers, *River,* pp. 161–62.

485   cross-examined colleagues nightly: Carson, *Struggle,* p. 209; int. Kwame Ture (Stokely Carmichael), Jan. 31, 1984.

485   familiar cotton fields and churches: Ibid.; Carmichael, *Ready,* pp. 505–6.

485   since Bob Moses dared to enter: Branch, *Parting,* pp. 633–34, 712–25; Branch, *Pillar,* pp. 66–74, 111–18; Dittmer, *Local People,* pp. 128–35.

485   lived and gone to jail there: Dittmer, *Local People,* pp. 276–79; Branch, *Pillar,* pp. 450–55.

486   "We'll put them up anyway": NYT, June 17, 1966, pp. 1, 33.

486   "just did not feel like Mississippi": Wiretap transcript of telephone conversation between Stanley Levison and "Bill LNU [probably Stein]," 7:20 P.M., June 16, 1966, FLNY-9-972a.

486   "who can be compared to": Paul Good, "The Meredith March," *New South,* Summer 1966, p. 5.

486   They reversed themselves to allow: Dittmer, *Local People,* p. 396.

486   Willie Ricks guided Carmichael: Ibid.; int. Kwame Ture (Stokely Carmichael), Jan. 31, 1984; int. Willie (Ricks) Mukasa, May 14, 1992; Carson, *Struggle,* pp. 209–10; Carmichael, *Ready,* pp. 506–7.

486   "This is the 27th time": Ibid.; NYT, June 17, 1966, p. 33; Paul Good, "The Meredith March," *New South,* Summer 1966, p. 8.

486   "We want black power!": Ibid.; CBS News Special Report, *The March in Mississippi,* June 26, 1966, MOB; *Citizen King,* a Roja Production for *The American Experience,* PBS, 2004.

486   Willie Ricks dueled Hosea Williams: NYT, June 18, p. 28.

487   tiny hamlet of Itta Bena: Branch, *Pillar,* pp. 111–17.

487   "What do you mean": *Citizen King,* a Roja Production for *The American Experience,* PBS, 2004.

487   "parts of it all over my new car": "Klansmen Linked to Negro's Death," NYT, June 18, 1966, p. 28.

487   Detroit's Cobo Hall: NYT, June 29, 1966, p. 17; Detroit LHM dated June 20, 1966, FSC-NR.

487   "Supremacy by Either Race": June 21, 1966, p. 30.

487   King and Ralph Abernathy detoured: Dittmer, *Local People,* p. 398; Paul Good, "The Meredith March," *New South,* Summer 1966, p. 11.

487   "Yes, it's me": Mars, *Witness,* p. 207.

487   "I wouldn't dirty": NYT, June 22, 1966, p. 25.

488   "King appeared to be shaken": Garrow, *Bearing,* p. 483.

488   King knew Deputy Price: Frank, *American Death,* pp. 68–69.

488   "Some 25 white men surged": NYT, June 22, 1966, p. 25.

488   "Whites and Negroes Trade Shots": "Philadelphia, Miss., Whites and Negroes Trade Shots," ibid., p. 1.

488   telegram to President Johnson: NYT, June 23, 1966, p. 23; Oates, *Trumpet,* p. 327.

489   "If I must die": CBS News Special Report, *The March in Mississippi,* June 26, 1966, MOB.

489   "Somebody said tonight": Ibid.; MLK rally speech in Yazoo City, Mississippi, June 21, 1966, A/KS.

489   "I'm sick and tired of violence": Ibid.; "Dr. King Scores Deacons," NYT, June 22, 1966, p. 25.

489   The leaders compromised on a pledge: Garrow, *Bearing,* pp. 484–85; Powers, *War,* p. 153.

489   Johnson's reply telegram: LBJ telegram to MLK, 10:46 A.M. CST, June 23, 1966, A/KP13f9.

489   through rainstorms into Canton: "Mississippi Police Use Gas to Rout Rights Campers," NYT, June 24, 1966, p. 1; *Jet,* July 7, 1966, pp. 14–20; Garrow, *Bearing,* pp. 485–86; Dittmer, *Local People,* pp. 399–400; int. James L. Moore, June 25, 1992; int. Edwin King, June 26, 1992.

490   Carmichael chopped the air: Ibid.; *Citizen King,* a Roja Production for *The American Experience,* PBS, 2004; WLBT news film, *The Meredith March,* Tape 0180/D46, MDAH.

490   "worse than Selma": Lewis, *King,* p. 328.

490   "They're gonna shoot again!": Paul Good, "The Meredith March," *New South,* Summer 1966, pp. 11–13.

490   leapt from the speakers' truck: Young, *Burden,* pp. 402–3.

490   "In light of this, Dr. King": CBS News Special Report, *The March in Mississippi,* June 26, 1966, MOB.

491   "And the very same men": MLK speech in Canton, Mississippi, June 1966, Hosea Williams Tape 133, King Library and Archives.

491   seeing faces in desperation so closely: Abernathy, *Walls,* pp. 412–13.

491   marchers regrouped in Canton: "Accord by Dr. King Angers Marchers," NYT, June 25, 1966, p. 1.

491   converged on Philadelphia: "Marchers Defy Crowd of Whites, Hold Rally in Philadelphia, Miss.," NYT, June 25, 1966, p. 15; Mars, *Witness,* pp. 211–12.

491   "We were brutalized here": WLBT news film, *The Meredith March,* Tape 0180/D46, MDAH.

491   federal lawsuit against Neshoba County: NYT, June 28, 1966, p. 22.

491   more fraternal than supposed: Carson, *Struggle,* p. 208; Sellers, *River,* pp. 168–69; Carmichael, *Ready,* pp. 509–14.

491   "terrible mistake": Wiretap transcript of telephone conference call among MLK, Stanley Levison, Clarence Jones, and Harry Wachtel, 9:10 P.M., June 22, 1966, FLNY-9-978a.

492   "Listen, Andy": Young, *Burden,* p. 398.

492   take freely from his closet in Atlanta: Int. Bernard Lee, June 19, 1985; int. Willie (Ricks) Mukasa, May 14, 1992. ("Willie Ricks loved Dr. King," recalled Lee. "Willie

and I were good friends, and are good friends. . . . He was always saying, 'Well, I knew I was ready when I got me some of them Dr. King shoes.' . . . They never saw what they were doing as hurting Dr. King. They thought they were enhancing the movement, they were enhancing the cause of black people. Stokely never had any problem with Martin King. It was that he thought it was time for black power. He thought that the nonviolent posture had just about run its course.")

492   "I have been used before": Garrow, *Bearing*, p. 485.

492   "I'm sorry, y'all": Int. Kwame Ture (Stokely Carmichael), Jan. 31, 1984.

492   Tougaloo College football field: Dittmer, *Local People*, p. 401.

492   Marlon Brando playfully slapped: WLBT news film, June 25, 1966, Tape 0181/D47, MDAH.

492   "You can't imagine": Ibid.

492   Ann Barth: NYT, June 19, 1966, p. 60.

492   Jim Leatherer and Henry Smith: NYT, June 18, 1966, p. 28.

492   an early staff purge against white people: Meier, *CORE*, pp. 392–408.

492   "I wanted to assure you": Peck to MLK, June 27, 1966, A/KP19f22.

493   final eight miles from Tougaloo: "Meredith Hailed at Rally at Mississippi's Capitol," NYT, June 27, 1966, p. 1; Dittmer, *Local People*, p. 402; WLBT news film, June 26, 1966, Tape 0184/D49, MDAH.

493   Newcomers included Walter Reuther: Ibid.; MLK to Walter Reuther, June 30, 1966, A/KP20f18; int. Al Raby, Feb. 20, 1985; int. Harry Wachtel, Nov. 29, 1983; wiretap transcript of Beatrice Levison telephone conversation, 12:49 P.M., June 26, 1966, FLNY-9-982a.

493   Al Raby with ten busloads: Int. Bernard Lafayette, May 29, 1990.

493   "I don't like the niggers": CBS News Special Report, *The March in Mississippi*, June 26, 1966, MOB.

493   A waitress on North Mill Street: Investigative report headed "Restricted, June 26, 1966, Jackson, Mississippi," MSSC.

493   blocked the southern front: NYT, June 27, 1966, p. 1; int. Edwin King, June 26, 1992.

493   Disjointed speeches wilted: Paul Good, "The Meredith March," *New South*, Summer 1966, p. 15; Garrow, *Bearing*, p. 487.

493   "The whole damn thing smells to me": NYT, June 25, 1966, p. 15.

493   "We thank thee, Oh God": CBS News Special Report, *The March in Mississippi*, June 26, 1966, MOB.

493   King's theology professor: Branch, *Parting*, pp. 92–94; Branch, *Pillar*, pp. 304–5, 375–78.

494   heard Andrew Young call his name: Int. Harold DeWolf, May 9, 1983.

494   "made it clear that a new philosophy": Gene Roberts, "Rights March Disunity," NYT, June 28, 1966, p. 23.

494   "We are faced now with a situation": NYT, July 31, 1966, p. IV-5; Wilmore, *Black Religion*, pp. 195–98. The forty-nine signatories included Episcopal Suffragan Bishop John M. Burgess of Boston, Rev. Charles E. Cobb of Springfield (father of SNCC's Charlie Cobb), Revs. Bryant George and Gayraud Wilmore of the United Presbyterian Church, Anna Hedgman and Benjamin Payton of the National Council of Churches' Commission on Religion and Race, Rev. James Hargett of Los Angeles AME Zion, Bishop Herbert Shaw of North Carolina, and Methodist Bishop James S. Thomas of Iowa.

494   "They're just going to die of attrition": Wiretap transcript of telephone conversation

between Stanley Levison and MLK [from Chicago], 12:20 A.M., July 1, 1966, FLNY-9-987.

495   "I've heard nothing from President Johnson": Dittmer, *Local People,* pp. 400–401.

495   "no specific reaction": NYT, June 25, 1966, p. 14.

495   "In the past, he had been able": Paul Good, "The Meredith March," *New South,* Summer 1966, p. 14.

495   public support numbers declining: Dallek, *Flawed,* pp. 371–75.

495   Johnson withheld approval: Ibid.; "President Hints Intensified War Effort; Ky Feels Junta Is 'Over Hump' in Crisis," NYT, June 19, 1966, p. 1.

495   "The choice is one of military lives": "Summary Notes of the 559th Meeting of the National Security Council," June 17, 1966, in FRUS, Vol. 4, p. 437ff.

496   "I don't see how you can go on": LBJ phone call with Robert McNamara, 7:59 A.M., June 28, 1966, Cit. 10266, Audiotape WH6606.06, LBJ.

496   security pact with McNamara: LBJ phone call with Robert McNamara, 5:33 P.M., June 28, 1966, Cit. 10273, Audiotape WH6606.06, LBJ.

496   lone dinner guest: PDD, June 28, 1966, LBJ.

496   "a lot of trouble to us": LBJ phone call with Robert McNamara, 10:05 A.M., April 27, 1966, Cit. 10049, Audiotape WH6604.04, LBJ.

496   grumbled against the war: Fite, *Richard Russell,* pp. 445–48.

496   Russell once proposed covert schemes: Branch, *Pillar,* pp. 308–10.

496   denying the strategic value: "Russell Favors a Poll in Vietnam on U.S. Presence/ Says 'We Can't Possibly Win' Against Vietcong if People Oppose American Help/ Rejects Domino Theory," NYT, April 26, 1966, p. 1. It was this story that LBJ said was "a lot of trouble to us," in a phone call to McNamara the next day.

496   "the vast chasm between our views": Russell to Honorable P. M. Watson, Jr., April 19, 1966, Series I, b15f26, RR, UGA.

496   predicted death by assassination: Russell, diary memo of June 28, 1966, Series XVIIIB, folder "Presidential (LBJ)", RR, UGA.

496   "He was obviously": Ibid.

496   resolved to endorse: Fite, *Richard Russell,* p. 449; "Bombing Evokes Criticism and Praise in Both Parties," NYT, June 30, 1966, p. 1. "I approve of it," said Russell. "It seems to me we have exhausted every effort to arrive at negotiations."

496   "The monks live in the church": Johnson, *Diary,* pp. 390–91; "President's Evening of Prayer for Pilots in 1966 Disclosed," NYT, May 13, 1967, p. 11.

497   "So it looks like we burned": LBJ phone call with Walt Rostow, 1:52 A.M., June 29, 1966, Cit. 10278, Audiotape WH6606.07, LBJ.

497   "Let's go to bed": LBJ phone call with Cyrus Vance, 2:47 A.M., June 29, 1966, Cit. 10283, Audiotape WH6606.07, LBJ.

497   Four of five Americans: Dallek, *Flawed,* p. 376.

497   flow of war matériel would recover: CIA "Appraisal of the Bombing of North Vietnam (Through 14 July 1966)," in FRUS, Vol. 4, p. 517ff; "An Appraisal of the Bombing of North Vietnam Through 11 August 1966," in ibid., p. 614ff; McNamara, *In Retrospect,* pp. 245–46.

497   The population of Hanoi dropped: Fall, *Reflections,* p. 160.

497   "They also know that nobody": LBJ phone call with Robert McNamara, 7:59 A.M., June 28, 1966, Cit. 10266, Audiotape WH6606.06, LBJ.

497   "And if we hurt them enough": Ibid.

497   Ho Chi Minh responded: Duiker, *Ho Chi Minh,* p. 555; Fall, *Reflections,* p. 160.

498 Ho advised Washington: Ambassador Charles Bohlen, Paris, to Secretary of State Rusk, July 21, 1966, in FRUS, Vol. 4, p. 508ff.

498 1.5 million North Vietnamese women: Turner, *Even the Women*, pp. 20–21.

498 two hundred missile sites: Appy, *Patriots*, p. 202.

498 Ngo Thi Tuyen: Turner, *Even the Women*, pp. 51–69.

498 *Nhan Dan:* Ibid., p. 125.

498 marched south with knapsacks: Ibid., p. 94.

498 Vu Thi Vinh said she defied: Appy, *Patriots*, pp. 103–4.

498 even though she loathed socialism: Turner, *Even the Women*, p. 84.

498 "Many of us temporarily lost our hair": Appy, *Patriots*, pp. 105–6.

498 700,000 wounded soldiers: Turner, *Even the Women*, p. 151.

498 8,558 U.S. aircraft lost: Appy, *Patriots*, p. 202.

498 "It was terrible": Turner, *Even the Women*, p. 99.

498 "When the helicopters dropped soldiers": Borton, *Sorrow*, p. 39.

499 A small caucus convened: Jo Freeman, "The Origins of the Women's Liberation Movement," *American Journal of Sociology*, No. 4, 1973, p. 30ff; Graham, *Civil Rights Era*, pp. 223–26.

499 "a woman as a dog warden": Rep. Martha Griffiths' floor speech, "Women Are Being Deprived of Legal Rights by the Equal Employment Opportunity Commission," *Congressional Record*, June 20, 1966, pp. 13689–94.

499 "Is it because the Commission": Ibid.

499 Pauli Murray among others proposed: Murray, *Song*, pp. 366–68.

499 "Get out! Get out!": Cohen, *Sisterhood*, pp. 133–37.

500 Friedan made up for shortcomings: Ibid.; Harrison, *Sex*, pp. 192–96.

500 drew no major press notice: Mills, *Place*, p. 9.

500 "Speaking in a gravelly alto": Lisa Hammel, "They Meet in Victorian Parlor to Demand 'True Equality'—NOW," NYT, Nov. 22, 1966, p. 44.

500 "If you are trying to run a whorehouse": Cohen, *Sisterhood*, p. 139.

30: CHICAGO

501 Hosea Williams stayed behind: "Dr. King Declares Rights Movement Is 'Close' to a Split," NYT, July 9, 1966, p. 1; "Mississippians Accused," ibid., p. 8. A July 14 undercover report to the segregationist Mississippi State Sovereignty Commission claimed that Stokely Carmichael and Hosea Williams met that day in Grenada and "almost had a fist fight over who was going to run the project there. (Carmichael is trying to take over.) Williams told him to get out of town, because that was his town and SCLC was running the show."

501 clubbed three hundred people: "Negroes Clubbed in Grenada, Miss.," NYT, July 11, 1966, p. 1.

501 "CORE Hears Cries": NYT, July 2, 1966, p. 24.

501 "Black Nationalists Gain": NYT, July 3, 1966, p. 1.

501 "NAACP Head Warns": *U.S. News & World Report*, July 18, 1966, p. 34.

501 "Dr. King and CORE Chief Act": NYT, July 11, 1966, p. 1.

501 trumpeted with warm-up music: Investigator's Report, "Rally and March, Southern Christian Leadership Conference/Coordinating Council of Community Organizations," July 11, 1966, File 940, RS, CHS.

501   three-year-old Bunny collapsed: King, *My Life,* p. 285.

501   King ceremoniously taped: Garrow, *Bearing,* pp. 491–92; Oates, *Trumpet,* p. 409.

502   repair 102,847 apartments: Cohen and Taylor, *Pharaoh,* p. 383.

502   hosted preliminary negotiations: Ibid., pp. 385–86; Anderson and Pickering, *Confronting,* pp. 208–9; NYT, July 12, 1966, p. 26.

502   drills for five hundred nonviolent volunteers: Ralph, *Northern,* p. 114.

502   a pothole intervened: Ralph, *Northern,* p. 109ff; Anderson and Pickering, *Confronting,* p. 212ff; SC, July 23–24, p. 2; Cohen and Taylor, *Pharaoh,* p. 387; NYT, July 13, 1966, p. 1.

502   detoured around jolting sights: King, *My Life,* p. 285ff.

502   release of six battered teenagers: MLK transcript, "West Side Riots," July 12, 1966, A/KS. "I think seven were originally arrested, and all of them were beaten. I went to the jail. This was in the jail. We went to the jail. They said to me as I talked with some of the groups that were very angry at that time, that if I could bring the fellows who had been arrested to them, that they would go home and end the disturbance. I said well if you wait right here, I'll go on down to the police station . . . and there we talked with the commander and were able to get them out on their own recognizance and took them back to the scene, I mean to the church."

503   "It's like improving the food": MLK transcript, "I Need Victories," July 12, 1966, A/KS.

503   Hundreds of young people stalked out: Ralph, *Northern,* p. 110; Anderson and Pickering, *Confronting,* p. 211.

503   At a roadblock of garbage cans: Bernard O. Brown, "WSO and the Riot on the Near West Side," LCMOC folder, West Side Christian Parish Papers, CHS.

503   refit the water hydrants: Ralph, *Northern,* p. 110.

503   sniper shots jumped a mile to housing projects: Anderson and Pickering, *Confronting,* p. 212.

503   more serious riots were spreading: "Armed Negroes Fight the Police in Chicago Riots," NYT, July 15, 1966, p. 1; Chicago LHM dated July 19, 1966, press summary, FSC-NR, p. 4.

503   "Get away from that window": King, *My Life,* p. 289.

503   claimed two fatalities: *Jet,* July 28, 1966, pp. 6–13; Cohen and Taylor, *Pharaoh,* pp. 389–90.

503   He blamed King's staff: Ibid.; *Chicago Tribune,* July 16, 1966, p. 1; Reynolds, *Jesse Jackson,* p. 58.

504   "Doctor King, I want to make": Anderson and Pickering, *Confronting,* p. 214.

504   "Now there was a program": Ibid., p. 215.

504   "We don't need sprinklers": "Troops Restoring Order in Chicago Negro Ghetto; 2 Dead, 57 Hurt in Rioting," NYT, July 16, 1966, p. 1.

504   dispatched two top assistants: Joe Califano to LBJ, 3:00 P.M., July 15, 1966, and Joe Califano to LBJ, 6:15 P.M., July 15, 1966, EX HU, Box 26, LBJ. "John Doar is in Chicago, as well as Roger Wilkins," Califano advised in the second memo. "I have talked to the various Cabinet Officers involved and told them that Katzenbach would be coordinating the Government's efforts."

504   a miniature Watts: Ralph, *Northern,* p. 112.

504   John Doar and Roger Wilkins: Wilkins, *Life,* p. 208; Garrow, *Bearing,* p. 496.

504   diverted from a canoe vacation: Int. John Doar, May 12, 1986.

504   "four *hot* hours": *Citizen King,* a Roja Production for *The American Experience,* PBS, 2004.

505   leader of the Roman Saints: "Chicago Calmer as Gangs Agree to End Violence/

Youths Heed Dr. King's Plea to Shift Tactics in Efforts to Achieve Their Aims," NYT, July 17, 1966, p. 1.

505   Internal deliberations reeled: Anderson and Pickering, *Confronting,* p. 233.

505   Stanley Levison thought most Americans: Wiretap transcript of telephone conversation between Stanley Levison and Andrew Young, 12:13 A.M., July 15, 1966, FLNY-9-1001.

505   King bemoaned the prior delays: Ralph, *Northern,* p. 113.

505   extra 650 deaths: "Record Hot Spell Lingers at 101; Death Rate Rises," NYT, July 14, 1966, p. 1.

505   eight student nurses systematically bound: "Survivor Says Killer of 8 Lulled Fears of Victims," NYT, July 16, 1966, p. 1.

505   mounted rebuilding demonstrations: Garrow, ed., *Chicago 1966,* pp. 20–21.

505   "We must move on": Anderson and Pickering, *Confronting,* p. 219.

505   "He's a goddam faker": LBJ phone call with Richard J. Daley, 7:10 P.M., July 19, 1966, Cit. 10414-15, Audiotape WH6607.02, LBJ.

506   he opposed the war: Cohen and Taylor, *Pharaoh,* pp. 445–50.

506   King called for an all-night vigil: Ralph, *Northern,* p. 119.

506   argued for a respite instead: Anderson and Pickering, *Confronting,* pp. 221–23.

506   "All housing should be available": Mary Lou Finley, "The Open Housing Marches Chicago Summer 1966," in Garrow, ed., *Chicago 1966,* p. 12.

506   debates essentially deferred to James Bevel: Ibid., pp. 6–12; Ralph, *Northern,* pp. 99–101.

506   cellmate Bernard Lafayette: Branch, *Parting,* pp. 412, 483–87; Branch, *Pillar,* pp. 53–56, 63–66, 81–84.

506   test nonviolent methods in Chicago: Int. Kale Williams, Feb. 21, 1985; int. James Lawson, Mar. 26, 1991; int. Bernard Lafayette, May 28, 1990.

507   yielded piecemeal results: Anderson and Pickering, *Confronting,* p. 217; *Jet,* Dec. 29, 1966, pp. 14–19.

507   Lafayette called the inner boundaries: Blackstone Productions, Inc., *Eyes on the Prize II, America at the Racial Crossroads—1965 to 1985,* Vol. 2, "Two Societies (1965–68)"; int. Bernard Lafayette, May 28, 1990.

507   Studies by his American Friends Service Committee colleagues: Cf. Bill Moyer, *An Analysis of the System of Housing Negroes in Chicago,* Feb. 18, 1966, West Side Christian Parish, LCMOC folder, CHS.

507   "All we are asking": Anderson and Pickering, *Confronting,* p. 217.

507   fifty volunteers set up Friday: Garrow, *Bearing,* p. 498; Garrow, ed., *Chicago 1966,* p. 24; Cohen and Taylor, *Pharaoh,* p. 393; Marx to "dear friend," Aug. 6, 1966, Courtesy of Jane Ramsey; int. Robert J. Marx, Sept. 19, 2005.

507   A column of 250: Ralph, *Northern,* p. 120; Cohen and Taylor, *Pharaoh,* pp. 392–93.

508   crescendo of neighborhood fury: Ibid.; "54 Hurt as Whites in Chicago Hurl Bricks at Rights Marchers," NYT, Aug. 1, 1966, p. 1; Karen Koko, "Chicago's Race March—A Walk on the Wild Side," *National Catholic Reporter,* Aug. 10, 1966, p. 1; "Dr. King Calls Chicago Police Lax in March Duty," NYT, Aug. 2, 1966, p. 12; *Jet,* Aug. 18, 1966, pp. 52–55; Anderson and Pickering, *Confronting,* pp. 223–24; Garrow, ed., *Chicago 1966,* pp. 63–64.

508   When a captain persuaded Raby: "Information Report, 8th District, 1 Aug. '66, 0030 Hours," File 940, RS, CHS.

508   Andrew Young saw the taillights: Young, *Burden,* p. 413.

508   "I don't know": Blackstone Productions, Inc., *Eyes on the Prize II, America at the Racial Crossroads—1965 to 1985,* Vol. 2, "Two Societies (1965–68)."

508   Rabbi Robert J. Marx: *Jet,* Sept. 8, 1966, pp. 46–47; Ralph, *Northern,* pp. 122–23.

509   "baited into a near-riot": *Chicago Tribune,* Aug. 5, 1966, cited in Anderson and Pickering, *Confronting,* p. 228.

509   community violence would only backfire: Ralph, *Northern,* pp. 129–30; Cohen and Taylor, *Pharaoh,* pp. 393–94.

509   The mayor sent his black alderman: Anderson and Pickering, *Confronting,* pp. 226–27.

509   mass meeting of 1,700 people: Garrow, *Bearing,* p. 499.

509   "If there is any doubt": Speech excerpts, "MLK Rally with Mahalia Jackson," Aug. 4, 1966, A/KS.

509   On Friday afternoon, August 5: Anderson and Pickering, *Confronting,* p. 228; Garrow, *Bearing,* pp. 499–500; Ralph, *Northern,* pp. 123–25; Oates, *Trumpet,* p. 414.

510   staggered King to the pavement: *Citizen King,* a Roja Production for *The American Experience,* PBS, 2004; Blackstone Productions, Inc., *Eyes on the Prize II, America at the Racial Crossroads—1965 to 1985,* Vol. 2, "Two Societies (1965–68)."

510   "There are at least twenty five hundred": Gene Roberts, "Rock Hits Dr. King as Whites Attack March in Chicago," NYT, Aug. 6, 1966, p. 1.

510   an undercover officer in one reported: Investigator's report dated Aug. 8, 1966, for Aug. 5 incident, File 940, RS, CHS.

511   Women poured sugar: Cohen and Taylor, *Pharaoh,* p. 396.

511   "The reinforcements came running": NYT, Aug. 6, 1966, p. 52.

511   King consoled a stunned: Investigators' reports dated Aug. 5 and 9, 1966, for Aug. 5 incident, File 940, RS, CHS.

511   "I have never in my life": *Jet,* Aug. 25, 1966, pp. 14–23; NYT, Aug. 7, 1966, p. 47.

511   gang marshals had batted down: NYT, Aug. 1, 1966, p. 1.

511   "I saw their noses being broken": Ralph, *Northern,* p. 137.

511   threatened to shoot Bevel: Investigator's report dated Aug. 2, 1966, File 940, RS, CHS.

511   closed New Friendship Baptist: Ralph, *Northern,* pp. 137–38; Garrow, ed., *Chicago 1966,* p. 16.

511   arraignment of Richard Speck: Breo and Martin, *Crime,* pp. 175–76.

512   helped save his life for trial: Ibid., pp. 106–26.

512   barricaded sniper Charles Whitman: Lavergne, *Sniper,* pp. ix–xvii.

512   "I don't really understand myself": Ibid., pp. 112–14.

512   "to have fun like the guys": Ibid., pp. 320–21.

512   Crime statisticians soon added: Ibid., pp. 327–28.

512   The news from Texas eclipsed: Ibid., pp. 294–95; Johnson, *Diary,* pp. 406–11.

512   "crime of the century": Breo and Martin, *Crime,* pp. 17, 73, 79.

512   King answered questions: WLBT news film, Aug. 8, 1966, Tape 3243/F2291, MDAH.

512   Neshoba County Fair: WLBT news film, August 3–4, 1966, Tapes 3225–36/F2274, MDAH.

513   "I flew over the scene": Ibid.; *Jackson Daily News,* Aug. 4, 1966, p. 10, attached in FBI files to Hoover memo of Aug. 11, 1966, FSC-1547.

513   keynote speaker, Edward Kennedy: Garrow, *Bearing,* p. 501; int. Edward Kennedy, April 12, 2004; int. William vanden Heuvel, Aug. 2, 2004.

513   FBI agents estimated three hundred pounds: SAC, Jackson, to Director, Aug. 9, 1966, FSC-1544.

513   "a young man on the way up": MLK introduction, Aug. 8, 1966, with handwritten changes, A/KS.

513   They stood to cheer when Kennedy asked: SC, Aug. 13–14, 1966, p. 1; LAT, Aug. 9, 1966; SP, Sept. 1966, p. 4.

513   A high fever sent King: Garrow, *Bearing,* pp. 500–501.

513   "his virus, the one he always got": Abernathy, *Walls,* p. 382; NYT, Aug. 11, 1966, p. 23.

513   "We're at a real turn": Wiretap transcript of telephone conversation between MLK and Stanley Levison, 7:56 P.M., Aug. 13, 1966, FLNY-9-1030a.

514   "Chicago has proven": MLK, President's Annual Report, Aug. 10, 1966, A/KS11.

514   ratified Al Lowenstein and Charles Morgan: Garrow, *Bearing,* pp. 500–501.

514   "non-existent structural and organizational foundations": MLK to Randolph T. Blackwell, Aug. 16, 1966, A/KP28f23. "These growing pains are still with us," King added in his farewell letter to Blackwell, "and they will probably last until we have the courage and aggressiveness to meet them head-on. So if we did not provide every aspect of the harmony that you expected, I do hope that you gained consolation from the fact that you started a process that will continue to lead us in the right direction."

514   integrate Grenada's public library: Investigative report on the SCLC convention dated Aug. 10, 1966, MSSC; Dittmer, *Local People,* p. 404.

514   lost, wrecked, or abandoned: David I. Schaffer, Corporate Counsel, Avis World Headquarters, to Andrew J. Young, Aug. 9, 1966, A/KP22f16. Schaffer reminded Young that Avis representatives had met with Blackwell in October of 1965 "to resolve various differences" over the conduct of Hosea Williams, which persisted nevertheless. His letter complained that the Memphis branch manager of Avis "was unable to convince Rev. Williams that her actions were anything but racially motivated. Miss Mitchell also informed us that, in the course of these rentals and meetings to and with members of your organization, she and her staff were subjected to much abusive, argumentative and impolite language and demeanor."

514   teased Andrew Young: Young, *Burden,* pp. 386–87.

514   staff prodigy had committed him: Anderson and Pickering, *Confronting,* p. 229; Abernathy, *Walls,* p. 383.

514   Jesse Jackson idolized: Frady, *Jesse,* p. 209.

514   Andrew Young among others: Young, *Burden,* pp. 386–87; Reynolds, *Jesse Jackson,* p. 54.

514   strategy papers for the Chicago movement: Cf. Jesse L. Jackson, "A Strategy to End Slums," May 31, 1966, A/SC149f35. "The giants of Chicago's Canaan are a mighty force. They have vast sums of money to keep us out. . . . Our battle plans call for us to march around the southwest side of Chicago until the walls of oppression come tumbling down."

515   "I have counted up the cost": Blackstone Productions, Inc., *Eyes on the Prize II, America at the Racial Crossroads—1965 to 1985,* Vol. 2, "Two Societies (1965–68)."

515   "would make Gage Park": Anderson and Pickering, *Confronting,* pp. 229–30.

515   teenager Jerome Huey: Ibid., p. 277; Cohen and Taylor, *Pharaoh,* pp. 397–98.

515   "They can buy tanks": Ralph, *Northern,* p. 139.

515   "with a heavy heart": NYT, Aug. 11, 1966, p. 23; Kathleen Connolly, "The Chicago Open-Housing Conference," in Garrow, ed., *Chicago 1966,* pp. 69–70.

516   Daley himself initiated: Anderson and Pickering, *Confronting,* p. 235; Ralph, *Northern,* pp. 149–52; Cohen and Taylor, *Pharaoh,* pp. 398–99.

516   Chicago Conference on Religion and Race: Branch, *Pillar,* pp. 24–32.

516   Rev. Robert Spike: Spike, *Photographs,* pp. 141–42, 192–93; Friedland, *Lift Up,* p. 190; NYT, Dec. 3, 1965, p. 35.

516   The American Nazi Party: Anderson and Pickering, *Confronting,* p. 232; NYT, Aug. 17, 1966, p. 23.

516   Bogan neighborhood on August 12: NYT, Aug. 13, 1966, p. 8.

516   John Lennon was apologizing: *Rolling Stone Rock Almanac,* p. 119.

516   three different neighborhoods: "Rights Leaders Schedule 3 Marches at Once in Chicago Today," NYT, Aug. 14, 1966, p. 48; Ralph, *Northern,* p. 148.

516   "We are here": Garrow, ed., *Chicago 1966,* p. 23; investigator's report dated Aug. 17, 1966, File 940, RS, CHS.

517   Men occupied all fifty-six seats: Garrow, ed., *Chicago 1966,* pp. 93–94.

517   Soaring hope collided: Chicago deliberations chiefly from minutes preserved by John McKnight, "The Summit Negotiations, Chicago, August 17–August 26, 1966," in Garrow, ed., *Chicago 1966,* pp. 111–45. Also Anderson and Pickering, *Confronting,* pp. 237–69; Ralph, *Northern,* pp. 152–71; Garrow, *Bearing,* pp. 503–25; Cohen and Taylor, *Pharaoh,* pp. 402–22; Fairclough, *Redeem,* p. 300ff.

517   When they reconvened: Ibid.

518   King implored exhausted negotiators: Garrow, ed., *Chicago 1966,* pp. 133–34.

518   News outlets considered: Ibid., pp. 78–79; Anderson and Pickering, *Confronting,* p. 254; "Dr. King Reports No Chicago Truce," NYT, Aug. 18, 1966, p. 31.

518   he exhorted a mass meeting: NYT, Aug. 19, 1966, p. 19.

518   "until every white person out there": Cohen and Taylor, *Pharaoh,* p. 412.

519   obtained within two hours a sweeping injunction: Ibid., pp. 413–14; "Chicago Injunction Limits Rights Drive; Dr. King May Defy It," NYT, Aug. 20, 1966, p. 1; Notice and Complaint, *City of Chicago v. Rev. Dr. Martin Luther King et al.,* Aug. 19, 1966, A/SC2fl.

519   "The issue is still justice": Anderson and Pickering, *Confronting,* p. 257.

519   *Meet the Press:* Transcript, *Meet the Press,* Aug. 21, 1966, reprinted in the *Congressional Record,* Aug. 29, 1966, pp. 21095–21102; "6 Rights Leaders Clash on Tactics in Equality Drive/ Meredith Asserts Negroes Should Take Law into Their Own Hands if Attacked/ Dr. King Hits Violence," NYT, Aug. 22, 1966, pp. 1, 36–37.

520   "Get your grandmother up from the South!": Ralph, *Northern,* pp. 162–63.

520   eighty-six-car caravan: Investigator's report dated Aug. 22, 1966, File 940, RS, CHS.

520   Alan Paton had recorded: Joravsky and Camacho, *Race,* p. 27.

520   "About 2,000 residents": "Dr. King and 500 Jeered in 5-Mile Chicago March," NYT, Aug. 22, 1966, p. 1.

520   "You are all good looking": Ralph, *Northern,* pp. 163–64.

520   George Lincoln Rockwell: Garrow, ed., *Chicago 1966,* p. 82; NYT, Aug. 22, 1966, p. 37.

520   anti-Jewish polemicist Connie Lynch: Lynch, founder of the National States Rights Party, delivered Klan-like speeches laced with sectarian beliefs of the Christian Identity movement, which held that Jesus had been of pure Aryan lineage, falsely claimed by Jews. With fellow supremacist J. B. Stoner, Lynch had mounted counterdemonstrations against King two years earlier in St. Augustine, Florida. Cf. Branch, *Pillar,* pp. 141–42, 377–78, 382.

520   satellite marches in two areas: Ralph, *Northern,* p. 163.

520   King himself announced: Ibid., p. 166; Garrow, *Bearing,* pp. 517–18.

520   "We've got commies": Garrow, ed., *Chicago 1966,* pp. 82–83.

520   "awfully close to a suicidal act": Anderson and Pickering, *Confronting,* p. 259.

521   While daily marches ventured: Ralph, *Northern,* p. 166.

521   "the present downhill course": NYT, Aug. 25, 1966, p. 36.

521   all seven black aldermen: Cohen and Taylor, *Pharaoh,* p. 415; Ralph, *Northern,* p. 165.

521   reconvened at the Palmer House: John McKnight, "The Summit Negotiations, Chicago, August 17–August 26, 1966," in Garrow, ed., *Chicago 1966,* pp. 136–45; Anderson and Pickering, *Confronting,* pp. 262–65; Cohen and Taylor, *Pharaoh,* pp. 418–19.

521   modest goal of at least one percent: Garrow, ed., *Chicago 1966,* p. 137; "Rights Aides Set Goal in Chicago/ Seek 1% Negro Occupancy in 75 Areas by April 30," NYT, Aug. 28, 1966, p. 50.

522   the ten-point Open Housing Summit Agreement passed unanimously: "Housing Pact Set, Dr. King Calls off Chicago Marches/ He Hails 10-Point Program and 'Defers' Rights Rally by 3,000 in Cicero/ Realty Men Back Plan/ But Several Negro Groups Dissent and Map Protest by 300 Tomorrow," NYT, Aug. 27, 1966, p. 1; Thomas G. Ayers, "The 'Summit Agreement,' " in Garrow, ed., *Chicago 1966,* pp. 147–54.

31: VALLEY MOMENTS

PAGE

523   "shown Chicago what it has known": Nicholas von Hoffman, "King Hails Accord but Problem Still Terrifies Chicago," WP, Aug. 29, 1966, p. 4.

523   "We are all, let us face it": Cited in Herbers, *Priority,* p. 123.

523   "King has hardly begun": Cited in Garrow, *Bearing,* p. 530.

523   "fanatical, indefensible violence": Rowland Evans and Robert Novak, "King's Chicago Pillow," WP, Aug 29, 1966, p. 13.

524   Angry white residents picketed: NYT, Aug. 30, 1966, p. 28; Cohen and Taylor, *Pharaoh,* p. 420.

524   Catcalls of "black power!": Alfred J. Slaughter, "Martin Luther King—'Mercy Killer,' " CDD, Sept. 10–16, 1966, p. 2; "Talk by Dr. King Disrupted," NYT, Sept. 1, 1966, p. 1; *Jet,* Sept. 15, 1966, p. 42; Chicago LHM dated Sept. 1, 1966, FSC-NR; Anderson and Pickering, *Confronting,* pp. 275–76; Ralph, *Northern,* p. 197. James Forman and Clayborne Carson spell the name "Sharpe" with a final "e" (Forman, *Making,* p. 470; Carson, *Struggle,* p. 234), both noting that the Chicago SNCC leader sought exile in Tanzania in 1967.

524   jettisoning the commitment: "Cicero Marchers Planning a Defense if Attacked," NYT, Aug. 29, 1966, p. 14.

524   "Prefers Action to Talk": NYT, Sept. 5, 1966, p. 8.

524   "I was pleased but also shocked": Travis, *Black Chicago,* pp. 252–54; Garrow, *Bearing,* p. 529.

524   "We are *not* marching into Cicero": Blackstone Productions, Inc., *Eyes on the Prize II, America at the Racial Crossroads—1965 to 1985,* Vol. 2, "Two Societies (1965–68)."

524   "Guards Bayonet Hecklers": NYT, Sept. 5, 1966, p. 1.

524   fulfilling their vow to fight: Ibid.; SC, Oct. 1–2, 1966, p. 3; comments of Glory Bryant in *Eyes on the Prize II.*

524   Stokely Carmichael offended the courtly mayor: Pomerantz, *Peachtree,* pp. 345–46.

524   anti-Vietnam picketing vigil: SNCC Atlanta Project, "Atlanta's Black Paper," Aug. 25, 1966, Reel 37, SNCC.

525   Depression-era black defendant Angelo Herndon: Branch, *Parting,* p. 210.

525   Atlanta's worst riot in sixty years: "Atlanta Negroes Riot After Police Wound a Suspect," NYT, Sept. 7, 1966, p. 1; *Jet,* Sept. 22, 1966, pp. 8–11; Pomerantz, *Peachtree,* pp. 344–50; Allen, *Mayor,* p. 181ff.

525   "the guts of a lion": Pomerantz, *Peachtree,* p. 348.

525   "SNCC members are not responsible": Bayor, *Race,* pp. 139–40.

525   Coca-Cola magnate Robert Woodruff: Pomerantz, *Peachtree,* pp. 343–44.

526   pointing his gun at Barbara Aaron: *Jet,* Aug. 25, 1966, pp. 54–55; Sept. 8, 1966, p. 24.

526   Carmichael had summoned: Anne Braden, "Slums Cause Outbreak," SP, Oct. 1966, p. 1; Sellers, *River,* pp. 174–77.

526   "S.N.C.C. Assailed": NYT, Sept. 8, 1966, p. 1.

526   "Negroes didn't have any clear idea": Cited in Sellers, *River,* p. 177.

526   rioters spat on its correspondent: NYT, Sept. 7, 1966, p. 38.

526   Atlanta police arrested Carmichael: "Carmichael Held in Riot Aftermath," NYT, Sept. 9, 1966, p. 1; "Carmichael Denies in Court That He Began Atlanta Riot," NYT, Oct. 2, 1966, p. 82.

526   "I think it's only fair": Roy Reed comments, April 1987, at the National Symposium on the Media and the Civil Rights Movement, at the Center for the Study of Southern Culture, University of Mississippi.

526   shooting death of a black teenager: "White in Atlanta Held in Slaying," NYT, Sept. 14, 1966, p. 33; "Georgian Guilty in Negro's Death," NYT, Feb. 9, 1967, p. 27.

526   "a hired hand": Garrow, *Bearing,* p. 530.

526   King was in Memphis: SAC, New York, to Director, Sept. 10, 1966, FK-NR.

526   retreat about staff morale: Int. James Lawson, Nov. 9, 1983.

526   "Big Lester" Hankerson: Branch, *Pillar,* p. 125.

527   "We screamed for help": Notes of Memphis retreat, Sept. 1966, A/SC49f14.

527   The Grenada staff had revolted: Garrow, *Bearing,* p. 531.

527   counseling of young workers: Int. James Lawson, Nov. 14, 1983; minutes of July 26, 1966, board meeting of the American Foundation on Nonviolence, Lowenstein Papers, File 1268, Box 50, UNC.

527   King called Stanley Levison: Wiretap transcript of telephone conversation between MLK and Stanley Levison, 6:51 P.M., Sept. 9, 1966, FLNY-9-1057a; NYT, Sept. 12, 1966, p. 49.

527   Julian Bond's departure from SNCC: Carson, *Struggle,* p. 231.

527   Schools opened in Grenada: Dittmer, *Local People,* pp. 403–7.

527   general assault on those behind: Ibid.; NYT, Sept. 13, 1966, p. 1; telephone conversation between MLK and Stanley Levison, 6:51 P.M., Sept. 9, 1966, FLNY-9-1057a; NYT, Sept. 12, 1966, p. 49; int. Willie Bolden, May 14, 1992. ("They had me stretched out over here," said Bolden, "and they were hitting a young boy. . . . I saw this guy put his foot between his crotch and twist his leg and broke his leg in two places. We finally got them, after they stopped, and went to Grenada Hospital. They wouldn't wait on us.")

528   "You get the Highway Patrol": Dittmer, *Local People,* p. 405.

528   Andrew Young flew in: NYT, Sept. 14, 1966, p. 1.

528   mustered eighty-seven black children: NYT, Sept. 15, 1966, p. 1.

528   "virtually abdicated their responsibility": NYT, Sept. 17, 1966, p. 26; SC, Sept. 24–25, 1966, p. 4.

528   FBI agents arrested thirteen men: NYT, Sept. 18, 1966, p. 1.

528   a short-lived drive to impeach: Johnston, *Defiant Years,* pp. 324–25.

528   "I can tell you my heart": Homer Bigart, "A Church Voices Sorrow in Grenada Over Mob Violence," Sept. 19, 1966, p. 1.

528   Folksinger Joan Baez arrived: Baez, *Voice,* pp. 107–10; Sandperl, *Kinder,* pp. 121–22, 131–39.

529   Baez and Sandperl joined escorts: NYT, Sept. 20, 1966, p. 34.

529   fourteen volunteer tutors: NYT, Dec. 28, 1966, p. 23.

529   "His speech was fiery": NYT, Sept. 20, 1966, p. 34.

529   Andrew Young summoned Baez: Baez, *Voice,* pp. 101–03; int. Joan Baez, Jan. 7, 1984.

529   he escorted two young girls: NYT, Sept. 21, 1966, pp. 1, 32.

529   Civil Rights Act of 1966 failed: NYT, Sept. 20, 1966, p. 1.

530   "We have received no word": "Pessimism Grows in White House over Rights Bill," NYT, Sept. 10, 1966, p. 1; "Dr. King Fearful for Rights Bill," NYT, Sept. 12, 1966, p. 49.

530   All eight Grenada defendants: SC, June 10–11, 1967, p. 1; Dittmer, *Local People,* p. 406.

530   Diana Freelon: Int. Bruce Hartford, Sept. 18, 2005; www.crmvet.org/vet/foster=f.htm.

530   "The Senate has an obligation": NYT, Sept. 14, 1966, p. 46.

530   "now that others' oxen": Graham, *Civil Rights Era,* p. 262.

530   "a package of mischief": Ralph, *Northern,* p. 192.

530   agreement in Chicago was stronger: Cf. "Giant Step," NYT editorial, Aug. 27, 1966, p. 28: "What Congress has thus far failed to confer adequately by law, the Rev. Dr. Martin Luther King, Jr., and his associates have now achieved in Chicago by their repeated demonstrations."

531   reimprison him for the Birmingham jail campaign: Fred P. Graham, "High Court to Weigh Dr. King Conviction in '63 Rights Rally," NYT, Oct. 11, 1966, p. 1; Lewis, *King,* p. 367; Westin, *Trial,* p. 205.

531   "Don't you find": *Citizen King,* a Roja Production for *The American Experience,* PBS, 2004.

531   influential front-page series: The conservative news weekly *U.S. News & World Report,* which seldom praised the *Times* on its civil rights coverage, recapped the entire series in the October 3 issue, p. 46.

531   "How deep does white disengagement go": NYT, Sept. 19, 1966, pp. 1, 36.

531   "Housing Equality Hits": NYT, Sept. 20, 1966, p. 1.

531   "We are witnessing": Wiretap transcript of telephone conversation between Stanley Levison and Rachelle [Horowitz], 3:35 P.M., Sept. 20, 1966, FLNY-9-1068a.

531   "It's fear": NYT, Sept. 21, 1966, pp. 1, 33.

531   "These are a new breed of cats": Ibid.

531   Katzenbach blocked a proposed White House summit: Katzenbach to Harry McPherson, Sept. 17, 1966, McPherson Papers, Box 22, LBJ. Katzenbach was responding to McPherson's short memo of September 14: "When the civil rights bill goes down the drain, I think something like this [attached proposal] should be done. When you have a chance, please give me your views on it. The pencil notations are the boss's." LBJ's penciled notations approved the proposed agenda and roster, which excluded the SNCC and CORE leadership, adding, "Subject to Nick's approval & I suggest he call meeting & bring them by later."

531   "The President does not strengthen": Ibid.

532   most Americans still identified: McPherson probably knew of a Gallup poll, cited in Dallek, *Flawed,* p. 327.

532   "Surely, the next generation": McPherson to Katzenbach, Sept. 20, 1966, McPherson Papers, Box 22, LBJ.

532   "You are stuck with it": McPherson to LBJ, Sept. 12, 1966, McPherson Papers, Box 7, LBJ.

532   Carmichael himself made bail: NYT, Sept. 16, 1966, p. 34.

532   "It shows how the press cultivated": Elizabeth Sutherland, New York SNCC office, "Press Survey—May 17–August 17, 1966," Sept. 15, 1966, Reel 16, SNCC.

532   "Everything seemed to go": Carmichael, *Ready,* p. 520.

532   "His style dazzles": Bernard Weinraub, "The Brilliancy of Black," *Esquire,* Jan. 1967, pp. 130–35.

532   "A shiver of nervous exhilaration": Lerone Bennett, Jr., "Stokely Carmichael: Architect of Black Power," *Ebony,* July 1966.

532   "Who could have thought it": Carmichael, *Ready,* pp. 523–24.

533   " 'When I use a word' ": Cited in Eldridge Cleaver, "My Father and Stokely Carmichael," *Ramparts,* April 1967, p. 14.

533   "He says that LBJ killed": Ibid.

533   "a fraudulent bunch of words": Carmichael press statement of July 1, 1966, A/KP3f25. "The Civil Rights Act of 1966 as reported by the House Judiciary Committee is totally useless and totally unnecessary," it began. "If passed, it will function both as a fraudulent bunch of words to convince black people of this country that Congress has taken action to deal with their problems, and as a smokescreen to obscure President Johnson's failure to enforce earlier civil rights legislation."

533   "hypocrisy which attempts to delude": Carmichael to MLK, July 4, 1966, attaching the July 1 press statement, A/KP3f25.

533   "You have displayed more backbone": SNCC telegram to MLK, Aug. 3, 1966, answering a telegram of the same date to Carmichael from Roy Wilkins, A. Philip Randolph, Whitney Young, and [approved by telephone] MLK, A/KP23f18; "Negroes Assail S.N.C.C. Protest," NYT, Aug. 5, 1966, p. 11.

533   "All those people who are calling us friends": Carmichael speech in Chicago, July 28, 1966, Reel 20, SNCC. In a speech two days later at Detroit's Cobo Hall, Carmichael said, "The white college friends say they are fighting with us, but they are only fighting to smoke 'pot' while the Negro is fighting for his life." Detroit FBI report dated Jan. 5, 1968, FSN-13.

533   "No, not one": NYT, Aug. 5, 1966, cited in Powers, *War,* p. 150.

533   "We cannot be expected": Stokely Carmichael, "What We Want," *New York Review of Books,* Sept. 22, 1966.

533   publicized summer meetings: NYT, July 29, 1966, p. 13; NYT, July 30, 1966; NYT, Aug. 29, 1966, p. 13; MS, Aug. 12, 1966, p. 4.

534   "You're different": Int. Richard Morrisroe, Feb. 20, 22, 2002.

534   Morrisroe managed his first sworn testimony: *Chicago Daily News,* Sept. 13, 1966, in file #940, RS, CHS.

534   "Father, may I ask a question?": Int. Richmond Flowers, Aug. 9, 1990; int. Richard Morrisroe, April 9, 2003, and May 22, 2003; Hayman, *Bitter,* pp. 223–26.

534   descended into disgrace: Hayman, *Bitter,* pp. 258–99.

534   curse Flowers again when Junior scored: Int. Richmond Flowers, Aug. 9, 1990; Mike Sielski, "Flowers: 'Fastest White Boy Alive,' " ESPN Classic Biography, ESPN.com.

535   Tennessee fielded its first black player: Peter Schrag, "Tennessee's Lonesome End," *Harper's,* March, 1970, pp. 59–67.

535   Gloria Larry reported: SNCC field reports, September 28–October 8, 1966, Reel 16, SNCC.

535   too enmeshed in politics: Morrisroe speech, "Jonathan Myrick Daniels, Seminarian and Martyr," 1999, courtesy of Richard Morrisroe.

535   legal career after his 1973 marriage: Jim Procter, "Richard Morrisroe's Journey Home," Hammond, Indiana, *Compass,* reprinted in *Congressional Record,* Dec. 3, 1975, p. S20967.

535   bride's four-year-old nephew: Int. Richard and Sylvia Morrisroe, April 9, 2003.

535   Thagard dismissed all charges: SC, Oct. 1–2, 1966, p. 1; Eagles, *Outside Agitator,* p. 252.

535   *Black Power, White Backlash:* Transcript, CBS Reports, Sept. 27, 1966, MOB.

535   "a stunning upset": NYT, Sept. 29, 1966, p. 1.

535   won by Lester Maddox: Reese Cleghorn, "Meet Lester Maddox of Georgia, 'Mr. White Backlash,' " NYT Magazine, Nov. 6, 1966, p. IV-27ff.

536   "The seal of the great state of Georgia": Maddox, *Speaking,* pp. 81–82. Maddox included Allen's attack in his memoir as a trophy.

536   "Georgia is a sick state": Ibid.; NYT, Sept. 26, 1966, p. 35.

536   "wouldn't be shocking enough": Wiretap transcript of telephone conversation between MLK and Stanley Levison, 11:40 P.M., Sept. 29, 1966, FLNY-9-1077a; Garrow, *Bearing,* p. 532.

536   "I do think we stand": MLK press statement in Chicago, Sept. 30, 1966, A/KS.

32: BACKLASH

PAGE

537   58 percent of party supporters: "G.O.P. Will Press Racial Disorders as Election Issue," NYT, Oct. 4, 1966, p. 1; "In the Tight Races, the Backlash Vote May Mean Victory," NYT, Oct. 17, 1966, p. 1.

537   begged the tavern keepers of Baltimore: NYT, Oct. 5, 1966, p. 51.

537   tea at the governor's mansion: NYT, Oct. 15, 1966, p. 15.

537   "we could win the war in Vietnam": NYT, Oct. 14, 1966, pp. 1, 18, 20.

537   "FDR passed five major bills": Dallek, *Flawed,* pp. 335–39.

538   Nicholas Katzenbach had just left: Katzenbach oral history by Paige Mulhollan, Nov. 23, 1968, pp. 1–2, LBJ. Katzenbach's photograph in Saigon at the end of the scouting trip appears on the front page of the Oct. 12, 1966, NYT.

538   complaints to Jewish War Veterans: "Jewish War Plea Vexes President/ Opposition to Vietnam Aims Proves Worry to Johnson," NYT, Sept. 11, 1966, p. 4; "Jewish Leaders Deny Johnson Linked Israel and War Support," NYT, Sept. 13, 1966, p. 4.

538   "Goldberg Mollifies Jews": NYT, Sept. 15, 1966, p. 1; "Goldberg Backs Right of Dissent/ He Says Criticism 'Can Only Benefit' Foreign Policy," NYT, Nov. 7, 1966, p. 4.

538   "If Abraham had no hesitation": *Nation,* Sept. 26, 1966, pp. 268–69.

538   invitations to visit Israel and Jordan: Dora McDonald to Bayard Rustin, Aug. 31, 1966, with attached press item about a planned MLK pilgrimage of "5,000 Negroes" to holy sites in Israel and Jordan, A/KP20f37.

538   "I implore all of you to remember": Bayard Rustin reading a draft letter, from the wiretap transcript of a conference call with MLK, Stanley Levison, Harry Wachtel,

Ralph Hellstein, Clarence Jones, Cleveland Robinson, Lawrence Reddick, and Walter [Fauntroy?], 11:45 P.M., Sept. 6, 1966, FLNY9-1054a.

538   Rustin drafted instead: Freeman, *Mule Train,* p. 456; White House memo, Clifford Alexander to Harry McPherson ("Bayard Rustin called today . . ."), Oct. 3, 1966, MLK Name File, Box 144, LBJ.

538   "racial justice by democratic process": NYT, Oct. 14, 1966, p. 27.

538   Still, King resisted entreaties: Garrow, *Bearing,* pp. 532–33; D'Emilio, *Lost Prophet,* p. 456.

539   "Dr. King Weighing Plan": NYT, Oct. 10, 1966, p. 1.

539   "Crisis and Commitment": NYT, Oct. 14, 1966, p. 35.

539   "7 Negro Leaders Issue": Ibid., p. 27. The seven signers were Roy Wilkins, Whitney Young, A. Philip Randolph, Dorothy Height, Bayard Rustin, Amos T. Hall of the Prince Hall Masons, and Hobson Reynolds, Grand Exalted Ruler of the Elks.

539   He carefully reprised his written critiques: Garrow, *Bearing,* p. 533.

539   "Violence as a strategy for social change": MLK, "Nonviolence: The Only Road to Freedom," *Ebony,* Oct. 1966, cited in Washington, ed., *Testament,* pp. 54–61.

539   "King Endorses Racial Statement": NYT, Oct. 15, 1966, p. 14.

540   "a serious misstep": Garrow, *Bearing,* p. 534.

540   Wiretapped phone lines buzzed: HQ LHM dated Oct. 17, 1966, FK-NR; NY LHM dated Oct. 17, 1966, FK-NR.

540   Rustin called Stanley Levison: Wiretap transcript, 2:40 P.M., Oct. 15, 1966, FLNY9-1093a.

540   "Bayard did this to us": Wiretap transcript of a telephone conversation between Andrew Young and Stanley Levison, 3:10 P.M., Ibid.

540   "What bothers me": Wiretap transcript of a telephone conversation between MLK and Stanley Levison, 4:14 P.M., Ibid.

540   McNamara and Katzenbach: Sheehan, *Bright,* pp. 628–31. Sheehan notes that Daniel Ellsberg, who in 1971 would disclose the historic Pentagon Papers on Vietnam, was assigned to Katzenbach for this trip as a Defense Department staff adviser.

540   After only thirty-six hours home: McPherson, *Political,* pp. 303–16; NYT, Oct. 18, 1966, pp. 1, 16.

540   "I know that I can wave no wand": LBJ departure statement, Dulles International Airport, Oct. 17, 1966, Department of State Bulletin, Nov. 6, 1966, p. 698.

540   "a little less pessimistic": McNamara to LBJ, Oct. 14, 1966, in FRUS, Vol. 4, pp. 727–35; Gravel, ed., *Pentagon Papers,* Vol. 4, pp. 348–54.

540   infiltration up threefold: Ibid.; also CIA intelligence memorandum to LBJ, Nov. 5, 1966, in FRUS, Vol. 4, pp. 801–4.

540   "has if anything gone backward": McNamara, *In Retrospect,* pp. 262–63. Quoting this memo in his 1995 memoir, McNamara revised its description of "the important war," pacification, from a quest "for the complicity of the people" in the 1966 original to one "for the [hearts and minds] of the people." This tiny shift covered up a strange and perhaps telling choice of the term "complicity" rather than consent as the desired political stance for the Vietnamese.

540   "the unceasing, backbreaking toil": Katzenbach to LBJ, Oct. 15, 1966, in FRUS, Vol. 4, pp. 746–52. The acronyms in Katzenbach's quotation stand for the following: MACV (Military Assistance Command, Vietnam), USAID (United States Agency for International Development), JUSPAO (Joint United States Public Affairs Office), GVN (Government of [South] Vietnam), ARVN (Army of the Republic of [South]

Vietnam), PF (Popular Forces), RF (Regional Forces), PFF (Police Field Forces), CIDG (Civilian Irregular Defense Group), PAT (Political Action Team), RD (Revolutionary Development).

541 "non-group": Katzenbach oral history by Paige Mulhollan, Nov. 23, 1968, pp. 19–21, LBJ.

541 neglected outlook of ordinary Vietnamese: More than three decades later, in his collection of Vietnamese and American war memories, author Christian Appy amplified Katzenbach's point about the gaping hole in public attention during the conflict: "No subject was more strikingly inaccessible than the experience of ordinary Vietnamese on all sides." Appy, *Patriots,* p. 239.

541 "Charlie zapped a slick": Radio interview by Dick Hubert, Nov. 21, 1966, in Fall, *Reflections,* pp. 27–28.

541 found Rev. Robert Spike bludgeoned: "Theologian, a Rights Advocate, Slain at Ohio State," NYT, Oct. 18, 1966, p. 28.

541 the family received telegrams: Spike, *Photographs,* pp. 187–88, 215–220.

541 News stories reviewed: "Robert Spike: The Movement Loses a Voice," SC, Oct. 29–30, 1966, p. 5.

541 "one of the best thinkers": "Prof Was Famed Rights Leader/ Murder Shocks Colleagues Thruout U.S.," *Chicago's American,* Oct. 18, 1966, File 940, RS, CHS.

541 "the last thing": Int. Jack Pratt, March 25, 1991.

542 "This staggers my mother": Spike, *Photographs,* pp. 223–25.

542 Mother and son fought an undertow: Ibid., pp. 135–37, 171–82.

542 church officials shut down inquiry: Int. Jack Pratt, March 25, 1991; int. James Hamilton, July 30, 1991.

542 Willful avoidance sealed Spike: Findlay, *Church People,* p. 176.

542 Andrew Young always feared: Young, *Burden,* pp. 472–73. Stokely Carmichael's posthumous memoir of 2003 lists Spike with King, Malcolm X, Robert Kennedy, and several other victims marked by lingering allegations of political conspiracy, in Carmichael, *Ready,* pp. 436–37.

542 with Spike's internecine rivals: In a haunted memoir about his father, Paul Spike records that Art Thomas of the Delta Ministry shared far-fetched suspicions even of Office of Economic Opportunity director Sargent Shriver, who in 1966, under pressure from Mississippi politicians, undercut a Mississippi movement poverty program that Robert Spike vigorously defended. Spike's trenchant criticisms of the Labor Department report on the Negro family also generated a feud with Daniel Moynihan, who tried to enlist the White House on his side. "Spike has been a leader of the effort to discredit me, which has been an organized effort," Moynihan wrote Harry McPherson. "The people involved in this are precisely those persons who have been the most vicious about the President and Viet Nam." Moynihan to McPherson, April 15, 1966, McPherson Papers, Box 21, LBJ; Spike, *Photographs,* pp. 199–204; [on the Mississippi poverty dispute] Greenberg, *Devil,* passim, especially pp. 601–25.

542 prosecutors considered him insane: NYT, Dec. 13, 1966, p. 15; Findlay, *Church People,* p. 176.

542 A harbinger series: Dick Hebert, "Atlanta's Lonely 'Gay' World," AC, Jan. 2–8, 1966.

542 "would cut off their left arms": Ibid., Jan. 7, 1966, p. 1.

542 Richard Nixon captured: NYT, Oct. 24, 1966, p. 1.

542 "playing the backlash issue": Transcript, *Meet the Press,* Vol. 10, No. 43, Oct. 23, 1966, courtesy of NBC News.

543   "as a fugitive": Powers, *War*, pp. 208–9.

543   "that's what *they* do": Tom Wolfe, "The Electric Kool-Aid Acid Test," in Library of America Anthology, *Reporting Vietnam*, pp. 198–207; Gitlin, *Sixties*, p. 209.

543   "turn on, tune in": "Dr. Leary Starts New 'Religion' with 'Sacramental' Use of LSD," NYT, Sept. 20, 1966, p. 33.

543   a Yellow Submarine prop: DeBenedetti, *Ordeal*, p. 161.

543   teach-in activist Jerry Rubin: Menashe and Radosh, eds., *Teach-Ins*, pp. 28–32; Zaroulis and Sullivan, *Who Spoke Up?*, pp. 84–85.

543   "in the Marxist tradition": *Rolling Stone Rock Almanac*, p. 126.

543   "a major cultural-political watershed": Dallek, *Right Moment*, p. 223.

543   call to old-fashioned morality: Ibid., pp. 190–91.

543   repeal the state's fair housing law: NYT, Aug. 14, 1966, p. 43.

544   "Every day the jungle": Dugger, *On Reagan*, p. 199.

544   "orgies so vile": Cannon, *President Reagan*, p. 148.

544   recruit ex-CIA Director John McCone: " 'White Backlash' Becomes a Major Coast Issue/ It Helps Reagan Even When He Doesn't Mention It, His Supporters Say," NYT, Sept. 28, 1966, p. 28.

544   "appeasement of campus malcontents": Reagan speech of Sept. 9, 1966, cited in Seth Rosenfeld, "The Governor's Race," *San Francisco Chronicle,* June 9, 2002.

544   "dresses like Tarzan": Gitlin, *Sixties*, p. 217.

544   telegram to Stokely Carmichael: Edwards, *Reagan*, pp. 168–69.

544   "hell, no": "Carmichael Asks Draft's Defiance/ Ridicules Johnson and Rusk at Rally in Berkeley," NYT, Oct. 30, 1966, p. 63.

544   Lyndon Johnson landed: "Johnson Is Home, 'More Confident' on Goals in Asia," NYT, Nov. 3, 1966, p. 1.

544   longest presidential trip in history: Dallek, *Flawed*, p. 384.

544   two white kangaroos: NYT, Nov. 3, 1966, p. 14.

544   bath from a silver spigot: McPherson, *Political*, p. 310.

544   since FDR at Casablanca: *U.S. News & World Report,* Nov. 7, 1966, pp. 19–20.

544   favorable rating on Vietnam to 63 percent: Dallek, *Flawed*, p. 385.

544   "could last five years": "Nixon Criticizes Manila Results," NYT, Nov. 4, 1966, p. 1; Powers, *War*, p. 131.

544   "chronic campaigner": "Johnson Derides Nixon's Criticism of Manila Stand," NYT, Nov. 5, 1966, pp. 1, 10.

544   Johnson canceled plans: Transcript of news conference, Question 10, ibid.; Edwards, *Reagan,* p. 169; Shesol, *Contempt,* pp. 346–47.

545   "I was the song leader": LBJ remarks, Nov. 7, 1966, PPP, 1966, pp. 1347–50; "Johnson Given Tests; Surgery Due Friday," WP, Nov. 8, 1966, pp. 1, 4.

545   meticulous observance of state law: Cf. John Hulett letters of notice to Judge Harrell Hammonds and the Alabama secretary of state, August 30, 1966, and Judge Harrell Hammonds letter of acknowledgment dated September 2, 1966, Box 1, A/RM; legal presentation by lawyer Morton Stavis at the twenty-fifth anniversary of the 1965 Selma march, in Selma, March 3, 1990.

545   5,806 names: Carmichael, *Black Power,* p. 112.

545   "We have enough registered people": Michael S. Lottman, "High Hopes in Lowndes," SC, Nov. 5–6, 1966, p. 1.

545   "We have never tried": Jeffries, "Freedom Politics," p. 127.

545   Carmichael no longer lived: J. M. McFadden, "Real Test Nears for Original 'Black Panther,' " WP, Sept. 18, 1966, p. 3.

545   deferred to local citizens: Cf. Robert Analavage, "What They're Saying in Lowndes County," SP, Oct. 1966, p. 3; Viola Bradford, "Freedom Candidates Campaign in Lowndes," SC, Oct. 22–23, 1966, p. 1.

545   "The help they have given us": SC, Nov. 5–6, 1966, p. 1.

545   observing a SNCC policy: Minutes of the central committee meeting, Knoxville, Oct. 22 and 23, 1966, p. 5, A/SN6.

545   arrested with Stuart House: "Selma Court Fines SNCC Worker $77," SC, Nov. 26–27, 1966, p. 1.

545   "I saw some Negroes aroused": "City of Selma vs. Carmichael: A Wild Day in Recorder's Court," SC, Dec. 3–4, 1966, p. 1; "Carmichael Gets 60-Day Sentence," NYT, Nov. 30, 1966, p. 23.

546   final mass meeting Monday night: Viola Bradford, "Lowndes," SC, Nov. 12–13, 1966, p. 1; Carmichael, *Black Power,* pp. 114–15.

546   "PULL THE LEVER": SC, Nov. 19–20, 1966, p. 1; int. Jennifer Lawson, Nov. 13, 2004.

546   "We have worked so hard": John Benson, "Freedom Party Wins Legal Ballot Status in Lowndes County Vote," *Militant,* Nov. 21, 1966.

546   His speech ranged: Terence Cannon, "Lowndes County," *Movement,* Dec. 1966, pp. 1, 8, 9; Sellers, *River,* pp. 152–54; Jeffries, "Freedom Politics," pp. 129–33.

546   On election day in Lowndes: Ibid.; Carmichael, *Black Power,* pp. 116–17; *Militant,* Nov. 21, 1966.

546   Driver Andrew Jones: Robert Analavage, "Lowndes Party Girds for Future," SP, Dec. 1966, p. 1; "Alabama Election Reports," Nov. 16, 1966, Reel 16, SNCC; Viola Bradford, "Lowndes," SC, Nov. 12–13, 1966, pp. 1, 4.

547   "cracked the hide on my head": Int. Andrew Jones, April 11, 2003.

547   "the first shot": Carmichael, *Ready,* pp. 474–75; *Movement,* Dec. 1966, p. 9.

547   Jennifer Lawson wielded: Int. Jennifer Lawson, Nov. 13, 2004.

547   Scott B. Smith wore military fatigues: Int. Scott B. Smith, April 11, 2003.

547   All seven nominees: SC, Nov. 12–13, 1966, p. 1; Jeffries, "Freedom Politics," pp. 135–38.

547   "was reflecting on him": SP, Dec. 1966, p. 1.

547   forfeited both paying jobs: Int. Andrew Jones, April 11, 2003.

547   Mark Comfort would lead: *Movement,* Dec. 1966, pp. 2, 9; Beth Wilcox, "Californians Bring Supplies to 'Brothers, Sister' in Lowndes," SC, Sept. 9–10, 1967, p. 7.

547   "Even though we lost": SC, Nov. 19–20, 1966, p. 1.

547   always expected to lose: Ibid.

547   "I think the cat did well": *Militant,* Nov. 21, 1966.

548   "We have a party now": SC, Nov. 19–20, 1966, p. 1.

548   no more than a token presence: Carmichael report in minutes of the central committee meeting, Oct. 23, 1966, p. 6, A/SN6; int. Silas Norman, June 28, 2000; int. Gloria Larry House, June 29, 2000; Branch, *Pillar,* pp. 611–13.

548   A phenomenon took root: Carmichael, *Stokely Speaks,* p. 187; Hilliard and Cole, *This Side,* pp. 115–16; Huey P. Newton jail interview of March 8, 1968, in Bracey, et al., *Black Nationalism,* pp. 534–51; Carmichael, *Ready,* pp. 474–76; int. Bob Mants, Sept. 8, 2000.

548   "The Battle of Fort Deposit": Int. Mike Miller, June 24, 1994; int. Bob Mants, Sept. 8, 2000; int. Jimmy Rogers, March 8, 2000; int. Scott B. Smith, April 11, 2003; int. Jennifer Lawson, Nov. 13, 2004; postings on the SNCC e-mail exchange, sncc@honors.olemiss.edu, by Scott B. Smith and by Michael (Wright) Oshoosi, March 15, 2002, and Eric Morton, March 16, 2002.

548   "propensity toward violence": Director to New York, Chicago, Cleveland, Detroit, Los Angeles, Mobile, Newark, Philadelphia, and Washington field offices, Sept. 9, 1966, FBPA-8. "Information available to the Bureau concerning formation of a Black Panther Party by Max Stanford, a New York Revolutionary Action Movement (RAM) leader, would indicate a completely separate organization is contemplated by Stanford," wrote Hoover. "Due to the propensity toward violence by Stanford and other RAM members as well as indications that Stokely Carmichael has offered to help Stanford to organize a New York based Black Panther Party, this matter should receive intensive investigative efforts. . . . There does not appear to be any actual connection between the Lowndes County Freedom Organization, a legitimate political party, and the formation of a Black Panther Party in New York by Stanford."

RAM had been founded in 1963 by the expatriate NAACP leader Robert Williams, on a platform that Stanford described as "revolutionary nationalism, black nationalism or just plain blackism." Stanford and Carmichael had known each other in New York, but quarreled in 1966 over what Carmichael thought was a surreptitious effort by Stanford to infiltrate SNCC with rigid RAM ideology. Cf. Tyson, *Radio Free,* pp. 290, 297; Bracey et al. *Black Nationalism,* pp. 508–17; Carson, *Struggle,* p. 261; Carmichael, *Ready,* pp. 567–69.

548   Beginning that fall: Marable, *Race,* p. 121.

548   "I don't think I lost": Handwritten notes of LBJ remarks by Bill Moyers, undated, [Nov. 1966], Office of the President, Box 8, LBJ.

549   net loss to Republicans: NYT, Nov. 10, 1966, p. 1; Mary White Ovington, "The National Association for the Advancement of Colored People, *Journal of Negro History,* Vol. 9, 1924, p. 339; Edwards, *Reagan,* p. 176.

549   "I just don't have the answer to it": NYT, Nov. 11, 1966, p. 18.

549   "It'll move beyond George Wallace": Lemann, *Promised,* p. 196.

549   "He *used* to be a liberal": "Wallace Doubts Reagan's Beliefs," NYT, Nov. 10, 1966, p. 30.

549   Reagan deflected instant clamor: "Reagan Emerging in 1968 Spotlight," NYT, Nov. 10, 1966, p. 1.

549   "very flattering that anyone": NYT, Dec. 1, 1966, p. 1.

549   won by 993,739 votes: Edwards, *Reagan,* pp. 171–72.

549   "It seems to be all over": Ibid.

549   He discounted white backlash: NYT, Nov. 10, 1966, p. 29; AC, Nov. 10, 1966, p. 7.

550   "For me," said Reagan: Edwards, *Reagan,* p. 176.

550   only 5 percent of the black vote: Ibid.; NYT, Nov. 19, 1966, p. 30.

550   "Whether we like it or not": Matusow, *Unraveling,* p. 214.

550   "unequivocal stand in favor": NYT, Nov. 9, 1966, p. 29; NYT, Nov. 6, 1966, p. 60.

550   18,000 patronage jobs: Cohen and Taylor, *Pharaoh,* pp. 426–27, 484.

550   troublemaker bent on creating backlash: *Chicago Tribune,* Nov. 2, 1966, p. 1; NYT, Nov. 2, 1966, p. 25.

550   "There were only certain suggestions": Cohen and Taylor, *Pharaoh,* p. 427.

550   "idea of affirmative action": Ibid., p. 146.

550   400,000 to 470,000 troops: McNamara to Joint Chiefs of Staff, Nov. 11, 1966, and McNamara to LBJ, Nov. 17, 1966, in Gravel, ed., *Pentagon Papers,* Vol. 4, pp. 364–78.

551   "leveling off": Ibid.; McNamara, *In Retrospect,* p. 263.

551   5,000 of the 6,644: NYT, Jan. 6, 1967, p. 2; Zaroulis and Sullivan, *Who Spoke Up?,* p. 98; DeBenedetti, *Ordeal,* p. 160.

551   filched from other Pentagon accounts: Cf. McNamara's explanation of war financing to LBJ: "But what I'm doing is taking money that I had planned to use, let's say, next April and May, for one purpose and drawing it forward now for another purpose. This is all legal, but it means that I've got a clear deficit condition developing next year." LBJ phone call with Robert McNamara, 9:48 A.M., June 16, 1966, Cit. 10241, Audiotape WH6606.04, LBJ.

551   supplemental appropriation of $12.4 billion: Powers, *War,* p. 157; FRUS, Vol. 4, p. 850ff.

551   prices had jumped 125 percent: National Intelligence Estimate, Dec. 15, 1966, in FRUS, Vol. 4, p. 942.

551   "Runaway inflation can undo": McNamara to General Earle Wheeler, Chairman, Joint Chiefs of Staff, Nov. 11, 1966, in ibid., pp. 826–27.

551   asked for an income tax surcharge: NYT, Jan. 11, 1967, p. 1; Johnson, *Vantage,* p. 446.

551   "stand firm": Karnow, *Vietnam,* p. 516.

551   "melancholy law of human societies": Dallek, *Flawed,* p. 449.

551   reintroduced the failed omnibus: Graham, *Civil Rights Era,* p. 267.

551   "intensify our efforts": Johnson, *Vantage,* p. 82.

551   every word the late President Kennedy said: LBJ to Bob Kintner, Nov. 24, 1966, and Fred Panzer response to Jake Jacobsen, Nov. 26, 1966, WE9, Box 28, LBJ.

551   economists compiled impressive statistics: HEW Secretary John Gardner to LBJ, Dec. 28, 1966, and "The War on Poverty: An Overall View," Dec. 27, 1966, WE9, Box 28, LBJ.

551   stalled at roughly $1.5 billion: Dallek, *Flawed,* p. 404.

551   "The poor will feel": Powers, *War,* p. 156.

551   Rustin's freedom budget: "10-Year Plan Aims at Poverty's End/ Rights, Religious and Labor Leaders Ask $185-Billion U.S. 'Freedom Budget,' " NYT, Oct. 27, 1966, p. 1.

551   fell dormant with its plan: D'Emilio, *Lost Prophet,* pp. 431–35.

551   Martin Luther King discreetly complained: Clifford Alexander to LBJ, Jan. 11, 1967, MLK Name File, Box 144, LBJ.

551   "Our work was just beginning": Johnson, *Vantage,* p. 82.

552   "the best minds are now": Henry H. Wilson, Jr., to LBJ, Dec. 10, 1966, WE9, Box 28, LBJ.

552   "You have a tired cabinet": Harry McPherson to LBJ, Dec. 19, 1966, McPherson Papers, Box 7, LBJ.

552   "I think it is unfair to take your leader": Tom Johnson to LBJ, Dec. 22, 1966, with attached meeting notes of Dec. 21, 1966, Tom Johnson Notes, Box 1, LBJ; Dallek, *Flawed,* p. 390.

552   "A miasma of trouble": Johnson, *Diary,* p. 469.

552   retreat on the coastal island: Garrow, *Bearing,* pp. 536–37; Power, *I Will,* pp. 3–5.

552   James Lawson and Ira Sandperl conducted: SC, Nov. 26–27, 1966, p. 3.

552   "The only time I have ever been hit": Power, *I Will,* p. 17.

552   Rival factions loyal to Bevel and Hosea Williams: Int. Hosea Williams, Oct. 29, 1991; int. Willie Bolden, May 14, 1992; int. James Bevel, May 13, 1985; int. Frank Soracco, Sept. 13, 1990; int. Andrew Young, Oct. 26, 1991; int. Bernard Lafayette, May 28, 1990.

552   "Dr. King, we love you": Int. Hosea Williams, Oct. 29, 1991.

553   "Remember, we are a nonviolent organization": Power, *I Will,* p. 14.

553   "All right, forget it": Garrow, *Bearing,* n. 14, p. 382.

553   King rebuked Andrew Young: Young, *Burden,* pp. 416–17.

553   On Monday evening, November 14: Garrow, *Bearing,* pp. 536–37; Fairclough, *Redeem,* pp. 324–27.

553   "Whether I have anything to say or not": Transcript, "Dr. King's Speech," Nov. 14, 1966, A/SC28f26.

554   David Garrow later identified: David J. Garrow, "Where Martin Luther King, Jr. Was Going: *Where Do We Go from Here* and the Traumas of the Post-Selma Movement," *Georgia Historical Quarterly,* Vol. 75, No. 4, Winter 1991, p. 726.

554   "While this period represented": Transcript, "Dr. King's Speech," Nov. 14, 1966, A/SC28f26.

555   "All that I have said boils down": Branch, *Pillar,* pp. 542–43.

555   "Now Hosea, I want you to hear this": Transcript, "Dr. King's Speech," Nov. 14, 1966, A/SC28f26.

556   a radical leap in the language of steadfast commitment: Fairclough, *Redeem,* pp. 324–25; Lewis, *King,* p. 364. Authors Fairclough and Lewis interpret the change as a shift within King, away from optimism. My view is that King had been realistic about race in the North at least since graduate school in Boston, and that the agenda for his last years reflected adverse trends in national politics more than a change in his core beliefs.

556   "about the 50-yard line": Ibid.

556   Andrew Young returned: Young, *Burden,* pp. 417–18; *Jet,* Dec. 15, 1966, p. 5.

557   "scared to death": Wiretap transcript of telephone conversation among Stanley Levison, Andrew Young, and Dora McDonald, 12:11 P.M., Dec. 1, 1966, FLNY-9-1140a; New York LHM dated Dec. 6, 1966, FSC-1694.

557   Operation Shredder: Oren, *Six Days,* pp. 33–35.

557   cancel his visit to the region in 1967: Wiretap transcript of telephone conversation between Stanley Levison and Rev. Moore, 9:18 P.M., Nov. 23, 1966, FLNY-9-1132a; wiretap transcript of telephone conversation between Stanley Levison and MLK, 7:48 P.M., Nov. 30, 1966, FLNY-9-1139a.

557   relief of Jews persecuted in the Soviet Union: Cf. Rabbi Israel Miller to MLK, Nov. 11, 1966, with attached telethon script in MLK's handwriting dated Dec. 11, 1966, A/KS.

557   Stanley Levison thought it would take genius: Wiretap transcript of telephone conversation among Stanley Levison, Andrew Young, and Dora McDonald, 12:11 P.M., Dec. 1, 1966, FLNY-9-1140a; New York LHM dated Dec. 6, 1966, FSC-1694.

557   "hammering at black power": Wiretap transcript of telephone conversation between Stanley Levison and Adele [LNU], Dec. 21, 1966, FLNY-9-1160a.

557   "calls him 'brother Marx' ": Ibid.

558   "too subtle to dramatize": Remarks to the Chicago staff of the American Friends Service Committee, Dec. 4, 1966, in Ralph, *Northern,* p. 233.

558   "was certainly far stronger": Ralph, *Northern,* p. 170; Lewis, *King,* pp. 352–53.

558   The Metropolitan Chicago Leadership Council for Open Housing: Cohen and Taylor, *Pharaoh,* p. 422; cf. "Realty Men Weigh Appeal in Chicago," NYT, Aug. 6, 1967, p. 42.

558   "We should have known better": Abernathy, *Walls,* pp. 362–63.

558   "I knew he had to fall": D'Emilio, *Lost Prophet,* p. 455.

559   "Great White Switch": Black and Black, *Rise,* p. 205.

559   "The beginning of the modern rise": Lemann, *Promised,* p. 200.

559   "He was a liberal": Dallek, *Right Moment,* pp. 238–39.

33: SPY VISIONS

PAGE

563   *Bond v. Floyd:* Fred P. Graham, "Supreme Court Voids Refusal of Georgia House to Seat Bond," NYT, Dec. 6, 1966, p. 1; *Bond v. Floyd* (385 U.S. 116); Neary, *Julian Bond,* pp. 140–41; Morgan, *One Man,* pp. 160–61.

563   "We are not persuaded": "Supreme Court Upholds Bond," AC, Dec. 6, 1966, pp. 1, 9.

563   "Fight in Congress to Bar Powell": NYT, Dec. 1, 1966, p. 1.

563   "Powell's Just Too Blatant": WP, Jan. 8, 1967.

564   third such case recently discovered: Cf. *Black v. United States* (385 U.S. 26), at 26; "Baker Aide Sues U.S. for Bugging by FBI," NYT, Feb. 25, 1967, p. 12; "FBI Ordered to Release Bugged Data on Tax Case," NYT, Feb. 24, 1968, p. 15.

564   "U.S. Reviews Cases": NYT, Dec. 1, 1966, p. 1.

564   "an issue of great emotion": Nicholas Katzenbach oral history by Paige E. Mulhollan, Nov. 12, 1968, p. 36, LBJ.

564   "As you know, this is a damn important matter for me": RFK to Katzenbach, handwritten, July 13, 1966, RFK Senate Papers, Box 5, Corr: Personal File 64-68, JFK; Schlesinger, *Robert Kennedy,* pp. 817–18.

564   managed to trace and shut down: Garrow, *FBI and King,* pp. 178–79; Dallek, *Flawed,* pp. 408–9; Nicholas Katzenbach oral history by Paige E. Mulhollan, Nov. 12, 1968, p. 45, LBJ.

564   "You got that little situation prohibited?": LBJ phone call with Nicholas Katzenbach, 9:15 P.M., July 15, 1966, Cit. 10410-11, Audiotape WH6607.02, LBJ.

565   frayed beyond civil respect: Int. Nicholas Katzenbach, June 14, 1991; Kalman, *Abe Fortas,* p. 316.

565   "We do not obtain authorization": Sullivan to DeLoach, July 19, 1966, Section 36, FHOC. Hoover's handwritten instruction appears at the end of the memo: "No more such techniques must be used."

565   "I note that requests": Hoover to Tolson and DeLoach, Jan. 6, 1967, Section 36, FHOC.

565   to ask Teamsters president Jimmy Hoffa: Garrow, *FBI and King,* p. 179; "Informative Note," Nov. 3, 1966, FSC-1628; SAC, New York, to Director, Nov. 3, 1966, FSC-1626; NYT, Nov. 8, 1966, p. 23.

565   Hoover authorized Deke DeLoach: Baumgardner to Sullivan, Oct. 28, 1966, FK-2779.

565   Katzenbach had left in place: LBJ phone call with Nicholas Katzenbach, 9:15 P.M., July 15, 1966, Cit. 10410-11, Audiotape WH6607.02, LBJ.

565   "Yike, does it really say that?": Wiretap transcript of telephone conversation between Stanley Levison and Clarence Jones, Nov. 8, 1966, FLNY-9-1117a.

565   an embarrassed Hoffa: LHM dated Nov. 14, 1966, FK-2775; DSS to Tolson, Nov. 14, 1966, FK-2780.

565   "our counterintelligence aim to thwart": Wick to DeLoach, Nov. 9, 1966, FK-2771.

566   harness satellite communications technology: Friendly, *Circumstances,* pp. 302, 308–25; Kabaservice, *Guardians,* pp. 276–77; Dallek, *Flawed,* p. 296; McGeorge Bundy, "The President's Review," Ford Foundation Annual Report 1966, pp. i–xi.

566   "full equality for all American Negroes": NYT, Aug. 3, 1966, p. 19; Kabaservice, *Guardians,* pp. 167–68, 277.

566   Bundy quietly hired two of their contacts: Int. Clarence Jones, Oct. 25, 2004. The Ford Foundation contacts were Douglas Pugh and Michael Miller.

566   grant negotiations progressed: Cf. wiretap transcripts of telephone conversations among Stanley Levison, Clarence Jones, Andrew Young, and Martin Luther King dated July 21, 1966 (FLNY-9-1007), Oct. 1, 1966 (FLNY-9-1079), Oct. 11, 1966 (FLNY-9-1089), Oct. 18, 1966 (FLNY-9-1096).

566   virtually to join the SCLC staff: Cf. wiretap transcript of Stanley Levison's telephone conversations with Mike Miller of the Ford Foundation, Nov. 23, 1966 (FLNY-9-1132a), MLK, Dec. 6, 1966 (FLNY-9-1145), Joan Daves, Dec. 6, 1966 (FLNY-9-1145), Clarence Jones, Dec. 11, 1966 (FLNY-9-1149a), MLK, Dec. 12, 1966 (FLNY-9-1151).

566   rescue the movement's financial base: Wiretap transcript of telephone conversation between Stanley Levison and Martin Luther King, July 12, 1966, FLNY-9-998a; Robert L. Green to MLK, July 16, 1966, A/SC47f10; *Jet,* Jan. 19, 1967, p. 46.

566   "I don't want five million dollars": Wiretap transcript of telephone conversation between Stanley Levison and Andrew Young, Oct. 15, 1966, FLNY-9-1093a.

566   DeLoach recruited an intermediary: Sullivan to Baumgardner, Oct. 24, 1966, reprinted in Hearings, House Select Committee on Assassinations, Vol. 6, pp. 279–80.

566   "I personally feel that Bundy": DeLoach to Tolson, Oct. 26, 1966, FSC-NR.

566   "We would get nowhere": Handwritten notation on ibid.

566   confidential mission with DeLoach: Int. Cartha A. DeLoach, June 1, 1984.

567   H. R. Gross to sign: Gross to Hoover, Dec. 5, 1966, Pearson file, Box G273, LBJ. DeLoach said his office drafted Gross's letter to Hoover as well as Hoover's reply, both for Hoover's advance approval.

567   Hoover's ad hominem reply: Hoover to H. R. Gross, Dec. 7, 1966, Pearson file, Box G273, LBJ.

567   "Hoover Asserts Robert Kennedy": NYT, Dec. 11, 1966, p. 1.

567   Kennedy offered a statement of rebuttal: Ibid., p. 84.

567   counterattack at precisely 2:25 P.M.: Wick to DeLoach, Dec. 12, 1966, FRFK-1893.

567   "absolutely inconceivable": FBI news release, Dec. 11, 1966, FRFK-1801; NYT, Dec. 12, 1966, p. 1.

567   "for the use and assistance": Director SAC letter marked "Personal Attention," Dec. 15, 1966, FRFK-1896.

567   gave way to sensational headlines: Hoover to the Acting Attorney General (Ramsey Clark), Dec. 23, 1966, FRFK-1894; WSJ, Dec. 22, 1966; "Who Knew About 'Bugging' . . . RFK's Story—and the FBI's," *U.S. News & World Report,* Dec. 26, 1966, pp. 32–35.

567   "a town which relishes": Robert Cahn, "Wiretap Dispute Flares," *Christian Science Monitor,* Dec. 13, 1966.

567   "President Aloof in Bugging Feud": Max Frankel, NYT, Dec. 13, 1966; Miller, *Lyndon,* pp. 568–69.

567   bombarded with FBI allegations: Hoover to White House aide Marvin Watson, Dec. 29, 1966, FRFK-1897; Hoover to the Acting Attorney General (Ramsey Clark), Dec. 19, 1966, FRFK-1892.

567   DeLoach brief Justice Fortas: Kalman, *Abe Fortas,* pp. 315–16.

567   "forty or fifty of them": LBJ phone call with Ramsey Clark, 11:39 P.M., July 13, 1966, Cit. 10407-08, Audiotape WH6607.01, LBJ.

567   "nobody in Washington could be sure": James Reston, "Washington: The Kennedy-Hoover Controversy," NYT, Dec. 14, 1966, p. 14.

567   Senate hearings on poverty, in which King cited: Garrow, *Bearing,* pp. 539–40.

568   "The error alone": MLK testimony in "Federal Role in Urban Affairs," hearings before the U.S. Senate Subcommittee on Executive Reorganization, Committee on Government Operations, Dec. 15, 1966, pp. 2967–99.

568   dialogue about why nonviolence: Ibid., pp. 2990–95.

568   "Dr. King 'Assumes' Phone Is Tapped": NYT, Dec. 15, 1966, p. 64.

568   Stanley Levison said: SAC, New York, to Director, Dec. 16, FK-2804; wiretap transcript of telephone conversation between Stanley Levison and Chauncey Eskridge, Dec. 16, 1966, FLNY-9-1155; Branch, *Parting,* pp. 833–41.

568   "When you have a guy": Wiretap transcript of telephone conversation between Stanley Levison and Harry Wachtel, Dec. 22, 1966, FLNY-9-1161a.

568   "the biggest publishing story": Thomas, *Robert Kennedy,* pp. 330–32; "Widow Dismayed by Kennedy Book," NYT, Dec. 11, 1966, p. 1; "Mrs. Kennedy Will Seek an Injunction," NYT, Dec. 15, 1966, p. 1.

568   forthcoming book on the Kennedy assassination: Manchester, *Death;* Dallek, *Flawed,* pp. 520–22; Schlesinger, *Robert Kennedy,* pp. 817–22.

568   remove his opening chapter: Manchester moved an abbreviated hunting story to page 118.

568   "to suppress my bias": Shesol, *Contempt,* p. 355.

568   Gossip oozed into the press: Cf. "Growing Rift of LBJ and Kennedys," *U.S. News & World Report,* Jan. 2, 1967, pp. 22–27; "Manchester Recounts Battle," WP, Jan. 23, 1967.

568   President Johnson fulminated to Fortas: Shesol, *Contempt,* pp. 355–59.

568   "I don't think I called Mrs. Kennedy": LBJ phone call with Bill Moyers, 10:17 A.M., Dec. 26, 1966, Audiotape K66.02, LBJ.

569   Moyers had just resigned: NYT, Dec. 15, 1966, p. 1.

569   push Moyers closer to Robert Kennedy: Miller, *Lyndon,* p. 556; Johnson, *Diary,* p. 469; "T.R.B. from Washington," *New Republic,* Dec. 24, 1966.

569   Harrison Salisbury: Salisbury, *Behind;* FRUS, Vol. 4, pp. 973–74.

569   "The cathedral tower looks out": Harrison E. Salisbury, "U.S. Raids Batter 2 Towns; Supply Route Is Little Hurt," NYT, Dec. 27, 1966, pp. 1, 3.

569   denounced the reports and then conceded: Neil Sheehan, "Washington Concedes Bombs Hit Civilian Areas in North Vietnam," NYT, Dec. 27, 1966, p. 1; Powers, *War,* pp. 171–72.

569   *Washington Post* impugned: "Hanoi Dispatches to Times Criticized," NYT, Jan. 1, 1967, p. 3; "Harrison Salisbury's Dastardly War Crime," *I. F. Stone's Weekly,* Jan. 6, 1967, pp. 1, 4; Karnow, *Vietnam,* pp. 503–4.

569   Jack Ruby: Manchester, *Glory,* p. 1272; Manchester, *Death,* p. 634.

569   first conspiracy indictment: Max Holland, "The Demon in Jim Garrison," *Wilson Quarterly,* Spring 2001, pp. 10–17.

570   Operation Cedar Falls: "Allies Press Attack," NYT, Jan. 13, 1967, p. 6; Schell, *Village, passim;* Karnow, *Vietnam,* pp. 454, 477–78; Appy, *Patriots,* pp. 202–9.

570   weekly record at 1,194: NYT, Jan. 20, 1967, p. 1.

570   "North Vietnam Spirit Found High": NYT, Jan. 15, 1967, pp. 1, 42.

570   drive to bar Adam Clayton Powell: "Democrats Vote to Oust Powell As House Committee's Chairman/ He May Be Kept from Seat Today," NYT, Jan. 10, 1967, p. 1; "Powell Denied House Seat Pending Five-Week Inquiry/ Vote Is 364–64," NYT, Jan. 11, 1967, p. 1; Jacobs, *Powell,* pp. 6–7.

570   "documents proving Bobby was lying": Jones to Wick, Jan. 10, 1967, FACP-NR.

570   *"None* of this misinformation": Hoover statement, "FBI Use of Electronic Listening

Devices," Jan. 10, 1967, before the Subcommittee on Administrative Practice and Procedure, Committee of the Judiciary, U.S. Senate, Section 129, FHOC (emphasis in original).

570   Robert Kennedy had signed: Ibid., p. 27.

570   He conflated wiretaps with bugs: Ibid., pp. 9, 30.

570   He argued at length that Kennedy: Ibid., pp. 15–35.

570   small portion of his private lodestar: Ibid., p. 10.

570   "It is quite clear that in the *Irvine* case: Brownell to Hoover, May 20, 1954, reprinted in Macy and Kaplan, *Documents,* pp. 41–43. See also Belmont to Boardman, May 21, 1954 (Section 114, FHOC), which announces the FBI's practical interpretation of the memo: "the Attorney General is giving us the go ahead on microphones whether or not there is trespass at the same time suggesting that discretion be used in certain areas."

571   William Manchester scarcely mentioned: Manchester, *Death,* p. 631.

571   "The Director told Manchester": DeLoach to Mohr, June 4, 1964, FRFK-1536.

571   straw polls from a 53–47 percent Kennedy lead: Shesol, *Contempt,* pp. 363–64.

571   Walter Lippmann asked whether Kennedy: Thomas, *Robert Kennedy,* pp. 354–55.

571   "a man of compassion": "Kennedy Defends Johnson on Poor," NYT, Dec. 13, 1966, p. 1.

571   "grave reservations": Shesol, *Contempt,* p. 363; "Kennedy Charms Oxford Students," NYT, Jan. 29, 1967, p. 6; "Aide Terms White House Puzzled by Kennedy Remark on the War," NYT, Jan. 31, 1967, p. 3.

571   he coldly advised Kennedy not to ruin: Schlesinger, *Robert Kennedy,* p. 824; int. William vanden Heuvel, Dec. 15, 2004.

572   "affectionate, admiring": Alsop to "Bobby," Feb. 1, 1967, RFK/Senate Correspondence, Personal File, Box 1, JFK. Alsop's letter summarized: "All this is merely intended to lead up to the observation that, for practical reasons, you really must give more weight to the support of what people call the 'establishment' than I think you do."

572   turn military victory: Joe Alsop, "The Biggest News," WP, Feb. 1, 1967, and "An End in Sight," WP, Feb. 3, 1967, columns attached to ibid.

572   Kennedy confronted a tempest: "Kennedy Sees President; Denies Bringing 'Feelers,' " NYT, Feb. 7, 1967, p. 1; Schlesinger, *Robert Kennedy,* pp. 825–28; Shesol, *Contempt,* pp. 363–66; Dallek, *Flawed,* pp. 447–48; Thomas, *Robert Kennedy,* pp. 332–33.

572   "a perfectly ridiculous episode": Nicholas Katzenbach oral history by Paige E. Mulhollan, Nov. 23, 1968, pp. 27–29, LBJ.

572   Kennedy saw an unstable warmonger: Allard Lowenstein oral history by Larry J. Hackman, April 23, 1969, pp. 55–56, JFK.

572   battered second for each contender: Nicholas Katzenbach oral history by Paige E. Mulhollan, Nov. 12, 1968, pp. 34–37, LBJ; Katzenbach oral history by Larry J. Hackman, Oct. 8, 1969, p. 48ff, JFK; int. Nicholas Katzenbach, June 14, 1991.

572   The play *MacBird!:* Mel Gussow, "Much Ado About Mac," *Newsweek,* Feb. 27, 1967, p. 99.

573   "At each male birth": Ibid.

573   "Two opposing Americas": Robert Brustein, "MacBird on Stage," *New Republic,* March 11, 1967, pp. 30–32; Nicholas Tomalin, "MacBird!—A British View," *National Review,* June 27, 1967, pp. 702–3.

573   "total catharsis of satire": *Newsweek,* March 6, 1967, p. 79.

573   "a crackpot consensus": NYT, Feb. 23, 1967, p. 38.

573   "The cruelty and vulgarity": "Off Broadway," *New Yorker*, March 11, 1967, p. 127.

573   refused a theater advertisement: NYT, April 5, 1967, p. 72.

573   conference in upstate New York: Forman, *Making*, pp. 475–79; Carson, *Struggle*, pp. 236–38; Sellers, *River*, pp. 178–82; Lyon, *Memories*, pp. 174–76; Fleming, *Soon*, pp. 178–81.

573   unwise to contest black solidarity: Int. Dorothy Zellner, Dec. 12, 1991; int. James Forman, Feb. 13, 2001; int. Jack Minnis, April 8, 2001; int. Ivanhoe Donaldson, June 30, 2000; int. Jennifer Lawson, Nov. 13, 2004; int. Kwame Ture (Stokely Carmichael), Jan. 31, 1984; Carmichael, *Ready*, pp. 566–71; Greenberg, ed., *Circle*, pp. 168–69.

574   Peg Leg Bates Country Club: Cf. NYT, Dec. 8, 1998, p. 28.

574   herded suddenly to a concrete bunker: "Hanoi During an Air Alert; Waitresses Take up Rifles," NYT, Dec. 28, 1966, p. 1.

574   delegation sponsored by peace groups: NYT, Dec. 17, 1966, p. 5; NYT, Dec. 24, 1966, p. 8; NYT, Dec. 26, 1966, p. 3; DeBenedetti, *Ordeal*, pp. 169–70.

574   "There are no innocent civilians": *Chicago Tribune*, Jan. 9, 1967, p. 3.

574   companion Barbara Deming: NYT, Jan. 10, 1967, p. 5; NYT, Jan. 11, 1967, p. 1; McWhorter, *Carry*, p. 386.

574   "President Ho did not ask us": Robinson, *Abraham*, pp. 218–19.

575   Nash delayed her return: NYT, Jan. 18, 1967, p. 9; NYT, Jan. 21, 1967, p. 3; *Jet*, Jan. 12, 1967, p. 51.

575   antiwar mobilization planned for spring: Cf. minutes of the Spring Mobilization Committee to End the War in Vietnam, Jan. 3, 1967, Jan. 9, 1967, and Jan. 13, 1967, all in Mobe Papers, Series 1, Box 1, SCPC; Dellinger, *From Yale*, pp. 275–77.

575   watching a load of diapers: Int. James Bevel, Aug. 13, 1992.

575   peculiar sign favoring the protest job: Wells, *War Within*, p. 116.

575   deadline to produce a book manuscript: "Dr. King Will Write Book During Leave," NYT, Dec. 14, 1966, p. 42; wiretap transcript of telephone conversation between Stanley Levison and Tom Offenburger, Dec. 20, 1966, FLNY-9-1159a.

575   three thousand words a day: Wiretap transcript of telephone conversation between MLK and Stanley Levison, 1:05 P.M., Jan. 5, 1967, FLNY-9-1175a.

575   showdown over Adam Clayton Powell: Cf. wiretap transcript of telephone conversation between Stanley Levison and Clarence Jones, 8:04 P.M., Jan. 6, 1967, FLNY-9-1176a.

575   "From my personal relationships": Wiretap transcript of telephone conversation between MLK and Stanley Levison, 12:38 A.M., Jan. 9, 1967, FLNY-9; SAC, New York, to Director, Jan. 9, 1967, FK-2814.

575   "unpalatable as it is": Wiretap transcript of telephone conversation between Stanley Levison and Bernard Lee, 11:28 P.M., Jan. 8, 1967, FLNY-9-1178a.

575   telegram of personal sympathy: *New York Post*, Jan. 13, 1967, p. 3; wiretap transcript of telephone conversation between Stanley Levison and Adele Kanter, 1:05 P.M., Jan. 13, 1967, FLNY-9-1183a.

575   King agreed with Levison: Wiretap transcript of telephone conversation between MLK and Stanley Levison, 8:40 P.M., Jan. 5, 1967, FLNY-9-1175a.

575   Lowenstein already had told him: Wiretap transcript of telephone conversation between MLK and Stanley Levison, 1:05 P.M., Jan. 5, 1967, FLNY-9-1175a.

576   dropped the word segregation: "Maddox Sounds Moderate Note," NYT, Jan. 12, 1967, pp. 1, 22.

576   "I see you finally got your seat": NYT, Jan. 14, 1967, p. 29.

576   " 'Weak-kneed' Wilkins": WP, Jan. 11, 1967, p. 1; NYT, Jan. 14, 1967, p. 29.

576   "Because Adam will turn right around": Wiretap transcript of telephone conference call among MLK, A. Philip Randolph, Bayard Rustin, Andrew Young, Stanley Levison, and Ralph Abernathy, 8:28 A.M., Jan. 14, 1967, FLNY-9-1184.

576   Ocho Rios on the coast of Jamaica: Garrow, *Bearing,* pp. 542–43; NYT, Jan. 16, 1967, p. 22; wiretap transcript of telephone conversation between Stanley Levison and [rewrite assistant for MLK's book] Hermine Popper, 9:40 A.M., Jan. 14, 1967, FLNY-9-1184.

576   "I don't like Chicago": "Dr. King Plagued by Resistance and Apathy in Chicago Slums," Jan. 16, 1967, p. 22.

576   "I mean the movement is entitled": Wiretap transcript of telephone conversation between MLK and Stanley Levison, 1:05 P.M., Jan. 5, 1967, FLNY-9-1175a; wiretap transcript of telephone conversation between Andrew Young and Stanley Levison, 12:27 P.M., Jan. 17, 1967, FLNY-9-1187a.

576   "I got so upset about it": Wiretap transcript of telephone conference call among MLK (from Jamaica), Stanley Levison (from New York), and Andrew Young and Ralph Abernathy (from Chicago), 3:05 P.M., Jan. 19, 1967, FLNY-9-1189a.

576   "Bevel is here": Int. Bernard Lee, June 19, 1985.

576   "Why are you teaching nonviolence": Int. James Bevel, Aug. 13, 1992.

577   on January 19: Ibid.; Garrow, *Bearing,* p. 543; Young, *Burden,* pp. 425–26.

577   "Bevel sounds like he's off his rocker": Wiretap transcript of telephone conference call among MLK (from Jamaica), Stanley Levison (from New York), and Andrew Young and Ralph Abernathy (from Chicago), 3:05 P.M., Jan. 19, 1967, FLNY-9-1189a.

577   "A million children": William F. Pepper, "The Children of Vietnam," with preface by Dr. Benjamin Spock, *Ramparts,* Jan. 1967, pp. 44–67; Zaroulis and Sullivan, *Who Spoke Up?,* pp. 104–5. Pepper cites the work of veteran war correspondent Martha Gellhorn, whose article, "Suffer the Little Children," appeared the same month in *Ladies' Home Journal,* reprinted in Library of America Anthology, *Reporting Vietnam,* pp. 287–97.

577   No food would taste good: Garrow, *Bearing,* p. 543; int. Bernard Lee, June 19, 1985.

577   "Thich Nhat Hanh offers": MLK to Nobel Institute, Jan. 25, 1967, www.iamhome.org/mlkletter.htm.

577   Al Lowenstein pursued many avenues: Chafe, *Never,* pp. 251–52; Powers, *War,* p. 178; Coffin, *Once,* pp. 209–23.

577   open letter from fifty Rhodes Scholars: "War Aim Questioned by Rhodes Scholars," NYT, Jan. 27, 1967, p. 1; Bob (Spearman) to Lowenstein, with London press release of Jan. 27, 1967, Folder 106, Box 54, AL, UNC.

577   "Student Leaders Warn President": NYT, Dec. 30, 1966, p. 1.

577   "Well, somebody's going to get hurt": Wells, *War Within,* pp. 118–19; Kabaservice, *Guardians,* pp. 298–99.

577   "462 on Yale Faculty": NYT, Jan. 16, 1967, p. 8.

577   Reinhold Niebuhr to make a declaration: "Niebuhr Calls for an End to the War in Vietnam," NYT, Jan. 19, 1967, p. 4; Niebuhr letter to the NYT, March 14, 1967, p. 46.

577   Robert McAfee Brown: Int. Robert McAfee Brown, July 1, 1991.

578   two thousand religious leaders gathering: Friedland, *Lift Up,* pp. 177–81; int. Richard Fernandez, Jan. 10, 1991; draft address by Eugene J. McCarthy, Feb. 1, 1967, Series 3, Box 8, CALCAV, SCPC. Background documents on the CALCAV mobilization include minutes of the Sept. 27, 1966, executive committee meeting, Series 1, Box 1, CALCAV, SCPC; Richard Fernandez memo of Oct. 4, 1966, Series 3, Box 8, CAL-

CAV, SCPC; Richard Fernandez memo of Dec. 21, 1966, Series 2, Box 2, CALCAV, SCPC.

578   250 Catholic bishops: Robert McAfee Brown, "An Open Letter to the U.S. Bishops," *Commonweal,* Feb. 17, 1967.

578   McNamara parried them: Hall, *Because,* pp. 33–38; Coffin, *Once,* pp. 224–29; int. John Bennett, Sept. 15, 1990; int. William S. Coffin, July 16, 1991; int. Robert McAfee Brown, July 17, 1991. Along with Heschel, Coffin, and Brown, the CALCAV delegation to McNamara consisted of Union Theological Seminary president John Bennett, Rabbi Jacob Weinstein of Chicago's Temple KAM, Catholic layman Michael Novak, and Lutheran priest Richard John Neuhaus.

578   Andrew Young relieved Bernard Lee: Wiretap transcript of telephone conversation between Stanley Levison and Dora McDonald, Feb. 3, 1967, FLNY-9-1204a.

578   Levison warned King: Wiretap transcript of telephone conversation between MLK and Stanley Levison, Feb. 4, 1967, FLNY-9-1205a.

578   "unable to comprehend their opportunity": Daniel P. Moynihan, "The President and the Negro: The Moment Lost," *Commentary,* Feb. 1967, p. 32.

578   "An era of bad manners": Ibid., p. 45.

578   King transferred his book operation: Garrow, *Bearing,* p. 544.

578   abruptly felled A. J. Muste: Robinson, *Abraham,* pp. 218–23.

578   "the American Negro might never": Ibid., p. 5.

579   "Though he slay me": Ibid., p. 192 (Job 13:15).

579   "If it does not have the spiritual connection": Ibid., p. 113.

579   King initiated a conference call: Wiretap transcript of telephone conference call among MLK and Andrew Young (from Miami), Stanley Levison (from New York City), and Cleveland Robinson (from New Rochelle, NY), 12:13 P.M., Feb. 18, 1967, FLNY-9-1219a; New York LHM dated Feb. 21, 1967, FK-2836.

579   Levison persuaded him to nestle: Ibid. Levison had recommended earlier that King accept the February 25 speaking invitation from Carey McWilliams of the Nation Institute. Wiretap transcript of telephone conversation between MLK and Stanley Levison, 1:05 P.M., Jan. 5, 1967, FLNY-9.

579   conference at the Beverly Hilton Hotel: Garrow, *Bearing,* pp. 545–46; Los Angeles LHM dated March 1, 1967, FK-NR.

579   "We should hesitate to waste": NYT, Feb. 26, 1967, p. 10.

579   "For nine years we vigorously supported": MLK address to the Nation Institute, "The Casualties of the War in Vietnam," Feb. 25, 1967, A/SC28f33.

580   "Dr. King Advocates": NYT, Feb. 26, 1967, p. 1.

34: RIVERSIDE

PAGE

581   Wharlest Jackson punched off duty: "Negro Leader Killed by Blast in Natchez," NYT, Feb. 28, 1967, p. 1; *Jet,* March 16, 1967, pp. 16–24; SC, March 4–5, 1967, p. 1; Dittmer, *Local People,* p. 417.

581   Perry Wallace of Vanderbilt: Fitzpatrick, *Walls,* pp. 232–39.

581   bomb ruined the new Head Start: NYT, March 14, 1967, p. 35.

581   Wharlest Jackson's murder would remain unsolved: Bullard, *Free,* pp. 94–95.

581   confessed the random murder of Ben Chester White: Ibid., pp. 92–93; NYT, April 7, 1967, p. 22; NYT, April 12, 1967, p. 51.

581   "Jury Told of Plot": NYT, April 8, 1967, p. 7.

582   reindictment that same February 27: NYT, Feb. 28, 1967, p. 40; McIlhany, *Klandestine,* p. 71; Mars, *Witness,* p. 225.

582   "has done more toward destruction": Transcript, WLBT, *Ten O'Clock News,* March 29, 1967, exhibit in Case 16663, Vol. 9, FCC.

582   political drama climaxed on March 1: "House Excludes Powell, 307–116; Rejects Inquiry's Censure Move, Overriding Two Parties' Leaders," NYT, March 2, 1967, p. 1; Jacobs, *Powell,* pp. 209–31; Hamilton, *Adam Clayton Powell,* pp. 461–63; Coleman, *Adam Clayton Powell,* p. 125; Haygood, *King,* pp. 357–59.

582   A few defenders objected: Remarks of Rep. John Conyers, *Congressional Record,* March 1, 1967, pp. 5004–5008; remarks of Rep. Elmer J. Holland, ibid., pp. 5028–29; Hamilton, *Adam Clayton Powell,* p. 462.

582   Gerald Ford coyly observed: *Congressional Record,* March 1, 1967, pp. 5018–19; Jacobs, *Powell,* pp. 210, 228–29.

582   threatened to impeach: Jacobs, *Powell,* p. 66.

582   "Mr. Speaker, I have a reasonably strong stomach": *Congressional Record,* March 1, 1967, p. 5012; Hamilton, *Adam Clayton Powell,* p. 462.

582   Only Drew Pearson: Drew Pearson and Jack Anderson, "Powell Accuser Had Long Police Record," WP, Feb. 14, 1967, p. B11. Washington physician Montague Cobb, uncle of SNCC's Charlie Cobb, scolded Pearson in a letter of February 17: "It seems to me that this comes a little late. Since you must have known these things all along it was hardly fair to keep bludgeoning Adam while you withheld the other side."

582   Powell refused to pay the libel judgment: Branch, *Parting,* pp. 314–16; Haygood, *King,* pp. 252–55.

582   Esther James had a record: Ibid.; Haygood, *King,* pp. 252–55, 319–22.

582   nor the select committee: Int. Ronald Goldfarb (counsel, select committee on Powell), May 16, 1991.

582   ten extraordinary House speeches: Branch, *Parting,* pp. 314–16; Branch, *Pillar,* pp. 41–46. Powell reviewed and extended his description of underworld corruption in a speech during King's Selma campaign, *Congressional Record,* Feb. 18, 1965, pp. 3006–38.

583   beneficiary rather than the victim: Hamilton, *Adam Clayton Powell,* p. 457.

583   "a 66-year-old domestic": Branch, *Pillar,* p. 44.

583   Powell shrugged: *Jet,* March 9, 1967, pp. 6–12.

583   Robert Kennedy proposed to suspend the bombing: "Kennedy Asks Suspension of U.S. Air Raids on North; Administration Unmoved," NYT, March 3, 1967, p. 1; Schlesinger, *Robert Kennedy,* pp. 828–33; Shesol, *Contempt,* pp. 370–75; Thomas, *Robert Kennedy,* pp. 333–37.

583   the President tried vainly to overshadow: Ibid.; Roy Reed, "Johnson Affirms His Commitment to Helping Negro," NYT, March 3, 1967, p. 1.

583   Richard Russell promised: LBJ phone call with Richard Russell, 3:15 P.M., March 2, 1967, PNO 5, Audiotape WHF67.08, LBJ, in FRUS, Vol. 5, pp. 221–25.

583   ordered a compilation of FBI secrets: Shesol, *Contempt,* p. 132; Russo, *Sword,* pp. 400–402.

583   "backfired against his late brother": Thomas, *Robert Kennedy,* pp. 334–35; Russo, *Sword,* p. 403.

584   "prolonging the war": Schlesinger, *Robert Kennedy,* p. 833.

584   consultation at Harry Wachtel's law office: Garrow, *Bearing,* pp. 546–47; wiretap tran-

script of telephone conversation between Stanley Levison and an unidentified party, March 6, 1967, FLNY-9-1235a; int. Harry Wachtel, Nov. 29, 1983, May 17, 1990; int. Andrew Young, Oct. 26, 1991.

584 Andrew Young joked: Int. Andrew Young, Oct. 26, 1991.

584 allowed him to tell King alone: Cf. Wiretap transcript of telephone conversation between Stanley Levison and Martin Luther King, Feb. 27, 1967, FLNY-9-1228a.

584 "squabbling pacifist, socialist": Wiretap transcript of telephone conversation between Stanley Levison and Rachel [?], March 1, 1967, FLNY-9-1230a.

584 an hour late to an evening fund-raiser: Garrow, Bearing, p. 547; Drew Pearson, "RFK Aide Linked to King Fund Raising," WP, April 26, 1967, p. B-15; int. Harry Wachtel, Nov. 29, 1983; int. William vanden Heuvel, Aug. 2, 2004, and Dec. 15, 2004; MLK to "Mr. and Mrs. Carter Burton [sic]," MLK to William and Jean vanden Heuvel, Andrew Young to William and Jean vanden Heuvel, all dated March 10, 1967, A/SC38f19; wiretap transcript of telephone conversation between MLK and Stanley Levison, 11:59 P.M., March 7, 1967, FLNY-9-1236a. The fund-raiser took place at the apartment of Carter and Amanda Burden. King told Levison that he had been introduced by historian Arthur Schlesinger, Jr., and that the event had raised $50,000 for SCLC's tax-exempt American Foundation on Nonviolence. Levison advised King to be careful of one $15,000 pledge until its donor could be vouched for by Africa specialist George Hauser, warning that industrialist Charles Englehard had extensive holdings in South Africa and "could be using us to take some of the curse off him."

584 counteroffensive by Hosea Williams: Garrow, Bearing, pp. 547–48.

584 "Our staff problems": Hosea Williams to MLK, March 8, 1967, A/KP35f18.

584 abruptly canceled an appointment: Marvin Watson to LBJ, March 13, 1967, MLK Name File, Box 144, LBJ. King had requested the appointment just before his Vietnam speech in Los Angeles. Marvin Watson to LBJ, Feb. 24, 1967, MLK Name File, Box 144, LBJ.

585 1,617 American war casualties: NYT, March 10, 1967, p. 1.

585 "Discussion with Johnson Bitter": NYT, March 14, 1967, p. 3; NYT, March 20, 1967, p. 24.

585 "raided their arsenals": Shesol, Contempt, p. 375.

585 mission was to broaden: Minutes of the working committee of the Spring Mobilization, 9:00 A.M., March 10, 1967, Series 1, Box 1, MOBE, SCPC, p. 1.

585 "over-simplifier": Wiretap transcript of telephone conversation between Stanley Levison and Rachel [?], March 1, 1967, FLNY-9-1230a.

585 Bernard Lafayette and Paul Brooks: Int. Bernard Lafayette, May 28, 1990; James Bevel to Spring Mobilization Committee, March 7, 1967, Series 4, Box 6, MOBE, SCPC; minutes of the working committee of the Spring Mobilization, 8:00 P.M., March 24, 1967, Series 1, Box 1, MOBE, SCPC.

585 "way of shaking cobwebs": Halstead, Out Now!, p. 271.

585 "must take the position of the folks": NYT, Feb. 26, 1967, p. 3; NYT, Jan. 28, 1967, p. 3.

585 "emphasis on 'mass murder' ": Steering committee of New York Women Strike for Peace to James Bevel, Feb. 24, 1967, Series 3, 4, Box 5, MOBE, SCPC.

585 novel shock theater: Hall, Because, p. 32; int. Richard Fernandez, Jan. 10, 1991.

585 "Jim Bevel has scared": Richard Fernandez, executive secretary of CALCAV, to Tom Nichols, Series 2, Box 3, CALCAV, SCPC. Also Fernandez to Bevel, Feb. 27, 1967, ibid. ("Rabbi Heschel informed me that he had had a long conversation with you and from his side, it did not seem too fruitful.")

585   his contrary resolve on March 14: Andrew Young to James Bevel and Dave Dellinger, March 14, 1967 (with copies to Al Lowenstein, Norman Thomas, Benjamin Spock, Donald Keys, William Coffin, John Bennett, and Bayard Rustin), March 14, 1967, b33f408, AL, UNC; Minutes of the Working Committee of the Spring Mobilization, March 16, 1967, Series 1, Box 1, MOBE, SCPC, p. 3.

586   pitched them into disbelief: "Dr. King Will Join a Vietnam Protest on April 15 at U.N.," NYT, March 16, 1967, p. 4; int. Harry Wachtel, Nov. 29, 1983, May 17, 1990; int. Andrew Young, Oct. 26, 1991.

586   scrambled with colleagues to limit the damage: Ibid.; int. John Bennett, Sept. 15, 1990; Young, *Burden,* pp. 427–28.

586   Fernandez was an awkward career misfit: Int. Richard Fernandez, Jan. 10, 1991.

586   When interviewed in 1966: Ibid.; Hall, *Because,* pp. 26–31; Goldstein, *Coffin,* p. 70; int. Balfour Brickner, Feb. 4, 1991; int. William Sloane Coffin, July 16, 1991.

586   *"This would give us a maximum"*: Richard R. Fernandez to Andrew Young, March 21, 1967, Series 2, Box 3, CALCAV, SCPC.

586   "I lost": Wiretap transcript of Stanley Levison telephone conversation, March 24, 1967, FLNY-9-1253.

586   King departed for Chicago: "Dr. King to Press Antiwar Stand," NYT, March 24, 1967, p. 1; Ralph, *Northern,* pp. 212–14; Anderson and Pickering, *Confronting,* pp. 315–17; Garrow, *Bearing,* pp. 549–50; Cohen and Taylor, *Pharaoh,* p. 436.

587   leaving Young only a four-part outline: Wiretap transcript of telephone conversation between MLK and Stanley Levison, April 8, 1967, FLNY-9-1268a.

587   Young to farm out the drafting assignment: Int. Andrew Young, Oct. 26, 1990; int. Richard Fernandez, Jan. 10, 1991; int. Vincent Harding, Dec. 30, 2004; Garrow, *Bearing,* p. 711, note 30; Zaroulis and Sullivan, *Who Spoke Up?,* p. 42; Goldstein, *Coffin,* p. 181.

587   "I have made it clear over and over": MLK press conference, Liberty Baptist Church, Chicago, March 24, 1967, A/KS.

587   SCLC's local Operation Breadbasket: MLK speech, Operation Breadbasket meeting at Chicago Theological Seminary, March 25, 1967, A/KS.

587   A few hecklers: Investigators' reports dated March 26 and 27, 1967, File 1021, RS, CHS.

587   "This war is a blasphemy": MLK address, Chicago Peace Parade and Rally, March 25, 1967, A/KS.

587   "I don't understand it": "Ask Louis Martin why he hasn't brought him in. He's canceled two engagements with me, and I don't understand it." LBJ note dictated to Marie Fehmer, 9:30 P.M., March 24, 1967, attached to memo from DNC chairman John Criswell to Marvin Watson, March 23, 1967, and to a memo from Louis Martin to Criswell, March 23, 1967, Box 2, EX LG/PR8-1K*/DNC/PR4, LBJ.

587   Pentagon figures of March 23: Cited in "North Vietnam Under Siege," *Life,* April 6, 1967. The photograph essay on bomb damage, published a month after the death of the magazine's pro-war founder Henry Luce (NYT, March 1, 1967, p. 1), included pictures of several of the 143 American POWs then held by North Vietnam.

587   Arnold Toynbee declared victory: NYT, March 19, 1967, p. 5.

587   North Vietnam released worldwide: NYT, March 22, 1967, p. 1.

587   exchange of secret letters: LBJ to Ho Chi Minh, Feb. 8, 1967, in FRUS, Vol. 5, pp. 91–93.

587   "Vietnam is thousands of miles": Ho Chi Minh to LBJ, Feb. 15, 1967, in ibid., pp. 173–74.

588   another 200,000 soldiers: Westmoreland telegram to Admiral Ulysses Sharp, Commander in Chief, Pacific, March 18, 1967, in ibid., pp. 253–55; McNamara, *In Retrospect,* pp. 264–65.

588   "I anticipated some of this": Wiretap transcript of telephone conversation between MLK and Stanley Levison, 1:43 A.M., March 25, 1967, FLNY-9-1254; New York LHM dated March 28, 1967, FSC-1829.

588   "You can't be identified with that": Wiretap transcript of telephone conversation between MLK and Stanley Levison, 4:50 P.M., March 27, 1967, FLNY-9-1256a; New York LHM dated March 29, 1967, FK-2963.

588   Muhammad Ali: Ali, *Greatest,* pp. 163–65; Hauser, *Ali,* pp. 161–66; Remnick, *King,* pp. 288–89; Robert Lipsyte, "I'm Free to Be Who I Want," NYT Magazine, May 28, 1967, p. 28ff.

589   King escaped the tempestuous SCLC board: Agenda, SCLC board meeting, March 29–30, 1967, b53f412, AL, UNC; Abernathy to Board of Directors, March 29, 1967, A/SC58f7; MLK to Al Lowenstein, March 22, 1967, b33f408, AL, UNC.

589   meet privately with Ali: Garrow, *Bearing,* p. 550; "World Wide Protest Rips Champ's Unjust Draft Call," MS, April 7, 1967, p. 9.

589   "My position on the draft": Tape snippet, MLK and Muhammad Ali being interviewed, March 29, 1967, A/KS.

589   "Black people should seek dignity": *Jet,* April 13, 1967, p. 46.

589   publicity from Hosea Williams: Ralph, *Northern,* pp. 214–15.

589   "We can start by planning": Powers, *I Shared,* p. 151.

589   "Martin has been thinking about you": Ibid., p. 146.

590   "I had no choice": Ibid., p. 148.

590   "This is no Methodist Church!": Excerpts, SCLC board meeting, Louisville, Kentucky, March 30, 1967, Tape 147, Hosea Williams tapes collection, King Archives.

590   Hosea Williams would recall: Garrow, *Bearing,* pp. 552, 711 (note 29).

590   a weaker version passed: John Herbers, "Dr. King's Aides Score Asia War," NYT, March 31, 1967, p. 1; Morgan, *One Man,* pp. 162–63.

590   "a major policy paper": NYT, April 2, 1967, p. 76.

590   interview appeared on the front page: "Dr. King to Weigh Civil Disobedience if War Intensifies," NYT, April 2, 1967, p. 1.

590   changes past the deadline crunch: Int. Richard Fernandez, Jan. 10, 1991; int. Andrew Young, Oct. 26, 1991; int. Vincent Harding, Dec. 30, 2004; int. Barry Johnson, Jan. 4, 2005; Garrow, *Bearing,* p. 552; Hall, *Because,* p. 42; Goldstein, *Coffin,* p. 181.

590   Henry Steele Commager: John C. Bennett to Henry Steele Commager, March 22, 1967, Series 3, Box 7, CALCAV, SCPC.

590   promotional releases drew a full turnout: Fernandez to CALCAV executive committee, March 27, 1967, "Arrangements for Martin Luther King Meeting on Vietnam," March 30, 1967, and CALCAV press release dated April 2, 1967, all in Series 3, Box 7, CALCAV, SCPC; Powers, *War,* p. 161.

590   suite at the Americana Hotel: New York FBI report dated Jan. 29, 1968, SFC-NR, pp. 6–7.

590   Levison and Harry Wachtel: Int. Harry Wachtel, Nov. 29, 1983, and May 17, 1990.

591   same charged moments to absorb: Wiretap transcript of telephone conversation between MLK and Stanley Levison, 4:34 P.M., April 8, 1967, FLNY-9-1267a.

591   overflow line stretched toward 120th Street: Ibid.; NYT, April 5, 1967, p. 1; Branch, *Parting,* pp. 38–39.

591   acute foreboding sent Levison: Wiretap transcript of telephone conversation between Stanley Levison and Alice Loewi, 11:24 A.M., April 5, 1967, FLNY-9-1265.

591   "I come to this magnificent house of worship": King's prepared text for the April 4, 1967, speech at Riverside Church was distributed beforehand by CALCAV sponsors under the title "Beyond Vietnam," Series 3, Box 7, CALCAV, SCPC. The same text appears under the title "A Time to Break Silence," in Washington, ed., *Testament,* p. 231ff. The address as actually delivered, which includes new beginning and ending paragraphs, plus minor changes from the body of the text, was recorded by WRVR (Radio Riverside) and preserved in Box 23, A/KS.

592   "greatest purveyor of violence in the world": Ibid.

592   "They must see Americans as strange liberators": Ibid.

593   "The world now demands a maturity": Ibid. This phrase and those cited above come from the comprehensive twenty-two-page speech draft submitted to King by Vincent Harding, "Suggested title; *Beyond Vietnam,*" Vincent Harding Papers, courtesy of Vincent Harding.

593   "barefoot and shirtless people": Ibid. For MLK's Nobel Prize Acceptance Speech, Dec. 10, 1964, and Nobel Lecture, Dec. 11, 1964, see NYT, Dec. 11, pp. 1, 33; Washington, ed., *Testament,* p. 224ff; "Outline for Nobel Prize Lecture" in Nobel Prize speech drafts, A/KP18f33 and A/KP12f67; Branch, *Pillar,* pp. 540–43.

594   "roll down like waters": Amos 5:24.

594   "There is no one who can speak": CALCAV pamphlet, *Speak on the War in Vietnam,* 1967, p. 19.

594   "I am not aware that Dr. King": Transcript, "Question and Answer Period Following Dr. Martin Luther King's address, Riverside Church, 4/4/67," Series 3, Box 7, CALCAV, SCPC.

594   musician Robert Williams: Branch, *Parting,* pp. 60–63, 201, 312.

594   friend now euphoric with relief: Int. Robert Williams, April 3, 1984; Garrow, *Bearing,* pp. 552–53; wiretap transcript of telephone conversation between Stanley Levison and Alice Loewi, 11:24 A.M., April 5, 1967, FLNY-9-1265.

594   distorted news coverage for a rude shock: Garrow, *Bearing,* pp. 553–55; Young, *Burden,* pp. 429–30; *Jet,* April 20, 1967, pp. 8–9; Hall, *Because,* pp. 43–44.

594   "almost universal condemnation": Friedland, *Lift Up,* p. 183.

594   "any attack on you": Wiretap transcript of telephone conversation among Stanley Levison, Harry Wachtel, and MLK, 5:35 P.M., April 9, 1967, FLNY-9-1269a; "Dr. King Upheld As Critic of War/ Rabbi Notes Rights Leader Received Nobel Prize," NYT, April 23, 1967, p. 15.

594   Jewish war veterans: "Jewish War Veterans Attack Dr. King's Stand on War," NYT, April 6, 1967, p. 10.

594   pamphlet of the collected Riverside addresses: CALCAV pamphlet, *Speak on the War in Vietnam,* with "a foreword by Dr. Reinhold Niebuhr," dated April 11, 1967; Hall, *Because,* p. 43.

594   "it would help to clarify things": Wiretap transcript of telephone conversation between MLK and Stanley Levison, 1:33 P.M., April 12, 1967, FLNY-9-1272a.

594   Stanley Levison considered the speech itself: Wiretap transcript of telephone conversation between Stanley Levison and Alice Loewi, 11:24 A.M., April 5, 1967, FLNY-9-1265; Wiretap transcript of telephone conversation between Stanley Levison and Harry Wachtel, 11:03 P.M., April 6, 1967, FLNY-9-1266a.

594   "I do not think it was a good expression": Wiretap transcript of telephone conversation between MLK and Stanley Levison, 4:34 P.M., April 8, 1967, FLNY-9-1269a.

595   "What on earth can Dr. King": Frank Getlein, "Sen. Brooke—Rev. King Contrast," WS, April 5, 1967, p. 18.

595   "crown prince of the Vietniks": Harry McPherson to LBJ, 6:30 P.M., April 4, 1967, McPherson Papers, Box 14, LBJ.

595   "has thrown in with the commies": John P. Roche to LBJ, April 5, 1967, White House Conference, Box 56, LBJ.

595   called King to argue in detail: Clifford L. Alexander, Jr., to LBJ, 5:07 P.M., April 7, 1967, EX SP2-4/1967, LBJ; int. Clifford Alexander, Dec. 17, 2004.

595   Alexander and others mobilized: Ibid.; Garrow, Bearing, pp. 554–56; George Christian to LBJ, 12:30 P.M., April 8, 1967, MLK Name File, Box 144, LBJ.

595   Carl Rowan angrily told King: Rowan, Breaking, pp. 246–48; Carl Rowan, "Martin Luther King's Tragic Decision," Reader's Digest, Sept. 1967, p. 37ff.

595   "N.A.A.C.P. Decries Stand": NYT, April 11, 1967, p. 1.

595   "Bunche Disputes Dr. King": NYT, April 13, 1967, p. 1.

595   text supplied by J. Edgar Hoover: Hoover to Mildred Stegall, April 11, 1967, Box 32, OFMS, LBJ.

595   press conference at the Biltmore: Wiretap transcript of telephone conference call among MLK, Andrew Young, Stanley Levison, Ralph Abernathy, and Tom Offenburger, 10:54 A.M., April 11, 1967, FLNY-9-1271; wiretap transcript of telephone conversation between Stanley Levison (dictating) and Dora McDonald, 1:32 P.M., April 11, 1967, FLNY-9-1271a; MLK statement, Biltmore Hotel, Los Angeles, April 12, 1967, A/SC28f35; NYT, April 13, 1967, p. 32.

596   "The war in Vietnam is a much graver injustice": Transcript of MLK press conference, April 12, 1967, A/KS.

596   "I felt sorry for him": Wiretap transcript of telephone conversation between MLK and Stanley Levison, 12:55 P.M., April 13, 1967, FLNY-9-1273a.

596   promising to make clear: Ibid.; NYT, April 14, 1967, p. 21; NYT, April 26, 1967, p. 14.

596   "in every movement we have started": Wiretap transcript of telephone conversation between MLK and Stanley Levison, 8:20 P.M., April 12, 1967, FLNY-9-1272a.

596   "This was very true in Birmingham": Wiretap transcript of telephone conversation between MLK and Stanley Levison, 12:55 P.M., April 13, 1967, FLNY-9-1273a.

596   "It will be harder than Birmingham": Ibid.

596   "those who are ashamed": Young, Burden, p. 422.

597   "Many who have listened": "A Tragedy," WP, April 6, 1967, p. 20.

597   "Dr. King's Error": NYT, April 7, 1967, p. 36.

597   broke down more than once into tears: Int. Harry Wachtel, Nov. 29, 1983; Wofford, Kennedys and Kings, p. 223; Young, Burden, p. 429; Garrow, Bearing, p. 554.

597   U.S. marshals escorted him: NYT, April 10, 1967, p. 13.

597   ballroom of the Hotel Heidelburg: NYT, April 11, 1967, p. 18.

598   "We have children": Hearings, U.S. Senate Subcommittee on Unemployment, Manpower, and Poverty, April 10, 1967, Y4.L11/2:P86/4/pt.2, p. 585.

598   "He is wrong": Ibid., p. 646ff; int. Marian Wright Edelman, March 5, 1985.

598   A few subcommittee members ventured: NYT, April 12, 1967, p. 29.

598   "What did you have for breakfast?": Jet, May 4, 1967, pp. 14–22.

598   Kennedy pushed into places: Schlesinger, Robert Kennedy, pp. 854–55; Stein, Journey, pp. 278–79; Dittmer, Local People, pp. 382–88; Shesol, Contempt, pp. 329–30; Thomas, Robert Kennedy, pp. 339–40; int. Edwin King, June 26, 1992.

598   "have been implemented in the best way": WLBT television news footage, April 11, 1967, Tape 3414/F2469, MDAH.

598 All nine members of the subcommittee: Joseph S. Clark et al. to LBJ, April 27, 1967, RFK Senate Papers, Subject File Hunger, 4/67-5/67, Box 59, JFK.

599 "I cannot agree with you more": RFK to MLK, April 28, 1967, RFK Senate Papers, Subject File Hunger, 4/67–5/67, Box 59, JFK.

599 Rabbi Heschel: Wiretap transcript of telephone conference call among MLK, Stanley Levison, and Harry Wachtel, 6:18 P.M., April 9, 1967, FLNY-9-1269a.

599 "I don't want to be up on that stage": Ibid.

599 "and I know that scared the hell": Wiretap transcript of telephone conference call among MLK, Stanley Levison, Harry Wachtel, Andrew Young, Harry Belafonte, and Cleveland Robinson, 6:28 P.M., April 12, 1967, FLNY-9-1272a.

599 Stanley Levison persuade King to adjust: Wiretap transcript of telephone conversation between MLK and Stanley Levison, 8:20 P.M., April 12, 1967, FLNY-9-1272a.

599 His revision sheltered: Wiretap transcript of telephone conversation between Stanley Levison and Clarence Jones, 10:46 A.M., April 14, 1967, FLNY-9-1274; wiretap transcript of telephone conversation between Stanley Levison and Harry Wachtel, 12:42 A.M., April 14, 1967, FLNY-9-1275. Levison complained to Wachtel that King was relying too much on Al Lowenstein, who was a newcomer to the team of speech contributors.

599 King flew overnight: Ibid.; MLK itinerary, April 1967, A/SC47f20.

599 April 15 Mobilization: Zaroulis and Sullivan, *Who Spoke Up?,* pp. 98, 111–14; Powers, *War,* pp. 181–83; Dellinger, *From Yale,* pp. 284–86; Wells, *War Within,* pp. 132–35; Williams, *King God Didn't Save,* p. 104; Hall, *Because,* p. 44; minutes of the working committee of the Spring Mobilization, 8:00 P.M., March 30, 1967, Series 1, Box 1, MOBE, SCPC; int. Ivanhoe Donaldson, Nov. 30, 2000.

600 "Stop the bombing!": Garrow, *Bearing,* pp. 556–57; King speech, April 15, 1967, A/KS; Marvin Watson to LBJ, April 19, 1967, MSF, LBJ.

600 singer's assistant expressed chagrin: Wiretap transcript of telephone conversation between Stanley Levison and Gloria Cantor, 12:40 P.M., April 17, 1967, FLNY-9-1277a.

600 "Dr. King, yesterday you led": Transcript, *Face the Nation,* Vol. 10, No. 16, April 16, 1967, A/KP6f25.

600 Press disputes clouded: Mike McGrady, "The Press and the Protest," *Newsday,* May 13, 1967; Wells, *War Within,* p. 133; NYT, April 16, 1967, p. 1; NYT, April 17, 1967, pp. 1, 26; NYT, April 19, 1967, p. 3; NYT, June 4, 1967, p. 49; Young, *Burden,* p. 429.

601 "F.B.I. Is Watching 'Antiwar' Effort": NYT, April 16, 1967, p. 1.

601 "would cause extreme embarrassment": Brennan to Sullivan, March 8, 1967, FK-2867.

601 reached even the prestige newspapers: Cf. "Dr. King and the War/ His Opposition to the U.S. Role in Vietnam Said to Hurt His Position As Rights Leader," NYT, April 14, 1967, p. 21; *Richmond News-Leader* editorial, "Vietnam Day," April 14, 1967; Memphis *Commercial-Appeal* editorial, "An Answer to Demonstrators," April 16, 1967; Marquis W. Childs, "Course of U.S. History Hinges on Decision by the Rev. Dr. King," *St. Louis Post-Dispatch,* May 12, 1967, p. 1.

601 "The Struggle to Sway King": WP, April 16, 1967, p. 1.

601 "is an instrument in the hands": Hoover "BY LIAISON" to Mrs. Mildred Stegall (keeper of LBJ's most sensitive papers), April 19, 1967, FSC-NR; Garrow, *FBI,* pp. 183–84.

602 "operated with far less discipline": DeLoach, *Hoover's FBI,* p. 218.

602 to announce Vietnam Summer: "Dr. King Starts Peace Crusade," NYT, April 24,

1967, p. 14; press release, Vietnam Summer Committee, April 23, 1967, "Join Harvard Students Ringing Doorbells," Series C, Box 1, SCPC.

602 "I think the war in Vietnam": Transcript, Vietnam Summer press conference by MLK, Gar Alperovitz, Chester Hartman, Carl Oglesby, Benjamin Spock, Greg Craig, and Robert Scheer, April 23, 1967, Series 5, Box 13, SCPC. The folder includes telegrams of support for Vietnam Summer from Archbishop Paul J. Hallinan of Atlanta, Robert McAfee Brown, Abraham Heschel, and Sam Brown of the National Student Association.

602 founding of Negotiation Now: "Dr. King and A.D.A. Aide Join New Group for Vietnam Peace," NYT, April 25, 1967, p. 16.

602 reporters besieged King about news leaks: Ibid.; "Dr. King Declines Peace Candidacy," NYT, April 26, 1967, p. 19; "Dr. King Considers Kennedy and Percy Best '68 Candidates," NYT, April 27, 1967, p. 38; press statement by MLK, April 25, 1967, A/KS.

602 "I begin to see why Spock": Wiretap transcript of telephone conversation between MLK and Stanley Levison, 12:53 P.M., April 22, 1967, FLNY-9-1282a; Library of America Anthology, *Reporting Civil Rights,* p. 585. Related conversations in the same file run from serials 1279–1285. King's aides complained about the "aggressiveness" of William F. Pepper and other leaders of the National Conference for New Politics.

602 "No senator is suggesting": "McGovern Leads a Senate Attack upon Escalation," NYT, April 26, 1967, pp. 1, 8, 9.

602 "They believe in what they are doing": "Westmoreland Tells Congress U.S. Will Prevail," NYT, April 29, 1967, pp. 1, 10; "Westmoreland Before Congress," T79:0321, MOB.

602 George Wallace declared that he would run: NYT, April 27, 1967, p. 36; Lesher, *George Wallace,* pp. 389–90.

603 "Lord, would two twenties": David Halberstam, "The Second Coming of Martin Luther King," *Harper's,* Aug. 1967, in Library of America Anthology, *Reporting Civil Rights,* p. 571.

603 "You're the most important man": Ibid., pp. 586–87; Harris, *Dreams,* p. 183.

603 agreement with Jewel food stores: Garrow, *Bearing,* p. 559.

603 three-hour stopover in Greenville: Wiretap transcript of telephone conversation between Stanley Levison and Clarence Jones, 5:40 P.M., April 27, 1967, FLNY-9-1287a; Columbia, South Carolina, LHM dated May 3, 1967, FK-2947.

603 "I really am a writer": Powers, *I Shared,* p. 160.

603 hit by rocks during sporadic demonstrations: Garrow, *Bearing,* pp. 560–61; Fairclough, *Redeem,* p. 351; NYT, April 14, 1967, p. 21; April 27, 1967, p. 36.

603 stripped Muhammad Ali of his title: "Clay Refuses Army Oath; Stripped of Boxing Crown," NYT, April 29, 1967, p. 1; Hauser, *Ali,* pp. 168–72.

603 cover story in *Sports Illustrated:* April 10, 1967, p. 30ff; May 8, 1967, p. 19ff.

603 King ran into his neighbor: Int. Vincent Harding, Dec. 30., 2004.

604 He startled Carmichael: Int. Kwame Ture (Stokely Carmichael), Jan. 31, 1984; "Dr. King Accuses Johnson on War," NYT, May 1, 1967, p. 1; Carmichael, *Ready,* p. 515.

604 "They applauded us on the freedom rides": MLK sermon, "Why I Am Opposed to the War in Vietnam," Ebenezer Baptist Church, April 30, 1967, A/KS21.

35: SPLINTERS

PAGE

605   Cleveland Sellers intercepted King: Int. Cleveland Sellers, Dec. 14, 1983.

605   "Don't let them get to you": Sellers, *River,* p. 190.

605   "Rights Leader Refuses": NYT, May 2, 1967, p. 7; "CR Workers Defy Draft in Jackson, Montgomery," SC, May 13–14, 1967, p. 1.

606   organizational disintegration already far advanced: Carson, *Struggle,* p. 251.

606   One feud snapped over car keys: Minutes, SNCC central committee meeting, March 4, 1967, pp. 4–6, A/SN6.

606   "You have been fired": Sellers, *River,* pp. 185–87.

606   "most of the equipment has been stolen": Stokely Carmichael to central committee, Jan. 19, 1967, A/SN6.

606   caught his live-in girlfriend: Sellers, *River,* pp. 178–82.

606   staff member Hubert G. Brown: Carson, *Struggle,* p. 252.

607   "Lightning hit over here": Michael S. Lottman, "Lowndes County Folks Get Plenty of Advice," SC, April 1–2, 1967, p. 5.

607   vigilante mystery stirred: Ibid.; SC, March 18–19, 1967, p. 1; SC, March 25–26, 1967, p. 1; int. Scott B. Smith, April 11, 2003; int. Jennifer Lawson, Nov. 13, 2004.

607   "Yeah, lightning": SP, May, 1967, p. 2.

607   "Black people are now serving notice": SC, March 25–26, 1967, p. 1.

607   "We'll all worship in one church": BAA, April 15, 1967, p. 1.

607   Some students at Miles College: NYT, April 5, 1967, p. 37; "Carmichael on Campus," NYT, April 14, 1967, p. IV-3; SC, Oct. 15–16, 1966, p. 1; SC, April 1–2, 1967, p. 1; SC, April 8–9, 1967, pp. 1, 5.

607   "Why are you here?": Carmichael, *Stokely Speaks,* p. 73.

608   three days of altercation: Carson, *Struggle,* pp. 245–48; "Rioting Nashville Negroes Fire on Cars, Stone Police," NYT, April 10, 1967, p. 1; NYT, April, 11, 1967, p. 16; *Jet,* April 27, 1967, p. 20ff.

608   " 'Black Power' in Nashville": NYT, April 11, 1967, p. 46.

608   to appeal his far-fetched conviction: SC, April 29–30, 1967, p. 1.

608   Commotion riveted the California Assembly: "Armed Negroes Enter California Assembly in Gun Bill Protest," NYT, May 3, 1967, p. 24; Gitlin, *Sixties,* pp. 348–49.

609   "colossal event": Hilliard and Cole, *This Side,* p. 122.

609   "We don't give up our guns": Ibid., pp. 122–23.

609   outside a crack cocaine house: Ibid., pp. 1–17, 432–38; Huey P. Newton biography, Africawithin.com; Stanley Crouch, "Huey Newton, R.I.P.," *New Republic,* Sept. 18 and 25, 1989, pp. 10–11.

609   "A Gun Is Power": NYT, May 21, 1967, p. 66.

609   introduced the poster photograph: Sol Stern, "The Call of the Black Panthers," NYT Magazine, Aug. 6, 1967, p. 10ff.

609   "The New Left Turns": NYT, May 7, 1967, p. 1; Sale, *SDS,* pp. 359–60.

610   Reagan soon would sign new firearm restrictions: NYT, July 29, 1967, p. 16.

610   "Rifle Club Sees Guns": NYT, May 7, 1967, p. 1.

610   roiling his political base: Edwards, *Reagan,* pp. 200–201; Cannon, *President Reagan,* p. 130ff; Boyarsky, *Rise,* pp. 188–92. Reagan signed the Therapeutic Abortion Act of 1967 on June 13, 1967.

610   "I had been led to believe": Boyarsky, *Rise,* p. 176.

610   "central casting anarchists": Cannon, *President Reagan,* p. 150.

610   town forum televised from London: Transcript, CBS Town Meeting of the World, May 15, 1967, Box 368, WHCF-PR, LBJ; "Town Meeting," T78:0450, MOB; Edwards, *Reagan,* pp. 221–22.

610   "stepping down": Carson, *Struggle,* p. 251; Sellers, *River,* pp. 184, 192; Carmichael, *Ready,* pp. 564–65.

611   "The white woman's not queen": SC, April 8–9, 1967, p. 5.

611   SNCC women in particular: Minutes, central committee meeting, May 1967, pp. 17–25, A/SN7f13; int. Jennifer Lawson, Nov. 13, 2004; int. Fay Bellamy, Oct. 29, 1991; int. Gloria Larry House, June 29, 2000; int. Bob Fletcher, Feb. 8, 2004.

611   Ruby Doris Smith: Fleming, *Soon,* pp. 177–78, 183–89; Forman, *Making,* pp. 479–81.

611   H. Rap Brown: Carson, *Struggle,* p. 252; SP, June 1967, p. 1.

611   no prior FBI information: Atlanta FBI report dated June 12, 1967, FSN-1281, pp. 4–8.

611   "Hopefully not": NYT, May 13, 1967, p. 20.

611   Rap Brown presided over a review: Sellers, *River,* pp. 193–97; Lyon, *Memories,* p. 140.

611   "It was difficult to get her": Minutes, central committee meeting, May 1967, A/SN7f13, p. 3.

611   "I think I have gotten over the emotional stage": Ibid., p. 31.

612   had beaten Zellner into jail with Bob Moses: Dittmer, *Local People,* pp. 110–13; Carson, *Struggle,* pp. 48–55; Branch, *Parting,* pp. 512–14.

613   "I think it is a mistake": Minutes, central committee meeting, May 1967, A/SN7f13, p. 52.

613   worst experience of her life: Int. Dorothy Zellner, Dec. 12, 1991.

613   A raw egg splattered: NYT, May 18, 1967, p. 5.

613   Spock kept vigil for three days: Zaroulis and Sullivan, *Who Spoke Up?,* p. 116.

613   jammed against locked gates: Nathaniel Davis to National Security Adviser Walt Rostow, with attached petition to LBJ signed "Delegation from the April 15th Mobilization to End the War in Vietnam," May 17, 1967, McPherson Papers, Box 28, LBJ.

613   "Bevel made numerous inflammatory remarks": Thomas L. Johns to LBJ, May 12, 1967, McPherson Papers, Box 28, LBJ.

613   The Mobilization leaders scheduled: Powers, *War,* p. 232; DeBenedetti, *Ordeal,* p. 180.

613   "Dr. King may well have": Fred Panzer to LBJ, May 19, 1967, MLK Name File, Box 144, LBJ.

613   Russell counseled that all such: Russell, "Notes on White House visit, May 12, 1967," Folder "Presidential (LBJ)," RR.

614   volunteered to inspect the southern war zone: McPherson, *Political,* p. 404.

614   "an air strike in progress": Harry McPherson to LBJ, 8:15 P.M., June 13, 1967, McPherson Papers, Box 29, LBJ.

614   first raided within the city limits of Hanoi: NYT, May 20, 1967, p. 1.

614   antiaircraft ground fire so thick: Appy, *Patriots,* pp. 212–15.

614   "The war in Vietnam is acquiring": McNamara to LBJ, "Future Actions in Vietnam," May 19, 1967, in FRUS, p. 423ff; Gravel, ed., *Pentagon Papers,* Vol. 4, pp. 169–77; McNamara, *In Retrospect,* pp. 266–71; Langguth, *Our Vietnam,* p. 445.

614   The CIA supported him: Richard Helms to LBJ, "North Vietnam Bombing," May 22, 1967, in FRUS, Vol. 5, p. 441; supplementary CIA reports cited in ibid., pp. 442–44; McNamara, *In Retrospect,* p. 238.

615   "increasingly hostage to the dead": Powers, *War,* p. 170.

615   Gamal Abdel-Nasser of Egypt closed the Straits of Tiran: NYT, May 23, 1967, p. 1; Oren, *Six Days,* pp. 82–89; Dallek, *Flawed,* pp. 425–27.

615   "the mood of the American Jewish community": Hertzberg, *Being Jewish,* p. 210; Califano, *Triumph,* pp. 204–5.

615   offered his confidential military judgment: Oren, *Six Days,* p. 110; "Johnson Backing Cautious Tactics/ Goal Is Face-Saving Means to End Aqaba Blockade," NYT, May 29, 1967, p. 2.

615   retreat at the Frogmore Center: Power, *I Will,* pp. 19–20; Garrow, *Bearing,* pp. 563–64; NYT, May 23, 1967, p. 38.

616   Jesse Jackson's office telephones: Jesse Jackson to MLK and Andrew Young, May 13, 1967, A/KP5f34.

616   "We control ourselves in public": "Frogmore Evaluation Session, Wednesday," A/SC49f13.

616   "I backed up a little when I came out": MLK Frogmore speech, May 22, 1967, A/KS.

616   King flew to Geneva: Garrow, *Bearing,* p. 565; *Jet,* June 15, 1967, pp. 26–28; NYT, May 26, 1967, p. 29; MLK statement, *Pacem in Terris* II convocation, A/KP19f8.

616   "prayer meeting": NYT, May 30, 1967, p. 6.

616   "is suffering badly because half": Wiretap transcript of telephone call between Stanley Levison and Adele Kanter, 3:32 P.M., May 31, 1967, FLNY-9-1321a.

616   Harry McPherson gamely continued westward: McPherson, *Political,* pp. 413–17; Oren, *Six Days,* pp. 145, 186.

616   preemptive Israeli strikes: Oren, *Six Days,* p. 176.

616   "War has broken out!": Ibid., p. 198.

616   jangled alive at 7:47 A.M.: Ibid., p. 196; McNamara, *In Retrospect,* pp. 278–79.

616   blow up both Muslim structures: Oren, *Six Days,* p. 246.

617   "The spirit of the army": McPherson to LBJ, June 11, 1967, History of the Middle East Crisis, Box 18, NSF, LBJ, cited in ibid., p. 307.

617   retreated pell mell across the Nile: Oren, *Six Days,* pp. 178, 305.

617   offer of sanctuary in Hanoi: Fall, *Reflections,* pp. 85–86.

617   "doomed to ignominious defeat": Oren, *Six Days,* p. 213.

617   ideological force of Pan-Arab nationalism: Ibid., p. 310.

617   For the Soviet Union: Ibid., pp. 8, 27.

617   "The whole world fell in love with us": Shipler, *Arab and Jew,* p. 142.

617   "There is great astonishment": Heschel, *Israel,* p. 5.

617   "remote to the synagogue": Hertzberg, *Being Jewish,* p. 219.

617   emergency tables: Kaufman, *Broken Alliance,* p. 201.

618   Hyman Bookbinder was struck: Int. Hyman Bookbinder, March 21, 1991.

618   "We grew so fast": Shipler, *Arab and Jew,* p. 143.

618   "I'm going to decorate my office": Kalman, *Abe Fortas,* p. 302.

618   plainly marked U.S.S *Liberty:* Oren, *Six Days,* pp. 262–71.

618   shrouded in secrecy: "Israel, U.S. Blamed in '67 Spy Ship Incident," WP, Jan. 13, 2004, p. 13; "NSA Tapes Offer Clues in '67 Attack on U.S. Spy Ship," *Baltimore Sun,* July 16, 2003, p. 1.

618   "muscular Judaism": Kaufman, *Broken Alliance,* pp. 200–202, 230–31.

618   "Both Israelis and Arabs": I. F. Stone, "Holy War," *New York Review of Books,* Aug. 3, 1967, pp. 6–14; Middleton, *I. F. Stone's Weekly Reader,* pp. 287–91.

619   "I was still afraid of Negroes": Norman Podhoretz, "My Negro Problem—And Ours," *Commentary,* Vol. 35, No. 2 (Feb. 1963), p. 93ff.

619   "Negroes Are Anti-Semitic": NYT Magazine, April 9, 1967, p. 26ff.

619   "Negroes Are Anti-Semitic": NYT Magazine, April 23, 1967, p. 28ff; "Anti-Semitic Role of Negro Is Noted," NYT, May 21, 1967, p. 114.

619   Irving Kristol traced: Kristol, *Neoconservatism, passim.*

619   extraordinary arc of Max Shachtman: Max Shachtman oral history by Stephen Chodes, Aug. 1, 1962, CU/OH; Drucker, *Max Shachtman, passim;* Isserman, *Hammer,* p. 35ff; Harrington, *Fragments,* pp. 71–77; Michael Massig, "Trotsky's Orphans," *New Republic,* June 22, 1987, pp. 18–22; Branch, *Parting,* p. 292.

619   "a brilliant red light": Drucker, *Max Shachtman,* p. 25.

619   Shachtman stunned the regulars: Int. Michael Harrington, Aug. 31 and Oct. 27, 1983; int. Irving Howe, Jan. 28, 1983; Harrington, *Fragments,* pp. 200–206.

620   made notes on Rustin's misery: Ibid.; D'Emilio, *Lost Prophet,* pp. 431–39, 442–48.

620   idolized Rustin for years: Carmichael, *Ready,* pp. 158–71, 252–58.

620   coined the word "neoconservative": Kristol, *Neoconservatism,* p. 33.

620   lending his name with Reinhold Niebuhr: NYT, May 29, 1967.

620   As he hopscotched between Cleveland and Chicago: MLK itinerary, June 1967, A/SC47f20; NYT, June 10, 1967, p. 19.

620   "the *Times* played it up": Wiretap transcript of telephone conference call among MLK, Andrew Young, Stanley Levison, and Harry Wachtel, 11:47 A.M., June 8, 1967, FLNY-9-1329.

620   "settles nothing": Wiretap transcript of telephone call between MLK and Stanley Levison, June 6, 1967, FLNY-9-1327a.

620   J. Edgar Hoover rushed to the White House: Marvin Watson to LBJ, with attached Hoover to Mildred Stegall, "BY LIAISON," June 9, 1967, OFMS, LBJ.

620   Rabbi Heschel endured mounting criticism: Int. Balfour Brickner, Feb. 4, 1991; int. Harry Wachtel, May 17, 1990; "Orthodox Jews Back U.S. on War," NYT, Nov. 25, 1966, p. 16.

620   "and now Israel faces the danger": Wiretap transcript of telephone call between Stanley Levison (quoting MLK) and Harry Wachtel, 12:10 P.M., June 11, 1967, FLNY-9-1332a.

620   several times they gathered secretly: Int. Harry Wachtel, May 17, 1990; int. John Bennett, Sept. 15, 1990; int. Balfour Brickner, Feb. 4, 1991; int. William Sloane Coffin, July 16, 1991; int. Barry Johnson, Jan. 4, 2005.

621   Heschel and the priest Daniel Berrigan: Friedland, *Lift Up,* pp. 186–87.

621   John Bennett sent Al Lowenstein: Bennett to Lowenstein, June 16, 1967, attaching Bennett to Heschel, June 15, 1967, f10f371, Collection 4340, UNC; *Christianity and Crisis,* June 26, 1967, pp. 141–42; "McGovern Backs Goals of Israel/Contrasts Mideast Situation with That in Vietnam," NYT, June 23, 1967, p. 2. Bennett's letter to Heschel acknowledged troublesome points: "Certainly it is one thing to support the government of Israel and another thing to support the Saigon government. I am reluctant to make this the main point. I do not think we should necessarily decide that a people threatened with catastrophe have to have a good government before we will help them. The situation in Vietnam, however, is such that the effort to help the nation to overcome its civil conflict turns out to be a self-defeating operation."

621   separate treatment: "Rabbi Urges U.S. Bar Israeli Deal/Asks Johnson Not to Link Vietnam to Mideast Pact," NYT, June 20, 1967, p. 20.

621   "All men are created equal": Heschel, *Israel,* p. 9.

621   "When the Egyptians": Ibid., p. 214 (citing Megillah 10b).

621   "It has given Johnson the little respite": Wiretap transcript of telephone call between MLK and Stanley Levison, June 6, 1967, FLNY-9-1327a.

621   "Before I came out here": Harry McPherson to LBJ, 8:15 P.M., June 13, 1967, Harry McPherson Papers, Box 29, LBJ.

622   "such person as has no trace whatever": *Loving Et Ux. v. Virginia,* 388 U.S. 1 (1967), at p. 5.

622   Mildred Loving's ancestry: "When Marriage Was Illegal," WP, June 15, 1992; *Jet,* June 29, 1967, pp. 18–20.

622   Virginia's appellate courts: "Va. High Court Backs Miscegenation Laws," WP, March 8, 1966, p. 1. For a vivid sample of congressional passion against miscegenation, cf. Remarks of Florida Senator William H. Milton, *Congressional Record,* March 1, 1909, p. 3480ff: "Mixture of the two races will never create a new race, but the Caucasian will be lost, for one drop of negro blood makes a negro. No matter how white the skin or straight the hair, if either party or both parties to an intermarriage have any negro blood, the resulting offspring of such union may revert and be born a child of the jungle."

622   "the corruption of blood": Ibid., at p. 7.

622   Most Americans within a generation": "Race, Sex and Forbidden Unions," NYT, Dec. 14, 2003, p. IV-4; "Bans on Interracial Unions Offer Perspective on Gay Ones," NYT, March 17, 2004, p. 16.

622   *Walker v. City of Birmingham:* 388 U.S. 307 (1967); "Dr. King Loses Plea; Faces 5 Days in Jail," NYT, June 13, 1967, p. 1.

622   grew from the pivotal Good Friday decision: Ibid.; Westin, *Trial, passim,* esp. p. 243ff; Branch, *Parting,* pp. 727–31.

622   Andrew Young noted: Wiretap transcript of telephone conference call among MLK, Andrew Young, Stanley Levison, and Harry Wachtel, 2:31 P.M., June 12, 1967, FLNY-9-1333a.

623   "entirely superior in the meantime": Westin, *Trial,* p. 249.

623   "is profoundly embarrassing": Ibid., p. 255; NYT, June 14, 1967, p. 46.

623   Prattville, Alabama jail: "Violence in Alabama," NYT, June 12, 1967, p. 88; "For the People of Prattville," SC, June 17–18, 1967, p. 1; Carson, *Struggle,* p. 254; int. (*Southern Courier* photographer) James Peppler, Jan. 24, 2005.

623   Rap Brown issued a press statement: Sellers, *River,* p. 199; SNCC press release, June 13, 1967, A/SC45f14.

623   Alabama National Guardsmen: NYT, June 13, 1967, p. 39; int. James Peppler, Jan. 24, 2005.

623   "Fault is on both sides": SC, Jan. 20–21, 1968, p. 1.

623   integrate the Supreme Court: NYT, June 14, 1967, pp. 1, 18, 32; Williams, *Thurgood Marshall,* pp. 330–31; Dallek, *Flawed,* pp. 438–42; Clifford Alexander oral history by Joe B. Frantz, Nov. 1, 1971, pp. 38–40, LBJ; *Jet,* June 29, 1967, pp. 14–16.

624   "The whole world and all people": Transcript, *Issues and Answers,* June 18, 1967, A/KS11.

624   "uncertain president": NYT, April 16, 1967, p. 3.

624   "knowing his abhorrence": Russell private notes, "White House Meeting, June 19, 1967," Folder "Presidential (LBJ)," Series XVIIIB, RR, UGA.

625   three days at Glassboro, New Jersey: FRUS, Vol. 5, pp. 521–23, 547–52.

625   U.S. battle deaths: Karnow, *Vietnam,* p. 525; Southern Methodist University, *The War in Vietnam 1965–68,* http://faculty.smu.edu/dsimon/Change-Viet2b.html.

625   "running all over the country": Wiretap transcript of telephone call between MLK and Stanley Levison, 12:50 P.M., June 24, 1967, FLNY-9-1345a.

625   published an excerpt: Martin Luther King, Jr., "Martin Luther King Defines 'Black Power,' " NYT Magazine, June 11, 1967, p. 26ff.

625   "I am opposed to violence": Transcript, *The Merv Griffin Show,* June 19, 1967, Tape 69, A/KS.

625   King argued from the book: Ibid.; King, *Where,* pp. 48–49, 64, 176–82.

626   Reviews of the book: Garrow, *Bearing,* pp. 567–68; David J. Garrow, "Where Martin Luther King Jr., Was Going: *Where Do We Go from Here* and the Traumas of the Post-Selma Movement," *Georgia Historical Quarterly,* Vol. 75, No. 4, Winter 1991, p. 719ff.

626   "return to nonviolence": NYT, July 12, 1967, p. 41.

626   "like a pre-historic relic": WP Book Week, July 9, 1967, p. 1.

626   "standing up strongly now": AC, June 27, 1967, p. 4.

626   "The Negro male, too": NYT Book Review, Sept. 3, 1967, p. 3.

626   "It is as if he is misdefining": *Commonweal,* Nov. 17, 1967, pp. 215–16.

626   "He had simply, and disastrously": "Soul Power," *New York Review of Books,* Aug. 24, 1967, p. 3ff.

626   peaked at seventy million: Jones, *Expectations,* pp. 75, 213.

626   featured the Beatles from London: Martin, *With a Little Help,* pp. 159–60.

626   music festival from Monterey: *Rolling Stone Rock Almanac,* p. 131.

626   A jury convicted Richard Speck: Breo and Martin, *Crime,* p. 439.

626   A court-martial sentenced Captain Howard Levy: NYT, June 4, 1967, p. 1.

626   "Brutality is a way of life": NYT, May 31, 1967, p. 2.

626   Attorney Charles Morgan represented Levy: Morgan, *One Man,* pp. 114–48.

627   on June 20 received the maximum sentence: NYT, June 21, 1967, p. 1; *Sports Illustrated,* July 3, 1967, p. 19; Hauser, *Ali,* p. 179.

627   official revelation of government surveillance: Morgan, *One Man,* pp. 166–82; Branch, *Pillar,* pp. 478–79.

627   A *Life* magazine story: William Lambert, "The Help-Hoffa Campaign of the U.S. Senator from Missouri," *Life,* May 26, 1967, p. 24ff.

627   "There is—or should be": "The F.B.I.'s 'Seal of Approval' ", NYT, June 2, 1967, p. 40.

627   charged with beating Grenada children: SC, June 10–11, 1967, p. 1.

627   Southern Baptists reserved judgment: NYT, June 2, 1967, p. 4; NYT, June 3, 1967, p. 31.

627   Southern Presbyterians voted: "Church Liberals Quell 2 Revolts," NYT, June 11, 1967, p. 46.

627   Northern Presbyterians completed: John Wilkinson, "Edward A. Dowey, Jr. and the Making of the Confession of 1967," *Journal of Presbyterian History,* Spring 2004, p. 5ff; Rogers, *Presbyterian Creeds,* pp. 212–19.

627   "The church, in its own life": United Presbyterian Church (U.S.A.), "The Confession of 1967," Paragraph 9:45.

627   grip of chronic alcoholic depression: Powers, *I Shared,* pp. 176–77; Young, *Burden,* p. 467; Abernathy, *Walls,* p. 479; Lewis, *King,* p. 15.

628   "I want to thank God for sleep": "Ingratitude," MLK sermon at Ebenezer Baptist Church, June 18, 1967, A/KS.

36: KING'S CHOICE

PAGE

629   "replenish their empty larders": DeLoach to Tolson, July 10, 1967, FK-NR.

629   "I assume we have to do it": Hoover's handwritten note on ibid.

629   "There is not a military stalemate": Meeting notes, Cabinet Room, 1:05–2:38 P.M., July 12, 1967, "Literally Eyes Only," Tom Johnson meeting notes, Box 1, LBJ; "Joint Chiefs Back Troop Rise Asked by Westmoreland," NYT, July 3, 1967, p. 1.

630   taxi driver John Smith: Kerner, *Report,* pp. 60–62.

630   "Racial Violence Erupts": NYT, July 13, 1967, p. 1; Kerner, *Report,* pp. 56–59.

630   "a meeting of the minds": "Generals Agree with President on Build-up Issue," NYT, July 14, 1967, p. 1.

630   state forces could handle Newark: Califano, *Triumph,* pp. 209–10; "Newark's Mayor Calls in Guard as Riots Spread," NYT, July 14, 1967, p. 1.

630   fires and generalized looting: NYT, July 15, 1967, p. 1; NYT, July 19, 1967, p. 1; Kerner, *Report,* pp. 66–69.

631   dozen spent bullets in a coffee can: "Victims' Kin Face a Lonely Future," NYT, July 19, 1967, p. 23.

631   "America's obsession with integration": NYT, July 20, 1967, p. 14.

631   Detroit police raided five "blind pigs": Kerner, *Report,* pp. 84–94.

631   "the ultimate riot": Comments of *Time* reporter Wallace Terry, Ole Miss Media Conference, April 3–5, 1987, MDAH.

631   "I got that in Germany": NYT, July 24, 1967, p. 15.

631   Ramsey Clark woke President Johnson: "The Detroit Riots Chronology," Office of the President, Box 3, LBJ.

631   "There were dark days before": Wiretap transcript of telephone conference call among MLK, Andrew Young, Stanley Levison, and Harry Wachtel, 1:20 P.M., July 24, 1967, FLNY-9-1375a; also, conference call among the same parties, 11:50 P.M., July 25, 1967, FLNY-9-1376a.

632   support federal intervention: "Dr. King Supports Troops in Detroit," NYT, July 26, 1967, p. 19.

632   "Well, I guess it's just": "Notes of the President's Activities During the Detroit Crisis, Crisis Period, 10 P.M. to 12:30 A.M., July 24, 1967," Tom Johnson meeting notes, Box 1, LBJ; Hoover to Tolson, DeLoach, and Sullivan, July 25, 1967, FCT-NR.

632   Democrats jockeyed with Republicans: "Army's Entry into Detroit; How Decision Was Made," NYT, July 30, 1967, p. 1; "Romney Accuses Johnson on Riots," NYT, Aug. 1, 1967, p. 1; Califano to LBJ, 7:30 P.M., Aug. 2, 1967, Office of the President, Box 3, LBJ; Califano to LBJ, 7:55 P.M., Sept. 11, 1967, with attached report of Vance to McNamara, Box 56, WHCF, LBJ; Dallek, *Flawed,* pp. 414–15; Califano, *Triumph,* pp. 213–20.

632   The President went on national television: NYT, July 25, 1967, p. 1.

632   Two thousand Army paratroopers: Kerner, *Report,* pp. 100–108.

632   "Two National Guard tanks ripped": Ibid., p. 104.

633   "We deplore the few who rely": NYT, July 28, 1967, pp. 1, 11.

633   toll from Newark and Detroit fell far beneath: NYT, July 29, 1967, p. 24; "U.S. Combat Loss in Vietnam Drops to Six-Month Low," NYT, Aug. 4, 1967, p. 1.

633   interrogation in a motel: Hersey, *Algiers Motel,* pp. 40–41; "Detroit Negroes Charge Atrocity," NYT, Aug. 1, 1967, p. 17.

633   "mad dogs against the people": NYT, July 26, 1967, p. 19; Dugger, *On Reagan,* p. 200.

633   stormed the Muslim mosque: NYT, July 30, 1967, p. 50; see above p. 295.

633   Eisenhower accused him of failing: Hoover to Tolson et al., 12:06 P.M., July 26, 1967, FCT-NR; NYT, July 27, 1967, p. 17.

633   Hoover called Johnson with electrifying reports: Hoover to Tolson et al., 10:35 A.M., July 25, 1967, FCT-NR; enciphered Teletype from Hoover to LBJ, DIA, WH Situation Room, 3:05 P.M., July 25, 1967, FK-NR; Hoover to LBJ, 5:30 P.M., July 31, 1967, Box 32, OFMS, LBJ; Garrow, *Bearing,* p. 570.

633   "I don't want to foreclose": Minutes of Cabinet meeting, Aug. 2, 1967, Cabinet Papers, Box 9, LBJ.

633   "a necessary phase of the black revolution": NYT, July 27, 1967, p. 18.

633   Rap Brown became famous: Carson, *Struggle,* pp. 253–56; "An Affable but Angry Rights Leader: Hubert Geroid Brown," NYT, July 28, 1967, p. 14.

633   "guerrilla war on the honkie": NYT, July 19, 1967, p. 42.

633   President Johnson called Hoover: Hoover to Tolson et al., 12:06 P.M., July 26, 1967, FCT-NR.

633   "If you give me a gun": "Burning Capital Urged, if Needed," NYT, July 28, 1967, p. 14.

633   "American as cherry pie": Ibid.; Kabaservice, *Guardians,* p. 344.

633   Some fourteen charges of incitement: Forman, *Making,* p. 504.

634   manhunt located the SNCC chairman: "Chief of S.N.C.C. Hunted by FBI," NYT, July 26, 1967, p. 1; "Leader of S.N.C.C. Seized in Virginia," NYT, July 27, 1967, p. 1.

634   "I took occasion to have a Negro Agent": Hoover to Tolson et al., 10:16 A.M., July 26, 1967, FCT-NR.

634   "We are preparing groups": FBI HQ LHM dated July 28, 1967, Box 73b, OFMS, LBJ.

634   on a televised news panel: Transcript of *Face to Face* news interview from Washington, D.C., July 28, 1967, in Washington, ed., *Testament,* pp. 394–414; NYT, July 29, 1967, p. 9.

634   harsh summer news on August 3: NYT, Aug. 4, 1967, p. 1; DeBenedetti, *Ordeal,* p. 191.

634   It provoked Johnson enough: Dallek, *Flawed,* pp. 474–75.

634   "Vietnam: The Signs of Stalemate": NYT, Aug. 7, 1967, p. 1; Maraniss, *They Marched,* p. 142. The Apple dispatch appeared beneath a front-page riot story: "Rap Brown Calls Riots 'Rehearsal for Revolution.' "

634   "The tragedy is that we are today engaged": Transcript, NBC News, *Meet the Press,* Vol. 11, No. 33, Aug. 13, 1967.

634   clarify a new strategic role: "Dr. King's Group to Restudy Role," NYT, July 11, 1967, p. 17.

634   He flew to San Francisco: Travis, *Black Chicago,* p. 166; transcript of MLK address to the National Association of Real Estate Brokers, Aug. 10, 1967, in San Francisco LHM dated Aug. 31, 1967, FK-3081.

634   "No one knows the importance": MLK address to the National Association of Radio Announcers, Atlanta, Aug. 11, 1967, tape recording courtesy of Lex Gillespie and Maurice Hundley.

635   SCLC banquet on August 14: Program, SCLC Tenth Anniversary Convention, Aug. 14–17, 1967, b33f412, AL, UNC.

635   Mayor Ivan Allen welcomed: NYT, Aug. 19, 1967, p. 12.

635   Aretha Franklin performed: *Rolling Stone Rock Almanac,* pp. 131–33.

635   "a new man in an old world": SC, Aug. 19–20, 1967, p. 1.

635   "Black Is Beautiful": NYT, Aug. 19, 1967, p. 12.

635   "A decade ago, not a single Negro": MLK address, "Annual Report of the President,"
        Aug. 16, 1967, A/KS11.

636   he could not understand a word: SC, Aug. 19–20, 1967, p. 1.

636   John Lewis stayed up all night: Int. Charles S. Johnson III by Archie E. Allen, Aug. 16,
        1968, AAP.

636   Personal disputes and alcohol: Wiretap transcript of telephone call between Stanley
        and Bea Levison, 11:40 A.M., Aug. 16, 1967, FLNY-9-1398.

636   modest rat-control bill: Dallek, *Flawed*, p. 415; Califano, *Triumph*, p. 212; "Rat Dam-
        age Is Put at Billion a Year," NYT, July 29, 1967, p. 9.

636   "Dr. King Planning Protests": NYT, Aug. 16, 1967, p. 1.

636   "Formula for Discord": NYT, Aug. 17, 1967, p. 36.

636   King's own staff confessed shock: Tom Offenburger oral history by Kay Shannon,
        July 2, 1968, RJB; int. Tom Offenburger, May 30, 1984.

637   mild public reaction to the riots: "Some at Capitol Get Heavy Mail; But Most Were
        Braced for an Avalanche of Protests That Did Not Come," NYT, July 29, 1967, p. 9.

637   King scheduled a retreat: MLK to Lowenstein, Aug. 28, 1967, b10f374, AL, UNC.

637   Levison urged King not to attend: Wiretap transcript of telephone call between MLK
        and Stanley Levison, 12:09 P.M., Aug. 22, 1967, FLNY-9-1404; Brennan to Sullivan,
        Aug. 28, 1967, FK-3075.

637   National Conference for New Politics: DeBenedetti, *Ordeal*, pp. 191–93.

637   One board member resigned: Wiretap transcript of telephone call between MLK and
        Stanley Levison, 11:36 P.M., Aug. 24, 1967, FLNY-9-1406a, regarding notice from
        board member Dick Russell.

637   "the ancient corruptions of populism": Arthur Waskow to Members of the NCNP
        Board, Aug. 17, 1967, "Vietnam Summer," Series 2, Box 5, SCPC.

637   Harvard instructor Martin Peretz: Kaufman, *Broken*, pp. 207–11.

637   "What rubs off on you": Wiretap transcript of telephone call between MLK and Stan-
        ley Levison, 4:40 P.M., July 9, 1967, FLNY-9-1360a; also, wiretap transcript of tele-
        phone call between Stanley Levison and Andrew Young, 12:10 A.M., July 10, 1967,
        FLNY-9-1361.

637   supported his notion of civil disobedience: Brennan to Sullivan, Aug. 21, 1967,
        FK-3064.

637   "Kill whitey, kill whitey": Zaroulis and Sullivan, *Who Spoke Up?*, p. 129.

637   Ralph Abernathy confided: "New Politics Convention," Chicago police surveillance
        report dated Sept. 1, 1967, File 1047, RS, CHS.

637   having resolved that calls for negotiations: Wiretap transcript of telephone conference
        call among MLK, Stanley Levison, Harry Wachtel, Andrew Young, and Walter
        Fauntroy, 9:15 P.M., Aug. 12, 1967, FLNY-9-1394a.

638   "'hate Johnson' thing": Wiretap transcript of telephone call between MLK and Stan-
        ley Levison, 4:40 P.M., July 9, 1967, FLNY-9-1360a.

638   Pickets carried banners: Clark, *Ready*, p. 75.

638   "Make way for Rap Brown!": Renata Adler, "Letter from the Palmer House," *New
        Yorker*, Sept. 23, 1967, p. 71.

638   "The black nationalists gave me trouble": Wiretap transcript of telephone call be-
        tween MLK and Stanley Levison, Sept. 1, 1967, FLNY-9-1414.

638   "afraid, worried and tired": "Convention Rally," Chicago police surveillance report
        dated Sept. 1, 1967, File 1047, RS, CHS.

638   Hyde Park Methodist Church: "Black Liberation Rally, Hyde Park Methodist
        Church," Chicago police surveillance report dated Sept. 5, 1967, File 1047, RS, CHS;

NYT, Sept. 2, 1967, p. 10; NYT, Sept. 3, 1967, p. 1; "Black Power in Action?," SC, Sept. 23–24, 1967, p. 4; "The 13 Propositions of the Black Caucus," *Militant,* Sept. 12, 1967.

638   "a thousand liberals thought": Sanford Gottlieb, "Report on the National Conference for New Politics Convention," b33f404, AL, UNC, p. 6.

638   "We are just a little tail": Ibid.; Powers, *War,* pp. 263–64; NYT, Sept. 4, 1967, p. 1.

638   "The only difference between Lyndon Johnson": Transcript, Rap Brown speech of Sept. 3, 1967, in Chicago Office FBI report dated Dec. 6, 1967, FSN-3410, p. 23ff.

638   James Forman rammed through resolutions: Powers, *War,* p. 266; "Panel on Black Liberation," Chicago police surveillance report dated Sept. 7, 1967, File 1047, RS, CHS, pp. 4–8; Forman speech of Sept. 2, 1967, to the Black Caucus of the National Conference for New Politics Convention, Reel 51, SNCC.

638   When two women moved: Evans, *Personal,* pp. 196–99.

639   "I am here to remind you": "Plenary Meeting of September 1," Chicago police surveillance report dated Sept. 5, 1967, File 1047, RS, CHS, p. 9.

639   "masochistic fascists": Adler, "Letter from the Palmer House," *New Yorker,* Sept. 23, 1967, p. 86.

639   promised to kill him if he opposed: Wiretap transcript of telephone call among Andrew Levison, Stanley Levison, and Bea Levison, 9:30 P.M., Sept. 19, 1967, FLNY-9-1432a.

639   "The organizers *are* 'the movement' ": Andrew Kopkind, "They'd Rather Be Left," *New York Review of Books,* Sept. 28, 1967, p. 3ff.

639   "Throughout the convention": Adler, "Letter from the Palmer House," *New Yorker,* Sept. 23, 1967, p. 56.

639   "I am afraid that many": Peretz to Young, Sept. 18, 1967, A/SC39f11.

639   "the most significant gathering": Zaroulis and Sullivan, *Who Spoke Up?,* p. 129.

639   thirty letters from rabbis: Wiretap transcript of telephone call between Stanley Levison and Adele Kanter, Sept. 19, 1967, FLNY-9-1432a.

639   King busily disclaimed: MLK press release beginning, "Serious distortions by the press," Sept. 2, 1967, A/KS; MLK to Morris B. Abram, Sept. 28, 1967, A/KP1f2.

640   "Coalitions are virtually impossible": Young to Dr. and Mrs. Martin Peretz, Sept. 6, 1967, A/SC39f10.

640   gathered at the Airlie House: Garrow, *Bearing,* p. 578; Hoover to Mildred Stegall, Aug. 29, 31, and Sept. 21, 1967, Box 32, OFMS, LBJ; NYT, Sept. 10, 1967, p. 40.

640   James Bevel enjoyed a prodigal's welcome: Tom Offenburger oral history by Kay Shannon, July 2, 1968, RJB.

640   celebrations turned into a strategic dispute: Ibid.; Young, *Burden,* p. 437ff; Frady, *Jesse,* p. 215ff; int. Harry Wachtel, Nov. 29, 1983; int. Joan Baez, Jan. 7, 1984; int. Marian Wright Edelman, March 5, 1985, and April 1, 2005; int. Hosea Williams, Oct. 29, 1991; int. Willie Bolden, May 14, 1992; int. James Bevel, Dec. 10, 1998.

641   how to dramatize poverty from remote: Wiretap transcript of telephone call between MLK and Stanley Levison, 12:09 P.M., Aug. 22, 1967, FLNY-9-1404.

641   gist of her idea from Robert Kennedy: Int. Marian Wright Edelman and Peter Edelman, March 5, 1985; Schlesinger, *Robert Kennedy,* pp. 937–38.

641   Historian Lawrence Reddick: Wiretap transcript of telephone call between MLK and Stanley Levison, 9:05 P.M., Jan. 20, 1968, FLNY-9-1555a.

642   "a mighty fine thing": *San Francisco Examiner,* Sept. 22, 1967, p. 6, FK-3106.

642   Secretary of State need not resign: Rusk, *As I Saw It,* pp. 579–82; McNamara, *In Retrospect,* p. 282; SC, Sept. 30–Oct. 1, 1967, p. 2.

642   several pioneer weddings: NYT, July 22, 1967, p. 11; NYT, Aug. 13, 1967, p. 31.

642   covered George Washington's portrait: Moore to Sullivan, Oct. 4, 1967, FK-3107.

642   George Bush pronounced himself satisfied: Sargent Shriver to LBJ, Sept. 15, 1967, WHCF, WE9, Box 98, LBJ; Bush floor speech of Aug. 14, 1967, *Congressional Record,* p. H22447.

642   precede every football game: SC, Aug. 26–27, 1967, p. 1.

642   convince the mild-mannered Bernard Lafayette: Int. Bernard Lafayette, May 28, 1990, March 18, 2005; MLK to Lafayette, undated, ca. Sept. 1967, A/SC4f26.

642   King and Harry Belafonte launched: Garrow, *Bearing,* pp. 578–79; San Francisco LHM dated Oct. 16, 1967, FK-3121.

642   performers even quarreled on stage: Int. Joan Baez, Jan. 7, 1984; *Rolling Stone Rock Almanac,* p. 135; Maraniss, *They Marched,* p. 313.

643   a showcase federal trial: "All-White Jury Picked as Trial of 18 in Slaying of 3 Rights Workers Begins in Mississippi," NYT, Oct. 10, 1967, p. 21.

643   "young male Negroes to sign": Ibid.; Cagin and Dray, *Not Afraid,* p. 445ff; Mars, *Witness,* p. 228ff; Whitehead, *Attack,* p. 260ff; McIlhany, *Klandestine,* p. 81ff.

643   "It was the first time that Christians": Cagin and Dray, *Not Afraid,* p. 447.

644   historic Arlington Street Unitarian: Zaroulis and Sullivan, *Who Spoke Up?,* pp. 133–34; Coffin, *Once,* pp. 238–44; Mendelsohn, *Martyrs,* pp. 173–74; Friedland, *Lift Up,* pp. 193–94.

644   "Are we to raise conscientious men": Goldstein, *Coffin,* p. 197.

644   Across the country in Oakland: Powers, *War,* pp. 236–37; DeBenedetti, *Ordeal,* p. 196; Viorst, *Fire,* p. 413.

644   a demonstration in Wisconsin: DeBenedetti, *Ordeal,* p. 196; Maraniss, *They Marched,* passim.

645   author David Maraniss: Maraniss, *They Marched,* pp. 322–28, 348–56, 363ff.

645   traced a sharp transformation: Ibid., p. 381.

645   "I'm a radical!": Ibid., p. 397.

645   "It was a brutal business": Wiretap transcript of telephone call between Stanley Levison and an unidentified party, 2:04 P.M., Oct. 21, 1967, FLNY-9-1464a.

645   King complained of a "vicious" editorial: Moore to Sullivan, Oct. 16, 1967, FK-3119; Hoover to SAC, Houston, Oct. 17, 1967, FK-3113.

645   Hoover approved: Handwritten note on Moore to Sullivan, Oct. 18, 1967, FK-3129.

645   "Midnight murder in the rural area": Whitehead, *Attack,* pp. 278–79.

645   raised finger at Deputy Sheriff Cecil Price: NYT, Oct. 19, 1967, p. 37.

646   "What I say": Cagin and Dray, *Not Afraid,* p. 449.

646   government officials braced: "Thousands Reach Capital to Protest Vietnam War," NYT, Oct. 21, 1967, pp. 1, 8; Califano, *Triumph,* pp. 198–99; Dallek, *Flawed,* pp. 487–89.

646   "are not going to run me out of town": Tom Johnson notes, LBJ meeting with Rusk, McNamara, Rostow, CIA Director Richard Helms, and Press Secretary George Christian, Oct. 3, 1967, in FRUS, Vol. 5, p. 840.

646   "You must not go down": Ibid., p. 845.

646   "If history indicts us for Vietnam": LBJ interview with Robert Manning of *The Atlantic Monthly,* cited in Dallek, *Flawed,* p. 486.

646   "Dr. Coffin, am I being tendered something?": NYT, Oct. 21, 1967, p. 8; Coffin, *Once,* pp. 244–51; Powers, *War,* pp. 193–94; Goldstein, *Coffin,* pp. 199–200.

647   "the Friday after Friday": Cagin and Dray, *Not Afraid,* p. 451.

647   "John Doar gave thanks and soon retired: Int. John Doar, May 12, 1986; NYT, Nov. 30, 1967, p. 35.

647   "a first step in a thousand-mile journey": NYT, Oct. 21, 1967, p. 18.

647   White Knights had intensified terror attacks: Whitehead, *Attack,* pp. 285–88; Nelson, *Terror,* pp. 64–82; Evans, *Provincials,* p. 221ff; Perkins, *Brother,* pp. 78–81; Tarrants, *Conversion,* pp. 48–61.

647   "preacher of Jesus the Galilean": Marsh, *Summer,* pp. 71–72.

647   It would be another twenty-two years: Jerry Mitchell, "Justice Delayed, Not Denied," *Jackson Clarion-Ledger,* Jan. 8, 2005, p. 1; NYT, April 2, 1995, p. 18; NYT, May 29, 1998, p. 1; WP, July 22, 1998, p. D-1.

647   seventy-nine-year-old Edgar Ray Killen: Jerry Mitchell, "Preacher Helped Conceal Klan Killings, Friend Says," *Jackson Clarion-Ledger,* July 19, 2001, p. 1; Jerry Mitchell, "Grand Jury Indicts Killen in '64 Slayings," *Jackson Clarion-Ledger,* Jan. 7, 2005, p. 1; NYT, Jan. 8, 2005, p. 1.

647   "sprinkling of Negroes": NYT, Oct. 22, 1967, pp. 1, 58.

647   "We don't want to play Indian": Zaroulis and Sullivan, *Who Spoke Up?,* p. 137.

647   vigils, skirmishes, and bonfires: Ibid., pp. 136–42; John C. Diamante, "Federal Troops Stop March at Pentagon," SC, Nov. 4–5, 1967, p. 4; DeBenedetti, *Ordeal,* p. 198; Dellinger, *From Yale,* pp. 302–7; Langguth, *Our Vietnam,* pp. 459–60.

648   none of the two hundred Wisconsin students: Maraniss, *They Marched,* pp. 428–29, 443, 460–66, 475–76.

648   "almost enough to retrieve": James Reston, "Everyone Is a Loser," Oct. 23, 1967, p. 1.

648   His testimony before the Kerner Commission: NYT, Oct. 24, 1967, p. 33; NYT, Jan. 14, 1968, p. 71.

648   "I think that the time has come": MLK statement, ABC Radio News, Oct. 23, 1967, A/KS.

648   "appeal to anarchy": "King's Camp-In," WP, Oct. 26, 1967, p. 20; Garrow, *Bearing,* p. 579.

648   Dora McDonald asked Levison: Wiretap transcript of telephone call between Stanley Levison and Dora McDonald, 2:55 P.M., Oct. 23, 1967, FLNY-9-1466a.

648   "will be lucky to break even": Wiretap transcript of telephone call between Stanley Levison and Chauncey Eskridge, Oct. 30, 1967, FLNY-9-1473a. An accounting in the files showed that the series lost $9,000 above overall revenues of $86,000: "Balance Sheet, Belafonte-Franklin Show," Nov. 15, 1967, ACS10f4.

648   "I thought you were coming": Int. Bernard Lafayette, March 22, 2005.

648   convocation at tiny Grinnell College: Mays, *Born,* pp. 269–70.

648   final court orders to surrender: NYT, Oct. 10, 1967, p. 40; NYT, Oct. 19, 1967, p. 41; Garrow, *Bearing,* pp. 579–80.

649   "a small price to pay": MLK statement of Oct. 30, 1967, attached to Atlanta office LHM dated Oct. 31, 1967, FK-3136.

649   "As we leave": SC, Nov. 4–5, 1967, pp. 1, 2.

649   hauled off by police cars: Ibid.; Westin, *Trial,* pp. 1–2.

649   "coherent voice to a catastrophe": NYT, Oct. 3, 1967, p. 45.

649   "I absorbed by osmosis": NYT, Aug. 5, 1967, p. 13.

649   diverted King to a facility: NYT, Oct. 31, 1967, pp. 1, 30; NYT, Nov. 1, 1967, p. 33; NYT, Nov. 2, 1967, p. 34.

649   four prisoners were transferred: SAC Birmingham to Director, Nov. 1, 1967, FK-3130.

649   Harry Wachtel to reconvene at Union Seminary: Harry Wachtel to Al Lowenstein, Nov. 8, 1967, Box 11f377, #4340, UNC.

650   passed over President Franklin Roosevelt's veto: Dickson and Allen, *Bonus Army,* pp. 252–53.

650   tuition grants for 11 million: Ibid., pp. 273–77.

650   King began an opinion piece: MLK, "A Bill of Rights for the Disadvantaged," NYT, Nov. 12, 1967, p. IV-11.

650   gossip about Birmingham authorities: Int. Edward Gardner, Jan. 21, 1986.

650   cut short the sentence: NYT, Nov. 4, 1967, p. 21; Birmingham LHM dated Nov. 6, 1967, FK-NR.

650   "This looks like '63!": SC, Nov. 11–12, 1967, p. 1.

650   Cleveland for the off-year elections: NYT, Aug. 27, 1967, p. 64; NYT, Oct. 4, 1967, p. 1; Garrow, *Bearing,* pp. 578–81; Young, *Burden,* pp. 436–37; Abernathy, *Walls,* pp. 485–88.

650   "Stokes, the great-grandson of a slave": *Newsweek,* Nov. 20, 1967, p. 66.

651   consultation in Chicago: MLK speech, University of Chicago, Nov. 11, 1967, Series 4, Box 1, CALCAV, SCPC; wiretap transcript of telephone call between Jesse Jackson and Bea Levison, Nov. 9, 1967, FLNY-9-1483a; wiretap transcript of telephone call between Stanley and Bea Levison, 11:40 a.m., Aug. 16, 1967, FLNY-9-1398; wiretap transcript of telephone call between MLK and Stanley Levison, 12:41 a.m., Oct. 9, 1967, FLNY-9-1452.

651   "I feel presumptuous even in asking questions": WP, Nov. 13, 1967, p. 1; NYT, Nov. 13, 1967, p. 1.

651   "turned to stone on the outside": Johnson, *Diary,* pp. 587–89.

651   postlude into a tempest: NYT, Nov. 14, 1967, p. 6; WP, Nov. 14, 1967, p. 10; NYT, Nov. 16, 1967, p. 8; NYT, Nov. 19, 1967, p. 2; NYT, Nov. 19, 1967, p. IV-12.

651   King departed for northern England: Garrow, *Bearing,* p. 581.

652   "psychologic elaboration": NYT, Nov. 12, 1967, p. 70.

652   openly proclaiming an advocacy stance: "Newsweek Drops Its Policy of Avoiding 'Advocacy' ": NYT, Nov. 11, 1967, p. 31; full-page advertisement signed by *Newsweek* editor Osborn Elliott, NYT, Nov. 13, 1967, p. 96; "Newsweek Urges Wide Aid to Negro," NYT, Nov. 13, 1967, p. 55.

652   special issue on the crisis of race: "The Negro in America: What Must Be Done," *Newsweek,* Nov. 20, 1967, p. 32ff.

652   King let Stanley Levison draft arguments: Wiretap transcript of telephone call between MLK and Stanley Levison, 10:45 a.m., Nov. 16, 1967, FLNY-9-1490; wiretap transcript of telephone call between Stanley Levison and Andrew Young, 1:26 a.m., Nov. 19, 1967, FLNY-9-1493.

652   "I'm on fire about the thing": MLK, "Why a Movement," Nov. 28, 1967, A/SC28f42.

652   At the week-long retreat: NYT, Nov. 27, 1967, p. 53.

652   "Violence has been the inseparable twin": MLK, "The State of the Movement," Nov. 28, 1967, A/SC28f42.

652   had just met with Olympic athletes: Ibid.; NYT, Nov. 24, 1967, p. 30.

653   "So I say to you tonight": MLK, "The State of the Movement," Nov. 28, 1967, A/SC28f42, p. 12.

653   Bevel disputed King's constitutional basis: Int. Bernard Lafayette, May 28, 1990 and March 22, 2005.

653   FBI intelligence reports of leadership friction: FBI HQ LHM dated Dec. 7, 1967, Box 32, OFMS, LBJ.

653   "his ability to confront without repelling": The Rev. G. H. Jack Woodard, Jr., to MLK, Nov. 28, 1967, A/SC2f19.

653   "I can't support you": Int. Hosea Williams, Oct. 28, 1991.

653   "That nigger don't know nothin' about niggers!": Int. William Rutherford, Dec. 7, 2004.

654   "The great burden of this": Notes, SCLC Frogmore Retreat, Nov. 1967, with a cover note from Stanley Levison to Dora McDonald, A/SC14f42.

654   "I figure our riots": Ibid.

654   check for culture shock in Rutherford: Int. William Rutherford, Dec. 7, 2004; int. Bernard Lafayette, March 22, 2005.

654   sell or license his businesses: Rutherford to Andrew Young, Sept. 1, 1967, A/SC39f10; Rutherford to MLK, Sept. 21, 1967, A/SC5f15; Rutherford to Andrew Young, Oct. 24 and Oct. 25, 1967, A/SC39f13.

654   greeted Rutherford with two secret assignments: Garrow, *Bearing,* pp. 584–85.

655   "Even Lillian?": Int. William Rutherford, Dec. 7, 2004.

655   "Public preoccupation with Vietnam": Rutherford to Andrew Young, Oct. 24, 1967, A/SC39f13.

655   "The day of the demonstration": MLK, "Why a Movement," Nov. 28, 1967, A/SC28f42.

655   this might be the last campaign: Int. Bernard Lafayette, March 22, 2005.

655   "I got really upset": Int. Hosea Williams, Oct. 29, 1991.

655   "There is something in the book of Revelation": MLK, "Why a Movement," Nov. 28, 1967, A/SC28f42. King's verse is apparently a paraphrase of Revelation 3:2: "Awake, and strengthen what remains and is on the point of death, for I have not found your works perfect in the sight of my God."

656   twelfth anniversary of his debut speech: Branch, *Parting,* pp. 138–42.

656   "The Southern Christian Leadership Conference": MLK press conference, Dec. 4, 1967, A/KS.

656   "The Negro leader's mood": NYT, Dec. 5, 1967, pp. 1, 32.

37: NEW YEAR TRIALS

PAGE

657   "We're killing innocent people": NYT, Nov. 27, 1967, pp. 1, 15.

657   "I don't know what I can do": Thomas, *Robert Kennedy,* p. 351.

657   He welcomed a potential quest: NYT, Nov. 19, 1967, p. 1.

657   "Dump Johnson" activist: Steven V. Roberts, "The Dump-Johnson Movement," *Commonweal,* Oct. 27, 1967, p. 106; Arnold S. Kaufman and Allard Lowenstein, "The Time Is Ripe to Dump Johnson," *Michigan Daily,* Nov. 2, 1967; "The Move to 'Dump' Johnson," *Newsweek,* Nov. 20, 1967; int. Curtis Gans, Oct. 23, 1991.

657   "Aren't you still waiting for Bobby?": Transcript, *Meet the Press,* Dec. 3, 1967, Box 54f109, AL, UNC.

658   Conference of Concerned Democrats: Press agenda, Box 54f109, AL, UNC; keynote address by Rep. Don Edwards, Dec. 2, 1967, Box 54f109, AL, UNC; Harris, *Dreams,* pp. 218–19; Chafe, *Never,* pp. 278–81.

658   candidate-in-waiting seethed offstage: NYT, Nov. 3, 1967, p. 1; NYT, Dec. 1, 1967, p. 1; "McCarthy Denies a Kennedy Plot," NYT, Dec. 3, 1967, p. 42; NYT, Dec. 4, 1967, p. 41.

658   McCarthy's poetic detachment: Powers, *War,* pp. 284–92; cf. Wilfred Stone to McCarthy, Jan. 15, 1968: "I heard you today at Stanford . . . I want you to *win* the nomi-

nation . . . but I think your speech was, in a political sense, ineffective . . . a kind of plaintive note, almost a note of self-pity." Box 54f91, AL, UNC.

658   Lady Bird Johnson bemoaned: Johnson, *Diary*, pp. 591–92.

658   he came alone to Johnson with appeals: McNamara cover note to LBJ, Nov. 1, 1967, Meeting Notes File, Box 2, LBJ; McNamara to LBJ, Nov. 1, 1967, in FRUS, Vol. 5, p. 943ff; McNamara, *In Retrospect*, pp. 305–11. McNamara began the cover note of November 1 as follows: "Yesterday at lunch I stated my belief that continuation of our present course of action in Southeast Asia would be dangerous, costly in lives, and unsatisfactory to the American people. The attached memorandum outlines an alternative program."

658   "we could even have another Forrestal": Califano, *Triumph*, p. 249.

658   Wise Men rejected it: McNamara, *In Retrospect*, p. 309; Kalman, *Abe Fortas*, p. 304; Clifford, *Counsel*, pp. 457–58; Taylor, *Swords*, pp. 377–78; Rostow to LBJ, Nov. 2, 1967, in FRUS, Vol. 5, p. 971; Rostow to LBJ, Nov. 4, 1967, in ibid., p. 986; Clifford to LBJ, Nov. 7, 1967, in ibid., p. 992; Rusk to LBJ, Nov. 20, 1967, in ibid., p. 1037.

658   "I can think of nothing *worse*": Fortas to LBJ, Nov. 5, 1967, in FRUS, Vol. 5, p. 991.

658   off to head the World Bank: Califano to LBJ, Nov. 27, 1967, Name File—Wiggins, LBJ; NYT, Nov. 28, 1967, p. 1; Dallek, *Flawed*, pp. 494–96.

659   "I do not know to this day": McNamara, *In Retrospect*, p. 311.

659   "I am beginning to agree": Tom Johnson notes of LBJ meeting with Vietnam advisers, Nov. 21, 1967, in FRUS, Vol. 5, p. 1055.

659   Johnson simply demanded: Dallek, *Flawed*, pp. 497–98.

659   "show some progress": Notes, meeting with foreign policy advisers, Nov. 2, 1967, in FRUS, Vol. 5, p. 959.

659   "deaths and dangers to the sons": Ibid., p. 958.

659   General Westmoreland publicly predicted: NYT, Nov. 16, 1967, p. 1; NYT, Nov. 20, 1967, p. 1.

659   "Oh, hell no": Sheehan, *Bright*, pp. 646–47.

659   President Johnson restrained an impulse: Cf. "Johnson Retorts to Critics of War; Scores Rowdyism/ Backs 'Responsible' Dissent at News Conference, but Not 'Storm Trooper Acts,' " NYT, Nov. 18, 1967, p. 1.

659   "Nonviolence can be adapted": MLK letter to "Dear Friend," sent "BY LIAISON" from Hoover to Mildred Stegall, Nov. 8, 1967, Box 32, OFMS, LBJ.

659   scrawled specific instructions: On ibid., next to MLK's signature, LBJ wrote: "M[arvin Watson]—Show this to Abe F[ortas] and to Carol + then to Sheldon [Cohen] + report to me."

659   "for the last three or four years": Unsigned note dated Nov. 20, 1967, attached to Marvin Watson to LBJ, 5:33 P.M., Nov. 20, 1967, identifying IRS director Sheldon Cohen as author of the unsigned note, Box 32, OFMS, LBJ.

660   would announce a grant of $230,000: "Ford Aid Is Given to Negro Clergy," NYT, Jan. 6, 1968, p. 18; UPI dispatch, Jan. 3, 1968, FSC-2069.

660   When the President asked Hoover: LBJ note, "Let's see if this can be checked," on Hoover to Stegall, Nov. 30, 1967, with attached DC LHM marked "Secret," Nov. 30, 1967, and Stegall reply to LBJ, Dec. 1, 1967, Box 32, OFMS, LBJ.

660   "to expose, disrupt, misdirect": Hoover, "PERSONAL ATTENTION TO ALL OFFICES," Aug. 25, 1967, FBNH-1.

660   third full-scale COINTELPRO: Powers, *Secrecy*, pp. 339–41, 413–15, 422–25; De-

Loach, *Hoover's FBI*, pp. 270–71; O'Reilly, *"Racial,"* pp. 104–5, 195–205, 261–92. Hoover had initiated the earlier COINTELPRO actions secretly against the Communist Party in 1956 and the Ku Klux Klan in 1964.

660   "FBI's Report on King Ready": Northern Virginia *Sun,* Aug. 24, 1967, p. 4; Chicago's *American,* Aug. 22, 1967, with handwritten note by Hoover, "This is the article!!!," FK-NR; Hoover to Tolson, 9:14 A.M., Aug. 24, 1967, FCT-NR.

660   lengthy congressional speech: Remarks by Rep. John Ashbrook, *Congressional Record,* Oct. 4, 1967, p. H27814ff.

660   Hoover explored ways to revive the King wiretaps: Moore to Sullivan, Dec. 13, 1967, FSC-2042. DeLoach wrote a note on the wiretap proposal: "I doubt that the Attorney General will approve such an installation, but believe we should try, for the record."

660   litany of faith, hope, and love: I Corinthians 13.

660   "You may desire a new beautiful house": MLK sermon in Montgomery, Alabama, Dec. 10, 1967, Tape 45, A/KS.

661   "The kingdom of God is in you": Ibid.; Luke 17:21.

661   Ku Klux Klan rally: SC, Dec. 16–17, 1967, pp. 1, 4; NYT, Dec. 11, 1967, p. 32; Mobile LHM dated Dec. 12, 1967, FK-NR.

661   King rushed to Chicago: Garrow, *Bearing,* p. 589.

661   At a Wednesday press conference: NYT, Dec. 14, 1967, p. 39.

661   "He's done in a week": Wiretap transcript of telephone call between MLK and Stanley Levison, 5:14 P.M., Dec. 13, 1967, FLNY-9-1517a.

661   Rutherford dismissed the daughter: Int. William Rutherford, Dec. 7, 2004; Chauncey Eskridge to MLK, "Re: Hotel Bills," Dec. 21, 1967, A/KP10f5; wiretap transcript of telephone call between Chauncey Eskridge and Stanley Levison, 1:40 P.M., Dec. 26, 1967, FLNY-9-1530a.

661   flurry of memos: Hosea Williams to Rutherford, re: Subsistence Workers, Dec. 15, 1967, A/SC57f3; Hosea Williams to Rutherford re: Mr. King Tyler, Dec. 15, 1967, A/SC57f3; Hosea Williams to Rutherford re: Automobile Rental, Dec. 15, 1967, A/SC57f2; Rutherford to Hosea Williams, Dec. 19, 1967, A/SC48f4; Rutherford to Hosea Williams, Dec. 19, 1967, A/SC57f3.

662   "You promised me your full cooperation": Rutherford to Jesse Jackson, Dec. 11, 1967, A/SC39f15.

662   Locks now secured: Int. William Rutherford, Dec. 7, 2004.

662   suspected that Harrison: Ibid.

662   informant account coded AT-1387-R: King scholar David Garrow revealed Harrison's role as an FBI informant in his 1981 book, *The FBI and Martin Luther King, Jr.,* pp. 175–79, 299; McKnight, *Crusade,* p. 23.

662   forum of one hundred intellectuals: "Violence As a Weapon of Dissent Is Debated at Forum in 'Village,' " NYT, Dec. 17, 1967, p. 16.

662   "Generally speaking": Klein, ed., *Dissent,* p. 99.

662   "All politics is a struggle": Arendt, *On Violence,* p. 35.

663   "violence is the best way of insuring": Klein, ed., *Dissent,* p. 104.

663   "whether we in this room": Ibid., p. 121; Young-Bruehl, *Hannah Arendt,* pp. 412–15.

663   "A White Liberal Shift": NYT, Dec. 17, 1967, p. 1.

663   "war may be the last of the tonics": NYT, Sept. 18, 1967, p. 2.

663   "You may put me in the position": NYT, Dec. 17, 1967, p. 16.

663   Hayden had gone to jail: "Improbable Radical," NYT, Nov. 13, 1967, p. 2; Branch, *Parting,* pp. 533–37.

663   "It seems to me": Klein, ed., *Dissent*, p. 127.

664   "Power and violence are opposites": Arendt, *On Violence*, p. 56.

664   President Johnson composed a unique: "Memorandum for the File by President Johnson," 1:40 P.M., Dec. 18, 1967, in FRUS, Vol. 5, p. 1118.

664   left the next day for an odyssey: Ibid., pp. 1120–23; Dallek, *Flawed*, pp. 500–501.

664   war talks in Melbourne: NYT, Dec. 21, 1967, p. 1.

664   "A mere handful of you men": McPherson, *Political*, p. 323.

665   "We're not going to yield": NYT, Dec. 23, 1967, p. 1.

665   reporters infuriated over the blind itinerary: Valenti, *Human*, pp. 223–26.

665   "My right hand keeps the pressure steady": Notes, "Meeting of the Pope and the President," Dec. 23, 1967, Meeting Notes File, Box 2, p. 2, LBJ.

665   "By terror they are recruiting": Ibid., p. 13; Valenti, *Human*, pp. 228–32.

666   "a Phineas Fogg adventure": McPherson, *Political*, p. 322.

666   news reports from Vatican sources: "Johnson Confers with Pope Paul on Vietnam War," NYT, Dec. 24, 1967, p. 1; Valenti, *Human*, pp. 232–38.

666   two hundred million citizens: Jones, *Expectations*, p. 190.

666   without a legal execution: Hauser, *Ali*, p. 174; U.S. Dept. of Justice, Bureau of Justice Statistics, "Number of persons executed in the United States, 1930–1997," www.ojp.usdoj.gov/bjs/glance/exe.txt (March 1998).

666   first-class postage stamp: *Baltimore Sun*, Feb. 7, 1990, p. 1.

666   military effort in Vietnam became six years old: LBJ and the *New York Times* dated the Vietnam War from the death of Specialist 4 James T. Davis on December 22, 1961, but others put the earliest American fatality as Air Force Sergeant Richard Fitzgibbon on June 8, 1956, and the earliest combat deaths as Major Dale Buis and Master Sergeant Chester Ovnand on July 8, 1959. Cf. NYT, June 23, 1968, p. 2; http://www.virtual-wall.org/dd/DavisJT01a.htm.

666   cumulative toll at 15,900: NYT, Jan. 2, 1968, p. 4; Terry, *Bloods*, p. 296; McNamara, *In Retrospect*, p. 321.

666   1968 alone would approach those totals: U.S. soldiers killed in 1968 numbered 14,589, the highest yearly total for the war. Cf. Sheehan, *Bright*, p. 670.

666   Westmoreland sent six thousand Marines: Karnow, *Vietnam*, pp. 552–53; Langguth, *Our Vietnam*, pp. 478–79; Braestrup, *Big Story*, pp. 258–65; Wheeler to McNamara, Jan. 13, 1968, in FRUS, Vol. 6, p. 30.

666   January message on civil rights: Graham, *Civil Rights Era*, pp. 270–72.

666   "full non-discrimination may take": Califano to LBJ, Jan. 21, 1968, Joseph Califano Papers, Box 8, LBJ.

667   Robert G. Clark: SC, Jan. 6–7, 1968, p. 1; SC, Jan. 20–21, 1968, p. 1; Dittmer, *Local People*, p. 416; Parker, *Black Votes*, pp. 74–75; Mills, *Light*, p. 190.

667   opened 1968 with hearings: NYT, Jan. 17, 1968, p. 42; NYT, Jan. 18, 1968, p. 28.

667   "Immediately following World War II": Hearings in New York, NY, U.S. EEOC, Jan. 15–18, 1968, pp. 125, 353, 438, 477.

667   CBS hired its first black: Clifford Alexander oral history by Joe B. Frantz, Feb. 17, 1972, p. 6.

667   "white Gentile secretary": NYT, Jan. 19, 1968, p. 19.

667   accredited its first black member: Bell, *In the Black*, pp. 45–46, 65–69.

667   secure Alexander's early resignation: Int. Clifford Alexander, Dec. 17, 2004.

668   "can look back on 1967": "Hoover Says Reds Use Black Power," NYT, Jan. 6, 1968, p. 1.

668   requested new wiretaps on King: Garrow, *FBI and King,* p. 184.

668   sent President Johnson a classified blueprint: Hoover to Mildred Stegall, with attached FBI HQ LHM dated Jan. 3, 1968, Box 32, OFMS, LBJ.

668   operation coded POCAM: McKnight, *Crusade,* pp. 22–24; Kotz, *Judgment,* p. 387.

668   "SPOCK INDICTED": *New York Post,* Jan. 6, 1968, p. 1; Spock, *Spock on Spock,* p. 199.

668   "I wish I did not have": MLK sermon, Jan. 7, 1968, A/KS.

668   King resisted overtures: MLK log, A/SC47f21; wiretap transcript of telephone call between Stanley Levison and Tudja Crowder, Jan. 8, 1968, FLNY-9-1543; wiretap transcript of telephone call between MLK and Stanley Levison, 11:03 A.M., Jan. 10, 1968, FLNY-9-1545.

669   Coffin at least initially agreed: Coffin, *Once,* pp. 260–65; Goldstein, *Coffin,* pp. 207–11; int. William Sloane Coffin, July 16, 1991.

669   "I can't tell another man": Int. Harry Wachtel, Nov. 29, 1983 and May 17, 1990.

669   reporters lost interest: Ibid.

669   "Dr. King Calls for Antiwar Rally": NYT, Jan. 13, 1968, p. 4; Hoover to SACs, Atlanta, New York, and Washington, Jan 17, 1968, FCLCV-4.

669   James St. Clair: Goldstein, *Coffin,* pp. 218–19.

669   "somebody brought up as goody-goody": Spock, *Spock on Spock,* p. 202.

669   Marcus Raskin collapsed: Ibid., p. 204; Coffin, *Once,* pp. 271–85.

669   chained to eight adult supporters: Barry Johnson, "Seminarian in 'The Resistance,' " *Christian Century,* Jan. 3, 1968, pp. 15–17; Hall, *Because,* p. 53; int. Barry Johnson, Jan. 4, 2005.

670   drove to the Santa Rita Rehabilitation Center: San Francisco LHM dated Jan. 18, 1968, FK-NR; Baez, *Voice,* pp. 111–12; Sandperl, *Kinder,* pp. 113–15; int. Joan Baez, Jan. 7, 1984.

670   "Doctor, you all be sure": MLK remarks to Atlanta staff retreat, Jan. 17, 1968, p. 7, A/KS.

670   "I might say that I see": News recording, Jan. 14, 1968, Tape 37, A/KS.

670   midnight flight through Dallas: MLK log, Jan. 14–15, 1968, A/SC47f21.

670   morning presentation at Ebenezer: Agenda, staff workshops, Jan. 14–16, 1968, A/KP34f15; FBI HQ LHM dated Jan. 18, 1968, Box 32, OFMS, LBJ; Moore to Sullivan, Jan. 24, 1968, FK-3191; Garrow, *Bearing,* p. 592.

670   Bill Rutherford's summons: Rutherford and Bernard Lafayette to "All SCLC Staff Members," Jan. 4, 1968, A/SC48f4.

671   "I say all of these things": MLK remarks to Atlanta staff retreat, "Why We Must Go to Washington," Jan. 15, 1968, A/KS.

671   "Talk about Peter": *Citizen King,* a Roja Production for *The American Experience,* PBS, 2004.

672   "patterned after the bonus marches": MLK press conference, Jan. 16, 1968, A/KS.

672   James Bevel and Jesse Jackson maintained: Garrow, *Bearing,* pp. 592–94; Frady, *Jesse,* pp. 215–16; minutes, executive staff committee meeting, Dec. 27, 1967, A/SC49f11.

672   "at this time consists of one person": Hosea Williams to executive staff committee, Jan. 22, 1968, A/KP35f18.

672   "I couldn't hardly get gas money": Int. Hosea Williams, Oct. 29, 1991.

672   Organizers also confessed: Fairclough, *Redeem,* p. 362; int. Bernard Lafayette, March 25, 2005.

672   "What's gonna happen": *Citizen King,* a Roja Production for *The American Experience,* PBS, 2004.

672   "I don't want to psychoanalyze": MLK remarks to Atlanta staff retreat, Jan. 17, 1968, p. 7, A/KS.

673   "we never would have had": Fairclough, *Redeem,* p. 363.

673   the Jeannette Rankin Brigade marched: Swerdlow, *Women,* pp. 135–41; Zaroulis and Sullivan, *Who Spoke Up?,* pp. 149–50; Wells, *War Within,* p. 228.

674   President Johnson entered the House chamber: Johnson, *Diary,* pp. 616–20; Califano, *Triumph,* pp. 253–57; Dallek, *Flawed,* pp. 513–18.

674   "Why then this restlessness?": NYT, Jan. 18, 1968, pp. 1, 16, 17.

674   "mutinous cries below decks": NYT, Jan. 19, 1968, p. 46.

674   "a spiritless message": Garrow, *Bearing,* p. 594.

675   he pared federal expenditures: Johnson, *Vantage,* pp. 445–61, 550–52; Dallek, *Flawed,* pp. 515, 554; " 'Red Ink' to Flood Government's Books?," *U.S. News & World Report,* May 29, 1967, p. 31; NYT, Jan. 30, 1968, pp. 1, 16; Califano to LBJ, Dec. 4, 1967, Box 31, WE9, LBJ; Califano to LBJ on budget message from Sargent Shriver, Jan. 9, 1968, Box 98, WE9, LBJ.

675   last surplus for the next twenty-nine years: U.S. Government Printing Office, *The Budget for Fiscal Year 2004,* pp. 21–22.

675   "radically vicious": *New Yorker,* Nov. 30, 1968, pp. 51–52.

675   pioneer 1964 sweepstakes in New Hampshire: Branch, *Pillar,* p. 241.

675   teller windows of duly licensed banks: "What's Wrong with the Lottery?," *New England Monthly,* January 1990, pp. 41–49; "Legislature Sits 21 Hours in Finale/ Votes 12 Lotteries a Year," NYT, April 3, 1967, p. 1.

675   "It seems incomprehensible": Hearings, U.S. Senate Banking Committee, "Prohibit Financial Institutions As Lottery Agencies," Aug. 19, 1967, p. 19.

675   chief sponsor of the bonus bill: Dickson and Allen, *Bonus Army,* pp. 30–35, 132.

675   bid to impeach Treasury Secretary Andrew Mellon: Ibid., pp. 46–51.

676   passed over FDR's veto in 1936: Ibid., pp. 230–53.

676   consulting firm would recommend: "State Lotteries," *Consumer Reports,* Feb. 1974, pp. 177–79.

676   new voice of state governments: "Lotto Baloney," *Harper's,* July 1983, p. 15ff; "Lotto-mania," *Forbes,* March 6, 1989, p. 92ff.

676   "The De Ville Made Me Do It": *New England Monthly,* January 1990, p. 42.

676   "The way to sell lottery tickets": Ibid., p. 43.

676   full-scale siege struck Khe Sanh: Braestrup, *Big Story,* pp. 256–67; Dallek, *Flawed,* pp. 502–3; Langguth, *Our Vietnam,* pp. 478–79; Zaroulis and Sullivan, *Who Spoke Up?,* p. 151; "5,000 Men Massed at Khesanh by U.S.," NYT, Jan. 24, 1968, p. 1.

676   lacked no support provision for military success: "Notes of the President's Tuesday National Security Lunch," Jan. 23, 1968, in FRUS, Vol. 6, p. 58ff.

676   "unusually good press": "Notes of Meeting of the National Security Council," Jan. 24, 1968, in FRUS, Vol. 6, p. 65ff.

676   "seem to have run temporarily": Braestrup, *Big Story,* p. 66.

676   "dramatic decline": "2-Year Drive in Saigon Cuts Terrorism Sharply," NYT, Jan. 19, 1968, p. 12.

676   pacification chief Robert Komer: "Pacification Gains Reported by Komer," NYT, Jan. 25, 1968, p. 7.

677   he fined three workers: Rutherford to James Harrison, Jan. 26, 1968, A/SC57f4.

677   "effective immediately": Rutherford to Meredith Gilbert, Jan. 25, 1968, A/SC56f10.

677   King had told each he was with the other: Garrow, *Bearing,* pp. 586–88.

677   King bristled against tampering: Int. Bernard Lee, June 19, 1985; int. Harry Wachtel, Nov. 29, 1983; int. William Rutherford, Dec. 7, 2004.

677   quietly diverted staff members: Int. William Rutherford, Dec. 7, 2004.

678   "confess all our stuff to our wives": Int. James Bevel, May 17, 1985, Nov. 23, 1997, Dec. 10–11, 1998.

678   psycho-biologist Wilhelm Reich: Ibid.; Young, *Burden,* p. 444.

678   Abernathy was gone: Garrow, *Bearing,* p. 594; Abernathy to MLK, Jan. 18, 1968, A/KP1f1.

678   Coretta underwent surgery: Wiretap transcript of telephone call between Stanley Levison and Joan Daves, 2:08 P.M., Jan. 24, 1968, FLNY-9-1559a; wiretap transcript of telephone call between Stanley Levison and Andrew Young, 2:26 P.M., Dec. 31, 1967, FLNY-9-1535a; Garrow, *Bearing,* p. 594.

678   The result was painful disaster: Confidential interviews.

679   he canvassed the regular mistresses: Int. Ralph Abernathy, Nov. 19, 1984.

679   he exhorted his New York advisers: Harry Wachtel invitation to members of the Research Committee, Jan. 17, 1968, A/SC39f19; Garrow, *Bearing,* p. 594; Lewis, *King,* p. 373; Fairclough, *Redeem,* p. 364.

679   "can only lead to further backlash": Rustin to MLK, "Strategy and Tactics," Jan. 1, 1968, in Rustin, *Down,* pp. 202–5; Williams, *King God Didn't Save,* pp. 109–13.

679   "mystical bullshit": Int. Bayard Rustin, Nov. 28, 1983.

679   "showed his true colors": Wiretap transcript of telephone call between Stanley Levison and William Rutherford, 10:55 P.M., Jan. 31, 1968, FLNY-9-1566a.

679   Rustin would be sensitive: Longenecker, *Peacemaker,* pp. 305–7; D'Emilio, *Lost Prophet,* pp. 457–71.

679   "that in 1968 I rejected the philosophy": Bayard Rustin, "Ally to the End in Dr. King's Philosophy of Nonviolence," letters to the editor, NYT, Sept. 18, 1995.

679   "He felt let down": Wachtel to Rustin, Sept. 25, 1995, courtesy of Harry Wachtel.

679   "We didn't know we were poor": Harrington, *Fragments,* pp. 128–29; int. Michael Harrington, Oct. 27, 1983.

680   "cutting down": Beifuss, *River,* pp. 27–29; Honey, *Black Workers,* pp. 302–5.

680   Robert Kennedy told reporters: Schlesinger, *Robert Kennedy,* pp. 902–4; Thomas, *Robert Kennedy,* pp. 356–57.

680   Allard Lowenstein reportedly accosted Kennedy: Ibid.; Chafe, *Never,* pp. 282–84.

680   "Besides the columnists": Fred Dutton to RFK, Jan. 31, 1968, Personal Correspondence, RFK Senate Papers, Box 3, JFK.

680   swamped the declared rival Eugene McCarthy: DeBenedetti, *Ordeal,* p. 209.

680   suspended for the three-day Buddhist celebrations: "Marines at Khesanh Sure a Big Attack Is Near," NYT, Jan. 29, 1968, p. 6; "Saigon Marks Tet, but Without G.I.'s," NYT, Jan. 30, 1968, p. 2.

680   "active candidates for employment": Langguth, *Our Vietnam,* p. 479.

680   spy ship *Pueblo* with all her crew: Rusk, *As I Saw It,* p. 391; Manchester, *Glory,* p. 1377.

680   "we are being heavily mortared": Notes of LBJ meeting with Rusk, McNamara, Clifford, Wheeler, Helms, Rostow, Christian, and note-taker Tom Johnson, 1:08–2:50 P.M., Jan. 30, 1968, in FRUS, Vol. 6, p. 79ff.

681   "This could be very bad": Ibid.

681   chauffeur nicknamed Satchmo: Karnow, *Vietnam,* pp. 536–39.

681   too late for some network broadcasts: Braestrup, *Big Story,* pp. 116–18.

681   "In one of the strangest scenes": Charles Mohr, "U.S. Aide in Embassy Villa Kills Guerilla with Pistol," NYT, Jan. 31, 1968, p. 1.

681   showed a Vietcong corpse: Appy, *Patriots,* p. 291.

681   Seventy thousand guerrillas launched: Ibid., pp. 285–88; Oberdorfer, *Tet!,* pp. 2–33, 116–34: Braestrup, *Big Story,* pp. ix–xi; Dallek, *Flawed,* p. 503.

681   hidden in more than four hundred homes: Langguth, *Our Vietnam,* pp. 468–71.

681   calamitous intelligence failure: CIA intelligence memorandum, "The Communist Tet Offensive," Jan. 31, 1968, in FRUS, Vol. 6, p. 92; CIA memorandum, "Vietnam— Operation Shock," Feb. 2, 1968, in ibid., p. 98; William J. Jorden to Walt Rostow, "Situation in Vietnam," Feb. 3, 1968, in ibid., p. 111.

681   "Saigon's 4 million people": Langguth, *Our Vietnam,* p. 474.

681   The plans left massive carnage: Karnow, *Vietnam,* p. 547; Dallek, *Flawed,* p. 504.

682   General Loan marched him: Karnow, *Vietnam,* pp. 462, 542; Braestrup, *Big Story,* pp. 347–49; Langguth, *Our Vietnam,* p. 475.

682   most decisive single drop: Oberdorfer, *Tet!,* pp. 161–71; McPherson, *Political,* pp. 424–25; Dallek, *Flawed,* pp. 505–6.

38: MEMPHIS

PAGE

683   Elvis Presley's escape: Goldman, *Elvis,* pp. 479–81.

683   Assistant Police Chief Henry Lux announced: MCA, Feb. 2, 1968, p. 1.

683   "Tell him I moved for him": MCA, Feb. 3, 1968, p. 7.

683   P. J. Ciampa flew in for a stopover: Beifuss, *River,* pp. 29–30; P. J. Ciampa oral history, Feb. 3, 1972, pp. 3–8, MVC.

684   Blackburn politely withheld: Ibid.; Charles Blackburn oral history, May 29, 1968, pp. 5–14, MVC.

684   Loeb answered all fifty-four citizens: MCA, Feb. 2, 1968, p. 9.

684   two Public Works vans startled Jones: T. O. Jones oral history, Jan. 30, 1970, pp. 11–12, MVC.

684   Willie Crain's five-man crew: Beifuss, *River,* p. 30; Lewis, *King,* p. 378; "Garbage Truck Kills 2 Crewmen," MCA, Feb. 2, 1968, p. 1.

684   city rules barred shelter stops: Honey, *Black Workers,* pp. 294–96, 302–5; Young, *Burden,* p. 449.

685   Television newscasts ignored them: News scripts, Memphis WMC-TV Channel Five, Feb. 1–3, 1968, MVC.

685   "fortress of discrimination": "Women Mistreated at P.O., Says NAPE," *Memphis Tri-State Defender,* Feb. 17, 1968, p. 1.

685   emphasized technical efforts: "Garbage Vehicles Suspended by City," MCA, Feb. 3, 1968, p. 25.

685   "Tom's boy mus' be": MCA, Feb. 2, 1968, p. 21.

685   "unclassified workers": Beifuss, *River,* p. 30; McKnight, *Crusade,* p. 34; T. O. Jones oral history, Jan. 30, 1970, pp. 16–18, MVC.

685   pregnant widow Earline Walker: "Worker's Final Check Pays on His Funeral," *Memphis Tri-State Defender,* Feb. 10, 1968, p. 1.

685   cheap burial across the Mississippi line: Int. Constance Cury, Feb. 16, 1993; Curry to the author with enclosed photographs, March 13, 1993.

685 "The Drum Major Instinct": MLK sermon at Ebenezer, Feb. 4, 1968, A/KS11; Washington, ed., *Testament,* p. 259ff; Carson and Holloran, eds. *Knock,* p. 165ff.

685 He freely adapted a sermon published: Miller, *Voice,* pp. 1–8; Lischer, *Preacher King,* pp. 99–100. No sources have yet come to light about King's attitude toward footnotes and attributions in formal scholarship, which might help explain the clear instances of plagiarism disclosed by 1990 in his 1954 doctoral dissertation at Boston University. As for the pulpit, however, some records do indicate that King viewed preaching to audiences as a collaborative art like improvisational jazz, and openly treated the words and rhetorical techniques of other orators as fair game in developing his repertoire. Cf. Miller, *Voice,* pp. 60–61; Warren, *King Came,* p. 134.

685 Yet Jesus in the Bible account: Mark 10:35–45.

686 "a conspicuous thread": Branch, *Parting,* p. 183.

686 recording played at his funeral: King, *My Life,* pp. 343–45.

686 "bring back Hosea Williams": Int. Hosea Williams, Oct. 29, 1991; int. Bernard Lafayette, March 22, 2005.

686 "a grand piece of psychological warfare": Kotz and Kotz, *Passion,* pp. 248–49.

686 waited in the Chicago YMCA: SAC, Chicago, to Director, Feb. 5, 1968, FK-3207; NYT, Feb. 6, 1968, p. 28.

687 "jumped on Martin": Kotz and Kotz, *Passion,* p. 252.

687 Bernard Lafayette rebelled: Int. Bernard Lafayette, May 28, 1990.

687 George Wiley: Kotz and Kotz, *Passion,* pp. 34–40, 53–59, 169–73, 238–42.

687 considered a position with SCLC: Wiretap transcript of telephone call between MLK and Stanley Levison, Sept. 9, 1967, FLNY-9-1057a.

687 Wiley soon wrote Young: Wiley to Young, March 25, 1968, A/SC40f3.

687 second nationwide mobilization: Hall, *Because,* pp. 62–64; Friedland, *Lift Up,* pp. 200–202; "Agenda for National Mobilization, February 5 & 6, 1968," Series 3, Box 8, CALCAV, SCPC.

687 "absolutely unsupportable": "Clerics Accuse U.S. of War Crimes," NYT, Feb. 4, 1968, pp. 1, 6; Melman, *America, passim;* press release for Feb. 4, 1968, Series 3, Box 8, CALCAV, SCPC, pp. 1–5.

687 protested the CALCAV mass meeting: NYT, Feb. 6, 1968, p. 15; WP, Feb. 6, 1968, p. B-1; FBI HQ LHM Feb. 6, 1968, FCLCV-15.

687 "to preserve freedom": *Washington Evening Star,* Feb. 6, 1968, p. 1.

687 "hardening of the heart": "In Whose Name?," a CALCAV pamphlet of speeches delivered Feb. 5 and 6, 1968, CALCAV papers, SCPC, p. 8.

688 "Guerilla warfare in the ghettos": Ibid., pp. 12–13.

688 Legal maneuvers intensified: "Clerics Rebuffed on a Protest Site," NYT, Feb. 3, 1968, p. 5; *Washington Evening Star,* Feb. 6, 1968, p. 1; WP, Feb. 6, 1968, p. B-1; NYT, Feb. 6, 1968, p. 15.

688 Two rabbis rushed off: Int. Balfour Brickner, Feb. 4, 1991.

688 News stories translated: NYT, Feb. 7, 1968, p. 17; WP, Feb. 7, 1968, p. B-1; "Clergy in the Capitol," *Christianity and Crisis,* March 4, 1968, pp. 36–37.

688 Book of Psalms: Mark 15:34 and Psalms 22:1.

688 King shuttled: SAC WFO to Director, Feb. 6, 1968, FK-3193; FBI HQ LHM dated Feb. 6, 1968, FCLCV-15.

688 laid aside the drafted speech: Int. Robert McAfee Brown, July 17, 1991; int. Barry Johnson, Jan. 4, 2005; MLK speech text released Feb. 6, 1968, Series 3, Box 8, CALCAV, SCPC; press release correction ["The speech was *not* (repeat) *not* delivered"], Feb. 6, 1968, Series 3, Box 8, CALCAV, SCPC.

688   King spoke extemporaneously: Ibid.

688   "I said some time ago": MLK remarks at New York Avenue Presbyterian Church, Feb. 6, 1968, A/KS10.

689   "seemed preoccupied with plans": *Newsweek,* Feb. 19, 1968, p. 58.

689   William Sloane Coffin closed: "In Whose Name?," a CALCAV pamphlet of speeches delivered Feb. 5 and 6, 1968, CALCAV papers, SCPC, pp. 15–20.

689   "You corrupted your wisdom": Ezekiel 28:17.

689   Washington's Black United Front: NYT, Dec. 12, 1967, p. 14; NYT, Jan. 16, 1968, p. 22; Chuck Stone, "He Was Our Balm in Gilead," *Philadelphia Daily News,* Jan. 16, 1986.

689   digest of his strident comments: Marvin Watson to LBJ, Dec. 28, 1967, with attached FBI special memorandum, dated Dec. 15, 1967, Box 73B, OFMS, LBJ.

689   "SNCC/Black Power": Hoover to Mildred Stegall, and Marvin Watson to LBJ, Aug. 23, 1967, with attached FBI monograph, "SNCC: Black Power," Box 73B, OFMS, LBJ.

689   "commandos occupying the place": Wiretap transcript of telephone call between Stanley Levison and William Rutherford, 10:30 P.M., Feb. 8, 1968, FLNY-9-1579a.

689   "serious tactical error": Carmichael, *Ready,* pp. 646–50.

689   "Well, if you are against this": Int. William Rutherford, Dec. 7, 2004; int. Jefferson Rogers, June 14, 2005.

690   banished the word "Negro": NYT, Feb. 26, 1968, p. 31.

690   King berated them: Garrow, *Bearing,* p. 596.

690   "Martin got very upset": Wiretap transcript of telephone call between Stanley Levison and William Rutherford, 10:30 P.M., Feb. 8, 1968, FLNY-9-1579a.

690   "And if I can leave you": MLK rally speech, Vermont Avenue Baptist Church, Feb. 7, 1968, A/KS10.

691   self-interest of wealthy Americans: NYT, Feb. 8, 1968, p. 30.

691   nearly missed his national appearance: Int. Harry Belafonte, March 7, 1985.

691   sensitive transitions in media history: "Belafonte Power," *Newsweek,* Feb. 19, 1968; *Tonight Show* notice for Feb. 8, 1968, A/KP4f17; Belafonte segment on CBS *60 Minutes,* Sept. 28, 1997; Dates and Barlow, eds., *Split Image,* pp. 288–89.

691   signal tragedy in Orangeburg: Nelson and Bass, *Massacre, passim;* Sellers, *River,* pp. 208–28; Marsh, *Summer,* pp. 185–88.

691   "during a heavy exchange of gunfire": Nelson and Bass, *Massacre,* pp. 99–105.

691   Two reporters would write: Ibid., *passim.*

691   Justice Department lawyers intervened: Ibid., pp. 115–18.

692   laconic sense of recovery: Paul Good, "The American Dream of Cleveland Sellers," *New South,* Spring 1973; int. Cleveland Sellers, Dec. 14, 1983.

692   "Being locked up for something": Sellers, *River,* p. 272.

692   "We demand that you act now": Undated statement with MLK signature in the hand of Andrew Young, A/SC39f23.

692   three FBI agents hamstrung: Nelson and Bass, *Massacre,* pp. 168–70; Nelson, *Terror,* p. 88. Authors Nelson and Bass conclude that the agents likely were motivated by their desire not to have to testify against South Carolina law enforcement officials. Declassified documents also show that, within hours of the shooting, the FBI disseminated to the White House and other agencies false reports that the students precipitated the incident with gunfire: "Several Negroes, while fleeing, reportedly opened fire with handguns and one highway patrolman struck in face by object later determined not to

be gunshot. Police guarding fire truck returned fire and three Negroes known to have been hit. . . . One Negro, who was shot, was reported to be Cleveland Louis Sellers, Jr. . . . He was later arrested by S.C. Law Enforcement Division." FBI Director to LBJ, 4:00 A.M., Feb. 9, 1968, WH Confidential Files, Box 56, HU2/ST40, LBJ.

692   Saturday in Philadelphia: NYT, Feb. 11, 1968, p. 60.

692   "I throw this out to get us shocked": "Action Committee Meeting," Paschal's Motor Hotel, Feb. 11, 1968, A/KP34f15; Garrow, *Bearing,* p. 597; Fairclough, *Redeem,* p. 366.

692    $6.97 payroll deduction: Charles Blackburn oral history by Selma Lewis, Bill Thomas, and David Yellin, May 29, 1968, pp. 16–21, MVC.

692   "Well, the men want": Beifuss, *River,* pp. 31–35.

693   "This was a strike": Honey, *Black Workers,* pp. 293–98.

693   sanitation workers walked off: McKnight, *Crusade,* p. 34.

693   P. J. Ciampa dampened the euphoria: Beifuss, *River,* pp. 34–35; Goulden, *Wurf,* pp. 148–50.

693   "Let no one make a mistake": "Loeb Issues Order to Stop Garbage Strike," MCA, Feb. 13, 1968, p. 1.

693   second week of Tet rattled experts: Clifford, *Counsel,* pp. 476–77.

693   "I do not want to argue": Notes of LBJ breakfast meeting with Democratic congressional leadership, Feb. 6, 1968, Box 2, Tom Johnson Papers, p. 4, LBJ; see also LBJ's discussion of the Byrd dissent with national security advisers the same day in FRUS, Vol. 6, p. 135ff.

693   "reinforcements at any time": Westmoreland to Wheeler, Feb. 9, 1968, in FRUS, Vol. 6, p. 153ff.

693   "strange contradiction": Notes of LBJ meeting with the Joint Chiefs of Staff, Feb. 9, 1968, Tom Johnson Papers, Box 2, p. 13, LBJ; "Johnson Says Foe's Raids Are a Failure Militarily," NYT, Feb. 3, 1968, p. 1.

693   The Sunday war council puzzled: Notes of meeting, 4:25–6:15 P.M., Feb. 11, 1968, in FRUS, Vol. 6, p. 175ff.

693   back-channel exchanges with the Pentagon: Karnow, *Vietnam,* pp. 562–64; FRUS, Vol. 6, p. 153, footnotes 1–3.

693   "We are now in a new ball game": Westmoreland to Sharp and Wheeler, Feb. 12, 1968, in FRUS, Vol. 6, p. 183ff.

694   President Johnson regathered his advisers: Notes of meeting, 1:45–3:08 P.M., Feb. 12, 1968, in FRUS, Vol. 6, p. 188ff.

694   News of the surprise escalation: "U.S. rushes 10,500 to Meet Threat of Vietnam Foe," NYT, Feb. 14, 1968, p. 1.

694   "More exploding rockets": "At Khesanh: Life on the Bullseye," NYT, Feb. 13, 1968, p. 1; Library of America Anthology, *Reporting Vietnam,* p. 576ff.

694   "Wheeler Doubts Khesanh": NYT, Feb. 15, 1968, p. 1.

694   "Westmoreland doesn't know": Notes of LBJ Meeting with Foreign Policy Advisors," 1:05–2:50 P.M., Feb. 20, 1968, Tom Johnson Papers, Box 2, LBJ.

694   The President also toured military installations: NYT, Feb. 18, 1968, p. 1; Schandler, *Unmaking,* p. 103; McPherson, *Political,* pp. 425–27; notes of LBJ breakfast on the carrier USS *Constellation,* Feb. 18, 1968, Tom Johnson Papers, Box 2, LBJ.

694   543 killed and 2,547 wounded: NYT, Feb. 23, 1968, p. 1; Langguth, *Our Vietnam,* p. 480.

694   twin-engine Cessna 406: Jackson LHM dated Feb. 16, 1968, FK-3215.

695   "I'm here to solicit": SC, Feb. 24–25, 1968, pp. 1, 3.

695   packed house at Selma's Tabernacle Baptist: Int. L. L. Anderson, May 27, 1990; int. Marie Foster, Aug. 8, 1990; int. Jean Jackson, May 27, 1990.

695   "Believe in your heart": MLK speech at Tabernacle Baptist Church, Feb. 16, 1968, A/KS.

695   Rev. M. C. Cleveland discreetly presented: Cleveland to MLK, Feb. 16, 1968, A/KP21f15.

695   Holt Street Baptist: Branch, *Parting,* pp. 138–42.

695   "and I see Brother Marlow": MLK speech to mass meeting in Montgomery, Feb. 17, 1968, Tape 25, A/KS; NYT, Feb. 18, 1968, p. 61.

695   favorite ecumenical parable: Luke 16:19–31.

695   deacon R. D. Nesbitt: SC, Feb. 24–25, 1968, pp. 1, 3; Branch, *Parting,* pp. 5–6, 103–4.

696   King described his two scariest memories: *Citizen King,* a Roja Production for *The American Experience,* PBS, 2004; "Assassination Attempt, in Plane," 1968, A/KS.

696   "Well, it came time to pray": Jose Iglesias, "Dr. King's March on Washington, Part II," NYT Magazine, March 31, 1968, p. 30ff.

696   parable of the Good Samaritan: Luke 10:25–37.

696   "And until mankind rises above race": MLK sermon, "Who Is My Neighbor?," Feb. 18, 1968, A/KS.

696   air of frantic melancholy: Barrett, *News,* p. 598.

696   "plush new Sheraton–Four Ambassadors Hotel": Hoover to Mildred Stegall, Feb. 21, 1968, with attached FBI HQ LHM and handwritten instructions for Rostow, Box 32, OFMS, LBJ.

696   major shift by the Ford Foundation: NYT, Feb. 18, 1968, p. 1.

696   "The first conclusion I offer": "The Ford Foundation Annual Report 1967," p. 2, AFF.

696   "The problem is that the rising": MLK remarks to the Ministers Leadership Training Program, Feb. 19, 1968, A/SC28f51.

697   convinced King to miss two days: Miami LHM dated Feb. 23, 1968, "RE: Washington Spring Project," FSC-NR; McKnight, *Crusade,* p. 69; Samuel B. (Billy) Kyles oral history, June 12, 1968, MVC; Garrow, *Bearing,* p. 598; Fairclough, *Redeem,* pp. 366–67.

697   James Lawson declined the trip: Int. James Lawson, Nov. 9, 1983, and Nov. 14, 1983.

697   Local editorials rallied behind city government: Beifuss, *River,* p. 45.

697   "The city hired 47 new sanitation workers": Lead story, WMC-TV Memphis, *Six O'Clock News,* Feb. 15, 1968, MVC.

697   "CIAMPA GO HOME": Beifuss, *River,* pp. 40–41.

697   Jerry Wurf, AFSCME's international president, assumed command: Goulden, *Wurf,* pp. 148–57.

697   Loeb stood a head taller: Frank, *American Death,* pp. 10–11.

698   public forum on Thursday, February 22: Beifuss, *River,* pp. 75–83; McKnight, *Crusade,* pp. 36–37.

699   total mechanization of cotton farms: Honey, *Black Workers,* pp. 286–87.

699   "The men were on their feet cheering": Beifuss, *River,* p. 82.

699   sanitation workers arrived: Bailey, *Mine Eyes,* p. 37.

699   "as if it were a raid by barbaric Visigoths": Goulden, *Wurf,* pp. 160–61.

699   Council members entered long enough: Beifuss, *River,* p. 83ff; MCA, Feb. 24, 1968, pp. 1, 3.

700   "could you give us a microphone?": James Lawson oral history, Sept. 24, 1969, p. 1, MVC.

700   Blanchard retained a stab of conscience: Jerred Blanchard oral history, pp. 5–8, 16–20.

700   "Well, the police have their gas masks on": Beifuss, *River,* p. 87.

700   order to disperse the procession: Frank Holloman oral history, Aug. 14, 1973, pp. 14–15, MVC.

700   Seventy-two-year-old O. B. Hicks: *Memphis Tri-State Defender,* March 2, 1968, p. 12; McKnight, *Crusade,* 40.

700   dragged toward jail on their bellies: *Citizen King,* a Roja Production for *The American Experience,* PBS, 2004.

701   P. J. Ciampa came there late: Goulden, *Wurf,* pp. 163–64.

701   strange sight of polished spats: P. J. Ciampa oral history, Feb. 3, 1972, pp. 12–15, MVC.

701   "This happened to me": Beifuss, *River,* pp. 92–93; H. Ralph Jackson oral history, pp. 1–10, MVC; McKnight, *Crusade,* pp. 40–41.

701   Rev. Bill Aldridge: Beifuss, *River,* pp. 180–81.

701   "who breathes fire and smoke": Bryant George, "Report to the Ford Foundation," Feb. 25, 1968, p. 3, Grant 67-580, FFA. The FBI sent the White House and major government agencies sketchy intelligence on Bevel's controversial rhetoric in Miami: "Concerning religion, Reverend Bevel advised he did not believe in the virgin birth of Christ. He advised he was firmly convinced that 'Mary' was raped by a Roman soldier." G. C. Moore to W. C. Sullivan, Feb. 26, 1968, FK-3227.

701   Daniel Moynihan had the misfortune: Ibid., p. 4; Moynihan to Bundy, Feb. 27, 1968, Grant 67-580, FFA; int. Marion Bascom, Jan. 19, 1995.

702   "I have shouted until my garter-holders": Address by C. T. Vivian, "Creative New Ministries," Feb. 22, 1968, transcript in Grant 67-580, FFA.

702   "And the valley calls us": MLK speech, "Pre-Washington Campaign," Feb. 23, 1968, A/KS.

702   "Oh Lord, all hell's broke": Beifuss, *River,* p. 96.

702   the Sheraton's piano: Samuel B. (Billy) Kyles oral history, June 12, 1968, MVC; Gwen Kyles oral history, May 28, 1968, MVC.

702   hundredth-birthday celebration: Lewis, *King,* p. 396; Garrow, *FBI and King,* p. 185; New York LHM dated Feb. 27, 1968, FK-NR.

703   "civilization virtually collapsed": MLK speech, "Honoring Dr. Du Bois," Feb. 23, 1968, *Freedomways,* Spring 1968, p. 104ff.

703   "I've never heard Martin": Wiretap transcript of telephone call between Stanley Levison and Clarence Jones, 2:28 P.M., Feb. 24, 1968, FLNY-9-1590a.

703   "Prime Minister of the Black Nation": Carson, *Struggle,* pp. 278–82; Carmichael, *Ready,* p. 641; jail interview with Huey P. Newton, March 8, 1968, in Bracey et al., *Black Nationalism,* p. 534ff.

703   "The vote in this country is": Carmichael, *Stokely Speaks,* pp. 111–30.

703   he turned also against any "white" Marxist anchor: Carmichael, *Ready,* p. 600; Carson, *Struggle,* p. 282; Gitlin, *Sixties,* p. 349.

704   "The sky is the limit": Forman, *Making,* pp. 526.

704   menaced himself by Black Panthers: Ibid.; int. Ivanhoe Donaldson, Nov. 30, 2000; int. James Forman, Feb. 13, 2001.

704   Newton wanted Carmichael: Hilliard and Cole, *This Side,* pp. 170–77.

704   "suitcase full of African souvenirs": Eldridge Cleaver, "Open Letter to Stokely," *Black Panther* newspaper of Aug. 16, 1969, in FBI report dated Oct. 31, 1969, p. 54, FBI HQ File 100-446080-2370.

704   "SNCC people were the bad niggers": Carson, *Struggle,* p. 283.

704   requesting 205,179 more U.S. soldiers: Wheeler to LBJ, Feb. 27, 1968, in FRUS, Vol. 6, p. 263ff.

704   "This is unbelievable and futile": Meeting notes, Feb. 27, 1968, in FRUS, Vol. 6, p. 260ff; Califano, *Triumph,* pp. 262–64.

704   Cronkite asked his viewers: *CBS Evening News,* "Walter Cronkite Report from Vietnam: Who? What? When? Where? Why?," Feb. 27, 1968, T79:0331, MOB; NYT, Feb. 28, 1968, p. 95; Dallek, *Flawed,* pp. 503–6; Appy, *Patriots,* p. 293; Karnow, *Vietnam,* p. 561.

704   Wheeler's manner was graver: Karnow, *Vietnam,* pp. 564–65; Clifford, *Counsel,* pp. 485–86.

705   "Buzz, we are very thankful": White House meeting notes, 8:35–11:15 A.M., Feb. 28, 1968, in FRUS, Vol. 6, p. 267ff.

705   Mendel Rivers irascibly said: NYT, March 1, 1968, p. 15.

705   Henry "Scoop" Jackson warned that he would balk: Clifford, *Counsel,* pp. 497–99.

705   "Well, did he call my name?": LBJ phone call with Richard Russell, 4:10 P.M., March 7, 1968, Audiotape F6802.04, in FRUS, Vol. 6, p. 345.

705   "Panel on Civil Disorders": NYT, March 1, 1968, p. 1.

705   The President steadfastly ignored: Cálifano, *Triumph,* pp. 260–62; Dallek, *Flawed,* pp. 515–16.

705   "What white Americans": Kerner, *Report,* pp. 2, 203.

705   Aides bravely warned: McPherson to Califano, March 1, 1968, McPherson Papers, Box 32, LBJ; Louis Martin to Califano, March 5, 1968, Califano Papers, Box 9, LBJ.

705   stealthy new travel regimen: "Johnson Berates Vietnam Critics," NYT, March 2, 1968, p. 21; "On the Trail: Johnson Has Answers," NYT, March 3, 1968, p. 1.

706   740,000 paperback copies sold: NYT, March 14, 1968, p. 49.

706   Potentates in Congress: NYT, March 2, 1968, p. 1.

706   *What Happened to the Riot Report?:* NYT, April 24, 1968, p. 95.

706   "Our nation is moving": Kerner, *Report,* p. 1.

706   "I'd be a hypocrite": Lemann; *Promised,* pp. 190–91.

706   Lawson made King laugh: Int. James Lawson, Nov. 9, 1983; Beifuss, *River,* p. 137.

707   turned out in Atlanta on Monday: NYT, March 5, 1968, p. 28.

707   backup force of ten thousand MPs: NYT, March 4, 1968, p. 22.

707   he escaped to Mexico: Garrow, *Bearing,* p. 600.

707   "We want arrest": Beifuss, *River,* pp. 156–59.

707   NAACP leader Maxine Smith: Ibid.; Maxine Smith oral history, June 13, 1968, pp. 1–16, MVC.

707   he had invited King to Memphis: News script, Memphis WMC-TV Channel Five, March 5, 1968, MVC. The newscast reported that King's Atlanta office said he was leaving the country until Saturday.

707   "Unfulfilled Dreams": MLK sermon at Ebenezer Baptist Church, March 3, 1968, A/KS; Carson and Holloran, eds., *Knock,* p. 191ff.

707   "You did well that it was in your heart": I Kings 8:18.

707   Ralph Abernathy soon wangled rooms: Int. Ralph Abernathy, Nov. 19, 1984.

708   He stared alone from a high balcony: Ibid.; Frank, *American Death,* pp. 90–93.

708   Hoover circulated another secret report: Garrow, *FBI and King,* pp. 185–86.

708   Richard Harwood disclosed: "J. Edgar Hoover: A Librarian with a Lifetime Lease," WP, Feb. 25, 1968, p. D-1.

708   a few journalists would regret: Haynes Johnson, "A Generation-Old Crusade to Destroy King's Name at Any Cost," WP, Oct. 16, 1983; AJC, Nov. 21, 2004, p. D-1.

708   "I didn't do my job": Paul Clancy, "The Bureau and the Bureaus," *Quill,* Feb. 1976, p. 15.

708   "Not a complete file": T. E. Bishop to DeLoach, Feb. 29, 1968, FK-NR.

708   "no possibility of embarrassment": Hoover to SAC, Albany, and forty SACs, March 3, 1968, FBNH-17, p. 6.

708   "a grave threat to peace": "Outlook for Racial Violence in Washington, D.C.," FBI study attached to R. W. Smith to W. C. Sullivan, March 6, 1968, FBI File 157-6-53, Serial 1284, p. 17.

709   "King would be a very real contender": Hoover to SAC, Albany, and forty SACs, March 3, 1968, FBNH-17, p. 3.

709   forty black rookies among six thousand agents: McKnight, *Crusade,* p. 96.

709   the approved COINTELPRO actions: Carson, *Struggle,* pp. 260–62; Garrow, *FBI and King,* p. 188; Powers, *Secrecy,* pp. 425–26; O'Reilly, *"Racial,"* pp. 80–86; McKnight, *Crusade,* pp. 26–27.

709   "each movement as they squirmed": Hoover to SAC, Albany, and all offices, Aug. 5, 1968, FBNH-233.

709   wars against the Communist Party: Cf. "FBI to Pay Widow After Targeting Communist Mate," *Baltimore Sun,* Oct. 27, 1989.

709   "Mrs. Carmichael appeared shocked": SAC, New York, to Director, Sept. 9, 1968, FBNH-[serial illegible].

709   "Show this to [Labor Secretary] Bill Wirtz": LBJ handwritten note on March 14, 1968 summary [by Marvin Watson], with Hoover note to Mildred Stegall and attached "Martin Luther King, Jr.—A Current Analysis," March 12, 1968, Box 32, OFMS, LBJ.

710   shock passed visibly through the ballroom: Clifford, *Counsel,* pp. 500–501.

710   "Westmoreland Requests": NYT, March 10, 1968, p. 1.

710   Paar told viewers: McCarthy for President, transcript of Jack Paar interview, March 11, 1968, Lowenstein Papers, Box 54, Folder 138, UNC.

710   McCarthy confounded political observers: Powers, *War,* pp. 290–91; transcript of nine LBJ ads run in New Hampshire, McCarthy for President, n.d., March 1968, Lowenstein Papers, Box 54, Folder 106, UNC.

710   "on an overwhelming scale": Braestrup, *Big Story,* pp. 492–93; NYT, March 14, 1968, p. 87.

710   139,801 American casualties: NYT, March 15, 1968, p. 1; Zaroulis and Sullivan, *Who Spoke Up?,* p. 159.

710   Robert Kennedy's tormented new offer: Clifford, *Counsel,* pp. 504–5; Shesol, *Contempt,* pp. 420–21; NYT, March 18, 1968, p. 1.

710   Kennedy formally challenged: Schlesinger, *Robert Kennedy,* pp. 910–21; transcript, "Kennedy Announcement," March 16, 1968, RFK Senate Papers, Box 4, JFK.

710   "blood oath" commitments: Mike Manatos note, March 16, 1968, Marvin Watson Papers, "Robert Kennedy" Folder, Box 25, LBJ; Marvin Watson to LBJ, March 15, 1968, Watson Papers, Box 25, LBJ.

710   "I can't afford to lose Russell": LBJ phone call with Clark Clifford, 8:44 A.M., March 20, 1968, Audiotape F6805.02, in FRUS, Vol. 6, p. 428ff.

711   offer from McGeorge Bundy: Ibid.; notes of LBJ meeting, March 19, 1968, in FRUS, Vol. 6, pp. 412–18; Clifford, *Counsel,* pp. 507–8.

711   civil rights bill from 1966: NYT, March 12, 1968, p. 1; Graham, *Civil Rights Era,* pp. 270–71; Kotz, *Judgment,* p. 391.

711   invoke cloture for the eighth time: NYT, March 5, 1968, pp. 1, 28.

711   "pulling it out of the fire": NYT, Feb. 28, 1968, pp. 1, 30.

711   wholesale segregation of state prisons: Morgan, *One Man,* pp. 48–56.

711   rules requiring flight attendants: Graham, *Civil Rights Era,* pp. 231–32.

711   "We would like to recruit": Beifuss, *River,* pp. 127–28.

712   "be-in" at New York's Grand Central Station: NYT, March 24, 1968, p. 1.

712   South African Government introduced: NYT, March 27, 1968, p. 16.

712   pelted four State Department visitors: SC, March 9–10, 1968, p. 1; Forman, *Sammy Younge,* pp. 264–67.

712   "It was the first time a state jury": Jack Nelson, "Klansman Given Life Sentence in Negro's Fire-Bomb Murder," LAT, March 16, 1968, p. 1; NYT, March 16, 1968, p. 17.

712   whittled on the bench: SC, March 23–24, 1968, p. 1.

712   "because I done what I done": LAT, March 15, 1968, p. 4.

712   reporter Jerry Mitchell noticed: Cf. Jerry Mitchell front-page stories, *Jackson Clarion-Ledger,* Jan. 17, 18, 26, 28, and Feb. 10, 1998.

712   atonement prosecutions revived: Cf. NYT, April 2, 1995, p. 18; NYT, May 29, 1998, p. 1; WP, July 22, 1998, p. C-1; *Baltimore Sun,* Dec. 20, 1998, p. C-1; AC, Feb. 21, 1999, p. M-1; NYT, May 18, 2000, p. 23; WP, Sept. 26, 2000, p. 3; NYT, Jan. 24, 2001, p. 17; NYT, May 11, 2004, p. 1; NYT, Jan. 8, 2005, p. 1; NYT, June 12, 2005, p. 16; NYT, June 24, 2005, p. 11; Branch, *Parting,* p. 611.

713   His elite Tiger Force platoon: Michael D. Sallah and Mitch Weiss, "Buried Secrets, Brutal Truths," *Toledo Blade,* Oct. 19–22, 2003; WP, Oct. 20, 2003, p. 2; NYT, Dec. 28, 2003, p. 18; NYT, Feb. 16, 2004, p. 9.

713   "They shot and wounded her": Hersh, *My Lai,* pp. 37–38.

714   My Lai: Hersh, *My Lai, passim;* Langguth, *Our Vietnam,* pp. 495–502, 579–80; Appy, *Patriots,* pp. 343–53.

715   "American troops caught": NYT, March 17, 1968, p. 1.

715   Ron Ridenhour: Hersh, *My Lai,* pp. 103–10; Langguth, *Our Vietnam,* pp. 495–96, 502; Appy, *Patriots,* pp. 349–53; Ridenhour letter of March 29, 1969, at www.law .umkc.edu/faculty/projects/ftrials/mylai/ridenhour_ltr.html; "The Heroes of Mylai," transcripts from the Tulane University My Lai conference in December 1994; NYT, May 11, 1998, p. 15; int. Mary Howell, July 17, 2005. The Ron Ridenhour associated with My Lai is not the Freedom Summer volunteer of the same name mentioned in Branch, *Pillar,* p. 371.

715   Soldier's Medal for Gallantry: NYT, March 15, 1998, p. 10.

715   Colburn was dumbfounded: Appy, *Patriots,* p. 349.

715   summit meeting with seventy-eight: NYT, March 15, 1968, p. 36; Garrow, *Bearing,* p. 601; Greenberg, *Crusaders,* pp. 431–32; George A. Wiley to Andrew Young, March 25, 1968, A/SC40f3; int. Bernard Lafayette, May 28, 1990, March 22, 2005, June 15, 2005; int. William Rutherford, Dec. 7, 2004; int. Tom Houck, June 23, 2005, July 12, 2005.

716   "Are they poor?": Int. Bernard Lafayette, March 22, 2005.

716   "that smart aleck nigger come out of jail": Peggy Terry oral history by Studs Terkel, 1990, "Conversations with America," http://www.studsterkel.org/race.php.

716   ribbed young Tom Houck: Gilliard, *Living,* p. 279ff.

716   "First he was Coretta's boy": Int. Tom Houck, July 12, 2005.

716   made note of hushed deliberation: Int. Vincent Harding, Dec. 30, 2004.

717   Tijerina proposed: Tijerina, *They Called Me,* pp. 101–4.

717   "I believe we caught a glimpse": Fairclough, *Redeem,* p. 369.

717   Grosse Point: Garrow, *Bearing,* p. 601; Detroit LHM dated March 15, 1968, FK-3239; WP, March 16, 1968, p. 6.

717   Robert Kennedy left a message: Schlesinger, *Robert Kennedy,* p. 930; wiretap transcript of telephone call between Stanley Levison and Harry Wachtel, 11:58 A.M., March 19, 1968, FLNY-9-11614a.

717   Burke Marshall persisted: Burke Marshall oral history by T. H. Baker, Aug. 14, 1983; int. Burke Marshall, Sept. 26, 1984.

717   noncommittal to reporters: SAC, Los Angeles, to Director, March 16, 1968, FK-3235.

717   "The government is emotionally committed": MLK speech to California Democratic Council, March 16, 1968, A/KS.

717   "We love nothing more": NYT, March 19, 1968, p. 1.

718   He sent a telegram to César Chávez: www.ufw.org/mlk00.html.

718   Robert Kennedy had just visited Chávez: Thomas, *Robert Kennedy,* p. 359.

718   change Michael Harrington's draft call: Wiretap transcript of telephone call between Stanley Levison and William Rutherford, 4:15 P.M., March 23, 1968, FLNY-9-1618a.

718   visits to Indian reservations: Ibid.; ADW, March 15, 1968, p. 2.

718   James Lawson tracked him down: Int. James Lawson, Nov. 9, 1983; Blackside, Inc., *Eyes on the Prize II—America at the Racial Crossroads, 1965 to 1985,* Vol. IV, "The Promised Land (1967–68)"; James Lawson oral history, July 1, 1968, MVC; Beifuss, *River,* p. 190; itinerary for MLK and Andrew Young, March 14–18, 1968, A/SC48f12.

718   "No one else can get": Fairclough, *Redeem,* p. 371; Frank, *American Death,* pp. 16–17.

718   into the cavernous Mason Temple: Beifuss, *River,* pp. 193–96; Frank, *American Death,* pp. 16–18; Young, *Burden,* p. 450; Goulden, *Wurf,* p. 173; Garrow, *Bearing,* pp. 605–6; James Lawson oral history, July 1, 1968, MVC; SAC, Memphis, to Director, March 19, 1968, FK-NR.

718   "NOT BY MIGHT": Zechariah 4:6.

719   "You are demanding that this city": MLK address at Mason Temple, March 18, 1968, A/KS.

720   "You could touch him": Walter Bailey oral history, July 10, 1968, MVC.

720   Into the night: Garrow, *FBI and King,* p. 189; Beifuss, *River,* p. 196; NYT, March 18, 1968, p. 28.

720   Tuesday morning in Batesville: Itinerary for MLK tour, March 19–23, 1968, A/KP12f67; SAC Jackson to Director, March 19, 1968, FK-[illegible]; King, *My Life,* p. 606.

720   old funeral parlor calendars: NYT, March 20, 1968, p. 18.

720   "Statistics reveal": MLK rally speech, Marks, Mississippi, March 19, 1968, A/KS.

720   pulled out a hundred-dollar bill: Ibid.; int. Curtis Wilkie, April 11, 1995.

721   "morning noon and night": Blackside, Inc., *Eyes on the Prize II—America at the Racial Crossroads, 1965 to 1985,* Vol. IV, "The Promised Land (1967–68)."

721   Abernathy and Andrew Young: Young, *Burden,* pp. 450–51; Abernathy, *Walls,* pp. 412–13. Abernathy puts this scene in Marks during the Meredith march of 1966, but the circumstances match the 1968 visit.

721   "He's here! He's here!": Int. David Jordan, June 25, 1992.

721   "I wept with them as I heard": MLK rally speech in Greenwood, Mississippi, March 19, 1968, A/KS.

721   landed after midnight in Hattiesburg: SAC Jackson to Director, March 20, 1968, FK-3260.

722   resentment of Indian and Hispanic groups: Ibid.; Garrow, *Bearing,* p. 607.

722   "You can pass all the riot laws": SC, March 30–31, 1968, p. 1.

722   cancel several Alabama stops: Birmingham LHM dated March 22, 1968, FK-NR.

722   Hoover reported secretly: Hoover to Stegall, with attached White House summary and FBI HQ LHM dated March 22, 1968, OFMS, LBJ.

722   The President was consumed: Dallek, *Flawed,* pp. 509–12; Clifford, *Counsel,* pp. 508–11; Langguth, *Our Vietnam,* pp. 487–88.

722   relieve General Westmoreland: Dallek, *Flawed,* pp. 509–12; Clifford, *Counsel,* pp. 508–11; Langguth, *Our Vietnam,* pp 487–88; FRUS, Vol. VI, pp. 451–53.

722   complained to Senator Russell: LBJ phone call with Richard Russell, 4:49 P.M., March 22, 1968, Audiotape F6803.02, in FRUS, p. 447ff.

722   "our own sensitivity to criticism": Fortas remarks in White House meeting of March 20, 1968, in ibid., p. 432ff.

722   Lawson called King: Beifuss, *River,* pp. 203–04; Garrow, *FBI and King,* p. 191.

722   "The Lord sent the snow": McKnight, *Crusade,* p. 52.

39: REQUIEM

723   "I'd feel like a bird in a cage": Garrow, *Bearing,* pp. 606–7.

723   "Now Marty and Dexter": MLK rally speech, Albany, Georgia, March 23, 1968, A/KS; report of Rev. Samuel B. Wells, A/KP34f3.

723   vision of dry bones: Ezekiel 37:1–14.

723   service for Rev. Wyatt Tee Walker: Garrow, *Bearing,* p. 608; int. Wyatt Tee Walker, Aug. 20, 1984; Dora McDonald to Wyatt Tee Walker, Dec. 6, 1967, A/KP36f4.

723   Adam Clayton Powell marched outside: *New York Daily News,* March 25, 1968, p. 3.

724   Powell's fugitive return: NYT, March 25, 1968, p. 1; Hamilton, *Adam Clayton Powell,* pp. 465–66; New York LHM dated March 25, 1968, FACP-361; wiretap transcript of telephone call between Stanley Levison and William Rutherford, March 23, 1968, FLNY-9-1618a.

724   "Nonviolence Tactic Defended by King": NYT, March 25, 1968, p. 46.

724   King's advisers gathered Monday: Garrow, *Bearing,* p. 608; Frances Allison to "Action Committee Members," March 20, 1968, A/SC48f7.

724   King's commitment to detour again into Memphis: "Dr. King Reschedules March for Strikers in Memphis," NYT, March 25, 1968, p. 46.

724   support in Washington from religious groups: WP, March 16, 1968, p. B-2; New York LHM dated March 26, 1968, "Washington Spring Project/Racial Matters," FK-NR.

724   Harry Wachtel broke away: Oates, *Trumpet,* p. 475.

725   "Where in America today": Transcript, "Conversation with Martin Luther King," March 25, 1968, in *Conservative Judaism,* Vol. 22, No. 3, Spring 1968, p. 1.

725   King returned Heschel's salute: Ibid.; Cf. Branch, *Pillar,* pp. 21–32.

725   jail witness long ago in Albany: Cf. Gentry, *Hoover,* pp. 630–31.

725   "if they couldn't protect Kennedy": Int. Harry Wachtel, Nov. 29, 1983.

726   quarrel lay with Logan's wife: Garrow, *Bearing,* p. 609; Frank, *American Death,* pp. 39–42; int. Marian Logan, April 24, 1984; int. Clifford Alexander, Dec. 17, 2004.

726   memo arguing that King should abort: Marian Logan to MLK, March 8, 1968, A/SC40f3.

727   "I am still so excited": NYT, March 27, 1968, p. 24.

727   "We do not fear": "Notes of Meeting," 1:15–3:05 P.M., March 26, 1968, in FRUS, Vol. 6, p. 466ff.

727   President Johnson invited the generals: Ibid.; PDD, March 26, 1968, pp. 4–8, LBJ.

727 McGeorge Bundy chilled the Cabinet Room: "Summary of Notes," Cabinet Room meeting, 3:15–4:32 P.M., March 26, 1968, in FRUS, Vol. 6, p. 471ff; McGeorge Bundy handwritten notes, March 26, 1968, Meeting Notes File, Box 2, LBJ.

727 repeat performances would demonstrate: LBJ briefings by General William DePuy and CIA official George Carver, March 27, 1968, in FRUS, Vol. 6, p. 481ff.

727 "Who the hell is there left": Isaacson, *Wise Men,* pp. 698–706; Langguth, *Our Vietnam,* pp. 488–90.

728 war loyalists stifled alarm: Clifford, *Counsel,* pp. 512–13.

728 "impregnated them with their doubts": Taylor, *Swords,* p. 391.

728 "deny military victory": Rusk, *As I Saw It,* p. 478.

728 "Then what in the name of God": Clifford, *Counsel,* p. 517; Langguth, *Our Vietnam,* pp. 491–92.

728 "What we want to do": FRUS, Vol. 6, p. 474.

728 "I know there is a lot of dying men": Ibid., p. 476.

729 "We have set our face": Clifford, *Counsel,* p. 510.

729 polls had shifted nearly 20 percent: DeBenedetti, *Ordeal,* pp. 211–13; Karnow, *Vietnam,* pp. 558–60.

729 "deepening disenchantment": O'Brien to LBJ, March 27, 1968, in FRUS, Vol. 6, p. 479.

729 lose to Eugene McCarthy: Powers, *War,* p. 302; Viorst, *Fire,* p. 419.

729 "I don't give a damn": Notes of LBJ meeting with Earle Wheeler and Creighton Abrams, 10:30 A.M.–12:15 P.M., March 26, 1968, in FRUS, Vol. 6, p. 46.

729 Tuesday's stops in Harlem: NYT, March 27, 1968, p. 24.

729 Hoover rushed: Hoover to Mildred Stegall, April 1, 1968, Box 32, OFMS, LBJ; NYT, March 24, 1968, p. 40.

729 "We'll make him Secretary of State": Wiretap transcript of telephone call between MLK and Stanley Levison, 12:37 A.M., March 27, 1968, FLNY-9-1621a.

730 side trip to Boston: Wiretap transcript of telephone calls between Stanley Levison and William Rutherford (9:45 P.M.), Levison and unnamed women (11:00 P.M.), March 26, 1968, and Levison and Dora McDonald (12:20 A.M.), March 27, 1968, in FLNY-9-1621a.

730 "Memphis Protest Avoids Violence": NYT, March 24, 1968, p. 66.

730 Wednesday night fund-raiser: Wiretap transcript of telephone call between Stanley Levison and Adele Kanter, 12:10 P.M., March 15, 1968, FLNY-9-1610a; Frank, *American Death,* p. 25.

730 breakneck antipoverty rallies: NYT, March 28, 1968, p. 40.

730 nothing unconstitutional about starving: Fager, *Uncertain,* p. 18.

730 loggerheads with Young: Gardner, *Young,* pp. 139–40; Young, *Burden,* p. 451.

730 frustrated King until he slammed: Int. Harry Belafonte, March 6–7, 1985.

730 King back to Memphis: Beifuss, *River,* pp. 211–42; Garrow, *Bearing,* pp. 609–11; Garrow, *FBI and King,* pp. 191–93; Frank, *American Death,* pp. 22–27; McKnight, *Crusade,* pp. 53–55; Fairclough, *Redeem,* pp. 372–75; MCA, March 29, 1968, p. 1; AC, March 29, 1968, p. 1; NYT, March 29, 1968, p. 1; *Memphis Tri-State Defender,* April 6, 1968, pp. 1, 12.

731 I AM A MAN: Beifuss, *River,* pp. 217–18; Honey, *Black Workers,* pp. 307–8; Goulden, *Wurf,* p. 174; Bailey, *Mine Eyes,* pp. 80–81.

731 Lawson ran about fifty feet: David Caywood oral history, May 20, 1968, MVC.

731 Pandemonium greeted King: "Day's Log of Police Calls," MCA, March 29, 1968, p. 25.

731 "It's my fault": Abernathy, *Walls,* pp. 417–18; Hearings, House Select Committee on Assassinations, Aug. 14, 1978, Vol. 1, pp. 15–16.

732 park named for W. C. Handy: MCA, March 29, 1968, p. 25; NYT, March 29, 1968, p. 29; Bailey, *Mine Eyes,* p. 66.

732 storefront windows being smashed: Blackside, Inc., *Eyes on the Prize II—America at the Racial Crossroads, 1965 to 1985,* Vol. IV, "The Promised Land (1967–68)"; *Citizen King,* a Roja Production for *The American Experience,* PBS, 2004.

732 Shainberg's: Oral history by Councilman Fred Davis, May 22, 1968, MVC.

732 "It had come seven blocks": Beifuss, *River,* p. 225.

732 within twenty feet of King: Lux testimony in *City of Memphis v. Martin Luther King, Jr. et al.,* U.S. District Court for the Western District of Tennessee, Case. No. C-68-80, April 4, 1968, p. 106, transcript courtesy of Charles F. Newman.

732 lent his bullhorn in the emergency: James Lawson oral history, July 8, 1970, MVC.

732 Bernard Lee pulled King and Abernathy: Stokes, *Report,* pp. 361–62; Bailey, *Mine Eyes,* pp. 60–61; McKnight, *Crusade,* p. 61; SAC, Memphis, to Director, 12:56 A.M., March 29, 1968, FBI File 157-1094, Serial 1405.

733 Trouble radiated from wild looting: Bailey, *Mine Eyes,* pp. 64–67, 78–79.

733 Nine officers would be injured: Ibid., pp. 68–69; Beifuss, *River,* pp. 243–45; McKnight, *Crusade,* p. 55.

733 One patrolman cornered: *Memphis Tri-State Defender,* April 6, 1968, pp. 1, 12; Beifuss, *River,* pp. 241–42, 263; McKnight, *Crusade,* p. 56.

733 Fleet young rioters: Beifuss, *River,* pp. 233–37.

733 Tennessee legislature swiftly proposed and enacted: MCA, March 29, 1968, p. 1; AC, March 29, 1968, p. 1.

733 1866 Reconstruction riot: James Gilbert Ryan, "The Memphis Riots of 1866; Terror in a Black Community During Reconstruction," *Journal of Negro History,* July 1977, p. 243ff.

733 Trapped at the Rivermont: Garrow, *Bearing,* p. 611; Frank, *American Death,* pp. 27–29; Abernathy, *Walls,* pp. 419–20; Hearings, House Select Committee on Assassinations, Aug. 14, 1978, Vol. 1, p. 16.

733 "accidentally exposed to Mace": News script, WMC-TV Channel Five, March 28, 1968, MVC.

733 stories marshaled politicians: Beifuss, *River,* pp. 243–50; "White Memphis Unshaken by Riot," NYT, March 31, 1968, p. 66.

734 He sank beneath the bedcovers: Frank, *American Death,* p. 28; Garrow, *FBI and King,* p. 194; McKnight, *Crusade,* p. 64.

734 Young called Stanley Levison: Wiretap transcript of telephone call between Stanley Levison and Andrew Young, 8:10 P.M., March 28, 1968, FLNY-9-1623a.

734 Levison groped for triage: Wiretap transcript of telephone call between MLK and Stanley Levison, 9:15 P.M., March 28, 1968, FLNY-9-1623a; New York LHM dated March 29, 1968, FK-3272.

734 "Maybe we just have to admit": Garrow, *FBI and King,* p. 194.

734 "The violence in Memphis": Fairclough, *Redeem,* p. 375.

734 churned out operations against King: Garrow, *FBI and King,* p. 188; McKnight, *Crusade,* pp. 60–61.

734 King did not need contributions: Moore to Sullivan, March 26, 1968, FBNH-NR; New York LHM dated March 20, 1968, FK-NR.

734 "Prepare the letters": Director to SAC, Mobile, April 2, 1968, FBNH-63.

735 Headquarters subsidized the lecture tour: Jones to Bishop, re: Julia Brown, March 28, 1968, FSC-NR; O'Reilly, *"Racial,"* p. 107.

735 "a black folk hero": SAC, Chicago, to Director, March 21, 1968, FBNH-39; Director to SAC, Chicago, March 25, 1968, FBNH-33.

735 "the result of King's famous espousal": Moore to Sullivan, March 28, 1968, FK-NR.

735 "Like Judas leading lambs": Moore to Sullivan, March 29, 1968, FBNH-NR.

735 requested permission to reinstall wiretaps: Hoover to the Attorney General, April 2, 1968, FSC-2107, FK-3655.

735 "discredit King and his aides with poor Negroes": SAC, Jackson, to Director, April 4, 1968, FBNH-72.

736 "What's wrong with Bobby?": Califano, *Triumph,* p. 268; Schlesinger, *Robert Kennedy,* p. 930.

736 Such dispassion baffled wary aides: Califano, *Triumph,* pp. 265–66; McPherson, *Political,* pp. 427–28.

736 Defense Secretary Clifford scowled down: McPherson, *Political,* pp. 437–38.

736 Kennedy had voted with him: Bellinger to Fred Panzer, March 29, 1968, cited in Shesol, *Contempt,* p. 336.

736 foreign policy officials reviewed: Clifford, *Counsel,* pp. 519–21; Langguth, *Our Vietnam,* p. 493.

736 memoirs by McPherson and Clifford: Ibid.; McPherson, *Political,* pp. 433–35.

736 "Tonight I want to speak to you": FRUS, Vol. 6, pp. 483–84; NYT, April 1, 1968, p. 26.

736 Johnson decried the Memphis riot: "President Offers U.S. Aid to Cities in Curbing Riots," NYT, March 30, 1968, p. 1.

737 "redress by mob law": Ibid.; *CBS Evening News with Walter Cronkite,* March 29, 1968, VTR 236-B, LBJ.

737 working from the peace draft: Clifford, *Counsel,* p. 521; McPherson, *Political,* p. 437.

737 "Don' mak no diff'unce": MCA, March 29, 1968, p. 25.

737 sharp knocks at the Rivermont suite: Frank, *American Death,* pp. 30–33; Garrow, *Bearing,* pp. 612–13; Abernathy, *Walls,* pp. 420–21; Garrow, *FBI and King,* pp. 194–95; Hearings, House Select Committee on Assassinations, Vol. 6, pp. 516–17.

738 On their way out: McKnight, *Crusade,* pp. 65–66; Beifuss, *River,* pp. 253–55.

738 King told assembled reporters: Abernathy, *Walls,* pp. 421–22; Hearings, House Select Committee on Assassinations, Vol. 6, p. 17; AC, March 30, 1968, p. 1; MCA, March 30, 1968, p. 1; NYT, March 30, 1968, p. 31; videotape outtakes, March 29, 1968, MVC.

738 "Nonviolence can be as contagious": NBC, *Huntley-Brinkley Report,* March 29, 1968, VTR 236-A, LBJ.

739 "Martin Luther King is dead": Wiretap transcript of telephone call between MLK and Stanley Levison, 3:30 P.M., March 28, 1968, FLNY-9-1624a; New York LHM dated April 1, 1968, FK-3291.

739 like James Lawson: James Lawson oral history, Sept. 23, 1969, MVC.

740 Jerry Wurf escorted him to the airport: Goulden, *Wurf,* pp. 154, 175–76; Beifuss, *River,* pp. 256–59.

740 "We never had any problem": Beifuss, *River,* p. 227.

740 marchers stepped gingerly: MCA, March 30, 1968, p. 1; news script, WMC-TV Channel Five, March 29, 1968, MVC.

740 "The young people here": "Dr. King and the Militants," *Southern Patriot,* April 1968, p. 1.

740   "I think my answer": NBC, *Huntley-Brinkley Report,* March 29, 1968, VTR 236-A, LBJ.

741   Butler Street YMCA: Garrow, *Bearing,* p. 615.

741   "If I get some fish": Juanita Abernathy interview on *Citizen King,* a Roja Production for *The American Experience,* PBS, 2004; Hearings, House Select Committee on Assassinations, Vol. 1, pp. 17–18; Abernathy, *Walls,* pp. 422–24; Raines, *Soul,* pp. 519–20.

741   third-floor conference room at Ebenezer: Account of the meeting on March 30, 1968, drawn from Garrow, *Bearing,* pp. 616–17; Young, *Burden,* pp. 457–59; Frady, *Jesse,* pp. 224–25; Kotz, *Judgment,* pp. 406–7; Fairclough, *Redeem,* p. 378; Abernathy, *Walls,* pp. 424–27; Raines, *Soul,* pp. 520–21; Beifuss, *River,* pp. 255–56; Reynolds, *Jesse Jackson,* p. 85; Frank, *American Death,* p. 72; Jesse Epps oral history, pp. 37–38, MVC; int. Hosea Williams, Oct. 29, 1991; int. William Rutherford, Dec. 7, 2004; int. Bernard Lafayette, May 28, 1990, March 22, 2005, Aug. 10, 2005.

742   "He did something I've never": Wiretap transcript of telephone call between Stanley Levison and Adele Kanter, 1:52 P.M., April 1, 1968, FLNY-9-1627a.

743   Stanley Levison criticized King: Wiretap transcript of telephone call between Stanley Levison and Alice Loewi, 4:03 P.M., March 31, 1968, FLNY-9-1626a.

744   "He said very quietly": Wiretap transcript of telephone call between Stanley Levison and Adele Kanter, 1:52 P.M., April 1, 1968, FLNY-9-1627a.

744   the battered reconciliation: Tom Offenburger staff memo, April 1, 1968, A/KP34f15.

744   "How do you keep the looters out?": NYT, March 30, 1968, p. 30.

744   "emotional demonstrations in this time": Ibid., p. 32.

744   "Let us have a march": WP, April 23, 1968, p. 18.

745   "ran like a scared rabbit": Beifuss, *River,* p. 249.

745   "King's Credibility Gap": MCA, March 30, 1968, p. 6.

745   "Chicken a la King": MCA, March 31, 1968, p. 8; Beifuss, *River,* p. 248.

745   "The Real Martin Luther King": *St. Louis Globe-Democrat,* March 30–31, 1968, p. 2-C.

745   grotesque zombie labeled King: Ibid.

745   Congressional investigators would discover: Stokes, *Report,* pp. 575–80; "FBI Tried to Hide Ties with Globe-Democrat," *St. Louis Post-Dispatch,* Dec. 1, 1977, p. 1; "Aides Deny King Moved to Motel Because of FBI," *Louisville Courier-Journal,* Jan. 2, 1976, p. 3.

745   Three thousand people filled: NYT, April 1, 1968, p. 20; Blackside, Inc., *Eyes on the Prize II—America at the Racial Crossroads, 1965 to 1985,* Vol. IV, "The Promised Land (1967–68)".

745   "Behold I make all things new": Revelation 21:5. King mistakenly said his text came from the 16th chapter.

745   "I was in Marks, Mississippi": MLK sermon listed as "Sleeping Through a Revolution," March 31, 1968, A/KS; Washington, ed., *Testament,* pp. 268–78; "Martin Luther King at National Cathedral, March 31, 1968," Section 24, FHOC; Carson and Holloran, eds. *Knock,* p. 205ff.

746   "Oh, we're always willing": NYT, April 1, 1968, p. 20.

746   "King Threatens Demonstration": AC, April 1, 1968, p. 2.

746   "I'm committed to non-violence absolutely": MLK, "Showdown for Non-Violence," *Look,* April 16, 1968, pp. 23–25.

746   greet their daughter Lynda: PDD, March 31, 1968, LBJ; Johnson, *Diary,* pp. 642–43; int. Lynda Johnson Robb, June 18, 1991; Johnson, *Vantage,* pp. 431–37.

746   "Daddy, I want to ask you": NYT, July 9, 1968, p. 25.

747   "No, we have heard nothing from Hanoi": Busby, *Thirty-first,* pp. 8–9, 181–90.

747   "Don't let a soul know": Ibid., pp. 191–96.

747   thunderstruck Vice President: Ibid., pp. 205–6; Humphrey, *Education,* pp. 358–59.

747   Johnson met the four top managers: Miller, *Lyndon,* p. 619.

748   bottom in his Gallup approval: NYT, March 31, 1968, p. 50.

748   "Chuck will hear this": Johnson, *Diary,* p. 644; Busby, *Thirty-first,* pp. 209–13.

748   "I'm very sorry, Mr. President": McPherson, *Political,* pp. 438–39.

748   Less than an hour before: PDD, March 31, 1968, p. 8, LBJ; FRUS, Vol. 6, pp. 494–95.

748   "Nothing in my career": Clifford, *Counsel,* pp. 522–24.

748   "He said that the decision": Busby, *Thirty-first,* pp. 223–25.

748   "Finally, my fellow Americans": NYT, April 1, 1968, pp. 1, 26.

749   "Nobly done, darling": Miller, *Lyndon,* p. 624; "Move Called 'Completely Irrevocable,' " NYT, April 1, 1968, p. 28.

749   "Can I go to England now?": PDD, March 31, 1968, p. 13, LBJ.

749   lifted the whole country into euphoria: Busby, *Thirty-first,* pp. 226–29; Califano, *Triumph,* pp. 270–72; Dallek, *Flawed,* p. 530.

749   record for most shares traded: " '29 Mark Broken/ 17.73 Million Shares Are Sold Day After Johnson Peace Bid," NYT, April 2, 1968, p. 1.

749   new mark lasted only two days: "Stocks Spurred to Sales Record," NYT, April 4, 1968, p. 1.

749   "This is a defeat": FRUS, Vol. 6, pp. 510–11; NYT, April 4, 1968, p. 16.

750   "Your speech was magnificent": Charles S. Murphy notes of LBJ, RFK, Sorensen meeting, 10:07–11:41 A.M., April 3, 1968, Diary Back-up, Box 94, LBJ; Walt Rostow notes in same file.

750   received only twelve minutes earlier: LBJ received the Reuters bulletin at 9:55 A.M. ("Hanoi is ready to talk"), and he entered the Cabinet Room to begin the Kennedy meeting at 10:07. PDD, April 3, 1968, p. 2, LBJ.

750   White Mountain Apaches: NYT, March 31, 1968, p. 59.

750   Humphrey, in fact: Humphrey, *Education,* pp. 360–61; Walt Rostow notes of LBJ, HHH meeting, 12:29–1:29 P.M., April 3, 1968, Diary Back-up, Box 94, LBJ; Tom Johnson notes, in FRUS, Vol. 6, pp. 523–25.

751   "and you wouldn't have liked it either": Sorensen notes, in Middleton, *LBJ,* pp. 224–25.

751   "You are a brave and dedicated man": Ibid.; Schlesinger, *Robert Kennedy,* pp. 933–34; Dallek, *Flawed,* pp. 531–32; Shesol, *Contempt,* pp. 441–44.

751   single-race sports conferences: "U.S. Court Rules Out Alabama Race Curb in School Athletics," NYT, April 2, 1968, p. 14.

751   Missouri Athletic Club: *St. Louis Globe-Democrat,* March 30–31, 1968, p. 3. This edition of the *Globe-Democrat* featured the editorial cartoon of King as trigger man for the March 28 Memphis riot.

751   percentage of black recruits: "Negro Increase in Guard Sought," NYT, March 31, 1968, p. 1.

752   odd mix in weekly American casualties: NYT, April 5, 1968, p. 15.

752   Eastern Air Lines Flight 381: Stokes, *Report,* p. 363; McKnight, *Crusade,* pp. 66–67; Garrow, *Bearing,* p. 619; Washington, ed., *Testament,* p. 286.

752   J. Edgar Hoover's spiteful edict: Branch, *Parting,* p. 692; Branch, *Pillar,* pp. 195–98, 408–9.

752   "Your airline brought Martin Luther King": McKnight, *Crusade,* pp. 68–69.

752   James Harrison endured: Garrow, *FBI and King,* p. 198; McKnight, *Crusade,* p. 71; U.S. Department of Justice, Report of the Department of Justice Task Force to Review the FBI Martin Luther King, Jr. Security and Assassination Investigations, p. 139.

752   The Memphis police force: Beifuss, *River,* pp. 121–23; McKnight, *Crusade,* pp. 46–47.

752   "Had one in our meetin' ": Honey, *Black Workers,* p. 306.

752   William Rutherford made note: Int. William Rutherford, Dec. 7, 2004.

752   Lawson himself told police inspector Don Smith: Stokes, *Report,* pp. 546–52; U.S. Department of Justice, Report of the Department of Justice Task Force to Review the FBI Martin Luther King, Jr. Security and Assassination Investigations, pp. 26–27.

753   Robert Lewis stepped from a hearse: Frank, *American Death,* pp. 43–44.

753   Detective Ed Redditt: Pepper, *Orders,* pp. 249–51.

753   "We are not going to be stopped": MCA, April 4, 1968, p. 1.

753   Redditt by then had selected: Frank, *American Death,* pp. 45–47.

754   Marrell McCullough: Hearings, House Select Committee on Assassinations, Vol. 6, p. 413ff; McKnight, *Crusade,* p. 48; Melanson, *Murkin,* pp. 74–78.

754   "would have given their eye teeth": McKnight, *Crusade,* p. 48.

754   "Liberation School": U.S. Department of Justice, Report of the Department of Justice Task Force to Review the FBI Martin Luther King, Jr. Security and Assassination Investigations, p. 20.

754   King's top aides acknowledged: Garrow, *Bearing,* pp. 619–20; Hearings, House Select Committee on Assassinations, Vol. 6, p. 512; Fairclough, *Redeem,* p. 380; int. Bernard Lafayette, Aug. 10, 2005; Garrow, *FBI and King,* p. 199.

754   "How many people did you kill": Young, *Burden,* p. 460.

754   "About nine male coloreds": Frank, *American Death,* p. 47.

754   security detail left the motel: Stokes, *Report,* pp. 547–50.

754   delayed another week: NYT, April 4, 1968, p. 30.

755   Redditt had scarcely entered the Mason Temple: U.S. Department of Justice, Report of the Department of Justice Task Force to Review the FBI Martin Luther King, Jr. Security and Assassination Investigations, pp. 29–30.

755   orders to report elsewhere in the morning: Stokes, *Report,* pp. 555–57; McKnight, *Crusade,* p. 76; Beifuss, *River,* p. 288.

755   seven o'clock twister: "Tornado Strikes Near Millington/ At Least 30 Hurt," MCA, April 4, 1968, p. 1; Beifuss, *River,* pp. 276–77.

755   "I want you to go speak": Abernathy, *Walls,* pp. 430–32; Raines, *Soul,* p. 522; Stein, *Journey,* pp. 253–54; Garrow, *Bearing,* p. 620; Young, *Burden,* p. 461; Frank, *American Death,* pp. 48–49; Hearings, House Select Committee on Assassinations, Vol. 1, p. 18.

755   He was still testy about Jackson: Frady, *Jesse,* pp. 225–26; Abernathy, *Walls,* pp. 430–32; int. William Rutherford, Dec. 7, 2004.

755   James Lawson emphasized: News script, WMC-TV Channel Five, April 3, 1968, MVC.

756   His entrance caused an eerie bedlam: Int. James Lawson, Nov. 9, 1983; Beifuss, *River,* p. 277.

756   "His daddy is a preacher": Frank, *American Death,* p. 50.

756   "but he is the one who tells": "Pitch for Unity Made by King," MCA, April 4, 1968, p. 11.

756   "If I were standing at the beginning of time": MLK address, "I Have Been to the

Mountain Top," April 3, 1968, A/KS; Washington, ed., *Testament,* pp. 279–86; Frank, *American Death,* pp. 50–54; Beifuss, *River,* pp. 276–81; Fairclough, *Redeem,* pp. 380–81; Abernathy, *Walls,* p. 433; Young, *Burden,* p. 463; Kotz, *Judgment,* pp. 412–14; *Citizen King,* a Roja Production for *The American Experience,* PBS, 2004.

758   biblical story of Moses: Deuteronomy 32:48–52, 34:1–6.

758   a long night on the town: U.S. Department of Justice, Report of the Department of Justice Task Force to Review the FBI Martin Luther King, Jr. Security and Assassination Investigations, pp. 21–22; Abernathy, *Walls,* pp. 434–36; confidential interviews.

759   King followed Davis to her Room 201: U.S. Department of Justice, Report of the Department of Justice Task Force to Review the FBI Martin Luther King, Jr. Security and Assassination Investigations, pp. 21–22; Powers, *I Shared,* pp. 217–28.

759   neither the city nor King would be safe: Beifuss, *River,* pp. 272, 284–85.

759   "The white citizens of Memphis": Testimony of Frank C. Holloman in *City of Memphis v. Martin Luther King, Jr. et al.,* U.S. District Court for the Western District of Tennessee, Case No. C-68-80, April 4, 1968, p. 58, transcript courtesy of Charles F. Newman.

759   "I would rather local people": Remarks of the court and testimony of Chief J. C. MacDonald, in ibid., pp. 81–84, 94–95.

759   "drop your bags right here": Frank, *American Death,* p. 72.

760   "I don't negotiate with brothers": Int. Bernard Lafayette, Aug. 10, 2005.

760   Invaders stormed off: Ibid.; Fairclough, *Redeem,* p. 381; Garrow, *Bearing,* p. 622; Stokes, *Report,* p. 364; Garrow, *FBI and King,* p. 200; Frank, *American Death,* p. 56; Beifuss, *River,* p. 289; Hearings, House Select Committee on Assassinations, Vol. 6, p. 416.

760   fried Mississippi River catfish: Abernathy, *Walls,* pp. 436–37; Frank, *American Death,* pp. 56–57; Walter (Bill) Bailey oral history, July 10, 1968, MVC.

760   "In the next campaign": Int. Bernard Lafayette, March 22, 2005.

760   "Are you telling the Court": Testimony of James Lawson in *City of Memphis v. Martin Luther King, Jr. et al.,* U.S. District Court for the Western District of Tennessee, Case No. C-68-80, April 4, 1968, pp. 146, 166, transcript courtesy of Charles F. Newman.

761   went downstairs to meet his brother: U.S. Department of Justice, Report of the Department of Justice Task Force to Review the FBI Martin Luther King, Jr. Security and Assassination Investigations, p. 22; *I Shared,* pp. 228–29; Garrow, *Bearing,* p. 622.

761   "She's always happy": Frank, *American Death,* p. 57.

761   "Call her": Abernathy, *Walls,* p. 438; Hearings, House Select Committee on Assassinations, Vol. 1, p. 19; Raines, *My Soul,* p. 522; Stein, *Journey,* p. 254; U.S. House of Representatives, Report of the Select Committee on Assassinations, p. 365.

761   spoiled her husband's trick: Samuel B. (Billy) Kyles oral history, June 12, 1968, p. 8, MVC.

762   "They were really laying": Gwen (Mrs. S. B.) Kyles oral history, May 28, 1968, pp. 12–16, MVC.

762   Andrew Young withstood: Testimony of Andrew Young in *City of Memphis v. Martin Luther King, Jr. et al.,* U.S. District Court for the Western District of Tennessee, Case No. C-68-80, April 4, 1968, pp. 168–207, transcript courtesy of Charles F. Newman.

762   "I think history shows": Ibid., p. 205.

762   "I think of Mr. Wilkins": Ibid., p. 192.

763   removal of Detective Redditt: U.S. Department of Justice, Report of the Department of Justice Task Force to Review the FBI Martin Luther King, Jr. Security and Assassi-

nation Investigations, pp. 30–32; Stokes, *Report,* pp. 549–55; McKnight, *Crusade,* pp. 77–78; Frank, *American Death,* pp. 64–65; Melanson, *Murkin,* pp. 68–71.

763   escaped convict bought a pair of Bushnell binoculars: Stokes, *Report*, pp. 378–87; Frank, *American Death,* pp. 58–64; Posner, *Killing the Dream,* pp. 22–28, 324–31; Huie, *He Slew,* pp. 112–13; McMillan, *Making,* pp. 290–93, 297–302.

764   free-for-all pillow fight: Young, *Burden,* pp. 463–64; Blackside, Inc., *Eyes on the Prize II—America at the Racial Crossroads, 1965 to 1985,* Vol. IV, "The Promised Land (1967–68)"; *Citizen King,* a Roja Production for *The American Experience,* PBS, 2004; Garrow, *Bearing,* pp. 622–23; Posner, *Killing the Dream,* pp. 23–24; Kotz, *Judgment,* p. 414.

764   "death and destruction": News script, WMC-TV Channel Five, April 4, 1968, MVC.

764   Officer Richmond noted: Frank, *American Death,* pp. 58, 65.

764   long-scheduled spring revival: Hearings, House Select Committee on Assassinations, Vol. 1, pp. 19–20; Raines, *Soul,* p. 523; Stokes, *Report,* p. 365; Abernathy, *Walls,* pp. 438–39.

765   Hosea Williams loudly evicted: Hearings, House Select Committee on Assassinations, Vol. 6, pp. 466–67, 520–21; Pepper, *Act of State,* pp. 193–94.

765   Jesse Jackson rehearsed: Beifuss, *River,* pp. 289–90.

765   King chimed in to needle Kyles: Samuel B. (Billy) Kyles oral history, June 12, 1968, pp. 8–15, MVC; Stokes, *Report,* p. 366; Frank, *American Death,* pp. 67–70; Baldwin, *Balm,* p. 306; Posner, *Killing the Dream,* pp. 29–30.

766   Marrell McCullough parked: U.S. Department of Justice, Report of the Department of Justice Task Force to Review the FBI Martin Luther King, Jr. Security and Assassination Investigations, p. 25; Hearings, House Select Committee on Assassinations, Vol. 6, pp. 418–19; McKnight, *Crusade,* p. 71.

766   tussling with Bevel: Stokes, *Report,* p. 366; Young, *Burden,* p. 464.

766   "Jesse, I want you to come": Frady, *Jesse,* pp. 226–27.

766   Time on the balcony: Stokes, *Report,* p. 367; Beifuss, *River,* pp. 292–93; Frank, *American Death,* pp. 73–75; Raines, *Soul,* pp. 522–23; Abernathy, *Walls,* pp. 440–41; Posner, *Killing the Dream,* pp. 30–32.

EPILOGUE

PAGE

767   McCullough first reached the victim: Stokes, *Report*, pp. 368–69; Posner, *Killing,* p. 31.

767   knot from King's necktie: Beifuss, *River,* pp. 292–93.

767   "Somebody done hit": Walter "Bill" Bailey oral history, July 10, 1968, MVC.

767   "They got my brother": Beifuss, *River,* pp. 305–6.

767   Memphis Search for Meaning Committee: Ibid., pp. 352–53.

767   segment filmed outside the emergency room at St. Joseph's: "Film Cabinet—News Film, On-the-Air & Outtakes," April 4, 1968, Video 44–45, Container 52, MVC.

767   Riots erupted in 110 American cities: NYT, April 10, 1968, p. 37.

767   Congress passed the nondiscrimination bill: NYT, April 11, 1968, p. 1.

767   what amounted to a state funeral in Atlanta: Pomerantz, *Peachtree,* pp. 358–63.

768   settled the Memphis strike: Beifuss, *River,* pp. 348–49; Goulden, *Jerry Wurf,* pp. 178–81.

768   King died intestate: Estate of Dr. Martin Luther King, Jr., File No. 81048, Probate Court of Fulton County, Georgia.

768   $12,351.36 from the eccentric poet and essayist Dorothy Parker: Amended Affidavit of Assets filed July 2, 1979, by Coretta Scott King, in ibid.; NYT, June 27, 1967, p. 22; Levison to Dora McDonald, June 27, 1967, A/KP15f10; "Dorothy Parker: Wit's End/Poet's Ashes, Ideals Honored in Baltimore," WP, Oct. 21, 1988, p. D-1.

768   new sheriff, John Hulett: Eagles, *Outside Agitator,* p. 256; int. Judge John Hulett, Jr., Sept. 28, 2005.

768   slowly entered the dedication ceremony: Dallek, *Flawed,* pp. 620–23.

768   "whom I don't know so well": Pamphlet, "Equal Opportunity in the United States: A Symposium on Civil Rights," 1972, p. 162, LBJ.

768   sought out an awed Bond: Int. Julian Bond, Jan. 10, 2004; LBJ to Bond, Dec. 13, 1972, courtesy of Julian Bond.

768   "Christmas bombing": Karnow, *Vietnam,* pp. 667–69; Appy, *Patriots,* pp. 395–96; Langguth, *Our Vietnam,* pp. 614–24.

768   Pauli Murray knelt trembling: Murray, *Song,* pp. 430–31.

769   "God here and now as father": NYT, July 30, 1974, pp. 1, 17.

769   upheaval over the sanctity of male-only clergy: Cf. "History-Making 65th Convention Ends," Sept. 23, 1976, Episcopal News Service record 76299, AEC; "Union Council Rejects Convention Decision," Nov. 10, 1976, Episcopal News Service record 76341, AEC.

769   female priests ordained by official sanction: "Episcopal Priests Ordained," WP, Jan. 9, 1977, p. 3; Murray, *Song,* pp. 434–35.

769   Within days, they had traced the mark: Stokes, *Report,* pp. 584–87; Posner, *Killing,* pp. 37–41; FBI LHM dated April 6, 1968, "Murder of Martin Luther King, Jr.," Box 32, OFMS, LBJ.

769   Stokely Carmichael or Rap Brown ordered King killed: Unsigned memo dated April 12, 1968, with attached FBI LHM, "Assassination of Martin Luther King, Jr.," April 10, 1968, Box 32, OFMS, LBJ.

769   FBI officials planted a malicious story: Jack Anderson, "FBI Used King File in Killer Hunt," WP, Aug. 15, 1970; int. Jack Anderson, Oct. 7, 1983; FBI memorandum, "Martin Luther King, Jr.," April 9, 1968, FK-3415.

769   "their plaster saint": Wiretap transcript of telephone conversation between Stanley Levison and Tom Offenburger, 12:43 A.M., April 19, 1968, FLNY-9-1645.

770   "there is no way a ten-cent white boy": Bernard Lee oral history by Walter Burrell, June 23, 1968, RJB.

770   eerie wedding ceremony: Posner, *Killing,* p. 261.

770   Dennis Sweeney: Chafe, *Never,* pp. 453–60; King, *Freedom Song,* pp. 510–18.

770   sentenced to life for the baffling murder: "Ex-Black Panther Is Sought in Death of Sheriff's Deputy," NYT, March 18, 2000, p. 7; "Al-Amin Calls Slaying Case a 'Government Conspiracy,' " WP, March 22, 2000, p. 3; "Georgia Upholds Former Militant's Conviction," NYT, May 25, 2004, p. 16.

770   Dexter King publicly proclaimed James Earl Ray innocent: NYT, March 28, 1997, p. 22.

770   Reagan announced his belief: NYT, Oct. 20, 1983, p. 1; partial transcript of Reagan press conference, WP, Oct. 20, 1983, p. 8; Cannon, *President Reagan,* pp. 523–24; "Uneasy Holiday," *New Republic,* Feb. 3, 1986, pp. 22–27.

770   students spilling into the streets of South Korea: Glennon, ed., *Our Times,* p. 630.

770   Soviet empire suddenly dissolved: Ibid., pp. 640, 650, 654, 656.

770   inspired the world from Tiananmen Square: Ibid., p. 641.

771   "Universal suffrage on a common voters' roll": Ibid., pp. 661, 680.

BIBLIOGRAPHY

Abernathy, Ralph David. *And the Walls Came Tumbling Down.* Harper & Row, 1989.

Adler, Bill. *The Johnson Humor.* Simon & Schuster, 1965.

Ali, Muhammad. *The Greatest.* Random House, 1975.

Allen, Ivan, Jr. *Mayor: Notes on the Sixties.* Simon & Schuster, 1971.

Anderson, Alan B., and George W. Pickering. *Confronting the Color Line: The Broken Promise of the Civil Rights Movement in Chicago.* University of Georgia Press, 1987.

Applebome, Peter. *Dixie Rising: How the South Is Shaping American Values, Politics, and Culture.* Harcourt Brace, 1997.

Appy, Christian G. *Patriots: The Vietnam War Remembered from All Sides.* Viking, 2003.

Arendt, Hannah. *On Violence.* Harvest Books, Harcourt, Brace & Jovanovich, 1969.

Ashmore, Harry S. *Hearts and Minds: The Anatomy of Racism from Roosevelt to Reagan.* McGraw-Hill, 1982.

Associated Press, The. *The World in 1965: History as We Lived It.* The Associated Press, 1966.

Baez, Joan. *And a Voice to Sing With.* Summit, 1987.

Bailey, D'Army. *Mine Eyes Have Seen: Dr. Martin Luther King Jr.'s Final Journey.* Towery, 1993.

Baldwin, Lewis V. *There Is a Balm in Gilead: The Cultural Roots of Martin Luther King, Jr.* Augsburg Fortress, 1991.

Barrett, Marvin. *Rich News, Poor News.* Crowell, 1978.

Bass, Jack. *Ol' Strom: An Unauthorized Biography of Strom Thurmond.* Longstreet, 1998.

———. *Taming the Storm: The Life and Times of Frank M. Johnson, Jr., and the South's Fight over Civil Rights.* Doubleday, 1993.

———. *Unlikely Heroes.* Simon & Schuster, 1981.

Bayor, Ronald H. *Race and the Shaping of Twentieth-Century Atlanta.* University of North Carolina Press, 1996.

Bea, Augustin Cardinal. *The Church and the Jewish People.* Harper & Row, 1966.

Beifuss, Joan Turner. *At the River I Stand.* Memphis: B&W Books, 1985.

Bell, Gregory. *In the Black: A History of African Americans on Wall Street.* Wiley, 2002.

Berry, Jason. *Amazing Grace.* Saturday Review Press, 1978.

Beschloss, Michael. *Reaching for Glory: Lyndon Johnson's Secret White House Tapes, 1964–65.* Simon & Schuster, 2001.

———. *Taking Charge: The Johnson White House Tapes, 1963–64.* Simon & Schuster, 1997.

Bird, Kai. *The Color of Truth: McGeorge Bundy and William Bundy: Brothers in Arms.* Simon & Schuster, 1998.

Black, Earl, and Merle Black. *The Rise of Southern Republicans.* Harvard University Press, 2002.

Borton, Lady. *After Sorrow: An American Among the Vietnamese.* Viking, 1995.

Boyarsky, Bill. *The Rise of Ronald Reagan*. Random House, 1968.

Bracey, John H., August Meier, and Elliott Rudwick. *Black Nationalism in America*. Bobbs-Merrill, 1970.

Braestrup, Peter. *Big Story*. Anchor Press, 1978.

Branch, Taylor. *Parting the Waters: America in the King Years, 1954–1963*. Simon & Schuster, 1988.

———. *Pillar of Fire: America in the King Years, 1963–65*. Simon & Schuster, 1998.

Breo, Dennis L., and William J. Martin. *The Crime of the Century: Richard Speck and the Murder of Eight Student Nurses*. Bantam, 1993.

Brink, William J. *Black and White: A Study of U.S. Racial Attitudes*. Simon & Schuster, 1967.

Brinkley, Douglas. *Rosa Parks*. Viking, 2000.

Brooks, Tim, and Elaine Marsh. *The Complete Directory to Prime Time Network TV Shows*. Ballantine, 1980.

Broome, Homer F. *LAPD's Black History: 1886–1976*. Norwalk, Calif.: Stockton Trade Press, 1978.

Bullard, Sara. *Free at Last: A History of the Civil Rights Movement and Those Who Died in the Struggle*. Oxford University Press, 1993.

Busby, Horace. *The Thirty-first of March: An Intimate Portrait of Lyndon Johnson's Final Days in Office*. Farrar, Straus & Giroux, 2005.

Cagin, Seth, and Phil Dray. *We Are Not Afraid: The Story of Goodman, Schwerner, Chaney, and the Civil Rights Campaign for Mississippi*. Macmillan, 1988.

Califano, Joseph A., Jr. *The Triumph and Tragedy of Lyndon Johnson*. Simon & Schuster, 1991.

Callahan, Nancy. *The Freedom Quilting Bee*. University of Alabama Press, 1987.

Cannon, Lou. *President Reagan: The Role of a Lifetime*. Simon & Schuster, 1991.

———. *Reagan*. Putnam, 1982.

Carmichael, Stokely. *Stokely Speaks: Black Power Back to Pan-Africanism*. Random House, 1971.

Carmichael, Stokely, and Charles V. Hamilton. *Black Power: The Politics of Liberation in America*. Random House, 1967.

Carmichael, Stokely, with Ekwueme Michael Thelwell. *Ready for Revolution: The Life and Struggles of Stokely Carmichael (Kwame Ture)*. Scribner, 2003.

Caro, Robert A. *Master of the Senate*. Knopf, 2002.

———. *Means of Ascent*. Knopf, 1990.

———. *The Path to Power*. Knopf, 1982.

———. *The Power Broker: Robert Moses and the Fall of New York*. Knopf, 1974.

Carson, Clayborne. *In Struggle: SNCC and the Black Awakening of the 1960s*. Harvard University Press, 1981.

Carson, Clayborne, ed. *The Student Voice: 1960–1965*. Meckler, 1990.

Carson, Clayborne, and Peter Holloran, eds. *A Knock at Midnight: Inspiration from the Great Sermons of Reverend Martin Luther King, Jr.* Warner, 1998.

Carter, Dan T. *The Politics of Rage: George Wallace, the Origins of the New Conservatism, and the Transformation of American Politics*. Simon & Schuster, 1995.

Chafe, William H. *Never Stop Running: Allard Lowenstein and the Struggle to Save American Liberalism*. Basic Books, 1993.

Chaves, Mark. *Ordaining Women: Culture and Conflict in Religious Organizations*. Harvard University Press, 1997.

Chestnut, J. L., and Julia Cass. *Black in Selma: The Uncommon Life of J. L. Chestnut, Jr.* Farrar, Straus & Giroux, 1990.

Church, Senator Frank. *Supplementary Detailed Staff Reports on Intelligence Activities and the Rights of Americans, Report No. 94-755, U.S. Senate.* Government Printing Office, 1976.

Clark, Septima. *Ready from Within: A First Person Narrative.* Trenton: Africa World Press, 1990.

Clarke, Erskine. *Wrestlin' Jacob.* John Knox Press, 1979.

Clifford, Clark, with Richard Holbrooke. *Counsel to the President: A Memoir.* Random House, 1991.

Coffin, William Sloane, Jr. *Once to Every Man: A Memoir.* Atheneum, 1977.

Cohen, Adam, and Elizabeth Taylor. *American Pharaoh: Richard J. Daley: His Battle for Chicago and the Nation.* Little, Brown, 2000.

Cohen, Marcia. *The Sisterhood: The True Story of the Women Who Changed the World.* Simon & Schuster, 1988.

Coleman, Emmett. *Adam Clayton Powell.* Bee-Line, 1967.

Collier, Peter. *The Kennedys.* Summit, 1984.

Cone, James H. *Martin and Malcolm and America: A Dream or a Nightmare.* Orbis, 1991.

Couto, Richard A. *Ain't Gonna Let Nobody Turn Me Round: The Pursuit of Racial Justice in the Rural South.* Temple University Press, 1991.

Curry, Constance, et al. *Deep in Our Hearts: Nine White Women in the Freedom Movement.* University of Georgia Press, 2000.

Dallek, Matthew. *The Right Moment: Ronald Reagan's First Victory and the Decisive Turning Point in American Politics.* Free Press, 2000.

Dallek, Robert. *Flawed Giant: Lyndon Johnson and His Times, 1961–73.* Oxford University Press, 1998.

Dates, Jannette L., and William Barlow, eds. *Split Image: African Americans in the Mass Media.* Howard University Press, 1990.

Davis, Burke. *Sherman's March.* Random House, 1980.

Davis, Jack E. *Race Against Time: Culture and Separation in Natchez Since 1930.* Louisiana State University Press, 2001.

Deakin, James. *Straight Stuff: The Reporters, the White House, and the Truth.* Morrow, 1984.

DeBenedetti, Charles. *An American Ordeal: The Antiwar Movement of the Vietnam Era.* Syracuse University Press, 1990.

Dellinger, David. *From Yale to Jail: The Life Story of a Moral Dissenter.* Pantheon, 1993.

DeLoach, Cartha "Deke." *Hoover's FBI: The Inside Story by Hoover's Trusted Lieutenant.* Regnery, 1995.

D'Emilio, John. *Lost Prophet: The Life and Times of Bayard Rustin.* Free Press, 2003.

Dickson, Paul, and Thomas B. Allen. *The Bonus Army: An American Epic.* Walker, 2004.

Dittmer, John. *Local People: The Struggle for Civil Rights in Mississippi.* University of Illinois Press, 1994.

Draper, Theodore. *Abuse of Power.* Viking, 1967.

———. *The Dominican Revolt: A Case Study in American Policy.* Commentary, 1968.

Drucker, Peter. *Max Shachtman and His Left: A Socialist's Odyssey Through the "American Century."* Atlantic Highlands, N.J.: Humanities Press, 1994.

Dugger, Ronnie. *On Reagan: The Man and His Presidency.* McGraw-Hill, 1983.

Duiker, William J. *Ho Chi Minh.* Hyperion, 2000.

Eagles, Charles W. *Outside Agitator: Jon Daniels and the Civil Rights Movement in Alabama.* University of North Carolina Press, 1993.

Edwards, Lee. *Reagan: A Political Biography.* San Diego: Viewpoint, 1967.

Egerton, John. *Speak Now Against the Day: The Generation Before the Civil Rights Movement in the South.* Knopf, 1994.

Evans, Eli N. *The Provincials: A Personal History of Jews in the South.* Free Press, 1997.

Evans, Rowland, and Robert Novak. *Lyndon B. Johnson: The Exercise of Power.* New American Library, 1966.

Evans, Sara. *Personal Politics.* Knopf, 1979; Vintage, 1980.

Evans, Zelia S., ed. *Dexter Avenue Baptist Church: 1877–1977.* Montgomery, Ala.: Dexter Avenue Baptist Church, 1978.

Fager, Charles E. *Selma, 1965.* Scribner, 1974; 2nd ed., Beacon, 1985.

———. *Uncertain Resurrection.* Kimo, 1982.

Fairclough, Adam. *To Redeem the Soul of America: The Southern Christian Leadership Conference and Martin Luther King, Jr.* University of Georgia Press, 1987.

Fall, Bernard B. *Last Reflections on a War.* Stackpole, 2000.

———. *The Two Viet-Nams: A Political and Military Analysis.* Praeger, 1963.

Fenderson, Lewis H. *Thurgood Marshall: Fighter for Justice.* McGraw-Hill: Rutledge, 1969.

Findlay, James F., Jr. *Church People in the Struggle: The National Council of Churches and the Black Freedom Movement, 1950–1970.* Oxford University Press, 1993.

Fite, Gilbert C. *Richard B. Russell, Jr.: Senator from Georgia.* University of North Carolina Press, 1991.

Fitzpatrick, Frank. *And the Walls Came Tumbling Down: Kentucky, Texas Western, and the Game That Changed American Sports.* Simon & Schuster, 1999.

Fleming, Cynthia Griggs. *Soon We Will Not Cry: The Liberation of Ruby Doris Smith Robinson.* Lanham, Md.: Rowman & Littlefield, 1998.

Foner, Eric. *Reconstruction: America's Unfinished Revolution, 1863–1877.* Harper & Row, 1988.

Forman, James. *The Making of Black Revolutionaries.* Macmillan, 1972.

———. *Sammy Younge, Jr.: The First Black College Student to Die in the Black Liberation Movement.* Grove, 1968.

Frady, Marshall. *Jesse: The Life and Pilgrimage of Jesse Jackson.* Random House, 1996.

———. *Southerners: A Journalist's Odyssey.* New American Library, 1980.

Frank, Gerold. *An American Death.* Doubleday, 1972.

Freeman, Roland L. *The Mule Train: A Journey of Hope Remembered.* Rutledge, 1998.

Friedland, Michael B. *Lift Up Your Voice Like a Trumpet: White Clergy and the Civil Rights and Antiwar Movements, 1954–73.* University of North Carolina Press, 1998.

Friedman, Maurice. *Abraham Joshua Heschel and Elie Wiesel: You Are My Witnesses.* Farrar, Straus & Giroux, 1987.

Friendly, Fred W. *Due to Circumstances Beyond Our Control.* Vintage, 1967.

Frymer-Kensky, Tikva, et al., eds. *Christianity in Jewish Terms.* Boulder: Westview, 2000.

Fulbright, J. William. *The Vietnam Hearings.* Vintage, 1966.

Fursenko, Aleksandr, and Timothy Naftali. *"One Hell of a Gamble": Khrushchev, Castro, and Kennedy, 1958–1964.* Norton, 1997.

Gans, Herbert J. *Deciding What's News: A Study of CBS Evening News, NBC Nightly News, Newsweek and Time.* Pantheon, 1979; Vintage, 1980.

Garrow, David J. *Bearing the Cross: Martin Luther King, Jr., and the Southern Leadership Conference.* Morrow, 1986.

———. *The FBI and Martin Luther King, Jr.: From "Solo" to Memphis.* Norton, 1981.

———. *Protest at Selma: Martin Luther King, Jr., and the Voting Rights Act of 1965.* Yale University Press, 1978.

Garrow, David J., ed. *Chicago 1966: Open Housing Marches, Summit Negotiations, and Operation Breadbasket.* Brooklyn: Carlson, 1989.

Gentry, Curt. *J. Edgar Hoover: The Man and the Secrets*. Norton, 1991.

Giap, Vo Nguyen. *Unforgettable Days*. Hanoi: Foreign Languages Publishing House, 1975.

Gilbert, Arthur. *The Vatican Council and the Jews*. World, 1968.

Gilliard, Deric A. *Unsung: Living in the Shadows of a Legend: Heroes and 'Sheroes' Who Marched with Dr. Martin Luther King, Jr.* Gilliard Communications, 2003.

Gitlin, Todd. *The Sixties: Years of Hope, Days of Rage*. Bantam, 1987.

Glennon, Lorraine, ed. *Our Times: The Illustrated History of the 20th Century*. Turner Publishing, 1995.

Goldman, Albert. *Elvis*. McGraw-Hill, 1981.

Goldman, Eric F. *The Tragedy of Lyndon Johnson*. Knopf, 1969.

Goldstein, Warren. *William Sloane Coffin, Jr.: A Holy Impatience*. Yale University Press, 2004.

Good, Paul. *The Trouble I've Seen*. Howard University Press, 1974.

Goodwin, Richard N. *Remembering America: A Voice from the Sixties*. Little, Brown, 1988.

Gossett, Thomas F. *Race: The History of an Idea in America*. Oxford University Press, 1963.

Goulden, Joseph C. *Jerry Wurf: Labor's Last Angry Man*. Atheneum, 1982.

Governor's Commission. *Violence in the City—An End or a Beginning?* State of California, 1965.

Graham, Hugh Davis. *The Civil Rights Era: Origins and Development of National Policy*. Oxford University Press, 1990.

Graham, Katharine. *Personal History*. Knopf, 1997.

Gravel, Mike, ed. *The Pentagon Papers: The Defense Department History of United States Decisionmaking on Vietnam*. Beacon, 1972.

Greenberg, Cheryl Lynn, ed. *A Circle of Trust: Remembering SNCC*. Rutgers University Press, 1998.

Greenberg, Jack. *Crusaders in the Courts*. Basic, 1994.

Greenberg, Polly. *The Devil Has Slippery Shoes*. Macmillan, 1969.

Guthman, Edwin. *We Band of Brothers*. Harper & Row, 1971.

Halberstam, David. *The Powers That Be*. Knopf, 1979.

Hall, Mitchell K. *Because of Their Faith*. Columbia University Press, 1990.

Halpern, Rick, and Roger Horowitz. *Meatpackers: An Oral History of Black Packinghouse Workers and Their Struggle for Racial and Economic Equality*. Twayne, 1996.

Halstead, Fred. *Out Now! A Participant's Account of the American Movement Against the Vietnam War*. New York: Monad, 1978.

Hamilton, Charles V. *Adam Clayton Powell, Jr.: The Political Biography of an American Dilemma*. Atheneum, 1991.

Hampton, Henry, and Steve Fayer. *Voices of Freedom: An Oral History of the Civil Rights Movement from the 1950s Through the 1980s*. Bantam, 1990.

Handy, Robert T. *A History of Union Theological Seminary in New York*. Columbia University Press, 1987.

Harrington, Michael. *Fragments of the Century*. Saturday Review Press, 1973.

Harris, David. *Dreams Die Hard*. St. Martin's, 1982.

Harrison, Cynthia. *On Account of Sex: The Politics of Women's Issues, 1945–1968*. University of California Press, 1988.

Hauser, Thomas. *Muhammad Ali: His Life and Times*. Simon & Schuster, 1991.

Haygood, Wil. *King of the Cats: The Life and Times of Adam Clayton Powell, Jr.* Houghton Mifflin, 1993.

Hayman, John. *Bitter Harvest: Richmond Flowers and the Civil Rights Revolution*. Black Belt Press, 1996.

Heirich, Max. *The Beginning: Berkeley, 1964*. Columbia University Press, 1968.

Herbers, John. *The Lost Priority.* Funk & Wagnalls, 1970.

Hersey, John. *The Algiers Motel Incident.* Knopf, 1968.

Hersh, Seymour M. *My Lai 4: A Report on the Massacre and Its Aftermath.* Random House, 1970.

Hertzberg, Arthur. *Being Jewish in America: The Modern Experience.* Schocken, 1979.

Heschel, Abraham J. *Israel: An Echo of Eternity.* Farrar, Straus & Giroux, 1967.

Higginbotham, F. Michael. *Race Law: Cases, Commentary, and Questions.* Carolina Academic Press, 2001.

Hilliard, David, and Lewis Cole. *This Side of Glory: The Autobiography of David Hilliard and the Story of the Black Panther Party.* Little, Brown/Back Bay, 1993.

Hilton, Bruce. *The Delta Ministry.* Macmillan, 1969.

Hodgson, Marshall G. S. *The Venture of Islam.* University of Chicago Press, 1984.

Honey, Michael Keith. *Black Workers Remember: An Oral History of Segregation, Unionism, and the Freedom Struggle.* University of California Press, 1999.

Horne, Gerald. *Fire This Time: The Watts Uprising and the 1960s.* University of Virginia Press, 1995.

Howlett, Duncan. *No Greater Love: The James Reeb Story.* Harper & Row, 1966.

Huie, William Bradford. *He Slew the Dreamer: My Search for the Truth About James Earl Ray and the Murder of Martin Luther King.* Delacorte, 1968.

Humphrey, Hubert H. *The Education of a Public Man.* Doubleday, 1976.

Isaacson, Walter, and Evan Thomas. *The Wise Men.* Simon & Schuster, 1986.

Isserman, Maurice. *If I Had a Hammer: The Death of the Old Left and the Birth of the New Left.* Basic Books, 1987.

Jacobs, Andrew. *The Powell Affair: Freedom Minus One.* Bobbs-Merrill, 1973.

Jeffries, Hasan Kwame. "Freedom Politics: Transcending Civil Rights in Lowndes County, Alabama, 1965–2000." Ph.D. diss., Duke University, 2002.

Johnson, Charles, and Bob Adelman. *King: The Photobiography of Martin Luther King, Jr.* Viking Studio, 2000.

Johnson, Lady Bird. *A White House Diary.* Holt, Rinehart and Winston, 1970.

Johnson, Lyndon B. *The Vantage Point.* Holt, Rinehart and Winston, 1971.

Johnston, Earle. *Mississippi's Defiant Years: 1953–1973.* Forest, Miss.: Lake Harbor, 1990.

Jones, Bill. *The Wallace Story.* Northport, Ala.: The American Southern Publishing Co., 1966.

Jones, Charles C. *The Religious Instruction of Negroes in the United States.* Savannah, 1842.

Jones, Landon Y. *Great Expectations.* Coward, McCann & Geoghegan, 1980.

Joravsky, Ben, and Eduardo Camacho. *Race and Politics in Chicago.* Chicago Renewal Society, 1987.

Jordan, Winthrop D. *White Over Black: American Attitudes Toward the Negro, 1550–1812.* University of North Carolina Press, 1968.

Kabaservice, Geoffrey. *The Guardians: Kingman Brewster, His Circle, and the Rise of the Liberal Establishment.* Henry Holt, 2004.

Kalman, Laura. *Abe Fortas.* Yale University Press, 1990.

Karnow, Stanley. *Vietnam: A History.* Viking, 1983.

Kasher, Steven. *The Civil Rights Movement: A Photographic History, 1954–68.* Abbeville, 1996.

Kaufman, Jonathan. *Broken Alliance: The Turbulent Times Between Blacks and Jews in America.* Scribner, 1988.

Kerner Commission. *Report of the National Advisory Commission on Civil Disorders.* Bantam, 1968.

Ketcham, Ralph. *James Madison.* University of Virginia Press, 1990.

King, Coretta Scott. *My Life with Martin Luther King, Jr.* Holt, Rinehart and Winston, 1969.

King, Desmond. *Making Americans: Immigration, Race, and the Origins of the Diverse Democracy.* Harvard University Press, 2000.

———. *Separate and Unequal: Black Americans and the US Federal Government.* Oxford University Press, 1995.

King, Martin Luther, Jr. *Chaos or Community? Where Do We Go From Here?* Hodder & Stoughton, 1968.

King, Mary. *Freedom Song.* Morrow, 1987.

Klein, Alexander, ed. *Dissent, Power, and Confrontation.* McGraw-Hill, 1971.

Kotz, Nick. *Judgment Days: Lyndon Baines Johnson, Martin Luther King, Jr., and the Laws That Changed America.* Houghton Mifflin, 2005.

Kotz, Nick, and Mary Lynn Kotz. *A Passion for Equality: George Wiley and the Movement.* Norton, 1977.

Kristol, Irving. *Neoconservatism: The Autobiography of an Idea.* Free Press, 1995.

Langguth, A. J. *Our Vietnam: The War 1954–75.* Simon & Schuster, 2000.

Lavergne, Gary M. *A Sniper in the Tower: The Charles Whitman Murders.* University of North Texas Press, 1997; Bantam, 1998.

Lawson, Steven F. *In Pursuit of Power: Southern Blacks and Electoral Politics, 1965–82.* Columbia University Press, 1985.

Lemann, Nicholas. *The Promised Land: The Great Black Migration and How It Changed America.* Knopf, 1991.

Lesher, Stephan. *George Wallace: American Populist.* Addison Wesley, 1994.

Lewis, David L. *King: A Critical Biography.* University of Illinois Press, 1970, 1978.

Lewis, John. *Walking with the Wind: A Memoir of the Movement.* Simon & Schuster, 1998.

Lischer, Richard. *The Preacher King: Martin Luther King and the Word That Moved America.* Oxford University Press, 1995.

Litwack, Leon F. *Been in the Storm So Long: The Aftermath of Slavery.* Knopf, 1979.

Logevall, Fredrik. *Choosing War: The Lost Chance for Peace and the Escalation of the War in Vietnam.* University of California Press, 1999.

Longenecker, Stephen L. *Selma's Peacemaker: Ralph Smeltzer and Civil Rights Mediation.* Temple University Press, 1987.

Lopez, Ian F. Haney. *White by Law: The Legal Construction of Race.* New York University Press, 1996.

Lyon, Danny. *Memories of the Southern Civil Rights Movement.* Chapel Hill/Center for Documentary Studies, 1992.

Macy, Christy, and Susan Kaplan. *Documents.* Penguin, 1980.

Maddox, Lester Garfield. *Speaking Out: The Autobiography of Lester Garfield Maddox.* Doubleday, 1975.

Mailer, Norman. *Armies of the Night: History As a Novel: The Novel As History.* New American Library, 1968.

Malcolm X. *The Autobiography of Malcolm X.* Grove, 1964.

Manchester, William. *The Death of a President.* Harper & Row, 1967.

———. *The Glory and the Dream: A Narrative History of America, 1932–1972.* Little, Brown, 1973.

Manis, Andrew M. *A Fire You Can't Put Out: The Civil Rights Life of Birmingham's Reverend Fred Shuttlesworth.* University of Alabama Press, 1999.

Mann, Robert. *The Walls of Jericho: Lyndon Johnson, Hubert Humphrey, Richard Russell, and the Struggle for Civil Rights.* Harcourt, Brace, 1996.

Marable, Manning. *Race, Reform and Rebellion: The Second Reconstruction in Black America, 1945–1982.* University Press of Mississippi, 1984.

Maraniss, David. *They Marched into Sunlight.* Simon & Schuster, 2003.

Mars, Florence. *Witness in Philadelphia.* Louisiana State University Press, 1977.

Marsh, Charles. *God's Long Summer: Stories of Faith and Civil Rights.* Princeton University Press, 1997.

Martin, George. *With a Little Help from My Friends: The Making of Sgt. Pepper.* Little, Brown, 1995.

Matusow, Allen J. *The Unraveling of America: A History of Liberalism in the 1960s.* Harper & Row, 1984; Harper Torchbooks, 1986.

Mayer, Henry. *All on Fire: William Lloyd Garrison and the Abolition of Slavery.* St. Martin's, 1998.

Mays, Benjamin E. *Born to Rebel: An Autobiography.* Scribner, 1971.

McCarty, Clinton. *Reins of Power: Racial Change and Challenge in a Southern County.* Tallahassee: Sentry, 1999.

McIlhany, William H., II. *Klandestine: The Untold Story of Delmar Dennis and His Role in the FBI's War Against the Ku Klux Klan.* Arlington House, 1975.

McKnight, Gerald D. *The Last Crusade: Martin Luther King, Jr., the FBI, and the Poor People's Campaign.* Boulder, Col.: Westview, 1998.

McMillan, George. *The Making of an Assassin: The Life of James Earl Ray.* Little, Brown, 1976.

McNamara, Robert S. *In Retrospect: The Tragedy and Lessons of Vietnam.* Times Books, 1995.

McPherson, Harry. *A Political Education.* Houghton Mifflin, 1988.

McWhorter, Diane. *Carry Me Home: Birmingham, Alabama—The Climactic Battle of the Civil Rights Revolution.* Simon & Schuster, 2001.

Meier, August. *CORE: A Study in the Civil Rights Movement.* University of Illinois Press, 1973.

Melanson, Philip H. *The Murkin Conspiracy: An Investigation into the Assassination of Dr. Martin Luther King, Jr.* Praeger, 1989.

Melman, Seymour, and Richard Falk, eds. *In the Name of America.* Turnpike, 1968.

Menand, Louis. *The Metaphysical Club: A Story of Ideas in America.* Farrar, Straus & Giroux, 2001.

Menashe, Louis, and Ronald Radosh, eds. *Teach-Ins: U.S.A.: Reports, Opinions, Documents.* Praeger, 1967.

Mendelsohn, Jack. *The Martyrs: Sixteen Who Gave Their Lives for Racial Justice.* Harper & Row, 1966.

Middleton, Harry. *LBJ: The White House Years.* Abrams, 1990.

Middleton, Neil, ed. *The I. F. Stone's Weekly Reader.* Vintage, 1974.

Miller, Keith D. *Voice of Deliverance: The Language of Martin Luther King, Jr., and Itsa Sources.* Free Press, 1991.

Miller, Merle. *Lyndon: An Oral Biography.* Putnam, 1980.

Miller, William Robert. *Martin Luther King, Jr.* Avon Books, 1968.

Mills, Kay. *A Place in the News: From the Women's Pages to the Front Page.* Dodd, Mead, 1988.

———. *This Little Light of Mine: The Life of Fannie Lou Hamer.* Dutton, 1993.

Moore, Charles. *Powerful Days: The Civil Rights Photography of Charles Moore.* Stewart, Tabori & Chang, 1991.

Moore, Lt. Gen. Harold G., and Joseph L. Galloway. *We Were Soldiers Once—And Young: Ia Drang, the Battle That Changed the War in Vietnam.* Random House, 1992.

Morgan, Charles, Jr. *One Man, One Voice.* Holt, Rinehart and Winston, 1979.

Murray, Pauli. *Song in a Weary Throat: An American Pilgrimage.* Harper & Row, 1987.

Myers, Robert Manson, ed. *The Children of Pride.* Yale University Press, 1972.

Nadell, Pamela S. *Women Who Would Be Rabbis: A History of Women's Ordination, 1889–1985.* Beacon, 1998.

Neary, John. *Julian Bond: Black Rebel.* Morrow, 1971.

Nelson, Jack. *Terror in the Night: The Klan's Campaign Against the Jews.* Simon & Schuster, 1993.

Nelson, Jack, and Jack Bass. *The Orangeburg Massacre.* World, 1970.

Neusner, Jacob, ed. *To Grow in Wisdom: An Anthology of Abraham Joshua Heschel.* Lanham, Md.: Madison, 1990.

Nhat Hanh, Thich. *Lotus in a Sea of Fire.* Hill & Wang, 1967.

———. *Love in Action.* Berkeley: Parallax, 1993.

Oates, Stephen B. *Let the Trumpet Sound: The Life of Martin Luther King, Jr.* Harper & Row, 1982.

Oberdorfer, Don. *Tet!* Doubleday, 1971.

Olson, Lynne. *Freedom's Daughters.* Scribner, 2001.

O'Reilly, Kenneth. *"Racial Matters": The FBI's Secret File on Black America, 1960–1972.* Free Press, 1989.

Oren, Michael B. *Six Days of War: June 1967 and the Making of the Modern Middle East.* Oxford University Press, 2002.

Orfield, Gary. *The Reconstruction of Southern Education.* Wiley, 1969.

Ottley, Roi. *The Lonely Warrior.* Regnery, 1955.

Ovington, Mary White. "The National Association for the Advancement of Colored People," *Journal of Negro History,* Vol. 9, 1924.

Pacyga, Dominic A., and Ellen Skerrett. *Chicago, City of Neighborhoods.* Chicago: Loyola University Press, 1986.

Parker, Frank R. *Black Votes Count: Political Empowerment in Mississippi After 1965.* University of North Carolina Press, 1994.

Patti, Archimedes L. A. *Why Viet Nam? Prelude to America's Albatross.* University of California Press, 1980.

Payne, Charles M. *I've Got the Light of Freedom: The Organizing Tradition and the Mississippi Freedom Struggle.* University of California Press, 1995.

Pepper, William F. *An Act of State: The Execution of Martin Luther King.* Verso, 2003.

———. *Orders to Kill: The Truth Behind the Murder of Martin Luther King.* Carroll & Graf, 1995.

Perkins, John. *He's My Brother: A Black Activist and a Former Klansman Tell Their Stories.* Grand Rapids: Chosen, 1994.

Petras, James, ed. *We Accuse.* Berkeley: Diablo, 1965.

Pomerantz, Gary M. *Where Peachtree Meets Sweet Auburn: A Saga of Race and Family.* Scribner, 1996; Penguin, 1997.

Posner, Gerald. *Killing the Dream: James Earl Ray and the Assassination of Martin Luther King, Jr.* Random House, 1998.

Poulos, George. *A Breath of God: A Biography of Archbishop Iakovos.* Brookline, Mass.: Holy Cross Orthodox Press, 1984.

Power, J. Tracy. *I Will Not Be Silent and I Will Be Heard.* South Carolina Department of Archives and History, 1993.

Powers, Georgia Davis. *I Shared the Dream: The Pride, Passion, and Politics of the First Black Woman Senator from Kentucky.* New Horizon Press, 1995.

Powers, Richard Gid. *Secrecy and Power: The Life of J. Edgar Hoover.* Free Press, 1987.

Powers, Thomas. *The War at Home*. Grossman, 1973.

Raines, Howell. *My Soul Is Rested: Movement Days in the Deep South Remembered*. Putnam, 1977.

Rainwater, Lee and William L. Yancey. *The Moynihan Report and the Politics of Controversy*. The M.I.T. Press, 1967.

Ralph, James R., Jr. *Northern Protest: Martin Luther King, Jr., Chicago, and the Civil Rights Movement*. Harvard University Press, 1993.

Reddick, Lawrence D. *Crusader Without Violence: A Biography of Martin Luther King, Jr.* Harper, 1959.

Remnick, David. *King of the World: Muhammad Ali and the Rise of an American Hero*. Random House, 1998.

Reporting Civil Rights: American Journalism, 1963–1973. Library of America, 2003.

Reporting Vietnam: Part One: American Journalism 1959–69. Library of America, 1998.

Reynolds, Barbara. *Jesse Jackson: The Man, the Movement, the Myth*. Nelson-Hall, 1975.

Roberts, Charles Wesley. *LBJ's Inner Circle*. Delacorte, 1965.

Robinson, Amelia Boynton. *Bridge Across Jordan,* rev. ed. Schiller Institute, 1991.

Robinson, Jo Ann. *Abraham Went Out: A Biography of A. J. Muste*. Temple University Press, 1981.

Rogers, Jack. *Presbyterian Creeds: A Guide to the Book of Confessions*. Westminster Press, 1985.

Rolling Stone, Editors of. *Rolling Stone Rock Almanac*. Rolling Stone Press, 1983.

Rossiter, Clinton, ed. *The Federalist Papers*. New American Library, 1961.

Rowan, Carl T. *Breaking Barriers: A Memoir*. Little, Brown, 1990.

Rowe, Gary Thomas, Jr. *My Undercover Years with the Ku Klux Klan*. Bantam, 1976.

Rusk, Dean. *As I Saw It*. Norton, 1990.

Russo, Gus. *Live by the Sword: The Secret War Against Castro and the Death of JFK*. Baltimore: Bancroft, 1998.

Rustin, Bayard. *Down the Line: The Collected Writings of Bayard Rustin*. Quadrangle, 1971.

Sale, Kirkpatrick. *SDS*. Random House, 1973; Vintage, 1974.

Salisbury, Harrison E. *Behind the Lines—Hanoi*. Bantam, 1967.

Sandperl, Ira. *A Little Kinder*. Science and Behavior Books, 1974.

Schandler, Herbert Y. *The Unmaking of a President: Lyndon Johnson and Vietnam*. Princeton University Press, 1977.

Schell, Jonathan. *The Unconquerable World: Power, Nonviolence, and the Will of the People*. Metropolitan, 2003.

———. *The Village of Ben Suc*. Knopf, 1967.

Schlesinger, Arthur M., Jr. *Robert Kennedy and His Times*. Houghton Mifflin, 1978.

———. *A Thousand Days: John F. Kennedy in the White House*. Houghton Mifflin, 1965.

Schneider, William J. *American Martyr: The Jonathan Daniels Story*. Harrisburg: Morehouse, 1992.

Schuck, Peter H. *Diversity in America*. Belknap Press, Harvard, 2003.

Sellers, Cleveland. *The River of No Return: The Autobiography of a Black Militant and the Life and Death of SNCC*. Morrow, 1973.

Shaplen, Robert. *The Lost Revolution: The U.S. in Vietnam, 1946–1966*. Harper/Colophon, 1966.

Shattuck, Gardiner H., Jr. *Episcopalians and Race: Civil War to Civil Rights*. University of Kentucky Press, 2000.

Sheehan, Neil. *A Bright Shining Lie*. Random House, 1988.

Shesol, Jeff. *Mutual Contempt: Lyndon Johnson, Robert Kennedy, and the Feud That Defined a Decade*. Norton, 1997.

Shibata, Shingo, ed. *Phoenix: Letters and Documents of Alice Herz.* Amsterdam: B. R. Gruner, 1976.

Shipler, David K. *Arab and Jew: Wounded Spirits in a Promised Land.* Penguin, 1987.

Shulimson, Jack, and Charles M. Shulimson. *U.S. Marines in Vietnam: The Landing and the Buildup, 1965.* U.S. Government Printing Office, 1978.

Sikora, Frank. *The Judge: The Life and Opinions of Alabama's Frank M. Johnson, Jr.* Black Belt Press, 1992.

Sleet, Moneta, Jr. *The Photographs of Moneta Sleet, Jr.* Johnson, 1998.

Spike, Paul. *Photographs of My Father.* Knopf, 1973.

Spock, Benjamin. *Spock on Spock.* Pantheon, 1985.

Stanton, Mary. *From Selma to Sorrow: The Life and Death of Viola Liuzzo.* University of Georgia Press, 1998.

Steel, Ronald. *Walter Lippmann and the American Century.* Atlantic Monthly Press, 1980.

Stein, Jean. *American Journey: The Times of Robert Kennedy.* Harcourt Brace Jovanovich, 1970.

Stokes Committee. *The Final Assassinations Report: Report of the Select Committee on Assassinations, U.S. House of Representatives.* Bantam, 1979.

Sullivan, William C., with Bill Brown. *The Bureau: My Thirty Years in Hoover's FBI.* Norton, 1979.

Sumner, William Graham. *Folkways.* Ginn, 1906.

Swerdlow, Amy. *Women Strike for Peace.* University of Chicago Press, 1993.

Szulc, Tad. *Dominican Diary.* Delacorte, 1965.

Tarrants, Thomas A., III. *The Conversion of a Klansman: The Story of a Former Ku Klux Klan Terrorist.* Doubleday-Galilee, 1979.

Taylor, Maxwell D. *Swords and Plowshares.* Norton, 1972.

Terry, Wallace, ed. *Bloods: An Oral History of the Vietnam War.* Random House, 1984.

Theoharis, Athan G., and John Stuart Cox. *The Boss: J. Edgar Hoover and the Great American Inquisition.* Philadelphia: Temple University Press, 1988.

Thomas, Evan. *The Man to See: Edward Bennett Williams.* Simon & Schuster, 1991.

———. *Robert Kennedy: His Life.* Simon & Schuster, 2000.

Tijerina, Reies Lopez. *They Called Me "King Tiger": My Struggle for the Land and Our Rights.* Arte Publico, 2000.

Travis, Dempsey J. *An Autobiography of Black Chicago.* Urban Research Institute, 1981.

Turner, Karen Gottschang, with Phan Thanh Hao. *Even the Women Must Fight: Memories of War from North Vietnam.* Wiley, 1998.

Tuttle, William M., Jr. *Race Riot: Chicago in the Red Summer of 1919.* Atheneum, 1975.

Tyson, Timothy B. *Radio Free Dixie: Robert Williams and the Roots of Black Power.* University of North Carolina Press, 1999.

U.S. House of Representatives. *Hearings, Select Committee on Assassinations.* 12 vols. *U.S. Government Printing Office,* 1979.

U.S. Department of State. *Foreign Relations of the United States, 1964–68: Volume II Vietnam January–June 1965.* U.S. Government Printing Office, 1996.

———. *Foreign Relations of the United States, 1964–68: Volume III Vietnam June–December 1965.* U.S. Government Printing Office, 1996.

———. *Foreign Relations of the United States, 1964–68: Volume IV Vietnam 1966.* United States Government Printing Office, 1998.

———. *Foreign Relations of the United States, 1964–68: Volume V Vietnam 1967.* U.S. Government Printing Office, 2002.

———. *Foreign Relations of the United States, 1964–68: Volume VI Vietnam January–August 1968*. U.S. Government Printing Office, 2002.

Valenti, Jack, *A Very Human President*. Norton, 1975; Pocket Books, 1977, 1976.

Viorst, Milton. *Fire in the Streets*. Simon & Schuster, 1979.

Vorgrimler, Herbert, ed. *Commentary on the Documents of Vatican II*. Herder and Herder, 1967.

Wagy, Tom. *Governor LeRoy Collins of Florida: Spokesman of the New South*. University of Alabama Press, 1985.

Wallace, George C. *"Hear Me Out."* Droke House, 1968.

Warren, Marvyn A. *King Came Preaching*. InterVarsity, 2001.

Washington, James Melvin, ed. *A Testament of Hope: The Essential Writings of Martin Luther King*. Harper & Row, 1986.

Waskow, Arthur I. *From Race Riot to Sit-in: 1919 and the 1960s*. Doubleday, 1966.

Watkins, Mel. *On the Real Side*. Simon & Schuster, 1994.

Webb, Sheyann, and Rachel W. Nelson. *Selma, Lord, Selma: Girlhood Memories of the Civil-Rights Days*. University of Alabama Press, 1980.

Wells, Tom. *The War Within: America's Battle over Vietnam*. University of California Press, 1994.

Westin, Alan F., and Barry Mahoney. *The Trial of Martin Luther King*. Crowell, 1974.

Whitehead, Don. *Attack on Terror: The FBI Against the Ku Klux Klan in Mississippi*. Funk & Wagnalls, 1970.

Wilkins, Roger. *A Man's Life: An Autobiography*. Simon & Schuster, 1982.

Wilkins, Roy. *Standing Fast: The Autobiography of Roy Wilkins*. Viking, 1982.

Williams, John A. *The King God Didn't Save*. Coward-McCann, 1970.

Williams, Juan. *Thurgood Marshall: American Revolutionary*. Times Books, 1998.

Williams, Roger M. *The Bonds: An American Family*. Atheneum, 1971.

Wilmore, Gayraud S. *Black Religion and Black Radicalism*. 1st ed., Anchor Doubleday, 1972; 2nd ed., Orbis, 1983.

Wofford, Harris. *Of Kennedys and Kings*. Farrar, Straus & Giroux, 1980.

Wood, Gordon S. *The Radicalism of the American Revolution*. Random House, 1991; Vintage, 1993.

Woodward, C. Vann. *The Strange Career of Jim Crow*. Oxford University Press, 1955; 3rd ed., 1974.

———. *Tom Watson: Agrarian Rebel*. Macmillan, 1938.

Yoder, Edwin M., Jr. *Joe Alsop's Cold War: A Study of Journalistic Influence and Intrigue*. University of North Carolina Press, 1995.

Young, Andrew. *An Easy Burden: The Civil Rights Movement and the Transformation of America*. HarperCollins, 1996.

Young-Bruehl, Elisabeth. *Hannah Arendt: For Love of the World*. Yale University Press, 1982.

Yzermans, Vincent A., ed. *American Participation in the Second Vatican Council*. Sheed & Ward, 1967.

Zaroulis, Nancy, and Gerald Sullivan. *Who Spoke Up? American Protest Against the War in Vietnam, 1963–1975*. Doubleday, 1984.

INDEX

PHOTO CREDITS

ABOUT THE AUTHOR

Taylor Branch is the bestselling author of *Parting the Waters: America in the King Years, 1954–63* (which won the Pulitzer Prize for History) and *Pillar of Fire: America in the King Years, 1963–65*. Branch has won almost every major award. He lives in Baltimore with his wife, Christina Macy.